PAULINE CHRISTOLOGY

PAULINE CHRISTOLOGY

An Exegetical-Theological Study

GORDON D. FEE

HENDRICKSON PUBLISHERS

Pauline Christology: An Exegetical-Theological Study
© 2007 by Hendrickson Publishers, Inc.
P. O. Box 3473
Peabody, Massachusetts 01961-3473

ISBN 978-1-59856-035-0

Printed in the United States of America

Second Printing — April 2007

Nestle-Aland, *Novum Testamentum Graece*, 27th Revised Edition, edited by Barbara Aland, Kurt Aland, Johannes Karavidopoulos, Carlo M. Martini, and Bruce Metzger in cooperation with the Institute for New Testament Textual Research, Münster/Westphalia, © 1993 Deutsche Bibelgesellschaft, Stuttgart. Used by permission.

Library of Congress Cataloging-in-Publication Data

Fee, Gordon D.
    Pauline christology : an exegetical-theological study / Gordon D. Fee.
       p. cm.
    Includes bibliographical references and indexes.
    ISBN-13: 978-1-59856-035-0 (alk. paper)
    1. Bible. N.T. Epistles of Paul—Theology. 2. Paul, the Apostle, Saint.
  3. Jesus Christ—History of doctrines. I. Title.
    BS2651.F35 2007
    232.092—dc22
                             2006027753

For Rikk Watts
former student
present colleague
friend and fellow traveler
on the journey

Contents

PART II: SYNTHESIS

Abbreviations

General

ad loc.	at the place discussed
cf.	compare
ch(s).	chapter(s)
contra	against
e.g.	for example
i.e.	that is
esp.	especially
ET	English translation
Gk.	Greek
lit.	literally
𝔐	Majority text
MS(S)	manuscript(s)
n(n).	note(s)
pace	contrary to the opinion of
par(s).	parallel(s)
p(p).	page(s)
repr.	reprint
q.v.	which see
s.v.	under the word
v(v).	verse(s)

Secondary Sources

AB	Anchor Bible
ABR	*Australian Biblical Review*
ASBT	Acadia Studies in Bible and Theology
BAGD	Bauer, W., W. F. Arndt, F. W. Gingrich, and F. W. Danker. *Greek-English Lexicon of the New Testament and Other Early Christian Literature.* 2d ed. Chicago, 1979

BDAG	Bauer, W., F. W. Danker, W. F. Arndt, and F. W. Gingrich. *Greek-English Lexicon of the New Testament and Other Early Christian Literature.* 3d ed. Chicago, 1999
BECNT	Baker Exegetical Commentary on the New Testament
BETL	Bibliotheca ephemeridum theologicarum lovaniensium
BEvT	Beiträge zur evangelischen Theologie
BibSem	Biblical Seminar
BJS	Brown Judaic Studies
BSac	*Bibliotheca sacra*
BTB	*Biblical Theology Bulletin*
BZNW	Beihefte zur Zeitschrift für die neutestamentliche Wissenschaft
CBQ	*Catholic Biblical Quarterly*
ConBNT	Coniectanea biblica: New Testament Series
CTJ	*Calvin Theological Journal*
DJG	*Dictionary of Jesus and the Gospels.* Edited by J. B. Green and S. McKnight. Downers Grove, Ill., 1992
DPL	*Dictionary of Paul and His Letters.* Edited by G. F. Hawthorne and R. P. Martin. Downers Grove, Ill., 1993
EBib	*Etudes bibliques*
EDNT	*Exegetical Dictionary of the New Testament.* Edited by H. Balz and G. Schneider. 3 vols. ET. Grand Rapids, 1990–1993
EstBib	*Estudios biblicos*
ETL	*Ephemerides theologicae lovanienses*
ETR	*Etudes théologiques et religieuses*
EvQ	*Evangelical Quarterly*
ExpTim	*Expository Times*
FRLANT	Forschungen zur Religion und Literatur des Alten und Neuen Testaments
GTJ	*Grace Theological Journal*
HTR	*Harvard Theological Review*
HUCA	*Hebrew Union College Annual*
ICC	International Critical Commentary
JBL	*Journal of Biblical Literature*
JETS	*Journal of the Evangelical Theological Society*
JSJ	*Journal for the Study of Judaism in the Persian, Hellenistic, and Roman Periods*
JSNT	*Journal for the Study of the New Testament*
JSNTSup	Journal for the Study of the New Testament: Supplement Series
JTC	*Journal for Theology and the Church*
JTS	*Journal of Theological Studies*
LCL	Loeb Classical Library
LD	Lectio divina

LS	*Louvain Studies*
MHT	Moulton, J. H., W. F. Howard, and N. Turner. *A Grammar of New Testament Greek.* 4 vols. Edinburgh, 1996–1999
MM	Moulton, J. H., and G. Milligan. *The Vocabulary of the Greek Testament.* London, 1930. Reprint, Peabody, Mass., 1997
NA^{27}	Nestle-Aland, *Novum Testamentum Graece.* Edited by B. Aland et al. 27th ed. Stuttgart, 1993
NCB	New Century Bible
NICNT	New International Commentary on the New Testament
NICOT	New International Commentary on the Old Testament
NIDNTT	*New International Dictionary of New Testament Theology.* Edited by C. Brown. 4 vols. Grand Rapids, 1975–1985
NIGTC	New International Greek Testament Commentary
NovT	*Novum Testamentum*
NovTSup	Novum Testamentum Supplements
NT	New Testament
NTS	*New Testament Studies*
NTT	New Testament Theology
OBS	Oxford Bible Series
OT	Old Testament
PSB	*Princeton Seminary Bulletin*
RB	*Revue biblique*
RevExp	*Review and Expositor*
SANT	Studien zum Alten und Neuen Testaments
SBLDS	Society of Biblical Literature Dissertation Series
SBLMS	Society of Biblical Literature Monograph Series
SBT	Studies in Biblical Theology
SD	Studies and Documents
SJT	*Scottish Journal of Theology*
SJTOP	Scottish Journal of Theology Occasional Papers
SNTSMS	Society for New Testament Studies Monograph Series
SNTSU	Studien zum Neuen Testament und seiner Umwelt
SP	Sacra pagina
SVTQ	*St. Vladimir's Theological Quarterly*
TDNT	*Theological Dictionary of the New Testament.* Edited by G. Kittel and G. Friedrich. Translated by G. W. Bromiley. 10 vols. Grand Rapids, 1964–1976
TJ	*Trinity Journal*
TNTC	Tyndale New Testament Commentaries
TUGAL	Texte und Untersuchungen zur Geschichte der altchristlichen Literatur
TZ	*Theologische Zeitschrift*
UBS^4	United Bible Societies, *The Greek New Testament.* Edited by B. Aland et al. 4th ed. Stuttgart, 1994
UNT	Untersuchungen zum Neuen Testament

VE	*Vox evangelica*
WBC	Word Biblical Commentary
WBT	Word Biblical Themes
WMANT	Wissenschaftliche Monographien zum Alten und Neuen Testament
WTJ	*Westminster Theological Journal*
WUNT	Wissenschaftliche Untersuchungen zum Neuen Testament
ZNW	*Zeitschrift für die neutestamentliche Wissenschaft und die Kunde der älteren Kirche*
ZWT	*Zeitschrift für wissenschaftliche Theologie*

Bible Versions

ESV	English Standard Version
GNB	Good News Bible (= TEV)
JB	Jerusalem Bible
KJV	King James Version (Authorized Version)
LXX	Septuagint
Montgomery	Centenary Translation of the New Testament
MT	Masoretic Text
NAB	New American Bible
NASB	New American Standard Bible
NASU	New American Standard Bible, Updated Version
NET BIBLE	The NET Bible (online: http://net.bible.org/bible.php)
NIV	New International Version
NJB	New Jerusalem Bible
NLT	New Living Translation
NRSV	New Revised Standard Version
Phillips	The New Testament in Modern English
REB	Revised English Bible
RSV	Revised Standard Version
TCNT	Twentieth Century New Testament
TEV	Today's English Version
TNIV	Today's New International Version

Greek and Latin Works

Chrysostom	
Hom. Col.	*Homiliae in epistulam ad Colossenses*
Jos. Asen.	*Joseph and Aseneth*
Josephus	
Ant.	*Jewish Antiquities*

Justin Martyr
    Dial.   *Dialogue with Trypho*
Philo
    Agr.   *De agricultura*
    Cher.   *De cherubim*
    Conf.   *De confusione linguarum*
    Ebr.   *De ebrietate*
    Fug.   *De fuga et inventione*
    Leg.   *Legum allegoriae*
    QG   *Quaestiones et solutions in Genesin*
    Somn.   *De somniis*
Tertullian
    Marc.   *Adversus Marcionem*

Preface

THIS BOOK RESULTED FROM THE confluence of three streams of concern that fed into it for over a decade. The first stream was an invitation to present a paper on the theology of 1 Corinthians at the SBL seminar on Pauline theology (1991). The several years during which this seminar convened at the annual meeting of the Society were at once an experience of delight and frustration. The delight came from the energy experienced in sitting at table and talking about Paul's theology in four of the seven letters of unquestioned authenticity (1–2 Corinthians, Galatians, and Romans). The frustration came in our use of the word "theology," where at times a great deal of energy was expended on items that appeared to be more cultural and sociological than theological. So here I discovered that Christology as such was simply not an issue to be brought to this "theological" table, since Paul's *presupposed* theology tended to be ruled out of bounds.

The second stream was related to what I had experienced in the writing of *God's Empowering Presence*. Similar to that situation, where I had been asked to do a dictionary article on the Spirit and Paul and discovered that there was no existing book on the subject, in this case the invitation to present papers at the interconfessional "summits" on Paul's understanding of "the Trinity" and "the Incarnation" resulted in the discovery that neither did a full-fledged study of Pauline Christology as such exist. The two books on the subject that do exist in English are quite limited in what they attempt to do. Werner Kramer's *Christ, Lord, Son of God* (1966) is not a truly Pauline Christology, since over half the book is devoted to "The Pre-Pauline Material," even though that material is ferreted out of Paul himself; and Jennings Reid's *Jesus: God's Emptiness, God's Fullness* (1990) is more popular and very narrowly focused. There are, of course, as with the Spirit in Paul, several books on New Testament Christology with Pauline chapters, and now we also have J. D. G. Dunn's and Tom Schreiner's theologies of Paul, with chapters on Christology. So part of the reason for this book is an attempt to fill this void.

The third stream, directly related to the second, came from the actual writing of the papers for the two summits, held the week after Easter at St.

Joseph's Seminary in Dunwoodie, New York, in 1997 and 1999 respectively. Both of these were delightful experiences of learning and enjoyment, as we read and interacted with papers from the biblical, theological, philosophical, and practical disciplines in a context of uncommon collegiality. I am grateful to the conveners of these summits (Steve Davis, Dan Kendall, and Gerald O'Collins) for the privilege of being invited, and to the members of the summits for the kind and generous interaction with both of these papers.[1] But these papers also got me involved in christological questions in ways that I had not had opportunity or inclination to do theretofore. And thus these two streams, especially the lack of such a book, were the primary impetus that set this study in motion.

The nudge that abetted this impetus came from a deep sense of unease in the course of research for the two summits over what has appeared in the literature during the last quarter century. In some quarters of New Testament scholarship there had developed a strong tendency to play down or minimize Pauline Christology. That led to my twice offering a seminar at Regent College on Pauline Christology (spring term 2002 and 2004), the latter during my second year of "retirement." The 2004 seminar in particular gave a jump-start to the present book.

Having written the big book on the Holy Spirit in Paul also led to one of the several frustrations that I experienced along the way. I realized that a book modeled after the first one was simply not feasible. Even if I limited myself only to the exegesis of passages that appeared to have christological content/presuppositions, the size of the volume would make such a study prohibitive. Thus I knew from the outset that it would require a much more focused exegesis of the passages involved.

The question then was how to proceed at all. In the end, and under the influence of *God's Empowering Presence* as well as the SBL seminar, I chose to write a book that goes through the letters individually and tries to ferret out the Christology of each one before attempting a synthesis of the exegetical work. But unlike the seminar, I did not limit myself either to the "unquestioned seven" of Paul's letters or to any one of the letters in isolation from the others. That is, at any one time I was well aware of the whole corpus. Nonetheless, I tried to keep the exegesis to the contingencies of the letter under study. And unlike in *God's Empowering Presence*, I chose to group texts under various themes, as they seemed to be dictated by the individual letters—thus I do not always cover the same themes in each of the letters.

---

[1]Subsequently published as "Paul and the Trinity: The Experience of Christ and the Spirit for Paul's Understanding of God," in *The Trinity: An Interdisciplinary Symposium on the Trinity* (ed. S. T. Davis, D. Kendall, and G. O'Collins; Oxford: Oxford University Press, 1999), 49–72; and "St Paul and the Incarnation: A Reassessment of the Data," in *The Incarnation: An Interdisciplinary Symposium on the Incarnation of the Son of God* (ed. S. T. Davis, D. Kendall, and G. O'Collins; Oxford: Oxford University Press, 2002), 62–92.

Since I anticipate this will be a cause of frustration to some readers, and especially to those who try only to "consult" this work, I have offered a detailed table of contents at the beginning.

Those who take the time to read portions of the book may experience an unevenness in detail and presentation. In part this is related to the recognized significance of some passages over against others. But some discussions also grew a bit disproportionately when I finally consulted the literature. (It has been my lifelong habit to do the exegesis without consulting the secondary literature along the way, and then spending many days reading the literature and going back to the manuscript to make corrections or to note agreement or disagreement. In this case I read the literature for each letter at the conclusion of writing that chapter, while I waited until I had finished my own attempt at "synthesis" before reading more widely on the topic itself. This, then, has led to some obviously disproportionate handling of some texts over against others, and it is also the cause of some repetitions that I tried to weed out in the final reading, although I have no confidence that I did so thoroughly.)

I have tried my best to acknowledge helpful insights that have come to me from others, but I am not sure that I totally succeeded. The careful reader will recognize that I owe a good deal to two scholars in particular: Larry Hurtado, a close friend over many years, who was engaged in christological questions long before I have been, and whose masterful *Lord Jesus Christ* is a model of scholarly endeavor and gracious handling of different opinions; and Richard Bauckham, with whose small programmatic *God Crucified* I found myself in agreement over and again, and whose language regarding the divine identity I find especially helpful to get past the centuries-long difficulties in dealing with the ontological questions per se.

It will also be obvious that on the other side I find myself often in disagreement with another acquaintance (and friend) of long standing, James Dunn. In the second edition of *Christology in the Making* (1989), he had openly invited further conversation on this issue, which I do in this study, even though I am joining the conversation at a later stage. If at times it looks as if we are only sparring partners and not friends, I take the blame for that and apologize in advance to Jimmy himself if my rhetoric is too much, and especially if my reporting of his positions is inadequate.

I need here to thank others who have helped along the way. First, the members of the seminar, whose papers and enthusiasm helped to give the manuscript its needed push: David Cameron, Nathan Carson, Brenton Dickieson, Kevin Duffy, Bryan Dunagan, Joyce Forrester, Nikola Galevski, Matt Johnson, Jun Son Jung, Claire McLean, Scott Scruggs, and Aaron Sherwood. Three of these students (Dickieson, Galevski, Sherwood) also read a chapter or more during the rough-draft stage and offered helpful critique. As with all these projects, my wife, Maudine, read through every word on every page to see whether someone not trained in New Testament studies could read with a measure of understanding; she also contributed long hours gathering the material for the indexes. Her "longsuffering" through the year and a half during which this book was the only thing I was doing, and her patient listening to my occasional "ranting" during a meal, were both noticed and deeply appreciated.

In what turned out to be my penultimate reading of the manuscript, which was intended as the final one, I was a bit abashed by the frequent rhetoric that occasionally emerged when engaging in debate with some with whom I disagreed. Not only so, in my reading of the literature for the appendix on Wisdom, I was equally taken aback by how often what appeared to me as especially weak arguments by others were put forth as "clear," or with the adverbs "clearly" or "surely." This required a "spell check" of my own manuscript, where I had clearly (!) done the same thing. I do not suggest here that I have successfully removed all such rhetoric; therefore, knowing my own weaknesses and my bent toward overstatement for effect, I apologize in advance to any who might be offended by it, especially when the rhetoric appears in the context of their names. If this study has exegetical or theological merit, I wish that to be demonstrated in the exegesis and theology, and not to be pushed by putting down the opinions of others. It is all too easy for some of us to engage in such an enterprise in the same way as the preacher in the apocryphal story who made a note in the margin of a sermon manuscript: "Shout loud; point weak here!" (But I should point out that the nature of the enterprise has caused me very often to point out what I see as "Paul's high Christology." I do not intend that repetitiousness as a rhetorical ploy; it is rather an awareness that many may wish only to consult the book on a given passage, not to read much of it in a consecutive way.)

Since I have been dealing with things Pauline for much of my academic life, it is inevitable that I should have occasion to refer to earlier work at times, simply as a way of trying to keep from reinventing the wheel. Besides the two major commentaries (NICNT on 1 Corinthians and Philippians) and the large study of the Holy Spirit in Paul noted above, a number of textual, exegetical, and theological studies that appeared originally in a variety of places have been collected by Wm. B. Eerdmans Publishing Company and published in 2001 under the title *To What End Exegesis? Studies Textual, Exegetical, and Theological.* Whenever I have occasion to refer to one of these studies, I give only the publishing data in this volume; for anyone who might be interested in the original publication data for any of these studies, that can be found on pages ix–x in the volume of collected studies.

One of the joys of this enterprise was how much I learned along the way, since many of these texts I had not had occasion to work closely with before. This learning includes some surprises: for example, that 1 Corinthians not only has the largest amount of christological data but also joins Romans as the only letters in the corpus in which are found all the various "themes" taken up in chapters 11–16 of this book; and that, especially in light of their well-known christocentric nature, Galatians and Ephesians turned out to have the least.

Finally, a word or two to the reader. First, because I can hardly expect everyone to read a book such as this one straight through, from cover to cover, I have tried to make it user friendly from chapter to chapter, which involved a bit more repetition than one would ordinarily wish to have. This is also the reason for the unusual number of cross-references throughout. Second, while I was teaching a course at the Continental Theological Seminary (Brussels) during July of 2004, a student suggested that the reading of *God's Empowering Presence* would have been easier for the non-New Testament specialist if the Greek had been translated into English. I heard that as a good word of advice and have tried to do so consistently in this volume, in this case always in italics immediately following the Greek. Third, for my own sake and then also for the sake of the reader, in citing the Pauline texts I have regularly put references to Christ in **bold,** while those to God the Father are underlined (and in some cases those to the Holy Spirit are in *italics*). And finally, in what also began for my own sake but seemed helpful enough to pass on to the reader, I have included two appendices in each chapter: one that lists all the texts in the given letter where either God and/or Christ are mentioned; and a second that presents the statistical data in an analytical way.

I thus offer these probings with the express desire that they may be helpful to some and be finally to the glory of God.

With special delight I dedicate this work to Rikk Watts, whom I first met when he arrived from Australia with his wife, Katie, and their children, Stephen and Rebecca, to matriculate at Gordon-Conwell Seminary in the autumn term of 1984. Being fellow travelers in the Assemblies of God, we began a friendship that developed into a close and congenial one over the next two years. On my fifty-first birthday, which coincided with the final day of term in May of 1985, he engineered to have the (very large) class purchase and individually sign, as a departing gift, Kurt Aland's *Vollständige Koncordanz zum griechischen Neuen Testament*, which is now dog-eared from constant use. At the end of his first Gordon-Conwell year I had the joy of introducing him to baseball at Fenway Park; some years later, after he had finished his PhD in New Testament at Cambridge (1990) and returned home to teach in Australia, he returned the favor by introducing me to Australian "footie." It was with great joy that some years later (1996) I welcomed him as my junior colleague at Regent, and then as the senior New Testament professor on my retirement from full-time teaching three years ago. He is a colleague on whom I have learned to lean and from whom I have learned much. Thank you, Rikk.

1

Introduction

ANYONE WHO READS EVEN A smattering of Paul's writings recognizes early on that his devotion to Christ was the foremost reality and passion of his life. What he said in one of his later letters serves as a kind of motto for his entire Christian life: "For me to live is Christ; to die is [to] gain [Christ]" (Phil 1:21). Christ is the beginning and goal of everything for Paul, and thus is the single great reality along the way. So when one dares to attempt what I have tried to do in this book—offer a Pauline Christology—one needs a clear sense of what one is doing: after all, Christ appears on every page, as it were.[1] Our first task, then, is to clarify what is meant by the term "Christology" and at the same time to define the word "Pauline."

Pauline Christology: What Is It?

The word "Christology" in this study is used exclusively to refer to the *person* of Christ—Paul's understanding of *who* Christ *was/is*, in distinction to the *work* of Christ—*what* Christ *did* for us as Savior (soteriology). But this is also our first difficulty, since a distinction between Christology and soteriology is not one that Paul himself makes.[2] If Christ is the singular passion of

---

[1]Except for Rom 1:16–3:20, which is so remarkably theocentric that Christ is mentioned but once (2:16), and this with reference to Paul's gospel.

[2]Indeed, as pointed out in ch. 11, for Paul this is an artificial distinction; cf. S. Kim: "In Paul Christology and soteriology are not two separate doctrines but one, the former being the ground of the latter" (*The Origin of Paul's Gospel* [WUNT 2/4; Tübingen: Mohr Siebeck, 1981], 100); and H. Ridderbos: "Paul's Christology is a Christology of redemptive facts" (*Paul: An Outline of His Theology* [Grand Rapids: Eerdmans, 1975], 49). The (valid) recognition of this reality has led scholarship down one path that is appreciated but will not be taken in this book, that of attempting to do Christology by way of narrative. See, e.g., B. Witherington, *Paul's Narrative Thought World: The Tapestry of Tragedy and Triumph* (Louisville: Westminster John Knox, 1994), 86–214; M. L. Soards, "Christology of the Pauline Epistles," in *Who Do You Say I Am? Essays on Christology* (ed. M. A. Powell and D. R. Bauer; Louisville: Westminster John Knox, 1999), 88–109; F. Matera, *New Testament Christology*

Paul's life, the focus of that passion is on the saving work of Christ; and Paul spells this out often enough in intentional moments for at least a modest understanding of what it meant for him to say, "Christ died for our sins according to the Scriptures" (1 Cor 15:3).[3]

This in turn leads directly to the second difficulty: there is only one passage in the entire corpus, Col 1:15–17, that might be described as intentionally christological. Here, over against some who (apparently) were diminishing the role, and thus the person, of Christ by their fascination with the "powers," Paul intentionally sets out to put the "powers" in their place with respect to the eternal Son of the Father.[4] And if this passage is, as most NT scholars believe, the first "stanza" of a two-stanza "hymn," then the second stanza (vv. 18–20) returns altogether to Paul's primarily soteriological concerns.

Third, and in many ways the greatest difficulty of all, is the inevitable question of trying to ferret out a coherent Christology from the scores of contingent moments[5] in Paul's letters where his "theology" emerges by way of presupposition or affirmation but not by explication. My ultimate concern in this study is with coherence in Paul's thought concerning the person of

---

(Louisville: Westminster John Knox, 1999), 83–133. My appreciation lies with the attempt to try to do Pauline Christology without being dominated by "titles." But the difficulty lies with trying to do what is attempted in this book (rightly or wrongly): to look at Christology on its own right and not to have it overladen with soteriology, even though, as pointed out in chs. 4 (pp. 196–98) and 11, the latter deeply impacts the former.

The main difficulty with the narrative approach is that it has trouble in dealing with Paul's christological *presuppositions* (see n. 8 below). This emerges especially in Matera's discussion of the Christology of 1 Thessalonians (*New Testament Christology*, 90–91), where he fails to take into consideration the Christology that Paul presupposes between himself and his readers. Furthermore, both Witherington and Matera try to factor personified Wisdom into the narrative, to which any ordinary reading of Paul should play the lie, since outside the Wisdom literature itself (esp. Sirach and Wisdom of Solomon) "she" has no role of any kind in Israel's essential narrative, and certainly not in that of Paul, who neither cites nor alludes to these two works in his letters. See further appendix A.

[3] This is said too easily, of course, since centuries of debate have accumulated around this question, mostly, I am convinced, because Paul uses a variety of metaphors to express the saving results of Christ's death, depending on which aspect of "sin" is in purview. Our theological difficulties have stemmed from pressing the metaphors beyond Paul's own usage. See G. D. Fee, "Paul and the Metaphors of Salvation: Some Reflections on Pauline Soteriology," in *The Redemption: An Interdisciplinary Symposium on Christ as Redeemer* (ed. S. T. Davis, D. Kendall, and G. O'Collins; Oxford University Press, 2004), 43–67.

[4] Some may see this last phrase as presupposing a later christological emphasis. But as is pointed out in the exegesis of this passage in ch. 7 (pp. 293–95), the grammatical antecedent of the "who" in Col 1:15–20 is "the beloved Son" of v. 13, into whose "kingdom" the Gentile Colossians have entered. So my language is predicated on what Paul actually says in the passage.

[5] For the use of this language in dealing with Pauline theology, see J. C. Beker, *Paul the Apostle: The Triumph of God in Life and Thought* (Philadelphia: Fortress, 1980), 11–15.

Christ; but the approach one must take to get at this coherence is altogether by way of the contingencies of the several letters, which are decidedly not intentionally christological (in the sense of systematically laying out what Paul believed about the person of Christ).[6]

The difficulty here can be illustrated by a brief look at 1 Cor 1:9, 18–25. As the concluding word of his opening thanksgiving, a thanksgiving that is at the same time "loaded" with theological and behavioral issues that will be taken up in the letter, Paul affirms (in our v. 9) that the Corinthian believers' ultimately attaining the eschatological prize rests altogether on the faithfulness of God. The evidence, and thus the ground, of God's faithfulness on their behalf is the fact that God has "called [them] into κοινωνία with[7] *his Son, Jesus Christ our Lord.*" With these words Paul presupposes a common christological ground between himself and the Corinthians regarding the three designations here attached to the historical person named Jesus: "Son," "Christ," and "Lord." At the same time, this is language to which later Christians are so accustomed that we read the whole set of names/titles as a singular reality, which in fact in this case it was almost certainly intended to be.

But when we come to the beginning of the first argument in the letter (1:18–25), we find that both the Corinthians and we must make some singular adjustments to our preconceptions. For the designation "Christ," it turns out, still carries freight from Jewish messianism, but with a decidedly singular twist. Indeed, Jesus, "God's Son" and the now exalted "Lord," turned out to be a messiah whom no one was expecting and who was being evaded by the believers in Corinth. For a "crucified Messiah" is the ultimate scandal and folly for those expecting a bit more triumphalism in their messiah.

So whether one wishes it or not, this basic Christian affirmation of God's faithfulness (1:9) and this first exposition in the Pauline corpus of what it means for Jesus to be the Messiah (1:18–25) are filled with christological presuppositions that one must come to terms with if one is going to be fair to Paul. Our christological task is to try to tease out what Paul himself

---

[6]On this whole question cf. the proviso of M. Hengel: "We should not forget, that in the Corpus Paulinum we have only a minimal (and partially also accidentally preserved) extract of his *oral* preaching which spanned a period of almost thirty years, an extract which nevertheless reveals a thinker of fascinating greatness. The richness of his preaching must have been even more fascinating!" (" 'Sit at My Right Hand!' The Enthronement of Christ at the Right Hand of God and Psalm 110:1," in *Studies in Early Christology* [Edinburgh: T&T Clark, 1995], 163). Indeed!

[7]On the meaning of this difficult phrase, see G. D. Fee, *The First Epistle to the Corinthians* (NICNT; Grand Rapids: Eerdmans, 1987), 45; cf. A. T. Thiselton: "The Communal Participation of the Sonship of Christ" (*The First Epistle to the Corinthians: A Commentary on the Greek Text* [NIGTC; Grand Rapids: Eerdmans, 2000], 103–5); and D. Garland: "Into Common-Union with His Son" (*1 Corinthians* [BECNT; Grand Rapids: Baker Academic, 2003], 35–36).

understood *presuppositionally* about Christ, and to do so on the basis of his explicit and incidental references to Christ.[8]

And that leads to a few words about yet another, the fourth, of the primary difficulties with this exercise. One can hardly, nor should one be expected to, come to these letters with a *tabula rasa,* a clean slate that has no presuppositions. The difficulty lies in recognizing one's own presuppositions (another's presuppositions being more obvious!) and asking in every case whether our reading of Paul is based on what Paul himself believed or on what we have long assumed he believed. In any case, this book will regularly remind us that we are seldom reading Paul's *argued* Christology, but rather his *assumed* Christology, and in these letters a Christology that he also assumed on the part of his readers.[9]

Because this is a given for us and because all of Paul's letters are full of assumptions between him and his readers based on their contingent circumstances, one needs to exercise special caution in terms of how much theological grist one makes of singular, sometimes isolated, statements about Christ in his letters.[10] Our best hope for getting it right, as it were, is to focus on those kinds of statements that are repeated throughout the corpus in a variety of ways.

For these various reasons I have attempted a Pauline Christology that is primarily exegetical, looking for the Christology that emerges in each of the letters in turn and thus trying to analyze each letter on its own terms.[11]

---

[8] Noted also by L. Hurtado: "Paul characteristically seems to *presuppose* acquaintance with the christological convictions that he affirms" (*Lord Jesus Christ: Devotion to Jesus in Earliest Christianity* [Grand Rapids: Eerdmans, 2003], 98); cf. D. J. Moo regarding no explicit Christology in the earliest six letters: "First, . . . Paul and his churches apparently were in basic agreement about who Jesus was," and "second, Paul must have inherited a good deal of his understanding of Jesus' person . . . from Christians who had gone before him" ("The Christology of the Early Letters of Paul," in *Contours of Christology in the New Testament* [ed. R. N. Longenecker; Grand Rapids: Eerdmans, 2005], 169).

[9] See the preceding note. This point needs to be repeated and emphasized because one could be accused of finding what one is looking for (and in a sense that is arguably true); but the fact that Paul argues for *none* of this is especially significant in terms of his and their shared assumptions.

[10] This surfaces especially regarding an alleged Spirit Christology that some find in the apostle, which ultimately is based on a single text (1 Cor 15:47); but this finds its singular expression as the direct result of Paul's use of Gen 2:7 and his making a deliberate set of contrasts between Christ and Adam. See the discussion in ch. 3 (pp. 114–19) and in ch. 13.

[11] The advantage of this over a narrative approach (see n. 1 above) is that one is (hopefully) less likely to overlook or omit what does not fit the prior construction of the narrative. The primary disadvantage of an exegetical approach, as Moo has rightly pointed out ("Christology," 170), is that it can be "tediously repetitive" (*caveat lector!*). At the same time, however, the evidence of this study has verified his assertion that "significant development in Paul's christology over the course of the decade during which these letters were written does not seem to have taken place" (ibid.). Moreover, as argued in chs. 14–15, it is nearly impossible to understand Paul's two

What is avoided here is a Christology that is basically an analysis of titles, although one can scarcely avoid some of this because Paul himself designated Christ in a variety of ways, some of which are titular. In so doing I am trying to follow Leander Keck's admonition that we respect "the grammar of the theological discourse."[12] Because each letter tends to have its own christological emphases, I realized that ordering this volume canonically would cause the reader (not to mention the writer) to get even more "lost in the woods." So I have chosen to group passages under certain themes or kinds of usage, as these emerge in each letter, and explain at the beginning of each chapter the reason(s) for the arrangement. I have also chosen to include a detailed table of contents for those who wish to find where certain passages are discussed in detail.[13]

So Christology in this study has to do with Paul's understanding of the *person* of Christ, as it emerges in his letters both in explicit statements about Christ and in other statements full of shared assumptions between him and his readers. And it therefore must be emphasized at the outset that the issue in this book is not the doctrine of the incarnation (or preexistence) per se, but rather *Paul's* theology, whether or not *he* believed it and asserted it, regardless of whatever I or others may or may not believe about it. Whether I am successful in this regard—I am a believer, after all—I will leave to others to judge.

By choosing to go this way, I am at the same time making a commitment as to what I mean by "Pauline." In the exegetical chapters of this volume that word has to do with all the letters in the canonical Pauline corpus, and thus "Pauline Christology" here refers to the *canonical Paul.* By going this way, I am intentionally making several important methodological decisions. First, inherent to this choice is the assumption that one letter or set of letters is not more significant than others.[14] This way, Romans, for example, which

---

primary christological emphases if one does not keep them solidly within Israel's (and thus Paul's) basic narrative.

[12] L. E. Keck, "Toward the Renewal of New Testament Christology," *NTS* 32 (1986): 370.

[13] As another help, in the Scripture index I have put references in bold to indicate where they are actually discussed in some measure, as over against where they are merely referenced.

[14] Related to this is the inherent difficulty that one finds in those who have written chapters on the "real" Paul and the "deuterocanonical" Paul (e.g., Matera, *New Testament Christology;* cf. C. Tuckett, *Christology and the New Testament: Jesus and His Earliest Followers* [Louisville: Westminster John Knox, 2001]). The alleged differences are the result *only* of the arbitrary choice regarding authorship. The point is that if one began, e.g., with the view that Paul did not write Philippians, then one could easily show how "un-Pauline" its Christology is in relation to the others, and this would generally be true of all the letters. This whole scenario becomes highly suspect when Tuckett, e.g., can exclude from Pauline Christology things of actual Pauline authorship under the guise that the Christology (of, e.g., 1 Thess 1:10 or Rom 1:3–4) is really that of Paul's source and perhaps not fully assimilated into Paul's own sentence (*Christology,* 49–50). See further n. 16 below.

is somewhat idiosyncratic at this point,[15] does not set the agenda for what one is to find in the other letters.[16]

Second, and especially important exegetically, by analyzing the Christology of the letters as they come to us, assumably "written" by a colleague at Paul's dictation,[17] we thereby also affirm that the alleged "hymns" in Col 1:15–20 and Phil 2:6–11; 3:20–21 are "Pauline" in both senses of the word—the *canonical* Paul, who is the only Paul available to us, and the *historical* Paul in these cases. After all, when someone incorporates previous language into their own text without acknowledgment, they are thereby de facto taking ownership of what is said, whatever "meaning" it may be supposed to have had in an "original" source.

Third, by approaching the letters in an assumed chronological order,[18] I have also kept my eyes open to the possibilities of "development." On this latter question, there seemed to be nothing that could be legitimately so categorized. Indeed, to my own surprise, that was not even true between the church corpus (the ten letters, including Philemon, written to churches) and the three letters to Timothy and Titus.[19]

---

[15] See ch. 6. By "idiosyncratic" I do not mean "different from" in terms of substance; rather, the very nature of the argument puts different emphases forward. For example, (1) totally out of sync with the rest of the corpus, God is mentioned one and a half times more often than Christ (see the chart on p. 26); (2) of the 96 specific references to Christ, the title κύριος ("Lord") appears comparatively fewer times than in all the rest of the corpus except for Galatians; (3) 7 of the 17 references to "the Son" occur in Romans (while Romans and Galatians together have 11 of the 17).

[16] At some point NT scholarship needs to take ownership of the circularity of some of its reasoning. One commonly encounters statements such as "The use of the term [Son of God] in Paul's writings is slightly complicated by the fact that the phrase seems to have been current in the pre-Pauline tradition as well, and Paul's use of the term may represent a slight modification of this pre-Pauline usage" (Tuckett, *Christology*, 49) (in this case having bought into Käsemann's highly suspect argument regarding Rom 1:3–4 [see pp. 240–44 below]). What is done here is that we (1) determine that the language is not like the Paul whom we have reconstructed, and thus is pre-Pauline; then (2) take the pre-Pauline "statement"—which is available to us *only* in a Pauline sentence—and use it in *contrast* to the real Paul; and then (3) argue that Paul has *modified* this pre-Pauline material for his own purposes. We are an amazing lot, to be sure.

[17] See, e.g., Tertius's own "signature" at the end of Romans, where he designates himself as "the writer of this letter" (16:22), and Paul's signing off Galatians with "large letters in his own hand" (6:11); cf. 2 Thess 3:17; 1 Cor 16:21; Col 4:18; Phlm 19.

[18] At issue are two matters: whether Galatians is Paul's first letter or was written much closer to the time of Romans; and whether Philippians was written near the time of Romans or from the same imprisonment as Colossians. I have taken quite traditional stances on both of these matters, in both cases because the internal data of the letters have pushed me there. Thus the order of discussion is 1 and 2 Thessalonians, 1 and 2 Corinthians, Galatians, Romans, Colossians/Philemon, Ephesians, Philippians, 1 Timothy, Titus, 2 Timothy.

[19] This is even more remarkable when one considers that historical "logic" should demand that at least christologically this would be so; yet even the most avid proponents of pseudepigraphy recognize the opposite to be the case and thus

Pauline Christology: The Theological Difficulty

Besides the difficulties of exegesis and coherence just noted, when turning to the *theological* dimension of Pauline Christology, one is faced with two contingencies that make a resolution very difficult indeed.

First, whatever else is true about Paul (whichever "Paul" one is looking at), he was an avid monotheist. On this point he is unyielding, since this was one of the primary "sticking points" between Jew and Gentile in the Jewish Diaspora, in which he had been born and raised. And it would have been all the more so for him as a trained Pharisee. Thus the Shema, "Hear, Israel; Yahweh your God, Yahweh is one" (Deut 6:4),[20] probably recited regularly in Sabbath and home, would have been the very first distinguishing mark of the Jew in the Diaspora. For them it would have meant simultaneously that Yahweh himself is a single God, not a multiplicity of "gods," and that he alone is God; there are no others.

Second, as already noted, the primary focus in all the Pauline Letters is on *salvation in Christ,* including Spirit-empowered ethical life as the genuine outworking of such salvation. But in the process, Paul regularly speaks of Christ in ways that indicate that "the Son of God" is also included in the divine identity. Before being sent by the Father to be born of a Jewish woman (Gal 4:4–5), he was himself in "μορφὴ θεοῦ [*the 'form' of God*]," having an equality with God that he did not exploit; rather, he chose to share our humanity (Phil 2:6–7). But this conviction, expressed in very presuppositional ways as the common belief of Paul and his churches, puts considerable tension on the first conviction: that there is only *one* God. [21]

_____

argue circuitously on this issue. See the bibliography and critique in P. H. Towner, "Christology in the Letters to Timothy and Titus," in Longenecker, *Contours of Christology,* 219–21.

[20] This "translation" is arbitrary on my part, since at this point I have chosen to follow the (apparent) "interpretation" in the Septuagint. For the options, see the text and footnote in the NRSV.

[21] This tension lies behind every form of "adoptionism," from the Ebionite, through Arius, to New England Unitarianism and German liberalism, to *Christology in the Making* by J. D. G. Dunn, who candidly acknowledges that "the too quick resort to the 'obvious' or 'plain' meaning [of Paul's texts] actually becomes in some cases a resort to a form of bitheism or tritheism," and "if we take texts like Col. 1.15ff. as straightforward descriptions of the Jesus who came from Nazareth we are committed to an interpretation of that text which has broken clearly and irrevocably from monotheism" (*Christology in the Making: A New Testament Inquiry into the Origins of the Doctrine of the Incarnation* [2d ed.; Grand Rapids: Eerdmans, 1989], xxxii). So at issue for Dunn is that either Paul or we who interpret Paul in more traditional ways have given up monotheism. Dunn's apparent concern is to protect Paul, who is otherwise something of a theological hero for him, from that theological "error." But is that not to do theology in reverse? If Paul in fact asserts Christ's deity, while maintaining his rigid monotheism, as the evidence itself indicates that he has done, then our task is to ask a different theological question: "How could Paul do so within his

Thus these combined realities—Paul's historic monotheism and what he says about Christ in both intentional and incidental ways—create the tensions for us on this side of Nicea and Chalcedon. On the one hand, what Paul often says about Christ should fill a monotheist with anxiety, or even horror; indeed, along with the Johannine corpus and Hebrews, Paul's letters became a primary source for the Nicene "settlements" about God as triune (Nicea) and Christ as one person with two natures (Chalcedon). On the other hand, the questions with which these later councils wrestled were simply not addressed by our NT authors, including Paul. Rather, they provide the "stuff" for the later theological resolutions. Or to put it another way, what Paul the monotheist says about Christ as Son of God and Lord is what causes any of us to raise the issue of Pauline Christology.

But the even greater difficulty for us is the one already mentioned: the attempt to extract Christology from Paul's letters apart from soteriology is like asking a devout Jew of Paul's era to talk about God in the abstract, without mentioning his mighty deeds of creation and redemption. Although one theoretically may theologize on the character and "person" of God on the basis of the revelation to Moses on Sinai (Exod 34:6–8), a Jewish person of Paul's era would hardly imagine doing so. What can be known and said about God is embedded in the story in such a way that God's person can never be abstracted out of the story. Whatever else, God is always "the God of Abraham, and of Isaac, and of Jacob."

So it is with Paul, who brings this dimension of his Jewishness to his reflections on Christ in a thoroughgoing way. However one finally understands the (purposely?) ambiguous statement in 2 Cor 5:21, it stands as a kind of centerpiece of how Paul thought about the Father and the Son. Was it "God *was in Christ* reconciling the world to himself"? or was it "God *in Christ was* reconciling the world to himself"? At the end of the day, both are true of Paul's understanding. Everything that God has done for us human beings and our salvation has been done in Christ. And precisely because God was doing it *in Christ*, it would have been quite out of character for Paul to think of God and Christ in totally separate categories. Whatever else is true of Paul, his worldview is now utterly christocentric. The risen Christ, who confronted him on the way to Damascus, by Paul's own confession, had "taken hold of me" (Phil 3:12), and had done so in such a way that Paul had gladly suffered the loss of all things for the surpassing worth of "*knowing* Christ Jesus *my* Lord" (Phil 3:8). Thus his life motto: "To live is Christ; to die is gain" (Phil 1:21).

So thoroughgoing is Paul's christocentric worldview that he can hardly talk about God without also mentioning Christ. Even in 1 Corinthians, the

---

own Jewish worldview?" This is what the church historically has tried to do. But rather than revise what the church has done, Dunn chooses to revise what Paul has said. In so doing, he stands in strong contrast to nineteenth-century liberalism. For the latter, Paul was the christological "bad guy"; for Dunn, that charge should be leveled against the authors of Hebrews and John's Gospel.

letter that might be considered most given over to the correction of behavioral aberrations, he starts with "Paul, called to be an apostle *of Christ Jesus by the will of God*" (1:1). This picks up again immediately in the address proper: "To the church of God, *sanctified in Christ Jesus*, which is in Corinth" (1:2),[22] to which he adds, "called to be saints together with all those everywhere who *call on the name of our Lord Jesus Christ*," a phrase taken directly out of the Greek Bible (Joel 3:5 LXX) and applied specifically to Christ. And the salutation proper (1:3), as in all of his letters from this point forward, is "grace to you and peace, from God our Father and *the Lord Jesus Christ*," with one preposition holding both nouns together. And how does the letter end? "If anyone does not love *the Lord*, let that person be Anathema. *Marana tha* (Come, *Lord*). The *grace of our Lord Jesus* be with you" (16:22–23).

Thus, even a casual reading of Paul's letters reveals how christocentric his basically theocentric worldview has become. God the Father is always the "first cause" of everything and thus always appears in the primary position as the "prime mover"; nonetheless, the focus of Paul's life is on Christ himself.

All of that is to say that the term "Christology" in this book expresses a very focused theological concern. First, the issues of Chalcedon are simply not raised at all, since the question of the "two natures" arises only after one is convinced that the proper resolution of the biblical data about the "one God" and the "Three Divine Persons" has been resolved in a Trinitarian way. Second, the actual Trinitarian questions (about the One and the Three as one God) are not raised either, since that too lies beyond Paul's expressed concerns. At issue in this book is the singular concern to investigate the Pauline data regarding the person of Christ in terms of whom Paul understood him to be and how he viewed the relationship between Christ, as the Son of God and Lord, and the one God, as the Father of our Lord Jesus Christ, who is therefore now revealed as our Father as well.

Since these questions are often put in terms of a "high" or a "low" Christology, I need here to speak to that issue as well. Although this might be considered an oversimplification, the ultimate issue has to do with the Son's preexistence; that is, does an author consider Christ to have had existence as (or with) God before coming into our history for the purposes of redemption, which included at the end his resurrection and subsequent exaltation to "the right hand of God" in "fulfillment" of Ps 110:1? If the answer to that question is yes, then one speaks of an author (e.g., the Gospel of John, the author of Hebrews) as having a high Christology. If the answer is either no or ambiguous at best, then the author (e.g., James) is credited with a low Christology. The ultimate question of Pauline Christology, therefore, is where Paul fits on this spectrum; and my conviction after a careful analysis of all the

_____

[22]See the discussion of this passage on p. 127 n. 107 below, for the argument that this is Paul's original word order.

texts is that he fits at the high end, along with John and the author of Hebrews.[23]

The ultimate purpose of this study, therefore, is twofold. The first concern is to offer a close examination of the texts in the Pauline corpus that mention Christ, and especially to offer a careful but focused exegesis of those texts deemed to have or, in some cases, not to have christological significance. Here the evidence seems conclusive that Paul belongs on the "high Christology" end of the NT spectrum. The second part of the study will then offer a *thematic* analysis of these data with the ultimate goal of determining how we might best speak *theologically* about Paul's Christology in its first-century setting.

Pauline Christology in the Twentieth Century

One of the historical questions that needs an attempted answer is why in the history of NT scholarship *only one* study, Werner Kramer's *Christ, Lord, Son of God*, can legitimately be called a "Pauline Christology."[24] And Kramer's study is less interested in Paul per se than in Paul's role in the "development" of early Christology. Using Paul as his beginning point, Kramer devotes over half his study to digging out of Paul's letters what might be assumed to be "pre-Pauline Christology." He then devotes the rest to how Paul handles the pre-Pauline material—which is available only in Paul in any case! So even though Kramer deals with Paul in a significant way, what drives the study from beginning to end is the question that dominated most of the twentieth century, namely, that of "origins": where did Paul come by his Christology? And that question inevitably carries with it the primary issue of "high" or "low" with regard to that Christology.

---

[23] At the same time, one must admit that not only do the texts drive one to that conclusion but also the very notion of a "low Christology" seems to contain an inherent contradiction. Note, e.g., J. B. Reid: "A Christ who is merely equated with another human being, however great, be he 'John the Baptist, or Elijah, or Jeremiah, or one of the other prophets' (Mt 16:14), is not enough" (*Jesus, God's Emptiness, God's Fullness: The Christology of St. Paul* [New York: Paulist Press, 1990], 68). Reid then cites Donald Baillie: "A toned down Christology is absurd. It must be all or nothing—all or nothing on both the divine and human side. That is the very extreme of paradox" (from *God Was in Christ: An Essay on Incarnation and Atonement* [London: Faber & Faber, 1961], 132). After all, within the framework of true monotheism a developmental scheme would seem to be a logical impossibility. Either Christ was divine or he was not; and if divine, then of necessity he must be included in the divine identity. A *tertium quid* simply cannot be considered truly divine in any true sense of "deity" within the framework of monotheism.

[24] My emphasis on "legitimately" here is based on my definition of Christology as having to do with the person, not the work, of Christ. Thus the one other "Pauline Christology" of the century, Lucien Cerfaux's *Christ in the Theology of St. Paul* (trans. G. Webb and A. Walker; New York: Herder & Herder, 1959), covers the whole gamut of Christology and soteriology, with more emphasis on the latter than the former.

Thus the answer to the "why" question raised above does not seem terribly difficult to come by. Historically, the issue had been altogether a canonical one—the Christology of the NT—to which debate Paul's letters offered several key texts, especially Phil 2:6–11 and Col 1:15–17. Thus Paul was simply a part of the larger scene as the church wrestled with the data presented in its primary documents: how to reconcile Christ's humanity with the deity that also emerges in the texts. And "orthodoxy" did so by rejecting "adoptionism" on the one hand (a nonpreexistent Christ given "divine status" at his exaltation) and Arianism on the other (a preexistent Christ, who was not eternally so).

But with the Enlightenment all of that changed. What for centuries had been assumed because of the role of Scripture in the church was now being rejected within the framework of a historicism that was overlaid with antisupernaturalism. The "deity" of Christ could only have been the invention of the early church; and Paul was the leading culprit. Thus a line of inquiry developed that ran from Schleiermacher to Harnack and beyond, exemplified by a rejection of historic orthodoxy accompanied by a series of attempts on the part of some to find the "real Jesus" behind the "supernatural overlay," a Jesus that "modern man" could follow and try to emulate. With this a new kind of "historicism" arose that sought for "origins," since the biblical picture, with its inherent supernaturalism, could not be "true" as historical data.

This basically accounts for no Pauline Christology as such. A high Christology was simply assumed as a part of the biblical record; so at issue historically was how Paul, and the early church with him, came by this divinization of the merely human Jesus of Nazareth. Thus in all of this there was a standard basic assumption that Paul was one of the villains, if not *the* villain, who turned the historical Jesus into a divine being that had little or no relationship to the Jesus of history.

But much of that changed with the appearance of Wilhelm Bousset's *Kyrios Christos* in 1913, a work that heavily influenced a considerable sector of NT scholarship through much of the first half of the century and that picked up steam again when the English translation appeared in 1970. Bousset's own presuppositions are several and obvious. He held to the (common) view that only seven of Paul's epistles are genuine, so Pauline Christology means specifically that which comes to us through these seven letters. Philosophically, he was wedded to rationalism, with its concomitant historicism and thus antisupernaturalism. At the same time, he held a rather strictly Hegelian developmental scheme of history that saw early Christianity as emerging from Judaism but quickly influenced by Hellenism (certain sectors of Judaism itself already being influenced by Hellenism). And above all, Bousset was a thoroughgoing advocate of a *religionsgeschichtlich* ("history of religions") view of early Christian history.

Thus, for Bousset, Paul's Christology is best understood in light of Hellenistic influences, quite divorced from the Jewish synagogue in which he had been raised, which had no place in it in any case for a truly divine Christ. Paul is thus understood to have received his view of Christ as κύριος from the Hellenistic believers in Antioch, who had adopted it from their pagan background in the mysteries. At the end of his chapter on Paul (pp. 153–210), after surveying all of his allowable data, Bousset asserts, "In the Pauline communities the veneration of the Kyrios stands alongside the veneration of God in an unresolved actuality," but then adds, "After all this one may not actually speak of a deity of Christ in the view of Paul."[25] And with that a considerable shift took place with regard to Pauline Christology.

The influence of Bousset's study has been massive, receiving a midcentury boost from Rudolf Bultmann, who wrote a preface to the fifth edition that was translated into English. And although the pendulum has swung considerably in recent years, Bousset's search for "origins" thoroughly dominated the century, both implicitly and, frequently, explicitly.[26] But at the same time, his own conclusions made it clear that the long-assumed high Christology in Paul's writings could no longer be simply assumed.

The first major response to Bousset came after World War II in the form of Oscar Cullmann's *The Christology of the New Testament* (1957; ET, 1959),[27] which was in fact the first major NT Christology after Bousset's; and though Bousset obviously had set the agenda for the historical inquiry, Cullmann set the agenda of the subsequently dominating tendency to do Christology by way of titles. He begins with titles that speak of Christ's earthly work (Prophet, Suffering Servant, High Priest—none of which is Pauline) and

---

[25] W. Bousset, *Kyrios Christos: A History of the Belief in Christ from the Beginnings of Christianity to Irenaeus* (trans. J. E. Steely; Nashville: Abingdon, 1970), 209 n. 150, 210.

[26] All one need do is to observe many of the titles, beginning with F. Hahn, *The Titles of Jesus in Christology: Their History in Early Christianity* (trans. H. Knight and G. Ogg; London: Lutterworth, 1969); see I. H. Marshall, *The Origins of New Testament Christology* (Issues in Contemporary Theology; Downers Grove, Ill.: InterVarsity Press, 1976).

[27] Cullmann's book appeared in Switzerland at roughly the same time as Vincent Taylor's much more popular *The Person of Christ in New Testament Teaching* (1958) appeared in the United Kingdom. Taylor's book served as an excellent overview for many but lacks sufficient supporting evidence or interaction with the larger scene of NT studies to merit discussion here. Also excluded is F. Hahn's *Christologische Hoheitstitel: Ihre Geschichte im frühen Christentum* (1963; ET, *The Titles of Jesus in Christology: Their History in Early Christianity* [1969]), which focused on the Synoptic Gospels, thus showing little interest in Paul. In many ways Hahn's work marked the end of an era, since he pressed to an extreme the scheme of historical "layers" that marked much of twentieth-century German scholarship (Palestinian Jewish community; the Hellenistic Jewish community; and the Hellenistic community as such) but which by the end of the century had been generally discredited, especially by various studies by I. H. Marshall and Martin Hengel. So also with R. Fuller's *The Foundations of New Testament Christology* (1965), since even more than Kramer, who showed considerable interest in what Paul did with the "foundations," Fuller is interested only in the historical and cultural foundations on which the NT writers built.

then moves on to where Bousset began, dealing with Christ's future work (Messiah, Son of Man [eschatological figure]); here he also discusses Paul's Adam Christology (as the heavenly man). It is in the third and fourth sections that Cullmann deals with Pauline Christology: Christ's "present work" as Lord and Savior (section 3) and titles that refer to Christ's preexistence (Logos, Son of God). But for all that, Cullmann's main emphasis is that NT Christology focuses on "function," not "being," which is true, of course; but at some point one must wrestle with the "being" that underlies the function.

The next major player (after Kramer) to emerge on the twentieth-century scene was Martin Hengel, whose first interest was the dissolution of the "developmental" scheme of the *religionsgeschichtliche Schule*, which had become pervasive in much of German and American scholarship by way of the influence of Bousset and Bultmann. This was the basic concern of his massive study *Judaism and Hellenism*, indicated by the subtitle, *Studies in Their Encounter in Palestine during the Early Hellenistic Period*. When Hengel turned to Christology itself, he produced two works that are significant for our purposes. The first was *The Son of God* (1975; ET, 1976), where, with another frontal attack on the History of Religions school, he demonstrated how early and "high" this language was; and, of course, here Paul becomes the key player, not as the "inventor" but as one who carried on a very early tradition. Hengel's *Studies in Early Christology* (1995), which included some previously published papers, was composed mostly of lectures. Here in particular he demonstrated the significant role of Ps 110 in early Christology; however, he also argued for Jesus himself as the originator of Wisdom Christology. On this latter question his influence has been especially significant, even though the idea had been around since the beginning of the century.[28]

The next significant work involving Pauline Christology was James D. G. Dunn's *Christology in the Making* (1980), a book that is very important but in some ways disappointing.[29] With an especially adept ability both to analyze texts and to think outside the box, as it were, Dunn basically returned to an earlier era in two ways. First, the major thrust of the book was a return to the developmental scheme, but in this case built not on the prior philosophical agendas but rather on a careful analysis of the biblical texts. In this scheme Paul is the "halfway house" between an early low Christology and the full-blown high Christology of John and Hebrews. Second, in order to make this work, he set out to demonstrate that in Paul's thought there is no concept of a genuine preexistence of Christ himself; the texts that seem to say as much are either to be understood differently or, in the case of Col 1:15–17, to be understood as having to do with the preexistent Wisdom, with

[28] For a critique of this christological bypath, see appendix A in the present volume, pp. 594–619.

[29] A second edition appeared in 1989, published in the United States by Eerdmans, in which Dunn responded to his critics in a twenty-four-page foreword, while the substance of the first edition remained unchanged.

whom Paul identifies the nonpreexistent Christ. This leads him to argue for a form of adoptionism, but without using that language.[30]

That was followed the next year by Seyoon Kim's *The Origin of Paul's Gospel* (1981), the main thesis of which stood as the total antithesis to that of Dunn. Kim argued that the crucial matters of Paul's (very high) Christology and soteriology all stem from his encounter with Christ on the Damascus Road. Although this was quite overstated,[31] it offered a welcome corrective regarding a matter that by and large had been overlooked in Pauline studies: Paul's own conversion experience. Working especially from those passages that suggest "revelation" (e.g., 2 Cor 4:4–6), Kim first examines "Christ, Lord, Son of God" and then offers over 130 pages on the εἰκὼν τοῦ θεοῦ (*image of God*). At the heart of things, he argues for Paul's prior acquaintance with personified Wisdom as the key to his Christology, thus carrying Hengel's assertions forward with vigor.[32]

The most significant steps forward in work that impinges on Pauline Christology have been taken in the past decade by Richard Bauckham and Larry Hurtado, both of whose studies portend a new development in NT Christology in general and in Pauline Christology in particular. Bauckham's *God Crucified: Monotheism and Christology in the New Testament* (1998) represents some published lectures given in anticipation of a much larger study to be entitled *Jesus and the Identity of God.* Writing particularly in response to the many recent studies by Hengel, Kim, Dunn, and others, who see a divine mediatorial figure in Second Temple Judaism as the way forward (Hengel) or backward (Dunn), Bauckham argues that these studies are working backwards by using a small amount of questionable data to the exclusion of the

---

[30] To get there, Dunn also had to resort to several instances of circuitous exegesis of a kind that leaves one wondering how the first readers could possibly have understood Paul without Dunn's help. For an exegetical critique of his handling of the crucial passages, see in the present volume the excursuses in chs. 3 (pp. 102–5), 7 (pp. 317–25), and 9 (pp. 390–93), plus appendix A at the end.

[31] Indeed, when Kim revisits this question in ch. 5 of *Paul and the New Perspective: Second Thoughts on the Origin of Paul's Gospel* (Grand Rapids: Eerdmans, 2002), 165–213, not only does he not back off, but also he reasserts all of his questionable positions even more strongly. So, e.g., he continues to insist that "in the Wisdom of Solomon . . . the personified Wisdom . . . [is] spoken of as the εἰκών of God," which is patently untrue, as the exegesis in ch. 7 and appendix A in the present volume demonstrate (pp. 323–25; 594–619).

[32] Both of these books (Dunn's and Kim's), it should be noted, independently went after this subject with the issue of "origins" as their first concern (obvious in Kim's title; for Dunn, see p. 5: "The questions can be posed thus: *How did the doctrine of the incarnation originate?*"). One is led to think that the two of them arrived at such radically different conclusions in part because they were both driven by this issue, and they set out to prove their own positions from the texts rather than letting the chips fall where they may by a much more straightforward exegesis of the Pauline texts themselves. This becomes especially noticeable with Dunn in his commentary on Colossians, where he spends much of his time trying to demonstrate a Pauline position that is not explicitly in the text itself—and from my perspective, not implicitly either.

large amount of certain data. Instead, he argues, one should begin not with these figures but with Jewish monotheism as such. Using the language of "identity" instead of "being" (thus adopting a Jewish, rather than Greek, view of the world), Bauckham is concerned with *who* God is rather than *what* God is. In so doing, he points out that two things are absolutely consistent in Second Temple Judaism: it was self-consciously monotheistic, and it was self-consciously monolatrous (exclusive in its worship).

Bauckham's first concern is to demonstrate that Israel's understanding of God was always in terms of God's relationship to Israel and then to all other reality. Thus Yahweh was never thought of in Greek abstractions. His character is always described in terms of relationship to Israel, as in Exod 34:6: a God who is merciful and gracious, slow to anger, and abounding in steadfast love and faithfulness. In terms of God's relation to all other reality, he is constantly referred to as both the Creator of all that is and thus the Ruler of all that is. And precisely at these crucial points Yahweh's character and role are *unshared* with intermediate figures; that is, though they were his *agents*, they never shared his identity as such.

In taking up the issue of Christology per se, Bauckham shows that from the beginning Christ shared the divine identity at all the crucial points: with regard to the divine "Name," in relation to all other things, and in relation to Israel. Finally, he argues that as "God crucified," Christ's identity as God means that God's identity is now wrapped up in the work of Christ on earth.

Larry Hurtado comes out very much at the same place. He has been on a long journey arguing that devotion to Christ can be traced back to the very earliest communities[33] and that it is the kind of devotion that is elsewhere given only to God. In the overview chapter on Paul in his magisterial *Lord Jesus Christ: Devotion to Jesus in Earliest Christianity* (2003), his concern is less with what Paul *believes* than with what Paul's letters reflect about early Christian practices regarding *worship*, especially in their ways of expressing devotion to Jesus.

Even before Bauckham, Hurtado has long argued that Paul is an avid monotheist. Yet totally without precedent in the Judaism of which he is a product, Paul ascribes various forms of worship and devotion to Christ that would seem to put considerable tension on that monotheism. On the other hand, neither Paul nor his communities seem to be aware of the tension, in the sense that Paul, at least, never once speaks to it. Indeed, in Colossians, the one letter where he speaks to such issues at all, he is intent on maintaining a very high role for Christ against those who (apparently) would subordinate him to a lesser role vis-à-vis "the powers."

In many ways the present study hopes to follow in the train of these last two scholars, in this case by putting most of the emphasis on the exegesis of all the significant texts, while at the end pointing out the christological implications of the exegesis.

---

[33] See the various Hurtado entries in the bibliography, pp. 656–57.

Pauline Christology: Some Basic Matters

Before turning to the Pauline texts themselves, I need here to address some basic exegetical matters and, for the sake of the reader, to anticipate the primary conclusions to which the exegetical chapters have led. I begin with the latter.

Whither Pauline Christology?

At the end of the exegetical process it became clear to me that even though the cumulative evidence tells the story in full, there are, by anyone's reckoning, three key texts that put forward most of the issues: 1 Cor 8:6; Col 1:15–17; Phil 2:6–11. Here I isolate the primary christological data that emerge in these three passages, which are spelled out or assumed in all the rest of the data. In the section that follows this one I address the issue that surfaces in full measure in the earliest of the letters: Paul's application to Christ of the κύριος = *Adonai* = Yahweh of the Septuagint and whether Paul did indeed find this in the Greek Bible he knew.

1 Corinthians 8:6

The significance of this passage for the analysis of Pauline Christology is universally recognized, but not all are agreed on the nature of that significance. The conclusions drawn from the exegesis of this passage in ch. 3 (pp. 89–94) can be briefly summarized, since they set the pace for so much else in the letters that follow.

1. What turn out to be the two most significant features of Pauline Christology are already in place in this passage: Christ as Son of God and as Lord. The latter of these is explicit in the passage itself ("there is one κύριος, Jesus Christ"); the former is implied in the preceding "there is one θεός, the Father," where all the evidence of the letters indicates that by this usage Paul begins not with God as *our* Father but with the fact that God has been revealed as "the Father of our Lord Jesus Christ,"[34] which leads to his being our Father through Christ and the Spirit.

2. As the exegesis of all the crucial passages demonstrates, these basic distinctions, already in place in the Thessalonian correspondence, are maintained in an exclusive way throughout the entire corpus.[35] At issue here are two matters: (1) some instances where κύριος has been suggested

---

[34] For the evidence of this, see the discussions of 2 Cor 1:3 and Gal 4:4–7 (pp. 169–71, 217–20).

[35] The only exceptions are the twelve passages where Paul is citing the Septuagint and no point is made of the referent; so one may assume that Paul is simply carrying over the reference to Yahweh = God from his source. For the twelve passages, see n. 7 in ch. 3 (p. 87).

to refer to God the Father;[36] and (2) the two instances[37] where many have argued that Paul's use of θεός refers to Christ: Rom 9:5 and Titus 2:13. Because of the significance of these latter two passages, they receive extended discussion in their respective chapters (pp. 272–77, 440–46). In both cases, when one pares off all the modifiers to get to the basic noun itself, the evidence seems strongly in favor of consistency: θεός in each case refers to God the Father.

3. Along with the considerable earlier evidence in 1 and 2 Thessalonians (see ch. 2), this passage offers a classic example of Paul's use of the Septuagint's κύριος = *Adonai* = Yahweh as a reference to Christ as the "Lord" of these OT passages. For here the fundamental theological reality from Paul's Judaism, the Shema, has been divided up so to embrace the Son along with the Father.

4. This is the first passage in the corpus where Paul asserts, as something assumed between him and his readers, that Christ was both preexistent and the mediatorial agent of creation. This assumption of preexistence is expressed in a variety of ways hereafter in the corpus.

5. Despite what is plainly stated by Paul, this passage has also been the place of first and last resort with regard to finding a "Wisdom Christology" in his writings. To get there, one must argue (1) that Paul will expect his readers to read Wisdom into this sentence on the basis of what he had said back in 1:24, 30 about the *crucified Messiah* as God's "wisdom," and thus (2) that ὁ κύριος as agent of creation is here in fact to be identified with *personified* Wisdom, and (3) that in the Wisdom literature itself personified Wisdom is regularly seen as the *agent of creation*. Both the exegesis of these three passages in 1 Corinthians[38] and the lack of any kind of *verbal* correspondence between the Wisdom literature and these passages[39] should ring the death knell for this point of view.

Colossians 1:13–17

The fact that I include vv. 13 and 14 in this discussion says a lot about the significance of this passage for Pauline Christology. There are three matters of significance here.

1. This is the first of the two major christological passages in the corpus.[40] Here Paul has picked up the language he had used of Christ in

---

[36] See, e.g., discussion on 2 Thess 2:13; 3:3, 5 (pp. 64–65, 65–66, 71–72).

[37] A few would add a third from 2 Thess 1:12 (see n. 92 on p. 62).

[38] See pp. 100–102, 106–7, 89–94, and esp. the excursus on this matter on pp. 102–6. For a full discussion of this matter, see appendix A (pp. 594–619).

[39] Esp. the lack of a single instance of the crucial preposition διά (*through*), which here and elsewhere implies mediatorial agency.

[40] At least this is true for those who take seriously its relationship to Philemon; for the inherent difficulties and lack of genuine supporting evidence for denying Pauline authorship, see n. 2 in ch. 7 (p. 289).

1 Cor 8:6 and spelled it out in some detail. This means that many scholars are ready to find personified Wisdom in this passage as well, although as with 1 Cor 8:6, and despite assertions to the contrary, there is not a single genuine verbal correspondence between this passage and the Wisdom literature.[41]

2. This is also the first instance where scholarship has invested enormous capital trying to demonstrate that Paul is here citing a "hymn" that had prior existence in the church. While one must remain open to this likely possibility, the same does not hold true of what is sometimes alleged on the basis of this assumption, namely, that Paul is not in full agreement with what he cites. That is, it is frequently suggested that Paul has not fully assimilated the "citation" into his argument, so that one must be careful in using it to discover Paul's own Christology. But besides the fact that this assertion appears to have little merit on its own right—after all, the alleged "original" is the product of our own making—one should always begin with the assumption that a first-century author "cites" precisely because he is in agreement with what he incorporates from another source into his own sentences.

This is all the more the case with Paul, since we have a clear analogy in his use of the Greek Bible, from which he both cites and borrows on a regular basis. And when he "borrows" from the Greek OT, as he would presumably have "borrowed" from a "hymn" in this case,[42] he regularly makes the language his own, and means what *he* intends, not necessarily in the same way the original author intended. In fact, this is precisely what happens in his very first "citations" of the Greek Bible in the corpus (1 Cor 1:31; 2:16), where Paul has considerably "rewritten" the passages with his own concerns in view. The point is that one may be sure in the case of this Colossians passage that the sentence in its entirety is now from Paul[43] and has Pauline intent in all its parts, whatever its origin.

3. Besides the points already made above from 1 Cor 8:6, which Paul is here expanding in greater detail, my reason for including vv. 13 and 14 in the discussion is that the grammatical antecedent of all the (some eighteen) instances of the relative and personal pronouns in vv. 15–20 is "the Son of the Father's love" in v. 13, into whose "kingdom" the Colossian Gentiles have now been included. Thus in this crucial christological passage, where neither Κύριος nor Χριστός appears, the theme of Son of God does appear, and inherent to this usage is the Jewish messianism expressed in v. 13. Thus besides spelling out in greater detail what is said in couched form in 1 Cor 8:6, Paul quite matter-of-factly puts that Christology in the context of his Son of God Christology as well.

---

[41] On this matter, see the excursus on pp. 317–25 in ch. 7.

[42] The point is that Paul regularly "cites" the Greek Bible and indicates as much by his "it is written" formula.

[43] This assumes, of course, with Dunn, Wright, and many others, that Paul is the author of Colossians; see n. 2 in ch. 7 (p. 289).

Philippians 2:6–11

This "acropolis" of the christological passages in the Pauline corpus has also had a long history of discussion as to whether Paul is adapting a previously existing "hymn." And as with the alleged Colossians "hymn," one can neither prove nor disprove the assertion, nor can one assume that some of this is not really Paul's own point of view.[44] Its significance for our present purposes is that besides also asserting Christ's preexistence, now in even stronger language regarding his actual deity, Paul also asserts Christ's "*equality* with God the Father." Along with some points made from the two preceding texts, there are three further matters that need to be noted from this passage.

1. This is the primary passage in Paul's writings that will not allow one to assert Christ's divinity without taking seriously the full *humanity* of his incarnation. This is repeated often enough in the passage to fly full in the face of any attempt to try to work out Paul's Christology in Apollonarian terms. Fully God though he was asserted to be in v. 6, what he became when he "poured himself out" in order to redeem us was one who was equally fully human.

2. This emphasis, plus the possible "conceptual echo"[45] of Gen 1 in Christ's not considering his equality with God as something to be held onto selfishly, has caused a significant group of NT scholars to find an Adam Christology here as well. And although there are no good reasons to deny this somewhat distant "conceptual echo," there is every good reason to be wary when one watches some scholars push this analogy to extremes that the passage itself will not sustain.[46]

3. Finally, and back to the first point made regarding 1 Cor 8:6, here in particular Paul significantly spells out both the reason for, and the origins of,

---

[44] One can only sit in amazement at the frequency with which it is asserted that the passage in its present form does not reflect Pauline Christology as much as it does that of the "pre-Pauline hymn" that Paul is "citing." This is all the more puzzling when one notes exegetically that the *reason* for the narrative is to offer a paradigm (in vv. 6–8) for the Philippians to emulate (v. 5).

[45] This is my own language for the possibility of "hearing" an echo of Genesis in this passage, since there is not a single *verbal* echo. Those who try to create such by arguing that μορφή and εἰκών are verbal "equivalents" not only are in error on that score (see pp. 377–79) but also seem to be out of step with reality. Only the language itself could call forth a verbal echo. One may as well argue that "eighty-seven years ago" would cause someone to think of Lincoln's Gettysburg Address (which begins with "four score and seven years ago"). First, no one would ever think of echoing Lincoln without Lincoln's own archaic language; and second, the only reason for using Lincoln's words at all would be for the effect that those words alone would create. So also with Paul's "failure" to use εἰκών here if he intended his readers to catch an echo of Gen 1.

[46] On this matter, see the discussion on pp. 375–76, and esp. the excursus (pp. 390–93). For the broader discussion of the matters noted in this paragraph, see ch. 13 (pp. 513–29).

the risen and exalted Christ's having been given the "Name" Κύριος. This is further elaborated as "the Name above all names" and then substantiated by applying what is said of Yahweh in Isa 45:23 to the risen Lord. Thus this depiction of how the exalted Christ was given the "Name" explains how he had had transferred to him the exclusive use of this expression of the divine "Name," which had come to the Greek-speaking church by way of the Greek Bible and emerges in a thoroughly presuppositional way in Paul's earliest preserved letters. And this in turn, though appearing later in the corpus, is the certain evidence for Paul's exclusive use of this "Name" to refer to Christ and not to God the Father.

So although there are many more moments of significant Christology in Paul's writings and, as the following chapters will demonstrate in full measure, very much assumed Christology everywhere, these three primary christological texts have embedded in them all the key elements of that Christology. These are developed in the second part of this book, "Synthesis."

Paul and the Septuagint

There are some readers, however, who will (rightfully) wince at the confidence with which I have spoken of Paul's referring to Jesus as the κύριος = *Adonai* = Yahweh of the Septuagint. So I need to address this matter. At issue are two questions. First, did Paul know and use a form of the Greek Bible known to us on the basis of basically Christian manuscripts that come from nearly three centuries after Paul wrote his letters? Second, whatever form of the Greek Bible that he and they had in common, would his readers have caught both the fact and the significance of his so often applying to Christ the κύριος of these many texts? I take these two matters up in turn.

Did Paul Know and Use the Septuagint?

Although the question of the "origin" of the Septuagint and its relationship to the editions that we currently possess is not easily answered, there are good reasons from the Pauline corpus itself for us to use this term with regard to the Greek Bible that he himself used and that was assumed by him to be a text that he had in common with his Greek-speaking churches. At the least, even if this question cannot be decided with absolute certainty, the evidence that we do have seems strong enough to allow the term "Septuagint" with regard to Pauline usage without constantly offering a learned hesitation. The primary evidence for this is twofold.

First, Paul refers to the Greek Bible in a variety of ways. In some instances he "cites" texts that are verbally identical to the text of the Septuagint known to us. In other cases he "cites" with a degree of freedom, while in still others he echoes the language of the Septuagint with enough precision to give one confidence that it is the ultimate source of his own language.[47] When Paul actually "cites" what he calls "Scripture," even though he does not do so in the thoroughgoing way the author of Hebrews does, his wording is so closely that of the Septuagint that we have basically one of two options. Either he *accidentally* lands on the same wording, including word order, that the translator had used before him (which is doubtful in the extreme), or he *cites* the Bible commonly used in the Diaspora synagogue in which he himself had been raised. There are just enough idiosyncratic moments where Paul and the Septuagint agree against a more precise rendering of the Hebrew text to give us considerable confidence here.[48]

Second, there are enough instances where Paul agrees with the Septuagint's rendering of the Hebrew text in places where the translator had several choices, both with words and word order, to make one think that Paul is citing a common Bible rather than imagine that this happened independently in some way. The analogy would be to try to decide, when a writer in English is citing the Bible without indicating the translation, whether he or she was, for example, using the NASB. The woodenness of that translation would tend to stick out and make dependence obvious. And so it is with Paul's Greek rendering of the OT; his wording, including some unusual renderings, are too often that of the Septuagint to allow one to think that he did not regularly use a form of translation that has come down to us as the Septuagint.

But for some scholars the more crucial matter is Paul's use of Κύριος = *Adonai* = Yahweh: whether, or how much, Paul is indebted to the Septuagint for this use as a primary appellation of Christ, a usage that is so considerable that I have assembled all of the examples in appendix B at the end of this book. This question has arisen especially because of the Septuagint

---

[47] An illustration in point is Paul's use of Joel 2:32 (3:5 LXX) in Rom 10:13: πᾶς γὰρ ὃς ἂν ἐπικαλέσηται τὸ ὄνομα κυρίου σωθήσεται (*For whoever will call on the name of the Lord will be saved*). The γὰρ (*for*) in this instance serves as his "introductory" formula, while the rest is precisely the text of the Septuagint. On the other hand, earlier, in 1 Cor 1:2, he apparently echoes this "biblical" language by referring to fellow believers with the Corinthians as πᾶσιν τοῖς ἐπικαλουμένοις τὸ ὄνομα τοῦ κυρίου ἡμῶν Ἰησοῦ Χριστοῦ (*all who call on the name of the Lord of us, Jesus Christ*). Had we only the latter passage, there would still seem to be no serious question as to the source of Paul's *language*, even if a direct allusion to the Joel prophecy may no longer have been up front in his mind. But the actual citation in context indicates that this Joel passage had become common stock among early Christians regarding their place in the biblical story (see, e.g., Acts 2:21).

[48] This assertion is enough to make any good Septuagintalist squirm. But my concern is not that of the expert in Septuagintal studies; rather, it is to point out that Paul *and* his churches show evidence that a text very much *like* the Septuagint was in use in the Jewish Diaspora in the mid-first century of the Christian era. Moreover, it has been demonstrated by N. Dahl and A. Segal ("Philo and the Rabbis on the Names of God," *JSJ* 9 [1979]: 1–28) that Philo of Alexandria read Greek MSS that used κύριος for the Tetragrammaton at about the same time as Paul did in Asia Minor.

texts that were discovered at Qumran, plus other (extremely fragmentary) evidence from some isolated papyri, since some of these fragments do not have a Greek equivalent at all but simply carry over the Tetragrammaton itself.[49]

It is difficult, however, to see what real difference this makes. For even if our present Septuagint is the product of use among Christians, as it most likely is, the Qumran evidence says very little finally about Pauline usage, since both Qumran and Paul in fact bear witness to the phenomenon of not pronouncing the Divine Name. One can be sure that when these Greek texts with the Tetragrammaton were read in synagogue, the reader did not actually say "Yahweh." Something else would have been substituted for the name, and the evidence of Paul, whether from written or oral sources, is that κύριος was used in its place.[50] Or to put that another way, Paul, along with Hebrews, is evidence of the later "Septuagint" at these places whether or not his Greek texts actually had κύριος in them, since that would most likely have been the regular *oral* substitution for the Divine Name as the common "translation" of the *Adonai* that had been substituted in the Aramaic-speaking synagogue.[51]

Equally important are the scores of "intertextual" uses of κύριος in the Pauline corpus, where the language of the Septuagint has been taken over by Paul so as to become a part of his own sentence. It is one thing to imagine what the public reader of Paul might have done with passages that begin "as it is written," since that assumes a "citation" of the biblical text. How-

---

[49] On this matter, see J. Fitzmyer, "The Semitic Background of the New Testament *Kyrios*-Title," in *A Wandering Aramean: Collected Aramaic Essays* (SBLMS 25; Missoula, Mont.: Scholars Press, 1979), 115–42; and esp. the mild critique by A. Pietersma ("Kyrios or Tetragram: A Renewed Quest for the Original Septuagint," in *De Septuaginta: Studies in Honour of John William Wevers on His Sixty-Fifth Birthday* [ed. A. Pietersma and Claude Cox; Mississauga, Ont.: Benben, 1984], 85–101), whose evaluation of this evidence is noteworthy. Not only does he point out that only one of these pieces of evidence has actual value, but also he suggests (rightly, it would seem) that the use of the Tetragrammaton in Qumran and elsewhere probably reflects an *archaizing* tendency on the part of some to heighten emphasis on the Divine Name lest it be lost altogether through translation of a familiar, but not sacred, word.

[50] In any case, we lack any evidence that in the Greek-speaking synagogues the reader of the Bible in Greek would have substituted Aramaic *Adonai* for the Divine Name.

[51] Cf. the similar judgment by L. J. Kreitzer (*Jesus and God in Paul's Eschatology* [JSNTSup 19; Sheffield: Sheffield Academic Press, 1987], 109): "Indeed, one is tempted to ask what was actually *said* when one came to pronounce יהוה within the public reading of Paul's letters to the churches concerned." Furthermore, as noted above (n. 48), there is sufficient evidence that Paul's older contemporary Philo of Alexandria used a Greek Bible where this substitution had already taken place; see D. B. Capes, *Old Testament Yahweh Texts in Paul's Christology* (WUNT 2/47; Tübingen: Mohr Siebeck, 1992), 40–42 (who notes Josephus as well); and J. D. G. Dunn, *The Theology of Paul the Apostle* (Grand Rapids: Eerdmans, 1998), 249–52.

ever, it is quite another thing for Paul to use κύριος in, for example, no less than four instances in 2 Thess 1:7–12, where each is a substantial echo of a passage from the Greek Bible. At this point any argument to the contrary, that either Paul himself or his Gentile churches did not use κύριος as a substitute for the Divine Name, seems to implode.[52]

Would Paul's Readers Have Been Aware of This Usage?

If we can, then, be rather certain that Paul regularly used and cited a form of the Greek Bible known to him and his readers, the second issue is whether there was an intentionality on Paul's part in echoing its language that *he expected his Gentile readers to pick up on.*[53] I begin my basically positive answer to this question with two observations.

First, the considerable volume of these data speaks for itself. Paul can hardly help himself; his own life had been steeped in Scripture from the time of his youth. Once he had encountered the exalted Lord, the sacred text was transformed into a place where the long-awaited Christ could now be found everywhere. And since his reading of the texts had been so remarkably transformed and since he is writing letters that have "sacred matters" as their immediate concern, citations and echoes of the OT are found throughout his letters. After all, the issue of *continuity* with his past is equally as

---

[52] This is especially true of the argument by G. Howard, "The Tetragram and the New Testament," *JBL* 96 (1977): 63–83. Again see the critique in Kreitzer, *Jesus and God in Paul's Eschatology.*

[53] Here I face a considerable difficulty in nomenclature. At issue is what to call these many places in Paul's writings where there can be little question that he is using the language of the biblical text (almost always some form of the Septuagint). Throughout the present study one will find the language of "echoing," "intertextuality," or "borrowing language from" in a variety of contexts. What I intend always is that Paul is (usually deliberately) using language from the Septuagint to recall or reinterpret the biblical text in his own situation(s); cf. R. B. Hays, *Echoes of Scripture in the Letters of Paul* (New Haven: Yale University Press, 1989), 6. For a much more precise use of language with regard to this phenomenon, see V. K. Robbins, *Exploring the Texture of Texts: A Guide to Socio-Rhetorical Interpretation* (Valley Forge, Pa.: Trinity Press International, 1996).

For a view different from the one taken here and throughout this book, see C. D. Stanley, *Paul and the Language of Scripture: Citation Technique in the Pauline Epistles and Contemporary Literature* (SNTMS 74; Cambridge: Cambridge University Press, 1992) (cf. C. Tuckett, "Paul, Scripture and Ethics: Some Reflections," *NTS* 46 [2000]: 403–24). Stanley's focus is altogether on the capacity of these Gentile churches to pick up on Paul's biblical quotations and echoes. He (helpfully) divides his fictive congregation into three types of audience: the "informed," the "competent," and the "minimal." But what he fails to take into serious consideration is the capacity for memory of the spoken word, and especially the "word" that is spoken over and over again, by those who cannot read or write. This is evidenced in preliterate children. "Grandpa, that's not how that story goes!" they exclaim; but by the time they become teenagers, this capacity is lost almost altogether, regarding both oral and written speech.

important to him as the measure of discontinuity brought about through Christ and the Spirit.

Moreover, in an oral/aural culture, where only about 15 percent of the population was able to read, both the limited amount of reading and the significance of sacred texts would mean that many people in Paul's churches would be biblically literate in ways reminiscent of the echoes of the KJV that abound in seventeenth-to-nineteenth-century English literature. Such verbal remembrance of any text, let alone Scripture, has in modern Western society become a thing of the past even among most of those who are avid lovers of the Bible. But Scripture undoubtedly would have been the standard "reading" fare for all of Paul's congregations.[54]

Thus, Paul's letters are full of verbal echoes of a variety of kinds that he could expect many of his hearers to catch (even if contemporary readers might not), although undoubtedly not all hearers in every case or every text in the same way. A contemporary analogy is the way that the large majority of Americans of my generation would hear echoes of our national "sacred documents" if someone were to say publicly, "Four score and seven years ago" or "When in the course of human events,"[55] even though many in the next generation would not.[56]

Second, and as noted throughout the following exegetical discussions, these transfers of biblical language from Yahweh to Christ are a part of what Paul does regularly. None of this is argued *for*, as though some kind of christological innovation was a point Paul wanted to make. To the contrary,

---

[54] But see Stanley (*Paul and the Language of Scripture*), who offers a minimalist view in this regard that seems to stand in some tension with the narrative of Luke-Acts, written by a Gentile convert who had a rather thorough knowledge of the Greek Bible. Indeed, so much is this so that Luke himself engages in considerable intertextuality (as the birth narratives offer full evidence). Furthermore, not only is the two-volume work addressed to a Gentile who is assumed to know the Jewish Bible in some detail but also, beginning with Acts 13, Scripture is both known and studied in the Diaspora synagogues (13:15; 17:2, 11; 18:24, 28), and earlier a proselyte is actually reading the scroll of Isaiah on his journey from Jerusalem back to Ethiopia (8:30–35).

[55] For those outside my own historical culture, these are the opening words of Abraham Lincoln's Gettysburg Address and of Thomas Jefferson's Declaration of Independence.

[56] A telling example (pointed out to me by my colleague Bruce Waltke) is found in Martin Luther King Jr.'s "I Have a Dream" speech, delivered orally at the Lincoln Memorial on August 28, 1963, the centennial year of the Emancipation Proclamation. It is doubtful whether all of the many thousands who heard that (now famous) speech would have caught all of his (surely deliberate) intertextual echoes of (1) Lincoln's Gettysburg Address, (2) Jefferson's Declaration of Independence, (3) Steinbeck's *The Winter of Our Discontent*, (4) Amos 5:24, and (5) Isa 40:4, although almost all of them would have known and been able to sing the quoted first stanza of the patriotic hymn "America." I did not hear the speech that day, but in reading it, I found that all of these echoes were readily at hand (and there may have been more that I simply did not recognize!).

they are used in such a way that Paul assumes them to be common knowledge between him and his readers. Thus, they often occur in quite offhanded ways, as assumptions between them, and sometimes as something to argue *from*, as is the case in the very important Christian reformulation of the Jewish Shema in 1 Cor 8:6. At the end, therefore, both the volume and the nature of these biblical echoes give evidence of an assumed high Christology between Paul and his churches.[57]

For these reasons, and also because the Septuagint is the term and text of familiarity, this will be the term of choice throughout the study that follows, noting only that the reader needs mentally to put quotation marks around it at every point.

A Numerical Analysis of the Pauline Data

Before turning our attention to the christological data in the individual letters, and since "usage" appears as the first thing up in each of the chapters, one may find it helpful to have handy a place where all the data are presented together. The full presentation of these data for each letter, with this kind of analysis, can be found as appendix II at the end of each chapter. For the most part these data comport with the Greek text found in NA[27] and UBS[4], except in a few instances where I have offered text-critical arguments in a footnote for a different reading.[58] I also add the cautionary note that one should use these data with considerable circumspection because what is missing in this kind of "analysis" are innumerable pronouns and the unexpressed subject of verbs, especially the so-called divine passives, which always have "God" as the implied subject (e.g., the three verbs in 1 Cor 6:11). So one must be especially cautious in using the final column (θεός). As for the rest, my concern was not with how *often* Paul refers to Christ (that would require the inclusion of pronouns) but with the specific *language* he uses when so doing, since, as it turned out, this sometimes does appear to have a measure of significance. (The various combinations of K, I, and X represent the word order of the "names" Κύριος, Ἰησοῦς, and Χριστός.)

---

[57] Paul's use of the Septuagint should also be part of the discussion, though it seldom is, of Paul's alleged use of "pre-Pauline" hymns and creeds as though one could "reconstruct" the original hymn or creed on the basis of the "obvious Pauline constructions" within it. But the methodological issue is seldom faced, even though such an example is ready at hand in Paul's "adaptations" of the OT. When he cites, not every word in the citation is relevant; but when he adapts by intertextual usage, then the very changes to the Septuagint make it clear that one could not always (or even most of the time) reconstruct the OT text, and especially not reconstruct *its* theology on the basis of what *Paul* does.

[58] See, e.g., the textual notes on 2 Thess 2:8; Rom 8:34; 14:12.

Letter	KIX/IXK/ XIK	KI/IK	XI/IX	KX	Κύριος	Ἰησοῦς	Χριστός	υἱός	Totals	θεός
1 Thess	5	6	2	x	13	3	3	1	33	36 [-3]
2 Thess	9	3	x	x	10	x	1	x	23	18 [+5]
1 Cor	8 / 1 / 1	4 / 1	6 / 2	x	49[+2]	2	45	2	121	103 [+18]
2 Cor	4 / 1	3	1 / 3	x	18[+2]	7	38	1	75	78 [-3]
Gal	3	x	7 / 5	x	2	1	22	4	44	29 [+15]
Rom	6 / 3 / 2	2 / 1	12 / 7	1	18[+8]	3	34	7	96	149 [-53]
Col	1 / x / 1	1	3	1	10	x	19	1	37	22 [+15]
Phlm	2	1	3	x	2	x	3	x	11	2 [+9]
Eph	6 / x / 1	1	10 / 1	x	16	1	28	1	65	31 [+34]
Phil	4 / x / 1	1	12 / 3	x	9	1	17	x	48	22 [+26]
1 Tim	2 / x / 2	x	10	x	1	x	1	x	16	22 [-6]
Titus	x	x	1 / 3	x	x	x	x	x	4	13 [-9]
2 Tim	x / 1	x	11 / 1	x	16	x	x	x	26	11 [+15]
Totals	48/5/7	22/2	78 / 25	2	164 [+12]	18	211	17	599	536 [+63]

Some general observations about these data:

1. The two final columns represent the total number of explicit references to Christ in relationship to actual uses of θεός, with the differential between the two columns found in square brackets in the θεός column. These data are obviously a bit skewed because I have not included in the count the (very few) references to God as Father where the designation "Father" is not accompanied by "God." Furthermore, I have deliberately avoided the inclusion of pronouns, as the actual value thereby gained did not seem to merit the added effort involved.

2. The full designation Κύριος Ἰησοῦς Χριστός appears in the very first reference in each letter. Thereafter it occurs in all the letters, but not as frequently as shorter designations.

3. The individual names occur most often, but not consistently throughout the letters. Some of this seems likely to be related to the situation and kind of letter in each case, but in the final analysis no apparent patterns seemed to emerge in the corpus.

4. Regarding the combinations of two "names": Κύριος Ἰησοῦς occurs less than others, and the majority of these occur in the first four letters (hardly ever Ἰησοῦς Κύριος, which is almost certainly because Κύριος is titular rather than a "name"); for reasons that are not altogether clear, Χριστὸς Ἰησοῦς appears in a ratio of about 3:1 over Ἰησοῦς Χριστός. In any case, this suggests that by Paul's time what was originally a title had come to be used increasingly as a "name."

5. Excluding Titus, which has by far the fewest direct references to Christ in the corpus, each of the single "names" occurs in most of the letters (Ἰησοῦς being the exception), but without consistency.

6. The twelve bracketed items represent instances where Κύριος is found in a citation of the Septuagint in which it does not refer to Christ. One may safely assume that all other instances are references to Christ.

7. Since some things that do not seem to comport with the data have been suggested about the use/nonuse of the article with Κύριος, I have included an excursus on this matter in the next chapter (p. 35).

Part I

Analysis

2

Christology in the Thessalonian Correspondence

OUR 1 THESSALONIANS[1] PROBABLY WAS written within a year after Paul (and Silas) had been hurried out of town in the dead of night (Acts 17:10).[2] His anxiety about the status of the beleaguered community he had left behind, and his own thwarted attempts to return, had finally resulted in their sending Timothy, who had returned to Paul and Silas in Corinth with basically good news (1 Thess 2:17–3:10). But not everything was as it should be, so he sent this letter, most of which is a rehearsal, from his perspective, of the intervening year (chs. 1–3) but which also offers some correctives (4:1–12), plus information about the coming of the Lord in light of someone who had died in the meantime (4:13–5:11).

Not long after, news reached Paul that things had in fact not progressed as he had hoped; indeed, someone apparently had spoken prophetically—as though speaking for Paul—that the Day of the Lord had come (2 Thess 2:1–2, 15),[3] thus increasing anxiety in the midst of increased persecution. This resulted in our 2 Thessalonians.[4]

---

[1]Commentaries on 1–2 Thessalonians are listed in the bibliography (pp. 639–40); they are cited in this chapter by author's surname only. For reasons noted below, the vast majority of commentaries deal with both of these letters in the same volume, which is one reason for keeping them together in the same chapter. The other reason is that, having been written to the same believers probably within one year's span, the two letters reflect a very similar christological perspective.

[2]Given the clear angst that Paul reveals in 1 Thess 2:14–3:10 and the sense of suddenness in his departure, there is no good reason to doubt the basic historicity of the account in Acts 17. In this case, the makeup of the community is probably mostly Gentile (see 1 Thess 1:9–10), but with roots in the synagogue, which will account for their presupposed familiarity with the Septuagint.

[3]For this perspective on the difficulties of 2 Thess 2:2, see G. D. Fee, "Pneuma and Eschatology in 2 Thessalonians 2:1–2: A Proposal about 'Testing the Prophets' and the Purpose of 2 Thessalonians," in *To What End Exegesis? Essays Textual, Exegetical, and Theological* (Grand Rapids: Eerdmans, 2001), 290–308.

[4]Doubt about the authenticity of 2 Thessalonians has a long history (see esp. W. Wrede, *Die Echtheit des zweiten Thessalonicherbriefs* [TUGAL 9/2; Leipzig: Hinrichs,

The first thing to be noted, then, is that these two letters have a relationship to one another that is unique to the corpus. Unlike the relationship between 1 and 2 Corinthians, for example, which stands at the opposite end of the spectrum with regard to similarities between them, these two letters are (not surprisingly) especially similar in that Paul in the second letter feels the need once more to cover much of the same ground. At the same time, these similarities are such that it is very difficult to discuss what appears in one without noticing what appears in the other. Nevertheless, I have tried to avoid comparisons in the discussions in 1 Thessalonians, except for a few isolated instances. But this is nearly impossible to do with regard to 2 Thessalonians, especially with regard to its Christology, which is why I have chosen to look at the Christology of the two letters together in the same chapter.

The Christology that presents itself in these letters is especially noteworthy, first of all because there is not a self-consciously christological moment in either of them.[5] That is, there is no passage where Paul is deliberately trying either to set forth Christ as divine (or human, for that matter) or to explain the nature of his divinity. His interest in Christ, as we come to expect in his later letters, is primarily soteriological.[6] "Our Lord,

---

1903]), based mostly on 2:3–12, which is perceived as standing in unrelieved tension with 1 Thess 5:1–11. Other slight differences between the two letters are then also brought to bear (e.g., 2 Thessalonians has less warmth; there are a few stylistic differences and "breaks" from Pauline thought). But, as Marshall (34) has pointed out, "it is very doubtful whether a set of weak arguments adds up to one powerful one." Indeed, the considerable historical difficulties that one has to overcome to hold this view far outweigh any alleged differences. It also might be pointed out that if the same criteria that bring 2 Thessalonians under doubt were applied to Romans in light of Galatians or to 2 Corinthians in light of 1 Corinthians, one would have a difficult time arguing for the authenticity of either. The evidence of this chapter shows how much the two letters have in common, precisely as one would expect from the same mind, over the same issues, in such close proximity in time. The attempt by M. J. J. Menken to capitalize on the (relatively small) christological differences between the two letters seems in the end to belie what he sets out to prove ("Christology in 2 Thessalonians: A Transformation of Pauline Tradition," *EstBib* 54 [1996], 501–22). The "Pauline tradition" in this title refers exclusively to 1 Thessalonians! See also K. Donfried, *The Theology of the Shorter Pauline Letters* (Cambridge: University Press, 1993), 94–101, whose discussion seems to lead him to conclusions (the similarity of the Christology of both letters) opposite to his presuppositions about authorship.

[5] See R. Jewett, "A Matrix of Grace: The Theology of 2 Thessalonians as a Pauline Letter," in *Thessalonians, Philippians, Galatians, Philemon* (vol. 1 of *Pauline Theology;* ed. J. M. Bassler; Minneapolis: Fortress, 1991), 70. Implicit in this observation is the fact that the Thessalonians will also have been on the same page regarding Christ and do not need "proof."

[6] This also readily explains why there is so little interest in this topic in the literature, including in the commentaries. The exceptions (noted only if the interest is in Christology per se): "Note D" in Milligan, 135–40; R. F. Collins, "Paul's Early Christology," in *Studies on the First Letter to the Thessalonians* (BETL 66; Leuven: Leuven University Press, 1984), 253–84; L. Morris, chapter 2 ("Jesus Christ Our Lord") in *1, 2 Thessalonians* (WBT; Dallas: Word, 1989), 27–40. R. E. H. Uprichard's "The Person

Jesus Christ" is the divinely given Savior, who "died for us"[7] (1 Thess 5:9–10) and whose resurrection has assured us that "we will live with him" (5:10) because he has also secured our "rescue from the coming wrath" (1:10) and our sharing in the coming glory (2 Thess 2:14). Thus "the Lord" is also the one whom believers "imitate" in their present suffering (1 Thess 1:6).[8] In a similar manner, and as turns out to be the norm, Christ is therefore the basic content of the gospel (1 Thess 3:2; cf. 2 Thess 1:8), as well as the divine agent of much (the apostolic "instructions" [1 Thess 4:2]; the divine will [5:18]).

What is noteworthy, therefore, is the remarkably high Christology that one meets here, presupposed at every turn and in the most off-handed of ways. Thus, Jesus Christ, the present, reigning Lord, is understood to share in any number of divine prerogatives, yet Paul never loses sight of Christ's prior earthly existence. And although no point is made of it here, in his next letter (1 Corinthians) it appears quite clear that Paul does this while maintaining his rigorous monotheism (1 Cor 8:4–6).[9] Paul's "Christology" in these first two letters, therefore, is not a matter of christological assertions or explanations; rather, one is struck by the reality that this rigorous monotheist can speak about Christ in ways as remarkable as one finds here—statements that by their very nature would seem to put considerable pressure on that monotheism.

I. Christology in 1 Thessalonians

Christology in 1 Thessalonians sets the pace for the discussion of Christology in all the subsequent letters, not because all of Paul's christological emphases get a hearing here but because the major matters appear on the

---

and Work of Christ in 1 Thessalonians" (*EvQ* 53 [1981]: 108–14) has only a small portion devoted to the person of Christ.

[7] As early as 1 Thess 1:10 Paul sets a pattern that will continue throughout the twelve-to-fourteen-year span of his letters, where in the context of addressing the community in the second person plural ("*you* turned from idols"), he changes midstream to the first person plural ("Jesus, who rescues *us* from the coming wrath"), so as to include himself with them when speaking of the saving events. In 5:1–11 this switch takes place in v. 5 ("You are all children of the light and children of the day. We do not belong to the night").

[8] This is one of the rare instances where Paul uses the title ὁ κύριος in reference to Jesus' earthly life, although 1 Thess 2:15 might also qualify here ("they killed τὸν κύριον Ἰησοῦν"), as might 2 Thess 2:13, where "loved by the Lord" is probably a reference to his death on their behalf (see the discussion below). The usage noted here (1 Thess 1:6) is the kind of thing that should keep scholars from being too dogmatic about "Pauline usage." Every once in a while he surprises us. In this case the present exalted Lord is the one who also suffered in his earthly life. The same thing happens in 1 Thess 2:15, which implies that the earthly Jesus was a prophetic figure whose death was in the long line of prophets who were killed.

[9] But see the discussion of 1 Thess 1:10 below for a different kind of emphasis on Jewish monotheism.

first page of the first letter, as presupposition and without emphasis. The special emphases within the letter itself are to be found first of all in the data themselves.

A Preliminary Look at the Data

All of the texts that specifically refer to Christ in some way are given in appendix I (at the end of this chapter); an analysis of usage is given in appendix II. Several matters about this usage need to be pointed out.[10]

First, as just noted, all the ways that Paul will speak of Christ in the subsequent letters are already in place in this letter.[11] This is all the more remarkable, given both the nature of the letter itself (comfort and correction) and the apparent lack of "need" to say so many of the things that he does. Thus we find the two major aspects of Pauline Christology already in place as presupposition: Jesus as the messianic "son of God," who is now recognized as the eternal Son; and Jesus as the exalted Lord of Ps 110:1. The one reference to "the Son" (1:9) and the three uses of the earthly name "Jesus" alone are especially related to these realities.

Other usage phenomena also need to be singled out. First, although references to Christ appear slightly less than references to God the Father,[12] most noticeable is the frequency with which Christ and the Father are brought together in clauses and phrases, even though for Paul, as in all his letters, the Father is always seen as the "prime mover" with regard to the saving event.

Second, the fullsome combination of the title "Lord," the name "Jesus," and the former title-turned-name "Christ"[13] occurs slightly less (5x) than does the combination "Lord Jesus" (6x); the combination "Christ Jesus" occurs 2 times.

Third, the most striking feature of usage in this letter, which will stand out even more in 2 Thessalonians, is the predominance of the title κύριος over all other designations. It occurs either alone (13x) or in combination (11x) in all but 9 of the 33 specific references to Christ in this letter. This is probably related to the fact that the Thessalonians' persecution stems primarily from their affirmation of Christ as κύριος in a city where such allegiance was offered to the Roman emperor. This usage, therefore, will receive the greater attention in this chapter.

---

[10] See also Milligan, 135–40.

[11] κύριος Ἰησοῦς Χριστός (5x); κύριος Ἰησοῦς (6x); Χριστός Ἰησοῦς (2x); (ὁ) κύριος (13x); Χριστός (3x); Ἰησοῦς (3x); υἱός (1x).

[12] There are 33 specific references to Christ and 36 to God the Father; this ratio is slightly reversed in 2 Thessalonians (23 to 18).

[13] The fact that one of the occurrences of Χριστός alone is articular (1 Thess 3:2; cf. 2 Thess 3:5) has led some (e.g., Findlay, 65, 203; Milligan, 136) to think of it as titular (in both instances). While that is possible, it must be noted that both are genitives modifying a noun that is also articular, which casts considerable doubt on the suggestion.

Excursus: The Use of the Definite Article with Κύριος

In this first exegetical chapter we need to note one of the more subtle features of Pauline usage: his use or nonuse of the definite article with the various formulations of κύριος. It has been suggested that anarthrous κύριος is a referent to God the Father,[14] but that is patently not true in the vast majority of cases in the Pauline corpus, beginning with these letters. Indeed, the only certain cases of such are the twelve instances where anarthrous κύριος occurs in a *citation* of the Septuagint and no point is made regarding the identity of κύριος.[15]

But in these two letters, for example, anarthrous usage occurs at least once with every name and title and with every combination of them (see appendix II). Usage has nothing to do with the referent ("Christ" in *all* cases in these two letters) and everything to do with other discernible phenomena. For example, a habit of usage found in these letters, which remains fairly consistent throughout the corpus, is Paul's use of anarthrous κύριος with certain prepositions (especially ἐν and ὑπό). This happens also with some echoes of the Septuagint where κύριος in Paul's sentences now refers to Christ.[16]

This phenomenon is also one of those subtle moments that argue strongly for Pauline authorship of 2 Thessalonians, since this fluctuation of usage, which includes some constants as well, is exactly the same in both of these letters and quite in keeping with the rest of the corpus—a feature that a pseudepigrapher could hardly have been expected to imitate.

Jesus as Messianic/Eternal Son of God

Although there are no inherent reasons in these letters for Paul to make reference to Jesus as the Jewish Messiah, nonetheless there are good reasons to think that such lies behind what has become for most readers the most commonplace of all matters in the corpus: the Pauline salutations. At least such a view seems arguable from the data.[17]

---

[14] See, e.g., D. A. Carson, *From Triumphalism to Maturity: An Exposition of 2 Corinthians 10–13* (Grand Rapids: Baker, 1988), 147 n. 3.

[15] For these exceptions, see n. 7 in ch. 3 (p. 87).

[16] This phenomenon, we should note here, also serves to verify that Paul is indeed echoing the Septuagint at these places (see the discussion in the preceding chapter, pp. 20–25).

[17] In most of the following chapters I let the evidence itself lead me to what is discussed first; but since κύριος Christology dominates both Thessalonian letters, I have chosen to put the present secondary christological matter in first position, partly because it comes up first (1 Thess 1:10) but mostly to keep it from getting lost at the end of the longer analysis of κύριος Christology.

1 Thessalonians 1:1, 3 (God as Father)

1:1 Παῦλος καὶ Σιλουανὸς καὶ Τιμόθεος τῇ ἐκκλησίᾳ Θεσσαλονικέων
ἐν θεῷ πατρὶ **καὶ κυρίῳ Ἰησοῦ Χριστῷ**[18]
Paul and Silas and Timothy, to the church of the Thessalonians
in God the Father and the Lord, Jesus Christ[19]

1:3 καὶ τῆς ὑπομονῆς τῆς ἐλπίδος **τοῦ κυρίου ἡμῶν Ἰησοῦ Χριστοῦ**
ἔμπροσθεν τοῦ θεοῦ καὶ πατρὸς ἡμῶν
and endurance of hope in our Lord, Jesus Christ
in the presence of God, even our Father

In their very first appearance in the Pauline corpus (1:1), God and Christ
are joined together by a καί as the compound object of the preposition ἐν,
and they are given the basic designations that will appear in the majority of
side-by-side references in the corpus: "God the Father" and "the Lord, Jesus
Christ."[20] A sentence later (v. 3), again side by side but not joined by καί,
they are both independently qualified by ἡμῶν (*our*). In this second instance
we also meet for the first time the designation of θεός as τοῦ θεοῦ καὶ πατρὸς
ἡμῶν, which most likely is to be understood as a hendiadys (= "God, even
our Father"). The phenomenon of the possessive with both "Father" and
"Lord" in 1:3 occurs in the other two instances of the joined names in this
letter (3:11, 13).[21]
However, in the first occurrence of the compound in 2 Thessalonians
(1:1), Paul begins a habit that will recur regularly hereafter throughout the
"church corpus":[22] using the possessive with only the first designation,

---

[18] For further exposition of this passage, esp. the meaning of ἐν θεῷ πατρὶ καὶ
κυρίῳ Ἰησοῦ Χριστῷ and the implications of both divine persons as double object of
the single preposition, see pp. 48–50 below.

[19] Unless otherwise noted, the English translations throughout are my own, usually very "literal" so that the Pauline emphases or echoes of OT usage can be seen
clearly in an English rendition. As throughout this study, the items in boldface are
references to Christ, while any mention of God is underlined.

[20] The statistics are telling: πατήρ as a designation for God occurs 37 times in the
corpus; in 15 instances Christ is joined to "the Father" with a καί (1 Thess 1:1; 3:11;
2 Thess 1:1, 2; 2:16; 1 Cor 1:3; 2 Cor 1:2; Gal 1:1; 1:3; Rom 1:7; Phlm 3; Eph 1:2; 5:23;
1 Tim 1:2; Titus 1:4; 2 Tim 1:2); 5 times God is designated "the Father of our Lord,
Jesus Christ" (2 Cor 1:3; 11:31; Rom 15:6; Col 1:3; Eph 1:3); in 15 other instances Christ
occurs in immediate proximity (1 Thess 1:3; 3:13; 1 Cor 8:6; 15:24; 2 Cor 1:3; Gal 1:4;
4:6; Rom 6:4; Col 1:2, 12–13; 3:17; Eph 1:17; 2:18; 4:6; 5:20). Only in 2 Cor 6:18 (a citation of the Septuagint) and Eph 3:14 is God mentioned as "our Father" without immediate relationship to Christ. For the full list of passages, see the appendix to ch. 14
(pp. 554–57).

[21] As well as in 2 Thess 2:16, where the names occur in reverse order.

[22] This is my designation for the first ten letters (including Philemon, which is
also addressed to the church in Colossae and therefore was intended to be read aloud
in the church along with Colossians).

"Father." On the basis of the usage in 1 Thessalonians, one may rightly assume that the "our" in these later instances is intended to do double duty for both nouns ("Father" and "Lord").

At issue for us christologically is how the designation of "Father" for God, which appears in these first two instances in a fully presuppositional way, came to be Paul's most common way to refer to God when God and Christ are mentioned in conjunction with one another. The solution to this question does not seem hard to come by. Four strands of evidence suggest that God becomes, in Paul's thinking, "our" Father because he is first of all the "Father of our Lord, Jesus Christ," which in turn implies Christ as "the Son"[23]—all of which has its origins, I will argue, in Jewish messianism.[24]

First, even though by the time of these first letters ὁ Χριστός has moved from title to name, Paul will sometimes still use it in a titular way to refer to Jesus as the Jewish Messiah. This is most certainly true of Rom 9:5 and most likely true of 1 Cor 1:23, 30 (see pp. 100–102 below). Thus Jewish messianism not only accounts for its usage in early Christianity as referring to the risen Lord, Jesus, but alone accounts for the universality of this title-turned-name in the early church.[25]

Second, beginning in 2 Cor 1:3 and repeated in 11:31, the one God is now identified as "the Father of our Lord, Jesus Christ," a designation that will recur several more times in the corpus (Rom 15:6; Col 1:3; Eph 1:3). Inherent in such a designation is the understanding of Jesus as God's Son.

Third, in two later passages, 1 Cor 15:25–28 and Col 1:12–15, Jesus as "the Son" is specifically tied to his kingly reign, and in the latter instance so closely tied to Davidic themes that Jewish messianism can scarcely be gainsaid.

Fourth, and most importantly, God becomes "our Father" through the gift of the Holy Spirit, whom Paul explicitly identifies in Gal 4:6 as "the Spirit of the Son," whom God sent "into our hearts" and who is thus responsible

---

[23] On this implication see, e.g., R. F. Collins, "The Theology of Paul's First Letter to the Thessalonians," in *Studies on the First Letter to the Thessalonians* (BETL 66; Leuven: Leuven University Press, 1984), 232–34.

[24] At this point, one is faced with the primary difficulty in methodology for the "chronological" approach taken in this study: how much can one assume about Pauline presuppositions based on what we know from later texts? Although the issue of "Son of God" has been a considerable one over many years, it needs to be pointed out that in the next letter after these two (1 Cor 15:25–28), also written to a primarily Gentile community, the combination of "King" and "Son" occurs together in a context that suggests that whatever "Son" came to mean in the course of time, its origins as a messianic designation probably lay with the combination of Exod 4:22–23, 2 Sam 7:13–14, and Ps 2. For an even-handed response to the considerable skepticism regarding "Jewish messianism" and its role in early Christology, see W. Horbury, "Jewish Messianism and Early Christology," in *Contours of Christology in the New Testament* (ed. R. N. Longenecker; Grand Rapids: Eerdmans, 2005), 3–24.

[25] Indeed, it occurs in every document in the NT except 3 John (but it does occur in the companion 2 John).

for believers' crying out to God the Father in the language of the Son ("Abba"). And since the Son, as "God's *own* Son" (Rom 8:3), has been sent forth by the Father (Gal 4:4), the language of sonship does double duty for Paul: to refer in its first instance to Jesus as the Jewish Messiah, while at the same time referring to the eternal, preexistent Son of God.[26]

When this evidence is combined with the reality that contemporary Judaism rarely referred to God as "our Father," one is led to conclude that such a designation for the one God, commonplace though it is for later Christians, has lying behind it an implicit "Son of God" Christology. Evidence for this can be found throughout the Pauline corpus, the first instance of which occurs in 1 Thess 1:10, where, hard on the heels of the designation of God as "Father," Paul refers to Christ as "the Son."

1 Thessalonians 1:9–10 (Christ as Son)

1:9–10 ⁹πῶς ἐπεστρέψατε <u>πρὸς τὸν θεὸν</u> ἀπὸ τῶν εἰδώλων δουλεύειν <u>θεῷ</u>
<u>ζῶντι καὶ ἀληθινῷ</u> ¹⁰καὶ ἀναμένειν **τὸν υἱὸν** <u>αὐτοῦ</u> **ἐκ τῶν**
οὐρανῶν, ὃν <u>ἤγειρεν</u> ἐκ τῶν νεκρῶν, Ἰησοῦν τὸν ῥυόμενον ἡμᾶς
ἐκ τῆς ὀργῆς τῆς ἐρχομένης
⁹*how you turned <u>to God</u> from idols, to serve <u>the living and true God</u>*
¹⁰*and to await <u>his</u>* **Son from heaven, whom** <u>*he raised*</u> *from*
the dead, **Jesus, who rescues** *us from the coming wrath*

One of the singular characteristics of 1 Thessalonians as a letter is that it actually has the appearance of one, at the beginning at least. What begins as a (typical) prayer and thanksgiving report (1:2–3) soon evolves into a chronological narrative about Paul's relationship with the Thessalonians. He begins with a reminder about the Thessalonians' actual conversion under the apostles' ministry (1:4–6), a conversion that became so well known that it preceded Paul as he moved from Macedonia down the Achaian Peninsula to Corinth (1:7–10). For his own reasons, he next reminds them of the nature of his own ministry among them (2:1–12); and after returning momentarily to the thanksgiving (2:13), he then resumes the narrative, taking up in turn (1) what had happened to them in the meantime (2:14–16), (2) his own thwarted attempts to return (2:17–20), (3) the sending of Timothy instead (3:1–5), and finally (4) his great relief to receive basically good news about them from Timothy (3:6–10).

The present text occurs at the end of his report about the notoriety of the Thessalonians' conversion, which with obvious deliberation he also uses to score some important theological points.[27] What has been noised abroad,

---

[26] For the full argumentation for this perspective, see ch. 14.

[27] Scholarship in the latter half of the preceding century saw a flurry of activity devoted to finding pre-Pauline creedal moments in his letters, of which this passage is usually brought forward as the first. Whether this passage is pre-Pauline is moot. The present interest is not in pre-Pauline Christology but in Paul's. And here, as in

and reported to Paul, is "how you turned to God from idols to serve the living and true God, and to wait for his Son from heaven, whom he raised from the dead—Jesus, who rescues us from the coming wrath." Three points are made: (1) the contrast between their "before" and "after," with scarcely hidden Jewish scorn for idolatry and a typically Jewish designation of God as "the living and true God"; (2) that they are currently "between the times" and are waiting for the conclusion of their salvation, which includes escaping the coming wrath (that their persecutors will indeed experience); and (3) that the one responsible for their salvation is the risen Jesus, here designated as "the Son of God."

We begin by noting that the text breathes the perspective of Jewish monotheism. Both epithets, "the living God" and "the true God," reflect the language of such monotheism in Israel's long struggle against idolatry. Although the two terms appear together only in Jer 10:10 ("But Yahweh is the true God; he is the living God, the eternal King"),[28] they appear separately in a variety of polemical contexts.[29] Whatever else is true of the God of the Jews, he is "the *living* God," over against the *lifeless* idols of the pagan world; and precisely because he alone is the living God, he is therefore "the *true* God" over against the *false* gods of idolatry. Moreover, the living and true God is further identified, here for the first time in the corpus, as the God "who raised [his Son] from the dead." This remarkable way of identifying the one God of Israel occurs just often enough in Paul's writings for Hans Küng to remark that " 'he who raised Jesus from the dead' becomes practically the designation of the Christian God."[30]

What is striking, therefore, on further reflection, is the designation of Christ as "*his Son* from heaven,[31] whom he raised from the dead—*Jesus*, who

---

all such cases, one may assume that what Paul wrote (by dictation, presumably), he himself believed, whatever prior existence it may have had.

It should also be noted that some see this passage as the primary Christology of 1 Thessalonians. See the discussion in Collins, "Early Christology," 254–55. But Collins, in keeping with a long tradition, does not pursue the possible messianism of the title "his Son." In any case, here is an instance where the usage almost demands that Paul is picking up language with which the Thessalonians would have been familiar.

[28] But see also *Jos. Asen.* 11:9–10.

[29] For "the living God," see, e.g., the oath formula in Num 14:21, 28 ("as [surely as] I live"); cf. Hos 2:1 (cited by Paul in Rom 9:26). It became a standard formula in the polemics of Second Temple Judaism (Dan 5:23 LXX; Bel 5 [Theodotion]; Sir 18:1; *Jub.* 21:3–4; *Jos. Asen.* 11:9–10). In the NT, see esp. Acts 14:15, where the wording of conversion is just as it appears here; cf. 1 Tim 4:10; Heb 3:12; 9:14; 10:31; 1 Pet 1:23; Rev 7:2; 15:7. For "the true God," see Wis 12:27; Josephus, *Ant.* 11.55; and in the NT, see esp. the Johannine literature (e.g., John 7:18; 8:26).

[30] Hans Küng, *On Being a Christian* (Garden City, N.Y.: Doubleday, 1976), 361. Besides the present text, see 1 Cor 6:14; 2 Cor 4:4; Gal 1:1; Rom 4:24; (6:4); 8:11 (2x); 10:9; Col 2:12; Eph 1:20; cf. 1 Pet 1:21.

[31] A considerable literature has suggested that the "background" to this usage is Daniel's "son of man" (Dan 7:13). Understandable as this might be, given (1) Paul's

rescues us from the coming wrath." That is, the "living and true God" has a Son, who is currently "in heaven" by virtue of the Father's having raised him from the dead; and this Son is none other than the earthly Jesus, the one who also rescues[32] us from the wrath of God that will be poured out on all who do not obey him (cf. 2 Thess 1:6–10).

Our present concern is to note that what is assumed in 1:1 now becomes explicit. And since it is easy for Christians who read their Bibles canonically to hear the title "Son of God" in Johannine terms, we note here that this is its first actual occurrence in the NT.[33] And since it is not a frequent term for Paul, something more needs to be said about its probable meaning in this first occurrence, especially as to how the Thessalonians may have understood it.

Although Paul is quite prepared to use "Son" for the risen Christ, as he will again in 1 Cor 15:28, it occurs most often in Paul's letters with reference to the Son's "giving his life" for us (2 Cor 1:19; Gal 2:20; 4:4–5; Rom 8:3, 32; Col 1:13). He also designates Christ as "Son" when he thinks of salvation as effecting the new creation, in which we are being transformed back into the divine image that is found perfectly in God's Son (Rom 8:29–30). Nonetheless, several passages indicate that the presuppositional beginning point for this title is Jewish messianism: 1 Cor 15:23–28; Rom 1:3–4 (and 8:32 indirectly); Col 1:12–15[34] (on this matter, see the full discussion in ch. 14). For now, one needs to note that Paul's reference here to the Son as *in heaven with the Father* most likely (presuppositionally) carries the double sense of the Son's now reigning as *the Jewish Messiah,* who, through his resurrection and exaltation, has come to be understood as *the eternal Son,* who had been sent from the Father to redeem.[35]

But would this double sense have been available to the Thessalonians? Most likely so. Both the internal evidence of the rest of these letters (Paul's

---

language "await . . . from heaven" and (2) the fact that Jesus almost certainly used this Danielic "title" with reference to himself, there is nonetheless scarcely a hint of any kind in the Pauline corpus that Paul is influenced by this language. What can be demonstrated (see ch. 14) is that he associates "Son of God" with the Davidic kingship.

[32] Gk. τὸν ῥυόμενον; the present tense here is probably not so much trying to say something about the "time" of the rescue, which in 5:9–10 is expressed in the past tense to refer to the saving event itself, as it is putting emphasis on the now exalted Son as the "Rescuer."

[33] This assumes, of course, that Galatians is not Paul's earliest extant letter but was written between 2 Corinthians and Romans. See p. 6 n. 18 above.

[34] One of the disappointing features of M. Hengel's otherwise especially useful study of this title (*The Son of God: The Origin of Christology and the History of Jewish-Hellenistic Religion* [Philadelphia: Fortress, 1976]) is his rather complete disregard of the use of this title for the Davidic king of Israel, which all the NT evidence together points to as the basic source of early Christian understanding.

[35] See esp. the discussion of 1 Cor 15:23–28; Gal 4:4; Rom 8:3 below. See also D. Juel, *Messianic Exegesis: Christological Interpretation of the Old Testament in Early Christianity* (Philadelphia: Fortress, 1988), 174–75.

intertextual use of the Septuagint) and the external evidence from Acts 17:1–6 suggest that many of these former idolators had already attached themselves to the Jewish synagogue and thus formed the nucleus of the neophyte Christian community.[36] One may therefore also assume that they themselves had already been instructed in the (now) double sense of Jesus as the Son of God.

For our present purposes, we should also note that this single (explicit) reference to "the Son" is in connection with his earthly name "Jesus," where the emphasis is on his future "coming." This seems especially to be in anticipation of 4:13–18.[37] The significance of this is that in the latter passage Paul shifts in v. 14, after explicit reference to Jesus' resurrection, from the name "Jesus" to the title ὁ κύριος (*the Lord*). This combination indicates that the two most significant messianic "titles," Lord and Son, which occur together a little later in 1 Cor 15:23–28, were already in place when Paul wrote this letter.

It is worth noting further that the combination κύριος Ἰησοῦς (*the Lord Jesus*), which occurs more often in 1 and 2 Thessalonians than anywhere else, appears most often in contexts where the reference is to Christ's Parousia (1 Thess 2:11; 3:13; 2 Thess 1:7, 8, 12; 2:8). And this leads us to examine the use of κύριος in 1 Thessalonians.

Jesus as the Κύριος of Septuagint Yahweh Texts

The second messianic title, Jesus as the κύριος[38] of Ps 110:1,[39] plays by far the most important christological role in 1 Thessalonians, so much so that the rest of this discussion is given to an analysis of this usage.

---

[36] It is worth noting here that Acts 17 records Paul as entering the synagogue and for three Sabbaths reasoning with them "*from the Scriptures,* explaining and proving that the Messiah had to suffer and rise from the dead, saying 'This Jesus I am proclaiming to you is the Messiah.'" The content of this "reasoning" had been presented earlier in Acts 13:16–47. There is no justifiable *historical* reason to doubt the essential accuracy of these pictures. Paul's own letters, including this one, are full verification that these earliest converts are well acquainted with the arguments that the crucified and risen Jesus is indeed the promised Jewish Messiah, God's exalted Son.

[37] I say "especially" here because the emphasis on the "coming" is found throughout the letter (1:3; 2:12, 19–20; 3:13; 5:1–11, 23).

[38] On Paul's appropriation of Septuagintal κύριος = *Adonai* = YHWH passages to refer to Christ, see the initial study by L. Cerfaux, "'*Kyrios*' dans les citations pauliniennes de l'Ancien Testament," *ETL* 20 (1943): 5–17; and more recently the published dissertation by D. B. Capes, *Old Testament Yahweh Texts in Paul's Christology* (WUNT 2/47; Tübingen: Mohr Siebeck, 1992).

[39] For the evidence of this assertion, see the discussion in 1 Cor 15:23–28, where this psalm is first cited by Paul, in a clearly messianic context. One of the truly idiosyncratic moments in NT scholarship was W. Bousset's attempt to tie this title in Paul to the pagan mystery cults (see *Kyrios Christos* [Göttingen: Vandenhoeck & Ruprecht, 1913; ET, trans. J. E. Steely; Nashville: Abingdon, 1970]) and thus totally apart from any OT usage. See further the critique in Hengel, *Son of God,* 77–79 n. 135.

There is good reason to think that this predominance occurs in part because of the city of Thessalonica itself. Strategically situated astraddle the Egnatian Way and with a deep-sea port, the city was of special interest to the empire. More in its own interests than out of "love" for the Thessalonians, Rome had bestowed on them the status of a "free city." The Thessalonians in turn gave back to the emperor the loyalty that this astute move was intended to secure. The significance of this emerges in Luke's abbreviated report in Acts 17:1–10, where the explicit charge brought against Paul was *maiestas* (high treason)—that he was promoting "another king than Caesar." Since devotion to Caesar meant proclaiming him as "Lord and Savior," this is the most probable explanation for the frequency of κύριος in these letters. In the Thessalonians' current situation of suffering for Christ, Paul is constantly reminding them of who the true "Lord" really is.[40]

We begin by noting that the title ὁ κύριος is the special province of Christ in 1 Thessalonians (as throughout the corpus); it is never attributed to the Father,[41] who is always referred to either as θεός (*God*) or ὁ πατήρ (*the Father*). This can be demonstrated in any number of ways, beginning with the very first mention of both in 1 Thess 1:1 ("the church of the Thessalonians in God the Father and the Lord, Jesus Christ"), which is repeated in slightly different form in v. 3 ("your endurance inspired by hope in our Lord, Jesus Christ, in the presence of God the Father"). These designations are then singled out in vv. 4 and 6, where "loved by God" (v. 4) means "loved by God the Father," and where "you became imitators . . . of the Lord" (v. 6) can only refer to Christ, since it mentions his earthly sufferings.

This usage in 1 Thessalonians can be conveniently packaged under two headings: (1) the intertextual use of the Septuagint's κύριος, where the Tetragammaton (YHWH) has been so translated[42] but where the κύριος of those texts now refers specifically to Christ; (2) texts where Christ as κύριος shares in the divine purposes and activities with God the Father, especially where prayer is freely offered to Christ as it would be to God the Father. We begin with Paul's attribution to Christ of the Septuagint's κύριος = YHWH.

---

[40] This is especially so, given that coins minted in Thessalonica from ca. 27 B.C.E. proclaim Julius Caesar as a god. See K. P. Donfried, *Paul, Thessalonica, and Early Christians* (Grand Rapids: Eerdmans, 2002), 34–37.

[41] For a discussion of the passages in these two letters where some think otherwise, see the discussion on 1 Thess 4:6 and 2 Thess 2:13; 3:3, 5 below. But to think otherwise, first, needs reasonable justification and, second, simply does not comport with the clear and certain evidence of 1–2 Thessalonians, not to mention 1 Cor 8:6 and elsewhere.

[42] For the debate on this matter, see the discussion in ch. 1, pp. 20–25.

1 Thessalonians 3:13

The first instance in the corpus where Paul uses language from the Septuagint and applies the κύριος = YHWH directly to Christ appears in the context of the eschatological goal of Paul's prayer for the Thessalonians in 3:11–13. For the christological significance of the prayer itself, see the discussion below (pp. 53–55). Here our focus is on the final phrase, where, after Paul has prayed that ὁ κύριος (= Christ) will cause their love to increase and abound (in the present time), he offers as the goal of such love that "[the Lord] may strengthen your hearts so that you will be blameless and holy in the presence of our God and Father *at the coming of our Lord, Jesus, with all his holy ones.*"[43] Here Paul's intertextual appropriation of Zech 14:5 seems certain, since the language is too close to be merely accidental.[44] The two texts read:

1 Thess 3:13	ἐν τῇ παρουσίᾳ	**τοῦ κυρίου** ἡμῶν Ἰησοῦ
	μετὰ πάντων	τῶν ἁγίων **αὐτοῦ**
Zech 14:5	καὶ ἥξει	**κύριος** ὁ θεός μου
	καὶ **πάντες**	οἱ ἅγιοι μετ' αὐτοῦ.

1 Thess 3:13	*at the coming*	**of** our **Lord** *Jesus*
	with all	**his holy ones**
Zech 14:5	*And shall come*	**the Lord** *my God*
	and **all**	**the holy ones with him.**

The christological import of this sentence lies with the fact that the κύριος of the Septuagint is "Yahweh *my* God," who will himself come to the Mount of Olives and carry out his eschatological victory over the nations. In Paul's theology, the future coming of the *Lord* is always seen as the return of the present reigning Lord, Jesus Christ. What Paul has

---

[43] The meaning of πάντων τῶν ἁγίων αὐτοῦ is debated in the literature as to whether it means "angels" (as it surely does in Zechariah; so Best, 152–53; Marshall, 102–03; Wanamaker, 145; Richard, 177–78; Malherbe, 214; Green, 181), "his saints" (as it usually does for Paul; so Ellicott, 47; Findlay, 77), or both (Milligan, 46; Rigaux, 492; Bruce, 74; Morris, 111–12; Holmes, 116). The intertextuality of this sentence seems to make it tilt decisively in favor of "angels," especially since the usage of οἱ ἅγιοι to refer to "God's people" does not occur in 1 Thessalonians at all (and in 2 Thessalonians only in 1:10). Moreover, in 2 Thess 1:7, where the present phrase seems to be spelled out in some detail, Paul says that "the Lord Jesus will be revealed from heaven with the angels of his power [μετ' ἀγγέλων δυνάμεως αὐτοῦ]." In any case, Paul can very well expect many of them to hear the echo of Zech 14:5, since this would have been a well-used text among early Christians (on this matter, see the discussion in ch. 1, pp. 20–25).

[44] The primary differences are the case and word order of "all" and "the holy ones." But this is an echo, after all, not a citation; thus Paul has adapted it to his own sentence. The adaptation includes the article with κυρίου, in this case caused by his addition of the possessive pronoun "our."

done seems clear enough: the future coming of Yahweh is now to be understood as the future coming of *"our* Lord Jesus," who alone is κύριος in Paul's new understanding, resulting from his own encounter with the risen Lord (see 1 Cor 9:1). One can scarcely miss the ease with which Paul now reads the κύριος (= YHWH) of Zechariah as referring to Christ, the Lord. So much is this so that in 2 Thess 1:7–10, the coming Lord Jesus Christ has altogether assumed the role of judging God's enemies as well (see pp. 57–61 below).

1 Thessalonians 4:16

Although this next instance of intertextual echo is seldom noticed in contemporary literature,[45] the linguistic tie between Ps 47:5 (46:6 LXX) and Christ's ascension was well known in the early church,[46] which suggests that for the ancient reader these kinds of echoes were much more real than they are for us. But "ascent" is one thing; the present Pauline text has to do with Christ's final "descent." At issue is whether Paul is deliberately echoing the psalm and giving it a new twist with regard to Christ's Parousia. The following display would seem to suggest so:

1 Thess 4:16 ὅτι αὐτὸς **ὁ κύριος** ἐν κελεύσματι, **ἐν φωνῇ** ἀρχαγγέλου
　　　　　　　καὶ ἐν **σάλπιγγι** θεοῦ,
　　　　　　　　　　　καταβήσεται ἀπ᾽ οὐρανοῦ

Ps 46:6 LXX　　　　　　　　　　ἀνέβη　　ὁ θεὸς ἐν ἀλαλαγμῷ
　　　　　　　　　κύριος　　　　　　　　ἐν φωνῇ σάλπιγγος.

1 Thess 4:16　*for*　**the Lord** *himself with a shout,*　**with the voice**
　　　　　　　　　　　　　　　　　　　　　　　　　of an archangel
　　　　　　　and　*with* **the trumpet** *of God,*
　　　　　　　　　　　*will de****scend*** *from heaven*

Ps 46:6 LXX　　　　　　　　　　　**Ascended**　　*God with a shout,*
　　　　　　　　　　the Lord　　　**with the voice of a trumpet.**

What Paul has done seems clear enough. In the central doublet of a psalm celebrating Yahweh as King over all the earth, the psalmist refers to Yahweh's "ascent" to Mount Zion, after he had "subdued nations under us." The two lines of the first stich celebrate the ascent as accompanied with "shouts of joy" and the "voice of the trumpet." In Paul's version of what

---

[45] The notable exception is C. A. Evans, "Ascending and Descending with a Shout: Psalm 47.6 and 1 Thessalonians 4.16," in *Paul and the Scriptures of Israel* (ed. C. A. Evans and J. A. Sanders; JSNTSup 83; Sheffield: Sheffield Academic Press, 1993), 238–53, to whom I am indebted for much of the detailed information of this discussion. Juel (*Messianic Exegesis,* 159) has suggested another allusion to Zech 14:5 here, but that seems doubtful.

[46] See Evans, "Ascending and Descending," 242–46.

seems an obvious use of the language of the psalm, the κύριος = Yahweh of the Psalter is now the already ascended Christ, whose *return* will be accompanied by "the voice" of an archangel and with "the trumpet" of God. The emphatic αὐτὸς ὁ κύριος (*the Lord himself*) makes the connection with "the Lord" of the psalm even stronger.[47] The Lord (Jesus) who had previously ascended on high is the Lord who himself will return at the sounding of the trumpet.

Other Κύριος Phrases That Echo Septuagint Usage

Once one recognizes Paul's intertextual appropriation of the language of the Septuagint, whereby κύριος = Yahweh is now κύριος = Christ, one becomes aware of the many exclusively Yahweh-phrases from the Septuagint that are also applied to Christ. This happens throughout the Pauline corpus; one finds it already well in place in this earliest letter. They are listed here with minimal comment.

The Word of the Lord

1 Thess 1:8	ἀφ᾽ ὑμῶν γὰρ ἐξήχηται	ὁ λόγος τοῦ κυρίου
1 Thess 4:15	τοῦτο γὰρ ὑμῖν λέγομεν	ἐν λόγῳ κυρίου
1 Thess 1:8	*for from you has gone out*	**the word of the Lord**
1 Thess 4:15	*for we say this to you*	**by the word of the Lord**

The wooden translation of the Hebrew construct genitive as λόγος κυρίου occurs more than 50 times in the Septuagint of the Hebrew prophets, always as a translation of *d^ebar YHWH*. In most cases it is the prophet's way of indicating that the "word" he is about to speak comes directly from Yahweh (see, e.g., Joel 1:1). For Paul, "the word of the Lord" is now that which is spoken by (or about) the Lord Jesus. Indeed, it seems most likely that in the first passage here, where the phrase is articular, Paul intends it to stand for the gospel; that is, it is the "word" *about* the Lord.

The second passage, however, is most likely a reflection of the usage in the Septuagint, and thus it refers to a word that Christ himself has spoken (either, most likely, in the Jesus tradition that has come down to Paul, or as a prophetic word that Paul has received from Christ).[48] In either case, this well-known Yahweh-phrase has now been appropriated to refer to Christ.

---

[47] The addition of the αὐτός also accounts for the addition of the article with κύριος.

[48] See Hurtado, *Lord Jesus Christ*, 150–51; Donfried (*Shorter Pauline Letters*, 39–40) thinks it is the latter.

The Name of the Lord

1 Thess 5:27 ἐνορκίζω ὑμᾶς τὸν κύριον ἀναγνωσθῆναι τὴν ἐπιστολὴν
                                    πᾶσιν τοῖς ἀδελφοῖς.

Gen 24:3 καὶ ἐξορκιῶ σε κύριον τὸν θεὸν τοῦ οὐρανοῦ
                        [cf. Neh 13:25]

1 Thess 5:27 *I charge* *you* *by the Lord*[49] *that this letter be read*
                                              to all the brothers (and sisters).

Gen 24:3 *and I charge you* *by the Lord* *the God of heaven*

In the OT, God's revelation of his name, "Yahweh" (ὁ κύριος in the Septuagint), lies at the very center of Israel's existence. They are to be a people who bear and call upon his name; Jerusalem is to be the place where Yahweh's name dwells, while the temple is to be the dwelling for that name. Although Israel was not to misuse or profane Yahweh's name (Exod 20:7; Lev 19:12), they were in fact commanded to take their oaths in his name (Deut 6:13). The appropriation of the Greek form of the Divine Name is what is reflected in the present usage; and "the Name," of course, is that which Paul in a later passage (Phil 2:10–11) will point out had been bestowed on Christ at his exaltation. So what was formerly done in/by the name of Yahweh is now for Paul, as the basis of his charge, done through Christ the Lord.

The Day of the Lord

1 Thess 5:2 ὅτι **ἡμέρα κυρίου** ὡς κλέπτης ἐν νυκτὶ οὕτως ἔρχεται
cf. Joel 1:15 ὅτι ἐγγὺς **ἡμέρα κυρίου**
Joel 2:1 διότι πάρεστιν **ἡμέρα κυρίου**

1 Thess 5:2 *that* **the day of the Lord** *as a thief in the night thus comes*
cf. Joel 1:15 *that* *near (is)* **the day of the Lord**
Joel 2:1 *therefore present is* **the day of the Lord**

This well-known phrase, which is found again in 2 Thess 2:2 as something being abused, occurs elsewhere in Paul's writings in 1 Cor 1:8 and 5:5; later it becomes "the day of Christ" (Phil 1:6, 10). The phrase belongs altogether to the prophetic tradition, referring to the great future day of Yahweh. As both the usage in this letter and the later substitution of "Christ" for "Lord" indicate, Paul is again appropriating and applying to Christ a well-known Yahweh-phrase.

---

[49] The meaning of the accusative τὸν κύριον is clear enough, but it is not at all easy to put it into English. Most translations, including the KJV, have "by the Lord," but the NET BIBLE has "in the Lord," with a note offering the options "by the Lord" or "before the Lord" (the latter is found in the TNIV).

What is noteworthy is that the phrase continues to carry the eschatological freight that it did for the prophets. But in contrast to the primary usage in the prophets, where it points to future judgment, Paul's interest in this "day" is primarily as God's eschatological conclusion to the *salvation* that has been effected through Christ. Although it is true that in its first occurrence here in 1 Thessalonians it still carries the threat of judgment, in Pauline usage that threat is strictly for those outside Christ. Indeed, the whole argument of 1 Thess 5:1–11 is to reassure the Thessalonian believers that the Day of the Lord is *not* to be thought of as a threat for them.

The Lord as Avenger

1 Thess 4:6 διότι	ἔκδικος	κύριος	περὶ πάντων τούτων
Ps 93:1 LXX ὁ θεὸς	ἐκδικήσεων	κύριος	

1 Thess 4:6 *because*	**avenger** *(is)*	**the Lord**	*concerning all these*
Ps 93:1 LXX *the God*	**of vengeance** *(is)*	**the Lord**	

Here is a case where some are ready to make this occurrence of κύριος refer to God the Father.[50] However, this not only runs roughshod over Paul's clear distinctions, but also it fails to take seriously the ease with which Paul can substitute Christ as "Lord" in speaking of prerogatives that otherwise belong to God alone. After all, in Rom 14:10, referring to believers—and in a context where ὁ κύριος dominates the discussion—Paul speaks of "the judgment seat of God," while in a similar context in 2 Cor 5:10, again referring to believers, he says that "we must all appear before the judgment seat of Christ." In the present text, unique to the NT, the use of "avenger" occurs in a context of "taking advantage of a brother or sister" (TNIV), in which the Lord Jesus himself will take the side of the wronged person.

The Lord Our Hope

1 Thess 1:3 καὶ τῆς ὑπομονῆς **τῆς ἐλπίδος**

τοῦ κυρίου ἡμῶν Ἰησοῦ Χριστοῦ

    and endurance   **of hope**   **in our Lord Jesus Christ**

---

[50] See, e.g., Morris, 124; Richard, 204; Malherbe, 233—although the latter admits that Christ is also seen as "judge" by Paul (pp. 185–86, 212, on 1 Thess 2:19). Most others correctly see that Paul's (apparently) exclusive use of κύριος to refer to Christ should determine its meaning here, especially (as pointed out by Frame, 158; Best, 166; Marshall, 112) in light of the emphatic ὁ θεός that follows in v. 7. So also E. S. Steele, "The Use of Jewish Scriptures in 1 Thessalonians," *BTB* 14 (1984): 15. Marshall (112), Wanamaker (156), and Beale (122 [following Marshall]) are the few who note that Paul is here using the language of Ps 93:1 LXX (94:1 MT). Richard (204) makes the remarkable comment that it must refer to God because Paul is using OT language here—a comment that seems insensitive to Paul's regular application of OT (LXX) language to Christ.

This unusual genitive probably is the result of the repeated genitives in the present context. In any case, it is universally agreed that τοῦ κυρίου here is objective, that the Thessalonians are commended for their endurance that is predicated on their "hope *in* the Lord Jesus Christ." This seems to be another case of appropriating κύριος language from the Septuagint and applying it to Christ. Whatever else was true of Yahweh for Israel's faithful, he was "their hope" (e.g., Ps 31:24;[51] 33:22). Again, in a quite off-handed way, language that is ordinarily reserved for God in the OT finds expression regarding Christ as Lord.

God and ὁ Κύριος Share in Divine Purposes and Activity

Another remarkable feature of Pauline Christology also finds its first expression in this earliest Pauline letter: the joining of Christ as Lord with God the Father in several key moments of divine purpose and activity on the Thessalonians' behalf. This begins in the salutation.

The Church Exists in God and Christ (1 Thess 1:1 [cf. 2 Thess 1:1])

1:1 Παῦλος ... τῇ ἐκκλησίᾳ Θεσσαλονικέων   ἐν θεῷ πατρὶ
                                                καὶ κυρίῳ Ἰησοῦ Χριστῷ

Paul ... to the church of the Thessalonians   *in God the Father*
                                                and the Lord Jesus Christ

Here only in the Pauline corpus does Paul designate the church as being simultaneously *in* God and Christ.[52] Whatever else this phrase means, its first aim is to distinguish the Christian ἐκκλησία from the many other ἐκκλησίαι of Thessalonica—particularly the Jewish synagogue but also various civil or trade entities that would gather under this designation. Several options are possible as to the sense of ἐν[53] here: sphere of existence; constituted by; belonging to. The main objection to the first sense (sphere of existence) is that Paul does not speak so elsewhere of God the Father. On the other hand, this sense is so common for Paul when it is used of Christ that it seems most likely that he intended precisely that sense in its first appearance in his let-

---

[51] Ps 30:25 LXX, which reads: πάντες οἱ ἐλπίζοντες ἐπὶ κύριον (*all who hope in the* LORD).

[52] N. Richardson (*Paul's Language about God* [JSNTSup 99; Sheffield: Sheffield Academic Press, 1994], 260–62) correctly lumps this passage with others where God and Christ share the same preposition; unfortunately, he does not comment on it as such. The result is that it is subsumed under the discussion of 1 Cor 1:3, where Barrett suggests that the phrase probably means "the Father is the source, Christ the means or agent" of the grace and peace. But that interpretation simply will not work in this first occurrence of the phenomenon in the corpus.

[53] What Richard (38) aptly dubs "the 'maid-of-all-work' preposition."

ters.[54] After all, in a world whose philosphers could think in terms of "in him we live and move and have our being,"[55] why should one think it strange that the Christian Paul would think of the believers' existence in such terms? God and Christ together are the sphere of all, and especially of Christian, existence.[56]

If so (and even if not so), the compound object of the preposition is striking. The church exists simultaneously in relationship to the heavenly pair: God the Father and the (now exalted) Lord, who is none other than Jesus the Messiah. And when Paul thinks in these terms, he regularly joins them as one in purpose and activity by means of a single preposition.[57] Two further observations about this usage need to be made:

1. In this very first reference to God and Christ in the extant corpus, Paul is already using the basic designations that come from the Shema in Deut 6:4,[58] with θεός being used exclusively of God the Father[59] and κύριος being used equally exclusively to refer to Christ,[60] who had "the Name" bestowed on him at the exaltation.[61] This has become so commonplace to later Christians that it simply goes by unnoticed. But this is a remarkable event indeed, and it has happened very early (before 50 C.E.) and sets the pattern for usage throughout Paul's letters. Paul, of course, is not trying to make any such point in these salutations. My point here is that these common designations ("Father" and "Lord"), which meet us at the beginning of all his letters, are fixed—and now stereotypical—precisely because they had become so for Paul many years before he had written any of his extant letters.[62]

2. This is the first of the several instances in the corpus where one prepositional phrase has as its twofold object θεός and κύριος.[63] It is easy to be

---

[54] So also Donfried, *Shorter Pauline Letters*, 42.

[55] Acts 17:18, where in the Areopagus speech Luke reports Paul as using this language from Epimenides.

[56] On this matter, see esp. C. F. D. Moule, *The Origin of Christology* (Cambridge: Cambridge University Press, 1977), ch. 2, "The Corporate Christ" (pp. 47–96). The other side of this phenomenon occurs in Col 1:16, where Christ the Son is designated as the one "in whom all things in heaven and earth were created." Thus, here believers exist "in God," while in Colossians the universe was created "in the Son."

[57] Cf. Findlay (17): "Everything this ἐκκλησία Θεσσαλονικέων rests upon and exists for is centred in these two Names, which complement each other and are bound by the . . . single ἐν."

[58] See the discussion of 1 Cor 8:6 in ch. 3 (pp. 89–94).

[59] For the two possible exceptions, see the exegesis of Rom 9:5 and Titus 2:13 (pp. 272–77, 440–46).

[60] In this case the lone certain exceptions are in the twelve citations of the Septuagint where no point is being made about ὁ κύριος at all. See n. 7 in ch. 3 (p. 87).

[61] See the discussion of Phil 2:9–11 in ch. 9 (pp. 393–401).

[62] It is easy to forget that here is a Jew who in his younger years would not have dared breathe the name YHWH but who now as a matter of course puts θεός and Jesus together as the compound object in a single prepositional phrase. Such a phenomenon is most easily explained on the basis of Paul's encounter with the risen Lord Jesus.

[63] See, e.g., 2 Thess 1:2 and all subsequent salutations in his letters.

dismissive of this phenomenon. Instead, it should be taken with full seriousness, since Paul regularly brings them together in other contexts in which the divine "working" of each is expressed separately.[64] The point is that Paul intends both Father and Son together to be both the means of their constitution as God's people and the sphere of their new existence.[65] What is most remarkable about this present usage is that this is the first and only time such a preposition is used of God the Father. Hereafter it is used exclusively of Christ. It is difficult to get around the plain implications of this, yet another unself-conscious, way of speaking that puts Christ together with God the Father in the highest place.

God's Will in Christ Jesus (1 Thess 5:18)

As Paul moves toward the conclusion of this letter, he exhorts the Thessalonian believers with a series of "staccato imperatives" that have the appearance of a kind of general parenesis that could fit well in most of his letters. Nonetheless, they do fit especially well the present (for many, obviously difficult) circumstances of these believers. He begins with the well-known triadic exhortation that they should "rejoice always, pray constantly, and give thanks in all circumstances" (5:16–18a). Then, in order to keep these words from becoming simply nice but unrealistic platitudes, he insists that "this is God's will for you." But what is striking is the christological modification he makes regarding the divine will: "This is God's will *in Christ Jesus* for you."

This phrase serves as a sort of inclusio with the way the hortatory ("how you ought to live to please God" [4:1]) section of the letter begins.[66] After the opening reminder regarding these instructions (vv. 1–2), he begins, "For this is the will of God, your sanctification" (v. 3). Now that "will" is modified as being "in Christ Jesus."[67] But what does that mean? And what are the christological implications?

As to what it means, this is probably best understood as a genuinely christological modification of God's will rather than a locative regarding God's people. That is, this is Paul's way of modifying God's will so that it

---

[64]This can be found in any number of ways, beginning with 2 Thess 3:5: "into the love of God and the perseverance of Christ"; cf. 1 Cor 12:5–6; 2 Cor 13:13; and many others.

[65]At least that is what the normal reading of the preposition suggests and therefore how the majority of interpreters understand it. Because this is the only occurrence of ἐν with "God" as the object, Richard and others suggest that the ἐν is instrumental here, but that is most unlikely.

[66]An observation also made by Malherbe, 330.

[67]At least the word order would seem to require such an understanding. Paul's text reads θέλημα θεοῦ ἐν Χριστῷ Ἰησοῦ εἰς ὑμᾶς. Had he intended that this is God's will for those who themselves are in Christ Jesus, the word order would more naturally have been θέλημα θεοῦ εἰς ὑμᾶς ἐν Χριστῷ Ἰησοῦ. Most English translations (the NRSV is a notable exception) have "this is the will of God for you in Christ Jesus," where "in Christ Jesus" probably is still intended to modify "the will of God." But see Beale (171), who takes it in the former sense.

will not be perceived as a form of "law." Rather, it should be understood as gift, as God's will that finds expression in Christ himself, who makes possible such unlikely verbalizations by God's people in the midst of present difficulties. If so, the "in Christ Jesus" functions as both a soteriological modifier (= as something made available to God's people through Christ) and a christological one (= God's will now finds expression in Christ). Thus, this association of Christ with God's will has inherent christological ramifications. If not necessarily a "shared prerogative" as such, it is at least an expression of the christological focus of Paul's understanding of God and his purposes.

The Divine Presence at the Parousia

The assumed close relationship between the Father and the Son also emerges in this letter when Paul thinks in terms of finally obtaining the divine Presence at the Parousia. Depending on the point of emphasis at a given moment, Paul can speak first of being in Christ's presence at his coming:

1 Thess 2:19 τίς γὰρ ἡμῶν ἐλπὶς ἢ χαρὰ ἢ στέφανος καυχήσεως ἢ οὐχὶ καὶ
ὑμεῖς – ἔμπροσθεν τοῦ κυρίου ἡμῶν Ἰησοῦ
ἐν τῇ αὐτοῦ παρουσίᾳ

*For what is our hope or joy or crown of boasting—if not even
you—**in the presence of our Lord Jesus Christ
at his coming?***

Not many sentences later, the same language is used to refer to being in God's presence:

1 Thess 3:13 **εἰς τὸ στηρίξαι** ὑμῶν τὰς καρδίας . . . <u>ἔμπροσθεν τοῦ θεοῦ καὶ
πατρὸς ἡμῶν</u> **ἐν τῇ παρουσίᾳ τοῦ κυρίου ἡμῶν Ἰησοῦ
μετὰ πάντων τῶν ἁγίων αὐτοῦ**

to strengthen *your hearts*   <u>*in the presence of our God and*</u>
<u>*Father*</u>   **at the coming of our Lord Jesus
with all his holy ones**

In the OT the divine Presence is closely associated with the divine Glory, as the interchange of these terms regarding tabernacle and temple makes certain.[68] For Paul the final goal of everything is to be at last in the divine Presence, now shared equally by Father and Son.

Christ the Lord Invoked in Prayer

Our final two texts in this letter are perhaps the most significant of all with regard to Paul's assumed Christology. For here one is faced not simply

---

[68] See further the discussion of 1 Cor 2:8 (p. 136) and 2 Cor 3:16–4:6 (pp. 180–84).

with shared divine activities and purpose but shared divine prerogatives. Whatever else is true of the early Christian communities as reflected in Paul's letters, this very early (probably earliest) document demonstrates that they prayed to both the Father and the Son, together and separately, and did so with obvious ease and spontaneity and without any sense of putting pressure on their monotheism.[69] There are two such passages in this letter, which we examine in their reverse order.

The Grace Benediction (1 Thess 5:28)

One of the noteworthy phenomena in Paul's letters is his attribution of χάρις to both God and the Lord. What is striking is how this attribution happens. In almost all of his letters, Paul concludes with some form of a prayer-wish/benediction like the one that concludes this letter:[70]

5:28 ἡ χάρις τοῦ κυρίου ἡμῶν Ἰησοῦ Χριστοῦ   μεθ᾽ ὑμῶν.
      *The grace **of our Lord Jesus Christ** (be)*   *with you.*

Although this is technically not prayer directed *toward* Christ, the assumption is that Christ himself would supply the "grace" that Paul wishes for them by way of benediction. Indeed, had Paul said, "the grace of God be with you," this would be universally recognized as the prayer-benediction directed toward God that it is. The remarkable thing is that Paul never puts God in this role in his benedictions; rather, it is always "the grace of our Lord, Jesus Christ."[71]

What makes this further noteworthy is that in the body of his letters, Paul most often refers to χάρις as from God, either as the predicate of our existence in Christ (1 Cor 1:4; Gal 2:21; Rom 5:15; Col 1:6) or as the basis of Paul's apostolic gifting (1 Cor 3:10; 15:10; Eph 3:2, 7). Nonetheless, there are three notable exceptions: 2 Cor 8:9; 12:9; 1 Tim 1:14.

This simply demonstrates what is otherwise well known: when Paul thinks of God's saving work in our behalf, he can emphasize alternatively the role of the Father or the Son, depending on context. But at the end of all his letters, it is the "grace of Christ" that he desires to be present with God's

---

[69] For a close look at these matters and their significance, see the various studies by L. Hurtado noted in the bibliography, most recently succinctly brought together in *Lord Jesus Christ*.

[70] This includes Philemon, which is clearly a community document as much as it is intended to apply to one person. Not only is the church greeted in the salutation (vv. 2–3), but also the grace benediction (v. 25) ends μετὰ τοῦ πνεύματος ὑμῶν (*with your* [pl.] *spirit*). One must assume that both Philemon and Onesimus were present for the reading of both Colossians and Philemon, which also explains why a full one-half of the house code in Colossians (3:18–4:1) is addressed to slaves (a feature that puts unusual pressure on theories of pseudonymity).

[71] The one noticeable deviation from this pattern occurs at the conclusion of 2 Corinthians, where Paul adds, "the love of God and the fellowship of the Holy Spirit."

people. The point to be made here is that this interchangeability in mention of prayer seems both natural and presuppositional to Paul. On its own, one would make very little of it at all; but it is not on its own, as the following passage makes plain.

1 Thessalonians 3:11–13

Our final passage in this letter is christologically perhaps the most significant of all.[72] For here in particular, it is the ease with which Paul makes these kinds of interchanges, especially in prayer, that catches our attention. Thus:

3:11–13   [11]Αὐτὸς δὲ ὁ θεὸς καὶ πατὴρ ἡμῶν **καὶ ὁ κύριος ἡμῶν Ἰησοῦς κατευθύναι** τὴν ὁδὸν ἡμῶν πρὸς ὑμᾶς· [12]ὑμᾶς δὲ ὁ κύριος πλεονάσαι καὶ περισσεύσαι τῇ ἀγάπῃ εἰς ἀλλήλους καὶ εἰς πάντας καθάπερ καὶ ἡμεῖς εἰς ὑμᾶς, [13]εἰς τὸ στηρίξαι ὑμῶν τὰς καρδίας ἀμέμπτους ἐν ἁγιωσύνῃ ἔμπροσθεν τοῦ θεοῦ καὶ πατρὸς ἡμῶν ἐν τῇ παρουσίᾳ τοῦ κυρίου ἡμῶν Ἰησοῦ μετὰ πάντων τῶν ἁγίων αὐτοῦ.

[11]*May God, even our Father,* **and our Lord Jesus direct** *our way to you;* [12]*and you* **may the Lord cause to increase and abound** *in love for one another and for all, just as also ours for you,* [13]***so as to strengthen*** *your hearts blameless in holiness* before our God and Father **at the coming of our Lord Jesus with all his holy ones.**

With this prayer report, Paul concludes the narrative of his and the Thessalonians' past and present relationships on a note similar to, and thus forming a kind of inclusio with, the prayer of thanksgiving with which the letter began. Gratitude to God for their faith, love, and hope in 1:3 is now matched in 3:10–13 with a report of prayer regarding their faith (v. 10) and in vv. 12 and 13 the actual prayer regarding their love and hope. These latter concerns are apparently what cause the prayer in vv. 12 and 13 to be singularly addressed to "the Lord."

The prayer itself is in two parts. The first (v. 11) puts the emphasis on God the Father by means of the αὐτός (*himself*), but the singular verb indicates that Paul understands God and the Lord to be jointly involved in "directing our way to you." And here the compound subject with singular verb implies not so much that Paul was a Trinitarian in later terms but that

---

[72]On this prayer, see G. P. Wiles, *Paul's Intercessory Prayers: The Significance of the Intercessory Prayer Passages in the Letters of St. Paul* (SNTSMS 24; Cambridge: Cambridge University Press, 1974), which has the misfortune of limiting the "letters of Paul" to the seven accepted by all (and therefore excluding 2 Thessalonians). Wiles's term for these prayers is "wish-prayer," which he defines as "the expression of a desire that God take action regarding the person(s) mentioned in the wish" (p. 22). Unfortunately, he downplays the role of Christ in the prayer altogether (see further n. 75 below).

since both are together in heaven (1:9–10) and he desires both to be involved in the action, his apparent instinct was to think of them as working together as one.

The second part of the prayer picks up what he wants *the Lord* (= Christ) to accomplish among the Thessalonians in the meantime (in part through the rest of his letter). So now the focus is on Christ alone, that (1) he would cause the love that Paul has thanked God for in 1:3 to increase and abound both among themselves (picked up in 4:9–12) and for everyone else (including those who are giving them grief); but (2) he also wants them to be "blameless with regard to holiness" at Christ's Parousia (which is picked up in 4:3–8).[73]

Two christological matters need to be noted. First, I make the observation that Paul can pray (1) to both God the Father and the Lord Jesus together as one (v. 11), (2) to both together but single out one as the object (grammatical subject) of the concerns of prayer at a given time (vv. 12–13), and (3) to either separately (for the Father, see 1 Thess 1:2–3; 5:23; for the Lord, see 2 Thess 3:5, 16 below).

Second, even though the first emphasis in this case is on God the Father, the final focus of the prayer is altogether on the Lord Jesus, which makes the singular verb and compound subject in v. 11 seem to be more than Paul's simply taking over "conventional liturgical language to which [he] and his readers were accustomed."[74] Indeed this same phenomenon happens in reverse in 2 Thess 2:16–17, where Christ is mentioned first (including with the αὐτός) while the pickup is, exactly as in the present case, with prayer addressed to the second divine person mentioned at the outset, namely, God the Father. So one simply cannot be dismissive about the role of Christ in the present prayer.[75]

Together, these realities indicate the very high place that Christ has in Paul's understanding of God's identity. Here is a strict monotheist praying with ease to both the Father and the Son, focusing first on the one and then the other, and without a sense that his monotheism is being stretched or is in some kind of danger.

One can only conjecture as to why Paul directs the continuation of the prayer to Christ rather than the Father. Most likely it is related to an inherent

---

[73] So that the prayer in 3:11–12 and the first two items in ch. 4, where he "supplies what is lacking," end up in a chiastic form (AB BA). The emphasis in both cases (coming last and then first) is on their holiness.

[74] So Wiles, *Paul's Intercessory Prayers*, 30. What is noteworthy is that this phenomenon exists only in 1–2 Thessalonians in the NT, although wish-prayers continue to be found in Paul's letters.

[75] As Wiles does by implication in his discussion of this prayer (*Paul's Intercessory Prayers*, 54–55). Indeed, Wiles only begrudgingly allows a place for Christ in the prayer at all, despite the fact that he is explicitly called upon in vv. 12–13. Christ's role in fact is limited to a single note, in which it is suggested that "perhaps Jesus was regarded as the divine agent of the requested action, as in the following verse [v. 12!]" (p. 55 n. 3). That hardly takes seriously what Paul himself says.

difference for him between the two loves. In the next prayer (2 Thess 2:16–17), the focus is on God's love for them, which issued in their experiencing by his grace "eternal comfort and good hope." Here the emphasis would tend toward the one whose love was expressed historically in his death "for us" (see on 2 Thess 2:13 below; cf. Gal 2:20). Paul wants the Lord who so loved them to cause their love for one another to abound.

Some final remarks are needed regarding the actual content of the prayer to Christ in v. 13, where Paul reports that he prays that the Lord (= Christ) will cause their love to increase (περισσεύσαι) so as to "strengthen (εἰς τὸ στηρίξαι) your hearts [that you might be] blameless in holiness." First, the same verb for "cause to increase" is used in a nearly identical way of God the Father in 2 Cor 9:8, thus illustrating one more time the ease with which Paul can make this kind of interchange between God and Christ the Lord. Second, and for our present purposes more significantly, Paul will refer to this need of the Thessalonians to be "strengthened" two further times in 2 Thessalonians, in the prayer in 2:17 and as word of encouragement in 3:3, the first directed toward God the Father, the second regarding Christ the Son.[76]

Thus, not only does Paul here pray directly to Christ, as he does elsewhere to God, but also the express concern of the prayer is the equally shared prerogative of both Father and Son.

Taken together, all these various texts, with their equally varied emphases, point to a very high Christology for Paul that was shared between him and the Thessalonian believers. Rather than here offer a concluding word about the nature of those christological assumptions, I will reserve that to the end of the chapter itself, since these two letters, among many other things, also share a common Christology.

II. Christology in 2 Thessalonians

When turning to 2 Thessalonians, and keeping the focus on Christology only, three matters call for attention by way of introduction. First, and most obviously, the Christology of this letter simply picks up where things left off in the first one. So much is this so that one could rightly have combined the two letters in one discussion, except that that would run cross-purposes to one of the concerns of this study, namely, to treat each letter on its own terms as to the christological emphases that emerge. Second, even though it is one of the shorter letters in the corpus,[77] it has a surprisingly large, and significant, amount of christological data. Third, this is the one letter in the church corpus with very little variety in its christological affirmations and

---

[76] On this matter see the discussion below (pp. 72–73).

[77] Only Philemon and Titus are shorter.

presuppositions. From the opening greeting to the final grace-benediction, and everywhere in between, the letter is dominated by an unyielding κύριος Christology, especially by way of applying to Christ a significant number of κύριος = *Adonai* = Yahweh texts and phrases. The nature of this dominance can be seen first by a brief look at the data.

A Preliminary Look at the Data

The predominance of κύριος as the primary referent to Christ is borne out by the simple observation that of the 23 references to Christ, 22 contain the title κύριος. Ten of these stand alone, while the other twelve appear either in the threefold combination "Lord Jesus Christ" (9x) or the twofold "Lord Jesus" (3x). Thus in every mention of Christ except for the singular use of Χριστός in 3:5, the title κύριος either stands alone or fronts the mention of "Jesus" or "Jesus Christ." As with the first letter, but even more so here, this probably is related to the fact that there has been a steady increase of persecution, which most likely stems from the Thessalonians' affirmation of Christ as κύριος in a city where such allegiance was reserved for the Roman emperor. The other significant thing about this usage is that just over half of these occurrences of κύριος occur in moments of OT intertextuality of some kind.

We should also note that this is the first of the letters in the church corpus where Christ is specifically mentioned more often than God the Father (23x versus 18x)—a feature that will continue in the majority of the letters in the church corpus.[78] There is nothing especially significant here, except to note how thoroughly Pauline this usage is.

A Case of Messianic Intertextuality—2 Thessalonians 2:8

In a moment of rare intertextuality in the corpus, Paul in 2 Thess 2:8 uses κύριος to refer to Christ in a passage whose primary language carries overtones of Jewish messianism. As with 1 Thessalonians, we begin here so that this singular moment does not get lost at the end of the chapter. And just as in 1 Thess 1:10, this single allusion to Christ as Messiah speaks of him as presently in heaven awaiting his role in the final judgment of the wicked.

The primary purpose of 2 Thess 2:1–12 is to reassure these believers that "the day of the Lord" has not yet come (2:2). To do so, Paul reminds them of some things that he had previously communicated to them regarding an antecedent appearance of "the mystery of lawlessness" and of "the lawless one." With the "coming" of the latter, "the Lord Jesus" himself will return in order to destroy him. In making this point, Paul picks up the language of Isa 11:4:

---

[78]Romans being the major exception.

2 Thess 2:8 ὃν ὁ κύριος[79]   ἀνελεῖ   τῷ πνεύματι τοῦ στόματος
αὐτοῦ καὶ καταργήσει τῇ ἐπιφανείᾳ τῆς παρουσίας αὐτοῦ

Isa 11:4   καὶ πατάξει γῆν τῷ λόγῳ   τοῦ στόματος αὐτοῦ
καὶ ἐν πνεύματι   διὰ χειλέων   ἀνελεῖ ἀσεβῆ

2 Thess 2:8 *whom **the Lord**   **will slay**   **with the breath of his mouth***
and will abolish at the manifestation of his coming

Isa 11:4   *and he will strike the land with the word* ***of his mouth,***
and with the breath *of his lips*   ***will slay*** *the ungodly*

Here Isaiah has prophesied that the coming "shoot from the stump of Jesse" will be characterized by righteousness and justice that will include his slaying the wicked with "the breath of his mouth." With help from Ps 32:6 (for the form of the phrase τῷ πνεύματι τοῦ στόματος αὐτοῦ), Paul combines the two lines of Isaiah's poetry into one and attributes this messianic future judgment to "the Lord = Jesus."

Thus Paul ends up having it both ways. As we will see in the next section, he regularly appropriates Yahweh passages and applies them to Christ by means of the Greek translation κύριος; here he appropriates a messianic passage and does the same. The net result, therefore, is that Paul never loses sight of the fact that Jesus is indeed the Messiah. But by way of the Septuagint's use of κύριος to represent YHWH, to which we turn next, Paul can also appropriate all kinds of Yahweh texts and apply them to the risen Lord, Jesus.

Jesus as the Κύριος of Septuagint Yahweh Texts

Although some of these passages are of more import than others, for convenience they are discussed here in their canonical order.

2 Thessalonians 1:6–10

Paul's first thanksgiving in 2 Thessalonians evolves into the first of three major concerns in this letter: to encourage the Thessalonian believers in the face of increased "persecutions and trials" (1:4).[80] The major part of this

---

[79] A difficult textual choice occurs here. Very good evidence has "the Lord Jesus" (א A D F G P Ψ 0278 33 pc latt sy co Or Did), but equally good evidence (B 1739 1881 𝔐) lacks the Ἰησοῦς found in the rest. Since there can be little question that "the Lord" here is indeed Jesus, did some early scribes add "Jesus" in keeping with the frequency of this combination in these letters, or was the "Jesus" omitted because of parablepsis? Since the divine names were abbreviated very early in the copying tradition of the Greek NT, these two nouns would have sat side by side as ΚΣΙΣ. It is easy to see how scribes could have left the second word out. But since this combination occurs so often in these letters (see pp. 34 and 56 above) and since the omission of one or the other occurs so rarely, it seems more likely in this case that the addition is secondary.

[80] The other two are found in 2:1–12 (a misguided prophetic word that the Day of the Lord is already at hand) and 3:6–15 (the continuing problem of the disruptive idle).

very long and convoluted "thanksgiving" (vv. 3–10) is intended to demonstrate the justice of God in the face of the Thessalonians' present persecution. Beginning at v. 6, where he picks up the thrice-repeated verb ἀνταποδίδωμι (*pay back*), which encloses the oracle in Isa 66:4–6,[81] Paul spells out the just judgment of God that their present enemies will experience at the final revelation of Christ (vv. 6–7a). But it is Christ himself who will carry out the judgment at his coming (vv. 7b–10), most of which clause is couched in language from several OT judgment texts, where the Septuagint has κύριος = Yahweh as the administrator of judgment.[82] Thus Christ is now the κύριος of these intertextual echoes.

1. Paul begins his depiction of Christ's coming in vv. 7b–8 with three prepositional descriptors. The first two echo what he had earlier affirmed in his first letter: "the Lord Jesus" will be revealed "from heaven" (1 Thess 4:16; cf. 1:10) with "the angels of his power," thus interpreting Zechariah's "all his holy ones" (see 1 Thess 3:13) with concepts from Jewish apocalyptic. The third one, ἐν φλογὶ πυρός[83] (*in blazing fire*), is an echo of Isa 66:15, while the end of the clause includes language from Isa 66:4. Thus:

---

[81] I do not mean that Paul is necessarily *consciously* picking up this verb. But the fact that language from Isa 66 plays a significant role in vv. 8 and 12 suggests that this passage is in his head, as it were. See how the verb sits in the display that follows. On the possible influence of Isa 66 on this whole passage, see R. Aus, "The Relevance of Isaiah 66:7 to Revelation 12 and 2 Thessalonians 2," ZNW 67 (1976): 252–68. This view is picked up especially by Beale (186–91), who sees it as Paul's deliberately setting the believing Thessalonians in sharp contrast to their persecutors, who do not obey the gospel—just as in Isa 66 the "humble and contrite" stand in equally sharp contrast to those "who have chosen their own ways" (66:3).

[82] Although seldom noted by earlier commentators (e.g., Ellicott), this phenomenon has long been recognized by English commentators, beginning with Findlay (1904), and more extensively by Frame (1912), who notes (correctly) that although "the description abounds in reminiscences from the Septuagint, there is but one approximately exact citation [v. 9 citing Isa 2:10]." Since Best (1972), this has been more or less standard fare in the commentaries, some more cautiously than others. The christological implications have also often been noted, starting with Findlay, 148 (on v. 8: "Διδόντος transfers to the Lord Jesus the dread prerogative reserved in the O.T. for God alone"); cf. Marshall, 179–80 (on v. 9: "It is significant that language originally used of Yahweh is here applied to Jesus"), and Wanamaker, 229 ("The appropriation of texts originally written about God to describe Jesus as Lord was one of the most important developments of early christology and eventually led to the near-total identification of Christ with the nature and activities of God").

[83] My text here differs from the preferred reading in NA[27]. The textual evidence is divided between ἐν φλογὶ πυρός (*in flame of fire*) (B D F G Ψ 2464 *pc* a vg sy co Ir[lat] Tert), which would ordinarily be considered the stronger MS evidence, and ἐν πυρὶ φλογός [*in fire of flame*] (א A 0111 0278 33 1739 1881 𝔐 d m sy[hmg] Ambst). The same variation is found in Exod 3:2 (the former in A; the latter in B). At issue is whether Paul is here echoing Isa 66:15, as I believe, and scribes changed it to the reading of the more familiar text (for them) of Exod 3:2, or whether Paul himself was influenced by the B text of Exod 3:2. There can be no question that the latter is the more difficult reading from our perspective. But if some early scribes knew only the B text of Exod 3:2, they could easily have changed Paul here to conform to that more familiar phrasing. So in the end the better textual evidence should probably prevail.

2 Thess 1:7–8 ⁷τοῦ κυρίου Ἰησοῦ . . . ⁸ἐν φλογὶ πυρός, διδόντος
ἐκδίκησιν τοῖς μὴ εἰδόσιν θεὸν
καὶ   τοῖς μὴ ὑπακούουσιν τῷ εὐαγγελίῳ
τοῦ κυρίου ἡμῶν Ἰησοῦ

Isa 66:15   **κύριος** ὡς πῦρ ἥξει καὶ ὡς καταιγὶς τὰ ἄρματα αὐτοῦ
ἀποδοῦναι ἐν θυμῷ **ἐκδίκησιν** καὶ ἀποσκορακισμὸν
ἐν φλογὶ πυρός

Isa 66:4   λέγει **κύριος** [v. 2] . . . **ἀνταποδώσω** αὐτοῖς ὅτι ἐκάλεσα
αὐτοὺς **καὶ οὐχ ὑπήκουσάν μου**

2 Thess 1:7–8 ⁷*of the Lord Jesus . . .*   ⁸*in flaming fire, giving*
punishment to those who do not know God
and   to those who do not obey the gospel
of our Lord Jesus Christ

Isa 66:15   *the Lord as fire will come, and as a storm his chariots,*
to recompense with wrath, punishment and repudiation
in flaming fire

Isa 66:4   *Says the Lord (v. 2) . . . I will repay them because I called*
them and they did not obey me

Three matters are significant for our present purposes. First, the κύριος (*Lord*) in both Isaiah passages is Yahweh, while the κύριος in Paul's use of this language is specified as "the Lord, Jesus." This means, second, that the Lord who will come "in blazing fire" to mete out this judgment is "the Lord, Jesus Christ," who will thus assume Yahweh's role. Third, the reason for judgment in Isaiah is that "they do not obey me," where Isaiah's "me = Yahweh" is now expressed in terms of "the gospel of our Lord Jesus Christ."

In this case, therefore, not only does Paul identify the Lord Jesus with the "Lord = Yahweh" of Isaiah's oracle, but also the gospel of the Lord Jesus is what the wicked have not obeyed, and therefore they will be judged by him. One can hardly escape the christological implications of such an intertextual interchange.

2. The description of their judgment occurs in v. 9: they "will pay the penalty of everlasting destruction *from the face of the Lord and from the glory of his might.*" Although there are some inherent difficulties in understanding what precisely is meant by "destruction from the face of the Lord," there can be little question that the italicized part of this sentence is a direct, deliberate use of Isa 2:10.[84]

_____

[84] Noted as early as Tertullian (*Marc.* 3.16). The Septuagint translator in this case took some liberties with Isaiah's wording, probably in order to make clear what he assumed Isaiah had in mind. Thus "the fear of YHWH" has to do with seeing "his face." Paul, in turn, has kept the "face = presence" language and has omitted φόβου because that is precisely where his interests lie: the coming of the Lord, and the persecutors having to deal with being in the Lord's *presence.*

2 Thess 1:9	οἵτινες . . .	ἀπὸ προσώπου τοῦ κυρίου
	καὶ	ἀπὸ τῆς δόξης τῆς ἰσχύος αὐτοῦ
Isa 2:10	κρύπτεσθε . . .	ἀπὸ προσώπου τοῦ φόβουκυρίου
	καὶ	ἀπὸ τῆς δόξης τῆς ἰσχύος αὐτοῦ

2 Thess 1:9	who . . .	**from the face of the Lord**
	and	**from the glory of his might**
Isa 2:10	hide . . .	**from the face of the** fear of **the Lord**
	and	**from the glory of his might**

Here is a case where Paul not only has brought language straight across from the Septuagint but also has kept the sense of Isaiah's text, which appears in a "Day of the Lord" oracle of judgment against Judah. That judgment is their being cut off from the divine Presence, which is now assumed to be that of Christ the Lord. Again Paul has transferred language from "the Lord = Yahweh" to "the Lord = Jesus Christ." As such, it is a certain instance where a unique, unshared prerogative of Yahweh has now been appropriated to refer to Christ.[85]

3. In v. 10, at the conclusion of his long sentence, Paul continues what he has said about Christ in v. 9 with further appropriation of language from the Septuagint—a collage of language from Ps 89:7 (88:8 LXX)[86] and Ps 68:35 (67:36 LXX).[87] In this case the word κύριος appears neither in the immediate sentences of the Psalter nor in Paul's sentence at this point. Nonetheless, the intertextual appropriation of the language of the Psalter seems certain in a passage where Yahweh is referred to as ὁ θεός:

| 2 Thess 1:10 | ὅταν | ἔλθῃ ἐνδοξασθῆναι | ἐν τοῖς | ἁγίοις αὐτοῦ |
| Ps 88:8 LXX | ὁ θεὸς | ἐνδοξαζόμενος | ἐν βουλῇ ἁγίων | |

| 2 Thess 1:10 | when | **he comes to be glorified** | **among his saints** |
| Ps 88:8 LXX | God | **being gloried** | **in** the council **of the saints** |

| 2 Thess 1:10 | καὶ | θαυμασθῆναι | ἐν πᾶσιν τοῖς πιστεύσασιν |
| Ps 67:36 LXX | | θαυμαστὸς ὁ θεὸς | ἐν τοῖς ἁγίοις αὐτοῦ |

| 2 Thess 1:10 | and | **to be marveled at** | **among all** who believe |
| Ps 67:36 LXX | | **marvelous** is God | **among his holy ones** |

---

[85] On the use of "glory" with reference to Christ, see pp. 70–71 (on 2 Thess 2:14) and pp. 180–84 (on 2 Cor 3:18; 4:4).

[86] For Paul's further christological appropriation of the psalm, see the discussion of Col 1:15–17 in ch. 7 (p. 301).

[87] These echoes may seem a bit more tenuous than the others in this series. Indeed, were they the only echoes of the Septuagint in this passage, they would scarcely be noted in this study, especially since they lack the word κύριος. They are included here precisely because they belong to a larger complex of such usage of the OT. Cf. Best, 264–65; Marshall, 180; Bruce, 153; Wanamaker, 231; Malherbe, 404; Green, 294–95; Beale (190), however, prefers to see it as still reflecting Isa 2 and 66.

As before, it is the collocation and amount of such unusual language (for Paul) that makes the intertextuality seem certain. Paul apparently modified the prepositional phrase from "in the *council* of the holy ones" in Ps 89:7 (88:8 LXX) to "in his holy ones" from Ps 68—and that most likely because of his addition of "to be marveled at" (from Ps 68:35, which the NRSV and TNIV render as "awesome" [67:36 LXX]) at the end of his sentence. Indeed, it is precisely the intertextuality that has made the prepositional phrase such a difficult one for interpreters and translators.[88] What is striking in this case is Paul's deliberate use of this language from two places in the Psalter where the psalmists are extolling the unparalleled grandeur and greatness of Yahweh. For Paul, that language perfectly fits the eschatological coming of Christ.

Thus, with a series of echoes of "judgment" texts from the OT, where Yahweh will "come" and mete out judgment, Paul, by way of the Septuagint's use of κύριος, now places Christ in God's role as judge.

4. We should also note that Paul concludes with the prepositional phrase "on that day" (ἐν τῇ ἡμέρᾳ ἐκείνῃ), which sits especially awkwardly at the end of this now very long sentence. On Paul's appropriation of this OT language, see discussion on 1 Thess 5:2 above (pp. 46–47). For our present purposes, two matters are noteworthy. First, the very awkwardness of the phrase calls the reader's attention to it.[89] Very likely it serves with its companion ἐν τῇ ἀποκαλύψει τοῦ κυρίου Ἰησοῦ (*at the revelation of the Lord Jesus*) in v. 7b as a deliberate framing device, thus making the whole of vv. 7b–10 a kind of "Day of the Lord" oracle in its own right. Second, at the same time, its emphatic position at the end is almost certainly a deliberate response to the issue to be raised next: someone in Paul's name has declared among them that "the day of the Lord has already come."

2 Thessalonians 1:12

When Paul turns from "thanksgiving" to prayer for the Thessalonians, he focuses not so much on their sure future as on their living in the present so as to bring glory to the name of the Lord. In so doing, he appropriates language from Isa 66:5, thus concluding with an echo from the same Isaianic oracle with which he began in v. 7:

_____

[88]Both the preposition and the word ἁγίοις present a measure of difficulty. The latter is almost certainly to be understood as referring to God's people (traditionally, "the saints"). Most likely the ἐν is a deliberate "in your face" word against the Thessalonians' persecutors. At the same eschatological event when the latter will be "punished with everlasting destruction and shut out from the presence of the Lord [Jesus]," the people of God in Thessalonica will be among those who will bring eternal glory to Christ by being present among the redeemed. Thus Christ the Lord is "glorified in them" on that day.

[89]Indeed, so awkward is it that even the KJV translators, in choosing to keep Paul's word order (as was their style), inserted a parenthesis around "because our testimony among you was believed," so that "in that day" could be seen by the reader (properly so) to modify the first part of v. 10.

2 Thess 1:12 ὅπως ἐνδοξασθῇ τὸ ὄνομα τοῦ κυρίου ἡμῶν Ἰησοῦ
                      ἐν ὑμῖν

Isa 66:5 ἵνα τὸ ὄνομα κυρίου
             δοξασθῇ

2 Thess 1:12 so that **might be glorified the name** **of our Lord Jesus**
                      among you

Isa 66:5 *so that* **the name** **of the Lord**
             might be glorified

Although at first sight this usage may seem more tenuous as a case of genuine "intertextuality,"[90] there are especially good reasons for viewing it as such. First, Paul's language is that of the Septuagint Isaiah, a book with which Paul shows thoroughgoing acquaintance.[91] His wording therefore differs considerably from the Hebrew, since the Septuagint translator here was trying to make sense of some difficult lines in the Hebrew text. Original words of taunt by the postexilic "aristocratic religious" to Yahweh's faithful ones ("Let the LORD be glorified that we may see your joy!") had been turned into a promise to the latter that "the name of the LORD will be glorified" and their persecutors thus will be brought to shame.

One should not miss the similarity of this context with that of the Thessalonians. Toward the end of his "thanksgiving" Paul had set forth the demonstration of God's justice (vv. 7–10) with echoes from this same Isaianic oracle. At the same time, he also picked up language from Isa 2 and from the Psalter to emphasize the contrasting eschatological future between the Thessalonian believers and their tormentors. Indeed, God intends for Christ "to be glorified in his saints." Now Paul prays for the fulfillment of that promise by returning to Isa 66, with language spoken into a context similar to theirs. And again "the Name = YHWH" now belongs to Christ Jesus through the Septuagint's ὁ κύριος, thus continuing Paul's substitution of Christ Jesus for Yahweh, with his (not argued for) attribution to Christ of clearly divine prerogatives.

We should also note, finally, that Paul's concluding phrase, κατὰ τὴν χάριν τοῦ θεοῦ ἡμῶν καὶ κυρίου Ἰησοῦ Χριστοῦ (*according to the grace of our God and Lord Jesus Christ*), stands ambiguously in the Greek. Did Paul intend "the grace of our God and Lord, Jesus Christ" or, as almost all English translations have it, "the grace of our God and of the Lord Jesus Christ"? If Paul intended the former, of course, he not only substitutes Christ the Lord for Yahweh when citing the Septuagint but also even calls the Lord Jesus θεός (*God*). Although Greek grammar ordinarily would favor this option,[92] Pauline

---

[90] Although not mentioned in earlier commentaries (e.g., Ellicott, Findlay, Milligan), from Frame (1912) on, it is generally noted—but see the slight hesitation in Best (271) because of the word order.

[91] For evidence of this, see appendix IV in NA[27], 789–93.

[92] That is, there is only one Greek article (τοῦ) controlling both nouns (θεοῦ and κυρίου), thus coming under Granville Sharp's Rule. This view is espoused by Findlay,

usage must prevail here. That is, Paul regularly associates God the Father and the Lord Jesus Christ together in single prepositional phrases[93] like this one; and even though he does so with a bit more grammatical precision elsewhere, it is difficult to imagine that this "inclusio" with v. 2 is now intended to identify Christ with God the Father.[94]

2 Thessalonians 2:13–14

2:13–14 ¹³ἡμεῖς δὲ ὀφείλομεν εὐχαριστεῖν τῷ θεῷ πάντοτε περὶ ὑμῶν, ἀδελφοὶ **ἠγαπημένοι ὑπὸ κυρίου,**[95] ὅτι εἵλατο ὑμᾶς ὁ θεὸς ἀπαρχὴν[96] εἰς σωτηρίαν ἐν ἁγιασμῷ πνεύματος καὶ πίστει ἀληθείας, ¹⁴εἰς ὃ καὶ[97] ἐκάλεσεν ὑμᾶς διὰ τοῦ εὐαγγελίου ἡμῶν **εἰς περιποίησιν δόξης τοῦ κυρίου ἡμῶν Ἰησοῦ Χριστοῦ.**

> ¹³We ought always to give thanks to God for you, brothers (and sisters) **beloved by the Lord,** because God has chosen you as firstfruits for salvation through the sanctifying work of the Spirit and your faith in the truth, ¹⁴unto which (salvation) he (God) also called you through our gospel, so that you might share **in the glory of our Lord Jesus Christ.**

Here is the first of the many proto-Trinitarian[98] soteriological moments in Paul's letters,[99] which ordinarily have the following "grammar" of salvation (see, e.g., Rom 5:1–8):

157; Green, 299–300; it is rejected by Ellicott, 105; Milligan, 94; Frame, 242; Rigaux, 643; Best, 272–73; Bruce, 156–57; Wanamaker, 236; Morris, 211; Richard, 311; Malherbe, 412; Beale, 196–97; D. B. Wallace, *Greek Grammar Beyond the Basics: An Exegetical Syntax of the New Testament* (Grand Rapids: Zondervan, 1996), 271.

[93] See, e.g., 1 Thess 1:1; 2 Thess 1:1, 2; and throughout the corpus.

[94] Furthermore, as Milligan (94) points out, an anarthrous κύριος is a regular feature of Pauline usage—a usage first of all related to the larger issue at hand, where Paul cites an anarthrous usage from the Septuagint, but also because very likely by now the title "the Lord" is moving very close to being an actual name.

[95] The wording here has been conformed to the θεοῦ of 1 Thess 1:4 in D* b m vg.

[96] For this textual choice (NRSV, TNIV [contra NIV]), see Fee, *To What End Exegesis?* 75–76.

[97] The textual choice of add/omit the (ascensive?) καί has proved to be a difficult one for interpreters. I think that the burden of probability rests with inclusion as original here (supported by ℵ G P 81 365 2464 al vg syʰ), since it is difficult to see why anyone would have added it, and its very difficulty is reason enough for some scribes to let it go.

[98] In light of some (legitimate) objections to my use of "Trinitarian" in *God's Empowering Presence: The Holy Spirit in the Letters of Paul* (Peabody, Mass.: Hendrickson, 1994) as proper nomenclature for Pauline theology—mostly because the word carries too much of the baggage of later discussions that are concerned with how the three divine "persons" cohere in unity of being—I have chosen to use "proto-Trinitarian" throughout this study. It is borrowed from Stanley Porter (in I. H. Marshall, *Beyond the Bible: Moving from Scripture to Theology* [ASBT; Grand Rapids: Baker, 2004], 122 n. 59) as a way of designating those texts where Paul himself, rigorous monotheist though he was, joins Father, Son, and Spirit in ways that indicate the full identity of the Son and Spirit with the Father without losing that monotheism.

[99] For a full listing of these passages, see Fee, *God's Empowering Presence*, 48 n. 39.

Salvation is *predicated* on the love of God;
   it is *effected* by Christ through his death and resurrection;
   and *made effective* through the work of the Holy Spirit.

But here it takes an unusual form:

The Thessalonians have been *chosen and called by God* as firstfruits for
   salvation;
   evidenced by the fact that they are *loved by the Lord*
   [ἠγαπημένοι ὑπὸ κυρίου];
   and are thus *saved through the sanctifying work of the Spirit.*

What is striking here is not what is said about God—indeed, throughout
the Pauline corpus both "election" and "calling" are regularly attributed to
God the Father—but rather that language usually reserved for God the
Father is here freely attributed to "the Lord"[100] and that language usually attributed to Christ is here the special province of the Holy Spirit. Our interest
lies with the middle line.[101]

In the five other instances where Paul speaks of Christ's love (Gal 2:20; 2
Cor 5:14; Rom 8:35; Eph 3:19; 5:2), it is usually tied explicitly to the love expressed in his redemptive death[102] (e.g., Gal 2:20: "the Son of God, . . . who
loved me and gave himself for me"). More commonly, Paul speaks of the love
of God (θεός), which serves for him as the predicate for salvation. Indeed,
two (Greek) sentences later (2:16) this is precisely what is said: "God our
Father who loved us, and by his grace gave us eternal encouragement and
good hope" (cf. 1 Thess 1:4). And even when one grants that the phrase
"loved by the Lord" is probably in this case an allusion to his saving work on
the cross,[103] rather than the predicate of their salvation as when it is said of
the Father, it is nonetheless remarkable that this particular attribution takes
place in one of Paul's triadic ways of speaking about salvation.[104]

---

[100]That this refers to Christ and not to God (contra Rigaux, 371; Malherbe, 436;
Green, 325 [?]; Beale, 225) seems certain on the basis of both Pauline usage and the
grammar of the present sentence. Had Paul intended ὑπὸ κυρίου to equal the preceding τῷ θεῷ, then the simple, ordinary composition of such a sentence would have
been: τῷ θεῷ . . . ἠγαπημένοι ὑπὸ αὐτοῦ, ὅτι εἵλατο ὑμᾶς ἀπαρχὴν (*to God, . . . loved by
him, because he chose you as firstfruits*). Thus the awkward repetition of "God" as the
subject of Paul's sentence occurs precisely because in the meantime he has mentioned a second subject ("the Lord"), thus necessitating his return to the first noun
(cf. Lightfoot, 119; Best, 311; Marshall, 206). This grammatical reality, plus the fact
that Paul makes a considerable point in these two letters of identifying Jesus Christ
as ὁ κύριος, would seem to far outweigh the contextual considerations that Malherbe
brings forward to suggest otherwise.
[101]For a full discussion of the third line, see Fee, *God's Empowering Presence*, 77–79.
[102]The notable exception is Eph 3:19.
[103]Cf. Frame, 279; *contra* Morris (238), who suggests that "there is probably no
significance in the change."
[104]Both Morris (238) and Marshall (206) suggest that the reason for it might be to
stand in contrast to what the Lord Jesus does to the wicked in the preceding passage.

At the same time, this is another moment where Paul echoes distinct language from the Septuagint, where κύριος had served to translate the Tetragrammaton (YHWH). In this case the language is precisely that of Deut 33:12, where of Benjamin it is said: ἠγαπημένος ὑπὸ κυρίου. If this were the only one of these in 1–2 Thessalonians, then one perhaps could dismiss it as coincidental (although not easily![105]). But it is the sheer volume of them, plus the OT context for this one, that makes it quite certain as well. Thus in its second appearance in the corpus, God's love for his elect people is expressed in terms of their being loved by Christ the κύριος, an attribute that in Paul's thinking is thus equally shared by Father and Son—by presupposition and without argumentation.[106]

2 Thessalonians 3:5

The next instance of intertextuality appears at the end of a brief transitional appeal in 2 Thess 3:1–5. Here Paul has first urged that they pray for him (vv. 1–2; as he has just done for them [2:16–17]); but then he turns once more toward the Thessalonians with a threefold expression of confidence: that the "faithful Lord" (Jesus [see pp. 71–72 below]) will also strengthen them and protect them from evil (v. 3); that they will also carry out what Paul is about to command them in 3:6–14 (v. 4); and finally with a prayer (v. 5) that the Lord will direct their hearts in both of these matters (love, anticipating vv. 6–14 [cf. 1 Thess 4:9–12], and perseverance, picking up the urgencies of the two preceding chapters). The latter is yet one more prayer in these letters (see below), and it has ὁ κύριος as the one prayed to and thus as the subject of the actions prayed for.

Some think that ὁ κύριος in this case refers to God the Father,[107] but that would stand in considerable tension with Paul's usage elsewhere in these letters, where "God" is always identified as ὁ θεός and Christ as

---

[105] After all, Paul himself takes some measure of pride in his Benjaminite ancestry (Rom 11:1; Phil 3:6); is it even imaginable that this "blessing" of his ancestral tribe was not well known to the apostle? That Paul is echoing the Septuagint in this case seems to be made the more certain by the anarthrous use of κυρίου. It is therefore remarkable that the majority of commentators have missed this certain echo of the Septuagint, which was first noted by Westcott-Hort and has been in the Nestle(-Aland) margin at least since 1950 (but see Findlay, 188; others [Frame, 279; Best, 312; Malherbe, 436] reference the Septuagint but see little or no connection).

[106] Thus reflecting what L. J. Kreitzer calls a "functional and conceptual overlap between Christ and God" (Jesus and God in Paul's Eschatology [JSNTSup 19; Sheffield: Sheffield Academic Press, 1987], e.g., 165, 170).

[107] See Malherbe, 447, and (apparently) Beale, 243–48. Most (correctly) see it as picking up from 2:16–17, where Christ has been specifically identified once more as ὁ κύριος. There was, after all, no chapter or verse break in Paul's text, so how could the Thessalonians possibly think that in the very next sentences (vv. 3, 5) ὁ κύριος suddenly changes identity? Most of the early Greek fathers argued that this is a reference to the Holy Spirit, since God and Christ are mentioned in what follows. But that is an interpretation driven by Trinitarian theology, not by Pauline usage.

ὁ κύριος. Indeed, it would make little sense of Pauline usage to make this ὁ κύριος refer to God when in the preceding prayer report in 2:16–17 Paul has chosen to place Christ first as the one addressed in prayer and identified him as ὁ κύριος—and used the intensive pronoun in so doing—and then followed with ὁ θεός, who is identified as ὁ πατήρ. Only our own familiarity with referring to God as "the Lord" and a resistance to Paul's own language patterns and deliberate designations would make this ὁ κύριος refer to God the Father.

Our immediate interest in this prayer is with its (apparently) deliberate intertextual use of 1 Chr 29:18.[108] In David's prayer in conjunction with the gifts brought for the construction of the temple, he prays, "Lord, God of our Fathers, . . . direct their hearts to you."

2 Thess 3:5   ὁ δὲ **κύριος**   **κατευθύναι**   ὑμῶν **τὰς καρδίας**
             εἰς τὴν ἀγάπην τοῦ θεοῦ

1 Chr 29:18   **κύριε** ὁ θεὸς . . . καὶ **κατεύθυνον**   **τὰς καρδίας** αὐτῶν
             πρὸς σέ

2 Thess 3:5   *May the Lord*   *direct*   *your* *hearts*
             into the love of God

1 Chr 29:18   *Lord* *God* . . .   *also* *direct*   *their* *hearts*
             toward you

Three items make one think that this is deliberate intertextuality. (1) The locution is both striking and unusual—in fact, the verb is found elsewhere in Paul's writings only in the prayer in 1 Thess 3:11. Moreover, (2) the phrase "the Lord direct their/your hearts" toward God is *unique to these two passages* in the Bible.[109] And (3) the phrase is found in the mouth of the great king of Israel, David himself—and in prayer!—so that it is not a merely passing phrase used by a more obscure figure. Again Paul attributes the Septuagint's translation of the Tetragrammaton to Christ.[110]

2 Thessalonians 3:16

The final moment of (seldom noted)[111] intertextuality in these letters occurs after the "peace" and before the final "grace" at the end of 2 Thessalonians. In a singular moment in his letters, Paul dips into his Jewish heritage

---

[108] So most commentators (e.g., Findlay, 202; Rigaux, 699; Best, 329–30; Marshall, 217; Bruce, 202; Richard, 372; Malherbe, 447; Green, 339).

[109] That is, these are the only two places where "the Lord" is the subject of this verb with "the heart" as the object. Hereafter, in 2 Chronicles, the king himself does or does not "direct his own heart" to follow Yahweh (e.g., 12:14; 19:3).

[110] What is further noteworthy in this case is that both 1 Thess 3:11 and this passage are expressed as *prayer;* and Paul's prayer is directed toward Christ as Lord (see further on the "prayer" texts below).

[111] Exceptions are Marshall (230) and Richard (385).

with the blessing "The Lord be with you"; only in this case, given the nature of the letter, it becomes, "The Lord be with *all* of you." In so doing, he appropriates language that in the OT was seen as evidence of faithfulness to Yahweh, as the author of Ruth is keen to point out. Thus Boaz greets his workers, "The LORD be with you," to which they respond, "The LORD bless you!" (Ruth 2:4).[112] Paul's greeting once again reflects the (in this case verbless) text of the Septuagint:

| 2 Thess 3:16 | ὁ κύριος | μετὰ πάντων ὑμῶν. |
| Ruth 2:4 | κύριος | μεθ' ὑμῶν· |

| 2 Thess 3:16 | **The Lord (be)** | **with** *all of* **you.** |
| Ruth 2:4 | **The Lord (be)** | **with** **you.** |

Thus once more, again in an especially significant way, Paul has appropriated what strictly belonged to Yahweh in an OT passage and applied it directly to Christ.

Κύριος Phrases That Echo Septuagint Usage

Along with these several (what appear to be) certain intertextual moments in this letter, where Paul has appropriated κύριος passages from the Septuagint and applied them to Christ, there are also a few instances where he has done the same with significant Yahweh phrases, some of which are repeated from 1 Thessalonians.

The Name of the Lord

2 Thess 3:6 παραγγέλλομεν δὲ ὑμῖν, ἀδελφοί,
ἐν ὀνόματι τοῦ κυρίου ἡμῶν Ἰησοῦ Χριστοῦ

We command you, brothers (and sisters),
in the name of our Lord, Jesus Christ

On the significance of this use of "the Name of the Lord," see above on 1 Thess 5:27 (p. 46). While in this case one could perhaps get around Paul's co-opting of "the Name" as referring to Christ, by suggesting that the name in this case is not "the Lord" but "Jesus Christ," which stands in apposition to "the Lord," that simply will not do in Rom 10:9–13 (q.v.), where the whole point is that Christ is "the Lord" upon whom people now call for salvation. Thus the text from Joel 2:32 (3:5 LXX) cited there probably functions for Paul as the basis for this terminology throughout the corpus.

That is surely the case here, where "Jesus Christ" simply defines the name of the Lord. Although this is not an oath as such, it functions very much like

---

[112]For this phenomenon, see also Judg 6:12 and Luke 1:28, both of which are preceded (as here) with the wish of peace.

one. Paul is going to command the disruptive idle to work with their own hands. The authority behind this command is "the name of the Lord," the same name that he prayed would be glorified among them as they live in a manner worthy of their calling (1:11–12). This understanding is further supported by a similar phenomenon that occurs later in this same passage:

2 Thess 3:12   παραγγέλλομεν καὶ παρακαλοῦμεν **ἐν κυρίῳ Ἰησοῦ Χριστῷ**
        We command   *and urge (them)*   **in the Lord Jesus Christ**

Here, "in the Lord Jesus Christ" functions in the same way as "the name of our Lord Jesus Christ" in v. 6. As before, the christological significance of this phrase lies with the fact that this use of "the Name" is an appropriation to Christ of what belonged exclusively to Yahweh in the Hebrew Bible.

The Word of the Lord

2 Thess 3:1   ἵνα   **ὁ λόγος τοῦ κυρίου** τρέχῃ
      in order that   **the word of the Lord** *might run*

For this usage, see above on 1 Thess 1:8 and 4:15 (p. 45). It could be argued that this is another intertextual moment, this time echoing Ps 147:15 [147:4 LXX], "his word runs swiftly." But in this case the Septuagint has translated the verb as future, δραμεῖται ὁ λόγος αὐτοῦ, so this one remains doubtful as true intertextuality. That is, Paul may be reflecting this passage, but the language is now his own.

The Day of the Lord

2 Thess 2:2 ὡς ὅτι   **ἐνέστηκεν**   **ἡ ἡμέρα τοῦ κυρίου**
       that   **has come**   **the day of the Lord**

For this usage, see the discussion of 1 Thess 5:2 above (pp. 46–47).

We might note, finally, that this extraordinary number of intertextual moments in both of the Thessalonian letters suggests at least two things. First, the evidence from Acts 17:1–6 seems to be a basically reliable account of the beginnings of this congregation. Whether Paul expected the church to catch all these echoes from the Bible is a moot point; that they could have done so, Gentiles though most of them were, seems highly likely if in fact the nucleus of the origins of the church in this city was composed partly of God-fearing Gentiles who would have regularly attended the synagogue and heard these texts read over and over again.

Second, very early on, and long before he wrote these first extant letters, Paul had already begun to connect the risen Lord, Jesus Christ, whom he had encountered on the Damascus Road, with the κύριος of the Septuagint. How much he intended by that christologically may also be a moot point, but what is not debatable, it seems, is that he regularly did so without impinging on his strict monotheism. The "Lord" of these texts, whom he surely knew to refer to God the Father, was now seen to refer to Christ. This can best be explained, I will argue in later chapters, in light of (1) his own reworking of the Shema—as he does in 1 Cor 8:6 (see pp. 89–94 below), so that the one Lord God now embraces both the Father (as θεός) and the Son (as κύριος)—and (2) his understanding that God, in exalting Christ to his "right hand," also bestowed on him "the Name" = ὁ κύριος, as Paul asserts in Phil 2:9–11. By any reasonable reckoning this reflects a very high Christology indeed.

God and ὁ Κύριος Share in Divine Purposes and Activity

Another christological feature of 2 Thessalonians that carries on what began in the first letter is the joining of Christ as Lord with God the Father in several key moments of divine purpose and activity on the Thessalonians' behalf. In this letter it begins with the salutation.

The Peace of the Lord (2 Thess 1:2; 1:12)

2 Thess 1:2   χάρις ὑμῖν καὶ εἰρήνη ἀπὸ θεοῦ πατρὸς[113]
                καὶ κυρίου Ἰησοῦ Χριστοῦ.

2 Thess 1:12   κατὰ τὴν χάριν   τοῦ θεοῦ ἡμῶν
                καὶ κυρίου Ἰησοῦ Χριστοῦ

2 Thess 1:2   *Grace to you and peace*   *from God the Father*
                and the Lord Jesus Christ.

2 Thess 1:12   *according to the grace*   *of our God*
                and the Lord Jesus Christ

The elaborated greeting in the second letter (1:2) begins a practice that becomes generally consistent in Paul's subsequent letters. As with the salutation proper (see pp. 48–50 above), here again we have one preposition controlling both nouns, so that "grace" and "peace" are understood to come from Father and Son together. That this understanding lies behind what Paul says is demonstrated by his further use of "grace" and "peace" in these

---

[113] The usual ἡμῶν has been added in B D P 33 1739 1881 *pc;* but here is a case where the rules of transcriptional probability override the "better evidence." First, there is no analogy to the "omission" of this pronoun in the other Pauline salutations, so why here only, one wonders; second, the regular usage would be so well known to scribes that they would quite independently add it, and do so without thinking. It should also be noted that the absence of the pronoun puts considerable pressure on the theory of pseudepigraphy. Would a pseudepigrapher have thus botched the borrowing of this phrase from the rest of the corpus?

two letters. We have already noted[114] how he freely attributes "grace" as coming from both Father and Son. Here we note that the same is true with "peace," where the evidence from the two letters together indicates the easy interchangeability between God and Christ on this matter. Note especially how the two letters conclude:

1 Thess 5:23	αὐτὸς δὲ ὁ θεὸς	τῆς εἰρήνης ἁγιάσαι	ὑμᾶς ὁλοτελεῖς
2 Thess 3:16	αὐτὸς δὲ ὁ κύριος	τῆς εἰρήνης δῴη	ὑμῖν τὴν εἰρήνην

1 Thess 5:23	*May the God*	*of peace himself sanctify you entirely;*
2 Thess 3:16	**May the Lord**	**of peace himself give** *you peace*

The intensive pronoun in both cases, which is a common feature in the prayers of these two letters, makes it certain that the 2 Thessalonians passage can refer only to Christ.[115] Indeed, only if one were predisposed to think otherwise, and only with some difficulty, could one get around the strong implications of these texts: God the Father and Christ the Son share equally in these divine attributes as benefits for God's people.

The Divine Glory (2 Thess 2:14)

At the end of his second thanksgiving in this letter (2:13–14 [see pp. 63–65 above]), Paul speaks of the goal of salvation in terms of "obtaining the glory of our Lord Jesus Christ." It is true that on two other occasions Paul speaks of Christ in terms of "glory,"[116] but when this word is used as the eschatological goal of Christian redemption, it ordinarily refers to "the glory of God the Father," as in 1 Thess 2:12 (cf. Phil 1:11; 2:11). Thus:

1 Thess 2:12	εἰς τὸ περιπατεῖν ὑμᾶς <u>ἀξίως τοῦ θεοῦ τοῦ καλοῦντος ὑμᾶς</u> <u>εἰς τὴν ἑαυτοῦ βασιλείαν καὶ δόξαν</u>
2 Thess 2:14	εἰς ὃ καὶ <u>ἐκάλεσεν</u> ὑμᾶς διὰ τοῦ εὐαγγελίου ἡμῶν **εἰς περιποίησιν δόξης τοῦ κυρίου ἡμῶν Ἰησοῦ Χριστοῦ**

[1 Thess 2:12	*that you walk* <u>*worthy of the God who calls you*</u> <u>*into his own kingdom and glory*</u>
2 Thess 2:14	*unto which also he called you through our gospel* **unto obtaining the glory of our Lord Jesus Christ**]

---

[114] See pp. 52–53 above.

[115] So most interpreters. Malherbe (461), who is disposed to think that κύριος in 2 Thess 3 has "God" as its referent, allows that "Christ" is "a possible, but not necessary" understanding of this phrase. But the burden of proof rests with him, since Paul explicitly identifies Christ as κύριος and nowhere uses this title unambiguously to refer to God.

[116] 1 Cor 2:8: "crucified the Lord of glory"; 2 Cor 3:18/4:4: "we all with unveiled faces behold the glory of the Lord" / "the glory of Christ, who is the image of God"; see the discussions in chs. 3 and 4 below (pp. 136, 180–84).

This common OT word gives expression to the sheer majesty of the eternal God, unshared by any other, and to the wonder evoked by that majesty. It is Yahweh's "glory" that Moses desired to see (Exod 33:18), and that then filled the tabernacle (Exod 40:35) and the temple (1 Kgs 8:11). Indeed, Yahweh expressly says that he will *not* share his glory with another (Isa 42:8; 48:11 [here referring to other "gods"]). But precisely because the divine Son already shares that glory, Paul can easily speak in such terms. In this instance, to be sure, the phrase most likely has to do with Christ's own present exaltation to glory, following his humiliation in death, an exaltation in which the Thessalonians will have a share. But even so, this attribution to Christ of language usually reserved for God is a remarkable way of speaking of the final goal of the Thessalonians' redemption.

Perhaps even more striking is the language of the thanksgiving in 2 Thess 1:3–10, with its strong affirmation of God's justice noted above (pp. 57–61). In that case, through his intertextual use of Isa 2:10, Paul has straight across attributed God's unshared glory—"the glory of his might"—to the Lord Jesus.[117]

The Divine Faithfulness (2 Thess 3:3)

One of the hallmarks of Yahweh is that he is a faithful God, true to himself and his own character. And because he is so—always—God's people can count on him and trust him at all times and in all circumstances. Yahweh is so revealed in Deut 7:9 ("the faithful [πιστός] God, keeping his covenant of love to a thousand generations of those who love him"), whose faithfulness means he can do no wrong (Deut 32:4). And it is Yahweh's faithfulness to which psalmists (Ps 145:13) and prophets (Isa 49:7) appeal. And so, too, does Paul.

Its first occurrence in Paul's letters is in 1 Thess 5:24, πιστὸς ὁ καλῶν ὑμᾶς, ὃς καὶ ποιήσει (*faithful is the one who called you, who will also do it*).[118] Although not frequent thereafter, this expression does occur 3 times in his correspondence with (less than faithful) Corinth: 1 Cor 1:9; 10:13; 2 Cor 1:18. In each case, as in the OT, it is God (θεός) who is faithful. But in 2 Thess 3:3, Paul attributes such faithfulness to Christ: Πιστὸς δέ ἐστιν ὁ κύριος, ὃς στηρίξει ὑμᾶς καὶ φυλάξει ἀπὸ τοῦ πονηροῦ (*Faithful is **the Lord, who will strengthen** you and **keep** you from the evil one*).

To be sure, there are some who, on the basis of usage elsewhere, argue that Paul has God the Father in mind here as well.[119] But two things seem to

---

[117] On the question of Christ as God's "glory," see the discussions of 2 Cor 4:4, 6 (ch. 4) and Titus 2:13 (ch. 10).

[118] That "the one who called" is a reference to God is not disputed by anyone; "calling," after all, is the special province of θεός, as is made plain in 1 Thess 2:12; 4:7.

[119] See, e.g., Malherbe, 445. However, his reasons seem less than weighty: that (in his reckoning) κύριος in this letter sometimes refers to God (see, e.g., n. 107 above); and that God is the one ordinarily so designated. But that scarcely stands up against the rather certain evidence going the other way. To be sure, if this were the

militate against such a view. First, just two sentences before this (2:16), Paul has once again, and this time with the intensive αὐτός, identified ὁ κύριος as Jesus Christ, which designation he then picks up 4 times in the sentences that follow (3:1–5). One would need extraordinary evidence to the contrary to overrule Paul's own identification. Second, in the other instances of this phrase in Paul's writings, God (θεός) is the express subject of faithfulness; one wonders why Paul would not have said the same if that is what he intended here. These data, plus the fact that Paul has so many of these kinds of interchanges in these two letters, seem to make certain that such is the case in this instance as well.

The One Who Strengthens Believers (2 Thess 3:3)

In the same passage (2 Thess 3:3), Paul goes on to describe the Lord's = Christ's faithfulness in terms of "who will strengthen [στηρίξει] you and protect [φυλάξει] you from the evil one." Earlier, in the prayer in 1 Thess 3:12–13, he likewise prayed that the Lord = Christ will cause their love to increase so as to "strengthen [εἰς τὸ στηρίξαι] your hearts (that they might be) blameless in holiness." Thus his two sentences read,

2 Thess 3:3   πιστὸς δέ ἐστιν ὁ κύριος, ὃς στηρίξει ὑμᾶς καὶ φυλάξει ἀπὸ τοῦ πονηροῦ.

           ***Faithful is the Lord, who will strengthen** you and **keep** you from the evil one.*

1 Thess 3:12–13   [12]ὑμᾶς δὲ ὁ κύριος πλεονάσαι καὶ περισσεύσαι τῇ ἀγάπῃ εἰς ἀλλήλους καὶ εἰς πάντας καθάπερ καὶ ἡμεῖς εἰς ὑμᾶς, [13]εἰς τὸ στηρίξαι ὑμῶν τὰς καρδίας ἀμέμπτους ἐν ἁγιωσύνῃ

        [12]*And you **may the Lord cause to increase and abound** in love for one another and for all, just as also ours for you, [13]**so as to strengthen** your hearts blameless in holiness*

But in between these two uses of στηρίζω in prayer and affirmation regarding Christ, Paul uses the same verb with God the Father as the subject:[120]

2 Thess 2:16–17   [16]θεὸς ὁ πατὴρ ἡμῶν ὁ ἀγαπήσας ἡμᾶς καὶ δοὺς παράκλησιν αἰωνίαν καὶ ἐλπίδα ἀγαθὴν ἐν χάριτι, [17]παρακαλέσαι ὑμῶν τὰς καρδίας καὶ στηρίξαι ἐν παντὶ ἔργῳ καὶ λόγῳ ἀγαθῷ.

        [16]*May God our Father, who loved us and gave (us) eternal encouragement and good hope in grace, [17]encourage and strengthen your hearts in every good deed and word.*

---

only instance of this kind of thing in these two letters, one would have good reason to pause. But this interchange of attributes and activities between the Father and the Son is one of the striking features of the two letters.

[120]These three instances of the verb στηρίζω (*strengthen*) account for half of the occurrences in the Pauline corpus; it occurs one other time in these letters (1 Thess 3:2) and twice in Romans (1:11; 16:25).

One should further note that the verb περισσεύω (*abound*) used of the Lord = Christ in 1 Thess 3:13 is attributed to God the Father in 2 Cor 9:8.

Again, it is the ease with which Paul makes these kinds of interchanges, and especially so in prayer, that catches our attention.

The Gospel of God and of Christ (2 Thess 1:8)

Finally, in the overview of these kinds of interchange between κύριος and θεός in these two letters, one should perhaps note a phenomenon that will occur frequently in later letters: the interchange between "the gospel of God" in 1 Thess 2:2, 8, 9 and "the gospel of Christ" in 1 Thess 3:2. As is often pointed out, this is most likely an interchange between God as the source of the gospel and Christ as its basic content.

However, in the long thanksgiving-turned-announcement of judgment against the Thessalonians' persecutors in 2 Thess 1:3–10, Paul refers to the latter as "not knowing God and not obeying the gospel *of our Lord Jesus*" (v. 8). This is a unique moment in the NT, and it seems obviously shaped to fit the immediate context. The final demonstration of God's justice will be accomplished at the Parousia of the Lord Jesus, who will himself carry out the just judgment against those who are persecuting the Thessalonian believers. This phrase is but one more adaptation of common language to fit that setting. Even though the καί (*and*) in this case is probably not a straightforward hendiadys, where the second member elaborates the first, obeying "the gospel of our Lord Jesus" is almost certainly intended as an explanation of what "knowing God" means in the present era.

Christ the Lord Invoked in Prayer

Paul's readiness to address prayer to Christ, noted in 1 Thessalonians, continues in this letter in an even more pronounced way. Besides the grace-benediction (3:18),[121] there are three more such prayers in this letter. The first of these (2:16–17) calls for considerable discussion, since it has some striking similarities to, and equally striking differences from, the prayer in 1 Thess 3:11–13.

2 Thessalonians 2:16–17 (cf. 1 Thess 3:11–13)

Here are the two texts together:

_____

[121] Which is identical to 1 Thess 5:28 except for the addition of πάντων ("be with you *all*").

2 Thess 2:16–17   [16]**Αὐτὸς δὲ ὁ κύριος ἡμῶν Ἰησοῦς Χριστὸς** <u>καὶ ὁ θεὸς ὁ</u> <u>πατὴρ ἡμῶν ὁ ἀγαπήσας ἡμᾶς καὶ δοὺς</u> παράκλησιν αἰωνίαν καὶ ἐλπίδα ἀγαθὴν ἐν χάριτι, [17]<u>παρακαλέσαι</u> ὑμῶν τὰς καρδίας καὶ <u>στηρίξαι</u> ἐν παντὶ ἔργῳ καὶ λόγῳ ἀγαθῷ.

1 Thess 3:11–13   [11]<u>Αὐτὸς δὲ ὁ θεὸς καὶ πατὴρ ἡμῶν</u> **καὶ ὁ κύριος ἡμῶν** **Ἰησοῦς κατευθύναι** τὴν ὁδὸν ἡμῶν πρὸς ὑμᾶς· [12]ὑμᾶς δὲ ὁ **κύριος πλεονάσαι καὶ περισσεύσαι** τῇ ἀγάπῃ εἰς ἀλλήλους καὶ εἰς πάντας καθάπερ καὶ ἡμεῖς εἰς ὑμᾶς, [13]**εἰς** **τὸ στηρίξαι** ὑμῶν τὰς καρδίας ἀμέμπτους ἐν ἁγιωσύνῃ <u>ἔμπροσθεν τοῦ θεοῦ καὶ πατρὸς ἡμῶν</u> **ἐν τῇ παρουσίᾳ** τοῦ **κυρίου ἡμῶν Ἰησοῦ μετὰ πάντων τῶν ἁγίων αὐτοῦ.**

2 Thess 2:16–17   [16]***And may our Lord Jesus Christ*** <u>*and God our Father, who loved*</u> <u>*us and gave us*</u> *eternal encouragement and good hope in grace,* [17]<u>*encourage*</u> *your hearts and* <u>*strengthen*</u> *(you) in every good deed and word.*

1 Thess 3:11–13   [11]<u>*May God, even our Father,*</u> ***and our Lord Jesus direct*** *our way to you;* [12]*and you* ***may the Lord cause to increase and abound*** *in love for one another and for all, just as also ours for you,* [13]***so as to*** ***strengthen*** *your hearts blameless in holiness* <u>*before our God and*</u> <u>*Father*</u> ***at the coming of our Lord Jesus with all his holy*** ***ones.***

First the similarities, since looking at them together will settle some of the grammatical questions that have been raised.

1. Both prayers are directed toward θεός and κύριος together.

2. Both have the compound subject ("God" and "Lord") with a singular verb. Some have argued that one cannot make too much theologically of this phenomenon,[122] but what must be noted here is that the same phenomenon occurs in both cases, even though the subjects are in reverse order in the present instance.[123]

---

[122]See, e.g., J. A. Hewett, "1 Thessalonians 3.13," *ExpTim* 87 (1975–1976): 54–55; Lightfoot, 48 (cf. Wanamaker, 142); and Bruce (71), who suggests that "with two subjects the verb commonly agrees with the nearer of the two." But the texts brought forward do not seem to be true illustrations. That is, "wind and sea" (Mark 4:41), "moth and rust" (Matt 6:19), and "silver and gold" (Jas 5:3) do not seem to make this point; rather, they are analogous to Paul's use here, where the two are thought of not individually but collectively. Richard (167–68) solves this "problem" by postulating an early scribal corruption to Paul's original text, which he reconstructs as "Now may God our Father himself, as also our Lord Jesus, direct." Better, it would seem, to take Paul himself seriously, since he can pray to both together and to one or the other separately. Richard's concern, it should be noted, is a legitimate one: not to read Paul in light of later Trinitarian formulations. On the other hand, it is the very kind of phenomenon that played a role in the later formulations.

[123]Wiles (see n. 72) and Richard (see preceding note), as with many others, it should be noted, reject Pauline authorship of 2 Thessalonians, which makes more difficult the task of accounting for this phenomenon in 1 Thessalonians.

3. Both begin with the intensive αὐτός, which in each case must be grammatically understood to go with the first subject,[124] although, given the singular verb, it may very well also be thought of as a collective singular.[125]

4. In both cases the elaboration of the prayer is directed toward the second addressee of the prayer (but grammatical subject of the sentence): "the Lord" in 1 Thessalonians, "God" in 2 Thessalonians. This phenomenon in turn seems to stand in some tension with the previous one. That is, the αὐτός would seem to put the emphasis on the first member, yet the elaboration focuses only on the second.

5. Both prayers share as a basic concern that the Thessalonians will be "strengthened," expressed with στηρίξαι, a verb that occurs 4 times in these letters and only 2 times elsewhere in the Pauline corpus (Rom 1:11; 16:25).[126]

The singular significant difference, of course, is that the two grammatical subjects are reversed in 2 Thess 3:16, so that if there were no elaboration at all, the emphasis might seem to lie with the first member, especially since in both cases this member is accompanied by the intensive αὐτός (*himself*): "May our God and Father *himself* and the Lord Jesus Christ"; "May our Lord Jesus Christ *himself* and God our Father." And so it does in a way. Indeed, had we only one of these prayers, one could argue[127] by extrapolation that the emphasis in prayer for Paul is on the first one being addressed. But having both prayers, with their reversal of order and with the continuation prayer addressed only to the *second* member, would seem to prevent that.

As to the prayer itself, one needs to note that it brings conclusion to all of 2:1–17, Paul's concern for the grossly mistaken eschatology that someone among them has put forward and that is therefore more deeply unsettling an already unsettled community. At the same time it concludes vv. 13–15, where Paul exhorts the Thessalonian believers to stay with what they have already been taught (v. 15), after setting them (vv. 13–14) in stark contrast to those who believe the lie and will be condemned with the man of lawlessness (vv. 10–12).

Here we are confronted with prayer that is quite different from the former one. As noted, it still has the plural subject with singular verbs, but the

---

[124] Wiles suggests that "this must have been taken over from the conventional liturgical language to which the apostle and his readers were accustomed" (*Paul's Intercessory Prayers*, 30). But "must have been" falls far short of actual demonstration. What is noteworthy is that the phenomenon exists only in 1–2 Thessalonians in the NT, although wish-prayers continue to be found in Paul's letters (Wiles lists Rev 21:3 as well, but this is affirmation, not prayer).

[125] So, e.g., Frame, 136–37; Best, 147.

[126] In Thessalonians three of the four have to do with divine strengthening, two of which have Christ as the subject (see above on 2 Thess 3:3), while the other (1 Thess 3:2) has to do with apostolic encouragement of God's people. So also in Romans: 16:25 is divine; 1:11 is apostolic.

[127] As Wiles does (see n. 72 above).

αὐτός now goes with the Lord Jesus Christ. The mention of God the Father is then elaborated as the one who "in grace has loved *us* and has given us eternal comfort and good hope." But then the two verbs that make up the actual prayer are (grammatically) assumed to be the joint action of the Lord and God the Father. The result, whether intended or not, is that the first verb (παρακαλέσαι) picks up the second phrase about God that has just preceded ("eternal παράκλησις"), while the second verb (στηρίξαι) is used of Christ in 1 Thess 3:12 and is picked up again in 2 Thess 3:3 as affirmation about what Christ will do for them.

2 Thessalonians 3:5

3:5 Ὁ δὲ κύριος κατευθύναι ὑμῶν τὰς καρδίας <u>εἰς τὴν ἀγάπην τοῦ θεοῦ</u> καὶ εἰς τὴν ὑπομονὴν τοῦ Χριστοῦ.

May the Lord direct *your hearts* <u>into the love of God</u> and **into the patience of Christ.**

This prayer concludes the transitional passage (3:1–5), which began with Paul urging reciprocal prayer from the Thessalonians with regard to his own ministry (vv. 1–2).[128] But with that, Paul turns his attention to them once again, in this case by means of three brief sentences that look both backward and forward, especially now in anticipation of the strong warning to the ἄτακτοι (*disruptive idle*) in vv. 6–16. First (v. 3), picking up from the preceding prayer, he assures them that "the faithful Lord will both strengthen them and protect them from the evil one." Second (v. 4), he expresses his "confidence in the Lord" that they are both doing and will do what he has commanded them (referring now especially to 1 Thess 4:9–12). Third (v. 5), he offers yet one more prayer, this time that "the Lord (Jesus) will direct your hearts into God's love and Christ's[129] perseverance," both of which will be needed for what he has to say next.

As with the prayer in 1 Thess 3:12–13, this one is directed to the Lord alone; but at the same time Paul picks up the verb from 1 Thessalonians 3:11, which was addressed to God and Christ together.

2 Thessalonians 3:16

3:16 αὐτὸς δὲ ὁ κύριος τῆς εἰρήνης δῴη ὑμῖν τὴν εἰρήνην

May the Lord of peace himself give *you peace*

---

[128] For the intertextual use of 1 Chr 29:18 in the formulation of the prayer, see the discussion on pp. 65–66 above. Our concern here is with the fact that the prayer is directed toward Christ alone.

[129] This is the only instance in 2 Thessalonians where the name "Christ" occurs by itself. Here it seems most likely the result, in part, of Paul's not wanting to repeat the subject of the sentence in this statement of the goal of the prayer. The actual referent of "perseverance" is unclear, but most likely it is the perseverance that Christ showed in his suffering and that he can now give to the Thessalonians.

This passage was noted above (p. 65) in the discussion of shared activities. I bring it into focus again at the end of this chapter to point out that it functions as yet one more *prayer* addressed to Christ alone. It should be noted that this prayer concludes the long warning to the disruptive idle in the same way the preceding prayer concluded that transitional paragraph. I have already called attention to the interchange of "the Lord of peace" with "the God of peace" in the similar prayer at the end of 1 Thessalonians. Here we simply note that Paul continues his directing prayer to Christ alone found in v. 5. And what a conclusion it is: Christ, as "the Lord of peace," is the Lord who can bring *shalom* into the Thessalonian community, disrupted by those who have refused to work and are living off the largesse of others. Paul's focus on the need of the believing community itself is thus expressed in a prayer that focuses on the Lord of the community himself.

The data from these prayers together point to a considerably high understanding of the person and role of Christ. Paul is addressing prayer, a prerogative that Jews reserved for God alone, to the present reigning Lord, Jesus Christ. And he does so apparently unself-consciously, which suggests that this has long been a part of his life of devotion.[130]

Conclusion

Since conclusions have been regularly drawn throughout this chapter, at the end of our look at 2 Thessalonians I simply bring together the two main points regarding the Christology that has emerged in the two letters.

First, clear distinctions are regularly made between God the Father and the Lord Jesus Christ, beginning with the opening salutation. They are neither confused nor conjoined in such a way that they are not thought of individually. And in many respects their "spheres" of activity can be isolated. God is always seen as the prime mover, and therefore as the one whose love lies behind all that believers experience (1 Thess 1:4), including their election and calling. Christ, on the other hand, is seen as the one who has effected their salvation (1 Thess 1:10; 5:10–11) and who therefore is the one actively engaged in their ongoing life as a community of faith and the one to whom Paul prays that such activity in their behalf will continue. Christ Jesus therefore is the exalted Lord, whose "name" is taken directly from the Septuagint's translation of Yahweh as κύριος and who thus assumes all kinds of roles that God alone has in the OT story.

Second, precisely because Christ as the messianic Son of God is also seen as the present reigning Lord in heaven, Paul can speak of either God or

---

[130] One of the difficulties with F. Matera's narrative approach to Christology is that it tends toward a minimalist view of the Christology of these letters. The difficulty lies not with what is said—"Jesus enjoys a godly status" (*New Testament Christology*, 91)—but with what is left unsaid, such as the data in these final two sections.

Christ in ways that reflect their shared purposes and activities. At the same time, however, he feels quite free to pray to both together or to one or the other, depending on the perceived need and situation. And Paul can do this as a thoroughly monotheistic Jew, for whom the living and true God is the one and only God over against all pagan idolatries.

If these two sets of realities bring tension for us in the later church, the way through that tension is not by denying or minimizing what Paul says and does; rather, it requires us to expand our own understanding of the identity of the one God, which can embrace both Father and Son while still being only one God. In N. T. Wright's language, what we are confronted with in these earliest letters is a "christological monotheism."[131] Faithful to his own heritage, Paul remains a strict monotheist. The Jewish God is God alone, the "living and true God." Yet there is, at the same time, a plainly christological modification of this monotheism. The one God has a Son, who, as the exalted Lord, shares the divine identity and the divine prerogatives. God's will now finds its expression "in Christ Jesus" (1 Thess 5:18).

It is this set of tensions that turns our attention to the Christology of the next letter, 1 Corinthians, where Paul plainly asserts as much about the one God, who is now both θεός (God the Father) and κύριος (the Lord, Jesus Christ).

Appendix I: The Texts

(double brackets [[ ]] indicate texts with references to God alone)

1 Thessalonians

1:1 Παῦλος καὶ Σιλουανὸς καὶ Τιμόθεος τῇ ἐκκλησίᾳ Θεσσαλονικέων ἐν θεῷ πατρὶ καὶ κυρίῳ Ἰησοῦ Χριστῷ,

[[1:2 Εὐχαριστοῦμεν τῷ θεῷ πάντοτε περὶ πάντων ὑμῶν μνείαν ποιούμενοι ἐπὶ τῶν προσευχῶν ἡμῶν,]]

1:3 . . . καὶ τῆς ὑπομονῆς τῆς ἐλπίδος τοῦ κυρίου ἡμῶν Ἰησοῦ Χριστοῦ ἔμπροσθεν τοῦ θεοῦ καὶ πατρὸς ἡμῶν,

[[1:4 εἰδότες, ἀδελφοὶ ἠγαπημένοι ὑπὸ τοῦ θεοῦ, τὴν ἐκλογὴν ὑμῶν,]]

1:6 καὶ ὑμεῖς μιμηταὶ ἡμῶν ἐγενήθητε καὶ τοῦ κυρίου, δεξάμενοι τὸν λόγον ἐν θλίψει πολλῇ μετὰ χαρᾶς πνεύματος ἁγίου,

1:8 ἀφ' ὑμῶν γὰρ ἐξήχηται ὁ λόγος τοῦ κυρίου οὐ μόνον ἐν . . . ἀλλ' ἐν παντὶ τόπῳ ἡ πίστις ὑμῶν ἡ πρὸς τὸν θεὸν ἐξελήλυθεν,

---

[131] See *The Climax of the Covenant: Christ and the Law in Pauline Theology* (Minneapolis: Fortress, 1992), 129.

1:9–10 ⁹... πῶς ἐπεστρέψατε <u>πρὸς τὸν θεὸν</u> ἀπὸ τῶν εἰδώλων δουλεύειν <u>θεῷ</u>
<u>ζῶντι καὶ ἀληθινῷ</u> ¹⁰καὶ ἀναμένειν **τὸν υἱὸν** <u>αὐτοῦ</u> **ἐκ τῶν οὐρανῶν**, ὃν
ἤγειρεν ἐκ τῶν νεκρῶν, **Ἰησοῦν** τὸν **ῥυόμενον ἡμᾶς ἐκ τῆς ὀργῆς τῆς**
ἐρχομένης.

[[2:2 ... ἐν Φιλίπποις ἐπαρρησιασάμεθα <u>ἐν τῷ θεῷ ἡμῶν</u> λαλῆσαι πρὸς
ὑμᾶς <u>τὸ εὐαγγέλιον τοῦ θεοῦ</u> ἐν πολλῷ ἀγῶνι.]]

[[2:4 ἀλλὰ καθὼς δεδοκιμάσμεθα <u>ὑπὸ τοῦ θεοῦ</u> πιστευθῆναι τὸ εὐαγγέλιον,
οὕτως λαλοῦμεν, οὐχ ὡς ἀνθρώποις ἀρέσκοντες ἀλλὰ <u>θεῷ τῷ δοκιμάζοντι</u>
<u>τὰς καρδίας ἡμῶν.</u>]]

[[2:5 ... οὔτε ἐν προφάσει πλεονεξίας, <u>θεὸς μάρτυς,</u>]]

[[2:7 δυνάμενοι ἐν βάρει εἶναι ὡς **Χριστοῦ ἀπόστολοι**, ἀλλὰ ἐγενήθημεν
νήπιοι ἐν μέσῳ ὑμῶν.

[[2:8 ... εὐδοκοῦμεν μεταδοῦναι ὑμῖν οὐ μόνον <u>τὸ εὐαγγέλιον τοῦ θεοῦ</u>
ἀλλὰ καὶ τὰς ἑαυτῶν ψυχάς,]]

[[2:9–10 ⁹... ἐκηρύξαμεν εἰς ὑμᾶς <u>τὸ εὐαγγέλιον τοῦ θεοῦ</u>. ¹⁰ὑμεῖς μάρτυρες
<u>καὶ ὁ θεός</u>, ὡς ὁσίως καὶ δικαίως καὶ ἀμέμπτως ὑμῖν ...]]

[[2:12 ... μαρτυρόμενοι εἰς τὸ περιπατεῖν ὑμᾶς <u>ἀξίως τοῦ θεοῦ τοῦ</u>
<u>καλοῦντος ὑμᾶς εἰς τὴν ἑαυτοῦ βασιλείαν καὶ δόξαν.</u>]]

[[2:13 Καὶ διὰ τοῦτο καὶ ἡμεῖς εὐχαριστοῦμεν <u>τῷ θεῷ</u> ἀδιαλείπτως, ὅτι
παραλαβόντες <u>λόγον ἀκοῆς παρ' ἡμῶν τοῦ θεοῦ</u> ἐδέξασθε οὐ λόγον
ἀνθρώπων ἀλλὰ καθώς ἐστιν <u>ἀληθῶς λόγον θεοῦ</u>, ὃς καὶ ἐνεργεῖται ἐν ὑμῖν
τοῖς πιστεύουσιν.]]

2:14 ὑμεῖς γὰρ μιμηταὶ ἐγενήθητε, ἀδελφοί, <u>τῶν ἐκκλησιῶν τοῦ θεοῦ</u> τῶν
οὐσῶν ἐν τῇ Ἰουδαίᾳ **ἐν Χριστῷ Ἰησοῦ**, ὅτι τὰ αὐτὰ ἐπάθετε καὶ ὑμεῖς ὑπὸ
τῶν ἰδίων ...

2:14–15 ¹⁴... συμφυλετῶν καθὼς καὶ αὐτοὶ ὑπὸ τῶν Ἰουδαίων, ¹⁵τῶν **καὶ τὸν**
κύριον ἀποκτεινάντων Ἰησοῦν καὶ τοὺς προφήτας καὶ ἡμᾶς ἐκδιωξάντων
καὶ **θεῷ** μὴ ἀρεσκόντων καὶ πᾶσιν ἀνθρώποις ἐναντίων,

2:19 τίς γὰρ ἡμῶν ἐλπὶς ἢ χαρὰ ἢ στέφανος καυχήσεως ἢ οὐχὶ καὶ ὑμεῖς
ἔμπροσθεν τοῦ κυρίου ἡμῶν Ἰησοῦ ἐν τῇ αὐτοῦ παρουσίᾳ;

3:2 καὶ ἐπέμψαμεν Τιμόθεον, τὸν ἀδελφὸν ἡμῶν καὶ <u>συνεργὸν τοῦ θεοῦ</u> ἐν
τῷ εὐαγγελίῳ τοῦ Χριστοῦ, εἰς τὸ στηρίξαι ὑμᾶς καὶ παρακαλέσαι ὑπὲρ
τῆς πίστεως ὑμῶν

3:8 ὅτι νῦν ζῶμεν ἐὰν ὑμεῖς στήκετε **ἐν κυρίῳ.**

[[3:9 τίνα γὰρ <u>εὐχαριστίαν δυνάμεθα τῷ θεῷ</u> ἀνταποδοῦναι περὶ ὑμῶν ἐπὶ
πάσῃ τῇ χαρᾷ ᾗ χαίρομεν δι' ὑμᾶς <u>ἔμπροσθεν τοῦ θεοῦ ἡμῶν,</u>]]

3:11–13 ¹¹<u>Αὐτὸς δὲ ὁ θεὸς καὶ πατὴρ ἡμῶν</u> **καὶ ὁ κύριος ἡμῶν Ἰησοῦς**
κατευθύναι τὴν ὁδὸν ἡμῶν πρὸς ὑμᾶς· ¹²ὑμᾶς δὲ **ὁ κύριος πλεονάσαι καὶ**

περισσεύσαι τῇ ἀγάπῃ εἰς ἀλλήλους καὶ εἰς πάντας καθάπερ καὶ ἡμεῖς εἰς ὑμᾶς, [13]εἰς τὸ στηρίξαι ὑμῶν τὰς καρδίας ἀμέμπτους ἐν ἁγιωσύνῃ ἔμπροσθεν τοῦ θεοῦ καὶ πατρὸς ἡμῶν **ἐν τῇ παρουσίᾳ τοῦ κυρίου ἡμῶν Ἰησοῦ μετὰ πάντων τῶν ἁγίων αὐτοῦ.**

4:1 Λοιπὸν οὖν, ἀδελφοί, ἐρωτῶμεν ὑμᾶς καὶ παρακαλοῦμεν **ἐν κυρίῳ Ἰησοῦ,** ἵνα καθὼς παρελάβετε παρ᾽ ἡμῶν τὸ πῶς δεῖ ὑμᾶς περιπατεῖν καὶ ἀρέσκειν θεῷ,

4:2 οἴδατε γὰρ τίνας παραγγελίας ἐδώκαμεν ὑμῖν **διὰ τοῦ κυρίου Ἰησοῦ.**

[[4:3 τοῦτο γάρ ἐστιν θέλημα τοῦ θεοῦ, ὁ ἁγιασμὸς ὑμῶν,]]

[[4:5 . . . καθάπερ καὶ τὰ ἔθνη τὰ μὴ εἰδότα τὸν θεόν,]]

4:6 τὸ μὴ ὑπερβαίνειν καὶ πλεονεκτεῖν ἐν τῷ πράγματι τὸν ἀδελφὸν αὐτοῦ, διότι **ἔκδικος κύριος** περὶ πάντων τούτων, καθὼς καὶ προείπαμεν ὑμῖν καὶ διεμαρτυράμεθα.

[[4:7–8 [7]οὐ γὰρ ἐκάλεσεν ἡμᾶς ὁ θεὸς ἐπὶ ἀκαθαρσίᾳ ἀλλ᾽ ἐν ἁγιασμῷ. [8]τοιγαροῦν ὁ ἀθετῶν οὐκ ἄνθρωπον ἀθετεῖ ἀλλὰ τὸν θεὸν τὸν καὶ διδόντα τὸ πνεῦμα αὐτοῦ . . .]]

[[4:9 . . . αὐτοὶ γὰρ ὑμεῖς θεοδίδακτοί ἐστε εἰς τὸ ἀγαπᾶν ἀλλήλους,]]

[[4:14–17 [14]εἰ γὰρ πιστεύομεν ὅτι **Ἰησοῦς** ἀπέθανεν καὶ ἀνέστη, οὕτως καὶ ὁ θεὸς τοὺς κοιμηθέντας **διὰ τοῦ Ἰησοῦ ἄξει σὺν αὐτῷ.** [15]Τοῦτο γὰρ ὑμῖν λέγομεν **ἐν λόγῳ κυρίου,** ὅτι ἡμεῖς οἱ ζῶντες οἱ περιλειπόμενοι **εἰς τὴν παρουσίαν τοῦ κυρίου** οὐ μὴ φθάσωμεν τοὺς κοιμηθέντας· [16]ὅτι **αὐτὸς ὁ κύριος** ἐν κελεύσματι, ἐν φωνῇ ἀρχαγγέλου καὶ ἐν σάλπιγγι θεοῦ, **καταβήσεται ἀπ᾽ οὐρανοῦ** καὶ οἱ νεκροὶ **ἐν Χριστῷ** ἀναστήσονται πρῶτον, [17]ἔπειτα ἡμεῖς οἱ ζῶντες οἱ περιλειπόμενοι ἅμα σὺν αὐτοῖς ἁρπαγησόμεθα ἐν νεφέλαις **εἰς ἀπάντησιν τοῦ κυρίου** εἰς ἀέρα· καὶ οὕτως **πάντοτε σὺν κυρίῳ ἐσόμεθα.**

5:2 αὐτοὶ γὰρ ἀκριβῶς οἴδατε ὅτι **ἡμέρα κυρίου** ὡς κλέπτης ἐν νυκτὶ οὕτως ἔρχεται.

5:9–10 [9]ὅτι οὐκ ἔθετο ἡμᾶς ὁ θεὸς εἰς ὀργὴν ἀλλὰ εἰς περιποίησιν σωτηρίας **διὰ τοῦ κυρίου ἡμῶν Ἰησοῦ Χριστοῦ** [10]**τοῦ ἀποθανόντος** ὑπὲρ ἡμῶν, ἵνα εἴτε γρηγορῶμεν εἴτε καθεύδωμεν **ἅμα σὺν αὐτῷ** ζήσωμεν.

5:12 Ἐρωτῶμεν δὲ ὑμᾶς, ἀδελφοί, εἰδέναι τοὺς κοπιῶντας ἐν ὑμῖν καὶ προϊσταμένους ὑμῶν **ἐν κυρίῳ** καὶ νουθετοῦντας ὑμᾶς

5:18 ἐν παντὶ εὐχαριστεῖτε· τοῦτο γὰρ θέλημα θεοῦ **ἐν Χριστῷ Ἰησοῦ** εἰς ὑμᾶς.

5:23 Αὐτὸς δὲ ὁ θεὸς τῆς εἰρήνης ἁγιάσαι ὑμᾶς ὁλοτελεῖς, καὶ ὁλόκληρον ὑμῶν τὸ πνεῦμα καὶ ἡ ψυχὴ καὶ τὸ σῶμα ἀμέμπτως **ἐν τῇ παρουσίᾳ τοῦ κυρίου ἡμῶν Ἰησοῦ Χριστοῦ** τηρηθείη.

[[5:24 πιστὸς <u>ὁ καλῶν ὑμᾶς</u>, <u>ὃς καὶ ποιήσει</u>.]]

5:27 Ἐνορκίζω ὑμᾶς τὸν **κύριον** ἀναγνωσθῆναι τὴν ἐπιστολὴν πᾶσιν τοῖς ἀδελφοῖς.

5:28 Ἡ χάρις **τοῦ κυρίου ἡμῶν Ἰησοῦ Χριστοῦ** μεθ᾽ ὑμῶν.

2 Thessalonians

1:1 Παῦλος καὶ Σιλουανὸς καὶ Τιμόθεος τῇ ἐκκλησίᾳ Θεσσαλονικέων <u>ἐν θεῷ πατρὶ</u> ἡμῶν **καὶ κυρίῳ Ἰησοῦ Χριστῷ**,

1:2 χάρις ὑμῖν καὶ εἰρήνη <u>ἀπὸ θεοῦ πατρὸς</u> [v.l. + <u>ἡμῶν</u>] **καὶ κυρίου Ἰησοῦ Χριστοῦ.**

[[1:3 <u>Εὐχαριστεῖν ὀφείλομεν τῷ θεῷ</u> πάντοτε περὶ ὑμῶν,]]

[[1:4 ὥστε αὐτοὺς ἡμᾶς ἐν ὑμῖν ἐγκαυχᾶσθαι <u>ἐν ταῖς ἐκκλησίαις τοῦ θεοῦ</u> ὑπὲρ τῆς ὑπομονῆς ὑμῶν . . .]]

[[1:5–6 ⁵ἔνδειγμα <u>τῆς δικαίας κρίσεως τοῦ θεοῦ</u> εἰς τὸ καταξιωθῆναι ὑμᾶς <u>τῆς βασιλείας τοῦ θεοῦ</u>, ὑπὲρ ἧς καὶ πάσχετε, ⁶εἴπερ δίκαιον <u>παρὰ θεῷ</u> ἀνταποδοῦναι τοῖς θλίβουσιν ὑμᾶς θλῖψιν]]

1:7–10 ⁷καὶ ὑμῖν τοῖς θλιβομένοις ἄνεσιν μεθ᾽ ἡμῶν, **ἐν τῇ ἀποκαλύψει τοῦ κυρίου Ἰησοῦ** ἀπ᾽ οὐρανοῦ μετ᾽ ἀγγέλων δυνάμεως αὐτοῦ ⁸ἐν πυρὶ φλογός, διδόντος ἐκδίκησιν <u>τοῖς μὴ εἰδόσιν θεὸν</u> καὶ τοῖς μὴ ὑπακούουσιν **τῷ εὐαγγελίῳ τοῦ κυρίου ἡμῶν Ἰησοῦ**, ⁹οἵτινες δίκην τίσουσιν ὄλεθρον αἰώνιον **ἀπὸ προσώπου τοῦ κυρίου καὶ ἀπὸ τῆς δόξης τῆς ἰσχύος αὐτοῦ**, ¹⁰ὅταν **ἔλθῃ ἐνδοξασθῆναι ἐν τοῖς ἁγίοις αὐτοῦ** καὶ **θαυμασθῆναι ἐν πᾶσιν τοῖς πιστεύσασιν**, ὅτι ἐπιστεύθη τὸ μαρτύριον ἡμῶν ἐφ᾽ ὑμᾶς, ἐν τῇ ἡμέρᾳ ἐκείνῃ.

1:11–12 ¹¹εἰς ὃ καὶ προσευχόμεθα πάντοτε περὶ ὑμῶν, ἵνα ὑμᾶς <u>ἀξιώσῃ</u> τῆς κλήσεως <u>ὁ θεὸς ἡμῶν καὶ πληρώσῃ</u> πᾶσαν εὐδοκίαν ἀγαθωσύνης καὶ ἔργον πίστεως ἐν δυνάμει, ¹²ὅπως **ἐνδοξασθῇ τὸ ὄνομα τοῦ κυρίου ἡμῶν Ἰησοῦ ἐν ὑμῖν, καὶ ὑμεῖς ἐν αὐτῷ**, <u>κατὰ τὴν χάριν τοῦ θεοῦ ἡμῶν</u> **καὶ κυρίου Ἰησοῦ Χριστοῦ.**

2:1–2 ¹Ἐρωτῶμεν δὲ ὑμᾶς, ἀδελφοί, **ὑπὲρ τῆς παρουσίας τοῦ κυρίου ἡμῶν Ἰησοῦ Χριστοῦ** καὶ ἡμῶν ἐπισυναγωγῆς **ἐπ᾽ αὐτὸν** ²εἰς τὸ μὴ ταχέως σαλευθῆναι ὑμᾶς ἀπὸ τοῦ νοὸς μηδὲ θροεῖσθαι, μήτε διὰ πνεύματος μήτε διὰ λόγου μήτε δι᾽ ἐπιστολῆς ὡς δι᾽ ἡμῶν, ὡς ὅτι **ἐνέστηκεν ἡ ἡμέρα τοῦ κυρίου·**

[[2:4 . . . ὥστε αὐτὸν <u>εἰς τὸν ναὸν τοῦ θεοῦ</u> καθίσαι ἀποδεικνύντα ἑαυτὸν ὅτι ἔστιν θεός.]]

2:8–9 ⁸καὶ τότε ἀποκαλυφθήσεται ὁ ἄνομος, ὃν **ὁ κύριος** [v.l. + Ἰησοῦς] **ἀνελεῖ τῷ πνεύματι τοῦ στόματος αὐτοῦ καὶ καταργήσει τῇ ἐπιφανείᾳ τῆς παρουσίας αὐτοῦ**, ⁹οὗ ἐστιν ἡ παρουσία . . .

[[2:11 καὶ διὰ τοῦτο <u>πέμπει αὐτοῖς ὁ θεὸς</u> ἐνέργειαν πλάνης εἰς τὸ πιστεῦσαι αὐτοὺς τῷ ψεύδει,]]

2:13–14 [13]Ἡμεῖς δὲ ὀφείλομεν <u>εὐχαριστεῖν τῷ θεῷ</u> πάντοτε περὶ ὑμῶν, ἀδελφοὶ **ἠγαπημένοι ὑπὸ κυρίου**, ὅτι <u>εἵλατο ὑμᾶς ὁ θεὸς</u> ἀπαρχὴν εἰς σωτηρίαν ἐν ἁγιασμῷ πνεύματος καὶ πίστει ἀληθείας, [14]εἰς ὃ καὶ <u>ἐκάλεσεν</u> ὑμᾶς διὰ τοῦ εὐαγγελίου ἡμῶν **εἰς περιποίησιν δόξης τοῦ κυρίου ἡμῶν Ἰησοῦ Χριστοῦ**.

2:16–17 [16]**Αὐτὸς δὲ ὁ κύριος ἡμῶν Ἰησοῦς Χριστὸς** <u>καὶ [ὁ] θεὸς ὁ πατὴρ ἡμῶν ὁ ἀγαπήσας ἡμᾶς καὶ δοὺς</u> παράκλησιν αἰωνίαν καὶ ἐλπίδα ἀγαθὴν ἐν χάριτι, [17]**παρακαλέσαι** ὑμῶν τὰς καρδίας καὶ **στηρίξαι** ἐν παντὶ ἔργῳ καὶ λόγῳ ἀγαθῷ.

3:1–5 [1]Τὸ λοιπὸν προσεύχεσθε, ἀδελφοί, περὶ ἡμῶν, ἵνα **ὁ λόγος τοῦ κυρίου** τρέχῃ καὶ δοξάζηται καθὼς καὶ πρὸς ὑμᾶς, [2]καὶ ἵνα ῥυσθῶμεν ἀπὸ τῶν ἀτόπων καὶ πονηρῶν ἀνθρώπων· οὐ γὰρ πάντων ἡ πίστις. [3]**Πιστὸς δέ ἐστιν ὁ κύριος**, ὃς στηρίξει ὑμᾶς καὶ φυλάξει ἀπὸ τοῦ πονηροῦ. [4]πεποίθαμεν δὲ **ἐν κυρίῳ** ἐφ᾽ ὑμᾶς, ὅτι ἃ παραγγέλλομεν [καὶ] ποιεῖτε καὶ ποιήσετε. [5]Ὁ δὲ **κύριος κατευθύναι** ὑμῶν τὰς καρδίας <u>εἰς τὴν ἀγάπην τοῦ θεοῦ</u> καὶ **εἰς τὴν ὑπομονὴν τοῦ Χριστοῦ**.

3:6 Παραγγέλλομεν δὲ ὑμῖν, ἀδελφοί, **ἐν ὀνόματι τοῦ κυρίου ἡμῶν Ἰησοῦ Χριστοῦ** στέλλεσθαι ὑμᾶς ἀπὸ παντὸς ἀδελφοῦ ἀτάκτως περιπατοῦντος καὶ μὴ κατὰ τὴν παράδοσιν ἣν παρελάβοσαν . . .

3:12 τοῖς δὲ τοιούτοις παραγγέλλομεν καὶ παρακαλοῦμεν **ἐν κυρίῳ Ἰησοῦ Χριστῷ**, ἵνα μετὰ ἡσυχίας ἐργαζόμενοι τὸν ἑαυτῶν ἄρτον ἐσθίωσιν.

3:16 **Αὐτὸς δὲ ὁ κύριος τῆς εἰρήνης δῴη** ὑμῖν τὴν εἰρήνην διὰ παντὸς ἐν παντὶ τρόπῳ. **ὁ κύριος μετὰ πάντων ὑμῶν**.

3:18 ἡ χάρις **τοῦ κυρίου ἡμῶν Ἰησοῦ Χριστοῦ** μεθ᾽ πάντων ὑμῶν.

Appendix II: An Analysis of Usage

(* = anarthrous; + = with possessive pronoun; [LXX] = Septuagint echo/ citation)

1 Thessalonians
θεός   36
Christ   33

2 Thessalonians
θεός   18
Christ   23

The Data
1. κύριος Ἰησοῦς Χριστός (5 / 9)
   1 Thess 1:1   D* (w/ θεός)
   1 Thess 1:3   G+
   1 Thess 5:9   G+ (διά)
   1 Thess 5:23   G+
   1 Thess 5:28   G+
   2 Thess 1:1   D* (w/ θεός)
   2 Thess 1:2   G* (w/ θεός)
   2 Thess 1:12   G* (w/ θεός)
   2 Thess 2:1   G+
   2 Thess 2:14   G+
   2 Thess 2:16   N (w/ θεός)
   2 Thess 3:6   G+
   2 Thess 3:12   D* (ἐν)
   2 Thess 3:18   G+
2. κύριος Ἰησοῦς (6 / 3)
   1 Thess 2:15   A
   1 Thess 2:19   G+
   1 Thess 3:11   N+ (w/ θεός)
   1 Thess 3:13   G+
   1 Thess 4:1   D* (ἐν)
   1 Thess 4:2   G (διά)
   2 Thess 1:7   G
   2 Thess 1:8   G+
   2 Thess 1:12   G+
3. Χριστὸς Ἰησοῦς (2 / 0)
   1 Thess 2:14   D* (ἐν)
   1 Thess 5:18   D* (ἐν)

4. κύριος (13 / 10)
   1 Thess 1:6   G
   1 Thess 1:8   G
   1 Thess 3:8   D* (ἐν)
   1 Thess 3:12   N
   1 Thess 4:6   N* [LXX]
   1 Thess 4:15   G* [LXX]
   1 Thess 4:15   G
   1 Thess 4:16   N
   1 Thess 4:17   G
   1 Thess 4:17   D* (σύν)
   1 Thess 5:2   G* [LXX]
   1 Thess 5:12   D* (ἐν)
   1 Thess 5:27   A
   2 Thess 1:9   G [LXX]
   2 Thess 2:2   G [LXX]
   2 Thess 2:8   N [tc + Ἰησοῦς]
                    [LXX]
   2 Thess 2:13   G* (ὑπό) [LXX]
   2 Thess 3:1   G
   2 Thess 3:3   N
   2 Thess 3:4   D* (ἐν) [LXX]
   2 Thess 3:5   N
   2 Thess 3:16   N
   2 Thess 3:16   N [LXX]
5. Ἰησοῦς (3 / 0)
   1 Thess 1:10   A* (appositive to
                    υἱός)
   1 Thess 4:14   N*
   1 Thess 4:14   G (διά)
6. Χριστός (3 / 1)
   1 Thess 2:7   G*
   1 Thess 3:2   G
   1 Thess 4:16   D* (ἐν)
   2 Thess 3:5   G
7. υἱός (1 / 0)
   1 Thess 1:10   A (αὐτοῦ)

3

Christology in 1 Corinthians

IN A LETTER WRITTEN A few years after 2 Thessalonians (ca. 54 C.E.), Paul spends most of his energy trying to correct behavioral aberrations that have emerged in the Corinthian community, some of which, apparently, have been argued for in their letter to him (1 Cor 5:9).[1] Paul's letter is thus primarily argumentation—over matters where the apostle and the church are at odds—so that its only specifically theological item has to do with the future bodily resurrection (ch. 15); everything else has to do with the Corinthians' behavior in some form or another. And even the argument in ch. 15 is probably a theological issue raised by the Corinthians to support their actions.[2]

It is not surprising, therefore, that the many christological moments in this letter appear in incidental ways, in that they are never argued *for*— although sometimes they are argued *from*. On closer examination, however, one wonders whether both Corinthian letters do not reflect an early crisis in Christology, even though Paul himself neither says as much nor pursues the issue in a direct way. In any case, that such a "crisis" serves as an undercurrent in much of the letter appears to be a live option when one considers the following details.

Although Paul addresses eleven different matters, more than 55 percent of the letter is made up of lengthy responses to just three issues. First, 1:10–4:21 takes up the matter of internal divisions in the name of different leaders based on σοφία (*wisdom*). Paul's initial response to this is primarily to reframe their (now false) view of Christ and the meaning of the cross. Second, 8:1–11:1 takes up the Corinthians' insistence, based on γνῶσις (*knowledge*), on the right to attend idol feasts, since "there is only one God," hence "an idol is not a real god." And since food is a matter of indifference to the one God, why should Paul forbid their attendance at the temple feasts? Paul's initial response to this is to broaden their understanding of the "one God" so as to include the

---

[1] Commentaries on 1 Corinthians are listed in the bibliography (p. 640); they are cited in this chapter by author's surname only. Since I have written a commentary on this letter, my bibliographic focus here will be on commentaries and studies that have appeared since the writing of the commentary (i.e., from 1985 and on).

[2] For this perspective on this letter, see Fee, 4–15.

"one Lord," whose death for the person with a "weak conscience" is being brushed aside. Third, in 12:1–14:40 the issue is manifestations of τὸ πνεῦμα (*the Spirit*), especially speaking in tongues. Paul's initial response to this is to contrast true Spirit speech as that which acclaims "the Lord is Jesus" over against speech that is not of the Spirit, that acclaims "cursed is Jesus."[3]

Add to these observations three other realities:

1. In none of Paul's other letters is there even a hint that his churches celebrated the Lord's Supper, yet in this letter he speaks of it no less than three times, and in three interestingly different contexts with quite different points (5:6–8; 10:14–16; 11:17–34). Although the *concern* in the latter two instances is with the bread = the body of Christ, and thus with the Corinthians' relationships with one another through Christ, in all three of them the *focus* is nonetheless on Christ himself. Christ is our Passover lamb who has been sacrificed (5:7); participation at the meal is participation in the blood and body of Christ (10:16); and the meal itself is designated as a κυριακὸν δεῖπνον (*a meal belonging to [or in honor of] the Lord*) (11:20). Thus, the failures and differences within the community are reflected in their dishonoring Christ himself at the meal in his honor.

2. This letter concludes in a most unusual fashion. After his own personal greeting (16:21), and without breaking stride, Paul pronounces an *anathema* on anyone "who does not love *the Lord*." Several features of this phenomenon are noteworthy. First, the fact that he would conclude in this fashion is in itself attention-getting. Second, this is almost certainly a pickup of 12:3, where the basic Christian confession κύριος Ἰησοῦς (*the Lord is Jesus*), spoken especially as an utterance of the Spirit, is preceded by the strange contrast "no one speaking by the Spirit can say ἀνάθεμα Ἰησοῦς [*cursed is Jesus*]." Thus the concluding word in 16:21 may suggest, more strongly than some of us have been willing to allow, that some believers in the Corinthian community were saying this very thing and that Paul at the end of the letter reverses the curse: it rests on those who do not *love the Lord*.[4] Third, this is the only place in the Pauline corpus where Paul speaks of loving Jesus, and he does so in terms of "loving *the Lord*" (who is Jesus). And finally, fourth, with assonance that is typical of the apostle, he immediately follows the *anathema* with *Maranatha*, a prayer for the Lord to come,

---

[3]It is of further interest regarding this structural phenomenon that when Paul tries in 12:8–10 to broaden their perspective on Spirit gifting, the first two items on the list pick up the words that drive the first two major sections: "to one through the Spirit is given λόγος σοφίας [*a word of wisdom*]; to another λόγος γνώσεως [*a word of knowledge*] by the same Spirit." Since such "gifts" are mentioned nowhere else in Paul's writings, it looks very much as if these are ad hoc moments in which he includes their favorite themes in the process of trying to put them into a much broader perspective.

[4]That is, as many have noticed, the designatee of both the confession and the curse is "Jesus," not "Christ." Thus this curse might be related in some way to those who are denying a future bodily resurrection of believers and doing so by "cursing" the Jesus who bore such a body in the first place.

which probably serves as both encouragement and warning. In sum: this exceedingly strange curse formula may exist in the letter because a faulty Christology lies behind it.

3. If all of this represents a latent christological crisis, then one can make good sense of the further christological emphases in 2 Corinthians—Christ as Son of God, bearer of the Father's image and glory—in a context where some are preaching "another Jesus" (11:4).

Although none of this can be made certain, it does make sense of the christological data of the present letter, even though that emphasis comes more indirectly rather than as an up-front attempt to straighten them out christologically. That is, the emphasis throughout, as all have recognized, is in fact on the Corinthians' misguided behavior. My point is that one can make a lot of sense of some of these aberrations if at the same time they reflect a diminished view of who Christ is. In any case, precisely because the Christology itself comes to us in a less direct way, the data are thus of considerable importance. After all, what Paul argues *from* and various kinds of *presuppositional* statements both serve as certain evidence of what Paul believed about the person of Christ. Furthermore, one must assume that this belief was held in common in the early church, including Corinth, since Paul never gives the impression that he or they believed anything different from what was believed by others.

At the same time, it is especially difficult in 1 Corinthians to abstract Christology from soteriology, since whatever else is true about the letter, it is thoroughly christocentric. Christ is the central focus at every turn, from beginning to end. Since Paul's soteriology is all about what Christ has done on our behalf, one can make sense of what this means for him only in light of his basic presupposition about who Christ is: the crucified Messiah, whose death and resurrection procured eternal redemption for us, who is now reigning as Lord in heaven awaiting his Parousia, the Day of the Lord. But the Son of God is also from eternity—co-creator of the universe and present with Israel in the desert—whose reign as Lord means that believers "call upon his name," that they are sent and equipped by him for ministry, that they go or stay in keeping with his will, and that they will be judged by him at the end. This is hardly the stuff of adoptionism! Indeed, it is Paul's utter devotion to Christ that must catch our attention, since it is the devotion that a devout Jew could give only to his God.[5]

In this chapter, then, we examine Paul's references to and statements about Christ in 1 Corinthians, with an eye toward his presuppositional understanding of the person of Christ. As before, we will proceed in a basically thematic way, beginning with one of the more significant christological moments in the entire corpus (8:6) and then branching out to a variety of other

---

[5] On this matter, see L. W. Hurtado, *Lord Jesus Christ: Devotion to Jesus in Earliest Christianity* (Grand Rapids: Eerdmans, 2003), passim; see also, in the present chapter, pp. 120–22, 125–27.

kinds of christological phenomena that appear in the letter.[6] And as it finally turns out, this letter not only contains the most christological data of the entire corpus (hence this is the longest of the exegetical chapters in the present volume) but also is one of the two letters (along with Romans) in which every item taken up in the thematic chapters of the present volume (11–16) is present in some significant way.

A Preliminary Look at the Data

The various references to Christ and to God are found in appendix I at the end of this chapter; likewise, an analysis of the different ways of referring to Christ is found in appendix II. What one discovers is that the patterns of usage already in place in the Thessalonian letters continue here, with one notable exception: the *relative* frequency of the appellation κύριος in comparison with other "names." While κύριος occurs more than others (64x),[7] it does so now only one more time than Χριστός (63x)—a pattern that will continue throughout the corpus, as "Christ" more and more becomes Paul's primary "name" for the Savior. Also as before, Christ is mentioned by name more often than θεός (*God*) or πατήρ (*Father*), 18 times in this case.

At the same time, although the number of compounds of any two of the three names now leans more heavily toward "Christ Jesus/Jesus Christ" (6x/2x) as over against "the Lord Jesus" (4x), the appellation "the Lord" alone (49x) continues to occur more frequently than "Christ" alone (45x). It should also be noted that patterns begin to emerge as to where and how often one name occurs more than the other. Where frequency of κύριος does emerge (7:10–39 [12x to 1 Χριστός]; cf. 10:21–22; 11:20–32 [9x]), the emphasis is on his lordship; where the frequency goes toward "Christ" (e.g., 15:3–23 [13x]), the emphasis reflects soteriological concerns.

Finally, we should note that the various combinations such as "the Lord, Jesus Christ" remain the same as in 1–2 Thessalonians, occurring most often up front in the letter (5 of 10 occurrences in the salutation and thanksgiving [1:1–9]).

---

[6] In contrast to the preceding chapter, many of these texts will require more exegetical attention, since there has also been considerably more scholarly discussion of them.

[7] This does not include the Septuagint citations in 3:20 and 14:21, where κύριος seems clearly to refer to God, since no point is made of it otherwise; cf. Rom 4:8; 9:28, 29; 10:16; 11:34; 15:11, and the λέγει κύριος formula apparently added by Paul to the citations in 2 Cor 6:17, 18; Rom 11:3; 12:19 (for convenience, these twelve texts are given in appendix B [pp. 637–38]). The citation of Isa 45:23 in Rom 14:11 is excepted here (see ch. 6, pp. 259–67), since (1) the "formula" is not the same as the others; rather, Paul uses an oath formula from Isa 49:18, etc. ("As I live, says the LORD") to preface the quotation; and thus (2) a very decided christological point is being made of the κύριος in the citation. Together these points make this one "citation" stand apart from the others listed here.

Christ: Preexistent Lord and Agent of Creation

The proper starting point for examining the Christology of this letter is 1 Cor 8:6, which could well serve as the starting point for any discussion of Pauline Christology.[8] And here in particular the context is of considerable importance for what Paul states so boldly about Christ.

The Corinthian Context (1 Cor 8:1–13)

At issue in 1 Cor 8:1–11:1 is an ongoing argument between Paul and the Corinthians over their insistence on the right to attend festive meals in pagan temples.[9] Apparently, Paul had already forbidden such practice (5:9), but in their return letter they argued vigorously for their right (ἐξουσία) to continue to do so (8:9). Their argument can be reconstructed with a measure of confidence from Paul's citations from their letter: "We all have knowledge"[10] (8:1) that "an idol has no reality" because "there is only one God" (v. 4); therefore, since food is a matter of indifference to God (v. 8), neither what we eat nor where we eat it (v. 10) matters to God. Crucial to this argument is their affirmation of the Jewish Shema, that there is only one God (Deut 6:4), as fundamental to Christian faith and behavior.

Paul's response to this specious reasoning is especially noteworthy. For even though he will eventually condemn their misunderstanding of idolatry—as to its essentially demonic nature (10:14–22)—he begins by appealing to the nature of Christian *love* that should forbid such casual destruction of the faith of others (8:2–3, 9–13). But even at this early stage he offers a preliminary "correction" to their "theology" per se (vv. 5–6), noting that the world is full of "gods" and "lords." In so doing, Paul is acknowledging the

---

[8] The bibliography on this passage is large. Among others, see C. H. Giblin, "Three Monotheistic Texts in Paul," *CBQ* 37 (1975): 527–47; R. Kerst, "1 Kor 8.6—Ein vorpaulinisches Taufbekenntnis?" *ZNW* 66 (1975): 130–39; R. A. Horsley, "The Background of the Confessional Formula in 1 Kor 8:6," *ZNW* 69 (1978): 130–35; J. Murphy-O'Connor, "I Cor. VIII,6: Cosmology or Soteriology?" *RB* 85 (1978): 253–67; D. R. deLacey, " 'One Lord' in Pauline Christology," in *Christ the Lord: Studies in Christology Presented to Donald Guthrie* (ed. H. H. Rowdon; Leicester: Inter-Varsity Press, 1982), 191–203; N. T. Wright, "Monotheism, Christology and Ethics: 1 Corinthians 8," in *The Climax of the Covenant: Christ and the Law in Pauline Theology* (Minneapolis: Fortress, 1992), 120–36; Richardson, *Paul's Language about God*; A. Eriksson, *Traditions as Rhetorical Proof: Pauline Argumentation in 1 Corinthians* (ConBNT 29; Stockholm: Almqvist & Wiksell, 1998), 97–99, 120–27, 135–73.

[9] For the full argumentation for this perspective, see G. D. Fee, "Εἰδωλόθυτα Once Again—An Interpretation of 1 Corinthians 8–10," in *To What End Exegesis? Essays Textual, Exegetical, and Theological* (Grand Rapids: Eerdmans, 2001), 105–28; cf. Fee, 357–63. For a modification of this perspective, see A. T. Cheung, *Idol Food in Corinth: Jewish Background and Pauline Legacy* (JSNTSup 176; Sheffield: Sheffield Academic Press, 1999); Garland, 347–362—although we differ on some details.

[10] There is good reason to believe that the Corinthians came to this view of "knowledge," as they did of "wisdom" in 1:10–4:21, by way of their experience of the Spirit, since these two are the first items that Paul picks up in his listing of Spirit manifestations in 12:8.

subjective reality[11] of idols for those who once believed in them. In v. 7 he thus spells out the disastrous consequences of this reasoning on "weaker" believers, for whom the subjective reality of idolatry still outweighs the objective reality being denied by those "in the know." But to get there, Paul does an even more remarkable thing: he insists that their understanding of the "one God" must now include Christ as well (v. 6), and he does this for basically soteriological, not christological, reasons. The attitudes and actions of the "knowing ones" who assert their "rights" serve potentially to destroy the work of Christ in others (vv. 10–13) and thus to destroy the Christian community as well.

1 Corinthians 8:6

Given this context and Paul's primarily soteriological interest, what he says in v. 6 is an extraordinary christological moment, where he offers a deliberate Christian restatement of the Shema, the basic theological confession of the Judaism in which Christian faith has its deep roots. In nicely balanced clauses Paul affirms,

(A) ἀλλ' ἡμῖν   εἷς θεὸς   ὁ πατὴρ,
                              ἐξ οὗ   τὰ πάντα
                 καὶ   ἡμεῖς   εἰς αὐτόν,

(B) καὶ   εἷς κύριος Ἰησοῦς Χριστὸς,
                              δι' οὗ   τὰ πάντα
                 καὶ   ἡμεῖς   δι' αὐτοῦ.

(A) *But for us*   *one God*   *the Father,*
                                from whom   *all things*
                  and   *we*   *for him,*

(B) *and*   **one Lord**   **Jesus Christ**
                                 through whom   *all things*
                  and   *we*   **through him.**

Deut 6:4   ἄκουε Ισραηλ   **κύριος**   **ὁ θεὸς ἡμῶν**   **κύριος**   **εἷς** ἐστιν.
          Listen, Israel,   *the* LORD   *our God*   *the* LORD   *one is.*

[11] This is my own term for the nature of Paul's argumentation, a view that recently has been challenged by J. Woyke, *Götter, "Götzen," Götterbilder: Aspekte einer paulinischen "Theologie der Religionen"* (BZNW 132; Berlin: de Gruyter, 2005). Verse 5a very likely expresses the view of those with weak consciences. In 10:14–22 Paul asserts in effect that despite "idols being nothing," they have an objective reality as the habitation of demons. In the present argument (ch. 8), besides v. 5, where he affirms that for pagans there are "gods many and lords many," Paul acknowledges in v. 7 that some with weak consciences do not have the "knowledge" the others have. This can hardly mean that they do not understand the truth that God is one and therefore that idols have no reality as gods; rather, because "the weak" had long attributed reality to the idols, when they became believers, they were unable to shake themselves free from these former associations, which is why it would be so deadly for them to return to the temples for festive meals that honored a "god" (vv. 11–12). And as has been recently pointed out (Thiselton, 632; Garland, 373–74), the "reality" of idolatry was everywhere in ancient Corinth.

What Paul has done seems plain enough. He has kept the "one" intact, but he has divided the Shema into two parts, with θεός (*God*) now referring to the Father, and κύριος (*Lord*) referring to Jesus Christ the Son.[12] Because Paul's interests here are pastoral, he identifies the "one Lord" as none other than the historical "Jesus Christ," the one who died for all, especially those with a weak conscience (v. 11).[13]

Thus, over against the "gods many" of paganism, the Shema rightly asserts—as the Corinthians themselves have caught on—that there is only one God. The Shema also asserts, typical of Paul's Jewish monotheism, that the one God stands over against all pagan deities at two crucial, interrelated points: as *Creator* of all that is and concomitantly as the one *Ruler* of all that is created. Nothing—absolutely nothing—lies outside the realm of the one Creator-Ruler God.[14] Thus God the Father is ἐκ/εἰς (*from/for*) in relation to everything that exists; that is, he is its source and goal (or purpose) of being—although the final phrase ("we for him"), noticeably Pauline, moves easily from creation to redemption, where God is the goal of his people in particular.[15]

The surprising moment comes in line B. Over against the "lords many" of paganism, there is only *one* Lord, Jesus Christ, whose relation to creation is that of effective agent. Thus the Father has created all things through the agency of the Son, who as the one Lord is also—and now Paul's second

---

[12] For the high probability that one should recognize "Son of God" implications in this reference to God as "Father," see the section that follows below, "Jesus as Messianic/Eternal Son of God" (pp. 99–114). Cf. Collins, 315–18; M. Hengel, *The Son of God*, 13–14.

[13] For a strong critique of Bousset's *Kyrios Christos* and others up through W. Kramer, *Christ, Lord, Son of God* (SBT 30; London: SCM Press, 1966), who prefer to find the background for this usage in the mystery cults, see Hengel, *Son of God*, 77–79 n. 135. That Paul's use of this title should be located in the mysteries, when over a score of instances in his writings are, like this one, direct borrowings from the Septuagint, is itself one of the mysteries of twentieth-century NT scholarship.

[14] For a helpful overview of this crucial point, that this combination of God as Creator and Ruler of the universe is the absolutely unique feature of Jewish belief, see R. Bauckham, *God Crucified: Monotheism and Christology in the New Testament* (Grand Rapids: Eerdmans, 1999), 1–22.

[15] Because of this, and because he is enamored with the text as a pre-Pauline creed, K.-J. Kuschel (*Born before All Time? The Dispute over Christ's Origin* [trans. J. Bowden; London: SCM Press, 1992], 285–91) argues that this passage has to do only with soteriology (as did Murphy-O'Connor before him ["I Cor. VIII,6"]). But that is to misread the passage in context; the analogy for Pauline usage here is Rom 11:36, not 2 Cor 5:18, as argued by Kuschel. What seems to make the creational reading of 8:6 certain is (1) the identical use of τὰ πάντα δι' αὐτοῦ in Col 1:16, which Kuschel gets around by denying Pauline authorship to Colossians (a circular argument that assumes what is questionable), and (2) the observation that if we had only the first line, with God as the source (Creator) of τὰ πάντα and "we" as the goal of everything, it seems unlikely that anyone would deny that this line refers to creation; it is then hard to conceive that the second use of τὰ πάντα would differ in meaning from the first, when both lines pick up the same two realities of creation and redemption. Cf. the critique in J. D. G. Dunn, *The Theology of Paul the Apostle* (Grand Rapids: Eerdmans, 1998), 268 n. 5.

point is being established—the agent of their redemption ("and we through him"). The whole passage therefore, typically for Paul, encloses the work of the Son within that of the Father; that is, the two διά phrases regarding the one Lord's role as agent of creation and redemption are (logically) framed by the ἐκ and εἰς phrases regarding the Father as the ultimate source and goal or purpose of all things—both creation and redemption.

It need hardly be pointed out—but it will be because of what is said in the literature—that this second line is a plain, undeniable expression of Paul's presuppositional conviction about Christ's preexistence as the Son of God: *preexistence*, because of the assertion that "through him are τὰ πάντα [*all things*]," with creation in view;[16] *Son of God*, because of Paul's identity of the "one God" as "the Father" (see the discussion on 1 Thess 1:1 in ch. 1, pp. 36–38).

All of this seems deliberate on Paul's part. That is, he is reasserting for the Corinthians that their theology has it right: there is indeed only *one* God, over against all other "gods many and lords many." But at the same time, he insists that the identity of the one God also includes the one Lord; and ultimately he does so because (1) this *is* the now shared Christian perspective about the one God and (2) it is the inclusion of Christ as Lord in God's identity that will give Paul the leverage to forbid attendance at pagan festive meals. Not only does that practice lack love toward those for whom Christ died (8:10–13), but also their own sacred meal is eaten in honor of/in the presence of the one Lord (10:16–22). Furthermore, they have radically misunderstood the nature of idolatry. That the idols are not "gods" is a given; what the Corinthians have failed to reckon with is that the idols are in fact the habitation of demons (see, e.g., Deut 32:17). And Paul's final point in this argument is that because there is only one Lord, and because the idols are the habitation of demons, they may not under any circumstances sit at both tables. For that is in fact a denial of the one Lord (10:19–22). Hence the reason for this elaboration of the Shema at the very beginning of Paul's attempt to correct their behavior—and theology—on this matter.

However, because of what one finds in the literature, three additional things must be noted about this passage. First, although the *conceptual* frame for this construction (ἐκ-διὰ-εἰς) can be found elsewhere in the NT,[17] there is nothing quite like this use of prepositional phrases apart from Paul himself. Indeed, the only other known use of this specific scheme of prepositions in ancient literature is in Rom 11:36, where the full phrase ἐξ αὐτοῦ καὶ δι' αὐτοῦ καὶ εἰς αὐτόν τὰ πάντα (*from him and through him and for him [are] all*

---

[16] Richardson (*Paul's Language*, 297) argues that the whole of the second line refers to redemption = "through Christ 'all things having to do with redemption' and 'we ourselves' through him"; but there is no Pauline analogy for such an understanding of τὰ πάντα.

[17] Most notably Heb 1:1–2, where God has "appointed the Son" as "heir of all things, *through* whom also he made the universe."

things) appears in a doxology without this christological modification.[18] It is of significant theological interest to note here that in the Romans doxology God (θεός) is the one "*through* whom" are all things, while in Col 1:16 *the Son* is the one "*for* whom" are all things. As Bauckham has recently argued in a slightly different way, this interchange of prepositions in itself indicates full identity of Christ with God.[19]

Second, this assertion is striking because at one level it seems quite unnecessary to the present argument, since nothing christological is at stake. That is, Paul is not here trying to *demonstrate* Christ's creative agency; he simply *assumes* it by assertion. Nonetheless, at a deeper level this is precisely the assertion that will make both the theological and ethical dimensions of the argument work. By naming Christ as the "one Lord" through whom both creation and redemption were effected, Paul not only broadens the Corinthians' perspective on the Shema, but at the same time he anticipates the role that Christ is to play in the argument that follows (esp. 8:11–12; 10:4, 9, 16–22), where everything hinges on their ongoing relationship to Christ. What is important for our present purposes is (1) Paul's deliberate use of κύριος for Christ, language that in the Septuagint was substituted for the Divine Name of the one God (see pp. 20–23 above), and (2) the presuppositional nature of the *historical* person, Jesus Christ, as preexistent and the personal agent of creation itself. There is nothing like this to be found in Paul's Jewish heritage as such. That is, he has no prior frame of reference into which this modification of the Shema can be fitted.[20] As is pointed out on 1 Cor 9:1 below (pp. 125–27), this adjustment most likely had its origins for Paul in his own encounter with the risen Christ.

---

[18] In his commentary on Romans, J. D. G. Dunn comments that "the use of prepositions like [these three] when speaking of God and the cosmos . . . was widespread in the ancient world and typically Stoic" (*Romans 9–16* [WBC 38B; Dallas: Word, 1988], 701). But apart from the three Pauline texts (Rom 11:36; 1 Cor 8:6; Col 1:16–17), he lists only six others, in none of which is there another instance of all three prepositions occurring together. Elsewhere, Dunn has further suggested that one of the texts (Philo, *Cher.* 125–127) serves as an illustration of one who has made "a similar division in the 'by, from, and through' formulation, between the originating role of God . . . and the instrumental role of the Logos" (*Theology of Paul*, 269). This is true, but Philo's concerns and language differ from Paul's. Apparently picking up Aristotelian usage (see the note by Colson and Whitaker, LCL, vol. 2, pp. 486–87), Philo's prepositions are ὑφ' οὗ (*by which*), ἐκ οὗ (*from which*), δι' οὗ (*through which*), δι' ὁ (*for which*), three of which apply to God, while the Logos is involved only in the third ("through whom"). Thus, although there are conceptual similarities, in fact the combination of prepositions found here (and Rom 11:36; Col 1:16–17) is apparently unique to Paul in antiquity.

[19] Bauckham, *God Crucified*, 37–40.

[20] On the attempt by some to find the background in Greco-Roman (Hellenistic) religion(s), see n. 13 above. The problem with this view, of course, is that the Pauline texts themselves do not support it. His use of the Septuagint, examined in the preceding chapter, indicates how thoroughgoingly his, and his earliest converts', "religious world" was altogether steeped in Hellenistic Judaism. See further the section "Jesus as the Κύριος of Septuagint Passages" below.

Third, there is nothing in this passage or in its surrounding context that would even remotely suggest that Jewish wisdom lies behind Paul's formulation.[21] At issue in the present context is illicit behavior predicated on γνῶσις (*knowledge*), not σοφία (*wisdom*). It is of some surprise, therefore, to note how often—and with a kind of "of course" attitude[22]—it is asserted that Paul is here identifying Christ with personified Wisdom.[23] But such an assertion will have to remain in the category of scholarly discovery, not Pauline disclosure. And one should not expect readers of Paul's text, including the Corinthians themselves, to catch such extreme subtlety.[24]

Thus, this (in one sense) quite uncalculated[25] statement—Christ as "Lord" (and Son) in the context of the "one God" of the Jewish Shema—

---

[21] Nevertheless, despite all evidence to the contrary (see below, pp. 102–5), this is now a common assertion in the literature (although Collins [320], at least, approaches this more hesitantly). The "logic" by which one arrives at this assertion is especially questionable, since it actually requires a four-step process, which seems perfectly clear to its proponents but much less so to anyone who lacks their interpretive keys: (1) it is acknowledged by almost all (see n. 16 above for an exception) that Christ is asserted to be the agent of creation; (2) then it is argued (quite wrongly, as it turns out) that personified Wisdom is seen as the *agent of creation* in the Wisdom literature (see n. 23 and appendix A); thus (3), since Paul calls Christ "the [personified] Wisdom of God" in 1:24 (which is altogether mistaken [see pp. 102–5 below]), therefore (4) Christ as preexistent and agent of creation must be picking up this (alleged) motif from Jewish wisdom. But it is difficult to have confidence in this logic when at least two of its premises (nos. 2 and 3) are patently not true. As Hurtado puts it succinctly, "The problem with this view [that Christ here = Wisdom] is that it is not what the Pauline passage says" (*Lord Jesus Christ*, 126)!

[22] Dunn makes bold to say, "Few issues in recent NT theology have commanded such unanimity of agreement as the source of the language and imagery used in these two passages [wisdom in 1 Cor 8:6 and 1:24]" (*Theology of Paul*, 269). While this appears to be a true statement, that hardly makes the point of agreement true. Given the lack of *hard evidence* in its favor, this sounds like special pleading. Indeed, it is refreshing to read Garland's recent (and excellent) commentary on this passage and not find the word "wisdom" mentioned at all; after all, why would one do so, given that there is not a hint here of any kind that one should read this through a lens that is so foreign to Paul in every way.

[23] The basis for this assertion is twofold: (1) Wisdom's alleged role in creation, coupled with (2) the further assertion that Paul intends an identification of Christ with personified Wisdom in 1:24. However, not a single text in the Wisdom tradition uses the preposition διά regarding Wisdom's presence at creation. The closest thing to it is in Solomon's prayer in Wis 9:1–2, where the dative is not instrumental but associative (a straight dative, in contrast to the instrumental ἐν in the preceding line). Here the author in a prayer has momentarily abandoned personification and says *to* God that τῇ σοφίᾳ σου κατασκευάσας ἄνθρωπον (*in your wisdom you fitted humankind [to rule . . .]*). See the full discussion in appendix A.

[24] See further the excursus on 1:24, 30; 10:4 below (pp. 102–5).

[25] That is, Paul is not trying to formulate a new Christology here; rather, he asserts something that he does not argue for but argues from. On the other hand, N. T. Wright is quite right that this is a "stunning theological innovation," which is "one of the greatest pioneering moments in the entire history of christology" ("Monotheism, Christology and Ethics," 136).

could well serve as the basic text from which all Pauline christological discussion should flow. That at least will be the case for the rest of our discussion in this chapter. From here the data are basically grouped under three heads: (1) texts that pick up on the theme of Christ's preexistence; (2) texts that reflect a "Son of God" Christology with roots in Jewish messianism; (3) texts that reflect the κύριος Christology that dominates the Thessalonian correspondence. At the same time, we will look at the issues of Wisdom Christology, Adam Christology, and Spirit Christology as these are argued for from various texts, and thus we will anticipate some matters taken up in the final chapters, as well as appendix A, of this book. We will conclude by examining two miscellaneous texts (3:23; 11:3) that do not easily fit these three major categories.

Christ as Preexistent with Israel

On his way toward a final word of prohibition regarding attendance at temple meals (10:20–22), Paul sets out to establish the Corinthians' spiritual connectedness with biblical Israel, who are seen to have experienced God in a "baptism" and "Lord's Supper" analogous to their own. Thus "our fathers"[26] were "baptized"—unto Moses in the cloud and the sea (vv. 1–2), and they too had "spiritual food and drink" in the wilderness—manna and water from the rock (vv. 3–4). But God had not been pleased with them and overthrew them in the desert (v. 5), which story is to serve as a warning to the Corinthians (v. 6). From there, Paul launches into four specific ways Israel had sinned, which had brought about their demise: idolatry (v. 7); sexual immorality (v. 8); testing God (v. 9); and grumbling against God and Moses (v. 10)—all of which sins are being repeated in Corinth.

Our present interest is with the two instances where Paul places Christ himself in the desert: as the Rock who was with Israel, supplying them with "spiritual water" (v. 4), and as the one whom Israel thus put to the test (v. 9). Both passages reflect not just analogies but, from Paul's perspective, actualities. That is, the same Christ who now supplies the Corinthians with the Spirit, and whom they are testing by going to pagan feasts, had already experienced such "testing" by Israel; and the Israelites had been overthrown in the desert so that they did not reach their goal. It is precisely the presence of *Christ* in Israel's story that will make all of this work as a warning to the Corinthians.

But since both of these passages have created difficulties for later interpreters, we need to look at them more closely and thus point out that Paul did indeed place the preexistent Christ in the desert experience of Israel.

---

[26] The (debated) use of ἡμῶν here actually seems clear enough. Paul sees believers in Christ as in continuity with the story that began with Abraham and Moses. It is this understanding that makes the argument work at all; and it is why the overlap of stories continues all the way through to the end (v. 22). See further on 10:20–22 below.

1 Corinthians 10:4

In retelling Israel's story, Paul alludes to the double narrative of water from the rock (Exod 17:1–7; Num 20:7–11), and he does so by picking up a rabbinic tradition that "they drank from the (spiritual) rock that followed them."[27] But he replaces that tradition by interpreting the "spiritual rock" as the presence of Christ himself: ἡ πέτρα δὲ ἦν ὁ Χριστός (*and the rock was Christ*).

It has often been suggested that Paul is here employing a rabbinic interpretive strategy, of the kind he uses elsewhere in 2 Cor 3:17 and Gal 4:25. But the difference between these latter two examples and what Paul does here is considerable. The standard form of the strategy is precisely as it occurs in 2 Corinthians and Galatians, where he starts with the definite article of the word that is to be interpreted, followed by a δέ, and then the word itself. He then follows with the "new meaning" for that word, followed by ἐστιν (*present* tense of "to be"). In the present text, while still following the same interpretive scheme, Paul makes three adjustments that put his interpretation "back there" rather than "here and now." Thus:

2 Cor 3:17	ὁ δὲ	κύριος	πνεῦμά	ἐστιν
Gal 4:25	τὸ δὲ	Ἁγὰρ	Σινᾶ ὄρος	ἐστίν
1 Cor 10:4	ἡ πέτρα	δὲ	ἦν	ὁ Χριστός

First, Paul here keeps the ἡ πέτρα together, so that the interpretive signal δέ not only does not come between them but also causes the δέ to function somewhat differently. Instead of meaning something similar to what it does in 2 Cor 3:17 ("*now* the Lord [just referred to] is [for our present purposes to be understood as] the Spirit"), Paul seems here to intend the δέ as the conjunctive signal for his new clause, as it relates to what has preceded.[28] By doing so, second, and especially with the use of the past tense of "to be," he firmly puts the present interpretation "back there."[29] That is, this interpretation is not about how the biblical passage applies in the present but with how the Corinthians are to understand what was actually going on with ancient Israel. This is further confirmed by the third difference, the reversal of

---

[27] On the (apparently) rabbinic background to this matter, see Fee, 448 n. 34; cf. Garland, 470. Thiselton's unfortunate attempt to bring personified Wisdom into the picture as well (pp. 727–30) makes for one of the less precise moments in his commentary. For his misreading of Wis 11:4, see n. 31 below.

[28] It should be noted that scribes did not care for this anomaly, so that as early as 𝔓46—and eventually the majority of mss—they reversed the order to the expected ὁ δὲ πέτρα. The original text is preserved in ℵ B D* 1739 et al.

[29] So also R. G. Hamerton-Kelly, *Pre-existence, Wisdom, and the Son of Man: A Study of the Idea of Pre-existence in the New Testament* (SNTSMS 21; Cambridge: Cambridge University Press, 1973), 132.

the order of verb and predicate noun, so that the emphasis now lies on the last word, "Christ," whom Paul is insisting was the actual source of water for Israel in the desert.

Given what seems to be rather clear in this case, one is thus mildly suprised to find that some see this as a reference *not* to Christ per se but to personified Wisdom, which in itself is problematic, since "Christ" is explicitly mentioned in the text itself. But if finding Wisdom in 8:6 was accomplished by a piece of circuitous reasoning,[30] how much more so for this passage, which requires the additional step that personified Wisdom had already been associated with the rock in Jewish Wisdom literature. Although Philo does this very thing,[31] it is patently not true of the Wisdom literature itself. The text brought forward is Wis 11:4,[32] where *in direct address to God* the author says, "When they were thirsty they called upon *you,* and water was given them out of the flinty rock."[33] The "you" here picks up the vocative from 10:20,[34] where the author has turned to God and sung hymns to him for his wisdom that has accompanied Israel from the beginning. The rest of the book, beginning with this passage, evolves into a series of antitheses between Egypt and Israel, where the same element (water in this first instance) is an expression of God's goodness to Israel but a source of punishment for Egypt. From here on (over half the book), the Lord who has done all these

---

[30] See n. 21 above. For an analysis of the Wisdom passages that have bearing on this discussion, see appendix A, pp. 594–619.

[31] In a thoroughly allegorical reading of the text, Philo says, "For the flinty rock is the wisdom of God, which he marked off highest and chiefest from His powers, and from which He satisfies the thirsty souls that love God" (*Leg.* 2.86). Whether Paul knew Philo is moot; in any case, Paul is not allegorizing.

[32] Some have occasionally suggested that Sir 24:21 reflects such a view; but a careful reading of "The Praise of Wisdom" in Sir 24 demonstrates that this is a creation out of whole cloth.

[33] In a considerable misreading of Wis 11:4, based on Philo's allegorical reading of Deut 8:15 (n. 31), it is often asserted that the "you" in this text refers to Wisdom (e.g., Barrett, 223; Hays, 161; Collins, 369; Horsley, 137; Tuckett, *Christology,* 63 n. 50. For example, B. Witherington says, "Here [Paul] draws on sapiential ideas about the role of personified Wisdom in Israel (cf. Wis 11:2–4), 'They journeyed through the uninhabited wilderness. When they were thirsty, they called upon [Wisdom] and water was given them out of the flinty rock'" ("Christology," *DPL* 103). But that is *not* what the author of Wisdom says, since personified Wisdom in fact drops out of the narrative at 11:1. Indeed, a careful exegesis of Wis 9–11 suggests that those who associate wisdom with the rock are "proof-texting," not taking the context of Wisdom seriously at all. This includes Thiselton, whose excursus on "the rock" (727–30) is a rare instance in his commentary where the use of ancient texts seems quite confused. Cf. the analysis and rejection of this idea in Garland, 456.

[34] "Therefore the righteous plundered the ungodly; they sang hymns, *O Lord, to your holy name,* and praised with one voice *your defending hand;* for wisdom opened the mouth of those who were mute, and made the tongues of infants speak clearly" (Wis 10:20–21 NRSV, emphasis mine). For a walk through the meaning of "wisdom" in Wis 7–10, see the exegesis in appendix A, pp. 594–619.

things (cf. 11:13–14) is repeatedly addressed in the second person singular, while personified Wisdom is mentioned only once more (14:2). And even there, though she is the "artisan" responsible for boats on the sea, it is God who is addressed (v. 3: "but it is your providence, O Father, that steers its course"). The fact is that personified Wisdom is never *addressed* in this book, only God the Father. Thus, personified Wisdom simply is not associated with the water from the rock in any of the Wisdom literature.[35]

To the contrary, in an ad hoc discourse related to the situation in Corinth, Paul is insisting that by their idolatrous actions, the Corinthians are in grave danger of repeating Israel's folly. Despite *Christ's* supplying Israel with "spiritual" water, they fell in the desert. Paul's point in making this association for the church in Corinth—placing the preexistent Christ in Israel's own history—seems clear enough. The Corinthians, too, face the same danger of testing Christ by their idolatry.

1 Corinthians 10:9

The second instance where Paul asserts Christ's preexistence is equally striking. In this case, however, the early copying tradition had some difficulty with it, so it was moderated to fit expectations. Paul's original text[36] reads, "Let us not put *Christ* to the test [μηδὲ ἐκπειράζωμεν τὸν Χριστόν], as some of them tested [him] and were destroyed by the snakes."

This is an allusion to the event in Num 21:4–7,[37] where Israel complained against God and Moses about the length, nature, and provisions of their long stay in the wilderness. Although the Numbers text does not have the verb ἐκπειράζω (*put to the test*), it does occur in the poetry of Ps 78:18, which refers to the similar events recorded in Num 14, 16, 20. Paul's use of this verb seems to be a deliberate echo of the Septuagint of Deut 6:16, "You shall not put the LORD your God to the test as you put him to the test at *Peirasmos*"[38] (οὐκ ἐκπειράσεις κύριον τὸν θεόν σου ὃν τρόπον ἐξεπειράσασθε ἐν τῷ Πειρασμῷ). This well-known text, cited also by Jesus

---

[35] In any case, it is highly unlikely that Paul was acquainted with the Wisdom of Solomon, as an examination of all the possible points of reference between Paul and this book demonstrates (see addendum I to appendix A, pp. 594–619). And if Paul cannot be shown to have been acquainted with the book, how could the Corinthians have known it so well as as to pick up a (nonexistent) allusion, when nothing in Paul's text itself offers the reader a clue? Although it is not crucial to my point, one might note further that on the basis of Wis 14:12–21, D. Winston dates the book ca. 37 C.E., well after Paul had become a follower of Christ (*The Wisdom of Solomon* [AB 43; Garden City, N.Y.: Doubleday, 1987], 20–25).

[36] See the discussion in n. 39 below. Unfortunately, the NIV, which is based on NA[25] and whose translators were generally insensitive to textual issues, perpetuated the secondary reading "Lord," which has been corrected in the TNIV (cf. NRSV, ESV).

[37] This is made clear by Paul's reference to their being "destroyed by the snakes."

[38] The Greek Πειρασμός is a translation of the *Massah* of the Hebrew text, both words meaning "The Testing."

in the Gospel tradition, most likely led early scribes to change Paul's "Christ" to "Lord."[39]

As with v. 4, Paul's point in context seems clear. By insisting on their "right" (ἐξουσία) to go to the temple meals (see 8:9–10), the Corinthian believers are putting Christ himself to the test, as Paul concludes in 10:21–22. Thus he is once more tying the situations of Israel and of the Corinthians together christologically. Paul has no qualms in pointing out that the "Lord" whom *they* are putting to the test is the same Christ whom Israel tested in the desert and that the Israelites were overthrown because of it. It is the presuppositional nature of this assertion that is so striking, since Christ's preexistence is what makes such an argument possible at all.

Excursus: 1 Corinthians 15:47 and Preexistence

First Corinthians 15:47 has sometimes also been brought forward[40] as evidence for Paul's view of Christ as preexistent, based on the KJV's "the second man is the Lord from heaven."[41] However, a careful analysis of the text in context indicates that such is not the case. Paul's sentences in 1 Cor 15:47–48 read,

15:47–48 ὁ πρῶτος ἄνθρωπος ἐκ γῆς χοϊκός, **ὁ δεύτερος ἄνθρωπος** ἐξ οὐρανοῦ. οἷος ὁ χοϊκός, τοιοῦτοι καὶ οἱ χοϊκοί, καὶ οἷος ὁ ἐπουράνιος, τοιοῦτοι καὶ οἱ ἐπουράνιοι·

*The first man (was) of dust of the earth, **the second man** (is) of heaven. As the earthly (man), such also (are) those of earth; and as the heavenly man, such also (are) those of heaven.*

At issue here is the *nature* of the resurrection body. Paul asserted in v. 45 that there are two kinds of bodies, one that is ψυχικόν (= adapted to the present earthly life characterized as having a ψυχή) and one that is πνευματικόν (= adapted to the final life of the Spirit through resurrection). To support this assertion, Paul returns to the Adam/Christ anal-

---

[39] Plus the fact that by the second century the divine names were abbreviated in the NT textual tradition, so that the change in this case was from χ̄π̄ to κ̄π̄. Thus scribes, seeing one thing but anticipating another, made the change. Χριστόν is found in 𝔓⁴⁶ D F G Ψ 1739 1881 𝔐 latt sy co; Κύριον in ℵ B C P 33 *pc*. See further C. D. Osburn, "The Text of 1 Corinthians 10:9," in *New Testament Textual Criticism—Its Significance for Exegesis: Essays in Honour of Bruce M. Metzger* (ed. E. J. Epp and G. D. Fee; Oxford: Clarendon, 1981), 201–12.

[40] See, e.g., Grosheide, 388; Barrett, 375–76; more recently it is suggested by Hurtado, *Lord Jesus Christ*, 119.

[41] This, however, reflects a very early understanding of the passage, given the otherwise totally inexplicable insertion of κύριος in the later Greek text (A Ψ 075 1881 𝔐), which is not found in any early Greek MS or in the earliest versions, Latin and Coptic. It seems unfortunate, therefore, that this translation (but without "the Lord") continues to be found in the English tradition dependent on the KJV (RSV, NRSV, NASB, ESV).

ogy from vv. 20–22. Adam had, and by implication all of us have, a σῶμα ψυχικόν; Christ in his resurrection was the first to assume the σῶμα πνευματικόν. The rest of the argument through v. 49 is an attempt to spell out the how and why of these two "bodies."

Thus in v. 47 Paul reaffirms the *source* of these two kinds of bodies: the first man's body was formed ἐκ γῆς χοϊκός (*of the dust of the earth*); the second man's body is ἐξ οὐρανοῦ (*of heaven*).[42] This understanding is made certain by the explanation that follows in v. 48, which has to do with believers already having the one body and being destined for the second. Since the issue is altogether the "resurrection body" that believers will assume and since the firstfruits of such a resurrection body happened at Christ's *resurrection,* the passage has nothing to do with Christ's being preexistent and coming from heaven (as the KJV had it).

Jesus as Messianic/Eternal Son of God

Besides affirming Christ's preexistence, 1 Cor 8:6 also assumes that he is the eternal Son of the Father. Also assumed with this *language,* although not in 8:6 itself, is the Son's role as the Jewish Messiah, Israel's hoped-for eschatological king. We turn next, then, to those texts that point to or assume the substratum of Jewish messianism that we noted in ch. 2, since it is also at work, even more visibly so, in this letter. Several texts are significant in this regard. We begin with the two that show a degree of similarity to early assertions in 1 Thessalonians (see pp. 35–40 above).

1 Corinthians 1:3, 9

Although not the first mention of Christ in this letter, both the greeting proper (v. 3), which concludes the salutation (vv. 1–3), and v. 9, which brings the thanksgiving to a conclusion, assume the closest kind of relationship between Christ and God and do so in "Father/Son" language. Thus:

1:3 χάρις ὑμῖν καὶ εἰρήνη <u>ἀπὸ θεοῦ πατρὸς</u> ἡμῶν καὶ **κυρίου Ἰησοῦ Χριστοῦ.**

1:9 <u>πιστὸς ὁ θεός, δι᾽ οὗ</u> ἐκλήθητε εἰς κοινωνίαν τοῦ υἱοῦ <u>αὐτοῦ</u> **Ἰησοῦ Χριστοῦ τοῦ κυρίου ἡμῶν.**

1:3 *Grace to you and peace from <u>God our Father</u> and (our)* **Lord Jesus Christ.**

1:9 <u>*Faithful is God, through whom*</u> *you were called into fellowship with <u>his</u>* **Son, Jesus Christ our Lord.**

---

[42] Thus the TNIV rightly translates, "The first man was of the dust of the earth; the second man is of heaven."

Although Paul is not trying to make a christological point here, his assertions assume the larger implications of the Jewish messianism and eternal sonship noted in the preceding chapter, which find clear expression later in Gal 4:4–7 (and Rom 8:3, 16–17) and especially in Col 1:13–16. Thus "the 'faithful' God" of v. 9 is "*our* Father" (v. 3) because he is first of all "the Father of our Lord Jesus Christ" (2 Cor 1:3). As such, God has called the Corinthians εἰς κοινωνίαν τοῦ υἱοῦ αὐτοῦ Ἰησοῦ Χριστοῦ τοῦ κυρίου ἡμῶν (*into fellowship with his Son, Jesus Christ our Lord*). Here is a place where the presupposition of the Son's present tenure is in heaven, as in 1 Thess 1:9–10, so that whatever is intended by κοινωνία, it involves a relationship with the now exalted eternal Son of God.

But what might be the reason for this considerable addition to what it means for God to be "faithful" in his calling of the Corinthians? How does this bring climax to a thanksgiving that began by noting the Corinthians' own Spirit gifting yet concluded on the twin notes of eschatological affirmation? One's answer can be only tentative, but the lack of an article with κοινωνία suggests that the sense is a calling "into a sharing/participation" both with the Son himself and especially into the much larger "fellowship" of all those who belong to the Son.[43] That is, whatever else, they are a part of the eschatological (messianic) community of believers who have been made so because they belong to the Messiah himself, who at the same time is the eternal Son of the Father.[44]

It may also be of more than passing interest to note that this concluding affirmation about Christ as Son gives way immediately to an emphasis on the *nature* of the Son's messianic destiny: humiliation by way of crucifixion. It is very likely, then, that this singling out of Christ as "the Son" presupposes the "sending" motif of Gal 4:4–5 and Rom 8:3—thus anticipating what comes next (1:18–31)—as well as his present reign, which is picked up at the end of the letter (15:23–28).

1 Corinthians 1:13–2:16

This passage serves as the first part of a three-part response to some Corinthians' rejection of Paul's apostleship, which they were doing under the guise of "wisdom," wherein he fared poorly in contrast to Apollos. But Paul recognizes this issue for what it really is: a radical misunderstanding of the

---

[43] Thus this concluding affirmation is only partly reassurance to the Corinthians that they are destined to be part of the glorious (but still future) Day of the Lord; it may also be a reminder that the κοινωνία embraces far more than just themselves, as Paul has already emphasized in v. 2 ("along with all those in every place who call on the name of our Lord Jesus Christ").

[44] Some may object to my seeing all this here. My point is that this otherwise quite unnecessary affirmation at the end of the thanksgiving is not a "throwaway" on Paul's part; as with everything in the letter, such moments seem to have ulterior purposes.

gospel (1:17–2:16) and of the church and the role of its intinerant teachers (3:1–23). He thus takes these issues up in this order, so that the actual presenting issue comes second, while the real issue for him—his own authority as apostle to the Gentiles—is addressed at the end (4:1–21). But what is ultimately at stake is the pure gospel itself; thus Paul begins his response here.

The issue is presented as a contest between their "wisdom" and God's, in which all human pretensions to wisdom are radically called into question. In the process, 1:18–25 turns out to be one of the two places in Paul's letters where the Greek word Χριστός probably should be rendered by the Jewish title "Messiah" rather than the title-turned-name "Christ."[45]

However, its first occurrences in this passage are in vv. 13, 17. If there is some mystery involved as to what precisely Paul meant by his rhetorical "Is Christ divided?"[46] at least he intended to respond to their quarreling by putting up front its christological/soteriological implications. I simply note here that the use of "Christ" as a title-turned-name, which begins in v. 12, continues right up to the Jeremiah citation in v. 31, where Christ is then identified with the Septuagint's ὁ κύριος = *Adonai* =Yahweh.

But the *perspective* of this usage shifts in midstream, in v. 17, to be exact. That is, the references to "Christ" in vv. 12, 13, and 17a all presuppose the risen and exalted Christ, made especially plain in v. 17, where Paul asserts that "Christ . . . sent me to preach the gospel." But the gospel he was sent to preach is "the gospel of Christ," which has to do with Christ as its content. And with that midsentence shift, the rest of the argument through 2:5 is about the *human Jesus as God's crucified Messiah*.

At stake for Paul is his proclamation of Χριστὸν ἐσταυρωμένον (*a crucified Messiah*), an inherent (deliberate) affront to both Jewish and Greek worldviews. To the one (the Jew who awaits displays of messianic power), a crucified Messiah is the ultimate scandal; to the other (the Greek who pursues "wisdom"), it is the height of folly. Nonetheless, Paul asserts, we so preach because what is folly and scandal to Jew and Greek is in fact "God's power and God's wisdom" at work in the world—*God's* power to those "seeking signs"; *God's* wisdom to those "looking for wisdom" (v. 22).

Thus, although this is a primarily soteriological moment, it is also christological by implication. Indeed, it is one of the relatively few places where Paul's interest in Christ puts considerable emphasis on the reality of his humanity. Thus, the (now) heavenly Christ, who sent Paul to preach (v. 17), is in fact God's earthly Messiah, who experienced the ultimate

---

[45]The other is Rom 9:5; contra N. Dahl, *Jesus the Christ: The Historical Origins of Christological Doctrine* (Minneapolis: Fortress, 1991), 16. N. T. Wright is prepared to argue that Χριστός should regularly be translated "Messiah" (see "ΧΡΙΣΤΟΣ as 'Messiah' in Paul: Philemon 6," in *Climax of the Covenant*, 41–55).

[46]In context it most likely is intended as a *reductio ad absurdum*, that Christ is now being apportioned out so that each group lays claim to Christ (even if not overtly so) or has its own "Christ" as the result of their present quarreling.

humiliation and rejection of those he came to save. Such passages thus make it impossible to read Paul's Christology in any way that might border on Doceticism.

Excursus: The Crucified Messiah and Jewish Wisdom

Despite the singularly soteriological focus of this passage, there are many who would make vv. 24 and 30 christological as well by using them as the basis for the sapiential interpretation of 1 Cor 8:6 noted above. Thus, regarding 8:6, one regularly reads something such as this: "At this point we need to recall that Paul in fact already explicitly identified Christ as God's Wisdom—in 1 Cor 1:24 and 30."[47] But such an understanding of 1:24 is altogether suspect, especially if one reads the passage on its own terms, without a prior agenda with respect to wisdom. At issue is whether—or how—the Corinthians could have made the association with personified Wisdom that NT scholarship (especially in recent decades) so easily asserts at this point. How is it, one wonders, that this purely *ironic* application of "wisdom" to the crucified One could have been understood by the Corinthians as also carrying *positive* value, pointing toward Christ as assuming the role of personified Wisdom, and *preexistent* Wisdom at that, as Dunn and others assert?[48] That seems to ask more of readers, both ancient and modern, than can be legitimately expected. Indeed, several matters stand altogether over against it.

1. Paul does not say in isolation that "Christ is the wisdom of God." "Christ" in this clause (v. 24) is an appositional pickup of "Christ crucified" at the beginning of the sentence (v. 23). Whatever else, Paul cannot have intended "We preach a crucified Messiah: a stumbling block to Jews and foolishness to Gentiles, but to those who are called, both Jews and Greeks, *the person of* Christ as God's power and as *personified Wisdom*," and then to go on in the next sentence to explain the irony at the beginning: "For the foolishness of God [i.e., personified Wisdom] is wiser than human wisdom, and the weakness of God is stronger than human strength." That is to talk nonsense, and it needs to be recognized as

---

[47] Dunn, *Theology of Paul*, 274. This is an invariable in all such discussions because without it no one could possibly have seen "Wisdom" as lying behind 8:6. In fairness to Dunn, as over against many others (e.g., A. M. Hunter, *The Gospel according to Paul* [Philadelphia: Westminster, 1966], 67–68; J. Ziesler, *Pauline Christianity* [rev. ed.; OBS; Oxford: Oxford University Press, 1990], 34; Matera, *New Testament Christology*, 94), he at least recognizes that Paul turns divine wisdom into the proclamation of Christ crucified; but even so, he treats v. 24 altogether as a christological, rather than soteriological, statement. Note especially the capitalization of "Wisdom" in Dunn's sentence, which no one who was exegeting 1:18–31 on its own terms would ever imagine doing.

[48] See Dunn, *Theology of Paul*, 274: "Is there then a thought of preexistence in 1 Cor. 8:6, not to mention 1:24 and 30? Of course there is." "Of course" works well for 8:6, but how is it even imaginable in 1:24 and 30, which refers to the crucifixion?

such. It is simply irresponsible scholarship to turn this pickup of the crucified Messiah from v. 23 into some form of identification with *personified* Jewish wisdom.

2. It is especially doubtful whether "wisdom" is a truly *Pauline* word at all and whether, therefore, Paul ever thinks of Christ in terms of Jewish wisdom.[49] The linguistic data tell much of the story: The noun σοφία and its cognate adjective σοφός occur 44 times in the Pauline corpus—28 in 1 Corinthians, 26 of these in chs. 1–3,[50] and most of them pejorative. Of the remaining 16, 1 occurs in a similarly pejorative way in 2 Cor 1:12, while 10 occur in Colossians and Ephesians, where the "heady" nature of the false teaching again calls forth this language. This means that in the rest of the corpus this word group appears just 5 times, only one of which is the noun (Rom 11:33, where it echoes OT usage referring to God's *attribute* of wisdom). These statistics therefore, not to mention the argument itself, indicate that "wisdom" is a *Corinthian* thing and that Paul is trying to counter it by appealing to God's foolishness[51] as the certain evidence that the gospel that saved them is not to be confused with σοφία *in any form.*[52]

3. Furthermore, in this context "wisdom" is clearly placed *on the Greek side of things, not the Jewish.* In fact, nothing in the argument suggests that those in Corinth enamored with "wisdom" had any interest in the Jewish wisdom tradition.[53] Not "wisdom and folly" but "power and weakness" are on the Jewish side of things, as vv. 20 and 22–24 make plain. That is, it is the Greek in pursuit of wisdom who would be most highly bemused by Paul's preaching a crucified Messiah. So when Paul

---

[49] Contra Witherington, for example, who (typical of many) is bold here: "[Paul] saw Christ as Wisdom come in the flesh (cf. 1 Cor 1:24)" ("Christology," 103); cf. S. Kim, regarding the Damascus Road experience: "Paul [himself] . . . 'identified' Christ with Wisdom . . . from the very beginning!" (*Origin of Paul's Gospel,* 135 n. 3).

[50] And the remaining two (6:5; 12:8) hark back to the issue raised here. In 6:5, the question "Can it be that there is no one *wise* enough to adjudicate between brothers?" is straight irony, predicated on the Corinthians' own position as it has emerged in chs. 1–3; while in 12:8, in his listing of Spirit manifestations in the community, Paul begins with the two that held high court in Corinth (λόγος σοφίας and λόγος γνώσεως) so as to recapture them for the vital life of the Spirit within the community ("for the common good" [12:7]).

[51] First, by saving through a crucified Messiah (1:18–25); second, by choosing the Corinthian "nobodies" to be among his new eschatological people (1:26–31); third, by calling them through Paul's preaching in personal weakness (2:1–5). For details, see Fee, ad loc.

[52] In fact, Paul asserts categorically that "in the wisdom of God [as attribute] the world through wisdom [διὰ τῆς σοφίας] did *not* know God" (v. 21). It seems altogether unlikely that he would then turn about and say that Christ is "wisdom" and, by implication, suggest that one can know God through Wisdom after all.

[53] Contra J. A. Davis, *Wisdom and Spirit: An Investigation of 1 Corinthians 1.18–3.20 against the Background of Jewish Sapiential Traditions in the Greco-Roman Period* (Lanham, Md.: University Press of America, 1984).

speaks of God's response to the Greek sense of folly and the Jewish scandal, it is altogether unlikely that he now intends for the Greek (not to mention the Jew) to turn to personified *Jewish* wisdom as the place where God's wisdom is at work in the world. Rather, the whole argument is full of irony. God's wisdom lies precisely in the folly of a *crucified* Messiah. How is it possible, one wonders, that the Corinthians would have seen this language at the same time as a christological affirmation, when it is so confrontational regarding the sheer folly of the Greek pursuit of wisdom?

4. What is frequently missed[54] in the discussion of this phrase is the fact that Paul does *not* actually call the crucified One "the wisdom of God." What he says, rather, is that the *proclamation* of the crucified One is "*God's* power and *God's* wisdom"—over against all human efforts to discover God. Two points need to be made here. First, this use of the "vernacular possessive" puts the primary emphasis on God, not on power or wisdom.[55] That is, Paul is not saying that Christ is the (now personified) Wisdom of God. Rather, he is asserting that a *crucified* Messiah, folly and weakness from a merely human point of view, is in fact *God's* power and *God's* wisdom in the world, despite all appearance to the contrary! This is exactly in keeping with how Paul uses the vernacular possessive elsewhere.[56]

Second, the phrase must be kept together as a single expression, since it is in direct response to vv. 22–23. If Paul had intended something christological here (signaling Christ as "the Wisdom of God"), then one may legitimately ask, Why find a "σοφία Christology" and not also a "δύναμις Christology," in which Christ is recognized as the Divine Power personified? After all, it is in each instance the first thing up, until the

---

[54]But not by Richardson (*Paul's Language*, 122–23), who goes on to argue that God's true εἰκών is revealed in the crucified One.

[55]A point, interestingly enough, scarcely made in the literature, even though it is demonstrably Paul's concern. But see Richardson (*Paul's Language*, 108–9), who makes note of it as the result of his interest in "Paul's language about God." For the term "vernacular possessive," see E. A. Abbott, *Johannine Grammar* (London: A. & C. Clark, 1906), 401. In this case, note especially the difference between this phrase (θεοῦ σοφίαν) and the way Paul introduces the term in v. 21: "the wisdom of God" (ἐν τῇ σοφίᾳ τοῦ θεοῦ / διὰ τῆς σοφίας τοῦ θεοῦ). The latter makes clear the meaning of the former, namely, that Paul is talking about an attribute of God that finds expression in the crucifixion. There is not a hint of personification in these phrases.

[56]See esp. 1 Cor 3:9 (θεοῦ γάρ ἐσμεν συνεργοί, θεοῦ γεώργιον, θεοῦ οἰκοδομή ἐστε), where Paul emphatically stresses God's possession: "*God's* co-workers we are [meaning: as co-workers, we together are expressions of God's activity in bringing about the church in Corinth]; and *God's* field, *God's* building you are." The whole context makes it plain why Paul used the vernacular possessive in this case: to assert in conclusion that *everything* belongs to God, not to Paul or Apollos or to the Corinthians. Cf. the less emphatic but equally clear possessive Χριστοῦ δοῦλος ("*Christ's* servant I would not be") in Gal 1:10.

chiasm of v. 25. The reason, of course, is that there are *no outside reasons* for someone wanting to do so. To put it plainly, finding personified Wisdom here comes not from a straightforward reading of this text but from an agenda that lies outside the text altogether: to have a Pauline basis for finding "Wisdom" in 1 Cor 8:6. But to separate out only part of this phrase, where Paul asserts that the crucified Messiah is *God's* wisdom unto salvation vis-à-vis the *Greeks,* and then to turn that into a christological affirmation allegedly derived from Jewish Wisdom (the [noncrucified] Christ is ἡ σοφία τοῦ θεοῦ = *the* Wisdom of God) is an illegitimate use of Paul's language to serve the outside agenda.

5. If Paul had intended this alleged sapiential identification from Jewish wisdom, such a usage would stand in solitary isolation in the entire Pauline corpus.[57] The evidence from Paul's demonstrable use of this literature does not lend any confidence that he would use speculative wisdom in the way he is alleged to have done. Because Paul's interests in the OT lie for the most part with the primary biblical story, he seldom cites or alludes to the wisdom tradition.[58] And when he does do so, it is for the same purposes that are expressed in the literature itself.[59]

Finally, it should be pointed out that if Jewish wisdom were to lie behind this at all, the use of δύναμις and σοφία here would seem most likely to echo a passage such as Job 12:13,[60] having to do with God's *attributes* of "power and wisdom." These divine attributes, Paul argues with the Corinthians, have been put on full display in the ultimate oxymoron of a "crucified Messiah." But this way of referring to God in the Wisdom literature itself seems to correspond to Paul only accidentally. One must remember throughout that the word "wisdom" in this case comes out of the Corinthians' agenda, not Paul's.

In the end, therefore, there is very little Christology as such in this passage, except the inherent scandal that God's Messiah in his humanity would be subjected to such shame, thus turning the tables on Jewish messianic expectations.[61] In this regard, Paul himself has come to understand the

---

[57] Some would argue that personified Wisdom also stands behind Col 1:15–17, but as I will point out in the exegesis of that passage, such an identification is even more tenuous there, where the word σοφία does not occur at all and where the alleged use of wisdom vocabulary is simply not true. See the excursus, pp. 317–25.

[58] For the full data and discussion, see appendix A, pp. 594–619.

[59] That is, moral (or sinful) behavior (Rom 3:10; 12:20); the greatness of God, who alone has wisdom (Rom 11:33); the folly of trying to match wits with God (1 Cor 3:19).

[60] Job 12:13: παρ᾽ αὐτῷ σοφία καὶ δύναμις, αὐτῷ βουλὴ καὶ σύνεσις (*with him are wisdom and power, to him belong counsel and understanding*). The significance of this text is not so much that Paul would be echoing it as that these two words occur together in an expression of Jewish wisdom in which wisdom is not personified—very much the same way it is found in Prov 3:19–20 ("The LORD in wisdom laid the earth's foundations . . .").

[61] On this matter, see the discussion in ch. 14, pp. 532–36.

Messiah as belonging to the long tradition, deeply embedded in the biblical story, that God scandalously kept choosing the barren woman and the younger, weaker son to be the bearer of the divine seed. The triumphalism apparently craved by the Corinthians—who have had an unfortunately numerous progeny in the history of the church—is simply not God's agenda. As the story of Christ that Paul rehearses in Phil 2:6–8 makes plain, Paul came to recognize very early on that "the foolishness of God" is wiser than our (merely human) wisdom. Thus, even though no christological point is made of it here, the "humiliation" of the divinely given Messiah, who came from heaven to earth "in the form of a slave," is Paul's thoroughgoing perspective (see also 2 Cor 8:9; cf., e.g., Gal 4:5–6; Rom 8:3). As he indicates here in v. 25, only God has wisdom and power sufficient to pull off such a scandal and thus eliminate all human pretensions for boasting.

1 Corinthians 1:30; 2:7

A soteriological, and thus nonchristological,[62] understanding of 1:24 is further confirmed by v. 30, where, at the end of the ad hominem argument of vv. 26–31, Paul restates what he had said in v. 24:

1:30 ἐξ αὐτοῦ [θεοῦ] δὲ ὑμεῖς ἐστε ἐν Χριστῷ Ἰησοῦ, ὃς ἐγενήθη σοφία ἡμῖν ἀπὸ θεοῦ, δικαιοσύνη τε καὶ ἁγιασμὸς καὶ ἀπολύτρωσις.
But of him (God) are you *in Christ Jesus, who became wisdom for us from God, that is, righteousness and sanctification and redemption.*

Having affirmed once more that God has made Christ to be "wisdom for us," Paul immediately qualifies it in such a way that the Corinthians could not possibly have imagined that he had personified Wisdom in mind. "Wisdom for us" is again clarified in terms of Christ's saving work: righteousness/justification, sanctification, and redemption[63]—three nouns that appear later in the letter as "saving verbs" (6:11) or as metaphor (6:20).

---

[62] Always with the demurral, of course, that one can never truly dissociate Christology from soteriology in Paul's thought. See ch. 11 below.

[63] B. Witherington (*Jesus the Sage: The Pilgrimage of Wisdom* [Minneapolis: Fortress, 1994], 310–11) tries to circumvent this by (1) making the ἐν Χριστῷ Ἰησοῦ instrumental (a possible but unusual sense for this phrase), (2) making the relative clause, toward which the whole sentence is pointing, parenthetical (!), and (3) thus turning the three nouns, which sit in apposition with σοφία, into predicate nouns with "you are." Thus, "But from God *you* are through Christ (who was made Wisdom for us by God), righteousness and sanctification and redemption" (italics and comma Witherington's). Rather than the "natural sense of the grammar," as he asserts, this looks like a "translation" intended to get around the plain implications of the text. Where in Paul's writings, one wonders, can one find another *parenthetical* ὅς-clause, and especially one that comes immediately after its obvious antecedent?

Finally, after a strong denial that his own ministry that brought them to faith had anything to do with the kind of "wisdom" that now fascinates them, Paul in 2:7 argues again that wisdom can indeed be found in the gospel that he preached; but it is (formerly) "hidden wisdom," so contradictory to merely human wisdom that it can be known only by revelation from the Spirit (v. 10). Again, the whole context, and v. 12 in particular (by use of χαρίζομαι), indicates that God's wisdom is to be found in the cross. That is, it was "hidden" in the sense of Jewish apocalyptic, waiting to be revealed at its proper time. But Christ *as person* is not in purview here at all.[64] What Paul is setting out to do is to recapture "wisdom" from his Corinthian critics by showing that God's foolishness found in the cross can in fact be recognized as wisdom, but now in terms of God's attribute of wisdom—and this only by those who have received the Spirit of God. Thus, at the end of the day, Christ is God's wisdom for Paul only in sharp *contrast* to the Corinthians' present fascination with wisdom, not as a positive way of setting forth the meaning of Christ that he will later capitalize on (in 8:6, where wisdom is not even mentioned) to his and their advantage. That simply does not happen either in 1 Corinthians or elsewhere in the corpus. The net result of a close look at this passage, therefore, with personified Wisdom in view brings only negative results. Paul neither here nor anywhere else in his letters makes even the remotest allusion to "her." She simply is not on his radar screen.

1 Corinthians 15:23–28

Although 1 Cor 8:6 and 1:24, 30 do not lend themselves to a "Wisdom Christology," together they do suggest a background in Jewish messianism. In the former passage it lay inherent in the appellation of God as "Father," implying that Christ is his "Son." In the latter, the entire passage is predicated on the divine modification of Jewish messianic expectations and of Greco-Roman abhorrence of that modification: a "crucified Messiah." Now toward the end of the letter, Paul returns to messianic themes once more, this time—and in stark contrast to 1:24, 30—reflecting the role that Christ as messianic king and Son of God plays in Paul's understanding of present and future eschatology.

At issue in 1 Cor 15 is a singular matter that has arisen on the Corinthians' end of things: a denial of a *future bodily* resurrection of believers. Paul's first response is simply a recapitulation of the eyewitness evidence, including himself, as to *Christ's* bodily resurrection (vv. 5–11). What he argues next is that Christ's resurrection set something in motion that makes ours both necessary and inevitable (vv. 20–28), an argument that both began

---

[64] Thus Ziesler's comment that "1 Cor 2:7 says there is something hidden and mysterious about Christ as the wisdom of God" (*Pauline Christianity*, 34) is especially far removed from Paul. God's wisdom is not here personified; it is found precisely in the absurdity (from a human point of view) of a crucified Messiah, which Paul will now go on to argue can be known only by the help of the Spirit.

(vv. 12–19) and concluded (vv. 29–34) in strikingly ad hominem fashion. In vv. 35–58 he takes up the second part of their denial: the "bodily" nature of the resurrection of the believing dead.

The present paragraph (vv. 20–28) is a resounding "but now!" (νυνὶ δέ) to the detailed set of "if not, then" expressions in vv. 12–19. If the dead are not raised, then Christ has not been raised; and if Christ has not been raised, then nothing counts for anything: our preaching and your faith is in vain; we are still in our sins and without hope; and God turns out to be a liar. "But now" Christ has indeed been raised from the dead, as the "firstfruits" of the final harvest to come. The singular concern in the present passage, then, is the *future* resurrection of believers, both its necessity and inevitability. Everything else is subordinate to this concern. And both its necessity and inevitability are predicated on the Adam/Christ contrast with which the paragraph begins. Adam's sin let something loose in the world—death—that is contrary to God and his nature. Christ's death and resurrection also let something loose in the world that will necessarily and inevitably overturn what Adam began. This is Paul's singular concern, not the temporal sequencing of events related to this concern.[65]

For our present purposes, three preliminary matters about usage interest us.[66] First is the predominance in this passage of Paul's use of the title-turned-name Χριστός (*Christ*). Indeed, from vv. 1 through 27, Paul uses the name "Christ" exclusively—13 times in all (over one-fourth of the total for the entire letter). Moreover, "Christ" is the assumed subject of the five pas-

---

[65]Indeed, one expression of interpretation suggests that Paul here envisions a temporal messianic reign between the two adverbs ἔπειτα / εἶτα; but that is to throw a red herring into the argument. Whether Paul believed in such cannot be known, since he never speaks to the question. But to find it in his use of these two adverbs is to read foreign matter *into* the text, not Paul's concerns *out of* it; and then to suggest that the messianic reign itself lies *between* these two adverbs, so that it is not currently in place, requires a considerable stretch of the imagination, not to mention of Paul's own concerns in the passage. Although there can be little question that the εἶτα carries with it an inherent temporal sequence, Paul's concern at this point is with the "logical" more than the temporal sequence of things. That is, the "then" is related to what happens next at the time of the Parousia. At that time, the resurrection of the dead will take place, and that means that the last of God's enemies has been subdued. What is left is for the Son to hand the "kingdom" back to the Father, so that he can be all and in all. For the contrary view, including a discussion of the literature (over what appears to be a nonissue for Paul), see Kreitzer, *Jesus and God*, 134–54. On the other hand, his christological reading of the text, which is not dependent on the temporal sequencing of things, is quite useful.

[66]For discussion of the Adam/Christ analogy/contrast in vv. 21–22, see pp. 114–16. The latter is separated out from the present discussion in part because it is not a messianic theme, and in part because this analogy/contrast emerges explicitly two further times in Paul's letters (1 Cor 15:45–49; Rom 5:12–17 [some would also suggest Phil 2:6–7]). Thus it is arguable that this theme was something that Paul regularly reflected on and thus needs its own separate analysis, especially since the usage is subtly different in each case.

sive verbs in vv. 4–8 ("was buried," "was seen"), and he is the "he/him/his" of the six pronouns in vv. 23–27. Second, at the end of the paragraph, where the antecedent of the pronouns begins to get a bit fuzzy, the specified referent becomes "the Son himself." Third, in our paragraph, between the predominant use of "Christ" and the use of "Son" in v. 28 (that Christ as Son will "turn over the kingdom" to "God the Father") there is the intriguing statement in vv. 24–25 that for now "he must reign" until "the end," when the final enemy, "death," is defeated through resurrection.

Add to this the predominant role that the combined "citations" from Ps 110:1 (v. 25) and Ps 8:6 (v. 27) play in the argument, and it becomes clear that, even though the future bodily resurrection of believers is the primary focus here, the whole paragraph is placed squarely within the framework of Jewish messianism.[67] It is therefore noteworthy that the only other place in this letter where this predominant use of "Christ" appears is in 1:13–25, where in at least one instance (1:22) Χριστός is titular before it is nominal.[68]

What Paul pictures here is a twofold temporal sequence, the second of which has his primary concern in the paragraph attached to it. Christ's resurrection as "firstfruits" guarantees the harvest that is to come; and that "harvest" will take place at the Parousia, which will be accompanied by the resurrection of the dead, thus subduing the "last enemy." Once that happens, then what is promised about the Messiah in Ps 110:1, that all his enemies will be subdued under his feet, will have taken place (vv. 25–26). The only thing left will be for the Son then to hand over the "kingdom" to the Father (vv. 27–28). Everything else in the passage is an elaboration in some way or another of this twofold sequence of resurrection: Christ's and, at his coming, those who are his. This alone is Paul's concern; and it is within this concern that several christological observations are to be made.

1. We begin by noting that Christ is the grammatical subject of all the verbs in vv. 24–26. The three preceding phrases in v. 23 are verbless, serving grammatically in apposition to the πάντες ζῳοποιηθήσονται (*all will be made alive*) in v. 22, where the conceptual subject of the passive verb is God. Thus in order: Christ the firstfruits; those who are Christ's at his coming, which also marks the end. The rest of v. 24 is composed of a pair of coordinate temporal clauses (ὅταν . . . ὅταν), which describe, without concern for sequence, the two features of the end that here interest Paul.[69] As part of the larger event of his Parousia, Christ (1) turns over the kingdom to God his Father, and (2) at the same time he abolishes all the "powers" that stand against him

---

[67] That is, Christ (= Messiah) is now the Son of God in heaven, who reigns in the heavenly realm. On "Son" as a messianic designation having to do with Israel's king, see the discussion on Col 1:13 (p. 297), and esp. ch. 14 on Jesus as messianic king.

[68] Thus 43 percent of the instances of Χριστός by itself occur in these two brief passages.

[69] See Fee, 752; Garland, 710; Thiselton, 1230–31; Keener, 127.

and his people. The last of the "powers," it turns out, is death itself (v. 26). But before coming to that point, which is the ultimate point of concern, Paul interrupts himself (v. 25) to offer a biblical explanation[70] about "the powers." By his abolishing the "powers," Christ has himself "fulfilled" Ps 110:1, which speaks of "putting all his *enemies* under his feet."

Thus in turn Paul asserts that Christ is the currently reigning King, who at his return will abolish all of the powers that stand over against him (and thus against God the Father), and will do so in fulfillment of the messianic Ps 110:1. Therefore, what in the psalm is the activity of God is now read by Paul as the activity of the presently reigning Christ. Some of this needs further elaboration.

2. Paul speaks of "the kingdom of God/Christ" only 13 times in his extant letters (including the Pastoral Epistles).[71] In most cases he uses the traditional language "the kingdom of God." Only here and in Col 1:13, plus the two instances in 2 Timothy, is Christ named as the King. Of these four, Col 1:13 uses the language "Son" as the referent of the King, as does the present passage at the end (v. 28). In both cases Paul is referring to the Messiah's *present* reign.[72] The other nine occurrences have "God" as the ruling one, and in these cases the usage fluctuates between the kingdom as a present reality and as a future event, the latter being clearly designated by the future tense and the language of "inheritance."[73]

The christological point, of course, is the ease with which Paul can interchange this kingdom language. On the one hand, this perhaps should be no surprise, since in Jewish messianism the Messiah would rule over God's coming kingdom. On the other hand, the radical change to traditional messianism that one finds in Paul's thought—the kingdom is now and the Son of God currently reigns (cf. Col 1:13)—changes the playing field considerably, since the "king" who reigns does so from on high, thus assuming the role of God himself in so doing.

3. This passage also offers us certain evidence that Paul had already joined with others (the author of Hebrews, for example) who understood Ps 8 in light of Ps 110, and thus both psalms together as messianic.[74] The key connection between them is the phrase ὑπὸ τοὺς πόδας αὐτοῦ (*under his feet*) found in Ps 110:1 (109:1 LXX) and Ps 8:6 (8:7 LXX). Thus in Ps 110 (109 LXX), Yahweh tells "my lord" the king to "sit at my right hand until I make your

---

[70] The γάρ (*for*) in this case is explanatory, not causal.

[71] In their assumed chronological order: 1 Thess 2:12; 2 Thess 1:5; 1 Cor 4:20; 6:9–10; 15:24; 15:50; Gal 5:21; Col 1:13; 4:11; Eph 5:5; 2 Tim 4:1; 4:18.

[72] As over against a yet future reign in an intermediate kingdom (see n. 65 above).

[73] So, e.g., in 1 Cor 6:9–10, "shall not inherit the kingdom of God"; cf. 15:50; Gal 5:21; Eph 5:5. This is probably true also of "being worthy of the kingdom of God" in 2 Thess 1:5, while the usage in 1 Thess 2:12 is more ambiguous.

[74] On this question and Paul's own role in the combination, see Hengel, " 'Sit at My Right Hand!' " 163–65.

enemies a footstool *under your feet."* Understanding this in a messianic way then caused Ps 8:7 LXX, with its similar language (plus "son of Man"), to be intrepreted in the same way (cf. Eph 1:20). And all of this is very likely already in place for Paul when he writes this letter. Thus:

Ps 109:1 LXX ἕως ἄν	**θῷ**	τοὺς ἐχθρούς σου		
		ὑποπόδιον	τῶν ποδῶν σου	
1 Cor 15:25 ἄχρι οὗ	**θῇ** πάντας	τοὺς ἐχθροὺς		
		ὑπὸ	τοὺς πόδας αὐτοῦ	

Ps 109:1 LXX *until*	***I put***	*your* **enemies**		
		under	***your feet***	
1 Cor 15:25 *until*	***he puts*** *all*	*[his]* **enemies**		
		under	***his feet***	

Ps 8:7 LXX	**πάντα**	ὑπέταξας	ὑποκάτω	τῶν ποδῶν αὐτοῦ
1 Cor 15:27	**πάντα** γὰρ	ὑπέταξεν	ὑπὸ	τοὺς πόδας αὐτοῦ

Ps 8:7 LXX	***all things***	***having put***	*under*	***his feet***
1 Cor 15:27	*for* ***all things***	***he has put***	*under*	***his feet***

Paul's unique contribution to this scheme is to interpret the "enemies" of Ps 110:1 in terms of *"all* enemies,"[75] the last and greatest of whom is death itself. So when death is defeated by resurrection, this psalm will then have reached its ultimate fulfillment. Moreover, the "citation" of Ps 110:1 in v. 25 is yet another place where, for Paul, Christ has assumed the role that God plays in the psalm itself. By changing from the first person, where Yahweh is speaking, to the third person, to conform to Paul's use of the psalm, he thus has attributed to Christ the role of "putting the enemies under his (own) feet."

4. But having made that point, Paul then goes on to reflect on this anticipated reality in terms of the even grander scale of things: the resurrection of the dead being the pivotal moment that marks the end of the present scheme of things. And here is where the language of "subject all things" under his feet comes into the picture. Paul is interpreting the psalm not only as messianic but also now as the final event on the Messiah's kingly agenda. He does this by referring to the currently reigning Christ as the Son (v. 28). That "Son" is here to be understood first of all as a messianic designation is made evident in two ways: first, by its sudden appearance in a context where it refers back to "the *one who must reign* until all his enemies are under his feet"; and second, by the use of the intensive αὐτός (*himself*) in v. 28, which in this case is an emphatic pickup of his being the one who rules in the earlier sentence (v. 25). That is, the one eventually designated as "the Son himself"

_____

[75] Several MSS, including A F G 33 629 a r, "fill out" the citation by adding αὐτοῦ (*his*) to represent the σου (*your*).

(v. 28) is the one who in v. 25 was said to rule until he himself has put all his enemies under his own feet, where "all enemies" refers especially to the final enemy, death itself. Thus, when God's kingly Son has subjected death "under his feet" through resurrection, his role as Messiah has been accomplished.[76] So he in turn "will be made subject to him who put everything under him, so that God may be all in all."[77]

5. It is this sequence of "events" and concerns that leads to the unmarked change of grammatical subject in vv. 27–28. At issue is where that change takes place. Unfortunately, our present versification muddies the waters; but if we follow Paul's own (repeated) structural signals, this is easier to determine than is often allowed. Paul's sequence goes like this:

A. "The end" (the destruction of death by resurrection) is marked by two events:
    1. The Son hands over the "rule" to his God and Father (v. 24a).
    2. At the same time, he destroys all the "powers," especially "death" (v. 24b).

B. The first biblical explanation (v. 25):
    1. He must reign until all enemies are under his feet (Ps 110:1).
    2. The last of these is death (v. 26)—what the passage is all about!

C. The second biblical explanation (v. 27a, citing Ps 8:6):[78]
    1. First elaboration: the "all things" excludes the one doing the subjecting.
    2. Second elaboration: when this happens, even the Son becomes "subject" to the Father.

Given Paul's own structural signals, not only does the whole argument makes good sense, but also one can see a modified set of chiasms going on. That is, the A1 and A2 clauses are picked up in reverse order in the two biblical explanations in vv. 25 and 27a: the first has to do with the destruction of

---

[76] On this understanding, see Wright, *Climax of the Covenant*, 30.

[77] On the difficult issue of the subtle shift of referents regarding "he/him" in vv. 26–28, see Fee (757–59), and now esp. Kreitzer (*Jesus and God*, 149–55), whose careful refutation of J. Lambrecht ("Paul's Christological Use of Scripture in 1 Cor 15:20–28," *NTS* 28 [1982]: 502–27) seems decisive in favor of a "subtle shift" (so most recent interpreters: Blomberg, Witherington, Hays, Collins, Thiselton, Garland).

[78] Note that this is followed by a compounded ὅταν δέ . . . ὅταν δέ, which in this case functions quite differently from the previous set. Here the δέ (*but*), although probably "consecutive," nonetheless in each case responds to what immediately precedes; and in both cases the ὅταν *begins* a clause with a subordinating introductory clause, "whenever (in time) this happens, then . . ." It is this feature that seems also to mark the intended break in grammatical subject. On this as the proper place to see the change of subject, see Hengel (" 'Sit at My Right Hand!' " 165), who likewise suggests that "Paul offers a rationale for the entire argument in the . . . quotation from Ps. 8:7."

"the powers," especially "death"; the second has to do with the relationship of the Son's present reign to the Father's eternal reign. And this in turn also indicates where the grammatical change of pronominal subject takes place, at C1, where Paul will explain biblically what it means for the Son to hand over the rule to the Father. Thus (substituting the assumed antecedents for the pronouns):

> *Then the end, when the Son hands over the rule to God the Father, when the Son destroys every rule and every authority and power. For the Son must rule until "he [the Son] places his enemies under his (own) feet" [Ps 110:1]. The final "enemy" to be destroyed is death. For "He [God] has subjected all things under his [the Son's] feet." Now when it says "all things have been subjected,"[79] this clearly excludes the one [God] who has subjected all things to him [the Son]. So when he [God] has subjected all things to him [the Son], then even the Son himself is subjected to the one [God the Father] who subjected all things to him [the Son], in order that God might be all in all.*

If this does not make smooth, or necessarily logical, reading for us, we can be fairly sure that this is Paul's "logic," which is based finally on the same "tension" between, on the one hand, his understanding of Christ as participating in the divine identity as in 8:6 and, on the other hand, his unrelenting monotheism, so that there is only "one God" even while at the same time there is now also only "one Lord."

Although it could easily be argued that this implies some form of "eternal subordination" of the Son to the Father, it is unlikely that Paul is thinking in terms of Christ's *person* here, but rather of his *role* in salvation history. The Son obviously does not cease to exist, nor is he here being placed eternally under the Father's authority;[80] rather, in the event described in this passage, his functional subordination in his role as Messiah, and thus as currently reigning messianic Lord, is now completed,[81] so that the "one God"

---

[79] This switch from the aorist active in the psalm to the explanatory perfect passive should be the giveaway as to what is going on and makes it certain (so it would seem) that God is now to be understood as the subject of the verb "to subject."

[80] In some evangelical circles the discussion of the eternal subordination of the Son to the Father came into existence altogether as an attempt to bring women under subjection to men. See esp. S. D. Kovach and P. R. Schemm Jr., "A Defense of the Doctrine of the Eternal Subordination of the Son," *JETS* 42 (1999): 44–76; but see the refutation by Kevin Giles, "The Subordination of Christ and the Subordination of Women," in *Discovering Biblical Equality: Complementarity without Hierarchy* (ed. R. W. Pierce and R. M. Groothuis; Downers Grove, Ill.: InterVarsity Press, 2004), 334–52.

[81] Cf. Wright, *Climax of the Covenant*, 30. O. Cullmann (*The Christology of the New Testament* [trans. S. C. Guthrie and C. A. M. Hall; Philadelphia: Westminster, 1959], 226–27, 293) suggests that Christ's lordship and sonship have a terminal point: that they exist only as long as the church exists on earth. But that seems out of step with the kind of Christology revealed in Phil 2:9–11, where "Lord" is the "name" given to Christ, apparently without end.

from whom and for whom are all things (1 Cor 8:6) is "all in all." The whole universe finds its meaning once more in the final glory of the one God.

6. We should note, finally, although no point is made of it here, that this is the first of four instances where Paul alludes to Ps 110:1, the most frequently cited/echoed text in the NT as a whole (see Rom 8:34; Col 3:1; Eph 1:20). For the early Christians this became the crucial text for their Κύριος Christology, which, according to the Gospels, finds its origins in Jesus himself (Mark 12:36 and pars.). Although each instance in Paul's writings comes with a slightly different emphasis, common to them all is Christ's present exalted status at the Father's "right hand."[82] The striking feature of the present one is that it seems to bookend the inherent scandal set forth in 1:22–25, that the Messiah who had died by crucifixion is the now exalted Lord at the Father's right hand.

Jesus as Second Adam

One of the striking features of the preceding argument is found at its beginning, in 1 Cor 15:21–22, where Paul, without prior hint or anticipation, draws an analogy between Christ and Adam in order to demonstrate the inevitability of our resurrection inherent in the metaphor ἀπαρχή (firstfruits). The Adam/Christ analogy has created a flurry of interest in its own right,[83] but our concern here is to tease out Paul's christological presuppositions in its two appearances in this letter. See the more complete discussion in ch. 13.

1 Corinthians 15:21–22

As noted, there has been nothing to prepare the reader for Paul's first reference to Adam in his extant letters. Paul's point is nonetheless easily discerned. The topic is the future bodily resurrection of believers; its premise has been stated in the "topic sentence" (v. 20): Christ has been raised as the "firstfruits" of those who are "sleeping." Therefore, just as the firstfruits of a harvest are the harbinger of the whole crop, so Christ's resurrection as firstfruits points to the certainty of the resurrection of those who are

---

[82] On this matter, see the seminal work by D. Hay, *Glory at the Right Hand: Psalm 110 in Early Christianity* (SBLMS 18; Nashville: Abingdon, 1973), which is still the starting point for the study of this psalm for Paul and other NT writers.

[83] See, e.g., M. Black, "The Pauline Doctrine of the Second Adam," *SJT* 7 (1954): 70–79; J. Jervell, *Imago Dei: Gen. 1,26f. im Spätjudentum, in der Gnosis und in den paulinischen Briefen* (FRLANT 58; Göttingen: Vandenhoeck & Ruprecht); E. Brandenburger, *Adam und Christus: Exegetisch-religionsgeschichtliche Untersuchung zu Röm. 5, 12-21 (1.Kor 15)* (WMANT 7; Neukirchen-Vluyn: Neukirchener Verlag, 1962); R. Scroggs, *The Last Adam: A Study in Pauline Anthropology* (Philadelphia: Fortress, 1966); J. D. G. Dunn, "1 Corinthians 15:45—Last Adam, Life-Giving Spirit," in *Christ and Spirit in the New Testament: Studies in Honour of Charles Francis Digby Moule* (ed. B. Lindars and S. S. Smalley; London: Cambridge University Press, 1973), 127–41.

Christ's. The "logic" is also easily discerned: resurrection presupposes death;
so just as death had its origins with a man, resurrection also has its origins
with another man (v. 21). This is then spelled out by naming the two "men,"
Adam and Christ, while at the same time Paul "locates" the Corinthian
believers in both "Adam" and "Christ" (v. 22).

The reason for the analogy, therefore, is twofold. First, Paul uses it to
point out that death is the result of sin—sin that was let loose in the world
through "a man"—so that all are heirs of our human progenitor in that we
all die. But second, the main point of the analogy and now as an interpretation of the "firstfruits" metaphor, the divine response to our death is resurrection, a resurrection that all who are Christ's[84] will equally share, just as
they shared equally in the "death" of Adam. Hence, the emphasis in this first
instance is on Christ's real humanity. Whatever else is true of Christ, in his
incarnation he was a true human being, who died as Adam died; otherwise,
the analogy does not work at all.

It is of some interest, therefore, that this passage leads into the
messianism that follows in vv. 23–28, where Christ's present role since his

------

[84] This, of course, is not precisely what Paul *says;* but it is almost certainly what
he means. Since Paul's letters were intended to be read aloud, not silently, it is typical
of Paul's prose to express contrasts or analogies by way of balanced, poetic lines like
these. In so doing, Paul often keeps the rhetoric intact, even if what is said is not precise. So, e.g., in 1 Cor 6:13, he cites the "poetry" of the Corinthians' slogan:

Food for the stomach,
and the stomach for food;
   and God will destroy both the one [food] and the other [stomach].

He then follows this with his theological denial that their slogan works with regard
to the body, as they apparently were arguing. Thus he asserts, following the same
pattern but making a necessary temporal adjustment to line 3:

The body for the Lord,
and the Lord for the body;
   and God both raised the Lord,
   and will raise us by his power.

By using poetically balanced lines, and in favor of the aural contrast over precision,
the second line of this construction (on its own) would appear to border on theological nonsense. Whatever else, the Lord does not exist simply for the sake of our bodies, which is what Paul says but hardly what he means. The same thing has
happened here, and it happens again in the much-debated 15:45 (see p. 117 below).
Paul's poetic instincts simply win out over precision, and he expects his hearers to
read the imprecision within the context of their known theology. Thus:

ὥσπερ γὰρ	ἐν τῷ Ἀδὰμ	πάντες ἀποθνήσκουσιν,
οὕτως καὶ	ἐν τῷ Χριστῷ	πάντες ζῳοποιηθήσονται.
Just as	*in Adam*	*all die,*
so also	*in Christ*	*all shall be made to live.*

Although there can be no question about the universal nature of the first πάντες,
there is every good reason, in light of the whole of the Pauline corpus, not to make
the second πάντες equal the first in meaning.

own resurrection is that of messianic king, who is now exalted and "ruling" in heaven.

1 Corinthians 15:44–49

The second occurrence of the Adam/Christ analogy/contrast in 1 Cor 15 comes at the end of his response to the second issue in the chapter: the *nature* of the resurrection body. With a series of analogies, one leading to yet another, Paul argues that (1) the resurrected body will have genuine continuity with the present body but (2) it will undergo significant change so as to be adapted to the life of the future. Toward the end of the argument, this change is expressed by means of the words ψυχικόν (*belonging to the soul*) and πνευματικόν (*belonging to the spirit*). But in doing so—that is, by describing the two expressions of *bodily* existence this way—he created a considerable oxymoron, σῶμα πνευματικόν (*"spiritual" body*). Most likely, in light of how he used these two adjectives in 2:6–16, he here intends to describe a "body adapted to the final life of the Spirit," whereas the first "body" is that which is adapted to the present earthly life, characterized by ψυχή.

And here is where Paul picks up once again on the Adam/Christ analogy, but now by sharp contrast only. Paul's present usage seems to have been determined by two matters: (1) the Septuagint's use of the word ψυχή to describe what Adam became in creation, and (2) his conviction that what is essential to our final life is Spirit (πνεῦμα). What is different in this second use of the analogy is that Paul is no longer emphasizing Christ's humanity as in common with Adam; rather, in sharp *contrast* to Adam, whose body was subject to decay and death, Christ's *risen body* is quite the opposite. It is now "of heaven" (even though it began on earth) and is therefore without the possibility of decay. So even though the contrast is maintained by the language of the "first man Adam" and the "last Adam/second man," the emphasis on Christ is no longer on his humanity but on his present heavenly existence in *a raised/transformed body*.

Paul's way of saying this, especially his playing on the language of the Gen 2:7, has caused some to read Paul as advocating a "Spirit Christology." But as is pointed out in ch. 16, the support for such a view is especially weak, so much so that one could assume it not to exist at all.[85] In a passage whose

---

[85] The recent, and most influential, presentation of this perspective is by Dunn ("1 Corinthians 15:45"; cf. Ziesler [*Pauline Christianity*, 46–47], who bought into it totally). Even though Dunn recognizes that the crucial clause about Christ has been shaped by the former one about Adam, he insists that Paul nonetheless intends something quite christological in this passage. Moreover, Dunn's statement on the basis of Paul's use of "life-giving πνεῦμα," that the "*believer's experience of the life-giving Spirit* is for Paul proof that the risen Jesus is σῶμα πνευματικόν" ("1 Corinthians 15:45," 131 [emphasis mine; Dunn emphasizes the whole sentence]), is an assertion pure and simple. In fact, this quite turns Paul's own point on its head, namely, that Christ's now assuming a "supernatural body" is the certain evidence that the Corinthian believers, too, will eventually "bear such a body" (v. 49).

whole point is soteriological-eschatological, Paul is intent on one thing: to demonstrate from Christ's own resurrection that there must be a future, *bodily* resurrection of believers as well. Thus he begins by citing the Septuagint of Gen 2:7, in a kind of midrash pesher:[86]

| 1 Cor 15:45 | ἐγένετο | ὁ πρῶτος ὁ ἔσχατος | ἄνθρωπος | Ἀδὰμ Ἀδὰμ | εἰς ψυχὴν ζῶσαν, εἰς πνεῦμα ζῳοποιοῦν |
| Gen 2:7 | καὶ | ἐγένετο | ὁ ἄνθρωπος | | εἰς ψυχὴν ζῶσαν |

| 1 Cor 15:45 | **became** | *the first the last* | **man** | Adam Adam | *a living soul,* *a life-giving spirit* |
| Gen 2:7 | *and* | **became** | *the* **man** | | *a living soul* |

Several observations about this citation-turned-interpretation are needed:

1. Paul's *modifications* of the Septuagint in the first line—the additions of the adjective "first" and of the name "Adam"—seem specifically designed to lead to the second line, where his real concern lies.

2. The two words that describe Adam and Christ respectively (ψυχή and πνεῦμα) are the cognate nouns for the adjectives ψυχικόν and πνευματικόν in v. 44. This in fact is the *only* reason both for the Genesis citation and for the language used to describe Christ. This clear linguistic connection implies that the *original* bearers of the two kinds of bodies mentioned in v. 44 are Adam and Christ.[87] That is, the two Adams serve as evidence that even as there is a ψυχικόν body (as the first Adam demonstrates [Gen 2:7]), so also Christ, the second Adam, by his resurrection is evidence that there must be a πνευματικόν body.[88]

3. Not only so, but Paul's basic reason for saying that Christ became "a *life-giving* πνεῦμα" is that the Septuagint had said of Adam that he became "a *living* ψυχή." That is, the language of the citation alone called for the parallel language about Christ. This is as typically Pauline as one can get, where he makes wordplays in contrasting clauses that would never have existed without the preceding contrast. It is of some interest, therefore, to note that

---

[86] Cf. E. Earle Ellis, *Paul's Use of the Old Testament* (Edinburgh: Oliver & Boyd, 1957; repr., Grand Rapids: Baker, 1981), 141–43; it is doubtful, however, whether Paul is here citing a midrash that had already taken hold in Christian circles (95–97). Paul himself is perfectly capable of such pesher. Dunn argues that the whole sentence "stands under the οὕτως γέγραπται—including verse 45b, as the absence of δέ indicates" ("1 Corinthians 15:45," 130). Yes and no. This is true of the pesher as such, but Paul scarcely intends the second clause to be understood as Scripture, even in a targumic way, in the same sense that the first line is.

[87] As Dunn ("I Corinthians 15:45," 130) also notes.

[88] This is the point that Max Turner makes especially strongly ("The Significance of Spirit Endowment for Paul," *VE* 9 [1975]: 62); cf. Wright: "Adam and Christ as individuals are not the main subjects of discussion, but a buttress to the anthropological assertions of vv. 42–44, 46–47" (*Climax of the Covenant*, 32).

every alleged "Spirit Christology" turns to this text at some point for support. But to create a theological construct from a wordplay, when straightforward statements of all kinds stand on the other side of such an idea, is to derive Christology from a highly suspect methodology.[89]

4. Even though the content of Paul's second line is neither present nor inferred in the Genesis text, it nonetheless reflects the language of the prior clause in the Septuagint, "and [God] *breathed* into his face the *breath of life* [πνοὴν ζωῆς]." Now in speaking about Christ, Paul makes a play on this language. The one who will "breathe" new life into these mortal bodies—with life-giving πνεῦμα (as in Ezek 37:14)—and thus make them immortal is none other than the risen Christ himself.

5. The language "life-giving" thus repeats the verb used of Christ in the previous Adam/Christ analogy in v. 22, indicating decisively, it would seem, that the interest here, as before, is in Christ's resurrection as the ground of our resurrection ("in Christ all will be made alive"). Therefore, the argument as a whole, as well as the immediate context, suggests that even though Christ has now assumed his exalted position in a σῶμα πνευματικόν and is thus a "life-giving πνεῦμα," his function in this particular role will take place at the resurrection of believers, when he "makes alive" their mortal bodies so that they too assume a σῶμα πνευματικόν like his.

The concern of line 2, therefore, is not christological in the sense that Christ and the Spirit were somehow now interchangeable terms for Paul. Indeed, despite the combination of "life-giving" and πνεῦμα, he almost certainly does not intend to say that Christ became *the* life-giving Spirit, but rather *a* life-giving spirit.[90] Christ is *not* the Spirit; rather, in a play on the Genesis text, Paul says that Christ, through his resurrection, assumed his new existence in the spiritual realm, the realm, of course, that for believers is the ultimate sphere of the Spirit, in which they will have "spiritual" bodies, adapted to the final life of the Spirit.

Nonetheless, if there is not a "Spirit Christology" at work in this passage, and that does seem to be foreign to everything that Paul is actually arguing here, it does have two significant christological moments that need to be isolated and thus highlighted.

The first of these occurs in the second line of v. 45. In referring to Christ as a "life-giving πνεῦμα," Paul envisions the risen Christ as assuming the *eschatological* role that God played at the beginning. As God breathed life into the first Adam, so that Adam (and all his progeny) would become living be-

---

[89] Cf. the critique in Wright, *Climax of the Covenant*, 31–35; see the further discussion of this issue in ch. 16 below, pp. 589–91.

[90] Grammar must still have its day in court. Paul tends to be very precise and generally unambiguous with his use or nonuse of the definite article with "Spirit." In the nominative, both as subject or as predicate noun (as here), when Paul intends the Holy Spirit, he always uses the article. For a full analysis of Pauline usage, see Fee, *God's Empowering Presence*, ch. 2.

ings, created in God's image, so Christ is now asserted to be the one who will breathe life into the dead so that they too shall live. Thus the risen Christ is seen to share in an otherwise unshared divine prerogative, as the Living One who gives life to others.

The second of these, on the other hand, in v. 49 actually offers us a significant moment of genuine Adam Christology, where Paul picks up the εἰκὼν θεοῦ (*image of God*) language from Gen 1:26–27 and 9:6. At the conclusion of this passage, where he is contrasting the two ἄνθρωποι (*men*) as earthly and heavenly, Paul urges that since believers have borne the "image" of the man of earth, they should also now (because they will) bear the image of the man of heaven.[91] The christological significance of this text is its certain emphasis in context on Christ's humanity and thus on his being the second Adam, the one who has most truly borne the divine image in his human life.

At the same time, because the present emphasis is on the new expression of the earthly body that he now bears, the assumption is that the eschatological goal of his redemptive work lies with our being transformed into that same image, so that the goal of the first creation will be finally realized in the second.

Thus, we should note that this is the first occurrence of "image" language in the corpus, and it seems designed here once again to emphasize Christ's genuine humanity. That is, Christ himself is seen as the one who, in his humanity, has been the one true bearer of the divine image, vis-à-vis the first Adam. And just as the Corinthians have borne the image of the fallen man in their "earthiness" and thus their sinfulness leading to death, Paul is urging them now to live in such a way that just as they through Christ bear the divine image now, so they will also bear his image when they are raised to life immortal.

---

[91] This reflects the textual decision argued for in my commentary (794–95, and the textual n. 5 on p. 787), which in this case, despite its being chosen by a minority of scholars and translators, has the overwhelming textual evidence, both external and internal, in its favor. Although it is true that Paul has been carefully arguing with them about the reality of the future eternal expression of the current body, which is subject to decay and death, it is also true that he has done so by a continual contrast between the body that the first Adam bore and that which the second Adam now bears. And if the sudden switch to exhortation comes as a bit of a surprise, it should not really be so for one well acquainted with Paul; nor does the exhortation really put their future in doubt, as some fear might happen if they were to choose to go with Paul's original text. Paul is simply being Paul, and he concludes first with the affirmation common to our being human: "just as we have borne the *image* of the earthly man" (note the past tense [!]; had Paul intended a simple contrast between present and future, one would expect him to have continued to use the present here). But his concern throughout this letter has been for them to live in keeping with the new life that has been given to them in Christ; so he concludes, "let us also bear the image of the heavenly man." And with that, the net gets thrown a little wider, so as to include their living now in conformity to the One whose new kind of body they are in fact destined to bear. See further ch. 13, pp. 538–39.

Jesus as Κύριος

As noted at the beginning of this chapter, Paul's primary way of speaking about Christ in this letter is with the title ὁ κύριος (*the Lord*), which once more brings us back to 8:6 as our point of departure. And as with the Thessalonian letters, the usage is both wide-ranging and christologically loaded. But in this case we begin at the end, since one of the more significant uses of this title in the entire corpus occurs here.

1 Corinthians 16:22—The Lord and Early Christian Devotion

The closing matters in this letter (16:19–24) are highly unusual[92] and probably reflect the tensions that exist between the church and Paul. On the one hand, much is recognizable. Verses 19–20 offer the standard exchange of greetings, while vv. 21 and 23 are recognizable from 1–2 Thessalonians: "I, Paul, write this greeting in my own hand"; and "the grace of the Lord Jesus be with you" (which becomes a standard item). On the other hand, each of these (vv. 21 and 23) is followed by a note about love, different from anything else in his letters and therefore startling when compared with the others. The unusual final sign-off item (v. 24) will not detain us here ("My love to all of you in Christ Jesus. Amen"), although there seems to be an emphasis on "all of you" that probably reflects some of the inherent tensions in the community itself.

More striking is v. 22: "If anyone does not love the Lord [φιλεῖ τὸν κύριον], let that person be *anathema. Maranatha.*" The assonance of these final two Aramaic words could hardly have been missed by those who would have heard the letter read aloud in their oral, and therefore aural, culture. As such, these words serve as the centerpiece of this epistolary conclusion; and as has been recently pointed out, they most likely are to be understood in the covenantal context of the *anathema.*[93] That is, in many ways these two words together serve simultaneously as invitation and warning—*invitation* to covenant loyalty by "loving the Lord" through obedience to what Paul has here written and is now signing off with his own hand; but also *warning*, if they are disobedient, of God's cursing them at the end when the Lord comes.

Whatever else, this *anathema* stands in striking contrast to the "*anathema Jesus*" of 12:3 that Paul adamantly denies can be an utterance of the Spirit. Although this is often seen as a hypothetical contrast to the basic Christian confession of "κύριος Jesus," the concluding warning of the present passage suggests that there might be more to the way the issue was raised in 12:3 than is often allowed. And while this is not the place to specu-

---

[92] See J. A. D. Weima, *Neglected Endings: The Significance of the Pauline Letter Closings* (JSNTSup 101; Sheffield: JSOT Press, 1994), 201–8.

[93] See esp. Eriksson, *Traditions as Rhetorical Proof,* 279–98; cf. Thiselton (1348–53), who endorses Eriksson's conclusions.

late on its specific nature, it is not a long stretch for one to relate such an *anathema* to Paul's adamant stance in 1:13–31 regarding his own proclamation of a crucified Messiah, which some in Corinth seem less enthusiastic about. In any case, and whatever the specifics might be in 12:3, the *anathema* there stands in stark contrast to the confession of Jesus as Lord. And so it is again in the present passage, where Paul reverses the "curse" so that it now rests on those who fail to "love the Lord." It is therefore of more than passing interest that both of the contrasting uses of *anathema* in this letter focus on a possible attitude toward the lordship of Christ in this early Christian community. And thus in each case Paul both asserts that lordship and urges love for the Lord as absolutely basic to Christian existence.

This carries its own christological weight. Elsewhere Paul can speak of "loving God" (Rom 8:28, with ἀγαπάω); only here does he speak of loving Christ. The fact that Paul can make such an interchange is in itself a noteworthy christological moment; that he does so here simply highlights the central role that Christ plays throughout the letter, most likely because the Corinthians by attitude and action are subordinating him to a much lesser role. Disobedience to what Paul says, who has "the mind of Christ" (2:16), is to put oneself under the curse of covenant disloyalty.

But equally important is the other side of the assonance, *Maranatha*. Our present concern is not to engage in the long debate as to whether this term is basically indicative or vocative ("The Lord comes" or "Come, Lord").[94] Whatever else, it is to be understood first of all as the response to *anathema*, so that either indicative or vocative works well: either disobedience means "curse," so take notice because "the Lord is coming"; or rather than experience the "curse" associated with disobedience, join in the Christian longing, "Come, Lord" (cf. Rev. 22:20). The general consensus of NT scholarship is that the latter is intended, as is evidenced by the majority of English translations that gloss the phrase in English rather than simply transliterate it (as in the KJV).

The significance of this cry for our purposes is twofold. First is the fact that an untranslated Aramaic phrase, written in Greek for a Greek-speaking Christian community, is still in use some twenty-three or more years after Christ's death and resurrection. Why would this be so? Almost certainly because they learned it from Paul or his companions as a phrase that had meaning to him/them in its original tongue.[95] This further means that the cry must go back before Paul himself became a believer, since by his own testimony (Gal 1:15–24) he had very little contact with the Aramaic-speaking church for most of the years following his conversion. Thus he would have learned it either from his earliest association with Aramaic-speaking followers of Jesus in

---

[94] On this matter, see the recent helpful overview in Thiselton, 1348–53.
[95] This is very similar, therefore, to the *Abba* cry in Gal 4:6 and Rom 8:16, which can only be explained as having come into the early church by way of Jesus himself and thus became devotional language even for those who did not know Aramaic.

Damascus or from his time in Antioch—but in this case from Greek-speaking Christians who themselves had already kept the "sacred language." In any event, this prayer (or affirmation) goes back to the very earliest time in the church, meaning that prayer to Christ as "Lord" is something Paul inherited, not something he created.[96]

The second (very significant) point is that this cry serves as evidence that almost from the very beginning the early church, because of Christ's resurrection and exaltation, had come to think of him in terms of Ps 110:1.[97] He is now the Lord, seated at the right hand of the Father, to whom they pray. It is not surprising, therefore, that even the Greek-speaking church had an attachment to this "foreign" phrase that signified so much—about both Christ himself and their longing for his return.

Most scholars assume that this first text examined reflects the church at worship. It is fitting, therefore, that we turn next to three further such texts that find expression in contexts where Paul is trying to bring some corrections to what is transpiring during Corinthian worship. We take these in their canonical order.

1 Corinthians 5:6–8; 10:16–17; 11:17–34—The Lord of the Eucharistic Meal

One of the more certain realities of the Jesus tradition is that in anticipation of his forthcoming death, he instituted a meal with his disciples that would be in his honor, whereby they would remember him—especially his death for them—on an ongoing basis. Significant for our present purposes is the historical reality that meals in honor of a deity were a part of the entire ancient Near Eastern world, including Israel. For example, Egyptian and Canaanite meals in honor of a god are reflected in Exod 32:7; Num 25:1–3, while practices contemporary with Paul and the Corinthians are seen in the more than twenty-five extant papyrus invitations to such meals.[98] The same is true with Israel, where the legislation for both their three annual feasts (Exod 23:14–19) and their festive celebration of the tithe (Deut 14:22–27) included requirements to eat in the presence of Yahweh (κύριος [Deut 14:26]; Exod 23:14–17). And the Passover in particular, though eaten in homes, was specifically referred to as "celebrating the Passover to the LORD" (ποιῆσαι τὸ πασχα κυρίῳ [Exod 12:48]).

It is in this latter context of eating "the Passover to the LORD" that Jesus instituted what the apostle Paul came to call κυριακὸν δεῖπνον (a meal in honor of the Lord [1 Cor 11:20]), which in ch. 10 he had referred to as "participation in the blood and body of Christ," the latter specifically intrepreted in terms of the church (10:16–17). But in 5:6–8 he keeps all the imagery of

---

[96] On this question, see Hurtado, Lord Jesus Christ, 21, 110.

[97] On the probability that they learned to do so because Jesus himself did so, see ch. 14.

[98] On this matter, see Fee, "Εἰδωλόθυτα Once Again," 113–18.

the Exodus intact: "Christ our Passover has been sacrificed. Therefore let us keep the festival . . . with the unleavened bread of sincerity and truth." This combination makes three matters certain: (1) that the κυριακὸν δεῖπνον of 11:20 is the Christian celebration of Passover; (2) that the primary point of reference is Christ's "sacrifice" as the eternal paschal lamb; (3) that the meal was universally celebrated in the early church (which is the assumption of the final exhortation). Most historical interest in this meal has had to do with its meaning and significance, but my goal here is simply to point out the considerable christological supposition that resides in Paul's descriptions of this meal, which exist primarily because of some abuses in Corinth.

What seems certain, then, on the basis of the passing reference in 5:7, is that Paul and the early church understood *this* meal as a replacement of the Passover meal, so that Christ the Lord has assumed the role of honoree that in Judasim had for centuries belonged to Yahweh alone and that in surrounding cultures belonged to the various "gods" and "lords" of the pagan cults. See further on 10:19–22; 11:32 (pp. 131–33, 138).

1 Corinthians 12:3—The Lord and the Earliest Christian Confession

To conclude his (for us) complex opening salvo regarding the Corinthians' overly zealous fascination with speaking in tongues,[99] Paul sets forth the ultimate criterion for all Spirit activity within the gathered community: does it coincide with the basic Christian confession, κύριος Ἰησοῦς (*the Lord is Jesus*). Indeed, his way of putting it is that this confession can be made only by one speaking through the agency of the Spirit. Significantly, this confession will occur two more times in Paul's letters,[100] always in this order, even though in three quite different contexts.[101]

Three things seem to be at play with this confession, which account both for the word order and for Paul's insistence here that it can be spoken only by those who have received the Spirit. This is obviously both the truly radical early Christian confession and the one therefore that served as the ultimate demarcation of followers of Jesus from all other peoples on the planet.

First, there is the significance of the word order, where the emphasis lies on the fact that "the Lord" is none other than Jesus. On the one hand, this

---

[99] On the complications of this passage, see Fee, 58–82, and now esp. Thiselton, 911–27; Garland, 564–73.

[100] See below on Rom 10:9 and Phil 2:11, in the latter instance with the addition of Χριστός.

[101] Interestingly, in Rom 10:9 it is evidence of conversion and therefore is the hallmark of the true follower of Christ; here it is understood as the ongoing confession that marks off from all others those who have the Spirit; in Phil 2:11 the thrust is eschatological, when the whole universe of created beings, including Caesar himself, will finally acknowledge what Christians now affirm as an ongoing reality: the Lord is none other than Jesus.

picks up the reality noted above on 8:6, where Paul's reshaping of the Shema presupposes that Christ has assumed the role of "Lord" at the right hand of the Father (Ps 110:1) and that he is thus the "Lord" who is at work in many of the Septuagint texts where κύριος stands for the Tetragrammaton (YHWH). Although this connection with the Tetragrammaton is not part of the present context, it is the crucial matter in the next two occurrences of this confession (Rom 10:9; Phil 2:10–11).[102] The "Lord" (Adonai = κύριος) of the Shema is Jesus; and confessing him as such is the primary line of demarcation between followers of Christ and all others in the present age. The devotion that was once the special province of Yahweh alone is now to be directed toward Christ himself: the Lord is Jesus.

Second, its final appearance in Phil 2:11 probably is intended in part to be a subversion of the empire with its emperor worship/devotion.[103] This is quite likely to be the case very early on. That is, the basic reason for its being a word given to believers by way of the Spirit is precisely that this confession radically marks off God's new covenant people from the rest of the empire, where loyalty to the emperor is expressed in terms of Caesar's being lord and savior.

Third, this confession, therefore, whatever else, was the acknowledgment—and thus included tacit submission to—the ultimate lordship of the risen Christ. Such submission assumed that one's loyalty in every aspect of life did not belong to any earthly "lord," be it the emperor or a householder or one of the "lords many or gods many" that surrounded them; rather, such submission was to be given to the one and only Lord, Jesus Christ. Hence this confession presupposes not just Paul's high Christology but that of the entire early church.

1 Corinthians 12:4–6—The Lord and the Divine Triad

Following his declaration that only by the Spirit can one confess Jesus as κύριος, Paul launches immediately into his first concern with regard to Spirit gifting in the assembly: unity does not require uniformity (all speaking in tongues), but it does require diversity. To get there, he does a most astounding thing: he marks the diversity itself as consonant with the divine Triad of Spirit, Lord, and Father.

There are over twenty soteriological texts in Paul's letters[104] that speak of salvation directly or indirectly in triadic terms: as the work of the Father

---

[102] On this matter, see esp. the discussion in C. E. B. Cranfield, *A Critical and Exegetical Commentary on the Epistle to the Romans* (2 vols.; 6th ed.; ICC; Edinburgh: T&T Clark, 1975–1979), 2:529–30.

[103] Although Cullmann (*Christology*, 219–21) probably was wrong in giving this matter priority regarding Pauline usage, one would disregard it to one's exegetical peril in light of its use in 1–2 Thessalonians and Philippians, where it seems certain to play a secondary role. Cullmann's strength lies in his emphasis on the contrast, "Cursed is Jesus," which may point to a recanting to avoid martyrdom.

[104] For the references, see Fee, *God's Empowering Presence*, 48 n. 39.

(predicated upon his love), of the Son (whose death and resurrection secured it), and of the Spirit (who implemented it and made it effective). But the present text, along with 2 Cor 13:13(14) and Eph 4:4–6, stands apart from these. Here Paul is not at all speaking of the role of the three in effecting our salvation; rather, he is asserting that the diversity necessary for a healthy body is precisely the diversity found in the identity of God himself. Thus in identical sentences Paul begins with the Spirit, since that is where the present concern lies. But he will not allow them to divorce the work of the Spirit from that of the Son and the Father. The poetic structure of the whole itself seems to demand such an understanding:

12:4–6 διαιρέσεις δὲ   χαρισμάτων εἰσίν,   τὸ δὲ αὐτὸ πνεῦμα·
       καὶ διαιρέσεις διακονιῶν εἰσιν,   **καὶ ὁ αὐτὸς κύριος·**
       καὶ διαιρέσεις ἐνεργημάτων εἰσίν, <u>ὁ δὲ αὐτὸς θεὸς ὁ ἐνεργῶν</u>
                                          <u>τὰ πάντα ἐν πᾶσιν.</u>

       But diversities of *giftings there are,*   but the same Spirit;
       and diversities of *ministries there are,*   **but the same Lord;**
       and diversities of *workings there are,*   <u>but the same God, who works</u>
                                                       <u>all things in all people.</u>

In a way that becomes typical throughout the corpus, Paul simultaneously includes the Spirit and the Lord within the divine identity, while placing their work within the larger context of God the Father. Our present concern is to point out the considerable christological implications of such a text. In this letter in particular, where Christ's preexistence is explicitly put forth as presuppositional to our present understanding of God (8:6), this passage assumes this reality, just as it does of the Spirit; and thus it becomes the kind of passage that will cause later generations to work out the implications of God's oneness in terms of his being, by expounding a Trinitarian understanding of God. Thus, in its own way this text and its companions join with the authors of John's Gospel and of Hebrews to lay the foundation for the Christian doctrine of the Trinity. A high Christology is simply presuppositional in such texts.

These first four passages together account for the significance that this title had in the life of Paul and of his churches. The next text offers us an understanding of the origins of this confession for Paul himself.

1 Corinthians 9:1—Paul's Encounter with the Risen Lord

In one of the more significant (for us) moments in 1 Corinthians, Paul sets out to justify his apostleship to those in the church who were calling his authority into question, or at least were having their doubts. "Am I not an apostle?" he asks; and then in immediate response to his own rhetorical question he responds, οὐχὶ Ἰησοῦν τὸν κύριον ἡμῶν ἑόρακα (*Jesus the Lord of us have I not seen?*). Almost everything about this question carries christological weight.

First, the order of the words gives the question a double emphasis, with "Jesus our Lord" in first position and "I have seen" in final position. Second, the introductory οὐχί is emphatic, insisting on the affirmative response that it requires; this is especially so since the surrounding questions all have the simple οὐ(κ). Thus, as the primary evidence of his apostleship Paul asks rhetorically, "Surely I have seen Jesus, our Lord, have I not?" Third, the reference to Christ also comes in the emphatic expression "Jesus, the Lord of us," which means (when unpacked, but not necessarily with full intent here) "the earthly Jesus who by resurrection has assumed his place of lordship, and that lordship is over us as well." Indeed, the only other place in the corpus where this exact combination occurs—both Jesus and Lord, followed by "our"—is Rom 4:24, which is likewise a reference to the risen Lord.

The point of Paul's rhetoric is that he is here asserting that Christ's appearing to him, "abnormal" as it was (15:8), fulfills for him the first criterion of authentic apostleship, as 15:5–8 seems to make certain. In that passage he first lists Christ's appearance to Cephas and the Twelve.[105] After noting that Christ also appeared to over five hundred brothers and sisters (v. 6), Paul then returns to those who were being commissioned as apostles by these resurrection appearances: James, all the apostles,[106] and finally Paul himself. This listing and the use of the same verb in each case indicate that Paul understood his encounter with the risen Christ to be the same in kind as the others. The difference in his case was the timing: it happened after such appearances had ceased.

There can be little question that this experience, which, according to Luke's account, happened on the road to Damascus, was for Paul both earth-shaking and life-changing. Having seen the risen One, he now had to rethink everything that he had come to believe about Jesus of Nazareth: instead of cursing *Jesus* by having him hung on a tree (pole), God had laid the curse that *we* deserved on him and by resurrection had affirmed his death as "for us." It is nearly impossible to understand Paul's radical turnabout, as he himself expresses it in Phil 3:4–8 and Gal 1:13–17, apart from an encounter with the living Jesus. And along with the other early followers of Jesus, he had come to believe that Christ was the "Lord" of Ps 110:1, who is now seated in the place of authority at the Father's right hand. All of this is spelled out in various forms of detail elsewhere (e.g., Phil 2:9–11). But here the issue is a simple one; what verifies Paul's apostleship is twofold: he himself had seen the risen Lord and had thus been commissioned by him; and he founded new churches (the point of the next rhetorical question).

Thus in many ways this bit of rhetoric, intended to bring the Corinthians up short with regard to their attitude toward him (or at least that of

---

[105] This latter term is a title, not a precise number, since there were only eleven who actually saw him.

[106] Who they were, and how many, is forever unknown to us; but perhaps it would have included, for example, Andronicus and Junia (Rom 15:7).

some of them), serves for us as the primary key to our understanding Paul's passion for the gospel and his utter devotion to Christ. It also serves as a primary cornerstone to our understanding of what it means for him constantly, and exclusively, to use ὁ κύριος as his primary title for the risen Jesus.

Jesus as the Κύριος of Septuagint Passages

As with 1–2 Thessalonians, the most common place where Paul's understanding of Christ as Lord emerges is his designation of Christ as the κύριος of OT texts where the Divine Name Yahweh had been so rendered in the Septuagint. But in contrast to the two earlier letters, in this case Paul also *cites* such texts as applying directly to Christ. This happens twice in this letter: in 1:31 and 2:16 as the clinching matter to end the first two parts of the argument of chs. 1–4. In both cases Paul is shifting ground from a *soteriological* understanding of the Jewish Messiah as the crucified One to a *christological* affirmation of the crucified Christ as κύριος. As with the preceding chapter, we will examine these echoes and citations in their canonical order.

1 Corinthians 1:2

At the very outset, as in most of his letters, Paul has a variety of ways of anticipating the issues to be taken up later. Although this comes out most clearly in the thanksgiving (vv. 4–9), it actually begins in v. 2. In this, the longest salutation in Paul's extant letters, three matters are pressed in this order:[107] (1) they are God's church because they have been sanctified[108] in Christ Jesus; (2) as his church in Corinth, they have been called to be ἁγίοις (= his *holy* people); (3) they are called to be such along with God's people everywhere.

Our present interest is in the third item, which is the first of several instances in the letter in which Paul is trying to broaden the Corinthians' perspective: they are in Christ with scores of other people in churches all over the empire.[109] Paul's way of describing this large body of people who belong

---

[107] At least this is the order of the best and (widespread) earliest evidence (𝔓46 B D*.2 F G b m Ambst). On the canon "the more difficult reading is most likely to be original" (since scribes tended more to ease difficulties in the text than to create them), this is easily the more difficult reading, and it also accounts for the rise of the text found in NA27. For the full argumentation of this point of view, see G. D. Fee, "Textual-Exegetical Observations on 1 Corinthians 1:2, 2:1, and 2:10," in *To What End Exegesis?* 43–56.

[108] Gk. ἡγιασμένοις ἐν Χριστῷ Ἰησοῦ; in 1 Corinthians the verb used here, ἁγιάζω, is used elsewhere as a metaphor for salvation itself (see 6:11; cf. 1:30). That is, God's saving act in Christ set them apart as his holy people in their very pagan surroundings.

[109] See 1 Cor 4:17; 11:16; 14:33, esp. 36.

to Christ is what interests us. They are "those who in every place call on the name of our Lord Jesus, their Lord and ours."

In using this language to describe God's new eschatological people, Paul has dipped into the OT in a very significant way. This language is found first in Gen 4:26. But with Abraham it became a key way of distinguishing God's people, hence its significance as a framing device for Abraham's failure in Egypt. As he first set out toward the south, he stopped at Bethel and "called on the name of Yahweh" (ἐπεκαλέσατο ἐπὶ τῷ ὀνόματι κυρίου [Gen 12:8]); following the Egypt narrative, he returns to Bethel and once again "calls on the name of Yahweh" (Gen 13:4). This then becomes a distinguishing feature of the people of God; they are those who "call on the name of Yahweh."

This language is picked up later by Joel in his well-known description of the eschatological Day of the Lord. When God pours out his Spirit on all people, Joel prophesies, πᾶς ὃς ἂν ἐπικαλέσηται τὸ ὄνομα κυρίου σωθήσεται (*everyone who calls on the name of the LORD will be saved*) (Joel 2:32 [3:5 LXX]). This is the passage that Paul later cites in Rom 10:13 as fulfilled when anyone, Jew and Gentile alike, believes with the heart in the resurrection of Jesus and confesses with the mouth that "Jesus is Lord," thus evidencing that this person has been saved. And this is the language that Paul now echoes at the beginning of this letter, as the reality that identifies those who are Christ's own people worldwide and that later in this letter he will attribute, as in the Joel passage, to the presence of the Spirit in their lives:

1 Cor 1:2	σὺν πᾶσιν **τοῖς ἐπικαλουμένοις**	**τὸ ὄνομα τοῦ κυρίου ἡμῶν Ἰησοῦ Χριστοῦ**
Gen 12:8	καὶ	**ἐπεκαλέσατο ἐπι** τῷ ὀνόματι κυρίου[110]
Joel 2:32	πᾶς ὃς ἂν	**ἐπικαλέσηται** τὸ ὄνομα κυρίου σωθήσεται

1 Cor 1:2	*with all those*	**who call on**	**the name of our Lord, Jesus Christ**
Gen 12:8	*and*	**he called on**	**the name of the LORD**
Joel 2:32	*everyone*	**who calls on** *will be saved*	**the name of the LORD**

In Deuteronomy this formula serves as the primary way of distinguishing Jerusalem. It is the place where God will choose "to have his name dwell," an expression that is regularly glossed in the Septuagint as "the place where the LORD your God has chosen for his name to be called upon" (e.g., 12:11: καὶ ἔσται ὁ τόπος ὃν ἂν ἐκλέξηται κύριος ὁ θεὸς ὑμῶν ἐπικληθῆναι τὸ ὄνομα αὐτοῦ ἐκεῖ). It is not surprising, therefore, that the phrase also occurs regularly in the Psalter and the prophets.

---

[110] See also Gen 13:4; 21:33 (Abraham); 26:25 (Isaac); 33:20 LXX (Jacob).

This Corinthians passage is the first of three where this phrase appears in the Pauline corpus (see Rom 10:9–13 and 2 Tim 2:22 below); and in each instance there can be little question that the "name of the Lord," which in the OT texts refers to the Divine Name "Yahweh," has now been transferred to Jesus, enthroned as the heavenly Lord. That is, God's people are still distinguished as those who "call on the name of the Lord"; but the Lord on whom they call is Christ himself, risen from the dead and exalted to the Father's right hand.[111]

Given this beginning of 1 Corinthians, one is not surprised to meet the several other instances of this same phenomenon, not to mention other instances where Paul speaks of Christ in ways he elsewhere speaks only of God.

1 Corinthians 1:31

This passage, signaled by its introductory γέγραπται (*it is written*),[112] is the first direct Yahweh/κύριος citation in Paul's letters where he has explicitly applied an OT κύριος passage to Christ. The paragraph itself (1:26–31) is a kind of midrash on Jer 9:23–24 (9:22–23 LXX), applied directly, somewhat ironically, to the Corinthians and their present fascination with and boasting in "wisdom." Thus, where Jeremiah underscores the "boasting" (= putting confidence in) of the wise, the strong, and the wealthy, Paul points out that the believers in Corinth are none of these. Rather, at the time of their calling they were among those who were not "wise," not "strong," and not "well-born"; indeed, he points out, God chose them precisely to bring to nothing those who could be characterized in this way. So at the end Paul returns to Jer 9 and cites a truncated version of v. 24 (v. 23 LXX), emphasizing the Corinthian believers' need to "boast" in the Lord = Jesus. Thus:

1 Cor 1:31	ἵνα καθὼς γέγραπται·	**ὁ καυχώμενος,** **ἐν κυρίῳ καυχάσθω**
Jer 9:23 LXX		ἐν τούτῳ **καυχάσθω** **ὁ καυχώμενος** συνίειν καὶ γινώσκειν ὅτι **ἐγώ εἰμι κύριος**
1 Cor 1:31	*so that as it is written:*	**the one who boasts,** **in the Lord let him boast**
Jer 9:23 LXX		*in this* **let him boast** **the one who boasts,** *to understand and know that* **I am the LORD**

---

[111] Hurtado notes that this usage "both explicitly indicates the christological appropriation of the biblical phrase and also makes this cultic reverence of Jesus the universal description of Christian believers" (*Lord Jesus Christ*, 143).

[112] This phenomenon is limited to three letters in the corpus: 1 and 2 Corinthians and Romans (with only 2 occurrences in both 1 and 2 Cor).

With a measure of freedom in actual wording, but in faithfulness to Jeremiah's concern, Paul now applies the text directly to Christ himself.[113] He whom God set forth as the ironic expression of his wisdom, whose crucifixion provided righteousness, santification, and redemption, is now "the Lord" in whom the Corinthians are to put their entire trust and boast. The irony, of course, is that the Lord in whom they are to boast is none other than God's foolishness, the crucified Messiah.[114]

The christological implication of such a claim is striking indeed, since the context in Jeremiah[115] has to do with Yahweh's absolute claim to loyalty over all other gods. That Lord, now Jesus Christ, is the one in whom the Corinthians are to boast. Here alone is God's wisdom on display.

1 Corinthians 2:16

Paul does a similar thing at the end of the next section of the argument (2:6–16), where he has set out to explain why the Corinthian believers should be able to see God's wisdom in what the world perceives as utter foolishness. They have received the Spirit of God, who knows and reveals the hidden things of God. At the end of this argument Paul makes a distinction between the person with the Spirit (ὁ πνευματικός), who is thus able to discern all things (= what God has done in Christ), and the person without the Spirit (ὁ ψυχικός), who is incapable of understanding the cross as God's wisdom. With an explanatory γάρ (for), Paul concludes his argument about this capability on the part of the person with the Spirit by citing Isa 40:13:

---

[113]See Gail R. O'Day, "Jer 9:22–23 and 1 Cor 1:26–31: A Study in Intertextuality," *JBL* 109 (1990): 259–67; Stanley, *Paul and the Language of Scripture*, 186–88. This is the common view and would seem hardly to need demonstration, given that this citation, loose as it might seem to be, serves as the climactic word to a very christocentric passage that began with clear echoes of Jer 9:22 LXX. After all, it is *Christ* whom God has set forth as "wisdom" for us, precisely so that God's people will boast in the crucified Messiah as the Lord.

[114]Richardson's comment on this passage seems confused (*Paul's Language*, 284–85). First, he acknowledges that "to boast 'in the Lord' (that is, in Christ) is the equivalent of boasting of the sovereign reality of God." But then he denies that this is "a transfer of language used in the Old Testament of God to Jesus." One can only wonder how that is so, since "the Lord" has already been identified by Paul as "Jesus Christ," who will next be identified as "the Lord of glory" who has been crucified by the Romans (2:7). Richardson's concern is the right one: Christ is not here and elsewhere identified as God himself; but one of Paul's reasons for using the κύριος of the Septuagint in such passages seems to be that Christ is thereby *included* in the divine identity, but without a straightforward, total identification so that the Son becomes, or takes the place of, God, as it were. That is, by these transfers of OT language from the Father to the Son, Paul is not saying that Jesus *is* the Yahweh in the OT passage itself but that the κύριος = *Adonai* = Yahweh of that passage *has now been applied* to Jesus Christ, who at his exaltation has been given "the Name" (Phil 2:10).

[115]Hays (34–35) brings 1 Sam 2:10 LXX (a Septuagint addition to Hannah's prayer, based on Jer 9:22–23) into the picture as well; but that seems unnecessary, since Paul's wording is closer to Jeremiah than 1 Samuel.

1 Cor 2:16 τίς γὰρ ἔγνω νοῦν κυρίου, ὃς συμβιβάσει αὐτόν;
ἡμεῖς δὲ νοῦν Χριστοῦ ἔχομεν.
Isa 40:13 τίς ἔγνω νοῦν κυρίου, καὶ τίς αὐτοῦ
σύμβουλος ἐγένετο, ὃς συμβιβᾷ αὐτόν;

1 Cor 2:16 *For **who** **has known** **the mind of** the Lord,*
who will advise him?
But we ***the mind of Christ*** *have.*
Isa 40:13 ***Who*** **has known** **the mind of** the LORD, *and who his*
adviser became, ***who will advise him?***

In context, the κύριος of this passage could possibly have a double referent. First, it takes the reader back to vv. 10–11, where the Spirit whom they
have received is the very one who "searches the deep things of God." Thus it
is the Spirit who has revealed *the mind of God,* the God who has chosen the
foolishness of the cross as the ultimate demonstration of his eternal wisdom.
So in response to Isaiah's rhetorical questions, "Who has known the mind of
the LORD? Who will advise him?"[116] one could easily argue for a reference to
God the Father.[117]

Paul's ultimate concern, however, is not simply that they get it right
with regard to the crucified One, but that they also come to terms with what
it means for *them* to be followers of such a one. So in typical fashion he concludes his answer to Isaiah's twofold question by including them in that answer. Even though Paul's "we" first of all means "I," he deliberately includes
the Corinthians as also being among those who (now) "have the mind of
Christ." Thus, God's mind is at the same time "the mind of Christ," meaning
that our (proper) understanding of what God has done in Christ is the work
of Father, Son, and Spirit.[118] The Spirit has revealed God's wisdom—God's
"mind," if you will—which at the same time is the mind of Christ.

And none of this is argued for; it is simply assumed by Paul. And he obviously expects the Corinthians to get on board—not as new revelation but
as the proper spelling out of what they already know about who Christ is.

1 Corinthians 10:19–22

Here, and now with outright prohibition, Paul concludes his long argument with the Corinthians about their insistence on attendance at temple
feasts.[119] He begins by picking up on what could be perceived as the (wrong)

---

[116] The subtle changes to the Septuagint here reflect Paul's immediate concerns.
Since Paul's Corinthian opposition has *not* known the mind of the Lord (after all, in
3:1–4, he will accuse them, Spirit people though they are, of acting precisely like those
without the Spirit), how is it that they now have the temerity to offer him advice?
[117] All the more so in light of the "citation" of this passage in Rom 11:34, where
it clearly refers to Yahweh. Cf. Hurtado (*Lord Jesus Christ,* 112), who is ambivalent.
[118] On this point, see Fee, *God's Empowering Presence,* 107–10.
[119] See pp. 88–89.

implications of his argument. By this somewhat circuitous (but absolutely crucial) form of argumentation regarding temple feasts,[120] they are not to understand him to have suggested either that idol food is actually sacrificed to a "god" or that the idols themselves are "gods" (v. 19). On that point, he and they are in total agreement (see above on 8:6).

Their problem, it turns out, is that they lack a truly *biblical* understanding of idolatry, that the idols and their temples are the habitation of demons. Paul's point, therefore, is that believers who are joined to the Lord cannot be joined equally to demons (v. 20). Hence the argument now concludes, first, with the absolute prohibition of attending such feasts, on the grounds that believers in Christ may neither eat the food nor share the table of demons (v. 21). The clincher, second, lies in the rhetorical questions of v. 22: "Are we trying to arouse the Lord's jealousy? Are we stronger than he?"

Of interest for our present purposes is that in so arguing, Paul continues the motif of Israel's disobedience in the desert (vv. 7–10) by applying to the Corinthians' situation the Song of Moses (Deut 32:1–34), where Yahweh remonstrates with disobedient Israel. Paul thus begins in v. 20 with an intertextual echo of Deut 32:17:

1 Cor 10:20	ἀλλ᾽ ὅτι ἃ **θύουσιν, δαιμονίοις καὶ οὐ θεῷ θύουσιν**[121]
Deut 32:17	**ἔθυσαν δαιμονίοις καὶ οὐ θεῷ**
1 Cor 10:20	*but what* **they sacrifice, to demons and not to God**
	they sacrifice
Deut 32:17	**they sacrificed to demons and not to God**

In keeping with the Septuagint, Paul's sentence has the idolators not sacrificing "to a god [θεός]" at all, either Yahweh or one of the gods; rather, their idol gods were to be understood as the locus of demons.

With that in hand, Paul moves directly to the prohibition (vv. 20b–21), and in so doing, he contrasts the ποτήριον κυρίου and the τραπέζης κυρίου with the "cup" and "table" of the demons. One must choose between what is

_____

[120] In turn Paul has (1) used his own denial of certain apostolic rights for the sake of others as exemplary for them (9:1–23), (2) spoken to the value of self-denial (9:24–27), (3) used the example of Israel's rejection of the Lord in the wilderness (10:1–13), and (4) appealed to the nature of their own "feast" in honor of the Lord as participation in him and his body (10:14–18). He does all of this, it would seem, so that there are sufficient grounds for the absolute prohibition with which he concludes.

[121] Paul's text has suffered at the hands of scribes, probably as the result of this "repetition" of θύουσιν. Apparently as early as 𝔓46 the text was modified to be more specific as to who was sacrificing to whom. Thus the later Majority Text (supported by the early Latin evidence) rewrote it to read: ἀλλ᾽ ὅτι ἃ θύουσιν τὰ ἔθνη, δαιμονίοις θύουσιν καὶ οὐ θεῷ (*but what the Gentiles sacrifice, to demons they sacrifice and not to God*). The NA27 text given here, and found in ℵ A B C P Ψ 33 81 1739 *pc*, is almost certainly Paul's original.

the Lord's and what is demonic; participation in both is absolutely forbidden ("You cannot do this!"). That leads then to the clinching moment. Returning to the language of Deuteronomy once more, Paul concludes the argument with a pair of rhetorical questions. The first one reads,

1 Cor 10:22	ἤ	παραζηλοῦμεν	τὸν κύριον;	
Deut 32:21	αὐτοὶ	παρεζήλωσάν	με	ἐπ᾽ οὐ θεῷ

1 Cor 10:22	or **are we**	**making jealous**	**the Lord?**	
Deut 32:21	*these*	**made jealous**	**me**	*at what is not a god*

In asking whether they are trying to make "the Lord" jealous, Paul thus applies what happened to Yahweh in the OT to what the Corinthians are doing to Christ. Just as Israel made the Lord = Yahweh jealous by sacrificing to "no god" demons, so the Corinthians, by attendance at pagan feasts, are sharing in what is demonic and thus making jealous their Lord = Christ, in whose death and resurrection they participate when they eat and drink at his table.

As always, Paul distinguishes between θεός and κύριος. Nonetheless, they also have shared identity, so that the "Lord" whom Israel was provoking to jealousy is, in the Corinthians' case, to be understood as the risen Lord, Jesus Christ.

1 Corinthians 10:26

Having concluded the long argument that led finally to a prohibition of attendance at temple meals, Paul turns in v. 23 to pick up the issue of temple food available for purchase in the marketplace. And here we find a quite different answer, which seems to make it certain that at issue has not been the food per se but, rather, eating the food in the presence of and in participation with what is demonic. On the matter of food per se, Paul shows no ambivalence whatsoever, even though, as in 9:19–22, he will argue for abstinence if food causes difficulty for someone else. Freedom to indulge also means freedom not to indulge.

To support his assertion (v. 25) that they may buy and eat anything sold in the marketplace, Paul cites Ps 24:1 (23:1 LXX):

1 Cor 10:26	τοῦ κυρίου γὰρ	ἡ γῆ καὶ τὸ πλήρωμα αὐτῆς
Ps 23:1 LXX	τοῦ κυρίου	ἡ γῆ καὶ τὸ πλήρωμα αὐτῆς

1 Cor 10:26	**of the Lord** *(for)*	*(is)* **the earth and its fullness**
Ps 23:1 LXX	**of the LORD**	*(is)* **the earth and its fullness**

Because of the familiarity of this text, one may assume that Paul intended the Corinthians to recognize what he was doing: offering scriptural support for the preceding assertion.[122] At issue for us is whether Paul in "cit-ing" the psalm is leaving the text as it sits in the OT, and thus letting the κύριος unconsciously stand for God,[123] or whether, given the immediate con-text, we should assume that once more he intends κύριος = Yahweh now to refer to Christ.

On the one hand, since the present argument concludes (v. 31) with the necessity of doing all things to the glory of God (θεός) and since Paul does not seem to be making a christological point here, it is arguable that in this case he is simply carrying over the meaning of the psalm in toto.

On the other hand, favoring the probability that Paul once more in-tended κύριος = Christ are (1) the close proximity of the citation to v. 22, which concluded the preceding argument; (2) the fact that Paul began the entire argument by highlighting the preexistent Son's mediatorial role in creation, who thus assumes the role of κύριος over both creation and those whom he has redeemed; (3) the overwhelming evidence that in freestanding sentences Paul always preserved this designation for Christ (in any case, such a usage is fully in keeping with Paul's regular patterns noted in this chapter and the preceding one).[124]

Κύριος Jesus and Divine Prerogatives

As in 1–2 Thessalonians, this letter also has several instances where Jesus as κύριος is understood in roles that are otherwise in Scripture always attributed to God (θεός). This happens in a variety of ways. We take them up in their order of appearance in 1 Corinthians (except for two items in ch. 7, where, for conceptual reasons, "the command of the Lord" and the "law of Christ" are discussed back-to-back).

The Grace of Our Lord (1 Cor 1:3; 16:23)

In the preceding chapter we have already dealt with the actual theologi-cal issues involved in the standard Pauline salutation, that grace and peace are seen as coming from both God the Father and the Lord Jesus Christ. Here I simply note how "grace" plays out in the rest of this letter.

First, in the letter body "grace" is expressed only in terms of God the Father. Thus in 1:4; 3:10; 15:10, 57, "grace" is either "of God" or is "given by God." But at the end of the letter, Paul's (typical) benedictory prayer is, "the

---

[122] And this despite its lack of γέγραπται. This is an instance where Paul's γάρ (for) tends to function in the place of "as it is written."

[123] As Paul often does when the text functions in a supporting role and no point is made of κύριος at all. See n. 7 above.

[124] Cf. Capes (Old Testament Yahweh Texts, 140–45), who takes an even stronger position than this one; Cullmann (Christology, 222) takes a more cautious stance.

grace of our κύριος Jesus be with you." Thus the interchange between God and the Lord noted in 1–2 Thessalonians continues here as well.

The Day of the Lord (1 Cor 1:8)

Toward the end of his long thanksgiving, in which Paul touches on many of the items to be taken up in the letter, he speaks of the believers' certain future as "the day of our Lord Jesus Christ." On this adoption of a Yahweh phrase from the OT that Paul now attributes to Christ, see the discussion on 1 Thess 5:2 (pp. 46–47).

In the Name of the Lord (1 Cor 1:10; 5:3–4)

1:10 παρακαλῶ δὲ ὑμᾶς, ἀδελφοί, **διὰ τοῦ ὀνόματος**
        τοῦ κυρίου ἡμῶν Ἰησοῦ Χριστοῦ,

5:3–4 ³ἐγὼ μὲν γάρ . . . ἤδη κέκρικα ὡς παρὼν τὸν οὕτως τοῦτο
        κατεργασάμενον· ⁴**ἐν τῷ ὀνόματι τοῦ κυρίου Ἰησοῦ,**

1:10 *I beseech you, brothers and sisters,* **through the name**
                                         of our Lord Jesus Christ

5:3–4 *³I for my part . . . already have judged, as being present, the one
        who has perpetrated this deed,* **⁴in the name of the Lord Jesus**

In keeping with another phenomenon observed in 1–2 Thessalonians, Paul in this case begins the letter body by making his appeal "in the name of our Lord Jesus Christ" (1:10). Although this is not an oath as such, Paul is using Christ's "name" as the authority behind the appeal that he is about to make. The point, of course, is that he uses "the name of ὁ κύριος," which in the Septuagint is the Divine Name for Yahweh. Here "the name of the Lord" has been transferred altogether to Christ. On this matter, see the discussion on 2 Thess 3:6 (pp. 67–68).

The usage of "in the name of our Lord Jesus" in 5:4 is more complex, since it is related to the larger question of the syntax of the entire sentence. But for several good reasons, including especially the fact that there is no known instance in the NT where a prepositional phrase *precedes* the participle and subject in a genitive absolute, the rendering of the NRSV and the TNIV probably have it correct, that Paul has already pronounced judgment on the man "in the name of our Lord Jesus."[125] What is significant christologically is that a judgment pronounced in the Lord's name belongs uniquely to Yahweh, the God of Israel; for Paul, it belongs equally to Christ Jesus. This understanding is also in keeping with Paul's use of the name in the mild oath of 2 Thess 3:12. For the expression "the power of the Lord Jesus" in this sentence, see the discussion on 1 Cor 5:4 (pp. 139–40).

---

[125] For details, see Fee, 203–8.

Sent/Commissioned by Christ (1 Cor 1:1, 17)

One of the recurring themes in the OT is the fact that God "sends" messengers and prophets to his people. The verb used in the Septuagint for this "sending" is ἀποστέλλω, which appears in the classic "commissioning" passage in Isa 6:8. God asks, "Whom shall I send [ἀποστείλω]?" To which the prophet replies, "Here I am; send me [ἀπόστειλόν με]." So also it is with the "sending" of the Servant of Yahweh in Isa 48:16 and the sending of Ezekiel in Ezek 2:4. In Paul's letters Christ now assumes this role by sending Paul to proclaim the gospel (γὰρ ἀπέστειλέν με **Χριστὸς** . . . εὐαγγελίζεσθαι [*for* **Christ** *sent me . . . to preach the gospel*]; 1:17); thus, above all else Paul is "an apostle of *Christ Jesus*" (1:1).

The Lord of Glory (1 Cor 2:8)

In one of the more striking moves in all of his letters, and with considerable irony, Paul speaks of "the rulers of this age" as having crucified "the Lord of glory." Although this is not a phrase found in the OT, the language rings with OT motifs. After all, "the Lord of glory" is not far removed from "the King of Glory" in the great divine coronation hymn, Ps 24.

But even more significant is the fact that "glory" in Paul's letters is primarily a way of speaking about God. He is the "Father of glory" (Eph 1:17), who dwells in glory (Phil 4:19), for whose glory all things are and should be done (1 Cor 10:31), and the one to whom glory is offered in benedictions and praise (Gal 1:5; Phil 4:20). And now "the Lord" who shares that glory with God the Father (2 Thess 2:14; 2 Cor 4:4) is the one whom the rulers of this age have crucified. Paul's use of such a unique phrase is to point out to the Corinthians that the one whom the powerful people of the world crucified is none other than "the Lord of glory" himself. Thus the scandal of the cross was not simply perpetrated by wicked people; what they did was predicated on divine wisdom. Hence, what they did not, indeed could not, know was that their act of brutality was against the very Lord of glory himself, whose "glory" was not diminished by the shame of the cross. And, of course, inherent in such language is that the crucified One is also the presently reigning Lord of glory. So their crucifying the Lord of glory was a win-win matter as far as the eternal God is concerned.

The Lord Has Given/Assigned (1 Cor 3:5; 7:17)

In a context of stressing both the unity and the differing gifts between himself and Apollos, Paul speaks of each ministry in terms of "as the Lord has given/assigned to each" (ἐκάστῳ ὡς **ὁ κύριος** ἔδωκεν). Elsewhere in Paul's writings it is ὁ θεός who "gives" such ministry (e.g., 2 Cor 5:18). In the OT, by way of the Septuagint, such gifting is always seen as the prerogative of κύριος = Yahweh.[126] And even though in the rest of the present paragraph Paul puts all the emphasis on God's activity, he begins by asserting that the specific gifting itself has come from the Lord = Christ.

In a similar way, but in a quite different context, in 7:17 Paul joins the activity of Christ and the Father in a single sentence and attributes to each his perception of the divine "division of labor": ἑκάστῳ ὡς ἐμέρισεν ὁ **κύριος**, ἕκαστον ὡς κέκληκεν **ὁ θεός**, οὕτως περιπατείτω (*to each as **the Lord** assigned; each as God has called, let them walk*). At issue here is a concern over those who would seek a change of status in life because of their new life in Christ.[127] The combination here reflects what is standard for Paul. Both election and calling are the activity of God (θεός);[128] but within that calling it is sometimes Christ who "assigns" the individual giftings/tasks (as in 3:5 above) or, in this case, station in life. On the other hand, this latter is also clearly a divine prerogative, as in 2 Cor 10:13; Rom 12:3. In the OT this kind of language is reserved altogether for κύριος = Yahweh.

Thus, in 1 Cor 12:4, in one of the three triadic moments of this kind in his letters,[129] and in a clause quite unnecessary to his primary concern, Paul asserts that "the same Lord" is responsible for the wide variety of διακονιῶν (*ministries*) that abound in the community of faith.

The Lord Judges (1 Cor 4:4–5; 11:32)

In a way similar to what is said in 1 Thess 4:6, Paul in 4:4–5 is again ready to assign to κύριος = Christ the activity both of examining Paul and of bringing hidden things to light at his coming:

4:4–5   [4]... ὁ δὲ ἀνακρίνων με **κύριός** ἐστιν. [5]ὥστε μὴ πρὸ καιροῦ τι κρίνετε ἕως ἂν ἔλθῃ ὁ **κύριος**, ὃς καὶ **φωτίσει** τὰ κρυπτὰ τοῦ σκότους καὶ φανερώσει τὰς βουλὰς τῶν καρδιῶν·

> [4]... **He who examines** me is **the Lord**. [5]So not before the time judge anything, **until the Lord comes, who will light up** the hidden places of darkness and reveal the plans of hearts.

Here Paul is simultaneously playing on the fact that the Corinthians are "judging" him by "examining"[130] him (v. 3) and warding off their "examina-

---

[126] So, e.g., Exod 31:2–5; 36:1–2 (of Bezalel).

[127] Or at least that is what seems to be the case. For details, see Fee, 308–9.

[128] See 1:9 above; cf. 1 Thess 2:12; 4:7; 5:24; 2 Thess 2:14; Gal 1:6, 15; Rom 8:30; Col 3:15.

[129] See also on 2 Cor 13:13(14) and Eph 4:4–6.

[130] The verb ἀνακρίνω occurs 10 times in Paul's letters, all of them in 1 Corinthians, where it is mostly pejorative in terms of the Corinthians' attitude toward Paul (besides v. 3, see 2:14–15 [probably; see Fee, 118–19] and 9:3). Although the analogy is not precise, the verb suggests the kind of "inquiry/examination" that a modern grand jury (which may conduct investigations and may decide whether there is probable cause to indict, but does not try anyone with respect to guilt or innocence of the charges contained in the indictment) might conduct.

tion" by putting it into the hands of "the Lord." Thus, in direct response to their attitude toward him, he makes three statements that are full of christological presuppositions. First, he asserts that the only one who has the right to "examine" him is ὁ κύριος[131] = Christ, so they should back off with regard to their own attitude toward him. Second, and now by implication, when the Lord does come, he will also function as the eschatological judge. And third, he tells them that when ὁ κύριος comes, he will assume the divine prerogative of "bringing to light what is hidden in darkness and will expose the motives of people's hearts."

This final clause is a play on the (apocalyptic) language of Daniel's prayer in Dan 2:20–23, where he affirms that the "[God of his ancestors] reveals deep and hidden things, [who] knows what is in the darkness, and light dwells with him"—a theme that is then repeated by Nebuchadnezzar in 2:47. For Paul, that revelation will take place at Christ's Parousia, and Christ himself will be the judge and will thus expose the human heart for what it is—this action being an exclusively divine prerogative again assigned to Christ as Lord. Christ is thus not merely the agent of divine authority; he himself is understood in a fully divine way as the one who knows all things, including "the hidden things" in the human heart. No merely exalted human figure could ever have been imagined to play such a role in Paul's Jewish world.

Similarly, in the context of the Corinthians' abuse of the Lord's Table (11:17–34), Paul sees the illness and death of some members of the community as evidence of God's present discipline of the Corinthian believers (vv. 30–32). With a considerable play on "judgment" language and themes, Paul (as a Christian prophet) first asserts that they are to understand some illness and deaths among them to be the direct result of their abuse of "the body" (= the church) at the table of the Lord, where they should rather be affirming that they together belong to the one Lord. Thus,[132] "if we were **διεκρίνομεν** [= discerning the body], we would not be **ἐκρινόμεθα** [= experiencing judgment]." On the other hand, he goes on, "in our presently being **κρινόμενοι** [judged] (in this way), we are in fact **παιδευόμεθα** ὑπὸ τοῦ κυρίου [being brought under discipline by the Lord = Christ]."

Here again, but now in considerable contrast to the eschatological judgment expressed in 4:3–5, Paul asserts that the "judgment" they are presently experiencing at the hand of God is in fact coming directly from the Lord, Jesus Christ.

---

[131] Here is a case where Colwell's Rule seems to be in effect, where an anarthrous predicate that precedes the verb "to be" is intended to be articular (not "a lord" but "the Lord"). In this case the unusual word order is itself a form of emphasis (= the only one who has authority to "examine" me is the Lord himself, who will judge at the appropriate time).

[132] In this instance the boldface type highlights the play on "judgment" language.

If the Lord Wills/Permits (1 Cor 4:19; 16:7)

In these two striking moments Paul assigns to Christ as κύριος what is elsewhere the absolute prerogative of God. Even in our letter, Paul begins by noting that his apostleship is "by the will of God," a phrase that occurs some thirteen times in his letters.[133] But here, in an absolutely off-handed way, he twice asserts that he will come and/or stay with the Corinthians "if the Lord wills/permits." Some could argue that such a casual reference might therefore be a reference to God the Father, but that is highly unlikely, since Paul consistently distinguishes between θεός and κύριος throughout this letter (see esp. 1:1; 8:6) and since the immediate context is all about Christ, especially vv. 14–17.

Again, this appears to be another instance where Paul, almost casually, assumes that Christ shares equally in prerogatives that otherwise belong to God alone.

The Power of the Lord Jesus (1 Cor 5:4)

Almost all of Paul's response to the serious situation of a man living in an incestuous relationship with his father's wife is directed toward the church itself, whose members have condoned this activity among them by having done nothing about it. In light of their inaction, Paul has done something. As already present among them by the Spirit, he has passed judgment on the man in the name of the Lord, Jesus; now they must carry it out. His description of that gathering is what catches our attention. Paul understands both himself and Christ to be present by the Spirit; and in that context they are to put the man outside the believing community. Paul's way of describing Christ as present is what is significant. "When I am present in the Spirit," he says, probably through a prophetic word, and "the power of our Lord Jesus is present," you are to put this man back out into Satan's sphere.

With this unusual terminology, "the power of our Lord Jesus," Paul is most likely making another oblique reference to the Spirit.[134] If so, then this is also another moment of considerable christological import. In the first place, it is another instance where Paul recognizes that the Spirit of God is at the same time the Spirit of the Lord Jesus.[135] But in this case, and because of

---

[133] Including 2 Timothy in this case, where it occurs in 1:1 in a thoroughly Pauline way. The count is 17 if one includes the occurrences with αὐτοῦ where θεός is the certain antecedent. The texts: 1 Thess 4:3; 5:18; 1 Cor 1:1; 2 Cor 1:1; 8:5; Gal 1:4; Rom 1:10; 12:2; 15:32; Col 1:1; (1:9 [αὐτοῦ]); 4:12; Eph 1:1; (1:5, 9, 11 [αὐτοῦ]); 6:6; 2 Tim 1:1. Only in Eph 5:17 does τὸ θέλημα τοῦ κυρίου appear; and as with most things in Ephesians, this could be argued to cut either way! It certainly is in keeping with our present passage.

[134] For the full discussion of this point of view, see Fee, God's Empowering Presence, 122–27.

[135] On this matter, see the discussions of 2 Cor 3:17 (pp. 190–92); Gal 4:6 (p. 220); Rom 8:9 (pp. 269–70); Phil 1:19 (p. 407).

the unusual nature of the situtation, Paul refers to the Spirit in terms of God's power being present. But God's power in this case is located in the Lord, Jesus, who is thus present by his Spirit, now designated in terms of "the power of our Lord Jesus."

Thus, in this pregnant setting, full of implications of the presence of God in their midst, Paul twice refers to Christ in terms of the divinely bestowed Name, "the Lord," who is then identified with the risen Jesus.[136] On the one hand, the judgment has been pronounced in *the name* of the Lord, Jesus; on the other hand, it is to be carried out with *the power* of the Lord, Jesus. Thus, just at the risen Lord will come with "the angels of his power" to execute eschatological judgment on his enemies (2 Thess 1:7), so now in the gathered community in Corinth, Paul expects the power of the exalted Lord, Jesus, probably by means of his Spirit, to be present as well to aid them in carrying out this judgment. All of this is replete with christological implications.

Striving to Please the Lord (1 Cor 7:32)

In his discussion of what he perceives as the advantages of singleness over marriage, Paul asserts that a single person can devote all energy to one thing: πῶς ἀρέστῃ τῷ κυρίῳ (*how to please the Lord*). Here is yet another OT concern[137] that has been taken over by Paul and that in most other instances has to do with "pleasing τῷ θεῷ (*God*)"[138] but is here directly applied to the Lord = Christ (cf. 2 Cor 5:9).

The Command of the Lord (1 Cor 7:10, 12, 25; 9:14; 14:36–37)

As already noted, in 1 Cor 5:3–5 Paul assumes himself to be present by the Spirit in the gathered community when his letter is read to them;[139] and in that context the Corinthians are to carry out the judgment on the incestuous man that he has already pronounced "in the name of the Lord." This in turn is most likely the framework for his pronouncement in 14:37: ἃ γράφω ὑμῖν ὅτι κυρίου ἐστὶν ἐντολή (*what I am writing to you is the Lord's command*). It also explains why he can make a pronouncement regarding a "mixed marriage" in 7:10 when he has no "word from the Lord"; thus "I say, not the Lord" (λέγω ἐγὼ οὐχ ὁ κύριος). Likewise, in 9:14 he refers back to a saying of the earthly Jesus as "the command of the Lord."

What is striking in this set of texts is the fact that Paul can so easily attribute to the risen Lord the kind of commandment language that is the special province of κύριος = Yahweh in the Septuagint. This is especially

---

[136] See the full discussion of this understanding of "the Lord, Jesus," based on Phil 2:10–11, in ch. 9 (pp. 396–98), and its larger christological implications in ch. 15 (pp. 558–85).

[137] See, e.g., Exod 33:13, 17; Num 14:8; Job 34:9; Ps 41:11; 69:13.

[138] See 1 Thess 2:15; 4:1; Rom 8:8; 12:1–2; 14:18; Phil 4:18.

[139] For this perspective, see Fee, *God's Empowering Presence*, 122–27.

true of "the Lord's command" in 14:37. Here is Septuagintal language, especially in Deuteronomy, for God's law given to Israel. With perfect ease Paul uses this language for what he himself says on behalf of the Lord.

More remarkable yet is the next item.

Under Christ's Law (1 Cor 9:21)

Here is a text that has caused not a little grief for those who read Galatians and Romans through the eyes of Luther and Calvin. But this wordplay on "law" is typical of Paul. In the rhetoric of "becoming all things to all people so that by all possible means he might save some" (v. 22), he asserts that when in the company of those who do not have the law, he himself conforms to their not having the law (τοῖς ἀνόμοις ὡς ἄνομος [*to those without the law as without the law myself*]). In context, one may rightly assume that this has to do with eating foods forbidden by the law of Moses and would include the expansion of those laws in the Judaism of Paul's day.

Such a pronouncement on its own, however, could come back to haunt the apostle, as he well understands, since he himself has been under siege on this matter.[140] So he immediately qualifies this expression of "becoming all things" with this remarkable clause: μὴ ὢν ἄνομος θεοῦ ἀλλ᾽ ἔννομος Χριστοῦ, which is nearly impossible to put into simple English. Playing on his description of Gentiles as ἄνομος (= not having the law), he says that in conforming to their "without the law" eating habits, Paul himself is not truly "without the law" as far as God is concerned; rather, under the new covenant he is "in-lawed to Christ," a phrase that F. W. Danker rightly glosses as "not, of course, being outside God's jurisdiction, but being inside Christ's."[141]

Our interest here is with the christological implications of this remarkable disclaimer. Although it is true that it conforms to Paul's consistent attitude toward the believer's (non)relationship to the Mosaic law, it puts ethical life on a new, and higher, plane, marked in Gal 5:22–23 as the fruit of the Spirit, for which there is no law in the old sense; rather, they are an expression of being "under Christ's law." Thus in this off-the-cuff disclaimer that Paul does not live a "lawless" life because he conforms to "the law" as it now finds expression through Christ and the Spirit, he has once more given evidence of his assumed high Christology. The "law of God" is in fact to be understood as "the (non)law of Christ," since conforming to Christ's character and behavior is now the way of being "under God's law."

With this passage, we come to the end of Paul's attribution to Christ as κύριος a large number of exact phrases or otherwise divine prerogatives that

---

[140] See the somewhat defensive nature of his sudden personal response to criticism in 10:29–30, which comes toward the end of an argument of which the present passage is a part.

[141] See BDAG, s.v. ἔννομος.

in the OT belong to God alone, not to angels or to human beings. Although several, or any one, of them might seem incidental and relatively unimportant, their cumulative affect is considerable. And as I have pointed out regularly, most of this is neither thought through nor designed to convince; rather, much of it is said so unself-consciously that one can only conclude that Paul's devotion to Christ as Lord had been in place for a long time before this letter was written.

Texts That Imply Subordination

Finally, we need to examine carefully the two other texts in this letter[142] that specifically suggest the Son to be in a subordinate relationship to the Father: 1 Cor 3:23; 11:3. And one must be especially careful here because the issue of "being" is simply not a part of Paul's epistolary discourse; his concern is always with the role or function of the Son in the divine plan of redemption. That is, the economy of salvation noted earlier on 2 Thess 2:13 (pp. 63–64) and recognized above in 1 Cor 8:6 holds true throughout the Pauline corpus. So these texts offer no surprises. They simply express that reality in ways that seem to border more on the issue of divine relationship than on Christ's saving function alone.

1 Corinthians 3:23—"Christ Is of God"

To sum up his argument against the presenting issue in 1 Cor 1–4, namely, divisiveness predicated on "belonging" to different leaders, Paul urges that despite differing functions in God's vineyard or temple, their leaders first of all belong to God (3:9). Because of this—and because the Corinthian believers themselves belong to Christ (v. 23a)—that means that all their leaders (Paul, Apollos, Cephas) also belong to them.[143] Thus, he concludes, "all things are yours" not because you are self-sufficient or important in your own right but precisely because "you belong to Christ."

But never one to leave such argumentation at that point, Paul concludes with a climaxing crescendo, pointing to God as the ultimate goal of all things. Just as they belong to Christ through his redemptive work, so Christ in that same redemptive work "belongs to God." This statement therefore maintains a motif found throughout the Pauline corpus: in his work of redemption Christ was carrying out the will of the Father. But such statements fall far short of speaking to his essential being or eternal relationship with the Father. That is, such statements as these reflect functional subordination

---

[142]Besides 15:28, noted above, p. 113.

[143]Thus, in a piece of nice irony, he has taken their slogans (e.g., "I am of Paul") and turned them upside down, so that "Paul is of you," in the sense that all things are yours, since you are of Christ.

and have to do with Christ's function as Savior, not with his being as such. Moreover, a good case can be made that this phrase is directed specifically toward those who say ἐγὼ Χριστοῦ (*I am of Christ* [1:13]),[144] so as to redirect their singular "I" to the plural "you" and thus to keep Christ within the bounds of what God has done, and is doing, in the world.

So what is of ultimate christological significance in this phrase is not its expression of subordinationism but its affirmation that Christ, in all that he has done and does for "us sinners," is ultimately an expression of what God is doing on our planet. As always for Paul, and especially in the primary christological assertion in this letter (8:6), God is the source and goal of everything, both creation and redemption, while Christ is the divine agent of creation and redemption. In this sense, "Christ is of God."

1 Corinthians 11:3—God as the "Head" of Christ

The final text we need to examine is Paul's metaphorical use of "head" in 11:3, where, in the third member of a triplet of relationships, Paul says that "the head of Christ is God." Thus:

11:3 παντὸς ἀνδρὸς ἡ κεφαλὴ ὁ **Χριστός** ἐστιν,
      κεφαλὴ δὲ γυναικὸς ὁ ἀνήρ,
      κεφαλὴ δὲ τοῦ Χριστοῦ ὁ θεός.

*Of every man the head is **Christ**;*
the head of the woman is the man;
***the head of Christ is* <u>God</u>.**

Unfortunately, the second member of this triplet has set off a considerable debate in recent years over the meaning of this metaphor regarding male and female relationships, a debate that has often produced as much heat as light.[145] Without rehashing that debate, we may here safely isolate several things about Paul's use of this metaphor, so as to understand the (probable) intent of what is said about the relationship of Christ and God.[146]

1. This is both the first occurrence of this metaphor in the Pauline corpus and its only appearance in a context where σῶμα (*body*) is not mentioned or assumed. That is, elsewhere when Paul speaks of, for example, Christ as "head" in relationship to his "body" the church, it is a metaphor not for "lordship" but for the supporting, life-sustaining role that the head was understood to have in relationship to the body (Col 2:19; Eph 4:15–16).

---

[144] So Richardson, *Paul's Language*, 113–15.

[145] See the especially helpful overview in Thiselton's excursus (812–23), and his equally useful bibliography (806–9), although it does not include the follow-up interchange between Grudem and Cervin.

[146] The substance of what is said here is adapted from G. D. Fee, "Praying and Prophesying in the Assemblies: 1 Corinthians 11:2–16," in Pierce and Groothuis, *Discovering Biblical Equality*, 149–55.

2. In the first line of this passage Christ's relationship to the church is *not* in view, but specifically his relationship to the man (= male human being). And whatever the relationship of Christ to the man envisioned by the metaphor in this context, most likely it is to be viewed in a way that is similar to Paul's understanding of the relationship of God the Father to Christ.

3. What we also know from the evidence is that when the Jewish community used this metaphor, as they did frequently in the OT, it most often referred to a leader or clan chieftain. On the other hand, although something close to this sense can be found among Greeks, they had a broader range of uses, all of which can be shown to arise out of their anatomical understanding of the relationship of the head to the body (its most prominent or important part; the "source of supply/support" for the body's working systems, etc.).[147]

4. The first extant interpretation of this passage in the early church is by Cyril of Alexandria (d. ca. 444), who very explicitly interprets in terms of the Greek metaphor: "Thus we can say that 'the head of every man is Christ.' For he was made by [διά] him . . . as God; 'but the head of the woman is the man,' because she was taken out of his flesh. . . . Likewise 'the head of Christ is God,' because he is of him [ἐξ αὐτοῦ] by nature" (*Ad Arcadiam et Marinam* 5.6). Cyril appears to go this way because (a) prompted by v. 8 ("the woman is ἐξ ἀνδρός"), it was also a natural metaphor in the Greek world and (b) it supports his christological concerns.

The question for us, then, is whether Paul was speaking out of his Jewish heritage or whether, in speaking into the Corinthians' Greek setting, he used a metaphor that would have been familiar to them.[148] Before settling that question for line 3, at issue in the passage itself is what kind of relationship between the "man" and the "woman" is envisaged here and how this plays out in the discussion that follows. For several reasons, it seems most likely that something very much like Cyril's understanding was in Paul's mind.

1. Despite repeated assertions to the contrary, nothing that is said following this verse hints at a subordination/submission relationship. Most often those who advocate this view have either a "husband/wife" or a "church order" relationship in view. But the latter is to read something into the text

---

[147] The clearest evidence for the real differences between the Jewish and Greek metaphorical use is to be found in the Septuagint. In the hundreds of places where the Hebrew רֹאשׁ is used for the literal head on a body, the translators invariably used the only word in Greek that means the same thing, κεφαλή. But in the approximately 180 times it appears as a *metaphor* for leader or chieftain, the many translators across the board usually eliminated the metaphor altogether and translated it ἀρχή (*leader*), which is evidence that they were uncomfortable with (unfamiliar with?) the Jewish metaphor and simply translated it out. The few instances (six in all) where they do not do this (Judg 11:11; 2 Sam 22:44; Ps 18:43; Isa 7:8, 9; Lam 1:5) are simply the exceptions that prove the rule.

[148] And, of course, one cannot appeal to the OT usage as a place of familiarity for them, since they would not know Hebrew and their Greek Bible already had the metaphorical usage basically translated out.

that is not there; and although the former may be intended, nothing inherent in the discussion that follows requires such a view. Moreover, the final wrap-up in vv. 13–15 is about men and women in general and therefore offers no further help in understanding the metaphor.

2. In the one instance in our passage where Paul might be picking up some dimension of the metaphor (vv. 8–9), the relationship envisaged is not one of subordination to the man as "leader." Paul is setting out to explain his assertion that "the woman is the *glory* of man." The answer lies in the Genesis narrative: she came from man (in the sense that she was taken from his side) and was created for his sake; this is what makes her the man's "glory." If this is an extension of the metaphor in v. 3, then it would seem to point to "man" as metaphorical head in the sense Cyril maintains. Moreover, there is no usage of "glory" anywhere in Scripture that would suggest that Paul is here advocating a subordinating relationship by means of this word—any more than his assertion in 2 Cor 4:6 that "knowledge of the glory of God" is to be seen "in the face of Jesus Christ" implies a subordinating relationship.

3. One of the ongoing puzzles for all interpreters is why Paul should include this third member in his opening sentence, since "God as the head of Christ" is not picked up again in any way. Most likely this is because the "saying" had prior existence and Paul is simply appealing to it. But if so, what was its point? Although one cannot be certain here, most likely it was a useful metaphor to express something of a chronology of "salvation history." According to 1 Cor 8:6, all things (including Adam) were created "through Christ"; the man then became the "source" of the woman's being, while God was the "source" of Christ's incarnation. In any case, this view of the saying can make sense of all three members in a way that seeing the metaphor to express "subordination" does not.

4. It is common to appeal to Paul's later use of this metaphor in Colossians and Ephesians and then to import here a meaning from there. But much confusion seems to be at work here, since in these two later (companion) letters the metaphor is used in three distinct ways: to point to (a) Christ's relationship with the church,[149] (b) Christ's relationship to "the powers,"[150] and (c) a householder's relationship to his wife.[151]

---

[149] See Col 1:18; 2:19; Eph 4:15–16; 5:23.

[150] See Col 2:10; Eph 1:22.

[151] Eph 5:23. I use the language "householder" here because the entire passage in Ephesians (5:21–6:9) assumes the Greco-Roman villa, not relationships within other settings (after all, Colossians, at least, was written at the same time as Philemon and assumes the reading of both letters in the context of that household). For example, if there were a married slave couple in the household, Philemon would be the "head" of the slave wife in the same way he would be of Apphia. Paul's point in using the metaphor in Ephesians is that the householder is the "savior" of his wife, in the sense of his being the one on whom the entire household is dependent for their well-being. See further G. D. Fee, "The Cultural Context of Ephesians 5:18–6:9," *Priscilla Papers* 16 (winter 2002): 3–8.

This imagery seems to stem ultimately from Paul's view of the church as the "body of Christ," celebrated at every Lord's Supper, according to 1 Cor 10:16–17; 11:29. What is at issue in Colossians, for example, are some people who are moving in clearly heretical directions, who are "not holding fast to the head" (2:19 = cutting themselves off from the "body" altogether and by implication being "joined" to the "powers" to whom they now give undue significance). This alone, it would seem, can explain the earlier occurrence of the metaphor in 1:18—as the "janus" between the two stanzas of the hymn in 1:15–20: "And he [the Son of God] is the head of the body, that is, the church."[152] This otherwise unnecessary insertion into the hymn/poem of 1:15–20 seems intended—as does the whole hymn/poem itself—to anticipate some things that will be said later as to Christ's relationship both to the powers and to the church in the main argument of 2:6–19.

First, he claims that Christ is "head of every power and authority" (2:10), and is so, he adds in Eph 1:22, *for the sake of* the church. These two instances are in fact the only certain places where Paul uses the imagery in this clearly Jewish way. Second, the key to the imagery in relationship to the church is the elaboration in Col 2:19, where the false teachers have "lost connection with the head" (TNIV). This obviously is a metaphor not for subordination or "lordship" but for the maintenance of life, as the rest of the sentence makes plain. To lose connection to the head means to lose life itself, since the church functions as Christ's body only as it maintains connection with the head. This is also how the head/body imagery is elaborated in Eph 4:15–16. Now in a positive context, the imagery encourages the life and growth of the church as a unity, which is why in Colossians those who cease to "hold fast" to the head cease to live and in fact are moving the church itself toward death.

This relationship seems also to be the point of the analogical use of the metaphor in Eph 5:22–24.[153] Precisely because Paul is deliberately using an *analogy*, not reality,[154] the *point* of the analogy takes us back to 4:15–16, *not*

---

[152] I say "janus" (= looks both ways) here because this line is otherwise unrelated to the content of the first stanza (vv. 15–17), where the emphasis is on the Son as the "firstborn over the whole created order"; in him all things, including the powers, were created; indeed, they were created by him and for him; and in him all things hold together. The balancing second stanza begins in v. 18b, "he [the Son] is the beginning, the firstborn from the dead," and then moves on to speak of his redemptive work that makes him so. Line 18a, "the Son is the head of the body, the church," joins these two stanzas. See further ch. 9, pp. 305–7.

[153] It should be pointed out that the metaphor is *not* used for the other two relationships with the householder (children and slaves), where "lordship" is plainly expressed. The change of verbs from ὑποτάσσω (*submit*) (where the middle voice suggests a form of volunteerism that is expected of all but also in a special way of wives) to ὑπακούω (*obey*) for children and slaves (in both letters) suggests that Paul would never have used the latter for wives and that there is therefore a basic difference between them despite occasional semantic overlap.

[154] That is, the husband is *not* the savior of his wife in the same way as Christ is of the church!

to the relationship of Christ to the "powers." And this point is the apt one: just as the church is totally dependent upon Christ for life and growth, so the wife in the first-century household was totally dependent on her husband as her "savior," in the sense of being dependent on him for her life in the world.

All of this is to say, then, that the importation into 1 Cor 11:3 of the *later* use of the imagery is probably suspect at best. But if it is deemed appropriate, then the relationship envisioned is not so much "head = leader" as it is "head = source of being," as Cyril rightly understood it.

What this means for us christologically, therefore, is that the relationship most likely in view here is the one that is standard in Paul, which derives primarily from Paul's soteriological concerns. Although it is true that the metaphor seems to imply the *priority* of the one to the other, that is to be taken not in a subordinating way but in a way that comports with Paul's consistent "grammar" of salvation, found in 8:6 and expressed regularly elsewhere. Everything is predicated on the "love of God," which then finds expression in the "grace of Christ," which is then made effective in the life of the believer and the church through the "participation/sharing in the Spirit" (2 Cor 13:13[14]; see also, e.g., Rom 5:3–8). Thus, just as in 1 Cor 15:28, the apparently "subordinating" expression of this passage and others is an expression not of person or being but of their individual roles in the economy of salvation.

Conclusion

As in the preceding chapter, since conclusions have been offered throughout, here I simply point out the more significant features of the Christology of this letter.

First, most of the features already present in the Thessalonian correspondence emerge here as well: the exalted Christ as messianic King and Son; Christ as "the Lord" of ever so many Septuagint texts where "the Lord" is Yahweh; Christ's sharing with the Father a great many divine prerogatives. The only real difference is that the first of these finds more definition here than in 1–2 Thessalonians.

Second, what is found explicitly, and boldly, for the first time in the corpus are affirmations of Christ's preexistence. In Paul's remarkable restatement of the Jewish Shema, Christ the Son assumes a role alongside the Father in God's identity, as the preexistent divine agent of creation as well as the historical agent of redemption. Thus he is also seen as present with Israel in the wilderness, as the One who supplied Israel with water and as the One whom they spurned in their rebellion.

At the same time, third, one also finds alongside these strong affirmations the first clear instances of the divine economy of salvation, which has its source in God the Father and its historical expression in the death and resurrection of Christ. In this role, Christ is regularly seen as subordinate to the Father.

Fourth, here also for the first time one finds very strong expressions of Christ's genuine humanity. Preexistent though he was and exalted King/ Lord though he is, his life on earth was fully human, finding ultimate expression in the scandal of a crucified Messiah.

As before, these various expressions regarding Christ's person are merely asserted or alluded to; they are never a point of argumentation as such. But this means that they also reflect our inherent christological difficulties: Christ is seen as coexistent with the Father in a framework of absolute monotheism, and the divine Redeemer was truly human in his incarnation. It has thus been the province of later theologians to wrestle with the data that Paul provides but never resolves.

And finally, the most challenging matter of all remains: the danger of analysis without adequate appreciation for the absolute centrality of Christ for Paul, an analysis of what Paul believed about Christ by way of what he says about his Lord that fails to comprehend and communicate his utter and total devotion to Christ—a devotion that a good Jew could give only to his God. The reason Christ is mentioned more often than God in this letter, and in most of Paul's letters, is not that Paul is not consistently theocentric in his thinking—he is indeed. Rather, his whole world had been radically reoriented by his encounter with the risen and exalted Lord, Jesus Christ. There is no longer any way that Paul can talk about God without at the same time automatically talking about what God has accomplished in and and through his Son. And at the end of the day, however one handles the language of Paul's express statements about Christ, there is no genuine Christology that does not account for Paul's utter devotion to and longing for Christ, which finds expression here and in all of his letters.[155]

Thus, by reason of his upbringing and continuing theological reflection, Paul can rightly be described as theocentric; but by experience and in proclamation he is utterly christocentric. All theological reflection must either come to terms with these twin realities or fail to understand the apostle at all.

Appendix I: The Texts

(brackets [[ ]] indicate texts with references to God alone; triple brackets [[[ ]]] with italics indicate citations from the LXX, where κύριος refers to Yahweh)

1:1 Παῦλος κλητὸς ἀπόστολος **Χριστοῦ Ἰησοῦ** <u>διὰ θελήματος θεοῦ</u> καὶ Σωσθένης ὁ ἀδελφὸς

---

[155] See further discussion of this matter in chs. 4 (pp. 196–98) and 9 (pp. 412–13).

1:2 τῇ ἐκκλησίᾳ τοῦ θεοῦ τῇ οὔσῃ ἐν Κορίνθῳ, ἡγιασμένοις ἐν Χριστῷ
Ἰησοῦ, κλητοῖς ἁγίοις, σὺν πᾶσιν τοῖς ἐπικαλουμένοις τὸ ὄνομα τοῦ
κυρίου ἡμῶν Ἰησοῦ Χριστοῦ ἐν παντὶ τόπῳ, αὐτῶν καὶ ἡμῶν·

1:3 χάρις ὑμῖν καὶ εἰρήνη ἀπὸ θεοῦ πατρὸς ἡμῶν καὶ κυρίου Ἰησοῦ
Χριστοῦ.

1:4–9 ⁴Εὐχαριστῶ τῷ θεῷ μου πάντοτε περὶ ὑμῶν ἐπὶ τῇ χάριτι τοῦ θεοῦ τῇ
δοθείσῃ ὑμῖν ἐν Χριστῷ Ἰησοῦ, ⁵ὅτι ἐν παντὶ ἐπλουτίσθητε ἐν αὐτῷ, ἐν
παντὶ λόγῳ καὶ πάσῃ γνώσει, ⁶καθὼς τὸ μαρτύριον τοῦ Χριστοῦ
ἐβεβαιώθη ἐν ὑμῖν, ⁷ὥστε ὑμᾶς μὴ ὑστερεῖσθαι ἐν μηδενὶ χαρίσματι
ἀπεκδεχομένους τὴν ἀποκάλυψιν τοῦ κυρίου ἡμῶν Ἰησοῦ Χριστοῦ· ⁸ὃς
καὶ βεβαιώσει ὑμᾶς ἕως τέλους ἀνεγκλήτους ἐν τῇ ἡμέρᾳ τοῦ κυρίου
ἡμῶν Ἰησοῦ Χριστοῦ. [ᵛ·ˡ·-Χριστοῦ] ⁹πιστὸς ὁ θεός, δι' οὗ ἐκλήθητε εἰς
κοινωνίαν τοῦ υἱοῦ αὐτοῦ Ἰησοῦ Χριστοῦ τοῦ κυρίου ἡμῶν.

1:10 Παρακαλῶ δὲ ὑμᾶς, ἀδελφοί, διὰ τοῦ ὀνόματος τοῦ κυρίου ἡμῶν
Ἰησοῦ Χριστοῦ, ἵνα τὸ αὐτὸ λέγητε πάντες καὶ μὴ ᾖ ἐν ὑμῖν σχίσματα, ἦτε
δὲ κατηρτισμένοι ἐν τῷ αὐτῷ νοῒ καὶ ἐν τῇ αὐτῇ γνώμῃ.

1:12–13 ¹²λέγω δὲ τοῦτο ὅτι ἕκαστος ὑμῶν λέγει· ἐγὼ μέν εἰμι Παύλου, ἐγὼ
δὲ Ἀπολλῶ, ἐγὼ δὲ Κηφᾶ, ἐγὼ δὲ Χριστοῦ. ¹³μεμέρισται ὁ Χριστός; μὴ
Παῦλος ἐσταυρώθη ὑπὲρ ὑμῶν, ἢ εἰς τὸ ὄνομα Παύλου ἐβαπτίσθητε;

[[1:14 εὐχαριστῶ [ᵛ·ˡ· +τῷ θεῷ] ὅτι οὐδένα ὑμῶν ἐβάπτισα εἰ μὴ Κρίσπον καὶ
Γάιον,]]

1:17 οὐ γὰρ ἀπέστειλέν με Χριστὸς βαπτίζειν ἀλλὰ εὐαγγελίζεσθαι, οὐκ
ἐν σοφίᾳ λόγου, ἵνα μὴ κενωθῇ ὁ σταυρὸς τοῦ Χριστοῦ.

[[1:18–21 Ὁ λόγος γὰρ ὁ τοῦ σταυροῦ τοῖς μὲν ἀπολλυμένοις μωρία ἐστίν,
τοῖς δὲ σῳζομένοις ἡμῖν δύναμις θεοῦ ἐστιν. ¹⁹γέγραπται γάρ· ἀπολῶ τὴν
σοφίαν τῶν σοφῶν καὶ τὴν σύνεσιν τῶν συνετῶν ἀθετήσω. ²⁰ποῦ σοφός; ποῦ
γραμματεύς; ποῦ συζητητὴς τοῦ αἰῶνος τούτου; οὐχὶ ἐμώρανεν ὁ θεὸς τὴν
σοφίαν τοῦ κόσμου; ²¹ἐπειδὴ γὰρ ἐν τῇ σοφίᾳ τοῦ θεοῦ οὐκ ἔγνω ὁ κόσμος
διὰ τῆς σοφίας τὸν θεόν, εὐδόκησεν ὁ θεὸς διὰ τῆς μωρίας τοῦ κηρύγματος
σῶσαι τοὺς πιστεύοντας·]]

1:23–25 ²³ἡμεῖς δὲ κηρύσσομεν Χριστὸν ἐσταυρωμένον, Ἰουδαίοις μὲν
σκάνδαλον, ἔθνεσιν δὲ μωρίαν, ²⁴αὐτοῖς δὲ τοῖς κλητοῖς, Ἰουδαίοις τε καὶ
Ἕλλησιν, Χριστὸν θεοῦ δύναμιν καὶ θεοῦ σοφίαν· ²⁵ὅτι τὸ μωρὸν τοῦ θεοῦ
σοφώτερον τῶν ἀνθρώπων ἐστὶν καὶ τὸ ἀσθενὲς τοῦ θεοῦ ἰσχυρότερον τῶν
ἀνθρώπων.

[[1:27–29 ²⁷ἀλλὰ τὰ μωρὰ τοῦ κόσμου ἐξελέξατο ὁ θεός, ἵνα καταισχύνῃ
τοὺς σοφούς, καὶ τὰ ἀσθενῆ τοῦ κόσμου ἐξελέξατο ὁ θεός, ἵνα καταισχύνῃ
τὰ ἰσχυρά, ²⁸καὶ τὰ ἀγενῆ τοῦ κόσμου καὶ τὰ ἐξουθενημένα ἐξελέξατο ὁ
θεός, τὰ μὴ ὄντα, ἵνα τὰ ὄντα καταργήσῃ, ²⁹ὅπως μὴ καυχήσηται πᾶσα σὰρξ
ἐνώπιον τοῦ θεοῦ.]]

1:30–31 [30]ἐξ αὐτοῦ δὲ ὑμεῖς ἐστε **ἐν Χριστῷ Ἰησοῦ, ὃς ἐγενήθη σοφία** ἡμῖν ἀπὸ θεοῦ, δικαιοσύνη τε καὶ ἁγιασμὸς καὶ ἀπολύτρωσις, [31]ἵνα καθὼς γέγραπται· ὁ καυχώμενος **ἐν κυρίῳ** καυχάσθω.

[[2:1 . . . ἦλθον οὐ καθ᾽ ὑπεροχὴν λόγου ἢ σοφίας καταγγέλλων ὑμῖν τὸ μαρτύριον τοῦ θεοῦ.]]

2:2 οὐ γὰρ ἔκρινά τι εἰδέναι ἐν ὑμῖν εἰ μὴ **Ἰησοῦν Χριστὸν καὶ τοῦτον ἐσταυρωμένον.**

[[2:5 ἵνα ἡ πίστις ὑμῶν μὴ ᾖ ἐν σοφίᾳ ἀνθρώπων ἀλλ᾽ ἐν δυνάμει θεοῦ.]]

2:7–8 [7]ἀλλὰ λαλοῦμεν θεοῦ σοφίαν ἐν μυστηρίῳ τὴν ἀποκεκρυμμένην, ἣν προώρισεν ὁ θεὸς πρὸ τῶν αἰώνων εἰς δόξαν ἡμῶν, [8]ἣν οὐδεὶς τῶν ἀρχόντων τοῦ αἰῶνος τούτου ἔγνωκεν· εἰ γὰρ ἔγνωσαν, οὐκ ἂν **τὸν κύριον τῆς δόξης** ἐσταύρωσαν.

[[2:9–14 . . . ἃ ἡτοίμασεν ὁ θεὸς τοῖς ἀγαπῶσιν αὐτόν. [10]ἡμῖν γὰρ ἀπεκάλυψεν ὁ θεὸς διὰ τοῦ πνεύματος· τὸ γὰρ πνεῦμα πάντα ἐραυνᾷ, καὶ τὰ βάθη τοῦ θεοῦ. [11]τίς γὰρ οἶδεν ἀνθρώπων τὰ τοῦ ἀνθρώπου εἰ μὴ τὸ πνεῦμα τοῦ ἀνθρώπου τὸ ἐν αὐτῷ; οὕτως καὶ τὰ τοῦ θεοῦ οὐδεὶς ἔγνωκεν εἰ μὴ τὸ πνεῦμα τοῦ θεοῦ. [12]ἡμεῖς δὲ οὐ τὸ πνεῦμα τοῦ κόσμου ἐλάβομεν ἀλλὰ τὸ πνεῦμα τὸ ἐκ τοῦ θεοῦ, ἵνα εἰδῶμεν τὰ ὑπὸ τοῦ θεοῦ χαρισθέντα ἡμῖν· . . . [14]ψυχικὸς δὲ ἄνθρωπος οὐ δέχεται τὰ τοῦ πνεύματος τοῦ θεοῦ·]]

2:16 τίς γὰρ ἔγνω νοῦν **κυρίου**, ὃς συμβιβάσει **αὐτόν**; ἡμεῖς δὲ **νοῦν Χριστοῦ** ἔχομεν.

3:1 Κἀγώ, ἀδελφοί, οὐκ ἠδυνήθην λαλῆσαι ὑμῖν ὡς πνευματικοῖς ἀλλ᾽ ὡς σαρκίνοις, ὡς νηπίοις **ἐν Χριστῷ.**

3:5–7 [5]τί οὖν ἐστιν Ἀπολλῶς; τί δέ ἐστιν Παῦλος; διάκονοι δι᾽ ὧν ἐπιστεύσατε, καὶ ἑκάστῳ ὡς **ὁ κύριος** ἔδωκεν. [6]ἐγὼ ἐφύτευσα, Ἀπολλῶς ἐπότισεν, ἀλλὰ ὁ θεὸς ηὔξανεν· [7]ὥστε οὔτε ὁ φυτεύων ἐστίν τι οὔτε ὁ ποτίζων ἀλλ᾽ ὁ αὐξάνων θεός.

[[3:9–10 θεοῦ γάρ ἐσμεν συνεργοί, θεοῦ γεώργιον, θεοῦ οἰκοδομή ἐστε. [10]Κατὰ τὴν χάριν τοῦ θεοῦ τὴν δοθεῖσάν μοι ὡς σοφὸς ἀρχιτέκτων θεμέλιον ἔθηκα, ἄλλος δὲ ἐποικοδομεῖ. ἕκαστος δὲ βλεπέτω πῶς ἐποικοδομεῖ.]]

3:11–12 [11]θεμέλιον γὰρ ἄλλον οὐδεὶς δύναται θεῖναι παρὰ τὸν κείμενον, **ὅς ἐστιν Ἰησοῦς Χριστός.** [12]εἰ δέ τις ἐποικοδομεῖ **ἐπὶ τὸν θεμέλιον** χρυσόν, ἄργυρον, λίθους τιμίους, ξύλα, χόρτον, καλάμην,

[[3:16–17 οὐκ οἴδατε ὅτι ναὸς θεοῦ ἐστε καὶ τὸ πνεῦμα τοῦ θεοῦ οἰκεῖ ἐν ὑμῖν; [17]εἴ τις τὸν ναὸν τοῦ θεοῦ φθείρει, φθερεῖ τοῦτον ὁ θεός· ὁ γὰρ ναὸς τοῦ θεοῦ ἅγιός ἐστιν, οἵτινές ἐστε ὑμεῖς.]]

[[3:19 ἡ γὰρ σοφία τοῦ κόσμου τούτου μωρία παρὰ τῷ θεῷ ἐστιν.]]

[[[3:20 (LXX) . . . <u>κύριος γινώσκει</u> τοὺς διαλογισμοὺς τῶν σοφῶν ὅτι εἰσὶν μάταιοι.]]]

3:23 ὑμεῖς δὲ **Χριστοῦ**, **Χριστὸς** δὲ <u>θεοῦ</u>.

4:1–5 ¹Οὕτως ἡμᾶς λογιζέσθω ἄνθρωπος ὡς ὑπηρέτας **Χριστοῦ** καὶ οἰκονόμους <u>μυστηρίων θεοῦ</u>. ²ὧδε λοιπὸν ζητεῖται ἐν τοῖς οἰκονόμοις, ἵνα πιστός τις εὑρεθῇ. ³ἐμοὶ δὲ εἰς ἐλάχιστόν ἐστιν, ἵνα ὑφ᾽ ὑμῶν ἀνακριθῶ ἢ ὑπὸ ἀνθρωπίνης ἡμέρας· ἀλλ᾽ οὐδὲ ἐμαυτὸν ἀνακρίνω. ⁴οὐδὲν γὰρ ἐμαυτῷ σύνοιδα, ἀλλ᾽ οὐκ ἐν τούτῳ δεδικαίωμαι, ὁ δὲ ἀνακρίνων με **κύριός ἐστιν**. ⁵ὥστε μὴ πρὸ καιροῦ τι κρίνετε ἕως **ἂν ἔλθῃ ὁ κύριος**, ὃς **καὶ φωτίσει** τὰ κρυπτὰ τοῦ σκότους καὶ φανερώσει τὰς βουλὰς τῶν καρδιῶν· καὶ τότε <u>ὁ ἔπαινος γενήσεται ἑκάστῳ ἀπὸ τοῦ θεοῦ</u>.

[[4:9 δοκῶ γάρ, <u>ὁ θεὸς ἡμᾶς τοὺς ἀποστόλους ἐσχάτους ἀπέδειξεν</u> ὡς ἐπιθανατίους,]]

4:10 ἡμεῖς μωροὶ **διὰ Χριστόν**, ὑμεῖς δὲ φρόνιμοι **ἐν Χριστῷ**·

4:15 ἐὰν γὰρ μυρίους παιδαγωγοὺς ἔχητε **ἐν Χριστῷ** ἀλλ᾽ οὐ πολλοὺς πατέρας· **ἐν γὰρ Χριστῷ Ἰησοῦ** διὰ τοῦ εὐαγγελίου ἐγὼ ὑμᾶς ἐγέννησα.

4:17 διὰ τοῦτο ἔπεμψα ὑμῖν Τιμόθεον, ὅς ἐστίν μου τέκνον ἀγαπητὸν καὶ πιστὸν **ἐν κυρίῳ**, ὃς ὑμᾶς ἀναμνήσει τὰς ὁδούς μου τὰς **ἐν Χριστῷ Ἰησοῦ**, καθὼς πανταχοῦ ἐν πάσῃ ἐκκλησίᾳ διδάσκω.

4:19 ἐλεύσομαι δὲ ταχέως πρὸς ὑμᾶς ἐὰν **ὁ κύριος** θελήσῃ, καὶ γνώσομαι οὐ τὸν λόγον τῶν πεφυσιωμένων ἀλλὰ τὴν δύναμιν·

[[4:20 οὐ γὰρ ἐν λόγῳ <u>ἡ βασιλεία τοῦ θεοῦ</u> ἀλλ᾽ ἐν δυνάμει.]]

5:3–5 ³ἐγὼ μὲν γάρ . . . ἤδη κέκρικα ὡς παρὼν τὸν οὕτως τοῦτο κατεργασά-μενον ⁴**ἐν τῷ ὀνόματι τοῦ κυρίου** [ἡμῶν] **Ἰησοῦ**, [v.l. + Χριστοῦ] **συναχθέντων ὑμῶν καὶ τοῦ ἐμοῦ πνεύματος σὺν τῇ δυνάμει τοῦ κυρίου ἡμῶν Ἰησοῦ**, [v.l. + Χριστοῦ] ⁵**παραδοῦναι** τὸν τοιοῦτον τῷ σατανᾷ εἰς ὄλεθρον τῆς σαρκός, ἵνα τὸ πνεῦμα σωθῇ **ἐν τῇ ἡμέρᾳ τοῦ κυρίου**. [v.l. + Ἰησοῦ]

5:7 ἐκκαθάρατε τὴν παλαιὰν ζύμην, ἵνα ἦτε νέον φύραμα, καθώς ἐστε ἄζυμοι· καὶ γὰρ **τὸ πάσχα ἡμῶν ἐτύθη Χριστός**.

[[5:12–13 τί γάρ μοι τοὺς ἔξω κρίνειν; οὐχὶ τοὺς ἔσω ὑμεῖς κρίνετε; ¹³τοὺς δὲ ἔξω <u>ὁ θεὸς κρινεῖ</u>. ἐξάρατε τὸν πονηρὸν ἐξ ὑμῶν αὐτῶν.]]

[[6:9–10 ἢ οὐκ οἴδατε ὅτι <u>ἄδικοι θεοῦ βασιλείαν οὐ κληρονομήσουσιν</u>; μὴ πλανᾶσθε· οὔτε πόρνοι οὔτε εἰδωλολάτραι οὔτε μοιχοὶ οὔτε μαλακοὶ οὔτε ἀρσενοκοῖται ¹⁰οὔτε κλέπται οὔτε πλεονέκται, οὐ μέθυσοι, οὐ λοίδοροι, οὐχ ἅρπαγες <u>βασιλείαν θεοῦ κληρονομήσουσιν</u>.]]

6:11 καὶ ταῦτά τινες ἦτε· ἀλλὰ ἀπελούσασθε, ἀλλὰ ἡγιάσθητε, ἀλλὰ ἐδικαιώθητε **ἐν τῷ ὀνόματι τοῦ κυρίου Ἰησοῦ Χριστοῦ** καὶ <u>ἐν τῷ πνεύματι τοῦ θεοῦ ἡμῶν</u>.

6:13–17 ¹³τὰ βρώματα τῇ κοιλίᾳ καὶ ἡ κοιλία τοῖς βρώμασιν, ὁ δὲ θεὸς καὶ ταύτην καὶ ταῦτα καταργήσει. τὸ δὲ σῶμα οὐ τῇ πορνείᾳ ἀλλὰ τῷ κυρίῳ, καὶ ὁ κύριος τῷ σώματι· ¹⁴ὁ δὲ θεὸς καὶ τὸν κύριον ἤγειρεν καὶ ἡμᾶς ἐξεγερεῖ διὰ τῆς δυνάμεως αὐτοῦ. ¹⁵οὐκ οἴδατε ὅτι τὰ σώματα ὑμῶν μέλη Χριστοῦ ἐστιν; ἄρας οὖν τὰ μέλη τοῦ Χριστοῦ ποιήσω πόρνης μέλη; μὴ γένοιτο. ¹⁶[ἢ] οὐκ οἴδατε ὅτι ὁ κολλώμενος τῇ πόρνῃ ἓν σῶμά ἐστιν; ἔσονται γάρ, φησίν, οἱ δύο εἰς σάρκα μίαν. ¹⁷ὁ δὲ κολλώμενος τῷ κυρίῳ ἓν πνεῦμά ἐστιν.

[[6:19–20 ¹⁹ἢ οὐκ οἴδατε ὅτι τὸ σῶμα ὑμῶν ναὸς τοῦ ἐν ὑμῖν ἁγίου πνεύματός ἐστιν οὗ ἔχετε ἀπὸ θεοῦ, καὶ οὐκ ἐστὲ ἑαυτῶν; ²⁰ἠγοράσθητε γὰρ τιμῆς· δοξάσατε δὴ τὸν θεὸν ἐν τῷ σώματι ὑμῶν.]]

[[7:7 . . . ἀλλὰ ἕκαστος ἴδιον ἔχει χάρισμα ἐκ θεοῦ, ὁ μὲν οὕτως, ὁ δὲ οὕτως.]]

7:10 τοῖς δὲ γεγαμηκόσιν παραγγέλλω, οὐκ ἐγὼ ἀλλὰ ὁ κύριος, γυναῖκα ἀπὸ ἀνδρὸς μὴ χωρισθῆναι,

7:12 Τοῖς δὲ λοιποῖς λέγω ἐγὼ οὐχ ὁ κύριος·

[[7:15 . . . ἐν δὲ εἰρήνῃ κέκληκεν ὑμᾶς ὁ θεός.]]

7:17 Εἰ μὴ ἑκάστῳ ὡς ἐμέρισεν ὁ κύριος, ἕκαστον ὡς κέκληκεν ὁ θεός, οὕτως περιπατείτω.

[[7:19 ἡ περιτομὴ οὐδέν ἐστιν καὶ ἡ ἀκροβυστία οὐδέν ἐστιν, ἀλλὰ τήρησις ἐντολῶν θεοῦ.]]

7:22–24 ὁ γὰρ ἐν κυρίῳ κληθεὶς δοῦλος ἀπελεύθερος κυρίου ἐστίν, ὁμοίως ὁ ἐλεύθερος κληθεὶς δοῦλός ἐστιν Χριστοῦ. ²³τιμῆς ἠγοράσθητε· μὴ γίνεσθε δοῦλοι ἀνθρώπων. ²⁴ἕκαστος ἐν ᾧ ἐκλήθη, ἀδελφοί, ἐν τούτῳ μενέτω παρὰ θεῷ.

7:25 Περὶ δὲ τῶν παρθένων ἐπιταγὴν κυρίου οὐκ ἔχω, γνώμην δὲ δίδωμι ὡς ἠλεημένος ὑπὸ κυρίου πιστὸς εἶναι.

7:32–35 ³²θέλω δὲ ὑμᾶς ἀμερίμνους εἶναι. ὁ ἄγαμος μεριμνᾷ τὰ τοῦ κυρίου, πῶς ἀρέσῃ τῷ κυρίῳ· ³³ὁ δὲ γαμήσας μεριμνᾷ τὰ τοῦ κόσμου, πῶς ἀρέσῃ τῇ γυναικί, ³⁴καὶ μεμέρισται. καὶ ἡ γυνὴ ἡ ἄγαμος καὶ ἡ παρθένος μεριμνᾷ τὰ τοῦ κυρίου, ἵνα ᾖ ἁγία καὶ τῷ σώματι καὶ τῷ πνεύματι· ἡ δὲ γαμήσασα μεριμνᾷ τὰ τοῦ κόσμου, πῶς ἀρέσῃ τῷ ἀνδρί. ³⁵τοῦτο δὲ πρὸς τὸ ὑμῶν αὐτῶν σύμφορον λέγω, οὐχ ἵνα βρόχον ὑμῖν ἐπιβάλω ἀλλὰ πρὸς τὸ εὔσχημον καὶ εὐπάρεδρον τῷ κυρίῳ ἀπερισπάστως.

7:39–40 ³⁹ . . . ἐὰν δὲ κοιμηθῇ ὁ ἀνήρ, ἐλευθέρα ἐστὶν ᾧ θέλει γαμηθῆναι, μόνον ἐν κυρίῳ. ⁴⁰μακαριωτέρα δέ ἐστιν ἐὰν οὕτως μείνῃ, κατὰ τὴν ἐμὴν γνώμην· δοκῶ δὲ κἀγὼ πνεῦμα θεοῦ ἔχειν.

[[8:3 εἰ δέ τις ἀγαπᾷ τὸν θεόν, οὗτος ἔγνωσται ὑπ᾽ αὐτοῦ.]]

[[8:4–5 Περὶ τῆς βρώσεως οὖν τῶν εἰδωλοθύτων, οἴδαμεν ὅτι οὐδὲν εἴδωλον ἐν κόσμῳ καὶ ὅτι <u>οὐδεὶς θεὸς εἰ μὴ εἷς</u>. ⁵καὶ γὰρ εἴπερ εἰσὶν λεγόμενοι θεοὶ εἴτε ἐν οὐρανῷ εἴτε ἐπὶ γῆς, ὥσπερ εἰσὶν θεοὶ πολλοὶ καὶ κύριοι πολλοί,]]

8:6 ἀλλ᾽ ἡμῖν <u>εἷς θεὸς ὁ πατὴρ ἐξ οὗ</u> τὰ πάντα καὶ ἡμεῖς <u>εἰς αὐτόν</u>, καὶ **εἷς κύριος Ἰησοῦς Χριστὸς δι᾽ οὗ** τὰ πάντα καὶ ἡμεῖς **δι᾽ αὐτοῦ**.

[[8:8 βρῶμα δὲ ἡμᾶς οὐ παραστήσει <u>τῷ θεῷ·</u>]]

8:11–12 ¹¹ἀπόλλυται γὰρ ὁ ἀσθενῶν ἐν τῇ σῇ γνώσει ὁ ἀδελφὸς δι᾽ ὃν **Χριστὸς ἀπέθανεν**. ¹²οὕτως δὲ ἁμαρτάνοντες εἰς τοὺς ἀδελφοὺς καὶ τύπτοντες αὐτῶν τὴν συνείδησιν ἀσθενοῦσαν **εἰς Χριστὸν** ἁμαρτάνετε.

9:1–2 ¹Οὐκ εἰμὶ ἐλεύθερος; οὐκ εἰμὶ ἀπόστολος; οὐχὶ **Ἰησοῦν τὸν κύριον ἡμῶν** ἑόρακα; οὐ τὸ ἔργον μου ὑμεῖς ἐστε **ἐν κυρίῳ**; ²εἰ ἄλλοις οὐκ εἰμὶ ἀπόστολος, ἀλλά γε ὑμῖν εἰμι· ἡ γὰρ σφραγίς μου τῆς ἀποστολῆς ὑμεῖς ἐστε **ἐν κυρίῳ**.

9:5 μὴ οὐκ ἔχομεν ἐξουσίαν ἀδελφὴν γυναῖκα περιάγειν ὡς καὶ οἱ λοιποὶ ἀπόστολοι καὶ οἱ **ἀδελφοὶ τοῦ κυρίου** καὶ Κηφᾶς;

[[9:9 ἐν γὰρ τῷ Μωυσέως νόμῳ γέγραπται· οὐ κημώσεις βοῦν ἀλοῶντα. μὴ τῶν βοῶν μέλει <u>τῷ θεῷ</u>;]]

9:12 εἰ ἄλλοι τῆς ὑμῶν ἐξουσίας μετέχουσιν, οὐ μᾶλλον ἡμεῖς; ἀλλ᾽ οὐκ ἐχρησάμεθα τῇ ἐξουσίᾳ ταύτῃ, ἀλλὰ πάντα στέγομεν, ἵνα μή τινα ἐγκοπὴν δῶμεν **τῷ εὐαγγελίῳ τοῦ Χριστοῦ**.

9:14 οὕτως καὶ **ὁ κύριος διέταξεν** τοῖς τὸ εὐαγγέλιον καταγγέλλουσιν ἐκ τοῦ εὐαγγελίου ζῆν.

9:21 τοῖς ἀνόμοις ὡς ἄνομος, μὴ ὢν <u>ἄνομος θεοῦ</u> ἀλλ᾽ **ἔννομος Χριστοῦ**, ἵνα κερδάνω τοὺς ἀνόμους·

10:4 καὶ πάντες τὸ αὐτὸ πνευματικὸν ἔπιον πόμα· ἔπινον γὰρ ἐκ πνευματικῆς ἀκολουθούσης πέτρας, ἡ πέτρα δὲ **ἦν ὁ Χριστός**.

[[10:5 ἀλλ᾽ οὐκ ἐν τοῖς πλείοσιν αὐτῶν εὐδόκησεν <u>ὁ θεός</u>, κατεστρώθησαν γὰρ ἐν τῇ ἐρήμῳ.]]

10:9 μηδὲ ἐκπειράζωμεν **τὸν Χριστόν**, [v.l. **κύριον**] καθώς τινες αὐτῶν ἐπείρασαν καὶ ὑπὸ τῶν ὄφεων ἀπώλλυντο.

[[10:13 πειρασμὸς ὑμᾶς οὐκ εἴληφεν εἰ μὴ ἀνθρώπινος· πιστὸς δὲ <u>ὁ θεός, ὃς οὐκ ἐάσει</u> ὑμᾶς πειρασθῆναι ὑπὲρ ὃ δύνασθε ἀλλὰ <u>ποιήσει</u> σὺν τῷ πειρασμῷ καὶ τὴν ἔκβασιν τοῦ δύνασθαι ὑπενεγκεῖν.]]

10:16 τὸ ποτήριον τῆς εὐλογίας ὃ εὐλογοῦμεν, οὐχὶ κοινωνία ἐστὶν **τοῦ αἵματος τοῦ Χριστοῦ**; τὸν ἄρτον ὃν κλῶμεν, οὐχὶ κοινωνία **τοῦ σώματος τοῦ Χριστοῦ ἐστιν**;

10:20–22 ²⁰ἀλλ᾽ ὅτι ἃ θύουσιν, δαιμονίοις καὶ <u>οὐ θεῷ</u> [θύουσιν]· οὐ θέλω δὲ ὑμᾶς κοινωνοὺς τῶν δαιμονίων γίνεσθαι. ²¹οὐ δύνασθε **ποτήριον κυρίου** πίνειν καὶ ποτήριον δαιμονίων, οὐ δύνασθε **τραπέζης κυρίου μετέχειν** καὶ τραπέζης δαιμονίων. ²²ἢ παραζηλοῦμεν **τὸν κύριον;** μὴ ἰσχυρότεροι **αὐτοῦ** ἐσμεν;

10:26 (LXX) **τοῦ κυρίου** γὰρ ἡ γῆ καὶ τὸ πλήρωμα αὐτῆς.

10:31–11:1 ³¹εἴτε οὖν ἐσθίετε εἴτε πίνετε εἴτε τι ποιεῖτε, πάντα <u>εἰς δόξαν θεοῦ</u> ποιεῖτε. ³²ἀπρόσκοποι καὶ Ἰουδαίοις γίνεσθε καὶ Ἕλλησιν καὶ <u>τῇ ἐκκλησίᾳ τοῦ θεοῦ</u>, ³³καθὼς κἀγὼ πάντα πᾶσιν ἀρέσκω μὴ ζητῶν τὸ ἐμαυτοῦ σύμφορον ἀλλὰ τὸ τῶν πολλῶν, ἵνα σωθῶσιν. ¹¹·¹ μιμηταί μου γίνεσθε καθὼς **κἀγὼ Χριστοῦ.**

11:3 θέλω δὲ ὑμᾶς εἰδέναι ὅτι παντὸς ἀνδρὸς ἡ κεφαλὴ **ὁ Χριστός** ἐστιν, κεφαλὴ δὲ γυναικὸς ὁ ἀνήρ, **κεφαλὴ δὲ τοῦ Χριστοῦ** <u>ὁ θεός</u>.

[[11:7 ἀνὴρ μὲν γὰρ οὐκ ὀφείλει κατακαλύπτεσθαι τὴν κεφαλὴν <u>εἰκὼν καὶ δόξα θεοῦ ὑπάρχων</u>·]]

11:11–12 ¹¹πλὴν οὔτε γυνὴ χωρὶς ἀνδρὸς οὔτε ἀνὴρ χωρὶς γυναικὸς **ἐν κυρίῳ**· ¹²ὥσπερ γὰρ ἡ γυνὴ ἐκ τοῦ ἀνδρός, οὕτως καὶ ὁ ἀνὴρ διὰ τῆς γυναικός· τὰ δὲ πάντα <u>ἐκ τοῦ θεοῦ</u>.

[[11:13 ἐν ὑμῖν αὐτοῖς κρίνατε· πρέπον ἐστὶν γυναῖκα ἀκατακάλυπτον <u>τῷ θεῷ προσεύχεσθαι;</u>]]

[[11:16 Εἰ δέ τις δοκεῖ φιλόνεικος εἶναι, ἡμεῖς τοιαύτην συνήθειαν οὐκ ἔχομεν οὐδὲ <u>αἱ ἐκκλησίαι τοῦ θεοῦ</u>.]]

11:20 Συνερχομένων οὖν ὑμῶν ἐπὶ τὸ αὐτὸ οὐκ ἔστιν **κυριακὸν δεῖπνον** φαγεῖν·

[[11:22 μὴ γὰρ οἰκίας οὐκ ἔχετε εἰς τὸ ἐσθίειν καὶ πίνειν; ἢ <u>τῆς ἐκκλησίας τοῦ θεοῦ</u> καταφρονεῖτε, καὶ καταισχύνετε τοὺς μὴ ἔχοντας; τί εἴπω ὑμῖν; ἐπαινέσω ὑμᾶς; ἐν τούτῳ οὐκ ἐπαινῶ.]]

11:23–27 ²³Ἐγὼ γὰρ παρέλαβον **ἀπὸ τοῦ κυρίου**, ὃ καὶ παρέδωκα ὑμῖν, ὅτι **ὁ κύριος Ἰησοῦς** ἐν τῇ νυκτὶ ᾗ παρεδίδετο ἔλαβεν ἄρτον ²⁴καὶ εὐχαριστήσας ἔκλασεν καὶ εἶπεν· τοῦτό **μού ἐστιν τὸ σῶμα** τὸ ὑπὲρ ὑμῶν· τοῦτο ποιεῖτε εἰς τὴν ἐμὴν ἀνάμνησιν. ²⁵ὡσαύτως καὶ τὸ ποτήριον μετὰ τὸ δειπνῆσαι λέγων· τοῦτο τὸ ποτήριον ἡ καινὴ διαθήκη ἐστὶν **ἐν τῷ ἐμῷ αἵματι**· τοῦτο ποιεῖτε, ὁσάκις ἐὰν πίνητε, εἰς τὴν ἐμὴν ἀνάμνησιν. ²⁶ὁσάκις γὰρ ἐὰν ἐσθίητε τὸν ἄρτον τοῦτον καὶ τὸ ποτήριον πίνητε, **τὸν θάνατον τοῦ κυρίου** καταγγέλλετε ἄχρι οὗ ἔλθῃ. ²⁷Ὥστε ὃς ἂν ἐσθίῃ τὸν ἄρτον ἢ πίνῃ **τὸ ποτήριον τοῦ κυρίου** ἀναξίως, ἔνοχος ἔσται **τοῦ σώματος καὶ τοῦ αἵματος τοῦ κυρίου.**

[[11:29 ὁ γὰρ ἐσθίων καὶ πίνων κρίμα ἑαυτῷ ἐσθίει καὶ πίνει μὴ διακρίνων τὸ σῶμα. ^[v.l. + τοῦ κυρίου]]]

11:32 κρινόμενοι δὲ ὑπὸ [v.l. + τοῦ] κυρίου παιδευόμεθα, ἵνα μὴ σὺν τῷ κόσμῳ κατακριθῶμεν.

12:3 διὸ γνωρίζω ὑμῖν ὅτι οὐδεὶς ἐν πνεύματι θεοῦ λαλῶν λέγει· Ἀνάθεμα Ἰησοῦς, καὶ οὐδεὶς δύναται εἰπεῖν· Κύριος Ἰησοῦς, εἰ μὴ ἐν πνεύματι ἁγίῳ.

12:4–6 ⁴Διαιρέσεις δὲ χαρισμάτων εἰσίν, τὸ δὲ αὐτὸ πνεῦμα· ⁵καὶ διαιρέσεις διακονιῶν εἰσιν, καὶ ὁ αὐτὸς κύριος· ⁶καὶ διαιρέσεις ἐνεργημάτων εἰσίν, ὁ δὲ αὐτὸς θεὸς ὁ ἐνεργῶν τὰ πάντα ἐν πᾶσιν.

12:12 Καθάπερ γὰρ τὸ σῶμα ἕν ἐστιν καὶ μέλη πολλὰ ἔχει, πάντα δὲ τὰ μέλη τοῦ σώματος πολλὰ ὄντα ἕν ἐστιν σῶμα, οὕτως καὶ ὁ Χριστός·

[[12:18 νυνὶ δὲ ὁ θεὸς ἔθετο τὰ μέλη, ἓν ἕκαστον αὐτῶν ἐν τῷ σώματι καθὼς ἠθέλησεν.]]

[[12:24 τὰ δὲ εὐσχήμονα ἡμῶν οὐ χρείαν ἔχει. ἀλλὰ ὁ θεὸς συνεκέρασεν τὸ σῶμα τῷ ὑστερουμένῳ περισσοτέραν δοὺς τιμήν,]]

12:27–28 ²⁷Ὑμεῖς δέ ἐστε σῶμα Χριστοῦ καὶ μέλη ἐκ μέρους. ²⁸Καὶ οὓς μὲν ἔθετο ὁ θεὸς ἐν τῇ ἐκκλησίᾳ πρῶτον ἀποστόλους, δεύτερον προφήτας, τρίτον διδασκάλους, ἔπειτα δυνάμεις, ἔπειτα χαρίσματα ἰαμάτων, ἀντιλήμψεις, κυβερνήσεις, γένη γλωσσῶν.

[[14:2 ὁ γὰρ λαλῶν γλώσσῃ οὐκ ἀνθρώποις λαλεῖ ἀλλὰ θεῷ· οὐδεὶς γὰρ ἀκούει, πνεύματι δὲ λαλεῖ μυστήρια·]]

[[14:18 εὐχαριστῶ τῷ θεῷ, πάντων ὑμῶν μᾶλλον γλώσσαις λαλῶ·]]

[[[14:21 (LXX) ἐν τῷ νόμῳ γέγραπται ὅτι ἐν ἑτερογλώσσοις καὶ ἐν χείλεσιν ἑτέρων λαλήσω τῷ λαῷ τούτῳ καὶ οὐδ᾽ οὕτως εἰσακούσονταί μου, λέγει κύριος.]]]

[[14:25 τὰ κρυπτὰ τῆς καρδίας αὐτοῦ φανερὰ γίνεται, καὶ οὕτως πεσὼν ἐπὶ πρόσωπον προσκυνήσει τῷ θεῷ ἀπαγγέλλων ὅτι ὄντως ὁ θεὸς ἐν ὑμῖν ἐστιν.]]

[[14:28 ἐὰν δὲ μὴ ᾖ διερμηνευτής, σιγάτω ἐν ἐκκλησίᾳ, ἑαυτῷ δὲ λαλείτω καὶ τῷ θεῷ.]]

[[14:33 οὐ γάρ ἐστιν ἀκαταστασίας ὁ θεὸς ἀλλὰ εἰρήνης, ὡς ἐν πάσαις ταῖς ἐκκλησίαις τῶν ἁγίων.]]

14:36–37 ³⁶ἢ ἀφ᾽ ὑμῶν ὁ λόγος τοῦ θεοῦ ἐξῆλθεν, ἢ εἰς ὑμᾶς μόνους κατήντησεν; ³⁷Εἴ τις δοκεῖ προφήτης εἶναι ἢ πνευματικός, ἐπιγινωσκέτω ἃ γράφω ὑμῖν ὅτι κυρίου ἐστὶν ἐντολή·

15:3–8 ³παρέδωκα γὰρ ὑμῖν ἐν πρώτοις, ὃ καὶ παρέλαβον, ὅτι Χριστὸς ἀπέθανεν ὑπὲρ τῶν ἁμαρτιῶν ἡμῶν κατὰ τὰς γραφὰς ⁴καὶ ὅτι ἐτάφη καὶ ὅτι ἐγήγερται τῇ ἡμέρᾳ τῇ τρίτῃ κατὰ τὰς γραφὰς ⁵καὶ ὅτι ὤφθη Κηφᾷ εἶτα τοῖς δώδεκα· ⁶ἔπειτα ὤφθη ἐπάνω πεντακοσίοις ἀδελφοῖς ἐφάπαξ, ἐξ ὧν οἱ πλείονες μένουσιν ἕως ἄρτι, τινὲς δὲ ἐκοιμήθησαν· ⁷ἔπειτα **ὤφθη** Ἰακώβῳ εἶτα τοῖς ἀποστόλοις πᾶσιν· ⁸ἔσχατον δὲ πάντων ὡσπερεὶ τῷ ἐκτρώματι **ὤφθη** κἀμοί.

[[15:9–10 ⁹Ἐγὼ γάρ εἰμι ὁ ἐλάχιστος τῶν ἀποστόλων ὃς οὐκ εἰμὶ ἱκανὸς καλεῖσθαι ἀπόστολος, διότι ἐδίωξα τὴν <u>ἐκκλησίαν τοῦ θεοῦ</u>· ¹⁰<u>χάριτι δὲ θεοῦ</u> εἰμι ὅ εἰμι, καὶ ἡ <u>χάρις αὐτοῦ</u> ἡ εἰς ἐμὲ οὐ κενὴ ἐγενήθη, ἀλλὰ περισσότερον αὐτῶν πάντων ἐκοπίασα, οὐκ ἐγὼ δὲ ἀλλὰ <u>ἡ χάρις τοῦ θεοῦ</u> [ἡ] σὺν ἐμοί.]]

15:12–19 ¹²Εἰ δὲ **Χριστὸς** κηρύσσεται ὅτι ἐκ νεκρῶν ἐγήγερται, πῶς λέγουσιν ἐν ὑμῖν τινες ὅτι ἀνάστασις νεκρῶν οὐκ ἔστιν; ¹³εἰ δὲ ἀνάστασις νεκρῶν οὐκ ἔστιν, οὐδὲ **Χριστὸς** ἐγήγερται· ¹⁴εἰ δὲ **Χριστὸς** οὐκ ἐγήγερται, κενὸν ἄρα [καὶ] τὸ κήρυγμα ἡμῶν, κενὴ καὶ ἡ πίστις ὑμῶν· ¹⁵εὑρισκόμεθα δὲ καὶ <u>ψευδομάρτυρες τοῦ θεοῦ</u>, ὅτι ἐμαρτυρήσαμεν <u>κατὰ τοῦ θεοῦ</u> ὅτι <u>ἤγειρεν</u> τὸν **Χριστόν**, ὃν οὐκ ἤγειρεν εἴπερ ἄρα νεκροὶ οὐκ ἐγείρονται. ¹⁶εἰ γὰρ νεκροὶ οὐκ ἐγείρονται, **οὐδὲ Χριστὸς** ἐγήγερται· ¹⁷εἰ δὲ **Χριστὸς** οὐκ ἐγήγερται, ματαία ἡ πίστις ὑμῶν, ἔτι ἐστὲ ἐν ταῖς ἁμαρτίαις ὑμῶν, ¹⁸ἄρα καὶ **οἱ κοιμηθέντες ἐν Χριστῷ** ἀπώλοντο. ¹⁹εἰ ἐν τῇ ζωῇ ταύτῃ **ἐν Χριστῷ** ἠλπικότες ἐσμὲν μόνον, ἐλεεινότεροι πάντων ἀνθρώπων ἐσμέν.

15:20–28 ²⁰Νυνὶ δὲ **Χριστὸς** ἐγήγερται ἐκ νεκρῶν **ἀπαρχὴ** τῶν κεκοιμημένων. ²¹ἐπειδὴ γὰρ δι᾽ ἀνθρώπου θάνατος, καὶ **δι᾽ ἀνθρώπου** ἀνάστασις νεκρῶν. ²²ὥσπερ γὰρ ἐν τῷ Ἀδὰμ πάντες ἀποθνήσκουσιν, οὕτως καὶ **ἐν τῷ Χριστῷ** πάντες ζῳοποιηθήσονται. ²³Ἕκαστος δὲ ἐν τῷ ἰδίῳ τάγματι· **ἀπαρχὴ Χριστός**, ἔπειτα **οἱ τοῦ Χριστοῦ ἐν τῇ παρουσίᾳ αὐτοῦ**, ²⁴εἶτα τὸ τέλος, ὅταν **παραδιδῷ** τὴν βασιλείαν <u>τῷ θεῷ καὶ πατρί</u>, ὅταν καταργήσῃ πᾶσαν ἀρχὴν καὶ πᾶσαν ἐξουσίαν καὶ δύναμιν. ²⁵δεῖ γὰρ αὐτὸν βασιλεύειν ἄχρι οὗ θῇ πάντας τοὺς ἐχθροὺς **ὑπὸ τοὺς πόδας αὐτοῦ**. ²⁶ἔσχατος ἐχθρὸς καταργεῖται ὁ θάνατος· ²⁷πάντα γὰρ ὑπέταξεν **ὑπὸ τοὺς πόδας αὐτοῦ**. ὅταν δὲ εἴπῃ ὅτι πάντα ὑποτέτακται, δῆλον ὅτι ἐκτὸς τοῦ ὑποτάξαντος αὐτῷ τὰ πάντα. ²⁸ὅταν δὲ **ὑποταγῇ αὐτῷ** τὰ πάντα, τότε [καὶ] **αὐτὸς ὁ υἱὸς** ὑποταγήσεται τῷ ὑποτάξαντι <u>αὐτῷ</u> τὰ πάντα, ἵνα ᾖ <u>ὁ θεὸς</u> [τὰ] πάντα ἐν πᾶσιν.

15:31 καθ᾽ ἡμέραν ἀποθνήσκω, νὴ τὴν ὑμετέραν καύχησιν, ἣν ἔχω **ἐν Χριστῷ Ἰησοῦ τῷ κυρίῳ ἡμῶν**.

[[15:34 ἐκνήψατε δικαίως καὶ μὴ ἁμαρτάνετε, <u>ἀγνωσίαν γὰρ θεοῦ τινες ἔχουσιν</u>, πρὸς ἐντροπὴν ὑμῖν λαλῶ.]]

[[15:38 <u>ὁ δὲ θεὸς</u> δίδωσιν αὐτῷ σῶμα καθὼς ἠθέλησεν, καὶ ἑκάστῳ τῶν σπερμάτων ἴδιον σῶμα.]]

15:45–49 ⁴⁵οὕτως καὶ γέγραπται· ἐγένετο ὁ πρῶτος ἄνθρωπος Ἀδὰμ εἰς ψυχὴν ζῶσαν, **ὁ ἔσχατος Ἀδὰμ εἰς πνεῦμα ζῳοποιοῦν**. ⁴⁶ἀλλ᾽ οὐ πρῶτον τὸ πνευματικὸν ἀλλὰ τὸ ψυχικόν, ἔπειτα τὸ πνευματικόν. ⁴⁷ὁ πρῶτος

ἄνθρωπος ἐκ γῆς χοϊκός, ὁ δεύτερος ἄνθρωπος [v.l. ὁ κύριος] ἐξ οὐρανοῦ.
⁴⁸οἷος ὁ χοϊκός, τοιοῦτοι καὶ οἱ χοϊκοί, καὶ οἷος ὁ ἐπουράνιος, τοιοῦτοι καὶ
οἱ ἐπουράνιοι· ⁴⁹καὶ καθὼς ἐφορέσαμεν τὴν εἰκόνα τοῦ χοϊκοῦ, φορέσομεν
καὶ **τὴν εἰκόνα τοῦ ἐπουρανίου**.

[[15:50 Τοῦτο δέ φημι, ἀδελφοί, ὅτι σὰρξ καὶ αἷμα βασιλείαν θεοῦ
κληρονομῆσαι οὐ δύναται οὐδὲ ἡ φθορὰ τὴν ἀφθαρσίαν κληρονομεῖ.]]

15:57–58 ⁵⁷τῷ δὲ θεῷ χάρις τῷ διδόντι ἡμῖν τὸ νῖκος **διὰ τοῦ κυρίου ἡμῶν
Ἰησοῦ Χριστοῦ.** ⁵⁸″Ωστε, ἀδελφοί μου ἀγαπητοί, ἑδραῖοι γίνεσθε,
ἀμετακίνητοι, περισσεύοντες **ἐν τῷ ἔργῳ τοῦ κυρίου** πάντοτε, εἰδότες ὅτι
ὁ κόπος ὑμῶν οὐκ ἔστιν κενὸς **ἐν κυρίῳ**.

16:7 οὐ θέλω γὰρ ὑμᾶς ἄρτι ἐν παρόδῳ ἰδεῖν, ἐλπίζω γὰρ χρόνον τινὰ
ἐπιμεῖναι πρὸς ὑμᾶς **ἐὰν ὁ κύριος ἐπιτρέψῃ**.

16:10 Ἐὰν δὲ ἔλθῃ Τιμόθεος, βλέπετε, ἵνα ἀφόβως γένηται πρὸς ὑμᾶς· **τὸ
γὰρ ἔργον κυρίου** ἐργάζεται ὡς κἀγώ·

16:19 Ἀσπάζονται ὑμᾶς αἱ ἐκκλησίαι τῆς Ἀσίας. ἀσπάζεται ὑμᾶς **ἐν κυρίῳ**
πολλὰ Ἀκύλας καὶ Πρίσκα σὺν τῇ κατ᾽ οἶκον αὐτῶν ἐκκλησίᾳ.

16:22–24 ²²εἴ τις οὐ φιλεῖ **τὸν κύριον**, ἤτω ἀνάθεμα. **μαράνα θά.** ²³ἡ **χάρις
τοῦ κυρίου Ἰησοῦ** μεθ᾽ ὑμῶν. ²⁴ἡ ἀγάπη μου μετὰ πάντων ὑμῶν **ἐν Χριστῷ
Ἰησοῦ.**

Appendix II: An Analysis of Usage

(* = anarthrous; + = with possessive pronoun; [LXX] = Septuagint echo/
citation)

1 Corinthians

θεός	103 + 2 κύριος LXX
	citations
Christ	121

The Data

1. κύριος Ἰησοῦς Χριστός (8)
   - 1:2   G+
   - 1:3   G*
   - 1:7   G+
   - 1:8   G+ [v.l.-Χριστοῦ]
   - 1:10   G+
   - 6:11   G
   - 8:6   N
   - 15:57 G+ (διά)

1a. Ἰησοῦς Χριστὸς κύριος (1)
   - 1:9   G (appositive to υἱός)

1b. Χριστὸς Ἰησοῦς κύριος (1)
   - 15:31 D + (ἐν)

2. κύριος Ἰησοῦς (4)
   - 5:4   G+ [v.l. + Χριστοῦ]
   - 5:4   G+ [v.l. + Χριστοῦ]
   - 11:23 N
   - 16:23 G [v.l. + Χριστοῦ]

2a. Ἰησοῦς . . . κύριος (1)
   - 9:1   A+

3. Χριστὸς Ἰησοῦς (6)
   - 1:1   G*
   - 1:2   D* (ἐν)
   - 1:4   D* (ἐν)

1:30   D* (ἐν)
4:15   D* (ἐν)
16:24   D* (ἐν)
3a. Ἰησοῦς Χριστός (2)
2:2   A*
3:11   N*
4. κύριος (49 + 15 = 64
            [+ 2 = God])
1:31   D* (ἐν) [LXX]
2:8   A
2:16   G* [LXX]
3:5   N
[3:20   N* LXX = God]
4:4   PredN* [Colwell's Rule]
4:5   N
4:17   D* (ἐν)
4:19   N
5:5   G [v.l. + Ἰησοῦ]
6:13   D
6:13   N
6:14   A
6:17   D
7:10   N
7:12   N
7:17   N
7:22   D* (ἐν)
7:22   G*
7:25   G*
7:25   G* (ὑπό)
7:32   G
7:32   D
7:34   G
7:35   D
7:39   D* (ἐν)
9:1   D* (ἐν)
9:2   D* (ἐν)
9:5   G
9:14   N
10:21   G*
10:21   G*
10:22   A
10:26   G [LXX]
11:11   D*
        (11:20 κυριακόν)

11:23   G (ἀπό)
11:26   G
11:27   G
11:27   G
11:32   G* [v.l. + τοῦ] (ὑπό)
12:5   N
[14:21 N* LXX = God]
14:37   G*
15:58   G
15:58   D* (ἐν)
16:7   N
16:10   G*
16:19   D* (ἐν)
5. Ἰησοῦς (2 + 24 = 26)
12:3   N*
12:3   PredN*
6. Χριστὸς (45 + 18 = 63)
1:6   G
1:12   G*
1:13   N
1:17   N*
1:17   G
1:23   A*
1:24   A*
2:16   G*
3:1   D* (ἐν)
3:23   G*
3:23   N*
4:1   G*
4:10   A* (διά)
4:10   D* (ἐν)
4:15   D* (ἐν)
5:7   N*
6:15   G*
6:15   G
7:22   G*
8:11   N*
8:12   A* (εἰς)
9:12   G
9:21   G*
10:4   PredN
10:9   A [v.l. κύριον]
10:16   G
10:16   G

11:1	G*
11:3	N
11:3	G
12:12	N
12:27	G*
15:3	N*
15:12	N*
15:13	N*
15:14	N*
15:15	A
15:16	N*
15:17	N*
15:18	D* (ἐν)
15:19	D* (ἐν)

15:20 N*
15:22 D (ἐν)
15:23 N*
15:23 G

7. υἱός (2)

1:9 G (w/ appositive Ἰησοῦς Χριστὸς κύριος)

15:28 N

8. Others

15:45 ὁ ἔσχατος Ἀδάμ
15:47 ὁ δεύτερος ἄνθρωπος
[v.l. ὁ κύριος]
16:22 μαράνα

4

Christology in 2 Corinthians

PAUL'S SECOND CANONICAL LETTER TO the believers in Corinth has much less christological data than does 1 Corinthians.[1] The reason for this is basically twofold: first, it is by far the most personal of all his letters, dealing primarily with defense and/or explanations of his most recent relations with them;[2] second, it is for this reason ad hoc at the very highest level,[3] which makes interpretation always a bit tenuous. Thus, while the personal nature of the letter tends to call for fewer references to Christ, Paul nonetheless tends to bring Christ into the picture simply because that is who Paul is; and since he can hardly speak about himself without speaking of Christ, we get presuppositional christological moments of all kinds and in many ways. The net result is that looking at the Christology of 2 Corinthians after that of 1 Corinthians is at some points like moving onto new ground.[4]

To begin with, 2 Corinthians has a more theocentric feel to it than do the earlier three letters, evidenced in part by the fact that God is mentioned more often than Christ. The letter itself begins on a theocentric note, blessing the God who is the Father of our Lord Jesus Christ and then concentrat-

---

[1]Commentaries on 2 Corinthians are listed in the bibliography (pp. 640–41); they are cited in this chapter by author's surname only.

[2]By way of contrast, 1 Corinthians focuses primarily on the Corinthian believers themselves, especially on the many behavioral/ethical matters that need serious attention, and apart from ch. 9 very little on Paul himself.

[3]It is a simple reality of life that the more a writer and recipient are on the same page with regard to shared experiences, the less the writer needs to inform the recipient about the known details. Since 2 Corinthians has so much of this kind of content, interpreters are basically left on the outside listening in on one side of a very intense conversation. Hence we are also left with a great deal more scholarly guesswork than in, for example, Galatians or Romans. See G. D. Fee and D. Stuart, *How to Read the Bible for All Its Worth* (3d ed.; Grand Rapids: Zondervan, 2002), 56–59.

[4]Indeed, there are so many items that would be considered "contradictory" if they appeared in, for example, Colossians or 2 Thessalonians that they would be proposed as further evidence for Paul's not having written those letters. The fact that many of the same kinds of alleged inconsistencies and linguistic differences exist between 1 and 2 Corinthians as between Colossians and the rest of the corpus reveals how much subjectivity goes into decisions about authenticity.

ing on God's mercies that spared Paul from what appeared to be certain death. This emphasis is then found at several places throughout, even in the great soteriological moment in 5:18–6:2 and its following catalogue of Paul's ministry and hardships (6:3–10). So while the emphasis on Christ that we have seen in 1–2 Thessalonians and 1 Corinthians continues to some degree, it is here much more noticeably placed within the larger context of God's purposes and will than before.

Furthermore, after the high level of intertextual use of the Septuagint in the earlier three letters, where κύριος = Yahweh has been taken over and applied to Christ, in this chapter on 2 Corinthians such a heading does not appear at all. What does carry over are the many Septuagint phrases of this kind,[5] plus some new ones, that have obviously become a part of Paul's theological vocabulary when speaking of Christ.

Nonetheless, despite these noticeable differences, 2 Corinthians has its own significant christological moments that add to the full-orbed picture, especially 8:9 and 3:16–4:6. And what does emerge reflects something of the same undercurrent of christological crisis that marked much of 1 Corinthians, where the significance of the person of Christ is tending to be diminished in some way. Here in particular Paul now spells out what it means for Christ to be the true bearer of the divine image and thus to reflect the divine glory. And as before, it is in t   and Son that one sees Pauline Christology   letter. At the same time, Paul continues to s   he has done in the three earlier letters. His primary interest in Christ continues to be the same: soteriological. What God has done in Christ is always Paul's primary theological focus. Thus the relational aspect of Christian life continues to focus on one's relationship with Christ, in ever so many ways and kinds of contexts.

As with previous chapters, the present chapter proceeds in a basically thematic way, beginning with one of the more significant christological moments in the corpus (8:9) and then branching out to a variety of other kinds of christological phenomena that appear in the letter. Items that have appeared in the earlier letters are simply listed and cross-referenced toward the end.

A Preliminary Look at the Data

The various references to Christ and to God are found in appendix I at the end of this chapter; likewise, an analysis of the different ways of referring to Christ is found in appendix II. In comparison with the first three letters, two matters stand out. First, for the second time[6] references to God (θεός) outnumber references to Christ (78x to 75x), including Χριστός

---

[5] See the discussion on 2 Cor 3:16–18; 8:21.
[6] Cf. 1 Thessalonians (see n. 12 in ch. 2).

(*Christ*), κύριος (*Lord*), Ἰησοῦς (*Jesus*), and υἱός (*Son*) in all of their various combinations. This stands in some contrast to 1 Corinthians, where Christ is mentioned by name 18 times more than God the Father (121x to 103x). Second, the most striking feature regarding references to Christ is the predominance of the title/name Χριστός (47x) in comparison with κύριος (26x)[7] and Ἰησοῦς (19x), including the number of times each occurs alone (Χριστός, 38x; κύριος, 18x; Ἰησοῦς, 7x). In fact, this begins a pattern that carries through the rest of the extant letters to churches (including Philemon).

With regard to the specific names/titles, the sudden high incidence of the name Ἰησοῦς in ch. 4 is easily explained by the subject matter: Paul is contemplating his sufferings in light of those of the earthly Jesus (Paul has Jesus' death in view, to be sure, but the focus is on Jesus' sufferings, not redemption brought about by his death). What is less clear is the reason for the sudden high incidence of the use of Χριστός as the primary "name" in this letter. But that is indeed what has happened, and it will continue so in the rest of the corpus.[8]

Christ: Preexistent and Incarnate Redeemer

As often happens in his letters, some of Paul's most profound christological moments appear in places where one might least expect them—further evidence that his Christology lies deeply rooted as presuppositional to his understanding of Christ and is not something that needed proof or explication. This was true of his first mention of Christ's preexistence in 1 Cor 8:6; it finds expression in this letter in a plea for the Corinthians to follow through on an unfulfilled promise of giving to the poor. At the same time, the "heavenly redeemer" lived a truly human life, yet without sin; and even if Paul does not speak of it often, a further moment in this letter reminds the Corinthians that Paul's own "weaknesses" are in keeping with the character of the earthly Jesus.

2 Corinthians 8:9—Incarnation as Paradigm for Giving to the Poor

In this thoroughly metaphorical passage, in which one wordplay follows another, Paul is exhorting the Corinthians toward selfless giving for the sake of the (literally) poor in Jerusalem.[9] He begins by telling the story of Mace-

---

[7] This does not include the two occurrences of κύριος in the λέγει κύριος formula taken over from citations of the Septuagint in 6:17–18. On this matter, see n. 7 in ch. 3.

[8] From here on, except for the clear instance in Rom 9:5, "Christ" seems to have become the Lord's *name;* but see the considerable argument by N. T. Wright on Phlm 6 suggesting otherwise (*The Climax of the Covenant: Christ and the Law in Pauline Theology* [Minneapolis: Fortress, 1992], 41–55).

[9] We actually learn this in a later letter (Rom 15:25–32).

donia: how they (also literally poor) have exemplified especially selfless generosity. To score this point in the strongest possible way, he concludes by reminding them of the basic story of Christ, doing so with metaphor and wordplay that are intended to remind the Corinthians that their very lives are totally dependent on the kind of "grace" similar to that in which he wishes them to engage. The text reads,

8:9 γινώσκετε γὰρ **τὴν χάριν**	τοῦ κυρίου ἡμῶν Ἰησοῦ Χριστοῦ,		
1. (a)	ὅτι	δι' ὑμᾶς	**ἐπτώχευσεν**
(b)			**πλούσιος ὢν**,
2. (a)	ἵνα	ὑμεῖς	**τῇ ἐκείνου πτωχείᾳ**
(b)			**πλουτήσητε.**
For you know	*"the grace"*	*of our Lord,*	*Jesus Christ,*
	that	*for you*	*he became "poor"*
			being "rich,"
	so that	*you*	*by his "poverty"*
			might become "rich."

Several christological observations are in order. First, it needs to be repeated that this is metaphor, expressive and powerful metaphor, that appears suddenly and without explanation either before or after. Thus the power lies in the metaphor itself. To argue that this is literal[10] in some way is to remove both the power and the poetry of this sentence. The same is true of an interpretation that does not presuppose preexistence.[11]

Second, Paul reminds them that what follows is something they "know." Whether this relates to the actual metaphor itself may be questionable; but at the least it has the incarnation as its referent. This is a theological point on which he and they are agreed; and we noted in the preceding chapter that their common understanding of Christ as preexistent lay behind some of Paul's argumentation in 1 Cor 8 and 10.

Third, the word "grace" appears here as a considerable wordplay. In the immediately preceding sentences this has been Paul's language to refer to the Macedonians' own giving for the poor. This is the "grace" that God has given them (v. 1), spelled out in vv. 2–5 as an overflow of their joy in Christ that demonstrated itself in "giving as much as they were able, and even beyond their ability." And this is the "grace" that in v. 6 Paul now urges on the

---

[10] As does G. W. Buchanan, "Jesus and the Upper Class," *NovT* 7 (1964): 195–209. Cf. Furnish's comment that Buchanan—"contrary to his own intention—succeeds in showing only how futile it is to argue for a literal interpretation" (417). Nonetheless, one finds a more literal approach to this text scattered throughout the literature; note, e.g., Hunter: "His earthly lot was that of a poor man (II Cor. 8.9)" (*Gospel according to Paul*, 59), which mixes this metaphor with the known reality of his earthly life.

[11] As, e.g., J. D. G. Dunn, *Christology in the Making: A New Testament Inquiry into the Origins of the Doctrine of the Incarnation* (2d ed.; Grand Rapids: Eerdmans, 1989), 121–23. See n. 13 below.

Corinthians, as a matter of bringing to completion something already begun. Indeed, he wants them to excel in "this grace," just as they have in other Christian virtues (v. 7).

So when Paul uses this word as his introduction to the "Christ story," this continues to be its first meaning. What "our Lord Jesus Christ" exemplified in his incarnation was the kind of "grace" of giving for the sake of the "poor" already noted among the Macedonians; but in this case, of course, the "poor" were the Corinthians,[12] who had been impoverished by the wretchedness of sin. At the same time, since the Corinthians know the story well, it is hard to imagine they will not also have heard the second level of meaning—Paul's more predominantly theological one—that God's grace toward the (sinful) needy was played out to the full in Christ's ultimate "impoverishment" on our behalf: death on the cross.

Thus it was through Christ's "impoverishment" that the Corinthians have become "rich"—not wealthy in worldly goods but wealthy as those redeemed from their former pagan idolatries and thus fitted for life eternal. Their true wealth came by way of the great reversal: the truly "rich" one becomes "poor" so that the truly "poor" ones might become "rich."

Third, the crucial christological point lies in the first (b) line, that it was the one who in his *preredemptive existence* was "rich" who became "poor." The modifying participial phrase with which the first clause concludes has "rich" as its predicate adjective (= "being rich"), thus creating a metaphor that expresses the glory inherent in Christ's preexistent state. The main verb then expresses the enormity of his grace: for your sakes he "became poor"— from the "richness" of eternity to the "impoverishment" of our humanity. The reason for this "impoverishment" is redemptive, to elevate us to his "richness." The power of the metaphor, as a way of expressing Christ's grace, lies precisely in the presupposition of preexistence and incarnation, which at the same time implies choice on the part of the preexistent One. It is difficult to imagine how such a metaphor could ever have come to mind if Paul had been speaking about one who had merely human beginnings.

In fact, however, it sometimes has been argued that this metaphor does not require us to think in terms of personal preexistence, that this metaphor would work for one who thought of Christ's earthly life as having only normal human beginnings.[13] But that is to read texts in isolation from one an-

---

[12] Note the emphatic positioning of the δι᾽ ὑμᾶς (*for your sakes*) and ὑμεῖς (*you*) in the two (a) lines: "how that for *your* sakes he became poor," "so that *you* by his poverty."

[13] Dunn (*Christology in the Making*, 121–23) begins the discussion by showing that the various parts of the sentence do not necessarily require the assumption of preexistence, always asking whether the Corinthians themselves would have assumed as much (see ch. 3, pp. 102–5 above for his view that 1 Cor 8:6 should be read as having to do not with Christ but with Wisdom!). He then offers that what more likely lies behind the metaphor is Jesus as the second Adam, who "was rich" in a way far beyond the first Adam but became "poor" in his suffering and death.

other; after all, the author of this text also wrote 1 Cor 8:6, insisting that "the one Lord, namely, Jesus Christ," is also the one "through whom all things" were created. And he is the same author of the later Phil 2:6–8, which tells this same story but with more detail. Granted that one must always use caution when looking at one passage in light of another; granted further that if we did not have these other texts, this passage, given its metaphorical nature, could be read in a way that does not necessarily lead to a view of personal preexistence. Nevertheless, the plain sense of the metaphor in this case carries all the freight in a *presuppositional* way of the normal sense of the language and theology of Phil 2:6–7.

2 Corinthians 5:21—He Who Knew No Sin

As Paul moves toward the conclusion of a long digression in which he has explained, and thus defended, his apostleship, including especially his physical weaknesses, he also moves toward an appeal for reconciliation between himself and them (5:18–21). But he does so, typically, by putting it into the context of the larger work of reconciliation that Christ has effected for the sake of the world.[14] I will discuss this whole passage at greater length in the section "Christ Devotion and Soteriology—2 Corinthians 5:14–6:2"; for now, we need especially to note that Paul understood Christ in his incarnation to be sinless.

Verse 21 serves as the wrap-up to this part of the long digression. What is striking is how apparently unrelated to the preceding sentences it seems to be. That is, Paul's concern from v. 14 has been with the radical new thing that Christ has effected in the world, bringing about God's "new creation." The reason for pressing this so hard on the Corinthians is that their present

_____

Although this view has rightly been found wanting by those who have written on this passage (e.g., Furnish, 417; Betz, 62; Martin, 263; Thrall, 533; Barnett, 407; Lambrecht, 137; Matera, 191; idem, *New Testament Christology*, 95), Dunn continues to maintain it in *Theology of Paul*, 290–92. One can only wonder how the Corinthians could have been party to such an oblique metaphorical referent as "rich" and "poor" having to do with Adam before and after the fall, since the only reference to Adam in 1 Corinthians has to do with his leading humanity into death (15:21–22) and thus having a body subject to decay in contrast to Christ's risen and glorified body (15:44–49).

[14]Because there is nothing else quite like this passage in the corpus, some have argued that Paul is here using "pre-Pauline" material; and often this claim is accompanied by the assumption that it is therefore somehow "non-Pauline." For a helpful overview of this discussion, see excursus VII in Thrall, 445–49; she rightly, though tentatively, rejects the theory as "by no means compelling." The point that needs to be made again (see, in the present volume, n. 27 in ch. 2) is that even if Paul was using prior material, it sits in its present context in Pauline sentences, dictated by him and aimed directly at the present tension between him and the Corinthians. The basic historical presupposition that should prevail in such moments is that what Paul wrote (even though by dictation), Paul himself believed and made his own; and therefore these sentences are as Pauline as anything else one finds in his letters.

view of him, he argues, has altogether to do with viewing things from an "old creation" point of view—that is, "from the perspective of the flesh." But this is no longer an option. Christ's death and resurrection have radicalized everything, so that viewing Paul's weaknesses from the "old age" point of view misses the point of everything that Christ has done for us and the world. The old has gone; the new has come (v. 17).

It is in this context that Paul brings in his own ministry as one of reconciliation, which in vv. 18–19 he describes in terms of the ministry that God has given to him; but in v. 20 he suddenly applies it directly to them: "We implore you on Christ's behalf: be reconciled to God." In context this means something like, "Accept God's way of doing things, and stop trying to remake the gospel to fit your own 'this-worldly' point of view"; and very near the surface lies an appeal to be reconciled to Paul as well.

The point is that Paul could easily have moved on to what he says in 6:1 and no one would have missed a thing in the argument itself. But he is never quite able to do things that way. What is crucial for him in this appeal is that the Corinthians recognize the enormity of the work of Christ that effected our reconciliation.[15] Thus, with a typical, very tight two-liner, with its very sharp contrasts (much like 8:9 above),[16] he sets forth the work of Christ in terms of the great exchange: the "sinless one" becomes "sin" for us so that we (the sinful ones) might in him (the sinless One) become the righteousness of God. Thus:

5:21 (a)   **τὸν μὴ γνόντα**   ἁμαρτίαν
     (b)   ὑπὲρ ἡμῶν   ἁμαρτίαν ἐποίησεν,
     (b')   ἵνα ἡμεῖς γενώμεθα   δικαιοσύνη θεοῦ
     (a') **ἐν αὐτῷ.**

      The one not knowing   sin
          for us   sin   [God] made,
          that we might become   the righteousness of God
      in him.

The very tightness of this kind of contrast has Paul saying things in a way that has led others to spill a great deal of ink over this passage, to give it a precision that removes some of our discomfort with what is said.[17] Our present concern is simply to note that the sinlessness of Christ in his incar-

---

[15] Or, in Barrett's words, "Paul has not yet explained to his own satisfaction how Christ crucified constitutes a message of reconciliation" (179).

[16] On this, see Barnett (407 n. 15), who sets out the two passages side by side.

[17] The ink has been spilled primarily over the two (b) lines, whose laconic nature has led to great concern as to what it means for God to "have made Christ [to become] sin" and us to "become the righteousness of God." I do not mean to take this debate casually—getting it right theologically is important, after all—but Paul's point seems clear without need of greater precision: Christ as the sinless One offered the "unblemished sacrifice" for our sins that we might be given righteousness and thus reconciled with God.

nation is here asserted as a nonnegotiable presupposition. That it is the earthly Jesus whom Paul had in view seems certain not only from the context but also from the typically Jewish way of putting it: Christ "knew no sin." This is the "knowing" that comes from experience, not from mental activity,[18] the kind of "knowing evil" that Adam and Eve experienced that led to human fallenness. It was the fact that Christ did not "know sin" in this way that made it possible for him to be offered as the perfect sacrifice on behalf of others.

Thus, at this point Paul joins the author of Hebrews (4:15) to express what was apparently the common point of view among the earliest Christians about the earthly life of Jesus: he was without sin.[19] These kinds of moments also disclose that Paul knew much more about that earthly life than many tend to believe; he simply did not have occasion often to make a point of it. But the next passage does in fact seem also to point in this direction.

2 Corinthians 10:1—Jesus' Attitudes as a Basis for Appeal

Although it is true that Paul rarely refers to Jesus' earthly life apart from the context of his death and resurrection, there are a few notable exceptions, this passage being one of them.[20] At the outset of what turns out to be an especially strong—to the point of being sarcastic—defense of his previous actions as an apostle, Paul begins by appealing to two qualities of Christ that seem to be the opposite of what is actually put on display in the argumentation that follows. That leads us to suspect, then, that these were the very kinds of things denounced in Corinth, as suggested by Paul's repeated references to his weaknesses as an apostle.

This is one of the issues that gives clear continuity between the two canonical letters to Corinth, as is made plain by Paul's strong defense in

---

[18] So most commentators. Thus it is unlikely that the similar phrase in Rom 3:20 and 7:7 has the same meaning as here (*pace* Bultmann, 164–65; Furnish, 339). In the two Romans passages, the law has caused people to become conscious of their sin as sin; here Paul is dealing with a different kind of "knowing" that comes by experience.

[19] This reality was anticipated regarding the Suffering Servant in Isa 53:9 ("though he had done no lawless deed [ἀνομία], nor was any deceit in his mouth"); according to *Pss. Sol.* 17:40–41; *T. Jud.* 24:1; *T. Levi* 18:9, this in turn became expected of the Messiah.

[20] At least this seems to be the most natural reading of the text (so Windisch, 292; Barrett, 246–47; Barnett, 459–60; Lambrecht, 153; Matera, 221–22; cf. G. N. Stanton, *Jesus of Nazareth in New Testament Preaching* [SNTSMS 27; Cambridge: Cambridge University Press, 1974], 198; Dunn, *Theology of Paul*, 193–94). Others have suggested that this is related to his preexistent humility in accepting the weakness of incarnation (see Bultmann, 182; Furnish, 460; Thrall, 600; see also Martin [302], who would have it both ways)—a view that arose from a much too skeptical approach to Paul's knowing anything about the historical Jesus. After all, Paul predicates his own ethical stance on his "imitating Christ" (1 Cor 11:1), and in doing so it is unlikely that he had the attitude of the preexistent Christ in view.

1 Cor 4, especially vv. 8–13.[21] In this second letter it is picked up regularly—beginning with 2:14 and then again in 4:7–12 and 6:3–10—and serves as the main piece of the argument against his opponents in chs. 10–13. At the outset of this final argument, Paul rests his appeal on the known character of Jesus himself.

Paul has been accused of being "weak" when present with them but "forceful" in his letters (v. 10). As he sets out to defend himself on this matter, he begins with something of a rhetorical coup: he makes his appeal on the basis of τῆς πραΰτητος καὶ ἐπιεικείας τοῦ Χριστοῦ (the meekness and gentleness of Christ). While these words could refer to Christ before his accusers in the Gospel crucifixion narratives, it is equally possible that Paul is reflecting the language of Jesus recorded in Matt 11:29:[22] "Learn of me, for I am πραΰς καὶ ταπεινὸς ἐν καρδίᾳ [gentle and humble in heart]." One might think so in part because these latter two words appear together in the virtue list of Col 3:12 and one (πραΰς) occurs among the fruit of the Spirit in Gal 5:23, and Paul insists elsewhere that he is an imitator of Christ (1 Cor 11:1).

In either case (and the latter seems more likely), Paul is appealing to what is known about the earthly Jesus as the foundation from which he himself will speak. In contrast to the strong language of his letters, Paul apparently has appeared "meek and gentle" while in Corinth. Here he is basing his own attitudes on what is known by both him and the church about the earthly Jesus. This kind of passing moment in his letters should be a constant reminder that Paul was no docetist; rather, the now reigning Christ lived a truly human life on this planet before his death and resurrection, and Paul from time to time is ready to appeal to that life.

Jesus Christ, the Son of God

A second point of correlation between 1 and 2 Corinthians is the appearance of a Son of God Christology. But in contrast to the preceding letters, God is here explicitly referred to as "the Father of our Lord Jesus Christ" (1:3; 11:31), and Christ in turn is explicitly called "the Son of God" (1:19), although this title is presupposed in the phrase "his Son" in 1 Thess 1:10; 1 Cor 1:9; 15:28. We begin this section, then, by examining these two texts (1:3, 19)

---

[21] See also 1 Cor 2:1–5; 15:8–11; the very fact that Paul raises this issue at points of contention with the Corinthians suggests that they had something of a triumphalist view of present Christian life that Paul failed to exemplify.

[22] The authenticity of this pericope (Matt 11:28–30) is often called into doubt because, while the preceding materials in vv. 25–27 have Q parallels in Luke, the rest of the passage is unique to Matthew. But that has the appearance of being overly skeptical. The present passage suggests that such an understanding of Christ was already a part of the church's tradition, being known by both Paul and the Corinthians, whether they knew the actual saying or not.

in turn, before turning to the very important christological passage in 4:4–6, where the title "Son of God" is presupposed, though not explicitly expressed.

2 Corinthians 1:3–5; 11:31—God as the Father of Our Lord Jesus Christ

In a remarkable departure from the thanksgiving that begins each of the first three letters—which in 1–2 Thessalonians also evolved into prayer— this letter begins with an expression of praise to God, in a Christianized form of the Jewish *berakah* ("blessing of God"), which Paul, from a young age, would have known in the Jewish synagogue.[23] This striking moment is another reflection of the differences between the two Corinthian letters. In the first letter the focus is on the Corinthians and their obvious need for change; hence the thanksgiving anticipates some of the very things that have gone astray in Corinth, good things that have gone sour. But here the focus is on Paul himself and his own relationship with them. The first thing up, then, is not thanksgiving and prayer but praise of God for his mercies and accompanying comfort.

But as is typical for Paul, he can scarcely mention God without including "our Lord Jesus Christ"; how he has done so in this case, however, has sometimes been seen as problematic with regard to the person of Christ and his relationship to God the Father. The text reads,

1:3   Εὐλογητὸς ὁ θεὸς καὶ πατὴρ **τοῦ κυρίου ἡμῶν Ἰησοῦ Χριστοῦ,**
    ὁ πατὴρ τῶν οἰκτιρμῶν καὶ θεὸς πάσης παρακλήσεως,

Blessed (be)[24] *the God and Father **of our Lord Jesus Christ,**
the Father of mercies and God of all comfort.*

At issue is how we are to understand the relationship of Christ to the name and title "God and Father." The problem is not with God's being "the *Father* of our Lord Jesus Christ"—that relationship has been set forth as presupposed from the very beginning (see discussion on 1 Thess 1:10 in ch. 2)— but with the possibility that it could be read that the Father is also "the *God* of our Lord Jesus Christ."[25] In the latter case one might be tempted to see this as a unique construction that came into existence for the chiastic effect of the whole phrase: (a) God and (b) Father . . . (b′) the Father of mercies and (a′) God of all comfort. But since this expression occurs again in 11:31 and in the similar *berakah* in Eph 1:3, it seems much more likely that the inclusion of the phrase "of our Lord Jesus Christ" is intended even in this first

---

[23] Even though these prayers in their contemporary synagogue form probably represent a later expression, Paul himself serves as evidence for their essential antiquity.

[24] There is no verb expressed in the sentence; at issue, therefore, is whether this is a call for praise ("May God be blessed") or an exclamation of praise (as I have rendered it).

[25] Especially so in light of Eph 1:17.

instance to give a christological identification of God the Father, unto whom Paul offers praise.[26]

That is, given what follows, where the focus is altogether on God the Father, the christological phrase that appears between the two names and their elaboration most likely occurs for two reasons: because (1) it is now Paul's habit to include Father and Son in the salutations of his letters and this "blessing" serves that function in this letter; and (2) this phrase is needed precisely to give a christological definition of the God whom Paul, the former worshiper in the synagogue, now, as a follower of the risen Christ, blesses. This is yet another instance where, akin to Midas of mythology, everything Paul's "hand" touches turns to gospel and reflects his utter devotion to Christ.

If these suggestions come close to the reasons for this (otherwise unnecessary)[27] prepositional phrase, then the phrase "God and Father" is not to be understood as a compound name (as in "Lord and Savior") of him who serves as the object of praise. Rather, given the way the *berakah* finally plays out, we are to understand the καί not as conjunctive but as ascensive, intended to give Christian definition to the God to whom Paul is now offering praise. Thus it means something like "blessed be God, even the Father of our Lord Jesus Christ."[28] That is, the God who is blessed in a variety of ways in the Jewish synagogue is now to be blessed as the God who is singularly known through revelation as "the Father of our Lord Jesus Christ," who is also known to us as "the Son of God," which is precisely what is picked up by Paul in v. 18, in the explanation of his changed itinerary with which the letter proper begins.

Thus, rather than being a moment to which one can point as evidence either of a diminished Christology or of an eternal subordination of the Son to the Father, this phrase turns out to be a significant christological moment in the letter, not to mention in the entire corpus. Here Paul appears to set

---

[26] Such an understanding seems all the more certain in light of Col 1:3, where the καί (*and*) is missing.

[27] "Unnecessary" in the sense that in what follows all the focus is on God; thus one might well have expected "Blessed be our God and Father, the Father of mercies and the God of all comfort." But this is Paul, after all, and as we have noted in earlier chapters (see discussion on 1 Thess 1:1, 10; 1 Cor 8:6), after Paul's encounter with the risen Lord, the God whom he knew as a boy and as a young man he had now come to know especially as "the Father of our Lord Jesus Christ."

[28] Or "blessed be the God whom we now know as the Father of our Lord Jesus Christ." This is the view held by most interpreters; as Barrett puts it, "Paul shows no interest in the personal religion of Jesus" (58). Thrall, however, prefers on grammatical grounds the possibility that Paul might be trying to "avoid any implication that Christ, as κύριος, is some kind of independent deity" (102). But that seems overly sensitive to how something "should have been written" and thus also to miss the fact that this letter is the fourth (or third) in a series between Paul and the Corinthians; and there is in fact nothing in either of the two canonical letters that would suggest such a need.

out the distinctively Christian understanding of God in a *berakah* that is set in apparently deliberate contrast to his former understanding as a faithful member of the Jewish synagogue.

The reason for the christological dimension of this blessing lies with the Son of God theology that emerges in vv. 18–22 as a way of legitimizing Paul's apostleship. Since this is a complex passage in terms of both its "why" and "what," we need in this case to spell out the argument in some detail so as to appreciate the role of the Son of God Christology that emerges here, which is quite different from the messianism presupposed in the former instances.

2 Corinthians 1:18–22—Jesus, the Son of God

1:18–22 ¹⁸<u>πιστὸς δὲ ὁ θεὸς</u> ὅτι ὁ λόγος ἡμῶν ὁ πρὸς ὑμᾶς οὐκ ἔστιν ναὶ καὶ οὔ. ¹⁹<u>ὁ τοῦ θεοῦ</u> γὰρ **υἱὸς Ἰησοῦς Χριστὸς ὁ** ἐν ὑμῖν δι᾽ ἡμῶν **κηρυχθείς,** δι᾽ ἐμοῦ καὶ Σιλουανοῦ καὶ Τιμοθέου, οὐκ ἐγένετο ναὶ καὶ οὒ ἀλλὰ **ναὶ ἐν αὐτῷ γέγονεν.** ²⁰<u>ὅσαι γὰρ ἐπαγγελίαι θεοῦ, ἐν αὐτῷ τὸ ναί·</u> διὸ καὶ **δι᾽ αὐτοῦ τὸ ἀμὴν** τῷ θεῷ πρὸς δόξαν δι᾽ ἡμῶν. ²¹<u>ὁ δὲ βεβαιῶν ἡμᾶς</u> σὺν ὑμῖν **εἰς Χριστὸν** <u>καὶ χρίσας ἡμᾶς θεός,</u> ²²<u>ὁ καὶ σφραγισάμενος ἡμᾶς καὶ δοὺς</u> τὸν ἀρραβῶνα τοῦ πνεύματος ἐν ταῖς καρδίαις ἡμῶν.

> ¹⁸*But <u>faithful is God,</u> because our word which came to you is not both "yes" and "no."* ¹⁹*For **the Son of God, Jesus Christ, the one preached** among you through us—through me and Silvanus and Timothy—did not become "yes" and "no"; rather, **it was "yes" in him.*** ²⁰*<u>For as many as are the promises of God,</u> **in (Christ) they are "yes."*** *For this reason also **through him the "Amen" is said** by us <u>to (God's) glory.</u>* ²¹*Now <u>it is God who establishes us</u> with you **in Christ** <u>and anointed us,</u>* ²²<u>*who also sealed us by giving us*</u> *the down payment of the Spirit in our hearts.*

Following the remarkable, very theocentric letter opening, Paul in v. 12 transitions to the first part of his appeal, which begins here and carries through to 7:16.[29] At issue is Paul's *integrity* as it relates to his relationship with the Corinthian community. Although Titus's return had indicated that there had been a measure of reconciliation between them and Paul (7:5–16), Titus probably had also to report that there was some lingering bad feeling. Some of this undoubtedly stems from an earlier time and is reflected in our 1 Corinthians.

In any case, Paul feels a decided urgency to explain his recent relations with them, and especially his recent change of itinerary, for a second time.[30]

---

[29] This, of course, recognizes that 2:14–7:4 forms a considerable (though understandable) break in this argument and in fact is also the longest single block of material in the letter.

[30] The combined evidence from 1 Cor 16:5–7; 2 Cor 1:15–17; 1:23–2:4 indicates that the visit mentioned in 2 Cor 1:15–16, 23–24 does *not* correspond to that proposed in 1 Cor 16:5–7 (thus one change in plans); Paul obviously has not followed through on the second plan mentioned in 2 Cor 1:15–16 as well. It is this latter change of

But at stake still more than his own integrity is his apostleship. This has been called into question by some of them for a considerable time, as 1 Cor 4:1–21 and 9:1–23 make plain. His change of announced plans to return to Corinth after traveling to Macedonia, returning to Ephesus instead, apparently has fueled the fires of his detractors, now supported by some outside opposition.[31] Paul can be no apostle of the truth that is in Christ, since he so obviously says both yes and no out of the same side of his mouth.

Therefore, precisely because his apostleship is at stake, Paul feels compelled not simply to explain himself but also to establish his integrity, ultimately on theological grounds. Thus arises the strange and (to us) convoluted nature of the present argument. He begins by giving the reason for the first change of plans (vv. 15–16),[32] insisting that that plan had not in fact been made with levity nor did changing it mean duplicity on his part (v. 17). "Are my plans made like a mere worldling,"[33] he asks rhetorically, "full of duplicity, meaning both 'yes' and 'no' at the same time?" The form of the rhetoric carries its own intended response: "Of course not."

But that is insufficient for Paul in this case, so he launches into a singular theological vindication of his integrity in which he is intent to tie his "words" (about itineraries, etc.) to his "word" (his preaching of the gospel) and thus to God's own faithfulness as that has been revealed in Christ his Son and in the gift of the Spirit. This is bold stuff indeed, based on the absolute conviction expressed in 1:1 that his apostleship is predicated altogether on God's will. Thus, the logic of the argument in its various parts can be readily traced out in six steps:

1. The first statement following the rhetorical denial of his duplicity is the boldest of all: "God is faithful" (v. 18a). Paul's own integrity is predicated first of all on God's faithfulness, or trustworthiness.

2. God's faithfulness is thus what guarantees Paul's "word" to them (v. 18b). An obvious wordplay is in progress here: in its first sense this guar-

---

plans that he is hereby explaining to them. See G. D. Fee, "ΧΑΡΙΣ in 2 Corinthians 1:15: Apostolic Parousia and Paul-Corinth Chronology," in *To What End Exegesis? Essays Textual, Exegetical, and Theological* (Grand Rapids: Eerdmans, 2001), 99–104; but see also the response by Furnish (142–45), who offers a different reconstruction of the proposed visits.

[31] These people, who are merely mentioned in chs. 1–9 (e.g., 2:14–4:6) but have come close to a "takeover" in chs. 10–13, seem to have seized on these doubts about Paul's authority as basic to their proclamation of "another Jesus" (11:4).

[32] In v. 15; in order that "they might have double opportunity for grace"—that is, the privilege of helping him on to Macedonia and of being the "sending church" for the mission to Jerusalem. For this interpretation of δευτέραν χάριν, see Fee, "ΧΑΡΙΣ."

[33] Gk. κατὰ σάρκα (lit., *according to the flesh*). Cf. 1:12, the accusation in 10:2, and especially the argument in 5:16 that he does not view anyone from this perspective, hence neither should they. This is a distinctively pejorative term that very often stands in contrast to the Spirit, as it seems to do here (v. 22). Thus it has to do with living from the perspective of the present age and its values. See on "worldly" wisdom in 1 Cor 2:6–16, and, especially for this contrast, Gal 5:16–6:8.

anteed "word" is that of vv. 15–17, but that is only first blush. The real "word" that validates all other "words" is his preaching of Christ, which is the true "word" that is "unto them" (v. 18) and was preached "among them" (v. 19).

3. And here is where Paul's Son of God Christology comes into play. The certain evidence that Paul's "word" is trustworthy is to be found in the faithful God's Son, whom Paul (and his companions) preached so effectively in Corinth. The "for" with which v. 19 begins is explanatory. Thus, "For the Son of God, Jesus Christ, whom we preached, is himself God's 'yes,'" not only to his own promises but by implication also to Paul's "word."

Here, then, is a genuine case of "like Father, like Son." The Father's faithfulness finds expression in the faithfulness—the "yes"—of his Son. Thus the Son is not simply an earthly Redeemer but a Savior who is also the guarantor of the Father's trustworthiness as that has found expression in the gospel through which the Corinthians were saved.

4. Indeed, Paul will explain further (v. 20a), almost certainly in anticipation of ch. 3 (and 11?), that all the promises of God made to Israel have found their divine "yes" in Christ. There is nothing more to be had. Thus, the Son is not only the guarantor of Paul's "word" but also the fulfillment of all the *promises* of God. This also suggests that Paul's Son of God Christology is deeply rooted in Jewish messianism, which ultimately goes back to the Davidic king as "God's Son."

5. Not only so, Paul adds (v. 20b), but also in our corporate worship it is "through Christ" that we (both Paul and the Corinthians) affirm God's trustworthy word, found in Christ and preached by us, by saying the "Amen" to God, unto his eternal glory. Thus God's Son is both the guarantor and the one who causes them to affirm the truth of the gospel, who by implication now also guarantees Paul's truthfulness in dealing with them.

6. Finally, he concludes (vv. 21–22), the same trustworthy God, whose Son is his "yes" to his promises, is the one who confirms us—and not only us but you as well. This present confirmation is the outflow of his having already "anointed" us—that is, his having "sealed" us by giving us the Holy Spirit himself as his down payment on our sure future.

It should be noted, finally, that this is one of the most God-centered, God-focused paragraphs in the Pauline corpus. As such, it is a concise expression of Paul's essential theology, the more telling precisely because it is such an off-the-cuff, nonreflective moment. Paul's integrity—and their own existence in Christ that is so integrally tied up with that integrity[34]—ultimately rests in the *character* of God (his trustworthiness), all of whose promises have been realized in his Son and thus in the *saving activity* of God, which is but an outflow of his character. Hence this passage seems to make certain that the proper understanding of the opening blessing is in praise of

---

[34] A point that is often made in the two extant letters to this congregation. See, e.g., 1 Cor 4:14–17; 9:1–2 and in our present letter esp. 3:1–3; 13:1–10.

the God who is now known to us as the Father of our Lord Jesus Christ, who is God's "yes" regarding Paul and his ministry.

Jesus, the Son of God: God's Glory and True Image

Part of the reality that the Lord Jesus is the Son of God is the fact that he is thereby the true bearer of the *divine image* and is thus the *Father's glory.* These twin realities are expressed explicitly in 2 Cor 4:4, 6 (picking up from 3:18), texts whose language and complexity have issued in a large variety of scholarly opinion. Hence this discussion needs to begin with an overview as to how they fit into the larger argument, since their complexity is related in part to the fact that 2:14–4:6 probably has more sudden shifts of metaphor, where one triggers another in rapid succession, than anywhere else in the Pauline corpus.[35]

The passage (2:14–4:6) stands at the beginning of a long "digression" (2:14–7:4)[36] in which four concerns are woven together into a continuous thread. At issue is (1) Paul's apostleship (and thereby his gospel), which (2) is characterized by suffering and weakness in keeping with Christ himself; nonetheless (3), it is full of the Spirit and therefore of glory, as is evidenced by the Corinthian believers themselves and their own experience of the Spirit, who therefore (4) should not succumb to the wiles of some outsiders, who, despite letters of commendation, are "peddlers of the word of truth." Thus it is absolutely crucial to a good reading of this long passage (2:14–7:4) to keep in mind that, despite an occasional digression, the whole is primarily a defense of Paul's apostleship, not so much the *fact* of it as its *character.* He seems especially concerned throughout to demonstrate, as in 1 Cor 4, that his apostolic "style" is quite in keeping with the message—marked by the cross but effective in its results. That at least seems to be the point of the beginning (2:14–17) and end (4:1–6) of this introductory section.

---

[35] For the considerable bibliography on this passage up to 1994, see Fee, *God's Empowering Presence,* 296 n. 46. To that list, and for the purposes of this study, I need to add ch. 4 ("A Letter from Christ") in Hays, *Echoes of Scripture,* 122–53, and to note that Wright's article is here cited from *Climax of the Covenant,* 175–92.

[36] Indeed, this is one of the classic "digressions" in ancient literature. This statement, of course, assumes several things: (1) that chs. 1–9 are to be understood as a single letter, not a later compilation by someone else (on the historical unlikelihood of such scissors-and-paste compilation, see G. D. Fee, "2 Corinthians 6:14–7:1 and Food Offered to Idols," in *To What End Exegesis?* 142–43); (2) that this is therefore a kind of "digression," as 2:13 and 7:5 reveal, although I would doubt that it is digressive in the ordinary sense of that word (hence the quotation marks), having had in this case a great deal of thought and intent to it; and (3) that Paul's letters were in fact a form of "literature," since they were intended to be read in the gathering of God's people and therefore had an intentionally public aspect to them from the beginning.

The net result is an argument that, while dealing with Paul's own ministry throughout, begins with a clear focus on Christ (and the gospel) and the ministry of the Spirit (2:14–4:6), set especially in contrast to some who, as outsiders, "peddle the word of God for profit" (2:17). Although Paul does not attack them directly at this point, as he will eventually in chs. 10–12, it seems probable from what is said here that their focus is on the continuing validity of the Jewish law.[37] So Paul is basically fighting on two fronts: (1) for the cruciform nature of his gospel and discipleship that the Corinthians disdain (or at least many of them), which still carries over from 1 Corinthians; and (2) now the added element of outsiders peddling a gospel with emphasis on the old covenant. At the same time, the latent christological crisis that was suggested to have emerged in 1 Corinthians seems also to be the reason for the "digression" in 3:7–4:6, whose beginning focus on the Spirit evolves into one of the more significant christological passages in the Pauline corpus.

Thus Paul's response to these peddlers, not surprisingly, concentrates first on the work of Christ. Picking up the metaphor of the Roman triumph (see 1 Cor 4:9), Paul begins by placing himself among the captives in Christ's triumphal procession (2:14). That in turn leads to his being the "aroma" of the incense (Christ himself) along the parade route, an aroma that leads either to life or to death (vv. 15–16). After the attack on the peddlers (v. 17), he begins another rapid shift of metaphors that moves in turn from a "letter of commendation" (3:1–2), to a "letter" from Christ, to the "letters" of the alphabet contained in words, written not on stone tablets but on human hearts (3:3). And with that echo of the giving of the law in Exodus, Paul launches into a comparison of the old covenant of "letter = law" to the new covenant effected by Christ and the Spirit (3:4–6), which comparison will now guide the contrasts that follow, taking the form of a "midrashic" interpretation of the Septuagint text of Exod 34:29–35.[38]

The keys to what immediately follows are two: (1) the word "glory," which dominates the Exodus passage, and (2) the realized experience of the Spirit, who is the effectual reality of the new covenant. The Exodus passage

---

[37] Several assumptions are at work in this sentence, of course: that the opponents in this passage are the same as those attacked in chs. 10–13; that they are Jewish believers; and that they are thus encouraging some form of Torah observance. Some movement in this direction can already be detected at various moments in 1 Corinthians (e.g., 7:18–19; 9:19–23; 15:56–57). If this is the correct scenario, then one must probably assume that the full nature of their activity has not yet been fully exposed; that emerges especially in the next letter, Galatians, where *insistence* on circumcision is now the heart of their mission. In this letter it is attacked simply as "another Jesus and another Spirit," which results in "another gospel" from the one the Corinthians had received (11:4).

[38] For a helpful analysis of the intertextuality of this passage that has brought some "uncommon" common sense to this issue, see Hays, *Echoes of Scripture*, 122–53. He rightly rejects calling this a midrash, comparing it with 1 Cor 10:1–13, which he dubs "an allusive homily based on biblical antecedents" (p. 132).

has to do with Moses' descent from the mount with the newly inscribed tablets of the law. The repeated reference in Exodus to the "glory" on Moses'
face drives the rest of the present passage. Apparently, the fact that this
"glory" is not mentioned in later passages (esp. Numbers) is interpreted by
Paul as being a "glory destined to perish."[39] This transitory glory has been
replaced in the new covenant by a much greater glory, effected by Christ and
made effective through the Spirit, so that believers, as they behold Christ by
the Spirit, are themselves transformed into the glory that is Christ's.

Our christological concerns emerge as Paul begins to apply the analogy
to the present situation (vv. 12–15), where the "veil" that covered Moses' face
(to hide the fact that the glory would come to an end) is now seen to cover
the hearts of those who hear Moses read in the synagogue, because the veil
is removed only through Christ (v. 14). With that, Paul reworks Exod 34:34
so as to illustrate the nature and reality of Christian conversion. And here is
where our (present) exegetical difficulties begin because, having brought
both Christ and the Spirit into the argument as crucial to effecting the new
covenant, Paul is going to apply the Exodus passage to the effective ministry
of each while at the same time the "removal of the veil"—first from Moses'
face but now also from the hearts of those who turn to the Lord—plays a
key role. Our concern from here is with what Paul says about Christ.[40]

The christological emphases in what follows are three, and they are especially important for the rounding out of Paul's Christology: (1) "the Lord"
in the Exodus passage refers first to the Spirit, who in the next clause is expressly identified as "the Spirit *of the Lord*"; hence Paul starts out with his
κύριος Christology intact; (2) the *glory* of the new covenant, picking up
the glory of the old from the Exodus passage, is now to be found *in the Lord
himself*, as believers in their own way "enter the presence of the Lord"; and
(3) by picking up the theme of Moses' being ἔναντι κυρίου (*before/in the presence of the Lord*) and speaking with him, Paul shifts images to one the Corinthians will fully understand: seeing one's *image* when gazing into a mirror.
But what one sees, by the work of the Spirit, Paul argues, is not one's *own*
image but that of *the Lord*,[41] into whose "image" we by the Spirit are also
being transformed. These latter two items are then picked up in the con-

---

[39] Traditionally, this has been interpreted as a "fading" glory; but there is no
warrant for this meaning of καταργέω, a word that occurs 4 times in this passage
with its ordinary Pauline sense of "coming to an end" (BDAG). For the difficulties involved in turning this Pauline word (25 of 27 NT occurrences) into the concept of
"fading," see Hays, *Echoes of Scripture*, 133–36.

[40] For the pneumatological emphasis of this passage, see Fee, *God's Empowering
Presence*, 309–20. It should be noted here that the work with all the κύριος texts of
Paul's letters for this study has brought about some slight changes to my view re-
garding Paul's application of the Exodus text to the Corinthian situation.

[41] At least that is what seems the most likely understanding of the metaphor; but
see Wright (*Climax of the Covenant*, 185–89), who argues that we see that glory in the
face of fellow believers.

cluding words of 4:4–6. We will examine each of these christological affirmations in turn.

Christ as Κύριος (2 Cor 3:16–18; 4:5)

Our first concern is to point out that for Paul, Christ has assumed the role of "the Lord" in the OT narrative. The way to see Paul's concerns is to first note what he has done in v. 16 with Exod 34:34:

Exod 34:34	ἡνίκα δ᾽ ἂν <u>εἰσεπορεύετο</u> Μωυσῆς <u>ἔναντι</u> **κυρίου**
	λαλεῖν αὐτῷ
	περιῃρεῖτο τὸ κάλυμμα ἕως τοῦ ἐκπορεύεσθαι,
2 Cor 3:16	ἡνίκα δὲ ἐὰν <u>ἐπιστρέψῃ</u> <u>πρὸς</u> **κύριον**,
	περιαιρεῖται τὸ κάλυμμα.

Exod 34:34	*But **whenever** Moses used to enter the presence of **the LORD***
	to speak with him,
	*he would **remove the veil** until he went out.*
2 Cor 3:16	*But **whenever** any one turns to **the Lord,***
	the veil is removed.

In this clear piece of intertextual use of the OT,[42] Paul has done four things to the Septuagint text to make it refer *simultaneously to the work of the Spirit and of Christ:*[43] (1) the subject "Moses" is (apparently deliberately) omitted so as to generalize the application to "anyone";[44] (2) the verb εἰσεπορεύετο (*used to go into*) is replaced with ἐπιστρέψῃ (*turn to*), which in Pauline and Lukan circles had become a quasi-technical term for "conversion";[45] (3) with the removal of the subject "Moses," Paul also therefore

---

[42] As Barrett (122) put it (before "intertextuality" became a buzzword in NT studies), "The closeness of this verse to the language of Exod. xxxiv. 34 lends it obscurity, but at the same time provides a necessary clue to its interpretation" (I would say, "*the* necessary clue").

[43] Missing this contextual reality, made clear (so it seems to me) by the twofold "interpretation" in v. 17, is what has brought about much of the diversity of interpretation in the two verses that follow.

[44] At least that appears to be the case. Our difficulty is that as Paul turns toward application, he begins a considerable wordplay on the text. Thus even though (based on the OT text and Paul's use of a verb in the singular) "Moses" *could* be the inferred subject, the veil that covers the hearts of those in the synagogue is the more immediate referent. Moreover, Paul will go on in v. 18 to make application to "we all" = he, the Corinthians, and all other believers.

[45] Pace D. A. Renwick, *Paul, the Temple, and the Presence of God* (BJS 224; Atlanta: Scholars Press, 1991), 151–54. For Paul, see 1 Thess 1:9; for Luke, see Acts 3:19; 9:35; 11:21; 14:15; 15:19; 26:20; 28:27. Cf. 1 Pet 2:25; Jas 5:20. Otherwise, see L. L. Belleville, *Reflections of Glory: Paul's Use of the Moses-Doxa Tradition in 2 Corinthians 3.1–18* (JSNTSup 52; Sheffield: Sheffield Academic Press, 1991), 252–53; Belleville sees it in terms of Septuagint usage, referring to the Jews themselves as "turning" to God (from their idols, etc.).

omitted the purpose clause, "to talk to him" (i.e., God); and (4) most significantly, he changed the verb from an imperfect middle with Moses as the grammatical subject ("he [Moses] used to remove") to a present passive[46] with "the veil" as the grammatical subject ("the veil is being removed"), which, by implication and in keeping with v. 14c, has been done by the work of Christ but now is effected by the Spirit.

The difficulty for us with regard to Paul's use of κύριος in this passage begins with his initial "interpretation" of the Septuagint text. Picking up the form of rabbinic interpretive strategy noted in the discussion of 1 Cor 10:4 (see ch. 3, p. 95), but in this case, as in Gal 4:25, staying true to the form itself, Paul makes the surprising identification of the κύριος in this passage as referring to the Spirit. But that is immediately qualified by the further interpretive word "and where the Spirit *of the Lord* [τὸ πνεῦμα κυρίου] [is], freedom [is]." So how does one handle this apparently contradictory kind of talk?

The resolution seems to lie both with the interpretive strategy itself and with the context, especially with Paul's emphasis on the work of the Spirit as the crucial reality that contrasts the new covenant with the former covenant and its transitory glory. First, let us note the interpretive strategy. The clue lies with the identical pattern that occurs in Gal 4:25, where Paul's ἐστιν (*is*) must not be taken literally, "this *is* that," but representationally, "this *represents* that." Thus, just as Hagar in Gal 4:25 is not in fact Mount Sinai but represents Mount Sinai, so here the κύριος in the Exodus passage now is *representative* of the Spirit. What this means, then, is that Paul interprets the *conversion* dimension of the Exodus text ("turning to the Lord") as having to do with the Spirit: " 'the Lord' is [= refers to the work of] the Spirit."[47]

But since it was Christ's death and resurrection that spelled death to the old, Paul immediately qualifies what he has just said by noting the Spirit's relationship with Christ: the Spirit who has been identified as at work in the present application of the Exodus passage is in fact the Spirit of Christ. An expanded version of his interpretation would go something like this: "The veil that covers the minds of those who hear the reading of the former covenant is removed by the work of Christ (vv. 13–15); so 'when anyone turns to the Lord,' that veil is removed. 'The Lord' in the Exodus passage refers to the work of the Spirit,[48] who alone brings people into freedom from law-keeping. And the Spirit, of course, is 'the Spirit *of the Lord*' = Christ."[49]

---

[46] Although Barrett (122) prefers to see it as a middle; thus "he [the Lord] takes away the veil." But either voice (passive or middle) comes out at the same point.

[47] Barrett comments, "It is in the realm of action . . . rather than of person . . . that the terms *Lord* and *Spirit* are identified" (123).

[48] That Paul must mean something like this, rather than a one-for-one equation of "the Lord" in the Exodus text with the Spirit, seems to be demanded by the further explication of that passage that follows.

[49] This is the first of four such moments of identification in the corpus; see below on Gal 4:6; Rom 8:9; Phil 1:19.

This means, then, that Paul is not intending to equate the κύριος of the Septuagint with the *person* of the Spirit but with the Spirit's *work* of moving believers into freedom from Torah observance.[50] After all, as always for Paul, the Holy Spirit is understood to be both "the Spirit of God" and "the Spirit of Christ."[51]

If this is the correct understanding of Paul's interpretive phrase, then the real issue is the identity of the "Lord" in the second phrase, τὸ πνεῦμα κυρίου (*the Spirit of the Lord*).[52] And here is where my mind has been changed. In *God's Empowering Presence* I argued (hesitantly, to be sure) that "the Lord" in this phrase is God the Father. That conclusion was predicated primarily on two grounds, which seem no longer valid after closer examination of all the κύριος texts in the corpus: (1) the unusual anarthrous use of κύριος in a phrase where the preceding noun is arthrous ("*the* Spirit of κυρίου"), which I recognized was the result of Paul's use of a Septuagintal phrase; and (2) the similar (also Septuagintal) phrase τὴν δόξαν κυρίου (*the glory of the Lord*) in v. 18, where I argued, on the basis of Christ himself being identified as God's glory in 4:6, that the "Lord" in this passage must also refer to God.

But in light of how Paul has been shown to apply these kinds of Septuagint phrases to Christ in 1–2 Thessalonians and 1 Corinthians (see chs. 2–3 above) and will be shown to do likewise in this letter (see the section "Christ as Sharer of Divine Prerogatives" below), neither of these earlier reasons now seems valid. In fact, three factors coalesce in this case to give one confidence that "the Lord" in these two phrases is Christ: (1) Paul regularly appropriates the Septuagint's κύριος = Yahweh as referring to Christ;[53] (2) Paul *consistently* uses κύριος in all other passages to refer to Christ; and (3) in concluding the present argument, Paul inserts a word (4:5) about his own ministry between the two concluding words about Christ as the image and glory of the Father; and here he explicitly says that he preaches Ἰησοῦν Χριστὸν κυρίον, using a word order that seems to demand the meaning "Jesus Christ as Lord."

---

[50] See n. 40 above regarding my own change of view from *God's Empowering Presence*, 311–15.

[51] For the christological implications of this interchange, see esp. discussion on Rom 8:9–10 in ch. 6 (pp. 269–70).

[52] The house is quite divided on this one: those who think it refers to Yahweh include Bernard, 58; Collange, 103–4; Harris, 339; Furnish, 213; Martin, 30; Belleville, *Reflections of Glory*; Thrall, 273; J. D. G. Dunn, "2 Corinthians iii.17—'The Lord Is the Spirit,'" *JTS* 21 (1970): 317; C. F. D. Moule, "2 Cor. 3.18b, καθάπερ ἀπὸ κυρίου πνεύματος," in *Neues Testament und Geschichte: Historisches Geschehen und Deutung im Neuen Testament* (ed. H. Baltensweiler and B. Reicke; Zurich: Theologischer Verlag, 1972), 235. Those who think that it refers to Christ include most of the older interpreters (e.g., Meyer, Hodge, Plummer, Strachan, Tasker) and many of the more recent: Bruce, 198; Barrett, 123; Bultmann, 89; Barnett, 200; Lambrecht, 55; Matera, 96–97.

[53] For this usage in 2 Corinthians, see pp. 188–95 below.

Thus, in 2 Cor 4:5 Paul is once more picking up what has become for him and his churches the primary Christian confession, noted above in 1 Cor 12:3, and named in Rom 10:9 as the true identifying mark that someone has been "saved": a verbal confession that κύριος Ἰησοῦς (*the Lord is Jesus*). In Phil 2:11 Paul asserts that this basic Christian confession will be offered by all created beings at the eschaton.[54] In the present passage the same confession is put in reverse, since here it is not "confession" but "proclamation." That is, Paul's preaching can be boiled down to this singular reality: Ἰησοῦς Χριστὸς κύριος (= *Jesus, the Jewish Messiah, is Lord of the universe*), to which the redeemed respond by way of the Spirit, "The Lord is Jesus Christ."

This means then that as elsewhere, in 3:16 Christ Jesus is being identified with "the Lord" = *Adonai* = Yahweh of the Septuagint, with all the christological implications being at hand here as well. This in turn leads us to the second matter: Christ as the incarnate expression of God the Father's "glory."

Christ, the Glory of the Lord (2 Cor 3:18; 4:4, 6)

2 Corinthians 3:18

Having now interpreted the Moses story in terms of Christian conversion with its greater glory—the gift of the Spirit and freedom from Torah observance—Paul moves on to describe, by way of application, the nature of this new freedom with its attendant glory. This transition to application is marked by the change of grammatical subject, back to the "we" of v. 13, now not as a "literary plural" (referring to himself)[55] but as an emphatic "we all" that includes the Corinthians. Here, Paul argues, is what the freedom of the Spirit means for all who are Christ's.

What follows is one of the more remarkable moments in the Pauline corpus. To make his point of application, Paul has joined two somewhat disparate images, but he has made them work magnificently. He begins with the Exodus imagery of "the unveiled face" from v. 16, and then he picks up the "mirror" imagery from his earlier letter (1 Cor 13:12), an imagery well suited to the believing community in a city renowned for its excellent bronze mirrors.[56] The concern in 1 Cor 12 was with the "indirect" nature of our present ability to "see God" in comparison with the full knowing that will be ours at the eschaton. The present concern is, first, with *who* is seen as we

---

[54] For the discussion of these three passages, see pp. 123–24 (1 Cor 12:3); pp. 257–59 (Rom 10:9); pp. 399–401 (Phil 2:11). But see also the discussion of Col 2:6 (pp. 326–27), where this same formula seems to be at work in Paul's speaking of the Colossians coming to faith ("as you have received τὸν Χριστὸν Ἰησοῦν τὸν κύριον" [= *the Messiah Jesus as Lord*]).

[55] On this matter, see the full discussion in Thrall, 105–7; she suggests, rightly I think, that in this former case, even though Paul is referring to himself, he is also intending what he says there to be exemplary of apostolic ministry.

[56] On this see Fee, *1 Corinthians*, 647–48 and n. 45.

look into the mirror and, second, with the transformative impact of such "beholding."[57] And it is at these two points that he joins the mirror imagery with the Exodus narrative that he has been expounding.

The result is that, by the empowering work of the Spirit, "we all" with our now "unveiled faces" have been brought into God's presence (as Moses of old); but in contrast to Moses, who longed to see the Lord's glory but could not (Exod 33:18–23), God's new covenant people are able to gaze on "the glory of the Lord." There are three important matters to notice here.

1. As noted, Paul is now applying the new understanding of the Exodus passage to himself and the believing community in Corinth;[58] and this is what has called forth his use of τὴν δόξαν κυρίου (the LORD's glory), a phrase implied in Exod 33 and 34 but explicitly used at the end of the narrative in Exod 40. When God's presence descends on the newly constructed tabernacle through the visible means of a cloud, we are told in 40:34 that δόξης κυρίου ἐπλήσθη ἡ σκηνή (with the glory of the LORD the tabernacle was filled).[59] So important is this final item in the narrative that not only is "the LORD's glory" put in the emphatic first position, but also the exact phrase is repeated as an inclusio at the end of the next sentence (v. 35), where we are told that "Moses was not able to enter" precisely because—to our great surprise, given the narrative of Exod 34—it had been filled with "the glory of the LORD."[60]

2. And now one can see the significance of the strange (for us) way that Paul has interpreted the sentence from Exod 34:34. What he has done is join the work of Christ and the Spirit in such a way that "the Lord" of that text is made to refer to Christ ("the Spirit of *the Lord*"), even though its first referent

---

[57] Gk. κατοπτριζόμενοι, a word that occurs only here in the NT. The noun κάτοπτρον is the most common word for "mirror" in Greek (see BDAG). On the issue as to whether it means "look at something in a mirror," assumed here as the meaning that makes the best sense of the argument, or "to reflect something as does a mirror," see *God's Empowering Presence*, 316–17.

[58] In a remarkable interpretation of this passage, Kim (*Origin of Paul's Gospel*, 128–29) reads all of 2 Cor 3:7–4:6, and especially 4:4, 6, as having to do with Paul's encounter with Christ on the Damascus Road, where "he perceived Christ as the true Wisdom." What makes it remarkable is that "wisdom" is mentioned but once in this letter (1:12), and that in a pejorative way, while the "echoes" of personified Wisdom that Kim finds here ("light, image") are more imaginative than substantive (see my excursus "On the Alleged Influence of Wisdom in 2 Cor 4:4, 6" below). To make this interpretation work, one would need to establish that Paul knew the Wisdom of Solomon at all and that such distant echoes were really front and center in his own thinking. On this whole question, see appendix A in the present volume (pp. 594–619).

[59] This same language is then repeated with regard to the descent of Yahweh's glory in Solomon's temple (1 Kgs 8:11).

[60] One might also compare Num 12:8: στόμα κατὰ στόμα λαλήσω αὐτῷ ἐν εἴδει καὶ οὐ δι᾿ αἰνιγμάτων καὶ τὴν δόξαν κυρίου εἶδεν (*Mouth to mouth I will speak to him, directly and not indistinctly, and he saw the glory of the LORD*). Although some (e.g., Furnish, 214) see this as the most likely referent, it seems more probable that the Exodus narrative itself supplies all that is needed by way of OT echo.

is to Christ's *Spirit*—as the way Christ the Lord leads us into this new free-dom and glory. The net result is that the word "glory," which has carried the narrative from v. 7 and which is specifically applied to Christ as the way we now see God's glory,[61] is ultimately transferred to believers. As "we" behold "the glory" that is Christ's—he being the incarnate manifestation of the di-vine glory—we by the Spirit are being transformed into Christ's own image, and that ἀπὸ δόξης εἰς δόξαν (*from glory to glory*).[62] Thus for the believer, the glory that is ours is the direct result of being brought face-to-face with "the glory of Christ" himself by means of the Spirit.

3. The first significant *christological* point in v. 18, therefore, is the identi-fication of Christ with "the glory of the LORD," an identification that turns out to be full of words and images from portions surrounding Exod 34. Paul thus continues to keep alive the contrast with Moses. In the immediately pre-ceding narrative (Exod 33:18–23), Moses has specifically requested of Yah-weh, "Show me your glory." The divine response is, "You *cannot see my face,* for no one may see me and live." Nonetheless, Moses is placed in the cleft of a rock from which he will see God's glory (from behind, as it were) as Yah-weh "passes by." By way of obvious contrast, God's new covenant people, when they turn to the Lord, are enabled by the Spirit to behold, as though looking into a mirror, "the glory of the Lord." So the glory that Moses was not allowed to see "we all" behold in Christ, where "the glory of the Lord"—both Christ's and the Father's—is fully revealed in the *face* of the Son, the perfect bearer of the divine image.

Thus, with this transformation of the Moses narrative of Exod 33–34 and 40 and his varied relationship to God's glory, believers are now under-stood to realize what was not available to Moses. In this move, Paul makes the same point that he will make later in Rom 8:29–30 and Col 3:10–11 with the εἰκών (*image*) language of Gen 1–2: the same Lord who is here the Fa-ther's glory into which believers are being transformed is there the true bearer of the divine image into which we are also being transformed.

All of this assumes a remarkably high Christology, where the Son of God is both the true expression of God the Father's glory and the true bearer of the divine image. And it is precisely at such points that Pauline Christology and soteriology merge, since with Christ as the Father's glory and image, through his death and resurrection and by the gift of his Spirit, the ultimate goal of redemption is finally actualized—which is not simply dealing with our sins and thus fitting us for heaven but actually re-creating us back into

---

[61] So also Barrett, 125.

[62] This is one of the more difficult phrases in the argument. The basic options are three: (1) ever-increasing glory; (2) from the glory of the old to that of the new; (3) from the glory that is Christ's to the glory that is ours. Each of these can be ar-gued as fitting the context, but each has a degree of difficulty also in terms of con-text. In *God's Empowering Presence* (318) I opted for the second, on the basis of v. 11. Although the third is attractive, Paul in other places uses ἐκ . . . εἰς to make a point of source and goal.

the divine image so besmirched by the fall. And this is the point that Paul makes next in the present narrative.

2 Corinthians 4:4, 6

Since the word "glory" has been the presenting word throughout the present narrative from 3:7, it is no surprise that Paul wraps up this part of his "defense" by picking up this theme in a passage that both concludes the introductory section (from 2:14) and serves as a turning point in the narrative (back to Paul's weaknesses). The two sentences (vv. 4, 6) are quite similar; their differences lie in their primary focus. First the texts:

4:4 ὁ θεὸς τοῦ αἰῶνος τούτου ἐτύφλωσεν τὰ νοήματα τῶν ἀπίστων εἰς τὸ μὴ αὐγάσαι **τὸν φωτισμὸν τοῦ εὐαγγελίου τῆς δόξης τοῦ Χριστοῦ,** **ὅς ἐστιν εἰκὼν** <u>τοῦ θεοῦ.</u>

4:6 <u>ὁ θεὸς ὁ εἰπών·</u> ἐκ σκότους φῶς λάμψει, <u>ὃς ἔλαμψεν</u> ἐν ταῖς καρδίαις ἡμῶν <u>πρὸς φωτισμὸν τῆς γνώσεως τῆς δόξης τοῦ θεοῦ</u> **ἐν προσώπῳ Ἰησοῦ Χριστοῦ.**

4:4 *The god of this age has blinded the minds of unbelievers so that they might not see **the light of the gospel of the glory of Christ,*** ***who is the image*** *of God.*

4:6 *The God who said, "Out of darkness light shall shine," has shined in our hearts to bring the light of the knowledge of the glory of God* ***in the face of Jesus Christ.***

Several things need to be noted about these companion sentences. First, picking up the evident movement from the christocentric discussion in 3:1–18 to the theocentric application that begins in 4:1, they deliberately set out in sharp contrast "the god of this age," who deals in darkness, with the God of creation, who spoke light into existence: whereas the first "god" blinded people's *minds,* the eternal God has shined light into their *hearts* = minds.

But, second, and in keeping with the whole argument, in both sentences the source of the light in the hearts of those who do believe is Christ, whose *own glory* is seen in the gospel (v. 4)[63] and who at the same time thus reveals the knowledge of *the glory of God* (v. 6).

---

[63] In one of their worst moments, the translators of the KJV (now followed by NET BIBLE!) took the genitive τῆς δόξης in the phrase τοῦ εὐαγγελίου τῆς δόξης τοῦ Χριστοῦ (*the gospel [having to do with] the glory of Christ;* cf. TNIV, "the gospel that displays the glory of Christ") as attributive (adjectival) and thus translated it "the glorious gospel of Christ." It is hard to imagine a more thoroughgoing misunderstanding of the passage in context. After all, δόξα (*glory*) is the presenting word in the entire argument of 2 Cor 3:7–4:6, where it occurs no less than 13 times in this intertextual exposition based on its occurrences in Exod 33:18–23; 34:29–35; 40:34–38. To make this one adjectival is to treat the argument itself in a cavalier fashion.

At the same time, third, in v. 4 Christ is now explicitly identified as "the image of God," while in the second instance God's glory is seen in the "*face* of Christ," which thus echoes the "image" motif in a slightly different way. So Christ the perfect bearer of the divine image is, by that very fact, himself also the revealer of the glory of God.

Thus, as earlier in the corpus, Christ simultaneously has his own glory—since he is himself divine, after all—and is the one in whom we also behold the Father's glory. This means further that although there is always clear distinction between them, Father and Son also share divine identity; and what one now knows about God has been revealed fully in the Son, whose image/face we behold as we gaze upon him by the Spirit.

Christ, the Bearer of the Divine Image (2 Cor 3:18; 4:4, 6)

With the use of εἰκών (*image*) in 3:18 and 4:4, several matters are brought into focus in this introductory passage; and since these three passages (3:18; 4:4, 6) obviously have been tied together by the apostle himself, we will look at the various components of the imagery as a package rather than verse by verse. Three matters call for elaboration.

1. The *impetus* for the language in this case lies *not* with Christ as the second Adam but with the mirror imagery that Paul uses in 3:18,[64] which in turn holds the three sentences together. God's people, as though looking into a mirror, now behold the glory of the Lord and are being transformed into "the same image." In 4:4 Paul then specifies what "the same image" refers to: Christ, the bearer of the divine glory, is himself the *imago Dei*. So believers are being re-created into the image of God as they by the Spirit behold the One who is himself the perfect bearer of the divine image, whose glory is seen in Christ's *face*.

2. The *goal*, or concern, of the passage, we need to remember, is not Christology as such but soteriology: God's new covenant people are themselves being redeemed (re-created, as it were) so as once more to bear the divine image. And here is where the analogy with Adam makes its way into the imagery. As Paul will state summarily, and emphatically, in Rom 8:30, this is what God's new people have been predestined for: to be conformed to the *image of his Son*, who himself has assumed the role of πρωτότοκος (*first-born*) among many brothers and sisters. Thus, lying behind the present passage is a *new-creation* theology,[65] in which God's new creation has a people who truly bear the divine image.

3. Paul's use of the phrase "image of God" in 4:4 indicates that he has himself intended to move beyond the mirror imagery toward the *biblical basis*

---

[64]So also Barrett, 125; Furnish, 215. Jervell (*Imago Dei*, 173–76) argues for Gen 1:26–27, but this has rightly been rejected by Barrett (125) and others.

[65]Which Paul will pick up in 5:14–21; see the discussion below on p. 197. See also the discussion of Col 3:10 in ch. 7 (pp. 303–4).

for this language: Gen 1:26, 27. There we have first the announcement (v. 26) and then the poetic narrative (v. 27) that "God created human beings in his own *image.*" The Septuagint translator used εἰκών to give expression to this divine "likeness" that human beings are to bear, who were to function as God's representatives on earth, which in turn is the most likely reason for the second commandment. It was not just that the one God by definition could not have rivals—that matter is taken up in the first commandment. At issue in the second commandment is making "*graven* images," images that are not living and therefore cannot reflect God's true likeness, which only his own people can do.

The first appearance of this language in Paul's writings is also in the Corinthian correspondence (1 Cor 15:49 [see p. 119 in ch. 3]), where Paul urges those who have borne Adam's image to press on to the eschaton so that they will also bear the image of Christ (the second Adam). Granted, Paul makes no further point of it there; but the fact that he picks it up again in the same correspondence suggests that he at least expected the Corinthians themselves to recognize the imagery, which in turn means that we have need to keep it within the bounds of this correspondence. Thus, it is highly unlikely that Paul is here suddenly bringing in imagery from Wisdom, as is suggested by so many.[66]

The christological point, of course, is that Christ himself in his humanity perfectly bore that image, so that as believers now behold him as the risen One, they are themselves being "transformed" back into that image/likeness. But the emphasis in these passages is not on Christ's humanity—that is assumed as inherent in the imagery itself. What we have, rather, is the true image being borne by the one *who shares the divine glory,* the one who, when turned to in devotion and obedience, transforms believers, by his Spirit, into the *image of God* that we had been created for in the first place.

Thus, whatever christological deviation was being promoted by the peddlers with their "another Jesus" (11:4), the end result of what Paul does in this response to them (mentioned again in 4:1–3) is to exalt Christ in his deity, whose own glory is the true manifestation of God's glory as well;[67] and where Paul touches on Christ's humanity, it comes by way of implication, not direct expression. Nonetheless, it is precisely because he shared our humanity, as he fully shares the Father's deity, that God's glory will be revealed in those who are being re-created and thus transformed into the divine image.

---

[66] See, e.g., Barrett, 133; Furnish, 239, 248; Thrall, 284, 310–11; as to why the imagery does not come from both sources (Genesis and Wisdom), see my excursus "On the Alleged Influence of Wisdom in 2 Cor 4:4, 6" below.

[67] That is, as Barrett points out (132), "through Christ as the image of God [people] come to comprehend the [divinity] of God," meaning that in the incarnation God has been most fully revealed; cf. the discussion on 1:3 above.

Excursus: On the Alleged Influence of Wisdom in 2 Corinthians 4:4, 6

One regularly reads in the literature that Paul is here reflecting Jewish Wisdom as expressed in Wis 7:25–26. Indeed, this is the *single* instance in the Pauline corpus that a direct influence might be suspected. Wisdom 7:25–26 reads,

²⁵ἀτμὶς γάρ ἐστιν τῆς τοῦ θεοῦ δυνάμεως καὶ ἀπόρροια τῆς τοῦ παντοκράτορος **δόξης** εἰλικρινής· διὰ τοῦτο οὐδὲν μεμιαμμένον εἰς αὐτὴν παρεμπίπτει.	²⁵For she is a breath of the power of God, and an emanation of the Almighty's pure **glory;** therefore nothing defiled gains entrance into her.
²⁶ἀπαύγασμα γάρ ἐστιν φωτὸς ἀιδίου καὶ ἔσοπτρον ἀκηλίδωτον τῆς τοῦ θεοῦ ἐνεργείας καὶ **εἰκὼν** τῆς ἀγαθότητος αὐτοῦ.	²⁶For she is a <u>reflection</u> of eternal *light,* and a spotless <u>mirror</u> of God's working; and an **image** of his goodness.⁶⁸

For the more complete exposition of Wisdom with regard to Pauline usage, see appendix A (pp. 594–619). Here we simply note that this passage appears in the author's encomium on Wisdom (7:22–8:1), intended for the "kings of the earth," that they themselves will desire wisdom so as to rule wisely (and thus ease up on the Jewish community in Alexandria). In v. 25 the author expresses her *relation* to God ("breath of his power; emanation of his glory"), which he then rhapsodizes with a triplet, using mirror imagery to indicate how she reveals aspects of God's character.

But there is nothing in this passage that requires, or even suggests, Paul either to have known it or to have borrowed its language, especially not the latter. The two actual verbal correspondences are quite coincidental and therefore incidental. Paul's use of "glory" comes not from Wisdom but from the Exodus passage that he has been interpreting. His use of "image" comes directly from his own "mirror" imagery in 3:18 (where there is not a wisp of Jewish wisdom present), and the imagery has to do with "looking into the mirror," while Wisdom's is the middle of three metaphors that deal with "reflection," not "beholding." Thus Wisdom's use of "image" also comes from the mirror imagery, as the third in the sequence of wordplays on the imagery. Moreover, she is not

---

⁶⁸For convenience, I have put in boldface the two words that actually correspond and italicized the one other related word (φῶς; cf. Paul's φωτισμός). The "mirror" imagery itself is incidental for Paul; he deliberately uses the verb κατοπτρίζω (v. 18) to make his point (the believer is doing the "looking into the mirror" with the goal of transformation); the author of Wisdom uses the noun, precisely because it is "reflection" that he has in view.

in fact said to be "the image of God," as Paul says of Christ; rather, she merely "images" his divine character of goodness.[69]

On the whole, therefore, it seems especially doubtful that Paul is here "echoing" this piece of Jewish wisdom speculation, for three reasons:[70] (1) Although there are some interesting linguistic correlations, Paul and Wisdom are in completely different worlds with regard to how they use the same words. (2) The key point of departure for Paul—the mirror imagery—comes from Paul himself, not from outside influences; after all, it occurs but twice in his letters, once in each of the letters to Corinth, a city that had renown as creator of mirrors for the world. This is a Pauline borrowing of local culture to make his point. (3) If this were an "echo" of Scripture, one would have to acknowledge that it is of a considerably different kind from those we have noted before, both in this chapter and in the preceding two chapters, where Paul's use of the OT texts is transparent and full of linguistic echoes of the texts themselves, not just incidental *conceptual* correspondences.

Christ as Sharer of Divine Prerogatives

One the most noticeable features of the Christology of 2 Corinthians is Paul's continuing to refer to Christ in a way that in his basic monotheistic worldview would ordinarily be reserved for speech about God. As with the earlier letters, this happens in two ways: in sentences that speak of Christ in ways normally reserved for God and in the use of Septuagint phrases where what is expressed about Yahweh in the OT text, translated as κύριος, has been taken over by Paul to refer to the "Lord, Jesus Christ." As before, these happen in the most off-handed of ways, totally presuppositional and therefore quite unrehearsed.

Some of these have been discussed in the earlier chapters, and so here they are merely listed with cross-references. But a whole variety of new ones emerge in this letter that make it certain that this is the "stuff" of Paul's understanding of the relationship of Christ the Son with God the Father: Christ fully shares divine prerogatives with the Father—and this without argumentation or ostentation.

First, then, the list of items (in canonical order) that we have looked at in the earlier letters:

---

[69] One reads with a sense of wonder that "there is *obviously* a close similarity between II Cor 3:18 and 4:4 and Wisdom 7:22–30. Wisdom as the 'image' of God is the mediator between God and man" (Hamerton-Kelly, *Pre-existence, Wisdom, and the Son of Man*, 145 [italics mine]). This amounts to "exegesis" pulled out of the air; it certainly is unrelated to the Wisdom of Solomon.

[70] On the unlikelihood that Paul even knew this work, see the discussion in appendix A (pp. 605–6).

1. On apostle of Christ (2 Cor 1:1), see on 1 Cor 1:17; 1:1 (p. 136).

2. On Christ's name being joined with the Father's by a single preposition at crucial moments in the letter (2 Cor 1:2), see on 1 Thess 1:1 (pp. 48–50); 1 Cor 1:3 (pp. 99–100).

3. On the Day of the Lord (2 Cor 1:14), see on 1 Thess 5:2 (pp. 46–47); 1 Cor 1:8 (p. 135).

4. On the gospel of Christ (2 Cor 2:10), see on 2 Thess 1:8 (p. 73).

5. On the love of Christ (2 Cor 5:14), see on 2 Thess 2:13 (pp. 64–65).

6. On the giving of the Lord (2 Cor 10:8; 13:10), see on 1 Cor 3:5; 7:17 (pp. 136–37).

In each of these cases what is said earlier of the christological significance of these phrases continues to be true of their appearance in 2 Corinthians. But what is striking regarding the present letter is the frequency of these kinds of items, many new and all carrying christological weight, in the sense that Paul says matter-of-factly about Christ what the OT says equally presuppositionally about Yahweh. Precisely because there is only one God, all divine power and attributes are found in him alone; thus when Paul applies these to Christ, he is again assuming Christ's fully divine status. Again, we examine them in their canonical order.

2 Corinthians 2:10—Forgiveness Offered in the "Presence of Christ"; 2 Corinthians 8:21—"In the Presence of the Lord"

1. One of the more common features of OT theology is the fact that the eternal God had from the beginning chosen to be present with those whom he had created in his own image. This motif finds its beginnings in the creation narrative, where the first result of the fall is that the man and his wife "hid themselves from the presence of the LORD God" and consequently were banished from that presence. Thus throughout the biblical narrative judgment often takes the form of being cut off from the divine Presence—a reality already cited by Paul in 2 Thess 1:9 and applied to those who were persecuting his people in Thessalonica. But the divine Presence, imaged as beholding "the face of the Lord," was also deeply embedded in Israel's devotion. The psalmists long to be in God's presence (= see his face) and thus express distress in terms of God's hiding his face from them.

What Paul has done in 2 Cor 2:10 is to pick up this motif, so essential to Israel's relationship with God, and apply it now to Christ. Thus, in order to move the Corinthians toward forgiveness of the one who has wronged Paul, he declares that "what he has been forgiven, I also have forgiven δι' ὑμᾶς ἐν προσώπῳ Χριστοῦ [for your sakes in the presence of Christ]." What he probably intends by this is similar to oaths taken in the Lord's name: Christ will serve as the divine witness to his integrity.[71]

2. This same language, and same transfer of divine prerogative to Christ, occurs again in 2 Cor 8:21, where Paul is safeguarding his integrity with regard to the gift for the Jerusalem poor. In this case, however, Paul lifts language directly out of Prov 3:4 and applies it to his own relationship to the churches and the world with regard to this collection. Thus:

2 Cor 8:21	προνοοῦμεν γὰρ **καλὰ** οὐ μόνον		**ἐνώπιον κυρίου** ἀλλὰ	
		καὶ	ἐνώπιον	**ἀνθρώπων.**
Prov 3:4	καὶ προνοοῦ	**καλὰ**	**ἐνώπιον κυρίου**	
		καὶ		**ἀνθρώπων.**

2 Cor 8:21	*For we* **consider what is good** *not only*		**before the Lord** *but*	
		also	*before*	**human beings.**
Prov 3:4	*And* **consider what is good**		**before the Lord**	
		and		**human beings.**

Here is another case where Paul borrows a κύριος phrase from the Septuagint[72] and applies it to Christ,[73] although in this case the Septuagint translator took a bit of liberty with the Hebrew text. In conjoining lines in the Hebrew Bible, the text has "God/Elohim" in v. 3 and "the LORD/Yahweh" in line 1 of v. 4. For reasons not clear to us, the translator reversed these two mentions of Israel's God. But in either case, the "Lord" = Yahweh before whose face Paul desires to do what is good is now the Lord, Jesus Christ. Thus by way of this identification of Christ with the Septuagint's κύριος = Yahweh, another divine prerogative is attributed to Christ as presupposition.

2 Corinthians 2:17; 12:19—Speaking as One "in Christ" in the "Presence of God"

Given what Paul has affirmed about being in Christ's presence, it is of some interest christologically that in this same letter he twice affirms the truthfulness of his speech as one who is "in Christ" in the "presence of God" (2:17; 12:19). Here the same divine prerogative is being assumed by God the Father. Of christological import is Paul's insistence that he stands "in Christ" in the presence of God. The most probable reason for such an assertion is to reinforce the sincerity (= integrity) of what he has said. Although probably

---

[71] So Windisch, 91; Barrett, 93; Furnish, 158; Martin, 39; Thrall, 180–81.

[72] It seems so obvious, in fact, that one is quite surprised to read in Betz (77) that the Septuagint text "reads quite differently from the New Testament." The only differences, in fact, are the (necessary) change of verb and the emphatic addition of "not only/but also," the latter thus requiring an additional ἐνώπιον. This, after all, is intertextuality, not citation as such.

[73] This is denied by Furnish (424), who asserts without evidence or argumentation that it refers to God, as also in the preceding v. 19; Thrall (552) allows the possibility. Lambrecht (139) mistakenly, and without textual evidence, turns "the glory of the Lord" in v. 19 into "the glory of God."

locative and having to do with Paul's relational standing before God (i.e., he can stand in God's presence precisely because his present existence is "in Christ"), in this instance the phrase "in Christ" seems intended to carry the force of an oath as well. In which case it stands in close relation to "the truth of Christ" being in Paul, as he puts it in 2 Cor 12:10.

2 Corinthians 3:17—The Spirit of the Lord

I do not here intend to repeat the exegesis of this passage given above (pp. 177–80) but rather to isolate the significance of this phrase for christological purposes. Although Paul three times elsewhere refers to the Holy Spirit as "the Spirit of [Christ],"[74] only here does he pick up the language of the Septuagint itself and refer to him as "the Spirit of the Lord." That this is an intentional referent to Septuagintal language is made certain by the unique expression τὸ πνεῦμα κυρίου, where there is a definite article with the first noun but not with the corresponding genitive.

The best explanation for this unique phenomenon (for Paul) is that the article is intentionally anaphoric, thus pointing back to (or picking up from) the immediately preceding "identification" of "the Lord" in the Exodus passage with "the Spirit." Paul's actual phrase reads, ὁ δὲ κύριος τὸ πνεῦμά ἐστιν (Now "the Lord" the Spirit represents). In the pickup of that clause, where he will now clarify who "the Spirit" is, he thus begins with an anaphoric "the" = "the Spirit just referred to." But when he actually identifies the Spirit, Paul reverts to the anarthrous κυρίου, the predominant way the Septuagint translators glossed the Adonai that had come to be used for Yahweh; and in turn this is the certain indication that they considered κύριος in these cases to be God's name, not a title.

What is significant for our present purposes is that here is yet another Septuagint phrase that singularly refers to Yahweh, which Paul now uses explicitly to refer to Christ. Thus the Spirit of Yahweh is, for Paul, the Spirit of the living Christ—a matter of considerable christological significance.

2 Corinthians 5:9—Living So as "to Please the Lord";
2 Corinthians 5:10—The "Judgment Seat of Christ";
2 Corinthians 11:2—To "Present You to Christ"

In a passage where Paul has been reflecting on the present "decay" of his body and his eager expectation of its new expression (4:7–5:5), he turns in 5:6 toward a conclusion that will also serve as a subtle form of exhortation to the Corinthians: they should join him to "make it our goal to please him [the Lord]" (v. 9). The paragraph as a whole is dominated by reference to "the Lord," which, as always for Paul, refers to Christ.

---

[74] See Gal 4:6 ("of his Son"); Rom 8:9 ("of Christ"); Phil 1:19 ("of Jesus Christ"). See the further discussion in ch. 16, pp. 589–91.

Although the specific language is not used, the first sentences continue the "presence" motif. Thus our present bodily existence is expressed in terms of our being "away from the Lord" (v. 6), which points toward our resurrected, eschatological life in his eternal presence; thus we presently live by faith and not by sight (v. 7). In the same way, our eschatological existence is then expressed in terms of our being "at home with the Lord" (v. 8). Paul shows little desire for "heaven," but every kind of desire to be eternally present with the Lord who saved him.[75]

With that, the narrative turns into a couched appeal in which the divine prerogative of final judgment regarding people's actions on earth is now assumed by Christ. Paul begins in v. 9 by asserting, "So we make it our goal εὐάρεστοι αὐτῷ εἶναι [to be pleasing to him (the Lord)]." Here is an OT concept having to do with one's relationship with God that is now expressed in terms of pleasing Christ[76]—a divine prerogative quite casually attributed to Christ as Lord (cf. on 1 Cor 7:32 in ch. 3, p. 140).

The reason for pleasing Christ by the way we live is given in v. 10, where another altogether divine prerogative is attributed to Christ as a matter of course and without argumentation. Whatever else is true of late Jewish understanding of God, his own justice and his role as the absolute ruler of the universe meant that he, and he alone, would mete out eschatological judgment on all people at the end. Even a sapiential book such as Ecclesiastes ends on this note: ὅτι σὺν πᾶν τὸ ποίημα ὁ θεὸς ἄξει ἐν κρίσει, ἐν παντὶ παρεωραμένῳ, ἐὰν ἀγαθὸν καὶ ἐὰν πονηρόν (For God will bring every deed into judgment, including everything that has been overlooked, whether it is good or evil) (12:14). Indeed, Paul is perhaps echoing the final phrase of this passage with his own concluding εἴτε ἀγαθὸν εἴτε φαῦλον.[77]

In any case, what is significant for our present purposes is that this same judgment in Rom 14:10 is referred to as "the bēma of God," although in this latter instance later scribes understandably changed the "God" into "Christ." My point is the frequently repeated one, that what is seen elsewhere as an exclusively divine prerogative is assumed by Paul to be carried out by the fully divine Son.[78]

---

[75] On this matter, see discussion in ch. 9, pp. 412–13.

[76] With two different (interchangeable) words (the adjective εὐάρεστος [used here] and the verb ἀρέσκειν), Paul ordinarily speaks of pleasing God (1 Thess 2:15; 4:1; Rom 8:8; 12:1–2; 14:18; Phil 4:18); but in 1 Cor 7:32 and here he speaks of "pleasing the Lord" = Christ.

[77] See, e.g., Kreitzer (Jesus and God, 107), who is more confident than I at this point (his "perhaps" evolves into "Paul's decision to allude to it"). My hesitation rests with two matters, both having to do with Paul's use of φαῦλος instead of the πονηρός of Ecclesiastes. First, Paul uses this same combination in Rom 9:11 regarding the yet unborn Isaac and Esau, which makes it look very much like a stock phrase, of a kind that may have had a long history, but not with the same words; second, in the present instance (but not in Rom 9) there is also textual variation, but the variant is κακόν, not the Septuagint's πονηρόν, which suggests that scribes did not have the Ecclesiastes passage in mind either.

Here is the place also to note the eschatological phrase in 2 Cor 11:2, where Paul speaks of his desire "to present you to Christ." The imagery here is that of the father of the bride, who in Jewish culture was responsible for guarding his betrothed daughter so as to present her "pure" to the groom at the time of their wedding. Paul now assumes the role of "father of the bride," while the "groom" is Christ rather than "God" as one might ordinarily expect.[79] In any case, it is yet another instance where Paul speaks in a matter-of-fact way of his and their appearing together in the eschaton before Christ rather than before God. While there are perfectly good contextual reasons for this, my point again has to do with the ease with which Paul makes this kind of statement with reference to Christ, which in the OT was imagery used of God with his people.

2 Corinthians 5:11—The "Fear of the Lord"

Still in the same context of argumentation, Paul with an inferential οὖν (*therefore*) now applies all that was said in 4:7–5:10 to his own situation; and since the most immediate context is v. 10, with its mention of "the judgment seat of Christ," his pickup phrase is "knowing τὸν φόβον τοῦ κυρίου [*the fear of the Lord*]." This phrase, which is a key idea in the canonical Wisdom literature, moves along a spectrum of meaning from being "fearful" to having proper "awe" before God, while the latter tends to dominate. Here the "fear of the Lord" does not mean to be fearful of him but, in light of his being the final judge, to live with proper reverence and awe in his presence. Thus, here is yet another key OT phrase where the κύριος = Yahweh of the Septuagint has been appropriated and applied to Christ. Since this is the only occurrence of the phrase in Paul's writings, it turns out to be used exclusively with reference to Christ.[80]

2 Corinthians 10:5—"Obedience to Christ"

Obedience to someone is not necessarily a divine prerogative as such. Indeed, obedience to God is rarely expressed in Scripture; rather, one is obedient to his commands.[81] But the obedience called for in this passage is the ultimate kind of obedience due God alone. What Paul is taking on here are the mis-

---

[78]Cf. Barrett, who includes Rom 2:16 in the discussion: "The lack of formal consistency [in this matter] is not insignificant Christologically. God carries out judgement, but he carries it out through Jesus Christ; Jesus Christ judges; and his judgement is the judgement of God" (160).

[79]That is, this is a familiar idiom in the OT, where Israel is often depicted as betrothed or wedded to Yahweh; cf. Isa 54:5–6; 62:5; Ezek 16:8; Hos 2:19–20.

[80]Given both the immediate context (v. 10, where the "judge" is Christ) and the preceding multiplied use of κύριος in vv. 6–9 as referring to Christ (cf. Bultmann [146], "the κύριος, of course, is Christ"), one meets with surprise that Furnish (306, emphatically) applies "the fear of the Lord" to God.

guided arguments and false teachings of those who oppose him. Those who are carrying on this "warfare" against Paul are seen by him to be setting themselves "up against the knowledge of God." Through his own spiritual weapons (v. 4) he intends to engage these enemies in a contest that has divine obedience as its goal. That obedience in this case is expressed as "obedience to Christ." Thus another divine prerogative is attributed to Christ.

2 Corinthians 11:10—Appeal Based on "the Truth of Christ" That Is in Paul

In previous letters, and in keeping with the biblical tradition, Paul has taken his oaths "in the name of the Lord," with the Lord now being Jesus Christ.[82] In a slightly different way, and not actually an oath itself,[83] Paul appeals in this case to "the truth of Christ" that is in him. This very likely refers to Paul's understanding of Christ as indwelling him (by the Spirit);[84] and if Christ, the Son of God in whom all the promises of God find their "yes" (= truthfulness, trustworthiness [1:18]), dwells in Paul, that truth that is Christ at the same time guarantees Paul's own word. This is the kind of language that in the biblical revelation is basically reserved for God; indeed, in Isa 65:16 God explicitly says that "all who invoke a blessing in the land will do so by the God of truth; those who take an oath in the land will swear by the God of truth." For Paul, the "truth" that guarantees the trustworthiness of his "boast" rests now with Christ, who by dwelling in Paul guarantees his own trustworthiness.

2 Corinthians 12:1—"Revelations of the Lord"

In one of the more complex moments in the Pauline corpus, he chooses momentarily to play the "Spiritual experiences game" with his opponents in order to deflate the significance of such experiences as a criterion for genuine apostleship.[85] Whereas his opponents have disdained his weaknesses, Paul boasts in them as reflecting the Christ whose gospel he proclaims. When he goes on to the criterion of "revelations," he obviously intends the

---

[81] For direct obedience to God, see, e.g., Deut 4:30; but throughout Deuteronomy (and elsewhere) the way one shows such obedience is by keeping his commands.

[82] On this matter, see ch. 2 on 1–2 Thessalonians (pp. 46, 67–68) and ch. 3 on 1 Cor 1:3 (pp. 135–36).

[83] Whether Paul intends this as an actual oath (most think so) is not especially crucial because, as Thrall (687) notes, what Paul says here functions like one in any case.

[84] Most see it as a subjective genitive (of "source" or "origins"), but that seems to make "truth" more objective than this oath would seem to warrant; in any case, Furnish (493) rightly objects to the view that it refers to the gospel. Paul is appealing not to some objective truth but to the fact that what he is about to say is absolutely trustworthy.

[85] For a more complete argumentation for this perspective, see Fee, God's Empowering Presence, 347–50.

narrative of an unrevealed revelation both to outflank his opponents and to help the Corinthians put such experiences into proper context.

At issue for us in this study is the sense of the phrase that serves generally as a heading for the narrative itself: ὀπτασίας καὶ ἀποκαλύψεις κυρίου (*visions and revelations of the Lord*). Although most have taken the genitive κυρίου as subjective[86]—that is, Christ is the source of these experiences—it seems more likely that he is their object.[87] Not only is this how Paul uses this phrase elsewhere (Rom 2:5; 8:19; 1 Cor 1:7; Gal 1:12), but also in the end it seems to be the point of concern. That is, despite how it has been viewed by many, it is not simply revelatory experiences themselves in which they boast; rather, it is seeing Christ in such revelatory experiences that makes their boast special.

And that leads to our reason for including this phrase in the present discussion. Here is another OT idea that has been taken over by Paul and applied to Christ. Thus Ezekiel begins his prophetic ministry by dating the beginning of what he called "visions of God" (ὁράσεις θεοῦ), where the "vision" that immediately follows is ultimately, though indirectly, of God himself. For Paul, Christ is now the one revealed in such experiences.

2 Corinthians 12:8–10—Prayer Directed "to the Lord"

In keeping with patterns well in place by the time he wrote his first letters,[88] Paul narrates his threefold prayer to "the Lord" for deliverance from a satanic "thorn in my flesh." That the Lord to whom he prays can only be Christ Jesus is made certain not only by Paul's consistent and basically exclusive use of κύριος as referring to Christ but in this case also by the immediate context. The response in this case is, "My grace is sufficient for you," language that in the concluding benediction is attributed to Christ, as "love" is attributed to God the Father. Moreover, in the ensuing explanation of his

---

[86] For translations, cf. NIV/TNIV, REB, NJB, GNB (TEV), NLT, and NET BIBLE (without explanation!). Cf. in the commentaries Bultmann, 219; Furnish, 524; Martin, 397 (with a considerable list of others who go this way); Barnett, 559. Barrett (307) and Matera (277) suggest that it goes both ways. For the reasons for rejecting this view, see the next note.

[87] See Fee, *God's Empowering Presence*, 150 n. 192; so also Hughes, 427 n. 97; Thrall, 775; Lambrecht, 200. Although this is the minority view, what is seen to stand against it is the fact that no such "revelation" is detailed in what follows. But that seems to be something of an irrelevancy, since the phrase is intended as a "heading" in this case and almost certainly comes from the opposition. The ordinary sense of this genitive, both in Paul's writings and in the Septuagint, is "the Lord" as the one who is seen in the vision or revelation. See now esp. the discussion in Thrall, 774–75.

[88] See ch. 2 on 1–2 Thessalonians, pp. 51–53, 73–77; Windisch (388) and Héring (93 n. 20) assert (the latter emphatically) that this is the only instance in the genuine Paul where prayer is directed toward Christ (Matera [284] cites Windisch with approval). But as the evidence of 1 Thessalonians and 1 Corinthians reveals, that is patently not true. On this matter, see Hurtado, *Lord Jesus Christ*, 138–43.

acceptance of the divine verdict, he refers to "Christ's power" at work in him and states that he endures such weaknesses "for Christ's sake."

What again is noticeable is the ease with which Paul both makes his prayer to Christ, as one praying to God,[89] and reports it without a sense of encroaching on his monotheism in so doing. Such a view of things reflects his basic supposition about the risen Christ as the "Lord," now "seated at the right hand of the Father" (Ps 110:1), making intercession for his own. This is divine prerogative whatever else.

2 Corinthians 13:13(14)—Christ in a Triadic Benediction

Closely related to the preceding text and to Paul's habits throughout, he brings his letter to a close by offering a benediction that the Corinthians may receive "the grace of the Lord Jesus Christ." But only here in his letters does he add the Father and the Spirit to the benediction, so that he ends up with a remarkable triadic prayer that includes Christ, the Father, and the Spirit. Thus we encounter the second of three such texts (see 1 Cor 12:4–6; Eph 4:4–6) where Paul explicitly places Christ and the Spirit in the same context with God the Father, and this time in a benedictory prayer. Thus:

13:13   **ἡ χάρις τοῦ κυρίου Ἰησοῦ Χριστοῦ**
    καὶ   <u>ἡ ἀγάπη τοῦ θεοῦ</u>
    καὶ   ἡ κοινωνία τοῦ ἁγίου πνεύματος
               μετὰ πάντων ὑμῶν.

13:14   ***The grace of our Lord Jesus Christ,***
    and   <u>*the love of God,*</u>
    and   *the participation in the Holy Spirit*
               (be) with all of you.

A lesser Christology would have subordinated the role of Christ and the Spirit to that of God the Father. But not so Paul; he desires each person in the divine Triad to bless the Corinthians with that person's own special attribute. In the present case, what is attributed to the divine threesome is what is most characteristic of their ongoing ministry in the church. Everything is ultimately predicated on God's love, which found expression historically through the grace of Christ in his death and resurrection and is now made available to his people through their common participation in the Holy Spirit, who is the Spirit of both the Father and the Son.

It is precisely such prayer as this that led the church finally to formulate its understanding of God in ontologically Trinitarian terms, in which it was following the lead taken by Paul in his understanding of Christ as fully divine.[90]

---

[89] Cf. Furnish, 530.

[90] So also Barrett, 311; Barnett, 619; most commentators note the significance of this early triadic prayer to the three "persons."

Christ Devotion and Soteriology—2 Corinthians 5:14–6:2

Up to this point, we have not had occasion to speak to the relationship between Paul's understanding of Christ himself (Christology) and his understanding of the death and resurrection of Christ as God's means of "salvation" (soteriology)—the new-covenant means of creating a people for God's name. It is not that Paul has not mentioned Christ's role in salvation heretofore; he has indeed.[91] However, what has not occurred to this point in the letters is some kind of *exposition* of the means and meaning of Christ's death as "for us." With the present passage, that begins to change considerably. One reason for bringing this passage into a discussion of Pauline Christology is that here we find plainly expressed what we must recognize as presuppositional elsewhere: *who* it is who died for us is absolutely crucial to Paul's understanding of the story.

Paul is still in the long narrative in which he is defending himself and the character of his apostleship (see pp. 174–77 above) when he launches into what turns out to be the first somewhat lengthy exposition of the gospel itself—in this instance, understandably enough, under the rubric of reconciliation.

Another reason for bringing this passage into focus in the present study is in anticipation of what comes next in Galatians, where the centrality of Christ reaches a kind of zenith in Paul's letters. We have already looked at this text in part, by noting the significance of the phrase "who knew no sin" (pp. 165–67). Here I begin by pointing out two features that are important for the purposes of this study. First, the entire passage from v. 14 is simultaneously christocentric and theocentric; how one finally comes down on this question relates in part to what one is looking for or, on which of the two emphases one wants to focus. Second, here we find absolutely intact Paul's grammar of salvation, which we first noted in 2 Thess 2:13 and then again in 1 Cor 8:6. God the Father is always seen as the ultimate source of everything; but all that God in his love has purposed for our salvation has been carried out by Christ. Thus, in a very true sense, if God is the first word in these passages, it is usually true also that Christ is the last word. That is especially (literally) true in the exposition of reconciliation in vv. 18–21. It begins, "all things are from God," and God is the ultimate source of everything Christ does; but the final word is ἐν αὐτῷ (*in him [Christ]*).

The net result of all this is likewise twofold. On the one hand, because our salvation is predicated both on God's will and on Christ's willing activity on our behalf, Paul can emphasize the role of either God or Christ at will, depending on context. But when he brings them together in the same context, the relationship between them is always as noted in the preceding para-

---

[91] See, e.g., 1 Thess 5:10–11; 1 Cor 1:30–31; 5:7; 6:11; 8:11; 11:25–26; 15:3–4.

graph. On the other hand, when he focuses especially on the work of Christ and Paul's own relationship to Christ, one can scarcely miss an emphasis that I will refer to as "Christ devotion." There is a christocentricity to Paul's understanding of the gospel that goes beyond mere historical reality or theological insight. What emerges finally in Philippians as utter devotion to Christ is already well in place in these earlier letters. I propose that there is an inherent Christology in such devotion that Paul shows toward Christ that is seldom, if ever, expressed about God the Father.[92] I conclude this chapter, then, by noting how this works out in this great passage, which comes in two noticeable parts, vv. 14–17 and 18–21.

Christ as the Bringer of the New Order (2 Cor 5:14–17)

In this first part only Christ is mentioned. As Paul's penultimate response to those in Corinth who have been calling into question both his gospel of a crucified Messiah and his cruciform apostleship, he asserts that it is "the love of Christ" that constrains or compels him. This compulsion was born out of a deep conviction about Christ's death and resurrection (v. 14): since his death was on behalf of all, this means that the whole human race has been brought under the sentence of death; and Christ's resurrection means that in the new order only what he brings to life is actually living. Thus, those who do live (in God's new order) may now live only for the One who died for them and was raised again (v. 15). Moreover, this new order brought about by Christ's death and resurrection nullifies one's viewing anything any longer from the Corinthians' present perspective, whose values reflect an "old age" (κατὰ σάρκα [*according to the flesh*]) point of view. To view either Christ or anyone/anything else from that perspective is no longer valid (v. 16). Why? Because being in Christ means that one belongs to the new creation: the old has gone, the new has come (v. 17). It does not take much reading of Paul to recognize that this radical, new-order point of view—resurrection life marked by the cross!—lies at the heart of everything he thinks and does (cf. Phil 3:4–14). It is also easy to see the "why" of his utter devotion to Christ, which in itself, I suggest, has considerable christological overtones.

Christ, the Means of God's Reconciliation (2 Cor 5:18–21)

Having begun with the *results* of Christ's love expressed in his death for us, Paul now offers an exposition of its *means;* and now God becomes the grammatical subject of all the sentences, except for the application in v. 20. Everything is from God, who reconciled "us" (you Corinthians and me) to himself through Christ and has given us (me especially) the ministry of reconciliation. And with that we come to the key text, v. 19. While "God" is still

_____

[92] See further in ch. 11, pp. 488–95.

the subject, the relationship between God and Christ is now left open-ended enough to leave us with a (purposeful?) measure of ambiguity, but the Christology is of considerable import. The crucial part of the text reads,

5:19 θεὸς ἦν ἐν Χριστῷ κόσμον καταλλάσσων ἑαυτῷ
God was **in Christ** *the world* reconciling to himself

At issue for us is how to punctuate this clause, which is left quite open-ended by the sentence structure itself. Paul's order separates the linking verb ("was") and its participle plus reflexive pronoun ("reconciling to himself") by the prepositional phrase ("in Christ") and the object of the reconciliation ("the world"). What did Paul intend by this order? Three options emerge:

1. In the incarnation, God was reconciling the world to himself, which would require a comma after "Christ." Thus: *God was in Christ, reconciling the world to himself.*

2. "In Christ" (i.e., through the work of Christ), God was reconciling the world to himself, which would put commas around "in Christ." Thus: *God was, in Christ, reconciling the world to himself.*

3. The major emphasis is on Christ, in terms of what God was doing in reconciling the world to himself. Here there would be no commas, so as to keep the ambiguity. Thus: *God was in Christ the world reconciling to himself.*

The first option made its way into the English-speaking world through the KJV, and it was the predominant view for centuries. The now prevailing view, found in most of the recent English translations, has moved toward the second option. But the difficulty with this view is that it tends to make the ἦν . . . καταλλάσσων a paraphrastic imperfect, of a kind that has no analogy in Paul's letters, where the form of "to be" is separated at some distance from the participle that completes the verb form. For this reason, I think that the third option is the most likely, that Paul was deliberately ambiguous by placing the ἐν Χριστῷ immediately following the ἦν. To be sure, the preposition most likely has the force of agency (as in the second option), but at the same time it allows the closest kind of relationship between Father and Son. God himself was active in Christ as he reconciled the world to himself.

Although this is not incarnation in the traditional sense, it does suggest that Paul saw the closest kind of relationship between the will of the Father and the saving work of the Son; and it is out of this recognition that Paul has become such an avid and devoted follower of the Son. Thus, at the end of the day, it is a precarious exercise to discuss Paul's Christology without constantly being reminded of Christ's primary role in redemption itself. And that leads us to the next chapter, "Christology in Galatians."

Appendix I: The Texts

(brackets [[ ]] indicate texts with references to God alone; triple brackets [[[ ]]] with italics indicate citations from the LXX, where κύριος refers to Yahweh)

1:1 Παῦλος ἀπόστολος **Χριστοῦ Ἰησοῦ** διὰ <u>θελήματος θεοῦ</u> καὶ Τιμόθεος ὁ ἀδελφὸς <u>τῇ ἐκκλησίᾳ τοῦ θεοῦ</u> τῇ οὔσῃ ἐν Κορίνθῳ σὺν τοῖς ἁγίοις πᾶσιν τοῖς οὖσιν ἐν ὅλῃ τῇ Ἀχαΐᾳ,

1:2 χάρις ὑμῖν καὶ εἰρήνη ἀπὸ <u>θεοῦ πατρὸς ἡμῶν</u> καὶ **κυρίου Ἰησοῦ Χριστοῦ.**

1:3–5 ³<u>Εὐλογητὸς ὁ θεὸς καὶ πατὴρ</u> **τοῦ κυρίου ἡμῶν Ἰησοῦ Χριστοῦ**, <u>ὁ πατὴρ τῶν οἰκτιρμῶν καὶ θεὸς πάσης παρακλήσεως</u>, ⁴<u>ὁ παρακαλῶν ἡμᾶς ἐπὶ πάσῃ τῇ θλίψει ἡμῶν</u> εἰς τὸ δύνασθαι ἡμᾶς παρακαλεῖν τοὺς ἐν πάσῃ θλίψει διὰ τῆς παρακλήσεως ἧς <u>παρακαλούμεθα αὐτοὶ ὑπὸ τοῦ θεοῦ</u>. ⁵ὅτι καθὼς περισσεύει **τὰ παθήματα τοῦ Χριστοῦ** εἰς ἡμᾶς, οὕτως **διὰ τοῦ Χριστοῦ** περισσεύει καὶ ἡ παράκλησις ἡμῶν.

[[1:9–10 ⁹ἀλλὰ αὐτοὶ ἐν ἑαυτοῖς τὸ ἀπόκριμα τοῦ θανάτου ἐσχήκαμεν, ἵνα μὴ πεποιθότες ὦμεν ἐφ᾽ ἑαυτοῖς ἀλλ᾽ <u>ἐπὶ τῷ θεῷ τῷ ἐγείροντι</u> τοὺς νεκρούς· ¹⁰<u>ὃς</u> ἐκ τηλικούτου θανάτου <u>ἐρρύσατο ἡμᾶς καὶ ῥύσεται, εἰς ὃν ἠλπίκαμεν</u> ὅτι καὶ ἔτι ῥύσεται,]]

[[1:12 Ἡ γὰρ καύχησις ἡμῶν αὕτη ἐστίν, τὸ μαρτύριον τῆς συνειδήσεως ἡμῶν, ὅτι <u>ἐν ἁπλότητι καὶ εἰλικρινείᾳ τοῦ θεοῦ</u>, [καὶ] οὐκ ἐν σοφίᾳ σαρκικῇ <u>ἀλλ᾽ ἐν χάριτι θεοῦ</u>, ἀνεστράφημεν ἐν τῷ κόσμῳ, περισσοτέρως δὲ πρὸς ὑμᾶς.]]

1:14 καθὼς καὶ ἐπέγνωτε ἡμᾶς ἀπὸ μέρους, ὅτι καύχημα ὑμῶν ἐσμεν καθάπερ καὶ ὑμεῖς ἡμῶν **ἐν τῇ ἡμέρᾳ τοῦ κυρίου ἡμῶν** [v.l.-ἡμῶν] **Ἰησοῦ.**

1:18–22 ¹⁸<u>πιστὸς δὲ ὁ θεὸς</u> ὅτι ὁ λόγος ἡμῶν ὁ πρὸς ὑμᾶς οὐκ ἔστιν ναὶ καὶ οὔ. ¹⁹ὁ <u>τοῦ θεοῦ</u> **γὰρ υἱὸς Ἰησοῦς Χριστὸς ὁ ἐν ὑμῖν δι᾽ ἡμῶν κηρυχθείς**, δι᾽ ἐμοῦ καὶ Σιλουανοῦ καὶ Τιμοθέου, **οὐκ ἐγένετο ναὶ καὶ οὒ ἀλλὰ ναὶ ἐν αὐτῷ γέγονεν.** ²⁰<u>ὅσαι γὰρ ἐπαγγελίαι θεοῦ</u>, **ἐν αὐτῷ τὸ ναί·** διὸ **καὶ δι᾽ αὐτοῦ** <u>τὸ ἀμὴν τῷ θεῷ</u> πρὸς δόξαν δι᾽ ἡμῶν. ²¹<u>ὁ δὲ βεβαιῶν ἡμᾶς</u> σὺν ὑμῖν **εἰς Χριστὸν** <u>καὶ χρίσας ἡμᾶς θεός</u>, ²²<u>ὁ καὶ σφραγισάμενος ἡμᾶς καὶ δοὺς</u> τὸν ἀρραβῶνα τοῦ πνεύματος ἐν ταῖς καρδίαις ἡμῶν.

[[1:23 Ἐγὼ δὲ μάρτυρα <u>τὸν θεὸν</u> ἐπικαλοῦμαι ἐπὶ τὴν ἐμὴν ψυχήν, ὅτι φειδόμενος ὑμῶν οὐκέτι ἦλθον εἰς Κόρινθον.]]

2:10 ᾧ δέ τι χαρίζεσθε, κἀγώ· καὶ γὰρ ἐγὼ ὃ κεχάρισμαι, εἴ τι κεχάρισμαι, δι᾽ ὑμᾶς **ἐν προσώπῳ Χριστοῦ**,

2:12 Ἐλθὼν δὲ εἰς τὴν Τρῳάδα εἰς **τὸ εὐαγγέλιον τοῦ Χριστοῦ** καὶ θύρας μοι ἀνεῳγμένης **ἐν κυρίῳ**,

2:14–17 ¹⁴Τῷ δὲ θεῷ χάρις τῷ πάντοτε θριαμβεύοντι ἡμᾶς **ἐν τῷ Χριστῷ** καὶ τὴν ὀσμὴν **τῆς γνώσεως αὐτοῦ** φανεροῦντι δι' ἡμῶν ἐν παντὶ τόπῳ· ¹⁵ὅτι **Χριστοῦ εὐωδία** ἐσμὲν τῷ θεῷ ἐν τοῖς σῳζομένοις καὶ ἐν τοῖς ἀπολλυμένοις, ¹⁶οἷς μὲν ὀσμὴ ἐκ θανάτου εἰς θάνατον, οἷς δὲ ὀσμὴ ἐκ ζωῆς εἰς ζωήν. καὶ πρὸς ταῦτα τίς ἱκανός; ¹⁷οὐ γάρ ἐσμεν ὡς οἱ πολλοὶ καπηλεύοντες τὸν λόγον τοῦ θεοῦ, ἀλλ' ὡς ἐξ εἰλικρινείας, ἀλλ' ὡς ἐκ θεοῦ κατέναντι θεοῦ **ἐν Χριστῷ** λαλοῦμεν.

3:3–6 ³φανερούμενοι ὅτι ἐστὲ **ἐπιστολὴ Χριστοῦ** διακονηθεῖσα ὑφ' ἡμῶν, ἐγγεγραμμένη οὐ μέλανι ἀλλὰ πνεύματι θεοῦ ζῶντος, οὐκ ἐν πλαξὶν λιθίναις ἀλλ' ἐν πλαξὶν καρδίαις σαρκίναις. ⁴Πεποίθησιν δὲ τοιαύτην ἔχομεν **διὰ τοῦ Χριστοῦ** πρὸς τὸν θεόν. ⁵οὐχ ὅτι ἀφ' ἑαυτῶν ἱκανοί ἐσμεν λογίσασθαί τι ὡς ἐξ ἑαυτῶν, ἀλλ' ἡ ἱκανότης ἡμῶν ἐκ τοῦ θεοῦ, ⁶ὃς καὶ ἱκάνωσεν ἡμᾶς διακόνους καινῆς διαθήκης, οὐ γράμματος ἀλλὰ πνεύματος· τὸ γὰρ γράμμα ἀποκτέννει, τὸ δὲ πνεῦμα ζῳοποιεῖ.

3:14 ... ἄχρι γὰρ τῆς σήμερον ἡμέρας τὸ αὐτὸ κάλυμμα ἐπὶ τῇ ἀναγνώσει τῆς παλαιᾶς διαθήκης μένει, μὴ ἀνακαλυπτόμενον ὅτι **ἐν Χριστῷ** **καταργεῖται·**

3:16–18 ¹⁶ἡνίκα δὲ ἐὰν ἐπιστρέψῃ **πρὸς κύριον**, περιαιρεῖται τὸ κάλυμμα. ¹⁷ὁ δὲ κύριος τὸ πνεῦμά ἐστιν· οὗ δὲ τὸ πνεῦμα κυρίου, ἐλευθερία. ¹⁸ἡμεῖς δὲ πάντες ἀνακεκαλυμμένῳ προσώπῳ **τὴν δόξαν κυρίου** κατοπτριζόμενοι **τὴν αὐτὴν εἰκόνα** μεταμορφούμεθα ἀπὸ δόξης εἰς δόξαν καθάπερ **ἀπὸ κυρίου** πνεύματος.

4:2–7 ²ἀλλὰ ἀπειπάμεθα τὰ κρυπτὰ τῆς αἰσχύνης, μὴ περιπατοῦντες ἐν πανουργίᾳ μηδὲ δολοῦντες τὸν λόγον τοῦ θεοῦ ἀλλὰ τῇ φανερώσει τῆς ἀληθείας συνιστάνοντες ἑαυτοὺς πρὸς πᾶσαν συνείδησιν ἀνθρώπων ἐνώπιον τοῦ θεοῦ. ³εἰ δὲ καὶ ἔστιν κεκαλυμμένον τὸ εὐαγγέλιον ἡμῶν, ἐν τοῖς ἀπολλυμένοις ἐστὶν κεκαλυμμένον, ⁴ἐν οἷς ὁ θεὸς τοῦ αἰῶνος τούτου ἐτύφλωσεν τὰ νοήματα τῶν ἀπίστων εἰς τὸ μὴ αὐγάσαι **τὸν φωτισμὸν τοῦ εὐαγγελίου τῆς δόξης τοῦ Χριστοῦ**, ὅς ἐστιν εἰκὼν τοῦ θεοῦ. ⁵Οὐ γὰρ ἑαυτοὺς κηρύσσομεν ἀλλὰ **Ἰησοῦν Χριστὸν κύριον**, ἑαυτοὺς δὲ δούλους ὑμῶν **διὰ Ἰησοῦν.** ⁶ὅτι ὁ θεὸς ὁ εἰπών· ἐκ σκότους φῶς λάμψει, ὃς ἔλαμψεν ἐν ταῖς καρδίαις ἡμῶν πρὸς φωτισμὸν τῆς γνώσεως τῆς δόξης τοῦ θεοῦ **ἐν προσώπῳ Ἰησοῦ** [v.l.-Ἰησοῦ] **Χριστοῦ.** ⁷Ἔχομεν δὲ τὸν θησαυρὸν τοῦτον ἐν ὀστρακίνοις σκεύεσιν, ἵνα ἡ ὑπερβολὴ τῆς δυνάμεως ᾖ τοῦ θεοῦ καὶ μὴ ἐξ ἡμῶν·

4:10–15 ¹⁰πάντοτε **τὴν νέκρωσιν τοῦ Ἰησοῦ** ἐν τῷ σώματι περιφέροντες, ἵνα καὶ **ἡ ζωὴ τοῦ Ἰησοῦ** ἐν τῷ σώματι ἡμῶν φανερωθῇ. ¹¹ἀεὶ γὰρ ἡμεῖς οἱ ζῶντες εἰς θάνατον παραδιδόμεθα **διὰ Ἰησοῦν,** ἵνα καὶ **ἡ ζωὴ τοῦ Ἰησοῦ** **φανερωθῇ** ἐν τῇ θνητῇ σαρκὶ ἡμῶν. ¹²ὥστε ὁ θάνατος ἐν ἡμῖν ἐνεργεῖται, ἡ δὲ ζωὴ ἐν ὑμῖν. ¹³Ἔχοντες δὲ τὸ αὐτὸ πνεῦμα τῆς πίστεως κατὰ τὸ γεγραμμένον· ἐπίστευσα, διὸ ἐλάλησα, καὶ ἡμεῖς πιστεύομεν, διὸ καὶ λαλοῦμεν, ¹⁴εἰδότες ὅτι ὁ ἐγείρας **τὸν κύριον Ἰησοῦν** καὶ ἡμᾶς **σὺν Ἰησοῦ** ἐγερεῖ καὶ παραστήσει σὺν ὑμῖν. ¹⁵τὰ γὰρ πάντα δι᾽ ὑμᾶς, ἵνα ἡ χάρις πλεονάσασα διὰ τῶν πλειόνων τὴν εὐχαριστίαν περισσεύσῃ εἰς τὴν δόξαν τοῦ θεοῦ.

[[5:1 Οἴδαμεν γὰρ ὅτι ἐὰν ἡ ἐπίγειος ἡμῶν οἰκία τοῦ σκήνους καταλυθῇ, οἰκοδομὴν ἐκ θεοῦ ἔχομεν,]]

[[5:5 ὁ δὲ κατεργασάμενος ἡμᾶς εἰς αὐτὸ τοῦτο θεός, ὁ δοὺς ἡμῖν τὸν ἀρραβῶνα τοῦ πνεύματος.]]

5:6–10 ⁶Θαρροῦντες οὖν πάντοτε καὶ εἰδότες ὅτι ἐνδημοῦντες ἐν τῷ σώματι ἐκδημοῦμεν **ἀπὸ τοῦ κυρίου**· ⁷διὰ πίστεως γὰρ περιπατοῦμεν, οὐ διὰ εἴδους· ⁸θαρροῦμεν δὲ καὶ εὐδοκοῦμεν μᾶλλον ἐκδημῆσαι ἐκ τοῦ σώματος καὶ ἐνδημῆσαι **πρὸς τὸν κύριον.** ⁹διὸ καὶ φιλοτιμούμεθα, εἴτε ἐνδημοῦντες εἴτε ἐκδημοῦντες, **εὐάρεστοι αὐτῷ** εἶναι. ¹⁰τοὺς γὰρ πάντας ἡμᾶς φανερωθῆναι δεῖ ἔμπροσθεν **τοῦ βήματος τοῦ Χριστοῦ,** ἵνα κομίσηται ἕκαστος τὰ διὰ τοῦ σώματος πρὸς ἃ ἔπραξεν, εἴτε ἀγαθὸν εἴτε φαῦλον.

5:11–21 ¹¹Εἰδότες οὖν **τὸν φόβον τοῦ κυρίου** ἀνθρώπους πείθομεν, θεῷ δὲ πεφανερώμεθα· ἐλπίζω δὲ καὶ ἐν ταῖς συνειδήσεσιν ὑμῶν πεφανερῶσθαι. . . . ¹³εἴτε γὰρ ἐξέστημεν, θεῷ· εἴτε σωφρονοῦμεν, ὑμῖν. ¹⁴**ἡ γὰρ ἀγάπη τοῦ Χριστοῦ** συνέχει ἡμᾶς, κρίναντας τοῦτο, ὅτι **εἷς ὑπὲρ πάντων ἀπέθανεν,** ἄρα οἱ πάντες ἀπέθανον· ¹⁵καὶ **ὑπὲρ πάντων ἀπέθανεν,** ἵνα οἱ ζῶντες μηκέτι ἑαυτοῖς ζῶσιν ἀλλὰ **τῷ ὑπὲρ αὐτῶν ἀποθανόντι καὶ ἐγερθέντι.** ¹⁶Ὥστε ἡμεῖς ἀπὸ τοῦ νῦν οὐδένα οἴδαμεν κατὰ σάρκα· εἰ καὶ ἐγνώκαμεν **κατὰ σάρκα Χριστόν, ἀλλὰ νῦν οὐκέτι γινώσκομεν.** ¹⁷ὥστε εἴ τις **ἐν Χριστῷ,** καινὴ κτίσις· τὰ ἀρχαῖα παρῆλθεν, ἰδοὺ γέγονεν καινά· ¹⁸τὰ δὲ πάντα ἐκ τοῦ θεοῦ τοῦ καταλλάξαντος ἡμᾶς ἑαυτῷ **διὰ Χριστοῦ** καὶ δόντος ἡμῖν τὴν διακονίαν τῆς καταλλαγῆς, ¹⁹ὡς ὅτι θεὸς ἦν **ἐν Χριστῷ** κόσμον καταλλάσσων ἑαυτῷ, μὴ λογιζόμενος αὐτοῖς τὰ παραπτώματα αὐτῶν καὶ θέμενος ἐν ἡμῖν τὸν λόγον τῆς καταλλαγῆς. ²⁰**Ὑπὲρ Χριστοῦ** οὖν πρεσβεύομεν ὡς τοῦ θεοῦ παρακαλοῦντος δι᾽ ἡμῶν· δεόμεθα **ὑπὲρ Χριστοῦ,** καταλλάγητε τῷ θεῷ. ²¹**τὸν μὴ γνόντα ἁμαρτίαν** ὑπὲρ ἡμῶν **ἁμαρτίαν ἐποίησεν,** ἵνα ἡμεῖς γενώμεθα δικαιοσύνη θεοῦ **ἐν αὐτῷ.**

[[6:1 Συνεργοῦντες δὲ καὶ παρακαλοῦμεν μὴ εἰς κενὸν τὴν χάριν τοῦ θεοῦ δέξασθαι ὑμᾶς·]]

[[6:4 ἀλλ᾽ ἐν παντὶ συνίσταντες ἑαυτοὺς ὡς θεοῦ διάκονοι,]]

[[6:7 ἐν λόγῳ ἀληθείας, ἐν δυνάμει θεοῦ·]]

6:15 **τίς δὲ συμφώνησις Χριστοῦ** πρὸς Βελιάρ, ἢ τίς μερὶς πιστῷ μετὰ ἀπίστου;

[[6:16 τίς δὲ συγκατάθεσις ναῷ θεοῦ μετὰ εἰδώλων; ἡμεῖς γὰρ ναὸς θεοῦ ἐσμεν ζῶντος, καθὼς εἶπεν ὁ θεὸς . . .]]

[[6:16–18 (LXX)¹⁶ . . . ὅτι ἐνοικήσω ἐν αὐτοῖς καὶ ἐμπεριπατήσω καὶ ἔσομαι αὐτῶν θεὸς καὶ αὐτοὶ ἔσονταί μου λαός. ¹⁷διὸ ἐξέλθατε ἐκ μέσου αὐτῶν καὶ ἀφορίσθητε, *λέγει κύριος*, καὶ ἀκαθάρτου μὴ ἅπτεσθε· *κἀγὼ εἰσδέξομαι* ὑμᾶς [18]*καὶ ἔσομαι ὑμῖν εἰς πατέρα* καὶ ὑμεῖς ἔσεσθέ *μοι* εἰς υἱοὺς καὶ θυγατέρας, *λέγει κύριος παντοκράτωρ*.]]

[[7:1 Ταύτας οὖν ἔχοντες τὰς ἐπαγγελίας, ἀγαπητοί, καθαρίσωμεν ἑαυτοὺς ἀπὸ παντὸς μολυσμοῦ σαρκὸς καὶ πνεύματος, ἐπιτελοῦντες ἁγιωσύνην ἐν φόβῳ θεοῦ.]]

[[7:6 ἀλλ᾽ ὁ παρακαλῶν τοὺς ταπεινοὺς παρεκάλεσεν ἡμᾶς ὁ θεὸς ἐν τῇ παρουσίᾳ Τίτου,]]

[[7:9–11 νῦν χαίρω, οὐχ ὅτι ἐλυπήθητε ἀλλ᾽ ὅτι ἐλυπήθητε εἰς μετάνοιαν· ἐλυπήθητε γὰρ κατὰ θεόν, ἵνα ἐν μηδενὶ ζημιωθῆτε ἐξ ἡμῶν. [10]ἡ γὰρ κατὰ θεὸν λύπη μετάνοιαν εἰς σωτηρίαν ἀμεταμέλητον ἐργάζεται· ἡ δὲ τοῦ κόσμου λύπη θάνατον κατεργάζεται. [11]ἰδοὺ γὰρ αὐτὸ τοῦτο τὸ κατὰ θεὸν λυπηθῆναι πόσην κατειργάσατο ὑμῖν σπουδήν,]]

[[7:12 . . . ἀλλ᾽ ἕνεκεν τοῦ φανερωθῆναι τὴν σπουδὴν ὑμῶν τὴν ὑπὲρ ἡμῶν πρὸς ὑμᾶς ἐνώπιον τοῦ θεοῦ.]]

[[8:1 γνωρίζομεν δὲ ὑμῖν, ἀδελφοί, τὴν χάριν τοῦ θεοῦ τὴν δεδομένην ἐν ταῖς ἐκκλησίαις τῆς Μακεδονίας,]]

8:5 καὶ οὐ καθὼς ἠλπίσαμεν ἀλλὰ ἑαυτοὺς ἔδωκαν πρῶτον **τῷ κυρίῳ** καὶ ἡμῖν διὰ θελήματος θεοῦ

8:9 γινώσκετε γὰρ **τὴν χάριν τοῦ κυρίου ἡμῶν Ἰησοῦ Χριστοῦ**, ὅτι δι᾽ ὑμᾶς **ἐπτώχευσεν πλούσιος ὤν**, ἵνα ὑμεῖς **τῇ ἐκείνου πτωχείᾳ** πλουτήσητε.

[[8:16 χάρις δὲ τῷ θεῷ τῷ δόντι τὴν αὐτὴν σπουδὴν ὑπὲρ ὑμῶν ἐν τῇ καρδίᾳ Τίτου,]]

8:19 οὐ μόνον δέ, ἀλλὰ καὶ χειροτονηθεὶς ὑπὸ τῶν ἐκκλησιῶν συνέκδημος ἡμῶν σὺν τῇ χάριτι ταύτῃ τῇ διακονουμένῃ ὑφ᾽ ἡμῶν **πρὸς τὴν αὐτοῦ** [v.l.-αὐτοῦ] **τοῦ κυρίου δόξαν** καὶ προθυμίαν ἡμῶν,

8:21 προνοοῦμεν γὰρ καλὰ οὐ μόνον **ἐνώπιον κυρίου** ἀλλὰ καὶ ἐνώπιον ἀνθρώπων.

8:23 εἴτε ὑπὲρ Τίτου, κοινωνὸς ἐμὸς καὶ εἰς ὑμᾶς συνεργός· εἴτε ἀδελφοὶ ἡμῶν, ἀπόστολοι ἐκκλησιῶν, **δόξα Χριστοῦ**.

[[9:7–8 [7]ἕκαστος καθὼς προῄρηται τῇ καρδίᾳ, μὴ ἐκ λύπης ἢ ἐξ ἀνάγκης· ἱλαρὸν γὰρ δότην ἀγαπᾷ ὁ θεός. [8]δυνατεῖ δὲ ὁ θεὸς πᾶσαν χάριν περισσεῦσαι εἰς ὑμᾶς,]]

9:11–15 [11]ἐν παντὶ πλουτιζόμενοι εἰς πᾶσαν ἁπλότητα, ἥτις κατεργάζεται δι᾽ ἡμῶν εὐχαριστίαν τῷ θεῷ. [12]ὅτι ἡ διακονία τῆς λειτουργίας ταύτης οὐ μόνον ἐστὶν προσαναπληροῦσα τὰ ὑστερήματα τῶν ἁγίων, ἀλλὰ καὶ περισσεύουσα διὰ πολλῶν εὐχαριστιῶν τῷ θεῷ. [13]διὰ τῆς δοκιμῆς τῆς διακονίας ταύτης δοξάζοντες <u>τὸν θεὸν</u> ἐπὶ τῇ ὑποταγῇ τῆς ὁμολογίας ὑμῶν **εἰς τὸ εὐαγγέλιον τοῦ Χριστοῦ** καὶ ἁπλότητι τῆς κοινωνίας εἰς αὐτοὺς καὶ εἰς πάντας, ¹⁴καὶ αὐτῶν δεήσει ὑπὲρ ὑμῶν ἐπιποθούντων ὑμᾶς διὰ τὴν ὑπερβάλλουσαν <u>χάριν τοῦ θεοῦ</u> ἐφ᾽ ὑμῖν. ¹⁵<u>χάρις τῷ θεῷ</u> ἐπὶ τῇ **ἀνεκδιηγήτῳ αὐτοῦ δωρεᾷ.**

10:1 Αὐτὸς δὲ ἐγὼ Παῦλος παρακαλῶ ὑμᾶς **διὰ τῆς πραΰτητος καὶ ἐπιεικείας τοῦ Χριστοῦ**, ὃς κατὰ πρόσωπον μὲν ταπεινὸς ἐν ὑμῖν, ἀπὼν δὲ θαρρῶ εἰς ὑμᾶς·

10:4–8 ⁴τὰ γὰρ ὅπλα τῆς στρατείας ἡμῶν οὐ σαρκικὰ ἀλλὰ <u>δυνατὰ τῷ θεῷ</u> πρὸς καθαίρεσιν ὀχυρωμάτων, λογισμοὺς καθαιροῦντες ⁵καὶ πᾶν ὕψωμα ἐπαιρόμενον <u>κατὰ τῆς γνώσεως τοῦ θεοῦ</u>, καὶ αἰχμαλωτίζοντες πᾶν νόημα **εἰς τὴν ὑπακοὴν τοῦ Χριστοῦ**, ⁶καὶ ἐν ἑτοίμῳ ἔχοντες ἐκδικῆσαι πᾶσαν παρακοήν, ὅταν πληρωθῇ ὑμῶν ἡ ὑπακοή. ⁷Τὰ κατὰ πρόσωπον βλέπετε. εἴ τις πέποιθεν ἑαυτῷ **Χριστοῦ εἶναι**, τοῦτο λογιζέσθω πάλιν ἐφ᾽ ἑαυτοῦ, ὅτι **καθὼς αὐτὸς Χριστοῦ**, οὕτως καὶ ἡμεῖς. ⁸ἐάν [τε] γὰρ περισσότερόν τι καυχήσωμαι περὶ τῆς ἐξουσίας ἡμῶν ἧς **ἔδωκεν ὁ κύριος** εἰς οἰκοδομὴν καὶ οὐκ εἰς καθαίρεσιν ὑμῶν, οὐκ αἰσχυνθήσομαι.

[[10:13 ἡμεῖς δὲ οὐκ εἰς τὰ ἄμετρα καυχησόμεθα ἀλλὰ κατὰ τὸ μέτρον τοῦ κανόνος οὗ <u>ἐμέρισεν ἡμῖν ὁ θεὸς</u> μέτρου, ἐφικέσθαι ἄχρι καὶ ὑμῶν.]]

10:14 οὐ γὰρ ὡς μὴ ἐφικνούμενοι εἰς ὑμᾶς ὑπερεκτείνομεν ἑαυτούς, ἄχρι γὰρ καὶ ὑμῶν ἐφθάσαμεν **ἐν τῷ εὐαγγελίῳ τοῦ Χριστοῦ**,

10:17–18 ¹⁷Ὁ δὲ καυχώμενος **ἐν κυρίῳ** καυχάσθω· ¹⁸οὐ γὰρ ὁ ἑαυτὸν συνιστάνων, ἐκεῖνός ἐστιν δόκιμος, ἀλλὰ ὃν **ὁ κύριος συνίστησιν**.

11:2–4 ²ζηλῶ γὰρ ὑμᾶς <u>θεοῦ ζήλῳ</u>, ἡρμοσάμην γὰρ ὑμᾶς ἑνὶ ἀνδρὶ παρθένον ἁγνὴν παραστῆσαι **τῷ Χριστῷ**· ³φοβοῦμαι δὲ μή πως, ὡς ὁ ὄφις ἐξηπάτησεν Εὕαν ἐν τῇ πανουργίᾳ αὐτοῦ, φθαρῇ τὰ νοήματα ὑμῶν ἀπὸ τῆς ἁπλότητος [καὶ τῆς ἁγνότητος] **τῆς εἰς τὸν Χριστόν**. ⁴εἰ μὲν γὰρ ὁ ἐρχόμενος **ἄλλον Ἰησοῦν κηρύσσει ὃν οὐκ ἐκηρύξαμεν**, ἢ πνεῦμα ἕτερον λαμβάνετε ὃ οὐκ ἐλάβετε, ἢ εὐαγγέλιον ἕτερον ὃ οὐκ ἐδέξασθε, καλῶς ἀνέχεσθε.

11:7 Ἢ ἁμαρτίαν ἐποίησα ἐμαυτὸν ταπεινῶν ἵνα ὑμεῖς ὑψωθῆτε, ὅτι δωρεὰν <u>τὸ τοῦ θεοῦ εὐαγγέλιον</u> εὐηγγελισάμην ὑμῖν;]]

11:10 ἔστιν **ἀλήθεια Χριστοῦ** ἐν ἐμοὶ ὅτι ἡ καύχησις αὕτη οὐ φραγήσεται εἰς ἐμὲ ἐν τοῖς κλίμασιν τῆς Ἀχαΐας.

[[11:11 διὰ τι; ὅτι οὐκ ἀγαπῶ ὑμᾶς; <u>ὁ θεὸς οἶδεν</u>.]]

11:13 οἱ γὰρ τοιοῦτοι ψευδαπόστολοι, ἐργάται δόλιοι, μετασχηματιζόμενοι **εἰς ἀποστόλους Χριστοῦ**.

11:17 ὃ λαλῶ, **οὐ κατὰ κύριον λαλῶ** ἀλλ᾽ ὡς ἐν ἀφροσύνῃ, ἐν ταύτῃ τῇ ὑποστάσει τῆς καυχήσεως.

11:23 **διάκονοι Χριστοῦ** εἰσιν; παραφρονῶν λαλῶ, ὑπὲρ ἐγώ·

11:31 ὁ θεὸς καὶ πατὴρ **τοῦ κυρίου Ἰησοῦ** οἶδεν, ὁ ὢν εὐλογητὸς εἰς τοὺς αἰῶνας, ὅτι οὐ ψεύδομαι.

12:1–3 ¹Καυχᾶσθαι δεῖ, οὐ συμφέρον μέν, ἐλεύσομαι δὲ εἰς ὀπτασίας καὶ **ἀποκαλύψεις κυρίου**. ²οἶδα ἄνθρωπον **ἐν Χριστῷ** πρὸ ἐτῶν δεκατεσσάρων, εἴτε ἐν σώματι οὐκ οἶδα, εἴτε ἐκτὸς τοῦ σώματος οὐκ οἶδα, ὁ θεὸς οἶδεν, ἁρπαγέντα τὸν τοιοῦτον ἕως τρίτου οὐρανοῦ. ³καὶ οἶδα τὸν τοιοῦτον ἄνθρωπον, εἴτε ἐν σώματι εἴτε χωρὶς τοῦ σώματος οὐκ οἶδα, ὁ θεὸς οἶδεν,

12:8–10 ⁸ὑπὲρ τούτου τρὶς **τὸν κύριον** παρεκάλεσα ἵνα ἀποστῇ ἀπ᾽ ἐμοῦ. ⁹καὶ **εἴρηκέν** μοι· ἀρκεῖ σοι **ἡ χάρις μου**, ἡ γὰρ δύναμις ἐν ἀσθενείᾳ τελεῖται. ἥδιστα οὖν μᾶλλον καυχήσομαι ἐν ταῖς ἀσθενείαις μου, ἵνα ἐπισκηνώσῃ ἐπ᾽ ἐμὲ **ἡ δύναμις τοῦ Χριστοῦ**. ¹⁰διὸ εὐδοκῶ ἐν ἀσθενείαις, ἐν ὕβρεσιν, ἐν ἀνάγκαις, ἐν διωγμοῖς καὶ στενοχωρίαις, **ὑπὲρ Χριστοῦ**· ὅταν γὰρ ἀσθενῶ, τότε δυνατός εἰμι.

12:19 Πάλαι δοκεῖτε ὅτι ὑμῖν ἀπολογούμεθα. κατέναντι θεοῦ **ἐν Χριστῷ** λαλοῦμεν·

[[12:21 μὴ πάλιν ἐλθόντος μου ταπεινώσῃ με ὁ θεός μου πρὸς ὑμᾶς καὶ πενθήσω πολλοὺς τῶν προημαρτηκότων καὶ μὴ μετανοησάντων ἐπὶ τῇ ἀκαθαρσίᾳ καὶ πορνείᾳ καὶ ἀσελγείᾳ ᾗ ἔπραξαν.]]

13:3–7 ³ἐπεὶ δοκιμὴν ζητεῖτε **τοῦ ἐν ἐμοὶ λαλοῦντος Χριστοῦ**, ὃς εἰς ὑμᾶς **οὐκ ἀσθενεῖ ἀλλὰ δυνατεῖ** ἐν ὑμῖν. ⁴καὶ γὰρ **ἐσταυρώθη ἐξ ἀσθενείας, ἀλλὰ ζῇ** ἐκ δυνάμεως θεοῦ. καὶ γὰρ ἡμεῖς ἀσθενοῦμεν ἐν αὐτῷ, ἀλλὰ ζήσομεν **σὺν αὐτῷ** ἐκ δυνάμεως θεοῦ εἰς ὑμᾶς. ⁵Ἑαυτοὺς πειράζετε εἰ ἐστὲ ἐν τῇ πίστει, ἑαυτοὺς δοκιμάζετε· ἢ οὐκ ἐπιγινώσκετε ἑαυτοὺς ὅτι **Ἰησοῦς Χριστὸς** ἐν ὑμῖν; εἰ μήτι ἀδόκιμοί ἐστε. ⁶ἐλπίζω δὲ ὅτι γνώσεσθε ὅτι ἡμεῖς οὐκ ἐσμὲν ἀδόκιμοι. ⁷εὐχόμεθα δὲ πρὸς τὸν θεὸν μὴ ποιῆσαι ὑμᾶς κακὸν μηδέν,

13:10 διὰ τοῦτο ταῦτα ἀπὼν γράφω, ἵνα παρὼν μὴ ἀποτόμως χρήσωμαι κατὰ τὴν ἐξουσίαν ἣν **ὁ κύριος ἔδωκέν** μοι εἰς οἰκοδομὴν καὶ οὐκ εἰς καθαίρεσιν.

[[13:11 λοιπόν, ἀδελφοί, χαίρετε, καταρτίζεσθε, παρακαλεῖσθε, τὸ αὐτὸ φρονεῖτε, εἰρηνεύετε, καὶ ὁ θεὸς τῆς ἀγάπης καὶ εἰρήνης ἔσται μεθ᾽ ὑμῶν.]]

13:13 **ἡ χάρις τοῦ κυρίου Ἰησοῦ Χριστοῦ** καὶ ἡ ἀγάπη τοῦ θεοῦ καὶ ἡ κοινωνία τοῦ ἁγίου πνεύματος μετὰ πάντων ὑμῶν.

Appendix II: An Analysis of Usage

(* = anarthrous; + = with possessive pronoun; [LXX] = Septuagint echo/ citation)

2 Corinthians
θεός   78 + 2 LXX citations
Christ   75

The Data
1. κύριος Ἰησοῦς Χριστός (4)
   1:2   G*
   1:3   G+
   8:9   G+
   13:13 G
1a. Ἰησοῦς Χριστός κύριος (1)
   4:5   A*
2. κύριος Ἰησοῦς (3)
   1:14   G+ [v.l.-ἡμῶν]
   4:14   A
   11:31 G
3. Χριστὸς Ἰησοῦς (1)
   1:1   G*
3a. Ἰησοῦς Χριστός (3)
   1:19   N (appositive to υἱός)
   4:6   G* [v.l.-Ἰησοῦ]
   13:5   N* [v.l.-Χρ. Ιης.]
4. κύριος (18 + 8 = 26 [+ 2 =
                        Yahweh])
   2:12   D* (ἐν)
   3:16   A* (πρός)
   3:17   G*
   3:18   G*
   3:18   G* (ἀπό)
   5:6   G (ἀπό)
   5:8   A (πρός)
   5:11   G
   (6:17 N* [LXX = Yahweh])
   (6:18 N* [LXX = Yahweh])
   8:5   D
   8:19   G (w/ αὐτοῦ) [v.l.-αὐτοῦ]
   8:21   G* (ἐνώπιον)
   10:8   N
   10:17 D* (ἐν)

10:18 N
11:17 A* (κατά)
12:1   G*
12:8   A
13:10 N
5. Ἰησοῦς (7 + 12 = 19)
   4:5   A* (διά)
   4:10   G
   4:10   G
   4:11   A* (διά)
   4:11   G
   4:14   D* (σύν)
   11:4   A*
6. Χριστὸς (38 + 9 = 47)
   1:5   G
   1:5   G (διά)
   1:21   A* (εἰς)
   2:10   G*
   2:12   G
   2:14   D (ἐν)
   2:15   G*
   2:17   D* (ἐν)
   3:3   G*
   3:4   G (διά)
   3:14   D* (ἐν)
   4:4   G
   5:10   G
   5:14   G
   5:16   A*
   5:17   D* (ἐν)
   5:18   G* (διά)
   5:19   D* (ἐν)
   5:20   G* (ὑπέρ)
   5:20   G* (ὑπέρ)
   6:15   G*
   8:23   G*
   9:13   G
   10:1   G
   10:5   G

10:7	G*	12:10	G* (ὑπέρ)
10:7	G*	12:19	G* (ἐν)
10:14	G	13:3	G
11:2	D		7. υἱός (1 [+ 2])
11:3	A (εἰς)	1:19	N (τοῦ θεοῦ)
11:10	G*	[1:3	implied: ὁ θεὸς καὶ πατήρ
11:13	G*		τοῦ . . .]
11:23	G*	[11:31	implied: ὁ θεὸς καὶ πατήρ
12:2	D* (ἐν)		τοῦ . . .]
12:9	G		

5

Christology in Galatians

TURNING TO GALATIANS[1] FROM THE first four letters in the Pauline corpus is like entering a new world. Instead of taking up several concerns, Galatians is intensely single-focused on the issue of Gentile observance of the law, especially the basic matters that distinguished Diaspora Jews from their Gentile neighbors: circumcision, Sabbath, and food laws.[2] Paul's churches in Galatia have been invaded by some Jewish Christian intinerant missionaries—"agitators" Paul calls them—bent on bringing the Galatian Gentiles into obedience on these matters, thus "completing" their conversion. Paul's singular and passionate "no" to this issue comes to us as his letter to the churches of Galatia.

For this reason, Galatians is specifically and singularly given over to the question of soteriology—salvation in Christ, made effective by the Spirit. For the same reason, it is one of the most intensely christocentric letters in the corpus. But as was noted in the concluding word to the preceding chapter, this focus on Christ is always kept within the larger framework of Paul's undiminished Jewish monotheism. Thus, at every turn the focus is on the *work* of Christ, while God the Father is ultimately responsible for everything.

This double focus appears at the very beginning in the (considerably expanded) salutation: Paul's apostleship (v. 1) is "through Christ Jesus," to which Paul immediately appends, "and God the Father who raised him from the dead." The salutation proper (v. 3), with its wish of grace and peace, is, as always, "from God our Father and the Lord Jesus Christ." But in this case it is then expanded in terms of Christ's "giving himself for our sins, in order that he might deliver us from this present evil age," which is immediately qualified with "in keeping with the will of our God and Father," who is then the object of the concluding doxology. And so it goes throughout, especially

---

[1] Commentaries on Galatians are listed in the bibliography (pp. 641–42); they are cited in this chapter by author's surname only.

[2] Circumcision is always the predominant issue, since it was the ultimate covenant marker in Israel and was so abhorrent to Gentiles. Thus it is the issue that carries the argument throughout. The observance of "days" is mentioned in 4:10, and the narrative about food laws in 2:11–13 launches Paul directly into the primary argument of the letter.

at the key soteriological moments: God is the one who was pleased to reveal his Son in Paul (1:15–16); God sent first his Son and then the Spirit of his Son in order to redeem and certify Gentile adoption into God's family (4:4–7).

The net result of this singular focus on the saving work of Christ in the context of the Father's will is that we find much less in Galatians that is explicitly christological. But what we do find, as we have come to expect, are several presuppositional christological moments in which a high Christology is simply assumed, not made a point of argumentation.

A Preliminary Look at the Data

The various references to Christ and to God are found in appendix I at the end of this chapter; as throughout, an analysis of the different ways Paul speaks of Christ is found in appendix II. The data speak for themselves in terms of the emphases of the letter. Christ is referred to by name or title forty-five times, while θεός (*God*) is mentioned specifically only twenty-nine times. The most striking features with reference to Christ end up being two sides of the same coin. First, there is the sudden, thoroughly diminished use of the title ὁ κύριος (*the Lord*). Apart from the four instances of the combined name "the Lord Jesus Christ," which occur basically at the expected places, Jesus is referred to as "Lord" only twice: 1:19, where James is called "the brother of our Lord," and 5:10, in the very Pauline asseveration "I am persuaded ἐν κυρίῳ [*in the Lord*]." This means also that for the first time in the corpus there are no intertextual allusions or echoes from the OT where the Septuagint's κύριος = Yahweh refers to Christ.

Second, the title/name Χριστός (*Christ*), which occurs a total of thirty-eight times, is easily the most common referent in the letter, itself occurring nine times more than explicit mention of God. Twenty-two of these occur alone, and all but three of these (1:7; 6:2, 12) are without the definite article,[3] indicating that by now it is the primary name by which the Lord is mentioned. He is simply "Christ," not "the Christ = Messiah."

Along with these several observations, one should note the sudden increase of references to Christ as "the Son" (4x), where in each case he is specifically called "God's [his] Son."[4] Since this is the crucial christological item in this letter, we begin our analysis here.[5]

---

[3] The 3 exceptions occur in genitive combinations (τὸ εὐαγγέλιον τοῦ Χριστοῦ / τὸ νόμου τοῦ Χριστοῦ / τῷ σταυρῷ τοῦ Χριστοῦ) where the article is required by the controlling noun, which is articular.

[4] "The Son of God" in 2:20; "his Son" in the other three references (1:16; 4:4, 6).

[5] It is of some importance to note here that the two letters where "Son of God" Christology dominates in Paul are the two letters where he argues most vigorously within a more strictly Jewish frame of reference (Galatians and Romans). Indeed, it is the very first thing up in Romans (1:2–4). This in itself should have caused some hesitation among those who argued for Hellenistic origins of this motif.

Christ, God's Messianic Son: Preexistent and Incarnate

In the discussion of 1 Thess 1:1, 10, we noted that in the first occurrence of θεός in the corpus God is called "the Father" (1:1), and this in close proximity to the first occurrence of the designation of Jesus as "his Son" in 1:10, in this case as the exalted One whose coming will be accompanied by God's wrath, from which his people will be rescued. A similar thing happens again in 1 Cor 1:1, 9, where the Christian community is thought of in terms of "the κοινωνία [*fellowship*] of/with God's Son." This occurs yet again at the beginning of 2 Corinthians, where in 1:3 God is now specifically identified, and hereafter to be known, as "the Father of our Lord Jesus Christ," whose Son in v. 19 is then described as the divine "yes" to all of the promises of God (the Father).

We further observed regarding 1 Cor 15:23–28 that the designation "Son" comes at the end of a passage where Christ is noted as the presently reigning heavenly "king." At the resurrection of the believing dead, when the soteriological cycle is thus completed, "the Son himself" turns everything back into the hands of the Father. This text in particular, which ties "the Son" with the "king," reflects Jewish messianic expectations, which again are explicitly in evidence in Col 1:12–16.[6]

These data indicate that even though it is not Paul's most frequent designation for his Savior, Jesus as Son of God does in fact carry considerable weight for him, both theologically and christologically. The reasons for this emerge in the three "Son of God" passages in this letter, where Paul first refers to his own conversion in terms of "God . . . revealing his Son *in me*" so that he (Paul) might proclaim the Son to the Gentiles. This is followed in 2:20 by a passage full of "Christ devotion," where Paul speaks of the one who lives in him as "the Son of God, who loved *me* and gave himself for *me*." All of this climaxes in 4:4–7, where Paul speaks of the Son as "having been sent" by the Father in order to "redeem those under the law, so that we might receive adoption to sonship." This is not only the crucial christological passage in this letter but also one of the more important in the corpus.

But before looking at these three passages in some detail, we begin by noting a significant moment in the argument of 3:1–4:7, where implicit messianism is also in view: Christ as Abraham's true seed (3:16).

Galatians 3:16—Abraham's "Seed," Who Is Christ

Paul's passion in the long argument of 2:15–4:7 is to convince the Galatians that "doing law" is no longer an option for those redeemed by Christ and living by the Spirit. After an opening foray in which the issue

---

[6] See pp. 293–98 below.

is presented and the logical absurdity of their position demonstrated (2:15–19),[7] Paul then appeals to their own experience of the Spirit as being quite apart from "works of law" (3:1–5). To offer biblical evidence in support of the experience of Christ and the Spirit (3:6–9), Paul settles on the Abraham narrative in Gen 12:1–25:11, for obvious reasons: Abraham is simultaneously (1) the father of the Jewish nation, (2) the recipient of the promise that through him God will bless the "nations" (= Gentiles), (3) the recipient of the covenant of circumcision, which is the major issue being fought over in this letter, and (4) the one of whom Scripture says that "his faith [in God] was credited to him as righteousness." Paul's subsequent argument based on this narrative (3:10–4:7) turns out to be a thing of wonder, as he keeps all of these balls in the air without losing any, while all the time bringing the argument to the climactic moment in 4:4–7.

At an early moment in the argument, Paul takes up the crucial issue: who are Abraham's true "children," his "seed" who will inherent the promise that includes the blessing of the Gentiles? The final answer to this question is given in 3:29: "those who are of Christ" are Abraham's true descendants ("seed") and thus "heirs in keeping with the promise." It is this conclusion that is elaborated in 4:4–7. In the process of getting to this point, Paul identifies *Christ* as the true "seed" of Abraham, so that those who are "of Christ" in turn are Abraham's true descendants. How Paul gets there needs some unpacking.

Near the beginning of the biblical story, Israel as a whole is/are identified as God's "son" (Exod 4:22–23); at a later time in the story their king, who represents the people, is likewise identified as God's "son" (Ps 2:7). Thus, after the (apparent) demise of the Davidic dynasty, "Son of God" becomes a messianic symbol. In the Gospel narratives, Jesus himself steps into this role as messianic King, who assumes Israel's identity[8] and becomes its deliverer, so that he in turn can make his people once more "the sons of God."

---

[7] Although Paul's sentences are tight (2:15–19), the logic is manageable. First premise: believers in Christ, both Jew and Gentile, have not been observant; second premise: if the agitators are right, that we must also keep (certain aspects of) the law, then by our not keeping the law at these points we in effect are lawbreakers, thus sinners (like the Gentiles, who by nature do not keep the law); conclusion: since we are not keeping the law because of our faith in Christ, yet we are found now to be lawbreakers, which means that Christ is responsible for our being sinners (Χριστὸς ἁμαρτίας διάκονος = Christ has become the servant of sin). No wonder his response is μὴ γένοιτο, "God forbid!"

[8] Thus he goes into the water (of baptism), where he is designated by the heavenly voice as "God's beloved Son" (echoing the Septuagint of Gen 22:2 and Ps 2:7); he then comes out to be tested forty days in the wilderness, during which he cites passages from Deuteronomy where Israel had failed the test, and then enters his public ministry by gathering *twelve* men around him. On this matter, see further N. T. Wright, *Jesus and the Victory of God* (Minneapolis: Fortress, 1996), 474–539.

This is the messianic vision that Paul is picking up in 3:6–4:7. Thus early on he moves in this direction by identifying Christ as the (singular) "seed" of Abraham (3:16), who is thus the true heir to the promise as well (which is now available to God's people, as they are "of Christ"). In something of a wordplay on "seed," a collective singular in Greek as in English, Paul makes a deliberate point of its being singular and therefore (prophetically) pointing forward to the Messiah.[9] God's promise to Abraham was to his "seed" (e.g., Gen 13:15), not "seeds," and the messianic "seed" is Christ.[10] This, then, is the messianic "Son of God" Christology that lies behind the concluding affirmations of 4:4–7.

Galatians 4:4–7 (and Gal 1:19)

4:4–7 ⁴ὅτε δὲ ἦλθεν τὸ πλήρωμα τοῦ χρόνου, ἐξαπέστειλεν ὁ θεὸς τὸν υἱὸν αὐτοῦ, γενόμενον ἐκ γυναικός, γενόμενον ὑπὸ νόμον, ⁵ἵνα τοὺς ὑπὸ νόμον ἐξαγοράσῃ, ἵνα τὴν υἱοθεσίαν ἀπολάβωμεν. ⁶Ὅτι δέ ἐστε υἱοί, ἐξαπέστειλεν ὁ θεὸς[11] τὸ πνεῦμα τοῦ υἱοῦ[12] αὐτοῦ εἰς τὰς καρδίας ἡμῶν κρᾶζον· αββα ὁ πατήρ. ⁷ὥστε οὐκέτι εἶ[13] δοῦλος ἀλλὰ υἱός· εἰ δὲ υἱός, καὶ κληρονόμος διὰ θεοῦ.[14]

---

[9] This is very similar to what happens in the OT with the word "Son" itself, which in Exod 4:22–23 is a collective designation for the whole of Israel but in later kingship materials finds its singular focus on the king himself (e.g., Ps 2:7). See further the discussion of Col 1:12–15 below (pp. 293–98).

[10] For a messianic understanding of this passage, cf. Lightfoot, 142–43, Longe-necker, 132; Hansen, 98; Dunn, 184; Martyn, 340.

[11] The expressed subject of the sentence ("God") has been omitted in B 1739 sa. Given this attestation and the tendency on the part of scribes to add subjects, the "omission" could easily be argued for as original. On the other hand, it is far more likely that Paul himself is responsible for the perfect symmetry of this sentence in relationship to v. 4 and therefore that the subject was omitted in B, or its nearest relative, which was then picked up in the other two very closely related witnesses.

[12] Quite missing the Pauline parallel, 𝔓⁴⁶ and Marcion (probably independently) omit the words τοῦ υἱοῦ, which produces a text that reads "God sent forth his Son" (v. 4); "God sent forth his Spirit" (v. 6). If this was a deliberate omission (as it most likely was, although it could have been produced by homoeoteleuton), then it was either for theological reasons (to avoid confusion about the Spirit, that he is the Spirit of God, not the Spirit of Christ) or for less theological reasons (simply trying to "clean up" what they assumed to be an awkward way of stating Paul's point, i.e., that God sent both the Son and the Spirit). But the omission simply misses too much; see the discussion below.

[13] Only here in this letter does Paul switch to the second person *singular* when addressing the whole people, probably as a way of individualizing his point.

[14] This θεοῦ is found in 𝔓⁴⁶ ℵ* A B C* 1739*ᵛⁱᵈ lat bo; that this is the original text is made certain by (1) its early and excellent support and (2) the fact that its very difficulty is what has led to the five variations found in the textual tradition, all of which can be explained on the basis of this as the original reading, which is not the case for any other of the variant readings.

> [4]*But when the fullness of time came, <u>God sent forth</u> **his Son, born**[15] *of a* **woman, born under law,** [5]*in order that* **he might redeem** *those under law, in order that we might receive adoption as "sons";*[16] [6]*and because you are "sons," <u>God sent forth</u>* **the Spirit of** *his* **Son** *into our hearts,* **crying out** *"Abba, Father."* [7]*So then you are no longer a slave but a "son"; and if a "son," then an heir through God.*

This sentence offers the christological-soteriological basis for Paul's singular interest throughout the letter: because they are in Christ Jesus (3:26, 28) and Christ is being "formed" in them (4:19), the Galatian Gentiles do not need to come "under Torah." It begins with language that ties what is about to be said to the preceding analogy (vv. 1–2) and its application (v. 3). In contrast to a former time when God's people were no better off than "a minor," still under the tutelage of a slave-pedagogue, God's time for them to reach their "majority" has now arrived.[17] God's time, as Paul has argued throughout, came with Christ, especially through his redemptive work on the cross. Although Paul's emphases in what follows are thus primarily soteriological, there also emerges a variety of "Son of God" affirmations (Jewish messianism, preexistence, incarnation, knowledge of the historical Jesus), which are crucial to Paul's special interests and therefore cause for close scrutiny.

1. The substratum of *Jewish messianism* in this passage lies with the middle lines of what turns out to be a piece of a-b-b'-a' chiasm,[18] enclosed in turn by the two primary declarations of God's having sent his Son and the Spirit of his Son. Thus:

---

[15]Gk. γενόμενος (in both clauses), which literally means "having become." In light of the similar usage in Phil 2:7b–8, these participles express "narrative action" (to borrow R. B. Hays's terminology [*The Faith of Jesus Christ: An Investigation of the Narrative Substructure of Galatians 3:1–4:11* (SBLDS 56; Chico, Calif.: Scholars Press, 1983), 105]). Thus, when one "has become" from a woman, one is "born." Unfortunately, this common (and correct) translation into English (and most other languages) causes the English reader to miss its parallels in the similar narrative in Phil 2:7b–8a. See the further discussion in 2(c) below.

[16]This word is a technical term for the adoption of a male heir into a Roman home (see the note in the TNIV), thus creating a wordplay on the language of "son" (God's Son and we as "sons"), which is, unfortunately, difficult to put into contemporary English without appearing to be gender exclusive. To render it "children" here (legitimate though it is in meaning) is to lose the wordplay. For this reason, I have chosen to translate it as "sons" as a way of signaling the wordplay and trying to avoid the gender difficulty.

[17]Note Hansen's (114–16) helpful headings for these two sections: "When sons were the same as slaves"; "When slaves became sons."

[18]Noted as early as Lightfoot (168) and regularly picked up in the commentaries.

(A)			God sent his Son,
	(a)		born of a woman
		(b)	born under the law,
		(b′)	to redeem those under the law,
	(a′)		that we might be adopted as "sons"
			[and to effect this]
(B)			God sent the Spirit of his Son

The two "b" lines together affirm: (1) the Son was born in the context of Judaism; and (2) his purpose in coming was "to redeem" those who are in present bondage. Thus, just as Moses functioned as "redeemer" of Israel, leading them, under God's power and jurisdiction, out of bondage to slavery in Egypt, so now the "kingly Son of God" has come from God to effect "redemption" for those enslaved to the law.

2. But now it turns out that the new "Redeemer King [God's Son]" is also the eternal Son of God, who was sent from heaven to redeem. In this move, Paul states explicitly what was presupposed in 1 Cor 8:6 (in terms of his preexistence) and expressed metaphorically as Christ's own action in 2 Cor 8:9 (in terms of his incarnation). Thus, in language that seems deliberately chosen[19] so as to tie together the work of Christ and the Spirit, Paul begins by saying that "God ἐξαπέστειλεν his Son."

Despite an occasional voice to the contrary,[20] three matters indicate that this assertion assumes Christ's *preexistence*,[21] that Christ is himself divine and came from God to effect redemption: (a) the use of the verb "he sent

---

[19] These are the only two occurrences of this word in Paul. For this reason, and because of the "fomulaic" feel to the whole, it has been popular to find here a pre-Pauline soteriological formula, which Paul used even if he did not fully integrate it into his own theology (!). Much of this discussion stems from several articles by E. Schweizer, who created such a "formula" on the basis of the Wisdom of Solomon and a passage in Philo (see esp. "Zum religionsgeschichtlichen Hintergrund der 'Sendungsformel' Gal 4,4f., Rm 8,3f., Joh 3,16f., 1 Joh 4,9," *ZNW* 57 [1966], 455–68 [for a shortened version in English, see his entry on υἱός in *TDNT* 8:354–57, 363–92]); cf. the view of his former student W. Kramer: "The influence of Wisdom speculation on [Paul's] formulation is not to be doubted" (!) (*Christ, Lord, Son of God*, 121 n. 406). On the particularly doubtful nature of this very speculative study, and especially its relationship to Wisdom, see Fee, *God's Empowering Presence*, 911–13; cf. Dunn (*Christology in the Making*, 39–43), who rightly rejects it and (correctly, I would argue) sees Jesus' parable of the Tenants in the Vineyard (Mark 12:1–12) as the proper place to look for "origins" of the language. But at the same time, Dunn substitutes an equally dubious Adam Christology in its place. Although Dunn has rightly caught the Pauline emphasis on the Son's humanity, there is no analogy for Adam to be equated with "Son of God" traditions.

[20] See, e.g., Bousset, *Kyrios Christos*, 208–20; and esp. Dunn, *Christology in the Making*, 38–44, followed by Tuckett, *Christology and the New Testament*, 51–52.

[21] For a different set of three reasons, see Matera, *New Testament Christology*, 106. Besides "born of a woman," he adds that Christ's "Sonship" was unique and that his being preexistent Son "endows his work with salvific value."

forth," especially in light of its parallel in v. 6 about *sending forth* the Spirit; (b) the otherwise unnecessary clause γενόμενον ἐκ γυναικός (*"born" of a woman*); and (c) the use of the participle γενόμενος (*having come to be*) rather than γεννώμενος, the ordinary verb for "birth." Each of these needs further comment.

(a) It must be acknowledged up front that the compound ἐξαποστέλλω on its own does not necessarily imply the sending forth of a preexistent being.[22] After all, in a different context in Rom 8:3 Paul himself repeats what is said here and uses πέμπω, the ordinary verb for "sending," which has no implication that the one sent had prior existence. So also ἐξαποστέλλω appears, for example, regularly in Acts for the "sending away" of people (9:30; 17:14) or of "sending" someone on a mission (11:22); and on the divine side, it is used of God's "commissioning" human servants without concern for their "origins" (7:12; 22:21). But it is also true that in other contexts God "sends forth" angels as divine messengers on earth (e.g., Gen 24:40; Acts 12:11) or prayer is made for God to "send forth" his (now personified) Wisdom to Solomon (Wis 9:10). At issue in the present case, then, is not what the verb *could* possibly mean but what Paul himself was presupposing and what the Galatians were expected to pick up by its use in these two sentences.

Here is where the twin usage about the Spirit in v. 6 becomes relevant. Using language that echoes Ps 104:30 (103:30 LXX),[23] and in a clause that is both parallel with and intimately related to what is said in vv. 4–5, Paul says that "God sent forth *the Spirit of his Son*" into our hearts with the *Abba*-cry. With this second sending, God thus verifies the "sonship" secured by the Son, whom God had previously "sent forth." It is this double sending, where in the second instance God's sending forth the Spirit of his Son can only

---

[22] Although this has been commonly assumed (note, e.g., Lightfoot: "The word assumes the preexistence of the Son" [168]). But see Burton (217), who recognized that this was not the case but pointed out that the logic of the sentence itself seemed to demand such a view. Dunn (*Christology in the Making*, 39) makes far too much of this point; in an attempt to "divide and conquer," much of his case against preexistence rests on his scouring the literature to show evidence that this verb does not itself carry the case, a point to which most will readily accede. But what one must be careful not to imply, as Dunn seems to, is that because it does *not necessarily* refer to such a sending forth, it therefore *probably* does not. The overall evidence of the passage suggests exactly the opposite. Since it *may* refer to a sending forth of a heavenly being, the overall context and language of this passage, especially the following two phrases, suggest that here *it does indeed.* Dunn's argument fails especially to take into account the significance of the parallel language of the Spirit in v. 6. Thus, although it certainly is true that the concern for Paul is not in fact Jesus' origins, the cumulative weight of the evidence and the way all of this is expressed certainly *presuppose* preexistence. Cf. W. Kasper, *Jesus the Christ* (trans. V. Green; New York: Paulist Press, 1976), 173, and most commentaries.

[23] Gk. ἐξαποστελεῖς τὸ πνεῦμα σου, καὶ κτισθήσονται (*You will send forth your Spirit, and they will be created*).

refer to the preexistent *Spirit of God*, now understood equally as the Spirit of the Son, that makes certain that in the first instance Paul is also speaking presuppositionally about Christ's preexistence.[24]

(b) In keeping with his whole argument to this point, for Paul, the work of Christ is a historical and objective reality. At one point in human history, when God's set time had arrived, the messianic Son of God entered human history (γενόμενον [*born*] from a woman) within the context of God's own people (γενόμενον [*born*] under the law) so as to free people from the slave tutor—Torah observance—by giving them "adoption as 'sons.'" What is striking about the phrase "born of a woman" is how unnecessary it is to the argument as a whole.[25] Paul's concern lies precisely in the next two items of his sentence ("born under the law, in order to redeem those under the law"). His first mentioning Christ as γενόμενον ἐκ γυναικός (*born of a woman*) seems understandable only if one recognizes the presuppositional nature of Christ's preexistence that is the predicate of the whole sentence. Or to put it another way, the fact that both γενόμενος phrases emphasize the Son's *human* condition seems to suggest that the sending word *presupposes* a prior existence that was not human.[26]

(c) Finally, the choice of the participle γενόμενον for these two subordinate clauses would seem to carry more significance than it is usually given, especially as twin modifiers of ἐξαπέστειλεν. While it is true that γίνομαι *can* mean "born,"[27] and for the purposes of making sense in English almost

[24] So also Burton, 217; cf. Bruce: "If the Spirit was the Spirit before God sent him, the Son was presumably the Son before God sent *him*" (195). It is of some interest that Dunn's analysis of this verb is strictly limited to v. 4; for obvious reasons, he simply avoids any discussion of its possible meaning in v. 6 (see the critique in Fee, *God's Empowering Presence*, 402 n. 127).

[25] The fact that nothing in the argument is picked up from this phrase, thus indicating a lack of *necessity* in the argument in context, is one of the factors that has led many to think that Paul is here using a pre-Pauline "sending formulation" (see n. 18 above); cf. Betz, 207; Longenecker, 166–67. It is a remarkable piece of historical investigation to argue that a sentence found *only* in Paul in all of ancient literature, by its very uniqueness within the Pauline corpus, thus becomes grounds for looking for a pre-Pauline formula. This, of course, can be neither proved nor disproved; but when it is further suggested that one can find the Pauline "additions" to the prior formula, which only exists by excising parts of Paul's sentence (!), then it looks very much as though the formula is a "unique" scholarly creation.

[26] Cf. Burton: "Both [b] clauses are evidently added to indicate the humiliation . . . to which the Son was in the sending forth subjected, the descent to the level of those whom he came to redeem" (217). Thus, rather than implying that the emphasis lies only on Jesus' *humanity*, not his preexistence (as Tuckett, *Christology*, 52–53), this should be seen rather as emphasizing his humanity precisely *because* the presuppositional common ground is his preexistence, thus not allowing a "docetic" Christ.

[27] Indeed, it is of some interest that this is the first meaning offered in BDAG ("to come into being through process of birth"); but in this case, putting this meaning first stands over against Danker's ordinary way of handling such verbs, where the first meaning usually given is the one from which all others evolve. In this case, that comes second, "to come into existence." Moreover, of his five examples under this

demands such a rendering here, the fact is that the verb has the primary sense of "coming to be, coming into existence," and therefore is one of the more flexible verbs in the language (often simply a substitute for "to be"). The point to be made is that its use here is demanded neither by context nor meaning. In fact, later in the chapter, when referring to the birth of Ishmael (and Isaac, by implication), Paul uses the ordinary verb for "to be born" (γεννάω [4:23, 24, 29]).

Furthermore, and more importantly, the two clauses are most likely intended to be posterior to the main verb, and thus they demand a sequence that implies the Son's preexistence followed by his "coming to be" from a human mother within the context of Judaism. Otherwise, the participles would need to be expressed as antecedent to the main verb: having been born of a woman and under the law, the Son was sent by God to redeem those under the law. That is grammatically possible, but it seems to make light of the very point of the sentence itself: God's Son was sent into our human condition precisely because only thus could redemption be effected.[28] Thus, "birth" from Mary in this case is expressed in terms of Christ's "coming into earthly existence" through a human mother. And this leads to our third christological observation.

3. Paul's emphasis with this phrase ("born of a woman"), in passing though it seems to be, is on the *incarnation* of Christ, who thereby stands in stark contrast to the ahistorical, atemporal στοιχεῖα τοῦ κόσμου (*elemental spiritual forces of the world* [v. 3 TNIV]) to which these former pagans had been subject. That is, if this clause makes certain that the main clause, "God sent his Son at the right time in history," implies his preexistence, then in its own way it puts special emphasis on his genuine humanity:[29] "the Son of God" was no docetic Christ but shared fully in our humanity, preexistent Son of God though he was.

Thus, in the interest of his argument to this point—Gentiles by the Spirit have become God's people through faith in Christ Jesus and are thus *not obligated to observe Torah*—Paul at the same time emphasizes that they nonetheless fit into God's ongoing story. In becoming God's children through Christ and the Spirit, they are thereby also Abraham's children and thus heirs to the promise that God made with Abraham. And here is the reason for emphasis on the incarnation. It was precisely because Christ himself entered history

---

first heading, two have to do with plant life (Matt 21:19; 1 Cor 15:37), while the other three, including this one (John 8:58; Rom 1:3), focus not on birth as such but on Abraham's or Christ's appearing in the world.

[28] On this whole question note the emphasis in Martyn (406–8) that Paul's apocalyptic worldview nearly demands such an understanding of these clauses.

[29] So most interpreters; cf. Betz: "This anthropological definition [born of a woman, born under the law] is given a christological purpose, indicating that Christ's appearance was that of a human being in the full sense of the term" (207–8); cf. Longenecker: "As a qualitative expression 'born of a woman' speaks of Jesus' true humanity and representative quality, i.e., that he was truly one with us" (171).

within the context of Israel's story that he eliminated for historical Israel "the curse" of having to live by the law, which thus excludes living by faith (3:12–14). Thus the twofold focus of the two "was born" clauses: God's Son was both truly human and born within the context of Israel.

4. In this same vein, one should note further the significance of the *Abba*-cry with regard to Christ's humanity. Here is another certain instance[30] where Paul shows knowledge of the *historical Jesus*;[31] a second one occurs earlier in this same letter where he refers to James as "the brother of the Lord" (Gal 1:19). And since by Paul's own testimony he spent a fortnight with Peter (and James) in Jerusalem, it is myopic skepticism of the highest order to suggest that Paul knew next to nothing of the historical Jesus.[32] If what he knows comes to him from others, it is nonetheless that knowledge of the historical Jesus that he demonstrates.

In the present instance, there is simply no reasonable historical explanation for the Aramaic *Abba*-cry to be found on the lips of Gentiles some quarter of a century after the death and resurrection of Jesus unless it goes back to Jesus himself, as the Gospels themselves report. That is, we need to take seriously that believers "cried out" *Abba* to God within the gathered Christian community, that they did so with full awareness that the Spirit was moving them to do so, and that they were thus using Jesus' own word of intimate relationship with the Father.[33]

---

[30] See, e.g., 1 Cor 11:23–25, where Paul clearly knows the historical context of the institution of the Lord's Supper.

[31] I do not mean by this that he had direct knowledge, although some would (incorrectly, I think) read 2 Cor 5:16 as implying such. After all, it is not Christ who is κατὰ σάρκα in that passage; rather, it is Paul's way of viewing the world. Hence the TNIV rightly has it, "regard [anyone] from a worldly point of view" (= from the perspective of the old order that has been radically eliminated as an option through the death and resurrection of Christ, who has ushered in the new creation).

[32] This is skepticism born out of another time when it was popular to believe that Paul is a kind of second creator of Christianity and therefore that he cared almost nothing for, and was unacquainted with, the historical Jesus. Such skepticism was fostered in the generation before mine by Bultmann's famous assertion "I do indeed think we can now know almost nothing concerning the life and personality of Jesus, since the early Christian sources show no interest in either" (*Jesus and the Word* [trans. L. P. Smith and E. Huntress; New York: Charles Scribners's Sons, 1934], 8). The general unlikelihood of such a position should have been evident to NT scholarship from the beginning. If Paul's emphases lie elsewhere (on the saving event), his passion for its ethical demands, in which he insists that he is following Christ (1 Cor 11:1), should have caused some degree of caution among those who were so ready to read Paul myopically. For the emerging new view, see Wright, *Jesus and the Victory of God*; cf. J. D. G. Dunn, *A New Perspective on Jesus: What the Quest for the Historical Jesus Missed* (Grand Rapids: Baker Academic, 2005).

[33] Perhaps the best analogy in the Pauline corpus is found in the confession "Jesus is Lord" in 1 Cor 12:3, which no one can make except by the Spirit. In both cases, it is not ecstasy that is in view but the presence of the Spirit, to whom such basic prayer and confession are ultimately attributable, as certain evidence that one is truly Christ's.

But more needs to be said about the language *Abba* itself, since in some ways this is what carries the argument for Paul and since a considerable amount of literature has grown up around this word. The landmark study in this regard was that of Joachim Jeremias,[34] who concluded, among other things, (1) that this was the address of intimacy, originating with small children in an Aramaic home, (2) that Jesus' use of this term to address God was unique to him in all of known Jewish literature, (3) that the prayer thus revealed the uniqueness of his own self-understanding as Son of the Father, and (4) that he invited his disciples to use this term as his own extension of grace to them. As with all such "landmarks" in NT scholarship, some correctives and advances are eventually made.[35] But when the dust has finally settled, and even if one were to assume the minimalist position of James Barr,[36] for example, much of this still remains. Indeed, it is this usage by Paul, as much as anything, that tends to verify the basic soundness of Jeremias's conclusions.

For our purposes, three matters are of significance.

(a) This usage by Paul both here and in Romans—written to a church that he had never visited!—presupposes the widespread usage of this prayer language in the Gentile churches.[37] Furthermore, these two passages together, and the argument of this one in particular, serve as primary evidence for its significance both in the life of Jesus and in the early church. Such widespread, presuppositional usage of this prayer language, in its *Aramaic original*, is most easily accounted for historically on the grounds that this was Jesus' own term and that he in fact invited his disciples to use his language after him.[38] Indeed, in the case of Paul's present argument, everything hinges on the fact that believers now, by the *Spirit of the Son*, are using

---

[34] As chapter 1 in *The Prayers of Jesus* (SBT 2/6; London: SCM Press, 1967), 11–65 (the German original appeared in 1966).

[35] Since Jeremias, see Dunn, *New Perspective on Jesus*, 21–26; C. E. B. Cranfield, *A Critical and Exegetical Commentary on the Epistle to the Romans* (2 vols.; 6th ed.; ICC; Edinburgh: T&T Clark, 1975–1979), 1:399–402; J. M. Oesterreicher, "'Abba, Father!' On the Humanity of Jesus," in *The Lord's Prayer and Jewish Liturgy* (ed. J. J. Petuchowski and M. Brocke; New York: Seabury, 1978), 119–36; G. Vermès, *Jesus and the World of Judaism* (London: SCM Press, 1983), 39–43; J. Fitzmyer, "Abba and Jesus' Relation to God," in *À cause de l'évangile: Mélanges offerts à Dom Jacques Dupont* (ed. R. Gantoy; LD 123; Paris: Cerf, 1985), 16–38; J. Barr, "'Abba' Isn't 'Daddy,'" *JTS* 39 (1988): 28–47; idem, "'Abba, Father' and the Familiarity of Jesus' Speech," *Theology* 91 (1988): 173–79; A. Mawhinney, "God as Father: Two Popular Theories Reconsidered," *JETS* 31 (1988): 181–89; E. Obeng, "Abba, Father: The Prayer of the Sons of God," *ExpTim* 99 (1988): 363–66; Dunn, "Prayer," *DJG* 617–25, esp. 618–19; L. W. Hurtado, "God," *DJG* 275–76.

[36] See previous note.

[37] This is evidenced all the more by Paul's switch to "our hearts" in this clause, which implies that for Paul this is the common experience of believers in all of his churches.

[38] See, among many, Dunn, *New Perspective on Jesus*, 22–26; Obeng, "Abba," 364; Hurtado, "God."

the *language of the Son.* To deny the origin of such usage to Jesus himself, and through him to the early church, is to push historical skepticism to its outer limits.

(b) The jury still seems to be out on the precise meaning, and therefore significance, of the term *Abba* itself. Jeremias had made a considerable case for intimacy on the grounds of its assumed origins as the word of infant children; Vermès and Barr have called that into question by offering evidence that it was the language of adult children as well. The latter may well be right on the question of origins; but its use by adult children in an Aramaic home does not thereby make it a more adult word.[39] Most likely, the word was in fact an expression of intimacy, used by children first as infants and later as adults, reflecting what is true in many such cultures where the terms of endearment for one's parents are used lifelong, which is generally not true in English-speaking homes. Thus, if "Daddy" is not a very good equivalent—and it almost certainly is not—the basic thrust of the term and the significance of Jesus' use of it in addressing God still carry considerable christological (as well as theological) weight. If the term cannot be demonstrated, as Jeremias supposed, to be unique to Jesus,[40] it certainly can be argued to be *distinctively* his form of address; and for Jesus, it is best understood as a term denoting his own sense of unique sonship, by his addressing God consistently in the language of the home. That he should invite his disciples to use his word after him was almost certainly an expression of grace on his part.

(c) Both the meaning of the term itself and the fact that such a cry comes from the heart suggest that for Paul, a form of intimacy with God is involved.[41] Here is the ultimate evidence that we are God's own children: we address God with the same term of intimate relationship that Jesus himself used. We are not slaves but children. The Spirit has taken us far beyond mere conformity to religious obligations. God himself, in the person of the Spirit— of both the Father and the Son—has come to indwell his people; and he has

---

[39] Barr ("'Abba' Isn't 'Daddy'") seems to miss the point here. Although he surely is correct that it did not *originate* with the babbling of children (after all, why these sounds and not others?), that these words (*abba* and *imma*) are the first words that most children would stammer needs to be noted. They do so because these are the first words that children are "taught," as it were (as in, "Say *abba*"). And in no language that I know are the more formal words for parents the first words that children are "taught" to speak. Thus "origins" as such are irrelevant, but not so with usage and significance.

[40] So Vermès, *Jesus and the World of Judaism;* Barr, "'Abba, Father'"; Mawhinney, "God as Father."

[41] So most who have written on the subject, contra Barr, who seems to overstep historical reality in this case in order to be done with a kind of "syrupy" relationality that is more about feelings than about a genuine encounter with the living God. On the other hand, "intimate" does not equal "individualistic." On the corporate nature of this cry in the present context, see M. M. Thompson, *The Promise of the Father: Jesus and God in the New Testament* (Louisville: Westminster John Knox, 2000), 116–32.

sealed that relationship by giving to them the language of his Son, the language of personal relationship. For Paul and for us, this is the ultimate expression of grace. No wonder Paul had such antipathy for Torah observance, because it invariably breaks this relationship of child to parent in favor of one that can only be expressed in terms of slavery—performance on the basis of duty and obligation, in which one "slaves" for God rather than being re-created in God's own likeness (cf. 4:20) which results in loving servant-hood toward all others (5:13). Christ the Son has effected such a relationship; the Spirit of the Son makes it work. The assumed Christology in these affirmations is thus thoroughgoing.

5. Paul's further elaboration in v. 6 of the soteriological reality asserted in vv. 4–5, in terms of the Galatians' having received the Spirit, also offers yet another kind of christological moment; for this is the second of four occurrences in the corpus where the Spirit of God is called "the Spirit of Christ, the Son." This interchange, already at work in 2 Cor 3:17, occurs most explicitly in Rom 8:9–10 and will appear again indirectly in Phil 1:19.[42] It is one of the most certain instances in Paul's writings of shared identity between the Father and the Son. In the Pauline corpus, the Holy Spirit is most often referred to as the Spirit of God, quite in keeping with Paul's OT roots. But the very fact that he can so easily and presuppositionally refer to the same Holy Spirit as "the Spirit of the Son" indicates that "divine" is the proper language for "the Son" as it is for the Father, whom the Son has revealed, thus indicating that the Son shares identity with the Father.

Finally, we should note the final prepositional phrase in the passage, "through God," which brings the whole passage full circle to its theocentric starting point. As significant as Paul's statements about Christ and the Spirit are for our Christology and pneumatology, Paul will frequently bring us back to his basic monotheistic roots: all of this, the work of the Son and the Spirit that effects and makes effective our salvation, is ultimately attributed to God the Father. In this case, therefore, the whole passage is enclosed by the phrases "God sent forth" and "through God." What needs to be noted further about the concluding expression of this framing device is that God is now seen as the "agent"—language that usually is reserved for Christ. Thus the "interchange" in this case goes the other direction: what Christ ordinarily does, God also does.

Galatians 1:16–17

The first issue that Paul takes up with the Galatians is the authenticity of his apostleship, since it was through his apostolic ministry that they were

---

[42]By "explicitly" and "indirectly," I mean that in Rom 8:9–10 the interchange between the Spirit as "the Spirit of God" and "the Spirit of Christ" happens in a single sentence, whereas the reference in Phil 1:19 to "the provision of the Spirit of Christ Jesus" occurs, as in the present text, in isolation from any mention of "the Spirit of God," Paul's more common way of speaking of the Spirit.

brought to faith. Although such a reminder actually begins the letter,[43] the narrative itself is picked up at 1:11, where he asserts again the divine origin of his gospel. After placing his story in the context of his former animosity toward Christ and his church (v. 13) and his considerable achievement as a young Pharisee (v. 14), he moves on in v. 15 to narrate his basic (post-conversion) lack of relationship with Jerusalem.[44]

In what must be considered one of the more surprising moments in Paul's letters, here he speaks of his "conversion" in terms of "God's[45] revealing his Son *in me.*" The surprise (in terms of our expectations) is twofold: (1) Paul thinks of his "conversion" in this case not in terms of what happened *to* me or, as in the next passage, in terms of what Christ lovingly did *for* me (and by implication for all others) but in terms of the revelation taking place *in* me; and (2) who is revealed in Paul is not "Christ" or "the Lord Jesus" but God's own Son. Both of these realities need brief discussion.

1. Despite the way a large number of scholars have read this sentence, one must take seriously that Paul's ἐν carries its ordinary locative force of "in." The point is that Paul is not trying to establish here that God revealed his Son *to* him, as though this were a different way of speaking of his encounter with the risen Lord noted first in 1 Cor 9:1–2. This is the point made earlier, in v. 12. He could have repeated that clearly and easily enough[46]; rather, Paul's point has ultimately to do with his apostleship and the true source of his gospel. Thus he emphasizes here that he himself is the locus of that revelation, meaning in context that the revelation of/from Christ that he has spoken of in v. 12 has taken place *in Paul* in such a way that both the gospel of Christ and Paul's apostleship should be visible to others as the

---

[43] See below on 1:1, 12.

[44] What Paul seems to be responding to here is the agitators' denial of his apostolic authority because he lacks proper credentials—that is, because he *does not* come from Jerusalem, while they do. But what they see as a liability he will capitalize on. The difference between him and the agitators is that they *do* come from Jerusalem, as it were, and in this argument that means that they have merely human authority. Paul distances himself from Jerusalem as a coup: his apostleship obviously cannot come δι' ἀνθρώπου; in fact, it comes directly from Christ and the Father.

[45] This, of course, is what Paul intends, even though it is highly unlikely that the ὁ θεός in v. 15 read by the majority of witnesses is authentic; it is missing in such early and diverse witnesses as 𝔓[46] B F G 0150 it[ar,b,f,g,o] vg sy[p] Ir[lat1/2] Epiph. An "omission" by even one witness is difficult to account for at this point; but here the omission would have to have happened at least twice for it to have appeared in both East and West so early. So also the dissenting voice of Metzger and Wikgren in B. M. Metzger, *A Textual Commentary on the Greek New Testament* (2d ed.; New York: United Bible Societies, 1994), 521–22.

[46] The evidence seems quite certain and consistent with regard to how Paul uses the verb ἀποκαλύπτω. When he speaks of the revelation as coming *to* someone, he uses the dative (1 Cor 2:10; 14:30; Eph 3:5; Phil 3:15); when he indicates the locus of the revelation, he uses ἐν (Rom 1:17 and here); the usage in 1 Cor 3:13 is probably a dative of means. The greater problem with the prevailing view is that there is no known instance where Paul uses ἐν to indicate the recipient of something.

revelation of the Son takes place in him.[47] That the implacable enemy is now a promoter of what he once sought to destroy is for Paul supreme evidence of "the grace of God."

2. In a letter in which Χριστός (*Christ*) is by far the most common way of referring to his Lord (6x to this point), it should probably catch our attention that Paul here refers to God as revealing *his Son* in Paul. This usage seems to set the stage for the next two occurrences (2:20; 4:4–6), which together suggest that near the heart of Paul's gospel is a Son of God Christology, which has Jewish messianism deeply embedded in it. Although the present usage could be simply off-handed, as it were, it is worth noting that this emphasis on Christ as "messianic Son" occurs in a letter in which Gentile believers are being cajoled by the agitators into accepting a degree of "Jewishness" in order to be completed as believers. The Jewish Messiah, Paul counters, has been revealed *in me;* how that revelation has taken place emerges in the next occurrence of Son of God language.

Galatians 2:20

In a passage that is thoroughgoing in its "Christ devotion," Paul begins by arguing that the alternatives "by faith in Christ Jesus"[48] and "by works of law" are mutually exclusive (v. 16). Indeed, if the Galatians were to add Torah observance to faith in Christ, this would imply that obedience to Torah is still necessary. That in turn would mean that people such as Paul and Peter are still "sinners," because, by putting their faith in Christ, they are no longer observant; and that, Paul argues vigorously, is tantamount to making Christ "a servant of sin" (since through him they are no longer observant and thus as "lawbreakers" have become "sinners"). After the proper renunciation of such an absurdity, Paul goes on to appeal to the fact that he has already died with respect to the law and thus he is living totally for God. And with that, Christ enters the story again, this time as the means of Paul's dying and coming to life.

Paul's death is expressed in terms of Χριστῷ συνεσταύρωμαι (*I have been crucified with Christ*), a very personal way of speaking about what Christ did for believers through his crucifixion. His death meant their death, which

---

[47]So also Lightfoot, 83; Dunn, 64; M. Hooker, *Pauline Pieces* (London: Epworth, 1979), 63; contra Burton, 50; Bruce, 93; Martyn, 158; Kim, *Origin of Paul's Gospel*, 56; Matera, *New Testament Christology*, 83, 105. Missing this point, unfortunately, seriously jeopardizes much of Matera's (otherwise helpful) discussion of the Christology of Galatians (105–7); similarly with Kim's use of this text to refer to Paul's Damascus Road experience without so much as noting the exegetical difficulty involved; cf. Ziesler (*Pauline Christianity*, 25), who lists this as the third of Paul's references to the Damascus Road experience; and U. Schnelle (*Apostle Paul: His Life and Theology* [Grand Rapids: Baker, 2005], 64–65), who by fiat, and against all evidence to the contrary, says that "ἐν ἐμοί (in me) is to be translated as the simple dative." Betz (71) sees it as referring to a "mystical experience," which seems especially doubtful in light of the concerns of this letter.

[48]On this choice for the meaning of ἐκ πίστεως Χριστοῦ, see the excursus that follows.

alone can lead to their being raised to a new life.[49] But in this case, instead of reflecting on the "new life" that results from Christ's resurrection,[50] Paul returns to the meaning of the crucifixion (anticipating what he will argue next) and expresses it in the most intimate terms yet, while at the same time picking up the Son of God language from 1:16–17: "The life I now live, I live in (the sphere of) faith in the Son of God, who loved me and gave himself up for me." This kind of personal language is rare in Paul (until Philippians); its significance for Pauline Christology needs a further word.

As noted at the conclusion of the preceding chapter, it is nearly impossible to explain Paul's Christology without taking seriously his utter devotion to Christ, who saved him, expressed here in terms of the Son of God's loving "me" and thus giving himself up for "me" (by death on the cross). The surprise in this sentence comes in the very personal way of speaking about the saving event. Ordinarily, Paul speaks of our salvation in terms of (1) its being rooted in the love of God[51] and (2) its being collectively for all of God's people. Here alone we find this expressed in terms of Paul personally, which in context, of course, is to be understood as also paradigmatic for the Galatians. But one simply cannot easily get past Paul's own sense of being loved personally by God's Son in his crucifixion. It is this same love that "constrains" Paul in 2 Cor 5:14. And this is most likely "the law of Christ" that is being "fulfilled" (6:2) as one carries the burdens of others. It is this love of Christ for him personally that causes so much of what Paul says to be so christocentric.

Excursus: Πίστις Ἰησοῦ Χριστοῦ ("Faith in Christ Jesus")

This present text, with its phrase "by faith in the Son of God" (TNIV), needs special discussion, since there is something of a groundswell in NT scholarship that interprets this phrase and its earlier version in v. 16 (πίστις Ἰησοῦ Χριστοῦ [faith in Christ Jesus]) as a subjective genitive and thus as referring to Christ's own faithfulness that led to his death for us. The reason for discussing it here is that if those who take it this way are correct, then this is another instance in this letter where Paul has Jesus' humanity in view. Since I stand on the other side of things on this issue, I hereby offer my reasons for so doing and thus for not including it as part of a discussion of Paul's Christology.

This use of πίστις (faith) with Christ in the genitive occurs four times in Galatians (2:16 [2x], 20; 3:22), twice in Romans (3:22, 26), and once in Philippians (3:9). In each case it occurs in direct contrast to doing "works of law." At issue is whether the genitive is "objective"

---

[49] See also Paul's argument with the Corinthians in 2 Cor 5:14–15.

[50] As he does in, e.g., 2 Cor 5:14–15; Rom 6:4–10.

[51] See, e.g., Rom 5:5–8; 2 Cor 13:13(14); this love, when expressed in terms of its relationship to Christ, is referred to as "the love of God which is in Christ" (Rom 8:39).

(Christ as the object of faith) or "subjective" (Christ as the one who lived "faithfully").[52] Although there are places where it might possibly refer to "the faithfulness of Christ" (e.g., Rom 3:22, on the pattern of "God's faithfulness" in 3:3 and Abraham's in 4:12, 16),[53] it is unlikely to do so here in Galatians and thus in its other (very few) occurrences. Here are the difficulties that I see:

1. Most damaging to the subjective-genitive view is its first occurrence (Gal 2:16), where it is immediately explained (with the cognate verb) in terms of "even we *believed* in Christ Jesus." The common appeal to tautology does not wash here, since the power of Paul's rhetoric lies in the threefold repetition of "works of law" and "belief in Christ." And in this case, the very phrasing and emphases of this second clause speak against the "new look" view. That is, when Paul immediately qualifies the phrase with καὶ ἡμεῖς εἰς Χριστὸν Ἰησοῦν ἐπιστεύσαμεν (*even we have believed in Christ Jesus*), the "even we" is a clear pickup from what precedes. Since "we know" that a person is not justified by works of law ἐὰν μὴ διὰ πίστεως Ἰησοῦ Χριστοῦ (*but through faith in Jesus Christ*), *even we ourselves* (= Paul, Peter, Barnabas, and the rest), law-keeping Jews though we were, *even we* put our trust in Christ. The "even we" makes very little sense following "Christ's own faithfulness."

2. It has been argued regarding the combination of πίστις with the genitive "that when πίστις takes a personal genitive it is almost never an objective genitive."[54] But almost all the alleged analogies are not true analogies at all, since the vast majority of them are the personal *possessive pronoun* and thus they all have the Greek definite article with the noun πίστις to specify precisely that the author is talking about "*the* faith that [you] have."[55] This means that the one analogy to this (pos-

---

[52] For a bibliography to 1980 of those who take it as subjective, see Longenecker, 87; for a more recent and influential advocacy, see R. B. Hays, *Faith of Jesus Christ;* M. D. Hooker, "ΠΙΣΤΙΣ ΧΡΙΣΤΟΥ," *NTS* 35 (1989): 321–42; and esp. the debate between Hays and Dunn in E. H. Lovering Jr., ed., *SBL Seminar Papers, 1991* (SBLSP; Atlanta: Scholars Press, 1991), 714–44. For advocacy of an objective genitive (besides Dunn), see A. J. Hultgren, "The *PISTIS CHRISTOU* Formulation in Paul," *NovT* 22 (1980): 248–63; V. Koperski, "The Meaning of *pistis Christou* in Philippians 3:9," *LS* 18 (1993): 198–216. For commentaries on Philippians that take it as subjective, see R. P. Martin, *The Epistle of Paul to the Philippians* (rev. ed.; TNTC; Grand Rapids: Eerdmans, 1987); P. T. O'Brien, *Commentary on Philippians* (NIGTC; Grand Rapids: Eerdmans, 1991).

[53] It is also to be noted, however, that πίστις carries a considerably different nuance in these latter two passages (*pace* Hays; O'Brien).

[54] The NET BIBLE, p. 2176 n. 52. The texts offered in support are Matt 9:2, 22, 29; Mark 2:5; 5:34; 10:52; Luke 5:20; 7:50; 8:25, 48; 17:19; 18:42; 22:32; Rom 1:8, 12; 3:3; 4:5, 12, 16; 1 Cor 2:5; 15:14, 17; 2 Cor 10:15; Phil 2:17; Col 1:4; 2:5; 1 Thess 1:8; 3:2, 5, 10; 2 Thess 1:3; Titus 1:1; Phlm 6; 1 Pet 1:9, 21; 2 Pet 1:5. This looks like an imposing list (thirty-six items in all), until one examines them carefully.

[55] This occurs in no fewer than thirty-two of the genitives. Two of the other four have Abraham as the subject (Rom 4:12, 16), and one "God's elect" (Titus 1:1). So the only possible analogy in this list is the one always appealed to, Rom 3:3.

sible) usage in Paul is Rom 3:3, which in fact is not a true analogy, since both nouns have the definite article, so as to make certain that Paul is referring to "*the* faithfulness of *the* [one and only] God." That God in this case is the subject of πίστις is evident by the use of the definite article with both words. But what is significantly overlooked in these discussions is the true analogy to this (double nonarticular) usage of πίστις with the genitive: Mark 11:22, where Jesus tells his disciples, ἔχετε πίστιν θεοῦ, and where no one would imagine translating, "Have God's faith(fulness)."

3. Moreover, the apparent analogies of Rom 3:3 and 4:16, where πίστις does mean "faithful," are not precise. In all seven instances of πίστεως Χριστοῦ both words occur *without the definite article,*[56] thus implying "through faith in Christ," exactly as Paul has it grammatically in 2 Thess 2:13 (ἐν . . . πίστει ἀληθείας [*by trusting in the truth*]). Indeed, this passage offers the real analogy to this phrase where Christ is in the genitive, but is overlooked in most of the discussions (cf. Mark 11:22 above). As with the usage in Galatians (see point 6 below), this unusual expression owes its existence to Paul's rhetoric, as a way of expressing a sharp contrast between the Thessalonian believers and those destined for perdition because they do not "love the truth" (2 Thess 2:10). Moreover, although the usage in Rom 4:16 regarding Abraham may seem to be "an exact parallel" (O'Brien, *Philippians*), in fact it is quite dependent on 4:12, where the defining article makes Paul's sense certain ("*the* faith/fulness of Abraham" [cf. Rom 3:3]).

4. Significantly, the "new look" rests altogether on an interpretation of this one phrase, which occurs but seven times in the entire corpus; and it does so by way of an understanding of the noun πίστις that can indeed be found (once at least) in Paul but is only a secondary meaning at best. That is, nowhere else does Paul in plain speech (rather than in a prepositional phrase with an unusual [for Paul] meaning) say anything about our salvation resting on Christ's faithfulness.

5. Not only so, but Paul does use a shortened version of the phrase (ἐκ πίστεως without a genitive qualifier) no fewer that seven times in Galatians alone,[57] and in each instance it refers to their "faith" in Christ, by which they were justified, not to the faithfulness of Christ that made such justification possible. Since ἐκ πίστεως by itself seems to be a pickup of the longer phrase, it would be especially strange for Paul to give it a *different* meaning from that intended in the two instances where

---

[56] Some might object that Paul uses the definite article in Gal 2:20, but this is not analogous, since the usage is appositional in this case, not truly articular. In typical fashion, Paul has phrased his contrasts in poetic chiasm: ὃ δὲ νῦν ζῶ ἐν σαρκί, ἐν πίστει ζῶ τῇ τοῦ υἱοῦ τοῦ θεοῦ, where the word order ζῶ ἐν σαρκί, ἐν πίστει ζῶ calls for the defining τῇ because of the intervening ζῶ.

[57] See Gal 3:7, 8, 9, 11, 12, 24; 5:5.

the same phrase occurs with "Christ" as the genitive qualifier (2:16; 3:22). That is, since ἐκ πίστεως means that we live "by faith" = trust in Christ Jesus, how is it that the longer version of the phrase makes Christ the subject of the "faith" rather than the object?

6. Finally, the phrase itself was most likely coined in its first instance (Gal 2:16) in antithesis to ἐξ ἔργων νόμου, where "works" can only refer to what we do. By analogy, and in total antithesis, ἐκ πίστεως Χριστοῦ is also what we "do"; we put our trust in Christ. Thus, the only reason this phrase exists at all in the Pauline corpus is rhetorical, as a way of expressing faith in Christ as the opposite, both grammatically and theologically, of "works of law."

Thus, given this high level of doubt that this phrase has to do with Christ's own faithfulness, it does not seem to add to our understanding of Paul's understanding of the *person* of Christ.

Christ and the Divine Prerogatives

As in each of the earlier letters, Paul in Galatians refers to Christ in quite incidental ways that presuppose his divine status and identity. Also as before, many of these are instances where Paul ascribes the same action or attribute to Christ as readily as he does to God, and in some cases vice versa. We examine these in their canonical order.

Galatians 1:1—The Agent of Paul's Apostleship

On this usage, see the discussion on 1 Cor 1:17; 1:1 in ch. 3 (p. 136). I bring it forward again in this case because of the unusual, but for the present circumstances necessary, qualifier regarding Paul's apostleship. In his concern to establish the origin of, and thus authority behind, his calling as an apostle, he joins the standard "of" (or in this case, "through") Christ with "God the Father, who raised him from the dead." As in other such moments,[58] a single preposition joins both "Jesus Christ," the messianic Son, with God the Father as compound objects of a single preposition.

Thus two points are established at the outset: (1) Paul's apostleship has divine origins, coming from both Christ and the Father; and (2) the heavenly Christ, who has called and empowered Paul, has now come by this divine authority through having been raised from the dead.

Galatians 1:3; 6:18—The Benedictory Grace of Christ

On the matter of Christ and the Father as the source of grace (in 1:3), which is picked up as from Christ alone in 6:18, see the discussion under

---

[58] See esp. the discussion of 1 Thess 1:1 in ch. 2 (pp. 48–50).

1 Cor 1:3 in ch. 3 (pp. 134–35). The benediction (6:18) is especially poignant in this case, since it follows hard on the heels of the final explicit reference in this letter to the historical Jesus. "I bear the *stigmata* of Jesus[59] in my body." That is followed by "The grace of our Lord Jesus Christ be with your spirits, brothers and sisters. Amen." Thus the standard benedictory "grace" is elaborated some;[60] but here it also comes from one who knows the sufferings of Jesus firsthand.

Galatians 1:6, 15; 2:21—The Grace of Christ/of God

As Paul can easily interchange "benedictory grace" as from both God and Christ, so also with the grace that "calls" or "saves." This reality as a shared divine prerogative finds remarkable expression in this letter, as can be seen from the following texts:

1:6   Θαυμάζω ὅτι οὕτως ταχέως μετατίθεσθε ἀπὸ <u>τοῦ καλέσαντος</u> ὑμᾶς ἐν χάριτι Χριστοῦ[61]

   I marvel that so quickly you are deserting <u>the one who called</u> you
   into the grace of Christ

1:15–16   [15]Ὅτε δὲ <u>εὐδόκησεν</u> [ὁ θεὸς] ὁ ἀφορίσας με ἐκ κοιλίας μητρός μου καὶ <u>καλέσας διὰ τῆς χάριτος αὐτοῦ</u> [16]ἀποκαλύψαι τὸν υἱὸν <u>αὐτοῦ</u>
                                                                          ἐν ἐμοί,

   [15]*When it <u>pleased God, who set</u> me <u>apart</u> from my mother's womb and <u>called</u> me <u>by his grace</u>, [16]to reveal his **Son** in me,*

2:21   Οὐκ ἀθετῶ <u>τὴν χάριν τοῦ θεοῦ·</u>
   I do not set aside <u>the grace of God.</u>

---

[59]This is the reading (surely Paul's original) of 𝔓[46] A B C* 33 629 1241 *pc*; later scribes at various times and in various ways moderated "Jesus" to read: "Christ," "the Lord Jesus," "the Lord Jesus Christ," or "our Lord Jesus Christ." All of these reflect tendencies to read Paul in ways that they had come to expect of him.

[60]This is the first instance of the addition "with your spirits," which occurs again in Philemon and Philippians.

[61]This is such an unusual expression for Paul that scribes instinctively modified it to fit their expectations. Thus "Christ" is omitted in F* G H[vid] a b Tert Cyp (an obviously "Western" phenomenon [the inclusion of 𝔓[46vid] in NA[27] is especially suspect here]); it is changed to "God" in a few late MSS. In a change of a different kind, but still showing evidence of its being the original text, some MSS have added "Jesus" before "Christ" (D 326 1241[s] *pc*); Bruce (80) is quite wrong to see this evidence as "rather evenly divided." Even though an "omission" is adopted by Martyn (109), here is a place where the brackets in NA[27]/UBS[4] need to be removed and the Χριστοῦ kept, since it is hard to imagine the circumstances in which a scribe would have added "Christ" to the phrase "in grace" in a sentence where God is the acting subject. That is, had the text read simply "the One who called you in grace," it is hard to imagine anyone *adding* the genitive "of Christ" to that—"*his* grace" following God as subject perhaps, but not "Christ's grace"! Note, e.g., the difficulty that Lightfoot (75–76) had

These latter two passages seem so "normal" to the reader that the expression "the grace of God" is read and scarcely noticed.[62] Exactly the opposite is true of "the grace of Christ" in 1:6. Although this expression serves as benediction to conclude most of the letters in the church corpus (Colossians is the lone exception), it occurs rarely in the body of the letters,[63] which is also the reason Χριστοῦ was omitted by the Western tradition in the present passage (see n. 61).

But what are we to make of it here? The choice is between a locative (the grace that is found by those who are in Christ) or means (that God called them by means of Christ's grace). Some commentators and most English translations prefer the latter,[64] but that runs contrary to Pauline usage elsewhere. That is, when the preposition ἐν modifies a verb of "calling," it is elsewhere only locative (1 Thess 4:7; 1 Cor 7:15, 18, 20, 22, 24; Col 3:15; Eph 4:4).[65] There is no good reason to think otherwise here, especially since in 1:15, when Paul wishes to express this concept in an instrumental way, he says διὰ τῆς χάριτος αὐτοῦ (*through* [= by means of] *his grace*). Thus Paul's point is that God's "call" to the Galatians was for them to exist continually as those who experienced Christ's grace. At this beginning point in this letter such a phrase seems intended to anticipate the rest of the letter: redeemed by God's grace, they are to continue to "live in the grace of Christ" from their conversion on.

Thus, even though this phrase is most likely a somewhat oblique reference to Christ's redemptive work, the ease with which Paul can attribute "grace" to Christ reflects his presuppositional Christology.

Galatians 1:12—Christ, the One Who Reveals

In one of the more difficult (for us) genitive constructions in this letter, Paul begins the personal narrative, in which he both affirms his own apostleship and "gospel" as coming directly from God and thus also distances himself from Jerusalem, by insisting that his gospel came to him δι᾽ ἀποκαλύψεως

---

with the original text, but he acknowledged its genuineness and then left it without further comment.

[62] Apart from the salutations and places where χάρις comes from both Father and Son (2 Thess 1:12), it occurs in both casual and careful ways in 1 Cor 3:10; 15:10 (2x); 2 Cor 1:12; 6:1; 8:1; 9:14; Col 1:6; Eph 3:2, 7; Titus 2:11 (and in these two places in Galatians).

[63] Apart from the combined moment in 2 Thess 1:12 (see ch. 2, pp. 61–63), it is found elsewhere only in 2 Cor 8:9, and as suggested regarding that passage, there it is picked up as a play on "the grace of giving" (see ch. 4, p. 164). It also occurs in Rom 5:15 in the contrast between Adam and Christ, but as "the grace of the one man."

[64] See Bruce, 80; Longenecker, 15; likewise most recent English translations (REB, NAB, NASB, NIV/TNIV, GNB, NET BIBLE [amazingly without explanation]); for the locative see NRSV, NJB, ESV.

[65] Noted also by Burton, 20–21; cf. Betz, 48; Fung, 44; Martyn, 109; Dunn (41) remains undecided.

Ἰησοῦ Χριστοῦ (*through revelation of/from Jesus Christ*). At issue is whether Christ is the object (content) of the revelation[66] or the (grammatical) subject, the one who did the revealing of the gospel to him. In the end, these probably come out very close to the same place (i.e., the revealer is also the revealed), but in this case it is more likely that the genitive is subjective (as TNIV: "I received it by revelation from Jesus Christ").[67] After all, at issue in this particular sentence is the source, not the content, of the revelation. It was not "handed down" to him from a human being,[68] nor did it come to him by way of (human) instructors; rather, he received his gospel by direct revelation from Christ himself.

Here, then, is yet another divine prerogative shared by Christ. In the Hebrew Bible Yahweh is consistently the source of revelation; so also in Paul, including the narrative that immediately follows (2:15–16).[69] But here Christ himself is the source of the revealing.

Galatians 4:14—Received Me as ἄγγελον θεοῦ, as Christ Jesus

In one of the more intriguing moments in this letter, Paul reminds the Galatians of their initial warm reception of him despite his physical disability. They did not disdain what he now calls "your trial in my flesh"—that is, the trial they had to endure regarding his illness. To the contrary, he says, they received him as ἄγγελον θεοῦ, as Christ Jesus. At issue in this case is the meaning of ἄγγελον θεοῦ, which in most modern English versions is rendered "an angel of God."[70]

Two matters need discussion here: (1) whether the phrase is generic and means "*an* angel *from* God" or whether it is specific, wherein Paul is picking up a common Septuagintal phrase and intends "*the* angel *of* God";[71] and (2)

---

[66] So Burton, 41–43; Bruce, 89; Betz, 63; Fung, 54; Morris, 51; Dunn, 53; Matera, 53; Martyn, 144.

[67] So also Lightfoot, 80; Longenecker, 24; Hansen, 41.

[68] Gk. οὐδὲ γὰρ ἐγὼ παρὰ ἀνθρώπου παρέλαβον αὐτό (*for I neither received it from a human source*), where the παρέλαβον is a semitechnical term for the passing on of tradition from generation to generation. In Paul's case, the "tradition" he received came directly from Christ himself, not from a merely human source.

[69] Although the verb ἀποκαλύπτω occurs most often in the "divine passive" (= [God] has revealed; see, e.g., Rom 8:18; Eph 3:5), Paul also expresses it in the active in 1 Cor 2:10; Phil 3:15.

[70] The NJB chooses to "modernize" the language and turn it into "a messenger from God." But that seems to miss a bit too much.

[71] For advocacy of the latter, see Wallace, *Greek Grammar beyond the Basics,* 252 n. 97, following N. Turner, *Syntax* (vol. 3 of J. H. Moulton, *A Grammar of New Testament Greek;* Edinburgh: T&T Clark, 1963), 180. For further discussion, see W. G. MacDonald, "Christology and 'the Angel of the Lord,'" in *Current Issues in Biblical and Patristic Interpretation: Studies in Honor of Merrill C. Tenney Presented by His Former Students* (Grand Rapids: Eerdmans, 1975), 324–35; D. Hannah, *Michael and Christ: Michael Traditions and Angel Christology in Early Christianity* (WUNT 2/109; Mohr Siebeck, 1999), 19–20.

the relationship between the two ὡς phrases—whether they are progressive and ascensive (one word leading to the next that is higher) or appositional (the second clarifying the first). It should be noted also that the second issue exists only if one decides that the phrase is specific. If it is generic, then it automatically means that the two phrases are progressive (and ascensive).

1. On the first matter, despite the fact that English translations have been loath to go this way, the evidence seems strongly to favor Paul's having picked up a common phrase from the Septuagint. Several things favor this choice. First, this is quite in keeping with Paul's habits that we have noted throughout this book, that he eats and breathes the Greek Bible, so that its language emerges in ever so many ways and in all kinds of contexts. Here the Septuagint evidence is both striking and a bit confusing. In the first place, one called "the angel of the LORD (or 'God')" regularly serves as the divine messenger in several OT narratives;[72] and in some of these narratives the "angel" turns out to be the Lord himself. This is especially true of the crucial narratives in Gen 18 and Exod 3–4, plus the Gideon narrative in Judg 6. In each case the first occurrence is anarthrous, as here, although it is certainly intended to be understood in an articular way.[73] That is, this "angel" is not "an angel" but is "the angel of the LORD." Paul's anarthrous use in this instance seems to point in the same direction,[74] since "an angel of God" has no certain Septuagint background.

Given the likelihood of the phrase's OT roots, scholarly distaste for what seems to be its natural sense is difficult to fathom, especially since Paul next speaks even more boldly: they accepted him as Jesus Christ himself. Thus it seems altogether likely that Paul is here reaching high as he acknowledges the level of acceptance that he received from them. "You received me as the angel of God."

But whether Paul's next phrase, "as Jesus Christ," is intended to stand in apposition to, and thus to identify, the angel of God is a different matter. That is, Christ may very well assume the role of the OT "angel of the LORD/God," but in light of the rest of the corpus, it seems unlikely that Paul is intending an absolute identification.

2. But if this is the case, that does not make the second matter easily resolved. In favor of "the angel of God" as equal to Christ himself is the fact that "the angel of the LORD" often turns out to be a representation of Yahweh himself, so that the two become one in some way.[75] On the other hand, there is simply no firm evidence that would lead us to believe that Paul had a

---

[72]This reality led to a great deal of speculation about angels in Second Temple Judaism, even to naming them and establishing a hierarchy (see the discussion in Hannah, *Michael and Christ*, 25–75).

[73]In the Genesis and Judges narratives, the subsequent occurrences have the article as an anaphora (= *the* angel referred to at the beginning).

[74]This is the point made especially by Turner and Wallace (see n. 71).

[75]On this matter, see, e.g., J. Durham, *Exodus* (WBC 3; Dallas: Word, 1987), 30–31.

kind of "angel Christology."[76] One is always wary of a christological perspective based on one or two texts that themselves are rather obscure.[77]

In any case, my interest here lies with the ease with which Paul can bring Christ into the picture as a divine presence in Galatia, as the ultimate kudo he can offer them regarding their receiving him in his visible weaknesses. Thus we seem in fact to be dealing with progression here rather than identification, which would mean that Christ is a full rung higher than the angelic theophanies of the OT.

Galatians 4:19—Until Christ Is "Formed" in You

Paul's longing for the Galatians to return to their senses on the issue at hand (no Torah observance for people of the Spirit) leads him to a striking mixing of images. His longing for them is so intense, and in some ways so distressing, that he pictures himself as experiencing "birth pangs" for them again. However, what is "being formed" takes place not within him but among them as they are transformed into the likeness of Christ and his character. The christological significance of this lies in the reality that for Christ to be "formed" in and among them[78] means they are to be taking on the divine image itself, which finds its ultimate expression in Christ. Thus this text reflects in its own incidental way the *imago Dei* Christology that lies behind texts such as 2 Cor 4:4, 6 and (especially) Rom 8:29, that God has predestined us to be "conformed to the image of his Son."

Galatians 6:2—The "Law" of Christ

In one of the more surprising moves in this letter, the man who has been strongly opposed to "the law" as needing to be observed by believers in Christ now opts to use this language as the ultimate expression of their being in servanthood to one another. If "the law" itself is no longer in place for those who live by the Spirit (5:18, 23), the same is not true of its replacement, "the law of Christ." By this wordplay, of course, Paul is pointing to how radical genuinely Christian ethics are over against "observance" ("doing law" is Paul's language).

The christological dimension of this phrase is considerable indeed and is related in concept to Christ's being "formed" in them (4:19). In the context

---

[76] Hannah's rejection of this suggestion remains the most cogent discussion of this issue.

[77] See esp. the discussion of "Spirit Christology" based on two unusual phrases in Paul, 1 Cor 15:47 and Rom 1:3–4, in Fee, *God's Empowering Presence*, 831–34. Such Christologies are suspect by the very fact that they are found in only one (barely possible) reading of a difficult text.

[78] This is one of Paul's uses of ἐν ὑμῖν that is difficult to pin down with precision. On the one hand, it is most likely at least distributive (each of them is to be so formed into Christ's likeness); on the other hand, such moments are usually also thought of in terms of their corporate sense (that they are to be communities of such image-bearing).

of a worldview (held by his opponents) where keeping God's law is the ultimate expression of godliness, Paul is prepared to shift the "law" to Christ himself. Thus Christ the Son, who is the perfect image of the Father, whom we now know as "the Father of our Lord Jesus Christ," gives ultimate definition to the law, where God's character finds expression in the language of 2:20, "who loved me and gave himself for me."[79] Thus, in some ways "the love of Christ" not only redefines the law but also sees the incarnate, crucified Christ as the divine expression, and thus replacement, of the law. Again, the presuppositional nature of an especially high Christology in Paul emerges in the most unexpected ways.

Conclusion

Since conclusions have been made throughout this chapter, we return at the end only to reinforce the observations made at the beginning and demonstrated throughout the chapter. The one major christological passage in this letter (4:4–7) touches a lot of christological bases. The language of "Son" is best understood first of all in terms of Jewish messianism, as Christ being designated as Abraham's true seed in 3:16; at the same time, the primary clause, "God sent his Son," implies the Son's preexistence even while it emphasizes his incarnation in terms of his genuine humanity. By implication, v. 6 also indicates knowledge of the historical Jesus. On the other hand, the entire passage is "enclosed" by Paul's basic theocentricity: God sent his Son, and at the end we become heirs "through God."

The other, more incidental, christological moments are all in keeping with what we have seen in the earlier letters, especially that Christ continues to share a variety of "divine prerogatives" with the Father. So there is very little that is new here, except for the way it is expressed in 4:4–7, and very much that reinforces what Paul has said in earlier letters.

Appendix I: The Texts

(double brackets [[ ]] indicate texts with references to God alone)

1:1 Παῦλος ἀπόστολος οὐκ ἀπ᾽ ἀνθρώπων οὐδὲ δι᾽ ἀνθρώπου ἀλλὰ διὰ **Ἰησοῦ Χριστοῦ** καὶ <u>θεοῦ πατρὸς τοῦ ἐγείραντος</u> **αὐτὸν** ἐκ νεκρῶν,

1:3–5 ³χάρις ὑμῖν καὶ εἰρήνη <u>ἀπὸ θεοῦ πατρὸς ἡμῶν</u> καὶ **κυρίου Ἰησοῦ Χριστοῦ** ⁴**τοῦ δόντος ἑαυτὸν** ὑπὲρ τῶν ἁμαρτιῶν ἡμῶν, **ὅπως ἐξέληται**

---

[79] For a similar interpretation, see R. B. Hays, "Christology and Ethics in Galatians: The Law of Christ," *CBQ* 49 (1987), 268–90; and J. M. G. Barclay, *Obeying the Truth: A Study of Paul's Ethics in Galatians* (Edinburgh: T&T Clark, 1988), 131–35.

ἡμᾶς ἐκ τοῦ αἰῶνος τοῦ ἐνεστῶτος πονηροῦ <u>κατὰ τὸ θέλημα τοῦ θεοῦ καὶ πατρὸς ἡμῶν</u>, ⁵<u>ᾧ ἡ δόξα εἰς τοὺς αἰῶνας τῶν αἰώνων</u>, ἀμήν.

1:6–7 ⁶Θαυμάζω ὅτι οὕτως ταχέως μετατίθεσθε ἀπὸ τοῦ καλέσαντος ὑμᾶς **ἐν χάριτι Χριστοῦ** εἰς ἕτερον εὐαγγέλιον, ⁷ὃ οὐκ ἔστιν ἄλλο, εἰ μή τινές εἰσιν οἱ ταράσσοντες ὑμᾶς καὶ θέλοντες μεταστρέψαι **τὸ εὐαγγέλιον τοῦ Χριστοῦ**.

1:10 Ἄρτι γὰρ ἀνθρώπους πείθω ἢ <u>τὸν θεόν</u>; ἢ ζητῶ ἀνθρώποις ἀρέσκειν; εἰ ἔτι ἀνθρώποις ἤρεσκον, **Χριστοῦ δοῦλος** οὐκ ἂν ἤμην.

1:12 οὐδὲ γὰρ ἐγὼ παρὰ ἀνθρώπου παρέλαβον αὐτὸ οὔτε ἐδιδάχθην ἀλλὰ **δι' ἀποκαλύψεως Ἰησοῦ Χριστοῦ**.

[[1:13 Ἠκούσατε γὰρ τὴν ἐμὴν ἀναστροφήν ποτε ἐν τῷ Ἰουδαϊσμῷ, ὅτι καθ' ὑπερβολὴν ἐδίωκον <u>τὴν ἐκκλησίαν τοῦ θεοῦ</u> καὶ ἐπόρθουν αὐτήν,]]

1:15–16 ¹⁵ὅτε δὲ <u>εὐδόκησεν [ὁ θεὸς]</u> ὁ ἀφορίσας με ἐκ κοιλίας μητρός μου καὶ <u>καλέσας διὰ τῆς χάριτος αὐτοῦ</u> ¹⁶ἀποκαλύψαι **τὸν υἱὸν αὐτοῦ ἐν ἐμοί**, ἵνα εὐαγγελίζωμαι **αὐτὸν** ἐν τοῖς ἔθνεσιν,

1:19 ἕτερον δὲ τῶν ἀποστόλων οὐκ εἶδον εἰ μὴ Ἰάκωβον **τὸν ἀδελφὸν τοῦ κυρίου**.

[[1:20 ἃ δὲ γράφω ὑμῖν, ἰδοὺ <u>ἐνώπιον τοῦ θεοῦ</u> ὅτι οὐ ψεύδομαι.]]

1:22 ἤμην δὲ ἀγνοούμενος τῷ προσώπῳ ταῖς ἐκκλησίαις τῆς Ἰουδαίας **ταῖς ἐν Χριστῷ**.

[[1:24 καὶ ἐδόξαζον ἐν ἐμοὶ <u>τὸν θεόν</u>.]]

2:4 διὰ δὲ τοὺς παρεισάκτους ψευδαδέλφους, οἵτινες παρεισῆλθον κατασκοπῆσαι τὴν ἐλευθερίαν ἡμῶν ἣν ἔχομεν **ἐν Χριστῷ Ἰησοῦ**, ἵνα ἡμᾶς καταδουλώσουσιν,

[[2:6 . . . ὁποῖοί ποτε ἦσαν οὐδέν μοι διαφέρει· πρόσωπον [ὁ] θεὸς ἀνθρώπου οὐ λαμβάνει]]

2:16–21 ¹⁶εἰδότες [δὲ] ὅτι οὐ δικαιοῦται ἄνθρωπος ἐξ ἔργων νόμου ἐὰν μὴ **διὰ πίστεως Ἰησοῦ Χριστοῦ**, καὶ ἡμεῖς **εἰς Χριστὸν Ἰησοῦν ἐπιστεύσαμεν**, ἵνα δικαιωθῶμεν **ἐκ πίστεως Χριστοῦ** καὶ οὐκ ἐξ ἔργων νόμου, ὅτι ἐξ ἔργων νόμου οὐ δικαιωθήσεται πᾶσα σάρξ. ¹⁷εἰ δὲ ζητοῦντες **δικαιωθῆναι ἐν Χριστῷ** εὑρέθημεν καὶ αὐτοὶ ἁμαρτωλοί, ἆρα **Χριστὸς ἁμαρτίας διάκονος**; μὴ γένοιτο. ¹⁸εἰ γὰρ ἃ κατέλυσα ταῦτα πάλιν οἰκοδομῶ, παραβάτην ἐμαυτὸν συνιστάνω. ¹⁹ἐγὼ γὰρ διὰ νόμου νόμῳ ἀπέθανον, ἵνα <u>θεῷ ζήσω</u>. **Χριστῷ συνεσταύρωμαι**· ²⁰ζῶ δὲ οὐκέτι ἐγώ, ζῇ δὲ **ἐν ἐμοὶ Χριστός**· ὃ δὲ νῦν ζῶ ἐν σαρκί, ἐν πίστει ζῶ τῇ **τοῦ υἱοῦ τοῦ θεοῦ** τοῦ ἀγαπήσαντός με καὶ παραδόντος ἑαυτὸν ὑπὲρ ἐμοῦ. ²¹οὐκ ἀθετῶ <u>τὴν χάριν τοῦ θεοῦ</u>· εἰ γὰρ διὰ νόμου δικαιοσύνη, ἆρα **Χριστὸς δωρεὰν ἀπέθανεν**.

3:1 ⁷Ω ἀνόητοι Γαλάται, τίς ὑμᾶς ἐβάσκανεν, οἷς κατ᾽ ὀφθαλμοὺς Ἰησοῦς Χριστὸς προεγράφη ἐσταυρωμένος;

[[3:6 καθὼς Ἀβραὰμ ἐπίστευσεν τῷ θεῷ, καὶ ἐλογίσθη αὐτῷ εἰς δικαιοσύνην·]]

[[3:8 προϊδοῦσα δὲ ἡ γραφὴ ὅτι ἐκ πίστεως δικαιοῖ τὰ ἔθνη ὁ θεός, προευηγγελίσατο τῷ Ἀβραὰμ ὅτι ἐνευλογηθήσονται ἐν σοὶ πάντα τὰ ἔθνη·]]

[[3:11 ὅτι δὲ ἐν νόμῳ οὐδεὶς δικαιοῦται παρὰ τῷ θεῷ δῆλον, ὅτι ὁ δίκαιος ἐκ πίστεως ζήσεται·]]

3:13–14 ¹³Χριστὸς ἡμᾶς ἐξηγόρασεν ἐκ τῆς κατάρας τοῦ νόμου γενόμενος ὑπὲρ ἡμῶν κατάρα, ὅτι γέγραπται· ἐπικατάρατος πᾶς ὁ κρεμάμενος ἐπὶ ξύλου, ¹⁴ἵνα εἰς τὰ ἔθνη ἡ εὐλογία τοῦ Ἀβραὰμ γένηται ἐν Χριστῷ Ἰησοῦ, ἵνα τὴν ἐπαγγελίαν τοῦ πνεύματος λάβωμεν διὰ τῆς πίστεως.

3:16 τῷ δὲ Ἀβραὰμ ἐρρέθησαν αἱ ἐπαγγελίαι καὶ τῷ σπέρματι αὐτοῦ. οὐ λέγει· καὶ τοῖς σπέρμασιν, ὡς ἐπὶ πολλῶν ἀλλ᾽ ὡς ἐφ᾽ ἑνός· καὶ τῷ σπέρματί σου, ὅς ἐστιν Χριστός.

[[3:17–18 ¹⁷τοῦτο δὲ λέγω· διαθήκην προκεκυρωμένην ὑπὸ τοῦ θεοῦ ὁ μετὰ τετρακόσια καὶ τριάκοντα ἔτη γεγονὼς νόμος οὐκ ἀκυροῖ εἰς τὸ καταργῆσαι τὴν ἐπαγγελίαν. ¹⁸εἰ γὰρ ἐκ νόμου ἡ κληρονομία, οὐκέτι ἐξ ἐπαγγελίας· τῷ δὲ Ἀβραὰμ δι᾽ ἐπαγγελίας κεχάρισται ὁ θεός.]]

[[3:20–21 ὁ δὲ μεσίτης ἑνὸς οὐκ ἔστιν, ὁ δὲ θεὸς εἷς ἐστιν. ²¹ὁ οὖν νόμος κατὰ τῶν ἐπαγγελιῶν τοῦ θεοῦ; μὴ γένοιτο. εἰ γὰρ ἐδόθη νόμος ὁ δυνάμενος ζῳοποιῆσαι, ὄντως ἐκ νόμου ἂν ἦν ἡ δικαιοσύνη·]]

3:22 ἀλλὰ συνέκλεισεν ἡ γραφὴ τὰ πάντα ὑπὸ ἁμαρτίαν, ἵνα ἡ ἐπαγγελία ἐκ πίστεως Ἰησοῦ Χριστοῦ δοθῇ τοῖς πιστεύουσιν.

3:24–29 ²⁴ὥστε ὁ νόμος παιδαγωγὸς ἡμῶν γέγονεν εἰς Χριστόν, ἵνα ἐκ πίστεως δικαιωθῶμεν· ²⁵ἐλθούσης δὲ τῆς πίστεως οὐκέτι ὑπὸ παιδαγωγόν ἐσμεν. ²⁶Πάντες γὰρ υἱοὶ θεοῦ ἐστε διὰ τῆς πίστεως ἐν Χριστῷ Ἰησοῦ· ²⁷ὅσοι γὰρ εἰς Χριστὸν ἐβαπτίσθητε, Χριστὸν ἐνεδύσασθε. ²⁸οὐκ ἔνι Ἰουδαῖος οὐδὲ Ἕλλην, οὐκ ἔνι δοῦλος οὐδὲ ἐλεύθερος, οὐκ ἔνι ἄρσεν καὶ θῆλυ· πάντες γὰρ ὑμεῖς εἷς ἐστε ἐν Χριστῷ Ἰησοῦ. ²⁹εἰ δὲ ὑμεῖς Χριστοῦ, ἄρα τοῦ Ἀβραὰμ σπέρμα ἐστέ, κατ᾽ ἐπαγγελίαν κληρονόμοι.

4:4–7 ⁴ὅτε δὲ ἦλθεν τὸ πλήρωμα τοῦ χρόνου, ἐξαπέστειλεν ὁ θεὸς τὸν υἱὸν αὐτοῦ, γενόμενον ἐκ γυναικός, γενόμενον ὑπὸ νόμον, ⁵ἵνα τοὺς ὑπὸ νόμον ἐξαγοράσῃ, ἵνα τὴν υἱοθεσίαν ἀπολάβωμεν. ⁶Ὅτι δέ ἐστε υἱοί, ἐξαπέστειλεν ὁ θεὸς τὸ πνεῦμα τοῦ υἱοῦ αὐτοῦ εἰς τὰς καρδίας ἡμῶν κρᾶζον· Αββα ὁ πατήρ. ⁷ὥστε οὐκέτι εἶ δοῦλος ἀλλὰ υἱός· εἰ δὲ υἱός, καὶ κληρονόμος διὰ θεοῦ.

[[4:8–9 ⁸Ἀλλὰ τότε μὲν οὐκ εἰδότες θεὸν ἐδουλεύσατε τοῖς φύσει μὴ οὖσιν θεοῖς· ⁹νῦν δὲ γνόντες θεόν, μᾶλλον δὲ γνωσθέντες ὑπὸ θεοῦ, πῶς ἐπιστρέφετε πάλιν ἐπὶ τὰ ἀσθενῆ καὶ πτωχὰ στοιχεῖα οἷς πάλιν ἄνωθεν δουλεύειν θέλετε;]]

4:14 καὶ τὸν πειρασμὸν ὑμῶν ἐν τῇ σαρκί μου οὐκ ἐξουθενήσατε οὐδὲ ἐξεπτύσατε, ἀλλὰ ὡς <u>ἄγγελον θεοῦ</u> ἐδέξασθέ με, **ὡς Χριστὸν Ἰησοῦν.**

4:19 τέκνα μου, οὓς πάλιν ὠδίνω μέχρις οὗ μορφωθῇ **Χριστὸς ἐν ὑμῖν·**

5:1–6 ¹τῇ ἐλευθερίᾳ ἡμᾶς **Χριστὸς** ἠλευθέρωσεν· στήκετε οὖν καὶ μὴ πάλιν ζυγῷ δουλείας ἐνέχεσθε. ²˝Ἴδε ἐγὼ Παῦλος λέγω ὑμῖν ὅτι ἐὰν περιτέμνησθε, **Χριστὸς** ὑμᾶς οὐδὲν ὠφελήσει . . . . ⁴κατηργήθητε **ἀπὸ Χριστοῦ,** οἵτινες ἐν νόμῳ δικαιοῦσθε, τῆς χάριτος ἐξεπέσατε. ⁵ἡμεῖς γὰρ πνεύματι ἐκ πίστεως ἐλπίδα δικαιοσύνης ἀπεκδεχόμεθα. ⁶ἐν γὰρ **Χριστῷ Ἰησοῦ** οὔτε περιτομή τι ἰσχύει οὔτε ἀκροβυστία ἀλλὰ πίστις δι᾽ ἀγάπης ἐνεργουμένη.

5:10 ἐγὼ πέποιθα εἰς ὑμᾶς **ἐν κυρίῳ** ὅτι οὐδὲν ἄλλο φρονήσετε·

[[5:21 φθόνοι, μέθαι, κῶμοι καὶ τὰ ὅμοια τούτοις, ἃ προλέγω ὑμῖν, καθὼς προεῖπον ὅτι οἱ τὰ τοιαῦτα πράσσοντες <u>βασιλείαν θεοῦ</u> οὐ κληρονομήσουσιν.]]

5:24 οἱ δὲ **τοῦ Χριστοῦ Ἰησοῦ** [v.l.-Ἰησοῦ] τὴν σάρκα ἐσταύρωσαν σὺν τοῖς παθήμασιν καὶ ταῖς ἐπιθυμίαις.

6:2 Ἀλλήλων τὰ βάρη βαστάζετε καὶ οὕτως ἀναπληρώσετε **τὸν νόμον τοῦ Χριστοῦ.**

[[6:7 Μὴ πλανᾶσθε, <u>θεὸς οὐ μυκτηρίζεται</u>.]]

6:12 ὅσοι θέλουσιν εὐπροσωπῆσαι ἐν σαρκί, οὗτοι ἀναγκάζουσιν ὑμᾶς περιτέμνεσθαι, μόνον ἵνα **τῷ σταυρῷ τοῦ Χριστοῦ** [v.l. Ιησου] μὴ διώκωνται.

6:14 ἐμοὶ δὲ μὴ γένοιτο καυχᾶσθαι εἰ μὴ ἐν τῷ σταυρῷ **τοῦ κυρίου ἡμῶν Ἰησοῦ Χριστοῦ, δι᾽ οὗ** ἐμοὶ κόσμος ἐσταύρωται κἀγὼ κόσμῳ.

6:15 [v.l. + ἐν γὰρ Χριστοῦ Ἰησοῦ] οὔτε γὰρ περιτομή τί ἐστιν οὔτε ἀκροβυστία ἀλλὰ καινὴ κτίσις.]]

[[6:16 καὶ ὅσοι τῷ κανόνι τούτῳ στοιχήσουσιν, εἰρήνη ἐπ᾽ αὐτοὺς καὶ ἔλεος καὶ <u>ἐπὶ τὸν Ἰσραὴλ τοῦ θεοῦ</u>.]]

6:17–18 ¹⁷Τοῦ λοιποῦ κόπους μοι μηδεὶς παρεχέτω· ἐγὼ γὰρ **τὰ στίγματα τοῦ** [v.l. + κυρίου] **Ἰησοῦ** ἐν τῷ σώματί μου βαστάζω. ¹⁸Ἡ **χάρις τοῦ κυρίου ἡμῶν Ἰησοῦ Χριστοῦ** μετὰ τοῦ πνεύματος ὑμῶν, ἀδελφοί· ἀμήν.

Appendix II: An Analysis of Usage

(* = anarthrous; + = with possessive pronoun)

Galatians

θεός   29
Christ   45

The Data

1. κύριος Ἰησοῦς Χριστός (3)
   1:3   G*
   6:14   G+
   6:18   G+
2. κύριος Ἰησοῦς (0)
3. Χριστὸς Ἰησοῦς (8)
   2:4   D* (ἐν)
   2:16   A* (εἰς)
   3:14   D* (ἐν)
   3:26   D* (ἐν)
   3:28   D* (ἐν)
   4:14   A*
   5:6   D* (ἐν)
   5:24   G [v.l.-Ἰησοῦ]
3a. Ἰησοῦς Χριστὸς (5)
   1:1   G* (διά)
   1:12   G*
   2:16   G*
   3:1   N*
   3:22   G*
4. κύριος (2 + 3 = 5)
   1:19   G
   5:10   D* (ἐν)
5. Ἰησοῦς (1 + 15 = 16)
   6:17   G [v.l. + κυρίου]

6. Χριστός (22 + 15 = 37)
   1:6   G*
   1:7   G
   1:10   G*
   1:22   D* (ἐν)
   2:16   G*
   2:17   D* (ἐν)
   2:17   N*
   2:19   D*
   2:20   N*
   2:21   N*
   3:13   N*
   3:16   N*
   3:24   A* (εἰς)
   3:27   A* (εἰς)
   3:27   A*
   3:29   G*
   4:19   N*
   5:1   N*
   5:2   N*
   5:4   G* (από)
   6:2   G
   6:12   G [v.l. + Ἰησοῦ]
7. υἱός (4)
   1:16   A+
   2:20   G
   4:4   A+
   4:6   G+

6

Christology in Romans

FOR THE PURPOSES OF THIS study, the most significant thing about Paul's letter to the Christian communities in Rome is that it was written to believers who were not among his own converts.[1] For this reason, one can expect a more deliberate presentation of Paul's basic urgencies. Thus, read on its own terms, the argument is clearly driven by Paul's ecclesiology rather than soteriology. From beginning to end it has to do with the inclusion of Gentiles with Jews in the one eschatological people of God, on the grounds of grace alone and apart from "doing law." This is made evident in a variety of ways, including how the letter begins, with a considerable elaboration of Paul's apostleship that spells out the gospel in terms of Christ as the messianic Son of God (of the seed of David and now the exalted Lord) (1:3–4), with the Gentile mission as its primary focus (1:5–6).

This in turn is how the argument itself begins in 1:16–17, that God's story of salvation, which began with the Jews, now includes the Gentiles on the equal grounds of "faith." The story of human fallenness that comes next (1:18–3:20) very purposefully includes both Gentile and Jew; and it concludes with the assertion that "all [= Gentile and Jew alike] have sinned"[2] and are thus in need of the righteousness that God has provided in Christ, which is received through faith. The story of Abraham that follows (4:1–25) deliberately presents him as the father of Jew and Gentile alike; and the argument of chs. 6–8 shows how this righteousness is effected for believers by Christ and the Spirit quite apart from the law. Since the Jewish community had generally rejected Christ by the time this letter was written, Paul also feels compelled to deal with their failure and ultimate inclusion (chs. 9–11), precisely because only as the two are brought together is the Abrahamic promise fulfilled.

Thus the argument in the early chapters focuses on circumcision, the primary matter of law-keeping that drove a wedge between Jew and Gentile.

---

[1] Commentaries on Romans are listed in the bibliography (pp. 642–43); they are cited in this chapter by author's surname only.

[2] As the TNIV now has it, "There is no difference between Jew and Gentile, for all have sinned."

But as the argument moves to its conclusion, Paul takes up the practical issue of how Jew and Gentile can live together with their differences regarding matters of food and "days" (= Sabbath) (14:1–15:6). The argument proper then ends with a passionate appeal for Jew and Gentile therefore to "accept one another" (15:7) so that the promises of Scripture might be fulfilled as Jew and Gentile together "with one mind and one voice . . . glorify the God and Father of our Lord Jesus Christ" (15:6). This is then followed by the citation of four OT passages that have the inclusion of the Gentiles into the one people of God as their common denominator (15:9–12). And with that, the argument ends by way of a benediction (15:13).

When the letter is thus read on Paul's terms, not Luther's, it seems certain that it has to do with the passion of his life, which is the Gentile mission: not Gentiles as a separate people of God but, rather, Jew and Gentile together as the one people of God. And here is where traditional Protestant concerns fit into the story. The only way this passion can be realized is for *both Jew and Gentile together* to come to terms with their respective need of "the righteousness of God." This has been made available quite apart from "doing law," namely, through the death and resurrection of Christ and subsequent gift of the Spirit, who is also received by faith alone.

This carefully crafted argument was thus very likely intended to heal a breach between Jewish and Gentile Christians in Rome by showing how God the Father, through the Son and the Holy Spirit, has brought about the fulfillment of the divine purposes that had included Gentiles from the beginning. In Paul's telling of the story, several distinct emphases emerge. For our present purposes, three things stand out. First, this is *God's* story; and therefore God is mentioned both by name and in other ways (pronouns, descriptors, etc.) almost one-half again as often as Christ. As throughout the corpus, God is always the prime mover of the saving activity accomplished by his Son and made effectual by the Spirit. In this letter, that emphasis stands out in bold print.

Second, also as throughout the corpus, Christ is the primary agent of God's saving activity, so much so that he often assumes the primary role in the saving activity itself. As a result, even though the concern regarding Christ's role is primarily soteriological, in this letter especially, one can scarcely miss the christological emphases as well.

Third, the passion of the letter—Jew and Gentile as one people of God and living Christianly by the Spirit and apart from the law—also dictates the primary christological emphases: Jesus is *the messianic Son of God* (who is also *the eternal Son* sent from the Father), who subsequent to his death and resurrection is now *exalted as Lord,* seated at the right hand of the Father in fulfillment of Ps 110:1. All other christological moments, including Paul's return to the theme of Christ as the "second Adam" in 5:12–21, find their ultimate locus in this Son of God/Messiah and exalted-Lord nexus. As before, we begin with a preliminary look at the data themselves, where the Pauline emphases become quite clear.

A Preliminary Look at the Data

The various references to Christ and to God are found in appendix I at the end of this chapter; an analysis of the ways Paul speaks of Christ is found in appendix II. As already noted, and as with most of the letters in the corpus, the special interests of the letter itself dictate both the way and the frequency that Christ is referred to.

The most striking feature of this letter in comparison with all the others is the predominance of references to God (θεός) vis-á-vis references to Christ (153x vs. 96x).[3] Whatever else, Romans is easily the most theocentric book in the corpus. Nonetheless, the heart of the story is the work of Christ, so that the 96 times that Christ is referenced are second in number only to 1 Corinthians (127x). At the same time, some of the distinctive features of usage carry over from Galatians. The clear concern to place Jesus within the story of Israel, and thus to be the divine means of fulfilling messianic hopes that include the Gentiles, most likely accounts for the twin facts that Χριστός is the most frequent referent (58x) and that Romans contains the one certain place in the corpus where ὁ Χριστός means "the Messiah" (9:5). These same realities also account for the continuation (from Galatians) of the high incidence of Son of God language (7x, the most in the corpus).

The second clear christological feature is the continuing emphasis on Christ as κύριος (Lord). However, quite in keeping with the argument as basically expounding God's story in its new covenant expression, the titular use of this designation does not emerge until its appearance at the crucial moment in 10:9, where the confession that "the Lord is Jesus" is what marks those who have come under the new covenant. Thereafter it occurs primarily in two large bunches: in the argument of 14:1–12 (about the observance/nonobservance of food laws and "days") and in the greetings in 16:3–16, where, interestingly, the two predominant titles appear together, as God's people in Rome are alternatively referred to as "in the Lord" or "in Christ."

Finally, we should note that one of the more intriguing moments in the corpus occurs in 9:5, where it is grammatically possible, and very many scholars think probable, that "the Messiah" is also called θεός ("God"). Since I think that the grammar should be understood otherwise, this text will receive special attention.

---

[3]This count is only of names or titles (θεός, Χριστός, κύριος, Ἰησοῦς, υἱός) and thus excludes pronouns and oblique references such as "the one who loved us," meaning Christ (8:37), as well as the citations of the Septuagint that have κύριος = God in which no referential point is being made by Paul. This latter phenomenon occurs 8 times in Romans (of its 12x in the corpus [see n. 7 in ch. 3]), not counting in 14:11, which is discussed in full below (pp. 272–77). In any other letter these phenomena would have been enough for some scholars to call its authenticity into question!

Jesus as Messianic/Eternal Son of God

The single most striking thing about the Christology of Romans is the significant role played by Paul's Son of God Christology, which, although rooted in Jewish messianism, is at the same time expressed in terms of eternal sonship, where the Son is understood as preexistent with the Father. The reason for this christological emphasis lies with the overall concern of the letter itself: Jew and Gentile together as one people of God. Thus, at several key points some form of Son of God Christology emerges; indeed, it is the very first thing up in the letter, in the highly elaborated salutation of 1:1–7.[4]

Romans 1:2–4

The surprisingly long salutation with which Romans begins is basically an elaboration of the phrase about Paul's "having been set apart for the gospel of God" (v. 1). The emphasis is threefold. (1) The gospel has continuity with the old covenant as the fulfilled promise—Christ is of royal David's lineage (vv. 2–3). (2) The content of the gospel is first of all christological, having to do with Christ's earthly ministry and his present exaltation in power (vv. 3–4). (3) Paul's own calling and apostleship for which he had been "set apart" were to bring about "the obedience of faith among all the Gentiles" (vv. 5–6).[5] Our interest lies in the first two of these emphases: Paul's opening, emphatic christological portrayal, where Christ Jesus is presented simultaneously as God's Son and Israel's Messiah.

Verses 3–4 turn out to be one of two places in the proemium (1:1–17) where the gospel is given content. The other, vv. 16–17, is strictly soteriological[6] and sets forth the themes of the argument of the letter itself. The present one is as obviously christological and seems intended from the outset to emphasize for the sake of Paul's Jewish readers that the gospel, which has Christ as its primary subject matter, is itself the fulfillment of God's promises

---

[4]See also the discussion of the messianic/eternal Son of God motif in the preceding chapters (1 Thess 1:9–10; 1 Cor 15:25–28; 2 Cor 1:3, 19; Gal 4:4–7). For a careful discussion of this matter in Romans, see L. W. Hurtado, "Jesus' Divine Sonship in Paul's Epistle to the Romans," in *Romans and the People of God: Essays in Honor of Gordon D. Fee on the Occasion of His 65th Birthday* (ed. S. K. Soderlund and N. T. Wright; Grand Rapids: Eerdmans, 1999), 217–33.

[5]In the thanksgiving/prayer report that follows, the emphasis lies singularly in Paul's desire to come personally to Rome so that he might be able to say in person what now he will write in a letter. The reason for both the unusual length and surprising content of this proemium seems related to its content: since the church in Rome is of some long standing and since it is not one of his own churches, Paul feels a special compulsion to justify the writing of this letter, which at the same time will pave the way for his own hoped-for soon arrival.

[6]The theocentric character of this letter is especially noticeable in this famous passage, inasmuch as Christ is not so much as mentioned, although his saving work, which will be spelled out in 3:21–26, is presupposed in the word "gospel."

in the OT (v. 2) and that Christ himself is the fulfillment of Jewish messianic
expectations (v. 3). The promises, of course, include God's blessing on the
Gentiles, which is what this letter is ultimately all about.

The christological concerns of this opening clause are best seen by noting its carefully crafted structure:

1:3–4	³περὶ τοῦ υἱοῦ αὐτοῦ	A		
	τοῦ γενομένου		B	
	ἐκ σπέρματος Δαυὶδ			C
	κατὰ σάρκα,			D
	⁴τοῦ ὁρισθέντος υἱοῦ θεοῦ ἐν δυνάμει		B	
	κατὰ πνεῦμα ἁγιωσύνης			D
	ἐξ ἀναστάσεως νεκρῶν,			C
	Ἰησοῦ Χριστοῦ τοῦ κυρίου ἡμῶν	A		

	³*concerning his Son,*	A		
	who came		B	
	from the seed of David			C
	according to his earthly life,			D
	⁴*who was declared Son of God with power*		B	
	according to the Spirit of holiness			D
	from the resurrection from the dead,			C
	Jesus Christ our Lord	A		

The whole is enclosed by the A lines, in which Christ is first set forth as
the Son of God and at the end identified appositionally as Jesus Christ our
Lord. The two main concerns are expressed in the B (+ C, D) lines, which are
set in deliberate contrast to each other.[7] First, as to his earthly life,[8] Christ,
being of the "seed of David," thus fulfilled Jewish messianic hopes. Second,
his earthly life was followed by his present exalted status as "Son of God with
power,"[9] predicated on his having been raised from the dead. Both clauses

_____

[7]Because of the tight and somewhat poetic nature of this passage, it is another
in which NT scholarship has found a pre-Pauline formula (cf. 1 Thess 1:10; Gal
4:4–5). This can be neither proved nor disproved (Cranfield remarks that while it
"seems highly probable," it is "hardly as certain as it is sometimes assumed to be"
[1:57]). Since the passage comes to us as a Pauline sentence with Pauline concerns
and nuances, one may assume that what Paul wrote (dictated) he himself believed.
In this case, the reason for the passage seems so obvious that finding a pre-Pauline
creedal moment is quite irrelevant. This is especially so in cases like Käsemann's
(10–13), where he is prepared to distinguish the theology of the pre-Pauline piece
from that of Paul himself—a view carried on at the popular level by Tuckett (*Christology*, 50–51).

[8]This is almost certainly what Paul intends here by κατὰ σάρκα (*according to the
flesh*), a phrase that will be repeated with the same sense in 9:5, where Paul singles
out Christ Jesus as "the Messiah, in terms of his earthly life."

[9]As with most commentaries (e.g., Cranfield, Dunn, Morris, Moo) and translations (TNIV, NRSV), I take the phrase ἐν δυνάμει (*with power*) to modify "Son of
God," not the participle ὁρισθέντος (*declared/appointed*) (Sanday and Headlam). The

are modified by twin prepositional phrases (ἐκ / κατά), expressed as Semitic parallels in poetically balanced contrasts.[10] Together, the two carefully balanced B lines and their modifiers express the heart of Paul's Son of God Christology in capsule form. Four matters need to be noted.

1. This passage is certain evidence that Paul's Son of God Christology is deeply rooted in Jewish messianism, which itself is rooted in the Davidic covenant.[11] The opening two clauses make this a certainty. First, the gospel, which is about God's Son, was "promised beforehand through his prophets in the sacred Scriptures" (v. 2). One can easily trace this messianic Son of God motif through a few key texts: Exod 4:22–23; 2 Sam 7:13–14; Ps 2:6–9; 89:3–4, 26–29. In its first occurrence, Moses is told to tell Pharaoh that Israel is Yahweh's "firstborn son." This language is later transferred to the Davidic king, both in the Davidic covenant and then especially in Ps 2, the enthronement psalm that serves with Ps 1 to introduce the entire Psalter. According to the Davidic covenant, the kingly "son of God" is to rule God's people in perpetuity; and this in turn is the cause of Ethan the Ezrahite's excruciating angst (Ps 89). But Ethan is also the one who now applies the language of both "firstborn" and "son" to the Davidic monarch. This is the biblical story of which Paul is fully aware; and the present passage, along with Rom 9:4–5, makes it equally clear that Paul is quite convinced that Ethan's yearning has been fulfilled in the earthly, and now heavenly, ministry of Jesus as Son of God and Messiah.[12]

2. Although nothing is said explicitly here about the Son's being preexistent, and thus the eternal Son, this does find expression later in the letter in 8:3. On the basis of this later explicit statement, one may also recognize preexistence as presuppositional here in the phrase τοῦ γενομένου ἐκ

---

contrast is between his being Son of God "in weakness" during his incarnation and his having received divine "appointment" as Son of God *with power* on the basis (or from the time) of the resurrection.

[10] Not necessarily intending, of course, by "contrast" that they are thereby "antithetical," which in this case they are not; *pace* J. D. G. Dunn, "Jesus—Flesh and Spirit: An Exposition of Romans i:3–4," *JTS* 24 (1973): 49 and passim. See further, Fee, *God's Empowering Presence*, 478–84.

[11] Cranfield notes that even though "some Jews of the NT period did not regard descent from David as an absolutely essential qualification of the Messiah, . . . the expectation that the Messiah would belong to the family of David was strongly established" (1:58). So most interpreters, and usually quite strongly; e.g., Dunn: "a clear assertion that Jesus was the anointed Son of David, the royal Messiah, the fulfillment of prophetic hopes long cherished among the people of Israel for the age to come" (1:12).

[12] That this is the proper starting point for Paul's Son of God Christology, cf. Schlatter: "He would not be the promised Son of God if he did not share in the flesh and thus belong to Israel and to the family of David" (9); and Stuhlmacher: "Verses 3 and 4 contain the history of Christ told in the Gospels in short form, and emphasize that the entire way of Jesus, from his birth to his exaltation, stands under the sign of the promises of God" (19). For the tendency to play down this rich Jewish heritage, see Käsemann, 11–13, and the response in Fitzmyer, 233.

σπέρματος Δαυὶδ κατὰ σάρκα (*who came from the seed of David according to the flesh*). Although the κατὰ σάρκα phrase is necessary to this whole presentation, it is quite unnecessary for this first point as such, as the similar construction in Gal 4:4–5 makes clear. So while the two κατά phrases deliberately set forth the "humiliation" and "exaltation" of Christ, the first one also puts emphasis on his earthly life, that the Son "came"[13] from heaven to "come" from the seed of David κατὰ σάρκα. The usage here is exactly that in the later, equally clearly, messianic passage in 9:5, where Paul refers to "the Messiah κατὰ σάρκα," which can only mean "as to his earthly life."[14] Behind such a phrase lies the assumption of his prior heavenly existence.

3. As always, and in this case probably without intent, such language strikes a blow against all docetic Christologies.[15] Although Paul does not generally emphasize the genuineness of Christ's humanity, phrases such as these, expressed in passing to point to his preexistence as eternal Son, at the same time land a death blow to all Christologies that would divest the incarnation of its genuineness.[16]

4. The climax of the Son of God Christology is expressed in v. 4, where, following his "humiliation," the eternal/messianic Son of God, through his resurrection from the dead, is now celebrated as "Son of God with power"— and this in keeping with the Spirit, who gives/supplies holiness.[17] And it is this exalted "Son of God with power" whose slave Paul is (v. 1) and who has called and empowered Paul for his own role in the inclusion of the Gentiles in the

---

[13]On γενόμενος in this context, see discussion on Gal 4:4–7 in ch. 5 (p. 215); cf. Lightfoot, who suggests that this word here "implies a prior existence of the Son before the Incarnation" (245).

[14]Cf. Cranfield: "Both here and there [1:3 and 9:5] it is best understood as meaning 'as a man,' 'so far as his Human nature is concerned' " (1:60); and most commentaries (e.g., Byrne, 44). Contra Dunn (1:13), who is enamored by the κατὰ σάρκα / κατὰ πνεῦμα contrast, of which he asserts that the "flesh" side of the contrast is always pejorative and thus lends itself to an understanding of "at least some negative connotation" regarding Christ himself—a view that stands in some tension with his acknowledgment that it is first of all about the Son's Davidic descent. And in any case, Paul does not always use the word σάρξ pejoratively, unless one thinks that being human itself is pejorative, which it is not for Paul.

[15]Cf. Schlatter: "Paul held the rejection of all docetic Christologies that divorce Jesus from Judaism and from the natural conditions essential to life, to be an essential characteristic of the message. It says: The Son of God lived in the flesh and, through his flesh was a son of David and thus a son of Abraham" (9).

[16]It is of some interest, therefore, to see Käsemann (10–12) move very close to such a position by (1) isolating the original "saying" from its now Pauline expression and (2) putting the emphasis on his humanity in the original confession but not in Paul. This simply denies that what Paul wrote/dictated he also intended.

[17]On this understanding of the unusual phrase κατὰ πνεῦμα ἁγιωσύνης, see Fee, *God's Empowering Presence*, 483. Although this could be understood as a periphrasis for "Holy Spirit," one must ask, Why do so here? After all, Paul regularly uses the term "Holy Spirit" as a primary designation for the Spirit; and in this letter in particular the Spirit is recognized as the one who by indwelling his people causes them to live in holiness before the Lord.

people of God (vv. 5–6). Later in the letter (8:32–34), the exalted Son is pictured as seated at the right hand of God, making intercession for his people.

We need to note finally that the final clause in v. 4 is another in a series of texts in which some have hoped to find a Spirit Christology.[18] But that is especially obtuse in this case. Indeed, far from supporting such a Christology, our passage refers to the Spirit in such a way that, although he is closely related to the Son—indeed, in 8:9–11 he will be declared to be the "Spirit of Christ"—he is clearly distinct from Christ. The passage does *not* say that Christ has now assumed Spirit existence. Furthermore, neither does our passage imply that the Spirit is the "means" whereby God raised Christ from the dead.[19] In keeping with the Pauline view as expressed everywhere in his letters, God himself raised Christ from the dead, with no reference to his having done so by his Spirit. Rather, the Spirit in the passage probably has to do with the heavenly, eschatological sphere of life, into which Christ himself by resurrection has now entered and into which all who are his will finally enter.

Romans 1:9

This next reference to Christ as the Son—the last reference of any kind to Christ until 2:16[20]—appears at the beginning of the thanksgiving period, where a sudden shift takes place from Paul's thanking "my God through Jesus Christ" for their faith to his own constant praying for them. Since he is unknown to most of them by face, he calls on God as witness to his speaking the truth in this matter; and the God whom he calls as witness is the "one whom I serve . . . in the gospel of his Son."

This is an obvious echo of the beginning of the salutation, where the gospel of God is "about his Son, who was descended from David." The probable reason for repeating it here is twofold. First, it gives the thanksgiving/prayer continuity with the salutation; that is, this is simply a pickup on the prior designation for Christ. At the same time, in a passage that now focuses on the Gentile recipients of the letter, this will also serve as a reminder that they have been brought into the biblical story through the work of the messianic Son of God, who is also the eternal Son.

---

[18] See, e.g., N. Q. Hamilton, *The Holy Spirit and Eschatology in Paul* (SJTOP 6; Edinburgh: Oliver & Boyd, 1957), 12–15; cf. in the present volume discussion in ch. 3 on 1 Cor 15:45 and in ch. 4 on 2 Cor 3:17.

[19] For this view see Hamilton, *Holy Spirit and Eschatology*; Hendriksen, 1:44; J. M. Scott, *Adoption as Sons of God: An Exegetical Investigation into the Background of ΥΙΟΘΕΣΙΑ in the Pauline Corpus* (WUNT 2/48; Tübingen: Mohr Siebeck, 1992), 240; cf. any number of scholars who assume that Paul has said as much in Rom 8:11, which in fact he neither does nor implies. See G. D. Fee, "Christology and Pneumatology in Romans 8:9–11—and Elsewhere: Some Reflections on Paul as a Trinitarian," in *To What End Exegesis? Essays Textual, Exegetical, and Theological* (Grand Rapids: Eerdmans, 2001), 230–34.

[20] And this passing reference turns out to be the *only* mention of Christ in the entire argument of 1:18–3:20.

Romans 5:10

Romans 5:6–11 seems designed both to elaborate the fact of God's love from 5:5 and to elaborate further on the effective nature of Christ's death as expressed in 3:21–26, by pointing out its reconciling dimension.[21] In so doing, Paul speaks of our being "reconciled to God through the death *of his Son*" (v. 10). This seems to be a deliberate attempt to bring his Son of God Christology into this mix of redemption metaphors. At the same time, he seems to be anticipating 8:32–34, where, echoing the Abraham narrative of Gen 22, Paul asserts, "God spared not his own Son, but freely gave him up for us all." The present passage, therefore, is christological only in a more distant sense; and the use of "Son of God" is soteriological rather than a reflection of either messianic or eternal-Son motifs, except to point out that in Pauline theology "the death of God's Son" is the first and foremost mission of the Son.[22]

Nonetheless, one can scarcely miss the implications of the "love of God" motif that is being explicated in this passage: it is *God's* love that is fully demonstrated in the death of his Son. One would have to work hard to avoid the deep personal relationship between the Father and the Son implied in this language. These are the kinds of statements that move us to think beyond soteriology to ontology: the Son is to be fully identified with God the Father.

Romans 8:3

In turning to this passage, we come to the next significant christological mention of the "Son of God" in the letter. But in contrast to the proemium, the messianic background to the usage of "Son" now gives way altogether to God's sending the eternal Son in order to do for us what the law was incapable of doing, namely, to deal with sin itself.

It is important to read this sentence in the context of the present argument in Romans, since it is an elucidation of 7:5–6 but now by way of the lengthy "digression" over the question of whether Torah itself is evil. This explanation is finally necessary not only because so much that has preceded comes down hard on the law but especially because in 7:4–5 Paul, remarkably indeed, has placed it on the same side of things as sin, the flesh, and death. Thus, Paul's primary objective in the present sentence (8:3–4) is to

---

[21] In the earlier passage Paul shifts metaphors no less than three times: justification, redemption, means of atonement. Each of these is in response to one of the ways of looking at the human condition in its fallenness (guilty, enslaved to sin, broken covenant); here reconciliation serves to overcome our enmity against God. See further, G. D. Fee, "Paul and the Metaphors of Salvation: Some Reflections on Pauline Soteriology," in *The Redemption: An Interdisciplinary Symposium on Christ as Redeemer* (ed. S. T. Davis, D. Kendall, and G. O'Collins; Oxford: Oxford University Press, 2004), 43–67.

[22] So Schlatter (124). Dunn (1:260) sees this view as Paul's distinctive contribution to earlier Son of God Christologies.

elaborate the "third law" (v. 2),[23] that of the Spirit who gives life, predicated on the redemptive work of Christ. It is in referring to Christ's role in making Torah observance obsolete that Paul speaks in terms of God's sending his Son to redeem.

The *work* of Christ is the obvious central concern of the sentence, whose basic subject and predicate assert that "God condemned sin in the flesh," which probably has a double referent: in Christ's own death "in the flesh" God condemned the sin that resides in our "flesh." How God did this is the point of the central modifier, "having sent his own Son in the likeness of the flesh of sin and as a sin-offering."[24]

That Christ's preexistence and incarnation are here asserted seems certain. Granted, Paul does not argue for such, nor, as has often been pointed out, is such an understanding essential to his present point.[25] Nonetheless, these realities are the natural *presupposition* of Paul's language. Despite some occasional demurrers to the contrary,[26] the threefold combination of "having sent," "his *own* Son," and "in the likeness of the flesh of sin" seems to bear witness in its own way to this perspective, since the natural assumption is that Christ had not experienced "flesh" before he was sent.[27] Indeed, one wonders what force the sentence could otherwise have had; that God sent a mere human being whom he chose as his Son to carry out his redemptive purpose seems to be leagues away from Paul's sense of *God's* triumph over the law's ineffectiveness.

First, to combine the first two matters, the sending language here is reflective of that which appears later in John. The aorist participle (πέμψας) implies an action that preceded the action of God's condemning sin in the flesh, so that the Son had been *sent* with this condemnation as its primary goal. What catches one's eye is the unique phrase "his *own* Son" (τὸν ἑαυτοῦ υἱόν), with "his own" in the emphatic position.[28] This emphasis seems to

---

[23] That is, in a clear play on the word νόμος, Paul asserts in 7:22–23 that the first "law" (torah) was ineffective precisely because it could do nothing about the second "law" (sin); thus in 8:2, enter the third "law," the effective one, that of the Spirit. For this reading, see Fee, *God's Empowering Presence*, 523–25.

[24] For this rendering of περὶ ἁμαρτίας, see Wright (*The Climax of the Covenant*, 220–25), who (correctly, it would seem) comes to this conclusion by noting that the Septuagint uses the phrase περὶ ἁμαρτίας to render "sin offering."

[25] E.g., Käsemann, 217; Moo, 510–11.

[26] See esp. Dunn (1:420–21), who thinks that the "Adam-christology" latent in some of this language rules against such a view; he argues this in greater detail in *Christology in the Making*, 38–40, 44–45. But this seems to do exegesis in reverse, where distant echoes are given priority over plain speech. Never in the biblical tradition as a whole or in Paul's letters in particular is Adam called "God's son"; and in Paul's letters, Adam is explicitly mentioned *only* as the beginning of human fallenness (Rom 5:12–21), thus making him the progenitor of death (1 Cor 15:21–22) and of the body that is destined to die (1 Cor 15:45–47).

[27] So most commentators; cf. Käsemann: "a liturgical statement which describes the incarnation of the pre-existent Son of God as the salvation of the world" (216).

[28] So also Cranfield, 1:379. Cf. τοῦ ἰδίου υἱοῦ later in the same chapter (v. 32).

point to the preexistent Son as having been sent to deal with the very sin that the law was unable to deal with in God's "son," Israel.

Second, the phrase "in the likeness of the flesh of sin" harks back to this combination that began in 7:14 ("I am *fleshly*, sold under *sin*"), picked up again in vv. 18–20. In 7:18 "in me" is defined as "in my flesh," which in v. 20 is expressed in terms of "the *sin* that dwells *in me* [= in my flesh]." Paul now says of Christ that he came "in the *likeness*" (ὁμοιώματι [cf. Phil 2:7]) of such, meaning that he was similar to our "flesh" in some respects but dissimilar in others.[29] That this is Paul's intent seems certain from the use of this word at all. Had Paul intended a more complete identification with us in our sinfulness itself, he could easily have said simply "in sinful flesh." But in fact all the words of this phrase are necessary here (i.e., "likeness," "flesh," "of sin") because of the preceding argument. Christ must effectively deal with sin, thus come in "our flesh" (which in our case is full of sin), but only in the "likeness" of such because, though "in the flesh," he was not in sin (as 2 Cor 5:21 makes clear).

Thus, despite the common use of the adjective "sinful" to translate the genitive ἁμαρτίας, Paul almost certainly did not intend it to be adjectival. Because he is speaking of Christ's incarnation, it is "flesh" characterized, in *our* case, by sin but not in *Christ's*. The similarity in this case is to be found in the flexibility of the word "flesh," which now has a slightly altered nuance from that in 7:14–20; that is, Christ came "in the flesh," to be sure, and thereby identified with us in our flesh, our humanness, even though ours was riddled with sin. But his was not "flesh" of this same kind, where "flesh" is now understood as fallen and opposed to God. Thus the Son came "in the *likeness* of the flesh *of sin*," meaning that he shared "flesh" with us all but only in the "likeness" of our "flesh," which was laden down with sin.

The upshot of all this is that in the very dense language of this passage Paul both assumes and expresses an eternal Son of God Christology that has soteriology as its goal.[30]

Romans 8:15–17

Toward the end of his argument that life in the Spirit both supersedes and is infinitely superior to life based on law observance, Paul moves to the

---

[29] Cf. BDAG (s.v. ὁμοίωμα): "It is prob[able] that [Paul] uses our word to bring out both that Jesus in his earthly career was similar to sinful humans yet not totally like them." See in ch. 9 of the present volume discussion on Phil 2:7 (p. 388).

[30] In light of all this, one is quite surprised by C. M. Pate's statement that "Romans 8:3 draws on the wisdom tradition" (*The Reverse of the Curse: Paul, Wisdom, and the Law* [WUNT 2/114; Tübingen: Mohr Siebeck, 2000], 233). This is followed by a series of alleged linguistic parallels that are so remote as to seem impossible to sustain, and these are followed in turn by five "conceptual parallels" with 8:3 that stagger the imagination, especially so when in fact there is not a single certain reference in the entire Pauline corpus to either Sirach or the Wisdom of Solomon. See in the present volume the discussion in appendix A (pp. 594–619), with its list of alleged parallels.

theme of the "sonship" provided by Christ and the Spirit over against the "slavery" of living under law. In so doing, he returns to the imagery from Gal 4:4–7, but he does so in this instance with considerable modifications. Most notable of these is that the thoroughly christocentric, and thus triadic, soteriological focus in Galatians is here replaced by a focus that is altogether on the Spirit, so much so that the "adoption of 'sons'" that Christ effected in Gal 4:5 is now referred to only in terms of the Spirit: he is "the Spirit of adoption as 'sons.'"

The present passage therefore reflects Paul's Son of God Christology only indirectly. As with all passages in Paul's writings where God is referred to as "Father," that is the direct result of Christ's being now known as "the Son." This is especially the case here, where the *Abba*-cry of believers is the Son's own language of address to God.[31] Moreover, the present passage is bookended by direct references to Christ as "the Son of God" (8:3 and 8:29, 32–34). Thus, even though Christ is not here directly referred to as "Son," this reality is finally expressed circuitously in v. 17: as "children," we are "fellow-heirs" with Christ, who is, of course, *the* Son.

Romans 8:28–39

It is easy to read Rom 8 in a way that loses sight of the fact that Paul is still arguing his case for Jew and Gentile as one people of God, made possible through Christ and the Spirit and thus apart from Torah observance. The main thrust of this part of the argument is, first, that God sent his Son to deal with the problem of sin itself (v. 3) and, second, that the subsequent gift of the Spirit enables the believer to live so as not to be enslaved any longer to either sin or the law. But that does not mean that God has also delivered his people from present suffering. Quite the opposite. It is only as we "suffer with Christ" that we will also "share in his glory" (v. 17). In making his case for the necessity and nature of present suffering/weakness, Paul argues that the same Spirit who serves as "firstfruits" guaranteeing our future resurrection (v. 23) also indwells us and makes intercession for us, thus helping us in our weaknesses (v. 26). And the good news is that God knows the mind of the Spirit, that the Spirit intercedes in keeping with God's own purposes (v. 27).

With that, Paul moves toward bringing closure to the long argument that began at 1:18. He does so by returning to the role of Christ in our present weaknesses, offering a set of conclusions intended to encourage his readers that God is on their side in every possible way, working in all things to accomplish his eternal purposes (v. 28). With a crescendo of tightly presented phrases (vv. 29–30), the first "conclusion" places our present circumstances within God's eternal purposes, first by placing them within the ultimate purpose of the Son's incarnation (v. 29), and that within God's purposes that result in our being "glorified" (v. 30), thus echoing the earlier cli-

---

[31] On this matter, see the full discussion of Gal 4:4–7 in ch. 5, pp. 218–20.

mactic moment in the argument at v. 17. Paul then moves to the final concluding word (vv. 31–39), one of the apostle's greatest moments. While the focus is still on God, thus keeping the theocentric nature of the argument intact, he also brings his two basic christological emphases together in vv. 32 and 34 ("Son" and "Lord"), where he presents Christ's past and present role in our behalf as we await the final glory. Each of the three key christological texts (vv. 29–30, 32, 34) needs detailed consideration—the first two here, and later v. 34 as the starting point of the discussion of Κύριος Christology in this letter (pp. 254–68 below).

Romans 8:29–30

In one of the truly exquisite moments of the corpus, Paul concludes the basic biblical and theological argument that began in 1:18 by stepping momentarily into the eschatological future and from that perspective looking back on the whole of what God has purposed and done in Christ. With a series of four identical clauses that begin with the relative pronoun οὕς and that thus modify "those who are called in keeping with [God's] purpose" (v. 28), he envisions the entire panorama of divine grace within the logic of five consecutive verbs: whom God foreknew, God thus predetermined, and then called, justified, and glorified. The first two of these verbs rest within the eternal purposes of God that can only be known as the next two verbs work their way out in history and the final verb brings eschatological conclusion to it all. In their barest form the sequence of verbs looks like this:

οὓς		προέγνω,	*whom*		*he foreknew,*
	καὶ	προώρισεν		*also*	*he determined beforehand*
οὓς	δὲ	προώρισεν,	*whom*		*he determined beforehand,*
τούτους	καὶ	ἐκάλεσεν·	*these*	*also*	*he called;*
καὶ οὓς		ἐκάλεσεν,	*and whom*		*he called,*
τούτους	καὶ	ἐδικαίωσεν·	*these*	*also*	*he justified;*
οὓς	δὲ	ἐδικαίωσεν,	*whom*		*he justified,*
τούτους	καὶ	ἐδόξασεν	*these*	*also*	*he glorified*

Structured this way, the long sentence looks like a theological construct per se; but that is hardly the case, for two reasons. First, Paul's concern is singular. These words come at the end of a long argument intended to reassure both Gentile and Jewish believers that despite present hardships and weaknesses, God is on their side; thus they offer the ultimate theological perspective as to why they can trust what God has done through Christ and the Spirit and therefore have no need to rely on Torah observance.

Second, the above structuring has (for now, deliberately) left out the key element in this recital of divine purpose: what God had in mind from the beginning was that human redemption should take the form of our being "conformed to the *image* of his *Son,* so that he [the Son] might be the *firstborn* among many brothers and sisters." So the first member of the structure actually looks like this:

8:29 οὓς προέγνω,
         καὶ προώρισεν συμμόρφους
                      τῆς **εἰκόνος** τοῦ **υἱοῦ** αὐτοῦ,
                      εἰς τὸ αὐτὸν εἶναι **πρωτότοκον**
                              ἐν πολλοῖς ἀδελφοῖς

  whom he foreknew,
      also he determined beforehand to be conformed
                      *to the **image** of his **Son,***
                  *so that he would be the **firstborn***
                           among many brothers
                           (and sisters)

I have put in boldface the three words that bear the weight of Paul's messianic "Son of God" Christology, which in turn also indicate at this concluding point (in the argument thus far) the nature of the Christology that was assumed at the beginning in 1:2–4. Moreover, what was said at the beginning of the present stage of the argument (8:3) verifies that for Paul, the messianic Son of God is none other than the eternal Son of God, who had been sent into the world for the ultimate purposes outlined here. Three matters are noteworthy about this combination of terms with reference to Christ.

1. All three of these terms will appear again in the series of ὅς (*who*) clauses in Col 1:13–15, thus indicating that they are a part of the substratum of Pauline Christology that emerges in various forms throughout the corpus. The divine *Son* is the Father's *firstborn*, who bears the Father's *image*. In Colossians, they further appear in a context where the Son is noted as having a "kingdom."

2. "Son" and "firstborn," which here appear together for the first time in Paul's writings, are in this instance best understood as a direct echo of Exod 4:22–23, where the Septuagint has τάδε λέγει κύριος, **υἱὸς πρωτότοκός** μου Ισραηλ (*Thus says the Lord, "Israel is my **firstborn son**"*). They are also reflected in a slightly different form in Ps 89:26–27 (88:27–28 LXX) with reference to David:

αὐτὸς ἐπικαλέσεταί με **πατήρ μου**   *He will call out to me, "**My Father**"*
. . . .
κἀγὼ **πρωτότοκον** θήσομαι αὐτόν   *And I will appoint him my **firstborn***

Thus this combination, especially in light of the addition of "kingship" language in Col 1:13, can scarcely be accidental. God's Son is also his "firstborn" (= has the rights of primogeniture), who in Paul's understanding has assumed the role of the messianic king, who in turn had come to stand in for God's people. As "firstborn among many brothers and sisters," therefore,

Christ is given the place of preeminence, while we at the same time are being fully identified with him in his "sonship."[32]

3. As noted in ch. 4 in the discussion of 2 Cor 3:18 and 4:4–6, the ultimate goal of God's redemptive work in Christ is the restoration of the divine image in humankind. Thus, he who as eternal Son perfectly bears that image, besmirched in us by Adam's fall, has come for the very purpose that we ourselves might be *transformed* and thus once more *conformed* to that image.[33] Thus, also inherent in the present passage is a modified form of Adam Christology, in which the one who as divine Son perfectly bears the divine image, in his humanity also perfectly bore the true image intended by God in creating human beings in the first place. The second Adam, in his becoming incarnate and through his death and resurrection, has restored what the first Adam defaced; and this is precisely what God has predetermined in our salvation that has been effected through God's call, Christ's justifying death and resurrection, and will be realized when we are finally glorified.

Romans 8:32

This next reference to Christ as God's Son is one of the bolder moves that Paul makes in this letter. For in his strong affirmative response to his equally bold rhetorical question "If *God* be *for* us, who can be against us?" he deliberately echoes the story of Abraham and Isaac from Gen 22. That the echo is real and deliberate seems certain, since God's word to Abraham was spoken twice, as Yahweh's ultimate affirmation of his loyalty:

Gen 22:12	σὺ καὶ	οὐκ ἐφείσω	τοῦ υἱοῦ σου	τοῦ ἀγαπητοῦ
Gen 22:16	καὶ	οὐκ ἐφείσω	τοῦ υἱοῦ σου	τοῦ ἀγαπητοῦ
Rom 8:32	ὅς γε	οὐκ ἐφείσατο	τοῦ ἰδίου υἱοῦ	

Gen 22:12, 16	*you also*	***did not spare***	*your **son**,*	***the beloved one***
Rom 8:32	*who*	***did not spare***	***his only Son***	

---

[32] On this last point, see esp. Fitzmyer, 525.

[33] Cf. Cranfield: "Paul is here thinking not only of their final glorification but also of their growing conformity to Christ here and now in suffering and obedience" (1:432); Barth, 223; and Schlatter (193), whose paragraph on what it means for the Son of God to be the perfect image of God and of God's intent in creating human beings is especially well articulated. The attempt by Dunn (483–84) to drive a wedge between the incarnate and risen Son at this point misses too much. The Son who is God's "image" and assumes the role of "firstborn" is the one who became incarnate for our redemption and is now risen as Lord of all; and especially in his incarnation he took the road to the cross and thus stamped the divine image in those who follow in his train. Being glorified obviously follows in this sequence. It is as the "firstborn" that the Son both precedes and guarantees the rest of his "brothers and sisters" their place as "glorified" ones.

Paul's boldness lies in his now attributing to God what God attributed to Abraham, in a story so well known that no one with even a modicum of biblical literacy could have missed it. At the same time, the ironical twist to his use of this language is that because Abraham did not spare his beloved son, God himself spared him by means of a ram. But now, in God's case, he did not spare his "only" Son, in that he freely gave him up—making him the ram, as it were—for us all. Although it is true that nothing inherent in this language demands divine status for the Son, the nature of the echo itself seems to require us to see the eternal Son as the presupposition to this usage.

But we need also to note Paul's use of ἰδίου (*his own/only*)[34] in place of the Septuagint's τοῦ ἀγαπητοῦ (*beloved*), which appears also at the beginning of the Genesis narrative (Gen 22:2).[35] Although Paul regularly cited or echoed the Septuagint, since that was the only Bible that would be known in his churches, he was also well acquainted with the Hebrew text, which emphasized that Isaac is Abraham's "only" son. One may conjecture that the Septuagint translator chose to refer to Isaac as Abraham's "beloved" son out of concern to "save" Moses from committing an error—Abraham had many sons. The point, of course, is not that Abraham had no other sons but that Isaac was the son of promise by way of (the barren) Sarah, hence the one who was thus exclusively "his only" son.

This echo of the Hebrew text, and the special relationship between Abraham and Isaac that lies behind this language, in the end suggests that the "Son" whom God did not spare on our behalf was the one who was truly "his only" Son in the same sense as Isaac was of Abraham.[36]

Romans 9:4–5

This passage will be discussed at some length at the end of the chapter (pp. 272–77), as to whether Paul refers to Christ as θεός. I bring it into the present discussion because it is the one certain passage in the entire corpus where Paul explicitly uses the Greek term ὁ Χριστός in a titular way to refer to the Jewish Messiah. The passage itself serves double duty for Paul: to offer the biblical-historical reasons for his own passionate longing for Jewish acceptance of Christ and to lead into the next part of the argument, where he explains their present failure and final future inclusion.

---

[34] Cf. BDAG 2, definition 2 under ἴδιος: "pert[aining] to a striking connection or an exclusive relationship."

[35] It is the language of the Septuagint that is found in the voice from heaven in the Synoptic tradition; cf. Mark 1:11 and pars.: σὺ εἶ ὁ υἱός μου ὁ ἀγαπητός (*You are my Son, the Beloved One*).

[36] On the drama, see on 8:3 above; cf. Cranfield: "The adjective serves to heighten the poignancy of the clause, emphasizing the cost to the Father of delivering up His dearest and most precious" (1:436).

Thus, in sequence Paul enumerates that to God's historic people belong "the adoption to sonship,"[37] the "glory,"[38] the "covenants," the "giving of the law," the "temple worship," and "the promises."[39] The list is then capped (or bookended, if you will) by his going back to "the Fathers" and culminating with "the Messiah." Thus in this enumeration of Jewish privileges, the Messiah is the climax, the ultimate privilege that God has given his ancient people.

Along with the Messiah as God's Son as the first thing expressed in the elaborate salutation (1:2–3), this climactic assertion of the gift of the Messiah as the ultimate Jewish privilege makes it clear that Paul's Son of God Christology is first of all rooted deeply in Jewish messianism: Christ is the long-awaited Davidic scion from the root of Jesse and thus of Judah. Although Paul had come to believe, probably through Christ's resurrection from the dead, that Christ is also the eternal Son (1:4), this part of the equation never eliminates the fact that this expression of Christology has its deepest roots in the history of God's people.

Moreover, just as in Rom 1:3, the qualifier τὸ κατὰ σάρκα (i.e., *according to the flesh*) and especially the use of the article τό[40] point unmistakably to Paul's presupposition that the earthly Messiah had preexistence that was *not* κατὰ σάρκα, and the κατὰ σάρκα here refers to his human nature. Thus this phrase expresses as presuppositional what Paul had said explicitly in 8:3.

Romans 15:6

This final "Son of God" text is expressed in terms already used in 2 Cor 1:3 and 11:31, that we now know the Father as Father because he is first of all "the Father of our Lord Jesus Christ." Thus the passion of this letter finds expression in this penultimate benedictory prayer for the Roman church(es), in a passage that anticipates a similar passion in Philippians: that God might give them the same mind-set toward one another (in this case, Jew and Gentile) that is in keeping with Christ, so "that together with one voice you might glorify the God who is (now known to us as) the Father of our Lord Jesus Christ."[41]

---

[37] Gk. υἱοθεσία, the identical word used of the "adoption to sonship" of believers in Christ in 8:15 (cf. Gal 4:5). Since this word reflects a Roman phenomenon of adopting a legal heir with all the rights of a freeborn son, it does not occur in the Septuagint. This is therefore a Pauline construct—his way of tying historic Israel with new-covenant Israel by suggesting that Israel's own beginnings were a form of "adoption," as implied in Exod 4:22–23.

[38] This choice of words is most likely metonymy for the whole experience of Sinai, esp. Exod 19, where God "adopted" them as his own treasured possession.

[39] This final one in the chronological enumeration is intended to point toward the present, with its fulfillment in Christ and the Spirit.

[40] Cf. Cranfield, 2:464.

[41] On this as the only viable option for this phrase, see the discussion in ch. 4 on 2 Cor 1:3 (pp. 169–71).

Jesus as Lord

As noted in the overview of usage, one of the more remarkable phenomena in the Pauline corpus occurs with regard to Paul's use of κύριος in Romans. What was the most frequent term in the earliest three letters ceases to be so in 2 Corinthians and continues that way until 2 Timothy at the end of the corpus, while in the preceding letter (Galatians) it had nearly disappeared altogether. In Romans, Paul has now returned to more normal usage with this title; what is striking is the fact that up through ch. 9 it occurs only in the threefold combination "Lord Jesus Christ"; after that, when it does appear on its own, it comes in bunches.

Although Paul's Κύριος Christology emerges first in this letter in 8:34 by way of his allusion to Ps 110:1, the actual use of κύριος as a christological title does not begin until he makes a point in 10:9 of the basic Christian confession, "The Lord is Jesus." This is then elaborated by means of a key text from Joel 3:5 LXX, already echoed in 1 Cor 1:2, that everyone who calls on the name of κύριος will be saved. Thereafter the title occurs basically in two significant passages (14:1–12; 16:1–16). We begin with 8:34.

Romans 8:34

We now return to Paul's conclusion (8:31–39) to the opening argument (1:18–8:30), which basically takes the form of a series of rhetorical questions. In response to the presenting question, "What, then, shall we say to these things?"[42]—and because rhetoric breeds rhetoric—he asks first, "If God be for us, who can be against us?" In response, Paul begins at the top: God? How could that be, when he "spared not his own Son but gave him up for us all? Will he not also [along with giving us Christ] freely give us all things?" That leads to the second rhetorical question: "Who will bring any charge against the elect of God?" And again he starts at the top: "God? The one who himself justifies?"[43] Which in turn leads to the third question: "Who is left to condemn?" to which the answer is fourfold and reflects the basic story of Christ. Starting again at the top, this time he asks, "Christ,[44] who died?[45]

---

[42] Gk. ταῦτα, which in this case refers at least to what has been said in ch. 8 but very likely is intended to pick up the argument from the beginning.

[43] At this point, the house is divided whether this is interrogative (as I think; cf. Barth, 328; Barrett, 172) or indicative (as most think); so also in n. 45 below.

[44] This reading (without Ἰησοῦς) is found in B D 0289 1739 1881 𝔐 a m syᵖ sa; the addition is found in 𝔓⁴⁶ ℵ A C F G L Ψ 6 33 81 104 365 1505 al syʰ lat bo. Although one can argue both ways in terms of scribal error (accidental omission due to homoioteleuton; addition due to familiarity), an addition as the cause of error seems more likely in this case than omission, particularly because Paul often uses "Jesus" when referring to his death as a historical rather than theological event.

[45] It is most common to take the rest of this verse as indicative (see Cranfield, 1:434; Käsemann [248] is characteristically dogmatic). I think that the rhetoric calls for a continuation of interrogatives (so Lietzmann, Barrett, Fitzmyer, Achtemeier).

Who rather has been raised? Who also[46] *is at the right hand of God?* Who also intercedes for us?"

With the italicized words in the final set of responses, Paul dips into the common pool of early Christian understanding of the risen Lord as the fulfillment of the messianic hopes expressed in Ps 110:1. This passage has already been cited by Paul in 1 Cor 15:27, where the emphasis lay on Christ's present heavenly reign as he awaits the eradication of our final enemy, death. Here, as will be the case also in Col 3:1, the echo is intended as comfort for those who believe in him. He is now Lord of all by virtue of his having "been raised," and he sits in the seat of divine authority as our heavenly intercessor. Paul obviously thinks that it simply cannot get any better than that. The Lord of all, seated at the Father's right hand, is at the same time the one who at all times pleads the cause of those who are his. How, Paul finally asks, can anyone or anything separate us from this love of Christ?

No wonder, after elaborating on the various exigencies that might cause such separation (vv. 35b–36), Paul simply bursts into rapturous final affirmation: nothing in the whole created order could possibly separate us from such love. Thus the good news: the Lord of the whole universe, Jesus Christ himself, loves his people and thus cares for them. And in so doing, his love is both independent of and identical with that of the Father in v. 39. That is, the love of God found its historical expression in Christ Jesus, whose love is still toward us in his now exalted place as Lord of all. Here, then, is the ultimate sharing of the divine nature.

Romans 10:5–13

Although probably not done by Paul's conscious design, it is of some interest that the first actual appellation of Christ as Lord in the argument of this letter appears in the middle of the next major section of the argument (chs. 9–11). Here, flowing directly out of the assurances of 8:31–39, Paul wrestles with God's faithfulness in the context of Israel's present unfaithfulness. Not counting the prologue (9:1–5) and confessional conclusion (11:33–36), the argument is in three clear parts. (1) In 9:6–29 it takes up the question of God's faithfulness in light of present Israel's unfaithfulness (regarding its Messiah): despite their rejection, God's word has not failed; rather, one needs a more biblical understanding of election. (2) In 9:30–10:21 it asserts that the people of Israel themselves are responsible for missing out, since they were seeking righteousness in Torah itself and missed the τέλος (*goal, fulfillment*) of Torah, Christ himself. (3) In 11:1–32 it

---

[46] This καί is surely original (although on the strength of its omission in א it was omitted in earlier editions of the Nestle text). Cranfield is ready to omit it as "certainly not required" but acknowledges that it "would hardly have been added deliberately," so therefore it must be added "by assimilation to the following clause" (2:458). But is that not "deliberate"? It seems more likely that it was omitted for the very reason of its being a bit awkward when followed by the second καί in the next clause.

raises the question, in light of Israel's rejection, Has God rejected Israel? to which the answer is a resounding no.

Our text, which lies at the heart of the second section, stands as the immediate response to Israel's misguided zeal. In pursuing righteousness based on Torah, they have missed out on the righteousness that God has provided through Christ. Thus, picking up a point made in Gal 3:11–12, Paul, by way of the Septuagint, contrasts those who live by Torah with those who live by faith. The former, he argues from Lev 18:5, are condemned to living by law, which by its very nature thus excludes living by faith (10:5).[47] But the contrast in this case finds its biblical roots in Deut 30:11–14,[48] and its christological basis in the death and resurrection of Christ. Thus, in a piece of inspired spiritual application of texts, Paul creates a collage that begins with Deut 9:4 ("Do not say in your heart"),[49] the content of which is Deut 30:12 ("Who shall ascend into heaven?"), which he interprets in terms of the *incarnation:* "that is, to bring Christ down." But then, instead of continuing with Deut 30:13, which pictures Israel as looking for the word beyond the sea, Paul substitutes language from Ps 107:26 (106:26 LXX) ("Who shall descend into the abyss?"), which is interpreted in terms of the *resurrection:* "that is, to bring Christ from the dead."[50] With that, he returns to Deut 30:14: "The word is near you; in your mouth and in your heart," which he interprets as "the word about faith which we preach."

Picking up "your mouth" and "your heart" from this latter passage, Paul makes the application in terms of the basic Christian confession, based on the basic Christian reality. The confession of "the mouth" is that "the Lord is Jesus," and the belief of "the heart" has to do with his resurrection. Applying these in chiastic order, he then avows that "believing with the heart" leads to justification and "confessing with the mouth" leads to salvation (10:10). And we must not miss the significance of what one "believes with the heart." By raising Jesus from the dead, God the Father exalted him to the highest place and thus bestowed on him *the Name,* which every tongue will one day confess (Phil 2:9–11). Paul's point here is that this is the

---

[47] For this view of this sentence, which is not the universal interpretation by any means, see also Cranfield, 2:521–22; Dunn, 2:601; and, in a more nuanced way, Moo, 648–49.

[48] It should be noted that this passage was well known to Israel, since it follows hard on the promise of a circumcised heart, which serves as the basis for the later prophetic promise of a new covenant (Jer 31:31–34; Ezek 36:24–32). Paul himself has already made use of the ideas and language from these texts earlier in this letter (2:28–29; 7:6).

[49] In his careful analysis of this text, Christopher Stanley suggests that Paul has here "substitute[d] the first line of Deut 9.4 for Deut 30.11" (*Paul and the Language of Scripture,* 129). That very well may be the case, since the whole is an "exposition" of Deut 30:11–14.

[50] For the view that Paul is referring to the incarnation and resurrection, see, e.g., Barrett, 199; Cranfield, 2:524–25; Murray, 53; Fitzmyer, 590–91; Byrne, 321; Moo, 655–56; Schreiner, 558; contra Käsemann, 288–90; Dunn, 2:605–6.

Name now confessed with the mouth (Jesus as the risen exalted Lord) that leads to salvation.

But Paul is not quite finished, as he makes a further series of biblical moves that are full of christological import. In 9:32–33 Paul had already cited Isa 28:16 with a collage from Isa 8:14 (in boldface):

> Behold, I lay in Zion a stone **of stumbling and a rock of offense;**
> and whoever believes in him will not be brought to shame.

Paul's concern in that case was with the first line, as that had played itself out in contemporary Israel's rejection of their Messiah. He now (10:11) returns to this passage by picking up the second line, where the Septuagint's "him" is now to be understood as Christ himself.

Since the passion of this letter is Jew and Gentile as *one* people of God in Christ Jesus, Paul next echoes his own language from 3:22–23, that "there is no distinction between Jew and Greek." But whereas in the former instance it had to do with Jew and Greek as both coming up short because both alike have sinned, the conclusion here is that "there is no distinction between Jew and Greek" in terms of salvation. For "the same Lord is over all [of them], showing himself rich toward all who call on him." The "Lord" in this case, of course, is the same as in the confession, "the Lord is Jesus." This final clause is then supported by a citation of Joel 3:5 LXX:[51]

πᾶς γὰρ ὃς ἂν ἐπικαλέσηται **το ὄνομα κυρίου** σωθήσεται.
*For everyone who calls on **the name of the LORD** will be saved.*

For our present purposes, three significant christological moments from this exposition need to be pointed out.[52]

1. Although Paul makes no special point of it, his christological interpretation of Deut 30:12 unmistakably presupposes his conviction regarding Christ's incarnation. This is made certain by the fact that the second clause (from Ps 107:26 [106:26 LXX]) is interpreted in terms of Christ's resurrection. It is altogether unlikely that Paul would have preceded this with reference to Christ's present exaltation in heaven and thus that in some oblique way it refers to Christ's future coming at his Parousia. After all, he needed to go outside Deuteronomy to make the point about the resurrection precisely because he intended the first clause to refer to Christ's coming to earth—sent by the Father, as he put it in 8:3—in order to redeem both Jew and Gentile on the

---

[51] Joel 2:32 in the English text, which follows the numbering in the Hebrew Bible.

[52] It is striking in the literature on this passage how few there are who point out the christological implications of what is said here. The one who sees it and articulates it most clearly (Dunn, 2:617–18) at the same time also tries to minimize it; Cranfield (2:529, 532) is a notable exception. Others occur after Dunn's commentary: Fitzmyer, 593 ("an eloquent witness to the early church's witness to Christ as *Kyrios*"); Moo, 659–60; Schreiner, 561.

same basis. Thus, present Judaism is at fault for still looking to heaven for Christ to come down, as it were, when he has already come down, "born of a woman, born under the law, to redeem those under the law," as he put it in Gal 4:4–5.

2. The basic Christian confession in v. 9, the first "stand alone" reference to "the Lord" in the letter, is in fact the second occurrence of the confession in the corpus. On its significance as picking up both the κύριος of the Jewish Shema and a Christian affirmation over against the reigning Caesar,[53] see the comment on 1 Cor 12:3 in ch. 3 (pp. 123–24) and the full elaboration in Phil 2:11 in ch. 9 (pp. 399–401).

3. Despite some opinions to the contrary,[54] the christological features at the end of the argument in vv. 12–13 point to Paul's presupposed high Christology. This happens in three ways and at the same time anticipates the practical outworking of this confession in 14:1–12.

(a) First, to begin at the end, the citation of Joel 2:32 (3:5 LXX) in v. 13 is the only certain instance in this letter[55] where ὁ κύριος = Yahweh of a Septuagint text is applied directly to Christ. On this phenomenon in Paul's letters, see especially the discussions in chs. 2 and 3 (on 1–2 Thessalonians and 1 Corinthians). Here again Paul simply posits that the role of the "Lord" in the Joel passage is now assumed by Christ the Lord, and the transfer is absolute and without argumentation. But in this case Paul is not merely borrowing the *language* of Joel; he undoubtedly sees this confession as the fulfillment of the eschatological promise inherent in that text. Here is the evidence that the promised Day of the Lord has come: the promised Spirit (Joel 2:28) has been outpoured, and Jew and Gentile together are "calling on the name of the Lord (Jesus)" and are thus being saved.

(b) But leading into that citation, Paul has already made the point that Jesus as "Lord" lies at the heart of God's aim to create one new people of God out of Jew and Gentile; thus the κύριος on whom both Jew and Gentile call is the "same Lord" over all. Here is one of the absolute divine prerogatives that is now seen as assumed by Christ through his resurrection to the "right hand of God." It is this point in particular that will be highlighted in 14:1–12.

(c) Finally, in connection with his being "Lord over all," Christ as Lord thus "is rich" toward all, in the sense that he lavishes all the divine wealth

---

[53] For this double focus, see Cranfield, 2:528, yet "it is not likely to have *originated* as a response to κύριος Καῖσαρ" (italics mine).

[54] See esp. Dunn, who articulates clearly what Paul has done in vv. 12–13 and then asserts (correctly) that Paul's point is "not . . . a Christological one; rather it is a salvation-history point" (2:617). But is not that in fact what makes the christological point so telling? Paul is *not* trying to *assert* something about Christ as divine; what he does, rather, is to *assume* it, and to do so in such an off-handed way that he expects common agreement on the part of all and with no fear of contradiction. Thus it is a moment of Christology of the highest kind.

[55] The only other possible such instance in this letter (Rom 14:11) lies more in the realm of probability than certainty. See the next section below.

generously on all those who do call on his name. Here Paul picks up the divine prerogative, noted already in 2 Cor 8:9, that the one who was previously rich made himself poor in his incarnation and crucifixion precisely so that he might bestow the wealth of God's mercy on them. Similarly in Phil 4:19, Paul turns over the reciprocity of friendship to God, who will supply every need of theirs in keeping with his "riches that are in Christ Jesus."

So indeed, Paul's point is soteriological, but the soteriology is expressed in terms that presuppose that the Son of God as Lord both is the fulfillment of the Joel prophecy and has himself assumed what are essentially divine prerogatives.

Romans 14:1–12

In this passage Paul reaches the practical climax to the argument of the letter. In a sense, everything has been aiming toward this very specific moment. Given that the time of Torah has come to an end, how, then, do Torah-observant Christian Jews and nonobservant Gentiles get along together as the one people of God? This is the sticky issue that Paul addresses here.[56]

The argument itself is both crucial and full of interest. The *goal* is expressed in 15:5–7: God will give both of them the grace to think along the same lines, so that *together,* with *one mouth,* they may glorify the God and Father of our Lord Jesus Christ. Therefore, he urges, "accept one another." This is why all of this is so crucial: the glory of God is at stake, and the gospel must work out in real life, right at this point of real differences among them, if it is going to count for anything at all.

How Paul gets there is what makes it so full of interest. On the issue itself, he obviously assumes the stance of the Gentiles; he still holds to what he has asserted elsewhere, "in Christ neither circumcision nor uncircumcision [and thus, neither food nor days] counts for a thing" (1 Cor 7:19; Gal 5:6).

---

[56] This is said more confidently than some will think warranted, since Jews and Gentiles are (carefully?) not mentioned until the end. Paul's own language is "the weak as to the/their faith" (14:1–2) and "the strong" (15:1). Many see connections with 1 Cor 8–10 and suggest that the food in question is the "idol meat" of the Corinthians passage (see esp. Ziesler, 124–27). This seems unlikely since (1) 1 Cor 8:1–10:22 has to do with attendance at idol temples and the issue is not food but idolatry, (2) the question of food per se is addressed only in 1 Cor 10:23–11:1 and there Paul vigorously defends his right to eat such food, although acknowledging a willingness to forbear in contexts outside his own lodgings, whereas (3) idolatry is not so much as mentioned here. On the other hand, the issue of food that is in view here is later called "clean" or "unclean" (14:14, 20); moreover, the final application in 15:5–12, which assumes Jew and Gentile, seems also to favor the position taken here. This is the most common view (most recently Cranfield, 2:694–95; Dunn, 2:795; Stuhlmacher, 219; Fitzmyer, 687; Moo, 829; Schreiner, 714–15; cf. M. B. Thompson, *Clothed with Christ: The Example and Teaching of Jesus in Romans 12:1–15:13* [JSNTSup 59; Sheffield: JSOT Press, 1991], 233–34 and passim). In light of the considerable debate, Morris (475) prefers to be noncommittal, but he also overlooks the clear Jewishness of much of the argument (e.g., 14:14, 20).

Nonetheless, the argument itself presumes to speak primarily *to* the Gentiles, to encourage love for the Jews by not forcing "Gentile freedom" on them. Even so, the very nature of the *theological* dimension of the argument, though addressed to the Gentiles, seems to be just as clearly intended to help the Jewish believers take a different view of things in light of Christ and the Spirit. Is this, then, his own rhetorical ploy, asking the Gentiles to back off while at the same time challenging the Jewish position?

In any case, the argument itself, which is in four parts,[57] begins (v. 3) with a word to Gentiles[58] but thereafter is an appeal to *both.* The issues are "food" (vv. 2–3, 6b) and "days" (vv. 5–6a). It is clear that God cares nothing at all about observance. But since both the observant and the nonobservant are accountable to God alone, any form of judgment (by the observant) or scorn (by the nonobservant) is out. In fact, both will appear before God in judgment, which serves as both warning and assurance—to both. The aim of all of this seems twofold: to remove these matters from the area of *genuine* righteousness and to demand that both peoples are responsible to God alone on such matters and therefore may not judge or scorn each other. Thus Paul simultaneously protects his gospel and those who would be abused by others.

What is striking in this section is its sudden christocentric focus, with Christ mentioned as ὁ κύριος (*the Lord*) no less than eight times and the verb κυριεύειν (*to rule over*) once. As such, Christ the Lord assumes the role of divine prerogative that in the Jewish world would be reserved for God alone. Thus, even though God is the one who has accepted the weak person (v. 3), that person stands or falls in terms of relationship to "his or her own Lord[59]

---

[57] Part 1 (14:1–12) presents the issue and its basic solution; part 2 (14:13–23) is directed primarily to the Gentiles: whatever their own personal practice might be before God, they are under obligation to love the Jews and thus not to offend or cause to stumble. Here in particular the whole is directed *practically* toward the Gentiles; nonetheless, it *theologically* also takes the side of the Gentiles and thereby in effect demolishes the position of the Jews; part 3 (15:1–6) is a final appeal to the Gentiles, supported by an appeal to the example of Christ, but it also brings in the Jews as well, by way of a final prayer; part 4 (15:7–13) serves as conclusion to the whole argument: first, with an appeal for both to accept each other, just as Christ has accepted *you* (surely both in this case); second, as a supporting argument to the appeal in v. 7, that the Christ who has accepted them both did so by way of Judaism but for the sake of Gentiles; and third, declaring the final result, which is Jew and Gentile as one people, together praising God, thus fulfilling the covenantal promises. All of which concludes with a final prayer.

[58] This seems to be made certain by the choice of the verb ἐξουθενέω here. Paul uses κρίνω and ἐξουθενέω ("to judge and "to scorn") with consistency throughout this passage as the two verbs that reflect the two attitudes involved—precisely the Jewish and Gentile attitudes toward each other regarding the religious requirements peculiar to the Jews in the Diaspora. Thus nonobservant Gentiles "scorn" the observant Jews, while the latter "judge" the former.

[59] Because the argument at this point begins by way of an analogy of the household, the tendency on the part of commentaries and translations is to represent this first use of κύριος at the metaphorical level; thus "before their own lord they stand

(= Jesus Christ)" (v. 4). To which Paul immediately appends, "and they will stand, for *the Lord*[60] is able to cause them to stand." Then in verse 6b, after mentioning the matter of observance/nonobservance of days, he concludes that on both matters those (the Jews) who regard days as special and those (the Gentiles) who eat everything[61] must do so in relationship to "the Lord" Jesus, since each gives thanks to God for their food, whether kosher[62] or nonkosher. Everything hinges on their belonging to the same Lord, not whether they are kosher.

With that, Paul then takes off on what may look like a Pauline excursion; but in fact, as the explanatory γάρ (*for*) makes certain, Paul is setting out to *justify* the prior assertion about their common Lord's not caring about kosher. At the same time, he anticipates the rest of the argument: even though food is a matter of indifference to God, their belonging to the same Lord also means that neither Jews nor Greeks live or die only to themselves, as it were (v. 7). In living, they live for the Lord, and in dying, they still belong to the same Lord; so they are the *Lord's* own people in both life and death. Indeed, Paul says in one of his more ad hoc theological moments, this is *why* Christ[63] died and returned to life,[64] so that he might have full lordship over both the dead and the living.

---

or fall" (NRSV; cf. TNIV: "to their own master"). But this is a bit tricky, since it is clear by the follow-on sentence that Paul already has Christ in mind; thus Paul is already pointing to Christ when he gets to this point in the analogy. After all, he noticeably does not use δεσπότης, which he well could have done in terms of the analogy itself. Hence my capitalized "Lord" here and the inclusion of this instance in the count. Some (e.g., Dunn, 2:796; Fitzmyer, 686, 690) would carry the analogy through to the next sentence ("his master can cause him to stand"), but this seems to make very little sense at the merely human level.

[60] The christological implications of this sentence are made plain by the later scribes who changed κύριος to θεός (D F G 048 33 1739 1881 𝔐), almost certainly because what is said would most commonly be attributed to God himself.

[61] This seems intended to keep the careful balance with which the argument began and has been maintained to this point; it is the Jewish Christian who will regard some days (esp. Sabbath) as sacred, while the Gentile believer will not be kosher.

[62] This anachronism is used simply as contemporary shorthand for Jewish food laws.

[63] One should note the change to "Christ" at this point, since, for Paul, ὁ κύριος is the exalted Lord and therefore did not die on the cross; rather, it was the Jewish Messiah who died for our sins. This change most likely was made simply by instinct.

[64] This is one of the more interesting moments where the Textus Receptus, translated by the KJV, has conflated the competing texts East and West. The Alexandrian reading found in the modern critical texts is supported by ℵ* A B C 365 1506 1739 1881 *pc* co; the "Western" reading, ἀνέστη, is read by F G 629. Beginning with D and from there on, the two were conflated to read ἀνέστη καὶ ἔζησεν, so that the KJV has the strange rendering "both died, and rose, and revived." But one can also see the reason for the Western reading. This is in fact the single instance in the corpus where Paul follows "Christ died" with this verb; in all other instances it is some form of "he rose." His choice here is predicated on the context, having to do with the fact that whether one lives or dies, one is still under the lordship of the One who "came to life."

Paul concludes by putting their present "judging" and "scorning" one another into its ultimate eschatological context. All of them will stand before the *bēma* of God (v. 10), where they each will give an account only for themselves (v. 12). But in between these sentences, which logically go together, Paul has inserted biblical evidence in support. But evidence for *what* is not totally clear. Is it for v. 9 ("Christ died and came to life so that he might exercise lordship over both the living and the dead"), which serves to conclude vv. 7–8? Or is it evidence for v. 10 ("we must all appear before the *bēma* of God"), which brings closure to the argument that began in v. 1, doing so by picking up the two negative verbs from v. 3 ("judge" and "scorn")? A first reading seems to favor the latter, but further reflection gives reason to pause because the nature of the citation itself and two significant variations in the textual tradition at the end of vv. 10 and 12. So in the end, I will argue, the citation is evidence for both: they may not judge/condemn each other because they must all appear before God's *bēma*, where every knee will bow to acknowledge Christ's lordship while with their tongues they will confess/praise God,[65] and this because the risen Lord has assumed lordship over both the living and the dead.

We begin with the two textual issues. In asserting in v. 10 that "we all" must stand before the divine *bēma*, Paul is picking up a metaphor that he first used in 2 Cor 5:10, where he asserted that all believers must appear before the *bēma* of *Christ*. But now he almost certainly refers to the same event as the *bēma* of *God*. The evidence:

θεοῦ   ℵ* A B C* D F G 630 1506 1739 1852 2200 *pc* lat co

Χριστοῦ   ℵ^c C² Ψ 048 0209 6 33 1175 𝔐 r vg^cl sy Mcion^T Ambst

In this case the evidence seems strongly to favor "God" as the original text. Both the earliest and the best evidence read θεοῦ; and a later change to Χριστοῦ is explicable as conforming to, and thus harmonizing with, what Paul said in 2 Corinthians.

Second, at the end of v. 12, Paul concludes that at this *bēma*, each of us will either (a) give an account of our *own selves* or (b) give an account of ourselves *to God*. Again the evidence:

+ τῷ θεῷ ℵ A C D Ψ 048 0150 0209 33 81 1175 1241 2127 𝔐 lat sy co

- τῷ θεῷ B F G 6 424^c 1739 1881 2200 it^{f,g,o,r} Cyp Ambst

This variation is not supported as strongly either way as with the former, and the two major early streams (Egypt and the Latin) have split evidence; nonetheless the heart of the Egyptian tradition (B 1739) and the

---

[65] On the meaning of ἐξομολογήσεται, see BDAG; it is very likely that here it takes on the additional sense of "praise," while in the Philippians usage (2:10) it seems to mean "confess."

earliest Latin evidence support the text without τῷ θεῷ. Moreover, so-called internal evidence is all on the side of the shorter text. It is the more difficult reading to account for as a sheer mistake, since there is nothing in the sentence that calls for an error of either sight or mind. At the same time, the sentence almost begs for an indirect object; and "God" is the obvious choice, given how both vv. 10 and 11 conclude. We may therefore safely determine that Paul concluded this paragraph by saying (simply), "Therefore, each of us shall give an account of ourselves."

But from this point on, nothing is easy. Indeed, when we turn to the citation in v. 11 itself, we are faced with a complexity that is much easier to describe than to explain, as to either how it happened or what it means. Our difficulties stem from three matters: (1) Paul's text is a collage of two Isaianic passages as they appear in the Septuagint (49:18; 45:23);[66] under ordinary circumstances one would simply assume that the "as I live, says the Lord" would refer to God, as in all other of Paul's citations of the Septuagint when it is introduced by the formula "It is written"; but (2) the entire passage to this point has had only to do with the Romans' relationship to Christ as Lord; and (3) the major part of the citation will appear again in Phil 2:10, where it is specifically interpreted in terms of "bowing the knee" to Christ as Lord.

So at issue is whether Paul intends "the Lord" in the first part of the citation (ζῶ ἐγώ, λέγει κύριος [*as I live, says the Lord*]), and thus the "to me" in the first line of the second citation, to refer to Christ or to God. And in a secondary way this will also determine how one sets out the poetry in an English translation, as two lines or three. Here are the texts themselves, and one will note that the only difference between Paul and the Septuagint is the word order of "every tongue confess":

Isa 49:18	ζῶ ἐγώ, λέγει κύριος,
Isa 45:23	ὅτι ἐμοὶ κάμψει πᾶν γόνυ καὶ ἐξομολογήσεται[67] πᾶσα γλῶσσα τῷ θεῷ
Rom 14:11a	ζῶ ἐγώ, λέγει κύριος,
Rom 14:11b–c	ὅτι ἐμοὶ κάμψει πᾶν γόνυ καὶ πᾶσα γλῶσσα ἐξομολογήσεται τῷ θεῷ

---

[66] This is said with a bit more confidence than is intended. In fact, the phrase "as I live, says the LORD" occurs 22 times in the Septuagint; for the sake of discussion, I have chosen simply to reference the one closest to Isa 45:23. It is the very commonness of the phrase that makes the issue of whether it is deliberate to be a bit tenuous.

[67] This is the reading of A and the corrector of ℵ; B and ℵ* read ὀμεῖται ("swear"). On the probability that Alexandrinus has the original of the Septuagint here, see G. D. Fee, *Paul's Letter to the Philippians* (NICNT; Grand Rapids: Eerdmans, 1995), 223 n. 28. There can be little question that the text that Paul cites here and in Phil 2:11 is the only one he had access to and is not his own creation. Although Paul is not always precise regarding his biblical citations, neither does he make a point based on a deliberate alteration.

1. On the one hand, there is much to be said in favor of "God" as the referent for λέγει κύριος. I note the following:

(a) The most immediately preceding divine person mentioned is God. Thus: "For everyone will appear before the *bēma* of God. For it is written: 'As I live, says the Lord (God), before me every knee will bow and every tongue confess to God.' " At the same time, the later scribes had it right by inserting "to God" at the end of v. 12, since the judgment is pictured only as appearing before God the Father.

(b) Probably the most telling matter on this side of things is the fact that "As I live, says the Lord" appears within a citation that begins with the formula "For it is written." Everywhere else in the corpus where Paul includes κύριος in such a citation, the referent is *incidental* to the point being made by the citation, so one might legitimately assume that Yahweh himself is intended simply by default.[68] Thus the "addition" of "as the Lord says" would simply be a Pauline way of emphasizing the divine oath that stands behind the certainty of final judgment.

(c) This view also has the advantage of keeping the poetry of Isaiah intact. In this case, the poetry would look like this:

14:11 ζῶ ἐγώ, λέγει <u>κύριος</u>,
  ὅτι <u>ἐμοὶ</u> κάμψει πᾶν γόνυ
  καὶ πᾶσα γλῶσσα ἐξομολογήσεται <u>τῷ θεῷ</u>.

  As I live, says <u>the Lord</u>,
    <u>before me</u> every knee will bow;
    and every tongue will confess <u>to God</u>.

The interpretation would then be straightforward, with only one divine person in view. God the Father, who is known throughout Scripture as "the Living One," swears by himself that they each will give an account only for themselves regarding the matter of food and days.

2. But the very uniqueness of this combination, plus the fact that Paul's use of the text in Phil 2:10–11 is altogether christological, gives legitimate reasons to pause. Thus, in favor of κύριος as referring to Christ are the following considerations:[69]

(a) The addition of the ζῶ ἐγώ, λέγει κύριος (by way of another passage in Isaiah) is to be understood as intentional and thus to offer support for what is stated clearly in v. 9: Christ died and ἐζήσεν (*returned to life*), with the definite purpose of assuming lordship over both the living and the dead. So

---

[68] For these citations, see n. 7 in ch. 3.

[69] As far as I can discern, the only two who actually adopt this interpretation are M. Black ("The Christological Use of the Old Testament in the New Testament," *NTS* 18 [1971–1972]: 8) and D. B. Capes (*Old Testament Yahweh Texts in Paul's Christology* [WUNT 2/47; Tübingen: Mohr Siebeck, 1992], 123–30); Hurtado (*Lord Jesus Christ*, 112) remains ambivalent.

the lead-in to the citation regarding universal judgment is, "As I [Christ] *live,* says *the Lord.*"[70]

(b) In this case it would most likely have been added so that both Christ the Lord and God the Father are understood to be present at this judgment, which is quite in keeping with 2 Cor 5:10. If so, then the first line of the citation of Isa 45:23 has to do with Christ as well. Thus, "every knee will bow before *me* [= the Lord Christ], and every tongue will confess to God."

(c) This is then further supported by the fact that Paul will pick up this passage again in Phil 2:10–11 in precisely this way. At his exaltation, Christ Jesus is given the Name above every name, which means that he is now the "Lord" of the κύριος = *Adonai* = YHWH text of the OT. Thus, before Christ every knee will bow and every tongue make confession: *The Lord* is Jesus Christ. At the same time, the τῷ θεῷ of the Septuagint appears at the end as "to the glory of God the Father," who has thus exalted Christ and bestowed on him the Name. This combination in Philippians is thus to be seen as fully echoing the usage first set forward here.

(d) This interpretation then also comports with the fact that the present passage is dominated unequivocally by ὁ κύριος = Christ Jesus, and would therefore keep this referent intact. In the entire passage the only exception to *Christ* as Lord over all is when Paul brings in "the *bēma* of God" in v. 12, precisely so that the final judgment is before both Christ, who as the risen One is thus "Lord" over both the living and the dead, and God the Father, before whom everyone will ultimately make "confession."

(e) This would further explain the textual confusion regarding *bēma.* Not only would scribes have been aware that this phrase is expressed as the "*bēma* of Christ" in 2 Corinthians, and so substituted "Christ" here (in v. 10), but also they could have been sensitive to the context. The same Lord whose lordship is over both the living and the dead is the one before whom they shall all appear at the final judgment.

(f) Finally—and this became decisive for me—this best explains why there is no indirect object at the end of v. 12. In this interpretation, everyone bows before Christ and praises God; and in so doing, everyone will give account only for oneself, not for the other who eats or does not eat, depending on people's point of view. And thus there is no emphasis on giving an account *to God* for how one lived regarding this matter.

If this understanding were in fact Paul's intent, then his citation would look like this (using the bold and underline as throughout this study):

14:11 ζῶ ἐγώ, λέγει **κύριος**, ὅτι **ἐμοὶ** κάμψει πᾶν γόνυ
καὶ πᾶσα γλῶσσα ἐξομολογήσεται τῷ θεῷ.

As I live, *says* **the Lord, before me** *every knee will bow;
and every tongue will confess <u>to God</u>.*

---

[70]Black sees this as decisive. As he put it, "This is Pauline hermeneutic: praise to God accompanies homage to Christ as Lord" ("Christological Use," 8).

In this case, and in keeping with what Paul says elsewhere, both the Father and the Son share position at the final judgment. Furthermore, it would be in keeping with the mood of v. 18 that follows: "anyone who **serves Christ** in this way is pleasing to God and approved by other people."

In the end, these various reasons seem considerably to outweigh the strongest argument for "God": Pauline usage in "citations" elsewhere, where mention of κύριος in the citation is quite incidental to the *point* of the citation.[71] Indeed, intentionality is the very factor that needs to be brought to bear here and makes this "citation" different from the others. There are two reasons for thinking so in this case. First, the "addition" of an oath formula to the citation is singular to this one instance in the corpus. Elsewhere Paul has simply added a λέγει κύριος to a citation (2 Cor 6:17, 18; Rom 11:3; 12:19); and in each case this is done to establish that what Paul cites is not simply Scripture but is in fact what Yahweh himself has spoken.

This suggests, second, that in this case it is more than simply an oath formula, although it also functions as such; rather, it is a deliberate, now scriptural, pickup of the astounding asseveration in v. 9, that the very reason Christ died and came to live again was so that he might assume lordship over both the living and the dead, both of whom will bow before him as Lord when they appear before the *bēma* of God.

That leads, then, to some summary observations about the very high Christology of this passage, where Paul speaks consistently of Christ as "the Lord."

1. The word "Lord" in this passage carries both its titular sense (as a referent to Christ as the divine "Lord" by virtue of his resurrection) and its functional sense (as the "Lord" to whom everyone is ultimately in servitude). The fact that the double sense of this language is used exclusively of God in the OT points to an exceptionally high Christology. People are subject to kings, rulers, or householders as their earthly "lords"; however, God alone has the ultimate lordship over all things and thus rightfully is called *Adonai Yahweh*. In this passage, Christ as Lord has already assumed this role for Paul.

2. In this case, Christ's lordship, on the basis of his own death and resurrection, is asserted to extend over both the living and the dead. Under any circumstances, in Jewish thought this is the prerogative of God alone; and in Paul's understanding, Christ thus shares this ultimate divine prerogative.

3. This understanding of Christ's ultimate lordship is thus the presupposition of the entire argument. The reason that one side or the other is not allowed to "win" the battle over food and days is that such things are ultimately irrelevant to the Lord Christ himself. Not only so, he is the one who will cause people to stand in their own times of weakness (v. 4).

4. Because of his present lordship over the living and the dead, Christ also appears with the Father at the final assize. The clear implication of ac-

---

[71] See n. 7 in ch. 3.

countability to the Son (both here and in 2 Cor 5:10) as well as to the Father indicates that both share alike in the divine identity and that there is therefore conceptual overlap as to their being.

5. Finally, if, on the basis of the more common interpretation, Christ is *not* here pictured as one of the divine persons involved in the final judgment, that is in fact said of him elsewhere (2 Cor 5:10). And since that is so, then the very fact that the text can be cogently argued as referring to Christ is in itself an acknowledgment of the high Christology assumed throughout the passage.

Romans 16:1–16, 18

This final set of κύριος texts in this letter have very little christological import; they are brought into the picture here because they make clear that the phrases "in Christ" (ἐν Χριστῷ) and "in the Lord" (ἐν κυρίῳ) are completely interchangeable. Thus Paul begins by urging that the Roman Christian communities receive Phoebe, the bearer of the letter, "in the Lord" in a manner worthy of the saints. Thereafter Paul alternates between believers' being "in the Lord" and being "in Christ." Prisca and Aquila are co-laborers "in Christ Jesus" (v. 3), as is Urbanus (v. 9); Epenetus is the firstfruits of Asia "for Christ" (v. 5); Andronicus and Junia, who are noted among the apostles, were "in Christ" (v. 7) before Paul was, while Apelles has proved trustworthy "in Christ" (v. 10).

Others are "in the Lord" in similar ways. Ampliatus is "my beloved in the Lord" (v. 8); Trophena and Tryphosa have "labored in the Lord," while Persis has "labored greatly in the Lord" (v. 12); Rufus is "elect in the Lord" (v. 13), while the members of the household of Narcissus are simply "in the Lord."

All of this to point out that for Paul, existence in the newly formed people of God means that all alike live in the same sphere of life in the Spirit, which means that they exist, live, and labor "in the Lord." This christocentric understanding of existence finds further expression in any number of ways in this letter, in which almost everything done by the believer is in some way related to Christ. I simply list them here and let their very number indicate how, for all the theocentric nature of the argument of this letter, Paul's understanding of life in the present age is thoroughly shaped by life in Christ:

1:1 Paul is an apostle "of Christ Jesus"

1:5 Paul's apostleship is "through him [Jesus Christ our Lord]"

1:6 The Roman believers have been called "of Christ" (= to be his "called ones")

1:8 Paul gives thanks through Christ Jesus (cf. 7:25)

2:16 God will judge the secrets of the heart "through Christ Jesus"

3:22	One's faith is "in Christ Jesus"
3:24	The source of redemption is Christ Jesus
5:1	Our peace with God comes "through our Lord Jesus Christ"
5:11	Our boast in God is "through our Lord Jesus Christ"
6:3	We were baptized "into Christ Jesus"
6:11	We are alive to God as we are "in Christ Jesus"
6:23	The gift of eternal life is "in Christ Jesus our Lord"
7:25	Our deliverance from condemnation is through "Jesus Christ our Lord"
8:1	Being "in Christ Jesus," therefore, means no condemnation
8:10	Christ himself lives in us (by his Spirit is implied)
8:35	Nothing can separate us from the love of Christ (cf. v. 37)
8:39	Indeed, God's own love is found "in Christ Jesus our Lord"
9:3	To be condemned would equal receiving Christ's anathema
10:4	Christ is himself the culmination of the law
10:17	The gospel itself is described as "the word about Christ"
13:14	The antidote to sinful behavior is to be "clothed with the Lord Jesus Christ"
14:14	The Lord Jesus is the source of Paul's persuasion that nothing is unclean in itself
14:18	Serving Christ by honoring a brother or sister is what pleases God
15:16	Paul's ministry to the Gentiles is "from Christ Jesus"
15:17	Therefore, Paul's only boast is "in Christ Jesus" regarding the things of God
15:18	Because it is Christ Jesus who has accomplished everything through him
15:29	Paul's coming to Rome would be in the "full measure of the blessing of Christ"
16:22	Tertius's own greeting is "in the Lord"
16:27	And the final doxology of glory to God is "through Jesus Christ"

This list leads us, then, to note at the end those few instances in this letter where Christ shares divine prerogatives with God the Father.

Christ and the Divine Prerogatives

As with all the preceding letters, and in equally presuppositional ways, in Romans Paul speaks of Christ as sharer in what are, for Paul, especially divine prerogatives. However, because of the basically theocentric character of the argument of this letter, there are fewer of these than one might expect, given its length.

The Spirit of Christ (Rom 8:9–11)

Four times in the corpus the Holy Spirit, whom Paul ordinarily denominates as "the Spirit of God," is called the "Spirit of Christ." We have already seen this at work in 2 Cor 3:17 and Gal 4:6, and we will see it again in Phil 1:19. But there is nothing else quite like what he does in Rom 8:9–10. Believers are "in the Spirit" because they have "the Spirit of God." In the very next breath, this same Spirit is called "the Spirit of Christ," which in turn is followed by "if Christ is in you."[72] It is precisely this kind of interchange in Paul's thought that led to the Trinitarian ontological discussions concerning the deity of Christ and the Spirit in the following centuries. Here I simply point out that this is the highest kind of shared prerogative that points with a steady bead toward Christ's full divinity. The one whom Paul identifies on two other occasions as "the same/one Spirit," in a context where he likewise identifies Christ as "the same/one Lord" and the Father as "the same/one God" (1 Cor 12:4–6; Eph 4:4–6), is at one and the same time the Spirit of both the Father and the Son.

But in this case more needs to be said because of the role that this passage has played in discussions of an alleged Spirit Christology[73] in Paul's thought. At issue is whether Paul intends a full identification of the risen Christ with the Spirit, so that in effect the two are the same in terms of "being."[74] There

---

[72]On the significance of this passage for Paul's pneumatology, see Fee, *God's Empowering Presence*, 543–54.

[73]This is one of most truly slippery terms to be found in the NT academy. By definition, it should mean that Christ and the Spirit are understood to be ontologically the same reality; and that is in fact what some are quite willing to assert. See, e.g., I. Hermann, *Kyrios und Pneuma: Studien zur Christologie der paulinischen Hauptbriefe* (SANT 2; Munich: Kösel, 1961), 132–26. On the other hand, similar things are said boldly by, e.g., Dunn (see the next note) and Hamilton (*Holy Spirit and Eschatology*, 3–16), who asserts distinction on p. 3 but then spends the rest of the chapter arguing vigorously for common identity.

[74]The language in the literature is especially confusing at this point. On the one hand, all would agree that in the present scene, the "not yet" of partly realized eschatology, one's experience of Christ is through the Spirit. On the other hand, one finds in support of this statements such as "Immanent christology is for Paul pneumatology; in the believer's experience there is *no* distinction between Christ and the Spirit. This does not mean of course that Paul makes no distinction between Christ and Spirit. But it does mean that later Trinitarian dogma cannot readily look to Paul for support at this point" (J. D. G. Dunn, "1 Corinthians 15:45—Last Adam, Life-Giving Spirit," in *Christ and Spirit in the New Testament: Studies in Honour of Charles Francis Digby Moule* [ed. B. Lindars and S. S. Smalley; London: Cambridge University Press, 1973], 139). The latter, of course, is patently not true, as the brief analysis of this chapter will point out. But this seems to be a strange

can be little question that for Paul, at the experiential level one actualizes the reality of the living Christ through the agency of the Spirit. But the same holds true with regard to the Spirit and God the Father; and in any case, the present passage hardly lends itself to a full identification. What Paul intends here is not something primarily ontological; rather, the final phrase, "if Christ is in you," is shorthand for what he has just said: "If anyone does not have the Spirit of Christ, that person does not belong to Christ." The pickup clause then puts that in brief, "but if Christ is in you," by which in context he intends, "if Christ *by his Spirit* is in you."[75] The italicized words are simply unnecessary to add because they should be clear enough to the reader from what has been said in the immediately preceding clause.

In the end, therefore, this passage is one of the more significant proto-Trinitarian texts in the Pauline corpus. Whatever else, Paul sees God's saving work as conjointly that of the Father, the Son, and the Spirit; and therefore the Spirit is understood by him to be the Spirit both of the Father and of the Son.

The Love of Christ (Rom 8:35)

In returning to this great conclusion to 1:18–8:30 discussed above, we note finally that in the same passage Paul speaks of Christ as loving us (vv. 35, 37) and then concludes the whole argument by referring to "the love of God that is in Christ Jesus our Lord." On its own, Christ's love could be understood simply as agency, but the entire passage indicates that the love that God has shown us, which resides in God's own character (Rom 5:5–8), is equally to be understood as Christ's own love toward us, which also rests in his equally divine character.[76] On this shared attribute, see discussion on 2 Thess 2:13 in ch. 2 (cf. 2 Cor 5:14).

---

confusion of terms. "Immanent Christology" has to do with ontology, Christ in his being; so Dunn's first statement subverts what he says in his second and third ones. If distinctions can indeed be made, then such distinctions must be worked out theologically; and whatever else is true in Paul, there is no confusion or fusion of the risen Christ with the Holy Spirit. As with God the Father, so with Christ: both are understood to be actively at work in the believer and in the world by means of the one Spirit. For a critique of "Spirit Christology" as such, see Fee, "Christology and Pneumatology."

[75] This is very much in keeping with the same kind of misreading of Paul that one finds in Dunn and others regarding 1 Cor 1:24, where it is asserted that Paul identifies Christ with personified Wisdom. That in fact is a serious misreading of Paul, where "Christ" in v. 24 is clearly and only an abbreviated pickup of "Christ crucified" in v. 23 (i.e., Paul intends, "Christ *crucified* is God's power and God's wisdom"). To read it otherwise is to read a foreign agenda into Paul's singularly soteriological sentence. See the discussion of this text in ch. 3 (pp. 100–106) and the discussion of the confusion with "Wisdom" in appendix A (pp. 594–619).

[76] Cf. Cranfield: Paul "can speak indifferently of the love of God and the love of Christ" (2:529).

An Appeal through Christ (Rom 15:30)

Finally, as also in preceding letters,[77] Paul bases an appeal "through our Lord Jesus Christ." The fact that this appeal is made to both Christ and the Spirit probably says more about the role of the Spirit in Pauline theology than that of Christ. Nonetheless, such an appeal comes very close to the kind of "oath-taking" that in the OT is commanded to be done in Yahweh's name alone. Again, that Paul can so easily appeal to Christ in such instances says something about the presuppositional nature of his Christology.

All the Assemblies of Christ (Rom 16:16)

At the end of the long series of greetings to various people known to Paul, he concludes, as he often does, with a reciprocal greeting from believers in the place where he is writing. In all other such moments Paul speaks of "the assembly/ies of God,"[78] and in each case the genitive is arguably both possessive and descriptive: the churches belong to God and exist for his purposes in the world. The phrase itself occurs a few times in the Septuagint, most often as "the Lord's [= Yahweh's] assembly" (ἐκκλησία κυρίου).[79] Thus, the various Greco-Roman towns and cities where Paul has established Christian communities have another "assembly" in their midst, one that belongs to the living God or, in this one instance, to the risen Christ. The interchange is remarkable for the very reason that it is basically unnoticeable, so that what is ordinarily understood as belonging to God is here designated as belonging to Christ, an obviously shared divine prerogative.

Jesus as Second Adam

For the third and final time in his letters, Paul in Rom 5:12–21 explicitly[80] contrasts Christ with Adam. In the two prior instances (1 Cor 15:21–22, 44b–49), Paul brought Adam into the picture within the context of the two parts of his argument with the Corinthians regarding the resurrection. In the first instance, the certainty of a *future* resurrection of believers is predicated

---

[77] See pp. 46 and 67 in ch. 2.

[78] See 1 Thess 2:14; 2 Thess 1:4; 1 Cor 1:2; 10:32; 11:16, 22; 15:9; 2 Cor 1:1; Gal 1:13; 1 Tim 3:5; 3:15; of these, 1 Thess 2:14; 2 Thess 1:4; 1 Cor 11:16; 1 Tim 3:5 are plural, as here.

[79] See Deut 23:1, 2; 1 Chr 28:8; Mic 2:5; in Neh 13:1, "assembly of God" (ἐκκλησία θεοῦ).

[80] I make this point because on the basis of these explicit references there is a tendency on the part of some to extrapolate this theme and find it in several instances where emphasis on Christ's humanity is in view (see esp. Dunn, *Christology in the Making*, 98–128; Wright, *Climax of the Covenant*, 57–62, 90–97). But there seems to be little warrant for such extrapolation, since Paul himself quite explicitly calls forth this imagery only in very specific situations; and he speaks of Christ's humanity in a variety of ways and situations. See further, in the present volume, chs. 12 and 13.

on Christ's own resurrection. Just as the first Adam brought sin and death into the world, which we inherited from him, so Christ as the second Adam has been raised to guarantee that resurrection life is God's response to our being destined for death. In the second instance, the contrast exists as part of the argument that the future resurrection will be *bodily*. Just as we bear the body subject to decay that is ours through Adam, so in the resurrection believers will bear a body like that of the risen Christ. Thus Adam serves in both instances as the progenitor of our race, now destined for death and decay.

In this third instance (Rom 5:12–21), the contrast is altogether on the issue of sin and righteousness. Just as sin entered the world through a man, so righteousness has been made available to the sinful through a man. And the interest in this instance is on the universality of both the sin and the righteousness: the righteousness that Christ has provided is for *all* who have sinned, Jew and Gentile alike, and thus countermands any necessity for Gentiles to "do law" as a way toward righteousness. One therefore should not make more of the use of τύπος than Paul himself does. Adam is a "type" in the sense of pattern only, not in some larger primordial theological sense.[81]

It should be noted that the common denominator of the three passages in which Adam is mentioned explicitly is twofold. First, Adam is brought into the picture only in cases where Paul's argument embraces the universal nature of human sinfulness that results in death. Second, and for our present purposes the crucial matter, in each case Paul brings Christ into the picture to emphasize his genuine humanity, a humanity that he shared fully with Adam and thus with us, but without sin.

It should be further noted here, therefore, that these three instances of contrast between Adam and Christ, where the issue is human sinfulness (Adam) and redemption (Christ), hardly warrant the overblown emphasis on a so-called Adam Christology that one finds in some quarters. The usage for Paul is altogether by way of analogy: Adam as sinner; Christ as second Adam nullifying the effects of Adam's heritage. The only other certain echo between Adam and Christ is that noted above on 8:29, where the Son is seen as bearing both the divine and therefore the true human εἰκών (*image*), thus deliberately picking up the language of the Septuagint of Gen 1:26–27. And although this is an echo of considerable significance, it hardly warrants an understanding of Christ as second Adam that often goes considerably beyond the biblical account itself and thus takes Paul's Christology where Paul himself does not go.

Does Paul Call the Messiah "God"?—Romans 9:5

Romans 9:5 presents us with one of the more difficult (possibly) christological texts in the corpus. The question is whether Paul intended the

---

[81] On this matter, see Schlatter, 129; cf. Barrett, 112.

doxologic moment at the end of his sentence to refer to the Messiah or to God the Father. At issue is a matter of punctuation, where the "normal" grammatical reading of the text and its actual content seem to stand at odds with each other.[82] The text reads (without any punctuation, as would be true in the manuscript tradition),

9:5 οἵτινές εἰσιν Ἰσραηλῖται . . . ὧν οἱ πατέρας καὶ ἐξ ὧν ὁ Χριστὸς τὸ
κατὰ σάρκα ὁ ὢν ἐπὶ πάντων θεὸς εὐλογητὸς εἰς τοὺς αἰῶνας ἀμήν

who are Israelites . . . whose are the Fathers and from whom the Messiah according to the flesh the one who is over all God blessed forever amen

The primary translational options (beginning with ὁ Χριστός) are three:[83]

(1) . . . the Messiah as to his earthly life, who is God over all, blessed forever;

(2) . . . the Messiah as to his earthly life, who is over all things. May God be blessed forever.

(3) . . . the Messiah as to his earthly life. May God who is over all things be blessed forever.

The point to be made is that if there were no issue with regard to *what* is said, one probably would read the ὁ ὢν as modifying ὁ Χριστός. But the *what* in this case seems heavily to outweigh our grammatical expectations, hence another equally acceptable grammatical option is preferred by many.

But we should also note that the *only* thing in favor of reading the final phrase as modifying "the Messiah" is the alleged "normal" way of reading the grammatical construction.[84] Since every other consideration seems to stand against it, here is a case where "normal" is probably in the eye of the beholder; indeed, "normal" does not mean that another way of punctuation

---

[82] So much so that as long ago as 1904, F. C. Burkitt commented that "the punctuation [of Rom 9:5] has probably been more discussed than that of any other sentence in literature" ("On Romans ix 5 and Mark xiv 61," *JTS* 5 [1904]: 451). The most recent and thorough discussions of the text are by B. M. Metzger ("The Punctuation of Rom. 9:5," in Lindars and Smalley, *Christ and Spirit*, 95–112) and M. J. Harris (*Jesus as God: The New Testament Use of Theos in Reference to Jesus* [Grand Rapids: Baker, 1992], 143–72), who argue the position opposite to the one presented here (cf. the succinct discussion in Cranfield, 2:464–70); others who favor the opposite view include Hodge, Godet, Sanday and Headlam, Schlatter, Murray, Fitzmyer, Moo, Schreiner.

[83] Metzger lists eight different punctuational options that have been argued for (cf. Cranfield [2:465–70], who works through a list of six). But in the end, as Metzger's summarization points out, all of them boil down to one of the three presented here.

[84] I do not intend the quotation marks to be pejorative; this is both the reality of the structure and the term that occurs over and again in Metzger's article to describe option 1.

is "not normal." Rather, in this case it simply means that without punctuation, one's *first instincts* are to read the text with the final clause modifying ὁ
Χριστός. But as everyone also acknowledges, when one comes to the word
θεός, there is every good reason to pause, since one's first instincts are confronted with a second circumstance, which stands contrary to those instincts. And in the end, I think that these reasons for pause far outweigh
what one might perceive as "normal" grammar, since in fact other ways of
punctuating equally conform to Pauline usage elsewhere. Here are my reasons for going with option 3, which at the same time stand over against
option 1.[85]

1. Very early on in his letters, in a passage of some significance and deliberation, Paul divided the Jewish Shema into two parts (1 Cor 8:6),[86] identifying the one θεός as the Father, and the one κύριος as Jesus Christ (the
Son); and so, using a Christian interpretation of the Shema as his point of
departure, he distinguished between θεός and κύριος while at the same time
including Christ in the divine identity. The "one Lord God" is now to be understood as *"God* the Father" and "the *Lord,* Jesus Christ."

The point to be made here is that these linguistic distinctions prevail
throughout the corpus, including the letters to Timothy and Titus. The only
exceptions are those citations from the Septuagint where no point is being
made as to who κύριος is.[87] I do not mean that all are agreed on this. But
those who disagree do so only in instances where they think that κύριος refers to God the Father and not to Christ; it is never the other way around.
And even in these cases, contextual considerations suggest otherwise, since
in every case one must run roughshod over Paul's own clear distinctions
that stand at the beginning of each of his letters, and do so without adequate contextual justification.[88] Moreover, Paul does not elsewhere interchange these two terms, so that one is left guessing as to whom κύριος and
θεός refer.

---

[85]So also the commentaries by Denney, Barth, Barrett, Käsemann, Dunn,
Stuhlmacher, Byrne; see also O. Kuss, "Zu Römer 9,5," in *Rechtfertigung: Festschrift
für Ernst Käsemann zum 70. Geburtstag* (ed. J. Friedrich, W. Pöhlmann, and P.
Stuhlmacher; Tübingen, Mohr Siebeck, 1976), 291–303; Richardson, *Paul's Language
about God,* 30–31.

[86]Metzger ("Punctuation of Rom. 9:5," 110) objects that "the decisive argument
[against the 'normal' reading] is one which is external to the passage under consideration." But he too appeals to supporting data in the corpus outside Romans. The first
point to be made here is that the identifications that Paul makes in 1 Cor 8:6 carry
through consistently elsewhere in Romans itself, so that if the alleged "normal"
reading is the correct one here, then this unique moment in Romans is also unique
to the entire Pauline church corpus and probably the entire corpus that includes the
Pastoral Epistles (for the possible exception, see the discussion of Titus 2:13 in ch. 10
of the present volume). So also Barth (330), who adds the point that this text never
played a role in the christological controversies of the early church.

[87]See n. 7 in ch. 3; cf. the discussion of Rom 14:10–11 above.

[88]See, e.g., the discussion of 2 Thess 2:13 and 3:1–5 in ch. 2.

2. The issue of Pauline (grammatical/syntactical) usage elsewhere is often brought into the picture; but this can be a mixed bag having to do finally with which analogies one considers the more significant. For me, the most telling of these is that found in the two other instances of Paul's doxologic use of εὐλογητός (Rom 1:25; 2 Cor 11:31); and of these, the one that stands toward the beginning of *the present letter* seems especially significant. Here are the two passages in parallel (plus 2 Cor 11:31):

Rom 1:25 παρὰ τὸν κτίσαντα, <u>ὃς</u> ἐστιν **εὐλογητὸς**
          εἰς τοὺς αἰῶνας. ἀμήν.

Rom 9:5   ὁ ὢν ἐπὶ πάντων   <u>θεὸς</u>   **εὐλογητὸς**
          εἰς τοὺς αἰῶνας, ἀμήν.

2 Cor 11:31 <u>ὁ θεὸς</u> καὶ πατὴρ **τοῦ κυρίου Ἰησοῦ** οἶδεν, ὁ ὢν **εὐλογητὸς**
          εἰς τοὺς αἰωνᾶς, ὅτι ...

Apart from the grammatical considerations that play into the present sentence, these two "blessings" of God are nearly identical, the blessing itself being identical in all three instances. The differences lie only with the lead-in, as to how θεός is identified in each case; and in each case the context is what calls for that lead-in. One will note that in both cases God is blessed as the Creator/Ruler of all that is.

3. Pauline emphases both in Romans as a whole and in the present passage in particular (chs. 9–11) are so thoroughly theocentric that one would seem to need more than simply a single grammatical option to overturn that emphasis in this letter. Even more is this so in the present passage itself, where the narrative of vv. 3–5 up to the doxology puts the Messiah as the climactic moment of Israel's privileges. The argument that follows keeps the same theocentric pattern, with Christ emerging as God's own way of bringing Torah observance to an end, so that the confession of "Jesus as κύριος" is the singular way Jew and Gentile together come into the blessing of God (9:30–10:21). It would seem strikingly strange for Paul, as a climax to this list of Jewish privileges in a very Jewish context, to bless *the Messiah* as God[89] when a doxology to God for all these privileges seems to be much more fitting.[90]

---

[89] This point is passed over far too casually by those who see the doxology as referring to Christ. Indeed, it is of some interest that most modern commentators correctly recognize the ὁ Χριστός as titular (= the Messiah) (cf. NRSV, NAB, REB, TNIV) but those who see the doxology as being to Christ then treat the title as a name, since it wrenches all Jewish (including NT) messianism to say "the Messiah is God"; see point 4 below.

[90] Cf. Käsemann: "A doxology [to God] is appropriate, since God has given the blessings and in so doing, as in blessings granted to the Christian community . . . , he has shown himself to be ὁ ὢν ἐπὶ πάντων, namely the one who directs history" (260).

Under this way of looking at things, both the introduction to the present section (9:1–5), which climaxes with the gift of the Messiah, and the long argument of the section[91] are brought to fitting climax with a final "blessing of God" in 11:33–36. Together, these "blessings" have the effect of bookending the argument of chs. 9–11; and since the latter is purely theocentric, the likelihood is that the former is as well, especially since Christ is simply not the focus of either the list of Jewish privileges (he is the climax but not the focus) or the argument that follows.

4. Along this same line, it is generally agreed that ὁ Χριστός in this case is titular. Granted that by now it also functions as a "name" for Jesus and thus here could be doing double duty, nonetheless, this titular use seems especially telling against the probability that ὁ ὢν . . . θεός is intended to stand in apposition with "the Messiah." It would be one thing for Paul to refer to Jesus Christ or to the Son as "God"; it would be quite another for him deliberately to put the coming of the Messiah as the climax of Jewish privileges and then suggest by way of doxology that the Messiah himself is God. This seems to stretch the bounds of probability by too much.

5. Finally, what seems to favor the "normal" reading does not necessarily do so. At issue are two matters: the appearance of ὁ ὤν, and the prepositional phrase ἐπὶ πάντων that immediately follows.

(a) The phrase ὁ ὤν, which occurs only two times in the corpus (here and 2 Cor 11:31), is often seen as the clinching grammatical point that favors option 1. But one should note that in its first occurrence (2 Cor 11:31), the phrase appears as a piece of straightforward prose. It sits in the sentence in such a way that its sense and meaning are clear, and the grammar itself allows no other meaning. Paul is here effecting an oath, the closest thing in the NT to the later common rabbinic insertion of "blessed be He" after the mention of God. Thus, "the God and Father of our Lord Jesus Christ knows—he who is blessed forever—that I am not lying." What is significant about the phrase ὁ ὤν is how unnecessary the participle ὤν is in this instance. In the stilted English of the NASU one reads, "The God and Father of our Lord Jesus Christ, He who is blessed forever, knows. . . ." But without the ὤν, one would read it exactly the same way and would not miss the participle if it were not there. On the other hand, the insertion of this (unnecesary) participle is probably intended to highlight that this interrupting phrase in fact goes back to the subject "our God and Father" and thus not to "our Lord Jesus Christ."

In the same way, the participle is equally unnecessary in the text under discussion if the blessing were to refer to Christ. Paul could simply have offered a straight appositive: ἐξ ὧν ὁ Χριστὸς τὸ κατὰ σάρκα, ὁ ἐπὶ πάντων θεὸς εὐλογητὸς εἰς τοὺς αἰῶνας, ἀμήν (*from whom is the Messiah as to his earthly life, God over all, blessed forever. Amen.*). Thus the appearance of the ὤν, which is often regarded as the clincher as referring to Christ, in fact does no such

---

[91] Which, somewhat ironically, given the argument of chs. 1–5, now has to do with the ultimate inclusion of Israel along with the Gentiles!

thing. To the contrary, it very likely occurs in this case precisely because Paul intended a change of subject.

(b) This is further confirmed by what is for me the clinching point: Paul's use of an "inclosed" word order, where the preposition "over all things" occurs between the ὁ ὢν and its noun, θεός. The reason for this is most likely for emphasis; and in so doing, Paul picks up the "blessing" from 1:25, where the emphasis was on God as *Creator*. At this later point in the argument Paul now puts his emphasis on the fact that the Creator God is himself *over all things*, including especially the list of Jewish privileges that climaxed with the gift of "the Messiah in his earthly life."

Thus, if we were to change this word order to the "normal" (unambiguous) one, ὁ θεὸς ὁ ὢν ἐπὶ πάντων εὐλογητός, then the ascription of the doxology to Christ simply would not have happened, or at least it would have happened less frequently. On the basis of Pauline usage elsewhere, one would put a full stop after κατὰ σάρκα and read the doxology in the "normal" Pauline way: "May God who is over all be blessed forever. Amen." And in doing so, one would both keep to Pauline usage elsewhere and recognize that this sudden blessing of God is typically Pauline, especially so in a passage where he has enumerated Jewish "privileges." The God who is over all things, including this history of his people that climaxes with the gift of the Messiah, is to be praised forever.

My point, then, is that the presence of the ὢν is ultimately irrelevant in terms of meaning but its occurrence is almost certainly responsible for the present word order.[92] Had Paul chosen to emphasize only that God should be blessed forever, then none of this discussion would have happened because there would have been no ὢν ἐπὶ πάντων. But since the emphasis is on God's being the ultimate source and ruler of "all things," especially the glorious history of his people, the word order comes out the way it does. It seems incongruous both to the letter as a whole and to the present context in particular—not to mention Paul's usage throughout the corpus—that Paul should suddenly call the Messiah θεός when his coming in the flesh is the ultimate expression of what God is doing in the world.

It should be pointed out at the end that even if this way of looking at things is deemed to be the less likely option here, it can hardly be questioned either as a possible or likely way of interpreting the grammar. And since that is the case, it means that there is in fact no *certain* instance where Paul calls Christ ὁ θεός, which is precisely what we should expect, given the clear distinctions that he presents both in his reworking of the Shema and in the salutations of all his letters. A "possible" reading of ambiguous grammar simply does not carry the same weight as certain usage does.

---

[92]Except for option 2, it should be noted. That is, the participle seems quite necessary for this option to have been considered at all. In this case the phrase would be in apposition to "the Messiah," as the climactic moment to the climactic reference to "the Messiah." In many ways this could be the most attractive option of all, except for the anarthrous use of θεός, which seems to be too great a hurdle to overcome.

Conclusion

Since conclusions have been forthcoming throughout this chapter, I need to go back to what was observed at the beginning, but now to note the significance of the considerably high Christology that emerges in this letter.

Whatever else is true of Romans, it is the most thoroughly theocentric epistle in the corpus. Written to a community that knows Paul only by reputation (1:11–13; 15:22–29), this letter has the appearance of being more carefully "composed" than many of the others. In such a letter, with its theocentric focus, one might also expect Paul to be more considered in the way he speaks of Christ as Son and Lord, which in fact seems to be the case. It is therefore of some significance that we find here, as elsewhere, both purposeful and presuppositional statements about Christ as Lord that indicate the same high Christology that has emerged in the earlier letters.

The primary focus on Christ is as the Son of God, and it is clear by the way he is introduced at the outset (1:2–4) that the messianic Son of God (as David's scion) is first of all the preexistent Son, who came to earth as the one sent by the Father. At the same time, both the messianic-Son aspect of this title (Messiah as to his earthly life [9:5; cf. 1:2]) and the comparison with Adam put full emphasis on the genuineness of his humanity. A docetic view of Christ is quite impossible on the basis of the evidence of this letter.

At the same time, the preexistent, incarnate Son of God has also fully assumed the role of "Lord" by virtue of his resurrection from the dead. Thus, as before, he is "the Lord" of the OT texts upon whom people now call for salvation (10:9–13), and he is now the Lord of both the living and the dead (14:9), who (probably) shares in the final judgment—the ultimate divine prerogatives.

Appendix I: The Texts

(brackets [[ ]] indicate texts with references to God alone; triple brackets [[[ ]]] with italics indicate citations from the LXX, where *kyrios* refers to Yahweh)

1:1–7 ¹Παῦλος **δοῦλος Χριστοῦ Ἰησοῦ**, κλητὸς ἀπόστολος ἀφωρισμένος <u>εἰς εὐαγγέλιον θεοῦ</u>, ²ὃ προεπηγγείλατο διὰ τῶν προφητῶν αὐτοῦ ἐν γραφαῖς ἁγίαις ³**περὶ τοῦ υἱοῦ** <u>αὐτοῦ</u> τοῦ γενομένου ἐκ σπέρματος Δαυὶδ κατὰ σάρκα, ⁴τοῦ ὁρισθέντος **υἱοῦ** <u>θεοῦ</u> **ἐν δυνάμει** κατὰ πνεῦμα ἁγιωσύνης ἐξ ἀναστάσεως νεκρῶν, **Ἰησοῦ Χριστοῦ τοῦ κυρίου ἡμῶν**, ⁵δι' οὗ ἐλάβομεν χάριν καὶ ἀποστολὴν εἰς ὑπακοὴν πίστεως ἐν πᾶσιν τοῖς ἔθνεσιν **ὑπὲρ τοῦ ὀνόματος αὐτοῦ**, ⁶ἐν οἷς ἐστε καὶ ὑμεῖς κλητοὶ **Ἰησοῦ Χριστοῦ**, ⁷πᾶσιν τοῖς οὖσιν ἐν Ῥώμῃ/ <u>ἀγαπητοῖς θεοῦ</u>, κλητοῖς ἁγίοις, χάρις ὑμῖν καὶ εἰρήνη <u>ἀπὸ θεοῦ πατρὸς ἡμῶν</u> καὶ **κυρίου Ἰησοῦ Χριστοῦ**.

1:8–10 ⁸Πρῶτον μὲν εὐχαριστῶ <u>τῷ θεῷ μου</u> **διὰ Ἰησοῦ Χριστοῦ** περὶ πάντων ὑμῶν ὅτι ἡ πίστις ὑμῶν καταγγέλλεται ἐν ὅλῳ τῷ κόσμῳ. ⁹μάρτυς γάρ <u>μού ἐστιν ὁ θεός</u>, ᾧ λατρεύω ἐν τῷ πνεύματί μου ἐν **τῷ εὐαγγελίῳ τοῦ υἱοῦ** <u>αὐτοῦ</u>, ὡς ἀδιαλείπτως μνείαν ὑμῶν ποιοῦμαι [10]πάντοτε ἐπὶ τῶν προσευχῶν μου δεόμενος εἴ πως ἤδη ποτὲ εὐοδωθήσομαι <u>ἐν τῷ θελήματι τοῦ θεοῦ</u> ἐλθεῖν πρὸς ὑμᾶς.

[[1:16–17 [16]Οὐ γὰρ ἐπαισχύνομαι τὸ εὐαγγέλιον, [v.l. + τοῦ Χριστοῦ] <u>δύναμις γὰρ θεοῦ</u> ἐστιν εἰς σωτηρίαν παντὶ τῷ πιστεύοντι, Ἰουδαίῳ τε πρῶτον καὶ Ἕλληνι. [17]<u>δικαιοσύνη γὰρ θεοῦ</u> ἐν αὐτῷ ἀποκαλύπτεται ἐκ πίστεως εἰς πίστιν, καθὼς γέγραπται· ὁ δὲ δίκαιος ἐκ πίστεως ζήσεται.]]

[[1:18–23 [18]Ἀποκαλύπτεται γὰρ <u>ὀργὴ θεοῦ</u> ἀπ᾽ οὐρανοῦ ἐπὶ πᾶσαν ἀσέβειαν καὶ ἀδικίαν ἀνθρώπων τῶν τὴν ἀλήθειαν ἐν ἀδικίᾳ κατεχόντων, [19]διότι <u>τὸ γνωστὸν τοῦ θεοῦ φανερόν ἐστιν</u> ἐν αὐτοῖς. ὁ θεὸς γὰρ αὐτοῖς <u>ἐφανέρωσεν</u>. [20]τὰ γὰρ ἀόρατα <u>αὐτοῦ</u> ἀπὸ κτίσεως κόσμου τοῖς ποιήμασιν νοούμενα καθορᾶται, <u>ἥ τε ἀΐδιος αὐτοῦ δύναμις καὶ θειότης</u>, εἰς τὸ εἶναι αὐτοὺς ἀναπολογήτους, [21]διότι γνόντες <u>τὸν θεὸν οὐχ ὡς θεὸν</u> ἐδόξασαν ἢ ηὐχαρίστησαν, ἀλλ᾽ ἐματαιώθησαν ἐν τοῖς διαλογισμοῖς αὐτῶν καὶ ἐσκοτίσθη ἡ ἀσύνετος αὐτῶν καρδία. [22]φάσκοντες εἶναι σοφοὶ ἐμωράνθησαν [23]καὶ ἤλλαξαν <u>τὴν δόξαν τοῦ ἀφθάρτου θεοῦ</u> ἐν ὁμοιώματι εἰκόνος φθαρτοῦ ἀνθρώπου καὶ πετεινῶν καὶ τετραπόδων καὶ ἑρπετῶν.]]

[[1:24–26 [24]Διὸ <u>παρέδωκεν αὐτοὺς ὁ θεὸς</u> ἐν ταῖς ἐπιθυμίαις τῶν καρδιῶν αὐτῶν εἰς ἀκαθαρσίαν τοῦ ἀτιμάζεσθαι τὰ σώματα αὐτῶν ἐν αὐτοῖς, [25]οἵτινες μετήλλαξαν <u>τὴν ἀλήθειαν τοῦ θεοῦ</u> ἐν τῷ ψεύδει καὶ ἐσεβάσθησαν καὶ ἐλάτρευσαν τῇ κτίσει <u>παρὰ τὸν κτίσαντα, ὅς ἐστιν εὐλογητὸς εἰς τοὺς αἰῶνας</u>. ἀμήν. [26]διὰ τοῦτο <u>παρέδωκεν</u> αὐτοὺς <u>ὁ θεὸς</u> εἰς πάθη ἀτιμίας,]

[[1:28 καὶ καθὼς οὐκ ἐδοκίμασαν <u>τὸν θεὸν</u> ἔχειν ἐν ἐπιγνώσει, <u>παρέδωκεν</u> αὐτοὺς <u>ὁ θεὸς</u> εἰς ἀδόκιμον νοῦν, ποιεῖν τὰ μὴ καθήκοντα,]]

[[2:2–6 [2]οἴδαμεν δὲ ὅτι <u>τὸ κρίμα τοῦ θεοῦ</u> ἐστιν κατὰ ἀλήθειαν ἐπὶ τοὺς τὰ τοιαῦτα πράσσοντες [3]λογίζῃ δὲ τοῦτο, ὦ ἄνθρωπε ὁ κρίνων τοὺς τὰ τοιαῦτα πράσσοντας καὶ ποιῶν αὐτά, ὅτι σὺ ἐκφεύξῃ <u>τὸ κρίμα τοῦ θεοῦ</u>; [4]ἢ <u>τοῦ πλούτου τῆς χρηστότητος αὐτοῦ</u> καὶ τῆς ἀνοχῆς καὶ τῆς μακροθυμίας καταφρονεῖς, ἀγνοῶν ὅτι <u>τὸ χρηστὸν τοῦ θεοῦ</u> εἰς μετάνοιάν σε ἄγει; [5]κατὰ δὲ τὴν σκληρότητά σου καὶ ἀμετανόητον καρδίαν θησαυρίζεις σεαυτῷ ὀργὴν ἐν ἡμέρᾳ ὀργῆς καὶ ἀποκαλύψεως <u>δικαιοκρισίας τοῦ θεοῦ</u> [6]ὃς ἀποδώσει ἑκάστῳ κατὰ τὰ ἔργα αὐτοῦ·]]

[[2:11 οὐ γάρ ἐστιν προσωπολημψία <u>παρὰ τῷ θεῷ</u>.]]

[[2:13 οὐ γὰρ οἱ ἀκροαταὶ νόμου δίκαιοι <u>παρὰ τῷ θεῷ</u> . . .]]

2:16 ἐν ἡμέρᾳ ὅτε <u>κρίνει ὁ θεὸς</u> τὰ κρυπτὰ τῶν ἀνθρώπων κατὰ τὸ εὐαγγέλιόν μου **διὰ Χριστοῦ Ἰησοῦ**. [v.l. Ἰησοῦ Χριστοῦ]

[[2:17 Εἰ δὲ σὺ Ἰουδαῖος ἐπονομάζῃ καὶ ἐπαναπαύῃ νόμῳ καὶ <u>καυχᾶσαι ἐν θεῷ</u>]]

[[2:23–24 ²³ὃς ἐν νόμῳ καυχᾶσαι, διὰ τῆς παραβάσεως τοῦ νόμου <u>τὸν θεὸν</u> ἀτιμάζεις· ²⁴<u>το</u> γὰρ <u>ὄνομα τοῦ θεοῦ</u> δι᾽ ὑμᾶς βλασφημεῖται ἐν τοῖς ἔθνεσιν,]]

[[2:29 . . . οὗ ὁ ἔπαινος οὐκ ἐξ ἀνθρώπων ἀλλ᾽ <u>ἐκ τοῦ θεοῦ.</u>]]

[[3:2–7² . . . πρῶτον μὲν γὰρ ὅτι ἐπιστεύθησαν <u>τὰ λόγια τοῦ θεοῦ.</u> ³τί γάρ; εἰ ἠπίστησάν τινες, μὴ ἡ ἀπιστία αὐτῶν <u>τὴν πίστιν τοῦ θεοῦ</u> καταργήσει; ⁴μὴ γένοιτο· <u>γινέσθω δὲ ὁ θεὸς ἀληθής,</u> πᾶς δὲ ἄνθρωπος ψεύστης, καθὼς γέγραπται· ὅπως ἂν <u>δικαιωθῇς</u> ἐν τοῖς λόγοις <u>σου</u> καὶ <u>νικήσεις ἐν τῷ κρίνεσθαί σε.</u> ⁵εἰ δὲ ἡ ἀδικία ἡμῶν <u>θεοῦ δικαιοσύνην</u> συνίστησιν, τί ἐροῦμεν; <u>μὴ ἄδικος ὁ θεὸς ὁ ἐπιφέρων</u> τὴν ὀργήν (κατὰ ἄνθρωπον λέγω); ⁶μὴ γένοιτο· ἐπεὶ <u>πῶς κρινεῖ ὁ θεὸς τὸν κόσμον;</u> ⁷εἰ δὲ <u>ἡ ἀλήθεια τοῦ θεοῦ</u> ἐν τῷ ἐμῷ ψεύσματι ἐπερίσσευσεν <u>εἰς τὴν δόξαν αὐτοῦ,</u> τί ἔτι κἀγὼ ὡς ἁμαρτωλὸς κρίνομαι;]]

[[3:11 . . . οὐκ ἔστιν ὁ ἐκζητῶν <u>τὸν θεόν.</u>]]

[[3:18 οὐκ ἔστιν <u>φόβος θεοῦ</u> ἀπέναντι τῶν ὀφθαλμῶν αὐτῶν.]]

[[3:19 . . . ἵνα πᾶν στόμα φραγῇ καὶ ὑπόδικος γένηται πᾶς ὁ κόσμος <u>τῷ θεῷ·</u>]]

3:21–26 ²¹Νυνὶ δὲ χωρὶς νόμου <u>δικαιοσύνη θεοῦ</u> πεφανέρωται μαρτυρουμένη ὑπὸ τοῦ νόμου καὶ τῶν προφητῶν, ²²<u>δικαιοσύνη δέ θεοῦ</u> **διὰ πίστεως Ἰησοῦ Χριστοῦ** εἰς πάντας τοὺς πιστεύοντας. οὐ γάρ ἐστιν διαστολή, ²³πάντες γὰρ ἥμαρτον καὶ ὑστεροῦνται <u>τῆς δόξης τοῦ θεοῦ</u> ²⁴δικαιούμενοι δωρεὰν <u>τῇ αὐτοῦ χάριτι</u> **διὰ τῆς ἀπολυτρώσεως τῆς ἐν Χριστῷ Ἰησοῦ·** ²⁵ὃν <u>προέθετο ὁ θεὸς</u> **ἱλαστήριον** διὰ τῆς πίστεως **ἐν τῷ αὐτοῦ αἵματι** εἰς ἔνδειξιν <u>τῆς δικαιοσύνης αὐτοῦ</u> διὰ τὴν πάρεσιν τῶν προγεγονότων ἁμαρτημάτων ²⁶<u>ἐν τῇ ἀνοχῇ τοῦ θεοῦ,</u> πρὸς τὴν <u>ἔνδειξιν τῆς δικαιοσύνης αὐτοῦ</u> ἐν τῷ νῦν καιρῷ, <u>εἰς τὸ εἶναι αὐτὸν δίκαιον καὶ δικαιοῦντα</u> τὸν **ἐκ πίστεως Ἰησοῦ.** [v.l.-Ἰησου]

[[3:29–30 ²⁹ἢ Ἰουδαίων <u>ὁ θεὸς μόνον;</u> οὐχὶ καὶ ἐθνῶν; ναὶ καὶ ἐθνῶν, ³⁰εἴπερ <u>εἷς ὁ θεὸς ὃς</u> δικαιώσει περιτομὴν ἐκ πίστεως . . .]]

[[4:2–3² . . . ἔχει καύχημα, ἀλλ᾽ <u>οὐ πρὸς θεόν.</u> ³τί γὰρ ἡ γράφει λέγει; ἐπίστευσεν δὲ Ἀβραὰμ <u>τῷ θεῷ</u> καὶ . . .]]

[[4:6 . . . ᾧ <u>ὁ θεὸς λογίζεται</u> δικαιοσύνην χωρὶς ἔργων·]]

[[[4:8 μακάριος ἀνὴρ οὗ οὐ μὴ λογίσηται <u>κύριος</u> ἁμαρτίαν.]]]

[[4:17 . . . κατέναντι οὗ ἐπίστευσεν <u>θεοῦ τοῦ ζωοποιοῦντος</u> τοὺς νέκρους καὶ <u>καλοῦντος</u> τὰ μὴ ὄντα ὡς ὄντα.]]

[[4:20 <u>εἰς δὲ τὴν ἐπαγγελίαν τοῦ θεοῦ</u> οὐ διεκρίθη τῇ ἀπιστίᾳ ἀλλ᾽ ἐνεδυναμώθη τῇ πίστει, δοὺς <u>δόξαν τῷ θεῷ</u>]]

4:24 ἀλλὰ καὶ δι᾽ ἡμᾶς, οἷς μέλλει λογίζεσθαι, τοῖς πιστεύουσιν <u>ἐπὶ τὸν ἐγείραντα</u> **Ἰησοῦν τὸν κύριον ἡμῶν** ἐκ νεκρῶν,

5:1–2 ¹Δικαιωθέντες οὖν ἐκ πίστεως <u>εἰρήνην ἔχωμεν πρὸς τὸν θεὸν</u> **διὰ τοῦ**
κυρίου ἡμῶν Ἰησοῦ Χριστοῦ ²**δι' οὗ** καὶ τὴν προσαγωγὴν ἐσχήκαμεν τῇ
πίστει εἰς τὴν χάριν ταύτην ἐν ᾗ ἐστήκαμεν καὶ καυχώμεθα ἐπ' ἐλπίδι <u>τῆς</u>
<u>δόξης τοῦ θεοῦ</u>.

[[5:5 . . . ὅτι <u>ἡ ἀγάπη τοῦ θεοῦ</u> ἐκκέχυται ἐν ταῖς καρδίαις ἡμῶν διὰ
πνεύματος ἁγίου τοῦ δοθέντος ἡμῖν.]]

5:6–11 ⁶ἔτι γὰρ **Χριστὸς** ὄντων ἡμῶν ἀσθενῶν ἔτι κατὰ καιρὸν ὑπὲρ ἀσεβῶν
ἀπέθανεν. . . . ⁸συνίστησιν δὲ <u>τὴν ἑαυτοῦ ἀγάπην εἰς ἡμᾶς ὁ θεός</u>, ὅτι ἔτι
ἁμαρτωλῶν ὄντων ἡμῶν **Χριστὸς ὑπὲρ ἡμῶν ἀπέθανεν**. ⁹πολλῷ οὖν μᾶλλον
δικαιωθέντες νῦν **ἐν τῷ αἵματι αὐτοῦ** σωθησόμεθα **δι' αὐτοῦ** ἀπὸ τῆς
ὀργῆς. ¹⁰εἰ γὰρ ἐχθροὶ ὄντες κατηλλάγημεν <u>τῷ θεῷ</u> **διὰ τοῦ θανάτου τοῦ**
υἱοῦ <u>αὐτοῦ</u>, πολλῷ μᾶλλον καταλλαγέντες σωθησόμεθα **ἐν τῇ ζωῇ αὐτοῦ**.
¹¹οὐ μόνον δέ, ἀλλὰ καὶ <u>καυχώμενοι ἐν τῷ θεῷ</u> **διὰ τοῦ κυρίου ἡμῶν**
Ἰησοῦ Χριστοῦ δι' οὗ νῦν τὴν καταλλαγὴν ἐλάβομεν.

5:15 . . . πολλῷ μᾶλλον <u>ἡ χάρις τοῦ θεοῦ καὶ ἡ δωρεὰ</u> ἐν χάριτι τῇ **τοῦ ἑνὸς**
ἀνθρώπου Ἰησοῦ Χριστοῦ εἰς τοὺς πολλοὺς ἐπερίσσευσεν.

5:17 . . . πολλῷ μᾶλλον οἱ τὴν περισσείαν τῆς χάριτος καὶ τῆς δωρεᾶς τῆς
δικαιοσύνης λαμβάνοντες ἐν ζωῇ βασιλεύσουσιν **διὰ τοῦ ἑνὸς Ἰησοῦ**
Χριστοῦ.

5:18–19, 21 ¹⁸ . . . οὕτως καὶ **δι' ἑνὸς δικαιώματος** εἰς πάντας ἀνθρώπους
εἰς δικαίωσιν ζωῆς. ¹⁹ . . . οὕτως καὶ **διὰ τῆς ὑπακοῆς τοῦ ἑνὸς** δίκαιοι
κατασταθήσονται οἱ πολλοί. . . . ²¹ . . . οὕτως καὶ ἡ χάρις βασιλεύσῃ διὰ
δικαιοσύνης εἰς ζωὴν αἰώνιον **διὰ Ἰησοῦ Χριστοῦ τοῦ κυρίου ἡμῶν**.

6:3–5 ³ἢ ἀγνοεῖτε ὅτι, ὅσοι ἐβαπτίσθημεν **εἰς Χριστὸν Ἰησοῦν**, εἰς τὸν
θάνατον αὐτοῦ ἐβαπτίσθημεν; ⁴συνετάφημεν οὖν **αὐτῷ** διὰ τοῦ
βαπτίσματος εἰς τὸν θάνατον ἵνα **ὥσπερ ἠγέρθη Χριστὸς ἐκ νεκρῶν** διὰ
<u>τῆς δόξης τοῦ πατρός</u>, οὕτως καὶ ἡμεῖς ἐν καινότητι ζωῆς περιπατήσωμεν.
⁵εἰ γὰρ σύμφυτοι γεγόναμεν τῷ ὁμοιώματι **τοῦ θανάτου αὐτοῦ**, ἀλλὰ καὶ
τῆς ἀναστάσεως ἐσόμεθα·

6:8–11 ⁸εἰ δὲ ἀπεθάνομεν **σὺν Χριστῷ**, πιστεύομεν ὅτι καὶ **συζήσομεν**
αὐτῷ ⁹εἰδότες ὅτι **Χριστὸς ἐγερθεὶς ἐκ νεκρῶν** οὐκέτι ἀποθνήσκει,
θάνατος **αὐτοῦ** οὐκέτι κυριεύει. ¹⁰ὃ γὰρ ἀπέθανεν, τῇ ἁμαρτίᾳ ἀπέθανεν
ἐφάπαξ. ὃ δὲ ζῇ, ζῇ <u>τῷ θεῷ</u>. ¹¹οὕτως καὶ ὑμεῖς λογίζεσθε ἑαυτοὺς εἶναι νεκροὺς μὲν τῇ ἁμαρτίᾳ ζῶντας δὲ <u>τῷ θεῷ</u> **ἐν Χριστῷ Ἰησοῦ**. [v.l. +τῷ κυρίῳ ἡμῶν]

[[6:13 . . . παραστήσατε ἑαυτοὺς <u>τῷ θεῷ</u> ὡσεὶ ἐκ νεκρῶν ζῶντας καὶ τὰ μέλη
ὑμῶν ὅπλα δικαιοσύνης <u>τῷ θεῷ</u>.]]

[[6:17 <u>χάρις δὲ τῷ θεῷ</u> ὅτι . . .]]

[[6:22 νυνὶ δὲ ἐλευθερωθέντες ἀπὸ τῆς ἁμαρτίας δουλωθέντες δὲ <u>τῷ θεῷ</u>
ἔχετε τὸν καρπὸν ὑμῶν εἰς ἁγιασμόν,]]

6:23 τὰ γὰρ ὀψώνια τῆς ἁμαρτίας θάνατος, <u>τὸ δὲ χάρισμα τοῦ θεοῦ</u> ζωὴ αἰώνιος **ἐν Χριστῷ Ἰησοῦ τῷ κυρίῳ ἡμῶν.**

7:4 ὥστε, ἀδελφοί μου, καὶ ὑμεῖς ἐθανατώθητε τῷ νόμῳ **διὰ τοῦ σώματος τοῦ Χριστοῦ,** εἰς τὸ γενέσθαι ὑμᾶς **ἑτέρῳ, τῷ ἐκ νεκρῶν ἐγερθέντι,** ἵνα καρποφορήσωμεν <u>τῷ θεῷ.</u>

[[7:22 συνήδομαι γὰρ <u>τῷ νόμῳ τοῦ θεοῦ</u> κατὰ τὸν ἔσω ἄνθρωπον,]]

7:25 <u>χάρις δὲ τῷ θεῷ</u> **διὰ Ἰησοῦ Χριστοῦ τοῦ κυρίου ἡμῶν.** ἄρα οὖν αὐτὸς ἐγὼ τῷ μὲν νοῒ δουλεύω <u>νόμῳ θεοῦ,</u> τῇ δὲ σαρκὶ νόμῳ ἁμαρτίας.

8:1–2 ¹Οὐδὲν ἄρα νῦν κατάκριμα **τοῖς ἐν Χριστῷ Ἰησοῦ.** ²ὁ γὰρ νόμος τοῦ πνεύματος τῆς ζωῆς **ἐν Χριστῷ Ἰησοῦ** ἠλευθέρωσέν σε ἀπὸ τοῦ νόμου τῆς ἁμαρτίας καὶ τοῦ θανάτου.

8:3 τὸ γὰρ ἀδύνατον τοῦ νόμου ἐν ᾧ ἠσθένει διὰ τῆς σαρκός, <u>ὁ θεὸς</u> **τὸν** <u>ἑαυτοῦ</u> **υἱὸν** <u>πέμψας</u> ἐν ὁμοιώματι σαρκὸς ἁμαρτίας καὶ περὶ ἁμαρτίας <u>κατέκρινεν</u> τὴν ἁμαρτίαν ἐν τῇ σαρκί,

[[8:7–8 διότι τὸ φρόνημα τῆς σαρκὸς <u>ἔχθρα εἰς θεὸν</u>, τῷ γὰρ <u>νόμῳ τοῦ θεοῦ</u> οὐχ ὑποτάσσεται, οὐδὲ γὰρ δύναται· ⁸οἱ δὲ ἐν σαρκὶ ὄντες <u>θεῷ ἀρέσαι</u> οὐ δύνανται.]]

8:9–11 ⁹ὑμεῖς δὲ οὐκ ἐστὲ ἐν σαρκὶ ἀλλὰ ἐν πνεύματι, εἴπερ <u>πνεῦμα θεοῦ</u> οἰκεῖ ἐν ὑμῖν. εἰ δὲ τις **πνεῦμα Χριστοῦ** οὐκ ἔχει, οὗτος οὐκ ἔστιν **αὐτοῦ.** ¹⁰**εἰ δὲ Χριστὸς** ἐν ὑμῖν, τὸ μὲν σῶμα νεκρὸν διὰ ἁμαρτίαν τὸ δὲ πνεῦμα ζωὴ διὰ δικαιοσύνην. ¹¹εἰ δὲ <u>τὸ πνεῦμα τοῦ ἐγείραντος</u> **τὸν Ἰησοῦν ἐκ νεκρῶν** οἰκεῖ ἐν ὑμῖν, <u>ὁ ἐγείρας</u> **Χριστὸν** ἐκ νεκρῶν ζῳοποιήσει καὶ τὰ θνητὰ σώματα ὑμῶν διὰ <u>τὸ ἐνοικοῦν αὐτοῦ πνεῦμα</u> ἐν ὑμῖν.

8:14–17 ¹⁴ὅσοι γὰρ <u>πνεύματι θεοῦ</u> ἄγονται, οὗτοι <u>υἱοὶ θεοῦ εἰσιν.</u> ¹⁵οὐ γὰρ ἐλάβετε πνεῦμα δουλείας πάλιν εἰς φόβον ἀλλὰ ἐλάβετε πνεῦμα υἱοθεσίας ἐν ᾧ κράζομεν· <u>ἀββα ὁ πατήρ.</u> ¹⁶αὐτὸ τὸ πνεῦμα συμμαρτυρεῖ τῷ πνεύματι ἡμῶν ὅτι ἐσμὲν <u>τέκνα θεοῦ.</u> ¹⁷εἰ δὲ τέκνα, καὶ κληρονόμοι· <u>κληρονόμοι μὲν θεοῦ</u>, **συγκληρονόμοι δὲ Χριστοῦ, εἴπερ συμπάσχομεν** ἵνα καὶ **συνδοξασθῶμεν.**

[[8:19 ἡ γὰρ ἀποκαραδοκία τῆς κτίσεως τὴν ἀποκάλυψιν <u>τῶν υἱῶν τοῦ θεοῦ</u> ἀπεκδέχεται.]]

[[8:21 ὅτι καὶ αὐτὴ ἡ κτίσις ἐλευθερωθήσεται ἀπὸ τῆς δουλείας τῆς φθορᾶς εἰς τὴν ἐλευθερίαν τῆς δόξης <u>τῶν τέκνων τοῦ θεοῦ.</u>]]

[[8:27 <u>ὁ δὲ ἐραυνῶν τὰς καρδίας οἶδεν</u> τί τὸ φρόνημα τοῦ πνεύματος, ὅτι <u>κατὰ θεὸν</u> ἐντυγχάνει ὑπὲρ ἁγίων.]]

8:28–30 ²⁸οἴδαμεν δὲ ὅτι <u>τοῖς ἀγαπῶσιν τὸν θεὸν</u> πάντα συνεργεῖ εἰς ἀγαθόν, τοῖς κατὰ πρόθεσιν κλητοῖς οὖσιν ²⁹ὅτι οὓς <u>προέγνω</u>, καὶ <u>προώρισεν</u> συμμόρφους **τῆς εἰκόνος τοῦ υἱοῦ** <u>αὐτοῦ</u>, **εἰς τὸ εἶναι αὐτὸν πρωτότοκον** ἐν πολλοῖς ἀδελφοῖς· ³⁰οὓς δὲ <u>προώρισεν</u>, τούτους καὶ ἐκάλεσεν· καὶ οὓς ἐκάλεσεν, τούτους καὶ ἐδικαίωσεν· οὓς δὲ ἐδικαίωσεν, τούτους καὶ ἐδόξασεν.

8:31–35 ³¹Τί οὖν ἐροῦμεν πρὸς ταῦτα; εἰ ὁ θεὸς ὑπὲρ ἡμῶν, τίς καθ᾽ ἡμῶν; ³²ὅς γε τοῦ ἰδίου υἱοῦ οὐκ ἐφείσατο ἀλλὰ ὑπὲρ ἡμῶν πάντων παρέδωκεν αὐτόν, πῶς οὐχὶ καὶ σὺν αὐτῷ τὰ πάντα ἡμῖν χαρίσεται; ³³τίς ἐγκαλέσει κατὰ ἐκλεκτῶν θεοῦ; θεὸς ὁ δικαιῶν· ³⁴τίς ὁ κατακρινῶν; Χριστὸς Ἰησοῦς ὁ ἀποθανών, μᾶλλον δὲ ἐγερθείς, ὃς καί ἐστιν ἐν δεξιᾷ τοῦ θεοῦ, ὃς καὶ ἐντυγχάνει ὑπὲρ ἡμῶν; ³⁵τίς ἡμᾶς χωρίσει ἀπὸ τῆς ἀγάπης τοῦ Χριστοῦ;

8:37 ἀλλ᾽ ἐν τούτοις πᾶσιν ὑπερνικῶμεν διὰ τοῦ ἀγαπήσαντος ἡμᾶς.

8:39 . . . οὔτε τις κτίσις ἑτέρα δυνήσεται ἡμᾶς χωρίσαι ἀπὸ τῆς ἀγάπης τοῦ θεοῦ τῆς ἐν Χριστῷ Ἰησοῦ τῷ κυρίῳ ἡμῶν.

9:1 Ἀλήθειαν λέγω ἐν Χριστῷ, οὐ ψεύδομαι, συμμαρτυρούσης μοι τῆς συνειδήσεώς μου ἐν πνεύματι ἁγίῳ,

9:3–5 ³ηὐχόμην γὰρ ἀνάθεμα εἶναι αὐτὸς ἐγὼ ἀπὸ τοῦ Χριστοῦ ὑπὲρ τῶν ἀδελφῶν μου τῶν συγγενῶν μου κατὰ σάρκα, ⁴οἵτινές εἰσιν Ἰσραηλῖται, ὧν ἡ υἱοθεσία καὶ ἡ δόξα καὶ αἱ διαθῆκαι καὶ ἡ νομοθεσία καὶ ἡ λατρεία καὶ αἱ ἐπαγγελίαι, ⁵ὧν οἱ πατέρες καὶ ἐξ ὧν ὁ Χριστὸς τὸ κατὰ σάρκα, ὁ ὢν ἐπὶ πάντων θεὸς εὐλογητὸς εἰς τοὺς αἰῶνας, ἀμήν.

[[9:6 Οὐχ οἷον δὲ ὅτι ἐκπέπτωκεν ὁ λόγος τοῦ θεοῦ. . . .]]

[[9:8 . . . οὐ τὰ τέκνα τῆς σαρκὸς ταῦτα τέκνα τοῦ θεοῦ . . .]]

[[9:11 . . . ἵνα ἡ κατ᾽ ἐκλογὴν πρόθεσις τοῦ θεοῦ μένῃ,]]

[[9:14 Τί οὖν ἐροῦμεν; μὴ ἀδικία παρὰ τῷ θεῷ; μὴ γένοιτο.]]

[[9:16 ἄρα οὖν οὐ τοῦ θέλοντος οὐδὲ τοῦ τρέχοντος ἀλλὰ τοῦ ἐλεῶντος θεοῦ.]]

[[9:20 ὦ ἄνθρωπε, μενοῦνγε σὺ τίς εἶ ὁ ἀνταποκρινόμενος τῷ θεῷ;]]

[[9:22 εἰ δὲ θέλων ὁ θεὸς ἐνδείξασθαι τὴν ὀργὴν καὶ γνωρίσαι τὸ δυνατὸν αὐτοῦ . . .]]

[[9:24 οὓς καὶ ἐκάλεσεν ἡμᾶς οὐ μόνον ἐξ Ἰουδαίων ἀλλὰ καὶ ἐξ ἐθνῶν,]]

[[[9:28–29 ²⁸λόγον γὰρ συντελῶν καὶ συντέμνων ποιήσει κύριος ἐπὶ τῆς γῆς. ²⁹καὶ καθὼς προείρηκεν Ἠσαΐας· εἰ μὴ κύριος σαβαὼθ ἐγκατέλιπεν ἡμῖν σπέρμα, ὡς Σόδομα ἂν ἐγενήθημεν καὶ ὡς Γόμορρα ἂν ὡμοιώθημεν.]]]

9:32 . . . προσέκοψαν τῷ λίθῳ τοῦ προσκόμματος,

10:1–4 ¹Ἀδελφοί, ἡ μὲν εὐδοκία τῆς ἐμῆς καρδίας καὶ ἡ δέησις πρὸς τὸν θεὸν ὑπὲρ αὐτῶν εἰς σωτηρίαν. ²μαρτυρῶ γὰρ αὐτοῖς ὅτι ζῆλον θεοῦ ἔχουσιν ἀλλ᾽ οὐ κατ᾽ ἐπίγνωσιν· ³ἀγνοοῦντες γὰρ τὴν τοῦ θεοῦ δικαιοσύνην καὶ τὴν ἰδίαν δικαιοσύνην ζητοῦντες στῆσαι, τῇ δικαιοσύνῃ τοῦ θεοῦ οὐχ ὑπετάγησαν. ⁴**τέλος γὰρ νόμου Χριστὸς** εἰς δικαιοσύνην παντὶ τῷ πιστεύοντι.

10:6–7 ⁶ . . . *μὴ εἴπῃς ἐν τῇ καρδίᾳ σου· τίς ἀναβήσεται εἰς τὸν οὐρανόν;* τοῦτ᾿ ἔστιν **Χριστὸν καταγαγεῖν**· ⁷*ἤ· τίς καταβήσεται εἰς τὴν ἄβυσσον;* τοῦτ᾿ ἔστιν **Χριστὸν ἐκ νεκρῶν ἀναγαγεῖν**.

10:9 ὅτι ἐὰν ὁμολογήσῃς ἐν τῷ στόματί σου **κύριον Ἰησοῦν** καὶ πιστεύσῃς ἐν τῇ καρδίᾳ σου ὅτι <u>ὁ θεὸς</u> **αὐτὸν** <u>ἤγειρεν</u> ἐκ νεκρῶν, σωθήσῃ·

10:12–13 ¹²οὐ γὰρ ἐστιν διαστολὴ Ἰουδαίου τε καὶ ῞Ελληνος, **ὁ** γὰρ **αὐτὸς κύριος πάντων**, **πλουτῶν** εἰς πάντας τοὺς ἐπικαλουμένους **αὐτόν**· ¹³*πᾶς γὰρ ὃς ἄν ἐπικαλέσηται τὸ ὄνομα κυρίου σωθήσεται.*

[[[10:16 . . . Ἠσαΐας γὰρ λέγει· <u>*κύριε, τίς ἐπίστευσεν τῇ ἀκοῇ ἡμῶν;*</u>]]]

10:17 ἄρα ἡ πίστις ἐξ ἀκοῆς, ἡ δὲ ἀκοὴ **διὰ ῥήματος Χριστοῦ**. [v.l. θεοῦ]

[[11:1–2¹Λέγω οὖν μὴ <u>ἀπώσατο ὁ θεὸς τὸν λαὸν αὐτοῦ</u>; μὴ γένοιτο· καὶ γὰρ ἐγὼ Ἰσραηλίτης εἰμί, ἐκ σπέρματος Ἀβραάμ, φυλῆς Βενιαμίν. *²<u>οὐκ ἀπώσατο ὁ θεὸς τὸν λαὸν αὐτοῦ</u>* ὃν <u>προέγνω</u>. ἢ οὐκ οἴδατε ἐν Ἠλίᾳ τί λέγει ἡ γραφή, ὡς ἐντυγχάνει <u>τῷ θεῷ</u> κατὰ τοῦ Ἰσραήλ;]]

[[[11:3 <u>*κύριε, τοὺς προφήτας σου ἀπέκτειναν,* . . .</u>]]]

[[[11:8 καθὼς γέγραπται· *ἔδωκεν αὐτοῖς <u>ὁ θεὸς</u> πνεῦμα κατανύξεως,*]]]

11:21–23 ²¹<u>εἰ γὰρ ὁ θεὸς</u> τῶν κατὰ φύσιν κλάδων <u>οὐκ ἐφείσατο</u> μή πως οὐδὲ σοῦ φείσεται. ²²Ἴδε οὖν <u>χρηστότητα καὶ ἀποτομίαν θεοῦ</u>· ἐπὶ μὲν τοὺς πεσόντας ἀποτομία, ἐπὶ δὲ σὲ <u>χρηστότης θεοῦ</u>, . . . ²³ . . . δυνατὸς γάρ ἐστιν <u>ὁ θεὸς</u> πάλιν ἐγκεντρίσαι αὐτούς.]

[[11:29–36 ²⁹ἀμεταμέλητα γὰρ <u>τὰ χαρίσματα καὶ ἡ κλῆσις τοῦ θεοῦ</u>. ³⁰ὥσπερ γὰρ ὑμεῖς ποτε <u>ἠπειθήσατε τῷ θεῷ</u>, νῦν δὲ ἠλεήθητε τῇ τούτων ἀπειθείᾳ ³¹οὕτως καὶ οὗτοι νῦν ἠπείθησαν τῷ ὑμετέρῳ ἐλέει, ἵνα καὶ αὐτοὶ νῦν ἐλεηθῶσιν. ³²<u>συνέκλεισεν γὰρ ὁ θεὸς</u> τοὺς πάντας εἰς ἀπείθειαν, ἵνα τοὺς πάντας <u>ἐλεήσῃ</u>. ³³῏Ω *βάθος πλούτου καὶ σοφίας καὶ γνώσεως θεοῦ·* ὡς *ἀνεξεραύνητα <u>τὰ κρίματα αὐτοῦ</u> καὶ ἀνεξιχνίαστοι αἱ ὁδοὶ αὐτοῦ.* ³⁴*τίς γὰρ ἔγνω <u>νοῦν κυρίου</u>; ἢ τίς <u>σύμβουλος αὐτοῦ</u> ἐγένετο;* ³⁵*ἢ τίς προέδωκεν <u>αὐτῷ, καὶ ἀνταποδοθήσεται αὐτῷ,</u>* ³⁶ὅτι <u>*ἐξ αὐτοῦ καὶ δι᾿ αὐτοῦ καὶ εἰς αὐτὸν τὰ πάντα·*</u> αὐτῷ ἡ δόξα εἰς τοὺς αἰῶνας, ἀμήν.]]

[[12:1–2 ¹Παρακαλῶ οὖν ὑμᾶς, ἀδελφοί <u>διὰ τῶν οἰκτιρμῶν τοῦ θεοῦ</u> παραστῆσαι τὰ σώματα ὑμῶν θυσίαν ζῶσαν ἁγίαν <u>εὐάρεστον τῷ θεῷ</u>, τὴν λογικὴν λατρείαν ὑμῶν· ²καὶ μὴ συσχηματίζεσθε τῷ αἰῶνι τούτῳ, ἀλλὰ μεταμορφοῦσθε τῇ ἀνακαινώσει τοῦ νοὸς εἰς τὸ δοκιμάζειν ὑμᾶς <u>τί τὸ θέλημα τοῦ θεοῦ</u>, τὸ ἀγαθὸν καὶ εὐάρεστον καὶ τέλειον.]]

[[12:3 . . . ἀλλὰ φρονεῖν εἰς τὸ σωφρονεῖν, ἑκάστῳ <u>ὡς ὁ θεὸς ἐμέρισεν</u> μέτρον πίστεως.]]

12:5 οὕτως οἱ πολλοὶ **ἓν σῶμά ἐσμεν ἐν Χριστῷ**, . . .

12:11 τῇ σπουδῇ μὴ ὀκνηροί, τῷ πνεύματι ζέοντες, **τῷ κυρίῳ δουλεύοντες**,

[[[12:19 . . . *γέγραπται γάρ· ἐμοὶ ἐκδίκησις, ἐγὼ ἀνταποδώσω, <u>λέγει</u> <u>κύριος</u>.*]]]

[[13:1–6¹Πᾶσα ψυχὴ ἐξουσίαις ὑπερεχούσαις ὑποτασσέσθω· οὐ γὰρ ἔστιν ἐξουσία <u>εἰ μὴ ὑπὸ θεοῦ</u>, αἱ δὲ οὖσαι <u>ὑπὸ θεοῦ τεταγμέναι εἰσίν</u> ²ὥστε ὁ ἀντιτασσόμενος τῇ ἐξουσίᾳ <u>τῇ τοῦ θεοῦ διαταγῇ</u> ἀνθέστηκεν, . . . ⁴<u>θεοῦ</u> γὰρ διάκονός ἐστιν σοὶ εἰς τὸ ἀγαθόν. ἐὰν δὲ τὸ κακὸν ποιῇς, φοβοῦ· οὐ γὰρ εἰκῇ τὴν μάχαιραν φορεῖ. <u>θεοῦ</u> γὰρ διάκονός ἐστιν ἔκδικος εἰς ὀργὴν τῷ τὸ κακὸν πράσσοντι. . . . ⁶ διὰ τοῦτο γὰρ καὶ φόρους τελεῖτε· <u>λειτουργοὶ</u> γὰρ <u>θεοῦ εἰσιν</u> εἰς αὐτὸ τοῦτο προσκαρτεροῦντες.]]

13:14 ἀλλὰ **ἐνδύσασθε τὸν κύριον Ἰησοῦν Χριστὸν** καὶ τῆς σαρκὸς πρόνοιαν μὴ ποιεῖσθε εἰς ἐπιθυμίας.

14:3–9 ³ . . . <u>ὁ θεὸς</u> γὰρ αὐτὸν προσελάβετο. ⁴σὺ τίς εἶ ὁ κρίνων ἀλλότριον οἰκέτην; **τῷ ἰδίῳ κυρίῳ** στήκει ἢ πίπτει. σταθήσεται δέ, **δυνατεῖ γὰρ ὁ κύριος στῆσαι** αὐτόν. ⁵ὃς μὲν γὰρ κρίνει ἡμέραν παρ᾿ ἡμέραν, ὃς δὲ κρίνει πᾶσαν ἡμέραν· ἕκαστος ἐν τῷ ἰδίῳ νοῒ πληροφορείσθω. ⁶ὁ φρονῶν τὴν ἡμέραν **κυρίῳ** φρονεῖ· καὶ ὁ ἐσθίων **κυρίῳ** ἐσθίει, εὐχαριστεῖ γὰρ <u>τῷ θεῷ</u>· καὶ ὁ μὴ ἐσθίων **κυρίῳ** οὐκ ἐσθίει, καὶ <u>εὐχαριστεῖ τῷ θεῷ</u>. ⁷οὐδεὶς γὰρ ἡμῶν ἑαυτῷ ζῇ καὶ οὐδεὶς ἑαυτῷ ἀποθνήσκει· ⁸ἐάν τε γὰρ ζῶμεν, **τῷ κυρίῳ** ζῶμεν. ἐάν τε ἀποθνήσκωμεν, **τῷ κυρίῳ** ἀποθνήσκομεν. ἐάν τε οὖν ζῶμεν ἐάν τε ἀποθνήσκωμεν, τοῦ κυρίου **ἐσμέν**. ⁹εἰς τοῦτο γὰρ **Χριστὸς ἀπέθανεν καὶ ἔζησεν**, ἵνα καὶ νεκρῶν καὶ ζώντων **κυριεύσῃ**.

14:10–12 ¹⁰σὺ δὲ τί κρίνεις τὸν ἀδελφόν σου; ἢ καὶ σὺ τί ἐξουθενεῖς τὸν ἀδελφόν σου; πάντες γὰρ παραστησόμεθα <u>τῷ βήματι τοῦ θεοῦ</u>. [v.l. **Χριστοῦ**] ¹¹γέγραπται γάρ· **ζῶ ἐγώ, λέγει <u>κύριος</u>** [or **κύριος**] ὅτι ἐμοὶ κάμψει πᾶν γόνυ καὶ *πᾶσα γλῶσσα ἐξομολογήσεται* <u>τῷ θεῷ</u>. ¹²ἄρα ἕκαστος ἡμῶν περὶ ἑαυτοῦ λόγον δώσει. [v.l. + <u>τῷ θεῷ</u>]

14:14 οἶδα καὶ πέπεισμαι **ἐν κυρίῳ Ἰησοῦ** ὅτι οὐδὲν κοινὸν δι᾿ ἑαυτοῦ, . . .

14:15 . . . μὴ τῷ βρώματί σου ἐκεῖνον ἀπόλλυε ὑπὲρ οὗ **Χριστὸς ἀπέθανεν**.

[[14:17 οὐ γὰρ ἐστιν <u>ἡ βασιλεία τοῦ θεοῦ</u> βρῶσις καὶ πόσις . . .]]

14:18 ὁ γὰρ ἐν τούτῳ δουλεύων **τῷ Χριστῷ** <u>εὐάρεστος τῷ θεῷ</u> καὶ δόκιμος τοῖς ἀνθρώποις.

[[14:20 μὴ ἕνεκεν βρώματος κατάλυε <u>τὸ ἔργον τοῦ θεοῦ</u>.]]

[[14:22 σὺ πίστιν ἣν ἔχεις κατὰ σεαυτὸν ἔχε <u>ἐνώπιον τοῦ θεοῦ</u>. . . .]]

15:3 καὶ γὰρ **ὁ Χριστὸς οὐχ ἑαυτῷ ἤρεσεν**, ἀλλὰ καθὼς γέγραπται· . . .

15:5–6 ⁵ὁ δὲ θεὸς τῆς ὑπομονῆς καὶ τῆς παρακλήσεως δῴη ὑμῖν τὸ αὐτὸ φρονεῖν ἐν ἀλλήλοις **κατὰ Χριστὸν Ἰησοῦν**, ⁶ἵνα ὁμοθυμαδὸν ἐν ἑνὶ στόματι δοξάζητε τὸν θεὸν καὶ πατέρα **τοῦ κυρίου ἡμῶν Ἰησοῦ Χριστοῦ.**

15:7–9 ⁷Διὸ προσλαμβάνεσθε ἀλλήλους, καθὼς **καὶ ὁ Χριστὸς προσελά-βετο ὑμᾶς** εἰς δόξαν τοῦ θεοῦ. ⁸λέγω γὰρ **Χριστὸν διάκονον γεγενῆσθαι** περιτομῆς ὑπὲρ ἀληθείας θεοῦ, εἰς τὸ βεβαιῶσαι τὰς ἐπαγγελίας τῶν πατέρων, ⁹τὰ δὲ ἔθνη ὑπὲρ ἐλέους δοξάσαι τὸν θεόν, καθὼς γέγραπται· . . .

[[[15:11 . . . *αἰνεῖτε, πάντα τὰ ἔθνη,* τὸν κύριον . . .]]]

[[15:13 ὁ δὲ θεὸς τῆς ἐλπίδος πληρῶσαι ὑμᾶς πάσης χαρᾶς καὶ εἰρήνης ἐν τῷ πιστεύειν, . . .]]

15:15–20 ¹⁵τολμηρότερον δὲ ἔγραψα ὑμῖν ἀπὸ μέρους ὡς ἐπαναμιμνῄσκων ὑμᾶς διὰ τὴν χάριν τὴν δοθεῖσάν μοι ὑπὸ τοῦ θεοῦ ¹⁶εἰς τὸ εἶναί με **λειτουργὸν Χριστοῦ Ἰησοῦ** εἰς τὰ ἔθνη, ἱερουργοῦντα τὸ εὐαγγέλιον τοῦ θεοῦ, ἵνα γένηται ἡ προσφορὰ τῶν ἐθνῶν εὐπρόσδεκτος, ἡγιασμένη ἐν πνεύματι ἁγίῳ.¹⁷ἔχω οὖν **τὴν καύχησιν ἐν Χριστῷ Ἰησοῦ** τὰ πρὸς τὸν θεόν· ¹⁸οὐ γὰρ τολμήσω τι λαλεῖν ὧν οὐ **κατειργάσατο Χριστὸς** δι᾽ ἐμοῦ εἰς ὑπακοὴν ἐθνῶν, λόγῳ καὶ ἔργῳ, ¹⁹ἐν δυνάμει σημείων καὶ τεράτων, ἐν δυνάμει πνεύματος θεοῦ. [ᵛ·ˡ·-θεοῦ] ὥστε με ἀπὸ Ἰερουσαλὴμ καὶ κύκλῳ μέχρι τοῦ Ἰλλυρικοῦ πεπληρωκέναι **τὸ εὐαγγέλιον τοῦ Χριστοῦ**, ²⁰οὕτως δὲ φιλοτιμούμενον εὐαγγελίζεσθαι οὐχ ὅπου **ὠνομάσθη Χριστός**, ἵνα μὴ ἐπ᾽ ἀλλότριον θεμέλιον οἰκοδομῶ,

15:29 οἶδα δὲ ὅτι ἐρχόμενος πρὸς ὑμᾶς **ἐν πληρώματι εὐλογίας Χριστοῦ** ἐλεύσομαι.

15:30 Παρακαλῶ δὲ ὑμᾶς, ἀδελφοί, **διὰ τοῦ κυρίου ἡμῶν Ἰησοῦ Χριστοῦ** καὶ διὰ τῆς ἀγάπης τοῦ πνεύματος συναγωνίσασθαί μοι ἐν ταῖς προσευχαῖς ὑπὲρ ἐμοῦ πρὸς τὸν θεόν,

[[15:32–33 ³²ἵνα ἐν χαρᾷ ἐλθὼν πρὸς ὑμᾶς διὰ θελήματος θεοῦ συναναπαύσωμαι ὑμῖν. ³³ὁ δὲ θεὸς τῆς εἰρήνης μετὰ πάντων ὑμῶν, ἀμήν.]]

16:2 ἵνα αὐτὴν προσδέξησθε **ἐν κυρίῳ** ἀξίως τῶν ἁγίων . . .

16:3 Ἀσπάσασθε Πρίσκαν καὶ Ἀκύλαν τοὺς συνεργούς μου **ἐν Χριστῷ Ἰησοῦ**,

16:5 . . . ἀσπάσασθε Ἐπαίνετον τὸν ἀγαπητόν μου, ὅς ἐστιν ἀπαρχὴ τῆς Ἀσίας **εἰς Χριστόν.**

16:7–13 ⁷. . . οἵτινές εἰσιν ἐπίσημοι ἐν τοῖς ἀποστόλοις, οἳ καὶ πρὸ ἐμοῦ γέγοναν **ἐν Χριστῷ.** ⁸ἀσπάσασθε Ἀμπλιᾶτον τὸν ἀγαπητόν μου **ἐν κυρίῳ.** ⁹ἀσπάσασθε Οὐρβανὸν τὸν συνεργὸν ἡμῶν **ἐν Χριστῷ** καὶ Στάχυν τὸν ἀγαπητόν μου. ¹⁰ἀσπάσασθε Ἀπελλῆν τὸν δόκιμον **ἐν Χριστῷ.** ἀσπάσασθε τοὺς ἐκ τῶν Ἀριστοβούλου. ¹¹ἀσπάσασθε Ἡρῳδίωνα τὸν συγγενῆ μου. ἀσπάσασθε τοὺς ἐκ τῶν Ναρκίσσου τοὺς ὄντας **ἐν κυρίῳ.** ¹²ἀσπάσασθε

Τρύφαιναν καὶ Τρυφῶσαν τὰς κοπιώσας **ἐν κυρίῳ**. ἀσπάσασθε Περσίδα τὴν ἀγαπητήν, ἥτις πολλὰ ἐκοπίασεν **ἐν κυρίῳ**. [13]ἀσπάσασθε Ῥοῦφον **τὸν ἐκλεκτὸν ἐν κυρίῳ** καὶ τὴν μητέρα αὐτοῦ καὶ ἐμοῦ.

16:16 . . . ἀσπάζονται ὑμᾶς **αἱ ἐκκλησίαι πᾶσαι τοῦ Χριστοῦ**.

16:18 οἱ γὰρ τοιοῦτοι **τῷ κυρίῳ ἡμῶν Χριστῷ οὐ δουλεύουσιν** ἀλλὰ τῇ ἑαυτῶν κοιλίᾳ,

16:20 <u>ὁ δὲ θεὸς τῆς εἰρήνης συντρίψει</u> τὸν σατανᾶν ὑπὸ τοὺς πόδας ὑμῶν ἐν τάχει. **ἡ χάρις τοῦ κυρίου ἡμῶν Ἰησοῦ** μεθ᾽ ὑμῶν.

16:22 ἀσπάζομαι ὑμᾶς ἐγὼ Τέρτιος ὁ γράψας τὴν ἐπιστολὴν **ἐν κυρίῳ**.

16:25–27 [25]<u>Τῷ δὲ δυναμένῳ ὑμᾶς στηρίξαι</u> κατὰ τὸ εὐαγγέλιόν μου **καὶ τὸ κήρυγμα Ἰησοῦ Χριστοῦ**, κατὰ ἀποκάλυψιν μυστηρίου χρόνοις αἰωνίοις σεσιγημένου, [26]φανερωθέντος δὲ νῦν διά τε γραφῶν προφητικῶν κατ᾽ ἐπιταγὴν <u>τοῦ αἰωνίου θεοῦ</u> εἰς ὑπακοὴν πίστεως εἰς πάντα τὰ ἔθνη γνωρισθέντος, [27]<u>μονῳ σοφῷ θεῷ</u>, **διὰ Ἰησοῦ Χριστοῦ**, <u>ᾧ ἡ δόξα εἰς τοὺς αἰῶνας</u>, ἀμήν.

Appendix II: An Analysis of Usage

(* = anarthrous; + = with possessive pronoun; [[LXX]] = Septuagint echo/citation)

Romans

θεός 147 + 9 κύριος [LXX] / 2 πατήρ

Christ 97

The Data

1. κύριος Ἰησοῦς Χριστός (6)
   1:7 G*
   5:1 G+ (διά)
   5:11 G+ (διά)
   13:14 A
   15:6 G+
   15:30 G+ (διά)

1a. Ἰησοῦς Χριστὸς κύριος (3)
   1:4 G+ (appositive to υἱός)
   5:21 G+ (διά)
   7:25 G+ (διά)

1b. Χριστὸς Ἰησοῦς κύριος (2)
   6:23 D+ (ἐν)
   8:39 D+ (ἐν)

2. κύριος Ἰησοῦς (2)
   14:14 D* (ἐν)

16:20 G+
[the use in 10:9 is predicate]

2a. Ἰησοῦς κύριος (1)
   4:24 A+

2b. κύριος Χριστός (1)
   16:18 D+

3. Χριστὸς Ἰησοῦς (12)
   1:1 G*
   2:16 G* (διά) [v.l. Ἰησοῦ Χριστοῦ]
   3:24 D* (ἐν)
   6:3 A* (εἰς)
   6:11 D* (ἐν) [v.l. + τῷ κυρίῳ ἡμῶν]
   8:1 D* (ἐν)
   8:2 D* (ἐν)
   8:34 N* [v.l.-Ἰησοῦς]
   15:5 A* (κατά)
   15:16 G*
   15:17 D* (ἐν)
   16:3 D* (ἐν)

3a. Ἰησοῦς Χριστός (7)

1:6	G*		5:8	N*
1:8	G* (διά)		6:4	N*
3:22	G*		6:8	D* (σύν)
5:15	G* (appositive to		6:9	N*
	ἄνθρωπος)		7:4	G
5:17	G* (appositive to εἷς)		8:9	G*
16:25	G*		8:10	N*
16:27	G* (διά)		8:11	A*

4. κύριος (19 + 15 = 34 [+9 LXX])

			8:17	G*
[[4:8	N* (LXX)]]		8:35	G
[[9:28	N* (LXX)]]		9:1	D* (ἐν)
[[9:29	N*(LXX) + σαβαώθ]]		9:3	G (ἀπό)
10:9	A*		9:5	N
10:12	N		10:4	N*
10:13	G* (LXX)		10:6	A*
[[10:16	V* (LXX)]]		10:7	A*
[[11:3	V* (LXX)]]		10:17	G* [v.l. θεοῦ] [v.l. omit]
[[11:34	G* (LXX)]]		12:5	D* (ἐν)
12:11	D		14:9	N*
[[12:19	N* (LXX)]]		14:15	N*
14:4	D		14:18	D
14:4	N		15:3	N
14:6	D*		15:7	N
14:6	D*		15:8	A*
14:6	D*		15:18	N*
14:8	D		15:19	G
14:8	D		15:20	N*
14:8	G		15:29	G*
[14:9	κυριεύσῃ]		16:5	A* (εἰς)
[[14:11	N*(LXX)]]		16:7	D* (ἐν)
[[15:11	A (LXX)]]		16:9	D* (ἐν)
16:2	D* (ἐν)		16:10	D* (ἐν)
16:8	D* (ἐν)		16:16	G
16:11	D* (ἐν)			

7. υἱός (7)

16:12	D* (ἐν)		1:3	G (αὐτοῦ)
16:12	D* (ἐν)		1:4	G (θεοῦ)
16:13	D* (ἐν)		1:9	G (αὐτοῦ)
16:22	D* (ἐν)		5:10	G (αὐτοῦ)

5. Ἰησοῦς (3 +14 = 17)

			8:3	A (ἑαυτοῦ)
3:26	G*		8:29	G (αὐτοῦ)
8:11	A		8:32	G (ἰδίου)
10:9	A*			

8. Others

6. Χριστός (34 +24 = 58)

			8:29	τὸν πρωτότοκον
5:6	N*		9:32	τῷ λίθῳ τοῦ προσκόμματος

7

Christology in Colossians (and Philemon)

IF MY CHRONOLOGY OF PAUL'S letters is correct, then in turning to Colossians from Romans, we come to the second consecutive letter written to a church that Paul did not found.[1] But in clear contrast with Romans, it is a church founded by one of his colleagues and therefore a church over which he assumes apostolic authority. What marks Colossians as unique in the corpus is that here Christology per se is a significant concern, not in isolation from soteriology, to be sure—then one could indeed make a case that it is not by Paul[2]—but Christology in its own right alongside soteriology. The reason for

---

[1]Commentaries on Colossians are listed in the bibliography (pp. 643–44); they are cited in this chapter by author's surname only. On the Christology of Colossians, see further F. O. Francis, "The Christological Argument of Colossians," in *God's Christ and His People: Studies in Honour of Nils Alstrup Dahl* (ed. J. Jervell and W. A. Meeks; Oslo: Universitetsforleget, 1977), 192–208.

[2]It remains one of the singular mysteries in NT scholarship that so many scholars reject Pauline authorship of Colossians yet affirm the authenticity of Philemon. These letters make especially good sense together if one takes seriously that both Philemon and Onesimus would have been present for the reading of both letters in Philemon's house church. On the one hand, the whole of Philemon is aimed toward what Paul seems quite confident that he will get: the forgiveness of Onesimus and his acceptance back into the community. On the other hand, given that over 50 percent of the "house code" of Col 3:18–4:1 is directed toward the behavior of slaves, Onesimus will have had his own moment to listen up carefully. That a pseudepigrapher could have cared to write such a letter in Paul's name, and with Philemon as his only certain source for "Paul" (contra M. Kiley, *Colossians as Pseudepigraphy* [BibSem 4; Sheffield: JSOT Press, 1986], 75–107), seems to put the option of pseudepigraphy at the lowest end of the scale of historical probability. And in fact, every alleged "deviation" from the Pauline "norm" (on what basis is such a thing determined, one wonders) can be accounted for in light of the historical situation in Colossae as that emerges in the letter. If Kiley's criteria, e.g., were used on the presupposition that 2 Corinthians or Romans were suspect (indeed, Romans has far more "deviations" from the Pauline "norm" as established by scholarship), then their respective relationship to 1 Corinthians and Galatians would absolutely condemn them as Pauline. Here is a clear case of "what goes in is what comes out."

this is almost certainly related to the situation in Colossae and the Colossian believers' fascination with, or anxiety about, "the powers" and magic.[3] If the issue is fascination, that would threaten to "dethrone" Christ as Lord of all; if the situation is anxiety, then "the powers" need to be placed in a christological context that would eliminate the fear.[4]

The result is that Paul's lifelong "Christ devotion" emerges in this letter in a very pronounced way; and as in Romans, it does so alongside an equally deep concern for these Gentile converts to recognize their own place in God's story. As long as they are enamored in any way with "the powers," they are in danger of missing out on what God has done in sending his Son. So what one finds in this letter are constant reminders of their place as Gentiles in the new-covenant expression of the story. At the same time, Paul constantly keeps before them both the person and the role of Christ, that he is none other than the eternal Son of God, in whose kingdom they now live and serve, and that whatever else, he is also their Redeemer and the head of his body, the church, of which they are a part. And the same Son of God who is their Redeemer, their deliverer from darkness, is the Creator of all things, including the unseen "powers," whose power has been altogether negated through Christ's death and resurrection.

Thus, in a letter where Christology emerges in its own right, one is not surprised that the primary emphases lie precisely where we have found them to lie in the more implied Christology of the corpus to this point: Christ as the messianic and eternal Son of God, and Christ as the exalted Lord seated at the right hand of the Father. As Son of God, who perfectly bears the divine image (1:15), he is also the Creator of all things (1:16–17) and is responsible for bringing about the new creation, where God's people are being restored into that same image (3:10), the image of their Creator, Christ.

At the same time, the central role attributed to Christ also brings to the fore new emphases: the Son as eternally preexistent, both Creator and sustainer of the universe; the Son as *incarnate* Redeemer, in whom all of God's fullness dwells in bodily expression; the Son as "head" *of* his body, the church, who is also "head" *over* the powers. The net result is a letter in which Christ, the Son of God and exalted Lord, holds the absolutely preeminent place—in "eternity past," in the present, and in "eternity future."

Nonetheless, the Son of God/exalted-Lord Christology, which seems obvious from a careful reading of what Paul actually says in Colossians, has in the academy regularly been sublimated or eliminated altogether in favor of

---

[3] For a convincing presentation that the "false teaching" was a syncretism of the gospel with folk religion (including magic and belief in intermediate beings), see C. E. Arnold, *The Colossian Syncretism: The Interface between Christianity and Folk Belief at Colossae* (Grand Rapids: Baker, 1996).

[4] Francis ("Christological Argument") makes a considerable case that Christology is a point of agreement between Paul and the Colossians; in this case, the "addition" to the "hymn" of the Son's lordship over "the powers" (1:16b) would be an up-front attempt to put the powers into christological perspective.

an alleged Wisdom Christology. So some of the following exegetical effort is directed toward the implausibility of the latter.[5]

A Preliminary Look at the Data

The various references to Christ and to God[6] are found in appendix I at the end of this chapter; as in earlier chapters, appendix II offers an analysis of the ways Paul speaks of Christ in these two letters. For a letter that was sent probably a few years after the letter to Rome, it is noteworthy that here Paul has returned to his earlier (normal?) patterns; and the patterns in Colossians can also be seen in Philemon, where no point of Christology is found at all.[7] As in the earlier letters, Christ is mentioned more often than God (37x / 29x), and this does not count the 16 pronouns in 1:15–22, all of which have υἱός (*the Son*) in v. 13 as their antecedent (the only use of υἱός in the letter), or the 8 pronouns in 2:8–15 that have Χριστός as antecedent. The most frequent designation for Christ is the title-turned-name Χριστός (25x), which occurs both in combination (6x) and by itself (19x) and is used rather than κύριος even in 3:1, where Paul echoes Ps 110:1. At the other end of the scale, the name Ἰησοῦς occurs only 6 times, always in combination with Christ and/or Lord.

On the other hand, while the title ὁ κύριος occurs 14 times, 4 of which are in combination, the usage in this case is remarkably similar to that in Romans, since seven of the 14 occurrences, and six of the ten occurrences of the title by itself, are bunched in one passage—in this case, in the "household code" of 3:18–4:1—and four of these in conjunction with mention of slaves.

Given these patterns of usage, it is not surprising to find that the two primary categories of Christology per se are the same as in Romans: Jesus as Son of God and exalted Lord, while the use of Χριστός that dominates occurs most frequently in soteriological or other kinds of contexts.

Jesus as Messianic/Eternal Son of God

One unfortunate result of having biblical texts with numbered chapters and verses is a tendency to take these often arbitrary divisions as actual reflections of the biblical author's own agenda. This is especially true of this letter's thanksgiving that starts in 1:9, which evolves first into a reminder of

---

[5] Cf. pp. 102–6 in ch. 3, where the same issue is dealt with in 1 Corinthians.

[6] For a different kind of analysis, using the same data, see Francis, "Christological Argument," 196–201.

[7] The data from Philemon are included for the sake of completeness, even though nothing in the letter seems to call for christological analysis; but see Wright, "ΧΡΙΣΤΟΣ as 'Messiah' in Paul," in *Climax of the Covenant*, 41–55.

the Colossians' place in God's story (vv. 12–14) and then (vv. 15–20) into a poetic exaltation of Christ,[8] as a way of confronting the Colossians with who they are in light of who Christ is.

Whether the latter passage had prior existence before it appeared here is debated;[9] in either case, Paul has deliberately incorporated this marvelous poetry into his now unmanageably long sentence.[10] What results is an ultimate blending of Paul's messianic Son of God Christology with the greater reality of Christ being the eternal Son of God—Creator and Lord of all. Since this passage is the first thing up in the letter and since it is also one of the more significant christological moments in the corpus, we will look at it in some detail. But before doing so, I offer a brief look at the first mention in the letter of God as Father.

Colossians 1:2–3—God Our Father and the Father of Our Lord Jesus Christ

One of the more idiosyncratic moments of this letter lies with the salutation, which begins as always, "Grace to you and peace from God our Father," but does not conclude with the usual "and the Lord Jesus Christ." This seems to be deliberate on Paul's part, as a way of anticipating the early part of the letter.

Thus, the greeting proper emphasizes that God is *our* Father, meaning of all believers, including those in Colossae; and only those who have read Paul's other letters would miss the Christ phrase here. But when we come to

---

[8] Present scholarly wisdom views this as a hymn; but see Wright (*Climax of the Covenant,* 99–106), who prefers simply to refer to it as poetry, and esp. the analysis by S. E. Fowl (*The Story of Christ in the Ethics of Paul: An Analysis of the Hymnic Material in the Pauline Corpus* [JSNTSup 36; Sheffield: Sheffield Academic Press, 1990], 31–45), who demonstrates rather conclusively that the passage is not a "hymn" in the sense that term is currently used in NT circles; rather, it and others are "hymns in the very general sense of poetic accounts of the nature and/or activity of a divine figure" (45). For the purposes of shorthand, I will use the term "hymn," with quotation marks, throughout this chapter.

[9] On this matter, see Fowl's summary in *Story of Christ,* 44–45. Unfortunately, NT scholarship still has not moved completely beyond the time where the "hymn" has been isolated from its Pauline moorings and then discussed as an entity of its own, as though that could actually be discovered and then discussed meaningfully apart from the only context in which it is actually known. On this matter, see in the present volume ch. 1, p. 6.

[10] Besides its obvious poetry, the primary evidence for the passage as a "hymn" is threefold: (1) the compounding of pronouns, all of which refer to the Son in v. 13 and which become more difficult for the reader the further one is removed from the original antecedent; (2) the fact that there are two quite recognizable "stanzas," which begin in similar ways; and (3) what seems to be an insertion into the "hymn" itself of the phrases regarding the powers that take up most of v. 16, none of which belong to the biblical tradition and which here seem to disrupt the poetry (but see Wright, 104–5). This latter phenomenon does indicate where the concern lies: the eternal Son of God is Lord over *all things,* including the powers.

the thanksgiving (v. 3), the reason for the "omission" makes perfectly good sense. Right up front in the letter, and returning to the way he "blesses" God at the beginning of 2 Corinthians (1:3), Paul identifies the God who is *our* Father as "the Father of *our Lord Jesus Christ*." However, in comparison with the Corinthians passage, his text in this case reads,

Col 1:3	εὐχαριστοῦμεν	<u>τῷ θεῷ,</u>[11] <u>πατρὶ</u> τοῦ κυρίου ἡμῶν Ἰησοῦ Χριστοῦ
2 Cor 1:3	εὐλογητὸς	<u>ὁ θεὸς καὶ πατὴρ</u> τοῦ κυρίου ἡμῶν Ἰησοῦ Χριστοῦ

Col 1:3	*We give thanks to*	<u>*God, the Father*</u> **of our Lord Jesus Christ**
2 Cor 1:3	*Blessed be*	<u>*the God and Father*</u> **of our Lord Jesus Christ**

In this letter, the phrase "Father of our Lord Jesus Christ" stands in demonstrable apposition to "God," which suggests that the καί (*and*) in the Corinthian *berakah* is to be understood as epexegetical (as I argued there). Also as in 2 Corinthians, this designation anticipates the Son of God Christology that becomes the central feature of the second thanksgiving, which begins in 1:12. On the meaning of this designation for God, see discussion on 2 Cor 1:3 in ch. 4 (pp. 169–71).

Colossians 1:12–17—Christ: Messianic and Eternal Son of God

The place to begin our analysis of the Christ story that dominates most of what follows is not with the "hymn" itself but with the long sentence that begins (basically) in v. 12, of which the "hymn" is an integral part. The reason for starting here, however, is not simply because Paul's own sentence demands it. In fact, the passage is so full of verbal echoes of Israel's essential story that the role of Christ in the story could otherwise be missed or considerably distorted.[12] Here is a place in particular where a visual representation of Paul's text seems useful.[13] I begin with a straightforward presentation of the text, in which for ease of observation mention of <u>the Father</u> is underlined and mention of **the Son** is in boldface, while the many echoes of the *OT story* are italicized.

_____

[11] The καί is missing in 𝔓[61vid] B C* 1739. It seems far more likely that this is the original text than otherwise. Although a deliberate omission could be accounted for here (the scribe is making clear that the phrase that follows is to be understood as in apposition to "God"), one must ask in such a case, Why only here in the corpus?

[12] On this matter, see esp. Wright, 61–64; cf. J. Behr, "Colossians 1:13–20: A Chiastic Reading," *SVTQ* 40 (1966): 247–64; F. Matera, *New Testament Christology* (Louisville: Westminster John Knox, 1999), 136–40.

[13] For the sake of convenience I offer a full structural analysis of 1:13–20 as appendix III, so that one can see how the various parts relate to each other.

1:12–16 ¹²εὐχαριστοῦντες <u>τῷ πατρὶ τῷ ἱκανώσαντι</u> ὑμᾶς εἰς *τὴν μερίδα τοῦ κλήρου τῶν ἁγίων ἐν τῷ φωτί·* ¹³<u>ὃς ἐρρύσατο</u> ἡμᾶς ἐκ τῆς ἐξουσίας τοῦ σκότους καὶ <u>μετέστησεν</u> εἰς *τὴν βασιλείαν* **τοῦ υἱοῦ** <u>**τῆς**</u> <u>*ἀγάπης αὐτοῦ,*</u> ¹⁴**ἐν ᾧ** ἔχομεν τὴν *ἀπολύτρωσιν,* τὴν ἄφεσιν τῶν ἁμαρτιῶν· ¹⁵**ὅς ἐστιν** **εἰκὼν** <u>τοῦ θεοῦ τοῦ ἀοράτου,</u> **πρωτότοκος** πάσης κτίσεως, ¹⁶**ὅτι ἐν αὐτῷ ἐκτίσθη** τὰ πάντα . . .

> ¹²thanking <u>the Father, who qualified</u> you to *share in the inheritance of the saints* in the light; ¹³<u>who *rescued*</u> us from the *power of darkness* and <u>transferred</u> us into *the kingdom **of the Son** <u>of his love,</u>* ¹⁴**in whom** we have *redemption,* the forgiveness of sins, ¹⁵**who is the *image*** <u>of the invisible God, *the firstborn*</u> over all creation, ¹⁶because **in him were created** all things . . .

At the outset, three matters are of primary importance. First, although the whole passage is a single sentence, one can easily detect the movement from (1) thanksgiving to God the Father for Gentile inclusion (note the ὑμᾶς [*you*] in v. 12), to (2) confession that includes Paul and Timothy, representing the Jewish community (note the shift to ἡμᾶς [*us*] in v. 13), to (3) the *what* and *how* of "our" redemption (vv. 13–14), to (4) an elaboration on the *one who* is responsible for it (vv. 15–17).

Second, just as there is movement from "you" to "us," where the latter includes Gentile and Jew together, so also there is movement from the role of the Father to that of the Son. Thus vv. 12–13 are all about what the Father has done: given you a share in the inheritance, by rescuing us from the rule of darkness and transferring us into the kingdom of the Son of his love. With the mention of the Son at the end of v. 13, the focus then shifts altogether to what the Son has done (v. 14) and finally to who the Son is in relation to the whole created order (vv. 15–16).[14] All of this can be easily seen by a modified display of the grammar:

<u>τῷ πατρὶ</u>
<u>τῷ ἱκανώσαντι</u> ὑμᾶς εἰς τὴν μερίδα τοῦ κλήρου τῶν ἁγίων ἐν τῷ φωτί,
   <u>ὃς ἐρρύσατο</u> ἡμᾶς ἐκ τῆς ἐξουσίας τοῦ σκότους
     καὶ
   <u>μετέστησεν</u> εἰς τὴν βασιλείαν **τοῦ υἱοῦ** <u>τῆς ἀγάπης αὐτοῦ,</u>
         ἐν ᾧ ἔχομεν   τὴν ἀπολύτρωσιν,
                    τὴν ἄφεσιν τῶν ἁμαρτιῶν,
         ὅς ἐστιν εἰκὼν <u>τοῦ θεοῦ τοῦ ἀοράτου,</u>
         πρωτότοκος πάσης κτίσεως,
         ὅτι
         ἐν αὐτῷ ἐκτίσθη τὰ πάντα

---

[14] H. C. G. Moule, in his *Colossian Studies* a century ago (London: Hodder & Stoughton, 1902) speaks of Paul's "thought . . . as it rises through prayer into worshipping confession" (75).

What this means, of course, is that English translations that start a new paragraph with v. 15 and put "Christ" as the substituted antecedent for the "who" (NIV, ESV,[15] NLT, GNB) miss Paul's own grammar and concerns by a considerable margin. And the same is true for commentators who treat vv. 15–20 as though by fiat they could be detached from Paul's own sentence and grammar.[16] Moreover, only by such an excision from Paul's own text could one find personified Wisdom in vv. 15–20; after all, the feminine figure of Sophia could hardly be either the Father's image or his firstborn!

Third, the first part of the narrative that includes the Colossians in the redemptive ministry of the Father and the Son is replete with echoes of Israel's primary story. Thus this brief recital, adapted as it is to the Colossians' own situation, also picks up the concerns of Romans that Gentile believers have, through Christ, been incorporated into God's story of redemption. We begin the christological analysis with this third item.

Colossians 1:12–14—The Messianic Son of God

When most of the attention given to this poetry begins with v. 15, one can easily miss the echoes of Israel's story in vv. 12–15, into which the Colossians themselves have been written by Christ, here celebrated by way of thanksgiving.[17] Although there are various ways one can configure the OT story, it would hardly be possible to do so without the following six elements, all of which appear regularly in various forms in the Pauline corpus:

---

[15] Although in the case of the NIV and ESV, the translators have simply kept the pronoun "he"; the problem lies with the insertion of a title before v. 15 that reads, "The Supremacy of Christ." That simply obstructs the ordinary reader from seeing what Paul is doing. The TNIV has kept the title but changed it to "The Supremacy of the Son of God," and (correctly) substituted "the Son" for the pronoun in v. 15.

[16] It is of some interest that this detachment of vv. 15–20 from their grammatical roots in vv. 12–14 begins at about the same time that NT scholarship began to refer to it as a "hymn"; and it becomes thoroughgoing when the "hymn" is understood to be pre-Pauline. Thus earlier studies (e.g., Lightfoot, 146; Moule, 71–72; Hendriksen, 71) recognize that the "hymn" is about the Son of God, while many of the later ones (although not all [see O'Brien, 42; Wright, 70; Barth and Blanke, 194]) tend to ignore altogether the actual grammatical antecedent (e.g., Lohse, 41, 46; Martin, 57–58; Schweizer, 63–69; Pokorný, 74–75; Dunn, 87, although not so in his *Theology of Paul the Apostle*, 268); cf. H. Ridderbos, *Paul: An Outline of His Theology* (Grand Rapids: Eerdmans, 1975), 70–71; Reid, *Jesus, God's Emptiness, God's Fullness*, 33; Kim, *Origin of Paul's Gospel*, 144. Indeed, Kim, by neglecting this important piece of grammar, makes bold to say, "In Col 1.15 Εἰκών-Christology is essentially Wisdom-Christology." How the Son of God becomes a female figure we are not told.

[17] Most commentators pay lip service to the basic biblical story in vv. 12–14 but then abandon it altogether when they begin comment on v. 15. The exceptions are rare; see Wright, 60–64; Barth and Blanke, 183–93.

1. creation

2. Abraham (with the promise of Gentile inclusion)

3. the exodus (deliverance from bondage and gaining the inherited land)

4. the giving of the law (especially Deuteronomy, with its anticipation of Israel's failure regarding the law)

5. the Davidic kingship

6. exile and the promised restoration (the eschatological consummation), which especially included Gentiles

All of these basic elements of the story occur in some form of linguistic or conceptual echo in the present passage, except for the giving of the law, which will become part of Paul's major concern when he directly addresses the Colossians' current situation in 2:13–23.

Our present interest is threefold, picking up Paul's own emphases on the third and fifth elements (exodus and Davidic kingship) of the basic story and then pointing out how messianic sonship evolves into concern over eternal sonship.

1. Even though our present passage begins with the theme of Gentile inclusion (v. 12)—after all, it is thanksgiving—Paul immediately celebrates that reality by echoing both dimensions of the exodus.[18] First, he starts with their "gaining the inheritance," where the phrase εἰς τὴν μερίδα τοῦ κλήρου τῶν ἁγίων (to share in the inheritance of the saints) has unmistakable linguistic ties to the several passages in Joshua where the words μερίς (share) and κλῆρος (inheritance) are used repeatedly regarding the apportioning of the land,[19] so much so that anyone who knows the biblical story at all could scarcely miss it. Moreover, κλῆρος also appears in other key texts regarding the exodus (see, e.g., Exod 6:6–8 below), always as a way of reminding Israel that God "brought them out" (of Egypt) in order to "bring them in" (to the promised land). Furthermore, expressing this "inheritance" in terms of τῶν ἁγίων (the saints) continues the exodus motif, since Israel in a programmatic way is called "a priestly kingdom and holy nation [ἔθνος ἅγιον]" at their initial constitution as God's people at Sinai (Exod 19:6)—a usage that most likely serves as the source of the term "the holy ones = saints" in later parts of the OT.[20]

---

[18] Cf. Wright (60–63), who entitles this section "the new exodus."

[19] E.g., starting in Josh 12:6, κλῆρος (share = inheritance) occurs 33 times with reference to inheriting the land, and μερίς (portion/share) occurs 13 times. They occur in proximity in 14:3–4; 18:6–8, 9–10; 19:9, 48–49; 24:30/32.

[20] On this question, see esp. Barth and Blanke, 185–86; that the phrase refers to the Colossian believers, see Schweizer, 47; O'Brien, 26; Bruce, 50; Dunn, 77. Lohse (followed by Martin, 54; Pokorný, 52; MacDonald, 50) makes the improbable suggestion, based on Qumran material, that the author here intends "the angels of heaven"

Second, Paul then picks up the first part of the exodus, the deliverance motif, by echoing language from one of its primary texts (Exod 6:6–8), where the Septuagint reads, ἐξάξω ὑμᾶς ἀπὸ τῆς δυναστείας τῶν Αἰγυπτίων καὶ ῥύσομαι ὑμᾶς ἐκ τῆς δουλείας καὶ λυτρώσομαι ὑμᾶς (*I will bring you out from under the domination of the Egyptians, and I will **deliver** you from slavery and **redeem** you*). In speaking of the saving work of Christ, Paul picks both of the key verbs from this passage ("deliver" and "redeem") and echoes the deliverance as from the "dominion" of darkness (τῆς ἐξουσίας τοῦ σκότους).

2. In Paul's narrative the final activity of God the Father is described as transferring "us" εἰς τὴν βασιλείαν τοῦ υἱοῦ τῆς ἀγάπης αὐτοῦ (*into the kingdom of the Son of his love*). Thus Paul asserts that the Redeemer is also the messianic King, of the seed of David. In speaking of the Son's "kingdom," he is using the primary language of this motif, which first finds expression in his letters in 1 Cor 15:24–27. As in that passage, so also here the Son is pictured as the currently reigning King, under whose kingly rule the Colossian Gentiles have now been transferred. And it is precisely at this point that the messianic Son merges with the eternal Son, which is then picked up in detail in v. 15.

The Davidic character of Christ's sonship is signaled by the qualifier "the Son of his love," which echoes the Septuagint of 2 Sam 7:14, 18. Here God speaks first to David about his son who will succeed him, ἐγὼ ἔσομαι αὐτῷ εἰς πατέρα, καὶ αὐτὸς ἔσται μοι **εἰς υἱόν** (*I will be to him a Father, and he will be to me* **a son**), to which the king responds, τίς εἰμι ἐγώ, κύριέ μου κύριε, καὶ τίς ὁ οἶκός μου ὅτι **ἠγάπηκάς με** ἕως τούτων; (*Who am I, LORD my Lord, and what is my house that **you loved me** this way?*).

In Paul's sentence the unusual phrase "the Son of his love" is perhaps deliberately ambiguous. On the one hand, it is a Semitism for "beloved Son"[21] and thus initially says something about the relationship of Father and Son: the Son himself is loved by the Father. At the same time, and probably more to Paul's immediate point, the Son who redeems through his own blood is the ultimate expression of God's love for us, as Paul says emphatically in Rom 5:5–9.[22]

What is especially significant for the rest of the narrative is that "the Son of his love" is the antecedent to all the subsequent pronouns through v. 22—even if by the time one gets to v. 18, Paul himself may have moved some distance from conscious recall of his antecedent. Nonetheless, the point that must be made is that in every case the pronouns could be replaced by their antecedent, "the Son."

---

(36). To look for a parallel in Qumran is surely to look in the wrong place, given the generally consistent usage of this term in the Pauline corpus (excepting 1 Thess 3:13, where Paul is "citing" the Septuagint), not to mention in this letter itself (see 1:2, 4, 26; 3:12) and the exodus motif that dominates this sentence.

[21] So, e.g., Bruce, 52; Dunn, 79.

[22] On this question, see Lightfoot, 142.

3. What happens next is full of interest. When Paul moves on to identify the Son's relationship to creation (vv. 15–17) and the church (vv. 18–20), he begins by picking up the two words that he had used of the Son in Rom 8:29, εἰκών (*image*) and πρωτότοκος (*firstborn*). There the focus was on the Son's relationship to redeemed humanity; here he keeps the Son of God imagery intact, but now he focuses on the Son's relationship to the Father. Stepping back into history, he names him as the One who perfectly bore the *image* of the unseen God and whose position of *firstborn* is now with regard not to our redemption but to the whole of creation. Thus the messianic Son (v. 13) is now set forth as the eternal Son, obviously preexistent and both the agent of and Lord over the whole created order, including the powers. What this means, in effect, is that the parts of the sentence that form our vv. 13b and 14a anticipate the two strophes of the "hymn": (1) God's beloved Son as kingly Lord ends up as the primary concern of vv. 15–17;[23] (2) God's beloved Son as Redeemer is then the focus of vv. 18–20.

My reason for noting all this here is that the shift between vv. 14 and 15 sometimes is regarded as so sharp that the relationship of the "hymn" to what has preceded is often disregarded altogether.[24] But Paul's own Christology, and the grammar of this now very long sentence, hardly allows such bifurcation. As we have seen right along, Son of God Christology has its origins with Christ's having been "sent," so that in his human life he was of the seed of David.[25] But the presupposition of this messianic Christology is ultimately predicated on the fact that the Davidic Son is none other than the eternal Son, whom the Father sent into the world. To this expression of Christology we now turn.

Colossians 1:15–17—The Eternal Son of God, Creator and Lord of All

Three significant features about the "hymn" as a whole (vv. 15–20) need to be noted at the outset before we look at the first strophe in more detail.[26]

---

[23] The insertion of v. 16b (the King's lordship over the powers) thus refocuses the emphasis of his role as preexistent Creator to present Ruler over all he has created.

[24] Or, as in the case of Tuckett (*Christology*) and others, minimized by fiat ("the opening relative clause . . . does not relate grammatically very easily to what comes just before" [75]). This is simply not true, since it is precisely the combination found in Rom 8:29 (Son, image, firstborn).

[25] See, e.g., discussion on Gal 4:4–5 in ch. 5; Rom 1:3–4; 8:3; 9:5 in ch. 6.

[26] As with most such passages, there is a considerable bibliography here; see the rather comprehensive list (through 1987) in Pokorný, 56–57. See also J. F. Balchin, "Colossians 1:15–20: An Early Christian Hymn? The Argument from Style," *VE* 15 (1985): 65–93; S. M. Baugh, "The Poetic Form of Col 1:15–20," *WTJ* 47 (1985): 227–44; Wright, *Climax of the Covenant*, 99–119; Fowl, *Story of Christ*, 103–54; several articles by L. L. Helyer: "Colossians 1:15–20: Pre-Pauline or Pauline?" *JETS* 26 (1983): 167–79; "Arius Revisited: The Firstborn over All Creation (Col 1:15)," *JETS* 31 (1988): 59–67; "Recent Research on Col 1:15–20 (1980–1990)," *GTJ* 12 (1992): 61–67; "Cosmic Christology and Col 1:15–20," *JETS* 37 (1994): 235–46.

First, just enough is said here that is picked up and spelled out in more detail later in the letter to make one think that the "hymn" serves as a kind of prelude (or overture) to the whole letter. This certainly seems to be the case with the "interruption" of the b^{1-4} lines in v. 16.[27] But it happens also in the second strophe (vv. 18–20), where one feature after another is presented (sometimes almost cryptically), only to be elaborated later on in a way that causes one to return to this passage and interpret it in light of the later elaboration.[28]

Second, one of the more striking features of Col 1:15–20 is its apparent relationship with what Paul has said in brief about the Son as "Lord" in 1 Cor 8:6. Indeed, whether intentional or not, vv. 15–20 look very much like an elaboration of the two διά phrases attributed to Christ in that text:

δι' οὗ τὰ πάντα	καὶ	ἡμεῖς	**δι' αὐτοῦ**
through whom all things	and	we	**through him**

Verses 15–17 of our passage poetically fill out "through him all things," a phrase that in fact sits at the center of the "hymn" (v. 16c). Likewise, vv. 18–20 poetically fill out "and we through him." Thus the two passages are concerned with the role of the Son in both creation and redemption.

Third, both *a* lines in the two strophes[29] present the Son with words that echo the creation narrative in Gen 1. In v. 15 the first thing said about the Son is that he is the εἰκών (*image*) of the invisible God; in a strophe that is all about the relation of the Son to the original creation, the first thing said about him is that he replaces Adam (Gen 1:26–27) as the true image-bearer of God. In the second strophe the first thing said about the Son is that he is the ἀρχή, which echoes the opening words of Gen 1:1, thus setting forth the Son as the "beginning"of the new creation.

We begin with the strophe regarding the original creation,[30] where the emphasis is on both the *act* of creation and the *fact* that the Son of God has absolute sovereignty over *what* has been created through his own agency.

---

[27] See the structural display below (next page) and the full display at the end of the chapter as appendix III.

[28] This is true of, e.g., (1) Christ the Son as "head" of his body, the church (cf. 2:19), which metaphor is also picked up with a different nuance in 2:10; (2) Christ as the ἀρχή (*beginning*), which anticipates the "new creation" motif in 3:10–11; (3) Christ as "firstfruit" of the resurrection, which guarantees life both now and forever (2:12–13; 3:1–4); (4) the use of "all the fullness" in v. 19, which is elaborated in 2:9 to mean "all the divine fullness"; and (5) "reconciliation [making peace] through the blood of the cross," spelled out in some detail in 2:13–15.

[29] See the structural analysis in appendix III at the end of this chapter.

[30] Not all will agree with my structural arrangement; in fact, it is often divided into three strophes. My reasons for this arrangement will become clear in the exegesis; however, my basic concern here is not to convince but simply to have a convenient display of the whole passage so as to comment briefly on its relevant parts.

Obviously, the Son is therefore himself not a part of the created order.[31] To aid in the following discussion, I offer here a display of the text, to which we will have frequent occasion to refer:

I. (a)   ὅς ἐστιν   εἰκὼν   <u>τοῦ θεοῦ τοῦ ἀοράτου</u>
   (a')   πρωτότοκος   πάσης κτίσεως,
   (b)   ὅτι   ἐν αὐτῷ   ἐκτίσθη   τὰ πάντα
   (b¹)   ἐν τοῖς οὐρανοῖς καὶ ἐπὶ τῆς γῆς
   (b²)   τὰ ὁρατὰ καὶ τὰ ἀόρατα
   (b³)   εἴτε θρόνοι   εἴτε κυριότητες
   (b⁴)   εἴτε ἀρχαὶ   εἴτε ἐξουσίαι,
   (b')   τὰ πάντα δι' αὐτοῦ καὶ   εἰς αὐτὸν   ἔκτισται.
   (c)   καὶ αὐτός ἐστιν   πρὸ πάντων
   (c')   καὶ τὰ πάντα   ἐν αὐτῷ   συνέστηκεν

I. (a)   **who is**   **the image**   <u>of the invisible God</u>
   (a')   **the firstborn**   over all creation,
   (b)   because   **in him**   were created   all things
   (b¹)   in heaven and on earth
   (b²)   things visible and invisible
   (b³)   whether thrones   or lordships
   (b⁴)   whether rulers   or authorities,
   (b')   all things **through him** and **for him**   were created.
   (c)   and **he is**   **before all things**
   (c')   and all things   **in him**   cohere

The strophe is expressed in three pairs of parallels, with a considerable expansion of the first line (line *b*) of the second pair. Together, these lines emphasize both the Son's precedence and his supremacy over the whole created order, including especially over the powers. Whatever was going on in the Colossians' church, their present fascination with, or anxiety about, the powers has resulted in the powers being given a much greater role than they deserve. Paul's point is the absolute superiority of Christ in every possible way. Not only did Christ preexist them, but also he himself is both Creator of and Lord over them.

   1. The first doublet (*a* / *a'*) affirms the two crucial matters regarding the Son's essential relationships: to the Father and to creation. First, the Son is

---

[31] I emphasize this point because it is common to see Paul as echoing motifs attributed to personified Wisdom (see pp. 317–25 below). But although Wisdom antedates the material creation, she herself is regularly noted to be the *first* of God's "creations," and thus, though preexistent, *personified* Wisdom is never visualized as eternal. Note, e.g., Prov 8:22–26 (the passage from which all others are derived): "The LORD brought me forth as the first of his works, before his deeds of old. I was formed long ages ago, at the very beginning, when the world came to be. When there were no oceans, I was given birth" (TNIV). Cf. Sir 1:4, 9: "Wisdom was created before all other things"; "The LORD himself created her." Nothing that Paul says even remotely resembles this with regard to the eternal Son of God.

the εἰκών (*image*)[32] of the only God, who is both unseen and unseeable.[33] It is through the Son, who alone by way of his incarnation perfectly bears the Father's image, that the unseen God is now known (cf. 2 Cor 4:4–6). Thus the eternal Son, whom the Father sent into the world (Gal 4:4), has restored the "image" of God that the first Adam bore but that was defaced by the fall. In the present context, therefore, where the rest of this first strophe is about the Son's supremacy over the created order, this first affirmation asserts in an especially Pauline way that the Father and Son bear the same identity.[34]

Second, and now turning to the immediate point in terms of the Colossian setting, the Son, who bears the Father's image, is thus also the πρωτότοκος of every created thing. Thus a word used earlier to emphasize the Son's relationship with the redeemed (Rom 8:29) in this case is used to point to the Son's holding the privileged position of "firstborn"—both heir and sovereign with regard to creation,[35] the point that will be elaborated in vv. 16–17. Paul's usage here is most likely derived from Ps 89:27 (88:28 LXX), where Yahweh says of the Davidic scion, "I will be a Father to him, κἀγὼ πρωτότοκον θήσομαι αὐτόν [*and I will appoint him my firstborn*]."[36]

---

[32] On the meaning of this word for Paul, see the discussion in ch. 4 of 2 Cor 3:18 and 4:4 (pp. 184–87), where the word first appears in his writings. On its nonuse in the biblical sense (from Gen 1–2) in the Wisdom of Solomon, see pp. 323–25 below.

[33] Gk. ἀοράτος (cf. Rom 1:20; Heb 11:27). The word occurs 3 times in the Septuagint, but not with regard to God or his attributes, in part perhaps because at various points in the OT it is implied that God has/can be seen (Exod 33:20–23; cf. Ps 63:2; Job 42:5). This latter, however, is almost certainly accommodating language. Thus God's "invisibility" becomes more common during Second Temple Judaism (see, e.g., Philo, *Somn.* 1.71–72; cf. Jesus in Matt 6:6, 18). Its usage here is most likely a deliberate contrast to the "unseen" things over which the Son also exercises absolute sovereignty (v. 16b).

[34] Note especially that the beloved Son is identified first of all as the One in whom we have redemption (v. 14). Thus the *nature* of the divine image is found not in creation but in redemption. That is, the one who bore that image and thus serves as co-creator of the universe is *also* the one in whom all the divine fullness has chosen to dwell so as to effect reconciliation "through the blood of his cross." Thus, as in 1 Cor 1:18–25 and Phil 2:8, God's own image (character) is on full display in Christ's death on the cross. To dehistoricize this into some distant, nonhistorical role played by personified Wisdom is to obliterate Paul's own concerns for outside concerns about the "origins" of this Christology (see the excursus below, pp. 317–25).

[35] It is sometimes alleged that for this usage Paul is indebted to the wisdom tradition. But that is simply not true. The word occurs once in Wisdom of Solomon (18:13, in the plural with reference to the slaughter of the Egyptian firstborn) and once in Sirach (36:17 [as a textual variant], echoing Exod 4:22–23, where Israel is called God's "firstborn"). See further pp. 320–21 below. The word, of course, would never have been used of personified Wisdom, since the word by definition implies "firstborn *son*."

[36] This passage was in fact so interpreted by Rabbi Nathan (cited in Lightfoot, 146): "God said, As I made Jacob a first-born (Exod. iv.22), so also will I make king Messiah a first-born (Ps. lxxxix.28)."

2. The ὅτι that begins the two *b* lines, typical of many psalms, gives reasons[37] for exulting in the one who is the "image" of God and holds primacy over creation. The two lines are synonymous and together emphasize that "all things" were created "in him," which is elaborated in the second line in terms of both "through him" and "for him." This elaboration indicates that the ἐν αὐτῷ in v. 16a (line *b*) is not causal[38] but dative of sphere, as in v. 17b (line *b¹*). Thus these two lines (*b* / *b'*) form an inclusio with regard to the Son's relationship to creation. What is enclosed is first of all the comprehensive nature of τὰ πάντα (*all things*), so that every imaginable created thing, whether in heaven or on earth, whether seen or unseen (including all "the powers" in the latter), exists "in him." As the eternal Son, he embraces the entire sphere of created existence, and nothing lies outside him or is independent of him. Thus "all things" were *created* "in him" (v. 16a) in the sense that "all (created) things" are *constituted* and *cohere* "in him" (v. 17b). The especially high christological affirmation involved in these enclosing lines can scarcely be denied—or deflected by making it simply another way of expressing agency. Just as there is nothing that lies outside God the Father's existence, so also there is no existing thing that lies outside the Son.

3. One should note further that line *b'* (v. 16f) begins as a direct echo of 1 Cor 8:6, thus explicitly repeating that the Son is the divine agent of creation. The second half of this line, however, now asserts that God's Son, who has the rights of primogeniture over all creation—none of which exists apart from him, and all of which in fact was created by him—is also the *goal* of creation (εἰς αὐτόν), the one *for* whom all creation exists and *toward* whom it points. In this case, therefore, the Son is also seen as stepping into the role played by God the Father in 1 Cor 8:6. Moreover, two (διά, εἰς) of the three all-encompassing prepositions in Rom 11:36 attributed exclusively to God are here attributed to the Son. And the ἐκ, which belongs to the Father alone in 1 Corinthians and is conceptually present in the divine passive (ἐκτίσθη, *were created*), is also moderated (remarkably so) by the assertion that all things were created *in him* (i.e., "in the Son").

---

[37] The ὅτι in this case is explanatory, not causal, as is often the case in the Psalter as well; cf. Eadie, 52; Lightfoot, 150.

[38] As in the NLT, GNB, NET BIBLE, NIV (now corrected in the TNIV); cf. the commentaries that take it as causal (Eadie, 52; Lohse, 50; Pokorný, 79; Barth and Blanke, 198; Dunn, 91), but not Lightfoot, 150; Moule, 76; Haupt, 30–31; O'Brien, 45; Bruce, 61–62; Wright, 71; Garland, 88. Martin (58) suggests that "in him" has the sense that in him "heaven and earth are 'joined,'" which he then likens to the role of "the divine word" in Sir 24:5 and Wis 18:16. But that is both to miss Paul and to misread Sirach and Wisdom. The passage cited in Sirach has nothing to do with Wisdom "joining heaven and earth"; rather, in this poetry Wisdom praises herself, whose first home is in heaven but who then sought out an earthly home and found it in Israel. And Wis 18:16 is about "the word" that destroyed Egypt's firstborn. To find a cosmic "Word" here that is even remotely similar to what Paul says of the Son in this passage seems to stretch the meaning of poetry beyond all legitimate bounds.

4. Line *c* (v. 17a) then reemphasizes what was implied in lines *a'*, *b*, and *b'*: the Son *is*, not "was," *before* all things, where the Greek preposition bears the same ambiguity (temporal and spatial) found in the English word *before*, thus emphazing both his existence prior to the created order and his having the position of primacy over it because he is the agent of its existence. In the final line (*c'*) the Son's role as the preexistent Creator of all things is furthered by the emphasis that they are currently "held together" in and through him.

The linguistic ties between this passage and 1 Cor 8:6, not to mention 2 Cor 4:4, suggest that the same christological point of view lies behind both of them, especially so since the next strophe (vv. 18–20) spells out in similar detail the καὶ ἡμεῖς δι᾽ αὐτοῦ (*and we through him*) of the earlier passage. The present passage thus expresses in greater detail what is already presupposed in 1 Corinthians. A higher Christology does not exist in the NT. Indeed, what is said here by Paul is also reflected in John and Hebrews; and since it is here asserted by Paul as something that the Colossians should also be in tune with, one has to assume that such a Christology existed in the church from a very early time. The relationship of this passage to 1 Cor 8:6 further indicates that "development" is hardly an adequate way to describe Paul's own christological assumptions that are more thoroughly articulated here.

Colossians 3:10—Christ and the New Creation: The Image Restored

Paul's second use of εἰκών (*image*) in this letter also occurs in a context of "creation" language, but now having to do with believers' being renewed into the "image" of the one who created them. Thus, in place of the "rules and regulations" that the Colossians feel compelled to come under, apparently both to keep in step with the "powers" and thus to secure their place with God (2:14–23), Paul urges them to live their lives in Christ in a way that reflects their belonging to the new creation effected by Christ (3:1–11). In the process, and moving toward a summation at the end, Paul picks up the baptismal terminology from 2:11–13 and urges the Colossians, since they have "taken off [their] old self with its practices" (3:9), to "put on the new self," which is in a constant renewal that is κατ᾽ εἰκόνα τοῦ κτίσαντος αὐτόν (*in accordance with the image of the one who created the new "man"*). Since this phrase echoes Gen 1:26, 28, at issue is the referent of τοῦ κτίσαντος, whether it is God the Father, who created the "first 'man'" (Adam), who through his fall became the "old man," or Christ the Son, who is understood to be responsible for the new creation.

Although there are frequent voices to the contrary,[39] in the context of this letter what at first reading may seem to be ambiguous should be seen on

---

[39] See, e.g., Lightfoot, 216; Moule, 213; Lohse, 143; O'Brien, 191; Dunn, 222; Jervell, *Imago Dei*, 249. Martin (107) and Schweizer (198) would have it both ways: the "image" is Chist, and the Creator is God. For the interpretation adopted here, see Chrysostom, *Hom. Col.*; Wright, 138–39; Barth and Blanke, 413–14.

closer reflection to refer to Christ the Son. Three contextual matters make
one think so. First, in the immediate context this clause is followed by the assertion "where [presumably in the new order presupposed by new-creation
language] there is neither Greek nor Jew [etc.], but *Christ* is 'all and in all' [=
the whole of everything and in all of them]." It is hard to imagine that one
should read "God," whose last mention was in terms of his "wrath" (v. 6),
into a sentence that concludes in such christocentric fashion.

Second, the same is true of the broader context, which began in 2:20,
along with 3:1–4. Here the baptismal terminology is especially pressed as the
foundation for a new and different kind of ethical life. The Colossians have
both "died with Christ" (2:20) (in the cross and realized in baptism) and
"have been raised with Christ" (3:1). Hence they should seek to live in keeping with their new position of life, a life located in Christ, who himself is
"seated at the right hand" of God and is thus their present source of "life"
(3:2–3). One should therefore naturally assume that Christ is both the Creator of this new life and the one into whose image they are being renewed.

And that brings us, third, back to the beginning of the letter, where the
Son of God is asserted to be both the bearer of the divine image and the one
"in whom, through whom, and for whom" all things came to be in the original creation. It would seem to make little sense in this letter for the
preexistent Son, who himself bears the divine image, to be Creator of the
whole universe and then for God the Father to be the Creator in the new
order, which finds its entire focus in Christ the Son.

What this means, further, is that with the present use of εἰκών, Paul has
returned to the usage of "image" and "firstborn" in Rom 8:29, his most recent
letter. There, Christ as Son was designated as "firstborn" among the many
brothers and sisters whom he has redeemed, whose redemption is expressed in
terms of their being predestined to bear the same εἰκών as the Son himself.
Thus here as well, in the new creation the Son restores the "image of God" in
humankind that was lost in the first creation through human sin.

The Son as Incarnate Redeemer

Given the emphasis in the first strophe of the hymn on the *preexistent*
Son as the divine image-bearer and the Creator of all that is, one is not surprised that in the second strophe there is also emphasis on his becoming *incarnate* when he assumed the role of Redeemer. But that emphasis does not
emerge until vv. 19–20, where both the incarnation and the Son's genuine
humanity are put forward as the means of his reconciling work. The latter
concern is then carried on into vv. 21–22, where Paul makes a considerable
point of the fact that this reconciling work took place "in his fleshly body."

But Paul does not begin there; rather, he begins where his primary concerns lie in this letter: the Colossian believers and their relationship to Christ.

And since that is not only the first thing up (v. 18) but also the main concern in the letter, we need first to note the christological moments in the "topical" sentence and their immediate ramifications. For here, without using κύριος language, Paul begins by asserting that the Son, by virtue of his resurrection, also holds the position of absolute primacy, and thus supremacy, with regard to "all things."[40]

Colossians 1:18—Christ the "Head" of the New Creation

In contrast to the first strophe of the "hymn," which focuses on the Son's relationship to the created order, this second strophe has primarily to do with the Son's relationship to the church and thus also to the powers for the sake of the church. The focus in this case, picking up from v. 14, is on the Son's redemptive work, particularly on the reconciliation that he has effected for the sake of the church in the context (apparently) of the powers. As before, the discussion is aided by seeing the structure as a whole:

(d)	καὶ **αὐτός ἐστιν**	**ἡ κεφαλὴ τοῦ σώματος,**	τῆς ἐκκλησίας·
II. (a)	ὅς ἐστιν	**ἀρχή,**	
(a')		**πρωτότοκος** ἐκ τῶν νεκρῶν,	
(a¹)		ἵνα **γένηται** ἐν πᾶσιν	**αὐτὸς πρωτεύων,**
(b)	ὅτι	**ἐν αὐτῷ** εὐδόκησεν <u>πᾶν τὸ πλήρωμα</u> κατοικῆσαι	
(b')	καὶ	**δι' αὐτοῦ** <u>ἀποκαταλλάξαι</u> τὰ πάντα **εἰς αὐτόν,**	
(b¹)		**εἰρηνοποιήσας διὰ τοῦ αἵματος τοῦ σταυροῦ αὐτοῦ**	
(b²)		**δι' αὐτοῦ**[41] εἴτε τὰ ἐπὶ τῆς γῆς εἴτε τὰ ἐν τοῖς οὐρανοῖς.	

(d)	and **he** is	**the head of his body**	the church;
II. (a)	**who** is	**the beginning,**	
(a')		**the firstborn** from the dead,	
(a¹)		so that **he might** in all things **have supremacy,**	
(b)	because	**in him** was pleased <u>all the fullness</u> to dwell	
(b')	and	**through him** <u>to reconcile</u> all things **to him,**	
(b¹)		**having made peace through the blood of his cross**	
(b²)		**through him** whether things on earth or things in heaven.	

---

[40] Gk. ἐν πᾶσιν; this is the single place in the poetry where the all-embracing τὰ πάντα is moderated in this way. Very likely this is because at issue now is not simply the created order as such but the new creation with its inclusion of the Colossian believers. Thus the Son who has "firstborn rights" with regard to the whole of creation, by means of his resurrection has the same rights "in all things," including the church, of which he is "the head."

[41] This apparently redundant δι' αὐτοῦ is not found in some of the earliest and best, as well as in some later, evidence (B D* F G I L 075 81 1175 1241 1739 1881 it bo arm eth); it occurs, however, in equally strong and early evidence that won the day as the Majority Text (𝔓⁴⁶ ℵ A C D¹ Ψ 048 0150 6 33 pler). Here is a case where the

The strophe has several features in keeping with, as well as in contrast to, what is said in vv. 15–17. Noteworthy is a somewhat similar structure, where the Son is now presented as "the head of the body." This is followed by a similar ὅς clause, again echoing Gen 1, where the Son is now the ἀρχή (the new *beginning*), which in turn is followed by the presentation of Christ as πρωτότοκος (*firstborn*), this time of the new creation by virtue of his resurrection from the dead; and again the third line (a^1) offers the purpose for his assuming this role, this time with a ἵνα (purpose)- clause. The final four lines are characterized by a repetition of the three primary prepositional phrases from the first strophe (ἐν, διά, εἰς; *in, through, for*), which in turn express the sphere/location where "all the (divine) fullness" dwells, plus the agency of reconciliation and its goal. Several christological moments need to be noted.

1. Paul has previously used the metaphor of the church as the body of Christ to emphasize the need for diversity within unity (1 Cor 12:12–25; cf. 10:17). But here, using the Greek sense of the metaphor "head,"[42] Paul emphasizes the church's utterly dependent relationship to Christ. Indeed, failure to be connected with the head, he says later (2:19), means total loss with regard to one's relationship with God. The church is thus to be understood as existing "in Christ" similarly to the way creation exists "in him": as the Son is the sphere of being for all that exists, so also the Son is the "head" of his body the church, which not only exists in him but also draws all necessary life from the "head" to which it is connected.

What is striking about this metaphor is the association between Christ and the people of God, newly constituted by Christ and the Spirit. In the OT story Israel is *God's* people, chosen by him, owned by him, dependent on him, and thus subservient to him. They live only in relationship to their God. With a metaphor drawn from the Greco-Roman understanding of the body politic,[43] Paul had already earlier associated the newly formed people of God as Christ's body, especially in connection with the bread of the Lord's Table (1 Cor 10:16–17). In his first elaboration of the metaphor (1 Cor 12:12–26) the emphasis was not on the body's relationship with Christ as such but on the

---

omission is easily accounted for, since the phrase seems so redundant. On the same grounds, one could hardly imagine the circumstances where it might have been added, except by sheer error; but the very fact that there is so much early and widespread evidence for the inclusion of the phrase would mean that the "error" would need to have happened more than once—a most unlikely probability. See the discussion in Metzger, *Textual Commentary*, 554. If the "repetition" is original, then it occurs for rhetorical purposes: to emphasize that the "all things" that have been "reconciled" through the "blood of the cross" includes both humankind and the powers (who in the latter case have been "disarmed," as Paul makes explicit in 2:14–15).

[42] The Greeks considered the head to be the ultimate necessary part of the body, since all its functions originate in and are sustained by the head; thus in metaphorical usage, the focus is on the body's dependence on the head.

[43] On this see G. D. Fee, *The First Epistle to the Corinthians* (NICNT; Grand Rapids: Eerdmans, 1987), 602.

needed diversity within unity that a functioning body must have (cf. Eph 4:10–16). But here the emphasis in on the *relationship* of the church to Christ, which turns out to be of far greater consequence than was Israel's relationship with Yahweh. Connected to Christ as "head" of the body, the Colossian believers are thus connected to the One who has total lordship *over* the powers (2:10).

2. Given this understanding of the janus, or presenting, clause (*d*), the relative pronoun ὅς (line *a*) probably should be understood in a way similar to that in line *a* in the first strophe. In that strophe the first thing up was a phrase clarifying the relationship of the incarnate Son to the unseen God, as the One who perfectly bore the divine image. In this strophe the first thing up, Christ as ἀρχή (*the beginning*), should likewise be understood in light of the immediately preceding reference to his body, the church. With an apparently deliberate echo of Gen 1:1,[44] the Son of God is asserted to be the "beginning" of the new creation,[45] just as he is the "cause" of the former creation; and he is so as the result of his being the "firstborn" with regard to the dead. In this case, however, πρωτότοκος carries both senses of the word: as the "first" to rise from the dead, he thus also has the rights of the "firstborn" with regard to his church. All belong to him, the author of the new creation, and all are thus totally dependent on him with regard to the life of the future.

3. The purpose (ἵνα) of Christ's being the "beginning" of the new creation (by means of his resurrection) is then expressed (line *a¹*) in terms that further echo what was said of him regarding the first creation. Just as he has the rights of primogeniture with regard to the original creation, so also as "firstborn" from the dead "he himself has the primacy/supremacy in all things."[46] Indeed, he was raised with this very goal in view. Thus, in this indirect way, Son of God Christology begins to move conceptually toward a Κύριος Christology, even though that title does not appear here.

Colossians 1:19–22—Incarnation and Redemption

With the opening *a* lines in first place—the Son as "head" in relationship to his body the church—Paul next focuses (in the series of *b* lines) on the *means* whereby the Son has assumed this role. This in turn leads us directly to Paul's assertion that the Son is none other than the incarnate Redeemer, which is stated twice: once in general terms in the "hymn" itself (vv. 19–20) and then in terms of specific application to the Colossian

---

[44] One is led to think so because this strophe is as much concerned with the new creation as the first strophe was with the original creation.

[45] This view can be traced back as far as Calvin; see Martin, 59; O'Brien, 50; Wright, 73; cf. Ridderbos: "He was . . . the Pioneer, the Inaugurator, who opened the way" (*Paul*, 56).

[46] Lightfoot notes regarding the phrase "in all things" that Paul now intends "not in the Universe only but in the Church also" (158).

believers (vv. 21–22). In both cases the metaphor for salvation is the reconciliation of God's enemies with himself (cf. 2 Cor 5:18–21); and in both cases the emphasis is put on the bodily reality of the One who became incarnate for their salvation. That much seems clear enough; but not all the details are equally clear, and therefore they require careful examination.

Colossians 1:19–20 (2:9)—Christ the Incarnate Reconciler

With an explanatory ὅτι, Paul picks up his assertion as to the Son's assumption of the place of absolute supremacy "in all things" and offers a twofold clarification as to *how* and *why* this came about. The "how" comes in line *b*, where he asserts that in his incarnation "all fullness" chose (or "was pleased")[47] to dwell.[48] The "why" comes in line *b'*: "all [God's] fullness" chose to dwell in the Son so that the Son might be the agent of the divine reconciliation of "all things." Again, that much seems clear enough; our difficulties stem from Paul's use of "all fullness"—*what* it means, *why* this language, and *how* it functions in the rest of the strophe. Since these questions are interrelated, I will take them up one by one.

1. As to the first matter (*what* "all fullness" means), Paul himself returns to this language in 2:9, where he adds the clarifying noun τῆς θεότητος (*of the deity*) plus the emphatic adverb σωματικῶς (*bodily*). The first of these is the abstract noun for divinity, which in 2:9 functions (apparently) as a periphrasis for "God." There can be little question that in our present passage, as in 2:9, Paul specifically refers to the Son as the divine incarnation. This is made certain in the latter reference with the addition of the emphatic "bodily."

In this passage, therefore, Paul is doing very much what one finds in John 1:1–18 and Heb 1:1–3. As the reader was set up to understand from vv. 13–14, Paul's primary concern is with the Colossians' *redemption* through the Son; with vv. 19–20 he has finally got there. But as with John and Hebrews, he begins by establishing that the incarnate Son, who came into the world to redeem, is first of all to be understood as the preexistent divine agent of the whole created order. And in keeping with the poetry of this passage, the incarnation is simply asserted. In the second instance (2:9) it is expressed emphatically as a matter of "bodily" existence—a point made less directly here.

---

[47] Cf. BDAG, which offers that εὐδοκέω leans first toward "to consider something as good and therefore worthy of choice" rather than simply "to take pleasure in." Thus the REB has "God in all his fullness *chose* to dwell," against most other English translations that have some form of the idea of "please/pleasure."

[48] Or at least a straightforward reading of the passage would seem to indicate this. The majority of interpreters, however, prefer to add an assumed outside referent, "God," as the subject of the sentence. But this view exists, as almost all readily admit, because of a prior commitment to understanding the εἰς αὐτόν at the end of the sentence as a reflexive pronoun ([ἑ]αυτόν) referring to the Father, not the Son. See the response below.

But what does need to be noted is that Paul here gives explicit, intentional expression to what he had said in earlier letters in more implicit ways. In straightforward language he asserts that all God's fullness found incarnational expression in the coming of Jesus, God's Son. What was presuppositional at several earlier, implicit moments in the corpus (e.g., 2 Cor 8:9; Gal 4:4–5; Rom 8:3) here finds explicit expression.

2. As to the *why* of this circumlocution, one can only speculate; nonetheless, a good reason can be given, having to do with Paul's consistent use of the word θεός. Throughout the corpus he reserves this word consistently to refer specifically to the Father.[49] Thus, even though Christ the Son shares the divine identity, the circumlocution "all the fullness of deity" allows Paul to think in terms of incarnation without specifying that θεός "dwelt" in him, lest that appear to circumscribe God's "dwelling" to a specific location as over against his inhabiting the whole universe that Father and Son have created.

3. But this very circumlocution, as a way of speaking about God's "dwelling" in the incarnate Son, has also created our difficulties in terms of *how* it functions in the rest of the sentence. At issue are three grammatical matters, which do not yield to ready solution. Each stems from the fact that Greek nouns have grammatical gender that requires grammatical agreement in subsequent related forms. In this case, the expression πᾶν τὸ πλήρωμα is neuter, even though it is a periphrasis for θεός (*God*), which is masculine. And since neuter nouns are identical in the nominative and accusative, one cannot always tell which is intended, especially in conjunction with the infinitive. Thus our three problems: (a) Is πᾶν τὸ πλήρωμα the subject of the main verb, εὐδόκησεν (*chose/was pleased*) or the subject of the following infinitive, and is an unexpressed θεός the subject of the main verb? (b) The participle εἰρηνοποιήσας (*having made peace*) in line *b¹* is masculine singular, but there is no preceding noun with which it agrees grammatically; does Paul intend us to read "God" as the subject of "chose," even though God has not been mentioned throughout the passage, or has he created a *grammatical* anomaly because "all the fullness" really does stand in for "God"? (c) The αὐτόν in the prepositional phrase εἰς αὐτόν (*to him*) at the end of line *b'* is a clearly personal pronoun, yet if the sentence were on its own (apart from this poetry), it would demand a reflexive (*to himself*), as most English translations arbitrarily make it, or else it really does refer to a second party ("God" in this case).

At stake for us christologically in the present discussion is this final item, as it is related to the earlier two. Did Paul intend "all things" to be reconciled to God, or to the Son? And this in turn affects one's understanding of the κατενώπιον αὐτοῦ (*in his sight*) at the end of v. 22. The discussion may be

---

[49] For the two instances that many consider to be exceptions to the "rule," see discussion on Rom 9:5 in ch. 6 (pp. 272–77) and Titus 2:13 in ch. 10 (pp. 442–46).

easier to follow if the two options are presented without pronouns, with the standard **boldface** for Christ and <u>underline</u> for God.

If an unexpressed "God" is the subject of the sentence, then the clauses would look like this:

> For **in the Son** <u>[God] chose to have all his fullness dwell</u>,
> and **through the Son** <u>to reconcile all things to Godself</u>,
> <u>having made peace</u> **through the blood of the Son's cross**,
> **through the Son**, whether things on earth or things in heaven.

If "all the fullness" is the subject of the sentence, then the clauses would look like this:

> For **in the Son** <u>all the fullness chose to dwell</u>,
> and **through the Son** <u>to reconcile all things</u> **to the Son,**
> <u>having made peace</u> **through the blood of the Son's cross**,
> **through the Son**, whether things on earth or things in heaven.

It should be noted at the outset that both of these face at least one grammatical anomaly. In the first instance, a personal pronoun is turned into a reflexive; in the second instance, a masculine participle is made conceptually to modify a (grammatically) neuter noun. But the real problem with the first (clearly majority) view is that it now shifts the emphasis from the Son to God the Father, who is not *explicitly* mentioned in the entire poem except in the opening prepositional phrase ("the image of the unseen God"). And this stance is taken primarily because of what Paul says in other letters about *reconciliation:* it has to do with being reconciled to God.[50] But this poem in its entirety is about the Son, not about the Father, who is brought into the picture only through the oblique referent "all the fullness" and who must be brought in at this point or the concept of incarnation does not work at all.

The issue, then, revolves around the prepositional phrases εἰς αὐτόν (*to him*) in v. 19 and κατενώπιον αὐτοῦ (*in his sight*) at the end of v. 22. To turn these into reflexives is to do something that, to the surprise of many,[51] was not once done in the long history of the textual tradition. This is all the more striking because the tendency in the history of interpretation and translation has been to do precisely that.[52] But to turn these personal pronouns into

---

[50] Indeed, the translators of the NET BIBLE put it baldly: "Since God is the one who reconciles the world to himself (cf. 2 Cor 5:19), he is *clearly* the subject of εὐδόκησεν" (italics mine). This is less clear to me.

[51] See esp. C. F. D. Moule, *An Idiom Book of New Testament Greek* (2d ed.; Cambridge: Cambridge University Press, 1959), 119 (cited in full in Meztger, *Textual Commentary,* 554).

[52] This is expressly so in translations that would come under the rubric of "functional equivalent" (e.g., NIV/TNIV: "for God was pleased"; cf. GNB, REB, NJB), but it is equally so of those that pride themselves as more "literal" (NASB, ESV, NRSV). The one

reflexives is a ploy that not only causes the second strophe to limp in terms of the whole being a poem/hymn about Christ but also causes the reader suddenly to have to make guesses about the pronouns, which up to this point consistently had "the Son" as their antecedent.

There is every good reason, however, to think that Paul was not at all confused as to what he was saying—and intending. Although it is true that "God," by way of the circumlocution "all the fullness," is the implied subject of the various verbs in the sentence, it is likewise true that the whole passage focuses on the work of the Son. It is the Son who stands as the "beginning" of the new creation, and the Son who through resurrection has assumed the place of absolute supremacy. So when Paul turns to emphasize his full deity by saying that "all the [divine] fullness chose/was pleased to dwell *in him*," he most likely does not thereby intend now to focus on God the Father. Rather, the very *periphrasis itself keeps the emphasis on the Son.*

But the more important reason for going this route exegetically is that it keeps all the pronouns intact, referring to the Son in this strophe as they did in the first one. This suggests that, just as in line *b¹* in v. 16, where the same two prepositional phrases ("through him" and "for/to him") focused on the Son, so also here.[53] And one should have no greater difficulty in seeing the Son as both the agent and goal of reconciliation (and thus the new creation) than one does in seeing him as the agent and goal of the first creation. Just as the original creation was "in him, through him, and for him," so also in the new creation, the divine fullness was pleased to dwell "in him," so that "through him," by means of his death on the cross, all things could now be reconciled "to him."

There are three further advantages of going this exegetical route. (1) It also keeps one from turning Paul's personal pronoun, εἰς αὐτόν (*to/for him*), into a reflexive pronoun, εἰς αὑτόν (*to himself*), a spelling of ἑαυτόν that does not occur elsewhere in the Pauline corpus. Indeed, Paul shows no aversion to the reflexive pronoun, which he uses regularly when the sense calls for it; thus one should perhaps assume that he did *not* intend this plainly personal pronoun to be turned into a reflexive. (2) Keeping the flow of the pronouns intact also means that when one gets to the τοῦ σταυροῦ αὐτοῦ (*of his cross*), one is not faced with the awkwardness of reverting to the δι᾽ αὐτοῦ (*through him*) at the beginning of line *b'* to find the proper antecedent. Instead, all the pronouns in this strophe are seen to refer to Christ, just as they did in the

known exception is the NAB, which reads, "and through him to reconcile all things for him." For the most part, this strategy has been employed in order (unnecessarily) to harmonize this passage with what Paul says elsewhere about reconciliation (2 Cor 5:18–21; Rom 5:10–11).

[53] Cf. Barth and Blanke: "The reference is to reconciliation with Christ; . . . attempts . . . to interpret *eis auton* (to him) by changing the accentuation to the reflexive and referencing it back to 'God,' are hardly convincing" (214–15). This view is taken also by Matera (*New Testament Christology*, 143), who likewise notes the parallel with v. 16.

first strophe. (3) Finally, the grammatical strategem of reading πᾶν τὸ πλήρωμα as the subject of the first infinitive ("to dwell"), but not the main verb "chose/was pleased," runs full in the face of what Paul says in 2:9. In this latter passage, Paul says the same thing in elaborated form that he says poetically in the present one; but he does so there in straightforward prose without the prepositional phrases and pronouns that dominate the present poetry. And there, πᾶν τὸ πλήρωμα is in fact the subject of the sentence, as it seems to be here.

It should be noted, finally, that by getting the pronouns right, one is not thereby "dethroning" God, as it were, since God the Father is not the focus at any point in the entire "hymn." Rather, what one does is properly to "enthrone" the Son. Through Christ's death on the cross "all the fullness" who was pleased to dwell in the Son has caused all things to be reconciled to the Son himself, having done so by the Son's having brought about peace through his death on the cross. And here, as noted above (n. 34), is the primary reason for εἰκών as the first thing up in the "hymn." The Son, who bears the divine image for purposes of redemption (Rom 8:30–31), is co-Creator of all things as well (cf. 1 Cor 8:6). What is going on here christologically, therefore, is what we have seen happen throughout the corpus thus far: Paul regularly understands Christ to share with God the Father what are otherwise explicitly divine prerogatives.

But what, then, does it mean for Paul to say that *all things* have been "reconciled" through and to him, especially since the first "who" clause modifying "the beloved Son" (1:14) speaks of his "redemption" in terms of "the forgiveness of sins"? This is all the more a significant question in light of the fact that what is said here is given specific application to the Colossians in the following verses, thus suggesting that this present clause has intentionally broader application. In that case, we should probably understand the τὰ πάντα of this strophe to be identical with the τὰ πάντα of the first strophe, so that the "all things" of both strophes refer to the whole creation, and especially "the principalities and powers." The reason for thinking so is that these are precisely the words picked up again in 2:10, 15, referring to "the powers" whom Christ has disarmed, making a public spectacle of them by triumphing over them in the cross.

This would further suggest that even though Paul also understands the "blood of the cross" to be God's means of forgiveness (2:13–14; cf. 1:14), he probably understands "reconciliation" in the present passage to go beyond forgiveness to the Son's role in subduing the powers for the Colossians' sakes as well.[54] If this is the case, then that further explains why both the cosmic creation (first strophe) and the new creation (second strophe) are being celebrated as "through and to/for the Son." As he is the one "through whom" all things were created and "through whom" all things are reconciled, so also

---

[54] For this view of the passage see, e.g., Lohse, 59; Bruce, 75; Martin, 60; O'Brien, 56; Wright, 76–77; Garland, 94–95; Dunn, 102–3.

he is the one who stands as the ultimate goal of his creating and reconciling work, so that in "all things" he might have the place of divine supremacy. Thus this moment of "reconciliation" is especially a christological assertion, which at the same time includes the saving work of Christ that Paul will now apply specifically to the believers in Colossae (vv. 21–22).

Finally, we should note that not only does this strophe emphasize the incarnation as such, but with line *b'* ("having effected peace through the blood of his cross") it also emphasizes the genuine nature of that humanity. The Son did not simply die for us; he shed his blood on the cross and thus effected peace. Since this is elaborated and expressed even more strongly in 2:14–15, we probably should take the "earthy" nature of Christ's death seriously. One can only speculate as to why there is this emphasis, but most likely it is related to the Colossians' current fascination with the "unseen powers," the very powers that Christ has triumphed over in his death. So even though it is not for later theological reasons that Paul presses this point, it does in fact further indicate that he was rightly concerned with the genuine humanity of Christ's incarnation.

Colossians 1:21–22—Application to the Colossians

For the purposes of this study, one could easily bypass this passage; however, the various English translations force us to take a look at it for the same reasons as with v. 20 above. Here again we are faced with the fact that translators have tended to let the prepositional phrase κατενώπιον αὐτοῦ (*in his presence*) dictate how they understand and thus render this sentence. But in this case the problem is increased because, by translating the text as it appears in our critical editions, they probably are not reflecting Paul's original text. Thus our difficulties lie at two levels: text and interpretation.

First one must resolve the matter of text, which comes to us in three basic forms:

ἀποκατήλλαξεν (*he reconciled*)	ℵ A C Dᶜ K and almost all others
ἀποκατηλλάγητε (*you were reconciled*)	𝔓⁴⁶ B (33) Hil Ephraem
ἀποκατηλλαγέντες (*having been reconciled*)	D* F G itᵇ·ᵈ·ᵍ vgᵐˢ Ir Ambst

Two major difficulties face the textual critic: (1) Two of the best manuscripts of the Pauline corpus (𝔓⁴⁶ and B) have a reading that is a grammatical anomaly (the preceding pronoun and participle are accusative, while the verb is passive and therefore cannot take an object). At the same time, the 𝔓⁴⁶ B text is the only one that can reasonably explain the existence of the others.[55] If original, then one would have to allow that Paul himself

---

[55] Indeed, the Western Text (D* et al) can *only* be explained as a corruption of the text of 𝔓⁴⁶ B. What the scribes created was also an anomaly: two participles without a main verb. This doubles the likelihood that the text of 𝔓⁴⁶ B is Paul's original.

started his sentence one way and then concluded it in another ("You, formerly being enemies, but now you have been reconciled").[56] (2) This has caused most textual critics to opt for the "grammatically correct" reading; but in so doing, they are able to offer no good explanation as to how the scribe of the *Vorlage* of such superior manuscripts as 𝔓[46] and B could have made such an egregious copying error. That is, from the perspective of a scribe copying a manuscript, it is nearly impossible to account for this reading if the other was original. Here seems to be a clear-cut case where the primary "rule" of textual criticism must take precedence: that reading which best explains how *all* the others came about is most likely the original.

For this reason, I have found myself on the side of J. B. Lightfoot and B. M. Metzger,[57] that the text of 𝔓[46] and B must be Paul's original, since (1) this text as a scribal error would be so difficult to account for even in lesser manuscripts and (2) the Western reading obviously presupposes this text as the one to which the Western scribe(s) made his (their) deliberate change to the text. Scribes do some strange things, to be sure, but this change can only have been deliberate; and it is far more likely that Paul's original text was ungrammatical and deliberately changed by scribes (who regularly try to "help out the author" in such moments) than that he wrote something as perfectly intelligible as the Majority Text reading and a scribe (or scribes) changed it to something so difficult to account for.

So I begin this discussion with the text of 𝔓[46] and B in hand as original and offer an interpretation that accords with what has preceded. The Greek text in this case reads,

1:21–22 Καὶ ὑμᾶς ποτε ὄντας ἀπηλλοτριωμένους καὶ ἐχθροὺς τῇ διανοίᾳ ἐν τοῖς ἔργοις τοῖς πονηροῖς, νυνὶ δὲ ἀποκατηλλάγητε **ἐν τῷ σώματι τῆς σαρκὸς αὐτοῦ διὰ τοῦ θανάτου παραστῆσαι** ὑμᾶς ἁγίους καὶ ἀμώμους καὶ ἀνεγκλήτους **κατενώπιον αὐτοῦ**.

*And you, once being alienated and enemies in your minds by means of your evil deeds, but now you have been reconciled **in the body of his flesh through death in order to present** you holy and unblemished and beyond reproach **before him**.*

---

[56] It is not difficult to see what may have happened. Paul started his sentence with an accusative that he intended to be the object of the verb, but when he came to the main clause, the emphasis on the *contrast* itself took over in the form of a νυνὶ δέ (*but now*), which then launched him into a contrast in which *they themselves* were still the focus.

[57] See Lightfoot, 252–53; cf. Metzger, *Textual Commentary*, 554–55. Interestingly, Dunn (105 n. 1) admits that this reading "meets all the criteria to be counted as original"; nonetheless, "since the second person passive fits so badly we may be justified in concluding that the early correction/improvement was wholly justified," he then proceeds to comment only on the acknowledged secondary text; cf. Barth and Blanke, 220–21.

Our difficulties are the same as before, and they would not be greatly different if the Majority Text were in fact original. As before, the antecedent of the pronoun in "the body of his flesh" is universally recognized to be the Son (or, for most, Christ), even though only pronouns have preceded this passage as far back as v. 14. At issue are the assumed subject of the infinitive "to present you" and who is the one "before whom" they are to be presented.

The majority of interpreters, on the other hand, are commenting on a text that reads, "*He has reconciled* in the body of *his* flesh in order to present you blameless [etc.] *before him.*" Again they are faced with enormous problems, since (an unexpressed) "God" is assumed to be the "he"; but they also recognize that the first pronoun cannot refer to the subject (even though all rules of grammar argue that it should), so it is translated "but now by **Christ's** death in **his body of flesh and blood** <u>God has reconciled</u> you <u>to himself</u>" (REB; cf. NIV/TNIV). And the reasons for doing so remain the same as in the preceding clause: for Paul, it is argued, God does the reconciling, and therefore the Son, who has died and risen, then presents believers before God at the eschaton. It should be pointed out, however, that even in this secondary (majority) text, this is not a necessary option.

In Paul's original text, this is even a lesser option. The passive most likely exists for the same reasons as Paul uses the periphrasis ("all the fullness") in the preceding clause: to keep the focus on Christ and the Colossians. This passive offers a similar kind of circumlocution: "you were reconciled" is a divine passive, which when made active would say, "God reconciled you." But that is not what Paul says. By means of the passive, he can keep his focus on the Son, who in this case did the reconciling by means of his (truly) bodily death; and he did this so that at the end the Colossians (and all other believers) might be presented before the heavenly court, and thus in the Son's own presence at the eschaton, blameless and holy.

As with the preceding clause, therefore, there are no *grammatical* grounds of any kind to change the referent of the pronoun from the Son to the Father. Not only has the Son been the grammatical referent of all seventeen of the masculine pronouns since v. 14—relative, personal, and intensive[58]—but also the only mention of God as the subject of a clause is the more oblique (and grammatically neuter) "all the fullness." Rather than change Paul's sentence to conform to what we might have been led otherwise to expect, we should recognize that here is yet one more instance in the corpus where Paul simply assumes that the Son shares divine prerogatives with the Father. Thus, as with the "judgment seat" itself, which alternatively

---

[58] And this is so even if one might argue that conceptually, Paul is not driving this point home all the way through the passage; that is, he might very well have lost sight of "the Son" as the explicit antecedent, since at the very end of the passage (v. 24) he has finally changed the referent to Christ. But there is no question that the one who is first called "the Son," whatever other designation ("Christ" or "the Lord") might fit the context better, is the constant referrent throughout the entire passage.

refers to Christ or God,[59] so also with this prepositional phrase that points to believers being in the divine Presence at the eschaton, Paul sees them as in the presence of both the Son and the Father.[60] In this case, the Son is pictured as presenting believers "before God," to be sure, but the focus is on their being in his own presence as well—the presence of the One who redeemed them.

Colossians 2:2–3

Rather than moving directly into an elaboration of his opening prelude (or overture) by applying it to the Colossians' own situation (which he finally does at 2:6), Paul begins with an explanation of his own role in proclaiming the gospel, especially for the sake of Gentiles (1:24–2:5). In so doing, he both co-opts some of the language that he used in the first thanksgiving (1:9–11) and elaborates it in such a way that one may be sure he is going right for the jugular with regard to the "heady" nature of the problem. Picking up the words σύνεσις (*understanding*), ἐπίγνωσις ([*real*] *knowledge*), and σοφία (*wisdom*) from 1:9 and the words μυστήριον (*mystery*) and ἀπόκρυφοι (*hidden*) from Jewish apocalyptic, Paul turns all of the Colossians' idle speculations into a focus on Christ. Thus, with a sentence that (apparently) tries to include all of their language, he states that his goal among the Gentiles is that "they may have the full riches of *complete understanding*, in order that they may *know* the *mystery* of God, Christ himself, in whom are *hidden* all the treasures of *wisdom* and *knowledge*." Thus the "mystery" is no longer hidden; it has been fully revealed in Christ.

In typical fashion, therefore, Paul has co-opted the language of his "opponents" and has transmuted it to serve his own purposes, which is to place Christ once more at the center of everything for the Colossians. In so doing, he also once again perceives Christ as being in the highest role. Everything that can be known about God, both his wisdom and knowledge about him, has now been revealed in Christ, in whom "all the fullness of the deity lives in bodily form" (2:9).

Thus, even though most of Paul's concern from this point on is with Christ as Redeemer, he has felt compelled at the beginning to present Christ as fully divine: preexistent, Creator, the one in whom all the fullness of the Deity dwells, and the ultimate revealer of "the mystery" of God. And all of this, apparently, is to defrock the powers and divest them of whatever hold they may have had on the Colossian believers. God himself has come present in Christ, who has delivered these Gentile believers not only from their sins but also from the burden of "doing the law" and is himself the source

---

[59] See discussion on 2 Cor 5:10 in ch. 4 (pp. 190–92) and Rom 14:10 in ch. 6 (pp. 262–67).

[60] On this matter, see esp. discussion on 2 Cor 2:10 and 8:21 in ch. 4 (pp. 188–89).

of life and righteousness in the new creation—thus he is sufficient for life now and forever.

And this calls for a final word. One of the tragedies of this kind of exegetical exercise occurs if we focus on the "meaning" of the passage and thus lose the Pauline focus altogether, which is on the utter greatness and glory of Christ. In trying to "get it right" with regard to *what* Paul says, we are in constant great danger of "getting it wrong" as to *why* he says it at all—the ever-present danger of doing with this grand passage what Jesus castigated the Pharisees for doing with the law: to turn from worship and adoration to fine-tuning our exegesis and thus never returning to worship and adoration. To do that, I would argue, would in the end defeat the Christology altogether. We simply have not entered into an understanding of Paul's understanding of his Lord if we are not drawn into his own absolute adoration and devotion. In the end, this passage should cause us to genuflect more than gesture.

Excursus: Christ and Wisdom in Colossians

What many scholars would find missing in the foregoing discussion of Col 1:15–17 is any mention of personified Wisdom as lying behind Paul's language in the "hymn." That absence, of course, was by design, since Wisdom does not obviously factor into Paul's presentation.[61] But since so many argue or simply assert otherwise,[62] we need to take a close look at the alleged evidence for this before bringing this section to a conclusion.

Given the exegesis presented above, where it is pointed out on the basis of grammar and usage that the whole passage fits presuppositionally within Paul's standard Son of God Christology, the question is, How did anyone ever come to see personified Wisdom as lying behind what Paul says? The answer is threefold. First, the relationship that was

---

[61]Ridderbos (*Paul*, 79–80) likewise rejects this notion in Colossians, which he characterizes as "vague reminiscences"—and even that is being kind.

[62]Indeed, Dunn (*Christology in the Making*, xix–xx) makes genuine interaction with him on this passage a bit difficult because he disallows such interaction at the very point where it must be done, namely, with his finding the "solution" to this text in Wisdom, which is neither linguistically nor conceptually present in this passage. He insists, rather, that further dialogue on the Colossians passage can move forward only if we allow his claim that "the identification of Christ with Wisdom . . . has been documented in sufficient detail in *Christology*" so as not to be "the issue in dispute" (xix). But this amounts to closing the door in advance on the very issue that must be in dispute. After all, (1) Paul himself identifies the person being celebrated in the "hymn" as God's beloved Son (v. 13); and (2) as will be pointed out here, his alleged verbal echoes of Jewish Wisdom are basically nonexistent (unless one considers such things to exist by fiat). So in order to carry on the conversation, one must deny that Paul's own grammar has any significance at all, and in its place one must assent to what are at best *distant verbal echoes* of words from texts that Paul cannot otherwise be demonstrated to have known.

pointed out between this passage and 1 Cor 8:6 is almost always the starting point.[63] Once one has discovered (nonexistent) personified Wisdom in that passage, based on Paul's (ironic) use of power and wisdom in 1 Cor 1:18–25 (!), the connection with this passage seems easy enough to make, given that the two parts of the Colossian "hymn" elaborate the two parts of the 1 Corinthians clause. Second, it has often been noted that the error in Colossae is something of a "heady" business, since the language of wisdom and knowledge creeps up several times; thus Paul can be seen to be rescuing "Wisdom" for the purposes of his gospel. Third, support for this view is then found in alleged verbal/linguistic connections in this passage to some isolated moments in the wisdom tradition, all of which are ultimately dependent on the Wisdom of Solomon. Since we have already noted favorably the connection of Col 1:15–17 with 1 Cor 8:6 (but without mentioning Wisdom, since Paul himself does not), we now investigate the other two items that have been seen to support a Wisdom Christology.

Paul's Actual Use of the Word Σοφία ("Wisdom")

One of the keys as to whether Paul has personified Wisdom as backdrop to his view of Christ in this letter is to see how, and how often, he actually uses the word σοφία (*wisdom*) itself, which he does in fact 6 times (for convenience, I have the language of "wisdom" underlined; the boldface is where Christ is specifically connected to wisdom).

1:9 πληρωθῆτε τὴν ἐπίγνωσιν τοῦ θελήματος αὐτοῦ ἐν πάσῃ σοφίᾳ καὶ συνέσει πνευματικῇ

1:28 καὶ διδάσκοντες πάντα ἄνθρωπον ἐν πάσῃ σοφίᾳ

2:3 ἐν ᾧ εἰσιν πάντες **οἱ θησαυροὶ τῆς σοφίας καὶ γνώσεως ἀπόκρυφοι**

2:23 ἅτινά ἐστιν λόγον μὲν ἔχοντα σοφίας ἐν ἐθελοθρησκίᾳ καὶ ταπεινοφροσύνῃ

3:16 ἐν πάσῃ σοφίᾳ διδάσκοντες καὶ νουθετοῦντες ἑαυτούς

4:5 ἐν σοφίᾳ περιπατεῖτε πρὸς τοὺς ἔξω τὸν καιρὸν ἐξαγοραζόμενοι

This high occurrence (for Paul) of the word σοφία may very well say something about the situation in Colossae, which is especially suggested by what Paul says in 2:23 about the church's gravitation toward being "observant" as having the "appearance of wisdom." However, this usage has to do not with personified Wisdom but with the attribute of wisdom. So also with his insistence that "all the treasures of wisdom and knowl-

---

[63]See above, pp. 299–303.

edge are hidden in Christ." This is the one place where Christ and wisdom are actually juxtaposed in the letter; but this is a far cry from Christ's assuming the role of personified Wisdom, since none of Paul's language belongs to that tradition. Finally, the three occurrences of ἐν πάσῃ σοφίᾳ are not designed to catch anyone's attention at all; Paul has taught—and they are to teach—others "with all wisdom," which has to do with the manner of teaching, not its content, and implies the same attributive understanding of the word. The same is true of their being filled with the knowledge of God's will, which will come by the Spirit's wisdom and insight (1:9).[64] To "walk in wisdom" toward outsiders (4:5) simply means to "walk wisely."

Paul's actual usage of σοφία in Colossians thus does very little to generate hope that in 1:15–17 he is thinking of God's Son in terms of *personified* Wisdom. Locating all the treasures of "wisdom and knowledge" in Christ, thus making Christ himself the depository of all the wisdom of God, is not the same things as identifying him with Lady Wisdom herself. Nor does the language of any of these uses appear in the Jewish Wisdom literature in contexts where wisdom is being personified. Although "wisdom" was part of the issue that Paul was rebutting, this says very little in favor of his alleged use of other language found in the wisdom tradition and applying it to Christ, which in fact he does not.

Paul's Alleged Use of "Wisdom" Vocabulary

The greater issue regarding Paul's vocabulary in Colossians is not in fact his use of the word σοφία but his use of *other* language that is alleged to be the special province not only of the Wisdom literature per se but also of Lady Wisdom in particular.[65] And here is where the argument ultimately is grounded regarding personified Wisdom as lying behind the first strophe of the "hymn" in 1:15–17. Thus it has been asserted by Dunn that Paul here uses "a sequence of correlation [between Paul and personified Wisdom that] can hardly be a matter of coincidence." Indeed, Dunn further claims that Paul's language in this passage (and in 1 Cor 8:6) offers "classic expressions of Wisdom christology."[66] But despite this assertion, there is a rather complete lack of both

---

[64] On this being the most likely meaning of this language, see Fee, *God's Empowering Presence*, 640–43.

[65] Note, e.g., C. H. Dodd: "Every point can be traced to Jewish Wisdom theology" ("The History and Doctrine of the Apostolic Age," in *A Companion to the Bible* [ed. T. W. Manson; Edinburgh: T&T Clark, 1947], 409); cf. Dunn: "The writer here is taking over language used of divine Wisdom and reusing it to express the significance of Christ" (89).

[66] Dunn, *Theology of Paul*, 269; the whole of his presentation, here rebutted, appears on pp. 268–70, concluding with "Clearly, then, Paul was attributing to *Christ* the role previously attributed to divine Wisdom." Such clarity, it would seem, as with beauty, is in the eye of the beholder!

linguistic and conceptual ties to this tradition. Dunn's "sequence of correlation" turns out to consist of five points (including Christ's role in creation, the crucial and controversial point that will be examined in appendix A [pp. 606–18]). The other four are primarily linguistic and require close scrutiny here, to which the word ἀρχή from v. 18 is added as well, since that word is also often brought into the discussion. Since only two of these (εἰκών and ἀρχή) actually occur in the wisdom tradition and εἰκών is the one with which all these conversations begin, these will be reserved for the end in order to give them their proper due. We begin here with the second one, Paul's use of πρωτότοκος in v. 15.

1. Personified Wisdom, it is commonly alleged, is called "God's 'firstborn' in creation."[67] But this is altogether misleading, since Paul's word (πρωτότοκος) occurs nowhere in the entire wisdom tradition.[68] The texts brought forward, Prov 8:22, 25, not only have quite different words in the Septuagint, but also their point (the fact that Wisdom is the first of God's "creations" so that she might be present to frolic as he creates all else) is something considerably different from Paul's use of πρωτότοκος here, where Christ *as Son* holds the rights of primogeniture with regard to every created thing, since they were all created *in* him and *through* him and *for* him.

The lack of this word in the Wisdom literature itself has caused scholars to turn to the Alexandrian Jewish philosopher Philo to bail them out at this point. But the word used by Philo with regard to the Logos is πρωτόγονος, where in each of its three occurrences it is *an adjective accompanying the word "son."*[69] Furthermore, in each case it carries

---

[67] See Dunn, *Theology of Paul,* 269; cf. Lohse, 48 (and his extensive n. 113); repeated often throughout the literature.

[68] At least not in Paul's sense (see n. 35 above). Besides the two dubious examples cited there, Dunn also gives two references to Philo as supporting this "parallel" (*Ebr.* 30–31; *QG* 4.97); but these are equally dubious. In the first passage, Philo speaks of God having union with "knowledge," who "bore the only beloved son who is apprehended by the senses, the world which we see" (LCL 3.335); "knowledge" is then equated with wisdom, at which point Philo "cites" Prov 8:22 in his own way: "God obtained me first [πρωτίστην] of all his works." But that is not even remotely related to Paul's use of πρωτότοκος, which has to do not with the Son's being *created* first but with his having the *role* of firstborn, heir and sovereign over all creation. The other passage exists only in an Armenian translation, which helps not at all here. It should be noted further that in any case, with this particular word, Philo stands altogether on the other side of things. The word πρωτότοκος occurs 45 times in Philo, always and only in the context of the OT narrative regarding an actual "firstborn" son or animal (never of a daughter!). On his actual word, πρωτόγονος, see the next note.

[69] *Agr.* 51; *Conf.* 146; *Somn.* 1.215; Philo's phrase πρωτόγονον υἱόν (*firstborn son*) means specifically "the first son out of the womb"; and in none of these three instances is God's wisdom mentioned. Dunn makes the astounding assertion that "the antecedent for use of the word πρωτότοκος . . . in relation to creation is *most obviously* Wisdom" (90 [italics mine]). In a footnote he lists four references in support (Prov 8:22, 25; Philo, *Ebr.* 30–31; *QG* 4.97), none of which contain this word. In an-

the sense of "the first male out of the womb" and thus none of the additional sense of having the rights of primogeniture or of inheritance. Thus, Philo does not offer even oblique help in finding the word πρωτότοκος in the Wisdom literature. Moreover, it is hard to imagine that even the most high-minded Jewish author of the first century could think of a *woman* in terms of a "firstborn *son*."[70] So not only does Paul's "titular" word not appear in the Wisdom literature with reference to personified Wisdom, but also it is altogether unlikely that the male authors of our texts could even have imagined as much.

2. It is also asserted that when Sir 1:4 speaks of Wisdom as "before all things," this "correlates" with what Paul says here of the Son. But this is particularly dubious, since not only does Sirach's phrase have a different word, but also he means something almost the opposite of Paul's meaning!

Col 1:17a   καὶ αὐτός ἐστιν πρὸ πάντων
         and he himself is before all things

Sir 1:4a   προτέρα πάντων ἔκτισται σοφία
         Wisdom *was created* before all things else

Sir 1:9a   κύριος αὐτὸς ἔκτισεν αὐτήν
         the Lord himself created her

In saying that "Wisdom *was created* before all things [προτέρα πάντων]," Sirach almost certainly means "before all things else."[71] Thus Sirach is simply reflecting on Prov 8:22–31, that the earth's "wise" design means that God in his own wisdom created the world; when Wisdom is then personified, she of necessity must have been "created before all things else." Paul, on the other hand, says that the Son ἐστιν πρὸ πάντων (*is before all things*), by which he means that the Son, through whom all things were created, *is* "before them" by virtue of his preexistence "temporally" and in terms of his primacy of rank. Thus this phrase from Sirach offers neither verbal nor conceptual correspondence to Paul's understanding of the Son as eternally preexistent.

3. Further, Paul's statement that "in him [the Son] all things hold together [συνέστηκεν]" is alleged to correspond to Wis 1:6–7, where the author speaks of "*that which* holds all things together [τὸ συνέχον],"

other footnote he then dismisses Ps 89:27 as "less relevant here," and this despite the fact that the actual antecedent of this word in Col 1:15 is the Davidic Son of God in v. 13. One should perhaps note that Philo's actual word, πρωτόγονος, occurs only twice in the Septuagint, one of which is with reference to Israel (Sir 36:17).

[70] This makes M. R. D'Angelo's rewriting of the hymn as to Sophia quite fanciful (see MacDonald, 66).

[71] See P. W. Skehan and A. A. di Lella, *The Wisdom of Ben Sira* (AB 39; Garden City, N.Y.: Doubleday, 1987), 136.

where "that which" in this case refers specifically to "the spirit" of the Lord. Again, here are the two texts:

Col 1:17b καὶ <u>τὰ πάντα ἐν αὐτῷ συνέστηκεν</u>

Wis 1:7 ὅτι <u>πνεῦμα κυρίου</u> πεπλήρωκεν τὴν οἰκουμένην,
καὶ <u>τὸ συνέχον τὰ πάντα</u> γνῶσιν ἔχει φωνῆς.

To find personified Wisdom here requires several leaps of faith.[72] First, there is the very complex issue regarding the translation of Wis 1:6; that is, when Pseudo-Solomon says that "wisdom is a kindly spirit," is the author equating Wisdom with the spirit of the Lord or—and this seems far more likely—referring to the "spiritual" quality of wisdom? Second, the personification of Wisdom in this book does not begin seriously until 6:12,[73] and except for a cameo appearance in 14:2, the personification ceases abruptly at 10:21, which means that personified Wisdom is not to be found in over two-thirds of the book. Third, the author does not in fact say that "Wisdom holds all things together";[74] rather, "the spirit" does. The only way this could be turned into a "source" for Wisdom Christology in Paul is to argue that for Pseudo-Solomon, "spirit" and "wisdom" are identical, which is not even a remote possibility. So even if Paul knew this passage, it could hardly have influenced him unless he himself would have understood the identity to be so—a most unlikely scenario.

---

[72] F. Thielman (*Theology of the New Testament: A Canonical and Synthetic Approach* [Grand Rapids: Zondervan, 2005]) acknowledges the strength of my prior argument against Wisdom Christology ("Wisdom Christology in Paul: A Dissenting View") but then proposes that "there is enough verbal and conceptual overlap between what Paul says about Christ in Col. 1:15–17 . . . and Wisd. 1:6–7 . . . to make a plausible case for Paul's *intentional* echo of some of them" (379 n. 15 [italics mine]). Indeed, to consider this text one such text would seem to make the case for Wisdom even weaker. This is an unfortunate blot on an otherwise superb study of Paul's theology.

[73] Σοφία is mentioned in an introductory way in the proem in 1:4, 6 but not as fully personified.

[74] Dunn also appeals to several instances in Philo where he says the same thing of Logos; but that is to assume what must be proven, not simply asserted, namely, that Logos and Sophia are interchangeable ideas for either author but especially for the author of Wisdom. This "interchange" is based primarily on the parallelism of Wis 9:1–2; but that is an especially doubtful understanding of this text, for two reasons: (1) this is the beginning of Solomon's prayer for wisdom, and throughout the prayer the guise of personification is basically dropped by the author; and (2) the doublet in vv. 1 and 2 is an example of "step," not "synonymous," parallelism. Thus, God created the world through his λόγος, and he fashioned human beings in his σοφία. These lines do not speak of creation twice but rather express two steps and plainly separate acts of creation, echoing day 1 and day 6; and the fashioning of human beings is not the same thing as creating the entire universe. See in the present volume appendix A, pp. 607–9.

Christology in Colossians (and Philemon)323

4. We turn then, finally, to the two words that Paul does share with the wisdom tradition; at issue is whether he also shares their meaning, so that one could argue that Paul was either *dependent* on this tradition or even *incidentally* used words in a way similar to the tradition. We begin with Paul's calling Christ ἀρχή in 1:18. Interestingly, this word occurs with reference to Wisdom only in Prov 8:22–23 and in Sir 24:9, which is simply an echo of Prov 8:23. And the likelihood that the Septuagint translator of Prov 8:23 intended to identify "Wisdom" with the word ἀρχή is especially remote. After all, the author's own elaboration of v. 22 in v. 23 specifically identifies her not with this word as such but with her being present "*at* the beginning," before the creation itself. And since this is the only way Sirach understood it (24:9; cf. 1:4), it is quite unlikely that Paul had Lady Wisdom in mind when he called the risen Son the "beginning." So the case rests altogether on a single usage in Philo, who does in fact speak of God's wisdom in this way (*Leg.* 1.43). But it is not at all clear that he is thinking in terms of personified Wisdom;[75] and Paul seems obviously to be reflecting Gen 1:1 and is thinking of Christ in terms of the new creation—an idea totally foreign to the wisdom tradition.

5. That leads us at last to εἰκών (*image*), the term that is always the first to be brought forward as an indication of Paul's dependence on Wisdom.[76] Indeed, C. K. Barrett made bold to say that "*image* is a word that belongs to the Wisdom literature," citing Wis 7:26 as evidence.[77] This is a plain overstatement of the case, since this is

---

[75] This is especially so since two paragraphs later he says similar things of virtue. Colson and Whitaker (LCL 1.175) certainly did not think so, and they are quite ready to capitalize these words when they are considered personification. Here they read, "By using many words for it Moses has already made it manifest that the sublime and heavenly wisdom is of many names," which include "beginning, image, and vision of God." And in any case, bringing Philo into a discussion of the Wisdom literature is itself somewhat problematic—all the more so when it is the *only possible referent* that one has.

[76] To be fair, this is because it comes first in Paul's presentation; but it is also clear from the literature that here is the one word where scholars are most confident of having a genuine *verbal* correspondence.

[77] C. K. Barrett, *Paul: An Introduction to His Thought* (Louisville: Westminster John Knox, 1994), 146–47. Cf. Dunn, "particularly Wis. 7:26" (88), which along with his second reference (Philo, *Leg.* 1.43) are the only two possible references in the literature; and whatever else, Wis 7:26 does not say that Wisdom is "the image of God." That this is rhetoric more than scholarship became evident when I asked my seminar (p. xxviii above), on the basis of Barrett's sentence and Dunn's "particularly," how many occurrences of this word one might expect in the literature. They were taken aback to learn that it appears only this one time. Unfortunately, Thielman (see n. 72 above) references this as the other "verbal and conceptual overlap" between Paul and Wisdom—unfortunate not only because the two authors are so far apart in their actual usage of this language but even more so because Paul is far more likely echoing Gen 1 and 2.

in fact the *only* occurrence of the word with this sense in the entire literature.[78]

More importantly, Paul and Pseudo-Solomon do not reflect truly parallel uses of language; for personified Wisdom is not "the εἰκών of God," nor is she seen to exist *in* the image of God. Rather, she is but "an image of his *goodness*" (εἰκὼν τῆς ἀγαθότητος αὐτοῦ)—one of the clear concerns of the author. Paul, on the other hand, is intending something very much like what he says in 2 Cor 4:4–6: the unseen God can now be known in his beloved Son (Col 1:13), who alone bears the true image of the Father, to whom Paul has been giving thanks (v. 12).

Moreover, the two authors share nothing in common as to the source of this usage. The further evidence from 3:10–11, where all agree that Paul is echoing Gen 1–2, argues strongly that Paul is doing the same in its first occurrence here and that it therefore has to do with the incarnate, now exalted, Son. Thus God's Son is the one who alone bears the "image" of the unseen God; and in Rom 8:29 God's predestining purpose is for the Son to conform those who are his into that same image, which had been defaced in the fall.

The usage in Wisdom, on the other hand, has no connection with the Genesis account at all; rather, the phrase is the last in a series of the twenty-eight descriptors regarding personified Wisdom, and in her case it has been triggered by the *metaphor of a mirror*, not by Gen 1–2. A look at the text of Wis 7:26 verifies this lack of correspondence. In a series of doublets and triplets that extol Wisdom's incomparable greatness, the third set appears thus:

<u>ἀπαύγασμα</u> γάρ ἐστιν φωτὸς ἀιδίου
>   For she is a *reflection* of eternal light,

καὶ <u>ἔσοπτρον ἀκηλίδωτον</u> τῆς τοῦ θεοῦ ἐνεργείας
>   *a spotless mirror* of the working of God,

καὶ <u>εἰκὼν</u> τῆς ἀγαθότητος αὐτου.
>   and *an image* of his goodness.

This is a threefold play on mirror imagery as such and is thus quite unrelated to Genesis. The middle member refers to the mirror itself, while the first and third lines indicate what Wisdom reflects of God's nature and character. First (line 1), as to God's nature, she merely reflects the light in which God dwells eternally; she is neither the light itself nor the source of light. Second (line 3), as to God's character, Wisdom is a mirror image of his goodness; again, she is neither goodness herself nor

---

[78] It is elsewhere found in Sir 17:3 and Wis 2:23 with direct reference to Gen 1:27, and in Pseudo-Solomon in several instances referring to idols (Wis 13:13, 16; 14:15, 17; 15:5) and once in a metaphorical way (17:21) referring to darkness. But these uses are so completely unrelated to personified Wisdom that they count for nothing.

the source of goodness. Whatever else may be true of this analogy, therefore, the imagery is not an echo of Genesis, nor does it come close to what Paul says in Col 1:15 of God's Son: he himself *is* the εἰκών of the otherwise unseeable God.

Thus, when Paul uses the term here, as in earlier instances the concern is that *the Son alone* bears the true likeness of the Father. In this way, although not explicitly stated, the Son also becomes the second Adam, bearing the *divine* image in his humanity;[79] at the same time, he also bears that image in *his own* humanity, the image that Adam and Eve had been intended to bear. It is hard to get around the supposition of incarnation in this clause, especially in light of the clauses that follow. Christ has made God known precisely because as God's Son he perfectly bore the divine image in his earthly life and crucifixion.

These various strands of questionable "parallels" therefore hardly constitute the kind of "sequence of correlation" asserted by Dunn and assumed throughout much of the literature. Indeed, there are no true *linguistic* ties in the Colossian passage with the Wisdom literature at all; and whether one can argue for *conceptual* ties without the linguistic ties seems to be a moot point. What Paul's sentences point to instead is a Son of God Christology, in which he uses *biblical* images from Genesis and the Davidic kingship. Some kind of clear *literary* or *conceptual* dependence of Paul on the Wisdom literature needs to be demonstrated—such as vv. 12–14 demonstrably have with Israel's basic story—in order for us to entertain the idea of a Wisdom Christology in Paul's thought. But that is precisely what is lacking, both here and elsewhere in the Pauline corpus.

Furthermore, what often is not said, but needs to be, is that even those who find Wisdom here are confronted by the reality that *most* of what Paul says in this "hymn" has no relationship to Wisdom at all. Indeed, as Martin, for example, points out about the second part of line *b'*, "No Jewish writer rose to these heights in daring to predict that wisdom was the ultimate goal of all creation."[80] And since the "parallels" are only in the mind of the beholder, the same could be said of all the alleged parallels, including that between Christ and Wisdom as the agent of creation, for, apart from this altogether dubious one, there simply is no parallel of any kind in Paul's writings between Christ and personified Wisdom. Since everything for this point of view ultimately hinges on the issue of Wisdom's agency in creation, that matter will be given full attention in appendix A at the end of this book.

---

[79] On this matter, see discussion in ch. 4 on 2 Cor 3:18; 4:4 and in ch. 6 on Rom 8:29.

[80] Martin, 58. This is said in a context where he quite misconstrues what Paul says about the Son in this poem. He is certainly not creation's "artificer" (Wis 8:6), as Martin asserts; the Son in fact is the sphere in which creation takes place ("in him"), and he himself is the one through whom it all happens.

Christ as Exalted Lord

Although the use of κύριος (*Lord*) is comparatively less frequent in Colossians than the mention of Christ or the Son, it occurs at precisely the same kinds of places as it did in Romans. In Colossians, however, Christ as Lord is also the assumption of an occasional argument, even though the title itself does not occur. We have already noted this regarding 1:18, where the Son by virtue of his resurrection has assumed the place of absolute supremacy in the universe. In that context the not-so-hidden agenda was on his role as Lord over the powers for the sake of the church. We now examine the several passages in which Christ as Lord is made explicit; what emerges is that κύριος occurs primarily with regard to ethical/behavioral concerns. This becomes clear as we take them in their order of appearance in the letter.

Colossians 1:10

In this first mention of Christ as κύριος after the opening thanksgiving (1:3), Paul prays that the Colossians will be filled with the Spirit's wisdom and understanding[81] so that they may "walk" in a way that is worthy of "the Lord." The ethical implications are clear. The christological presupposition is that their present life is to be seen as under Christ's lordship and therefore as accountable to him in all their actions. Thus once again, Christ as Lord assumes the role that in Paul's Judaism would belong to God alone.

Colossians 2:6

In this first sentence of the main body of the letter—in terms of Paul's concerns for the Colossians themselves—he starts by picking up the ethical/behavioral concern expressed in the περιπατῆσαι (*walk*) of the opening prayer (1:9). Here it is expressed plainly: just as they have received τὸν Χριστὸν Ἰησοῦν τὸν κύριον ([*the*] *Christ Jesus,* [*who is*] *the Lord*), so they are to "walk" *in* him, meaning "in the sphere of his lordship." Since this is the only occurrence of this unusual phrasing in Paul's letters,[82] there is every good reason to believe that he intended the phrase to be understood as here punctuated. If so, then those several English translations that have rendered it "receive Christ Jesus as Lord"[83] are very much on the mark, where the em-

---

[81]For this understanding of this phrase, see Fee, *God's Empowering Presence,* 641–43 (cf. now the TNIV).

[82]Up to this point, the order "Christ Jesus the/our Lord" has occurred only 3 times (1 Cor 15:31; Rom 6:23; 8:39); after this it will occur only in Phil 3:8 (with the unique addition of "my" with Lord). The totally unexpected feature of the present usage is the repeated definite article (once with "Christ" and once with "Lord").

[83]So NIV/TNIV, REB, GNB, NLT, NET BIBLE; cf. the NET BIBLE footnote: "Though the verb παραλάβετε does not often take a double accusative, here it seems to do so," which is then spelled out in a bit more detail.

phasis is on the Colossians' recognition of the lordship of the Christ whom they have "received." That is, in their becoming believers they not only believed in Christ Jesus but also revered him as their Lord, vis-à-vis all other "lords" in both the religious cults and the empire.

Thus, Christ's lordship assumed in the opening prayer is here expressed in terms of the Colossians' "receiving" Christ as their Lord, meaning that they have taken his lordship to be their primary frame of reference in this new life, which is then elaborated with a double shift of metaphors. As a tree, they are to be firmly rooted (ἐρριζωμένοι) in the Lord;[84] and as a temple,[85] they are to be built on him. This imperative is brought up front as the first matter in the letter probably because in Paul's view their current fascination with the Jewish law and their giving too great a role to the powers have had the twofold effect of dethroning Christ and of moving the Colossians onto the wrong ground for truly godly living. As always, Christ as Lord is a presupposed and dominant feature of Paul's Christology.

Colossians 3:1–4

In a passage that serves as a kind of inclusio with 2:6, this paragraph does several things at once. First, by means of its opening words, εἰ συνηγέρθητε τῷ Χριστῷ (*if you have been raised with Christ*), it stands in explicit relationship with 2:20–23, which begins, εἰ ἀπεθάνετε σὺν Χριστῷ (*if you have died with Christ*). Second, by these same clauses Paul also brings the Colossians back to their baptism, noted above in 2:11–13, where he reminded them that they "died" to their former life and "rose" to a new life. Third, and now especially with 2:20–23 in view, he is about to move on to explain *what* in the past they have died to (the sins of their former way of life [3:5–9]) and that their "doing law" in terms of not touching or tasting has no value at all with regard to such sins. What they need to learn is to live in keeping with their new life, a life now raised with Christ and hidden in him who is their life—a life therefore that will reflect his character and likeness (3:12–15).

In making this point at the outset (3:1), even though the word κύριος does not appear explicitly, it is again, as in Rom 8:34, assumed by Paul's echo of Ps 110:1. Christ is the messianic "Lord" seated at God the Father's right hand. But the emphasis in this case is not on his present ministry of intercession; rather, Paul places him in heaven "above," at the "right hand of

---

[84] This assumes that the antecedent of the ἐν αὐτῷ is in fact τὸν κύριον, not the whole phrase "Christ Jesus as Lord." Paul's emphasis seems to be on their receiving him *as* Lord, and thus in their being "rooted" in the Lord they now serve.

[85] This assumes that the building metaphor assumed by Paul is, as almost everywhere, the people of God as the new-covenant temple of God. This is explicitly stated in, e.g., 1 Cor 3:16–17; it is also especially the point made in the companion letter, at Eph 2:20–22, where the same verb appears specifically with regard to the temple (even if Paul did not write Ephesians, its author surely understood the passage in Colossians in this way).

God," primarily to refocus the Colossians' own worldview. Their minds are set on "earthly [below] things," and thus they are enamored with the powers and the law, and their "ethics" are earthbound, having to do with "handle, touch, taste" (2:21). They need to have their minds retooled so as to focus on Christ seated at the right hand of God.

In so doing, they not only acknowledge his current lordship, but also they thereby acknowledge that "in him" they have died to that former life; and their new life is "hidden in Christ," who is their life. So they are now both secure in him in the present (thus no need for the rules) and guaranteed with regard to the future. When Christ their life appears, they too will appear with him "in glory." Thus, in the present they are both rooted in and built on "the Lord" (2:6), and also they are hidden in him. In every way, the Lord now "seated at God's right hand" has absolute sovereignty both for now and for the future. The Christology of such affirmations is self-evident.

Colossians 3:13–17

Paul immediately follows the preceding introduction to the Colossians' new life in Christ by painting their pagan past in graphically strong terms (3:5–9). This is the way of life that they have died to; these are the garments of the old life that they have taken off by entering the waters of Christian baptism. Starting in v. 12, he goes on to describe the "garments" of the new life that is "hid with Christ in God" (vv. 12–15)—a description that looks and sounds remarkably like the words and life of Jesus himself.[86] One of the ways they are to live out their new life in Christ is by "forgiving" one another, just as "the Lord [= Christ][87] has forgiven you" (v. 13).[88] And since his forgiveness is assumed to be of wrongs committed against God himself, Paul thus once more easily and without argument attributes to Christ as Lord a divine role that belongs to God alone.[89]

In v. 15 he then urges that they let "the peace of Christ *rule* in your hearts," meaning not that they experience personal peace in the midst of difficulty but that Christ's peace rule among them collectively, since it is to this "peace" they have been called in the one body, the church. The very fact

---

[86] Note esp. Matt 11:29, where Jesus is recorded as saying, "And learn from me, that I am πραΰς καὶ ταπεινὸς τῇ καρδίᾳ [*gentle and humble in heart*]." These are two of the five words used by Paul in v. 12 regarding the new "clothing" of believers.

[87] This is the apparent understanding of the church, since a large section of the scribal tradition altered it to Χριστός (C K P Ψ 33 81 1739 𝔐 it), while only one MS (ℵ) altered it to θεός. The original is read by 𝔓⁴⁶ A B D* G vg *al.*

[88] Occasionally there are some who would read this κύριος as referring to God the Father on the basis of 2:13; but Pauline usage must prevail here (so Lohse, 148; Martin, 112; O'Brien, 202–3; Dunn, 231; Pokorný, 171; Barth and Blanke, 423).

[89] Cf. Barth and Blanke: "We can observe several times in Paul that God, as also Jesus, can be named as subject for one and the same action, and this represents no contradiction" (423).

that later scribes changed this to read "the peace of God"[90] serves as evidence that their expectations were that this is an attribute ordinarily spoken of God. On this matter, see in ch. 2 on the interchange of this phrase in 1–2 Thessalonians (pp. 69–70).

Paul concludes this passage with a brief admonition (v. 16) that focuses on the role of Christ in their worship, both in word ("the message about Christ") and song, led by the Spirit;[91] at the end he notes that such singing about Christ is ultimately addressed to God.[92] Thus, as the companion passage Eph 5:18–19 makes even more plain, Paul understands Christ to have the central role in both conversion and worship; but in so doing, Christ does not usurp the ultimate role always attributed to God the Father. Just as salvation in Christ is predicated on the love of God, effected through the death of Christ and made effective through the Spirit, so now in worship these roles are played in reverse: the Spirit inspires the singing that has the glory of Christ as its content, all of which is directed ultimately with thanksgiving to God the Father. Passages such as these are part of the mix that led Christians very early on to think of God in the triadic terms that eventually led to the articulation of God as Trinity.

This whole passage—the admonitions regarding both their life together (vv. 12–15) and their worship (v. 16)—is brought together in a single concluding word, which once again offers us insight noted elsewhere about the role of Christ in the new order. Whatever they do, whether it be in word (v. 16) or deed (vv. 12–15), they are to do "all things" in the name of the Lord, Jesus, and through him to offer their thanksgiving to God. On the christological significance of this phrase, see discussion in ch. 2 on 2 Thess 3:6 (pp. 67–68) and in ch. 3 on 1 Cor 1:10 (p. 135).

Colossians 3:18–4:1

At the end of the more general paranesis of 3:12–17, Paul hones in on the relationships within the Christian household (3:18–4:1)—one of the more remarkable moments in Colossians and Philemon. Since two of the four people named in Philemon reappear in the final greetings of this letter (Onesimus [3:9]; Archippus [3:17]), one may rightly assume that Colossians will first be read aloud in Philemon's house church, but so will the letter to Philemon, since it is equally addressed to the church that meets in Philemon's house (Phlm 2). What this means is that both Philemon and (the forgiven) Onesimus will be present for the reading of the present

---

[90] Although this reading became that of the Majority Text, it does not seem to have been known much before the eighth century (in codex Ψ).

[91] For this perspective on this passage, see Fee, *God's Empowering Presence*, 649–57.

[92] Although later scribes changed the θεῷ at the end of v. 16 to κυρίῳ, as a very late assimilation to Eph 5:19.

letter—the only letter besides its companion, Ephesians, where the so-called house rules appear.

The remarkable feature of this passage is the inordinate amount of it that is devoted to slaves.[93] But this is perhaps less remarkable if one considers that both Philemon and Onesimus are present for the first public reading of the letter—although Onesimus may well have been aware of its contents from the time of its writing (4:9). In any case, only four people are in view in the house code itself, and despite their now generalized plurals, they can also be assumed in their first instance to have names: Philemon is a husband (v. 19), father (v. 21), "master" (κύριοι [4:1]); Apphia is a wife (v. 18); Archippus (?) could be a son (v. 20); and Onesimus is a slave (vv. 22–25). What is noteworthy is that 56 out of a total of 116 words (48+ percent of the total) are devoted to the slaves alone while 74 of the 116 (64 percent of the total) are devoted to the relationship between master and slave.

Several things could be speculated regarding this imbalance, but in the end it appears to be a prophylactic against other slaves doing what Onesimus had done that required Paul to write to Philemon in the first place (and served as a secondary occasion for this letter as well). For our present purposes, these historical realities also account for over half the occurrences of the word κύριος (9 of 16) in this letter, where Paul plays on the word that describes the householder in a context where both householder (as κύριος of his household) and all the others in the household have Christ as their common κύριος.

Thus wives and children are to live out their respective roles as those who are ἐν κυρίῳ (*in the Lord*); and although this is a common designation in Paul's writings regarding Christian life in its various aspects, the believers in Colossae would scarcely know that. After all, they do not know Paul personally, and these are the first two occurrences (of four [see 4:7 and 17]) of this phrase in the letter. His point seems to be that despite the fact that a man like Philemon is the κύριος of his own household, his wife and children owe their obedience to him as those who with him live out their Christian lives "in the Lord," thus under Christ's lordship.

But it is the relationship between master and slave that receives top billing. The long word addressed to the slaves, which begins by requiring obedience to their "lords κατὰ σάρκα [*in keeping with their present earthly life*]," is then punctuated by constant reminders that in the end even this obedience is to be understood in light of their relationship to *their one and only* true Lord. Thus they are to serve their earthly "lords" not as "man-pleasers" but with sincerity of heart, "fearing the Lord [Christ]" (v. 22). This only instance

[93] On this passage, see also J. M. G. Barclay, "Ordinary but Different: Colossians and Hidden Moral Identity," *ABR* 49 (2001): 34–52; A. Standhartinger, "The Origin and Intention of the Household Code in the Letter to the Colossians," *JSNT* 79 (2001): 117–30.

of "fear" with Christ as the object is a clear pickup of language from the Septuagint, where the Lord = Yahweh; and here it is "fear" not so much in the negative sense but in the sense of awesome reverence—another moment of high Christology indeed.

Moreover, they are to consider all of the work for their earthly "lords" as working "for the Lord," who is their true Master (v. 23); indeed, Paul goes on, such service will receive what an earthly slave would not ordinarily expect: "an *inheritance* [!] from the Lord as reward." And this is then followed by (probably) the repeated indicative, "It is, after all, the Lord Christ you are serving"[94] even when it is done for your earthly "lord."

The net result is at once a striking play on the language of "lordship" that not only allows Paul to put the household *in toto* under Christ as Lord but also serves as a striking example of how Christ as Lord moderates all earthly relationships. By making a Christian out of the household "lord," God has not only put the householder under Christ's ultimate lordship but at the same time also has set the standard for the nature of that "lordship": Christ himself, who gave himself for those over whom he is the ultimate Lord. In so doing, Paul has so moderated the traditional household that a Christian master who is abusive becomes a total contradiction in terms. And lying behind all of this is Christ as the Lord of Ps 110:1, who is seated in the place of authority as the right hand of God the Father.

Colossians 1:27–29

One final christological moment needs to be noted in this letter that does not easily fit in the categories that have been set out: Col 1:27–29. In the paragraph where Paul is explaining his own role as "apostle to the Gentiles," he places that role totally within the context of the work of Christ, which at the end also has a moment of christological significance. Using the language of "mystery," Paul picks up his new way of understanding the term in light of what Christ has done. "Mystery" has nothing to do with currently "hidden" things; rather, it has to do with what was once "hidden" in God but is now openly manifested in Christ.[95]

At issue is Paul's understanding of the Gentile mission, which he declares in christological terms as having to do with "Christ in you [Gentiles]," who is their own specific hope of attaining the final glory of God (v. 27). When Paul turns to his own role in this mission, he personifies his proclamation in terms of "[Christ] whom we proclaim," the goal of which, whether it

---

[94] Even though the form δουλεύετε is quite ambiguous (either indicative or imperative), the vast majority of English translations and interpreters see it this way, mostly because of the word order (an imperative at the end of a sentence can and does occur, but it is much rarer than in first position).

[95] On this matter, see Fee, *First Epistle to the Corinthians*, 104–5.

be "admonishing" or "teaching," is to present everyone "complete in Christ" (v. 28). This, he adds at the end, is the primary reason for his labor and toil, which in turn are carried out "through the energy that Christ himself powerfully works in me."

Thus this rather complex sentence (vv. 26–29) is another moment of shared prerogative with God the Father. To be sure, the language of ἐνεργέω/ἐνεργεία (*powerful working*) can be attributed to inanimate realities (love, God's word, etc.); but when elsewhere Paul has attributed it directly to divine activity, the one at work is either God the Father (as in Col 2:12; cf. 1 Cor 12:6; Gal 2:8; Phil 2:13) or the Holy Spirit (1 Cor 12:11). Here that same powerful divine working is attributed to Christ.

Conclusion

We should not be surprised to find that the Christology that emerges in Colossians continues the trajectory already found in the earlier letters. But since the local concerns are different, so are Paul's emphases. At the behavioral, ethical level, Paul's Κύριος Christology predominates, just as it did in Romans. What is missing in this case for the second time in the corpus (see Galatians) are echoes of the Septuagint where κύριος = Yahweh.

On the other hand, Paul's messianic Son of God Christology emerges at the very beginning, as a way of including the Gentile Colossians into God's story, which has found its climax in Christ. But this immediately gives way to an eternal Son of God Christology of the most explicit kind found in Paul's letters. Thus, the Son's preexistence is not simply asserted; it is emphasized, as is his role as the divine mediator of creation, both old and new. The entire created order is first of all "in" the Son, as the sphere of its being; at the same time, it came into existence "through him" and "for him." And through his death and resurrection he not only brought redemption, but also he set in motion the *new creation* wherein his people are now being re-created back into the divine image.

Although much of what Paul says here presents some of the highest expressions of Christology in the NT, it is not herewith set forth by Paul for the first time. Rather, what has been implied and presupposed in any number of ways in the earlier letters is here explicitly spelled out as part of the corrective teaching. Thus, in Paul's own language, the Son of God has been raised from the dead so that he might be shown to have the supremacy in all things.

Appendix I: The Texts

(double brackets [[ ]] indicate texts with references to God alone)

Colossians

1:1–2 ¹Παῦλος **ἀπόστολος Χριστοῦ Ἰησοῦ** <u>διὰ θελήματος θεοῦ</u> καὶ Τιμόθεος ὁ ἀδελφὸς ²τοῖς ἐν Κολοσσαῖς ἁγίοις καὶ πιστοῖς **ἀδελφοῖς ἐν Χριστῷ**, χάρις ὑμῖν καὶ εἰρήνη <u>ἀπὸ θεοῦ πατρὸς ἡμῶν</u>.

1:3–4 ³Εὐχαριστοῦμεν <u>τῷ θεῷ πατρὶ</u> **τοῦ κυρίου ἡμῶν Ἰησοῦ Χριστοῦ** πάντοτε περὶ ὑμῶν προσευχόμενοι, ⁴ἀκούσαντες **τὴν πίστιν ὑμῶν ἐν Χριστῷ Ἰησοῦ** καὶ τὴν ἀγάπην ἣν ἔχετε εἰς πάντας τοὺς ἁγίους

1:6–8 ⁶ . . . καὶ ἐπέγνωτε <u>τὴν χάριν τοῦ θεοῦ</u> ἐν ἀληθείᾳ· ⁷καθὼς ἐμάθετε ἀπὸ Ἐπαφρᾶ τοῦ ἀγαπητοῦ συνδούλου ἡμῶν, ὅς ἐστιν πιστὸς ὑπὲρ ὑμῶν **διάκονος τοῦ Χριστοῦ**, ⁸ὁ καὶ δηλώσας ἡμῖν τὴν ὑμῶν ἀγάπην ἐν πνεύματι.

1:9–14 ⁹Διὰ τοῦτο καὶ ἡμεῖς, ἀφ᾽ ἧς ἡμέρας ἠκούσαμεν, οὐ παυόμεθα ὑπὲρ ὑμῶν προσευχόμενοι καὶ αἰτούμενοι, ἵνα πληρωθῆτε <u>τὴν ἐπίγνωσιν τοῦ θελήματος αὐτοῦ</u> ἐν πάσῃ σοφίᾳ καὶ συνέσει πνευματικῇ, ¹⁰περιπατῆσαι **ἀξίως τοῦ κυρίου** εἰς πᾶσαν ἀρεσκείαν, ἐν παντὶ ἔργῳ ἀγαθῷ καρποφοροῦντες καὶ αὐξανόμενοι <u>τῇ ἐπιγνώσει τοῦ θεοῦ</u>, ¹¹ἐν πάσῃ δυνάμει δυναμούμενοι κατὰ τὸ κράτος <u>τῆς δόξης αὐτοῦ</u> εἰς πᾶσαν ὑπομονὴν καὶ μακροθυμίαν, μετὰ χαρᾶς ¹²εὐχαριστοῦντες <u>τῷ πατρὶ τῷ ἱκανώσαντι ὑμᾶς</u> εἰς τὴν μερίδα τοῦ κλήρου τῶν ἁγίων ἐν τῷ φωτί· ¹³<u>ὃς ἐρρύσατο ἡμᾶς</u> ἐκ τῆς ἐξουσίας τοῦ σκότους <u>καὶ μετέστησεν</u> **εἰς τὴν βασιλείαν τοῦ υἱοῦ** <u>τῆς ἀγάπης αὐτοῦ</u>, ¹⁴**ἐν ᾧ ἔχομεν** τὴν ἀπολύτρωσιν, τὴν ἄφεσιν τῶν ἁμαρτιῶν·

1:15–20 ¹⁵**ὅς ἐστιν εἰκὼν** <u>τοῦ θεοῦ τοῦ ἀοράτου</u>, **πρωτότοκος πάσης κτίσεως**, ¹⁶**ὅτι ἐν αὐτῷ ἐκτίσθη τὰ πάντα** ἐν τοῖς οὐρανοῖς καὶ ἐπὶ τῆς γῆς, τὰ ὁρατὰ καὶ τὰ ἀόρατα, εἴτε θρόνοι εἴτε κυριότητες εἴτε ἀρχαὶ εἴτε ἐξουσίαι· **τὰ πάντα δι᾽ αὐτοῦ καὶ εἰς αὐτὸν ἔκτισται·** ¹⁷**καὶ αὐτός ἐστιν πρὸ πάντων καὶ τὰ πάντα ἐν αὐτῷ συνέστηκεν**, ¹⁸**καὶ αὐτός ἐστιν ἡ κεφαλὴ τοῦ σώματος** τῆς ἐκκλησίας· **ὅς ἐστιν ἀρχή, πρωτότοκος ἐκ τῶν νεκρῶν, ἵνα γένηται ἐν πᾶσιν αὐτὸς πρωτεύων**, ¹⁹**ὅτι ἐν αὐτῷ εὐδόκησεν πᾶν τὸ πλήρωμα κατοικῆσαι** ²⁰**καὶ δι᾽ αὐτοῦ ἀποκαταλλάξαι τὰ πάντα εἰς αὐτόν, εἰρηνοποιήσας διὰ τοῦ αἵματος τοῦ σταυροῦ αὐτοῦ, δι᾽ αὐτοῦ** εἴτε τὰ ἐπὶ τῆς γῆς εἴτε τὰ ἐν τοῖς οὐρανοῖς.

1:21–22 ²¹Καὶ ὑμᾶς ποτε ὄντας ἀπηλλοτριωμένους καὶ ἐχθροὺς τῇ διανοίᾳ ἐν τοῖς ἔργοις τοῖς πονηροῖς, ²²νυνὶ δὲ **ἀποκατήλλαξεν ἐν τῷ σώματι τῆς σαρκὸς αὐτοῦ** διὰ τοῦ θανάτου παραστῆσαι ὑμᾶς ἁγίους καὶ ἀμώμους καὶ ἀνεγκλήτους **κατενώπιον αὐτοῦ**,

1:24 Νῦν χαίρω ἐν τοῖς παθήμασιν ὑπὲρ ὑμῶν καὶ ἀνταναπληρῶ τὰ ὑστερήματα τῶν θλίψεων **τοῦ Χριστοῦ** ἐν τῇ σαρκί μου ὑπὲρ τοῦ σώματος αὐτοῦ, ὅ ἐστιν ἡ ἐκκλησία,

[[1:25 ἧς ἐγενόμην ἐγὼ διάκονος κατὰ <u>τὴν οἰκονομίαν τοῦ θεοῦ</u> τὴν δοθεῖσάν μοι εἰς ὑμᾶς πληρῶσαι <u>τὸν λόγον τοῦ θεοῦ</u>,]]

1:27–29 [27]οἷς <u>ἠθέλησεν ὁ θεὸς γνωρίσαι</u> τί τὸ πλοῦτος τῆς δόξης τοῦ μυστηρίου τούτου ἐν τοῖς ἔθνεσιν, ὅ ἐστιν **Χριστὸς ἐν ὑμῖν**, ἡ ἐλπὶς τῆς δόξης· [28]**ὃν** ἡμεῖς καταγγέλλομεν νουθετοῦντες πάντα ἄνθρωπον καὶ διδάσκοντες πάντα ἄνθρωπον ἐν πάσῃ σοφίᾳ, ἵνα παραστήσωμεν πάντα ἄνθρωπον **τέλειον ἐν Χριστῷ**. [v.l. + Ἰησοῦ] [29]εἰς ὃ καὶ κοπιῶ ἀγωνιζόμενος κατὰ τὴν **ἐνέργειαν αὐτοῦ τὴν ἐνεργουμένην** ἐν ἐμοὶ **ἐν δυνάμει**.

2:2–3 [2]ἵνα παρακληθῶσιν αἱ καρδίαι αὐτῶν συμβιβασθέντες ἐν ἀγάπῃ καὶ εἰς πᾶν πλοῦτος τῆς πληροφορίας τῆς συνέσεως, εἰς ἐπίγνωσιν <u>τοῦ μυστηρίου τοῦ θεοῦ</u>, **Χριστοῦ**, [3]**ἐν ᾧ εἰσιν** πάντες οἱ θησαυροὶ τῆς σοφίας καὶ γνώσεως ἀπόκρυφοι.

2:5 εἰ γὰρ καὶ τῇ σαρκὶ ἄπειμι, ἀλλὰ τῷ πνεύματι σὺν ὑμῖν εἰμι, χαίρων καὶ βλέπων ὑμῶν τὴν τάξιν καὶ τὸ στερέωμα **τῆς εἰς Χριστὸν πίστεως** ὑμῶν.

2:6–7 [6]Ὡς οὖν παρελάβετε **τὸν Χριστὸν Ἰησοῦν τὸν κύριον, ἐν αὐτῷ** περιπατεῖτε, [7]ἐρριζωμένοι καὶ ἐποικοδομούμενοι **ἐν αὐτῷ** καὶ βεβαιούμενοι τῇ πίστει καθὼς ἐδιδάχθητε, περισσεύοντες ἐν εὐχαριστίᾳ.

2:8–10 [8]Βλέπετε μή τις ὑμᾶς ἔσται ὁ συλαγωγῶν διὰ τῆς φιλοσοφίας καὶ κενῆς ἀπάτης κατὰ τὴν παράδοσιν τῶν ἀνθρώπων, κατὰ τὰ στοιχεῖα τοῦ κόσμου καὶ οὐ **κατὰ Χριστόν**· [9]ὅτι **ἐν αὐτῷ** κατοικεῖ <u>πᾶν τὸ πλήρωμα τῆς θεότητος</u> σωματικῶς, [10]καὶ ἐστὲ **ἐν αὐτῷ** πεπληρωμένοι, **ὅς ἐστιν ἡ κεφαλὴ** πάσης ἀρχῆς καὶ ἐξουσίας.

2:11–15 [11]**Ἐν ᾧ καὶ** περιετμήθητε περιτομῇ ἀχειροποιήτῳ ἐν τῇ ἀπεκδύσει τοῦ σώματος τῆς σαρκός, ἐν τῇ **περιτομῇ τοῦ Χριστοῦ**, [12]συνταφέντες **αὐτῷ** ἐν τῷ βαπτισμῷ, ἐν ᾧ καὶ συνηγέρθητε διὰ τῆς πίστεως <u>τῆς ἐνεργείας τοῦ θεοῦ τοῦ ἐγείραντος</u> **αὐτὸν ἐκ νεκρῶν**· [13]καὶ ὑμᾶς νεκροὺς ὄντας ἐν τοῖς παραπτώμασιν καὶ τῇ ἀκροβυστίᾳ τῆς σαρκὸς ὑμῶν, <u>συνεζωοποίησεν</u> ὑμᾶς **σὺν αὐτῷ**, χαρισάμενος ἡμῖν πάντα τὰ παραπτώματα. [14]<u>ἐξαλείψας</u> τὸ καθ᾽ ἡμῶν χειρόγραφον τοῖς δόγμασιν ὃ ἦν ὑπεναντίον ἡμῖν, καὶ αὐτὸ ἦρκεν ἐκ τοῦ μέσου <u>προσηλώσας</u> αὐτὸ τῷ σταυρῷ· [15]<u>ἀπεκδυσάμενος</u> τὰς ἀρχὰς καὶ τὰς ἐξουσίας <u>ἐδειγμάτισεν</u> ἐν παρρησίᾳ, <u>θριαμβεύσας</u> αὐτοὺς **ἐν αὐτῷ**.

2:17 ἅ ἐστιν σκιὰ τῶν μελλόντων, **τὸ δὲ σῶμα τοῦ Χριστοῦ**.

2:19 καὶ οὐ κρατῶν **τὴν κεφαλήν, ἐξ οὗ** πᾶν τὸ σῶμα διὰ τῶν ἀφῶν καὶ συνδέσμων ἐπιχορηγούμενον καὶ συμβιβαζόμενον αὔξει <u>τὴν αὔξησιν τοῦ θεοῦ</u>.

2:20 εἰ ἀπεθάνετε **σὺν Χριστῷ** ἀπὸ τῶν στοιχείων τοῦ κόσμου, τί ὡς ζῶντες ἐν κόσμῳ δογματίζεσθε;

3:1–4 [1]Εἰ οὖν **συνηγέρθητε τῷ Χριστῷ**, τὰ ἄνω ζητεῖτε, **οὗ ὁ Χριστός ἐστιν** <u>ἐν δεξιᾷ τοῦ θεοῦ</u> καθήμενος· [2]τὰ ἄνω φρονεῖτε, μὴ τὰ ἐπὶ τῆς γῆς. [3]ἀπεθάνετε γὰρ καὶ ἡ ζωὴ ὑμῶν κέκρυπται **σὺν τῷ Χριστῷ** <u>ἐν τῷ θεῷ</u>·

⁴ὅταν ὁ Χριστὸς φανερωθῇ, ἡ ζωὴ ὑμῶν, τότε καὶ ὑμεῖς σὺν αὐτῷ φανερωθήσεσθε ἐν δόξῃ.

[[3:6 δι᾽ ἃ ἔρχεται ἡ ὀργὴ τοῦ θεοῦ ἐπὶ τοὺς υἱοὺς τῆς ἀπειθείας.]]

3:10–11 ¹⁰καὶ ἐνδυσάμενοι τὸν νέον τὸν ἀνακαινούμενον εἰς ἐπίγνωσιν κατ᾽ εἰκόνα τοῦ κτίσαντος αὐτόν, ¹¹ὅπου οὐκ ἔνι Ἕλλην καὶ Ἰουδαῖος, περιτομὴ καὶ ἀκροβυστία, βάρβαρος, Σκύθης, δοῦλος, ἐλεύθερος, ἀλλὰ τὰ πάντα καὶ ἐν πᾶσιν Χριστός.

[[3:12 Ἐνδύσασθε οὖν, ὡς ἐκλεκτοὶ τοῦ θεοῦ ἅγιοι καὶ ἠγαπημένοι, σπλάγχνα οἰκτιρμοῦ χρηστότητα ταπεινοφροσύνην πραΰτητα μακροθυμίαν,]]

3:13–15 ¹³ἀνεχόμενοι ἀλλήλων καὶ χαριζόμενοι ἑαυτοῖς ἐάν τις πρός τινα ἔχῃ μομφήν· καθὼς καὶ ὁ [v.l. + Χριστὸς] κύριος ἐχαρίσατο ὑμῖν, οὕτως καὶ ὑμεῖς· ¹⁴ἐπὶ πᾶσιν δὲ τούτοις τὴν ἀγάπην, ὅ ἐστιν σύνδεσμος τῆς τελειότητος. ¹⁵καὶ ἡ εἰρήνη τοῦ Χριστοῦ [v.l. θεοῦ] βραβευέτω ἐν ταῖς καρδίαις ὑμῶν, εἰς ἣν καὶ ἐκλήθητε ἐν ἑνὶ σώματι·

3:16–17 ¹⁶ὁ λόγος τοῦ Χριστοῦ ἐνοικείτω ἐν ὑμῖν πλουσίως, ἐν πάσῃ σοφίᾳ διδάσκοντες καὶ νουθετοῦντες ἑαυτούς, ψαλμοῖς ὕμνοις ᾠδαῖς πνευματικαῖς ἐν τῇ χάριτι ᾄδοντες ἐν ταῖς καρδίαις ὑμῶν τῷ θεῷ. [v.l. κυρίῳ] ¹⁷καὶ πᾶν ὅ τι ἐὰν ποιῆτε ἐν λόγῳ ἢ ἐν ἔργῳ, πάντα ἐν ὀνόματι κυρίου Ἰησοῦ εὐχαριστοῦντες τῷ θεῷ πατρὶ δι᾽ αὐτοῦ.

3:18–4:1 ¹⁸Αἱ γυναῖκες, ὑποτάσσεσθε τοῖς ἀνδράσιν ὡς ἀνῆκεν ἐν κυρίῳ. ¹⁹Οἱ ἄνδρες, ἀγαπᾶτε τὰς γυναῖκας καὶ μὴ πικραίνεσθε πρὸς αὐτάς. ²⁰Τὰ τέκνα, ὑπακούετε τοῖς γονεῦσιν κατὰ πάντα, τοῦτο γὰρ εὐάρεστόν ἐστιν ἐν κυρίῳ. ²¹Οἱ πατέρες, μὴ ἐρεθίζετε τὰ τέκνα ὑμῶν, ἵνα μὴ ἀθυμῶσιν. ²²Οἱ δοῦλοι, ὑπακούετε κατὰ πάντα τοῖς κατὰ σάρκα κυρίοις, μὴ ἐν ὀφθαλμοδουλίᾳ ὡς ἀνθρωπάρεσκοι, ἀλλ᾽ ἐν ἁπλότητι καρδίας φοβούμενοι τὸν κύριον. [v.l. θεόν] ²³ὃ ἐὰν ποιῆτε, ἐκ ψυχῆς ἐργάζεσθε ὡς τῷ κυρίῳ καὶ οὐκ ἀνθρώποις, ²⁴εἰδότες ὅτι ἀπὸ κυρίου ἀπολήμψεσθε τὴν ἀνταπόδοσιν τῆς κληρονομίας. τῷ κυρίῳ Χριστῷ δουλεύετε· ²⁵ὁ γὰρ ἀδικῶν κομίσεται ὃ ἠδίκησεν, καὶ οὐκ ἔστιν προσωπολημψία. ⁴⁺¹Οἱ κύριοι, τὸ δίκαιον καὶ τὴν ἰσότητα τοῖς δούλοις παρέχεσθε, εἰδότες ὅτι καὶ ὑμεῖς ἔχετε κύριον ἐν οὐρανῷ.

4:3 προσευχόμενοι ἅμα καὶ περὶ ἡμῶν, ἵνα ὁ θεὸς ἀνοίξῃ ἡμῖν θύραν τοῦ λόγου λαλῆσαι τὸ μυστήριον τοῦ Χριστοῦ, δι᾽ ὃ καὶ δέδεμαι,

4:7 Τὰ κατ᾽ ἐμὲ πάντα γνωρίσει ὑμῖν Τύχικος ὁ ἀγαπητὸς ἀδελφὸς καὶ πιστὸς διάκονος καὶ σύνδουλος ἐν κυρίῳ,

[[4:11 καὶ Ἰησοῦς ὁ λεγόμενος Ἰοῦστος, οἱ ὄντες ἐκ περιτομῆς, οὗτοι μόνοι συνεργοὶ εἰς τὴν βασιλείαν τοῦ θεοῦ,]]

4:12 ἀσπάζεται ὑμᾶς Ἐπαφρᾶς ὁ ἐξ ὑμῶν, **δοῦλος Χριστοῦ Ἰησοῦ**, πάντοτε ἀγωνιζόμενος ὑπὲρ ὑμῶν ἐν ταῖς προσευχαῖς, ἵνα σταθῆτε τέλειοι καὶ πεπληροφορημένοι ἐν παντὶ θελήματι τοῦ θεοῦ.

4:17 καὶ εἴπατε Ἀρχίππῳ· βλέπε τὴν διακονίαν ἣν παρέλαβες **ἐν κυρίῳ**, ἵνα αὐτὴν πληροῖς.

Philemon

Phlm 1 Παῦλος δέσμιος **Χριστοῦ Ἰησοῦ** καὶ Τιμόθεος ὁ ἀδελφός . . .

Phlm 3 χάρις ὑμῖν καὶ εἰρήνη ἀπὸ θεοῦ πατρὸς ἡμῶν καὶ **κυρίου Ἰησοῦ Χριστοῦ**.

Phlm 4–6 ⁴Εὐχαριστῶ τῷ θεῷ μου πάντοτε μνείαν σου ποιούμενος ἐπὶ τῶν προσευχῶν μου, ⁵ἀκούων σου τὴν ἀγάπην καὶ τὴν πίστιν, ἣν ἔχεις **πρὸς τὸν κύριον Ἰησοῦν** καὶ εἰς πάντας τοὺς ἁγίους, ⁶ὅπως ἡ κοινωνία τῆς πίστεώς σου ἐνεργὴς γένηται ἐν ἐπιγνώσει παντὸς ἀγαθοῦ τοῦ ἐν ἡμῖν **εἰς Χριστόν**.
[v.l. + Ἰησοῦν]

Phlm 8–9 ⁸Διὸ **πολλὴν ἐν Χριστῷ παρρησίαν ἔχων** ἐπιτάσσειν σοι τὸ ἀνῆκον ⁹διὰ τὴν ἀγάπην μᾶλλον παρακαλῶ, τοιοῦτος ὢν ὡς Παῦλος πρεσβύτης νυνὶ δὲ καὶ **δέσμιος Χριστοῦ Ἰησοῦ**.

Phlm 16 . . . ἀδελφὸν ἀγαπητόν, μάλιστα ἐμοί, πόσῳ δὲ μᾶλλον σοὶ καὶ **ἐν σαρκὶ καὶ ἐν κυρίῳ**.

Phlm 20 ναὶ ἀδελφέ, ἐγώ σου ὀναίμην **ἐν κυρίῳ**· ἀνάπαυσόν μου τά σπλάγχνα **ἐν Χριστῷ**. [v.l. κυρίῳ]

Phlm 23 Ἀσπάζεταί σε Ἐπαφρᾶς ὁ συναιχμάλωτός μου **ἐν Χριστῷ Ἰησοῦ**,

Phlm 25 Ἡ χάρις **τοῦ κυρίου Ἰησοῦ Χριστοῦ** μετὰ τοῦ πνεύματος ὑμῶν.

Appendix II: An Analysis of Usage

(* = anarthrous; + = with possessive pronoun)

Colossians
θεός   22
Christ   37

Philemon
θεός   2
Christ   11

The Data
1. κύριος Ἰησοῦς Χριστός (1 / 2)
   Col 1:3   G+
   Phlm 3   G* (ἀπό)
   Phlm 25   G
1a. Χριστὸς Ἰησοῦς κύριος (1 / 0)
   Col 2:6   A
2. κύριος Ἰησοῦς (1 / 1)
   Col 3:17   G*
   Phlm 5   A (πρός)
2b. κύριος Χριστός (1 / 0)
   Col 3:24   D
3. Χριστὸς Ἰησοῦς (3 / 3)
   Col 1:1   G*
   Col 1:4   D* (ἐν)
   Col 4:12   G*
   Phlm 1   G*
   Phlm 9   G*
   Phlm 23   D* (ἐν)
4. κύριος (10 + 4 = 14 / 2 + 6 = 8)
   Col 1:10   G
   Col 3:13   N [v.l. + Χριστὸς]
   Col 3:18   D* (ἐν)
   Col 3:20   D* (ἐν)
   Col 3:22   A [v.l. θεόν]
   Col 3:23   D

   Col 3:24   G* (ἀπό)
   Col 4:1   A ("a lord")
   Col 4:7   D* (ἐν)
   Col 4:17   D* (ἐν)
   Phlm 16   D* (ἐν)
   Phlm 20   D* (ἐν)
5. Ἰησοῦς (0 / 0)
6. Χριστός (19 + 6 = 25 / 3 + 5 = 8)
   Col 1:2   D* (ἐν)
   Col 1:7   G
   Col 1:24   G
   Col 1:27   N*
   Col 1:28   D* (ἐν) [v.l. + Ἰησοῦ]
   Col 2:2   G* (appositive to μυστήριον)
   Col 2:5   A* (εἰς)
   Col 2:8   A* (κατά)
   Col 2:11   G
   Col 2:17   G
   Col 2:20   D* (σύν)
   Col 3:1   D
   Col 3:1   N
   Col 3:3   D (σύν)
   Col 3:4   N
   Col 3:11   N*
   Col 3:15   G [v.l. θεοῦ]
   Col 3:16   G
   Col 4:3   G
   Phlm 6   A* (εἰς) [v.l. + Ἰησοῦν]
   Phlm 8   D* (ἐν)
   Phlm 20   D* (ἐν) [v.l. κυρίῳ]
7. υἱός (1 / 0)
   Col 1:13   G (αὐτοῦ)

Appendix III: A Structural Analysis of Colossians 1:15–20

(**boldface** = the Son; <u>underline</u> = God the Father; *italics* = "all created things")

[context]
13 <u>ὃς ἐρρύσατο</u> ἡμᾶς ἐκ τῆς ἐξουσίας
                                τοῦ σκότους
    καὶ <u>μετέστησεν</u>   εἰς τὴν βασιλείαν [cf. strophe I]
                                τοῦ υἱοῦ <u>τῆς ἀγάπης αὐτοῦ</u>,
14   **ἐν ᾧ** ἔχομεν   τὴν ἀπολύτρωσιν, τὴν ἄφεσιν τῶν ἁμαρτιῶν·
                                        [cf. strophe II]
[the poem]
I   (*a*)   **ὅς ἐστιν εἰκὼν**   <u>τοῦ θεοῦ τοῦ ἀοράτου</u>,
     (*a′*)   **πρωτότοκος**   *πάσης κτίσεως*,
     (*b*)   ὅτι   **ἐν αὐτῷ** <u>ἐκτίσθη</u>   *τὰ πάντα*
       (*b¹*)   *ἐν τοῖς οὐρανοῖς καὶ ἐπὶ τῆς γῆς*,
       (*b²*)   *τὰ ὁρατὰ καὶ τὰ ἀόρατα*,
       (*b³*)   *εἴτε θρόνοι   εἴτε κυριότητες*
       (*b⁴*)   *εἴτε ἀρχαὶ   εἴτε ἐξουσίαι·*
     (*b′*)   *τὰ πάντα* **δι' αὐτοῦ καὶ εἰς αὐτὸν**   <u>ἔκτισται·</u>
     (*c*)   καὶ **αὐτός**   **ἐστιν**   *πρὸ πάντων*
     (*c′*)   καὶ *τὰ πάντα* **ἐν αὐτῷ** *συνέστηκεν*,
[janus] (*d*) καὶ **αὐτός ἐστιν**   **ἡ κεφαλὴ τοῦ σώματος**, τῆς ἐκκλησίας·
II   (*a*)   **ὅς ἐστιν ἀρχή**,
     (*a′*)   **πρωτότοκος** ἐκ τῶν νεκρῶν,   [cf. I(*a′*)]
       (*a¹*)   ἵνα γένηται *ἐν πᾶσιν* **αὐτὸς πρωτεύων**, [cf. I(*c*)]
     (*b*)   ὅτι   **ἐν αὐτῷ** εὐδόκησεν <u>πᾶν τὸ πλήρωμα</u>
                                        κατοικῆσαι [cf. I(*c′*)]
     (*b′*)   καὶ   **δι' αὐτοῦ**   <u>ἀποκαταλλάξαι</u> *τὰ πάντα* **εἰς αὐτόν**,
                                        [cf. I(*b′*)]
       (*b¹*)   **εἰρηνοποιήσας διὰ τοῦ αἵματος**
                                τοῦ σταυροῦ αὐτοῦ,
       (*b²*)   **δι' αὐτοῦ**   *εἴτε τὰ ἐπὶ τῆς γῆς*   [cf. I(*b¹*)]
                                εἴτε τὰ ἐν τοῖς οὐρανοῖς.
cf. 1 Cor 8:6
     (1)   ἀλλ'   ἡμῖν   <u>εἷς θεὸς</u>   <u>ὁ πατὴρ</u>
                                <u>ἐξ οὗ</u>   *τὰ πάντα* καὶ ἡμεῖς <u>εἰς αὐτόν</u>,
     (2)   καὶ   **εἷς κύριος Ἰησοῦς Χριστὸς**,
                                δι' οὗ   *τὰ πάντα* καὶ ἡμεῖς **δι' αὐτοῦ**.

8

Christology in Ephesians

WHEN TURNING TO EPHESIANS FROM Colossians, one has a sense of "the same but not the same."[1] Although clearly related to Colossians, this letter lacks the element of "correction" as such, and therefore it exhibits more deliberation than one is used to in the apostle Paul. Indeed, Ephesians appears to sustain a relationship with Colossians similar to that which Romans has with Galatians. In both cases, the first letters (Galatians and Colossians) are full of argumentation and correction, while the second (Romans and Ephesians) are far less impassioned and argumentative, while at the same time full of unique features not found elsewhere in the corpus.[2] Ephesians also has in common with Romans that the role of Christ is consistently expressed within the larger context of God the Father's working out of the divine plan. This feature caused Romans to be especially theocentric; that is less so in Ephesians, where the emphasis is so thoroughly on the role of Christ that it becomes emphatically christocentric.

The most unique feature of Ephesians is that it is so much less occasional than all the other letters of Paul.[3] Nothing within the letter itself seems to have called it forth. Moreover, it also goes considerably beyond Romans and Colossians—also written to churches that he had not founded—in that it is addressed to people who apparently do not know him personally,[4] although 6:21–22 assumes that his readers know of him in a secondary way. Very likely

---

[1] Commentaries on Ephesians are listed in the bibliography (pp. 644–45); they are cited in this chapter by author's surname only.

[2] It is of high interest that NT scholarship by and large has opted for pseudepigraphy with regard to Ephesians but has not done so with regard to Romans, which has far more idiosyncratic moments and differences from the rest of the corpus than does Ephesians. This is not to say that there are not serious problems to face in Ephesians, but it does suggest that authorship issues tend to lie in the eye of the beholder and thus they depend chiefly on one's stance at the beginning.

[3] This feature is very likely responsible for the several other features that cause it to be suspect as genuinely Pauline. For helpful analyses of the data that come down on either side of this issue, see Lincoln, lix–lxxiii; O'Brien, 4–47.

[4] As 1:15 and 3:1–2 make clear; not only so, it lacks any terms of endearment and any hint of specific knowledge of the recipients and their situation, except that

it was intended to be a circular letter, to be read in many of the churches of Asia. In any case, the letter reflects a considerable amount of shared assumptions between him and his readers, assumptions that are elaborated in a variety of ways and that indicate the central place that Christ Jesus held in these early Gentile communities.

However one views the provenance and reason for Ephesians, the letter comes to us as a remarkable blend of the passions that drive Colossians, on the one hand, and Romans, on the other. The *berakah* (blessing of God) with which Ephesians begins (1:3–14) reflects the primary concerns of Colossians, especially Christ's role as Redeemer, but now with the cosmic implications noted in Colossians (e.g., 1:20) spelled out in grand fashion. Thus, redemption is, as always, from human brokenness and sin. At the same time, in the thanksgiving and prayer that follow (1:15–23), through the Son's death and resurrection-exaltation the powers are also placed under his feet in the heavenly realm. However, when this is played out historically in ch. 2, the issue is that of Romans—Jew and Gentile as one people of God, made so through the reconciling work of the cross—while ch. 3 picks up Paul's apostolic role in this reconciling work.

Also as in Romans, the work of Christ that makes this letter so christocentric is much more soteriological throughout if one includes in Christ's saving work the ethical dimension of the Ephesian believers' being God's people in the world. The end result is that Ephesians, very much like Galatians, has fewer strictly christological moments than the rest of the corpus. But as always, this very emphasis on Christ as Savior and Redeemer becomes christological in its own right. So much is this so that at the end of the *berakah* and prayer of ch. 1, the Son, through whom God has offered redemption and under whom all things will ultimately find their unity (vv. 3–10), is seen in the place of sovereign authority at the Father's right hand as the one "who fills everything in every way" (v. 23). Thus, the implications of the "hymn" in Col 1:15–20 come to full, cosmic fruition in this letter.

But for all that, and despite these new turns, we still find here the same christological patterns and emphases that have emerged throughout the corpus. Christ as Son of God is the first thing up in the letter, and this is repeated in a variety of ways throughout. Only in this case, the movement from the Son of God of Jewish messianism to eternal Son is not so obvious—although it seems presupposed in 5:5 in the phrase ἐν τῇ βασιλείᾳ τοῦ Χριστοῦ καὶ θεοῦ (*in the kingdom of the Messiah and of God*), where the kingdom is related (probably) to Jesus as the messianic king. At the same time, the exaltation of the risen Son to the Father's right hand assumes his present role as κύριος of all. The result is that in this letter Son of God and κύριος Christologies tend to blend in a unique way.

---

they are Gentiles. Paul has friends or contacts in Rome and Colossae (Rom 16:1–16; Col 1:8; Phlm 1–3). The letter to the Ephesians lacks this element altogether.

A Preliminary Look at the Data

As before, all the texts where Christ and God are mentioned in the letter are found in appendix I; the analysis of usage is given in appendix II. The most striking feature of usage in Ephesians is that Christ is mentioned by name more than twice as often as God (65x / 31x); in fact, apart from Philemon (11x / 2x), this is the largest differential in usage in the corpus—a phenomenon that began in a moderate way in Colossians (37x / 29x) and will be found again in Philippians (48x / 23x). Thus, in a letter whose predicate is that it is the Father's activity that finds expression through the Son, Christ is nonetheless mentioned far more often than the Father—a result that would be the same even if one added in all the pronouns.

With regard to Christ himself, the title-turned-name, Χριστός, is by far the most commonly used language, occurring in 47 of the 65 mentions of the Lord by name. It is of some interest to observe at this point that there has been a gradual progression in the letters from the dominant use of κύριος in the two Thessalonian letters,[5] to a rather even mix in 1 Corinthians, to a predominance of the title Χριστός over κύριος in all the later letters (including the Pastoral Epistles) until 2 Timothy. In this matter, Ephesians has its closest affinities to Philippians, the next letter in the corpus.[6]

Two further notes are of interest regarding usage. First, as all have recognized, the letter comes to us in two very clear parts. Chapters 1–3 spell out both the fact and the soteriological implications of Christ's death and resurrection-exaltation, while chs. 4–6 spell out their ecclesiological and behavioral (ethical) implications. What is of interest is that distinctive usage also follows this pattern. The 10 occurrences of the combination Χριστὸς Ἰησοῦς (plus the one Ἰησοῦς Χριστός) occur exclusively in chs. 1–3, while all but one of the 14 occurrences of singular ὁ κύριος and the majority of singular (ὁ) Χριστός (17 of 28) occur in chs. 4–6. One is not sure what to make of this phenomenon, but probably it is related to the fact that chs. 1–3 focus on the person and work of Christ himself; that is, he is the "object" of the conversation. By contrast, in chs. 4–6 the focus is on the recipients and how they are to live in light of what Christ has done; hence, he becomes the active "subject" in the conversation. And Pauline usage thus tends to change accordingly.

Second, although the appellation "Son" occurs but once (4:13), the language of "Father" is attributed to God more often than in any other letter in

---

[5]In 1 Thessalonians κύριος occurs in 29 of the 36 references to Christ, while in 2 Thessalonians it is 22 of 23.

[6]It is of some interest, therefore, that in this probably less conscious matter of usage, Ephesians fits the Pauline patterns perfectly while it is difficult to conceive of a pseudepigrapher doing the same, especially when Colossians would have been the one certain letter known to the writer. Also of interest regarding this usage is that Ephesians has so much in common with Philippians—the next letter in the assumed chronology—with which it otherwise has so little in common.

the corpus (8x). And since this is the first thing up, both in the salutation and the *berakah*, this again is the logical place to begin our christological analysis.

Jesus as Messianic/Eternal Son of God

The Christology of Ephesians is played out altogether in the context of Christ's carrying out the will and purposes of God the Father. And since the readers' knowledge of God as Father is the result of his being "the Father of our Lord Jesus Christ," this combination of language and interest, noticeably present in the opening *berakah* and thanksgiving-prayer, will function throughout the letter, especially in the interest of Paul's readers. Lying behind this language is Paul's frequently occurring eternal Son of God Christology. But toward the end there is one text (5:5) that places this Christology also in the context of Jewish messianism. Here is a place, then, where we begin at the beginning.

Christ Jesus as the Son of the Father

The various passages that speak of God as Father in the context of his being the Father of the Son of God occur mostly in ch. 1, in the opening *berakah* and thanksgiving-prayer. These in turn will serve as the basis for Paul's referring to God as also the Father of himself and his readers.

Ephesians 1:2; 6:23

One of the unusual features of Ephesians, again attributable to the probability that it is a circular letter, is that it begins and ends on a very similar note: a wish of grace and peace. Thus:

1:2   χάρις ὑμῖν καὶ εἰρήνη
                  <u>ἀπὸ θεοῦ πατρὸς ἡμῶν</u>   καὶ **κυρίου Ἰησοῦ Χριστοῦ.**

6:23   εἰρήνη τοῖς ἀδελφοῖς καὶ ἀγάπη μετὰ πίστεως
                  <u>ἀπὸ θεοῦ πατρὸς</u>   καὶ **κυρίου Ἰησοῦ Χριστοῦ.**

1:2   *Grace to you and peace*
                  <u>*from God our Father*</u>   *and* ***the Lord Jesus Christ.***

6:23   *Peace to the brothers (and sisters) and love with faith*
                  <u>*from God the Father*</u>   *and* ***the Lord Jesus Christ.***

Although this closing benediction has a number of interesting features in its own right,[7] our immediate interest in both of these texts is again the

---

[7]Including: the interesting substitution of τοῖς ἀδελφοῖς for ὑμῖν; that "grace" and "peace" are now "peace" and "love" (but from whom to whom?); that the more

christological assumptions in the single preposition with a double object, which assumes that these divine qualities are to come to the readers simultaneously from both the Father and the Son. As before, one may assume that the "our" in 1:2 (missing in 6:23) does double duty: God is "our" Father, and Jesus Christ is "our" Lord. On the presupposed christological dimension of this greeting see the full discussion on 1 Thess 1:1, 3 in ch. 2 (pp. 36–38).

Ephesians 1:3, 6–7

Ephesians is the second letter (see 2 Cor 1:3) that begins with a *berakah*, an offering of praise to God, rather than the more common thanksgiving and prayer for the recipients. Thus:

Eph 1:3   εὐλογητὸς <u>ὁ θεὸς καὶ πατὴρ</u> **τοῦ κυρίου ἡμῶν Ἰησοῦ Χριστοῦ,** <u>ὁ εὐλογήσας</u> ἡμᾶς . . .

2 Cor 1:3   εὐλογητὸς <u>ὁ θεὸς καὶ πατὴρ</u> **τοῦ κυρίου ἡμῶν Ἰησοῦ Χριστοῦ,** <u>ὁ πατὴρ τῶν οἰκτιρμῶν</u> . . .

Eph 1:3   *Blessed be <u>the God and Father</u> **of our Lord Jesus Christ,** <u>who blessed</u> us . . .*

2 Cor 1:3   *Blessed be <u>the God and Father</u> **of our Lord Jesus Christ,** <u>the Father of mercies</u> . . .*

The difference from 2 Corinthians is that here the *berakah* is followed also by the more traditional thanksgiving and prayer, both of which have as their singular aim the encouragement of Paul's Gentile readers as to their place in the larger scheme of things. The theological result is that God the Father, who is the grammatical subject of the majority of the verbs in the *berakah*, receives the praise; however, the praise is for what the Father has done through the Son, resulting in adoration of the Son as the primary content of both passages (1:3–14, 15–23), with the redemption of both Jew and Gentile as its secondary content.

The reason for the *berakah* seems especially to be for the sake of Paul's readers, in this case to encourage and reassure his Gentile readers that they have been included in God's story by way of Christ and the Spirit. This becomes clear in 2:11–22, where the various shifts of imagery (citizens/foreigners, household, temple) all aim at emphasizing the inclusion of Gentile and Jew together in the newly constituted commonwealth of Israel. But it is already anticipated in ch. 1, as evidenced by the shift in personal pronouns throughout the *berakah* and thanksgiving-prayer. Thus in the first part of the *berakah* (1:3–10), the first person plural pronoun occurs throughout (7x plus one verb); and Paul's "we/us" minimally includes himself and his readers.

---

familiar triad of "faith, hope, love" here takes the expression of "peace, love, faith"; and the meaning of μετὰ πίστεως in a context of desiring this as coming from God and Christ.

The twofold application in vv. 11–14 is signaled by the thrice repeated "in whom also," which in its first occurrence means "we [Jews] also obtained an inheritance," thus using Exodus language to speak of the Jews' being first to be included in the story. But in v. 13, with an emphatic twofold "in whom also," there is a noticeable shift to the second person plural, so that through Christ and the Spirit "you [Gentiles] also" were marked by the divine seal of the promised Holy Spirit and thus included in the promises made to Israel.

The shift to the first person singular in the thanksgiving-prayer (vv. 15–23) brings them back to the salutation, where in v. 1 Paul had identified himself and his readers. The thanksgiving itself is then for "you (= Gentile believers)," which continues through v. 18; but, typically for Paul,[8] he shifts to the all-inclusive "us who believe" in v. 19, when the reality of which he speaks reaches out broadly to include all of God's people.

On the Christology of the *berakah* itself, see the discussion on 2 Cor 1:3–5; 11:31 in ch. 4 (pp. 169–71). Its content in this case, however, is about as far removed from the former as one can get, since in both cases they reflect the concerns of each letter (consolation and exaltation). Nonetheless, here, as in 2 Corinthians, the intent seems to be to offer a *christological identification of God the Father*, unto whom Paul now offers praise. The God of Israel, who is blessed in the synagogue, is now known and blessed as "the Father of our Lord Jesus Christ," thus once more bringing a Son of God Christology up front as the first thing that one meets in the letter.

This is further confirmed at the end of v. 6 and beginning of v. 7 by Paul suddenly bringing in the theme of Christ as "the beloved." After three prepositional phrases where "Christ" is the divine agent of God's activity, Paul echoes his own reference to the Davidic king in the thanksgiving of Col 1:12–14. It is in his "beloved [Son]" that God the Father has "graced us." Thus, even though not expressed explicitly, lying behind all this language is Paul's deeply rooted, presuppositional Son of God Christology.

Ephesians 1:4—The Son as Preexistent

Although eventually, in 2:11–21, Paul will spell out how historically God has included his Gentile readers in the story, in the opening *berakah* he places that historical reality within the ultimate divine purposes: God had chosen "us" for the praise of his glory from eternity past, namely, *in Christ before the foundation of the world*. Thus a sentence that begins by articulating God's present blessings of his people "in Christ with every spiritual blessing in the heavenly realm" immediately goes on to place this present reality in the context of God's eternal purposes. In so doing, and without trying to make a point of it, Paul once more articulates his presuppositional conviction of Christ's preexistence.[9] We were chosen in him before the foundation of the world.

---

[8]On this matter, see the discussion on Col 1:12–13 in ch. 7 (p. 294).

[9]It is so presuppositional, in fact, that a large number of commentaries in English do not mention it at all (the exceptions include Scott, 140; Hendriksen, 76;

At least that seems to be the plain sense of the passage. It is (remotely) possible that Paul, with the prepositional phrase "in him," was positioning Christ not so much temporally as personally. That is, the "choice" belonged to God before the worlds began, and Paul's use of "in him" at this point was simply an atemporal anticipation of the fact that it would happen "in Christ" at a given point in time.[10] But what makes that seem unlikely is the introductory καθώς (*just as*), which implies that v. 3 expresses the present (historical) reality, while the clause that begins v. 4 will spell out its antecedent reality in the divine purposes before time began; and Christ the Son was already, eternally a part of that divine plan.

Ephesians 1:17

The second instance of the *berakah* formula (v. 17) had a considerable history in the early christological debates, since on the surface it appears to reflect a much lower Christology than one finds ordinarily in Paul's writings. Indeed, were this the only way Paul expressed himself with this idiom, then the historical debate over its intent would seem to carry some weight.[11] But this is not the first instance of usage, since Paul here presupposes what he has said in v. 3, while at the same time emphatically identifying the Father with the thrice-repeated preceding phrase, "to the praise of his δόξα [*glory*]." Since he could not make this identification within the standard rubric,[12] Paul in this case simply reorders the way he speaks about the God to whom he prays. Thus:

1:3	εὐλογητὸς <u>ὁ θεὸς καὶ πατὴρ</u>	τοῦ κυρίου ἡμῶν Ἰησοῦ Χριστοῦ,
1:17	ἵνα[13] <u>ὁ θεὸς</u>	τοῦ κυρίου ἡμῶν Ἰησοῦ Χριστοῦ,
	<u>ὁ πατὴρ τῆς δόξης</u>	

1:3	*Blessed be* <u>*God, even the Father*</u>	***of our Lord Jesus Christ,***
1:17	*that* <u>*the God*</u>	***of our Lord Jesus Christ,***
	<u>*the Father of glory*</u>	

Bruce, 254; Lincoln, 24; Best, 121; O'Brien, 100; Hoehner, 108–9). In part that is because many commentators are more interested in dealing with the doctrine of election than with placing the text in its historical context of reassuring Gentile believers that their place in God's plan reaches back into eternity.

[10] Although this view is not articulated as such in the commentaries, one could read it out of Abbott's comment that "believers were viewed in God's purpose as being in Christ adopted as sons through Him" (6).

[11] For a brief overview of some of the early history, see Eadie, 78–80. The debate, which had its beginnings in the Arian controversy, gives evidence as to how often such debates were primarily theologically driven, so that text in context was not always on the screen.

[12] That is, not even in Greek could he meaningfully say, "that the God and Father of glory [and] of our Lord Jesus Christ"—although he could, of course, have repeated the πατήρ ("the God and Father of our Lord Jesus Christ, the Father of glory").

[13] This ἵνα functions here as a ὅτι, thus introducing the content of Paul's prayer; cf. Best, 161.

The concern in this present case seems to be twofold. First, Paul's interest in v. 3 was to say something not about the relationship of the Son to the Father but of the Father to the Son. That is, Paul's praise of God identifies God as the One whom we now know as "the Father of our Lord Jesus Christ." This is the God who has blessed us in Christ his Son. But now, second, he identifies the same God with his "glory" that was being praised in vv. 6, 12, 14.

Although the phrase "the Father of glory" might possibly mean "the glorious Father" (as in several contemporary translations),[14] that misses altogether the connection with the preceding *berakah*—a connection that Paul seems purposely to be making. And this in turn accounts for the present awkwardness of expression, since even in Greek he could not meaningfully have said, "the God and Father of glory of our Lord Jesus Christ." Thus Paul's present emphasis is on identifying the God who is now known to us as "the Father of our Lord Jesus Christ" as the one who also dwells in infinite and unfathomable glory, to the praise of whose glory all of the divine activity carried out by the Son has taken place.[15]

Paul's readers would know from the opening *berakah* that the present expression, "the God of our Lord Jesus Christ," is not about the God whom Christ worships[16]—such an idea is totally foreign to Paul—but is about the God who is now known to us as most truly revealed in his Son. At the same time, this God is "the Father who dwells in the context of infinite glory." Thus, even though he is the Father of glory as defined, and therefore the one to whom Paul can pray with great confidence, Paul's confidence in his prayer rests ultimately with the fact that the matters for which he prays are available to his readers because this God is first of all the Father of our Lord Jesus Christ.

Thus, once more in Paul's letters we are reminded of how much his encounter with the risen Lord, Jesus Christ, has affected the way he thinks about everything, including his understanding of God himself.

---

[14] See, e.g., the NIV/TNIV, NLT, GNB, REB. The problem with this translation is that the reader who knows no Greek could not pick up the connection with "to the praise of his glory" in vv. 3–14. These translations do the same with the next phrase, "the riches of his glorious inheritance in his people" (TNIV), which probably also should be rendered more literally, "the riches of the glory of his inheritance in his people," so as to keep this key word intact. Cf. Hoehner, 255.

[15] It is of some surprise how seldom this connection is made in the commentaries; but cf. Best, 161, for the phrase itself. For the OT background, cf. Ps 29:3 ("the God of glory") and Ps 24:7–10 ("the King of glory"). See also in the present volume the discussion on 1 Cor 2:8 in ch. 3 (p. 136).

[16] As a freestanding sentence on its own, of course—and Arius and others read texts "on their own" rather than in context—this would seem to be the plain meaning of the phrase, just as in "my God," or "your God," or "the god of the Gentiles." Both immediate context and usage throughout the Pauline corpus negate such an understanding.

Ephesians 4:13

That Paul's Son of God Christology lies behind all the preceding references to God as Father seems to be made certain by his reference to the Son of God in the middle of a long sentence (vv. 11–16) describing the role of those whom Christ himself has given to the church.[17] The reason such ministries (apostles, prophets, evangelists, pastor-teachers) have been given is ultimately for the church's full maturity. That maturity will include works of service so that the body of Christ may be built up, but its ultimate aim is for the body's unity in two matters: the faith itself and the "full knowledge[18] of the Son of God." Thus:

4:13 καταντήσωμεν οἱ πάντες εἰς τὴν ἑνότητα τῆς πίστεως
καὶ **τῆς ἐπιγνώσεως τοῦ υἱοῦ**[19] **τοῦ θεοῦ**
we all attain   *the unity of the faith*
*and of **the knowledge of the Son of God***

What is striking is this sudden appearance of the title "the Son of God" in a passage surrounded by references to Christ. This may be just for change of pace, but it seems far more likely to be a deliberate pickup of this theme from the opening praise of God and prayer for the readers in ch. 1, where God was deliberately designated as the Father of our Lord Jesus Christ, with the Son of God being present by presupposition. Full knowledge of the Son of God is, in this passage, the equivalent of full knowledge of God himself, since the word has to do not so much with the accumulation of facts and data but with the kind of knowing that people who know each other well have of one another. Thus, in this kind of usage we are dealing not with Jewish messianism but with Paul's Christian conviction that Jesus is the Son of God, whom the Father sent into the world.[20] The assumed high Christology in such a phrase is self-evident.

---

[17] For a critique of M. Barth's idiosyncratic view of this passage, as having to do with believers going out to meet Christ at his Parousia as king and bridegroom (484–96), see Lincoln, 255.

[18] Gk. ἐπίγνωσις; although "full knowledge" might appear to be "overtranslation," this is an attempt to distinguish it from γνῶσις itself. Here Paul intends something more, having to do with intimate acquaintance with, not just "knowledge about." For Paul's usage of the present word in this kind of setting, see G. D. Fee, *The First Epistle to the Corinthians* (NICNT; Grand Rapids: Eerdmans, 1987), 648–49, on 1 Cor 13:12, where the cognate verb appears.

[19] The words τοῦ υἱοῦ are missing in a few Western witnesses (F G b Clement[pt] Lucifer), most likely because of the four words in a row that have the same ending, which in their abbreviated form would appear as ΤΟΥ ΥΥ ΤΟΥ ΘΥ.

[20] Cf. Robinson: " . . . suggesting, as it would seem, the thought of His eternal existence in relation to the Divine Father" (100).

God as "Our" Father

The other several references to God as Father presuppose God as the Father of our Lord Jesus Christ, but now the emphasis lies with God as the Father of his people, redeemed by Christ Jesus. In each case Paul's emphasis is on Jew and Gentile together as the one people of God. There are five such moments.

Ephesians 2:18

In one of the more eloquent passages in his letters regarding Jew and Gentile together as the one, newly formed people of God (2:11–18), Paul's concluding word is that "we both by the Spirit have equal access *to the Father*."[21] And here again this referent to God as Father presupposes that it is through the Son that he also becomes our Father (as in Gal 4:4–6).[22] The reason for thinking so is not only because of what is said emphatically in the opening *berakah* but also because the present paragraph is altogether about the work of Christ, who is the Son of the Father. Using significant language from the OT sacrificial system, Paul presents Christ as the one who through his "blood" tore down the wall of hostility between Jew and Gentile by setting aside what divided them: the law "with its commands and regulations." Thus, Christ reconciled *both* (not just the Gentiles) to God through his death on the cross, and by so doing, he put to death their long history of hostility. Thus, at the end Paul points out that what Jew and Gentile now have in common is access *together* to the God who is the Father of their Lord Jesus Christ and who through him is also their common Father. Thus again, although Jewish messianism is not in view here, Paul's Son of God Christology—Christ as the messianic/now eternal Son—is the presupposition of the reference to God in this sentence.

Ephesians 3:14–16

This same thing happens again in Eph 3:14–16. Here Paul is intent on putting his own apostleship in the context of the reconciliation just narrated, the now disclosed "mystery" that through Christ "the Gentiles are heirs together with Israel, members together of one body, and sharers together in the promise [that is fulfilled] in Christ Jesus" (3:6). Given how Paul brought God the Father into that equation in ch. 2, it should not surprise us that he does a similar thing in the long prayer for his Gentile readers, that they will both comprehend and actualize this great reality. Thus the prayer that began in

---

[21] That the emphasis is still on Jew and Gentile together having access is made clear by Paul's word order, which (literally put) reads, "Because through him [Christ] we have access, the both of us, by the one Spirit to the Father." Not very good English, but showing how the Greek emphasizes Jew and Gentile together as one people.

[22] So also Eadie, 187; Lincoln, 149; O'Brien, 209.

v. 1, but was broken off to explain Paul's own role in what God was doing in Christ, is picked up again in v. 14 as Paul "bowing his knees" before the Father.

The context makes it certain here that God is the Father of his people—he is, after all, the one who has named everything in the entire universe[23]—but the larger context again indicates that this relationship exists between God and the universe not simply because he gave it birth, as it were (cf. v. 9), but because he has been praised at the very beginning of the letter (1:3) as the God whom we now know as the Father of our Lord Jesus Christ.[24]

Ephesians 4:6

Again, this same thing occurs in the triadic expression of God's identity in Eph 4:4–6, where in the interest of his immediate concern about ethical life that is to be lived by the power of the Spirit, Paul names God's threefold identity in the ascending order of the role of each in salvation. Because his immediate concern is for his readers to keep the unity of the Spirit (v. 3), picking up this emphasis from 2:18, 22, Paul places that unity ultimately in the "oneness" of (1) the one Spirit (v. 4), who formed the body and as God's down payment is the ground of their hope; (2) the one Lord (v. 5), who has become so for them through their common faith and baptism; and (3) the one God (v. 6), who is again identified as "the Father of all," which is then interepreted in terms of his being "over, through, and in" all things.[25] In so doing, Paul again picks up the emphasis from 2:18 and 3:14 on his being the Father of both Jew and Gentile and thereby the Father of all; and again that is so precisely because he is first of all the Father of our Lord Jesus Christ (1:3).[26]

Ephesians 5:1

In what seems to be at once a summary and transitional passage, Paul urges his readers, as God's dear children, to follow God's example of forgiveness. Even though God is not called "Father" here, it is implied in Paul's

---

[23] At least that seems to be the point of the "divine passive" ὀνομάζεται (*is named*) in this clause. The reason for the passive verb at the end is to emphasize that everything comes from the God who has "named" them all.

[24] This understanding of the text goes back very early, as is evidenced by the widespread addition of τοῦ κυρίου ἡμῶν Ἰησοῦ Χριστοῦ, found as early as the Old Latin and which eventually became the Majority Text. The shorter, original text is found in 𝔓46 ℵ* A B C P 6 33 81 365 1175 1739, plus Origen and the Coptic. Best (337) asserts that by rejecting this reading, one also rejects this understanding. But that is a quite unnecessary move; after all, it is Paul who is in prayer and who has just spoken of the Father as the one to whom Jew and Gentile have common access (2:18). Why the additional descriptor that sees God also as the Father of all should thus change the meaning is not at all clear. For the understanding suggested here, see also O'Brien, 255.

[25] Some recent commentators (Lincoln, 240; O'Brien, 284) have noted the relationship of this language to Paul's reworking of the Jewish Shema in 1 Cor 8:6.

[26] See pp. 355–56 below for the christological implications of the middle member, "one Lord."

calling them God's children. At stake is still the concern for Jew and Gentile as one people of God and thereby giving evidence of it by the way they live in unity with each other. Thus a passage that began in 4:1, urging them to "walk" in love, further urges them to make every effort to keep the unity of the Spirit through the bond of peace, since there is only one body (picking up from the assertion in 3:6 that Gentiles and Jews together form one body).

Most of the rest of the chapter spells out the means (through the gifts of ministry given them by Christ) and the nature of that unity. Thus, when Paul moves on in 4:25 to spell out the latter, he once more picks up the imagery of the church as "one body." One can hardly miss the fact that all the sins mentioned thereafter until 5:1 are sins that destroy the unity of the one body. To sum up what has preceded and to make the transition to other kinds of sins, which list begins in 5:3, Paul urges them to be "like Father, like child" by forgiving one another when wronged and in any case to "walk in love," of the kind demonstrated by *the* Son, who gave himself for them. With this word, Paul thus frames the entire passage from 4:1, but also he anticipates the movement toward corporate life that begins again in 5:15–20. It is in this latter passage that the final mention of God as "our" Father occurs.

Ephesians 5:20

Following a path already laid out in Colossians, Paul uses the teaching dimension of their singing as a way to transition from the prior ethical concerns to the concern for living Christ in the Christian household. Thus he urges that their Spirit-inspired worship be such that as they "speak to one another" through their various forms of sacred singing, they do so also as thanksgiving "in the name of our Lord Jesus Christ" but ultimately offered τῷ θεῷ καὶ πατρί (*to [our] God and Father*). Thus the basic hortatory section of the letter concludes on the same note with which the whole letter began. In 1:3 the God whom we praise is the one whom we now know as the Father of our Lord Jesus Christ; in 5:20 the God to whom we offer thanks in the Son's name (5:20) is the God who at the same time is "our" Father.

Together, all of these passages,[27] although focused more on God's people, elaborate on the reality that the God whom they serve and worship, the only God there is, is in fact their Father because he is first of all the Father of our Lord Jesus Christ. In all of this the focus is on Christ as the eternal Son of God. In our final passage in this section we turn to the one place where it is presupposed that the eternal Son has also assumed the messianic role of the Davidic Son of God.

Ephesians 5:5—Jesus the Messianic King

With yet another echo of his letter to the Colossians, but considerably reshaped to fit the broader context of the present letter, Paul refers to the fu-

---

[27] See the summary of uses in the letter in Robinson, 83.

ture kingdom of God as "the kingdom of the Messiah and of God." In both passages (Col 1:12–13 and this one) the setting has to do with Gentiles receiving their share of the "inheritance." In its original setting, this language had to do with Israel's inheriting the promised land, which eventually became the place where the Davidic king ruled God's people. In Colossians, Paul assures his Gentile readers that they have already received their share of the inheritance when they were transferred "into the [present] kingdom of the beloved Son of the Father." In the present passage, Paul is urging his readers to give up altogether the kind of behavior that, from Paul's Jewish perspective, characterized pagan Gentiles: sexual immorality, uncleanness, and avarice—the last being identified as a form of idolatry. Such people, Paul goes on, have no "inheritance in the [coming] kingdom of the Messiah and of God."

That τοῦ Χριστοῦ in this case is more the Son's title[28] than his new "name" seems likely for three reasons. First, the combination τοῦ Χριστοῦ καὶ θεοῦ (an articular ὁ Χριστός joined with a καί [and] to an anarthrous θεοῦ) is unique not only to this letter but also to the corpus as a whole. In fact, when such a phenomenon does appear (i.e., articular noun / καί / anarthrous noun), as in 1:3 and 5:20, the second noun is in apposition to the first ("God, that is, the Father"). Since that does not seem to be the case here, this unusual usage suggests that ὁ Χριστός means "the Christ/Messiah." Second, the more common expression in Paul's writings, as in the rest of the NT, is "the kingdom of God."[29] But the evidence from Col 1:13 (and 1 Cor 15:24) suggests that the present expression of God's kingdom has the messianic Son of God as King. Third, the very order of these nouns puts the emphasis on the Messiah's rule, which at the same time is God the Father's kingdom. This in itself not only is best expressed in terms of the messianic King but also indicates the assumed high Christology of the apostle. Thus the eternal Son of God, who presently rules in God's eternal kingdom, does so because in his earthly pilgrimage he assumed the role of the long-awaited Jewish Messiah.

All of this is to say, then, that with Paul's use of Son of God/God as Father language, he regularly presupposes that the eternal Son of God in his earthly life stepped into the role of the Davidic messianic King, who in 2 Sam 7:14 and Ps 2:7 is called God's Son (cf. Ps 89:26–27).

Christ as Κύριος

As with all the preceding letters, Paul can hardly speak about Christ without regularly using the title ὁ κύριος (the Lord). As indicated in the next

---

[28] Cf. Hoehner, 661–62 ("possibly").

[29] So much is this so that two (companion) manuscripts (F G) reverse Paul's order to what the scribe expected.

letter (Phil 2:10–11), from Paul's perspective this title was bestowed on Christ at his exaltation. Whereas this title dominated Paul's earlier letters, in Ephesians as in Colossians it tends to be found primarily in the ethical/behavioral section, in this case primarily in chs. 4–6. At the heart of Paul's—and the early church's—use of this title was the conviction that Christ's exaltation was to the Father's "right hand," thus in fulfillment of Ps 110:1 ("The LORD says to my Lord, 'Sit at my right hand until I make your enemies a footstool for your feet' "). The fourth of Paul's references to this reality[30] occurs in the thanksgiving-prayer in Eph 1:15–23, and in this instance, as in its first appearance (1 Cor 15:24–27), it is combined with language from Ps 8:6. And even though the title κύριος itself does not occur here, we begin this discussion of the title in Ephesians by looking at this passage because it plays such an important role in all subsequent uses of the title.

Ephesians 1:20–23—The Exalted One at the Right Hand

The dominating soteriological motif in this letter has to do with the reconciling work of Christ, whereby through his death he created a new ἄνθρωπος (*humanity*) out of Jew and Gentile, having abolished the barrier (the law) that separated them (2:11–22). Throughout chs. 3 to 5 this theme is carried forward through the metaphor of the church as Christ's body. But the secondary soteriological motif, which carries over from Colossians, is that Christ, through his death and resurrection-exaltation, has also subdued and thus subjugated "the powers," the spiritual forces that apparently played a considerable role in the lives of many believers in the Lycus Valley and beyond.

It is not surprising, therefore, that these two soteriological themes are played out with special force in the *berakah* (1:3–14) and thanksgiving-prayer (1:15–23) with which this letter begins. Christ's victory over the powers is hinted at in the *berakah* ("he has blessed us in the heavenlies" [v. 3]), but this theme is otherwise subordinated to the redemptive work of the cross, whereby we have been both forgiven of our sins and adopted as God's children (vv. 5–8). However, in the thanksgiving-prayer the focus is altogether on Christ's victory over the powers. With an extraordinary profusion of "power" language, Paul speaks of God's power both as at work in the raising of Christ from the dead and as his "inheritance" for these Gentile believers.

Our immediate interest lies with vv. 20–23, where Paul speaks of God's mighty power that raised Christ from the dead and exalted him to the highest place, having "seated him at his right hand" in the heavenly realm. That this is a deliberate echo of Ps 110:1 (109:1 LXX) can be seen by looking at the two texts together:

---

[30] For a more complete examination of this usage, see discussion in ch. 3 on its first occurrence in 1 Cor 15:24–27 (pp. 110–12); cf. Rom 8:34 and Col 3:1.

Ps 109:1 LXX εἶπεν ὁ κύριος **τῷ κυρίῳ μου**
               κάθου   **ἐκ δεξιῶν μου**
Eph 1:20   καὶ **καθίσας**   **ἐν δεξιᾷ αὐτοῦ** ἐν τοῖς ἐπουρανίοις

Ps 109:1 LXX   *Said the* LORD *to* **my Lord,**
               Sit   **at my right hand**
Eph 1:20   *and* **having seated him** **at his right hand** *in the heavenlies*

Paul's concern in this instance is with the second line in the psalm, that God has positioned Christ as Lord and thus far above all the other powers, which are named here with language from Colossians: πάσης ἀρχῆς καὶ ἐξουσίας καὶ δυνάμεως καὶ κυριότητος καὶ παντὸς ὀνόματος ὀνομαζομένου (*every rule and authority and power and lordship and every other name that is named*). This last phrase indicates that Paul's intent is to cast a wide net, so that by whatever name "the powers" are known to his readers, Christ has been exalted to a κυριότητος (*lordship*) far above, and therefore over, all of them.[31]

Paul then concludes his prayer with a final sentence in which he echoes the second strophe from Ps 110:1 (109:1 LXX), but now with the language of Ps 8:6 (8:7 LXX)—a phenomenon that had already occurred in 1 Cor 15:24–27. Thus, not only has Christ been *positioned* in the place of authority—at the Father's right hand—but also, in so doing, God has *subjected* the powers to his authority. Thus:

Ps 109:1 (LXX) ἕως ἂν θῶ τοὺς ἐχθρούς σου **ὑποπόδιον τῶν ποδῶν** σου
Ps 8:7 (LXX)   **πάντα ὑπέταξας**   **ὑποκάτω τῶν ποδῶν αὐτοῦ**
Eph 1:22   καὶ **πάντα ὑπέταξεν** **ὑπὸ τοὺς πόδας αὐτοῦ**

Ps 109:1 (LXX) *until I put your enemies* **under your feet**
Ps 8:7 (LXX)   **all things having**   **subjected under his feet**
Eph 1:22   *and* **all things he**   **subjected under his feet**

In Paul's understanding of the exalted One, therefore, Christ has been appointed to be the "Lord" of Ps 110:1 and thus to have all authority in heaven and on earth both in the present age and in the age to come. And all of this has happened, Paul reminds his readers, for their sakes. Thus, with a striking use of the metaphor of the body and its head (found only here and in Col 2:9–10), he uses the Jewish understanding of this metaphor by placing Christ as "head" *over* the powers.[32]

There can be no mistaking the very high Christology presupposed in this passage, which comes to a striking climax in the final clause, a clause whose

---

[31] Cf. Matera: " . . . Christ's enthronement, whereby God established his Messiah as ruler over spiritual as well as human beings" (*New Testament Christology*, 150).

[32] Interestingly, when Paul later uses this same metaphor for Christ's relationship to the church itself, he shifts to the Greek use of the metaphor, where Christ is

grammar seems clear enough but whose nuanced meaning is not quite so. The clause reads, ἥτις ἐστὶν τὸ σῶμα αὐτοῦ, τὸ πλήρωμα τοῦ τὰ πάντα ἐν πᾶσιν πληρουμένου (*which is his body, the fullness of him who fills all things in all places*). The grammar seems plain enough: the church, where Jew and Gentile have become the one people of God, is pictured as the body of Christ—the Lord, who now sits enthroned in the heavenlies and under whose feet all other powers have been subjected.

But Paul does not end there because he understands the church itself to be a part of this expansive role of the now exalted Christ. So in apposition to "the church" he adds the metaphor of the church as Christ's body, now understood as expressing his continuing presence on earth. And so he appends a final clause: the church, Christ's body, is to be the expression of the "fullness" of Christ, who is then described in language that ordinarily belongs to God alone. Through his church, Christ's own fullness now fills τὰ πάντα ἐν πᾶσιν (*all things in all places*).[33] This is precisely the kind of thing said over and again about God the Father—in this letter in 4:6, where God is "over all things, through all things, and in all things."

One can scarcely miss the christological implications. Through Christ's death and resurrection, there is no part of the created order that is not filled with his presence. And this is the most likely reason for such a high incidence of the phrase "in Christ / Christ Jesus / the Lord" in this letter. The church's entire existence is circumscribed as being "in Christ Jesus"; and thus while his people are an expression of his "fullness" on earth, they are at the same time "seated with [God] in the heavenly realms in Christ Jesus" (2:6). Thus, through his incarnation and exaltation, Christ himself fills "all things in all places"—a phrase that presupposes his full deity.

Ephesians 4:4–6—The One Κύριος and the Triadic Character of the One God

The second major christological passage in Ephesians occurs toward the beginning of the ethical/behavioral section of the letter; here it will be dis-

---

the "head" of the body, whose working parts are all dependent on, and supported by, the head. See discussion on 1 Cor 11:3 in ch. 3 (pp. 143–47) and the article where this analysis was first presented: G. D. Fee, "Praying and Prophesying in the Assemblies: 1 Corinthians 11:2–16," in *Discovering Biblical Equality: Complementarity without Hierarchy* (ed. R. W. Pierce and R. M. Groothuis; Downers Grove, Ill.: InterVarsity Press, 2004), 142–60.

[33] At least that is what the grammar seems to demand; at issue is the meaning of the participle πληρουμένου, which on its own could be either middle (with Christ as the assumed subject) or passive (with God as the assumed subject). The vast majority of interpeters view it as a middle; among those who argue for a passive, see esp. Best, 187–89; cf. J. A. T. Robinson, *The Body: A Study in Pauline Theology* (SBT 5; London: SCM Press, 1952), 68–69; R. Yates, "A Re-examination of Ephesians 1:23," *ExpTim* 83 (1972): 146–51; P. Benoit, "Body, Head and *pleroma* in the Epistles of the Captivity," in *Jesus and the Gospel* (trans. B. Weatherhead; 2 vols.; London: Darton, Longman & Todd, 1973–1974), 2:90; Hoehner, 298–99.

cussed in two parts (vv. 4–6, 7–13). As noted previously, chs. 4–6 of the letter spell out the practical implications of Christ's having created one new humanity of Jew and Gentile together. Thus Paul begins this section with his basic appeal: they should "walk worthy of their calling" (v. 1) by "bearing with one another in love" (v. 2) and thus making "every effort to keep the unity of the Spirit through the bond of peace" (v. 3). The next two matters brought forward are, first, the theological *basis* of their unity (vv. 4–6) and, second, the *source* of the gifting that will aid them in making that unity work (vv. 7–18). Our immediate interest is with the significant basis that he sets before them.

As Paul's beginning point, he once again reflects his understanding of the body as a matter of diversity within essential unity, first articulated in some detail in 1 Cor 12:12–26. In both cases the unity is found in the divine Triad: the one Spirit, the one Lord, and the one God, who is Father of all (vv. 4–6; cf. 1 Cor 12:4–6); and in both cases the order is Spirit, Christ, and God because the Spirit is the key to making the unity work. But there can be no real unity that does not embrace the body's essential diversity. In 1 Corinthians the urgency was on the diversity itself, where the Corinthians had confused uniformity with unity. Here the emphasis is primarily on the unity of the body. Their "oneness" in the context of their diversity, he postulates, is predicated on the "oneness" of the divine Triad—Spirit, Lord, Father. Thus he abruptly asserts, out of the blue, as it were,

ἓν σῶμα	one body,
καὶ ἓν πνεῦμα,	and one Spirit,
καθὼς καὶ ἐκλήθητε ἐν μιᾷ ἐλπίδι . . .	just as you were called with one hope . . .
εἷς κύριος,	one Lord
μία πίστις,	one faith
ἓν βάπτισμα,	one baptism
εἷς θεὸς καὶ πατὴρ πάντων,	one God and Father of all
ὁ ἐπὶ πάντων	who is above all things
καὶ διὰ πάντων	and through all things
καὶ ἐν πᾶσιν	and in all things

In making this bold assertion, particularly in the context of the one Spirit and one Lord, Paul emphasizes his readers' own "oneness" in terms of both their origins and what it means for them to be one body in Christ. The one Spirit has formed them into the one body, and also has "sealed" them as belonging to God, thus guaranteeing their future (1:13–14); so his readers' "one hope" is also associated with the "one Spirit." Associated with the one Lord is their "one faith" and "one baptism," the common denominator for both Jewish and Gentile incorporation into the body of Christ. And all of this takes place within the framework of the one God, who is the Father of all and through whom all things exist.

In making this kind of affirmation, Paul is in line with other early believers whose understanding of God's identity now includes both the Son and the Spirit (Peter, John, Hebrews). And it is this divine "oneness" and their unity within diversity that serves for Paul as the ultimate basis of the unity of Jew and Gentile in one body. On the considerable christological, not to mention theological, significance of such an assertion, see discussion on 1 Cor 12:4–6 in ch. 3 (pp. 124–25).

Ephesians 4:7–13—The Exalted Christ, the Giver of Gifts

Having thus offered the *basis* for their unity, Paul next describes the *means* for establishing that unity within their obvious diversity; and here Paul's high Christology again finds expression.

He begins with a thematic statement similar to that found in 1 Cor 12:7 and Rom 12:6: ἑνὶ δὲ ἑκάστῳ ἡμῶν ἐδόθη ἡ χάρις κατὰ τὸ μέτρον τῆς δωρεᾶς τοῦ Χριστοῦ (*to each one of us grace has been given according to the measure of the gift of Christ*).[34] On first reading, one might understandably assume that the verb ἐδόθη (*has been given*) is a "divine passive," with God as the implied subject. This seems especially so in light of the concluding prepositional phrase, which suggests that what has been given is "in keeping with the measure of the gift of Christ"; that is, God's present gifting in the church is in keeping with the "measure" found in God's giving Christ to us.

However, what follows gives us good reason to pause, so much so that most English translations treat the genitive τοῦ Χριστοῦ as subjective, thus understanding that Christ himself allots the gifts.[35] That this is most likely what Paul intended is borne out by the intriguing citation of Ps 68:18 (67:19

---

[34] This is the kind of sentence that should cause proponents of pseudepigraphy to have second thoughts, since it is both too Pauline and too much a combination of what he had said earlier in 1 Corinthians and Romans, and thus much too subtle for a pseudepigrapher, who would also need to have known both of the earlier letters to have written this sentence. Here are the three passages, with the ties to 1 Corinthians in boldface and to Romans in underline:

> 1 Cor 12:7   **ἑκάστῳ δὲ δίδοται** ἡ φανέρωσις τοῦ πνεύματος πρὸς τὸ συμφέρον
>
> Rom 12:6   ἔχοντες δὲ χαρίσματα κατὰ <u>τὴν χάριν τὴν δοθεῖσαν</u> ἡμῖν
>
> Eph 4:7   ἑνὶ δὲ **ἑκάστῳ** ἡμῶν <u>ἐδόθη</u> <u>ἡ χάρις</u> κατὰ τὸ μέτρον τῆς δωρεᾶς τοῦ Χριστοῦ

This is Paul simply making the same point three times and adjusting each to the particular setting.

[35] The NRSV, e.g., even though it adheres to a more literal translation, puts it in a way that is hardly ambiguous: "according to the measure of Christ's gift." Functional equivalence translations make it even clearer: "grace has been given as Christ apportioned it" (TNIV); "bestowed in whatever way Christ allotted it" (NJB); "in proportion to what Christ has given" (GNB). So also most commentaries, most recently Hoehner, 523.

LXX) that follows. The introductory διὸ λέγει (*therefore it [or he] says*) indicates that Paul is citing the psalm in order to secure his present point: Christ himself is responsible for the variety of giftings necessary for the building up of his church. Thus Paul, in a nearly verbatim citation of the Septuagint, writes,

Eph 4:8　　　ἀναβὰς εἰς ὕψος ᾐχμαλώτευσεν αἰχμαλωσίαν,
　　　　　　　ἔδωκεν　　　　　δόματα τοῖς ἀνθρώποις.

Ps 67:19 LXX　ἀνέβης εἰς ὕψος ᾐχμαλώτευσας αἰχμαλωσίαν,
　　　　　　　ἔλαβες　　　　　δόματα ἐν ἀνθρώπῳ.

Eph 4:8　　　***Having ascended on high, he took captives captive;***
　　　　　　　he gave　　　　***gifts*** *to* ***human*** *beings.*

Ps 67:19 LXX　***You ascended on high, you took captives captive;***
　　　　　　　you received　　***gifts*** *among* ***humanity.***[36]

The difficulty that many have had with Paul's citation is that, in contrast to most such citations, he seems deliberately to have altered the text of the psalm to suit his own purposes, which in turn seem to be the opposite of what the psalmist says. On the other hand, it is arguable that what Paul has done makes perfectly good sense in light of his (proper) understanding of the ancient Near Eastern setting. In a psalm that pictures Yahweh himself as the warrior-king who has ascended to his holy hill in Jerusalem, the psalmist notes that Yahweh, as with all such ancient warriors, has taken a great deal of spoils. But the main purpose of such spoils was for the warrior-king to benefit his people, not simply to increase his own wealth. Indeed, this is the picture presented in Exodus regarding Yahweh's contending with Pharaoh, and thus with Pharaoh's gods. In the Song of Moses, Pharaoh boasts, "I will pursue, I will overtake, I will divide the spoil" (Exod 15:9), which, of course, did not happen because Yahweh "threw him into the sea." But in the Exodus narrative itself it was previously noted that Yahweh himself would do this to Pharaoh and his people. Thus, "When you leave, you will not go empty-handed; every woman is to ask her neighbor . . . for articles of silver and gold and for clothing, which you will put on your sons and daughters. And so you will plunder the Egyptians" (Exod 3:21–22).

This phenomenon most likely lies behind Paul's citation of the psalm. As his own interpretation that follows indicates (vv. 9–10), his first concern is with Christ's having ascended to his throne, thereby stepping into the role of the ancient warrior-king and thus able to divide the spoils, as it were. Paul gets there with a christological interpretation of the text similar to that in Rom 10:6–8. There he interpreted Christ's death, resurrection, and ascension in light of Deut 30:12–14, using language from Ps 107:26 in the process (see

---

[36] This rendering into English is less an attempt at gender accuracy as it is to recognize that Paul and the Septuagint have the same word, although Paul keeps the plural of the Hebrew while the Septuagint has the singular.

ch. 6, pp. 255–59). Here he does the same thing with Ps 68:18; but in this case the citation serves a double purpose.

On the one hand, it provides the language "ascended on high," which originally referred to Yahweh's "ascent" to Mount Zion but now is applied to Christ and his ascent to the right hand of the Father (cf. 1:20–21), where he now has authority over all the powers, whether in heaven or on earth. And that in turn allows Paul to pick up the emphasis from ch. 1, in this case arguing by implication that the Christ who ascended to the right hand of the Father had previously "descended" to the depths by way of his death; but since he has conquered death through resurrection, there is no part of the universe that does not come under his divine lordship.[37]

On the other hand, and now the primary reason for the citation, Christ's victory over death and the grave means that he has not only taken the enemies' "spoils" as his own, but he has done so precisely so that he might thereby endow his church with all the gifts that are his to give, resulting from his "ascent" after his "descent." In making this move with regard to the psalm, Paul has simply captured the point of the psalm itself: Yahweh plundered Egypt (and Canaan) for the sake of his people. It is of some interest, therefore, that the Aramaic Targum on the Psalms makes precisely this same move quite independently of Paul, rendering the passage, "You captured captives; . . . you gave gifts to the sons of men."[38]

One can scarcely miss the christological implications. First, as with so many earlier texts in Paul's letters, an OT passage that has Yahweh as its referent has been appropriated and applied to Christ as Lord. Christ is now the

---

[37] This decidedly minority view goes back as far as Chrysostom; cf. Robinson, 180; Hendriksen, 192; Barth, 433–34; O'Brien, 295; Hoehner, 536. Most hold the view that the "descent" is simply a reference to his incarnation per se; see Eadie, 293 (who lists a large number of earlier interpreters); Westcott, 60; Mitton, 147–48; Bruce, 343–44; Best, 384–86; MacDonald, 290–91. The major difficulty with this view is the adjective κατώτερα (*lower parts*), which on the one hand is totally unnecessary if descent to the earth itself were intended and, on the other hand, when combined with the genitive "of the earth," seems unnecessarily redundant—either "to the lower parts = earth" or simply "to the earth," but why "lower parts *of* the earth"? Many have thus taken it to refer to descent into Hades (Tertullian, Irenaeus, Jerome; Alford, Ellicott, Scott), but that seems an unnecessary intrusion into this text. Finally, G. B. Caird argued vigorously for the "descent" at Pentecost, where Christ returned by his Spirit ("The Descent of the Spirit in Ephesians 4:7–11," in *Studia evangelica II* [ed. F. L. Cross; TUGAL 87; Berlin: Akademie, 1964], 535–45; Lincoln (247) also prefers it, as does W. H. Harris, "The Ascent and Descent of Christ in Ephesians 4:9–10, *BSac* 151 (1994): 198–214; cf. idem, *The Descent of Christ: Ephesians 4:7–11 and Traditional Hebrew Imagery* (Grand Rapids: Baker, 1998), 171–97.

[38] In light of the immediate context of v. 11, G. V. Smith ("Paul's Use of Psalm 68:18 in Ephesians 4:8," *JETS* 18 [1975]: 181–89) adds to this view the interesting possibility that Paul also had Num 18:6 in view, where Yahweh speaks of his having "taken" the Levites from among the people of Israel: "To you they are given as a gift for the Lord." O'Brien (292–93) is especially attracted to this view. The difficulty, of course, is that it lacks the warrior-king motif of the psalm.

warrior-king, who through his death and resurrection not only subdued all of God's enemies but also is the source of all gifting in his body, the church. Second, what are ordinarily, and rightly, understood as the prerogatives of God alone are now equally shared by Christ the Lord—and this without apology or explanation.

Christ and the Divine Prerogatives

Although the preceding passages represent the primary christological moments in this letter, as with all the preceding letters, this one is filled with all kinds of "incidental" moments that reflect Paul's high Christology as an assumed substratum. We look at them in canonical order.

Ephesians 3:19; 5:1–2, 25–27—The Love of Christ

As we have noted before (see 1 Thess 2:13; 2 Cor 5:14; Rom 8:35), Paul more often speaks of the love of God than of Christ; and when he does speak of the latter, it is usually (as in 5:2, 25) expressed in terms of the love demonstrated in his dying for us. But the three instances of usage in this letter call for further comment. In 3:19, as the climax to his profuse prayer for his readers, Paul's concern is that they will come to know Christ's love in all its fullness and thereby to be filled with God's fullness. Although perhaps an allusion to what he has said about Christ in 2:14–18, this in fact is the only time that Paul speaks of the love of Christ without tying it directly to Christ's death for us (as in 5:2). Indeed, here is an instance where one might have expected Paul to refer to "the love of God"; but for him, this love is an interchangeable reality with regard to the Father and the Son.[39]

The imperative in 5:1–2 calls for special attention because it reflects the kind of interchange between God's love and Christ's love that one finds in Rom 8:35, 39. In the present passage, God's love is expressed in terms of the recipients' being "beloved" *children* who are now called upon to imitate the *Father's* love in their relationships with one another. But when Paul goes on to offer the supreme example of such love—demonstrated in *the* Son—he speaks of "Christ [who] loved us and gave himself for us." Thus both the interchange and the specific way he speaks of Christ's love reflect what has been said in earlier letters.

Similarly in 5:25–27, Paul, urging the believing householder to love his wife, directs him to do so after the model of Christ. In language identical to 5:2, Paul urges love for one's wife of the same kind as "Christ [who] loved the

---

[39] There has been considerable discussion regarding "knowing this love that surpasses knowledge." Surely, Paul intends that this love can be comprehended in terms of its effects, but in the end it is beyond our human capacity fully to comprehend such love in Christ.

church and gave himself up for her to make her holy." The surprising christological twist comes at the end of this long sentence, where the bridegroom (Christ), through his cleansing of her, will "present her *to himself* as a radiant church." Paul does this, of course, to keep the analogy intact; but in so doing, he makes an easy shift away from what one might have expected, that Christ would "present the church to the Father," just as in an earlier use of this imagery Paul speaks of himself presenting the church to Christ (2 Cor 11:2). Rather, Christ here is both "presenter" and "receiver"; and thus Paul, again with perfect ease, places Christ in a role that ordinarily would belong to God the Father.

Ephesians 4:17—A Modified Oath Formula

In several previous moments in his letters when Paul wants to emphasize the importance or gravity of a certain point, he takes a mild oath in the name of the Lord.[40] This happens again in this letter, although it is less an oath and more the basis on which he will command the Ephesian believers to stop living like Gentiles. Thus:

4:17	τοῦτο οὖν λέγω	καὶ	μαρτύρομαι ἐν κυρίῳ
	This, therefore, I say;	*indeed*	**I insist on it in the Lord**

As before, the significance of this kind of oath-taking is that it was required of Israel to take their oaths in Yahweh's (= the Lord) name alone (Deut 6:13). Thus, when Paul urges his readers to abandon altogether their former way of life, he "insists on it in the Lord," where Christ as Lord assumes the role that was formerly the special province of Yahweh.

Ephesians 4:21—The Truth That Is in Jesus

4:21 ὑμεῖς δὲ οὐχ οὕτως ἐμάθετε **τὸν Χριστόν**, εἴ γε **αὐτὸν** ἠκούσατε καὶ ἐν **αὐτῷ** ἐδιδάχθητε, καθώς ἐστιν **ἀλήθεια ἐν τῷ Ἰησοῦ**,

But you did not thus learn **Christ**, *if indeed* **him** *you heard about and* **in him** *you were taught, just as is* **the truth in Jesus.**

In this remarkable sentence Paul once again asserts that an attribute that is essential to God's character (absolute truth) is to be found in Jesus. That God is not only the one true God but also therefore the God of truth is a standard OT staple, of which Ps 31:5b (30:6b LXX) is but one example: ἐλυτρώσω με, κύριε, ὁ θεὸς τῆς ἀληθείας (*Redeem me, Lord, the God of truth*). This kind of understanding is carried over by Paul with regard to God, who is both the living and the true God (1 Thess 1:9) and the one whose truth is represented in the gospel (Rom 15:8). In 2 Cor 11:10, how-

---

[40]See, e.g., discussion in ch. 2 on 1 Thess 5:27; 2 Thess 3:6, 12; in ch. 3 on 1 Cor 1:10; 5:3–4; in ch. 4 on 2 Cor 11:10; in ch. 6 on Rom 15:30.

ever, Paul speaks of "the truth of Christ" that is "in me" (see ch. 4, p. 193). In a very similar way, he now speaks of the content of his gospel as "the truth that is in Jesus."

Ephesians 5:8–14—Christ, the Source of Light

Whatever else is true about God in the OT, he is himself both the source of light (the first reality of creation [Gen 1:3]) and the one who dwells in inextinguishable light. It is in God's light that we see light (Ps 36:9b). Thus, one of the eschatological promises is that the sun will be needed no longer, since "the LORD will be your everlasting light" (Isa 60:19). In Ephesians this is yet another divine attribute now applied to Christ.

In a series of plays on light and darkness, as representing God's people in a dark world, Paul first notes that by their being ἐν κυρίῳ (in the Lord), his readers are themselves light (v. 8); and then after a considerable play on this concept as to how they live in the world, he cites from an unknown source that in their awakening from sleep, and thus rising from the dead, "Christ will shine on you" (v. 14).[41] Thus, what was thought of as a strictly divine prerogative is presuppositionally here attributed to Christ.

Ephesians 5:10—Living to Please the Lord

In the middle of the preceding passage, as the means whereby his readers will be children of the light, Paul urges that they learn to "determine (by proper examination) what is pleasing to the Lord." On this assumption of yet another divine prerogative by Christ, see in ch. 4 the discussion of 2 Cor 5:9 (pp. 190–91).

Ephesians 5:17 (and 1:1; 6:6)—The Lord's Will and God's Will

Although not found often in the OT, the concept of doing "God's will" most likely has its roots in texts such as Ps 40:8, a text cited and expounded in Heb 10:5–10 ("Here I am—it is written about me in the scroll—I have come to do your will, my God"). This concept occurs frequently in Paul's thought.[42] In this letter it finds expression both in the somewhat standard phrase regarding Paul's apostleship in 1:1 and regarding the conduct of slaves in 6:6. In light of this consistent way of speaking about the divine will, Paul's urging of his readers (in 5:17) to "know what the will of the Lord is" (ἀλλὰ συνίετε τί τὸ θέλημα τοῦ κυρίου) is another remarkable transfer of a notably divine prerogative to the Lord = Christ.

---

[41] On the possibility that this is an amalgam of OT texts (in the manner of 1 Cor 2:9), see Hendriksen, 234–36. It is more common to suggest that the source is an early Christian hymn; so Best, 497–98.

[42] See 1 Thess 4:3; 5:18 (accompanied by ἐν Χριστῷ Ἰησοῦ); 1 Cor 1:1; 2 Cor 1:1; 8:5; Gal 1:4; Rom 1:10; 12:2; 15:32; Col 1:1, 9; 4:12; 2 Tim 1:1.

Ephesians 5:19–20—Singing to the Lord and in the Lord's Name

In Col 3:16 Paul speaks of their worship in terms of singing the message about Christ, indicating that such singing is ultimately to God and offered with thanksgiving. In this companion passage the exhortation is slightly reconstructed so that its goal (teaching and admonishing one another), its content (the message about Christ), and its mode (with all wisdom) are no longer in view. This means that the recipient of such singing also changes, from God the Father to Christ the Lord, always at the same time offering thanksgiving to God "in the name of the Lord." Thus, in a very typical way, Paul makes the same kind of interchange with regard to the divine person to whom they sing as he does in the many other kinds of activities noted in this section of these chapters. And again, such an interchange carries significant christological implications,[43] since such singing is the worship of a deity.[44]

On Paul's use of offering thanks "in the name of the Lord," see the discussion in ch. 2 on 2 Thess 3:6 (pp. 67–68) and in ch. 3 on 1 Cor 1:10 (pp. 135–36).

Ephesians 6:5—Obedience to Christ, the Lord; Ephesians 6:8—The Lord Will Reward

In the "house rules" of the letter (5:21–6:9), which differ significantly from those in Col 3:18–4:1, Paul again urges slaves to treat their service to their earthly "lords" as service to God. On this matter, see the discussion in ch. 7 on the Colossians passage (pp. 330–31).

In this same passage, Paul tells the slaves that the end result of their serving their earthly masters as those serving their heavenly Lord is that each, whether slave or free, κομίσεται παρὰ κυρίου (*will receive recompense from the Lord*). This is the same language used of the outcome for those (all of us) who appear before "the judgment seat of Christ" in 2 Cor 5:10 (see ch. 4, pp. 190–92).

Ephesians 6:10—Being Strong in the Lord

For the concept of this passage, see the discussion in ch. 2 of 2 Thess 3:3 (pp. 71–72). Because the present passage comes as an imperative—what Paul's readers are themselves to do in this matter—the point is quite the same as the indicative addressed to the Thessalonians ("The Lord [= Christ]

---

[43]Eadie notes the imperatival nature of this text and thus remarks, "The early church, in obedience to the apostle's mandate, acknowledged His Divinity, and sang praises to Him as its God" (404).

[44]Cf. Hurtado, *Lord Jesus Christ*, 150–51.

is faithful, who will strengthen you"). Thus here, as in 2 Thess 3:3 and 1 Thess 3:12, Paul sees the Lord as in the divine role otherwise attributed to God the Father (2 Thess 2:17; Rom 16:25).[45]

But equally significant in the present passage is the way the phrase concludes: καὶ ἐν τῷ κράτει τῆς ἰσχύος αὐτοῦ (*and in the power of his might*). This is the same language used earlier in this letter (1:19) to speak of God's power by which he raised Christ from the dead (κατὰ τὴν ἐνέργειαν τοῦ κράτους τῆς ἰσχύος αὐτοῦ [*according to the working of the power of his might*]). Thus one more time, and obviously without thoughtful intent, Paul attributes to Christ as Lord what elsewhere he says of God.

Conclusion

What should be striking about the various phrases in the preceding passages in this final section is how much like the Paul of the other letters this phenomenon is. One wonders about the capacity of someone writing in Paul's name to be able to enter into his skin so thoroughly as to succeed in doing this. In any case, what emerges in the more incidental ways is in keeping with the fully Pauline character of the Christology that emerges throughout, even though, as it turns out, after Galatians this letter has the least amount of christological data in the church corpus. And this is in keeping with the similar concern of both letters: Jew and Gentile as one people of God through Christ and the Spirit. It is the second concern of this letter—the exalted Christ as Lord over the powers—that has increased the amount of christological data in this case.

These two concerns also account for the twofold christological emphases: Christ as Son of God, and the risen Christ as Lord. Thus the Christology of this letter is quite in keeping with that of the earlier letters and represents what is genuinely Pauline Christology.

---

[45] Of course, Rom 16:25 has come under suspicion of being non-Pauline because of the significant differences in the various ways the extant copies of Romans conclude. On this larger matter, see H. Y. Gamble, *The Textual History of the Letter to the Romans: A Study in Textual and Literary Criticism* (SD 42; Grand Rapids: Eerdmans, 1977); on the doxology as such, see the brief discussion in B. M. Metzger, *A Textual Commentary on the Greek New Testament* (2d ed.; New York: United Bible Societies, 1994), 476–77; also the much longer discussion by L. Hurtado, "The Doxology at the End of Romans," in *New Testament Textual Criticism—Its Significance for Exegesis: Essays in Honour of Bruce M. Metzger* (ed E. J. Epp and G. D. Fee; Oxford: Clarendon, 1981), 185–99.

Appendix I: The Texts

(double brackets [[ ]] indicate texts with references to God alone)

1:1–2 ¹Παῦλος **ἀπόστολος Χριστοῦ Ἰησοῦ** <u>διὰ θελήματος θεοῦ</u> τοῖς ἁγίοις τοῖς οὖσιν ἐν Ἐφέσῳ καὶ πιστοῖς **ἐν Χριστῷ Ἰησοῦ**, ²χάρις ὑμῖν καὶ εἰρήνη <u>ἀπὸ θεοῦ πατρὸς ἡμῶν</u> καὶ **κυρίου Ἰησοῦ Χριστοῦ.**

1:3–10 ³Εὐλογητὸς <u>ὁ θεὸς καὶ πατὴρ</u> **τοῦ κυρίου ἡμῶν Ἰησοῦ Χριστοῦ**, <u>ὁ εὐλογήσας</u> ἡμᾶς ἐν πάσῃ εὐλογίᾳ πνευματικῇ ἐν τοῖς ἐπουρανίοις **ἐν Χριστῷ**, ⁴καθὼς <u>ἐξελέξατο</u> ἡμᾶς **ἐν αὐτῷ** πρὸ καταβολῆς κόσμου εἶναι ἡμᾶς ἁγίους καὶ ἀμώμους <u>κατενώπιον αὐτοῦ</u>, ἐν ἀγάπῃ ⁵<u>προορίσας</u> ἡμᾶς εἰς υἱοθεσίαν **διὰ Ἰησοῦ Χριστοῦ** <u>εἰς αὐτόν</u>, κατὰ τὴν εὐδοκίαν <u>τοῦ θελήματος αὐτοῦ</u>, ⁶<u>εἰς ἔπαινον δόξης τῆς χάριτος αὐτοῦ ἧς ἐχαρίτωσεν</u> ἡμᾶς **ἐν τῷ ἠγαπημένῳ.** ⁷<u>ἐν ᾧ</u> ἔχομεν τὴν ἀπολύτρωσιν **διὰ τοῦ αἵματος αὐτοῦ**, τὴν ἄφεσιν τῶν παραπτωμάτων, κατὰ <u>τὸ πλοῦτος τῆς χάριτος αὐτοῦ</u> ⁸<u>ἧς ἐπερίσσευσεν</u> εἰς ἡμᾶς, ἐν πάσῃ σοφίᾳ καὶ φρονήσει, ⁹<u>γνωρίσας</u> ἡμῖν <u>τὸ μυστήριον τοῦ θελήματος αὐτοῦ</u>, <u>κατὰ τὴν εὐδοκίαν αὐτοῦ ἣν προέθετο</u> **ἐν αὐτῷ** ¹⁰εἰς οἰκονομίαν τοῦ πληρώματος τῶν καιρῶν, ἀνακεφαλαιώσασθαι τὰ πάντα **ἐν τῷ Χριστῷ**, τὰ ἐπὶ τοῖς οὐρανοῖς καὶ τὰ ἐπὶ τῆς γῆς **ἐν αὐτῷ.**

1:11–14 ¹¹**Ἐν ᾧ καὶ** ἐκληρώθημεν προορισθέντες <u>κατὰ πρόθεσιν τοῦ τὰ πάντα ἐνεργοῦντος κατὰ τὴν βουλὴν τοῦ θελήματος αὐτοῦ</u> ¹²εἰς τὸ εἶναι ἡμᾶς <u>εἰς ἔπαινον δόξης αὐτοῦ</u> τοὺς προηλπικότας **ἐν τῷ Χριστῷ.** ¹³**ἐν ᾧ καὶ** ὑμεῖς ἀκούσαντες τὸν λόγον τῆς ἀληθείας, τὸ εὐαγγέλιον τῆς σωτηρίας ὑμῶν, **ἐν ᾧ καὶ** πιστεύσαντες ἐσφραγίσθητε τῷ πνεύματι τῆς ἐπαγγελίας τῷ ἁγίῳ, ¹⁴ὅ ἐστιν ἀρραβὼν τῆς κληρονομίας ἡμῶν, εἰς ἀπολύτρωσιν τῆς περιποιήσεως, <u>εἰς ἔπαινον τῆς δόξης αὐτοῦ.</u>

1:15–23 ¹⁵Διὰ τοῦτο κἀγὼ ἀκούσας τὴν καθ᾽ ὑμᾶς πίστιν **ἐν τῷ κυρίῳ Ἰησοῦ** καὶ τὴν ἀγάπην τὴν εἰς πάντας τοὺς ἁγίους ¹⁶οὐ παύομαι εὐχαριστῶν ὑπὲρ ὑμῶν μνείαν ποιούμενος ἐπὶ τῶν προσευχῶν μου, ¹⁷ἵνα <u>ὁ θεὸς</u> **τοῦ κυρίου ἡμῶν Ἰησοῦ Χριστοῦ**, <u>ὁ πατὴρ τῆς δόξης,</u> δώῃ ὑμῖν πνεῦμα σοφίας καὶ ἀποκαλύψεως <u>ἐν ἐπιγνώσει αὐτοῦ</u>, ¹⁸πεφωτισμένους τοὺς ὀφθαλμοὺς τῆς καρδίας ὑμῶν εἰς τὸ εἰδέναι ὑμᾶς τίς ἐστιν ἡ ἐλπὶς <u>τῆς κλήσεως αὐτοῦ</u>, τίς ὁ πλοῦτος τῆς δόξης <u>τῆς κληρονομίας αὐτοῦ</u> ἐν τοῖς ἁγίοις, ¹⁹καὶ τί τὸ ὑπερβάλλον μέγεθος <u>τῆς δυνάμεως αὐτοῦ</u> εἰς ἡμᾶς τοὺς πιστεύοντας κατὰ τὴν ἐνέργειαν <u>τοῦ κράτους τῆς ἰσχύος αὐτοῦ</u>, ²⁰ἣν ἐνήργησεν **ἐν τῷ Χριστῷ** <u>ἐγείρας</u> **αὐτὸν ἐκ νεκρῶν** καὶ καθίσας <u>ἐν δεξιᾷ αὐτοῦ ἐν τοῖς ἐπουρανίοις</u> ²¹ὑπεράνω πάσης ἀρχῆς καὶ ἐξουσίας καὶ δυνάμεως καὶ κυριότητος καὶ παντὸς ὀνόματος ὀνομαζομένου, οὐ μόνον ἐν τῷ αἰῶνι τούτῳ ἀλλὰ καὶ ἐν τῷ μέλλοντι· ²²καὶ **πάντα ὑπέταξεν ὑπὸ τοὺς πόδας αὐτοῦ καὶ αὐτὸν ἔδωκεν κεφαλὴν ὑπὲρ πάντα τῇ ἐκκλησίᾳ**, ²³ ἥτις ἐστὶν **τὸ σῶμα αὐτοῦ**, τὸ πλήρωμα τοῦ τὰ πάντα ἐν πᾶσιν πληρουμένου.

2:4–10 ⁴<u>ὁ δὲ θεὸς πλούσιος ὢν ἐν ἐλέει</u>, διὰ τὴν πολλὴν ἀγάπην αὐτοῦ ἣν <u>ἠγάπησεν</u> ἡμᾶς, ⁵καὶ ὄντας ἡμᾶς νεκροὺς τοῖς παραπτώμασιν συνεζωοποίησεν **τῷ Χριστῷ**, χάριτί ἐστε σεσῳσμένοι – ⁶καὶ συνήγειρεν καὶ συνεκάθισεν **ἐν τοῖς ἐπουρανίοις ἐν Χριστῷ Ἰησοῦ**, ἵνα ἐνδείξηται ἐν τοῖς αἰῶσιν τοῖς ἐπερχομένοις τὸ ὑπερβάλλον πλοῦτος τῆς χάριτος αὐτοῦ ἐν χρηστότητι ἐφ᾽ ἡμᾶς **ἐν Χριστῷ Ἰησοῦ**. ⁸Τῇ γὰρ χάριτί ἐστε σεσῳσμένοι διὰ πίστεως· καὶ τοῦτο οὐκ ἐξ ὑμῶν, θεοῦ τὸ δῶρον· ⁹οὐκ ἐξ ἔργων, ἵνα μή τις καυχήσηται. ¹⁰αὐτοῦ γάρ ἐσμεν ποίημα, κτισθέντες **ἐν Χριστῷ Ἰησοῦ** ἐπὶ ἔργοις ἀγαθοῖς οἷς προητοίμασεν ὁ θεὸς, ἵνα ἐν αὐτοῖς περιπατήσωμεν.

2:12–18 ¹²ὅτι ἦτε τῷ καιρῷ ἐκείνῳ **χωρὶς Χριστοῦ**, ἀπηλλοτριωμένοι τῆς πολιτείας τοῦ Ἰσραὴλ καὶ ξένοι τῶν διαθηκῶν τῆς ἐπαγγελίας, ἐλπίδα μὴ ἔχοντες καὶ ἄθεοι ἐν τῷ κόσμῳ. ¹³νυνὶ δὲ **ἐν Χριστῷ Ἰησοῦ** ὑμεῖς οἵ ποτε ὄντες μακρὰν ἐγενήθητε ἐγγὺς **ἐν τῷ αἵματι τοῦ Χριστοῦ**. ¹⁴**Αὐτὸς γάρ ἐστιν ἡ εἰρήνη ἡμῶν, ὁ ποιήσας** τὰ ἀμφότερα ἓν καὶ τὸ μεσότοιχον τοῦ φραγμοῦ **λύσας**, τὴν ἔχθραν **ἐν τῇ σαρκὶ αὐτοῦ**, ¹⁵τὸν νόμον τῶν ἐντολῶν ἐν δόγμασιν **καταργήσας**, ἵνα τοὺς δύο κτίσῃ ἐν αὐτῷ εἰς ἕνα καινὸν ἄνθρωπον **ποιῶν εἰρήνην** ¹⁶**καὶ ἀποκαταλλάξῃ** τοὺς ἀμφοτέρους ἐν ἑνὶ σώματι τῷ θεῷ διὰ τοῦ σταυροῦ, **ἀποκτείνας τὴν ἔχθραν ἐν αὐτῷ**. ¹⁷καὶ **ἐλθὼν εὐηγγελίσατο εἰρήνην** ὑμῖν τοῖς μακρὰν καὶ εἰρήνην τοῖς ἐγγύς· ¹⁸ὅτι **δι᾽ αὐτοῦ** ἔχομεν τὴν προσαγωγὴν οἱ ἀμφότεροι ἐν ἑνὶ πνεύματι πρὸς τὸν πατέρα.

2:19–22 ¹⁹Ἄρα οὖν οὐκέτι ἐστὲ ξένοι καὶ πάροικοι ἀλλὰ ἐστὲ συμπολῖται τῶν ἁγίων καὶ οἰκεῖοι τοῦ θεοῦ, ²⁰ἐποικοδομηθέντες ἐπὶ τῷ θεμελίῳ τῶν ἀποστόλων καὶ προφητῶν, **ὄντος ἀκρογωνιαίου αὐτοῦ Χριστοῦ Ἰησοῦ**, ²¹**ἐν ᾧ** πᾶσα οἰκοδομὴ συναρμολογουμένη αὔξει εἰς ναὸν ἅγιον **ἐν κυρίῳ**, ²²**ἐν ᾧ καὶ** ὑμεῖς συνοικοδομεῖσθε εἰς κατοικητήριον τοῦ θεοῦ ἐν πνεύματι.

3:1–2 ¹Τούτου χάριν ἐγὼ Παῦλος **ὁ δέσμιος τοῦ Χριστοῦ Ἰησοῦ** [v.l.-Ἰησοῦ] ὑπὲρ ὑμῶν τῶν ἐθνῶν ²εἴ γε ἠκούσατε τὴν οἰκονομίαν τῆς χάριτος τοῦ θεοῦ τῆς δοθείσης μοι εἰς ὑμᾶς,

3:4 πρὸς ὃ δύνασθε ἀναγινώσκοντες νοῆσαι τὴν σύνεσίν μου **ἐν τῷ μυστηρίῳ τοῦ Χριστοῦ**,

3:6–7 ⁶εἶναι τὰ ἔθνη συγκληρονόμα καὶ σύσσωμα καὶ συμμέτοχα **τῆς ἐπαγγελίας ἐν Χριστῷ Ἰησοῦ** διὰ τοῦ εὐαγγελίου, ⁷οὗ ἐγενήθην διάκονος κατὰ τὴν δωρεὰν τῆς χάριτος τοῦ θεοῦ τῆς δοθείσης μοι κατὰ τὴν ἐνέργειαν τῆς δυνάμεως αὐτοῦ.

3:8–12 ⁸Ἐμοὶ τῷ ἐλαχιστοτέρῳ πάντων ἁγίων ἐδόθη ἡ χάρις αὕτη, τοῖς ἔθνεσιν εὐαγγελίσασθαι **τὸ ἀνεξιχνίαστον πλοῦτος τοῦ Χριστοῦ** ⁹καὶ φωτίσαι πάντας τίς ἡ οἰκονομία τοῦ μυστηρίου τοῦ ἀποκεκρυμμένου ἀπὸ τῶν αἰώνων ἐν τῷ θεῷ τῷ τὰ πάντα κτίσαντι, ¹⁰ἵνα γνωρισθῇ νῦν ταῖς ἀρχαῖς καὶ ταῖς ἐξουσίαις ἐν τοῖς ἐπουρανίοις διὰ τῆς ἐκκλησίας ἡ πολυποίκιλος σοφία τοῦ θεοῦ, ¹¹κατὰ πρόθεσιν τῶν αἰώνων ἣν ἐποίησεν **ἐν τῷ Χριστῷ Ἰησοῦ τῷ κυρίῳ ἡμῶν**, ¹²**ἐν ᾧ** ἔχομεν τὴν παρρησίαν καὶ προσαγωγὴν ἐν πεποιθήσει διὰ τῆς πίστεως **αὐτοῦ**.

3:14–17 ¹⁴Τούτου χάριν κάμπτω τὰ γόνατά μου <u>πρὸς τὸν πατέρα</u>, ^{[v.l. + τοῦ}
^{κυρίου ἡμῶν Ἰησοῦ Χριστοῦ]} ¹⁵<u>ἐξ οὗ</u> πᾶσα πατριὰ ἐν οὐρανοῖς καὶ ἐπὶ γῆς
ὀνομάζεται, ¹⁶ἵνα <u>δῷ</u> ὑμῖν κατὰ τὸ πλοῦτος <u>τῆς δόξης αὐτοῦ</u> δυνάμει
κραταιωθῆναι <u>διὰ τοῦ πνεύματος αὐτοῦ</u> εἰς τὸν ἔσω ἄνθρωπον
¹⁷**κατοικῆσαι τὸν Χριστὸν** διὰ τῆς πίστεως ἐν ταῖς καρδίαις ὑμῶν,

3:19 γνῶναί τε τὴν ὑπερβάλλουσαν τῆς γνώσεως **ἀγάπην τοῦ Χριστοῦ**, ἵνα
πληρωθῆτε <u>εἰς πᾶν τὸ πλήρωμα τοῦ θεοῦ</u>.

3:20–21 <u>Τῷ δὲ δυναμένῳ ὑπὲρ πάντα ποιῆσαι</u> ὑπερεκπερισσοῦ ὧν
αἰτούμεθα ἢ νοοῦμεν κατὰ τὴν δύναμιν τὴν ἐνεργουμένην ἐν ἡμῖν, ²¹<u>αὐτῷ ἡ</u>
<u>δόξα</u> ἐν τῇ ἐκκλησίᾳ καὶ **ἐν Χριστῷ Ἰησοῦ** εἰς πάσας τὰς γενεὰς τοῦ
αἰῶνος τῶν αἰώνων, ἀμήν.

4:1 Παρακαλῶ οὖν ὑμᾶς ἐγὼ ὁ δέσμιος **ἐν κυρίῳ** ἀξίως περιπατῆσαι τῆς
κλήσεως ἧς ἐκλήθητε,

4:5–7 εἷς κύριος, μία πίστις, ἓν βάπτισμα, ⁶<u>εἷς θεὸς καὶ πατὴρ πάντων</u>, ὁ ἐπὶ
<u>πάντων καὶ διὰ πάντων καὶ ἐν πᾶσιν</u>. ⁷Ἑνὶ δὲ ἑκάστῳ ἡμῶν ἐδόθη ἡ χάρις
κατὰ τὸ μέτρον **τῆς δωρεᾶς τοῦ Χριστοῦ**.

4:8–11 ⁸διὸ λέγει· ἀναβὰς εἰς ὕψος ᾐχμαλώτευσεν αἰχμαλωσίαν, ἔδωκεν
δόματα τοῖς ἀνθρώποις. ⁹τὸ δὲ **ἀνέβη** τί ἐστιν, εἰ μὴ **ὅτι καὶ κατέβη εἰς τὰ**
κατώτερα μέρη τῆς γῆς; ¹⁰**ὁ καταβὰς αὐτός ἐστιν καὶ ὁ ἀναβὰς** ὑπεράνω
πάντων τῶν οὐρανῶν, ἵνα **πληρώσῃ τὰ πάντα.** ¹¹**Καὶ αὐτὸς ἔδωκεν** τοὺς
μὲν ἀποστόλους, τοὺς δὲ προφήτας, τοὺς δὲ εὐαγγελιστάς, τοὺς δὲ ποιμένας
καὶ διδασκάλους,

4:12–16 ¹²πρὸς τὸν καταρτισμὸν τῶν ἁγίων εἰς ἔργον διακονίας, εἰς
οἰκοδομὴν **τοῦ σώματος τοῦ Χριστοῦ**, ¹³μέχρι καταντήσωμεν οἱ πάντες εἰς
τὴν ἑνότητα τῆς πίστεως καὶ **τῆς ἐπιγνώσεως τοῦ υἱοῦ τοῦ θεοῦ**, εἰς
ἄνδρα τέλειον, εἰς μέτρον ἡλικίας **τοῦ πληρώματος τοῦ Χριστοῦ**, ¹⁴ἵνα
μηκέτι ὦμεν νήπιοι, κλυδωνιζόμενοι καὶ περιφερόμενοι παντὶ ἀνέμῳ τῆς
διδασκαλίας ἐν τῇ κυβείᾳ τῶν ἀνθρώπων, ἐν πανουργίᾳ πρὸς τὴν μεθοδείαν
τῆς πλάνης, ¹⁵ἀληθεύοντες δὲ ἐν ἀγάπῃ αὐξήσωμεν **εἰς αὐτὸν** τὰ πάντα, **ὃς**
ἐστιν ἡ κεφαλή, Χριστός, ¹⁶<u>ἐξ οὗ</u> πᾶν τὸ σῶμα συναρμολογούμενον καὶ
συμβιβαζόμενον διὰ πάσης ἁφῆς τῆς ἐπιχορηγίας κατ' ἐνέργειαν ἐν μέτρῳ
ἑνὸς ἑκάστου μέρους τὴν αὔξησιν τοῦ σώματος ποιεῖται εἰς οἰκοδομὴν
ἑαυτοῦ ἐν ἀγάπῃ.

4:17–18 ¹⁷Τοῦτο οὖν λέγω καὶ **μαρτύρομαι ἐν κυρίῳ**, μηκέτι ὑμᾶς
περιπατεῖν, καθὼς καὶ τὰ ἔθνη περιπατεῖ ἐν ματαιότητι τοῦ νοὸς αὐτῶν,
¹⁸ἐσκοτωμένοι τῇ διανοίᾳ ὄντες, <u>ἀπηλλοτριωμένοι τῆς ζωῆς τοῦ θεοῦ</u> διὰ τὴν
ἄγνοιαν τὴν οὖσαν ἐν αὐτοῖς, διὰ τὴν πώρωσιν τῆς καρδίας αὐτῶν,

4:20–21 ²⁰Ὑμεῖς δὲ οὐχ οὕτως ἐμάθετε **τὸν Χριστόν**, ²¹εἴ γε αὐτὸν ἠκούσατε
καὶ ἐν αὐτῷ ἐδιδάχθητε, καθὼς **ἐστιν ἀλήθεια ἐν τῷ Ἰησοῦ**,

[[4:24 καὶ ἐνδύσασθαι τὸν καινὸν ἄνθρωπον τὸν κατὰ θεὸν κτισθέντα ἐν δικαιοσύνῃ καὶ ὁσιότητι τῆς ἀληθείας.]]

[[4:30 καὶ μὴ λυπεῖτε τὸ πνεῦμα τὸ ἅγιον τοῦ θεοῦ, ἐν ᾧ ἐσφραγίσθητε εἰς ἡμέραν ἀπολυτρώσεως.]]

4:32 γίνεσθε δὲ εἰς ἀλλήλους χρηστοί, εὔσπλαγχνοι, χαριζόμενοι ἑαυτοῖς, καθὼς καὶ ὁ θεὸς ἐν Χριστῷ ἐχαρίσατο ὑμῖν.

5:1–2 ¹Γίνεσθε οὖν μιμηταὶ τοῦ θεοῦ ὡς τέκνα ἀγαπητὰ ²καὶ περιπατεῖτε ἐν ἀγάπῃ, **καθὼς καὶ ὁ Χριστὸς ἠγάπησεν ἡμᾶς καὶ παρέδωκεν ἑαυτὸν** ὑπὲρ ἡμῶν προσφορὰν καὶ θυσίαν τῷ θεῷ εἰς ὀσμὴν εὐωδίας.

5:5 τοῦτο γὰρ ἴστε γινώσκοντες, ὅτι πᾶς πόρνος ἢ ἀκάθαρτος ἢ πλεονέκτης, ὅ ἐστιν εἰδωλολάτρης, οὐκ ἔχει κληρονομίαν **ἐν τῇ βασιλείᾳ τοῦ Χριστοῦ καὶ θεοῦ.**

[[5:6 Μηδεὶς ὑμᾶς ἀπατάτω κενοῖς λόγοις· διὰ ταῦτα γὰρ ἔρχεται ἡ ὀργὴ τοῦ θεοῦ ἐπὶ τοὺς υἱοὺς τῆς ἀπειθείας.]]

5:8 ἦτε γάρ ποτε σκότος, **νῦν δὲ φῶς ἐν κυρίῳ**· ὡς τέκνα φωτὸς περιπατεῖτε

5:10 δοκιμάζοντες τί ἐστιν **εὐάρεστον τῷ κυρίῳ,**

5:14 πᾶν γὰρ τὸ φανερούμενον φῶς ἐστιν. διὸ λέγει· ἔγειρε, ὁ καθεύδων, καὶ ἀνάστα ἐκ τῶν νεκρῶν, καὶ ἐπιφαύσει σοι **ὁ Χριστός.**

5:17 διὰ τοῦτο μὴ γίνεσθε ἄφρονες, ἀλλὰ συνίετε τί **τὸ θέλημα τοῦ κυρίου.**

5:19–20 ¹⁹λαλοῦντες ἑαυτοῖς ἐν ψαλμοῖς καὶ ὕμνοις καὶ ᾠδαῖς πνευματικαῖς, ᾄδοντες καὶ ψάλλοντες τῇ καρδίᾳ ὑμῶν **τῷ κυρίῳ,** ²⁰εὐχαριστοῦντες πάντοτε ὑπὲρ πάντων **ἐν ὀνόματι τοῦ κυρίου ἡμῶν Ἰησοῦ Χριστοῦ** τῷ θεῷ καὶ πατρί.

5:21–24 Ὑποτασσόμενοι ἀλλήλοις **ἐν φόβῳ Χριστοῦ,** ²²αἱ γυναῖκες τοῖς ἰδίοις ἀνδράσιν **ὡς τῷ κυρίῳ,** ²³ὅτι ἀνήρ ἐστιν κεφαλὴ τῆς γυναικὸς **ὡς καὶ ὁ Χριστὸς κεφαλὴ τῆς ἐκκλησίας, αὐτὸς σωτὴρ τοῦ σώματος·** ²⁴ἀλλὰ ὡς ἡ ἐκκλησία **ὑποτάσσεται τῷ Χριστῷ,** οὕτως καὶ αἱ γυναῖκες τοῖς ἀνδράσιν ἐν παντί.

5:25–27, 29–32 ²⁵Οἱ ἄνδρες, ἀγαπᾶτε τὰς γυναῖκας, **καθὼς καὶ ὁ Χριστὸς ἠγάπησεν τὴν ἐκκλησίαν καὶ ἑαυτὸν παρέδωκεν ὑπὲρ αὐτῆς,** ²⁶ἵνα αὐτὴν **ἁγιάσῃ καθαρίσας τῷ λουτρῷ τοῦ ὕδατος** ἐν ῥήματι, ²⁷ἵνα **παραστήσῃ αὐτὸς ἑαυτῷ** ἔνδοξον τὴν ἐκκλησίαν, μὴ ἔχουσαν σπίλον ἢ ῥυτίδα ἤ τι τῶν τοιούτων, ἀλλ᾽ ἵνα ᾖ ἁγία καὶ ἄμωμος. . . . ²⁹Οὐδεὶς γάρ ποτε τὴν ἑαυτοῦ σάρκα ἐμίσησεν ἀλλὰ ἐκτρέφει καὶ θάλπει αὐτήν, **καθὼς καὶ ὁ Χριστὸς τὴν ἐκκλησίαν,** ³⁰ὅτι μέλη ἐσμὲν **τοῦ σώματος αὐτοῦ.** . . . ³²τὸ μυστήριον τοῦτο μέγα ἐστίν· ἐγὼ δὲ λέγω **εἰς Χριστὸν** καὶ εἰς τὴν ἐκκλησίαν.

6:1 Τὰ τέκνα, ὑπακούετε τοῖς γονεῦσιν ὑμῶν **ἐν κυρίῳ** [v.l. omit] τοῦτο γάρ ἐστιν δίκαιον.

6:4 Καὶ οἱ πατέρες, μὴ παροργίζετε τὰ τέκνα ὑμῶν ἀλλὰ ἐκτρέφετε αὐτὰ ἐν παιδείᾳ καὶ **νουθεσίᾳ κυρίου.**

6:5–9 ⁵Οἱ δοῦλοι, ὑπακούετε τοῖς κατὰ σάρκα κυρίοις μετὰ φόβου καὶ τρόμου ἐν ἁπλότητι τῆς καρδίας ὑμῶν **ὡς τῷ Χριστῷ,** ⁶μὴ κατ᾽ ὀφθαλμοδουλίαν ὡς ἀνθρωπάρεσκοι ἀλλ᾽ **ὡς δοῦλοι Χριστοῦ** ποιοῦντες τὸ θέλημα τοῦ θεοῦ ἐκ ψυχῆς, ⁷μετ᾽ εὐνοίας δουλεύοντες **ὡς τῷ κυρίῳ** καὶ οὐκ ἀνθρώποις, ⁸εἰδότες ὅτι ἕκαστος ἐάν τι ποιήσῃ ἀγαθόν, τοῦτο κομίσεται **παρὰ κυρίου** εἴτε δοῦλος εἴτε ἐλεύθερος. ⁹Καὶ οἱ κύριοι, τὰ αὐτὰ ποιεῖτε πρὸς αὐτούς, ἀνιέντες τὴν ἀπειλήν, εἰδότες ὅτι καὶ αὐτῶν καὶ ὑμῶν **ὁ κύριός ἐστιν ἐν οὐρανοῖς** καὶ προσωπολημψία οὐκ ἔστιν παρ᾽ αὐτῷ.

6:10–11 ¹⁰Τοῦ λοιποῦ, ἐνδυναμοῦσθε **ἐν κυρίῳ** καὶ **ἐν τῷ κράτει τῆς ἰσχύος αὐτοῦ.** ¹¹ἐνδύσασθε τὴν πανοπλίαν τοῦ θεοῦ πρὸς τὸ δύνασθαι ὑμᾶς στῆναι πρὸς τὰς μεθοδείας τοῦ διαβόλου·

[[6:13 διὰ τοῦτο ἀναλάβετε τὴν πανοπλίαν τοῦ θεοῦ,]]

[[6:17 . . . ¹⁷δέξασθε καὶ τὴν μάχαιραν τοῦ πνεύματος, ὅ ἐστιν ῥῆμα θεοῦ.]

6:21 . . . Τύχικος ὁ ἀγαπητὸς ἀδελφὸς καὶ **πιστὸς διάκονος ἐν κυρίῳ,**

6:23–24 ²³Εἰρήνη τοῖς ἀδελφοῖς καὶ ἀγάπη μετὰ πίστεως ἀπὸ θεοῦ πατρὸς καὶ **κυρίου Ἰησοῦ Χριστοῦ.** ²⁴ἡ χάρις μετὰ πάντων τῶν ἀγαπώντων **τὸν κύριον ἡμῶν Ἰησοῦν Χριστὸν ἐν ἀφθαρσίᾳ.**

Appendix II: An Analysis of Usage

(* = anarthrous; + = with possessive pronoun)

Ephesians
θεός   31
Christ 65

The Data
1. κύριος Ἰησοῦς Χριστός (6 + 1 = 7)
    1:2   G* (ἀπό)
    1:3   G+ (w/ πατήρ)
    1:17   G+ (w/ θεός / πατήρ)
    [3:14 v.l. G+ (w/ πατήρ)]
    5:20   G+
    6:23   G* (ἀπό)
    6:24   A+

1a. Χριστὸς Ἰησοῦς κύριος (1)
    3:11   D+ (ἐν)
    [3:12 ἐν ᾧ]
2. κύριος Ἰησοῦς (1)
    1:15   D (ἐν)
3. Χριστὸς Ἰησοῦς (10 + 1 = 11)
    1:1   G*
    1:1   D* (ἐν)
    2:6   D* (ἐν)
    2:7   D* (ἐν)
    2:10   D* (ἐν)
    2:13   D* (ἐν)
    2:20   G* [genitive absolute]

3:1   G [v.l.-Ἰησοῦ]
3:6   D* (ἐν)
3:21 D* (ἐν)
3a. Ἰησοῦς Χριστὸς (1)
  1:5   G* (διά)
4. κύριος (16 + 8 = 24)
  2:21 D* (ἐν)
  [2:22 ἐν ᾧ]
  4:1   D* (ἐν)
  4:5   N*
  4:17 D* (ἐν)
  5:8   D* (ἐν)
  5:10 D
  5:17 G
  5:19 D
  5:22 D
  6:1   D* (ἐν) [v.l. omit]
  6:4   G*
  6:7   D
  6:8   G* (παρά)
  6:9   N
  6:10 D* (ἐν)
  6:21 D* (ἐν)
5. Ἰησοῦς (1 + 19 = 20)
  4:21 D (ἐν)

6. Χριστός (28 + 18 = 46)
  1:3   D* (ἐν)
  [1:4 ἐν αὐτῷ]
  1:10 D (ἐν)
  [1:10 ἐν αὐτῷ]
  [1:11 ἐν ᾧ]
  1:12 D (ἐν)
  [1:13 ἐν ᾧ]

[1:13 ἐν ᾧ]
1:20   D (ἐν)
2:5   D
2:12   G* (χωρίς)
2:13   G
[2:14 αὐτὸς . . . ἐστιν]
[2:18 δι' αὐτοῦ]
3:4   G
3:8   G
3:17   A
3:19   G
4:7   G
[4:11 αὐτὸς ἔδωκεν]
4:12   G
4:13   G
4:15   N* (appositive to κεφαλή)
4:20   A
4:32   D* (ἐν)
5:2   N
5:5   G
5:14   N
5:21   G*
5:23   N
5:24   D
5:25   N
5:29   N
5:32   A* (εἰς)
6:5   D
6:6   G*
7. υἱός
  4:13 G (τοῦ θεοῦ)
8. Other
  1:6   ἐν τῷ ἠγαπημένῳ

9

Christology in Philippians

HERE IS A LETTER IN the Pauline corpus without which we would have been impoverished indeed, especially when it comes to christological concerns.[1] As we have observed to this point, the only intentionally christological moment in the corpus is Col 1:15–17. Otherwise, Paul's Christology is simply assumed, and much of what is assumed is brought to bear on the primary concern of the letters: Christ's loving, redemptive sacrifice and the implications of that love for all relationships and behavior within the believing community. This is especially true of Paul's letter to the believers in Philippi, in which appears one of the more significant christological moments in the NT (2:6–11).

Written toward the end of Paul's active ministry, almost certainly from Rome,[2] this letter is full of friendship motifs expressed with genuine love and concern for the Philippians. At the same time, Paul tackles an emerging problem of possible dissension, which had arisen in the context of their suffering at the hands of the pagan population in this small outpost of Rome on the eastern end of the Macedonian plain.

As in earlier letters, two things stand out: the absolute centrality of Christ to Paul's life and worldview, and the high Christology that is assumed throughout, which emerges as a matter of course, not of theological deliberation. Indeed, what many consider the high-water mark of Pauline Christology (2:6–11) is offered to provide the ultimate paradigm of the humility and

---

[1] Commentaries on Philippians are listed in the bibliography (pp. 645–46); they are cited in this chapter by author's surname only.

[2] On this and other introductory matters, see Fee, 1–53 (in this case, 34–37), much of which is also confirmed, somewhat independently, in Bockmuehl, 25–32. Placing Philippians earlier, and from Ephesus, is one of the "assured results" of a recent generation of NT scholars that the hard data have unraveled. Not only is there no known imprisonment in Ephesus, but neither could there have been a Praetorium/Praetorian guard (1:13) or a contingent of Caesar's household worthy of note (4:22), since Asia was a senatorial, not imperial, province. The major difficulty with the traditional view has been the number of trips back and forth between Philippi and Rome that many assume; but a different way of reading the data allows for three such trips rather than five (see Fee, 36–37).

selflessness that Paul is urging on the community during this time of apparent tension.

But the Christology of this letter is not limited to this one grand narrative; in contrast to Galatians, for example, in which most of the Christology emerges in one passage, in Philippians the Christology is found throughout, and in a variety of ways. We begin as usual with a preliminary look at matters of language.

A Preliminary Look at the Data

As throughout this study, the various references to Christ and to God are found in appendix I at the end of this chapter; likewise, an analysis of the different ways of referring to Christ is found in appendix II.

The most notable feature of usage in Philippians is that Paul here continues patterns of usage that emerged in Colossians/Philemon and Ephesians, especially the latter. As in Ephesians, Christ is mentioned by name or title more than twice as often as God (49x / 23x).[3] But beyond that, there are no features of usage in Philippians that tend to stand out in a unique way. The triple designation κύριος Ἰησοῦς Χριστός occurs 5 times, but across the letter in this case (1:2; 2:11; 3:8, 20; 4:23). Double designations occur 16 times (Χριστὸς Ἰησοῦς or Ἰησοῦς Χριστός [15x]; κύριος Ἰησοῦς [1x]), mostly in prepositional phrases. Again, these are spread throughout the letter rather than bunched in any special way.

Regarding single names/titles, "Jesus" occurs once (2:10 [in the genitive and anarthrous]). Κύριος occurs 9 times, 8 of them in the phrase ἐν κυρίῳ, the single exception occurring in 4:5 in an echo of Ps 145:18. As with its companion letters, Χριστός is the most common referent (17x alone; 38x altogether); and this usage covers the whole range—subject or object of verbs; plus 4 times in prepositional phrases (but only two ἐν Χριστῷ). Whereas these latter two titles occur throughout the letter, the use of single Χριστός disappears after 3:18, and 5 of 9 single κύριος occurrences come in 4:1–10. On the other hand, for the first time since 2 Thessalonians there is no explicit reference to Christ as υἱός (Son); nonetheless, God is called πατήρ (Father) 3 times, always in close association with Christ.

Finally, this is the first (and only) time in the church corpus that the title σωτήρ (Savior) appears (3:20, with "Lord Jesus Christ" standing in apposition).[4] In this case, since it occurs in the context of "citizenship," it almost certainly stands in direct confrontation with the emperor (Nero, in this case), who is acclaimed throughout the empire as "Lord and Savior."

---

[3] Cf. Colossians (37x / 29x) and Ephesians (63x / 31x).
[4] Although see Eph 5:23, where it appears in a nontitular way, "the savior of the body."

We begin our investigation, then, with the two major christological passages in the letter, 2:6–11 and 3:20–21, in which Paul's (typical) Κύριος Christology finds ultimate expression; but in the former case we also have the clearest and strongest expression of Paul's belief in Christ as preexistent—fully divine and equal with the Father—who in his incarnation became fully human for the salvation of humankind.

Christ, Preexistent and Incarnate—Philippians 2:6–8

Since Phil 2:6–11 is one of the more significant christological passages in the corpus and since not all are agreed on a goodly number of matters related to it, some important preliminary words are needed at the outset,[5] especially some words about its structure and origin as well as its role in the context of the letter. We begin with the latter.

The immediate context (2:1–5) indicates that vv. 6–8 function primarily as paradigm.[6] At issue in Philippi is some degree of dissension within the be-

---

[5] For a full discussion and presentation of the argumentation for the positions taken here, see Fee, 191–218; cf. Bockmuehl, 114–40.

[6] That this is the plain sense of v. 5, see Fee, 199–201 (esp. n. 33). Indeed, one has to be taught to read it otherwise, since the context and grammar call for this traditional view. Nonetheless, there are two noteworthy exceptions: E. Käsemann, "A Critical Analysis of Philippians 2:5–11," *JTC* 5 (1968): 45–88; R. P. Martin, *A Hymn of Christ: Philippians 2:5–11 in Recent Interpretation and in the Setting of Early Christian Worship* (rev. ed.; Downers Grove, Ill.: InterVarsity Press, 1997). Käsemann's denial is in strong opposition to Lohmeyer and is thus predicated primarily on his theological aversion to anything that smacks of "imitating Christ," as though ethics were based finally on self-effort rather than on grace; for Martin, it also includes the "impossibility" of emulating Christ in vv. 9–11. But these objections are based on a fundamental misunderstanding of *imitatio* in Paul's thought, which does not mean "repeat after me" but rather (in the present context) "have a frame of mind which lives on behalf of others the way Christ did in his becoming incarnate and dying by crucifixion." One can appreciate the desire not to let this profound passage lose its power by making it simply an exemplary paradigm, but Paul himself seems to have done that very thing. He then follows up with his own story in 3:5–14 as one who lives out the Christ paradigm and urges the Philippians to follow his example of following the primary example (3:15–17) and thus to live in the present in a cruciform way.

The argument that vv. 9–11 are not paradigmatic seems to be tilting with windmills, since that is not in fact the majority view. Rather, these verses express God's *vindication* of Christ's living out the self-sacrificial humility set forth in vv. 6–8. L. W. Hurtado ("Jesus as Lordly Example in Philippians 2:5–11," in *From Jesus to Paul: Studies in Honour of Francis Wright Beare* [ed. P. Richardson and J. C. Hurd; Waterloo, Ont.: Wilfred Laurier University Press, 1984], 113–26), whose refutation of the Käsemann/Martin view is especially noteworthy, points out (125) that they object to a view that is overly simplistic (dubbed by Martin "naïve ethical idealism"), their caricature of which, one might add, is not the perspective of most who have written on the subject. See further the discussion in O'Brien, 253–62; S. D. Fowl, *The Story of Christ in the Ethics of Paul: An Analysis of the Function of the Hymnic Material in the Pauline Corpus* (JSNTSup 36; Sheffield: Sheffield Academic Press, 1990), 77–101.

lieving community at the very time they are also experiencing a degree of persecution from the local pagan population. These two matters are presented together in the opening appeal in 1:27–30, while the issue of dissension becomes front and center in 2:1–16. After a passionate appeal for them to "have the same mind-set,"[7] Paul indicates negatively the kind of mind-set that destroys unity: "Do nothing," he says, "out of selfish ambition [ἐριθεία] and vain conceit [κενοδοξία]," but rather in "humility" put concern for others before yourselves (vv. 3–4). At which point he then appeals to the "mind-set" of Christ (v. 5).

In the well-known telling of Christ's story that follows, and in direct contrast to the language of v. 3, Paul makes two basic points: As *God*, Christ "poured himself out" by becoming human (vv. 6–7a); as *a human*, he humbled himself by becoming obedient unto death (vv. 7b–8). Thus he demonstrated Godlikeness, over against "selfish ambition," by "pouring himself out" in assuming the role of a slave; and he demonstrated true humanness (what it means to be in God's own image), over against "vain conceit," by humbling himself in an obedience that led to the cross. Verses 9–11 then go on to relate his vindication through exaltation, by God's having bestowed on him *the Name* (= LORD). Thus everything in vv. 6–8 is aimed at offering the divine alternative to living selfishly in the context of Christian community.

At the same time, in telling the essential story of Christ, the passage is both self-contained and has an obvious poetic dimension to it. For some decades now it has therefore been a common denominator of NT scholarship to refer to this passage as "the Philippian hymn"; and what has often accompanied this "assured result" is that the "hymn" is probably non-Pauline, since there is so much said here that does not appear in quite this way at other points in the corpus.[8] But there is every good reason to be cautious at this point, since, as Stephen Fowl has pointed out, none of the alleged "hymns"

---

[7] Gk. φρονέω, a word that occurs 23 times in the Pauline corpus (of 26 in the NT), 9 times in Romans, and 10 times in this letter. In both of these letters it occurs most often in paraenetic passages having to do with "giving careful consideration to something" (BDAG), having one's mind set in a certain way, so as to be disposed toward a given way of thinking and living.

[8] This last argument seems especially specious. Paul is not writing systematic theology, after all, but letters intended to correct and encourage believers in ad hoc situations in his churches, which means that much of what they contain has been conditioned by the contingencies of the situation. Would any NT scholar, for example, believe that the Lord's Supper was celebrated in the Pauline churches if some Corinthians had not been abusing the poor at the table? And Rom 9–11 is so unlike anything else in the corpus, it sits as a constant reminder that we simply do not know all there is to know about the apostle's theology. Since the present passage is available to us only as a piece of Pauline prose and was written specifically to moderate the attitudes expressed in v. 3, one may correctly assume that what Paul wrote/dictated he had himself taken ownership of. Cf. D. J. Moo: "Methodologically it is necessary at least to assume that whatever Paul quotes, he himself affirms" (*The Epistle to the Romans* [NICNT; Grand Rapids: Eerdmans, 1996], 49 [on Rom 1:3–4]).

in the Pauline corpus fit what we know from other sources regarding this term.[9] Thus, since Paul is here telling the story of Christ as an exemplary paradigm, I will refer to it simply as "the Christ story."

Furthermore, although it is true that the passage has a decidedly poetic ring to it, it nonetheless comes to us in three (very Pauline) sentences.[10] Our immediate interest is with the first two sentences in (vv. 6–8), whose similar structure may be displayed thus:

I	a	ὃς ἐν μορφῇ θεοῦ ὑπάρχων
	b	[οὐχ ἁρπαγμὸν ἡγήσατο τὸ εἶναι ἴσα θεῷ,
	c	ἀλλὰ][11] ἑαυτὸν ἐκένωσεν
	d	μορφὴν δούλου λαβών,
	e	ἐν ὁμοιώματι ἀνθρώπων γενόμενος·
II	f	καὶ σχήματι εὑρεθεὶς ὡς ἄνθρωπος
	g	ἐταπείνωσεν ἑαυτὸν
	h	γενόμενος ὑπήκοος μέχρι θανάτου,
	i	θανάτου δὲ σταυροῦ.[12]

I	a	*Who in the "form" of God being,*
	b	*(not* harpagmon *did he consider the being equal with God.*
	c	*but) himself he poured out*
	d	*the "form" of a slave having taken,*
	e	*in the likeness of human beings having come.*
II	f	*And having been found in appearance as a "human being,"*[13]
	g	*he humbled himself*
	h	*having become obedient unto death,*
	i	*namely, death on a cross.*

Apart from the "not/but" contrast, the two sentences are nearly identical in structure, which in itself suggests that they are intended to correspond to each other. In fact, if one were to take out the bracketed line *b*, the two

---

[9]In *Story of Christ*, 31–45; cf. G. D. Fee, "Philippians 2:5–11: Hymn or Exalted Pauline Prose?" in *To What End Exegesis? Essays Textual, Exegetical, and Theological* (Grand Rapids: Eerdmans), 175–91.

[10]I say "very Pauline" because of (1) the "not/but" contrast in the first sentence, which is a thoroughly Pauline feature, as is (2) the inferential διὸ καί with which v. 9 begins; furthermore (3), the intertextual use of Isa 45:23 in v. 10 is especially Pauline (he actually cites the text in Rom 14:11), while (4) the Κύριος Christology of vv. 9–11 theologically reflects what Paul had done with the Jewish Shema in one of his early letters (1 Cor 8:6).

[11]These brackets are not intended to remove this material from the text but simply to aid in the discussion that follows.

[12]Although this arrangement is mine, the sentencing itself is that of NA[27]/UBS[4]. One of the idiosyncrasies of the Textus Receptus was a versification wherein v. 6 included lines *a-c*, v. 7 lines *d-f* (!), and v. 8 lines *g-i*; the KJV translators, however, adopted the versification known in the English Bible tradition.

[13]On the difficulty of rendering ἄνθρωπος in lines *e* and *f*, see n. 35 on 1 Tim 2:5 in ch. 10 (p. 429).

sentences end up being nicely balanced, the first indicating how Christ acted as God, the second how he acted in his humanity. But Paul does include line *b* in his sentence, and as always in his letters, the "not/but" contrast functions to heighten the effect of the "but" line—although in this case the two contrasting lines qualify negatively and positively what Christ's "being in the form of God" actually means.

It should further be pointed out that most of the difficulties with interpretation lie with the first of the two sentences (vv. 6–7), where the ideas are profound and full of theological grist, and the language not at all simple. On this matter, therefore, two further words are necessary. First, historically, the discussion has centered in four difficult wordings: ἐν μορφῇ θεοῦ (*in the "form" of God*), ἁρπαγμόν (*using to one's own advantage*), ἑαυτὸν ἐκένωσεν (*he emptied himself*), and ἐν ὁμοιώματι ἀνθρώπων (*in human "likeness"*). These difficulties, it should be noted, are concentrated in the sentence that deals with divine mysteries. That is, on the basis of what *was* known and came to be believed about Jesus' earthly life, Paul is here trying to say something about what could *not* be observed yet came to be believed about Christ's prior existence as God. Most of our difficulties stem from this reality, that Paul is expressing in narrative form what he and other early believers did not themselves experience but nonetheless believed to be a true account of Christ's own story before, during, and after his incarnation. Preexistence, therefore, is simply presuppositional to their understanding of his story.

Second, Paul's primary concern is not theological as such but illustrative,[14] what Christ Jesus did (in keeping with his "mind-set") in his prior existence as God (which, of course, does indeed say something theological). His stepping into human history is the singularly most profound display of Godlikeness that the human race has ever encountered—as profound as the ultimate oxymoron of Christian faith: a crucified Messiah.[15] Therefore, although not primarily intended as such, by its very nature the passage is full of Christology that must be dealt with.

Finally, we note that several scholars have seen Paul as here presenting Christ as the second Adam,[16] a view that has moved in two directions: first,

---

[14] A point that is too often missed in the discussions; on this matter, see Kennedy, 435.

[15] On this, see the discussion in ch. 3 on 1 Cor 1:13–2:16 (pp. 100–102).

[16] Although a possible association with Gen 2–3 was noted (but rejected) by Plummer (44), it has been much more widely accepted in recent years (e.g., Caird, 118; Houlden, 73; Kent, 127; Silva, 116 [partially]; Cullmann, *Christology*, 175; Ridderbos, *Paul*, 74; A. Bandstra, " 'Adam' and 'the Servant' in Philippians 2:5ff.," *CTJ* 1 [1966]: 213–16; M. Hooker, "Philippians 2:6–11," in *Jesus und Paulus: Festschrift für Werner Georg Kümmel zum 70. Geburtstag* [ed. E. E. Ellis and E. Grässer; Göttingen: Vandenhoeck & Ruprecht, 1978], 151–64; Dunn, *Christology in the Making*, 114–21; Wright, *Climax of the Covenant*, 90–97), with varying degrees of conviction as to how much the language has been purposely designed to represent this analogy, from Caird's "the context requires it" to Wright's more cautious "typically cryptic reference to Adam" (cf. Silva: "network of associations"). It is rejected by Collange, 88;

toward a diminished Christology that sees Christ as only human and not preexistent but whose self-sacrificial refusal to be like Adam was "rewarded" by final exaltation to God's right hand; second, toward a high Christology that sees an intentional contrast between Adam's failure and the divine Christ's stepping into that role with full success.[17] Since this has become a relatively common view despite the lack of actual *linguistic* ties between this passage and Gen 2–3, this option will be regularly evaluated in light of what Paul actually says or does not say.

Ἐν μορφῇ θεοῦ ὑπάρχων (Being in the "Form" of God) (v. 6a)

Paul's opening participial phrase, "who being[18] in the 'form' [μορφή] of God," presents us with two christological concerns: the meaning of μορφή and whether the phrase presupposes preexistence. We begin with the latter, noting that despite some recent interpreters, this language expresses as *presupposition* what the rest of the sentence assumes: it was the preexistent One who "emptied himself" at one point in our human history "by taking the 'form' of a slave, being made in the likeness of human beings." Several matters are decisive on this point.

First, Paul's use of the participle rather than the finite verb was most likely because of Christ's always "being" so.[19] Indeed, the participle ulti-

---

T. F. Glasson, "Two Notes on the Philippians Hymn (ii.6–11)," *NTS* 21 (1974–1975): 133–39; R. B. Strimple, "Philippians 2:5–11 in Recent Studies: Some Exegetical Conclusions," *WTJ* 41 (1979): 247–68; P. D. Feinberg, "The Kenosis and Christology: An Exegetical-Theological Analysis of Phil 2:6–11," *TJ* 1 (1980): 21–46; Fowl, *Story of Christ*, 70–73; Melick, 102–3; Bockmuehl, 131–33. See the useful current overview of this matter in O'Brien, 263–68.

[17] The major proponent for the first view is J. D. G. Dunn (*Christology in the Making*, 114–21, 310–13; cf. idem, *Theology of Paul*, 281–88; cf. J. Murphy-O'Connor, "Christological Anthropology in Phil. II, 6–11," *RB* 83 [1976]: 25–50). For the second view see Wright, *Climax of the Covenant*, 90–97. Because of their recognized importance, my interaction will be with these two major players.

[18] Gk. ὑπάρχων; although at times interchangeable with εἶναι (*to be*), in this case it very likely carries its primary sense of "to exist (really)" (cf. BDAG, contra BAGD). Earlier interpreters (e.g., Lightfoot, 110; Plummer, 42) argued that the word itself implies prior existence; but in the Koine period the word on its own will hardly bear that weight. See MM 650–51.

[19] On this usage of the participle in a very similar context, cf. 2 Cor 8:9. Dunn (*Christology in the Making*, 310–11) calls this point into question, since the participle by itself does not necessarily carry the connotation argued for and it may refer only to Christ's "state of being" at the time he οὐκ ἡγήσατο (*did not consider*). But this objection can be turned on its head in two ways: (1) the first verb (οὐκ ἡγήσατο) does not necessarily refer to a single moment in time but rather to his state of mind during the entire period he was ἐν μορφῇ θεοῦ; (2) had Paul intended the kind of Adam/Christ contrast that Dunn argues for, then the simple ὃς ἦν would have served his purposes better and without ambiguity. More importantly still, the participle most likely modifies the main verb of the sentence, ἐκένωσεν (*emptied*), just as the participle in v. 7b modifies ἐταπείνωσεν (*humbled [himself]*).

mately modifies, and thus stands in temporal contrast with, not the aorist of "he did not consider" but the main verb in the sentence, "he emptied himself." It was while in his state of "being one thing" that he at one point in time "emptied himself" by taking another "form," which is spelled out by the two aorist participles at the end of the sentence (lines *d* and *e*). Thus, *prior* to his "having taken the 'form' of a slave" he was in fact "in the 'form' of God." Moreover, it also stands in contrast in a substantive way with the final participle in the sentence, "*having come to be* in the likeness of human beings," which makes best sense only if "being in the μορφή of God" presupposes prior existence as God.[20] Thus, even if Paul might be contrasting Christ with Adam in this opening sentence, this phrase can scarcely be an allusion to Christ's *humanity* as being "in God's image." After all, it makes little sense to say that "being already in God's likeness [as a human being], Christ emptied himself by coming to be (or 'being born') in human likeness."[21]

That leads us, second, to the word μορφή,[22] where our difficulties are two:[23] discovering what Paul intended by this word and then translating it

---

This further suggests that much of the debate over the relationship of the participle "being" to the verb "did not consider" is moot—e.g., concessive (the majority; NRSV ["though he was in the form of God"]; cf. NASB; ESV; NAB; Lightfoot, 111; Vincent, 58; Michael, 85; Hendriksen, 103; Silva, 112) or causal (Hawthorne, 85; Wright [*Climax of the Covenant*, 83 n. 110], following C. F. D. Moule ["The Manhood of Jesus in the New Testament," in *Christ, Faith and History: Cambridge Studies in Christology* (ed. S. W. Sykes and J. P. Clayton; Cambridge: Cambridge University Press, 1972)], 97), thus "precisely because he was in the form of God . . . he recognized what it meant, etc." More likely, Paul's intent is circumstantial (in relation to the main verb): "who, in the circumstance of being in the μορφή of God (as he always was), poured himself out" (cf. GNB: "he always had the nature of God"; so also Meyer, 79).

[20] Dunn's way of handling this is to suggest that lines *a* and *d* and *b* and *e* form a double inclusio (*Christology in the Making*, 115). Thus "in the 'form' of God" in line *a* means "in the image of God"; in the inclusio of line *d* Jesus' willingness to bear the "image" of a slave is said to be parallel with Adam's having become a slave to sin. For the second contrast, which takes a lot more imagination, see point 2 in the section "The Role of the Participles in Verses 7–8" below (pp. 385–89).

[21] As Wright has correctly observed, "[The contrast] does not involve merely the substitution of one sort of humanity for another" (*Climax of the Covenant*, 92).

[22] The word occurs in only these two instances in the NT. The literature here is immense. The best of the dictionary articles are those in *TDNT* (4.759–62 [J. Behm]) and *EDNT* (2.442–43 [W. Pohlmann]), with a useful bibliography in the latter. The best of the earlier discussions in English (before the influence of the papyri) is by Kennedy (435–36 [cited in MM 417]), which supersedes that of Lightfoot (127–33), which was limited to classical usage (and, in spite of its usefulness in that regard, takes up issues probably not Pauline). See also the discussion by Martin (*A Hymn of Christ*, 99–133 [although he accepts its improbable identity with εἰκών and δόξα]), and the more recent commentaries (Hawthorne, 81–84; Silva, 113–16; O'Brien, 207–11; Fee, 204; Bockmuehl, 127).

[23] Others see another issue here as well: the cultural-historical "background" to this word (and to many other of the ideas found throughout the "hymn"). On this issue, see O'Brien, 193–98—except to point out that the influential view of Käsemann (n. 6 above), that it reflects a pre-Christian gnostic redeemer myth, is itself a piece of

into English, which lacks a precise equivalent.[24] The key to understanding the word lies with Paul's probable reason for choosing it, which in turn lies with what transpires in the sentence itself. His urgency is to say something about Christ's "mind-set," first as God and second as a man. But in the transition from Christ's "being God" (line *a*) to his "becoming human" (line *e*), Paul expresses by way of *metaphor* (line *d*) the essential quality of that humanity: he "took on the 'form' of a slave." Μορφή was precisely the right word for this dual usage, to characterize both the reality (his being God) and the metaphor (his taking on the role of a slave),[25] since it denotes "form" or "shape" not usually in terms of the external features by which something is recognized but of those characteristics and qualities that are essential to it. Hence, it means *that which truly characterizes a given reality.*[26] It turns out, therefore, that this is the only word in Greek that would serve Paul's purposes; and all attempts to understand ἐν μορφῇ θεοῦ in line *a* without at the same time considering line *d* are doomed to failure at the outset.[27]

This understanding of μορφή, it should be noted, puts considerable negative pressure on the view that this word has sufficient semantic overlap with εἰκών (*image*) so as to make possible a *semantic* allusion to Christ as second Adam. Whether the entire sentence allows for a *conceptual* allusion is more open-ended;[28] but the fact remains that there is not a single verbal

---

scholarly mythology, since there are no hard data (or soft, for that matter) for such a view in the first Christian century.

[24] Cf. Vincent: "'Form' is an inadequate rendering of μορφή, but our language affords no better word" (57). In the absence of a better alternative, I will stay with "form" but put it in quotation marks.

[25] Had it not been for the second phrase, therefore, Paul might have written something like φύσει θεός (*being God in nature*) or perhaps ἐν φύσει θεοῦ (*in God's nature*). But φύσις would not work in the second instance, where "slave" is metaphorical and needs the second participle (line *e*) to spell out what is intended. Nor would the σχῆμα of the final participial phrase in v. 7 work (UBS[4]; beginning of v. 8 in English translation), since that word emphasizes external features rather than substance or reality. As Meyer notes, "The μορφή θεοῦ presupposes the divine φύσις" (80).

[26] So MM: "a form which truly and fully expresses the being which underlies it" (417 [citing Kennedy]) (cf. Martin, 94; Hawthorne, 83; O'Brien, 210). As noted, the second occurrence is what makes it extremely unlikely that μορφή serves as a synonym for εἰκών (*image*). The second occurrence of μορφή (v. 7) also creates difficulties for the view, adopted in various forms (by, e.g., Meyer, Jones, Martin [95], Strimple ["Philippians 2:5–11"], Bockmuehl [128–29], Fowl [*Story of Christ*, 54]), that μορφή = δόξα (*glory*), a view that would have much going for it had we only the first instance (ἐν μορφῇ θεοῦ); but to apply "glory" to the role of the slave is to press words beyond their ordinary sense (cf. Collange, 97–98; Hawthorne, 82).

[27] Dunn does in fact take this into account, suggesting that it "probably refers therefore to what Adam became as a result of his fall: he lost his share in God's glory and became a slave" (*Christology in the Making*, 115). It is of some interest, of course, that this language is used neither in the OT nor by Paul with reference to Adam (it is imported into the discussion by way of Paul using it in Rom 6 with regard to believers being thus enslaved, but where Adam is no longer in purview).

[28] See the discussion of line *b* below.

connection of any kind between this passage and the Septuagint of Gen 1–3. The alleged semantic overlap between these two words is in fact a piece of scholarly mythology based on untenable semantics.[29] And whatever else, εἰκών does not carry the sense of being "equal with God," which the present phrase does, as the next line makes certain.

What the earliest followers of Christ had come to believe, of course, on the basis of his resurrection and ascension, was that the one whom they had known as truly human had himself known prior existence in the "form" of God—not meaning that he was "like God but really not" but that he was characterized by what was essential to being God. It is this understanding that (correctly) lies behind the TNIV's "in very nature God."[30] And it is this singular reality, lying in the emphatic first position as this phrase does, that gives potency to what follows and therefore to the whole.

Τὸ εἶναι ἴσα θεῷ ([the] Being Equal with God) (v. 6b)

That Paul by the first phrase intends "in very nature God" is further confirmed by the clause that immediately follows, which is also one of the more famous cruxes in the corpus. "Being in the 'form' of God," Paul begins. "Not *harpagmon* did Christ consider the being equal with God," he adds next. Besides finding an adequate meaning for ἁρπαγμόν, there are two significant matters of grammar, often overlooked, that require special attention: Paul's word order and (especially) his use of an anaphoric τό (*the*)[31] with the infinitive.

---

[29] See, e.g., Cullmann's "word study" on this matter: "It is interesting that we find [in Rom 8:30] the root μορφή closely followed by εἰκών, for this *confirms the fact that Phil 2.6 really refers to Gen 1.26*" (*Christology*, 177 [italics mine]). On this whole issue, see esp. D. H. Wallace, "A Note on *morphé*," *TZ* 22 (1966): 19–25; D. Steenburg, "The Case against the Synonymity of *MORPHE* and *EIKON*," *JSNT* 34 (1988): 77–86; Hurtado, *Lord Jesus Christ*, 121–22. The improbability of genuine semantic overlap can especially be seen in the fact that the two words never occur together in the several entries for each in Louw and Nida's *Greek-English Lexicon of the New Testament Based on Semantic Domains;* and as Hurtado points out, at issue is not simply the two words but the phrase itself (μορφή with the genitive θεοῦ), which does not exist anywhere in Jewish literature with this sense. The whole issue becomes even more problematic when one notes that Paul in several other instances uses εἰκών with regard to Christ as the Son of God to say something about his truly "imaging" God (2 Cor 4:4; Col 1:15), as well as his being the true divine image in human beings, who were intended from the beginning to bear that divine image (2 Cor 3:18; Rom 8:29; Col 3:10). Given this significant usage in earlier letters of the Septuagint's actual word, why now, one wonders, would Paul resort to μορφή if in fact he actually meant εἰκών, since he could have easily used a different noun in line *d.* Cf. Wright: "The asserted equivalence of μορφή and εἰκών in the LXX . . . seems to me illusory" (*Climax of the Covenant,* 72). Indeed!

[30] Cf. GNB: "he always had the nature of God"; NEB: "the divine nature was his from the first" (but changed back to the ambiguous "form" in the REB); cf. TCNT; Montgomery; Phillips.

[31] In form it is an articular infinitive; but since such infinitives are relatively rare in Paul's writings and since this one seems so clearly to stand in apposition to the

First, there is the word order. Paul's clause in fact is a form of indirect discourse, which, as in English, can be expressed by a verb of the mental processes followed by two accusatives on either side of an expressed or, in the case of "to be," implied infinitive. The first of the accusatives is the subject, and the second is the predicate noun or adjective.[32] In the present clause, the infinitive phrase τὸ εἶναι ἴσα θεῷ (*to be equal with God*) is the *subject* of the implied "to be," and ἁρπαγμόν is the predicate noun. Put into "ordinary" English word order, it would thus read, "[He] considered the being equal with God [to be] not *harpagmon.*"[33] But in this case, Paul fronts the predicate noun and thereby puts his first emphasis on what equality with God did *not* consist of:[34] Christ's being a grasping opportunist. Apparently, Paul did this so that in the next clause he could emphasize its stark, unexpected opposite—especially for a deity. At the same time, this also puts our present phrase ("the being equal with God") in the equally emphatic final position, thereby stressing Christ's full equality with God.

This word order also means that the infinitive phrase is not to be understood, as it often has been, as the object of a verbal idea inherent in ἁρπαγμόν, as though Christ neither had equality with God nor tried to seize what was not rightfully his. The meaning of the noun, the grammar itself, and the infinitive phrase together simply do not allow such a reading despite the frequency with which it has been suggested in the literature.[35]

---

first clause, its first function is anaphoric, however else it may be described; cf. Wright, 83. Contra the objection by D. B. Wallace, who suggests that the τό functions in this case "simply to mark it [the infinitive] out as the object" (*Greek Grammar beyond the Basics,* 220), this misses the mark by too much, since the whole seems rather to be a form of indirect discourse following ἡγήσατο (as in the example from Heliodorus in n. 33 below).

[32] It is a cause of some wonder that the association of this clause with v. 3 is so seldom noted, and yet it is the point of everything. There Paul says, ἀλλήλους ἡγούμενοι ὑπερέχοντας ἑαυτῶν, again a form of indirect discourse but in that instance fronting the subject of the assumed clause: "considering others [to be] above yourselves." This seems to be the obvious reason for the same verb in the present clause as well as for ἐταπείνωσεν in v. 8, which picks up the ταπεινοφροσύνη in v. 3.

[33] This grammatical point is often either blurred or misread in the literature, but it seems to be the only viable understanding of this combination of words and forms. Cf. Lightfoot (111), who gives several examples of the idiom, only one of which has the present combination of words (Heliodorus vii.20: οὐχ ἅρπαγμα οὐδὲ ἕρμαιον ἡγεῖται τὸ πρᾶγμα [*he does not consider the matter to be either a piece of plunder or a godsend*]); his own proposed translation of the phrase is "yet [he] *did not regard* it *as a prize,* a treasure to be clutched and retained at all hazards," where his "it" stands in for the infinitive phrase.

[34] This is further confirmed by the placement of the negative οὐχ, which in this case negates the noun, not the verb. On this matter, see J. Carmignac, "L'importance de la place d'une négation: ΟΥΧ ΑΡΠΑΓΜΟΝ ΗΓΗΣΑΤΟ (Philippiens II.6)," *NTS* 18 (1971–1972): 131–66.

[35] This is one of the more obvious difficulties with Dunn's assessment of the passage. It is of some interest that he does not speak to the grammatical question at all, thus his "translational" interpretation of the clause, "he chose [!] *not* as Adam . . . to

Second, there is the anaphoric τό (*the*). It is especially important to note that this definite article has the force of making a noun out of the verb "to be." And in this case it is almost certainly anaphoric; that is, it makes the present phrase an intentional pickup of the preceding "in the 'form' of God," thereby functioning in a nearly appositional way.[36] Thus, in telling Christ's story, to illustrate the divine "mind-set" that stands in stark contrast to "selfish ambition" and "empty glory," Paul now clarifies what "in the 'form' of God" means. This "being equal with God" just mentioned means that the God who has revealed himself in the Son exemplifies precisely the opposite mind-set of the deified "lord" Nero, not to mention of the deities in the Greco-Roman pantheon, who were often rapacious, whatever else.

The net result, therefore, is that these two phrases together make explicit what Paul has implied in a variety of ways throughout the corpus: Christ had preexistence as the Son of God, and his sonship was that of one who was fully and equally divine with the Father. The striking thing about this in the present telling of the story is his insistence that Christ's action as God in becoming incarnate stands in such stark contrast to what people ordinarily had come to expect of their deities. Thus a closer look at the word ἁρπαγμός gives us insight into how Paul's understanding of Christ as fully divine aids us in understanding how Christ shaped Paul's understanding of the character of God.

Οὐκ ἁρπαγμός (Not to His Own Advantage) (v. 6b)

The well-documented difficulties with our understanding the precise intent of this word boil down to two matters:[37] its rarity in Greek literature; and where it does appear, it tends to denote "robbery,"[38] a meaning that can hardly obtain here.[39] This means that scholars have been left to determine

---

grasp equality with God." But this disregards the grammar altogether, focusing on a given meaning of ἁρπαγμός and making the rest of the clause conform to it. Not only so, but Dunn's use of "chose" as an interpretation of ἡγήσατο not only fails to take Paul's sentence seriously but also disregards the verbal link with v. 3 (see n. 32 above), which is his apparent reason for using this verb at all.

[36] Cf. Fowl: "The emphasis of this clause is to assert Christ's disposition toward his equality with God" (94).

[37] Again, as with μορφή, the literature is immense. The best of the recent literature is that by Wright (*Climax of the Covenant*, 62–90), who both summarizes the preceding debate and offers a solution that is especially satisfactory in light of all the issues and to which I gladly acknowledge indebtedness. Wright basically adopts the view of R. W. Hoover ("The HARPAGMOS Enigma: A Philological Solution," *HTR* 64 [1971]: 95–119), moderated by the earlier insights of C. F. D. Moule ("Further Reflexions on Philippians 2:5–11," in *Apostolic History and the Gospel: Biblical and Historical Essays Presented to F. F. Bruce on His 60th Birthday* [ed. W. W. Gasque and R. P. Martin; Grand Rapids: Eerdmans, 1970], 264–76).

[38] The noun is formed from the verb ἁρπάζω, which means to "snatch" or "seize," usually with the connotation of violence or suddenness.

[39] Since it makes very little sense at all (despite the KJV and those who have tried to comment on the basis of this translation). J. C. O'Neill ("Hoover on *harpagmos*

its meaning on the basis of (1) perceived context, or (2) the formation of Greek nouns, or (3) finding parallels which suggest an idiomatic usage.[40]

Although for some the jury is still out on this question, the probable sense of this word is most likely to be found in one (or both) of two refinements—by Moule and Hoover—of earlier suggestions.[41] The former based his conclusions on the formation of Greek nouns, in which nouns ending in-μος do not ordinarily refer to a concrete expression of the verbal idea in the noun but rather to the verbal idea itself.[42] In this view, ἁρπαγμός is not to be thought of as a "thing" at all ("something" to be treated by the verbal idea in the noun); rather, it is an abstract noun, emphasizing the concept of "grasping" or "seizing." Thus, Christ did not consider "equality with God" to consist of "grasping" or being "selfish"; rather, he rejected this popular view of kingly power by "pouring himself out" for the sake of others. In Moule's terms, equality with God means not "grasping" but "giving away." This view has much to commend it,[43] and in any case, it

Reviewed, with a Modest Proposal concerning Philippians 2:6," *HTR* 81 [1988]: 445–49) argues against Hoover (see n. 37 above) that "robbery," which is "near nonsense," seems "to be the only choice left" (448); O'Neill's counsel of despair is to emend the text. But in so doing, he has called into question only *some* of Hoover's data (the evidence from Heliodorus [Hoover, 102–6] is especially noteworthy); by turning Hoover's findings into a "rule," O'Neill eliminates the "rule" by noting the exceptions. But that is not the same thing as eliminating Hoover's understanding of the idiom.

[40] Also involved is the question, already dealt with above, as to whether "equality with God" was something that Christ did not possess but might have desired, or something that he already possessed but did not treat in a ἁρπαγμόν way. The technical language for these distinctions as they have appeared in the literature is *res rapta* ("something grasped" = "robbery") or *res rapienda* ("something to be grasped"), both referring to what was not previously possessed, and *res retinenda* ("something to be clung onto"), referring to something already possessed.

[41] See n. 37 above. These two studies appeared nearly simultaneously (1971 and 1970 respectively). Hoover built especially on the work of W. W. Jaeger ("Eine stilgeschichtliche Studie zum Philipperbrief," *Hermes* 50 [1915]: 537–53), although its line goes back to Lightfoot (111). Moule gave a more solid philological base to the previous work of J. Ross ("ΑΡΠΑΓΜΟΣ [Phil. ii.6]," *JTS* 10 [1909]: 573–74), F. E. Vokes ("Ἁρπαγμός in Phil. 2:5–11," in *Studia evangelica II* [ed. F. L. Cross; TUGAL 87; Berlin: Akademie, 1964], 670–75), and S. H. Hooke (*Alpha and Omega: A Study in the Pattern of Revelation* [London: J. Nisbet, 1961]); see also J. M. Furness, "Ἁρπαγμός . . . ἑαυτὸν ἐκένωσε," *ExpTim* 69 (1957–1958): 93–94; H. Dean, "Christ's True Glory," *ExpTim* 71 (1960): 189–90. Although some have followed Moule (e.g., Hawthorne, 85), the general swing (adopted also in my commentary) is toward Hoover, while keeping Moule in view (so Martin, 96–97; Strimple, "Philippians 2:5–11"; Feinberg, "Kenosis and Christology"; Wright, *Climax of the Covenant*, 76–80; Silva, 118; Fowl, *Story of Christ*, 55–56; O'Brien, 214–15; Melick, 102–3); it was taken earlier by Käsemann, "Critical Analysis," 63 ("to use something for one's own benefit").

[42] See the discussion in MM 78.

[43] The common objection that it still requires an object—"*what* is not being seized or given away?"—has already been answered by Moule: such an "active" view of the noun does not require an object as such. And in any case, Dunn's "translation" is without grammatical warrant ("did not count equality with God as *something* to be grasped").

surely points in the right direction in terms of the overall sense of the noun in context.[44]

The alternative is to see the word as a synonym of its cognate ἅρπαγμα ("booty" or "prey"), which in idioms similar to Paul's[45] denotes something like "a matter to be seized upon," in the sense of "taking advantage of it." This view also has much to commend it, although it is arguable that the evidence for the interchangeability of ἁρπαγμός and ἅρπαγμα is not as strong as its proponents suggest.[46] In either case, it should be noted, the clause comes out very much at the same point. Thus, Paul insists, the true God-likeness that is found in Christ's mind-set has revealed God to be self-giving rather than self-serving, loving rather than exploiting.

We should further note that this word has played a key role for those who find an Adam/Christ analogy in this passage. But such a view requires an understanding of the word that does not seem to fit easily with the context or the emerging view as to its meaning. And since there is no linguistic tie to the Genesis narrative, and since the conceptual tie is one of our own making and not something made explicit by Paul, the intended contrast in the "not/but" clause seems far more likely to be a deliberate confrontation with the emperor and the capricious, rapacious "gods" of the Greco-Roman pantheon. That seems all the more to be the driving point at the end of the sentence of vindication in v. 11 ("the Lord" is not Nero Caesar, whose minions are causing the believers grief in Philippi, but rather the exalted Christ Jesus, before whom all the "gods" and Caesar himself will one day bow). And in any case, the present concern is with behavior among the Philippian believers. People become like the God they worship; and these Philippian believers are still on a transformational track, away from their previous devotion to other deities toward being reshaped into God's likeness as found in Christ.

Ἐκένωσεν ἑαυτόν (He Poured Himself Out) (v. 7a)

In coming to the main verb in Paul's sentence, we also come to a major crux in the Pauline corpus, as to what Paul intended with this language. At issue is whether the verb ἐκένωσεν is to be understood literally or metaphorically. Did Paul understand the divine Christ (literally) to have "emptied himself *of something*" in taking the "form" of a slave? Or is this a strong metaphor, giving pictorial expression to what is otherwise inexpressible and thus meaning something like "he made himself nothing" in becoming human?

---

[44] As Wright (*Climax of the Covenant*, 83) also points out.

[45] That is, when it occurs as part of a "double accusative" with a verb such as "think" (as here) or "do."

[46] Cf. the (much overstated) critique by O'Neill, "Hoover on *harpagmos*." The first objection to both suggestions (Moule's and Hoover's) is, of course, the lack of linguistic evidence as such for this word.

These questions cannot be answered definitively, but it is at least arguable, on the basis of the parallel structure of the *two* sentences in vv. 6–8,
that the participles very likely carry the same sense in both instances (vv. 6
and 8). And here, it would seem, one can make more sense of both of them
when understood as having a modal relationship to the main verb in each
clause. That is, this is the *way* Christ emptied himself and humbled himself:
by "becoming human" and by "becoming obedient." And if this is the case,
it would also seem more likely that the verb is an intentional, very powerful
metaphor, similar to Paul's usage of the verb regarding the cross in 1 Cor 1:17,
where the cross would lose its meaning and power if presented in the guise
of "wisdom of word."

The question, then, is not *what* Christ emptied himself *of,* but *how else*
Paul could possibly have expressed the divine mystery of God incarnate except by this kind of powerful imagery. Historically, far too much has been
made of the verb, as though, in becoming incarnate, he literally "emptied
himself" *of something.* However, just as ἁρπαγμόν requires no object for
Christ to "seize" but rather points to what is the opposite of God's character,
so also Christ did not empty himself *of* anything; he simply "emptied *himself,"* poured himself out, as it were.[47] Thus, the issue for Paul is the selflessness of God, expressed by the preexistent divine Son, whereby in "becoming
human" he took the μορφή of a slave—one who expressed his humanity in
lowly service to others.[48]

Such a meaning, it would seem, is finally demanded by the context,
since such a strong metaphor makes little sense at all of one who was already only human. What is thus being urged upon the Philippians is not a
new view of Jesus[49] but a reinforcement, on the basis of Paul's view of the
crucifixion, that in the cross God's true character—his outlandish, lavish expression of love—was fully manifested.[50] This is what Paul is calling them to
by way of discipleship. The phrase "not ἁρπαγμόν," after all, corresponds to
"not looking to your own interests" (TNIV) in v. 4. Here is Paul's way of saying that Christ, as God, did not act so. Thus, as he has just appealed to them

---

[47] Since my commentary was written, I have discovered that this view was advo-
cated as far back as 1911, by W. Warren ("On ἑαυτὸν ἐκένωσεν," *JTS* 12 [1911]:
461–63); it is noted favorably by Michael, 90.

[48] To be sure, theologically the former question needs to be asked, but in a quite
different way; and it moves us considerably beyond Paul's own concerns in choosing
such a metaphor. The nature of the self-limitations that Christ imposed upon himself
by becoming incarnate is simply not in Paul's purview.

[49] As a Pauline church, what is presented here is the view they would already
have known well.

[50] Which is why the "coda" to the final participle in v. 8, "even death on a cross,"
is expressed in such a way—so as to carry ultimate rhetorical effect. Here is the apo-
gee of true "Godlikeness," where the divine Christ gives himself away in the utterly
execrable "weakness" (humiliation) of crucifixion. For this understanding of the
cross, see esp. 1 Cor 1:18–25 in G. D. Fee, *The First Epistle to the Corinthians* (NICNT;
Grand Rapids: Eerdmans, 1987), 67–78.

to have a singular "mind-set" (τὸ αὐτὸ φρόνητε [v. 2]), which will express it-self in "humility" as they "consider" one another better than themselves, so now he has repeated the injunction to have this "mind-set" (φρονεῖτε [v. 5]), which they see in Christ Jesus, who did not "consider" (same verb as in v. 4) being equal with God as something to be taken selfish advantage of. Rather, he "poured himself out," with the salvation of humankind as his goal.

The Role of the Participles in Verses 7–8

That this is Paul's intent is made even more certain by the two explana-tory participial phrases that follow and the pickup participial phrase that be-gins v. 8, which together especially compound the emphasis *on the reality of Christ's humanity*.[51] So much is this so that it is extremely difficult to imagine that Paul considered Christ to be already human when he said of him at the beginning, "being in the form of God."

1. The first participle explains the *nature* of Christ's emptying himself, the way it expressed itself in our human history: μορφὴν δούλου λαβών (*by taking*[52] *on the "form" of a slave*). "Form" (μορφή) here means precisely what it did above: in his earthly existence he took on the "essential quality" of what it meant to be a slave. The combination μορφὴν δούλου here probably means something close to the corresponding verb in Gal 5:13 (= "perform the duties of a slave").[53] From Paul's perspective, this is how divine love manifests itself in its characteristic and profuse expression.

It is often suggested that δοῦλος carries a bit more weight here, that by using "slave," Paul had some other "background" in mind than simply a household servant. Two basic ones have been proffered. Altogether unlikely is the suggestion that by becoming human, Christ accepted "bondage" to the "powers" so that through death he might destroy them.[54] The obvious diffi-culty with such a view is that nothing in the text suggests as much; indeed, it is held basically by those who read the "hymn" as pre-Pauline, with this

---

[51] So much is this so, one would think that Dunn et al. would argue that Paul is deliberately trying to *counter* the view that Christ was preexistent as God. But if that were the case, then one would also need to acknowledge that Paul had left himself wide open to misunderstanding by the way he speaks of Christ elsewhere (e.g., 1 Cor 8:6; 10:4, 9; 2 Cor 8:9; Gal 4:4; Rom 8:3). It is of some interest that Dunn refutes preexistence in each of these texts by arguing *against* what he acknowledges that they seem to say.

[52] Gk. λαβών; ordinarily, the aorist participle indicates antecedent time. But de-spite Moule (*Idiom Book*, 100), who recognizes only two such uses in the NT (both in Acts), the majority of scholars understand this participle to express coincident time. Cf. Gal 4:6; Eph 1:9.

[53] On this meaning of the verb, see Fee, *God's Empowering Presence*, 425. To argue that he must be *enslaved to someone* ("God" [so Meyer, 91; Plummer, 45] or "the pow-ers" [see the next note]) is to press the metaphor and therefore to miss it.

[54] See Käsemann ("Critical Analysis," 67–68), followed by Beare, 82; Gnilka, 120; Caird, 121–22; G. Bornkamm, "Zum Verständnis des Christus-Hymnus, Phil. 2.6–11," in *Studien zu Antike und Urchristentum* (BEvT 28; Munich: Kaiser, 1959), 181.

meaning in the background of its prior existence there, which Paul has then imperfectly imported into its present context.

A more tenable "background" is the Servant of the Lord of Isa 42–53, where some interesting linguistic and conceptual links do exist.[55] In the Septuagint, however, Isaiah's Servant is designated by a quite different Greek word.[56] If such ties exist, therefore—and they are at least as viable as the "cryptic reference to Adam" in v. 6—they most likely do so as general background. After all, Jesus himself interpreted his death in light of Isa 53, and Paul and the early church were quick to see that Christ's "servanthood" was ultimately fulfilled in the "pouring out of his life unto death" (53:12) for the sake of others. It is hard to imagine that early Christians, therefore, would not rather automatically have heard this passage with that background in view, especially since the passage in Isaiah begins (52:13) the way this one ends, with the Servant's exaltation by God.[57]

But in the present context, the emphasis does not lie on Jesus' messianism or on his fulfilling the role of the Servant of the Lord; rather, it lies primarily on the servant nature of Christ's incarnation. He entered our history not as κύριος (Lord), which name he acquires at his vindication (vv. 9–11), but as δοῦλος (slave), a person without advantages, with no rights or privileges but in servanthood to all.[58] And all of this, surely, with an eye to vv. 3–4.[59] Thus the δοῦλος of this phrase serves as the nadir between the

---

[55] Especially the repeated εἰς θάνατον (53:8, 12) in the context of his being ἐν τῇ ταπεινώσι (v. 8). Note also the conceptual ties of "he emptied himself" and "he poured out his soul unto death" (53:12); and 52:13 ("my servant καὶ ὑψωθήσεται καὶ δοξασθήσεται σφόδρα [shall be exalted and glorified greatly]"). See, e.g., Michael, 90–91 (tentatively); Hendriksen, 109; Cerfaux, Christ in the Theology of Saint Paul, 288–98; J. Jeremias, "Zu Phil ii 7: ΕΑΥΤΟΝ ΕΚΕΝΩΣΕΝ," NovT 6 (1963): 182–88; Martin, A Hymn of Christ, 169–96; Strimple, "Philippians 2:5–11," 260–61; Feinberg, "Kenosis and Christology," 36–40; J. G. Gibbs, "The Relation between Creation and Redemption according to Phil. II.5–11," NovT 12 (1970): 170–83; and Reid, Jesus, God's Emptiness, God's Fullness, 58–60 (who reads it totally within the framework of Isa 53 with no mention of either Adam or Wisdom!). See the helpful discussion in O'Brien, 268–71, although he finally rejects it.

[56] He is the παῖς θεοῦ; Paul's word is δοῦλος. Some caution might be due here, since the Servant speaks of himself in a nontitular way as the Lord's δοῦλος (49:5) and he does the same of Israel in 42:19; 48:20; 49:3 (so Bockmuehl, 135); but all these are nontitular, and Paul never refers to Christ as "the slave of the Lord"—for good reason, since κύριος in Paul's thought is reserved strictly for Christ himself. This linguistic difference is the most frequently given reason for rejecting the idea altogether (e.g., Plummer, 45).

[57] Similarly Bockmuehl, 135–36; and Silva (125), who also cites in support J. Heriban, Retto φρονεῖν e κένωσις: Studio esegetico su Fil 2,1–5,6–11 (Rome: LAS, 1983), 160–62; G. Wagner, "Le scandale de la croix expliqué par le chant du Serviteur d'Isaïe 53: Réflections sur Philippiens 2/6–11," ETR 61 (1986): 177–87.

[58] Moule ("Further Reflexions," 268–69) suggests this as the primary motif; cf. Hawthorne, 87; Bruce, 78.

[59] So also Hurtado, "Jesus as Lordly Example"; cf. O'Brien, 223–24; E. Schweizer: "His oneness with man would then, it is true, be implied, but the emphasis would be

twin zeniths of his "being in the form of God" (v. 6a) and his being exalted
by God the Father and confessed by all as κύριος (v. 11).

2. The second participial phrase simultaneously (a) clarifies the first by
elaboration,[60] (b) especially emphasizes the reality of Christ's humanity,
and (c) concludes the present sentence by paving the way for the next
(v. 8). Together, these phrases give definition to Christ's "impoverishment."
The phrase "in the form of a slave" comes first for rhetorical reasons: to
sharpen the contrast with "in the form of God" and to set out the true nature of his incarnation. It thus reflects the "quality" or "nature" of his incarnation. This second phrase indicates its "factual" side. Thus, Christ
came "in the form of a slave"—that is, by his "having come[61] in the likeness of human beings."[62]

This phrase seems necessary only because of what Paul has said at the
beginning of the sentence, that Christ was "in the form of God." Here, and
now with explicit clarity, Paul asserts that (the in-the-form-of-God) Christ
"emptied himself" specifically by being born in the likeness of ἀνθρώπων
(*human beings* [note the plural]). If it had been intended that we understand the prior phrase as simply referring to Christ as human, then this
one—and the next—presents us with an intolerable redundancy (the one
already human now comes in the likeness of human beings [plural]). Dunn
tries to avoid the redundancy by means of a circuitous exegesis that makes
it refer to something beyond what is actually said, suggesting that it points
to Adam in his *fallen humanity* and now *subject to death*.[63] The difficulty
with such a view is, of course, that there are no signals in the text itself to
help us read it this way; indeed, it requires us to have a prior reconstructed

---

on his uniqueness by which he would be distinguised from all men" (*Lordship and
Discipleship* [SBT 28; London: SCM Press, 1960], 63).

[60] Cf. Meyer: "specifies" (90); Kennedy: "defines" (437); Vincent: "explains" (59).

[61] Gk. γενόμενος; on this word, see the discussion in ch. 5 of Gal 4:4 (pp. 215–16),
where a similar usage is most often translated "was born." Although that is seldom
the case here (the NRSV is a notable exception), there is in fact very little difference
between the present passage and that one, except that in Galatians his "coming to
be" is specified as "of a woman."

[62] Gk. ἀνθρώπων; the plural seems purposeful, implying his identity with the
whole human race, which is then particularized in the next phrase ("as a human
being [himself]").

[63] This, at least, is how Dunn (*Christology in the Making*, 115–16) interprets the
phrase; but this turns out to be a difficult read in Dunn, since he is clear enough as
to how this could refer to the *first* Adam but less clear as to how it might refer to
Christ. Thus, "the contrast . . . is between what Adam was and what he became
[what men now are in their fallenness], and it is this Adam language that is used of
Christ." But he carefully avoids suggesting *how* this fits Paul's telling the story of
Christ. This lack of clarity is compounded by two matters: Christ is elsewhere asserted by Paul to be sinless (2 Cor 5:21); and this passage is Christ's story—not
Adam's—yet Dunn seems to assume right along that Paul is narrating the story of
the *second* Adam, as though this were plain for all to see, when there is not a single
linguistic clue.

Adam paradigm as our basic way to look at Christ and then to apply that paradigm to this phrase.[64]

A final note is needed about the sometimes troubling word "likeness," a word that occurred in a similar way in Rom 8:3 (see p. 247). As with that passage, Paul's choice of ὁμοίωμα seems deliberate and is used because of his belief (in common with the rest of the early church) that in becoming human, Christ did not thereby cease to be divine. This word allows for the ambiguity, emphasizing that he is similar to our humanity in some respects and dissimilar in others. The similarity lies with his full humanity; in his incarnation he was "like" us in the sense of "the same as." The dissimilarity in this case has to do with his never ceasing to be "equal with God." Thus he came in the "likeness" of human beings because, on the one hand, he has fully identified with us and because, on the other hand, in becoming human, he was not human only. He was God living out a truly human life, all of which is safeguarded by this expression.[65]

In sum: This first sentence, the earliest of its kind in the NT, makes the two points that are crucial to NT Christology: (a) Christ was both in the "form" of God and equal with God, and therefore personally preexistent, when he chose to "empty himself" by taking the "form" of a slave; (b) he took the "form" of a slave by coming to be (γενόμενος) in the "likeness" (ὁμοίωμα) of human beings. Thus, in Christ Jesus, God has thus shown his true nature; this is what it means for Christ to be "equal with God": to pour himself out for the sake of others, and to do so by taking the role of a slave. Hereby Christ not only reveals the character of God but from the perspective of the present context also reveals what it means for us to be created in God's image, to bear his likeness and have his "mind-set." It means taking the role of the slave for the sake of others, the contours of which are what the next clause will spell out.

3. The third participial phrase in succession (line *f*) stands at the beginning of the second sentence, and thus it functions precisely as line *a* does in the opening sentence: to establish Christ's mode of being (God / human) when he did the action of the two main verbs ("emptied himself / humbled himself"). But it does so in this case by picking up where the previous sentence had left off, with his becoming human. The result is a twofold emphatic assertion as to the genuineness of Christ's humanity: now "found in human like-

---

[64] This, of course, is what Dunn attempts to do in the preceding chapter in *Christology in the Making* (pp. 107–13); but this further assumes *that the Philippians would have been privy to this reconstruction*, whereas nothing in this letter would otherwise make one think so. One of the inherent difficulties in assessing Dunn's perspective on this passage is that he never offers us a "translation" that clears away the ambiguities and lets the reader see where Paul's language is allegedly heading.

[65] Even so, one should not miss that this phrase is also part of the powerful contrasts being set up in the passage. Christ "made himself of no reputation" in becoming human—whether we humans like that or not!

ness," he chose the path of obedience.[66] The fact that three consecutive participial phrases press this same point suggests that Paul is emphasizing the contrast between who he "was" and who he "became" in his incarnation.[67]

The construction itself especially negates the interpretive option that would here see Christ as "becoming" human only in the sense of being like Adam in his fallenness and therefore subject to death. What Paul asserts is that he "was found to be"[68] in the recognizable appearance[69] of a human being. This assertion would seem to make little sense if Paul did not intend what the traditional view of this passage has regularly recognized: in his incarnation, Christ did a totally new thing, becoming what he had not been before—mystery though that might be for us theologically. At the end of the day, this now threefold emphasis on Christ "emptying himself" by becoming human makes sense only as a purposeful contrast, not simply between who he was and who he became but to emphasize the character of God, whose incarnation in Christ and subsequent obedience that led to the cross serve as the ultimate paradigm for all relationships within the believing community.

"He Humbled Himself" (v. 8)

The main clause in the second sentence of the story relates how the incarnate Christ acted in his humanity. Not surprisingly, it was precisely in keeping with how he acted as God in becoming incarnate. Since the emphasis now is on his humanity, two important christological points need to be noted: first, he lived out his humanity in obedience to God; second, his death on the cross was a deliberate choice, the fulfilling of the Father's will. It was not seen as something in which evil people took his life away from him.

Both of these points need to be stressed only because there is nothing in Pauline Christology that could lead one to an Apollonarian view of Christ—a view that tends to prevail in the church—where Christ's deity is understood as

---

[66] A point, one needs to note again, that seems intolerably redundant if ἐν μορφῇ θεοῦ ὑπάρχων in v. 6 was a simple referent to his already being human and in the image of God as Adam was.

[67] Dunn, on the other hand, argues that these three phrases are "all variant ways of describing the character of fallen Adam, all drawn from Adam theology" (*Christology in the Making,* 117), which in Christ's story means he "therefore is the man who undid Adam's wrong" by making the correct choices at the key points. But why, one wonders, would Paul have felt it necessary to make Dunn's point so many times? And how, one wonders further, can one speak intelligibly of one who is *only* human (as Dunn argues Paul's Christ to be) as taking on "human likeness" and then as "being found in appearance as a human being"?

[68] Gk. εὑρεθείς (aorist passive of εὑρίσκω), which can range from "coming upon something by purposeful search" to "finding in the sense of surprise or discovery," or, as in the present case, simply to "attain a state or condition" (BDAG).

[69] Gk. σχήματι; in Paul's writings only here and 1 Cor 7:31, where it refers to the world "in its present expression" that is passing away. Although perhaps simply a stylistic matter for the sake of variety, this word nonetheless puts emphasis on the external nature of something that makes it recognizable.

superimposing itself on his humanity. Paul's choice of the metaphor "emptied himself" is already a safeguard against such a christological perspective; the present verb simply reinforces the reality of a genuine incarnation: he humbled himself, becoming obedient to the point of death on the cross.

On the other side, this sentence also spells out in narrative form what is found throughout Paul: the cross was not a merely human activity that God made the best of. This sentence makes clear what also is found elsewhere in the corpus: the cross was the direct result of the divine will. Indeed, this sentence is the Pauline version of the prayer of Jesus in Gethsemane: "Not my will, but yours be done."

As before, Christ as second Adam has also been brought into this sentence, but much more circuitously. As Adam's *disobedience* led to his being subject to death (some 930 years later in the Genesis narrative), so Christ's *obedience* in this narrative leads to his actual death. But again, without the template in hand, how is one to have heard this "echo," since there is not a verbal connection of any kind? And the "obedience" motif must be imported from another Pauline letter (Rom 5:19) in order to work at all. Thus, the only way this works finally is to argue, as Dunn does, that the template in this case is Paul's primary way of viewing Christ; but that would also mean that the Philippians would know about it from personal contact with Paul, since it is unlikely that they knew 1 Corinthians or Romans.

Excursus: A Final Note on the Alternative View

Before moving on to the sentence of vindication (vv. 9–11), we need a final word regarding the alleged Adam Christology in these first two sentences, especially as this has been argued by Dunn, first in his *Christology in the Making*, whose essence is repeated without serious modification in his magisterial *Theology of Paul the Apostle*. Basic to this view is not what one finds explicitly stated anywhere in Philippians but a prior paradigmatic Adam Christology, which Dunn reconstructed in a prior chapter of *Christology in the Making*. Crucial to this enterprise is to read out of Paul any hint of a conviction of Christ's preexistence. On the basis of the prior paradigm, Dunn holds that in this present telling of the story "there are four or five points of contact with Adam tradition and Adam christology," of which he lists five of a kind for which he has "yet to see any alternative framework of thought into which the hymn 'fits' at so many points."[70] The five points are:

---

[70] *Theology of Paul*, 284 n. 77. This is a telling moment of presupposition, indicating that the story can be understood only in light of a prior precedent or analogy, which thus eliminates Paul's own encounter with the risen Christ as a primary source (and one can only wonder about what Paul might have been doing those many months in Arabia [Gal 1:17]). This is even more telling when one considers that preexistence is presuppositional for Paul, and thus for his churches, as well as for the author of Hebrews and John, and therefore was (apparently) independently widespread by the middle of the first Christian century.

1. v. 6a—in the form of God
2. v. 6bc—tempted to grasp equality with God
3. v. 7—took the form of a slave [to corruption and sin]
4. v. 8—obedient to death
5. vv. 9–11—exalted and glorified[71]

The problem with these is that not one of them is self-evident from a straightforward reading of the text, neither of Paul nor of the Genesis account.[72] We have pointed out above that point 1, the alleged semantic overlap of μορφή with εἰκών, exhibits semantic wishfulness, not reality. But even more difficult is the problem for the reader. Here is the one place where a *verbal link* seems absolutely necessary. One can understand how a scholar, impressed by the "conceptual" possibility of an echo of Adam, might know there is a (limited) semantic overlap between these two words. But how would the believers in Philippi come by this? The "overlap" is such that it would function very much for them as with the ordinary English reader, who on reading "form" is unlikely to think of its (limited) semantic overlap with "image" and therefore hear "image" while reading "form." Only a scholar could point this out either to the Philippians or to us.

Point 2 is the one that might be perceived to echo the Genesis story; but that is a purely conceptual echo, not a linguistic one, nor is it one that corresponds well with what is actually said in the Adam story or by Paul. The Genesis account deals primarily with Eve, not Adam;[73] they were not tempted to be equal with God but to "be like God" *regarding the knowledge of good and evil,* which the narrative says actually happened

---

[71]Each of these is "supported" by references, which, when consulted, tend to bring the whole enterprise under suspicion. Dunn seems to have made an easy shift from Gen 1–3 (which he cites with quotes for points 1 and 2) to Paul's use of Adam in 1 Cor 15 and Rom 5 (for items 3 to 5); but he does not reference Genesis and Paul *at the same time* except for point 4, where he references Gen 2:17 (which did not in fact happen to Adam in the literal sense). His other OT support for points 3 to 5 are Wis 2:23–24 (for 3 and 4) and Ps 8:5b–6 (for point 5). How, for example, does Wis 2:23 ("for God created *us* for incorruption, and made *us* in the image of his own eternity," which echoes Genesis but is interested in humanity as such, not in Adam per se) reflect point 3, that Christ "took the form of a slave"? Even his parenthesis that this has to do with "corruption and sin" is an imprecise admixture of Wisdom and Paul. So what we end up with on these points is not the Genesis account at all but *Adam as he appears in Paul's letters*—although nothing close to this language appears in either of the two passages that mention Adam. One is therefore tempted to wonder further how the Philippians could possibly have caught what Paul was doing.

[72]Indeed, this is a quintessential illustration of what D. Juel in another context calls "interpreting the clear by the obscure, [by] ignoring directions suggested by the text" (*Messianic Exegesis: Christological Interpretation of the Old Testament in Early Christianity* [Philadelphia: Fortress, 1988], 92 n. 4).

[73]This continues in the "judgment" scene as well (3:14–19), which takes the same order as in vv. 1–7: the serpent, the woman, Adam.

(3:22) and which therefore had nothing at all to do with attaining divine status.[74] As pointed out above, "equality with God" was something Christ had, not something he chose not to grasp after.[75] Finally, points 3 to 5 would require special assistance to understand even after one has read Dunn's exposition, and his references in the corresponding footnotes are especially obtuse.[76] Analogies, one would think, need to be made of sterner stuff.

So not only does this position fall short of demonstration in the biblical accounts themselves, but also, further against this view that the text is dealing with the earthly Jesus and not with preexistence, are the following points made in the preceding exegesis: (1) the grammar and language that do exist must be stretched nearly beyond recognition in order to make the analogy work; (2) the especially strong metaphor inherent in ἐκένωσεν (*he emptied himself*) seems strikingly inappropriate to refer to one who is already human; (3) the one described in v. 6 as "being in the form of God," which means further that he was "equal with God," is later said to "be made/born in human likeness" and is then "found in human appearance"; all of this is an exceedingly strange thing to say of a second Adam whose beginnings are to be understood as "from below"; (4) the structure of the whole narrative, where sentence 2 (v. 8), which begins, "and being found in appearance as a human being," stands in strong contrast to the beginning of sentence 1 ("who being in the 'form' of God"); such an emphasis makes almost no sense of one who was always and only a human being; (5) this view divests the first part of the narrative of its essential power, which rests in the pointed contrast between the opening participle ("being in the form of God") and the final coda ("death of the cross"); and (6) it takes a considerable stretch to find in the sentence of vindication any referent to Adam at all, except as vindication pure and simple, which is never a part of the Adam story either in the OT or in Paul's writings.[77]

---

[74] Dunn considers this objection to be pedantic, that "knowing good and evil" would make them equivalent to God; but that is not at all clear in the Genesis account, which limits "being as God" to one factor only: the self-determination of good and evil. And since that much actually happened (!)—without deification—one is left to wonder where the *equality* with God lay for Adam.

[75] Cf. Bockmuehl, 131–32.

[76] See n. 70 above.

[77] For further refutations, see Feinberg, "Kenosis and Christology"; L. D. Hurst, "Re-enter the Pre-existent Christ in Philippians 2:5–11?" *NTS* 32 (1986): 449–57; T. Y.-C. Wong, "The Problem of Pre-existence in Philippians 2,6–11," *ETL* 62 (1986): 167–82; C. A. Wanamaker, "Philippians 2.6–11: Son of God or Adamic Christology?" *NTS* 33 (1987): 179–93; Fowl, *Story of Christ*, 70–73; O'Brien, 263–68; Bockmuehl, 131–33. For a helpful overview, see L. W. Hurtado, "Pre-existence," *DPL* 743–46. Perhaps one should note finally how easily Paul could have expressed this alternative view without all the misleading language and grammar. For example, he could have used εἰκών instead of μορφή had he intended this echo; rather than the articular,

What this means, then, is that whatever degree of Adam-Christ analogy might be present in the first two lines, the analogy breaks down precisely at the point of the main verb and its twin modifiers ("He emptied himself, by having taken the 'form' of a slave, by having come in the likeness of human beings"), where the second modifier (line *e*) elaborates the first (line *d*) by emphasizing Christ's "becoming" human. Thus to turn a *possible* Adam/Christ analogy into a *full-blown* one and thereby dismiss or diminish preexistence and incarnation in this passage requires one to overcome one linguistic and conceptual difficulty after another.

On the other hand, Paul's nicely balanced sentences are written precisely to counter the two negative attitudes expressed in v. 3 ("selfish ambition" and "vain glory"), so that Christ as God "emptied himself by taking the form of a slave" and as man "humbled himself by becoming obedient to the point of death on the cross." All of this makes perfectly good sense in terms of Paul's understanding of Christ as preexistent and fully divine, but very little sense *in this context* as emphasizing his role in contrast to Adam and assuming a view of Christ that begins from below. As Barth put it with inimitable style, "There is no other Christ than this, God's Equal become man" (66).

Christ, Exalted Lord of All—Philippians 2:9–11

Although this third sentence serves to conclude the Christ story that began in v. 6—as vindication of the selfless humbling of the preexistent One—its christological emphasis of necessity moves in a different direction. And if the first two sentences are the high-water mark of Paul's understanding of Christ as preexistent and thus of the character of God revealed in his becoming incarnate, this sentence of vindication is likewise the high-water mark of Paul's Κύριος Christology. With this note of exaltation, Paul both affirms the rightness of the paradigm to which he has called the Philippians and keeps before their eyes the eschatological vindication that awaits those who are Christ's[78]—a concern that runs throughout the letter and the note

and therefore anaphoric, infinitive in line *b*, he had several nouns at his disposal that would have made his point quite easily; indeed, had he used different verbs altogether, especially in place of the strong metaphor "he emptied himself," he could have eliminated all the ambiguity that has caused the majority of scholars to think that Paul meant something very much in keeping with what the words and clauses would ordinarily mean.

[78]The first to note this view of vv. 9–11 among English commentaries was Michael (93); most neglect it altogether, usually because by the time they come to this verse, the context is forgotten in the interest of what Paul says about Christ himself. On the basis of his view of v. 5, Barth (66–67) sees the vindication come to the Philippians as a result of their being "in Christ." But such a view arose only for

on which this whole section concludes (2:16). For a suffering community whom Paul repeatedly reminds regarding the absolute centrality of Christ in everything, both present and future, here is the necessary concluding word.

Although the passage has the ring of doxology to it, it lacks the poetry that has preceded, which was abetted primarily by the participial constructions.[79] Indeed, everything has changed. In vv. 6–8, Christ is the subject of all the verbs and participles; here God is the subject and Christ the object, who is recipient both of the divine "Name" and of the worship offered by "every knee" and "every tongue," all to the glory of God. If this is part of a hymn, it has no known parallels, either in Judaism, Hellenism, or Paul's writings.[80] The parallelism that does exist (in vv. 10–11) is the direct result of another piece of "intertextuality" in this letter;[81] indeed, the whole has been formulated to echo the oracle in Isa 45:18–24, where the κύριος (Lord) of the Septuagint refers to Yahweh, Israel's Savior, where his exalted status over all gods and nations is strongly declared.

To guide the rest of our discussion, I set out the basic structure in "lines" as helps for easy reference.

a διὸ καὶ ὁ θεὸς αὐτὸν ὑπερύψωσεν
b καὶ   αὐτῷ ἐχαρίσατο τὸ ὄνομα τὸ ὑπὲρ πᾶν ὄνομα,
c ἵνα ἐν τῷ ὀνόματι Ἰησοῦ **πᾶν γόνυ κάμψῃ**
c^1 ἐπουρανίων καὶ ἐπιγείων καὶ
                                                καταχθονίων
d **καὶ πᾶσα γλῶσσα** ἐξομολογήσηται ὅτι **κύριος** Ἰησοῦς Χριστὸς
d^1 εἰς δόξαν θεοῦ πατρός.

a *Therefore also God him*   *has highly exalted*
b *and*   *to him*   *he has bestowed the Name that is above every name,*
c *that at the name of Jesus*   **every knee should bow**
c^1 *in heaven and on earth and*
                                                in the depths
d **and every tongue**   **confess** *that* **the Lord** *is Jesus Christ*
d^1 *to the glory of God the Father.*

---

theological reasons: to be done with a kind of *imitatio Christi* that seems to imply personal effort and therefore to circumvent grace—a totally unnecessary move in light of vv. 12–13, where it is God himself who is at work in them for his own purposes.

[79] Cf. Silva (127) and O'Brien (232), who recognize that this is a Pauline prose sentence and begin by describing its obvious parts but who then continue to use the language of hymnody.

[80] The lack of a Pauline parallel is highlighted when contrasted with Rom 11:33–36, a doxologic passage that appears in nicely balanced Semitic parallelism. Cf. the "addition" to the prescript in Galatians, where in v. 4 Paul says of Christ, "who gave himself for our sins, *in order that* he might deliver us . . . , *in keeping with* the will of God, to whom [God] be glory forever." As with the present passage, this is the stuff of creed, not hymn; it is expressed in the exalted language of praise but its "poetry" is incidental, not hymnic.

[81] See Fee, e.g., on 1:20 and 2:14–16; cf. 4:5 below (pp. 409–10).

Even a casual glance at this structural display confirms that there is nothing hymnic here. In fact, it is a thoroughly Pauline sentence, with Pauline idioms, Pauline use of the Septuagint (in bold), Pauline theology, and the basic Pauline confession that the Lord is none other than Jesus Christ.[82]

With an inferential "therefore also,"[83] Paul thus draws the preceding narrative to its proper conclusion, offering the divine vindication of Christ's emptying himself and humbling himself in obedience by dying on a cross. As God's "yes" to *this* expression of "equality with God," God the Father "exalted him to the highest place and gave him the Name, the Name above every other."[84] Although expressed as a twofold action, most likely Paul intends the two verbs to point to a single reality: God highly exalted Christ *by*[85] granting him "the Name." Nonetheless, both parts of the sentence raise issues that need closer examination.

God Highly Exalted Him (v. 9a)

In asserting (in line *a*) that God has "highly exalted"[86] Christ, Paul uses a compound of the ordinary verb for "exalt" with the preposition ὑπέρ, whose basic meaning is "above." On the basis of a certain understanding of v. 6 (what Christ did not "seize" was something *not previously his*), some see Paul as stressing that Christ has been rewarded for his humiliation by having been given a *higher* "position" than he had heretofore.[87] Others see an emphasis

---

[82] The third such in the corpus; see discussion on 1 Cor 12:3 in ch. 3 (pp. 123–24) and Rom 10:9 in ch. 6 (pp. 257–59). Given how thoroughly Pauline it is, and in an undisputed Pauline letter, it is a cause for some wonder that this sentence could be considered by some to be pre-Pauline and thus not by Paul (e.g., Käsemann, "Critical Analysis"; Beare, 77; Martin, 93).

[83] Gk. διὸ καί; the conjunction itself (διό) is always inferential and never slips into modified expressions, such as resumption, which is so characteristic of οὖν. The καί is best understood as intensifying the conjunction, which BDAG suggests "denot[es] that the inference is self-evident." For this usage in Paul's writings, see 2 Cor 1:20; 4:13 (2x); 5:9; Rom 4:22; 15:22.

[84] That Paul mentions neither the resurrection nor the ascension has been used to argue for non-Pauline authorship. But in fact, many of these kinds of creedal statements, most of which in Paul's letters are soteriological, do not mention the resurrection. In this case, as in others, these two realities are presupposed by what he does say.

[85] Thus reading the καί as epexegetic and the sentence as a hendiadys, where the second verb elaborates or fills out the meaning of the first. On this usage in Paul's writings, see esp. 1 Cor 11:22 ("or do you despise the church of God *by* humiliating the have-nots"; cf. the TNIV); so also Silva, 128–29.

[86] Gk. ὑπερύψωσεν, found only here in the NT

[87] E.g., Meyer, 99; Houlden, 77; Silva, 127–28. There might be a sense that in the "chronology" of heaven as it intersects with earth Christ has assumed a "new role," as it were (as sympathetic high priest, e.g., who knows our suffering from the inside out). But it is doubtful that one can mine "positional" significance out of that kind of understanding.

on his victory over the powers,[88] although that concern is foreign to the narrative and must be inferred on the basis of an (almost certainly) incorrect understanding of "in heaven and on earth and under the earth." But the verb "highly exalted" implies neither of these. In fact, Paul uses ὑπέρ compounds far more than do other NT writers, and in the vast majority of cases these compounds magnify, or express excess,[89] not position.[90] Likewise here, that God has "highly exalted" Christ means that he exalted him to the highest possible degree. The next clause then spells out what this means.

The Name, the One above Every Name (v. 9b)

The real concern in this clause has to do with the *way* God has exalted Christ to the highest place: by "gracing"[91] him with the Name. At issue is what Paul intended (in line *b*) by "the name, the one above every name." Since the next clause begins by reference to "the name of Jesus," it has been common to see "Jesus" as the name being referred to.[92] But neither the context nor historical reality supports such a view. After all, the name "Jesus" has especially to do with his earthly life, not his exalted, heavenly one. Hence the phrase ἐν τῷ ὀνόματι Ἰησοῦ (*in the name of Jesus*) refers not to someone hearing the name "Jesus" and thus bowing before him; rather, it is a direct pickup of what has preceded and means something like "the Name that now belongs to Jesus."[93]

What follows suggests that here at last we have Paul's own explanation of the recurring, and consistent, phenomenon of his transferring the Septuagint's κύριος (*Lord*) = Yahweh to the exalted Christ. This was already fully in place in Paul's earliest letters (1–2 Thessalonians). In his next letter (1 Cor 8:6) he explicitly divided the Jewish Shema into its two Greek parts, so that there is only one θεός (God the Father) and one κύριος (Jesus Christ), which is how Paul can simultaneously be an avid monotheist while including Christ is the divine identity.

The rest of this sentence makes it certain that this is "the name" Paul is referring to, hence the reason for it being capitalized and for emphasizing

---

[88] E.g., Käsemann, "Critical Analysis"; Beare, 86; Caird, 123.

[89] See MHT 2.326; as pointed out there, the English equivalent is our "over" compounds (e.g., "overjoyed, overburden, overdevelop"); or as many have put it, the emphasis is on the superlative, not comparative.

[90] Cf., e.g., ὑπερπερισσεύω ("superabound") in Rom 5:20; 2 Cor 7:4; or ὑπερνικάω ("prevail completely") in Rom 8:37.

[91] Gk. ἐχαρίσατο, the verb formed from the noun χάρις (*grace*), and a Pauline favorite; cf. 1:29.

[92] Understandably so, given how common the idiom is in Scripture (e.g., "the name of the Lord [your God]"); this was argued for by Moule, "Further Reflexions," 270; it can be found regularly in the literature.

[93] So (rightly) Plummer (48), who also (again rightly) rejects the common habit of turning Paul's ἐν into an "at." Rather, it is "in the name that now belongs to Jesus" that every knee shall bow; cf. Ps 63:4 (62:5 LXX).

the article, "*the* Name." Although it is not illegitimate to translate Paul's τὸ ὄνομα τὸ ὑπὲρ πᾶν ὄνομα as "the name that is above every name," his use of the anaphoric article indicates that the phrase τὸ ὑπὲρ πᾶν ὄνομα functions as an adjectival qualifier and thus means, "namely, the one above every name." Paul's point is that God the Father has at Christ's exaltation graced him with "*the* name-above-every-name Name," which can hardly be anything other than a reference to the Divine Name in the OT. This is the Name that was revealed to Moses at Sinai as the Name that was to be God's forever (Exod 3:13–15), the God who is one and whose Name is one (Deut 6:4), the God who chose Jerusalem as the place where his Name should dwell (Deut 12:5) and the place where all Israel was to call upon that Name (12:11). It is *this* Name, by way of the Septuagint's κύριος, that has now been given to the exalted Christ.

The certain evidence for this understanding comes in what follows. The exaltation of the one who poured himself out by becoming a human being and who humbled himself in obedience to death on the cross has as its final eschatological result[94] the total obeisance of the entire created world. To make this point, Paul borrows once more from the language of Isa 45:23.[95]

Phil 2:10–11   [10]**πᾶν γόνυ κάμψῃ** ἐπουρανίων καὶ ἐπιγείων καὶ καταχθονίων
                [11]**καὶ πᾶσα γλῶσσα ἐξομολογήσηται** ὅτι **κύριος**
                                                        Ἰησοῦς Χριστὸς

Isa 45:23   ὅτι ἐμοὶ **κάμψει πᾶν γόνυ**
               καὶ ἐξομολογήσεται πᾶσα γλῶσσα τῷ θεῷ

cf. Isa 45:18 οὕτως λέγει **κύριος** ὁ ποιήσας τὸν οὐρανόν . . .

Phil 2:10–11   [10]*every knee will bow* in heaven and earth and under the earth,
               [11]*and every tongue will confess* that *the Lord* is Jesus Christ

Isa 45:23   *that to me will bow every knee*
               and will confess every tongue to God

cf. Isa 45:18 *thus says the Lord, who made the heaven . . .*

_____

[94] Gk. ἵνα, which in classical Greek expresses purpose and still does for the most part in the NT, including Paul's letters. But there are several instances where for Paul the purpose seems to embrace result more than aim (cf. v. 2 above; see Fee, *God's Empowering Presence*, 434–37, on Gal 5:17); cf. O'Brien, 239. Most interpreters see it strictly as purpose.

[95] The certainty of the intertextuality is verified by Paul's citation of this same passage in Rom 14:11 (see discussion in ch. 6 [pp. 261–67]), which citation is especially noteworthy as demonstrating intertextuality in the present passage because in both instances he cites a form of the text with ἐξομολογήσεται rather than ὀμεῖται (see n. 67 in ch. 6 [p. 263]), thus indicating that in the present instance he is not "loosely reworking" or "alluding" to this passage, as suggested by, e.g., Kreitzer (*Jesus and God*, 115–16). This is a primary example of intertextuality, in which Paul purposely picks up the language of an earlier text, bringing with it the basic contextual concerns of that text, and now reapplies it to the present situation.

Both clauses stress that the whole creation will at the end offer Christ homage and worship. Thus the narrative that began in v. 6 covers the whole gamut: it begins in eternity past with Christ "*being* in the 'form' of God," then focuses on his incarnation, and finally expresses his exaltation as something already achieved (v. 9), thus presupposing resurrection and ascension; now it concludes by pointing to the eschatological future, when all created beings will own his lordship.[96] Both parts of this result clause need more detailed examination.

Every Knee Will Bow (v. 10)

Here in particular it is clear that Paul intends his readers to hear what is said about Christ in the context of what was said about Yahweh in Isa 45. In this stirring oracle (Isa 45:18–24a) Yahweh is declared to be God alone, over all that he has created and thus over all other gods and nations. And he is Israel's Savior, whom they can thus fully trust. In vv. 22–24a Yahweh, while offering salvation to all but receiving obeisance in any case, declares that "*to me* every knee shall bow." The "bowing of the knee" is a common idiom for doing homage, sometimes in prayer but always in recognition of the authority of the god or person to whom one is offering such obeisance.[97] Paul now asserts that through Christ's resurrection and at his ascension God has transferred this right of obeisance to the Son; he is the Lord before whom every knee eventually will bow.[98]

The significance of Paul's using the language of Isaiah in this way lies with his substituting "in the name of Jesus" for the "to me" of Isa 45:23, which refers to Yahweh, the God of Israel. There is in this language no hint that those who bow are acknowledging his salvation; on the contrary, they *will* bow to his sovereignty at the end, even if they are not now yielding to it. This, then, is another case where an OT passage expressing Yahweh's sovereignty over the nations has, by way of the κύριος of the Septuagint, been transferred to Christ.

---

[96] This seems so clearly the perspective of the whole that one is caught by surprise that there has been debate as to the "time" of this event (see Martin, *A Hymn of Christ*, 266–70). On this matter, Lohmeyer (97) had it right, that it speaks of the eschatological future from the perspective of "a present in God." This is nothing other than the "already/not yet" eschatological framework that informs the whole of Pauline theology.

[97] See, e.g., Ps 95:6; Mark 15:19; Luke 5:8; 22:41; Acts 7:60; 9:40; Eph 3:14; cf. the discussions in *NIDNTT* 2:859–60 (Schönweiss), and *EDNT* 1:257–58 (Nützel).

[98] N. Richardson makes the altogether unlikely suggestion (as an assertion) that "'bending the knee' at the name of Jesus is now the new way of acknowledging that Yahweh is God"; he then suggests further that there is here no "transfer of language used in the Old Testament of God to Jesus" (*Paul's Language about God* [JSNTSup 99; Sheffield: Sheffield Academic Press, 1994], 285). But that seems to miss altogether Paul's point regarding "the Name": the κύριος of the OT texts has now been transferred to Christ, and before *him* every knee will bow.

Also in keeping with the Isaianic oracle, but now interrupting the language of the citation itself, Paul declares the full scope of the homage that Christ will one day receive: every knee "of those in the heavenlies and of those on earth and of those under the earth" will bow to the authority inherent in his being κύριος. In keeping with the oracle, especially that "the Lord" is the Creator of the heavens and the earth (45:18), Paul is purposely throwing the net of Christ's sovereignty over the whole of created beings.[99] Those "of heaven" refer to all heavenly beings, angels and demons;[100] those of earth refer to all those who are living on earth at his Parousia, including those who are currently causing suffering in Philippi; and those "under the earth" probably refer to "the dead," who also will be raised to acknowledge his lordship over all. The high Christology inherent in this clause seems undeniable.

Every Tongue Will Confess (v. 11)

But there is more to the poetry of Isaiah's oracle. Not only will every creature bend the knee and offer the worship that is due Christ's name, but also "every tongue"[101] will express that homage in the language of the confessing[102] but currently suffering church: the Lord is Jesus Christ. In Isaiah (LXX) this is the final, obvious capitulation of all the nations to the singular lordship of Yahweh over them all. For Paul it becomes the third instance in his extant letters where this basic Christian confession is mentioned. In its

---

[99] But it seems unlikely that the three words are neuter and intend to imply "the whole range of creation," including inanimate creation, as Lightfoot (115) argues, followed by Plummer, 49; Silva, 133; W. Carr, *Angels and Principalities: The Background, Meaning and Development of the Pauline Phrase "hai archai kai hai exousiai"* (SNTSMS 42; Cambridge: Cambridge University Press, 1981), 86–89.

[100] So most interpreters. Although this language will surely include "the powers," there seems to be no particular emphasis on them, nor is there any reason to suppose that all three designations refer to "spirit powers" (as, e.g., Käsemann ["Critical Analysis"]; Beare, 86; Martin [*A Hymn of Christ*, 257–65], Traub [*TDNT* 5:541–42], Nützel [*EDNT* 1:258]). This view, which has been thoroughly refuted by O. Hofius (*Der Christushymnus Philipper 2,6: Untersuchungen zu Gestalt und Aussage eines urchristlichen Psalms* [WUNT 2/17; Tübingen: Mohr Siebeck, 1976], 20–40; cf. Carr, *Angels and Principalities*, 86–89), is the direct result of faulty methodology, which (1) presupposes that the "hymn" is pre-Pauline (and therefore non-Pauline), (2) seeks to root its "background" in gnostic or Hellenistic cosmology, and (3) then reads that alleged "background" into its present Pauline usage. Besides this methodological weakness, there is not a hint in the present letter that the Philippians were distressed by the "powers"; their problem is with people, whose opposition is bringing them considerable suffering.

[101] Gk. γλῶσσα. This word ordinarily refers to languages as such, but here it is distributive (= "every person, regardless of the language that person speaks" [BDAG]); thus Paul is picking up the sense of the Septuagint of Isa 45:23, that the "tongue of every person" will confess, which is also in keeping with the parallel, "knee."

[102] The ὅτι is a ὅτι-recitativum (used to introduce a quote), thus indicating, as elsewhere in Paul's writings, that these are the actual words of the confession.

Pauline occurrences the confession always takes the form "the Lord is Jesus," to which he here adds "Christ." For Paul, this confession is the line of demarcation between believer and nonbeliever (Rom 10:9). Such confession, he had argued earlier in 1 Cor 12:3, can come only by way of the Spirit; hence the crucial role of the Spirit in conversion. In Rom 10:9 this confession is linked with conviction about the resurrection of Jesus; that same combination is undoubtedly in view here. When at the end all creation beholds the risen Jesus, they will on that basis declare that κύριος is none other than the Jesus who was crucified and whom Christians worship. But the confession will then be not that of conversion but of final acknowledgement that "God has made this Jesus, whom you crucified, both Lord and Christ" (Acts 2:36).

Despite an occasional demurrer, there can be little question that this confession arose in the early Jewish Christian community,[103] as the Aramaic "Marana tha" in 1 Cor 16:22 bears striking evidence.[104] Thus, in the very earliest Aramaic-speaking communities, the language that belonged to God alone is now being addressed to Christ in corporate invocation. One can scarcely gainsay the christological implications of this confession in the present passage. On the one hand, in the Jewish synagogue the appellation "Lord" had long before been substituted for God's "name" (Yahweh). The early believers had now transferred that "name" (Lord) to the risen Jesus. Thus, Paul says, in raising Jesus from the dead, God has exalted him to the highest place and bestowed on him the name of God—in the Hebrew sense of *the Name*, referring to his investiture with God's power and authority.[105]

On the other hand, Paul's monotheism is kept intact by the final phrase, "unto the glory of God the Father."[106] Thus very much in keeping with 1 Cor 8:6, where there is only one Lord (Jesus Christ, *through* whom are all things and we through him), whose work is enclosed within that of the one God (the Father, *from* whom and *for* whom are all things, including ourselves), so here this final sentence begins with God's exalting Christ by bestowing on him *the Name* and concludes on a similar theological note, that all of this is to God the Father's own glory.[107]

Finally, we should note that this declaration of Jesus as "Lord" probably would not be lost on believers in a city whose pagan inhabitants were Roman citizens and devotees of "lords many," including "lord Caesar." Paul well knows to whom he is writing these words, especially since he is now one of the emperor's prisoners, and the Philippian believers are suffering at the hands of Roman citizens as well. All of them, Paul asserts, including

---

[103] On this question, see esp. Hurtado, "Lord," *DPL* 560–69.

[104] See the discussion on the passage in ch. 3 (pp. 120–22).

[105] Cf. Kreitzer (*Jesus and God*, 116), whose language I have here borrowed.

[106] Cf. ibid., 161; cited also by Hurtado, "Lord," 565. Cf. 1:11, where the fruit of righteousness comes "through Christ Jesus unto the glory and praise of God."

[107] That is, this phrase goes with the whole narrative (from v. 6), not just the final clause (so Meyer).

the emperor himself, will at the end acknowledge that all along there has been only one Lord.

Christ, Heavenly Savior and Lord—Philippians 3:20–21

Toward the end of the argumentation of this letter, and as the theological conclusion to the application of Paul's own story as he models Christ's story (3:4–14), Paul picks up the eschatological theme struck throughout the letter and puts everything into that perspective. In contrast to those who live as enemies of the cross, because their minds are set on what is only of the earth, Paul presents his final portrayal of the now exalted Lord and Savior as the eschatological goal of everything. Expressing it in terms of Christ's present reign and coming Parousia, he asserts that the believer's own eschatological existence is wholly determined by the presently reigning Christ.

The language of the passage is full of echoes of the Christ story in 2:6–11; nonetheless, it has its own unique role in the letter, serving simultaneously to conclude the argument that began in 3:1 and offering an immediate response to the "many" who "walk" contrary to the Pauline pattern (vv. 17–18). They ultimately are judged because "their minds are set on earthly things" (v. 19). At the same time, Paul also picks up the play on the believers' "dual" citizenship (cf. 1:27); as (present) citizens of Rome (by way of Philippi's being a Roman colony), they are reassured that their true citizenship is in heaven.[108] All of this[109] is said in a sentence that rises to extraordinary christological heights; not only is Christ the focus and center of everything, but also his activities here are those that in Pauline soteriological texts are ordinarily attributed to God the Father.[110] Three strictly christological matters concern us.

---

[108] On this matter, see A. T. Lincoln, *Paradise Now and Not Yet: Studies in the Role of the Heavenly Dimension in Paul's Thought with Special Reference to His Eschatology* (SNTSMS 43; Cambridge: Cambridge University Press, 1981), 97–101.

[109] Because of the exalted nature of this passage and its linguistic connections to 2:6–11, some find here another possible piece of pre-Pauline material; but as with the former passage, and even more so in this case, here is vintage Paul, whose thoroughly eschatological outlook and christological focus repeatedly merge in climactic moments such as this. See the discussion in Fee, 376–77.

[110] Which some see as "condemning it" as Pauline (e.g., G. Strecker, "Redaktion und Tradition im Christushymnus Phil 2 6–11," *ZNW* 55 [1964]: 63–78; J. Becker, "Erwägungen zu Phil. 3,20–21," *TZ* 27 [1971]: 16–29). This is a remarkable judgment, since Paul himself dictated what is said here; and as noted on 2:6–11, methodologically we must assume as self-evident that what the apostle dictates for the hearing of the Philippians he also affirms—all the more so, one would think, when the passage brings this hortatory section that began in v. 1 to its resounding conclusion. It is little wonder that the idea of a pre-Pauline, and therefore non-Pauline, hymn fragment has found such a small hearing in this case. For a more extensive rebuttal, see Kim, *Origin of Paul's Gospel*, 150–56.

Christ as "Savior" and "Lord"

The first point that Paul makes by way of conclusion to the present argument is that the Philippian believers' present citizenship is already "in heaven," from whence "we eagerly await [the coming of] our Savior."[111] He is none other than "the Lord Jesus Christ," the one who had the name "Lord" bestowed on him at his exaltation (2:9–10). Thus Paul focuses first of all on the coming of Christ as the eschatological Lord and Savior.

Significantly, both for his readers' context and for our understanding of Paul's Christology, the one whom we "eagerly await" is first of all designated as "Savior."[112] The significance of this is highlighted by its rarity in Paul's writings; only once heretofore (Eph 5:23) has he used this appellation of Christ, and in that case it was not fully titular.[113] He does so here almost certainly for the Philippians' sakes, since this is a common title for Caesar,[114]

---

[111] Although the language of this clause does not specify Christ's Parousia (coming), what Paul says does in fact presuppose it: first, that we eagerly await him "from heaven" can only mean his Parousia from heaven; and second, the verb ἀπεκδεχόμεθα (*we eagerly await*) is used exclusively by Paul in connection with the coming of Christ at the eschatological "wrap-up" (cf. 1 Cor 1:7; Gal 5:5; Rom 8:19, 23, 25 [elsewhere in the NT in Heb 9:28, also an eschatological context, and 1 Pet 3:20]). By this verb, Paul harks back to his own "eager pursuit" of the heavenly prize (vv. 12–14), likewise emphasizing how he lives in the present with his focus constantly on the goal.

[112] Gk. σωτῆρα, which stands in the emphatic first position (the object before the verb) and without the definite article. But it is doubtful that Paul intended merely "*a* Savior," as some contend. Rather, the anarthrous usage is emphatic, as with the anarthrous κύριον Ἰησοῦν Χριστόν that follows. This probably is a variation on "Colwell's Rule," that a definite predicate noun that precedes the verb is usually anarthrous (in this case, a definite direct object, followed by an apposition, seems to function analogously).

[113] Although it becomes more common in the letters that follow this one; see Titus 1:4; 3:6 (some would add 2:13, but see the discussion below, pp. 442–46); 2 Tim 1:10 (a context very much like this one). Many (e.g., Beare, 137; Collange, 140; O'Brien, 462–63) emphasize the usage as reflecting Paul's use of the verb "save," which, it is alleged, is used exclusively to refer to the future of eschatological salvation. But that is simply not so, as 1 Cor 1:21; 15:2; Rom 8:25; and Eph 2:5, 8 bear clear witness.

[114] Cf. Foerster, *TDNT* 7:1010–12. In its Hellenistic derivation the term refers to anyone who "saves" or delivers; thus it has nothing to do with being "saved from sin" but rather with being delivered and protected, either by the gods (thus it is variously applied to Zeus, Apollo, Poseidon, Heracles, Asclepius, and Sarapis) or by significant human figures (e.g., Pompey, the emperors). Caesar is thus called "the Savior of the World," Augustus himself being "the Savior of Humankind." K. H. Schelkle (*EDNT* 3:326–27) denies that the usage here has any reference to the emperor, but the fact that it occurs in a sentence that deliberately places their "commonwealth" in heaven, from whence they await their true "Savior," seems to weigh more heavily in favor of the view espoused here; cf. P. Perkins, "Philippians: Theology for the Heavenly Politeuma," in *Thessalonians, Philippians, Galatians, Philemon* (vol. 1 of *Pauline Theology*; ed. J. M. Bassler; Minneapolis: Fortress, 1991), 93–94.

often in conjunction with "Lord."[115] That this is a deliberate referent seems certain because of the equally deliberate assertion that their true "citizenship" is in heaven, not in Roman Philippi.

That Paul would designate Christ as "Savior" at all is especially significant christologically because the title occurs frequently in the OT to refer to "God our (my) Savior," which is almost certainly its first referent. Its significance is to be found in its Septuagint origins, where it occurs often and at key places, as an appellation for the God who had "saved" = "delivered" Israel from Egyptian bondage. Thus in the Song of Moses (Deut 32:15), "Jacob" is chastised because he "rejected God his Savior"; and at the heart of book 1 of the Psalter, "David" speaks of "God my Savior" (Ps 25:5; 27:9).

The clincher to all of this, as far as Paul's word of reassurance to the Philippians is concerned, is the final, otherwise unnecessary, appositive "the Lord Jesus Christ," in which he picks up the precise language (including word order) from 2:11—the only two absolute uses of this combination in the letter. The Savior, they are thus reminded, is none other than "the Lord Jesus Christ" himself, whose lordship every tongue will confess at the eschatological denouement.

The One Who Will Transform Our Bodies

Paul's second clause focuses on the way in which Christ will function as eschatological Savior. It begins,

3:21 ὃς μετασχηματίσει   τὸ σῶμα   τῆς ταπεινώσεως ἡμῶν
       σύμμορφον   τῷ σώματι   τῆς δόξης αὐτοῦ

     who will transform   *the body*   *of our lowly estate,*
       conforming (it)   *to the body*   *of his glory*

One can scarcely miss the wordplays, contrasts, and echoes of prior moments in the letter. The primary contrast is between our and Christ's present bodies: ours is an expression of "humility," which echoes the verb "he humbled himself" in 2:8; his is currently an expression of his "glory," a word that belongs to God the Father in 2:11.[116] At the same time, the word σύμμορφον can only be a deliberate echo of 3:10,[117] where the believer is to be συμμορφιζόμενος τῷ θανάτῳ αὐτοῦ (*conformed to Christ's death*), while

---

    [115] Cf. Bockmuehl, 235.

    [116] At the same time, it stands in deliberate contrast to the opponents who "glory" in (what should be to) their shame (3:19).

    [117] This is mostly because of its proximity to that passage and the fact that the verb in 3:10 is found only here in the Pauline corpus and its cognate noun only here and in Rom 8:29, where it also has to do with believers being "conformed" into the image of Christ.

μετασχηματίσει is a verbal construction from the noun σχήματι in 2:7b ("in human *likeness*").[118]

Although Paul's language is quite different here, the concept itself is to be understood in light of what he had written earlier to the Corinthians (1 Cor 15:42–57), in a context where some were denying a future, bodily resurrection of believers. The contrasts there were between our present bodies as perishable and "natural" (and, when dead, "sown in dishonor and weakness") and the transformed heavenly body as imperishable and "supernatural"[119] (and raised in "glory" and "power"); the present bodies are thus to be transformed into the "likeness" of the "man of heaven," who already bears such a body through his resurrection. And although the emphasis in that passage is on the resurrection per se, Paul concludes by emphasizing that the same transformation will occur for those living until the Parousia (1 Cor 15:52–53).

Two significant christological points are embedded in the present clause. First, along with 1 Cor 15:44b–49, this is a strong assertion of Christ's bodily association with us in his incarnation, which reality was stressed in 2:7–8 without the language of "body." This in turn is the certain evidence that Paul understood the incarnation forever to mark Christ, so that in his present exaltation at the Father's right hand, he is there in bodily form (although transformed for eternal existence). Thus, mystery though this might be for us, Paul seems clearly to have believed that the one who was always by nature God (2:6), in becoming one with us in his humanity, continues even in his present exaltation to glory to bear the reality of his having shared our bodily existence.

The point here, of course, is that the same future awaits those who are Christ's, which is Paul's present concern. The Philippians' present lot, he has argued in 1:29–30 and alluded to in 2:17, is to "suffer for Christ's sake." But they can "rejoice in the Lord" in the midst of such suffering (2:18; 3:1; 4:4) because that suffering itself is enabled by "the power of his resurrection" (3:10), which resurrection at the same time guarantees their certain future. Hence, in their present "humiliation" the believers in Philippi await the coming of the Savior and, with that coming, the transformation of their humiliation into the likeness of his glory.

Second, the most striking thing about the sentence is that Christ himself is its (grammatical) subject. Here is one of the more remarkable interchanges in the corpus, where an activity that is elsewhere either the express or implied activity of God the Father is attributed to Christ. Although the language of "transformation" does not appear earlier, this point has previ-

---

[118] For a more complete list of the verbal echoes between this passage and 2:6–11, see Lincoln, *Paradise Now*, 88.

[119] For this as the proper contrast between ψυχικόν σῶμα and πνευματικόν σῶμα, as bodies "adapted to the present, natural, life and to the final eschatological life of the Spirit," see Fee, *God's Empowering Presence*, 262–64.

ously been made several times by Paul. In 1 Cor 15:38 it is God who gives the new "body" to what is raised; in 2 Cor 5:2 the new body is "a building from God, a house not made with hands"; and in Rom 8:11 it is the God who raised Christ from the dead who "will also give life to your mortal bodies because of the Spirit who lives in you" (TNIV).[120] But in the present sentence this action is attributed to Christ, who will himself "transform" the body that in its present lowly estate is subject to death and, by doing so, will conform it to his own presently glorified body.

The Final Subjection of All Things

The third significant christological moment in this sentence is found in its final phrase. The power by which Christ will bring about this transformation, the Philippians are told, is κατὰ τὴν ἐνέργειαν τοῦ δύνασθαι αὐτὸν καὶ ὑποτάξαι αὐτῷ τὰ πάντα (*in keeping with the working of him who is able also to subject to himself all things*). In some ways, this is the most remarkable "transformation" of all, in that Paul here uses language about Christ that he elsewhere uses exclusively of God the Father.

First, it is "in keeping with[121] the working,"[122] which is then defined, "that enables him also to subject all things to himself." The phrase itself occurs exclusively in the so-called Captivity Letters, in Col 1:29; Eph 1:19; 3:7; 4:16; and here. In Colossians and Ephesians the "working" is exclusively that of God the Father. Here it is equally attributed to the Son.

Second, the phrase "able to subject all things to himself" is Paul's eschatological interpretation of Ps 8:7 LXX, where God will "subject all things" to his Messiah, who in turn, according to 1 Cor 15:28, will turn over all things to God the Father so that "God might be all and in all." Remarkably, in the present passage the "subjecting" of all things to Christ himself is said to be by Christ's own power.

---

[120] The TNIV has got this right (against most other English translations) that the Spirit is not the agent but the indwelling cause of a future bodily resurrection. On this textual matter and the meaning of this passage in context, see Fee, *To What End Exegesis?* 230–34, esp. n. 47.

[121] Gk. κατά. For a discussion and rejection of the view that this preposition ever functions in a purely instrumental way, see Fee, *God's Empowering Presence*, 481 n. 24. This is especially so here; not only does the preposition *not* denote instrumentality (*pace* TNIV, NASB, NRSV, NAB, REB, NJB), but also what it *does* convey is the "norm" or "standard" in keeping with which something is done. Hence, Paul intends not "*by* the working" but "in keeping with that working" that is already recognized to have been at work in his own resurrection/transformation.

[122] Gk. κατὰ τὴν ἐνέργειαν; cf. Eph 3:7, κατὰ τὴν ἐνέργειαν τῆς δυνάμεως αὐτοῦ (*in keeping with the working of his power;* also Eph 1:19, "in keeping with the working of his might," and 3:20, "in keeping with the power that is at work in us"—texts referring to the way God's power is (or will be) tangibly at work in the world. The verb occurred in Phil 2:13 of God's working all things in/among them for his good purpose.

Third, the little word "also" is much too important to be omitted, as in many English translations.[123] Here is the final word of assurance to the Philippians. By the same power that he will transform their present bodies that are suffering at the hand of opposition in Philippi, Christ will *likewise* subject "all things"[124] to himself, including the emperor and all those who in his name are causing the Philippians to suffer. As Paul has already said in 1:28 and implied in 3:19, their own salvation "from God" will at the same time result in the "destruction" of the opposition.

Paul's point here, of course, as in the entire sentence and most other such moments in the corpus, is not christological per se. That is, his christological affirmations are not intentionally, but incidentally, so; and this is what makes them so telling. Here is a man not bent on either demonstrating or proving the deity of Christ; rather, this is so fully assumed by Paul that he can regularly interchange between the Father and the Son such exclusively divine activities as these.

Other Christological Passages/Phrases

Given the significant amount of expressed and presupposed Christology in this brief letter, we should not be surprised at the considerable amount of other incidental expressions that have christological import. Most of these are of a kind with two categories of usage found throughout the corpus: Christ's assuming the role of the divine κύριος of Septuagint texts and Christ's sharing in some of the divine prerogatives. And many of these will by now have been noted in earlier chapters.

Christ as Κύριος = Yahweh in Septuagint Phrases

The Day of Christ (1:6, 10; 2:16)

One of the less obvious, but nonetheless certain, concerns that Paul has for the Philippian believers is that they not lose sight of the absolute certainty of their future hope. This concern is expressed in a variety of ways, beginning with the thanksgiving (1:6) and prayer (1:10–11), and then touched on throughout the letter. The result is that Paul reminds them of their sure future more often than he does in any other letter, which is not surprising in a letter that focuses so thoroughly on Christ.

---

[123] Cf. NIV, GNB, NAB, REB; translated "also" in NRSV, or "even" in RSV, NASB, NJB.

[124] Gk. τὰ πάντα, used by Paul when he wants to refer to the whole of the created universe or the whole of a given subject; for present usage, cf. 1 Cor 8:6 (2x); 15:27–28 (4x); Rom 11:36. The present passage is a direct reflection of the argument of 1 Cor 15:25–28.

In Paul's earliest two letters the prophetic language regarding the coming great "Day of Yahweh" had already been co-opted by the early church to refer to the future (second) coming of Christ. In those letters Paul had kept the language of the Septuagint intact (ἡμέρα κυρίου) and simply applied it to Christ. In 1 Cor 1:8 he identifies "the Lord" in this phrase as "the Lord Jesus Christ." Now toward the end of his life, and quite in keeping with his full-blown Christ devotion, Paul refers to this future hope simply as "the Day of Christ Jesus." But it still carries the obvious identification of Christ with the κύριος = Yahweh of the prophetic phrase.

The Spirit of Jesus Christ (1:19)

For the fourth time in his letters Paul speaks of the Holy Spirit as the Spirit of Christ (see 2 Cor 3:17; Gal 4:6; Rom 8:9). As was pointed out in the discussion of Rom 8:9, the Spirit, who elsewhere has his own identity, is on the basis of Septuagint usage more commonly called "the Spirit of God." As in the preceding three passages, the reason for the shift of language here is purely contextual. In a letter in which Paul presents Christ as the ultimate paradigm of Godlikeness, especially in his having become obedient unto death on the cross, he longs for the Holy Spirit to enable him to magnify Christ at his own tribunal.

What is significant christologically is that the one Holy Spirit (1 Cor 11:4; Eph 4:4), who is so often referred to as the Spirit of God, can also be so easily called the Spirit of Jesus Christ. Indeed, this kind of easy interchange had its own role in the eventual articulation of God as Trinity.

That Christ Be Magnified (1:20)

It should be noted further that the content of the previous phrase controls the rest of the sentence, so that through their prayers and the consequent "supply" of the Spirit of Jesus Christ, Paul expects to experience God's σωτηρία (*salvation/vindication*). With the phrase "this will turn out as 'salvation' for me," Paul has thus dipped into the Septuagint of Job 13:16, where Job longs to present his case before Yahweh, "even though he slay me." This option, Job recognizes, scary as it would be, is his only hope for vindication and thus salvation. With his coming tribunal in view, Paul asserts that it will be through "the Spirit of Jesus Christ" that he will know God's "salvation = vindication," whose end result will be an absence of "shame" as "Christ is magnified" in Paul's body (through life or death).

This final collocation of "shame" and Christ's being "magnified" echoes the beginning of Ps 34:2–3 (33:3–4 LXX) and the conclusion of Ps 35:26–27 (34:26–27 LXX). What Paul desires is that his tribunal will not be a cause for "shame"—not for himself personally but for Christ and the gospel. Rather, his longing is for God's "salvation/vindication," wherein Christ will be "magnified" whether it means life or death for Paul. Since this is the only instance of this combination (that "Christ be magnified") in Paul's writings and since it fits the whole context so well, one may assume that here again Paul has used biblical language that in the Septuagint is used of "the Lord" and has attributed it to Christ as Lord.

Thus the whole passage is replete with echoes of various kinds that reflect the language of OT texts where those in trouble cry out to the Lord for help. Only now "the Lord," whose Spirit will cause him to be magnified, is Christ Jesus.

Rejoice in the Lord (3:1; 4:4; cf. 4:10)

As with the preceding passage, Paul seems also to be echoing OT ideas when he frames the final warning/exhortation of the letter with the imperative χαίρετε ἐν κυρίῳ (*rejoice in the Lord* [3:1 and 4:4), which language he then picks up in 4:10 as his own response to having received their gift. Although the Septuagint translators use two different verbs (both different from Paul's),[125] this idiom occurs throughout the Septuagint as a primary expression of Israelite piety (most often in the indicative; see, e.g., Ps 32:11 [31:11 LXX]; 33:21 [32:21 LXX]; 35:9 [34:9 LXX]; 40:16 [39:17 LXX]). For reasons not known to us, they consistently avoided χαίρω for this idiom (but see Zech 10:7). Paul, on the other hand, uses their words only once (2 Cor 2:2),[126] not counting Septuagint citations. But given the flexible way this idiom is handled in the Septuagint and given Paul's linguistic preferences, it is difficult to imagine that this imperative is not his own rendering of this OT idiom, especially when, as with the Philippians, the context of the psalmist is most often one of duress or trouble. And again without forethought he simply attributes now to his Lord, Jesus Christ, what in the OT is the special province of Yahweh.

Boast in Christ Jesus (3:4); Know Christ Jesus My Lord (3:8)

In a context of distinguishing between those who promote circumcision (the κατα-τομή, "mutilators" of the flesh) and those who serve God by the Spirit (3:2–3), Paul adds that the true circumcision (the περι-τομή) are those who "boast in Christ Jesus" (3:4). This is such unusual language that one is led to believe that Paul is here once more echoing the (for him) crucial passage from Jer 9:23–24 (see discussion in ch. 3 on 1 Cor 1:31 [pp. 129–30]). The only legitimate "boasting" is in "the Lord"; and this boast rests in "knowing the Lord." Thus it seems more than coincidental that the single instance of "knowing the Lord" in the Pauline corpus (3:8)

---

[125] They regularly use ἀγαλλιάω or εὐφραίνω; the first word does not occur at all in Paul's letters, the second only in 2 Cor 2:2 plus in two Septuagint citations (Gal 4:27; Rom 15:10).

[126] The usage in the passage offers something of a clue to his choice of words, since here εὐφραίνω is strictly nonverbal (= "to gladden") whereas his use of χαίρω ordinarily implies verbal expression.

follows 3:4 as an elaboration/explanation of what it means to "boast in Christ Jesus," just as in Jeremiah God's word is, "Let those who boast *boast* in this, that they understand and *know* me" (9:24).

As with several such moments in Paul's writings, his Christ devotion results in his using Septuagint language that refers to Yahweh and applying it to Christ, and doing so with such ease.

The Lord Is Near (4:5)

The sudden appearance of this indicative (ὁ κύριος ἐγγύς [*the Lord is near*])[127] in the context of Paul's concluding exhortations is as surprising as its intent is obscure. The asyndeton typical of this kind of hortatory material also holds true for this indicative, so that one cannot tell whether Paul intends it to conclude what precedes or introduce what follows, and therefore whether it expresses future or realized eschatology. Does he intend "Rejoice in the Lord always; *and* let your gentle forbearance be known by all, *for* the [coming of] the Lord is near"?[128] Or is it *"Because* the Lord is [always] near, do not be anxious about anything, but let your requests be made known to God"?[129] Or—perhaps something as close to intentional double entendre as one finds in the apostle—does he intend a bit of both?[130]

On the one hand, this looks very much like another instance of intertextuality,[131] purposely echoing Ps 145:18, "the LORD is near all who call upon him."[132] In which case it introduces vv. 6–7 as an expression of "realized"

---

[127] The difficulty lies with the adverb ἐγγύς, which, as with the English "near," has either spatial or temporal connotations, depending on the context. On its own in a sentence like this, it is totally ambiguous; unfortunately, in context it can go either way as well.

[128] So Lightfoot (160), who notes the similarity with Jas 5:8, where μακροθυμία (*forbearance*) is called for in light of the Parousia; cf. Plummer, 93; Michael, 197; Lohmeyer, 168–69; Barth, 122; Beare, 146; Hendriksen, 194; Gnilka, 169; Houlden, 109; Martin, 155; Kent, 151; Silva, 227.

[129] So Calvin, 288; Caird, 150–51; C. Bugg, "Philippians 4:4–13," *RevExp* 88 (1991): 253–57; cf. the NEB, which starts a new paragraph with this indicative ("The Lord is near; have no anxiety [etc.]").

[130] So Ellicott, 101; Vincent, 133; Collange, 144; Bruce, 142–43; Hawthorne, 182; O'Brien, 490.

[131] Cf. Lohmeyer, 169; D. M. Stanley, *Boasting in the Lord: The Phenomenon of Prayer in Saint Paul* (New York: Paulist Press, 1973), 106; J. Baumgarten, *Paulus und die Apokalyptik: Die Auslegung apokalyptischer Überlieferungen in den echten Paulusbriefen* (WMANT 44; Neukirchen-Vluyn: Neukirchener Verlag, 1975), 205–8; O'Brien, 489. For this phenomenon in Philippians, see 1:19; 2:10, 15–16.

[132] Ps 144:18 LXX, ἐγγὺς κύριος πᾶσιν τοῖς ἐπικαλουμένοις αὐτόν; cf. 34:18 (33:19 LXX), ἐγγὺς κύριος τοῖς συντετριμμένοις τὴν καρδίαν (*the LORD is near the contrite in heart*); cf. 119:151 (118:151 LXX), where it appears in the second singular. Paul has ὁ κύριος ἐγγύς, whose word order, in contrast to the psalm, puts emphasis on "the Lord" more than "near." Baumgarten (*Paulus und die Apokalyptik,* 205–8) correctly emphasizes the implicitly high Christology in such language; cf. discussion of 2:10 above.

eschatology: "Because the Lord is ever present, do not be anxious, but pray." On the other hand (or perhaps at the same time), it also echoes the apocalyptic language of Zeph 1:7, 14 ("the Day of the LORD is near"), picked up by Paul in Rom 13:12, and found in Jas 5:8 regarding the coming of the Lord.

On the whole, it seems likely that this is primarily intended as the last in the series of eschatological words to this suffering congregation, again reminding them of their sure future despite present difficulties. Thus, it probably is a word of encouragement and affirmation.[133] Since their present suffering is at the hands of those who proclaim Caesar as Lord, they are reminded that the true "Lord" is "near." Their eschatological vindication is close at hand. At the same time, by using the language of the Psalter, Paul is encouraging them to prayer in the midst of their present distress, because the "Lord is near" in a very real way to those who call on him now. And, as always for Paul, "the Lord" who is ever near is now the Lord Jesus Christ.

Sharer of the Divine Prerogatives

Despite the comparative brevity of this letter, it contains several other phrases that speak of Christ in ways that Paul and other NT writers would ordinarily attribute to God the Father. There are four such in this letter that call for brief comment.

With the Compassion of Christ Jesus (1:8)

Paul concludes his rather complex thanksgiving, which focuses both on who the Philippians are and on their partnership with him in the gospel, by offering a mild oath as to how greatly he personally longs for them ἐν σπλάγχνοις Χριστοῦ Ἰησοῦ (*with the compassion of Christ Jesus*). This use of the entrails as a way of expressing deep feelings toward someone is a common Greek idiom; and though it is never used of God in the OT, it is a near synonym of the recurring οἰκτίρμων/-μος (*compassion*). Indeed, in 2:1 of this letter Paul appeals to this very deep feeling (which he hopes they have toward him) as the final basis for the exhortation of vv. 2–4.

In the OT this latter word is used of God's character, and thus his attitude toward Israel, in the key revelatory passage in Exod 34:4–6 ("the LORD, a God of οἰκτίρμων καὶ ἐλεήμων [*compassion and mercy*]"). In the present passage it is this same characteristic, now attributed to Christ, that serves as the basis of Paul's own strong affection for his Philippian friends.

Hope in the Lord Jesus (2:19); Confident in the Lord (1:14; 2:24)

The first thing up in the letter after the long exhortation of 1:27–2:18 is a commendation of two companions, Epaphroditus, the bearer of the letter

---

[133] It is possible, but less likely, that Paul intended a word of motivation—that is, "Be gently forbearing, because the Lord is near."

(2:25–30), and Timothy, who will come to them with news of the outcome of Paul's imprisonment (2:19–24). Since that outcome lies in God's presently unknown (to them) future, Paul begins with a qualified expression of what he expects to happen soon. Thus he says, "I hope in the Lord Jesus to send Timothy to you soon." In everyday contemporary English this would mean very little; but for Paul, it is in fact an expression of considerable confidence. He has already expressed himself as expecting to be released from his imprisonment (1:24), which he repeats again in 2:23–24. Thus, this is not simply a kind of wishful hopefulness regarding the future; for Paul, it borders more on certainty, as the pickup in 2:24 makes clear.

This "hope" is thus expressed in biblical language,[134] even if it does not mean quite the same thing here as it does in the OT texts. There it had to do with putting one's whole confidence in God for what he would do in the future; for Paul, it is simply another moment in which Christ is the one in whom he has confidence for a more everyday reality.

But in the two instances of "confident in the Lord," Paul moves much closer to genuine trust. The Greek idiom, which occurs regularly in the Septuagint, is a form of the verb πείθω (*persuade*), which in the perfect tense moves toward the idea of "being persuaded" about someone or something and thus to put one's confidence in that person. The first instance of this usage in Paul's letters is in 2 Thess 3:4, where Paul expresses total confidence in the Lord regarding the Thessalonians. There the source of this confidence is God himself, so that in the Septuagint various forms of "trust" language end up being glossed into Greek by πείθω. This is almost certainly the source of Paul's usage.

In the first instance (1:14) it has to do with those who have been aroused to proclaim Christ because of Paul's imprisonment; and such confidence is needed precisely because of that imprisonment, especially if they are to "dare all the more to proclaim the gospel without fear." In the second instance (2:24) it indicates how much Paul genuinely expected to be released from this imprisonment. What is striking is that language that in the Septuagint had to do with the psalmists' confidence in Yahweh is now expressed by Paul in terms of Christ.

The One Who Strengthens (4:13)

That God "strengthens" his people for various tasks is a recurring biblical theme. Paul has previously prayed for such in 1 Thess 3:13 (to Christ) and in 2 Thess 2:17 (to God). The only issue in the present text (Phil 4:13) is the assumed subject of the clause—God or Christ—which in this case must refer to Christ, since the context seems to demand it (see v. 10). That at least was

---

[134] See, e.g., Ps 4:5 [4:6 LXX], καὶ ἐλπίσατε ἐπὶ κύριον (*and put your hope in the Lord*), and throughout the Psalter, usually with ἐπί when the object is κύριος but ἐν with idioms such as "hope in the name [of the LORD]" (Ps 33:21 [32:21 LXX]).

the common view in the early church, where scribes added "Christ" to the manuscript tradition but not "God." This same verb will be used again with reference to Christ's strengthening the apostle in 1 Tim 1:12. In Paul's mind, Christ and the Father share this activity on behalf of God's people.

Thus, quite in keeping with the entire church corpus, not to mention the letters to associates that follow, Paul regularly attributes to Christ divine activities or prerogatives, and he does so in such a nonreflective way that the presuppositional basis of such language speaks volumes about his understanding of Christ. And that leads us to reflect once more on the central place Christ has in Paul's entire worldview, in which not everything that he thinks about Christ is strictly soteriological.

Paul and Christ Devotion

We had occasion in our look at the Christology that emerges in 2 Corinthians to note how Paul's Christ-centered soteriology especially spills over into his Christology. Any look at Paul's Christology in Philippians that did not take his utter devotion to Christ into account would seem to be a case of carrying on theology in the abstract, divorced from reality. For here, with wonderful assonance, Paul gives expression to the passion of his life: ἐμοὶ γὰρ τὸ ζῆν Χριστὸς καὶ τὸ ἀποθανεῖν κέρδος (for to me to live, Christ; to die, gain, 1:21). Whereas we find this kind of devotion sprinkled throughout the corpus, in this letter it sits in bold relief. And those of us who know Paul only through his written remains need to take seriously that this is what drives the apostle at every moment, of which the gospel as such is the most significant part. But it is not the whole part, as this letter and this motto make clear.

What is striking in Paul's letters is the rather complete lack of similar devotion expressed toward God the Father, who for Paul stands at the beginning and end of all things. And this from a thoroughgoing monotheist whose own devotional life has been molded in part by the Psalter, where such devotion to Yahweh regularly finds expression: "My soul thirsts for the living God" (42:2); "You, God, are my God, . . . I thirst for you, my whole being longs for you" (63:1); "My heart and my flesh cry out for the living God" (84:2). Such devotion in Paul's thought is directed altogether toward Christ his Lord.

The devotion takes two essential forms. On the one hand, there is here, as elsewhere, a deep love for Christ for soteriological reasons, both for salvation as such and for the new-creation dimension of that salvation. This latter finds expression especially when Paul uses his own story as a paradigm for the Philippians to imitate (3:4–14, 15, 17), a story that seems deliberately patterned after the main thrust of the Christ story in 2:6–11. Thus the penultimate goal of "knowing Christ Jesus my Lord" (v. 8) is, by the power of the resurrection, to be conformed into Christ's own likeness as that found expression in his sacrificial death for others (v. 10).

On the other hand, the devotion is especially toward Christ himself. This is where the motto fits in; for Paul, living is all about Christ, and dying means to "gain" Christ. And what disallows us to think of this as strictly soteriological is his elaboration of the "gain" to mean "to depart and *be with Christ*" (1:23), the better-by-far option, if options were to be had. In ordinary human discourse this can only be taken in a personal way.[135]

It is striking, therefore, that Paul consistently thinks of the eschatological goal in terms of "being with Christ." This begins as early as 1 Thess 5:10–11 ("that we might *live with him*"). It is picked up again in 2 Cor 5:8 ("we prefer to be away from the body and *at home with the Lord*"). It finds full expression in Philippians, first in 1:23 noted above and then especially in 3:8–9, where he echoes 1:21 by affirming that everything else is loss in comparison with the option of "gaining Christ, and being found in him." Contextual exegesis, therefore, suggests that this is both "the one thing" in 3:13 and thus the eschatological prize in v. 14; anything else would seem do an injustice to Paul.

Whatever else one may think of this kind of pure devotion to Christ, it must be acknowledged as devotion toward one's deity, not toward a merely exalted human being. And thus once more Paul's high Christology finds expression without being articulated in a purposefully theological way.

Conclusion

As in earlier chapters, the christological conclusions have been drawn throughout. By now it is no surprise that Paul's Κύριος Christology, which tends to be the dominant motif in most of the letters, takes pride of place in this one as well. Not only does the Christ story in 2:6–11 conclude with an extraordinary emphasis on this motif, but also the same Lord, Jesus Christ, will be responsible for the final transformation of our present bodies into ones that conform to his own present "body of glory." It is difficult not to see some of the emphasis on this motif as an indirect confrontation with the Roman emperor (Nero in this case), whose egomania by now may very well lie behind the outside pressures that the Philippian believers are experiencing.

This last matter is perhaps what lies behind the emergence in this letter of identifying Christ the Lord as "Savior" as well. This unusual (for Paul) designation for Christ, even though the language surely belongs to Paul's OT roots, makes a great deal of sense within such a setting.

If there is very little Son of God Christology in this letter—many would argue that there is none at all—it is of some interest that the doxological

---

[135]Otherwise it would be like a man getting married and thinking of his wife only in terms of her "being so good to verk," as an old German immigrant said of his wife in one of my pastor father's earliest parishes.

conclusion of the Christ story speaks of "the glory of God *the Father*" in a context where the preexistent, incarnate, and exalted Christ is the main thrust of the passage. Christ's strongly affirmed preexistence, which in other Pauline moments is expressed in terms of God sending his Son, is what leads one to think so. In any case, this letter offers the most straightforward presentation of Christ's preexistence and incarnation that one finds in the corpus.

Appendix I: The Texts

(double brackets [[ ]] indicate texts with references to God alone)

1:1 Παῦλος καὶ Τιμόθεος **δοῦλοι Χριστοῦ Ἰησοῦ** πᾶσιν τοῖς ἁγίοις **ἐν Χριστῷ Ἰησοῦ** τοῖς οὖσιν ἐν Φιλίπποις σὺν ἐπισκόποις καὶ διακόνοις,

1:2 χάρις ὑμῖν καὶ εἰρήνη <u>ἀπὸ θεοῦ πατρὸς ἡμῶν</u> καὶ **κυρίου Ἰησοῦ Χριστοῦ.**

[[1:3 Εὐχαριστῶ <u>τῷ θεῷ μου</u> ἐπὶ πάσῃ τῇ μνείᾳ ὑμῶν]]

1:6 . . . ὅτι ὁ ἐναρξάμενος ἐν ὑμῖν ἔργον ἀγαθὸν ἐπιτελέσει **ἄχρι ἡμέρας Χριστοῦ Ἰησοῦ·**

1:8 <u>μάρτυς γάρ μου ὁ θεός</u> ὡς ἐπιποθῶ πάντας ὑμᾶς **ἐν σπλάγχνοις Χριστοῦ Ἰησοῦ.**

1:10–11 [10]εἰς τὸ δοκιμάζειν ὑμᾶς τὰ διαφέροντα, ἵνα ἦτε εἰλικρινεῖς καὶ ἀπρόσκοποι **εἰς ἡμέραν Χριστοῦ,** [11]πεπληρωμένοι καρπὸν δικαιοσύνης τὸν **διὰ Ἰησοῦ Χριστοῦ** <u>εἰς δόξαν καὶ ἔπαινον θεοῦ.</u>

1:13–14 [13]ὥστε τοὺς δεσμούς μου φανεροὺς **ἐν Χριστῷ** γενέσθαι ἐν ὅλῳ τῷ πραιτωρίῳ καὶ τοῖς λοιποῖς πάσιν, [14]καὶ τοὺς πλείονας τῶν ἀδελφῶν **ἐν κυρίῳ πεποιθότας** τοῖς δεσμοῖς μου περισσοτέρως τολμᾶν ἀφόβως τὸν λόγον λαλεῖν.

1:15–18 [15]τινὲς μὲν καὶ διὰ φθόνον καὶ ἔριν, τινὲς δὲ καὶ δι' εὐδοκίαν **τὸν Χριστὸν κηρύσσουσιν·** [16]οἱ μὲν ἐξ ἀγάπης, εἰδότες ὅτι εἰς ἀπολογίαν τοῦ εὐαγγελίου κεῖμαι, [17]οἱ δὲ ἐξ ἐριθείας **τὸν Χριστὸν καταγγέλλουσιν**, οὐχ ἁγνῶς, οἰόμενοι θλῖψιν ἐγείρειν τοῖς δεσμοῖς μου. [18]Τί γάρ; πλὴν ὅτι παντὶ τρόπῳ, εἴτε προφάσει εἴτε ἀληθείᾳ, **Χριστὸς καταγγέλλεται**, καὶ ἐν τούτῳ χαίρω.

1:18–21 [18] . . . Ἀλλὰ καὶ χαρήσομαι, [19]οἶδα γὰρ ὅτι τοῦτό μοι ἀποβήσεται εἰς σωτηρίαν διὰ τῆς ὑμῶν δεήσεως καὶ ἐπιχορηγίας **τοῦ πνεύματος Ἰησοῦ Χριστοῦ** [20]κατὰ τὴν ἀποκαραδοκίαν καὶ ἐλπίδα μου, ὅτι ἐν οὐδενὶ αἰσχυνθήσομαι ἀλλ' ἐν πάσῃ παρρησίᾳ ὡς πάντοτε καὶ νῦν **μεγαλυνθήσεται Χριστὸς** ἐν τῷ σώματί μου, εἴτε διὰ ζωῆς εἴτε διὰ θανάτου. [21]Ἐμοὶ γὰρ **τὸ ζῆν Χριστὸς** καὶ τὸ ἀποθανεῖν κέρδος.

1:23 συνέχομαι δὲ ἐκ τῶν δύο, τὴν ἐπιθυμίαν ἔχων εἰς τὸ ἀναλῦσαι καὶ **σὺν Χριστῷ εἶναι**, πολλῷ [γὰρ] μᾶλλον κρεῖσσον·

1:26 ἵνα τὸ καύχημα ὑμῶν περισσεύῃ **ἐν Χριστῷ Ἰησοῦ** ἐν ἐμοὶ διὰ τῆς ἐμῆς παρουσίας πάλιν πρὸς ὑμᾶς.

1:27 Μόνον ἀξίως **τοῦ εὐαγγελίου τοῦ Χριστοῦ** πολιτεύεσθε,

[[1:28 καὶ μὴ πτυρόμενοι ἐν μηδενὶ ὑπὸ τῶν ἀντικειμένων, ἥτις ἐστὶν αὐτοῖς ἔνδειξις ἀπωλείας, ὑμῶν δὲ σωτηρίας, καὶ <u>τοῦτο ἀπὸ θεοῦ·</u>]]

1:29 ὅτι ὑμῖν ἐχαρίσθη **τὸ ὑπὲρ Χριστοῦ**, οὐ μόνον τὸ **εἰς αὐτὸν** πιστεύειν ἀλλὰ καὶ **τὸ ὑπὲρ αὐτοῦ πάσχειν**,

2:1 Εἴ τις οὖν παράκλησις **ἐν Χριστῷ**, εἴ τι παραμύθιον ἀγάπης, εἴ τις κοινωνία πνεύματος, εἴ τις σπλάγχνα καὶ οἰκτιρμοί,

2:5–11 ⁵Τοῦτο φρονεῖτε ἐν ὑμῖν ὃ καὶ **ἐν Χριστῷ Ἰησοῦ**, ⁶<u>ὃς ἐν μορφῇ θεοῦ</u> **ὑπάρχων** οὐχ ἁρπαγμὸν **ἡγήσατο** τὸ εἶναι <u>ἴσα θεῷ</u>, ⁷ἀλλὰ **ἑαυτὸν ἐκένωσεν** μορφὴν δούλου **λαβών**, ἐν ὁμοιώματι ἀνθρώπων **γενόμενος·** καὶ σχήματι **εὑρεθεὶς** ὡς ἄνθρωπος ⁸**ἐταπείνωσεν ἑαυτὸν** γενόμενος ὑπήκοος μέχρι θανάτου, θανάτου δὲ σταυροῦ. ⁹διὸ καὶ <u>ὁ θεὸς</u> **αὐτὸν** <u>ὑπερύψωσεν</u> <u>καὶ ἐχαρίσατο</u> **αὐτῷ** τὸ ὄνομα τὸ ὑπὲρ πᾶν ὄνομα, ¹⁰ἵνα **ἐν τῷ ὀνόματι Ἰησοῦ** πᾶν γόνυ κάμψῃ ἐπουρανίων καὶ ἐπιγείων καὶ καταχθονίων ¹¹καὶ πᾶσα γλῶσσα ἐξομολογήσηται **ὅτι κύριος Ἰησοῦς Χριστὸς** <u>εἰς δόξαν θεοῦ</u> <u>πατρός</u>.

[[2:13 <u>θεὸς γάρ ἐστιν ὁ ἐνεργῶν</u> ἐν ὑμῖν καὶ τὸ θέλειν καὶ τὸ ἐνεργεῖν ὑπὲρ τῆς εὐδοκίας.]]

[[2:15 ἵνα γένησθε ἄμεμπτοι καὶ ἀκέραιοι, <u>τέκνα θεοῦ ἄμωμα</u> μέσον γενεᾶς σκολιᾶς καὶ διεστραμμένης, ἐν οἷς φαίνεσθε ὡς φωστῆρες ἐν κόσμῳ,]]

2:16 λόγον ζωῆς ἐπέχοντες, εἰς καύχημα ἐμοὶ **εἰς ἡμέραν Χριστοῦ**, ὅτι οὐκ εἰς κενὸν ἔδραμον οὐδὲ εἰς κενὸν ἐκοπίασα.

2:19 Ἐλπίζω δὲ **ἐν κυρίῳ** Ἰησοῦ Τιμόθεον ταχέως πέμψαι ὑμῖν, ἵνα κἀγὼ εὐψυχῶ γνοὺς τὰ περὶ ὑμῶν.

2:21 οἱ πάντες γὰρ τὰ ἑαυτῶν ζητοῦσιν, οὐ **τὰ Ἰησοῦ Χριστοῦ**.

2:24 πέποιθα δὲ **ἐν κυρίῳ** ὅτι καὶ αὐτὸς ταχέως ἐλεύσομαι.

[[2:27 καὶ γὰρ ἠσθένησεν παραπλήσιον θανάτῳ· ἀλλὰ <u>ὁ θεὸς ἠλέησεν</u> αὐτόν, οὐκ αὐτὸν δὲ μόνον ἀλλὰ καὶ ἐμέ,]]

2:29–30 ²⁹προσδέχεσθε οὖν αὐτὸν **ἐν κυρίῳ** μετὰ πάσης χαρᾶς καὶ τοὺς τοιούτους ἐντίμους ἔχετε, ³⁰ὅτι **διὰ τὸ ἔργον Χριστοῦ** μέχρι θανάτου ἤγγισεν παραβολευσάμενος τῇ ψυχῇ,

3:1 Τὸ λοιπόν, ἀδελφοί μου, χαίρετε **ἐν κυρίῳ**.

3:3 ἡμεῖς γὰρ ἐσμεν ἡ περιτομή, οἱ <u>πνεύματι θεοῦ</u> λατρεύοντες καὶ καυχώμενοι **ἐν Χριστῷ Ἰησοῦ** καὶ οὐκ ἐν σαρκὶ πεποιθότες,

3:7–14 [7]Ἀλλὰ ἅτινα ἦν μοι κέρδη, ταῦτα ἥγημαι **διὰ τὸν Χριστὸν** ζημίαν. [8]ἀλλὰ μενοῦνγε καὶ ἡγοῦμαι πάντα ζημίαν εἶναι διὰ τὸ ὑπερέχον **τῆς γνώσεως Χριστοῦ Ἰησοῦ τοῦ κυρίου μου**, δι᾽ ὃν τὰ πάντα ἐζημιώθην, καὶ ἡγοῦμαι σκύβαλα, ἵνα **Χριστὸν κερδήσω** [9]καὶ εὑρεθῶ **ἐν αὐτῷ**, μὴ ἔχων ἐμὴν δικαιοσύνην τὴν ἐκ νόμου ἀλλὰ τὴν **διὰ πίστεως Χριστοῦ**, τὴν <u>ἐκ θεοῦ δικαιοσύνην</u> ἐπὶ τῇ πίστει, [10]τοῦ **γνῶναι αὐτὸν** καὶ τὴν δύναμιν **τῆς ἀναστάσεως αὐτοῦ** καὶ τὴν κοινωνίαν τῶν **παθημάτων αὐτοῦ**, συμμορφιζόμενος **τῷ θανάτῳ αὐτοῦ**, [11]εἴ πως καταντήσω εἰς τὴν ἐξανάστασιν τὴν ἐκ νεκρῶν. [12]Οὐχ ὅτι ἤδη ἔλαβον ἢ ἤδη τετελείωμαι, διώκω δὲ εἰ καὶ καταλάβω, ἐφ᾽ ᾧ καὶ κατελήμφθην **ὑπὸ Χριστοῦ Ἰησοῦ**. [v.l.-Ἰησοῦ] [13]ἀδελφοί, ἐγὼ ἐμαυτὸν οὐ λογίζομαι κατειληφέναι· ἓν δέ, τὰ μὲν ὀπίσω ἐπιλανθανόμενος τοῖς δὲ ἔμπροσθεν ἐπεκτεινόμενος, [14]κατὰ σκοπὸν διώκω εἰς τὸ βραβεῖον τῆς ἄνω <u>κλήσεως τοῦ θεοῦ</u> **ἐν Χριστῷ Ἰησοῦ**.

[[3:15 Ὅσοι οὖν τέλειοι, τοῦτο φρονῶμεν· καὶ εἴ τι ἑτέρως φρονεῖτε, καὶ τοῦτο <u>ὁ θεὸς</u> ὑμῖν ἀποκαλύψει·]]

3:18 πολλοὶ γὰρ περιπατοῦσιν οὓς πολλάκις ἔλεγον ὑμῖν, νῦν δὲ καὶ κλαίων λέγω, τοὺς ἐχθροὺς **τοῦ σταυροῦ τοῦ Χριστοῦ**,

3:20–21 [20]ἡμῶν γὰρ τὸ πολίτευμα ἐν οὐρανοῖς ὑπάρχει, ἐξ οὗ καὶ **σωτῆρα ἀπεκδεχόμεθα κύριον Ἰησοῦν Χριστόν**, [21]**ὃς μετασχηματίσει** τὸ σῶμα τῆς ταπεινώσεως ἡμῶν σύμμορφον **τῷ σώματι τῆς δόξης αὐτοῦ** κατὰ τὴν ἐνέργειαν τοῦ δύνασθαι **αὐτὸν** καὶ **ὑποτάξαι αὐτῷ** τὰ πάντα.

4:1 Ὥστε, ἀδελφοί μου ἀγαπητοὶ καὶ ἐπιπόθητοι, χαρὰ καὶ στέφανός μου, οὕτως στήκετε **ἐν κυρίῳ**, ἀγαπητοί.

4:2 Εὐοδίαν παρακαλῶ καὶ Συντύχην παρακαλῶ τὸ αὐτὸ φρονεῖν **ἐν κυρίῳ**.

4:4–7 [4]Χαίρετε **ἐν κυρίῳ** πάντοτε· πάλιν ἐρῶ, χαίρετε. [5]τὸ ἐπιεικὲς ὑμῶν γνωσθήτω πᾶσιν ἀνθρώποις. **ὁ κύριος ἐγγύς**. [6]μηδὲν μεριμνᾶτε, ἀλλ᾽ ἐν παντὶ τῇ προσευχῇ καὶ τῇ δεήσει μετὰ εὐχαριστίας τὰ αἰτήματα ὑμῶν γνωριζέσθω <u>πρὸς τὸν θεόν</u>. [7]καὶ <u>ἡ εἰρήνη τοῦ θεοῦ</u> ἡ ὑπερέχουσα πάντα νοῦν φρουρήσει τὰς καρδίας ὑμῶν καὶ τὰ νοήματα ὑμῶν **ἐν Χριστῷ Ἰησοῦ**.

[[4:9 . . . καὶ <u>ὁ θεὸς τῆς εἰρήνης</u> ἔσται μεθ᾽ ὑμῶν.]]

4:10 Ἐχάρην δὲ **ἐν κυρίῳ** μεγάλως ὅτι ἤδη ποτὲ ἀνεθάλετε τὸ ὑπὲρ ἐμοῦ φρονεῖν, ἐφ᾽ ᾧ καὶ ἐφρονεῖτε, ἠκαιρεῖσθε δέ.

4:13 πάντα ἰσχύω ἐν **τῷ ἐνδυναμοῦντί** με.

4:18–19 [18]ἀπέχω δὲ πάντα καὶ περισσεύω· πεπλήρωμαι δεξάμενος παρὰ Ἐπαφροδίτου τὰ παρ᾽ ὑμῶν, ὀσμὴν εὐωδίας, θυσίαν δεκτήν, <u>εὐάρεστον τῷ θεῷ</u>. [19]<u>ὁ δὲ θεός μου</u> πληρώσει πᾶσαν χρείαν ὑμῶν κατὰ τὸ πλοῦτος αὐτοῦ ἐν δόξῃ **ἐν Χριστῷ Ἰησοῦ**.

[[4:20 <u>τῷ δὲ θεῷ καὶ πατρὶ ἡμῶν</u> ἡ δόξα εἰς τοὺς αἰῶνας τῶν αἰώνων, ἀμήν.]]

4:21 Ἀσπάσασθε πάντα ἅγιον **ἐν Χριστῷ Ἰησοῦ**. ἀσπάζονται ὑμᾶς οἱ σὺν ἐμοὶ ἀδελφοί.

4:23 **Ἡ χάρις τοῦ κυρίου Ἰησοῦ Χριστοῦ** μετὰ τοῦ πνεύματος ὑμῶν.

Appendix II: An Analysis of Usage

(* = anarthrous; + = with possessive pronoun)

Philippians

θεός   22
Christ   48

The Data

1. κύριος Ἰησοῦς Χριστός (4 + 1 = 5)
   1:2   G*
   2:11   N*
   3:20   A* (w/ σωτήρ)
   4:23   G

1a. Χριστὸς Ἰησοῦς κύριος (1)
   3:8   G+ (w/ μου)

2. κύριος Ἰησοῦς (1)
   2:19   D* (ἐν)

3. Χριστὸς Ἰησοῦς (12 + 3 = 15)
   1:1   G*
   1:1   D* (ἐν)
   1:6   G*
   1:8   G*
   1:26   D* (ἐν)
   2:5   D* (ἐν)
   3:3   D* (ἐν)
   3:12   G* [v.l.-Ἰησοῦ] (ὑπό)
   3:14   D* (ἐν)
   4:7   D* (ἐν)
   4:19   D* (ἐν)
   4:21   D* (ἐν)

3a. Ἰησοῦς Χριστός (3)
   1:11   G* (διά)
   1:19   G*
   2:21   G*

4. κύριος (9 + 6 = 15)
   1:14   D* (ἐν)
   2:24   D* (ἐν)
   2:28   D* (ἐν)
   3:1   D* (ἐν)
   4:1   D* (ἐν)
   4:2   D* (ἐν)
   4:4   D* (ἐν)
   4:5   N
   4:10   D* (ἐν)

5. Ἰησοῦς (1 + 21 = 22)
   2:10   G*

6. Χριστός (17 + 20 = 37)
   1:10   G*
   1:13   D* (ἐν)
   1:15   A
   1:17   A
   1:18   N*
   1:20   N*
   1:21   N*
   1:23   D* (σύν)
   1:27   G
   1:29   G* (ὑπέρ)
   2:1   D* (ἐν)
   2:16   G*
   2:30   G*
   3:7   A (διά)
   3:8   A*
   3:9   G*
   3:18   G

10

Christology in the Pastoral Epistles

WHEN ONE TURNS TO THE three letters addressed to Timothy and Titus, several differences emerge between them and the preceding corpus.[1] The first, and most obvious, is that the earlier ten are primarily church documents—addressed to churches and intended to be read aloud[2] as a Spirit-inspired prophetic word to the community.[3] These three letters, on the other hand, are addressed to two of Paul's younger colleagues, who are to assume primary responsibility for carrying out the church correctives that they contain. The second set of differences has to do with language and style, plus what many perceive as an advanced concern for regulating church order.[4]

---

[1] Commentaries on these letters are listed in the bibliography (pp. 646–47); they are cited in this chapter by author's surname only. Because NT scholarship by and large has rejected these letters as being from Paul, their Christology (always grouped together) has received several specialized studies. They are listed here in chronological order: A. Klöpper, "Zur Christologie der Pastoralbriefe," ZWT 45 (1902): 339–61; H. Windisch, "Zur Christologie der Pastoralbriefe," ZNW 34 (1935): 213–38; V. Hasler, "Epiphanie und Christologie in den Pastoralbriefe," TZ 33 (1977): 193–209; H. Simonsen, "Christologische Traditionselemente in den Pastoralbriefen," in *Die paulinische Literatur und Theologie—skandinavische Beiträge: Anlässlich der 50. jährigen Gründungs-Feier der Universität von Aarhus* (ed. S. Pedersen; Teologiske studier 7; Århus: Forlaget Aros, 1980), 51–62; I. H. Marshall, "The Christology of the Pastoral Epistles," SNTSU 13 (1988): 157–77; K. Läger, *Die Christologie der Pastoralbriefe* (Hamburger theologische Studien 12; Münster: LIT, 1996); A. Y. Lau, *Manifest in the Flesh: The Epiphany Christology of the Pastoral Epistles* (WUNT 2/86; Tübingen: Mohr Siebeck, 1996); J. M. Bassler, "A Plethora of Epiphanies: Christology in the Pastoral Letters," PSB 17 (1996): 310–25; H. Stettler, *Die Christologie der Pastoralbriefe* (WUNT 2/105; Tübingen: Mohr Siebeck, 1998). There are also brief sections in various NT Christologies: most recently F. Young, *The Theology of the Pastoral Letters* (NTT; Cambridge: Cambridge University Press, 1994), 59–68; Matera, *New Testament Christology*, 158–72; Tuckett, *Christology*, 84–88; Towner, "Christology," 219–44.

[2] This is true even of Philemon, which, though intended specifically for Philemon, was also addressed to the church in Colossae and intended to be read aloud, along with Colossians, with both Philemon and Onesimus assumed to be present.

[3] For this view of Paul's letters, see the discussion of 1 Cor 5:3–5 and 14:36–38 in Fee, *God's Empowering Presence.*

[4] Full discussions of these matters will not detain us here; they can be found in the commentaries and NT introductions. The tensions between the first and second

Although the majority of NT scholars assume that Paul did not write these letters, the nature of this book requires that the present chapter be included. For at issue is whether the Christology of these letters varies significantly from what emerges in the acknowledged letters. In fact, one of their more striking features is what some see as a lessened christological emphasis in the very letters where one might expect the opposite.[5] Our first concern in this chapter, however, is not comparison but analysis.[6]

Many years ago I argued that lumping the three letters together as one entity is prejudicial at the outset[7] and simply misses far too much of their individual differences. This includes the striking and significant differences in *Sitze im Leben* as they emerge in the letters, where 1 Timothy and Titus assume Paul to be still in itinerant ministry while 2 Timothy assumes him to be in prison in Rome. These differences in turn affect the christological emphases in each letter. Indeed, so much is this so that these differences could serve as an argument against the same author having written all three letters.

What the three letters have in common is that each is addressed to a younger co-worker who had a long history with the apostle. In each case they have been left in (or sent to) Ephesus (Timothy) and Crete (Titus) to deal with the related matters of leadership and opposition to Paul's gospel. This means that 1 and 2 Timothy share much in common. Their primary differences are related to Paul's own circumstances:[8] an itinerant missioner in one and an imperial prisoner in the other. Thus, 1 Timothy was written primarily to authenticate and guide Timothy in a situation where some of

---

set of differences is what has caused a division of the house in NT scholarship over authorship. How one comes down on the question of authorship is ultimately a matter of whether one stresses their considerable Pauline character despite the acknowledged differences, or whether their Pauline chararcter is pushed aside in favor of the differences.

[5] See esp. the recounting of this history in Lau, *Manifest in the Flesh*, 1–17; for a brief but helpful overview, see Towner, "Christology," 219–21. Matera's survey also makes this very point: "His Christology may not rival that of the great apostle in whose name he writes, but it does represent an important contribution that is indebted to the Pauline tradition" (*New Testament Christology*, 158).

[6] But even "analysis" can hardly claim objectivity. All Christologies of the Pastoral Epistles tend to be determined by one's view of authorship. If one takes the letters at face value (as from Paul in some way), then one tends to read them in light of what has preceded; authors who think of them as pseudepigraphic invariably read them in contrast to Paul—even though the presupposition of pseudonymity in this case should begin with the similarities, since that is what the alleged "author" has set out to do.

[7] See Fee, 5–14. Indeed, the most troublesome datum for the theory of pseudepigraphy is the issue of "why three letters" and with such different *Sitze im Leben.* See now esp. Towner, 27–36.

[8] In 1 Timothy he has left/sent Timothy to curtail inroads of some serious deviations from the gospel that apparently are being promoted by some local elders; and Paul himself hopes to return at some point (3:14). In 2 Timothy the instructions are given in light of his pulling Timothy out of Ephesus to join him in Rome.

the leadership itself seems to have gone astray after false teaching. Second Timothy was written at a later time, when, even though the "heresy" was still very much alive in Ephesus, Paul was nonetheless turning that ministry over to Tychicus and calling Timothy to his side in Rome (2 Tim 4:9–13), since Paul does not expect a favorable outcome to his present imprisonment.[9]

The christological differences between these two letters lie with these two very different historical circumstances. The emphasis in 1 Timothy on Christ's humanity is almost certainly in response to the false teaching itself, while the emphasis in 2 Timothy on Christ as κύριος (Lord) is related to Paul's own circumstances of being on trial before Nero, the currently reigning Roman "lord and savior."

The most striking feature of the letter to Titus, on the other hand, is the relatively sparse amount of christological data—only four references to Christ in all. Here the primary concern is behavioral and soteriological, the latter intended to correct aberrations that have emerged within the churches of Crete. Thus Christ is mentioned in the body of the letter only in its two major soteriological summaries (2:11–14; 3:4–7). Nonetheless, these two passages offer significant christological data of a kind that requires considerable investigation.

These clear differences in emphases among the three letters, therefore, demand that the Christology of each letter be examined separately, while one is nonetheless also constantly alert to some obviously Pauline assumptions that each letter shares with the other two. At the same time, a constant eye will be cast backward on the Christology found in the earlier letters as well.[10] The analysis itself will proceed letter by letter in their assumed chronological order: 1 Timothy, Titus, 2 Timothy.

I. Christology in 1 Timothy

As in the preceding corpus, the Christology of 1 Timothy emerges not so much as an issue on its own but in service to the larger soteriological issues that are constantly present for Paul. In this letter these issues are very closely tied to a concern over the false teaching that has arisen in Ephesus. For our present purposes, precision about the nature of this teaching is not required except to note that celibacy and food restrictions are explicitly men-

---

[9]This stands in some contrast to what Paul says in Philippians (see 1:25–26; 2:23–24), which is also the main reason many suggest that this is a second imprisonment.

[10]For these reasons I have chosen to refer to Paul as the author, knowing full well the difficulties involved. But at stake here is *not* to demonstrate that the letters are from Paul himself. In the end, referring to the author as Paul seemed a better choice than either "the author" or "Paul" (with quotation marks).

tioned in 4:3–5, thus suggesting some sort of ascetic ideal.[11] But this, Paul objects, stands over against God as Creator of everything, with the inherent implication that everything that God created is good. This denial of the goodness of creation thus appears to lie behind the major christological emphasis in the letter.

In response, Paul simultaneously works on two fronts: (1) Christ came to save sinners by offering himself as a ransom (1:15; 2:6), thus shifting the ground from ascetic requirement to gracious acceptance; (2) Christ came in a genuine incarnation, thereby himself affirming the goodness of creation. All four of the major christological moments in the letter, therefore, emphasize Christ's humanity (1:15; 2:4–6; 3:16; 6:12–13), while the first and third also reflect/emphasize the incarnation. At the same time, three of them, either directly or indirectly, have soteriological implications.[12]

Preliminary Observations about Usage

A close look at the data in appendices I and II reveals that usage in 1 Timothy has a high level of similarity to what occurs in the preceding corpus. And as with the letters to churches, where each has its own idiosyncratic moments in comparison with the others, so it is with 1 Timothy.

The full threefold appellation occurs 4 times, twice each in the order "Christ Jesus our Lord" and "our Lord, Jesus Christ." What is new is the combination "Christ Jesus our hope" in the salutation, which occurs in conjunction with the formulation "God our Savior" as the twofold source of Paul's apostleship ("in keeping with the command of God our Savior and Christ Jesus our hope").

The most common designation (10 of 16 references) is the combination "Christ Jesus," which is the only double combination in the letter and occurs consistently in this order (cf. Galatians). This order is also the most common in the preceding corpus (61x to 20x). As with Romans and 1 Thessalonians, God (θεός) is mentioned more often than Christ (22/16)—a matter that changes radically in 2 Timothy (13/27).

The most striking feature of usage in 1 Timothy is the fact that Christ is referred to by single name/title only twice, ὁ κύριος (*the Lord*) in 1:14 and ὁ Χριστός (*Christ*) in 5:11. This, too, conforms to the corpus as a whole, since the use of "the Lord" fluctuates the most widely in the corpus (only 2x in

---

[11] These in turn seem to lie behind other features in the letter—e.g., the urging of marriage in 2:15 and 5:14 and urging Timothy to drink wine in 5:23.

[12] Only the hymn in 3:16 lacks clear reference to Christ's saving work. Many would argue that it is assumed in line 2 ("he was vindicated by the Spirit"), which presupposes his death, resurrection, and exaltation, and then again in lines 4 and 5, where he is preached among, and believed in, by the Gentiles. Even so, in contrast to the other passages, this one lacks *explicit* reference.

Galatians, for example)—a fairly good indicator that when this title occurs by itself (13x in 2 Timothy!), it is very often related directly to the subject matter.[13] In any case, there is nothing with regard to usage that argues against Pauline authorship, nor is there any highlight of usage per se that would give special direction to the analysis that follows.

Christ, the Incarnate Savior

The place to begin a christological analysis of this letter is with a straightforward, but christologically focused, exegesis of the four major passages, which will be taken up in their canonical order (1:11–17; 2:4–6; 3:16; 6:13–16). What these passages have in common is a strong affirmation of Christ's humanity, while two of them (1:15; 3:16) also presuppose his preexistence and thus reflect an understanding of Christ's human life as a divine incarnation.

1 Timothy 1:11–17

At the end of a very strong opening indictment of the false teachers (vv. 3–7), Paul refers to their desire to be teachers of the law. This in turn spins off into an affirmation of the law as a good thing, although not intended for believers. Rather, its intent, it is argued, was to curb the sins of the unrighteous, whose sins are then catalogued in a way that roughly echoes the Ten Commandments (vv. 8–10a). At the end, these sins (and thus the law itself) are set in sharp contrast to the "healthy teaching" found in the gospel, described here as a manifestation "of the blessed God's glory" and entrusted to Paul (vv. 10b–11). With that, Paul bursts into an outpouring of gratitude to his Lord (v. 12), while offering himself as Exhibit A of the reality of the gospel of grace (vv. 13–16).

Typically Pauline, the thanksgiving, while a genuine outflow of gratitude, is at the same time instructional, anticipating some matters later in the letter. The emphasis is on the immensity and wideness of Christ's mercy—an emphasis necessary because of the nature of sin, which is over against Christ and therefore not curable by doing the law. The result is that the singular focus throughout this thanksgiving-turned-testimony is on Christ. Indeed, beginning with v. 11 (the conclusion to the excursus on the true reason for the law), Paul presents a series of christological affirmations that climax in vv. 15–16 and lead to a concluding benediction of praise to God. Not all of these affirmations are equally obvious; indeed, some may very well be questioned, so we will look at them sentence by sentence.

---

[13]On this whole question, see the usage in 1–2 Thessalonians as a whole, plus Rom 14; Col 3:17–4:1; 2 Tim 4.

Verse 11

. . . τῇ ὑγιαινούσῃ διδασκαλίᾳ . . . κατὰ τὸ εὐαγγέλιον τῆς δόξης <u>τοῦ</u> <u>μακαρίου θεοῦ</u>, ὃ **ἐπιστεύθην** ἐγώ

. . . *the healthy teaching . . . which accords with the gospel of <u>the blessed God's</u> glory, with which I **was entrusted***

Our interest in these concluding words to vv. 8–11 lies with two matters: (1) the gospel has to do with "the blessed God's glory," a phrase that will be partially picked up again in Titus 2:13; (2) Paul himself was entrusted with this gospel. Ordinarily, little could be made of these items; however, the present passage is not ordinary, since what immediately follows is an elaborate thanksgiving *to Christ,* who appointed Paul to his apostleship. Thus, it is arguable that Christ is already the focus of these two phrases as well.

First, it seems highly likely that Paul already had Christ in view when he speaks of the gospel as a manifestation of God's glory.[14] This probability lies with what is said about Christ in Titus 2:13.[15] The language of "glory" with reference to what has been revealed about God through Christ's incarnation and redemption first occurs in the long argument of 2 Cor 3:7–4:6. In the Titus passage the reference is to the future manifestation of God's glory at Christ's Parousia. There is good reason to believe, therefore, that rather than simply using high-sounding language about God derived from the OT, Paul is at this point deliberately anticipating the christocentric nature of the gospel in the thanksgiving that follows.

The second issue is whether the implied subject of the "divine passive"[16] ἐπιστεύθην (*I was entrusted*) is "God" or "Christ Jesus." In favor of "God" is the fact that this passive immediately follows the mention of "the blessed God." Thus the TNIV's "which he [God] entrusted to me." But there are good reasons to think otherwise, since the thanksgiving that follows is directed specifically to Christ, who in turn is the subject of the repeated passive "I was shown mercy" in vv. 13, 16. Indeed, everything in the thanksgiving that follows focuses on both Christ's initiatory and his effective role in Paul's apostleship.

Thus, although neither of these matters in v. 11 can be settled definitively, their possible christological implications are at least suggested by the more certain matters in vv. 12–16.

---

[14] Cf. Kelly, 51; Knight, 91. This was suggested as early as Fairbairn, 90–91; it was noted by Lock and Bernard as a possibility but rejected by Marshall, 383.

[15] For this understanding of Titus 2:13, see the full discussion below, pp. 442–46. This understanding of "glory" at least alleviates the problem with its appearance here noted by Johnson, 172.

[16] It is the nature of the so-called divine passive that the grammatical subject of the sentence (ἐγώ [*I*]) is in fact the conceptual object. Rendered in the active voice, the clause would read, "he entrusted me with the gospel." At issue is the antecedent of the implied "he." On the "divine passive," see Wallace, *Greek Grammar beyond the Basics,* 437–38.

Verses 12–13

¹²Χάριν ἔχω τῷ ἐνδυναμώσαντί με **Χριστῷ Ἰησοῦ τῷ κυρίῳ ἡμῶν**, ὅτι πιστόν με **ἡγήσατο θέμενος** εἰς διακονίαν ¹³τὸ πρότερον ὄντα βλάσφημον καὶ διώκτην καὶ ὑβριστήν, ἀλλὰ **ἠλεήθην**, ὅτι ἀγνοῶν ἐποίησα ἐν ἀπιστίᾳ·

¹²*I give thanks **to him who empowered** me, **Christ Jesus our Lord,** because **he considered** me trustworthy **by appointing** me to this ministry* ¹³*—who was formerly a blasphemer and persecutor and a man of violence; but I **was shown mercy,** since I acted ignorantly in unbelief.*

Three significant christological matters catch one's attention in these opening words, significant in part because, as throughout the corpus, they do not appear to be intentionally christological.

1. With the single exception of Rom 16:4,[17] thanksgiving in Paul's writings is always directed toward God, both in thanksgiving reports[18] and in exhortations to give thanks (e.g., 1 Thess 5:18). Indeed, only here in the corpus is the kind of thanksgiving that is elsewhere directed toward God (τῷ θεῷ) now offered to Christ. That it is offered to Christ is made plain by both the grammar and the context.

Such an interchange between God and Christ is typically Pauline in two ways.[19] First, Paul has done this same thing with regard to *prayer reports*. For the most part, and as one would expect of a Jewish monotheist, prayer is directed to God the Father; but in 2 Cor 12:8 Paul reports that three times he "pleaded with the Lord" (= Christ) to take away a "thorn in his flesh."[20] To which request Christ answered, "My grace is sufficient for you." So also here with regard to thanksgiving; for case-specific reasons, what is ordinarily addressed to God the Father is now offered to Christ.

Second, one is struck by the thoroughly unrehearsed way this happens in both cases. How is it, one feels led to ask, that a rigorous monotheist[21] can offer prayer both as petition and as thanksgiving to Christ as though he were God?

2. Even more significant for christological purposes is the fact that Christ is the subject of all the verbs expressing divine activity that follow, activities that ordinarily belong to the province of God. In turn, Paul affirms that (a) Christ "enabled/empowered me" (ἐνδυναμώσαντί με);[22] (b) Christ "consid-

---

[17] In this case it is an expression of thanks to Prisca and Aquila on behalf of the churches.

[18] See, e.g., 1 Thess 1:2; 2:13; 1 Cor 1:4; Col 1:3; Phil 1:3.

[19] As with so many things in these letters, this datum can be seen to cut two ways. Thus, some (e.g., Quinn and Wacker, 122–23) find this singular instance a strike against Pauline authorship; on the other hand, a pseudepigrapher should be expected to be more careful, whereas this kind of interchange is thoroughly Pauline.

[20] See the discussion in ch. 4, pp. 194–95.

[21] The affirmation of "one God" in 2:5 makes this a certainty for this author, whether Paul or otherwise.

[22] This verb is used elsewhere by Paul of Christ's empowering; see Phil 4:13; 2 Tim 4:17. It appears as an imperative in Eph 6:10; 2 Tim 2:1. The concept of God as

ered me faithful/trustworthy" (πιστόν με ἡγήσατο);[23] and (c) Christ "appointed me to this ministry" (θέμενος εἰς διακονίαν).

Thus, even though later on Paul will emphasize the soteriological aspect of Christ's mercy toward him, that is not the case in this opening note of thanksgiving. Rather, he is referring to the divine activity of the reigning Lord, since these verbs all refer to the exalted Christ's role in Paul's becoming his apostle.

3. Without breaking stride, Paul moves on to describe the kind of person Christ had chosen for this ministry: one who up to the point of his call and conversion had steadfastly stood over against Christ in every way—blasphemer,[24] persecutor, violent in his opposition. His appointment, Paul asserts, was an act of *divine* mercy ("but I was shown mercy"), where the assumed subject of the divine passive once more is Christ. To think otherwise would be to miss Paul's point—mercy was shown by the very one against whom Paul had stood in such violent opposition—and would thus disrupt the christocentric nature of the testimony.[25] As before, under ordinary circumstances one might presume God to be the assumed subject of the verb, but both here and in v. 16 all the emphasis is on what Christ has done on Paul's behalf; and as 1 Cor 7:25 makes clear, Paul is not adverse to using this verb with reference to Christ.

Again, therefore, here is a divine attribute that is quite matter-of-factly attributed to Christ, not as something Paul is setting out to demonstrate but as something that is simply a matter of course.

Verse 14

ὑπερεπλεόνασεν δὲ ἡ χάρις τοῦ κυρίου ἡμῶν μετὰ πίστεως καὶ ἀγάπης τῆς ἐν Χριστῷ Ἰησοῦ.

But **the grace of our Lord** overflowed (to me) along with **the faith and love that are in Christ Jesus.**

Having described the kind of person he had been before his encounter with Christ, Paul now expands on Christ's mercy toward him. In doing so, he offers the christological basis of his divine appointment, which he does

---

the one who empowers his people is writ large in the biblical story, although other verbs are more often used.

[23] Cf. 1 Cor 7:25, where this is also said of Christ, whose mercy has made Paul "trustworthy" to offer guidance on a matter that has not otherwise been revealed.

[24] In this context the use of this word could also be seen to have christological import, since it is used here in a way that suggests blasphemy against a deity; and the context indicates that Christ is the one whose name has been blasphemed.

[25] While the context seems to demand such a view of this "divine passive," not all commentators think so; indeed, most posit God as the assumed subject without raising the contextual question: Johnson, 179; Towner, 140; Quinn and Wacker (129) are ambivalent. It is the lack of clarity on this verb that has led some to see "the Lord" in v. 14 as also referring to God (see the next note).

with a sentence that by its very intentional christocentricity—the repetition of reference to Christ—comes off awkwardly for us. Thus some are prepared to make "our Lord" in this case refer to God.[26] But that is to "clean up" for our sakes what was not messy to the author. Everything God has done for us in salvation has been effected through Christ, both in his sacrificial death and now as the reigning Lord on high. Thus both the "grace" that overflowed to Paul and its accompanying faith and love come directly from Christ himself.

As noted in ch. 2,[27] almost all of Paul's letters conclude with a benedictory prayer of "grace" from Christ; yet there are three places in the body of his letters, including this one,[28] where he expresses *current* grace as from Christ rather than from God. The striking feature of the sentence is the addition of "faith and love" as the "attendant circumstance"[29] of Christ's grace. As always for the apostle, our faith in Christ and love for others both have their locus in Christ and are together the necessary accompanying expressions of Christ's prior grace in our behalf. What is of christological import is that these "graces" in this case are pointing not to the historical work of the cross but to Paul's experience of grace in his personal encounter with the living, reigning Christ.

Verse 15

πιστὸς ὁ λόγος καὶ πάσης ἀποδοχῆς ἄξιος, ὅτι **Χριστὸς Ἰησοῦς ἦλθεν** εἰς τὸν κόσμον ἁμαρτωλοὺς σῶσαι, ὧν πρῶτός εἰμι ἐγώ.

*Trustworthy is the saying and worthy of acceptance by all: "**Christ Jesus came** into the world to save sinners," of whom I am foremost.*

The narrative is now interrupted in order to extol the divine antidote to human sinfulness, while at the same time keeping the focus on Paul's own reception of divine mercy as the ultimate exhibit of that mercy. Thus, what began in v. 12 as an expression of sheer gratitude to Christ his Savior now climaxes with a "trustworthy saying"—the first of three in this letter[30]—that offers the divine grounds and effective means of Christ's saving activity.

---

[26] See, e.g., Kelly, 53; Lea, 74; but most recent commentators take it the way suggested here (e.g., Spicq, 1:343; Knight, 97; Quinn and Wacker, 131; Marshall, 394 n. 100 ["clearly"]). So also, but hesitantly, Young, *Theology*, 59.

[27] See pp. 52–53.

[28] The other two are 2 Cor 8:9; 12:9. Thus Quinn and Wacker (131) are quite imprecise to suggest that this usage is non-Pauline because it does not occur elsewhere; and they completely disregard the closing benedictions.

[29] For this sense of the μετά, see BDAG A 3 b.

[30] See 3:1; 4:8; cf. 2 Tim 2:8; Titus 3:4–7. In this first instance, as well as in 4:8–9, the full description appears: "and worthy of full acceptance" (= worthy of acceptance by everyone). This is probably in part related to the contrastive nature of Paul's "testimony" vis-à-vis the false teachers' attraction to the Jewish law.

Despite an occasional demurrer to the contrary,[31] everything about this sentence, not to mention the larger context of this letter (esp. 3:16), points to preexistence and incarnation as its presuppositional base.[32] It would make almost no sense at all for our author to use the language "came into the world" of one who is merely human and whose birth is simply propitious; such people do not "come *into the world*," at least not in the language and worldview of our biblical authors. At issue ultimately is the assumed common ground between the author and his reader(s). That Christ's preexistence is a central Pauline construct is made certain by texts such as 1 Cor 8:6; 10:4, 9; 2 Cor 8:9; Col 1:15–20; Phil 2:6–7. And to argue that a post-Pauline author does not assume Paul's own affirmations of Christ's preexistence seems to be self-defeating. How, one wonders, could a "Paulinist" hope to palm off these letters as being by Paul and yet miss Paul so badly at this key christological moment?

So one can be rather certain that this very abbreviated "saying," which has human salvation as its main focus, at the same time has a preexistent, incarnational perspective on Christ's "coming into the world" as its primary presuppositional base. Here is what historically set in motion Christ's saving activity on Paul's (and others') behalf; here is the beginning point of the mercy that Paul himself, as the foremost of sinners, experienced historically from the risen Christ, who then appointed him to his apostolic ministry of the gospel. And in (mild) contrast to what Paul says elsewhere of the "coming," the perspective here is not on God's *sending* his Son (Gal 4:4; Rom 8:3) but on the Son's active role in coming into the world.

The point of this recitation, it needs finally to be noted, is precisely to exalt the gospel as a display of divine mercy on sinners, vis-à-vis the false teaching that apparently stresses law-keeping and advocates an ascetical ideal. Such a view of salvation requires no mercy at all; and Paul, who was overtaken by God's mercy in Christ, will have none of it. So the emphasis throughout continues to be on Christ as the active agent in all of God's saving activity.

Verse 16

ἀλλὰ διὰ τοῦτο **ἠλεήθην**, ἵνα ἐν ἐμοὶ πρώτῳ **ἐνδείξηται Χριστὸς Ἰησοῦς τὴν ἅπασαν μακροθυμίαν** πρὸς ὑποτύπωσιν τῶν μελλόντων πιστεύειν ἐπ' αὐτῷ εἰς ζωὴν αἰώνιον.

*But for this very reason I **was shown mercy,** so that in me, the foremost [of sinners], **Christ Jesus might display his immense forbearance** as an example for those who were going to believe **in him** unto eternal life.*

---

[31] See, e.g., Windisch, 222; Dibelius and Conzelmann, 29; Collins, 39; Dunn, *Christology in the Making,* 239, 345.

[32] Cf. Marshall, 398: "the context is the author's epiphany Christology," which, he adds, thus makes "preexistence . . . a likely implication." So also Fairbairn, 96; Bernard, 32; Spicq, 1:344; Hanson, 61.

In this final sentence of the thanksgiving Paul repeats from v. 14 the fact that Christ showed him mercy, but Paul does so now to emphasize the exemplary nature of his conversion. His point is that if Christ can so embrace his most brazen enemy, then there is abundant hope for all others as well. Here is the passage that makes certain that Christ is the implied subject of the divine passive "I was shown mercy," since his saving Paul was the ultimate display of Christ's own immense long-suffering. And this in turn is another significant christological moment, since the word μακροθυμία is for Paul an expression of God's character. This is explicitly stated in Rom 2:4 and 9:22 and is implied in texts such as 1 Cor 13:4 and Gal 5:22. Moreover, the verb ἐνδείκνυμι is an especially Pauline word in the NT, used often as a powerful demonstration of divine character.[33]

This incredibly profound divine attribute, which by the Spirit is to characterize believers' love for others, has been put on full display in Christ's coming into the world to save sinners—saving work that will be elaborated in the next christological passage (2:4–6). But before that, something must be said about the doxology with which it all concludes.

Verse 17

τῷ δὲ βασιλεῖ τῶν αἰώνων, ἀφθάρτῳ ἀοράτῳ μόνῳ θεῷ, τιμὴ καὶ δόξα εἰς τοὺς αἰῶνας τῶν αἰώνων, ἀμήν.

Now to the King of the ages, the immortal, invisible, only God, be honor and glory unto all possible ages, Amen.

Given the heavily christocentric nature of the preceding thanksgiving, one is not quite prepared for this equally startling theocentric doxology at the end.[34] With language that emphasizes the exclusively monotheistic nature of Paul's Jewish heritage, he offers praise to the one God, thereby reflecting the Shema of Deut 6:4 (cf. 1 Cor 8:4, 6), the absolute cornerstone of Jewish religion. Thus, in ways that reflect the bold Christian restatement of the Shema in 1 Cor 8:6, Paul once again embraces the divine work of Christ within his basic, absolute monotheism.

Although it might be argued that Paul is here trying to offer a "corrective" to the christocentricity of the preceding thanksgiving, there is good reason to think otherwise. Whatever else is true for Paul, and however we are finally to understand the ontological nature of Christ's divinity, he always views salvation as originating in God the Father's love and made available to all through the work of Christ and the Spirit. Hence, it is the very

---

[33] See Marshall, 260.

[34] Because of the christocentricity of the preceding paragraph, Mounce (60) suggests that this doxology is most likely addressed to Christ. But that is as unlikely a use of μόνος θεός in a Pauline letter (even if pseudepigraphic [see esp. 1 Cor 8:6]) as the suggestion by the majority that the substitution of κύριος for θεός in 2 Tim 2:19 refers to God the Father (see discussion on 2 Tim 2:19 below, pp. 455–58).

christocentricity that calls for such an exclamatory word at the end. On the one hand, the doxology emphasizes that Christ does not act independently of the Father; on the other hand, it serves as the divine punctuation of the christological centrality of all that has preceded. Christ did/does not work independently from the Father, nor is his work to be seen in isolation from what God is doing in the world.

1 Timothy 2:3–6

³. . . τοῦ σωτῆρος ἡμῶν θεοῦ, ⁴ὃς πάντας ἀνθρώπους θέλει σωθῆναι καὶ εἰς ἐπίγνωσιν ἀληθείας ἐλθεῖν. ⁵Εἷς γὰρ θεός, εἷς καὶ μεσίτης θεοῦ καὶ ἀνθρώπων, ἄνθρωπος Χριστὸς Ἰησοῦς, ⁶ὁ δοὺς ἑαυτὸν ἀντίλυτρον ὑπὲρ πάντων,

³. . . _God our Savior,_ ⁴_who wants all people to be saved_ and to come into a knowledge of the truth. ⁵For _there is one God_ and **one mediator** between _God_ and human beings, **Christ Jesus, himself human,** ⁶**who gave himself** a ransom for all people. (TNIV)[35]

This second christological passage in 1 Timothy is intended to offer theological support for the recurring emphasis on πάντας ἀνθρώπους (_all people_),[36] in a passage that encourages prayers of all kinds be made for all people. The theological basis for this appeal is that "God our Savior wants all people to be saved." God's efficacious way of being our Savior was to make his salvation available to all "men" through a "man," Christ Jesus, the emphasis being not on Christ's maleness but on his genuine humanity[37] and thus on the reality of his incarnation. The divine mediator was neither an angelic being of some kind nor a divine visitation who merely "appeared" to be human; rather, Paul's point is that Christ's ransom, though himself divine, was effected as a truly human being.

The result is a twofold christological emphasis: first, in his humanity Christ served the divine purposes of being a _truly human_ mediator between

---

[35] One faces a translational quandary in this passage as to how to render πάντας ἀνθρώπους, since the word "men/man" in current English tends to be limited to an adult male human being. In Greek, as in the English of an earlier day, the word ἄνθρωπος (_man_) could serve double duty, referring to an adult male as well as to humankind in general, which causes Paul's Greek to make perfectly good sense as a minor play on this word. That is, prayer is to be made for "all men = all humankind" because there is one mediator between God and "man = humankind," namely, the truly representative Man (= human person), Christ Jesus. The TNIV has nicely captured this sense of Paul's Greek, since there in no emphasis on Christ's maleness at this point.

[36] See vv. 1, 3, 6. It is difficult to escape the conclusion that this emphasis stands in direct opposition to the exclusivism of the false teaching that is circulating in Ephesus (see Fee, 6–10, 61–62).

[37] E.g., Fairbairn, 116–17; Marshall, 430; Mounce, 87; Johnson, 192; cf. P. Towner, _The Goal of Our Instruction: The Structure of Theology and Ethics in the Pastoral Epistles_ (JSNTSup 34; Sheffield: Sheffield Academic Press, 1989), 54–55.

God and humankind;[38] second, at the same time he came as a *divinely incarnate* mediator, who in his incarnation,[39] by "giving himself," thus offered a truly effective ransom[40] for human sinfulness.

In isolation this might be perceived as reading something into the text; but here is a clear case where one needs to keep the whole epistle in view when examining any of its parts.[41] Here indeed is the significance both of the first "saying," that "Jesus Christ *came into the world* to save sinners" (1:15), and of the first line of the hymn in 3:16, that "he appeared in the flesh." Thus the emphatic "*one* God" and "*one* mediator, the ἄνθρωπος Christ Jesus" seem intended to preserve, on the one hand, the inviolability of the author's monotheism and to press the issue, on the other hand, that the one mediator, though preexistent and thus divine, was nonetheless truly human.[42] Thus the divine nature of Christ implied in his incarnation does not negate the basic affirmation of the unity of God. What it does do, as Richard Bauckham has urged,[43] is to enlarge the boundaries of God's *identity* as the one God.

Thus what we have in this instance, where Christ's divinity is presupposed, is a twofold emphasis. First, Paul stresses the genuineness of Christ's humanity, an emphasis that makes most sense if that is somehow being downplayed by the ascetic worldview of the false teaching.[44] Second, even though the ultimate concern is soteriological, as is most often the case for Paul, he nonetheless is equally concerned to affirm that the human Savior is himself divine.

---

[38] Cf. Knight, who anticipated the rendering of the TNIV in his commentary: "The one God has provided one mediator between himself . . . and humans . . . , [Christ Jesus] who is himself human" (121).

[39] If this is not said directly, it is hard otherwise to discover a reason for the emphasis on Christ's humanness. Why the point of Christ's being "human," one wonders, if there is not here a presupposition about his first of all being divine? Cf. Fairbairn, 117; Bernard, 41; Lock, 28; Scott, 21–22; Spicq, 1:366; Mounce, 88.

[40] Given that the concern here is primarily soteriological, we should note in passing that the imagery of "ransom for all" echoes Mark 10:45 and thus points ultimately to the Suffering Servant of Isa 53:12 and through him back to God's redeeming his people from Egyptian bondage. The metaphor appears in its first instance in Paul's writings in 1 Cor 1:30 and is picked up again in 6:11 and Rom 3:24. In these letters it appears again in Titus 2:14, where it will carry additional christological import.

[41] One of the problems with commentaries is the tendency to discuss texts in isolation from others. Thus this emphasis on Christ's humanness vis-à-vis the false teachers is seldom noted in the literature; or even worse, when it is noted, the problem is seen to be some form of Gnosticism.

[42] See Marshall, "Christology," 173. Cf. Phil 2:7–8; it is therefore of some interest that emphasis on Jesus' humanity occurs in Pauline texts where Jesus' deity is also presupposed or expressed; cf. Knight, 121.

[43] See Bauckham, *God Crucified*, 25–42.

[44] On this matter, see especially the vigorous rebuttal of their position in 4:3–5, in which Paul emphasizes the essential goodness of the whole creation. It is surely arguable that this emphasis on Christ's true humanity fits squarely within this larger concern.

1 Timothy 3:16

ὃς[45] ἐφανερώθη ἐν σαρκι, ἐδικαιώθη ἐν πνεύματι, ὤφθη ἀγγέλοις,
ἐκηρύχθη ἐν ἔθνεσιν, ἐπιστεύθη ἐν κόσμῳ, ἀνελήμφθη ἐν δόξῃ.

He who appeared in the flesh, **was vindicated** *in the Spirit,* **appeared** *to angels,*
was preached *among the nations,* **was believed** *on in the world,* **was taken up**
in glory.

Until recent years, this passage had more ink spilled over it than any
other in this letter[46]—for good reason. Even when the text is put forward in
prose form, as above, one can scarcely miss the poetic nature of the whole.
And poetry has its own set of difficulties, in this case related (1) to the versification itself,[47] (2) to the meaning of some of the lines,[48] which is related in
part to the first issue, and especially (3) to its role in the immediate context.

For our present purposes, not all of these need to be resolved, especially
the issue of versification, since our christological interest lies primarily with
the first two lines and all are agreed that these stand in poetic parallel with
one another. Moreover, all are basically agreed that the parallelism in this

---

[45] That this ὃς (א* A* C* G 33 365 442 2127 sy co arm goth eth Or Epiph Jerome)
is the original text and not the corruption ὃ of D (thus making it agree with the preceding τὸ μυστήριον) or the θεός of the later majority of witnesses is made certain by
three facts: (1) it is the universal reading in all of the early witnesses, including the
Greek texts lying behind all the early versions; (2) it is easily the "more difficult reading" and therefore the one least likely to have arisen from the others; (3) it is hard to
imagine the circumstances under which "God" would, early and often, have been
changed to the ungrammatical "who." Thus later scribes are bold to say what Paul at
this earlier time was consistently not ready to do: use the word θεός (which he used
exclusively to refer to God the Father) when referring to Christ (see discussion of
1 Cor 8:6 in ch. 3, pp. 89–94; cf. the discussion of Titus 2:13 below, pp. 442–46, and of
Rom 9:5 in ch. 6, pp. 272–77).

[46] It has now been overtaken by the barrage of articles and books dealing with
1 Tim 2:11–15, brought on by the rift among evangelical Christians over the issue of
God's gifting women for ministry.

[47] As to whether it follows an AB, AB, AB or AB/C AB/C pattern; thus either:

Who appeared in flesh,	Who appeared in flesh,
was vindicated in the Spirit,	was vindicated in the Spirit,
Appeared to angels.	appeared to angels.
was preached among the nations,	Was preached among the nations,
Was believed on in the world,	was believed on in the world,
was taken up in glory.	was taken up in glory.

Several other schemes are also suggested, but getting this right lies beyond the concerns of this study.

[48] This is especially true of line 2, but it is also true of line 6, which seems to
offer a second reference to Christ's exaltation. For these reasons, I have argued that
one best understands the poem as having two stanzas, the first dealing with Christ's
earthly life, the second (lines 4–6) dealing with the spread of the gospel after his ascension (line 3), which concludes with a repetition of the ascension motif (line 6).
See Fee, *God's Empowering Presence,* 761–68.

case is a form of synonymy, not antithesis. But after that, a good deal of difference of opinion is to be found.

Since the issue of context is seldom addressed adequately,[49] that will be our starting point here. The clues lie in three areas. First, v. 14 is best understood not as a conclusion to chs. 2–3 but as the beginning of the instructions as to "how people ought to conduct themselves in God's household" (TNIV), and thus it anticipates the larger concerns that follow regarding truly Christian conduct.[50] Second, the δέ (*but*) in 4:1, often either left untranslated or rendered with a "now," is best understood as a true adversative to v. 16.[51] Thus after spelling out the content of the divine "mystery" found in the gospel, by citing from an (apparently) early Christian hymn, Paul next spells out by way of contrast the reason for reminding Timothy and the church in Ephesus of the basic elements of the story of Christ. Third, what holds the entire passage together is the word εὐσέβεια (*godliness*), which appears first at the beginning of v. 16 and then reappears as the controlling word in the application to Timothy in 4:7–10.

All of this suggests, therefore, that the content of the hymn exists precisely to prepare the way for the indictment of the false teachers in 4:1–5. The emphasis in the hymn is on Christ's true humanity (line 1), which received divine vindication both by the Spirit and angels (lines 2–3) and by the subsequent proclamation in the early church (lines 4–5), to which is appended the final vindication by Christ's thus being "taken up in glory." All of this stands squarely over against the hypocritical liars (about the truth of God) who are denying the goodness of creation by their insistence on certain forms of abstinence (4:3–5).

This emphasis also explains why in this case there is no mention of Christ's saving work as such—although it is obviously presupposed in lines 4 and 5. What is being preached and believed among the nations/Gentiles is that which has been expressly stated in the two earlier passages: "Christ Jesus came into the world to save sinners" (1:15), and he "gave himself a ransom for all people" (2:6). Such is always presupposed by Paul; it is not said here because in context the issue is not Christ's redemptive work as such, but rather the meaning of God and creation; and the incarnation of Christ, followed by his divine vindication by the Spirit, sets the stage at the outset for the vigorous denunciation of the ascetics that follows.

---

[49] Most often it is seen as bringing theological conclusion to chs. 2–3, but with very little hint as to *how* it does so (e.g., Knight, 186; Marshall, 522; Johnson, 236–37). See the fuller discussion in Fee, *God's Empowering Presence*, 762–63, with full documentation (up to 1992). The studies by Fowl (*Story*) and Towner (*Goal of Our Instruction*) were then, and still tend to be, the notable exceptions; but some recent commentaries have begun to pick up this point; see, e.g., Mounce, 218; Towner, 284–85.

[50] Thus the TNIV has rightly offered a new text heading at v. 14 that carries all the way through to 5:1, and thus with no major break at 4:1.

[51] But see now the NASU.

This larger contextual reading of the whole passage tends also to determine the meaning of its various parts. Line 1 is an emphatic declaration of the incarnation, since the language "Christ was ἐφανερώθη[52] ἐν σαρκί" allows for no other adequate understanding.[53] Despite the views of some scholars to the contrary,[54] this would seem like a strange thing to say of one whose origins were merely human. And the whole phrase puts special emphasis on both that Christ was "a divine manifestation" and the fact that this manifestation took place in the flesh of his genuine humanity.[55] Thus this line, because of the nature of the heresy being combated, emphatically eliminates the possibility of a docetic understanding of Christ's humanity.

It is also this use of ἐν σαρκί that calls for the corresponding ἐν πνεύματι in the second line. But to treat this as having to do with Christ's own spirit, as in some English translations,[56] seems to trivialize the first line. That is, Christ's vindication for having appeared in the flesh did not take place within his internal psyche; rather, through resurrection and exaltation he has now entered the realm of our final eschatological existence, the realm of the Spirit.[57] And the rest of the hymn simply emphasizes the further vindication of his "appearing in the flesh." His exaltation and the subsequent proclamation of the gospel, which has Christ as its absolute centerpiece, further emphasize the validity of his incarnation.

---

[52] This is the first appearance of this word group and its companions, ἐπιφαίνω/ ἐπιφάνεια (appear/appearance), in these letters; their very close relationship can be seen in 2 Tim 1:10, where they appear together as verb and noun (φανερόω/ ἐπιφάνεια) in close proximity, with their slightly differing nuances: "revealed through the appearing" (TNIV, NRSV), "manifested through the appearing" (ESV), where both words are used with reference to the incarnation. This passage in particular makes a nonpreexistence interpretation of this verb an especially difficult enterprise. In the two instances where it is used of Christ, it refers to his "first (earthly) appearing"; but the fact that the second word is used of both Christ's incarnation (2 Tim 1:10) and his Parousia (1 Tim 6:13; Titus 2:13; 2 Tim 4:1, 8) strongly suggests that both words in these letters imply a heavenly descent of the Redeemer.

[53] On this question, see esp. Lau, Manifest in the Flesh; cf. Bassler, "Plethora of Epiphanies."

[54] See, e.g., Dunn (Christology in the Making, 237), who tries to make this very case. But he does so by assertion, not by exegetical argumentation. This is a strange locution indeed—both verb and prepositional phrase—if the author were trying merely to contrast Jesus' pre-Easter earthly existence with his Easter exaltation to heaven. Why would someone merely human "appear in the flesh"? Or one might put the question the other way about. What other language might the author have used in a terse line of poetry to describe a "coming" that included preexistence and incarnation? Whereas he could easily have spoken quite differently if he were intending us not to think "incarnation."

[55] Thus, the emphasis is not on his "body" per se (as the NIV), but on his being "in flesh," thus sharing fully in our common humanity.

[56] See, e.g., the NRSV: "was vindicated in spirit."

[57] For the full explication of this understanding, see Fee, God's Empowering Presence, 765–67; cf. Knight, 184–85; Marshall, 525–26.

Thus the hymn makes explicit—as explicit as poetry allows—that Christ's beginnings are divine; and if the early scribes, taking their clue from John's Gospel, made that a bit too explicit by saying that "*God* was manifest in the flesh," they nonetheless understood correctly that such is the only real possibility for the first line, since that alone gives an adequate explanation for the citation of the entire hymn in this context.

1 Timothy 6:13–16

¹³παραγγέλω ἐνώπιον τοῦ θεοῦ ζῳογονοῦντος τὰ πάντα καὶ **Χριστοῦ Ἰησοῦ τοῦ μαρτυρήσαντος** ἐπὶ Ποντίου Πιλάτου τὴν καλὴν ὁμολογίαν, ¹⁴τηρῆσαί σε τὴν ἐντολὴν ἄσπιλον ἀνεπίλημπτον μέχρι **τῆς ἐπιφανείας τοῦ κυρίου ἡμῶν Ἰησοῦ Χριστοῦ,** ¹⁵ἣν καιροῖς ἰδίοις δείξει ὁ μακάριος καὶ μόνος δυνάστης, ὁ βαλιλεὺς τῶν βασιλευόντων καὶ κύριος τῶν κυριευόντων, ¹⁶ὁ μόνος ἔχων ἀθανασίαν, φῶς οἰκῶν ἀπρόσιτον, ὃν εἶδεν οὐδεὶς ἀνθρώπων οὐδὲ ἰδεῖν δύναται· ᾧ τιμὴ καὶ κράτος αἰώνιον, ἀμήν.

¹³*I charge you* before God who gives life to all things *and* **Christ Jesus who bore witness** *before Pontius Pilate to the good confession,* ¹⁴*that you keep this command without spot or blame until* **the manifestation of our Lord Jesus Christ,** ¹⁵*which (God) will reveal at the right time, who is the blessed and only ruler, King of kings and Lord of lords,* ¹⁶*who alone has immortality, dwelling in unapproachable light, whom no one has seen or can see; to whom be honor and might forever, Amen.*

Cf. 1 Timothy 5:21:[58]

διαμαρτύρομαι ἐνώπιον τοῦ θεοῦ καὶ **Χριστοῦ Ἰησοῦ** καὶ τῶν ἐκλεκτῶν ἀγγέλων, ἵνα ταῦτα φυλάξῃς χωρὶς προκρίματος,

I charge you   before God   *and* **Christ Jesus** *and the elect angles, that you keep (these instructions) without partiality.*

This fourth of the major christological passages in this letter occurs at the end of the final charge to Timothy (6:3–16), a charge that serves along with 1:3–7 as an inclusio to frame the entire letter. Only in this case, the charge involves Timothy's need not simply to stop the false teachers (vv. 3–10) but also to avoid the same kinds of entanglements (v. 11), and thus to give himself with all vigor to the pursuit of the gospel. The goal of the charge is that he keep "this command"[59] with purity until the final "manifestation" of Christ as his Parousia (v. 14).

At the same time, it functions as the second of three such instances in 1–2 Timothy where Paul places Timothy under solemn oath as one who receives the charge "in the presence of God and Christ." The first of these, 1 Tim

---

[58] See also discussion on 2 Tim 4:1 below (pp. 467–68).

[59] The antecedent of the "this" is not at all clear in this instance; most likely it embraces not simply the most recent charge but by the very nature of things also goes back to the beginning of the letter (1:3–7).

5:21, also includes "the elect angels," thus indicating a charge conducted in the presence of the entire heavenly tribunal. But in this current passage and in the later one in 2 Tim 4:1, the emphasis is altogether on the divine *persons* before whom Timothy is understood to be standing while receiving the charge.

The christological import of the present passage lies at four places. First, one should note that when Paul moves from the whole heavenly arena as witnesses (5:21) to the actual naming of the persons in whose presence the charge is made, he includes God and Christ together as the divine witnesses to the charge. That is, Paul here has moved from the heavenly scene as such to put Timothy under oath before God himself, and in this case he includes Christ as the compound object of the single preposition ἐνώπιον (*in the presence of*). Thus, with this phrase one sees a continuity of usage that goes back to the earliest letters in the corpus, 1–2 Thessalonians.[60] And as will be noted below (2 Tim 4:1), in the final case the emphasis rests specifically on Christ as the one before whom Timothy must receive the charge.

Second, the whole of vv. 13–16 expresses the charge in a single, very long, very complex sentence. But its parts are easily discernible and thus help to explain why it comes in one sentence. It is expressed in an a/b/b'/a' chiastic pattern: the witnesses to the charge are (a) the living God (implying creation) and (b) the historical Christ, who bore effective witness preceding his crucifixion; the goal of everything is (b') the coming of Christ, and the source of all things is (a') the eternal and only God. Thus, as happens elsewhere in the Pauline corpus,[61] the work of Christ is enclosed within the timeless and eternal verity of God the Father.

Third, quite in keeping with the emphases throughout this letter, what is said about Christ in this case puts all the emphasis on his earthly life.[62] There is an oblique allusion to his crucifixion (after all, his "witness" was not just verbal but was on open display in the cross), but the emphasis is on the witness that he bore in his own earthly life at the most crucial moment in that life. So here, as with the three previous texts, Paul simply will not let Timothy, and thus also the hearers of this letter in Ephesus, get away from the reality of Christ's incarnation. Which means further that this is the third instance where Paul focuses on the crucifixion, although more obliquely in this case.

Fourth, as with 1 Tim 1:12–17, the passage ends on the note of absolute monotheism, in this case with an especially strong emphasis on God's absolute sovereignty as well. However we are to understand Paul's understanding of the ontological relationship between God and Christ, Father and Son, he will not let the reality of Christ's genuine deity overrule his basic, absolute monotheism[63]—precisely the issue in any Pauline Christology.

---

[60] See discussion in ch. 2 on 1 Thess 1:1 (pp. 48–50).

[61] See, e.g., 1 Cor 8:6; 15:25–28.

[62] As before, this point is seldom noted in the literature.

[63] It is difficult in this case not to see an emphasis over against the Roman Caesar as well, not to mention the various κύριος cults that existed in Ephesus.

Other Christological Moments

Although the foregoing discussion covers most of the christological moments in 1 Timothy, there are a few scattered references to Christ that need brief noting as well, since they fit well within the scope of what we have discovered in the preceding chapters. Indeed, all but one of these reflect a usage discussed in previous chapters. They are simply noted here because they reflect Pauline usage, whether by Paul himself or by a Paulinist who has entered into the apostle's mind with unusual sensitivity.

God and Christ Together (1 Tim 1:1–2)

[1]Παῦλος ἀπόστολος **Χριστοῦ Ἰησοῦ** <u>κατ' ἐπιταγὴν θεοῦ σωτῆρος ἡμῶν</u> καὶ **Χριστοῦ Ἰησοῦ** τῆς ἐλπίδος ἡμῶν [2]Τιμοθέῳ γνησίῳ τέκνῳ ἐν πίστει, χάρις ἔλεος εἰρήνη <u>ἀπὸ θεοῦ πατρὸς</u> καὶ **Χριστοῦ Ἰησοῦ τοῦ κυρίου ἡμῶν**.

[1]*Paul, apostle **of Christ Jesus** according to <u>the command of God our Savior</u> and **Christ Jesus our hope**,* [2]*to Timothy, true son in faith, grace, mercy, and peace from <u>God the Father</u> and **Christ Jesus our Lord**.*

Quite in keeping with the rest of the corpus and with 6:13 in this letter, God and Christ appear together as the object of a single preposition and thus as the single source of Paul's apostleship (1:1)—indeed, in this case as the single source of the "command" that called him into apostleship.[64]

So also with the salutation. Although it includes the addition of "mercy" and appears without the common "our," its essential point is the same as in the earlier letters. The greeting desires for Timothy an outflow of grace, mercy, and peace, which are understood to come from both God the Father and Christ the Lord. Indeed, in its next occurrence in this letter (v. 14), grace is understood to have come to Paul specifically from "our Lord" (see pp. 425–26 above).

One should also note here that in v. 1, when referring to the source of his apostleship, Paul designates God as "our Savior" and Christ Jesus as "our hope." Although these are the first occurrences of such designations in the corpus, they are typically Pauline in the way that they deliberately anticipate special themes in the letter. Thus, "God our Savior" will be picked up again in 2:3 as the lead-in to the most significant soteriological passage in the letter; and at the end (6:14), Paul makes a special point of emphasizing the future appearing of Christ, even though little is made of this concern elsewhere in the letter.

Christ and the Apostle/Believers

One of the more striking features of 1 Timothy is the paucity of references to Christ apart from the salutation and the primary christological pas-

---

[64]On this matter, see the discussion in ch. 2 on 1 Thess 1:1 (pp. 48–50); cf. the discussion in Mounce, 8–9.

sages. Indeed, there are only four others (3:13; 4:6; 5:11; 6:3). In turn, they have to do with (1) Christ as both the object of faith and the one with whom one has a sustained relationship in that faith (3:13); (2) Christ as source of Timothy's ministry (4:6) (just as he is of Paul's [1:1]); (3) Christ as the one who is spurned when a Christian widow marries (presumably) outside Christ; and (4) Christ as the source and/or content of the "sound instruction" of the gospel (6:3).

Nothing could be more Pauline than these various unrehearsed mentions of Christ. What they do point to is the very strong christocentric predisposition of the author. If things like this are not said as often as they are in Galatians, for example, still they are said in a way that, combined with the whole of the evidence looked at in this letter, demonstrates the absolutely central role that Christ plays in the mind and heart of the author. Or to put that another way, the Christology of this letter is quite in keeping with the previous corpus of letters; indeed, it does not differ from them as significantly as, for example, 2 Corinthians does from 1 Corinthians, or Romans from Galatians.

II. Christology in Titus

There are three striking features about the christological data of this letter. (1) There is a paucity of direct references to Christ—only four in all,[65] and in each instance as either "Jesus Christ" or "Christ Jesus." (2) This is the only letter in the Pauline corpus where the title κύριος does not appear at all. (3) The appellation of σωτήρ, which occurs three times in 1 Timothy with reference to God the Father, in this letter is at least twice also attributed to Christ.[66]

The four references to Christ occur in three passages: twice in the salutation (1:1–4) and once each in the two major creedal moments in the letter (2:11–14; 3:4–7), which serve as compendia of Paul's gospel over against some Cretan aberrations. The analysis will take up each of these passages in turn.

Christ Jesus Our Savior—Titus 1:1–4

The two references to Christ in the salutation appear at standard places, and both in connection with God the Father. First, in v. 1 Paul identifies himself as δοῦλος θεοῦ, ἀπόστολος δὲ Ἰησοῦ Χριστοῦ (_God's slave and **Jesus Christ's**_[67] _apostle_). Although this exact combination is unique, it

---

[65] By way of contrast, and in keeping with Romans and 1 Timothy, θεός occurs 13 times.

[66] The third instance is the much disputed occurrence in 2:13.

[67] The unusual word order (for this combination) of "Jesus Christ" (found in all the early and best evidence both East and West [א* C D F G 33 326 1739 _pc_ latt], contra J. K. Elliott [_The Greek Text of the Epistles to Timothy and Titus_ (SD 36; Salt Lake

is in fact a modification of what Paul does elsewhere, a modification that almost certainly is related to the concerns that follow.[68] For our present purposes, we simply note that the Paul who identifies himself elsewhere as "Christ's slave" (Gal 1:10; Rom 1:1; Phil 1:1)[69] here identifies himself as *"God's* slave." In this letter, a title that could appear to be demeaning is most likely intended to force upon the Cretan believers that even though he is an apostle, Paul is first of all a "slave" under orders from God and therefore they should listen carefully to what he has to say because it comes from God his master.

The christological point, of course, is that elsewhere Paul says the same thing about his relationship to Christ. Thus, at the beginning of this letter we find the same kind of easy interchange between God and Christ that one meets throughout the corpus,[70] only this time it is God the Father assuming the role ordinarily attributed to Christ.

The second christological point to make is the ease with which Paul identifies himself, especially his calling and ministry, as simultaneously in relation to both God and Christ. The appellation "apostle of Christ Jesus" made its first appearance in 1 Cor 1:1, where Paul's authority was being questioned; it became standard thereafter (Philippians and Philemon excepted). Thus it appears in all three of these letters to his adjutants, almost certainly to establish their authority in the respective churches. On its christological significance, see the discussion under 1 Corinthians in ch. 3 (p. 136).

This first mention of God and Christ together in the salutation, as the ultimate source of Paul's authority to speak into the situation in Crete, is then bookended by their (standard) appearance together in v. 4, in the salutation proper. But there are enough unusual features—full of christological implications—about this salutation to require a more extended discussion. Here is the present salutation (second line) set in comparison with what is nearly universal[71] elsewhere:

City: University of Utah Press, 1968), 201], whose unusual kind of "eclecticism" leads him astray here) is one of the scores of phenomena in these letters that can cut two ways when brought forward on the question of authenticity. For reasons not at all clear, the order "Jesus Christ" occurs in three of the four occurrences in this letter (1:1; 2:13; 3:6).

[68] On the details of this feature and many others in this letter, see esp. the commentaries by Marshall and Towner.

[69] And in 2 Tim 2:24 he uses δοῦλος in reference to Timothy (but with κυρίου, not Χριστοῦ). Whether the present usage is also titular, as Mounce (378) suggests, is less certain, since this exact expression does not occur at all in the OT; and for it to be titular, one would think that it should have precedent (the OT passages cited by Mounce all have "my" or "his" as the genitive, not θεοῦ or κυρίου).

[70] See esp. the discussion of its earliest occurrences (1–2 Thessalonians) in ch. 2, pp. 45–48, 69–73.

[71] The exceptions are 1–2 Thessalonians and Colossians. In the case of Paul's first letter (1 Thessalonians), he has simply "grace to you and peace." In 2 Thessalonians this is elaborated for the first time by the compound source ("from God the

χάρις ὑμῖν καὶ εἰρήνη ἀπὸ <u>θεοῦ πατρὸς</u> ἡμῶν καὶ **κυρίου Ἰησοῦ Χριστοῦ.**

χάρις καὶ εἰρήνη ἀπὸ <u>θεοῦ πατρὸς</u> καὶ **Χριστοῦ Ἰησοῦ τοῦ σωτῆρος** ἡμῶν.

Grace to you and peace from <u>God our Father</u> and	**Lord Jesus Christ.**
Grace to you and peace from <u>God our Father</u> and	**Christ Jesus,** *our* **Savior.**

Everything that was noted earlier about Paul's bringing God and Christ together as the compound object with a single preposition also holds here.[72] The striking feature in this instance is the substitution of "Savior" for the more common "Lord." This has the added striking feature that Paul had just used this same appellation for God in the immediately preceding clause, "entrusted to me by the command of God our Savior." This same double appellation of "God our Savior" and "Jesus Christ our Savior" occurs again in 3:4, 6.[73] Two things about this usage are of interest for this study.

1. In the discussion of the phenomenon of referring to Christ by the title of "Savior" in Phil 3:20, where it appears for the first time in the corpus, we noted the significance of the twin appellation of Christ as "Lord and Savior." Although both terms find their basic roots in the OT story by way of the Septuagint, this was language also used in public acclamation of the emperor Nero; and since Philippi was a Roman colony with historical loyalty to the emperor, the transference of these titles to the risen Christ, whose "epiphany" is eagerly awaited, should almost certainly be understood as also over against the emperor and emperor worship.

This historical reality might still linger in the background of Paul's usage in this letter, but since he reserves this title ("Savior") strictly for God in 1 Timothy, it would seem much less likely to be the primary reason for so referring to Christ in this particular letter.[74] Rather, almost everything in Titus seems especially tailored to speak to the difficult situation of establishing the church on the island of Crete, where loyalty to the emperor would not have been an issue.[75] The issue in Crete, as always, must be reconstructed from what appears in the letter itself; and the key in this instance is the unusual way that in 1:10–16 Paul refers directly to Crete's infamous reputation of being a place populated by liars, where truth was not always held

---

Father and the Lord Jesus Christ"); thereafter this is the form that consistently appears, but with the addition of ἡμῶν (*our*) to "Father." In Colossians Paul has omitted "and the Lord Jesus Christ." It should be noted that in each of these instances, including this one in Titus, there is textual variation by later scribes in favor of total conformity.

[72] See the discussion under 1–2 Thessalonians in ch. 2 (pp. 48–50).

[73] This point has also been observed by Kelly, 229; Mounce, 382.

[74] Cf. Kelly: "There is no need to regard [the title] as a Christian correction of the growing custom of saluting the emperor as saviour" (40).

[75] On this matter, see the discussions of the history and character of Crete and its people and their relationship to the empire in the recent commentaries by Johnson, Marshall, and esp. Towner.

in high regard. At the same time, Paul further characterizes his opponents as dabbling in "Jewish myths," whose view of "purity" was seen not in terms of character but of ritual "cleanness."

These items together suggest that the primary background for the use of the title "God our Savior" in this letter, as in 1 Timothy, is to be found in its Septuagint origins, where it occurs regularly and at key places as an appellation for the God who had "saved" = "delivered" Israel from Egyptian bondage. Thus, in the Song of Moses (Deut 32:15), "Jacob" is chastised because he "rejected God his Savior"; and at the heart of book 1 of the Psalter, "David" speaks of "God my Savior" (Ps 25:5; 27:9). That this is the primary source for this appellation is made certain by the large number of intertextual echoes of Israel's primary story that occur in the two creedal passages in 2:13–14 and 3:4–7 (see discussion below). All of this suggests that Paul is trying to replace the Cretan believers' use of the OT for ritualistic purposes with his standard use of the OT to place God's new-covenant people within the framework of God's continuing story. It is not surprising, therefore, that in this letter—and for similar kinds of reasons in 1–2 Timothy as well—God regularly receives the appellation "God our Savior."

2. The key christological dimension of this usage is thus to be found in this passage and in 3:4–7, where Paul speaks first of "God our Savior" and immediately follows it by a reference to "Christ Jesus/Jesus Christ our Savior" (1:3–4; 3:4, 6). Such an interchange should by now not surprise us;[76] but it happens in this case almost certainly because Christ becomes the key player in the new-covenant fulfillment of the story. Thus, even though the two uses reflect Paul's standard perspective, where "God our Savior" refers to the ultimate source of salvation and "Jesus Christ our Savior" refers to the effective means of salvation,[77] as in Paul's earlier letters this interchange is made in a completely matter-of-fact way, without any attempt to *demonstrate* something about Christ and without the slightest sense of tension in making this kind of interchange within the same sentence(s).

Does Paul Call Jesus "God"?—Titus 2:11–14

This next christological moment in Titus has served for many as the second (or third) place in the corpus where Paul chooses to use the appellation θεός (*God*) with reference to Christ.[78] But as with Rom 9:5, this text is equally controverted, not just because of Pauline usage elsewhere—although, at the

---

[76] In passing, it might be noted that the very subtlety and ease of this interchange is thoroughly Pauline. Could a pseudepigrapher be expected to know and catch such things as this?

[77] So also Marshall, 135.

[78] See the discussions of 2 Thess 1:12 in ch. 2 (pp. 61–63) and Rom 9:5 in ch. 6 (pp. 272–77).

end of the day, that too will count for something—but because it is equally fraught with syntactical and grammatical issues that make final resolution somewhat tenuous.

The primary issue in this case results from the fact that the name Ἰησοῦ Χριστοῦ stands in apposition to a preceding genitive. But to which genitive? There are three options: (1) to "our Savior" alone, (2) to the combination "our great God and Savior," (3) to the word "glory" in the longer phrase "our great God and Savior's glory." The first of these is found in the KJV and thus has had a long history in the English-speaking church; here the phrases "our great God" and "our Savior Jesus Christ" were understood as a reference to the Father and the Son. The second is the currently "reigning" point of view, adopted by almost everyone in the NT academy[79] and found in most of the major English translations. The third was first proposed by F. J. A. Hort; it was adopted in the NEB and in my commentary (1984, 1988) and more recently in the commentary by P. H. Towner. It is the one that will be argued for again in this study. But before looking at this issue in some detail, we need to have a good sense of the sentence as a whole.

Part of our difficulty lies with the fact that all of 2:11–14 is one long sentence in Greek, whose primary subject and predicate is ἐπεφάνη . . . ἡ χάρις τοῦ θεοῦ (*the grace of God appeared*). The reason for the long sentence probably is related to Paul's present concerns, which are two: first, in light of what has been said to this point, he is concerned about the educative aspect of the basic Christian story for the situation in Crete; second, he is equally concerned to reinforce the fact that the story itself is centered in the person and work of Christ. The sentence as such revolves around the twofold "manifestation"[80] of Christ: (1) his first appearance, which is mentioned obliquely in v. 11 but finally explicated in v. 14; (2) his (coming) second appearance, expressed in v. 13 in terms of "our blessed/happy hope." This means that the *purpose* of Christ's "appearing" (salvation for all) is given first, in v. 12, while the *means* to that purpose is expressed in v. 14. The part of the sentence that concerns us is sandwiched between these statements of purpose and means, where Paul affirms the eschatological conclusion of Christ's appearing in a second "appearing/manifestation"— this time of God's glory that is to be revealed in full at the end. Thus the "logic" of the sentence can be easily traced, even if one can also easily get lost in its many details:

---

[79] See especially the argument in Harris, *Jesus as God,* 173–85.

[80] Gk. ἐπιφαίνω/ἐπιφάνεια. See n. 52 above. As a theological concept about the "appearing/coming" of Christ, this word group is found in the NT only in 2 Thess 2:8 and its several instances in the Pastoral Epistles (the verb in Titus 2:11; 3:4; the noun in Titus 2:13, plus 1 Tim 6:14; 2 Tim 1:10; 4:1, 8 [Luke uses the verb twice but not theologically]). This shift of language makes a good deal of sense as a response to Nero's assuming this language for himself as a divine manifestation.

v. 11—the *fact* of Christ's appearing is expressed in terms of God's grace being manifest

v. 12—the first *purpose* of his appearing is educative (so that people know how to live)

v. 13—the ultimate *conclusion* of this appearing is a second appearing

v. 14—the *means* to the purpose is redemption and purification through Christ's death

The net result is that there are two "appearings" of Christ mentioned. The first, begun in v. 11 and completed in v. 14, is the historical "manifestation" of God's *grace*. The second, brought into the story in v. 13, is the future "manifestation" of God's *glory* at Christ's second coming—or at least that is what seems to be the intent of the sentence.[81] But this second "manifestation" is the point of much difficulty and controversy.

Christ the Manifestation of God's Glory (v. 13)

Perhaps the easiest way to see the issues involved in this clause is by looking at each of the options in terms of how its structure is differently understood. At issue is whether Paul in this clause refers to two personages (God and Christ) or only one (Christ):

Option 1 ("two persons" [KJV, NRSV^mg]):

προσδεχόμενοι τὴν μακαρίαν ἐλπίδα
              καὶ
              ἐπιφάνειαν τῆς δόξης
                    τοῦ μεγάλου θεοῦ
                    καὶ
                    σωτῆρος ἡμῶν
                    Ἰησοῦ Χριστοῦ

= the blessed hope and glorious appearing of *the great God and our Savior Jesus Christ*

Option 2 ("one person" [NRSV, TNIV, ESV]):[82]

---

[81] This at least seems a more likely analysis than that by Mounce (431) as "past" (v. 12), "present" (v. 14), and "future" (v. 13), since v. 14 is still expressed in the past tense and seems intended to give content to what is said in vv. 11–12.

[82] By eliminating the comma after "Savior" (found in the NRSV and TNIV), the ESV has deliberately erased the possibility of understanding the text in the way argued for here. It is unambiguously "our great God and Savior Jesus Christ."

προσδεχόμενοι   τὴν μακαρίαν   ἐλπίδα
                            καὶ
                            ἐπιφάνειαν
                               τῆς δόξης
                                   τοῦ μεγάλου θεοῦ καὶ σωτῆρος ἡμῶν
                                   Ἰησοῦ Χριστοῦ

= the blessed hope and appearing of the glory of *our great God and Savior, Jesus Christ*

Option 3 ("two persons" [NEB; Hort, Fee, Towner]):

προσδεχόμενοι   τὴν μακαρίαν   ἐλπίδα
                            καὶ
                            ἐπιφάνειαν
                               τῆς δόξης
                                   τοῦ μεγάλου θεοῦ καὶ σωτῆρος ἡμῶν
                                   Ἰησοῦ Χριστοῦ

= the blessed hope and appearing of *our great God and Savior's glory, Jesus Christ*

So how shall we assess these options? First, we may dismiss as most highly unlikely the attempt by the translators of the KJV, followed by the NASB and NIV (and the NET BIBLE), to overcome some of the difficulty by viewing the genitive "of the glory" as adjectival ("the glorious appearing").[83] There is hardly a thing in favor of this view, and nearly everything against it. Not only is it out of sync with Paul's usage elswhere, but also it puts the present emphasis in the wrong place: on a description of the *nature* of Christ's coming rather than on the fact that God's own glory is what is going to be revealed at the second "manifestation."

We may likewise dismiss the attempt by the same translators to turn the long genitive phrase τοῦ μεγάλου θεοῦ καὶ σωτῆρος ἡμῶν (*of our great God and Savior*) into two personages.[84] This we do on the grounds of both grammar and the overall sense of the passage. Here is a case where "Granville Sharpe's Rule" comes into play: two nouns controlled by a single article are to be understood as one entity, not two. Not only so, but this formulation of "adjective-noun-and-noun-adjective" occurs elsewhere in Paul's writings[85]

[83]See also on 2 Cor 4:4, where the translators did the same thing ("the glorious gospel"), in a context dominated by the concept of "glory." To do so in the present passage is to obliterate the parallel with "the manifestation of grace" in v. 11 (cf. Marshall, 275) and thus to destroy the rhetoric of the sentence as a whole. It is also rightly rejected by, e.g., Knight, 322; Mounce, 421.

[84]The presentation of this option will be greatly abbreviated here, since it is the single option that almost all the literature argues against. For a more complete discussion, see Marshall; Towner; Harris, *Jesus as God*, 173–85.

[85]See, e.g., 2 Thess 2:17, ἐν παντὶ ἔργῳ καὶ λόγῳ ἀγαθῷ, which is rightly translated not "in every deed and good word," but "in every good deed and word."

as a convenient way of having two nouns be modified by two adjectives without having to repeat the two adjectives. Thus, both "great" and "our" modify the one reality, "God and Savior." Moreover, the KJV created a considerable anomaly with the suggestion that both God and Christ will be manifest at the second coming.

That leaves us then with a choice between options 2 and 3. For the most part, option 2 has tended to win the day by default. That is, it is simply assumed that "Jesus Christ" stands in apposition to the word or word cluster that it immediately follows. But that is precisely the assumption that needs to be called into serious question, on the basis both of the present argument and of Pauline usage elsewhere. Several points need to be made.

1. It is highly unlikely that anyone would have ever read the text as in option 2 had there not been a multiplication of modifiers. That is, had the present clause been given in its barest essentials, "awaiting the manifestation of the glory of God, Jesus Christ," no one would have imagined that "Jesus Christ" stood in apposition to God.

2. Evidence for this is the appearance of this very structure in Col 2:2, where Paul speaks of εἰς ἐπίγνωσιν τοῦ μυστηρίου τοῦ θεοῦ, Χριστοῦ (*for the knowledge of the mystery of God, Christ*), which the NIV tradition has made clear by inserting "namely" between "God" and "Christ." Indeed, had Paul chosen to elaborate this phrase as happens here, it would read, "the knowledge of the mystery of our great God and Savior, Christ," and then instinct would change the antecedent from "mystery" to "our great God and Savior."

3. Thus, it is only the *distance* from what it stands in apposition to, made so by the second appellation of God as "our Savior," that has caused us historically to read "Jesus Christ" as in apposition to either "our Savior" or "our great God and Savior."[86] So much is this so, Marshall has suggested that at this distance Paul would have needed to add some kind of pickup such as a relative pronoun to relieve the ambiguity.[87] But that is to assume that an author recognized the difficulty that he had created for others, when what he intended when he wrote (dictated) was perfectly clear to him. And in any case, when one puts Paul's phrase into ordinary English, it makes perfectly good sense: "awaiting the appearance of our great God and Savior's glory,

---

[86] I do not mean by this to downplay the obvious difficulty of the "distance factor." My point, rather, is that this is the *only* difficulty with the position argued for here; and when one thinks of the enormous difficulty of either Paul or someone writing in his name calling Christ "our *great God* and Savior," which stands over against Pauline (and Pastoral) usage in every way, it seems like the lesser of difficulties!

[87] See Marshall, 229. The "distance" factor in fact is the almost universal reason for rejecting this point of view; sometimes (e.g., Mounce, 431) it is rejected in part because "the Glory of God" is questioned as a title for Christ. I, too, would question such an interpretation. Christ is no more "the Glory of God" than he is "the Grace of God," as though titles were in view in either case. The passage has to do with the *manifestation* of God's glory.

Jesus Christ." This is precisely how several translations (e.g., NRSV, ESV) overcome the same awkwardness in Col 2:2 ("God's mystery, namely, Christ").

4. In *favor* of "glory" as the apposing word for "Jesus Christ" is the fact that this is very much a Pauline idea.[88] In 2 Cor 3:7–4:6 (see ch. 4, pp. 180–84), a passage where δόξα occurs no less than 13 times, even though Paul does not explicitly call Christ "God's glory," he makes it clear that Christ is indeed *the manifestation of God's glory*, since he is God's true "image." And it is into that glory (the glory of God as expressed in God's true image) that we ourselves are being transformed as (with the "veil" of Torah removed) we gaze by the Spirit into the face of Christ. Similarly in our present passage: Christ is the coming manifestation of God's glory precisely because he was first of all the manifestation of God's grace as the one who has stepped into the divine role of redeeming and cleansing "for himself a people for his name" (see discussion below).

Furthermore, it seems inexplicable for Paul (or someone writing in his name) to here refer to the personal coming of Christ as a manifestation of *Christ's* "glory." Of course his "glory" will be seen when he comes; but why say such a thing at all in this context? Indeed, it is to overcome this difficulty that some have chosen to turn this phrase into a descriptive genitive; but as already noted, that puts the emphasis at the wrong place.

5. There is the further difficulty for either Paul or a pseudepigrapher to have created the anomaly of referring to Christ as θεός. Two matters regarding Pauline usage create the difficulty. First, there is Paul's very early separation of the Jewish Shema into two parts in 1 Cor 8:6, where he explicitly identifies God the Father as the "*one* θεός" and Christ the Son as the "*one* κύριος." And throughout the numerous preceding pages we have seen how consistent Paul is with this explication of the Shema. One would therefore need considerably strong evidence to overturn that consistency, especially when it is quite unnecessary for our understanding of the present usage and passage as a whole.

Second, there is the double difficulty of Paul's not only referring to Christ as "God" but also, in this one instance where he might do so,[89] of adding to the appellation of God the well-known OT adjective, thus referring to him as "the great God."[90] One can make a great deal of sense of Paul's having added this appellation here with reference to God the Father, but why he

---

[88] See esp. C. C. Newman, *Paul's Glory-Christology: Tradition and Rhetoric* (NovTSup 69; Leiden: Brill, 1992).

[89] Or possibly second instance. See the similar discussion in ch. 6 of Rom 9:5 (pp. 272–77).

[90] It is sometimes argued that this singular appearance in the NT of "great" with God fits best with Christ; but the grounds for this are especially weak ("Great is the mystery of godliness" in 1 Tim 3:16 is hardly comparable). Against this is the use of this word group in the NT to refer exclusively to God ("greatness/majesty" [see Luke 9:43; Heb 1:3; 8:1; Jude 25]), and especially its multiplied occurrences in the OT to refer to God.

would do so with regard to Christ would remain a singular mystery. And especially this would be so in a letter in which a very high Christology is simply not an observable agenda.[91]

6. Finally, in all of this mix one must look again at whether the appellation "our Savior" fits best with Christ or God *in this setting,* noting that both God and Christ are unambiguously so called in this letter. On the basis of v. 14, it is arguable that this is another place where Christ himself receives this appellation. On the other hand, this passage is bookended by references to "God our Savior" (2:10; 3:4). And since the "grace of God" and the "glory of God" are what are being manifested in Christ's two "appearances," there is every good contextual reason to think that Paul in this passage has simply brought forward the previous reference in v. 10 to "God our Savior" in order to emphasize whose glory is being manifested in the coming of Christ.

At the end of the day, therefore, it is not simply the anomaly of calling Christ θεός that calls the new consensus into question but also the role of this phrase and appellation of God in the whole sentence that leads to a different reading. The believer's hope lies in our eager expectation of the final manifestation of God's glory, the coming of Jesus Christ himself. And that in itself is high Christology indeed, one wants to add emphatically at the end of this long discussion. The coming of Christ is the full and final manifestation of God's glory.

Christ the Manifestation of God's Grace (vv. 11, 14)

The christological data in these framing clauses are several. First, Christ's giving of himself for our sins (v. 14) gives content to the "manifestation" of "the grace of God" (v. 11). That is, "grace of God" in this sentence is not simply the attribute of God that serves as the theological predicate of the Cretans' salvation—although the term emphasizes this reality as well. Rather, this phrase, the grammatical subject of the sentence, is at the end given historical actualization in Christ's redemptive giving of himself for *us.* The "grace of God" has thus been manifested historically in the coming of Christ, "who gave himself for us to redeem us."

While this is quite in keeping with Paul's view of Christ's death found elsewhere, in this case the author has deliberately used language from the Septuagint, and in so doing, he has once again in a very Pauline way appropriated to Christ what in the OT is the activity of God. Although several OT texts carry this language, Paul's sentence especially echoes Ps 130:8 [129:8 LXX][92] (cf. Ezek 37:23 below):

---

[91] This view, of course, depends in part on how one interprets the present text; my point is that apart from *this* text, a high Christology is not an observable agenda.

[92] Some have also noted the similarities to the words of Jesus in Mark 10:45 // Matt 20:28 (δοῦναι τὴν ψυχὴν αὐτοῦ λύτρον ἀντὶ πολλῶν [*to give his life a ransom for many*]); see Knight, 327. But this is so clearly an echo of Isa 53:12 that the connection seems only incidental rather than direct.

Titus 2:14   ὃς ἔδωκεν ἑαυτὸν . . . ἵνα **λυτρώσηται** ἡμᾶς
                                      ἀπὸ **πάσης**   **ἀνομίας**

Ps 129:8 LXX   καὶ   αὐτὸς   **λυτρώσεται** τὸν Ισραηλ
                                      ἐκ **πασῶν τῶν ἀνομιῶν** αὐτοῦ

Titus 2:14   *who gave himself in order*   *to* **ransom** *us*
                                      from **all**   **iniquity**

Ps 129:8 LXX   *and   he himself* **will**   **ransom**   *Israel*
                                      from **all** *their*   **iniquities**

As elsewhere in the corpus, the "he himself" that in the psalm refers to
Yahweh is here appropriated directly to Christ, the historical manifestation
of God's grace (and the future manifestation of his glory). Here, then, is how
Paul's standard high Christology emerges in this passage. But even more so
in the next clause.

Besides "redemption" as ransom, and in the interest of the behavioral issues at stake in Crete, Paul adds that Christ redeemed us precisely so that
"he might purify for himself a people that are his very own" (TNIV). Here is
yet another passage full of OT intertextuality, in this case from several passages in Ezek 36–37. Much of the language of Paul's sentence can be found
especially in Ezek 37:23:[93]

Titus 2:14 ὃς ἔδωκεν ἑαυτὸν . . . ἵνα **λυτρώσηται**   ἡμᾶς
                                               ἀπὸ **πάσης ἀνομίας**
                            καὶ καθαρίσῃ   ἑαυτῷ λαὸν
                                               περιούσιον

Ezek 37:23 καὶ   ῥύσομαι αὐτοὺς ἀπὸ **πασῶν** τῶν
                                               ἀνομιῶν αὐτῶν,
              ὧν ἡμάρτοσαν ἐν αὐταῖς, **καὶ καθαριῶ** αὐτούς,
                                 καὶ ἔσονταί **μοι εἰς λαόν**

Titus 2:14 *who gave himself in order to* **ransom**   *us*
                                               from **all iniquity**
                            and cleanse   **for himself a people**
                                               of his own

Ezek 37:23 *and*   *I will rescue them from* **all**
                                               their **iniquities,**
              which they sinned among themselves **and I will cleanse** *them,*
                                 and they will be **for me a people**

As we have seen from the very beginning of the Pauline corpus, language that in the Septuagint refers to God alone has again been appropriated

_____

[93] See also Knight, 328, Marshall, 285; Towner, 762–63; the verbal exactness with
Ezekiel of much of Paul's sentence suggests that this is a bit more than merely "reminiscent" (Mounce, 431).

and applied to Christ. And the christological signficance must not be downplayed. The whole point of the OT story is that God is redeeming a people *for himself,* a people who by the way they live will reflect his glory among the nations. Although God is still seen as the prime mover in this sentence, Christ's role in the passage is not only to redeem this new people through giving himself but also to "cleanse" them for his own (divine) purposes as a *people* who are uniquely *his very own.* And they will do so as they are "eager to do what is good" (v. 14).

Christ the Giver of the Spirit—Titus 3:6

The final reference to Christ in the letter occurs in the second of the two soteriological summaries (3:4–7). As with the preceding passage, this one comes by way of another "manifestion" of God, this time of his "kindness and love." But now the focus is primarily on the Spirit, as the agent of "rebirth and renewal."[94] The role of Christ in this telling of the story is twofold, with both aspects carrying christological significance.

First, Christ is the giver of the Spirit. That is, believers are reborn and renewed by means of "the Spirit whom God has poured out on us generously *through Jesus Christ our Savior."* As with other such moments in the corpus, this exact expression does not occur elsewhere; but neither is it a surprise or out of sync with Paul's theology. Quite the opposite. On at least four occasions Paul refers to the Spirit as the Spirit of (Jesus) Christ,[95] so it is a small step from God's sending of "his Spirit" to Paul's expression of this reality in the more triadic fashion found here. And, of course, such an idea is quite in keeping with Peter's speech in Acts 2:33, where Luke articulates in full detail what was almost certainly the common understanding of the early church, that "exalted at the right hand of God, [the Messiah] has received from the Father the promised Holy Spirit and has poured out what you now see and hear."

The implied Christology, of course, is considerable. Not only does the saving work of God appear as the combined work of Father, Christ, and Spirit, but also an activity that throughout the OT is seen as the special province of God is now seen as accomplished through Christ the Son—and this without argumentation or apparently christologically conscious motivation.[96]

Second, the mention of Christ is further elaborated in terms of "having been justified by the grace of that one [= Christ],[97] we became heirs in keep-

---

[94] On this larger question, see the discussion in Fee, *God's Empowering Presence,* 777–84.

[95] 2 Cor 3:17 ("the Spirit of the Lord"); Gal 4:6 ("the Spirit of the Son"); Rom 8:9 ("the Spirit of Christ"); Phil 1:19 ("the Spirit of Jesus Christ").

[96] On this point, cf. Lock: "His work is at once placed on the level with God's" (155).

[97] Gk. τῇ ἐκείνου χάριτι. The question of the referent of the ἐκεῖνος is settled in BDAG in favor of Christ ("referring back to and resuming a word immediately preceding" [a β.]).

ing with the hope of eternal life." No surprises here. As already articulated in 2:13–14, Christ is both the agent of God's saving work and the one who guarantees the final goal of eternal life. But what is significant christo-logically, and again in keeping with what happens throughout the corpus, is that language that is ordinarily used with reference to the role of God the Father in our salvation is now matter-of-factly attributed to Christ. It is both "his [own] grace," thus tying this summary to the previous one (2:11–14), and through that grace his means of "justifying" us. Thus, language regu-larly used of, or attributed to, God is now brought directly into the service of Christ as the mediator of God's saving activity. It is, after all, an easy linguis-tic move to use language ordinarily attributed to the source of salvation for the agent of that salvation.

All of this to say, then, that the Christology of Titus, small though it is in quantity, is quite in keeping with that found in Paul's letters to churches as well as in 1–2 Timothy. On the understanding of 2:13 offered here, it is cer-tainly not "higher" than the corpus written to churches; on the other hand, neither is it "lower" in any way, even though the mention of Christ is sur-prisingly less frequent.

III. Christology in 2 Timothy

Paul's second letter to Timothy is chronologically the final letter in the corpus.[98] In many ways, small and otherwise, it is so much like the Paul of the letters to churches that had it been the only one of the Pastoral Epistles to have survived, it probably would well have vied for authenticity. The Christology of the letter is especially noteworthy in this regard, since here one finds much that looks like what one finds elsewhere throughout the cor-pus. Again we begin with some general observations about usage.

Preliminary Observations about Usage

Christ is mentioned by name/title a total of 29 times[99] in this letter, well over double the number of references to θεός (13x), thus bringing this usage phenomenon back in line with the majority of the letters to churches (Romans being the outstanding example contrariwise). Seventeen of these occurrences use the title κύριος (Lord),[100] and only one of these in combina-

---

[98] This is true whether by Paul or by someone writing in his name, in which case it probably would have been intended as a kind of last will and testament of Paul.

[99] This figure includes the textual decision that κυρίου rather than θεοῦ is the original text in 2:14 (see pp. 469–71 below).

[100] As elsewhere in the corpus, not all are agreed that κύριος refers to Christ in each instance; for the more debatable ones, see the discussion below on 1:18; 2:19;

tion with others (in the salutation [1:2]). The title is anarthrous 4 times, and in keeping with the preceding corpus, it occurs when the author is either citing the Septuagint or using a Septuagintalism.[101] The other 12 references are to "Christ Jesus" (11x) or "Jesus Christ" (1x).[102]

Although these statistical data suggest that the present discussion should begin with the use of κύριος, two other factors have determined the sequence of discussion here. First, the Christology of this letter has understandably close ties to concerns found in 1 Timothy; second, it also has remarkably close ties to the letters to churches in the preceding corpus. We begin with the singular close tie to 1 Timothy.

Jesus as Preexistent and Incarnate

Even though this letter is more personal than 1 Timothy, Paul still intends it to be read to the Ephesian congregations, the evidence for which is not only its ongoing concern over the false teachers but also especially the double grace at the end: ὁ κύριος μετὰ τοῦ πνεύματός σου (to Timothy), followed by ἡ χάρις μεθ᾽ ὑμῶν (to the whole church). The upshot of this is that the Christology of the letter tends to serve both parties. What is intended to bolster Timothy's courage at the same time serves to remind the community of Jesus' genuinely earthly life. We begin with the two passages in this letter that have a semicreedal ring to them, in both of which Christ's preexistence and incarnation are either asserted or implied.

2 Timothy 1:8–10

⁸μὴ οὖν ἐπαισχυνθῇς **τὸ μαρτύριον τοῦ κυρίου ἡμῶν** μηδὲ ἐμὲ τὸν δέσμιον **αὐτοῦ**, ἀλλὰ συγκακοπάθησον τῷ εὐαγγελίῳ <u>κατὰ δύναμιν θεοῦ</u>, ⁹<u>τοῦ σώσαντος</u> ἡμᾶς <u>καὶ καλέσαντος κλήσει ἁγίᾳ</u>, οὐ κατὰ τὰ ἔργα ἡμῶν ἀλλὰ κατὰ <u>ἰδίαν πρόθεσιν καὶ χάριν τὴν δοθεῖσαν</u>, ἡμῖν ἐν **Χριστῷ Ἰησοῦ πρὸ χρόνων αἰωνίων**, ¹⁰φανερωθεῖσαν δὲ νῦν **διὰ τῆς ἐπιφανείας τοῦ σωτῆρος ἡμῶν Χριστοῦ Ἰησοῦ, καταργήσαντος** μὲν τὸν θάνατον **φωτίσαντος δὲ ζωὴν καὶ ἀφθαρσίαν** διὰ τοῦ εὐαγγελίου

4:17–18. Indeed, Young (*Theology*, 60) speaks of "undoubted ambiguity" with regard to usage in this letter. But that is far too skeptical of a usage that is fully in keeping with the undoubted letters, as the following discussion seeks to point out. Surely, "identification" by the author himself (1:2), where Paul's clear distinction between θεός and κύριος is maintained, should have its day in court!

[101] Marshall sees each of these as a reference to God the Father rather than Christ. But that seems to miss the distinctly Pauline nature of this usage, where he regularly keeps the anarthrous usage of the Septuagint when applying the text or language to Christ. See, e.g., 1 Thess 4:6; 5:2; 2 Thess 2:13; 1 Cor 1:31; 2:16; Rom 10:13. See further on 2:19 below.

[102] This single exception is at 2:8.

[8]*Therefore do not **let witness for our Lord**[103] nor me **his** prisoner be a matter of shame; but join in suffering for the gospel, on the basis of [104] the power of God,* [9]*who saved and called us with a holy calling, not because of our works but in keeping with his own purpose and grace, which was[105] given to us* **in Christ Jesus before the ages began,** [10]*but has now been revealed* **through the appearing of our Savior, Christ Jesus, having destroyed** death and having **brought life and immortality to light** through the gospel.*

This passage functions as the heart of an opening appeal to Timothy to remain loyal to Paul and the gospel despite present (and future) hardships to be endured. The appeal itself is for Timothy to "join in suffering for the gospel," the presupposition of which is both the past sufferings of Christ (hence 2:8–13) and Paul's present suffering at the hands of the empire. It is framed by reference to the gift of the empowering Spirit of God (vv. 6–7, 14), who will make such steadfastness possible. The centerpiece of the appeal is a semicreedal telling of the gospel story,[106] which began in eternity past and found historical expression in the "appearing" of Christ Jesus our Savior. What Christ did in his coming was to destroy death itself (through his own death and resurrection) and thus to bring life immortal into clear visibility.

In so doing, Paul reminds Timothy of some of the basic matters of the Christian gospel, matters that in this case are carefully tailored to the setting in Ephesus and thus pick up concerns that emerged in 1 Timothy. Quite in keeping with the essential Pauline gospel, God the Father is the ultimate source and prime mover of everything. God (θεός) saved us by calling us into this new life, a reality that resides within his own purposes and grace. Also quite in keeping with the Pauline gospel, this redemptive will of God found its historical expression in "our Savior,[107] Jesus Christ." In

---

[103] The translation reflects a conviction that τοῦ κυρίου ἡμῶν is an objective genitive, rather than subjective as with most interpreters and translations. Despite Johnson (346), who allows either as possible, it is difficult to make sense of this as referring to the witness that Jesus bore as being a matter of shame.

[104] For this rendering of κατά, see BDAG B 5a δ (513A); the referent is back to the Spirit of God in v. 7 (see Fee, *God's Empowering Presence*, 790; Knight, 373; Marshall, 704).

[105] The translation assumes, with most interpreters, the antecedent of τήν to be "grace" (as the realized expression of God's purpose). Johnson (348–49) appears to stand alone in suggesting it picks up both words.

[106] This is another passage where most NT scholars believe that the author is appealing to a preexisting creed. Although sometimes used as evidence against Pauline authorship, such a view seems self-defeating, for two reasons: (1) semicreedal statements like this occur throughout the Pauline corpus, beginning with 1 Thessalonians (1:9–10 and 5:9–10); and (2) no two of them are alike (the closest are Gal 4:4–7 and Rom 8:15–16). To paraphrase Pierson Parker's quip about the use of sources by the author of John's Gospel: "If Paul used preexisting creeds, it looks as if he wrote them all himself"! Thus the present passage is thoroughly Pauline in both of the above senses. Only some of the language is new—but one must be careful here as well, since this is true of the large majority of these moments in Paul's letters.

[107] This is the only appearance of σωτήρ in this letter; for this usage, see esp. the discussion of Titus 1:3–4. The present creedal statement offers us the needed insight

making this point, Paul says several things about Christ that are of considerable christological significance, which also correspond to the emphasis in 1 Timothy regarding both Christ's preexistence and the genuineness of his incarnation.

1. With regard to Christ's *preexistence,* Paul insists that God's saving purposes already had their existence in Christ Jesus before the ages themselves had a temporal referent. In the mind and will of God, salvation had already "been given to us" in Christ. The historical event itself was set in motion by the *incarnation,* the "appearing"[108] in history of "our Savior, Christ Jesus." The noticeable absence of κύριος in this appellation, especially for this letter, is the result of the present emphasis, which is not on Christ's present reign/lordship resulting from his death and resurrection,[109] but on his having humbled death into oblivion (cf. 1 Cor 15:24–27), with his own death and resurrection as the presupposition.

2. Paul's own emphasis in this telling of the story is on the "life" that has been made available through Christ, thereby harking back to "the promise of life" in v. 1. Thus "the life" brought to light through the "appearing of Christ Jesus" has its focus on the future, as the addition of "and immortality" makes clear. Significant for our present purposes is the assumed presupposition lying behind this language. Whatever else is true of Yahweh, he is "the Living God," who gave/gives life to all that is. Life itself, echoed in his very name, belongs to him alone, and every living thing owes its borrowed life to the Giver of life. Paul's emphasis here is on the role of Christ in this gift of life, since by his resurrection he has "destroyed death" and thus assured life eternal for those who are his.

Therefore, although this narrative does not, as in 1 Timothy, emphasize Christ's earthly life per se, it presupposes it in every way. In his concern to bolster Timothy's fortitude, Paul reminds him of his certain future brought about by the work of Christ in history, a reminder that also functions to emphasize Christ's incarnation vis-à-vis the false teachers. Both of these concerns are picked up again in the next reference to the Christ narrative in 2:8–13.

---

regarding this usage in these letters as to why Paul can use the epithet of both God and Christ. God is "our Savior" (1 Tim 1:1; 2:3; Titus 1:3; 2:10, 13; 3:4) in the ultimate, originating sense; Christ Jesus is "our Savior" (Titus 1:4; 3:6; 2 Tim 1:10) as the one who effected salvation in human history.

[108] On this word, see n. 52 above. That this is a reference to Christ's incarnation is held almost universally. But here again Dunn (*Christology in the Making,* 237–38) has shown that one can read Pauline texts in a way that neither presupposes nor asserts preexistence and incarnation; as elsewhere, Dunn's presuppositional base (commitment to a "developmental Christological scheme") has dictated what the text is suggested to mean.

[109] See discussion in ch. 9 on Phil 2:9–11 (pp. 393–401), and on the emphasis in the present letter on Christ's kingdom (4:1) and thus his being "the righteous Judge" (4:8, 14).

2 Timothy 2:8–13

⁸μνημόνευε Ἰησοῦν Χριστὸν ἐγηγερμένον ἐκ νεκρῶν, ἐκ σπέρματος Δαυίδ, κατὰ τὸ εὐαγγέλιόν μου ⁹ἐν ᾧ κακοπαθῶ μέχρι δεσμῶν ὡς κακοῦργος, ἀλλὰ <u>ὁ λόγος τοῦ θεοῦ οὐ δέδεται</u>· ¹⁰διὰ τοῦτο πάντα ὑπομένω διὰ τοὺς ἐκλεκτούς, ἵνα καὶ αὐτοὶ σωτηρίας τύχωσιν **τῆς ἐν Χριστῷ Ἰησοῦ μετὰ δόξης αἰωνίου.** ¹¹πιστὸς ὁ λόγος·

εἰ γὰρ **συναπεθάνομεν, καὶ συζήσομεν·**
¹²εἰ ὑπομένομεν, καὶ **συμ**βασιλεύσομεν·
εἰ ἀρνησόμεθα, **κἀκεῖνος ἀρνήσεται** ἡμᾶς·
¹³εἰ ἀπιστοῦμεν, **ἐκεῖνος πιστὸς μένει, ἀρνήσασθαι** γὰρ ἑαυτὸν οὐ **δύναται.**

⁸*Remember **Jesus the Messiah, raised from the dead, of the seed of David,** according to my gospel, ⁹for which I am suffering to the point of being chained like a criminal. But <u>God's word is not chained</u>. ¹⁰Therefore, I endure all things for the sake of the elect, so that they themselves might obtain the salvation which resides **in Christ Jesus with eternal glory.** ¹¹The saying is trustworthy:*

*For if we died **together (with him), we shall also live together;***
*if we endure, we shall also reign **together;***
*if we deny **(him), he will also deny us;***
*if we prove faithless, **he remains faithful, for he cannot disown himself.***

With these words, Paul concludes the opening appeals to Timothy to join with him in enduring hardship for the sake of the gospel. The common denominator between the two appeals (1:6–14; 2:1–13) is that such hardship characterized the earthly life of the Lord himself. If that was merely presupposed in the first appeal, it is spelled out with some clarity in this second instance, in which the story of Christ and Paul's involvement in that story are typically interwoven.

And here especially the christological concerns that dominated 1 Timothy—the reality of Christ's incarnation and thus of his earthly life—are spelled out in striking detail. This emphasis begins with the single instance in this letter of the reversed order of the combined name:[110] "Remember *Jesus Christ,*" which here puts emphasis on Jesus' earthly life, as the two qualifiers that follow make clear. In keeping with the emphasis in the preceding narrative, Paul mentions Jesus' resurrection as the matter of first importance; but by referring to his Davidic descent as well,[111] Paul also puts emphasis on Jesus' being the Jewish Messiah.[112] Here is another instance in

---

[110] It is therefore remarkable that there is almost no "correction" of this word order in the textual tradition to the more common (for this letter) "Christ Jesus."

[111] On this matter, see further the discussion in ch. 6 of Rom 1:3–4 (pp. 240–44).

[112] The language is a conscious pickup from the Davidic covenant, expressed in 2 Kgs 7:12 (ἀναστήσω τὸ σπέρμα σου μετὰ σέ [*I will raise up your seed with you*]); cf. Ps 89:4, 29. See further the discussion in ch. 6 on Rom 1:3 (pp. 241–42).

the corpus[113] where the Greek Χριστός does double duty as both name and title.

With that, Paul then returns to his own suffering for the sake of the gospel, "the message that comes from God." And because it is God's thing, Paul gladly endures present suffering for the sake of "the elect," who are destined to obtain the salvation that has been afforded through Christ and that has "eternal glory" as it eschatological goal. But Paul's ultimate concern in this narrative is that "the elect" themselves, including Timothy, stay with the gospel to the end, which is the reason for citing the fifth and last of the "trustworthy sayings" in these letters.

The primary emphasis in the quatrain that follows is with the believer's "endurance" in the face of present pressures.[114] The options, of course, are two: faithful endurance to the end, or denial of Christ under pressure. The point of the quatrain is to reassert the eschatological results of the two options. But the whole ends up focusing on Christ even more than on the believer; and the "result" parts of lines 1 and 2 spell out the two christological emphases of the two opening narratives.

In line 1 Paul picks up on Christ as the bringer and giver of life from 1:10. In line 2 Paul picks up the messianic theme from 2:8. He whose origins are ἐκ σπέρματος Δαυίδ is the currently reigning King in heaven (cf. 1 Cor 15:25); the promise given to those who have died with him is that they will also reign with him. Not only is this motif itself demonstrably Pauline, but also the very way that this clause picks up and melds a variety of christological themes is typically Pauline.

Finally, in line 4 Christ's essential deity is once more assumed in the phrase "he remains faithful, for he cannot disown himself." Here is language that implies God's own eternal character of faithfulness to himself. As it is impossible for God as the embodiment of truth to lie, so God by definition cannot deny himself; now Christ is spoken of in language that could apply only to the Deity himself, which in turn is the presupposition behind the entire passage.

Jesus as the Κύριος of Septuagint Texts

The preceding text, with its echo of the Septuagint regarding the messianic king, leads us to turn to the use of κύριος in this letter. We begin with several texts—like the many in earlier letters—where κύριος = Yahweh in the Septuagint has been taken over by Paul and applied to Christ.[115]

---

[113] See discussion in ch. 3 on 1 Cor 1:20–25 (pp. 100–102); cf. Rom 9:5; Eph 5:5.

[114] For a discussion of a very minority position that the "saying" belongs to the section that follows, see Knight, 400–408. The position has almost nothing to commend it and everything against it.

[115] On this matter, see esp. in earlier chapters the relevant sections in 1–2 Thessalonians, 1 Corinthians, Romans, Colossians, Ephesians, and Philippians.

2 Timothy 2:7

In a somewhat enigmatic conclusion to the renewed charge in 2:1–7,
Paul concludes by urging Timothy to "think over what I say." Then by way
of encouragement he adds, "For the Lord will give you understanding in all
things." This final sentence is the first (apparent) instance of intertextuality
in this letter, where Paul seems to be echoing the Septuagint of Prov 2:6.
Thus:

2 Tim 2:7	δώσει	γάρ σοι ὁ κύριος	σύνεσιν ἐν πᾶσιν.
Prov 2:6		ὅτι κύριος δίδωσιν σοφίαν . . .	
			γνῶσις καὶ σύνεσις
2 Tim 2:7	*For* **will give** *to you* **the Lord**	**understanding** *in all things.*	
Prov 2:6	*for*	**the LORD gives** *wisdom . . .*	
		knowledge and **understanding**	

Although this might be more incidental than some of the others that
follow, it does reflect a common Pauline feature: where the apostle cites, alludes to, or echoes an OT κύριος = Yahweh text, the "Lord" for him is Jesus
Christ.[116] Thus we have yet another instance in the corpus where a divine
action attributed to God in the OT has for Paul now become the prerogative
of Christ as well.

2 Timothy 2:19

ὁ μέντοι στερεὸς θεμέλιος τοῦ θεοῦ ἔστηκεν, ἔχων τὴν σφραγῖδα ταύτην·
ἔγνω κύριος τοὺς ὄντας **αὐτοῦ**, καὶ· ἀποστήτω ἀπὸ ἀδικίας πᾶς ὁ
ὀνομάζων τὸ ὄνομα κυρίου.
Nonetheless, God's sure foundation stands, having this seal:
"The Lord knows *those who are* **his,"** *and,* "*Let everyone*
who names the name of the Lord *depart from iniquity.*"

After a second appeal for Timothy to remain loyal to Christ and the gospel and thus to Paul as Christ's apostle, Paul turns to an indictment of the
false teachers (2:14–23). The passage is full of both warning and appeal, in
which the primary perpetrators are actually named. Despite their apparent
success, however, the future, Paul affirms, lies not with them but with the
gospel. To make this point, he cites two κύριος passages from the Septuagint
and applies them to Timothy's current situation. He begins the affirmation
with temple imagery, which appears to echo the Septuagint as well. We look
at the three items in turn.

---

[116] Or at least this is so for most interpreters who speak to it at all (e.g., Bernard,
118; Marshall, 731; Quinn and Wacker, 624). Knight (396) thinks otherwise; Mounce
(511) is ambivalent.

1. Picking up the temple imagery from 1 Tim 3:16, Paul reassures Timothy (and the church through Timothy) that "God's sure foundation stands (firm)." The language "God's foundation" (θεμέλιος τοῦ θεοῦ) is a probable echo of Isa 28:16,[117] where "The Sovereign LORD says, 'Behold, I lay for the foundation [θεμέλιος] of Zion a tested stone, a costly cornerstone, a sure foundation [θεμέλιος]; the one who relies on it/him will not be dismayed.'" Part of the reason for thinking so is that Paul makes a considerable christological point of this text in Rom 9:33. In the present usage it seems most likely that "foundation" stands as a synechdoche for the temple, which in turn is a Pauline metaphor for the church,[118] the people of God.

The metaphor is intended to reassure Timothy that the church belongs to God; after all, it bears God's own "seal" (= mark of ownership). The "seal" in turn takes the form of the two "citations" that follow, the first one putting the emphasis on God and the second one on his people's necessary response. The christological import of the passage picks up at this point, since the divine side of the affirmation is now predicated on "the Lord" (κύριος) = Christ Jesus.

2. In emphasizing God's role in securing a people for his name, Paul cites Num 16:5 with his own christological modification, "the Lord knows those who are his." Thus:

2 Tim 2:19	ἔγνω κύριος[119]	τοὺς ὄντας αὐτοῦ
Num 16:5	ἔγνω ὁ θεὸς	τοὺς ὄντας αὐτοῦ

Here is a case of citation where the context of the OT passage is also in view: the Korah rebellion against Moses and Aaron in the desert is being replicated by the false teachers in Ephesus. It is also a case where the Septuagint has two important differences from the Hebrew text. The Hebrew has "in the morning *the* LORD [= Yahweh] will *make known* those who are his." The Septuagint translator rendered the Hebrew יֵדַע slavishly as "has known" (= "knows") and used ὁ θεός rather than the usual anarthrous κύριος for the Divine Name.[120]

---

[117] This view goes back at least to Bertil Gärtner, *The Temple and the Community in Qumran and the New Testament* (SNTSMS 1; Cambridge: Cambridge University Press, 1965), 71. Cf. Marshall, 755; and esp. Towner, 534–35.

[118] That is, the "foundation" functions as a part representing the whole, whereas "temple" as a metaphor for the church occurs several times in Paul's letters (1 Cor 3:16–17; 2 Cor 6:16; Eph 2:20).

[119] Two otherwise excellent MSS (א 1739) read θεός here, thus conforming Paul to the Septuagint that he is citing.

[120] This assumes, of course, that the translator was using a Hebrew text that looked like the MT; if in fact he was using a different Hebrew text, then Paul himself is not responsible for the differences. My point remains even if he is merely citing, which is the much less likely option in any case.

Paul's citation has its own significant christological twist. While keeping both the sense and word order of the Septuagint, he has at the same time re-introduced κύριος into the text. In doing so, he thus created a passage in which Christ the Lord is once more to be identified with Yahweh of the OT text.[121] Some would object to this, suggesting instead that Paul has intended "God" by this substitution.[122] But that makes little sense either of the context or of Pauline usage—a usage that is demonstrably in effect in this letter, clearly set forth in 1:2. As elsewhere throughout the corpus, Paul uses ὁ θεός exclusively for God, while Christ is regularly understood to be the κύριος of the OT texts where it serves as a circumlocution for Yahweh.

The christological point is that the people of God are Christ's own people as well. In the context of both loyalty (Onesiphorus [1:16–18]) and disloyalty (Hymenaeus and Philetus [2:14–18]), Timothy is reassured that, just as in the Korah rebellion, the Lord (Christ) knows who are his own—the first stone in the sure foundation of his church. This understanding seems to be made further certain by the next citation.

3. This final "citation" is something of a collage of Septuagint texts; the part that most interests us is how the people of God are identified as "those who name the name of the Lord." Here Paul is reshaping Isa 26:13,[123] a text that in its Greek translation especially emphasizes that God's true people will not "name the name of another," but will "name only the name of the LORD." Thus:

---

[121] At least one would think that this would be the ordinary way to read the text, given the author's use of κύριος throughout this letter (see pp. 449–50 above); but it turns out in fact to be a distinctly minority view. It is held by Lock, 97 (apparently); Hanson, 137 (who calls it a "loose version" of the Numbers text!); Capes, *Old Testament Yahweh Texts*, 145–49. Johnson (397) allows the possibility but rejects it. Marshall (757) implies that the burden of proof rests with those who think so; but on this matter he seems to have missed Pauline usage (including the Pastoral Epistles) by a wide margin, especially when Paul cites or echoes the Septuagint (see n. 101 above). And in this case, had Paul wanted to refer to God the Father, all he had to do was to keep the Septuagint text intact! His alteration of the Septuagint text, putting "Lord" in place of "God," would seem rather conclusively to put the burden of proof on the other side.

[122] This is based on two questionable assumptions: (1) the lack of the article suggests that Paul is intending "God" as the referent; (2) "God" is the referent in the immediate context. But in regard to the first assumption, the plain fact is that Paul is not consistent in this matter, since he hardly ever adds the article to an OT intertextual echo or citation where the OT referrent is Yahweh and Paul has appropriated it to Christ (cf. n. 101 above). And in regard to the second assumption, although it is true that "God" is the most recent divine person mentioned (v. 15), it is far more likely that "Christ" is the correct reading in v. 14 (see discussion below), and thus "Christ" otherwise predominates in the preceding appeals.

[123] The phrase itself is found elsewhere (Lev 24:16[2x]; Amos 6:10), but the immediate context, in which abandoning the Lord for another and an echo of Isa 26:18 seems already to be present, suggests that the Isaiah text is in mind. Knight (416) suggests Joel 3:5 (LXX), which is most likely true of the next passage (2:22), but the present usage looks much more like the Isaiah text.

2 Tim 2:19   ἀποστήτω ἀπὸ ἀδικίας[124] **πᾶς ὁ ὀνομάζων τὸ ὄνομα κυρίου.**

Isa 26:13   κύριε, ἐκτὸς σοῦ ἄλλον οὐκ οἴδαμεν   **τὸ ὄνομά σου**
                                                       ὀνομάζομεν.

2 Tim 2:19   *Let depart from evil*   ***everyone who names the name of***
                                            the Lord.

Isa 26:13   **LORD,** *apart from you, another we do not know;*   ***your name***
                                                                    we name.

The christological significance of this moment is to be found in the deliberate emphasis on "the name of the Lord," which in the OT is a referent to Yahweh but is now transferred to Christ.[125] That this is the case,[126] again against a large majority of scholars, seems to be made certain by the next intertextual echo. Thus once more in the corpus, by this interchange of the risen Lord for κύριος = Yahweh in the OT text, Paul is asserting that the one God's identity includes the Son.

2 Timothy 2:22

At the beginning of his personal exhortation to Timothy, Paul picks up an echo of the preceding passage (2:19 above), and in so doing, he also reflects the more common way of expressing it in the OT itself.[127] Thus, in light of the defections and failures of the false teachers, Paul urges Timothy to flee youthful passions and to pursue the Christian virtues of righteousness, faith, love, and peace, along with those who, with a pure heart, "call on the name of the Lord" (τῶν ἐπικαλουμένων τὸν κύριον). This phrase, as elsewhere in the corpus, is a reflection of one of the distinguishing features of God's chosen people in the Genesis narrative (see 12:8; 13:4 [Abraham]; 26:25 [Isaac]; 33:20 LXX [Jacob]); that it refers to Christ as elsewhere in the corpus (1 Cor 1:2; Rom 10:9–13) is a given for most interpreters.[128] Given the

---

[124] The NA[27] margin includes Sir 17:26 here as an actual citation with regard to these words; but that seems especially doubtful. Sirach reads,

ἐπάναγε ἐπὶ ὕψιστον καὶ **ἀπόστρεφε ἀπὸ ἀδικίας** καὶ σφόδρα μίσησον
βδέλυγμα.
*Return to the Most High and **turn away from iniquity;** and hate intensely what
he abhors.* (NRSV)

Had the verb been the same for each author, then one could at least allow the possibility of such; but with a different verb and completely different overall context, this "citation" is problematic. Far more likely, the two passages reflect similar (basically Jewish) concerns; so that the conceptual echo is there even if Paul did not know Sirach.

[125] This was also the obvious view of the later scribes who changed it to read Χριστοῦ, the reading that made its way into the Textus Receptus and thus into the KJV.

[126] So also Fairbairn, 351–52; Hanson, 138.

[127] Or at least that is what both usage and context should cause one to think (so also Lock, 100).

[128] So Bernard, 126 ("of course"); Lock, 101; Scott, 114; Kelly, 189; Spicq 2:763; Hanson, 141; and even in this case Knight, 422.

predominance of κύριος as the denominator for Christ, this usage is also to be understood as fully in keeping with Paul's use of this language for believers in Christ in the earlier corpus.[129]

2 Timothy 2:24

Following the exhortation of v. 21, that Timothy should avoid foolish arguments because they only produce quarrels, Paul offers by way of explanation that "the servant of the Lord" must not quarrel. In so doing, and in contrast to what occurs in the earlier corpus where it is always "the servant of Christ," he here uses the title given to Moses and Joshua in the books of Joshua and Judges, δοῦλος κυρίου (*the servant of the LORD*).[130] On its own, very little could be made of this usage. But of course it is not on its own; within the Pauline corpus this is simply another of many such OT Yahweh phrases that became κύριος in the Septuagint and have been appropriated by Paul with Christ as the referent.[131] The fact that the phrase is anarthrous and stands first in the sentence only adds to the certainty of what Paul is suggesting to Timothy. He is now "the servant of the Lord" who must bear this epithet as one fully aware of the Lord's own character that is being urged upon him.

2 Timothy 4:14

As Paul moves toward the end of the letter (4:8–22),[132] there is a sudden increase in the appearance of the title κύριος, mostly in the form of appeal or affirmation regarding the future. In each case, "the Lord" is to be understood as Christ Jesus, since in the first of these (v. 8) the sentence ends with the phrase "who love his (= the Lord's) appearing." In several of these, beginning with v. 14, there are clear echoes of Septuagint passages, in ways reminiscent of what Paul does throughout the corpus. This first one is in response to the evil done him by Alexander the metalworker. While Timothy is warned to be watching for Alexander when he (Timothy) comes to Troas, Paul also assures him, in the language of two different Septuagint texts, that "the Lord will repay him [Alexander] according to his deeds."[133] Thus:

---

[129] See esp. the discussion in ch. 3 of 1 Cor 1:2 (pp. 127–29).

[130] See Josh 7:14 (B text); 24:29; Judg 2:8. Some (e.g., Kelly) see the Suffering Servant of Isa 53 here; but in fact this phrase occurs neither in that passage nor in the whole of Isa 40–55. Dibelius and Conzelmann make the strange comment that " 'servant of the Lord' is reminiscent of 'man of God' in the parallel passages (1 Tim 6:11; cf. 2 Tim 3:17)" (113); this seems unrelated to actual usage.

[131] On this matter, see esp. discussion in ch. 2 (pp. 41–45, 57–69) and ch. 3 (pp. 120–34).

[132] See also p. 469 below.

[133] In Rom 2:6 Paul also cites this OT language with reference to God's "righteous judgment" on the wicked. See the note on this passage in the TNIV.

2 Tim 4:14	ἀποδώσει	αὐτῷ	ὁ κύριος	
			κατὰ τὰ ἔργα αὐτοῦ·	
Ps 61:13 LXX	κύριε, . . . σὺ	ἀποδώσεις	ἑκάστῳ	κατὰ τὰ ἔργα αὐτοῦ.
Prov 24:12	κύριος . . .	ὃς ἀποδίδωσιν	ἑκάστῳ	κατὰ τὰ ἔργα αὐτοῦ.

2 Tim 4:14	*will repay*	*him*	*the Lord*	
			according to his deeds.	
Ps 61:13 LXX	*LORD,* . . . *you*	*will repay*	*each one*	*according to (his) deeds.*
Prov 24:12	*The LORD* . . .	*who will repay*	*each one*	*according to (his) deeds.*

In so doing, Paul also echoes his own affirmation in v. 8 regarding the "crown of righteousness" that "the Lord will 'repay' me on that day." This internal echo is the certain evidence that ὁ κύριος in this second passage refers to Christ as well.[134] As is pointed out further in the discussion of 4:1, 8, 14 below, this is a clear instance where Christ the Lord shares fully in a divine prerogative that in biblical thought belongs to God alone.

2 Timothy 4:16–18

The letter body now ends with a final word of explanation about Paul's situation before the empire/emperor. He does so with a considerable play on and echo of Ps 22 (21 LXX), a passage that became front and center for early Christian understanding of the *Davidic* character of their Suffering Servant messiah. The Gospel tradition indicates that this understanding of Jesus' sufferings goes back to the Savior himself.[135] The present passage picks up echoes of this psalm in several ways.

Verse 16

| 2 Tim 4:16 | ἀλλὰ πάντες | με ἐγκατέλιπον· |
| Ps 21:2 LXX | ἵνα τί | ἐγκατέλιπές με; |

| 2 Tim 4:16 | *But all* | *me have abandoned.* |
| Ps 21:2 | *Why* | *have you abandoned me?* |

Paul begins the recital of his "first trial" (apparently a kind of grand jury investigation) by noting that "everyone has abandoned me." Here he seems to be echoing the language of Ps 22:2, thus also echoing the cry of his Lord when he was being executed by the empire. While this language is

---

[134] So also Knight, 468; Mounce, 593; Quinn and Wacker, 813. Marshall (822) allows for either, but that seems to miss the echo of v. 8 by too much. Otherwise Kelly, 280; Spicq, 2:817; Lea, 255.

[135] See esp. the word from the cross, which the Gospel tradition kept in its Aramaic original, ελωι ελωι λεμα σαβαχθανι (*My God, my God, why have you forsaken me?*) (Mark 15:34, citing Ps 22:2).

"symbolic of the cruciform path walked by the Messiah,"[136] for Paul, the abandonment itself takes a quite different turn. It was by believers of whom Paul apparently expected better things and therefore was not by God. Indeed, it was quite the opposite: "The Lord stood by me and empowered me."

With these last words Paul steps out of the context of Ps 22 momentarily and picks up familiar language from the Yahweh epiphany before Moses on Mount Sinai.

Verse 17 (cf. 2 Tim 3:11)

2 Tim 4:17	ὁ δὲ	**κύριός** μοι	**παρέστη** . . .
Exod 34:5	καὶ κατέβη	**κύριος** . . . καὶ	**παρέστη** αυτῷ ἐκεῖ·

2 Tim 4:17	*But*	***the Lord*** *me*	***stood beside*** . . .
Exod 34:5	*And came down*	***the LORD*** . . . *and*	***stood beside*** *him there.*

One could easily discount this as an accidental allusion, but in fact this first appearance of this theme in the OT (LXX) anticipates God's presence as a recurring theme throughout the biblical story. For Paul, it is Christ's own presence with him that "empowered" him for the witness that he bore at his tribunal. As always, Septuagint language that has Yahweh as its original referent has now become the special province of Christ the Lord.[137] In the larger context of Pauline theology, the presence motif ordinarily belongs to the Spirit;[138] but here it is the presently reigning Lord himself who stood by Paul and whom Paul trusts finally to rescue him from every evil design and bring him safely to his heavenly kingdom. Almost certainly, as in 1–2 Thessalonians and Philippians, this usage stands as a direct confrontation with κύριος Caesar. The "Lord Caesar" is the lion in the next clause, while the true Lord, Christ, stood by Paul in his trial.[139]

The final clause in this verse is what makes certain that the whole is a kind of Pauline "midrash" on Ps 22 (21 LXX). Referring to his divine deliverance at his first tribunal, Paul uses the "divine passive" ("I was rescued" = "he [the Lord] rescued me") to refer to his "deliverance" in the precise language of Ps 21:21–22 LXX:

2 Tim 4:17	καὶ **ἐρρύσθην**	ἐκ στόματος λέοντος.
Ps 21:21–22 LXX	[21]**ῥῦσαι** . . . [22]**με**	ἐκ στόματος λέοντος

2 Tim 4:17	*And* **I was rescued**	*from the mouth of the lion.*
Ps 21:21–22 LXX	[21]*to* **rescue** [22]*me*	*from the mouth of the lion*

---

[136] The language is borrowed from Towner, 639.
[137] So most commentators; otherwise Scott; Kelly.
[138] See Fee, *Paul, the Spirit and the People of God,* 9–23.
[139] See further, Young, *Theology,* 64–65.

Whatever "David" may have had in mind by "the lion," one can scarcely miss the very direct allusion to Nero himself in this bit of intertextuality. What was for the psalmist a prayer for deliverance becomes for Paul an affirmation of what Christ did for him in the very recent past. That the "divine passive" is an indirect reference to Christ as Lord seems to be made certain by two factors. First, this very language has already been used of Christ in 3:11, "but the Lord [ὁ κύριος] delivered me from them all," which all recognize as a direct reference to Christ. Second, the affirmation that follows in v. 18, which places a similar rescue in the future, still carries overtones from the larger context of Ps 22.

Verse 18a

In a case of striking asyndeton,[140] Paul repeats the verb for "rescue" from Ps 21:21 LXX, used above in the past tense, and affirms his strongest expectations about the future.

ῥύσεταί με ὁ κύριος ἀπὸ παντὸς ἔργου πονηροῦ καὶ **σώσει εἰς τὴν βασιλείαν αὐτοῦ τὴν ἐπουράνιον·**

The Lord will rescue me from every evil work and will save me in his heavenly kingdom.

Although some are prepared to argue that the author is now using "the Lord" to refer to God,[141] there are three pieces of combined evidence that point very strongly in the other direction. First, there is no certain evidence in this letter, or in the corpus as a whole, that Paul on his own ever uses ὁ κύριος to refer to God.[142] And in fact, all the evidence, including that of this letter—put forth in the salutation (1:2) and carrying forward throughout—argues for a reference to Christ.

Second, "the Lord" in this sentence can only refer to the same "Lord" who in v. 17 is said to have stood "by me." There is no analogy of any kind in Paul's writings or the rest of the NT that such language is ever used of God. In the "geography" of the NT writers, and especially of Paul, God the Father

---

[140]Despite Elliott (*Greek Text*, 210) to the contrary, whose form of "rigorous eclecticism" has a notable anti-Nestle-Aland bent, it is nearly impossible to account for an "omission" of a καί by early scribes, as though under Attic influence. On the other hand, the asyndeton is so harsh that one can easily account for the addition (and καί precisely for the reasons Elliott rejects it; it reflects the "Semitic" flavoring of the Septuagint echo). The original is read by all the earliest (and the best of the later) Greek evidence (א A C D* 6 33 81 104 1175 1739 1881 *pc*) as well as the Latin.

[141]See, e.g., Kelly, 280; but this is a decidedly minority position, contra Bernard, 141; Spicq, 2:821; Hanson, 162; Lea, 257; Knight, 473; Marshall, 826; Quinn and Wacker, 829; Mounce, 598.

[142]On the exceptions, where κύριος belongs to the citation with no point of identity being made, see n. 7 in ch. 3.

and Christ the Son are "in heaven," while the Spirit continues the work of Christ on earth.[143] For Paul, the earthly work of Christ and the Spirit can sometimes be expressed interchangeably,[144] but not so with God the Father, who is always viewed as in heaven.

Third, and for the present context decisively, the final clause ("he will save me into his heavenly kingdom") reflects a Pauline view that the risen Lord is currently reigning on high, which in this letter has already been alluded to in 2:12 and asserted in 4:1. For Paul, to be "absent from the body" is to be "present with the Lord" (2 Cor 5:8). It is into *Christ's* kingly reign that the apostle expects to enter when his present ordeal is played out to the end. Those who think otherwise[145] are for the most part influenced by the doxology that follows, which has "the Lord" of this preceding sentence as its antecedent. So to that text we must now turn.

Verse 18b

ᾧ ἡ δόξα εἰς τοὺς αἰῶνας τῶν αἰώνων, ἀμήν.

to whom be the glory forever and ever, Amen.

At issue here is the antecedent of the relative pronoun ᾧ (*to whom*). There are basically two options.

1. Many think that "the author" has lost track of himself and at some point has shifted the referent "the Lord" from Christ to God the Father. But as the discussion above would suggest, this is to do exegesis in reverse by letting a prior fixed opinion about doxologies dictate how one should read the κύριος that precedes it.

A slight modification of this option would be to allow that the doxology is a fixed phrase, so that the relative pronoun does not need a specific grammatical antecedent. The analogy would be the usage in 1 Tim 3:16, where the assumed (but unexpressed) antedecent of the ὅς is "he who = Christ." In the same way, God is here to be understood as the assumed antecedent. "To whom" thus means "to him = God."

---

[143]For Paul, see esp. Rom 8:26–34, where within the space of a very few short sentences he can refer to the Spirit as "interceding" for us from within our hearts (v. 27) and the exalted Christ "interceding" for us at "the right hand" of the Father. This same "geography" explains why the Spirit is never pictured as in heaven in the book of Revelation; he is symbolically present as "the seven eyes of the Lamb" and the sevenfold candelabra, but John explicitly says that the sevenfold Spirit (echoing Isa 11:2; Zech 4:1–10) has been "sent out into all the earth" (Rev 5:6).

[144]As in v. 17 above; cf. esp. Rom 8:9–10.

[145]See, e.g., Scott, 142–43; Kelly, 220. Hanson's prejudice against this author emerges in his insisting that this kingdom is only future in the Pastoral Epistles and thus here, vis-à-vis Paul (see 161–62). That misses the point of the affirmation by too much, since it is a reflection on Paul's view that to be absent from the body is to be present with the Lord.

2. The second option is simply to take the text as it comes to us and to allow that in this one instance[146] Paul offers such praise to Christ the Lord precisely because he is the presently reigning King on high.

In the end, option 2 seems to be the better choice, for two reasons. First, it does not require an interpretation "to get around the obvious." Such exegesis should always give us reason to pause. The fact is, second, that the only thing that stands against its referring to the preceding "Lord = Jesus Christ" is Pauline usage elsewhere. But why should this feature become fixed in a way that others are not? A Paul who prays to Christ as to God and who regularly offers benedictions in the name of the Lord,[147] which would ordinarily belong to God, would also seem capable of praising his Lord in form and language that would otherwise belong exclusively to God the Father.

If this is the correct understanding, then this is yet another moment of especially high Christology in the Pauline corpus. Whether it is also by Paul himself resides finally with one's view of authorship. Both the subtlety and consistency of the Pauline nature of the above discussion perhaps should cause some to rethink that issue. One might have good reason to pause as to whether it is a reasonable historical option for a pseudepigrapher to have entered into Paul's skin so thoroughly as to bring off these many moments of thoroughly Pauline citation and intertextuality.

Jesus ὁ Κύριος and the Divine Prerogatives

Finally, as with the preceding corpus, this brief letter also offers a variety of moments in which the author refers to Christ as ὁ κύριος in ways that presuppose deity—places where Christ assumes what in Jewish monotheism are exclusively divine prerogatives. One of these, of course, is the standard salutation in 1:2, where "grace, mercy, and peace" are assumed to come simultaneously from God the Father and Christ Jesus, the Lord.[148] But in this letter there are several instances where Christ alone is either the object of prayer and doxology or the grammatical subject of activities that are elsewhere regularly attributed to God. The ease with which this interchange has been made reflects a thoroughly Pauline way of doing things and, as with the church corpus, presupposes a considerably developed christological perspective.

---

[146] Although many would see Rom 9:5 as a Pauline antecedent; see pp. 272–77 above.

[147] Indeed, the present letter ends precisely this way. See the discussion of 4:22 below (p. 466).

[148] For the significance of this phenomenon, see the discussion in ch. 2 on its first occurrence, in 1 Thess 1:1 (pp. 48–50).

Jesus the Lord as the Object of Prayer and Doxology

In keeping with the entire corpus, Jesus "the Lord" appears in this letter as the object of prayer and doxology. The probability that this is the case with the doxology in 4:18b has been discussed above. Here we look at two other such texts where Christ is the κύριος to whom prayer is addressed.

2 Timothy 1:16, 18

Between Paul's two opening appeals to Timothy to remain loyal to Christ and the gospel and therefore also to Paul (1:6–14; 2:1–13), he presents two examples, one of disloyalty (Phygelus and Hermogenes [v. 15]) and the other of loyalty (Onesiphorus [vv. 16–18]). Our interest lies with the latter, where Paul twice offers prayer on his behalf, first for his household (v. 16) and second for Onesiphorus himself (v. 18).[149] In both cases the prayer is for mercy and is directed specifically to ὁ κύριος. What has been said about Christ prior to this point in the letter indicates that here "the Lord" can only be Christ. In the standard salutation in v. 2, as in most of the preceding letters, God is identified as "the Father" and Christ Jesus is "the Lord." And in the further occurrence of ὁ κύριος in v. 8, the context makes it certain that the identification established in v. 2 continues to be in place.[150]

Therefore, only the presupposition that prayer should be addressed only to God would ever cause one to read these next two occurrences of ὁ κύριος as referring to God the Father. To be sure, were this the only instance of prayer addressed to the Lord = Christ in the corpus, then such an assumption might hold. But that is precisely not what we have found elsewhere. Paul can offer prayer to Christ the Lord as easily as he can to God the Father;[151] after all, it is Paul himself who asserts that the exalted Son sits at the Father's right hand making intercession (Rom 8:34). Prayer to such an intercessor would be a natural phenomenon.

So we may conclude with a high level of certainty that the κύριος to whom both of these petitions are addressed is *the* Lord, Jesus Christ. More difficult, however, is the intended referent of the παρὰ κυρίου (*from the Lord*) in v. 18 ("may the Lord [Christ] grant that he will find mercy from *the Lord* on that day"). For most scholars, this redundancy is a bit too much, so it is suggested that the prayer itself is directed toward the Lord = Christ (the intercessor), while the source of mercy is the Lord = God the Father. This

---

[149] This is not the place to enter into the long debate as to whether Onesiphorus had died after he had rendered service to Paul (in Rome supposedly); see the major commentaries for a full discussion.

[150] The content of this paragraph should be enough to make the point here; the next paragraph points out that the phenomenon is thoroughly Pauline, whether our letter is directly from Paul or was written by a Paulinist.

[151] On this question, see esp. discussion in ch. 2 (pp. 51–55, 73–77).

possibility is seen to be furthered by the anarthrous use of κύριος in the prepositional phrase παρὰ κυρίου, a phrase that occurs several times in the Septuagint.[152]

Although this is the position that I opted for in my commentary, the present study has given me plenty of reason for pause. The problem is that this ploy in fact actually resolves very little, since the awkwardness remains under either circumstance: whether Paul prays "to the Lord (Jesus)" that he (Jesus) would grant Onesiphorus to find mercy "from the Lord (God the Father)" or whether he prays that the Lord Jesus would grant him to find mercy from the Lord Jesus himself. Since, in terms of awkwardness, nothing at all is gained by assuming a second "Lord" to be mentioned in the sentence and since a very similar "tautology" occurs in Gen 19:24,[153] one probably should stay with Pauline usage and assume that he created his own tautology in an attempt to reinforce the source of the mercy that he desires for his friend. The Christology, it needs to be pointed out, is high in either case, as Paul prays to Christ to grant mercy (either from himself or from the Father) on behalf of Onesiphorus.

2 Timothy 4:22

In one of the more remarkable moments in this letter, the author signs off with a double benediction—a phenomenon that does not occur in either 1 Timothy or Titus. We have already noted in the preceding chapters that a customary "grace-benediction" is found as the final word in most of the letters and that it tends to take the standard form of "the grace of our Lord [Jesus Christ] be with you (or, 'with your spirits')."[154] Only in Colossians is there no mention of Christ as the source of the "grace"; rather, it concludes simply with "grace be with you." This is the same form it takes in 1 Timothy and Titus, both times in the plural, as evidence that both letters were intended to be read in the churches.

In this final letter in the corpus, we get it both ways. "Grace" for all is the *last* word. Immediately preceding it is a "grace" to Timothy himself, but one that does not include the word "grace." Rather, it takes the form of benediction: ὁ κύριος[155] μετὰ τοῦ πνεύματός σου (*the Lord be with your spirit*). On the christological significance of this usage, which first appears in 1–2 Thessalonians, see discussion in ch. 2 (pp. 52–53).

---

[152]E.g., Ps 24:5; 27:4; 37:23; 118:23 (LXX: 23:5; 26:4; 36:23; 117:23).

[153]Καὶ **κύριος** ἔβρεξεν ἐπὶ Σοδομα καὶ Γομορρα θεῖον καὶ πῦρ **παρὰ κυρίου** ἐκ τοῦ οὐρανοῦ (*and the LORD rained down on Sodom and Gomorrah sulphur and fire from the LORD from heaven*).

[154]It is elaborated in 2 Corinthians into the well-known Trinitarian formulation; in Ephesians, a much more elaborate formulation occurs that in the end fails to take the form of an actual benediction.

[155]Scribes, who know well the way this is "supposed" to appear, have variously added either Ἰησοῦ or Ἰησοῦ Χριστοῦ.

Jesus the Lord as Heavenly King and Judge

One of the features of the earlier corpus that reappears in this letter is the latent Jewish messianism that is inherent in the concept of the risen Lord as having assumed the role of the (now heavenly) messianic king. This language emerges first in 1 Cor 15:23–24 and is found regularly, though spasmodically, throughout the rest of the corpus. No special point is ever made of Christ's kingly reign; it is simply mentioned as an assumption and thus serves as a presupposition of whatever other point Paul is trying to make. What is of special significance is that kingship is twice predicated of Christ in 2 Timothy (2:12; 4:1) by the same author who, in bursting into doxology to God the Father in 1 Tim 1:17, first calls him "the king of the ages." Thus, in the present passages kingship is a shared prerogative of Christ the Lord and God the Father.

But one element of OT kingship that is sometimes not noted in messianic discussions is that Israel's king was also understood to be Israel's primary judge.[156] Thus, the Messiah was often depicted as the bringer of divine judgment when he brought the kingdom. These two elements occur both together and separately in this letter. We take the various texts in the order of their appearance.

2 Timothy 2:12

εἰ ὑπομένομεν, καὶ **συμβασιλεύσομεν·**
εἰ ἀρνησόμεθα, **κἀκεῖνος ἀρνήσεται** ἡμᾶς·
*If we endure, we shall also reign **with him;***
*if we deny him, **he will also deny** us.*

This passage has been discussed above (pp. 453–54), where we noted, on the basis of the phrase "from the seed of David" in 2:8, that Jewish messianism lies as the unspoken presupposition behind these two lines in the quatrain. The second line above almost certainly presupposes the next item for discussion: Jesus the Lord as the heavenly judge. At the divine assize, Christ himself will pronounce his rejection of those who in earthly trials denied him.

2 Timothy 4:1

διαμαρτύρομαι ἐνώπιον <u>τοῦ θεοῦ</u> καὶ **Χριστοῦ Ἰησοῦ τοῦ μέλλοντος κρίνειν** ζῶντας καὶ νεκρούς, καὶ **τὴν ἐπιφάνειαν αὐτοῦ καὶ τὴν βασιλείαν αὐτοῦ·**
*I charge you before <u>God</u> and **Christ Jesus, who is going to judge** the living and the dead, and in view of **his appearing and his kingdom:***

---

[156] See esp. the narrative in 1 Kgs 3, where this reality is the presupposition of the entire narrative.

This is the third such charge to Timothy in the two letters that bear his name. In this case it is given to Timothy in light of Paul's expected departure from this life. The concern is that Timothy be absolutely loyal to Christ and the gospel and thus fulfill his own ministry and calling. As with the former two charges (1 Tim 5:21; 6:13), it comes in the expected standard order of God first and then Christ. But as with the twin prayer reports in 1 Thess 3:11 and 2 Thess 2:16–17, there is in this case a considerable elaboration of the second name. And a most remarkable elaboration it is indeed, but quite in keeping with statements in earlier letters.

First, one should note that the very elaboration puts all the present emphasis on Christ. Elaborations such as this occur for both God and Christ in the charge in 1 Tim 6:13; but here the focus is on Christ's "appearing,"[157] in this case as eschatological king and judge. Thus, the language of "appearing" (ἐπιφανεία) is used in this letter to refer both to Christ's incarnation (1:10) and to his final coming as eschatological king.

The theme of Christ as eschatological judge emerges first in 1 Thess 4:6; it is picked up again in 1 Cor 4:4–5; 11:32. In 2 Cor 5:10 Paul declares that all will appear before the eschatological judgment seat of Christ. Yet in Rom 14:10 this same judgment seat is said to be God's. Furthermore, in Rom 6:5–6 Paul speaks of "God's righteous judgment." In this present remarkable christological moment, Paul now refers to Christ as "the righteous judge," who will thus mete out these righteous judgments, while all are at the same time in the presence of God as well.

In the present instance, the judgment is expressed in its ultimate terms: Christ will judge both those who are alive at his coming and the dead, who will be raised to be judged as well. At the same time, this final judgment is placed in the context of Christ's eschatological appearing. As such, it anticipates the two expressions of judgment that follow: positively, with regard to Paul himself in v. 8; negatively, with regard to Alexander in v. 14.

At the same time, the eschatological appearing will usher in the final kingdom, the ultimate fulfillment of Jewish messianic hopes. This charge, therefore, picks up the theme of Christ's reign from 2:12 and spells it out in a very straightforward way. Likewise, it anticipates the two instances noted above where Paul assures Timothy (and the church) that Christ's judgment will be just.

2 Timothy 4:8

λοιπὸν ἀπόκειταί μοι ὁ τῆς δικαιοσύνης στέφανος, ὃν **ἀποδώσει μοι ὁ κύριος** ἐν ἐκείνῃ τῇ ἡμέρᾳ, **ὁ δίκαιος κριτής**, οὐ μόνον δὲ ἐμοὶ ἀλλὰ καὶ πᾶσι τοῖς ἠγαπηκόσι **τὴν ἐπιφάνειαν αὐτοῦ**.

*Finally, there is kept in reserve for me the crown of righteousness, which **the Lord, the righteous judge, will award** to me on that day, and not only to me but also to all those who love **his appearing**.*

---

[157] See the discussion above on 1 Tim 3:16 (esp. n. 52); 6:13; Titus 2:13.

With these words, Paul brings closure to the final charge to Timothy, a charge that began in 3:10 but picked up speed at 4:1. In effect, it serves as a kind of inclusio with 4:1, as Paul returns to the theme of Christ the judge, whose judgment will occur at his appearing. The present passage serves as Paul's final testimony regarding his own faithfulness and thus the expected outcome of his "judgment." At the same time, it also seems likely intended to serve as a paradigm for Timothy to strive toward.

Paul assures Timothy (and the church) that their Lord, Jesus Christ, who will judge the living and the dead at his coming, will ἀποδώσει (*repay*) Paul with the victor's wreath as a display of the righteousness of "the righteous judge." This unusual verb hardly moves in the direction of "works righteousness"; rather, it seems to be used here in anticipation of v. 14. Thus Paul here looks forward to the "just reward" that Christ will "repay" to those who have faithfully followed him.

2 Timothy 4:14

ἀποδώσει αὐτῷ **ὁ κύριος** κατὰ τὰ ἔργα αὐτοῦ.
The Lord *will repay him according to his deeds.*

We have already noted this passage under Paul's use of the Septuagint's ὁ κύριος as referring to Christ. I bring it forward here simply to note how it rounds out the "Christ as judge" passages that began in v. 1. It thus brings closure to Christ's judging the living and the dead at his appearing. Whereas Paul, and those who follow him as he has followed Christ, may expect "a crown of righteousness," the opposite will be reserved for those whose deeds, like Alexander's, have been evil; they will be paid back in keeping with their own misdeeds.

The christological point in all of this is that eschatological judgment, which by all biblical measure is the special province of God alone, is now seen as transferred to Christ, "the righteous judge."[158] One can scarcely get around the implied high Christology, as the risen Christ assumes the role of divine eschatological judgment.

Giving a Charge in the Presence of the Lord (2 Tim 2:14)

Although this passage is very closely related to those noted above where Paul charges Timothy "before God and the Lord" (1 Tim 5:21; 6:13; 2 Tim 4:1), it is slightly different from those in two significant ways. First, in this case, Timothy is now being told to "warn God's people before [the Deity]" to stop getting involved in controversies over words. Second, this is the only instance in these letters where there is only one divine person in whose

---

[158] One is a bit surprised by the ambivalence of Marshall here (822), who suggests that "the Lord" in this instance may be either "Christ or God"—especially so when he is quite definite about the usage in both 4:8 and 4:17–18.

presence the people are to be warned. Our difficulty here is compounded by the fact that there is a considerable textual variation with regard to which divine person is mentioned. So first some words are needed about the textual matter as such.

The textual evidence in this case is generally evenly divided between the reading θεοῦ (*God*) and κυρίου (*the Lord*), with a few late manuscripts reading Χριστοῦ (*Christ*). Whereas the "majority of the committee" of the UBS/NA editors chose to go with "God,"[159] there are good reasons to think otherwise in this case. First, then, the textual evidence itself:

θεοῦ   ℵ C F G I 614 629 630 1175 2495 *al* a vg[mss] sy[hmg] sa[mss] bo[pt]
κυρίου   A D K Ψ 048 𝔐 b vg sy sa[ms] bo[pt]
Χριστοῦ   206 429 1758 1799

Since the early and better evidence is fairly evenly divided, the issue here must be decided on internal grounds. Both the UBS/NA committee and Elliott have chosen to go with so-called intrinsic probability, having to do with what the author is deemed most likely to have written. In this case, that was determined by "the author's usage elsewhere."[160] But in making textual choices, this is easily the most subjective of the criteria and is therefore usually considered to be the third step in the process. It is an especially doubtful criterion in this case, since the only other examples of this idiom in the Pastoral Epistles have both τοῦ θεοῦ καὶ Χριστοῦ Ἰησοῦ (*God and Christ Jesus*) as the witnesses to the charge (1 Tim 5:21; 6:13; 2 Tim 4:1). The fact that God is always mentioned first has obviously tilted the scales here; but one wonders how that is significant in the present case, where only one of the divine persons is being called upon as witness, especially since this author can fluctuate between God and Christ in other significant roles (king, judge).

That leads us, then, to the criterion that would seem to be the more decisive in this case, so-called extrinsic probability, having to do with which of these two options is most likely the result of a *scribal* error—for example, the scribe's seeing one thing in his text and either accidentally or deliberately changing it to the other. And here is a case where the criterion "the more difficult reading is to be preferred as the original" should rule the day, since the error came from scribal activity, not from the author, and scribes are well known to have changed texts, either deliberately or by accident, toward conformity or familiarity.

---

[159] See Metzger, *Textual Commentary*, 579; it is also adopted (with hesitation, to be sure) by Elliott, *Greek Text*, 136–37; so also Knight, 410 (who suggests that in either case it means "God"!); Marshall, 744; Mounce, 522 (whose comment that "God" appears in 4:1 and 1 Tim 5:21 should perhaps have led to the opposite conclusion [see the discussion below]); Johnson, 383.

[160] Cf. Bernard, 115; indeed, Johnson (384) frankly admits that this is "the easier reading," which by all ordinary rules of textual criticism should have led to the opposite conclusion.

This criterion is certainly not foolproof,[161] but here is a case where the change from an original θεοῦ to κυρίου seems highly unlikely except by sheer accident while the other can be easily accounted for, for two reasons: first, because of familiarity and conformity to how the other three instances begin; second, and more importantly, if "God" were in the scribe's own text, it is difficult to imagine why in this context he would have changed it to "the Lord." That is, the title "the Lord" does not occur in the immediate context,[162] and since there is basically no christological advantage to be gained, Christian scribes would simply never have been bothered by the appearance of "God" at this point in the text so as to feel the need to change it. Whereas one can give several reasons for why they might have changed the unexpected appearance of "Lord" at this point in the letter: it conforms to usage elsewhere; it conforms to the sentence that immediately follows; it would be the more expected way of stating an oath.

If this reasoning is correct regarding the textual issue, then a christological point can in fact be made from this distance: the appearance of "the Lord" at this point would be quite in keeping with the christological emphases of this letter. The same Lord who is to judge the living and the dead is the Lord before whom Timothy is to charge the community to avoid wars over words. And if this is the correct understanding of the original text and its nuance, then this is but one more unrehearsed moment in which Paul's high Christology emerges in passing.

Christ the Lord as Source and Sustainer

I conclude the analysis of the Christology of this letter by simply noting a series of texts that on their own would hardly lead one to a view of Christ as divine. But they are not on their own; and together they attribute to Christ activities that ordinarily would be thought of as belonging more strictly to the province of God. As such, therefore, they add further to the awareness that Paul thinks of Christ as divine in ways that are not necessarily consciously brought forward but that nonetheless are basic to his assumed worldview. I present these texts here with little comment, since they tend to speak for themselves, except to note that they, while perhaps not significant in themselves, add to the total picture that indicates Paul's presupposition of the divine identity of Christ.

2 Timothy 1:1—"Apostle of Christ Jesus"

Although this phrase does not imply deity, it does imply that the one who commissioned Paul is the presently reigning Lord, Jesus Christ. See discussion in ch. 3 on 1 Cor 1:17; 1:1 (p. 136).

_____

[161] Especially in this case, since the text that was being copied would have been abbreviated (θ̅υ̅ or κ̅υ̅).

[162] The most recent mention is v. 7. What precedes, of course, is all about Christ but without the title "the Lord."

2 Timothy 1:1—"Promise of Life in Christ Jesus"

With this unusual phrase, Paul here (typically) anticipates some matters that are to come in the letter. From the outset it has a very decidedly future orientation to it. This phrase is perhaps primarily shorthand for the larger soteriological reality that Christ has "brought life and immortality to light through the gospel" (1:10), but also it is the case that here Paul implies that this life "resides in Christ Jesus" in a way that is characteristic only of God.

2 Timothy 1:12—"The One Trusted and the Guardian of the Present Deposit"

There is some measure of debate as to the implied antecedent of "the one I have trusted."[163] While it is true that God is the "one who has saved us" (v. 9), it is equally true that the entire passage (vv. 9–10) climaxes with emphasis on the saving work of "our Savior Christ Jesus." This nearer context seems more likely still to be in Paul's mind than the more distant reference to God the Father. In any case, the very debate can take place because all recognize that what Paul affirms here could be said of either God or Christ, which is why some simply refuse to come down on one side or the other.

2 Timothy 2:1—"Grace in Christ Jesus"

As with the preceding item, God's own quality of "grace" is asserted to reside in Christ Jesus, and it is in this grace that Timothy is urged to take his stand and be strong.

Conclusion

As before, conclusions have been drawn throughout this chapter. What needs to be drawn together at the end is the concern with which the chapter began: the Christology of these letters is very much in keeping with what has emerged in the letters to churches that have preceded. Although none of this on its own will determine how scholars come down on the matter of authorship, it needs to be underlined here that *nothing in these letters appears to be either more or less christologically aware than what appears in the earlier corpus.* On the one hand, if these really are letters written at a later time by another hand, one might have expected a more measured and heightened christological emphasis; but that is simply not the case. On the other hand, what does emerge is a Christology so like the earlier letters, and often so sub-

---

[163]Those who argue for "God" think that the context requires it; so Knight, 379; Johnson, 351; Mounce, 487. Marshall (710) leans toward "Christ" but is ambivalent.

tle and unrehearsed, that one could use these findings to argue rather strongly for Pauline authorship (as their ultimate source, whoever may have done the actually writing for him).

Any careful reading of this chapter makes clear that I come down on the latter side of things. When I began this study, I was quite ready in the "synthesis" chapters that follow to leave these letters to one side, but the evidence did not seem to lead me to go that route. Therefore, in the following chapters I will include this material as part of the evidence for "Pauline Christology," since, even if Paul did not write the letters, they are so thoroughly in line with what one meets elsewhere, it would seem to be mere prejudice alone that would exclude them.

On the other hand, neither am I comfortable in making a specific christological point based on the evidence of these letters alone. So their evidence will be part of the bigger picture, but that picture hopefully will not be distorted in one way or the other by anything found only in one of these letters.

Appendix I: The Texts

(double brackets [[ ]] indicate texts with references to God alone)

1 Timothy

1:1–2 ¹Παῦλος ἀπόστολος **Χριστοῦ Ἰησοῦ** <u>κατ᾽ ἐπιταγὴν θεοῦ σωτῆρος ἡμῶν</u> καὶ **Χριστοῦ Ἰησοῦ τῆς ἐλπίδος ἡμῶν** ²Τιμοθέῳ γνησίῳ τέκνῳ ἐν πίστει, χάρις ἔλεος εἰρήνη <u>ἀπὸ θεοῦ πατρὸς</u> καὶ **Χριστοῦ Ἰησοῦ τοῦ κυρίου ἡμῶν**.

[[1:4 . . . αἵτινες ἐκζητήσεις παρέχουσιν μᾶλλον ἢ <u>οἰκονομίαν θεοῦ</u> τὴν ἐν πίστει.]]

1:11 κατὰ τὸ εὐαγγέλιον τῆς δόξης <u>τοῦ μακαρίου θεοῦ</u>, ὃ ἐπιστεύθην ἐγώ.

1:12–17 ¹²Χάριν ἔχω **τῷ ἐνδυναμώσαντί με Χριστῷ Ἰησοῦ τῷ κυρίῳ ἡμῶν**, ὅτι πιστόν με **ἡγήσατο θέμενος** εἰς διακονίαν ¹³τὸ πρότερον ὄντα βλάσφημον καὶ διώκτην καὶ ὑβριστήν, ἀλλὰ ἠλεήθην, ὅτι ἀγνοῶν ἐποίησα ἐν ἀπιστίᾳ· ¹⁴ὑπερεπλεόνασεν δὲ **ἡ χάρις τοῦ κυρίου ἡμῶν** μετὰ πίστεως καὶ ἀγάπης **τῆς ἐν Χριστῷ Ἰησοῦ**. ¹⁵πιστὸς ὁ λόγος καὶ πάσης ἀποδοχῆς ἄξιος, ὅτι **Χριστὸς Ἰησοῦς ἦλθεν** εἰς τὸν κόσμον ἁμαρτωλοὺς σῶσαι, ὧν πρῶτός εἰμι ἐγώ. ¹⁶ἀλλὰ διὰ τοῦτο ἠλεήθην, ἵνα ἐν ἐμοὶ πρώτῳ **ἐνδείξηται Χριστὸς Ἰησοῦς** τὴν ἅπασαν μακροθυμίαν πρὸς ὑποτύπωσιν τῶν μελλόντων πιστεύειν **ἐπ᾽ αὐτῷ** εἰς ζωὴν αἰώνιον. ¹⁷<u>τῷ δὲ βασιλεῖ τῶν αἰώνων, ἀφθάρτῳ ἀοράτῳ μόνῳ θεῷ</u>, τιμὴ καὶ δόξα εἰς τοὺς αἰῶνας τῶν αἰώνων, ἀμήν.

2:3–6 ³τοῦτο καλὸν καὶ ἀπόδεκτον <u>ἐνώπιον τοῦ σωτῆρος ἡμῶν θεοῦ</u>, ⁴<u>ὃς πάντας ἀνθρώπους θέλει σωθῆναι</u> καὶ εἰς ἐπίγνωσιν ἀληθείας ἐλθεῖν. ⁵<u>Εἷς</u>

γὰρ θεός, εἷς καὶ μεσίτης θεοῦ καὶ ἀνθρώπων, ἄνθρωπος Χριστὸς Ἰησοῦς, ⁶ὁ δοὺς ἑαυτὸν ἀντίλυτρον ὑπὲρ πάντων, τὸ μαρτύριον καιροῖς ἰδίοις.

2:7 ἀλήθειαν λέγω, [v.l. + ἐν Χριστῷ] οὐ ψεύδομαι,

[[3:5 εἰ δέ τις τοῦ ἰδίου οἴκου προστῆναι οὐκ οἶδεν, πῶς ἐκκλησίας θεοῦ ἐπιμελήσεται;]]

3:13 οἱ γὰρ καλῶς διακονήσαντες βαθμὸν ἑαυτοῖς καλὸν περιποιοῦνται καὶ πολλὴν παρρησίαν ἐν πίστει τῇ ἐν Χριστῷ Ἰησοῦ.

[[3:15 ἐὰν δὲ βραδύνω, ἵνα εἰδῇς πῶς δεῖ ἐν οἴκῳ θεοῦ ἀναστρέφεσθαι, ἥτις ἐστὶν ἐκκλησία θεοῦ ζῶντος, στῦλος καὶ ἑδραίωμα τῆς ἀληθείας.]]

3:16 ... ὃς ἐφανερώθη ἐν σαρκι, ἐδικαιώθη ἐν πνεύματι, ὤφθη ἀγγέλοις, ἐκηρύχθη ἐν ἔθνεσιν, ἐπιστεύθη ἐν κόσμῳ, ἀνελήμφθη ἐν δόξῃ.

[[4:3–5 ³... ἀπέχεσθαι βρωμάτων, ἃ ὁ θεὸς ἔκτισεν εἰς μετάλημψιν μετὰ εὐχαριστίας τοῖς πιστοῖς καὶ ἐπεγνωκόσι τὴν ἀλήθειαν. ⁴ὅτι πᾶν κτίσμα θεοῦ καλὸν καὶ οὐδὲν ἀπόβλητον μετὰ εὐχαριστίας λαμβανόμενον· ⁵ἁγιάζεται γὰρ διὰ λόγου θεοῦ καὶ ἐντεύξεως.]]

4:6 Ταῦτα ὑποτιθέμενος τοῖς ἀδελφοῖς καλὸς ἔσῃ διάκονος Χριστοῦ Ἰησοῦ,

[[4:10 ... ὅτι ἠλπίκαμεν ἐπὶ θεῷ ζῶντι, ὅς ἐστιν σωτὴρ πάντων ἀνθρώπων μάλιστα πιστῶν.]]

[[5:4–5 ⁴... τοῦτο γάρ ἐστιν ἀπόδεκτον ἐνώπιον τοῦ θεοῦ. ⁵ἡ δὲ ὄντως χήρα καὶ μεμονωμένη ἤλπικεν ἐπὶ θεὸν ...]]

5:11 ... ὅταν γὰρ καταστρηνιάσωσιν τοῦ Χριστοῦ, γαμεῖν θέλουσιν

5:21 Διαμαρτύρομαι ἐνώπιον τοῦ θεοῦ καὶ Χριστοῦ Ἰησοῦ καὶ τῶν ἐκλεκτῶν ἀγγέλων, ἵνα ταῦτα φυλάξῃς χωρὶς προκρίματος,

[[6:1 ... ἵνα μὴ τὸ ὄνομα τοῦ θεοῦ καὶ ἡ διδασκαλία βλασφημῆται.]]

6:3 εἴ τις ἑτεροδιδασκαλεῖ καὶ μὴ προσέρχεται ὑγιαίνουσιν λόγοις τοῖς τοῦ κυρίου ἡμῶν Ἰησοῦ Χριστοῦ καὶ τῇ κατ᾽ εὐσέβειαν διδασκαλίᾳ,

[[6:11 Σὺ δέ, ὦ ἄνθρωπε θεοῦ, ταῦτα φεῦγε·]]

6:13–16 ¹³παραγγέλω [σοι] ἐνώπιον τοῦ θεοῦ ζωογονοῦντος τὰ πάντα καὶ Χριστοῦ Ἰησοῦ τοῦ μαρτυρήσαντος ἐπὶ Ποντίου Πιλάτου τὴν καλὴν ὁμολογίαν, ¹⁴τηρῆσαί σε τὴν ἐντολὴν ἄσπιλον ἀνεπίλημπτον μέχρι τῆς ἐπιφανείας τοῦ κυρίου ἡμῶν Ἰησοῦ Χριστοῦ, ¹⁵ἣν καιροῖς ἰδίοις δείξει ὁ μακάριος καὶ μόνος δυνάστης, ὁ βαλιλεὺς τῶν βασιλευόντων καὶ κύριος τῶν κυριευόντων, ¹⁶ὁ μόνος ἔχων ἀθανασίαν, φῶς οἰκῶν ἀπρόσιτον, ὃν εἶδεν οὐδεὶς ἀνθρώπων οὐδὲ ἰδεῖν δύναται· ᾧ τιμὴ καὶ κράτος αἰώνιον, ἀμήν.

[[6:17 . . . μηδὲ ἠλπικέναι ἐπὶ πλούτου ἀδηλότητι ἀλλ᾽ <u>ἐπὶ θεῷ τῷ παρέχοντι</u> ἡμῖν πάντα πλουσίως εἰς ἀπόλαυσιν,]]

Titus

1:1–4 ¹Παῦλος δοῦλος <u>θεοῦ</u>, ἀπόστολος δὲ **Ἰησοῦ Χριστοῦ** <u>κατὰ πίστιν</u> <u>ἐκλεκτῶν θεοῦ</u> καὶ ἐπίγνωσιν ἀληθείας τῆς κατ᾽ εὐσεβείαν ²ἐπ᾽ ἐλπίδι ζωῆς αἰωνίου, ἣν <u>ἐπηγγείλατο ὁ ἀψευδὴς θεὸς</u> πρὸ χρόνων αἰωνίων, ³ἐφανέρωσεν δὲ καιροῖς ἰδίος τὸν λόγον αὐτοῦ ἐν κηρύγματι, ὃ ἐπιστεύθην ἐγὼ <u>κατ᾽</u> <u>ἐπιταγὴν τοῦ σωτῆρος ἡμῶν θεοῦ,</u> ⁴Τίτῳ γνησίῳ τέκνῳ κατὰ κοινὴν πίστιν, χάρις καὶ εἰρήνη <u>ἀπὸ θεοῦ πατρὸς</u> καὶ [v.l. + κυρίου] **Χριστοῦ Ἰησοῦ τοῦ** **σωτῆρος** ἡμῶν.

[[1:7 δεῖ γὰρ τὸν ἐπίσκοπον ἀνέγκλητον εἶναι <u>ὡς θεοῦ οἰκονόμον,</u>]]

[[1:16 <u>θεὸν ὁμολογοῦσιν εἰδέναι,</u> τοῖς δὲ ἔργοις ἀρνοῦνται,]]

[[2:5 . . . ἵνα μὴ <u>ὁ λόγος τοῦ θεοῦ</u> βλασφημῆται.]]

[[2:10 . . . ἵνα <u>τὴν διδασκαλίαν τὴν τοῦ σωτῆρος ἡμῶν θεοῦ</u> κοσμῶσιν ἐν πᾶσιν.]]

[[2:11 Ἐπεφάνη γὰρ <u>ἡ χάρις τοῦ θεοῦ</u> σωτήριος πᾶσιν ἀνθρώποις]]

2:13–14 ¹³προσδεχόμενοι τὴν μακαρίαν ἐλπίδα καὶ ἐπιφάνειαν **τῆς δόξης** <u>τοῦ μεγάλου θεοῦ καὶ σωτρὸς ἡμῶν</u> **Ἰησοῦ Χριστοῦ,** ¹⁴**ὃς ἔδωκεν ἑαυτὸν** **ὑπὲρ ἡμῶν, ἵνα λυτρώσηται** ἡμᾶς ἀπὸ πάσης ἀνομίας **καὶ καθαρίσῃ** **ἑαυτῷ** λαὸν περιούσιον, ζηλωτὴν καλῶν ἔργων.

3:4–7 ⁴ὅτε δὲ <u>ἡ χρηστότης καὶ ἡ φιλανθρωπία ἐπεφάνη τοῦ σωτῆρος ἡμῶν</u> <u>θεοῦ,</u> ⁵οὐκ ἐξ ἔργων τῷ ἐν δικαιοσύνῃ ἃ ἐποιήσαμεν ἡμεῖς ἀλλὰ κατὰ τὸ αὐτοῦ ἔλεος <u>ἔσωσεν ἡμᾶς</u> διὰ λουτροῦ παλιγγενεσίας καὶ ἀνακαινώσεως πνεύματος ἁγίου, ⁶οὗ <u>ἐξέχεεν</u> ἐφ᾽ ἡμᾶς πλουσίως **διὰ Ἰησοῦ Χριστοῦ τοῦ** **σωτῆρος ἡμῶν, ἵνα δικαιωθέντες τῇ ἐκείνου χάριτι** κληρονόμοι γενηθῶμεν κατ᾽ ἐλπίδα ζωῆς αἰωνίου.

[[3:8 . . . ἵνα φροντίζωσιν καλῶν ἔργων προΐστασθαι <u>οἱ πεπιστευκότες</u> <u>θεῷ·</u>]]

2 Timothy

1:1–2 ¹Παῦλος **ἀπόστολος Χριστοῦ Ἰησοῦ** <u>διὰ θελήματος θεοῦ</u> κατ᾽ **ἐπαγγελίαν ζωῆς ἐν Χριστῷ Ἰησοῦ** ²Τιμοθέῳ ἀγαπητῷ τέκνῳ, χάρις ἔλεος εἰρήνη <u>ἀπὸ θεοῦ πατρὸς</u> καὶ **Χριστοῦ Ἰησοῦ τοῦ κυρίου** ἡμῶν.

[[1:3 Χάριν ἔχω <u>τῷ θεῷ, ᾧ λατρεύω</u> ἀπὸ προγόνων ἐν καθαρᾷ συνειδήσει,]]

[[1:6–7 ⁶Δι᾽ ἣν αἰτίαν ἀναμιμνήσκω σε ἀναζωπυρεῖν <u>τὸ χάρισμα τοῦ θεοῦ,</u> ὅ <u>ἐστιν ἐν σοὶ</u> τῆς ἐπιθέσεως τῶν χειρῶν μου. ⁷οὐ γὰρ <u>ἔδωκεν ἡμῖν ὁ θεὸς</u> πνεῦμα δειλείας ἀλλὰ δυνάμεως καὶ ἀγάπης καὶ σωφρονισμοῦ.]]

1:8–10 ⁸μὴ οὖν ἐπαισχυνθῇς **τὸ μαρτύριον τοῦ κυρίου ἡμῶν** μηδὲ ἐμὲ τὸν δέσμιον **αὐτοῦ**, ἀλλὰ συγκακοπάθησον τῷ εὐαγγελίῳ <u>κατὰ δύναμιν θεοῦ</u>, ⁹<u>τοῦ σώσαντος</u> ἡμᾶς <u>καὶ καλέσαντος</u> κλήσει ἁγίᾳ, οὐ κατὰ τὰ ἔργα ἡμῶν ἀλλὰ κατὰ <u>ἰδίαν πρόθεσιν καὶ χάριν</u>, τὴν δοθεῖσαν ἡμῖν **ἐν Χριστῷ Ἰησοῦ πρὸ χρόνων αἰωνίων**, ¹⁰φανερωθεῖσαν δὲ νῦν **διὰ τῆς ἐπιφανείας τοῦ σωτῆρος ἡμῶν Χριστοῦ Ἰησοῦ, καταργήσαντος** μὲν τὸν θάνατον **φωτίσαντος δὲ ζωὴν καὶ ἀφθαρσίαν** διὰ τοῦ εὐαγγελίου

1:12 . . . ἀλλ᾽ οὐκ ἐπαισχύνομαι, οἶδα γὰρ **ᾧ πεπίστευκα** καὶ πέπεισμαι ὅτι **δυνατός ἐστιν** τὴν παραθήκην μου **φυλάξαι εἰς ἐκείνην τὴν ἡμέραν.**

1:13 Ὑποτύπωσιν ἔχε ὑγιαινόντων λόγων ὧν παρ᾽ ἐμοῦ ἤκουσας ἐν πίστει καὶ ἀγάπῃ **τῇ ἐν Χριστῷ Ἰησοῦ**·

1:16 **δῴη ἔλεος ὁ κύριος** τῷ Ὀνησιφόρου οἴκῳ,

1:18 **δῴη** αὐτῷ **ὁ κύριος εὑρεῖν ἔλεος παρὰ κυρίου** ἐν ἐκείνῃ τῇ ἡμέρᾳ.

2:1 Σὺ οὖν, τέκνον μου, ἐνδυναμοῦ **ἐν τῇ χάριτι τῇ ἐν Χριστῷ Ἰησοῦ**,

2:3 Συγκακοπάθησον ὡς καλὸς **στρατιώτης Χριστοῦ Ἰησοῦ.**

2:7 νόει ὃ λέγω· **δώσει γάρ σοι ὁ κύριος** σύνεσιν ἐν πᾶσιν.

2:8–13 ⁸Μνημόνευε **Ἰησοῦν Χριστὸν ἐγηγερμένον ἐκ νεκρῶν, ἐκ σπέρματος Δαυίδ**, κατὰ τὸ εὐαγγέλιόν μου ⁹ἐν ᾧ κακοπαθῶ μέχρι δεσμῶν ὡς κακοῦργος, ἀλλὰ <u>ὁ λόγος τοῦ θεοῦ οὐ δέδεται</u>· ¹⁰διὰ τοῦτο πάντα ὑπομένω διὰ τοὺς ἐκλεκτούς, ἵνα καὶ αὐτοὶ σωτηρίας τύχωσιν **τῆς ἐν Χριστῷ Ἰησοῦ μετὰ δόξης αἰωνίου.** ¹¹πιστὸς ὁ λόγος· εἰ γὰρ **συναπεθάνομεν, καὶ συζήσομεν·** ¹²εἰ ὑπομένομεν, καὶ **συμβασιλεύσομεν·** εἰ ἀρνησόμεθα, **κἀκεῖνος ἀρνήσεται** ἡμᾶς· ¹³εἰ ἀπιστοῦμεν, **ἐκεῖνος πιστὸς μένει, ἀρνήσασθαι γὰρ ἑαυτὸν οὐ δύναται.**

2:14–15 ¹⁴Ταῦτα ὑπομίμνῃσκε διαμαρτυρόμενος **ἐνώπιον τοῦ κυρίου** [v.l. <u>θεοῦ</u>] μὴ λογομαχεῖν, ἐπ᾽ οὐδὲν χρήσιμον, ἐπὶ καταστροφῇ τῶν ἀκουόντων. ¹⁵σπούδασον σεαυτὸν δόκιμον <u>παραστῆσαι τῷ θεῷ</u>, ἐργάτην ἀνεπαίσχυντον,

2:19 (LXX) ὁ μέντοι στερεὸς θεμέλιος τοῦ θεοῦ ἔστηκεν, ἔχων τὴν σφραγῖδα ταύτην· **ἔγνω κύριος** τοὺς ὄντας **αὐτοῦ**, καί· ἀποστήτω ἀπὸ ἀδικίας πᾶς ὁ **ὀνομάζων τὸ ὄνομα κυρίου.**

2:22 . . . δίωκε δὲ δικαιοσύνην πίστιν ἀγάπην εἰρήνην μετὰ **τῶν ἐπικαλουμένων τὸν κύριον** ἐκ καθαρᾶς καρδίας.

2:24 **δοῦλον δὲ κυρίου** οὐ δεῖ μάχεσθαι ἀλλὰ ἤπιον εἶναι πρὸς πάντας,

[[2:25 . . . μήποτε <u>δώῃ αὐτοῖς ὁ θεὸς</u> μετάνοιαν εἰς ἐπίγνωσιν ἀληθείας]]

3:11–12 ¹¹ . . . οἵους διωγμοὺς ὑπήνεγκα καὶ ἐκ πάντων με **ἐρρύσατο ὁ κύριος** ¹²καὶ πάντες δὲ οἱ θέλοντες **εὐσεβῶς ζῆν ἐν Χριστῷ Ἰησοῦ** διωχθήσονται.

3:15 . . . τὰ δυνάμενά σε σοφίσαι εἰς σωτηρίαν **διὰ πίστεως τῆς ἐν Χριστῷ Ἰησοῦ.**

[[3:17 ἵνα ἄρτιος ᾖ <u>ὁ τοῦ θεοῦ ἄνθρωπος</u>, πρὸς πᾶν ἔργον ἀγαθὸν ἐξηρτισμένος.]]

4:1 Διαμαρτύρομαι <u>ἐνώπιον τοῦ θεοῦ</u> καὶ **Χριστοῦ Ἰησοῦ τοῦ μέλλοντος κρίνειν** ζῶντας καὶ νεκρούς, καὶ **τὴν ἐπιφάνειαν αὐτοῦ καὶ τὴν βασιλείαν αὐτοῦ·**

4:8 λοιπὸν ἀπόκειταί μοι ὁ τῆς δικαιοσύνης στέφανος, ὃν **ἀποδώσει μοι ὁ κύριος** ἐν ἐκείνῃ τῇ ἡμέρᾳ, **ὁ δίκαιος κριτής**, οὐ μόνον δὲ ἐμοὶ ἀλλὰ καὶ πᾶσι τοῖς ἠγαπηκόσι **τὴν ἐπιφανείαν αὐτοῦ.**

4:14 . . . ἀποδώσει αὐτῷ **ὁ κύριος** κατὰ τὰ ἔργα αὐτοῦ·

4:17–18 [17]**ὁ δὲ κύριός μοι παρέστη καὶ ἐνεδυνάμωσέν με**, ἵνα δι᾿ ἐμοῦ τὸ κήρυγμα πληροφορηθῇ καὶ ἀκούσωσιν πάντα τὰ ἔθνη, καὶ ἐρρύσθην ἐκ στόματος λέοντος. [18]**ῥύσεταί με ὁ κύριος** ἀπὸ παντὸς ἔργου πονηροῦ καὶ **σώσει εἰς τὴν βασιλείαν αὐτοῦ τὴν ἐπουράνιον· ᾧ ἡ δόξα εἰς τοὺς αἰῶνας τῶν αἰώνων**, ἀμήν.

4:22 **Ὁ κύριος** μετὰ τοῦ πνεύματός σου.

Appendix II: An Analysis of Usage

(* = anarthrous; + = with possessive pronoun; [LXX] = Septuagint echo/ citation)

Pastoral Epistles
θεός   47
Christ   46

1 Timothy
θεός   23
Christ   16

Titus
θεός   13
Christ   4

2 Timothy
θεός   11
Christ   26

The Data
1. κύριος Ἰησοῦς Χριστός (2 / **0** / *0*)

1 Tim 6:3   G+
1 Tim 6:14 G+
1a. Χριστὸς Ἰησοῦς κύριος (2 / **0** / *1*)
    1 Tim 1:2   G+
    1 Tim 1:12 D+
    2 Tim 1:2   G+
2. κύριος Ἰησοῦς (0 / **0** / *0*)
3. Χριστὸς Ἰησοῦς (10 / **1** / *11*)
    1 Tim 1:1   G*
    1 Tim 1:1   G*
    1 Tim 1:14 D* (ἐν)
    1 Tim 1:15 N*
    1 Tim 1:16 N*
    1 Tim 2:5   N*
    1 Tim 3:13 D* (ἐν)
    1 Tim 4:6   G*
    1 Tim 5:21 G*
    1 Tim 6:13 G*

Titus 1:4 G* [v.l. + κυρίου]
2 Tim 1:1 G*
2 Tim 1:1 D* (ἐν)
2 Tim 1:9 D* (ἐν)
2 Tim 1:10 G* (appositive to
                        σωτήρ)
2 Tim 1:13 D* (ἐν)
2 Tim 2:1 D* (ἐν)
2 Tim 2:3 G*
2 Tim 2:10 D* (ἐν)
2 Tim 3:12 D* (ἐν)
2 Tim 3:15 D* (ἐν)
2 Tim 4:1 G* (ἐνώπιον)
3a. Ἰησοῦς Χριστός (0 / **3** / *1*)
   Titus 1:1 G*
   Titus 2:13 G* (appositive to
                        δόξα)
   Titus 3:6 G* (διά) + σωτήρ
   2 Tim 2:8 A*
4. κύριος (1 / **0** / *16*)
   1 Tim 1:14 G+
   2 Tim 1:8 G+
   2 Tim 1:16 N
   2 Tim 1:18 N
   2 Tim 1:18 G* (παρά)
   2 Tim 2:7 N
   2 Tim 2:14 G [v.l. θεοῦ]
                        (ἐνώπιον)

2 Tim 2:19 N* [LXX]
2 Tim 2:19 G* [LXX]
2 Tim 2:22 A
2 Tim 2:24 G*
2 Tim 3:11 N
2 Tim 4:8 N
2 Tim 4:14 N
2 Tim 4:17 N
2 Tim 4:18 N
2 Tim 4:22 N
5. Ἰησοῦς (0 / **0** / *0*)
6. Χριστός (1 / **0** / *0*)
   1 Tim 5:11 G
7. υἱός (0 / **0** / *0*)
8. σωτήρ [= God]
   [1 Tim 1:1 G+]
   [1 Tim 2:3 G+]
   [[1 Tim 4:10
        PredN* after ὅς]]
   [Titus 1:3 G+]
   Titus 1:4 G+
   [Titus 2:10 G+]
   [Titus 2:13 G+]
   [Titus 3:4 G+]
   Titus 3:6 G+ (διά)
   2 Tim 1:10 G+

Part II

Synthesis

11

Christ, the Divine Savior

A MAJOR DIFFICULTY IN THIS study now faces us. How does one proceed in attempting to offer a reasonable synthesis of the many disparate parts that have preceded, especially since, apart from Col 1:15–17, Christology in terms of the person of Christ is never Paul's concern per se? Indeed, if we are to keep faith with the apostle himself, the beginning point will have to be Christ as Savior,[1] since that is clearly the central feature of Pauline theology, whatever else one may be investigating. Fortunately in this case, what is central also has considerable christological implications. So Christ as (divine) Savior will be our point of departure.

But we also need to put this reality into its larger theological context, since in much of North American Christendom salvation is conceived in a much more individualistic way than Paul himself would have understood. So this chapter begins with a brief overview of what "salvation in Christ" meant for the apostle, some of which will be picked up again in ch. 14; and at the end, we examine the christological implications of Paul's thoroughly christocentric worldview, especially as it emerges in his "Christ devotion."

That leads us in turn to ch. 12, in which we examine Paul's understanding of Christ as preexistent, since it is otherwise nearly impossible to account for such Christ devotion by an avid monotheist unless his understanding of the one God now included the Son of God in the divine identity. But preexistence as God also means that the Jesus of history must be understood in terms of an incarnation; and such an understanding by Paul must be taken seriously: the divine Son of God lived a truly human life on our planet. So ch. 13 picks up the question of Christ's humanity by way of Paul's use of "Adam" and the crucial word εἰκών (*image*) from Gen 1–2, pointing out that the ultimate concern in this analogy is emphasis both on

---

[1] This is true, even though the title itself is seldom used and does not occur until toward the end of the corpus (Phil 3:20); see ch. 9, pp. 402–3.

Christ's genuine humanity and on his bearing and restoring the divine image lost in the fall.

The final two chapters will pursue the two primary christological emphases that emerge regularly in the corpus and that arguably hold the keys to Paul's answer to the question "Who is Christ?" The suggested answer: Christ is, first of all, the messianic/eternal Son of God (ch. 14); and second, Christ is the messianic, now exalted "Lord" of Ps 110:1 (ch. 15), who for Paul has come to be identified with κύριος (Lord) = Yahweh, which was how the Septuagint handled the Divine Name. Since it is this (exclusive) usage of Christ as Lord that tends to dominate Paul's understanding of Christ in his present kingly reign, this chapter will conclude with a rehearsal of the many ways that Paul refers to Christ by way of presupposition, attributing to him activities that a monotheistic Jew would attribute to God alone.

Although these various aspects need to be examined separately,[2] one must also do so with the ultimate theological question in mind: how does Paul perceive the relationship of the Son to the Father, since he never abandons—indeed, he stoutly retains—his historic monotheism? On the one hand, there are those several texts where it appears certain that Paul, by presupposition, understands Christ in terms of eternal divinity; on the other hand, and whatever else, there are not two Gods. So in the end, the larger theological question must be raised (ch. 16). But before that, this and the following chapters will try to establish from the preceding data how best to understand Paul's understanding of the person of Christ. We begin, then, with Paul's primary concern: salvation in Christ.

The Central Role of Christ in Salvation

Although I have tried carefully in this study to avoid dealing with Pauline soteriology as such, in some cases, especially as in 2 Corinthians, it is nearly impossible to do so. That is, the role of Christ is often tied directly to Paul's presupposition about the person of Christ; and one would be remiss not to point that out from time to time. It is this concern that will be picked

---

[2]What some will find missing in this overview is the role of personified Wisdom in Paul's view of Christ, especially when it comes to Christ as the mediator of creation. Since I am convinced that "her" role in Paul's Christology is itself the creation of modern scholarship, not the result of exegesis of the Pauline texts, a full discussion and thus rebuttal of this position is offered in appendix A. See also the excursuses on this matter in ch. 3 (pp. 102–5); ch. 4 (pp. 186–87); ch. 7 (pp. 317–25).

up in this chapter; to get there, I first offer some brief observations about Pauline soteriology in general.

The phrase "salvation in Christ" might well serve as the basic summing up of Paul's central concern theologically. This phrase may be unpacked as follows. First, in the discussion of 2 Thess 2:13, the first passage of its kind in the corpus, it was pointed out that Paul has a rather consistent *grammar* of salvation,[3] which takes the following triadic form: salvation is predicated on the love of God the Father, it is effected through the death and resurrection of Christ the Son, and it is made effective through the Spirit of God, who is also the Spirit of the Son. Thus, whatever language one uses for this divine triadic phenomenon, one does justice to Paul only when recognizing that human salvation is grounded in and accomplished by the Father, Son, and Holy Spirit.

Second, the ultimate *goal* of salvation is not simply the saving of individuals and fitting them for heaven, as it were, but the *creation of a people for God's name*, reconstituted by a new covenant. That is, although people in the new covenant are "saved" one by one, the goal of that salvation is to form a people who, as Israel of old, in their life together reflect the character of the God who saved them, whose character is borne by the incarnate Christ and re-created in God's people by the Spirit.

Third, the *framework* of God's "salvation in Christ" is thoroughly eschatological, meaning that Christ's death and resurrection and the gift of the Spirit mark the turning of the ages, whereby God has set in motion the new creation, in which all things eventually will be made new at the eschatological conclusion of the present age.

Fourth, the *means* of "salvation in Christ" is Christ's death on the cross and his subsequent resurrection, whereby people are "redeemed" from enslavement to self and sin, and death itself has been defeated. A careful reading of Paul's letters reveals that all of his basic theological concerns are an outworking of his fundamental confession: "Christ died for our sins, according to the Scriptures; he was buried, and he was raised" (1 Cor 15:3–4; cf. Rom 4:25, "He was delivered over to death for our sins and was raised to life for our justification"; and many others).

Although the first of these foundational propositions reflects the ultimate concern of this book, in this chapter we will pursue the second and fourth of these items, especially since the second one is seldom brought up front in discussions of Pauline soteriology and since the role of Christ is not as immediately obvious here as in the other points.

_____

[3] See ch. 2, pp. 63–65; cf. the other semicreedal soteriological passages, such as 1 Cor 6:11; 2 Cor 1:21–22; 13:13[14]; Gal 4:4–7; Rom 5:1–5; 8:3–4; 8:15–17; Eph 1:13–14; 4:4–6; Titus 3:5–7. But see also many other such texts, soteriological or otherwise: 1 Cor 1:4–7; 2:4–5; 6:19–20; 2 Cor 3:16–18; Gal 3:1–5; Rom 8:9–11; 15:16; 15:18–19; 15:30; Col 3:16; Eph 1:3; 1:17–20; 2:17–18; 2:19–22; 3:16–19; 5:18–19; Phil 1:19–20; 3:3.

The Ultimate Goal of Salvation: Re-Creation into the Divine Image

One of the serious weaknesses of much traditional Protestant theology is its proclivity toward a soteriology devoid of ecclesiology. That is, the tendency is to focus on salvation in an individualistic way that loses the "people of God" dimension of Paul's soteriology. This is due in large part to a presuppositional emphasis on discontinuity between the two covenants, with very little appreciation for the significant dimension of continuity. To be sure, discontinuity resides in the not insignificant reality that entrance into the people of God under the new covenant happens one by one through faith in Christ Jesus and the gift of the Spirit.[4] But to embrace that point of emphasis to the neglect of the equally important "people of God" dimension to Christ's saving work is to miss Paul by too much.

Paul simply cannot help himself, since both his own history in the Jewish community and his calling as apostle to the Gentiles presuppose that the goal of God's saving work in Christ is to create an end-time people for God's name out of both Jew and Gentile together. This passion finds expression especially in Galatians and Romans,[5] where the issue is not primarily justification by faith but rather Jew and Gentile together as one people of God predicated on the work of Christ and the Spirit and realized by faith. After all, the whole argument of Romans climaxes in 15:5–13, "so that with one mind and one voice you [Jew and Gentile together] may glorify the God and Father of our Lord Jesus Christ" (v. 6), which is followed by a catena of four OT passages that focus on the inclusion of Gentiles. Similarly, Galatians concludes with a repetition of his aphorism "Neither circumcision nor uncircumcision means anything; what counts is a new creation" (6:15),[6] followed by a benediction on all who follow this "rule," who are then described as *"God's Israel."*

Paul's own calling is thus expressed in keeping with this concern: "But when God, who . . . called me by his grace, was pleased to reveal his Son *in me*[7] so that I might *preach him among the Gentiles* . . ." (Gal 1:15–16; cf. Rom

---

[4] This presupposes the reality that Paul's letters all were written to first-generation adult converts, who became so through faith in Christ and the gift of the Spirit. How second-generation believers become members of the household of God is an area of huge debate and division among later Christians, which has happened in part because Paul, not to mention the rest of the NT, simply does not speak specifically to this question.

[5] It is a primary driving concern in Ephesians as well, where the emphasis is more clearly on ecclesiology rather than soteriology as such.

[6] This aphorism occurs first in 1 Cor 7:19: "Neither circumcision nor uncircumcision means anything; what counts is keeping God's commands" (!). It also occurs in Gal 5:6, where it is followed by "What counts is faith expressing itself through love."

[7] For the both inadequate and erroneous turning of Paul's locative ἐν ἐμοί into a datival "to me," see ch. 5, pp. 220–22.

15:15b–19). Luke's version goes, "I am sending you to the [Gentiles] to open their eyes and turn them from darkness to light, and from the power of Satan to God, so that they may receive forgiveness of sins and a place among those who are sanctified by faith in me" (Acts 26:17–18). Although the language is Luke's, the content is fully Pauline. Thus Paul expresses his self-understanding by echoing the language of Isaiah, who had envisioned the inclusion of Gentiles in the eschatological people of God. This inclusion, which stands at the very beginning of Isaiah (2:1–5), finds expression several times thereafter.[8] Both Paul's and Luke's versions of Paul's call echo the second of Isaiah's Servant Songs (47:1–7).[9]

This vision, in turn, takes us back to Gen 12:2–3, where God makes a covenant with Abraham that "I will make you into a great nation," whose final goal is "and all peoples on earth will be blessed through you." Israel's failure in this regard is what is picked up eschatologically in the prophetic tradition—the tradition to which Paul is thoroughly indebted.

It is not surprising, therefore, that Paul's language for the people of God, which now includes Gentiles, is simply an extension of the language of the former covenant. The most common term is "saints," which is a direct borrowing of the language of Dan 7:18, 22, which in turn is itself an echo of Exod 19:5–6.[10] Crucial for Paul's use of this term is the fact that "the saints" included "all nations and peoples of every language" (Dan 7:14). The same sense of continuity is found in his usage of ἐκκλησία (assembly), which of course also has the advantage of being a term well known in the Greek world. But Paul's usage is determined by its appearance in the Septuagint as a translation of קהל, when referring to the "congregation" of Israel.

The same is true of his use of "election" and "new covenant" language.[11] Equally telling is Paul's use of "temple" imagery for the people of God in a given location (1 Cor 3:16–17; 2 Cor 6:16; Eph 2:20), which picks up the crucial "presence of God" motif from the OT and which in Eph 2:20–22 is explicitly applied to the reality of Jew and Gentile as one people of God.

This concern with the people of God is also found in other ways in Paul's thinking. It is of more than passing interest that most of his letters to

---

[8] See 11:10 (cited as the fourth and final passage in the catena of Rom 15:9–12); 42:6; 49:6. Since these latter two appear in the Servant Songs, it is not surprising that Paul sees Isa 54:1 (at the conclusion of the final Servant Song) as fulfilled by Gentile inclusion (Gal 4:27); cf. similarly his use of Isa 65:1 in Rom 10:20, and of Hos 2:20 and 1:10 in Rom 9:25–26. Gentile inclusion is found elsewhere in the prophetic tradition in Mic 4:1–2; Zeph 3:9; Zech 8:20–22; 14:16–19.

[9] Paul echoes both vv. 1 and 6: "Before I was born the Lord called me; from my birth he made mention of my name" (cf. v. 5, "he who formed me in the womb to be his servant"), and "I will make you a light for the Gentiles" (cf. 42:6). The latter is echoed in the Lukan version.

[10] See the discussion in ch. 7 of Col 1:12–14 (pp. 296–97).

[11] For "election," see 1 Thess 1:4; 2 Thess 2:12; Col 3:12; Eph 1:4,11; for "new covenant," see 1 Cor 11:25; 2 Cor 3:6–17; cf. Gal 4:24; Rom 2:29 (echoing Deut 30:6).

churches are addressed to whole congregations, not to a leader or leaders. Indeed, even when leaders (plural) are included in the salutation in Phil 1:1, they are so as an addendum ("*along with* the ἐπίσκοποι [*overseers*] and διάκονοι [*deacons*]"). Moreover, even when a problem in the church is the direct result of an individual's wrongdoings, Paul never addresses the wrongdoer directly, but rather calls on the whole church to deal with the issue as a community matter. See, for example, the arguments in 1 Cor 5:1–13; 6:1–12. At issue in each case is primarily the community as God's people in Corinth;[12] although the individual sinner(s) are not overlooked, they are to be dealt with by the community.

All of this is to point out, then, that for Paul, "salvation in Christ" has the creation of a people for God's name as its goal and that this concern is especially to be seen as being in continuity with the people of God as constituted by the former covenant.

For our present purposes, one further facet of this concern needs to be noted here: Paul's use of "new creation" terminology to speak of the *result* of God's saving event in Christ. Related to this is his use of "image of God" language. Two facets of this usage in Paul's letters are important to point out here: his use of "new creation" language in its own right but especially in light of his usage of "image of God" and "second Adam" language with regard to Christ. So important is this aspect of Pauline soteriology—and his Christology—that the bulk of ch. 13 will be devoted to it.

Paul articulates "new-creation" theology in two ways. First, as the key passage 2 Cor 5:14–21 demonstrates,[13] the death and resurrection of Christ have set in motion a radical, new-order point of view—resurrection life marked by the cross—which lies at the heart of everything that Paul thinks and does (cf. Phil 3:4–14). This leads, second, to a series of texts in his letters that pick up "second exodus" imagery from Isa 40–66: God is about to do a "new thing" (Isa 43:18–19), and in the end he will establish "new heavens and a new earth" (Isa 65:17; 66:22–23). In Paul's thinking, this theme is applied to believers, who through association with Christ's death and resurrection have themselves experienced death and are being raised to newness of life (Rom 6:1–14; 7:4–6; Col 3:1–11; Eph 4:20–24). Common to these texts, either explicitly (Rom 6:1–14) or implicitly (e.g., compare Col 3:1–11 with 2:9–12), is an association with Christian baptism. Colossians 3:1–11 is especially noteworthy, since it concludes, "Here there is no Greek and Jew, circumcised and uncircumcised, barbarian, Scythian, slave and free, but Christ

---

[12]For example, "When you are assembled and I am with you in Spirit, and the power of the Lord Jesus is present, hand this man over to Satan" (1 Cor 5:4–5); "Get rid of the old yeast so that you may be a new unleavened batch of dough" (v. 7); "Expel the wicked person from among you" (v. 13 [citing Leviticus]). Cf. 6:1–6, which focuses on the church's own failure to act on a deed that has been taken "before the ungodly." In this case, Paul finally speaks to the two litigants (in vv. 7–8, 9–10), but his focus is primarily on what this has meant as a failure for the whole community.

[13]See ch. 4, pp. 196–98.

is all, and is in all" (cf. Gal 3:28). That is, in the new order, already set in motion through Christ's death and resurrection, the value-based distinctions between people—ethnicity, status, gender—no longer maintain.

Crucial to this view of things is Paul's use of "image of God" language, where he echoes Gen 1:26–27. Since God's "image-bearers" are to be his vice-regents in "charge" of the creation, there is every reason to believe that behind this usage is a common feature of suzerainty in the ancient Near East. One way for a suzerain to remind subject peoples of his sovereignty was by placing "images" of himself throughout the land(s) as visual reminders of that sovereignty. Thus, God is expressing his own sovereignty over creation by placing it under his "image-bearers," man and woman. What was distorted in the fall was "the image of God" in humanity; and this is precisely where, in Paul's theology, Christ enters history as the one who is bringing about the new creation, restoring the image.[14] He is thus the "second Adam," the one who first of all *in his humanity is the perfect image-bearer* of the eternal God (2 Cor 4:4; Col 1:15), while at the same time he is the one who *restores that image in fallen humanity* (Rom 8:29).[15]

Equally significant for our present purposes is the fact that in saving a people for God's name, Christ is described as the πρωτότοκος, the "firstborn among many brothers and sisters," who have themselves been predestined to be "conformed into the image of [God's] Son" (Rom 8:29; cf. Col 2:10–11). Indeed, Paul says elsewhere, it is as though God's people by the Spirit were looking into a mirror and beholding not their own image but Christ's and thus are being transformed into that same image, from glory to glory[16] (2 Cor 3:17–18). By the Spirit, Christ thus effects the new creation by restoring humanity back into the divine image. And this is precisely why the law is out and "walking by/in the Spirit" is in (Gal 5:16) and therefore why so much in Paul's extant letters deals with ethical/behavioral matters. As Gal 5 and Rom 12–14 make abundantly clear, "salvation in Christ" includes behavior that reflects God's own character; otherwise there has been no salvation at all.[17] Thus Paul's longing for the Galatians is for "Christ [to be] formed in you" (4:19), which in Rom 13:14 takes the form of an admonition to "clothe yourselves with the Lord Jesus Christ."

In Pauline theology, therefore, Christ's saving work is not only (re-) creating a people for God's name, but also, at the same time, this people is to

---

[14] One should note at this point N. T. Wright's observation (in an oral presentation) that a second Adam became necessary in part because the first Adam gave birth to a son "in his own image" (Gen 5:1).

[15] See the further discussion below, pp. 518–22.

[16] Either "from present to final glory," or "from one measure of glory to another," or "from one moment of glory to another."

[17] It is the lack of this dimension of Pauline soteriology—understandably downplayed because of the role of "works" in prior theologies—that is the great theological weakness in many Lutheran and Reformed expressions of Pauline soteriology.

be part of the new creation, who in their own lives and in their life *together* are God's image-bearers on this planet. And this is why Paul's energies are given almost totally to exhorting and encouraging his congregations to live out this calling as God's people wherever they are.

Presupposed in all of the soteriological talk, therefore, are both the preexistence and the incarnation of the Son. His beginnings were not when he was "born of a woman";[18] rather, he was eternally the Son, whom the Father *sent* into the world, both to *bear* the image and to *restore* the image in us. And it is precisely here that Christology and soteriology intersect in Paul's thinking.

The Place of "Christ Devotion" in Pauline Christology

This intersection of Christology and soteriology also helps to explain one of the best-known, but seldom contemplated, realities in the Pauline corpus: the fact that this rigorous monotheist has become such a devoted follower and worshiper of Christ the Son. This "Christ devotion" in Paul's theology takes two forms: personal devotion to Christ himself and devotion in the sense of the community's offering worship to Christ as Lord—both are full of christological presuppositions.

Christ as Object of Personal Devotion

Having grown up in a devout Diaspora home, Paul would have known by rote the primary commandment for all Israel: "You shall love the LORD (= Yahweh) your God with all your heart." It is of some interest, therefore, that this kind of language seldom occurs in the Pauline Letters.[19] Nonetheless, despite the lack of this precise language, and especially so with regard to the christocentric worldview that emerged after his encounter with the risen Lord, the kind of devotion to God that is embraced in this primary commandment is generally now given over to Christ. This finds expression in a variety of ways in his letters; it is invariable whenever he speaks longingly of his and his church's eschatological future.

I begin by noting once again how thoroughly christocentric most of Paul's letters are. Indeed, in the ten letters in the church corpus, God is mentioned more often than Christ only in Romans (considerably so) and 2 Thessalonians and 2 Corinthians (slightly so); but overall, Christ is mentioned sixty-three times more than God (599/536), and very little of this appears to be by design. In fact, as we saw regularly in the exegetical chapters, what is striking

---

[18] On this question, see discussion in ch. 5 on Gal 4:4–6 (pp. 213–16).

[19] In fact, there are only three occurrences: Rom 8:28 and 1 Cor 2:9 speak of "those who love God"; the grace benediction in Eph 6:24 is for "all who love our Lord Jesus Christ."

is the way Paul so freely interchanges θεός and Χριστός in a variety of ways when speaking about divine activities. And given Paul's rather consistent "grammar of salvation," noted above[20] and carried through in Romans in such a thoroughgoing way, this somewhat incidental, more frequent mention of Christ than God is all the more striking.[21] In Paul's radically changed worldview, everything is done in relation to Christ. The church exists "in Christ," and everything that believers are and do is "for Christ," "by Christ," "through Christ," and "for Christ's sake." But these more generalized expressions of life totally devoted to Christ also at times find more explicit expression.

Take, for example, Paul's argument with the Corinthians about the advantages of the single life. Such people are "concerned about the Lord's affairs—how they can please the Lord" (1 Cor 7:32); their "aim is to be devoted to the Lord in both body and spirit" (7:34). Indeed, being single allows one the best of all options: "to live in a right way in undivided devotion to the Lord" (v. 35). It is not difficult to hear Paul speaking personally here, even though it is being presented as a viable option for the unmarried in Corinth.

Similarly, despite the OT precedent that puts emphasis on Israel's "knowing God," this kind of language appears in Paul's letters only with relation to Christ. This is especially so in Philippians, where the kind of "longing" that Paul has for these friends is placed "in the bowels [= affection] of Christ Jesus" (1:8). When he goes on in 3:4–14 to tell his own story as a model of living cruciform, he echoes Jer 9:24 by claiming that he "boasts in Christ Jesus," for whom he has gladly "suffered the loss of all things, for the surpassing worth of *knowing Christ Jesus my Lord*," where "the Lord" = Yahweh of the Jeremiah text is now transferred completely to Christ (see ch. 9, pp. 408–9). The christological significance of this can scarcely be gainsaid, since these words are written by one whose religious heritage includes the Psalter, where this kind of devotion is offered exclusively to Yahweh. For Paul, such devotion to God is reserved *primarily* for Christ.

It is in light of such "Christ devotion" that one needs to understand Paul's own longing for the arrival of God's final eschatological future. In Paul's letters this longing finds expression exclusively in terms of "being with Christ," never expressly "with God," although one may well assume that such an understanding is inherent in his longing for Christ. This phenomenon begins in the first two letters, where in 1 Thessalonians "we wait

---

[20] The "classic" expression of this is found in Paul's reworking of the Jewish Shema in 1 Cor 8:6, where the two prepositions used of God the Father (ἐκ–εἰς [*from–for*]) enclose the double use of διά (*through*) with Christ the Lord; see the discussion in ch. 3, pp. 90–92.

[21] For a NT perspective on this matter, cf. the similar christological interest that drives 1 Peter, yet there God is specifically mentioned 43 times (not counting OT citations), while Christ is explicitly mentioned in some way or another only 22 times. This is quite similar to what one finds in Romans; yet elsewhere in the corpus, even though the "grammar of salvation" remains the same, Christ is mentioned far more often than God.

for his Son from heaven" (1:10) so that "we may live with him" (5:10), whom "we will be with forever" (4:17); in 2 Thessalonians this is expressed in terms of "our being gathered to him" (2:1). In 2 Corinthians the "eternal glory that outweighs" present suffering (4:17) is expressed in terms of "being away from the body [in its present suffering] and at home with the Lord [with a body 'overclothed' for eternity]" (5:8). And in one of his latest letters this takes the form of "depart and be with Christ" (Phil 1:23). Nothing like this is ever said about being with God the Father.

Thus, one is hardly surprised that one of the later expressions of the standard benediction with which his letters conclude takes the form "Grace to all who love our Lord Jesus Christ" (Eph 5:24). All of this seems natural enough to those of us who have been raised on the Christian Scriptures; but careful reflection causes one to think again. Here is a thoroughgoing monotheist, raised in a context of absolute theocentrism, who now turns the larger part of his devotion to God toward the Lord Jesus Christ. This is Christology in evidence without Paul trying to make it so, and therefore it is all the more telling.

Christ as Object of Worship

Christ devotion as "worship" takes several forms in Paul's letters, mostly the result of the early church's devotion to the risen Christ that grew up around the Lord's Table.[22] Three expressions of such devotion that have christological implications are briefly noted here: the Lord's Table; the singing of hymns to and about Christ; and prayer addressed to Christ.

1. For the concerns of this study, the (apparently) central role that the Lord's Table assumed in the early church is a most remarkable christological innovation. Interestingly enough, it is something we know about in the Pauline churches only because of a Corinthian abuse; hence it is mentioned or alluded to only in 1 Corinthians in the entire corpus, and here no less than four times (10:2–3, 16–17; 11:17–34; 5:8). The first of these (10:2–3) alludes to the Christian table by way of the analogy of Israel's having food and drink divinely supplied in the desert. Almost certainly this is in anticipation of what Paul will say in 10:16–17, where he uses the Lord's Table as the exclusively Christian meal, which thereby forbids attendance at the meals in the idol-demon temples. Israel, Paul points out, had its own form of divinely supplied food and drink, yet that did not "secure" them with God; and because of their idolatries, they were overthrown in the desert (10:3–10). At the same time (v. 17), Paul interprets the bread as having to do with the church as Christ's body, and thus he anticipates the issue of unity and diversity that will be picked up in chs. 12–14. All of this puts the focus of the Christian meal squarely on the Lord Jesus Christ.

---

[22]On these matters, see the careful, more thorough analysis in Hurtado, *Lord Jesus Christ,* 134–53.

For obvious reasons, however, most subsequent interest in what Paul says about what came to be called the Eucharist has focused on the issue and remedy that he speaks to in the third passage, where (apparently) the rich are abusing the poor at the Lord's Table by turning it into their own private meal that excludes "those who have nothing."[23] To correct this abuse, he reminds them of the words of institution, which are nearly identical to those found in Luke's Gospel. Our present (christological) interest in this passage is to point out again (see ch. 3, pp. 122–23) that there can be very little question that this is *the Christian version of a meal in honor of a deity*. This finds expression in several ways in the passage.

First, Paul's language for the meal in this instance is κυριακὸν δεῖπνον (1 Cor 11:20), language that occurs only here in the NT and is probably a Pauline construct, deliberately chosen in contrast to the τὸ ἴδιον δεῖπνον (*your own private meal*) of the wealthier Corinthians. Here the adjective κυριακόν can mean either "pertaining to" (thus, "in honor of") the Lord or "belonging to," in the sense of that which is his own specifically instituted meal. But in either case, it puts the emphasis on the fact that this meal uniquely has to do with "the Lord," in whose name and honor it is eaten. Thus, as with the Passover in Israel, which this meal replaces, this is the only singularly Christian meal, and the focus and honor belongs to the "Lord," not to God the Father.

Second, according to Paul, this meal was instituted by Christ in the context of a Passover meal. Paul expresses this in two ways: (a) by his previous assertion (in 5:8) that "Christ our Passover was sacrificed; therefore let us celebrate the feast without the leaven of malice and wickedness" (thus without the incestuous man present); this can only be an allusion to the Lord's Table and thus to his understanding of the connection between what Christ did and the Christian "celebration" of their own "feast"; (b) by his use of the introductory phrase (in 11:23) "on the night that he was betrayed," an allusion to Jesus' institution of this meal in the context of the Passover. The point, of course, is that in the Christian community the Passover meal eaten annually in honor of Yahweh and in remembrance of his deliverance of his people from Egypt is now eaten regularly (weekly?) exclusively in honor of Christ as the Christian deity and thus in remembrance of his delivering his people from bondage to Satan.

Third, in the earlier passage in ch. 10, Paul deliberately set the "meal in honor of the Lord" as the Christian alternative to the temple meals, which some of the Corinthians were insisting on attending, since "there is no God but one"; and therefore, in their view, the pagan meals, even though in

---

[23] For this view, see G. D. Fee, *The First Epistle to the Corinthians* (NICNT; Grand Rapids: Eerdmans, 1987), 540–45; for further nuanced understanding, see A. T. Thiselton, *The First Epistle to the Corinthians: A Commentary on the Greek Text* (NIGTC; Grand Rapids: Eerdmans, 2000), 860–64; D. Garland, *1 Corinthians* (BECNT; Grand Rapids: Baker Academic, 2003), 539–44.

honor of a deity, were not *in reality* in honor of a deity, since the "god" did not actually exist. And although Paul grants them that, he nonetheless identifies the "deities" as demons. Thus Paul's clear setting out of the Lord's Table as the Christian alternative to these pagan meals assumes that Christ is the Christian deity who is honored at his meal. Such a meal would simply be unthinkable as in honor of a mere human being who sacrificed himself on behalf of others, and who was therefore highly honored by God through resurrection.

Fourth, the remainder of Paul's corrective puts the Corinthian abuse in the strongest possible christological framework. Abuse of the Lord's body (= church) at the Lord's Table has resulted in divine punishment; and the text makes plain that these present (temporal) judgments are seen as coming from the Deity who is being dishonored, namely, "the Lord" = Jesus Christ (v. 32).[24] The net result is that a meal in honor of the Lord calls for the Lord's judgment on those who would abuse his people at his table (who corporately bear the divine εἰκών). In Paul's Jewish worldview, such prerogatives belong to God alone.

Thus, everything about this passage assumes and asserts the highest kind of Christology; and all of this is in direct relationship to Christ as divine Savior.

2. In a similarly incidental way, we are told in Col 3:16 that hymn singing in Christian worship had the message *about* Christ as its primary focus. In the twin passage, Eph 5:18–19, such singing is indicated as being "*to* the Lord." Thus, singing lay at the heart of Christian worship from the very beginning, and such singing was full of assumed Christology. In Colossians the primary concern of the exhortation is with the "word of Christ"—that is, the message of the gospel with its central focus on Christ.[25] This, after all, is what the letter is all about: Christ the embodiment of God; Christ, Creator

---

[24] See the discussion in ch. 3, p. 123.

[25] This takes the genitive τοῦ Χριστοῦ (*of Christ*) as objective, expressing the content of the "word" (so E. Lohse, *Colossians and Philemon* [Hermeneia; Philadelphia: Fortress, 1971], 150; R. P. Martin, *Colossians and Philemon* [NCB; London: Oliphants, 1974], 115; P. T. O'Brien, *Colossians, Philemon* [WBC 44; Waco, Tex.: Word, 1982], 206–7; N. T. Wright, *Colossians and Philemon* [TNTC; Grand Rapids: Eerdmans, 1986], 144), not subjective, as some consider it (see T. K. Abbott, *A Critical and Exegetical Commentary on the Epistles to the Ephesians and to the Colossians* [ICC; Edinburgh: T&T Clark, 1897], 290: "most comm."; cf. F. F. Bruce, *The Epistles to the Colossians, to Philemon, and to the Ephesians* [NICNT; Grand Rapids: Eerdmans, 1984], 157 n. 148). This view alone seems to keep the whole letter intact. Most scholars consider 1:15–18, whose focus is altogether on Christ and his work, to be from an early Christian hymn, that is, what is taught through singing. Thus the concern here is neither with Christ speaking to them as they gather—although that too could happen through prophetic utterance—nor with his teachings but with their letting the concern of this letter, the message of gospel with its total focus on Christ and his work, dwell richly in their community life. See further the discussion in Fee, *God's Empowering Presence*, 648–57.

and Redeemer. Paul now urges that this "word of Christ," which in part he has already articulated in 1:15–23, "dwell in their midst" in an abundant way. In so doing, part of their activity will be directed toward one another ("teaching and admonishing one another"), and part toward God ("singing to God with your hearts"). Thus the "riches" of the gospel are to be present among them with great "richness." The structure of the sentence as a whole indicates that songs of all kinds are to play a significant role in that richness.

Significantly, Col 1:15–18 itself possibly reflects such a hymn about Christ.[26] If so, then that would also explain why Paul thinks of these various kinds of hymns and Spirit songs as a means of their "teaching and admonishing one another." Such songs are by their very nature creedal, full of theological grist, and thus give evidence of what the early Christians most truly believed about God and his Christ.

When we turn to the twin passage in Ephesians, we note that the exhortation has the hymns now being sung *to Christ.* The background to the two-dimensional worship expressed here and assumed in the Colossians passage—hymns that are at once directed toward the Deity and didactic for the participants—is to be found in the Psalter. There we find dozens of examples of hymns addressed to God in the second person, which also have sections in the third person, extolling the greatness or faithfulness of God for the sake of those singing to him.[27] The use of hymns in the NT documents indicates how much they also function in this two-dimensional way for the early church. For our present purposes, the significance lies in the fact that in the Pauline churches Christ often assumes the dual role of being sung to and sung about—precisely as in the Psalter, whose hymns are both addressed to and inform about God.

Thus, as with the Lord's Table, worship in the form of singing focuses on Christ as the centerpiece of the worship. The singing contains "the message about Christ," and it is seen at times as being sung to Christ. Such worship obviously includes Christ in the divine identity, while always maintaining unwavering monotheism.

3. The third form of the worship of Christ the Savior as Lord comes in the form of prayer directed toward Christ in precisely the same ways that prayer is also directed toward God the Father. This shows up in a large way in the first two letters in the corpus and continues right to the end if one considers 1–2 Timothy as the "end" of the Pauline corpus (see ch. 10, pp. 465–66 above).

---

[26] See the discussion of this passage in ch. 7, p. 292 n. 10.

[27] This happens throughout the Psalter. See, e.g., Ps 30, which offers praise to God in the second person in vv. 1–3, then encourages singing on the part of the "congregation" in vv. 4–5, predicated on the fact that "his favor lasts a lifetime," and returns to second-person address in vv. 6–9. Cf., e.g., Pss 32; 66; 104; 116; so also the many hymns that call on the congregation to praise God in light of his character and wondrous deeds.

The evidence for this is writ large in the corpus and covers most kinds of prayer. Although there has been a tendency on the part of some to play down the role of Christ in prayer,[28] this simply will not work in terms of Paul's own usage. The point to be made is that had Christ not been included as the object of prayer, then all would see these as true prayer addressed to God. And that, of course, is what one should do; but now the net has to be thrown a bit more widely because Paul includes prayer to Christ in precisely the same way he does to God the Father.

Thus, in his "benedictory" prayers, which occur most frequently in 1–2 Thessalonians, Paul's prayer is directed first to *God and Christ together* (with a singular verb), that they would "direct our way to you" (1 Thess 3:11). This is immediately followed by prayer to Christ alone (vv. 12–13), that he would cause them to increase and abound in love, both for one another and for all, and thus also "establish your hearts" toward blameless and holy living. In this next letter (2 Thess 2:16–17) this is said in reverse: the prayer is directed to *Christ and God together* (again with a singular verb), but this time the follow-up is directed toward God alone. But in the two concluding prayers of this kind (2 Thess 3:5, 16), only Christ is addressed.

Turning to prayer reports (Paul reporting his prayers, past and present), we find the same phenomenon. Thus in more direct prayer, Paul concludes 1 Corinthians (16:22) with the (apparently) universal language of early Christian prayer, *Marana tha* ("Lord, come"). And in 2 Cor 12:8–10 he reports that he specifically petitioned Christ as Lord to remove the "thorn in his flesh." And in this case he also reports the answer he received from Christ ("My grace is sufficient for you").

The point to make again is that Paul himself is *not* trying to make a point; he is simply doing what has become natural for him: to address prayer to Christ as often as he does to God the Father, sometimes to both together and sometimes to either alone. Deity is simply presupposed in such moments, and as Larry Hurtado has pointed out, such devotion to Christ is in many ways more telling theologically than actual "theological statements" themselves.[29]

The point of all this is that Christ as Savior is not just the *mediator of salvation;* he also emerges as the *object of devotion and worship* in the Pauline corpus, both for Paul and for his churches. And the worship is both because

---

[28] See, e.g., Wiles, *Paul's Intercessory Prayers* (see in the present volume discussion in ch. 2 on 1 Thess 3:11–13 [pp. 53–54, esp. nn. 72, 74, 75]), who has a variety of ploys to eliminate Christ from Paul's prayers; but this simply will not hold up under the scrutiny of careful exegesis.

[29] See Hurtado, *Lord Jesus Christ,* passim. His point is that such devotion to Christ was well in place before the earliest known statements about Christ emerged in the early Christian community. Both the acclamation by the Spirit that κύριος Ἰησοῦς ("The Lord is Jesus" [e.g., 1 Cor 12:3]) and the prayer *Marana tha* ("Come, Lord" [1 Cor 16:22]) precede any known attempts to express theologically the implications of such devotion; and the latter surely arise out of the former.

of *what* he did for us and especially because of *who* he is as divine Savior. And what becomes clear in Paul's letters is that Christ's significance as divine Savior did not *begin* with his earthly life as Jesus of Nazareth; rather, that earthly life was an expression of an incarnation of the preexistent Son of God.

So before we look at how Paul understood the exalted Son of God as Lord of all, we need to take a closer look at the various texts that assert as presupposition that the Savior "came to earth" to redeem. At issue for us, then, as the first matter of christological significance is to come to terms with Paul's understanding of the divine Savior as both preexistent and incarnate, and in that incarnation as truly human in every aspect of our humanity but without sin.

Appendix: The Pauline Soteriological Texts

(Texts in double brackets [[ ]] = allusions only)

1 Thess 1:10   and to wait for <u>his</u> **Son** from heaven, **whom** <u>he raised</u> from the dead—**Jesus, who rescues us from the coming wrath.**

1 Thess 5:9–10   [9]For <u>God did not appoint us to suffer wrath but to receive salvation</u> **through our Lord Jesus Christ.** [10]**He died for us** so that, whether we are awake or asleep, we may live together with him.

2 Thess 2:13   But we ought always to thank <u>God</u> for you, brothers and sisters **loved by the Lord,** because <u>God chose you</u> as firstfruits <u>to be saved through the sanctifying work of the Spirit</u> and through belief in the truth.

[[1 Cor 1:13   . . . Was Paul **crucified for you**?]]

[[1 Cor 1:17   . . . lest **the cross of Christ** be emptied of its power.]]

1 Cor 1:18   The **message of the cross . . . to us who are being saved . . . is** <u>the power of God</u>.

1 Cor 1:21   . . . <u>God was pleased</u> through the foolishness of what we preach <u>to save</u> those who believe.

1 Cor 1:23–24   [23]but we preach **a crucified Messiah** . . . [24]but to those whom <u>God has called</u> . . . <u>God's power and God's wisdom</u>.

1 Cor 1:30   . . . you are **in Christ Jesus, who has become for us** <u>wisdom from God</u>: **our righteousness, holiness, and redemption.**

1 Cor 2:2   I resolved to know nothing while I was among you except **Jesus Christ and him crucified.**

1 Cor 2:8   . . . they would not have **crucified the Lord of glory.**

1 Cor 5:7   . . . For **Christ, our Passover lamb, has been sacrificed.**

1 Cor 6:11   . . . <u>You were washed, you were sanctified, you were justified,</u> **in the name of the Lord Jesus** and by the Spirit <u>of our God.</u>

1 Cor 6:20   <u>you were bought</u> **at a price.**

1 Cor 7:22–23   [22]. . . **Christ's slaves.** [23]**You were bought at a price.**

1 Cor 8:6   . . . and there is but **one Lord, Jesus Christ, through whom** all things came and **we through him.**

1 Cor 8:11   . . . this weak brother or sister, **for whom Christ died,**

1 Cor 11:24–26   [24]. . . "This **is my body, which is for you;** do this in remembrance of me." [25]. . . "This cup is **the new covenant in my blood.** . . ." [26]For whenever you eat this bread and drink this cup, you proclaim **the Lord's death** until **he comes.**

1 Cor 15:2–4   [2]By this gospel you are saved, . . . [3]. . . that **Christ died for our sins** . . . [4]**that he was buried, that he was raised the third day** . . .

2 Cor 5:14–15   [14]For **Christ's love compels us,** because we are convinced that **one died for all, and therefore all died.** [15]**And he died for all,** that those who live should no longer live for themselves but **for him who died for them and was raised again.**

2 Cor 5:18–19   [18]All of this <u>is from God, who reconciled us to himself</u> **through Christ** . . . [19]<u>that God was</u> **in Christ** <u>reconciling the world to himself, not counting people's sins against them.</u>

2 Cor 5:21   <u>God made</u> **him who knew no sin to be sin** for us, so that **in him** we might become <u>the righteousness of God.</u>

2 Cor 8:9   For you know **the grace of our Lord Jesus Christ, that though he was rich, yet for your sake he became poor, so that you through his poverty might become rich.**

2 Cor 13:4   For to be sure, **he was crucified in weakness,** yet **he lives** <u>by God's power.</u>

Gal 1:3–4   [3]. . . and **the Lord Jesus Christ,** [4]**who gave himself for our sins to rescue us from the present evil age,** <u>according to the will of God the Father,</u>

Gal 2:20   I have been **crucified with Christ** . . . **the Son of God, who loved me and gave himself** for me.

Gal 3:1   . . . Before your eyes **Jesus Christ was clearly portrayed as crucified.**

Gal 3:13–14   [13]**Christ redeemed us from the curse of the law by becoming a curse for us,** . . . [14]**He redeemed us** . . .

Gal 4:4–5 . . . <u>God sent his</u> **Son, born of a woman, born under the law,** ⁵**to redeem** those under the law, that we might receive adoption . . .

Gal 5:1 It is for freedom that **Christ has set us free.**

Gal 6:14 May I never boast **except in the cross of our Lord Jesus Christ, through which the world has been crucified to me,**

Rom 3:24–25 ²⁴All are justified freely by <u>his grace</u> **through the redemption that came by Christ Jesus,** ²⁵**whom** <u>God presented</u> as a **means of atonement through the shedding of his blood** . . .

Rom 4:5 . . . but trusts <u>God, who justifies the ungodly,</u>

Rom 4:24–25 ²⁴. . . but believe in <u>him who raised</u> **Jesus our Lord from the dead.** ²⁵**He was delivered over to death for our sins and was raised to life for our justification.**

Rom 5:6 . . . while we were still powerless, **Christ died for the ungodly.**

Rom 5:8 But <u>God demonstrates his love for us in this</u>: while we were still sinners, **Christ died for us.**

Rom 5:9 Since we have now been justified **by his blood,** how much more <u>shall we be saved from God's wrath</u> **through him.**

Rom 5:10 For if, while we were <u>God's enemies, we were reconciled to him</u> **through the death of his Son,** how much more, <u>having been reconciled</u>, **shall we be saved through his life.**

Rom 5:11 . . . but we also boast <u>in God</u> **through our Lord Jesus Christ, through whom we have now received reconciliation.**

Rom 5:18 . . . so also **one righteous act resulted in justification and life for all.**

Rom 6:3 . . . all of us who were **baptized into Christ were baptized into his death**

Rom 6:6 . . . our **old self was crucified with him** so that the body ruled by sin might be done away with,

Rom 7:4 . . . you also died to the law **through the body of Christ,**

Rom 7:25 Thanks be <u>to God, who delivers me</u> **through Jesus Christ our Lord.**

Rom 8:3 What the law was powerless to do . . . <u>God did by sending</u> **his own Son in the likeness of sinful flesh as a sin offering.**

Rom 8:17 . . . then we are heirs—heirs <u>of God</u> and **co-heirs with Christ, if indeed we share in his sufferings** . . .

Rom 8:32   He who did not spare his own **Son,** but gave **him** up for us all
. . .

Rom 8:34   Who then can condemn? **Christ Jesus who died**? **Who** was raised to life? **Who is** at the right hand of God **and is also interceding for us?**

Rom 14:9   For this reason, **Christ died and returned to life** so that he might be **the Lord of both the living and the dead.**

Rom 14:15   . . . Do not destroy your brother or sister **for whom Christ died.**

Col 1:12–13   [12] . . . the Father, who qualified you to share in the inheritance of the saints **in the kingdom of light.** [13]For he has rescued us from the dominion of darkness and brought us **into the kingdom of the Son he loves, in whom we have redemption, the forgiveness of sins.**

Col 1:19–20   [19]For **in him** all the fullness was pleased to dwell, [20]and **through him** to reconcile all things **to him, . . . by making peace through his blood, shed on the cross.**

Col 1:21–22   [21]And you, once being alienated and enemies in your minds by means of your evil deeds, [22]but now **you have been reconciled in the body of his flesh through death** in order to present you holy and unblemished and beyond reproach **before him.**

Col 2:13–15   [13]. . . God made you alive **with Christ.** He forgave us all our sins, [14]having canceled the statement of indebtedness . . . ; he has taken it away, nailing it **to the cross.** [15]. . . he made a public spectacle of them, triumphing over them **by the cross.**

Col 3:13   . . . Forgive as **the Lord forgave you.**

Eph 1:4–7   [4]. . . In love [5]he predestined us for adoption to sonship **through Jesus Christ . . .** [7]**in whom we have redemption through his blood, the forgiveness of sins,**

Eph 2:4–5   [4]. . . God, who is rich in mercy, [5]made us alive **in Christ** even when we were dead in transgressions—it is by grace you have been saved.

Eph 2:14–16   [14]**For he is our peace,** who has made the two one . . . [15]**by setting aside in his flesh the law with its commandments . . . and in one body to reconcile both of them** to God **through the cross, by which he put to death their hostility.**

Eph 4:24   and to put on the new self, **created** to be like God in true righteousness and holiness.

Eph 5:2   . . . **just as Christ loved us and gave himself up for us as a fragrant offering and sacrifice** to God.

Eph 5:25–27   ²⁵. . . **just as Christ loved the church and gave himself up for her ²⁶to make her holy, cleansing her by the washing of water through the word, ²⁷and to present her to himself as a radiant church** . . .

Phil 2:8   . . . **he humbled himself, by becoming obedient to death—even death on a cross.**

Phil 3:10   I want to know **Christ, both the power of his resurrection and participation in his sufferings, becoming like him in his death,**

[[Phil 3:18   . . . they live as enemies **of the cross of Christ.**]]

1 Tim 1:15   . . . **Christ Jesus came into the world to save sinners** . . .

1 Tim 2:5–6   ⁵For there is <u>one God</u> and **one mediator between** <u>God</u> and human beings, **Christ Jesus, himself human,** ⁶**who gave himself as a ransom for all people.**

Titus 2:13–14   ¹³. . . **Jesus Christ,** ¹⁴**who gave himself for us to redeem us from all wickedness and to purify for himself a people of his very own** . . .

Titus 3:4–7   ⁴. . . <u>God our Savior</u> . . . ⁵. . . <u>saved us through the washing of rebirth and renewal by the Holy Spirit,</u> ⁶<u>whom he poured out on us generously</u> **through Jesus Christ our Savior,** ⁷**so that having been justified by his grace,** we might become heirs . . .

2 Tim 1:8–10   ⁸<u>God,</u> ⁹<u>who saved us</u> . . . <u>because of his own purpose and grace,</u> which was given to us **in Christ Jesus before the beginning of time** ¹⁰but has now **been revealed through the appearing of our Savior, Christ Jesus, who has destroyed death and brought life and immortality to light through the gospel.**

2 Tim 2:8–10   ⁸Remember **Jesus Christ, raised from the dead, descended from David.** . . . ¹⁰. . . **to obtain the salvation that is in Christ Jesus,**

2 Tim 2:11   . . . **If we died with him, we will also live with him;**

12

Christ: Preexistent and
Incarnate Savior

IN THE PRECEDING EXEGETICAL CHAPTERS there were several occasions to point
out that Paul either asserts or assumes the preexistence of Christ as the eternal Son of God. The major texts are 1 Cor 8:6; 10:4, 9; 2 Cor 8:9; Gal 4:4; Rom
8:3; Col 1:15–20; 2:9; Phil 2:6; 1 Tim 1:15; 3:16; 2 Tim 1:9–10. What is striking
about this collection of passages is that most of them speak of Christ in
terms of his saving activity and thus point to the reality that he is not simply
our Savior; he is, in fact, the divine Savior.[1] Our purpose here is not to repeat
the exegesis as such but rather to look at the passages as a group, gathered
under three headings. Together they demonstrate that Paul believed Christ
to be the preexistent Son of God, who had become incarnate in order to redeem. But before doing that, we need to stress the theological significance of
the *nature* of these various texts.

The Nature of Paul's Incarnational Christology

One of the more significant points that needs to be brought forward
from the preceding exegetical chapters is that Paul is not trying in these passages to demonstrate preexistence and incarnation as something to be argued for. Quite the opposite. In every case, Paul is arguing for something else
on the basis of a *commonly held belief* in Christ as the incarnate Son of God.
And it is precisely this reality that makes their cumulative effect carry so

---

[1] I note in passing that the identification of Christ with Wisdom fails especially at
this point, since Christ's preexistence is consistently, and thus primarily, related to his
role as Redeemer and only secondarily to his role as Creator. Whatever else is true of
Wisdom, she was never perceived as even a semidivine redemptrix. See the full discussion in appendix A, pp. 595–630; cf. A. H. I. Lee, *From Messiah to Preexistent Son:
Jesus' Self-Consciousness and Early Christian Exegesis of Messianic Psalms* (WUNT
2/192; Tübingen: Mohr Siebeck, 2005), 285–96.

much christological weight. Were Paul arguing *for* incarnation, then one would pursue him with regard to both the what and the how of his argumentation, as to whether it "works" or is weighty. But when it is something Paul repeatedly argues *from*, then at issue is not whether Paul and his churches believed in Christ as the divine, preexistent Savior but what was the nature of that belief.

Because this is the nature of the Pauline materials, it is conceivable—indeed, it has been done—to argue in several instances for a nonincarnational view of a given text.[2] But although that might work with some of these texts in isolation from the others, such an argument ultimately comes aground against both the cumulative effect of the several texts together and their presuppositional nature.[3] Indeed, by the very nature of presuppositional statements held in common, one is not always covering all the bases so as to prevent misunderstanding. The result is that not everything that could be said at any given point will be said, because an author who assumes his readers to be in agreement with him for that very reason does not try to reestablish the material content of what is held in common.[4]

---

[2]Dunn, e.g., in both *Christology in the Making* and *Theology of Paul the Apostle,* has shown how one can examine these various texts in isolation from each other and then argue that any one of them does not necessarily assert or assume preexistence (a view unfortunately "seconded" by assertion by Ziesler in *Pauline Christianity,* 40–41). But Dunn's way of denying preexistence in Paul's theology was by an exegetical process that can best be described as "divide and conquer." That is, rather than reading Paul's texts in light of each other, he set out to demonstrate that none of the texts in which the church—and scholars—have historically found preexistence necessarily require such a view; and therefore, by showing how they can be interpreted in other ways, it is argued that they probably do not affirm or even imply preexistence in Paul's thought. But exegesis whose goal in part is to "get around" what the texts appear to say is always suspect, especially when it is required of an accumulation of texts. That Dunn felt the sting of these objections is demonstrated by his partial retraction in the otherwise superb *Theology of Paul the Apostle,* where he affirms (regarding 1 Cor 8:6), "Is there then a thought of preexistence in 1 Cor. 8.6 . . . ? Of course there is. But it is the preexistence of divine Wisdom. That is, the preexistence of God." This, of course, is neither what Paul says nor means, and in effect it is a denial that the one whom Paul calls the "one Lord" (who is *not* divine Wisdom) is in fact preexistent (see in the present volume ch. 3, pp. 89–94, 102–5). See the preceding chapters in the present volume for the exegesis of these various texts. Cf. the stinging critique of Dunn's first edition by A. T. Hanson, *The Image of the Invisible God* (London: SCM Press, 1982), 59–76.

[3]On this matter, and in direct response to Dunn, see esp. A. T. Hanson, *Image,* 59–76.

[4]A good example of this phenomenon can be seen by comparing 1 Cor 8:6 and Col 1:15–20 (see below). While perfectly understandable in its barest form in 1 Cor 8:6, the elaboration in Colossians gives evidence not only that our understanding of the 1 Corinthians passage is correct but also that the presuppositional base is even stronger than one might assume merely from the earlier passage. For example, on the basis of Col 1:13–20, where God's "beloved Son" in v. 13 is the subject of all that is said in vv. 14–20, one may rightly surmise that 1 Cor 8:6 is also about the Son, on the basis of Paul's describing God as "the Father."

Given, then, the basic reality of the presuppositional nature of what Paul says regarding Christ as preexistent and incarnate, one is impressed by the variety of ways Paul reaffirms this commonly held ground. Its substance is always the same, thus giving it *coherence;* its variety is directly related to the *contingent* circumstance of each letter (or section within a letter).[5] Thus, both by straightforward statement and by metaphor, Paul reminds his churches of various implications for them regarding their common starting point: Christ preexisted as Son of God and became incarnate "for us human beings and our salvation."

Christ as Agent of Creation and Redemption

Two texts fit under this first category, 1 Cor 8:6 and Col 1:15–20, which have common language regarding the role of Christ in creation and redemption (both creation and redemption are δι' αὐτοῦ [*through him*]) but exist in their immediate contexts for quite different, but similarly pragmatic, reasons.

1 Corinthians 8:6; 10:4, 9

In the striking passage (1 Cor 8:6) where Paul reshapes the Jewish Shema to embrace both the Father and the Son while at the same time emphasizing his inherited monotheism, Paul asserts that the "one Lord" (= Yahweh) of the Shema is to be identified as the Lord Jesus Christ. And he does this in a context where he is both agreeing with and deliberately enlarging the perspective of the Corinthians, who in embracing a rigorous monotheism are arguing for attendance at pagan temples on the basis of that monotheism (the god does not exist, so why forbid it?). Paul, of course, is in full agreement with them on the first matter (rigid monotheism), but he will have none of their argument on the second matter. In time he will reject this spurious reasoning on theological grounds (10:14–22). At this point in the argument, the use and elaboration of the Shema was for the sake of those for whom the divine Son died and who cannot attend these temple meals without being "destroyed" (8:10–12).

At the same time, this present assertion—the same Christ who redeemed them had the role of preexistent Creator—prepares the way for Paul to pick up the latter theme again in his argument with them in 10:1–13. The Corinthians, he insists, are themselves in similar danger as were the Israelites whom God overthrew in the desert. After all, the preexistent Christ, the "one Lord" of the Shema, Paul argues, was with Israel as "the Rock that followed them" (10:4); and the same preexistent Christ whom Israel tested in

---

[5]For this significant distinction regarding Paul's theology, which unfortunately is often overlooked in discussions of the topic, see Beker, *Paul the Apostle,* 22–36.

the desert was responsible for their being destroyed by the snakes (10:9). So if having Christ present did not guarantee Israel's entrance into the promised land, then the Corinthians need to take heed regarding their own flirtation with idolatry.

In a still more profoundly theological way, by his inclusion of the preexistent Son[6] as the agent of creation, Paul has thus included him in the divine identity at its most fundamental point, since the one God of the Jews was regularly identified vis-à-vis all other "gods" as the Creator and Ruler of all things.[7] Thus, it is one thing for Christ to be the means of redemption, but for him likewise to be the divine agent of creation is what clearly includes him within Paul's now adjusted understanding of "the one God."

That Paul so easily and matter-of-factly enlarges the Shema to embrace Christ suggests that this view of God's "oneness" to include both Father and Son did not begin at this ad hoc moment. The very way these sentences are expressed—in perfect poetic parallel, which is both condensed and tight—suggests that this is not the first time Paul had found a way to embrace two significant realities at once: his fundamental monotheism and his understanding of it so as to include Christ in the divine identity.[8] But however and whenever its origins in Paul's theology, here is the earliest, and one of the most intriguing, instances of Paul's clear assertions of Christ as the preexistent Son of God. And the less-than-hidden reason for this assertion lies with Paul's soteriological concerns for the "weaker" believers in Corinth.

To be sure, there have been efforts to get around this plain assertion of Christ's preexistence.[9] But these denials face enormous exegetical difficulties,[10] and they exist primarily to sidestep the plain sense of the text and

---

[6] See n. 4 above. The appellation of God as Father has its origins for Paul not with God's being *our* Father but with God's own new identity as "the God who is the Father of our Lord Jesus Christ" (2 Cor 1:3; 11:31; Eph 1:3). Hence, Paul's identification of the "one God" in this passage as "the Father" presupposes Christ as "the Son."

[7] On this matter, see Bauckham, *God Crucified*, 9–13.

[8] See ibid., vii–x, 25–42. "Identity" leads one to think of the divine Triad as a matter of "choice," so that "ontology" as such is a derivative, not primary, idea.

[9] Some have done so by suggesting that the whole passage is soteriological only (see n. 15 in ch. 3); and others by identifying Christ with personified Wisdom, thus asserting that only Wisdom preexisted, while the human, now exalted Christ is merely identified here with Wisdom (see the excursus in ch. 3 [pp. 102–5] and the discussion in appendix A [pp. 599–601]). But there is not a hint of personified Wisdom in this passage; and to bring "her" into the picture here from Paul's assertion in 1:24 that a crucified Messiah is *God's* power and wisdom vis-à-vis the Corinthians' own fascination with Greek wisdom reflects an "exegesis" of this latter passage that is so questionable as to be irrelevant—if exegesis is understood in terms of an author's intent and the readers' capacity to understand. In effect, the (failed) argument that these texts are about "Wisdom" when in fact they are explicitly about Christ as Lord is a tacit admission that Paul and his churches believed that Christ was the preexistent Son of God.

[10] On the difficulty of denying that creation is in view, see ch. 3, p. 90 n. 15; see the preceding note for the difficulties of identifying Christ with Wisdom (esp. in

thus disregard the contextual reasons for Paul's making this assertion here. Moreover, they quite miss one of the reasons for naming Christ as "the Lord" = Yahweh of the Shema: to place Christ as already present with the Israel to whom the Shema was originally given. And, of course, this is a clear case where the later, fuller elaboration offered in Col 1:15–20 spells out with clarity how this earlier, more condensed version is thus to be understood.

Finally, we note how unnecessary (at one level) this striking christological assertion is to the present argument, since nothing *christological* is at stake here. Indeed, in Rom 11:36, in a doxology directed toward God the Father alone, the full phrase ἐξ αὐτοῦ καὶ δι᾽ αὐτοῦ καὶ εἰς αὐτόν (*from whom and through whom and for whom [all things]*) appears without this christological modification. But since Paul's christological assertion is what will make both the ethical and theological dimensions of the present argument work, we note again that it will work *only* if this is in fact a shared assumption between Paul and the Corinthians.

Colossians 1:15–20

In a poem of two stanzas that looks very much like an elaboration of the two lines of 1 Cor 8:6, Paul in Col 1:15–20 once again asserts that the Son of God is the divine agent both of creation and of redemption. But in this case both lines are elaborated in such a way as to place Christ at the beginning point of both the old and the new creations. Christ is also in this case explicitly identified as the "beloved Son of the Father" (1:13), who both bears the "image" of the unseen God (v. 15) and is the efficient cause and goal of the whole created order (v. 16). At the same time, he is God's own "firstborn"— first regarding creation (v. 15) and second regarding resurrection (v. 18). This Son, who is thus the "beginning" of the new creation (v. 18) as he was agent of the first, has reconciled all things *to himself*[11] by his "having made peace through the blood of his cross."

So intent is Paul in placing Christ as supreme, and thus above "the powers," that he elaborates the Son's role in creation in two ways: first, by using two of the three prepositions that in Rom 11:36 he had used of God the Father (διά/εἰς [*through/for*]); and second, by twice using the all-embracing ἐν αὐτῷ (*in him*) regarding the Son's role both in creation itself and in its currently being sustained. Christ the Son is thus both the Creator and the sphere in which all created things have their existence.[12] To put this em-

---

1:24); and in any case, as pointed out in the exegesis of the Wisdom passages in appendix A, "she" is never posited in the Wisdom literature as the actual *agent* of creation. Personified Wisdom is envisioned as only *present*, evidenced by creation's wise design.

[11] On this as the proper understanding of the reflexive εἰς ἑαυτόν in 1:19–20, see ch. 7, pp. 310–12.

[12] Since all of this is both plain and emphatic, some would deny preexistence in Paul's thought by denying Pauline authorship (on the improbability of this, see n. 2 in ch. 7). See the preceding notes for other forms of denial.

phatically and rhetorically: it is the Son who is the image of the unseen God; it is the Son who has the rights of primogeniture; it is the Son through whom and in whom all things came to be; and it is the Son who by virtue of his resurrection stands as the beginning of the new creation, effected through his reconciling death.

This christocentric emphasis continues on into the stanza regarding redemption. And in this case there is an equal emphasis on incarnation. Using the periphrasis "all the fullness," meaning all the divine fullness that is God himself, Paul asserts that this "fullness" dwelt in Christ so that, as the Incarnate One, Christ might reconcile all things to himself—and thus, by implication, to God.[13]

It should be noted that in this case, since Paul himself did not *found* this church, he spells out in some detail the more condensed assertion of 1 Cor 8:6. This presents the interesting phenomenon that while the passage as a whole has an assumptive ring to it—that is, Paul seems to expect the Colossian believers to share this common belief with him—at the same time it is the closest thing one finds in the Pauline corpus to a deliberate presentation of Paul's assumed Christology. Nonetheless, both its poetic nature and the obvious insertion of the phrases about the powers in v. 16b indicate that he is still presenting Christ in a way that assumes that Paul and his readers are on common ground.

Colossians 2:9

When Paul in 2:6 turns his attention to the Colossian situation itself, he begins typically with a series of imperatives. First, and positively, they are "to walk in the Messiah Jesus, the Lord," whom they have "received." Second, negatively, they are to beware the "vain philosophy" that is currently threatening them, which is in keeping with the στοιχεῖα (*elemental forces*) of the world and not "in keeping with Christ." In identifying what it means to be "in keeping with Christ," Paul returns to what he had said in 1:19, but now with special emphasis on the incarnation as such. "All the fullness of the deity," Paul asserts again, "dwells in Christ *bodily*." And since this is a clear pickup of 1:19, this kind of condensed phrase assumes the emphasis on preexistence expressed in 1:15–20 but now elaborates it by emphasizing the genuinely incarnational dimension of Christ as the divine Presence while on earth.

How this relates to the Colossian error itself has been a matter of some debate, not to mention speculation. My point here is simply to note again how emphatically this addition of "bodily" denies any "spiritual" understanding of Christ that does not embrace an actual "incarnation." Although not expressed here, the preceding passage, which places the Son as the agent of creation and redemption, affirms that preexistence is presupposed.

---

[13]For the full presentation of this position (Christ is reconciling all things to himself), see ch. 7, pp. 308–13.

Christ as "Impoverished" Redeemer

In two of the "preexistence" passages (2 Cor 8:9; Phil 2:6–8) Paul speaks of the incarnation with extraordinarily strong metaphorical language, where the emphasis of the metaphor is on the "impoverishment" that Christ experienced in becoming human. In both cases the passages exist to present Christ as an exemplary paradigm for the conduct being urged on Paul's readers; and in both cases the metaphors themselves are simply too strong, and the language itself too plain, to allow an interpretation that discounts preexistence and incarnation.

2 Corinthians 8:9

This text serves as Paul's final appeal to the Corinthians to follow through on their commitment to help care for the poor in Jerusalem. In trying to avoid any semblance of "command" or "coercion," he asserts that his concern in all of the prior comparisons is exactly the opposite: to test the sincerity of their love. Paul's final coup is to speak in metaphor of Christ's incarnation and redemption for their sakes: "For you know the grace of our Lord Jesus Christ, that for your sakes *he became poor, so that through his poverty* you might become rich." Thus, the "he became poor for your sakes" is metaphor for the incarnation;[14] "so that you through his poverty might become rich" is also metaphor for the crucifixion and its benefits for the Corinthians.

In keeping with the "money" issue at hand, and as Christ's own expression of "grace," Paul appeals directly to the enormous "generosity" of Christ's incarnation (which in turn leads inherently to his crucifixion). The incarnation of the one who was preexistent as God can only be expressed in terms of "his becoming poor," an "impoverishment" that meant untold "riches" for others (including the Corinthians). But, Paul argues, his aim is not their own "impoverishment"; rather, it is simply that, given the enormity of Christ's generosity, they should gladly follow through on their commitment to the poor, which will not in fact impoverish them in the same way.

Again, this metaphor works only because Paul and the Corinthians share the same presuppositional understanding of Christ as the preexistent One who became incarnate. After all, this very tight metaphorical sentence (which would be destroyed if elaborated!) was written to the same community to which he had written 1 Cor 8:6.

Philippians 2:6–8

It is of some significance theologically that the telling of the Christ story in Phil 2:6–11 exists primarily to reinforce by way of divine example some at-

---

[14] For the unlikelihood that this reflects Paul's "Adam Christology," see n. 13 in ch. 4.

titudinal concerns that Paul has regarding internal relationships in the believing community in Philippi. "Do nothing," he has urged, "out of selfish ambition or vain conceit" (v. 3); rather, they are to have the exact opposite mind-set, that which is exemplified by Christ through both incarnation (vv. 6–7) and crucifixion (v. 8).

With this as his goal, Paul tells Christ's story in particularly powerful and telling language. Beginning with Christ's prior existence "in the 'form' of God," Paul urges that this equality with God that was his by nature was not in Christ's case exemplified by his selfishly grasping or holding onto what was rightly his. To the contrary, and now with an especially strong metaphor, Paul asserts that Christ chose "to pour himself out [with regard to his equality with God] by assuming the 'form' of a slave [with regard to his incarnation]." And to clarify what this means, Paul then abandons the metaphors regarding his divine preexistence and says it plainly: "by coming to be in human likeness."[15]

With that in hand, Paul then emphasizes the reality of Christ's incarnation by starting the next sentence with an echo of the preceding one, which repeats the emphasis on the genuineness of his humanity. It was as the one who was "found" to be in the recognizable appearance of one who is truly human that he humbled himself to the Father in an obedience that led to death on a cross. And all of this on Paul's part is to impress on the Philippians their need "in humility [to] value others above yourselves, not looking to your own interests, but each of you to the interests of the others" (vv. 3–4). Any reading of this passage that does not take seriously its implied and expressed emphasis on Christ's incarnation is to read the text apart from the context in which Paul has told the story; and in any case, as we noted in ch. 9, both grammar and content disallow such a reading.[16] One who is already only and merely human does not "become human"!

Again, Paul can make use of Christ as the exemplary paradigm precisely because this is shared belief that he can point to without argumentation.

---

[15]In one of the more idiosyncratic moments of twentieth-century NT scholarship, Oscar Cullmann chose to argue that Christ was a preexistent heavenly *man,* "the God-man already in his preexistence" (*Christology,* 177). This has the earmarks of one holding a presuppositional theology about the impassability of God before reading the texts themselves.

[16]It should be noted further that such a metaphor, with its powerful expression of what it meant for God to become human, makes almost no sense at all as an echo of the story of Adam, who was never either in the "form" of God nor equal with God, so that in yielding to sin, he "poured himself out into the slavery" of his fallenness and thus found himself to be "human" in the negative sense. If an echo of Gen 2–3 is present at all, it is only conceptual: Christ, who had divine status, chose to become a human being, while Eve and Adam, who were *created* in the divine image, sought for a divine *privilege* that became their undoing. But to push the analogy further than that requires considerable ingenuity and the ability to read back into the Genesis narrative what is not explicit in the narrative itself. See further the excursus on this passage in ch. 9 (pp. 390–93).

When one considers that this church was founded in the late 40s of the first Christian century, one must further surmise that such belief was common stock in the much larger Christian community at a time considerably prior to the writing of this letter.

2 Timothy 1:9–10

By bringing this passage into the discussion, I am not arguing for or against Pauline authorship. The historical fact is that this letter exists in the NT solely because it was believed by the church up through the eighteenth century to be by Paul. And my point in bringing it into this discussion is to note that its Christology, despite its unique way of being expressed, is fully in keeping with Paul.[17]

Even though the "impoverishment" motif does not occur in this passage, the emphasis is once more on Christ's preexistence and the genuineness of his incarnation. Christ's preexistence is asserted by the clause "God saved us . . . in keeping with this own purpose and grace, which was given to us *in Christ Jesus before the ages began.*" His incarnation is then expressed as, "but has now been revealed *through the appearing of our Savior, Christ Jesus.*" Thus, this very Pauline concern finds expression in the corpus yet one more time. Christ preexisted with the Father, and at one point in human history he became incarnate in order to redeem.

The Son as the "Sent One"

Finally, it is in light of the quite explicit passages in 1 Cor 8:6 and Col 1:15–20 and the equally strong implications of 2 Cor 8:9 and Phil 2:6–8 that one must read the two "sending" passages in Gal 4:4–5 and Rom 8:3. As was pointed out in the exegesis of these two passages, even on their own, both grammar and context call for an incarnational reading of the text. Both passages are set in contexts where Paul's concern is that Christ and the Spirit have made Torah observance obsolete. Both passages are therefore altogether soteriological in terms of their reason for being: in both of them Paul asserts that God "sent his (own) Son" to free humankind from enslavement to both Torah and death.

Galatians 4:4–7

This passage offers the christological-soteriological basis for Paul's singular interest throughout the letter: because they are in Christ, the Galatian

---

[17] To argue that its vocabulary is unlike Paul's is quite circular in this case, since each of the passages under investigation in this chapter is unique in relationship to the rest, except for Gal 4:4–7 and Rom 8:3–4. So unique vocabulary and mode of expression mean very little here. At issue is the Christology expressed by this language.

Gentiles do not need to come "under Torah." Thus it has been shaped with this singular concern in view. As Paul has argued in a variety of ways throughout, God's time came with Christ, especially through his redemptive work on the cross.

In language that seems deliberately chosen to tie together the work of Christ and the Spirit, Paul says that "God ἐξαπέστειλεν [*sent forth*] his Son." Despite an occasional voice to the contrary,[18] two matters indicate that this is an assertion of Christ's preexistence, that the Son is himself divine and was sent from the Father to effect redemption.

First, although the verb ἐξαποστέλλω on its own does not necessarily imply the sending forth of a preexistent being,[19] here it is not on its own, since Paul begins his next sentence by saying exactly the same thing about God's "sending forth the Spirit of his Son." Using language reminiscent of Ps 104:30, and in a clause that is both parallel with and intimately related to what is said in vv. 4–5, Paul says that "God sent forth *the Spirit of his Son*" into our hearts with the *Abba*-cry, thus verifying the "sonship" secured by the Son whom God had previously "sent forth." It is this double sending, where in the second instance God's sending forth of the Spirit of his Son can only refer to the preexistence of *the Spirit of God* now understood equally as the Spirit of the Son, that makes certain that in the first instance Paul is also speaking presuppositionally about Christ's preexistence.[20]

Second, in keeping with his whole argument to this point, for Paul the work of Christ is an objective, historical reality. At God's own set time, Christ entered our human history (born of a woman) within the context of God's own people (born under the law) so as to free people from Torah observance by giving them "adoption as 'sons.'" It is the otherwise unnecessary phrase "born of a woman" that is so striking. Paul's primary concern lies with the next two phrases: "born under the law in order to redeem those under the law." That he first mentions Christ as "born of a woman" seems understandable only if one recognizes that Christ's preexistence is the predicate of the

---

[18] See esp. Dunn (*Christology in the Making*, 38–44), whose case builds on a series of (correct) observations that on its own, such language neither argues for (which certainly is true) nor necessarily presupposes preexistence; cf. Tuckett (*Christology*, 51–52), who appears to have followed Dunn uncritically on this matter. For the difficulty with this view, see the discussion in ch. 6, pp. 214–15; cf. Kasper, *Jesus the Christ*, 173; and most commentaries.

[19] As Dunn (*Christology in the Making*, 39) points out; indeed, much of his case rests on his scouring the literature to find evidence for this reality, to which all will readily accede. But what one must be careful not to imply, as Dunn seems to, is that because the verb does *not necessarily* refer to such a sending forth, it therefore *probably* does not. The overall evidence of the passage suggests exactly the opposite: since it *may* refer to a sending forth of a heavenly being, the overall context and language of this passage, especially its occurrence in v. 6, suggest that here *it does indeed*.

[20] Cf. F. F. Bruce: "If the Spirit was the Spirit before God sent him, the Son was presumably the Son before God sent *him*" (*The Epistle of Paul to the Galatians: A Commentary on the Greek Text* [NIGTC; Grand Rapids: Eerdmans, 1982], 195).

whole sentence. Paul's emphasis here, in passing though it seems to be, is on the incarnation of Christ, who thereby stands in stark contrast to the ahistorical, atemporal "elemental spirits of the universe" (v. 3) to which these former pagans had been subject.

Romans 8:3–4

In a sentence that at once both picks up the argumentation from 7:4–6 and concludes the lengthy "digression" over the question of whether Torah itself is evil, Paul sets out to elaborate the "third law" noted in v. 2 (cf. 7:22–23)—that of the Spirit who gives life, which itself is predicated on the redemptive work of Christ. In referring to Christ's role in making Torah observance obsolete, Paul speaks once more in terms of God sending his Son to redeem, and he does so in language reminiscent of Gal 4:4–5.

But in this case he speaks of the work of Christ in terms of God having thus "condemned sin in the flesh," which is almost certainly a piece of double entendre: in Christ's own death "in the flesh" God condemned the sin that resides in our "flesh." How God did this is the point of the central modifier: "having sent his own Son in the likeness of the flesh of sin and as a sin-offering."

On the matter of Christ's preexistence and incarnation, Paul does not argue for such, nor is such an understanding essential to his present point. Nonetheless, these two realities are the natural *presupposition* of Paul's language, especially the threefold combination of "having sent," "his *own* Son," and "in the likeness of sinful flesh." Together these phrases clearly assume that Christ had not experienced "flesh" before he was sent, especially so in light of Paul's certain belief in Christ's preexistence and incarnation from the other passages currently under purview. What catches the eye in this instance is the unique phrase "his *own* Son" (τὸν ἑαυτοῦ υἱόν), with "his own" in the emphatic position.[21] This is hardly the language of "adoption," and it assumes the unique relationship with the Father that is the prerogative only of the Son, while at the same time it anticipates the allusion to Abraham and Isaac in 8:32 (cf. Gen 22:16).

Furthermore, the phrase "in the likeness of the flesh of sin," as with the phrase "in human likeness" in Phil 2:7, means that he was similar to our "flesh" in some respects but dissimilar in others.[22] That this is Paul's intent seems certain from the use of this word at all, since if he intended a more complete identification with us in our sinfulness itself, he could easily have said simply "in sinful flesh." So in this case not only Christ's preexistence and incarnation are presupposed by what Paul says, but also his sinlessness.

---

[21] Cf. τοῦ ἰδίου υἱοῦ later in the same chapter (v. 32).

[22] Cf. BAGD (on ὁμοίωμα): "It is safe to assert that [Paul's] use of our word is to bring out both that Jesus in his earthly career was similar to sinful men yet not absolutely like them."

1 Timothy 1:15; 2:5; 3:16

In this later expression in the corpus of the reality of Christ as the "sent One," the "trustworthy saying" has narrowed the focus to Christ himself, without emphasis on his being "sent." Thus, "Christ Jesus came into the world to save sinners." As with the preceding texts, this sentence does not require that preexistence is in view. But as was pointed out in the exegesis of this passage, this is a strange way of referring to Christ's redemptive death if it does not in fact presuppose preexistence. Why not simply say, "Christ Jesus died to save sinners"? For that is the most "creedal" way of saying it, as 1 Cor 15:3 makes clear.

The emphasis on Christ "coming into the world" in this passage is then picked up in 2:5 and 3:16 with specific interest in the reality of the incarnation—an emphasis that makes the preceding understanding of 1:15 appear certain. The mediatorial work of the one mediator between God and humanity was accomplished by one who was himself fully human, thus implying both preexistence and incarnation. And such a view of these first two texts is fully confirmed by the first line in the poetry of 3:16: "he was manifested *in the flesh.*" As was pointed out in the exegesis of this latter passage, this emphasis is almost certainly in response to a kind of latent Docetism in the negation of the material world that lay behind the heresy that Paul is engaging. And that leads us to our final observations in this chapter.

The Importance of the Incarnation for Paul

What are we to make of this evidence that Paul and his churches held in common the conviction that their Savior, the Lord Jesus Christ, had pre-existed as God's Son and had been "sent into the world" to effect redemption? How does this reality affect our overall understanding of Paul's Christology?

The first and most obvious point to make is that Paul clearly understood Christ the Savior himself to be divine; he was not simply a divine agent. If most of Paul's christological emphases have to do with Christ's present postresurrection reign as Lord, these various sentences in Paul's letters make it clear that in Christ's coming, "all the divine fullness dwelt in him in a human body." Thus, the full deity of Christ is never something Paul argues for; rather, it is the constant presupposition of everything that he says about Christ as Savior. And surely it is this greater presupposed reality that accounts in large measure for Paul's "Christ devotion" noted in the preceding chapter. To be sure, Paul speaks only rarely of "the Son of God who loved me and gave himself for me" (Gal 2:20); but the very fact that in this case he identifies Christ as "the Son of God" suggests that what overwhelms Paul about such love is not simply Christ's death on his behalf. What lies behind such language is the overwhelming sense that the preexistent, and therefore divine, Son of God is the one who by incarnation as well as crucifixion "died for me." To put that another way, the deity of Christ is therefore for Paul no small matter; it is rather of central significance to his understanding of, and devotion to, his Lord.

At the same time, especially in the later letters, there is a considerable emphasis on Christ's genuine humanity—a factor that in itself argues for Paul's conviction about Christ's true identity as the divine Son. This emphasis comes in such a way in Colossians and the Pastoral Epistles as to make one think that by this time, a full generation after the death and resurrection of Christ, Paul is already needing to fight on a second front: against those whose understanding of Christ's *deity* might tend to minimize the reality of his having become *truly human*. Although none of these passages is overtly antidocetic, they nonetheless either speak to or anticipate that possibility. And Paul will have none of it. By saying that Christ came in "human likeness" or "in the likeness of our sinful flesh," he does not mean that Christ's flesh was not real (bodily) flesh like ours; rather, it is language that safeguards both dimensions of a genuine incarnation: in Christ, one who was truly God was living a truly human life.

If Paul does not put it quite that way, this nonetheless is almost certainly the assumed Christology that lies behind such statements. At the same time, one must hold together, along with these statements, Paul's twice-stated insistence that there is "only one Lord, and one Spirit, and one God" (1 Cor 12:4–6; Eph 4:4–6), along with his repeated emphasis on the divine Triad as being responsible for our salvation.[23] And it is precisely such statements that cause us at a later time in history to try to work through for ourselves how one can best express the conviction that there is ever and only but one God but that the one God must be understood to include Father, Son, and Spirit in his identity as the one God.

---

[23] On this matter, see Fee, *God's Empowering Presence* (see p. 48 n. 39 for a listing of the texts; pp. 827–45 for a discussion of the "Trinitarian" implications).

13

Jesus as Second Adam

THE PRECEDING CHAPTER CONCLUDED ON the note that in some later texts that speak of Christ's incarnation, Paul appears to move toward an emphasis on the reality of Christ's humanity. The primary purpose of the present chapter is to pursue this matter in more detail, especially since orthodox Christianity has historically had a tendency toward Apollonarianism, wherein one pays lip service to Christ's humanity but then emphasizes the deity in ways that often tend to negate the genuineness of the humanity. At the same time, the road into this discussion for many scholars has been by way of Paul's references or allusions to Christ as "second Adam" or "last Adam." Thus, much of this chapter is devoted to this issue, especially since neither the nature nor the extent of so-called Adam Christology is a matter on which all are agreed.

The primary issue regarding Christ and Adam is one's overall stance toward the Pauline data: whether one takes (1) a *minimalist* position, which deals only with the three passages where Adam is specifically mentioned (1 Cor 15:21–22, 44b–49; Rom 5:12–21); or (2) a *maximalist* position, such as one finds in the work of J. D. G. Dunn or N. T. Wright, who approach this in two quite different ways[1] but neither of whom take Paul's explicit references to Adam as the starting point;[2] or (3) a *middling* position, which does not limit itself only to explicit references but is less inclusive as to what else in Paul's writings actually makes a comparison of Christ with Adam viable, based on what appear to be *certain* connections made by Paul between Christ and the actual *language* of Gen 1–3.[3]

---

[1] See esp. Dunn, *Christology in the Making,* 98–128; idem, *Theology of Paul,* 199–204; on the other side, see Wright, *Climax of the Covenant,* 18–40, 57–62, 90–97.

[2] For Dunn, the starting point is the plight of "man" as the result of Adam's fall; thus Rom 1:18–34, e.g., is read in light of Gen 2–3 (rightly so) but then is extrapolated to say that the plural ἄνθρωποι of that passage *could* be read in the singular to refer to Adam, and therefore it *is* read that way. For Wright, the starting point (much more convincing to my mind) is the deliberate verbal connection in the Genesis narrative (and beyond) between Adam and Abraham and through Abraham to Israel.

[3] The primary reason for going this route is that Paul's own usage is quite limited and in each case the reason for the analogy is altogether soteriological, not christological; cf. Matera, *New Testament Christology,* 95. But Matera himself

The third option is the one that I find most compatible with the overall data. To demonstrate that, we need to return briefly to Paul's "new-creation" theology, since the crucial issue to be dealt with in this matter is his use of εἰκών (*image*) with reference to Christ. "New creation" will be our point of departure, after which we will examine the three explicit mentions of Adam in the corpus and then turn to the implied reference to Adam in the use of "image" language. The chapter will conclude with another look at what is perceived to be the Pauline emphasis: even though Paul understood Christ to be preexistent and now exalted to the Father's right hand as Lord of all, when he referred to Christ as Savior, he occasionally stressed, but in any case generally presupposed, his genuine humanity.

Paul and New-Creation Theology

On at least three occasions in Paul's letters, argument aimed toward behavioral change is predicated on the fact that with the coming of Christ Jesus, and especially as the result of his death and resurrection, God had inaugurated the "new creation" promised in Isa 65:17–25.[4] Two texts in particular serve as the proper starting point here. First, in 2 Cor 5:14–17 Paul confronts those in Corinth who are calling into question his gospel of a crucified Messiah as well as his own cruciform apostleship. The new creation, he argues, brought about by Christ's death and resurrection, nullifies viewing anything any longer from the old-age point of view (κατὰ σάρκα [*according to the flesh*]).[5] Christ's death means that the whole human race has come under the sentence of death (v. 14), so that those who have been raised to life (in God's new order) now live for the one who died for them and was raised again (v. 15). The result, he goes on, is that from this point on, to view either Christ or anyone/anything else from a perspective that is "according to the flesh" is no longer valid (v. 16). Why? Because being in Christ means that one belongs to the new creation: the old has gone, the new has come (v. 17). It does not take much reading of Paul to recognize that this radical new-order point of view—life marked by the cross—lies at the heart of everything that he thinks and does.

This leads to our second text, Gal 6:14–16, where again in a context of the cross (and assumed resurrection) Paul asserts that the old order that distinguished people on the basis of circumcision has yielded to the new. Earlier

---

(pp. 124–25) is willing to see Adam Christology in Phil 3:20–21, which is especially doubtful.

[4] All of this is in keeping with the thoroughgoing eschatological framework that characterizes Paul's theology as a whole and that is quite in keeping with the rest of the early church. For a brief overview of this essential position, see ch. 12 in Fee, *God's Empowering Presence*, 803–13; for some, a more accessible version is found in idem, *Paul, the Spirit, and the People of God*, 49–62.

[5] See the more complete exposition of this passage in ch. 4, pp. 196–98.

on (3:26–29), he had put that plainly: participation in Christ's death and resurrection through baptism had radicalized everything. In the new order neither religious ethnicity (Jew/Gentile), nor social status (slave/free), nor gender (male/female) counted for anything, not in the sense that one's status itself was changed (e.g., one remained a Gentile, free, woman) but that *value and privilege* based on status had been brought to nothing with the inauguration of the new creation.

These texts serve as crucial background to the third text, Col 3:9–11, which is important for our present discussion because here, by means of the crucial word εἰκών (*image*), which he had already used of Christ himself in 1:13–15, Paul presents Christ as the focal point of the new creation. In a passage that echoes Gal 3:26–28, that entrance into the new humanity is by way of Christ's death and resurrection evidenced by baptism, Paul also reiterates the radical new order that emerges as a result ("no Gentile or Jew, circumcised or uncircumcised, barbarian, Scythian, slave or free"). But in this passage, having earlier (1:15) identified Christ as the bearer of the divine image, he adds that the "new person is thus being newly created . . . in keeping with the εἰκών of him who has [thus] created the new person."

As was pointed out in ch. 7 regarding this passage (pp. 303–4), this language echoes the creation of Adam and Eve in Gen 1:26–27 (and 9:6) as well as vv. 15 and 18 of the Christ poem with which Colossians begins. And despite a majority of voices to the contrary, everything in the letter as a whole and in this passage in particular indicates that the Creator in this case is Christ himself.[6] The one who as the Son of God bears the divine image is also the one who by virtue of his death and resurrection is now re-creating a people into that same image. Significantly for our present purposes, this passage contains all three of the matters that here concern us: (1) the new creation, in which (2) God's new people are being restored into the divine image, and (3) that this is effected by Christ the divine image-bearer. It is this combination of ideas and language that is crucial christologically with regard to any real significance that Christ might have as the "second Adam." But first we need to look more carefully at the concerns of the three passages where Christ is explicitly identified with Adam by way of analogy.

Sin and Death—The Explicit Comparisons

All three of the explicit references to Christ as "second Adam" occur in contexts where Christ's humanity is in full view, not necessarily with

---

[6] Briefly, the reasons are that (1) Christ alone is in view in the immediate context as well as (2) this entire passage (2:20–3:11 [God is referred to only in terms of his wrath, in 3:6]) and (3) that in 1:15–20 Christ is both the divine image-bearer and the one through whom the original creation came to be, and is himself called the ἀρχή (*beginning*) of the new (1:18). See the full discussion in ch. 7, pp. 303–4.

emphasis on his being human but with that as the basic, thoroughgoing presupposition. Indeed, at issue in all three of the explicit contrasts between Christ and Adam are the two basic realities of our humanity: sin and death, which Adam let loose in our humanity and which Christ as "second Adam" overcame by his death and resurrection. A brief overview of the three passages makes this abundantly clear.

1 Corinthians 15:21–22

There is nothing earlier in this letter or in 1–2 Thessalonians that quite prepares us for the sudden mention of Adam in this passage. However, the fact that Paul picks it up again in the second phase of his argument with the Corinthians (over the matter of the future bodily resurrection of believers) and again in such a matter-of-fact way in Rom 5 suggests that he had previously reflected on this analogy before it here found its first expression in the extant letters.

In this first case, the analogy is simple and straightforward: death became a human reality because of the first ἄνθρωπος (*human being*); similarly, resurrection will become a future reality for believers because of the resurrection of the second ἄνθρωπος, Christ Jesus. This is then repeated with emphasis on its effects for other human beings: as in Adam all die, so in Christ will all (believers) be made alive. Since this is in direct response to a denial by some Corinthians of a future resurrection of believers, the emphasis is altogether on the fact that just as the "man" who stands at the beginning of the old creation brought death into the world, so also it is the "man" who stands at the beginning of the new creation who has brought bodily resurrection into the world.

The analogy is straightforward, and the emphasis is on Christ's human role in the new creation, even though that language is not used here.

1 Corinthians 15:44–49

The emphasis in this pickup of the Adam/Christ analogy is once again on the fact that Christ is the "last" ἄνθρωπος; but in this case the analogy gets a bit more complex because the issue itself has changed considerably. In 15:1–34 the issue had been singularly about the reality of the *future* resurrection of believers, which is predicated altogether on Christ's own resurrection. The issue in 15:35–49 is about the *bodily nature* of that future resurrection. And if Paul goes at this in a somewhat prolix way, that is because he is intent on emphasizing the fact that the risen Christ *continues to have a body that is related to his life as a human being.* Paul does this by way of the complex adjectives ψύχικος and πνευμάτικος, which in this case can only mean something like "natural" and "supernatural."[7] That is, the body that Christ bore was very much the

---

[7] On this issue and the somewhat ironical use of these adjectives, see G. D. Fee, *The First Epistle to the Corinthians* (NICNT; Grand Rapids: Eerdmans, 1987), 785–86.

same as the one we all bear, fully and completely adapted to life on planet earth; but the body that he has come to bear by way of resurrection has been "refitted" for the final life of the Spirit. Thus it is the same body but at the same time not quite the same. The various complexities of the present argument are all related to this phenomenon.

The result is that the "first ἄνθρωπος, Adam, had a body that was of the earth, and made of earthly stuff" (v. 47). The "second Adam," while once having borne this earthly body, now has a body fitted for heaven, thus "of heaven" (v. 47). The reason for this somewhat complex way of saying it turns out to be hortatory. Paul wants the Corinthians to live in such a way that they will be among those who at the resurrection will also bear the "heavenly body" of the second Adam (v. 49), since they do indeed already have a body like that of the first Adam.

If the direction of the argument in this case has changed a bit, Paul's emphasis on Christ's having been "truly human" continues from before. The difference is that Christ is now spoken of as the progenitor of the *new* humanity, just as Adam was of the *first*. Thus, in both instances of this analogy in 1 Cor 15, Paul's concern is singular: Christ in his humanity, through death and resurrection, has not simply identified with us as human beings but has set a future resurrection in motion—as the new creation with its eventual realization of a new body, fully adapted to the life of the future. And all of this because in his incarnation he bore a body that was truly in keeping with that of Adam.

Romans 5:12–21

The concern in both instances of the Adam/Christ contrast in 1 Cor 15 had to do with death and life as such. When Paul returns to this analogy in Rom 5, this is still a central concern. The issue now, however, is not death itself but rather the cause of death, sin. Nonetheless, despite the focus on sin and righteousness that led to this analogy—a focus that is repeated throughout and follows from it—Paul continues with this analogy to emphasize death and life. What Adam let loose in the world was sin, which led to death; what Christ brought into the world was righteousness, which leads to life; and as with 1 Cor 15, the emphasis throughout this passage is on the repeated use of ἄνθρωπος for both Adam and Christ.

What needs to be noted finally with regard to these three explicit mentions of Christ and Adam in the extant Pauline corpus is how narrowly focused they are. In all three cases the analogy has specifically to do with the one responsible for bringing death into the world through sin and the other bringing life into the world through his own death and resurrection. But nothing more is made of the analogy at all; hence, one can well understand why many take a minimalist position on this matter, even if they do not articulate it in this way. That is, if one stays only with what the texts specifically say, there is hardly a ground of any kind for such a thing as an Adam Christology.

But something more does need to be said, and this something also arises out of these three texts. In each of the three there is considerable emphasis on Adam and Christ as standing at the beginning of something, as the progenitors of the two "creations": one progenitor fallen, which has issued in sin and death, and the other crucified and risen, which has issued in a new creation. And it is this matter, implicit in these first texts, that becomes explicit in several other texts, to which we now turn.

Christ as the Image of God—The Implied Comparison

In light of the discussion to this point, there is every good reason to believe that Paul's references to the Son of God as bearing the divine "image" (Rom 8:29; Col 1:13–19; cf. 1 Cor 15:49; 2 Cor 3:18–4:6; Col 3:10) are intentionally contrasting Christ as "second Adam" with the first Adam. This seems especially to be so because, in Paul's first use of εἰκών in this way (1 Cor 15:49), he himself deliberately sets out this contrast in an Adam/Christ context.[8] But what is less clear in the scholarly literature is where one places the emphasis on Paul's use of εἰκών: is it on Christ's bearing of the divine image or on his replacing Adam as the one truly human person in whom the divine image has been restored? Or again, is it somewhat (deliberately?) ambiguous, since one cannot speak of Christ as εἰκών without recognizing that it simultaneously goes both ways? To resolve this matter, we return to these five texts with our focus altogether on this question. The texts are examined in their assumed chronological order, since there is much to learn from doing so.

1 Corinthians 15:49

With this sentence, Paul concludes his long argument for the future *bodily* resurrection of believers (15:35–49), and he does so by returning to the Adam/Christ analogy first set out in vv. 21–22. The point throughout this final paragraph (vv. 44b–49) is to contrast the two kinds of bodies: the earthly one that Adam (and thus also Christ) bore and the new heavenly ex-

---

[8]In a somewhat idiosyncratic discussion of this matter, Kim devotes well over one hundred pages to this motif, arguing that it had its origins in Paul's Damascus Road encounter (*Origin of Paul's Gospel*, 137–268). But that is to put enormous weight on ideas that must be brought together in circuitous fashion. Whether this would have been true for Paul can hardly be proved; by the same token, neither can it be disproved—although it seems highly unlikely, given that Paul himself puts very little overall christological weight on this theme. Much of Kim's discussion is mitigated by his confidence that Paul's εἰκών Christology is related to Wisdom Christology ("clearly"/"clear" [p. 117]), which is based on a single text in the Wisdom literature that in fact does *not* equate Wisdom with the "image of God" (see in the present volume the excursus in ch. 7, pp. 323–25; and the discussion in appendix A, pp. 601–2)!

pression of this body that the risen Christ alone bears at this point in time. It is the "same" body now adapted for the life of the future. At the end of this sentence Paul offers one final exhortation to the Corinthians, urging them to live so as also to bear this new body in the eschaton.

At least, exhortation is the point of the overwhelming majority of the best and earliest manuscript evidence.[9] As we noted in ch. 3, Paul is simply being Paul, and he concludes first with the affirmation common to our being human: "just as we have borne the *image* of the earthly man." But his concern throughout this letter has been for them to live in keeping with the new life that has been given to them in Christ; so he concludes, "let us also bear the image of the heavenly man." And with that, the net gets thrown a little wider, so as to emphasize their living *now* in conformity to the one whose new kind of body they are in fact destined to bear. With a kind of double entendre, therefore, the emphasis lies first on the bodily nature of the resurrection that Christ now bears and that all who are his will eventually bear. But, second, Paul cannot help himself—not with regard to the Corinthians, at least—so the certain future that awaits them is expressed by way of urging them to live with that future in view.

Thus, in this passage the emphasis lies primarily with Christ's bearing the *imago Dei* in his human life, even if the first emphasis is on his truly human, but now transformed, body. There is no emphasis here on the fact that he bore this image because he was divine; rather, in his coming as the "second Adam," he did what Adam failed to do: bear the divine image *in his humanity* and thus serve as the progenitor of all others who do the same, which has Christ's present eschatological existence as its final goal.

2 Corinthians 3:18; 4:4–6

The most striking thing about this series of sentences is that the first appearance of εἰκών (in v. 18) is generated not by Gen 1 but by the mirror imagery that Paul is using in writing to believers in a city famous for its bronze mirrors. But if that is said to catch their attention, the main thrust of the sentence has to do with Christ himself bearing the unfading divine glory (in contrast to the fading glory that Moses experienced). And, of course, in this first sentence the point that Paul makes for the sake of the Corinthians is that as they by the Spirit "gaze" on Christ as into a mirror, they themselves

---

[9]On this matter, see ch. 3, p. 119. The prevailing wisdom that the "error" is the result of an easy interchange between the letters *omega* (φορέσωμεν [*let us bear*]) and *omicron* (φορέσομεν [*we shall bear*]) simply does not hold. There are hundreds of places where in the great majority of early and late MSS there is no interchange between these two vowels; rather, such changes occur predominantly at points like this one, where later scribes and scholars had a hard time believing that Paul meant what he seems to have said. In this instance, the textual evidence is overwhelmingly on the side of a hortatory subjunctive, which alone accounts for the few MSS that have the future indicative.

are being transformed into that same "image," the image of God as that is
borne fully and perfectly by Christ.

When Paul returns to this twofold language in 4:4 ("image" and
"glory"), the emphasis is now on Christ himself. And because that is true,
the emphasis in this second instance is not so much on Christ's humanity as
such—that is assumed as inherent in the imagery itself. What we have,
rather, is the true image of God being borne by the one *who shares the divine
glory,* the one who, when turned to in devotion and obedience, transforms
believers by his Spirit into the image of God that humanity was created for in
the first place. But even with this different emphasis, the use of this language for Christ in itself always presupposes his humanity, which is the only
reason this language is used of Christ at all.

It is therefore of some interest that in the two places in the extant Corinthian correspondence where Paul uses the language of Gen 1 with reference
to Christ, in the first instance his central concern is with Christ's bearing
that image in his humanity while in the second instance the emphasis is on
the fact that he shares the divine glory with the Father. Thus he is the one
who, because he is also fully divine, bears the perfect image of God—the
image to which believers themselves are in the process of being conformed.

Romans 8:29

With this passage, we come to the first of the two εἰκών passages (with
Col 1:15) where Christ is explicitly referred to as "the Son" of the Father; and
in both cases the two-sided reality (human and divine) of the language of
Gen 1 is in play. Moreover, in both of these instances Paul also refers to the
Son as God's πρωτότοκος (*firstborn*), a word that is never used of Adam in
any of the Jewish literature.[10] Thus, in both cases, even though an Adam
Christology lies behind the *language,* the emphasis begins to move toward a
messianic Son of God Christology. It is therefore also of some interest that in
both cases the emphases differ considerably from each other.

The appearance of this combination in the present passage comes as the
climactic moment in Rom 8:1–30, where Paul's primary goal is to assure the
believers in Rome, both Jew and Gentile together, that the combination of
the work of Christ on their behalf and of God's gift of the Spirit—the Spirit
of both the Father and the Son (8:9–10)—is also the guarantee of ethical life
now and of eternal life to come. Thus, in a sentence that begins on the
double note of God's foreknowing them and thus predestining them, Paul interrupts to spell out the shape and the ultimate goal of that "predestina-
tion." God has foreordained that they are to be "conformed to the image of
his Son," who himself is God's "firstborn" among the many who are to
become his brothers and sisters.

---

[10] Nor of "Wisdom," I might add, since it is so often asserted to the contrary. See
ch. 7, pp. 320–21; and the full discussion in appendix A, p. 601.

Deeply embedded in such language are the twin emphases, first, that the eternal Son of God perfectly bears the divine image and, second, that he did so in his own identity with us in our humanity. This latter emphasis is immediately picked up in v. 32 by an echo of the Abraham narrative of Gen 22, where Paul points to the crucifixion by asserting, "God spared not *his own* Son" for our sakes.

This second matter—emphasis on Christ's humanity—is what is then picked up in our present passage with the phrase "the firstborn among many brothers and sisters." And thus, even though there is otherwise no direct echo of Gen 1 in this passage, the language of the latter passage is what ultimately gives meaning to this one. It would therefore seem fair to add that where Adam failed as God's "firstborn," Christ has succeeded altogether—something foreordained by God from eternity past.

Colossians 1:15

As was pointed out in the exegesis of this passage, both "strophes" of this Christ poem make sense precisely as one takes seriously that the *grammatical* antecedent of the "who" in vv. 15 and 18 is "God's beloved Son" in v. 13 and that it is in fact the intended *conceptual* antecedent as well. Thus Paul is here returning to what he had said in Rom 8:29, but now to a different church with considerably different concerns. These new concerns are to identify the Son as the *messianic* Son of God (v. 13),[11] who also has the rights of primogeniture with regard to the whole of creation, which also came into existence through him. Thus, Paul's emphasis with his use of εἰκών in this passage is on the incarnate Son of God as the *divine* image-bearer, who in eternity past was both the agent and the goal of the created order.

That Paul is here once again (indirectly but deliberately) echoing Gen 1 is confirmed by the way he begins the second "strophe" of the poem: "the Son is the ἀρχή [*beginning*]." This most unusual language is a direct echo of Gen 1:1; and as with the εἰκών that begins the first strophe, this ἀρχή is immediately followed by a second use of πρωτότοκος. But now the referent is his being the "firstborn" of the *new* creation, marked by his resurrection from the dead.

Thus, even though εἰκών does not occur in the second strophe, it is assumed throughout, so that the emphasis on the Son's bearing the *divine* image in the first strophe now moves toward his identity with us in his work of reconciliation. It is the one in whom all the divine fullness dwells (bodily) who has brought reconciliation through the blood of his cross. And that leads us directly to Paul's fifth instance in which he has used εἰκών with regard to Christ.

---

[11] This is confirmed in this case by his adding that the Son is also the Father's πρωτότοκος (thus echoing Ps 89:26–27 [88:27–28 LXX]).

Colossians 3:10

With this text, we bring the presentation of the present chapter full circle. For here the one who is himself the "image" of God, who is the Father's own "firstborn," and by virtue of his resurrection the "firstborn" with regard to the new creation, is now the one who "re-creates" broken and fallen humanity back into the divine image that he himself has perfectly borne. The Creator of the first creation, who himself bears the Father's image, now is seen as the Creator of the new creation, as he restores his own people back into the divine image[12]—that is, into his own image that he alone perfectly bears. Thus the emphasis is simultaneously on Christ's being the *divine* image-bearer who now also re-creates fallen *humanity* into that same image.

Philippians 2:6–8

I return to this passage (from the previous chapter) at the end of the analysis of Paul's actual use of εἰκών in his letters because there has been a veritable groundswell in the NT academy that has argued (or more often simply asserted) that Paul's use of μορφή in the opening phrase of the Christ story (v. 6) is virtually synonymous with εἰκών. But as was pointed out in the prior examination of this passage (ch. 9, pp. 377–79), this is a piece of scholarly mythology that needs to be laid to rest. The preceding discussion of Paul's actual use of εἰκών argues for this even more so, while at the same time it reinforces the fact that the presupposition of the phrase ἐν μορφῇ θεοῦ (*in the "form" of God*) emphasizes Christ's preincarnate divine existence.

Two things now make that even more certain. First, as was previously suggested, Paul's apparent reason for choosing μορφή was that this in fact is the only word available in the language that would serve equally well on both sides of his sentence: to define Christ's "mode" of preexistence with God and to indicate the extreme nature of the "mode" of his incarnation: coming into our history in the "form" of a slave.

Second, Paul's actual use of εἰκών elsewhere in his letters points out (1) the near folly of arguing that μορφή could actually serve as a nearly synonymous equivalent and (2) the fact that whatever "echo" the next phrase—about Christ "not selfishly grasping" his equality with God—has with reference to Adam, it cannot include the ἐν μορφῇ θεοῦ that has preceded. Whatever else, Paul did not intend to begin by saying, "Who, being in the image of God," with regard to his preexistent *divine nature.* The preceding analysis has shown that Paul uses this language with regard to Christ *only* with regard to his being the divine image-bearer in his incarnation, not with regard to his

---

[12]For the full argumentation of this understanding of the passage, see ch. 7, pp. 303–4.

preexistence, where it would make no sense as an echo of Gen 1–2. This further means, of course, that whatever "Adam" echo there might be in this grand telling of the story, it is altogether *conceptual*, since it lacks a single *linguistic* tie of any kind.

So Adam Christology there is in Paul's thought, to be sure; but in terms of actual language and echoes of Gen 1–2, it is limited to two kinds of passages: first, explicit contrasts between Christ and Adam, where Christ is seen as the progenitor of the *new creation*, who has overturned the effects of Adam's sin, which led to death; and, second, where the incarnate Christ is seen as the true bearer of the divine image, who is also re-creating a people who bear that image with him.

These, however, are not the only ways Paul refers to the earthly Jesus. The rest of this chapter will examine other Pauline evidence for emphasis on Christ's true humanity, including a side glance at Paul's knowledge of, or reference to, the historical Jesus.

The Pauline Emphasis—A Truly Human Divine Savior

At the beginning of the twentieth century, the extreme skepticism of nineteenth-century NT scholarship had produced a considerable harvest, so that it was common to find Paul accused of being the "bad guy" who had created a divine Savior out of a merely human Jesus. Related to this was an equally extreme skepticism regarding Paul's knowledge of the historical Jesus, except for his death by crucifixion. But by the end of the century, the pendulum had swung back considerably, so that it was possible for a major Christology to argue that Paul viewed Christ basically as coming from below and thought of Christ's "divine status" in terms of a human Savior now exalted to heaven because of his self-sacrificial death.[13]

In some ways, both of these views can be seen as in reaction to a kind of Christian "orthodoxy" that failed to take Jesus' full humanity with real seriousness, an orthodoxy that had come to believe on theological grounds that Jesus in his earthly life was *non posse peccare* ("not to be able to sin"). This is a view that many resist because it seems ultimately to turn Christ into a divine robot rather than his being a truly human person who was *posse non peccare* ("to be able not to sin") because, in Luke's language, God was with him. At issue for this kind of orthodoxy was to build a convincing case for Christ's true humanity that did not look as if he were merely acting out in his human life what was in fact not possible at all.

When one turns from later theologizing to the apostle Paul himself but with this debate in hand, one is struck first by the apparent paucity of the data. But the paucity in this case is related to the larger issue at hand. Paul

[13] See Dunn, *Christology in the Making*, 65–128.

nowhere tries to establish a Christology as such; rather, because for the most part he is dealing with issues in his churches that need correcting—and need good "theology" as the way of doing so—his references to Christ are either soteriological in their focus or put emphasis on his present reign as Lord. But all the same, Paul drops the curtain just often enough so that we can basically reconstruct what he and his churches believed about Christ— that he was the truly divine Savior but one who effected that salvation through an incarnation in which he had become a truly human person. Thus, I conclude this chapter by gathering these various data together as a package in support of this latter point. And at the end, I point out again how thoroughly presuppositional Christ's humanity was for Paul.

Paul and the Historical Jesus

It is not my purpose here to argue the case that Paul knew about the historical Jesus. The evidence for that is made certain by the following enumeration. Nor do I intend to argue the case for any of the items that follow. My concern is simply to list the evidence that Paul did indeed know the traditions about Jesus that are found in the Gospels, and thus to point out that the human life of Jesus was held to be presuppositional to everything else that he came to believe regarding Jesus' death and resurrection. Indeed, in a basically oral/aural culture, it is well nigh unthinkable that knowledge about Jesus did not circulate in ever so many ways that it would have made it nearly impossible for Paul not to have known about Jesus' life and teachings.[14] The Pauline data itself can be classified under two headings.

Knowledge of the "Life of Jesus"

That Paul knew the basic details of the "life of Jesus" can be seen from the following:[15]

1. According to Gal 4:4, Jesus was born of a woman within an observant Jewish family.[16] As such, he was believed to have been the long-awaited Jewish Messiah (Rom 9:5; 1:2–4; 1 Cor 1:22), which further meant that he had come to reign in God's eschatological kingdom (1 Cor 15:24; Col 1:13–14). Paul's repeated emphasis on Christ's death and resurrection can best be explained in light of the radical departure that this event was, in light of Jewish messianic expectations (1 Cor 1:20–25), so much so that its true nature could have been revealed only by the Spirit (1 Cor 2:6–10).

2. The historical reality that Jesus died by crucifixion, and thus by Roman hands, is writ large in the corpus; and in 1 Thess 2:14–15 it is seen as

---

[14] See now Dunn, New Perspective on Jesus, 35–56.

[15] Cf. a similar, brief paragraph in Hunter, Gospel according to Paul, 59.

[16] Some might object to the language "observant," but Paul's own language ("born under the law") and argument make very little sense if he did not consider Mary and Joseph to be observant Jews.

belonging to, and in keeping with, the tradition of "the killing of the prophets." Moreover, the allusion to Jesus' sufferings in 1 Thess 1:6, in the context of the Thessalonians' "much affliction," can hardly refer solely to his crucifixion. There is therefore no good reason to doubt the thoroughly Pauline nature of the historical affirmation in 1 Tim 6:13, that Jesus made a good confession before Pontius Pilate. On the other hand, and contrary to some, the fact that Paul focuses primarily on Jesus' death says next to nothing about his further knowledge of the life of Jesus as such.

3. If there are fewer explicit references to Jesus' earthly life than one might wish, those that do appear are all the more telling because of their incidental nature. Indeed, how much further knowledge must be assumed to lie behind the twofold notice (made quite in passing) that Jesus had biological brothers who were well-known members of the earliest Jewish Christian community (1 Cor 9:5; Gal 1:19).

4. If Paul does not explicitly say more about Jesus' earthly life, the nature of that life as one of servanthood was well known to him (Phil 2:7), which was as radical a departure from Jewish messianic expectations as was Jesus' being a crucified Messiah. It is within this framework that one best understands Paul's appeals to his own "imitation of Christ," which in turn Paul expects of his churches as they follow his own example. Although this appeal can refer to his living cruciform, as it surely does in Phil 3:15–17 and probably does in 1 Thess 1:6–7, this can hardly be the case in 1 Cor 11:1, where Paul's *imitatio* refers to his doing everything for the glory of God and thus becoming all things to all people for the sake of the many. Here is assumed knowledge of the life of Christ about which we could only speculate. But the speculation could well be grounded in the appeal to Christ's attitudes of "meekness and gentleness" in 2 Cor 10:1 and his "compassion" in Phil 1:8, especially since Paul lists two of these virtues in an appeal to the Colossians to "put on" the new self that is being renewed into the "image" of their Creator, Christ himself (3:10–11).[17]

That there are not more of these kinds of references in Paul's letters means very little, since what does exist is once again not argued for in terms of its historicity but rather is appealed to as common knowledge among early followers of Christ.

Knowledge of the Teaching of Jesus

Although there is likewise not much by way of Jesus' actual teaching that emerges in Paul's letters, what does appear is of such diverse nature that once again it suggests that we have only the tip of the iceberg.

1. The earliest reference to Jesus' teaching appears in Paul's earliest letter, at 1 Thess 4:15, where he appeals to "the Lord's word" but without citing it. Since Paul uses κύριος exclusively to refer to Christ, there can be little

[17] For this understanding of this passage, see ch. 7, pp. 303–4.

question that this is an appeal to something spoken by Jesus. Although it could possibly refer to a prophetic word from the risen Lord, more likely it is an appeal to something said by the earthly Jesus.

2. In both Gal 4:6 and Rom 8:16 Paul refers to Greek-speaking Gentile Christians as crying out to God as Father with the language of Jesus himself: *Abba*. Although the Gospel writers put this word into the mouth of Jesus himself (in Gethsemane), it is equally a part of his teaching, since it undoubtedly lies behind Jesus' own instructions in how to pray (Matt 6:9). The fact that this Aramaic language has been maintained even in the Greek-speaking church indicates that this word is bedrock history regarding the earthly Jesus.[18]

3. In the third letter in the corpus Paul twice appeals to a saying of Jesus as supporting the position that he is espousing. In the first case, 1 Cor 7:10, he appeals to a saying that can be found in the Gospels regarding a wife separating from her husband. Since Paul's version is adapted to the present situation, it is of little value to pursue the precise nature of its origins, but it reflects what appears in two forms in the Gospels (Mark 10:11 // Matt 19:9; Luke 16:16 // Matt 5:32).

4. In the second case, 1 Cor 9:14, Paul appeals to a command of Jesus as supporting his case that he has the right to the church's material support even though he has given it up. This same saying emerges again in a similar context in 1 Tim 5:18, that "workers deserve their wages," which appears in this instance in the language of Luke 10:7.

5. Finally, in his attempt to correct the abuse of the Lord's Table in Corinth, Paul appeals to the words of institution as something he had received from the Lord and had in turn handed on to them (11:23–25). Although there is a degree of ambiguity with regard to what he means by "I received from the Lord," the fact is that what Paul cites is almost verbatim with what appears in Luke's Gospel. It should not surprise us, therefore, that when the "form" of a saying can be traced to the Gospel tradition itself, it is the Lukan version that Paul cites.

Again, even though there are but few of these, those that do appear are sufficient evidence that there is a much deeper pool of Jesus tradition from which Paul could cite if he had been so inclined. Why he was overall less inclined to do so is a matter of historical speculation; that he knew about Jesus and that he knew his teachings are incontrovertibly attested in his letters.

Paul and the Earthly Jesus

I conclude this chapter by offering a summarizing overview of several other texts that either assert or assume the genuine humanity of Christ, besides those just noted that indicate Paul's knowledge of the historical Jesus.

---

[18]See the full discussion, and christological implications, of this word in ch. 5, pp. 217–20; ch. 6, pp. 247–48.

Philippians 2:6–8

In a passage that begins with the assertion that Christ existed "in the form of God" but did not selfishly grasp his "equality with God," Paul makes the strongest kinds of statements regarding the genuineness of Christ's incarnate humanity. This begins with the strong metaphor "he poured himself out by taking the 'form' of a slave," which is then interpreted nonmetaphorically as "coming to be (being born) in the likeness of human beings," meaning that even though he had prior existence as God, his incarnation involved being born just as all other human beings.

The second sentence deals with what Christ did as an ἄνθρωπος, a truly "human being": he accepted the path to the cross in obedience to his Father. As was pointed out in the exegesis of this passage, this language simultaneously assumes that at one point he had not been a human being but that when he did become one of us, he was fully and completely so.

1 Timothy 2:5; 3:16

In a similar way, in speaking of Christ as the divine mediator between God and human beings, "Paul" puts the stress on Christ being truly human. As the TNIV nicely puts it, "There is one mediator between God and human beings, Christ Jesus, himself human" (2:5). And also as in the preceding passage, what he did as a human being was "to give himself up as a ransom"— language that presupposes choice and obedience. Thus, even though 1 Timothy is a disputed letter, it is significant here to point out that this essential bit of theology is in fact very Pauline.

Given this earlier statement, one is not surprised that the "hymn" in 3:16, which tells the essential gospel story, begins, "He was manifest *in the flesh* [= as one who was truly human]."

Galatians 4:4–5; Romans 8:3

As was pointed out in the exegesis of Gal 4:4–5, the narrative of salvation found in this very brief summary has as its point the fact that Christ's death eliminated the need for Torah observance. Its essential parts say, "God sent his Son . . . to redeem those under the law." But the two middle members, which elaborate the first part of the sentence and anticipate the latter, at the same time emphasize his humanity: he was born of a woman; he was born under the law. The first of these eliminates any possibility of a divine Savior who was not truly human; the second places him squarely within a clearly identifiable historical context. So even though there is probably no intent here to emphasize Christ's humanity as such, Paul in fact does so without trying—precisely because this was the common understanding of the early church.

In the second instance of this "sending formula" (Rom 8:3), the emphasis is especially on Christ's humanity so that he could serve as an adequate sin offering. Thus, he came "in the 'likeness' of sinful flesh." His flesh itself was like all others, but in this case he did not yield himself to sin.

Galatians 3:16; Romans 1:3; 9:5; 2 Timothy 2:8

These several texts are part of a much bigger picture in Paul's thought where, as will be spelled out in some detail in the following chapter, the human origins of Jesus as the Jewish Messiah are explicitly presented. On the one hand, in Gal 3:16 he is identified as Abraham's "seed," where Paul deliberately presents him as the embodiment/culmination of Israel itself. On the other hand, and more specifically messianic, Rom 1:3 and 2 Tim 2:8 identify him as born of David's lineage, while Rom 9:5 explicitly refers to him as the Messiah, as the culminating expression of Jewish privileges.

Again, no point is made of his humanity; it is simply the assumption inherent in the language itself. And this is true as well of Paul's use of Χριστός (as his primary way of identifying the now risen Jesus). It has been argued that this "name" always carries with it its titular connotations of Jesus as the Jewish Messiah.[19] But in any case, this title-turned-name, even when it is a simple identifying referent, always harks back to the historical reality that the earthly Jesus lived and died as the Jewish Messiah, whom God raised from the dead to be Lord of all.

The Use of the Name "Jesus"

My concern here is to point out that the one unqualified reality that emerges in all of Paul's letters is that the name "Jesus" always has as its primary referent the historical person Jesus of Nazareth, whom the Romans crucified and whom the earliest Christians believed to be the Jewish Messiah and the now risen Lord. And in very many cases the use of the historical name by itself is specifically pointing back to his earthly, truly human life. Thus, Paul's use of the name in itself carries the assumption of Christ's genuine humanity.

The One Who "Died for Our Sins"

Finally, in this gathering of data I must mention the reality that Paul places all the emphasis on the Messiah's redeeming work in his "death on the cross." Although this language also has become a theological construct for Paul, it never loses its actual historical bearings. That is, when Paul speaks of "the Son of God who loved me and gave himself for me," he is not thinking simply of the theological outcome of that death. It is the historical event of the death itself—the excruciating death by crucifixion at the hands of the (very historical) Roman Empire—to which Paul is referring. And so it is with every mention of the cross and of Christ's death as "for us." This

[19] See Wright, *Climax of the Covenant*, 41–55.

event does not begin for Paul as theology; it begins as *history*, where a truly human Jesus died as the Jewish Messiah. What Paul came to see clearly is that this historical event that was humanity's loud "No!" to Jesus of Nazareth was in fact God's louder "No!" to human sin; but through resurrection, God pronounced an exclamatory "Yes!" to everything that the historical Jesus had done through his death for sinners.

The One Who Knew No Sin

But there is one text in Paul's letters that explicitly puts Christ's humanity outside the framework of what is common to all other human beings. On the one hand, in a variety of ways Paul is adamant about the universality of human sinfulness ("all have sinned and come short of God's [intended] glory"); on the other hand, this is the single aspect of our common humanity that Jesus did not know by experience. In a text (2 Cor 5:21) where the clause is otherwise unnecessary for the point Paul is trying to make, he asserts that "[Christ] knew no sin," by which he means "know" in the Jewish sense of knowing by experience.

Nonetheless, the very reason for this assertion is to place it in stark contrast with the climactic phrase "he became sin [or, 'a sin offering'] for us." This is the great exchange; and it could happen for Paul only because the sinless one was nonetheless truly one of us and he came to know our sinfulness not by his own experience of it but by bearing the weight of it in his death on the cross. And in all of this he never ceased to be God as well. It is this mystery that lies at the heart of the Christian faith; and Paul is one of its primary advocates.

Finally, and to repeat once again what has been noted throughout this study, part of the significance of this accumulation of data is that in the majority of these passages Paul is not trying to prove something about Christ's humanity. It is quite clear that he is writing to believers who already share this understanding of Christ as part of what is common to the faith of the early church. At issue, therefore and finally, is the nature of their equally shared conviction that the truly human Jesus had been sent by the Father in order to effect their redemption.

In Paul's case, as we will see in the next two chapters, that conviction was a combination of two realities. First, Jesus in his earthly life fulfilled the Davidic promises that David's greater Son would effect final redemption for God's people, but that messianic Son turned out to be an incarnation of God's eternal Son. Second, through his exaltation the eternal Son also assumed the role of the "messianic Lord" seated at the right hand of the Father, the Lord to whom all now are ultimately subject and before whom at the eschaton every knee will bow and whose lordship every tongue will confess.

14

Jesus: Jewish Messiah and Son of God

IN THIS CHAPTER AND THE next we turn finally to examine what the data suggest are Paul's primary categories for understanding the person of Christ—that is, *who* it was who functioned as Redeemer and Creator of the new humanity. The answer proposed here, and spelled out in detail in these two chapters, is twofold: (1) the risen Jesus was none other than the preexistent *Son of God*, who came present among us to redeem; and (2) the risen Jesus is the *exalted Lord* "seated at the right hand of God" in fulfillment of Ps 110:1. In the first instance, we will note that there is some awareness, if not emphasis, on the relationship of the Son to the Father. In the second instance, the emphasis is altogether on the exalted Christ's relationship to us and to the world.[1]

Both of these themes, it will be pointed out, have their deepest roots in Jewish messianism, based on the Davidic kingship. In the first instance, Jesus was recognized to be of the "seed of David," who was God's anointed One, his "son" *par excellence*, whose progeny would sit on his throne "forever." In the second instance, David's messianic progeny was understood to be "the Lord" seated at the LORD's (= Yahweh) right hand in Ps 110:1. Yet in both cases, Paul's understanding went considerably beyond these roots: the son of David was none other than God's eternal Son; and the risen Lord at his exaltation had God's own "name" bestowed on him as the one before whom all creation will eventually bow and do homage.

---

[1] There is nothing new here, since this turns out to be the direction taken by many scholars who have written on the subject; see, e.g., M. Hengel, *Son of God*, 13–15; H. Ridderbos, *Paul*, 68–90; L. W. Hurtado, "Paul's Christology," in *The Cambridge Companion to Paul* (ed. J. D. G. Dunn; Cambridge: Cambridge University Press, 2003), 191–95; Matera, *New Testament Christology*, 132–33; cf. Kramer (*Christ, Lord, Son of God*), who also recognizes that this is so but unfortunately separates "Son of God" from "Christ." These two motifs also hold a prominent place even for those who would broaden the perspective some; e.g., Ziesler (*Pauline Christianity*, 24–48), who not only separates "Messiah" from "Son of God" and fronts "Wisdom" before both "Lord" and "Son of God" but also adds "Spirit" at the end—an unusual reading of Pauline Christology indeed; and his discussion of "Lord" has little foundation in Paul.

The history of NT scholarship also forces us to engage in the question of "origins,"[2] especially where Paul came by his understanding of Christ as the eternal Son of God. It is therefore of more than casual interest to note that *both* of these primary understandings of Christ were already at work in the Aramaic-speaking Jewish community that preceded Paul, as is evidenced in Paul's own letters. On three occasions he uses two different transliterated Aramaic terms, which are thus presupposed as part of the devotional life of his congregations: Αββα = "Father" (Gal 4:6; Rom 8:15) and Μαρανα θα = "Come, Lord" (1 Cor 16:22). As was noted in the exegetical chapters on these texts,[3] both of these terms have considerable christological significance, not the least of which is that *they reflect at a very early stage in the Aramaic-speaking community the two primary christological motifs in Paul's letters:* Jesus as Son of God and Jesus as Lord. Thus, however Paul may have been affected by other factors, the basic "origins" of these two primary christological motifs were deeply rooted in the believing community that preceded him.

The concern of the present chapter, then, is to examine the twofold sense of the theme of Jesus as the Son of God—as Jewish Messiah and eternal Son. At the same time, I am also picking up a major concern from the preceding chapter: as the eternal Son, Jesus is the One who perfectly bears the divine image and who through his death and resurrection is in the process in the new creation of restoring the divine image in those who are his. Because of the complex way I have chosen to process this material, I here offer the "logic" of the presentation.

The first concern is to demonstrate that Jesus is "son of God" in terms of Jewish messianism. To get there, one must establish the significance for Paul that it was the *crucified* Jesus who was indeed the Jewish Messiah. Scandal though it was, Paul's later reflection on his own encounter with the risen Lord caused him to capitalize on the scandal rather than downplay it. With that in hand, I walk through the basic Jewish story to show how Paul now reread the story in light of Christ. That leads us to trace the theme of "son of God" in the basic story, including its development as a messianic theme in later Judaism, which Paul has picked up as the first point of contact between Jesus as Son of God and the biblical story. But that history, as crucial as it is to Paul's understanding, does not explain how he came also to understand Christ as the *eternal* Son of God; so this is taken up at the end of the chapter, with emphasis on his understanding of Christ as the preexistent (thus eternal) Son of God, agent of creation, and, in his incarnation, agent of redemption.

---

[2] Indeed, this question drives much of the christological discussion; however, it seems methodologically backwards to begin here. The first task, rather, is the descriptive one, which in turn leads to the historical one. This methodological failure—starting with "origins" and then analyzing Paul's Christology in light of one's presuppositions on this matter—alone accounts for the popularity of Wisdom Christology, since the texts themselves do not support it even minimally (see appendix A, pp. 597–99).

[3] See chs. 3, pp. 120–22; 5, pp. 217–20; 6, pp. 247–48.

Jesus as the Messianic Son of God

In order to examine the christological significance of Jesus as the Son of God, one needs first to look at Paul's reflections on the relationship of Jesus to Israel's primary story.[4] Here we take our lead from Romans, the least impassioned of Paul's letters but the one where the passion of his own apostolic calling is argued at length: Jew and Gentile as one eschatological people of God. For in Romans in particular, Paul spells out quite plainly Jesus' earthly origins as the Jewish Messiah. In fact, Rom 9:5 is the one place in the corpus where all agree that ὁ Χριστός is altogether titular, where Jesus as the Jewish Messiah is the climax of the biblical story and thus of all Jewish privileges. Indeed, this concern is the first thing up in the letter—in the salutation (1:2–4), where Jesus is introduced as the messianic son of God, who in his subsequent exaltation returns to his place as eternal "Son of God with power."[5] It is not surprising, therefore, as we noted in ch. 6, that "Son of God" is the primary christological motif in the letter.

The place to begin this examination, however, is not with "Son of God" language as such but rather with the role that this language played in Israel's basic story, since Paul himself regularly places Christ within the parameters of that story. In order to do this, we begin where Paul does, with his own encounter with the crucified Jesus as the exalted (messianic) Lord of Ps 110:1—an encounter that radically altered his own understanding of Jesus as the Messiah and the relationship of this reality to the crucifixion.

The Ultimate Scandal: Jesus as Crucified Messiah

Nils Dahl once observed that scholars historically could speak of Paul's Christology without ever referring to the messiahship of Jesus. He then rightly goes on to point out that in historical fact, however, "whether Jesus was the Messiah or not was crucial in the life of the onetime persecutor and later apostle."[6] The justification for this correct assessment of Paul's view of Christ lies ready at hand in several passages that appear somewhat early in the corpus, beginning with two in 1 Corinthians, followed by two in Galatians, which is easily his most impassioned letter.

---

[4] Historically, this has not been so obvious to some, especially those in the long history of German scholarship who have insisted that this "title" belongs to Paul's "Hellenization" of the faith. But that day has almost totally run its course; see esp. the critique in Hengel, *Son of God*, 4–5, 17–41.

[5] Although many would object to this way of putting it, I am only trying to take Paul at face value; and he is the one who insists that God the Father "sent his Son" into the world (Rom 8:3; cf. Gal 4:4). To object that Paul is here using a prior creedal statement that he may not have fully incorporated is to argue against what Paul actually does: he dictates all of this into his own sentence with a view toward its oral reading in the Roman communities—communities that have already had a considerable history of belief in Christ before this letter was penned.

[6] See Dahl, *Jesus the Christ*, 15.

1 Corinthians 15:3; 1:18–25

When in 1 Cor 15:3 Paul reminds the Corinthians of what he "handed down" to them, namely, that "Christ died for our sins," he undoubtedly intended this as the early and universal creedal formula that NT scholarship has come to believe that it is. But what is generally overlooked by that same scholarship is that this "formula" comes at the very *end* of the letter, where Paul finally takes on those who deny a future bodily resurrection of believers; and thus it serves as an inclusio with, and must be understood in light of, the *first* item addressed in the letter in 1:13–2:16.[7] And here Paul is adamant that the content of his preaching deliberately involved the reality that the one who died for our sins had been *crucified* (2:1–3)—by the Romans and probably as a messianic pretender. At issue for him regarding the Corinthian believers was that some of them were seeking to avoid this central reality. And Paul will have none of that.

Moreover, this earlier passage makes sense contextually *only* if "Christ crucified" in fact means "a crucified Messiah."[8] This was the ultimate scandal for the Jews, which at the same time would have been such utter folly to the Greeks that one can only wonder why Paul would so vehemently press this point. Why not simply let Christ be a proper name and put the emphasis on his *death* as "for us"? But no, Paul says, we preach a *crucified* Messiah, knowing full well how both Jew and Greek would respond. And why does he do this? Because, he maintains, God in his own infinite wisdom and power thereby undercut every imaginable human pretension to being able "to find out God."[9]

But one may still ask, "So what?" with regard to Pauline Christology, to which the answer is, "One will simply never understand Paul himself, nor the depth of his commitment and utter devotion to Christ, who does not start here." And here is why Dahl's observation noted above is the historically correct one, which in turn leads us to seek for Paul's own reasons for such a proclamation when he knows how people on both sides of the ethnic

---

[7] This "failure" to read 1 Corinthians as a whole is especially damaging to the way Kramer (*Christ, Lord, Son of God*) chose to go about examining Paul's Christology. By going after the so-called pre-Pauline material to be found in Paul, he conveniently isolates this passage out of Paul's own Christology, so that he never even mentions that according to Paul himself (in a rhetorical moment, to be sure), the only Christ he preached in Corinth was Jesus as "a crucified Messiah."

[8] See the more complete discussion in ch. 3, pp. 101–2.

[9] To miss the point made in this paragraph is to miss Paul by too wide a margin. E.g., Reid (*Jesus, God's Emptiness, God's Fullness*, 19–20) rightly sees the significance of Paul's encounter with the *risen Christ*, but he fails to note the radical turnabout with regard to the crucifixion. Rather than simply giving Paul new insight into the cross, his encounter with the risen Christ meant for him a total overthrow of his deeply held conviction of what *God* had done by having Christ crucified; and this required a radical paradigm shift at the deepest roots of his understanding of messianism.

"wall of separation" will instinctively resist it. And thus that leads us back once more to Paul's own story.

Galatians 1:14; Philippians 3:4–6

Early on in the argument of Galatians, in demonstrating that his version of the gospel was without human origins of any kind and was therefore not dependent on Jerusalem, Paul points to the radical nature of his conversion. According to him, he had advanced far beyond others in Judaism in two ways: as a persecutor of the church and as an avid student of Torah. Although the second of these is perhaps the more important overall, his being a persecutor of the church is mentioned first in this instance in part because it distanced him from the early Christian community. This both demonstrated his independence from them and put him altogether on the other side of any of those who had actually followed Jesus as the Jewish Messiah. Thus, there was simply nothing historically that would have led him to become a follower of Christ, and yet he had in fact become one, passionately so.

The sentence that follows this preconversion autobiographical moment begins in an especially significant way: "When the God who . . . called me by his grace was pleased . . . to reveal his Son *in me* . . . so that I might preach him among the Gentiles . . ." As was pointed out in the exegesis of this passage (ch. 5, pp. 228–29), Paul's point is that the revelation was not *to* Paul in this case (that is mentioned in v. 12) but *in* Paul. The absolutely radical nature of his own "conversion" (from a Christ hater to a Christ devotee) served for him as Exhibit A of the gospel of grace that included both Jew and Gentile.

That v. 14 was not an incidental moment, struck on the hot iron of controversy, seems certain from Paul's pressing of the same two points in his much later retelling of his story in Phil 3:4–6. Here again he sets forth his unquestioned Jewish credentials, first in terms of what had been given him at birth (circumcised, of the tribe of Benjamin, an Israelite of Israelites) and second in terms of his own achievements within Judaism (a zealous Pharisee who persecuted the church and adhered to the law perfectly).[10] So again he juxtaposes his being a persecutor of the church and a faithful adherent of the law; and in this case the surpassing worth of knowing Christ as Lord put all of these former privileges into the category of "dung."

---

[10] It is of some interest that in both of these retellings of his essential pre-Christian story he places violence against the church before his loyal adherence to the law. Most likely this is the result of his own controversies within Judaism, where he was wont to remind other Jews that he had once been where they were. Hurtado makes the further point that both of these emphases make most sense if Paul had "developed sufficient familiarity with Jewish Christians to become convinced that they were a very dangerous sect and that resolute efforts to destroy it were demanded. It is, therefore, reasonable to suggest that Paul's basic christological beliefs were very likely reflective of the beliefs he had previously opposed" ("Paul's Christology," 188).

Thus, the common denominator of Paul's pre-Christian life was that he was an avid follower of Torah, accompanied by an equally avid hatred of those who dared proclaim that the crucified Jesus was in fact the Jewish Messiah.

Galatians 3:13; 1 Corinthians 1:22

We learn the reason for this hatred for followers of Jesus a bit later in Galatians, when in 3:13 Paul associates Christ's death by crucifixion with the curse of Deut 21:23 (expressed in the language of the curses of ch. 27): "Cursed [by God] is anyone who is hanged on a pole." Since Jesus had been "hung on a pole" by the Romans, this for Paul was the sure evidence that God had cursed him; and he whom God had cursed could not possibly be honored as the Jewish Messiah. Thus it is no mere bit of cleverness but words spoken out of personal experience that had led Paul earlier to argue with the Corinthians that a crucified Messiah must be recognized as *God's* power and wisdom at work in the world, since such a historical event is an utter scandal even to the everyday Jew (1 Cor 1:21–24), let alone to a passionate one such as Saul of Tarsus.

That this lies at the heart of Paul's pre-Christian understanding of Jesus of Nazareth helps to explain his being described in 1 Tim 1:13 as at one time "a blasphemer, persecutor, and violent man." Such a prior commitment to violent opposition alone explains the radical nature of his conversion in the Damascus Road experience, which he relates in terms of "I saw the Lord" (1 Cor 9:1). After all, here is an undoubted case where the *effect* (Paul's utter and total devotion to Christ as Lord) must be commensurate with the *cause* (seeing the crucified One as the risen One). His encounter with Jesus risen from the dead radicalized Paul (cf. 1 Cor 15:8); it also explains his departure to Arabia (Gal 1:17), perhaps in part to sort out what had happened to him.

Thus Paul emerged from this experience as a passionate follower of God's true Messiah—Jesus, crucified and raised from the dead. What he came to realize, as the argument in Gal 3:10–14 indicates, is that Christ's having been hanged on a cross did indeed involve God's curse but not on Christ himself. Rather, the whole human race, in its sin and rebellion against the eternal God, came under God's curse and in effect was hung on the cross through the one perfect sacrifice. Thus, humankind's "No" to Christ was in fact God's "No" to our fallenness and rebellion, whereby he offered us grace and eternal glory. And by raising Christ from the dead, God said "Yes" to his Son and thus to humankind through the Son. The result, Paul argues, was that what for any good Jew was the ultimate oxymoron—a crucified Messiah—turns out to be the ultimate expression of God's own wisdom and power against every form of human machination.

Here is a sure instance, therefore, where "frequency of mention" is quite unrelated to theological significance.[11] That Paul does not refer more frequently either to his conversion or to Christ as a "crucified Messiah" has little or no bearing on the importance of this event for his subsequent theological understanding. Rather, what does emerge with a kind of frequency that is theologically compelling is the sheer volume of Paul's references to the risen Lord Jesus as (the) "Christ."[12] Even if one grants that by the time of his letters the title "the Christ" had moved very close to a name in its own right, the messianic origins of this "name" are probably never fully abandoned. In Paul's case, this is evidenced by the considerable frequency of every imaginable combination of names and titles in the corpus, including the Pastoral Epistles, except the combination "the Lord Christ," which appears but twice (Rom 16:18; Col 3:24). The fact that the combination occurs at all indicates that the title has in fact become something of a name; yet its infrequency in comparison with all the other combinations suggests that Paul comes to this slowly and rarely.[13]

Since this title-turned-name derives directly out of Paul's own understanding of the crucified and risen Jesus as the Jewish Messiah, it is of some importance to trace this understanding as best one can by way of Paul's relationship to the basic narrative of his deeply held commitment to historic Judaism. Whatever else is true of Paul's Christology, he himself was convinced that the crucified and now risen Christ is in fact the culmination of the basic Jewish story, as Rom 9:3–5 bears eloquent testimony.

Christ and the Basic Narrative of Judaism

We begin this inquiry by noting that Paul cites or echoes the OT, primarily in its Septuagintal form, in over two hundred instances[14] and in a variety

---

[11]This is another major shortcoming in Kramer's analysis of Pauline Christology (see n. 7 above). The end result of his limiting his study to "titles" is a thoroughgoing minimizing of Christ = Messiah. Although he recognizes that this would have been its *original* meaning, he expresses doubt as to whether it would carry meaning for the *Greek-speaking* Hellenistic communities (indeed, he concludes that "such a connection is completely unrecognized by the Gentile Christian church in the Pauline period" [pp. 213–14], which would seem to put any proper understanding of 1 Cor 1:22–25 and Rom 9:5 in considerable doubt!). To the contrary, one must take seriously that the original Pauline communities were mixed and that Paul himself had been their teacher. And in any case, the place to begin is with Paul's *own* understanding as that emerges in his letters.

[12]By actual count (using the text of NA[27]), "Christ" is used 343 times in the church corpus, plus 32 in the Pastoral Epistles; by way of contrast, the designation "Lord," which is only a title in Paul's writings, occurs 223 times, plus 22 in the Pastoral Epistles, and the actual name "Jesus" occurs 177 times, plus 31 in the Pastoral Epistles.

[13]For the statistics included in this paragraph, see the table in ch. 1, p. 26. Cf. Dahl, *Jesus the Christ*, 16.

[14]This is by actual count of appendix I in Ellis, *Paul's Use of the Old Testament*, 150–54.

of ways throughout the corpus. Although Paul tends to *cite* the OT primarily in argumentation,[15] the letters that are often regarded as having no citations (e.g., Thessalonians, Colossians, Philippians) are full of even more important kinds of materials where the OT is *echoed* in such crucial ways and with such frequency that one must assume his readers for the most part to have been able to hear these echoes.[16]

Thus when one turns to look at Paul's use of the OT in general, what stands out is the fact that his primary interest lies with the central features of Israel's essential story:[17]

1. Creation

2. Abraham (with the promise of Gentile inclusion)

3. The exodus (deliverance from bondage and gaining the inherited land)

4. The giving of the law (especially Deuteronomy, with its anticipation of Israel's failure regarding the law)

5. Davidic kingship

6. Exile and the promised restoration (the eschatological consummation), which especially included Gentiles

It is not surprising, therefore, that although Paul cites texts from all over the Greek Bible, the majority (over 70 percent) come from Genesis, Deuteronomy, Isaiah, and the Psalter.[18] What is most striking is the role that Christ plays in the story, as the story itself is now read so as to incorporate Christ crucified, raised, and exalted. Indeed, for Paul, Christ plays a major role in all six of the primary facets of the story. Even though our present interest is with the fifth and sixth items—the Davidic kingship and the eschatological consummation—a brief look at the role that Christ plays in the first four elements of the story serves to heighten the effect of the whole picture, that whatever else, Christ is first of all the messianic Son of God who at the same time is (especially) the eternal Son of God.

Creation

The role of Christ in creation is writ large in two major christological texts in the corpus: 1 Cor 8:6 and Col 1:15–16. To be sure, some have found these texts to be echoing personified Wisdom's alleged role in creation; but a careful examination of these texts demonstrates that this is a

---

[15] Thus the majority are in Romans, 1 Corinthians, Galatians, and 2 Corinthians.

[16] On this matter, see the discussion in ch. 1, pp. 20–25.

[17] On this matter, see the discussion of Col 1:12–14 in ch. 7, pp. 295–98.

[18] It is in light of this large use of the Greek Bible that we need also to note the considerable paucity of texts from the wisdom tradition, precisely because they are not part of the primary story (see the analysis in appendix A, pp. 602–5).

false path.[19] The point to repeat here from the exegesis of the two passages in their respective letters is that in both cases what is either implied (1 Corinthians) or explicit (Colossians) is that Jesus as *the Son of God* is in fact the divine agent of creation. That is, identifying God as Father in 1 Cor 8:6 and the specific identification of Christ as the Father's beloved Son in Col 1:13 place creation firmly in the context of Jesus as the messianic/eternal Son of God; indeed, Paul urges in Col 1:15–16, everything that exists came through the agency of the beloved (eternal) Son, who is expressly identified as the sphere, agent, and goal of the whole created order.

Abraham (with the Promise of Gentile Inclusion)

Abraham as progenitor of God's elect people plays a major role on two occasions where Paul refers to the story: Gal 3 and Rom 4. And as with creation, Christ himself plays the crucial role in the (now eschatological) retelling of the story. In Galatians, Christ is identified as the true "seed of Abraham" (v. 16), so that all who are "in Christ" become Abraham's true children (v. 29).

In the argument of Romans, the role of Christ with regard to Abraham is spelled out in a slightly different way, but in the end it comes out at the same place. Abraham again is the ancestor of all peoples, Jew and Gentile alike. But in this case, Abraham offers the key to much of the story: he is (1) the exemplary man of faith, in that (2) he trusted God *before* circumcision, and is thus the father of Gentiles who believe. Indeed, (3) he received circumcision as an expression of his faith and is thus also the father of the Jews, now especially of those who have similar faith. But most telling is (4) *how* he serves as the primary example of faith: through the birth of Isaac, whom he received as one raised from the dead (!), which in turn leads to our faith in the one who was truly raised from the dead.

On the matter of Christ and Abraham, one should note further the echo of Gen 22:16 in Rom 8:32, where Christ steps into the role of the promised Son. Just as God blessed Abraham because οὐκ ἐφείσω τοῦ υἱοῦ σου τοῦ ἀγαπητοῦ (*you did not spare your beloved son*), so God himself steps into the role of Abraham, ὅς γε τοῦ ἰδίου υἱοῦ οὐκ ἐφείσατο ἀλλὰ ὑπὲρ ἡμῶν πάντων παρέδωκεν αὐτόν (*[he] did not spare his own Son but freely gave him up for us all*). Thus every mention in Paul's letters of Abraham and his role in the basic story is explicitly tied to Christ. With Christ's coming, the promise to Abraham that all the nations will be blessed had found its fulfillment.

The Exodus (Deliverance from Bondage and Gaining the Inherited Land)

This part of the story comes through in ever so many ways, primarily in the soteriological texts, which are too many to note here. Indeed, every

---

[19] See appendix A (pp. 595–630), plus the excursuses in 1 Corinthians (pp. 102–15), 2 Corinthians (pp. 186–87), and Colossians (pp. 317–25).

metaphor for salvation in Christ except reconciliation comes directly from the Pentateuch, especially when the theme of "redemption" itself occurs. One passage in particular, Col 1:12–16, can be brought forward here, since it echoes so much of the story of the exodus, including gaining the inherited land, while at the same time it embraces item 5, the Davidic kingship. Here is the passage with the various key elements in the basic story underlined:

[12]*giving joyful thanks to the Father, who has qualified you to share in the inheritance of the saints in the kingdom of light. [13]For he has rescued us from the dominion of darkness and brought us into the kingdom of the Son he loves, [14]in whom we have redemption, the forgiveness of sins, [15]who is the image of the invisible God, the firstborn over all creation. [16]For in him all things were created . . . all things have been created through him and for him.*

Without repeating the exegesis of this text here, I simply note that every significant moment in the story except for the giving of the law is found echoed in some way in this passage; and Christ's replacing the law is what the argument and appeal of 2:6–23 is all about.[20] Thus:

1. Creation: He is both before all things,
               they were all created "in him" and "through him,"
               and they all exist "for him";
               and in v. 18 he is the "beginning" of the new creation.

2. Abraham: The language of "beloved son" begins here (Gen 22:2, 16).

3. Exodus: (a) The verb "rescued" (ἐρρύσατο) and noun "redemption"
                  (ἀπολύτρωσιν) echo Exod 6:6, a crucial text in the story.
              (b) The "deliverance" is from the power of darkness.
              (c) The result is "a share in the inheritance."

[4. The law: This emerges as the central issue in 2:6–23.]

5. Kingship: Several verbal echoes from David's story are present:
              (a) The Son is King (or the King is God's Son).
              (b) The Son is God's beloved.
              (c) The Son is God's "firstborn" (πρωτότοκος, as in Exod 4:22;
                  Ps 89:26–27).

6. The eschatological inclusion of the Gentiles, signaled by the interchange of "you/us."

And all of this is found in just one (very long) sentence. I simply note further that this basic narrative is thoroughgoing in Paul's thought. Christ is

_____

[20]On this matter, see G. D. Fee, "Old Testament Intertextuality in Colossians: Reflections on Pauline Christology and Gentile Inclusion in God's Story," in *History and Exegesis: New Testament Essays in Honor of E. Earle Ellis on His Eightieth Birthday* (ed. A. Son; London: T&T Clark, 2006), 203–23.

regularly seen as the way the new-covenant fulfillment of the story takes place, and thus he is understood as being in continuity with the first expression of the story. At the same time, in 1 Cor 10:4, 9 he is expressly understood to have been present with Israel in that first expression of the story.

The Giving of the Law

Here is the one element that all readily recognize as "fulfilled" with the coming of Christ. Nonetheless, it is of some interest to note that this emphasis occurs in Paul's writings in only four places, all of which have in common the threat of Gentiles capitulating to Torah observance (Romans; Galatians; Phil 3; Col 2). The key christological text at this point is Rom 10:4: τέλος γὰρ νόμου Χριστὸς εἰς δικαιοσύνην παντὶ τῷ πιστεύοντι (*For Christ is the end/goal of the law with regard to righteousness for everyone who believes*).

The point of this abbreviated review is simply to point out that for Paul, Christ both was present at key places in the first unfolding of the story and is the central feature of its present eschatological unfolding. Thus, one is not surprised to see Christ play the absolutely major role in the crucial fifth and sixth elements of the story, which at the same time serve as the key matters in Paul's Christology.

Jesus as the Davidic Son of God

In order to appreciate how Paul came to understand Christ as the eternal Son of God first of all in terms of the Davidic kingship, we need (selectively) to examine several key texts from the story itself,[21] including the role that the historical Jesus himself plays in the story.

Exodus 4:22–23

We begin by noting the primary text where Israel as a people is designated as God's son, Exod 4:22–23, where Moses is directed to speak with Pharaoh:

Then say to Pharaoh, "This is what Yahweh says, 'Israel is my <u>firstborn son</u> [υἱὸς πρωτότοκός μου], *and I told you, "Let <u>my son</u> go, so he may worship me." But you refused to let him go, so I will kill your firstborn son.'"*

Here, as a play on words in terms of what would happen to the Egyptians, *Israel* is designated both as God's "son" and "firstborn." This theme is echoed in Hos 11:1, "Out of Egypt I have called my son."

2 Samuel 7:13–14, 18 LXX

In time, this "son" designation falls on Israel's king, who was understood both as God's representative to Israel and especially as standing in for

---

[21] Traditionally, both the NT and early Christian writers saw many such texts as predicting a kingly messiah: Isa 9:6–7; 11:1–9; Jer 23:5–6; 33:14–16; Ezek 34:23–24; 37:24; Zech 9:9–10; Ps 132:11–18.

the people before God. Thus, as the story progresses, the king especially picks up this designation, and he does so at the crucial turning point in the story: the Davidic covenant. Note the Septuagint of 2 Sam 7:13–14 (regarding Solomon and his successors) and 7:18 (regarding David himself):

¹³αὐτὸς οἰκοδομήσει μοι οἶκον τῷ ὀνόματί μου καὶ ἀνορθώσω τὸν θρόνον αὐτοῦ ἕως εἰς τὸν αἰῶνα. ¹⁴**ἐγὼ ἔσομαι αὐτῷ εἰς πατέρα καὶ αὐτὸς ἔσται μοι εἰς υἱόν·** . . . ¹⁸καὶ εἰσῆλθεν ὁ βασιλεὺς Δαυιδ καὶ ἐκάθισεν ἐνώπιον κυρίου καὶ εἶπεν· τίς εἰμι ἐγώ, κύριέ μου κύριε, καὶ τίς ὁ οἶκός μου ὅτι **ἠγάπηκάς με** ἕως τούτων;

¹³*He will build a house for my name and I will establish his throne forever.* ¹⁴*I **will be a Father to him and he will be my son.** . . .* ¹⁸*And King David went in and sat before the* LORD *and said: Who am I,* LORD *my Lord, and what is my house that **you have loved me** in this way?*

Thus in the Davidic covenant, David's progeny will be called "God's son," while David himself responds (in the Septuagint only) that he is God's beloved.

Psalm 2:2, 7–8; 72:1 (71:1 LXX)

The theme of the king as God's "son" is especially picked up in the Psalter, serving in fact to frame the so-called Davidic Psalter (books 1–2). Indeed, Ps 2, which introduces books 1–2, was most likely a coronation hymn for the Davidic scion. Significantly, this is also the first instance in the OT where the "kingly son" is also called the Lord's "anointed," which in the Septuagint is translated χριστός (*Christ*). Thus in this psalm, which now introduces Israel's king as the one who stands in for the people with laments and praises to God, the psalmist declares both that the king is "God's Christ" and "God's son" and that the nations (Gentiles) will become his inheritance:

Ps 2:2:

οἱ ἄρχοντες συνήχθησαν ἐπὶ τὸ αὐτὸ	*The rulers have gathered together*
κατὰ τοῦ κυρίου	*against the* LORD
καὶ **κατὰ τοῦ χριστοῦ** <u>αὐτοῦ</u> . . .	*and **against** <u>his</u> **Anointed (Christ)** . . .*

Ps 2:7–8:

⁷διαγγέλλων τὸ πρόσταγμα κυρίου,	⁷*I will declare the* LORD'*s decree:*
<u>κύριος εἶπεν</u> **πρός με**·	<u>*The* LORD *said* **to me,**</u>
υἱός <u>μου</u> **εἶ σύ,**	**"You are** <u>*my*</u> **son;**
<u>ἐγὼ σήμερον γεγέννηκά</u> **σε**·	<u>*today I have begotten*</u> **you.**
⁸**αἴτησαι** <u>παρ' ἐμοῦ</u>, καὶ δώσω **σοι**	⁸**Ask** <u>*of me, and I will give*</u> **you**
ἔθνη **τὴν κληρονομίαν σου** . . .	*the nations **as your inheritance** . . ."*

Similarly, and with obvious thoughtfulness, the collector put a psalm of Solomon as the bookend to Ps 2, and thus as the framing device for the initial Davidic Psalter:

Ps 72:1 (71:1 LXX):
ὁ θεός, τὸ κρίμα σου **τῷ βασιλεῖ** δὸς,
    καὶ τὴν δικαιοσύνην σου **τῷ υἱῷ τοῦ βασιλέως**.
God, give your justice **to the king,**
    and your righteousness **to the royal son.**

Psalm 89:26–27 (88:27–28 LXX)

It was the "eternal" nature of this covenant that in turn elicited Ethan the Ezrahite's plaintive cry in Ps 89, composed during the exile in light of the apparent demise of both the king and Jerusalem. In the part of the psalm where he is reciting the promises of God's covenant with David (vv. 20–38), he reminds God of his own declaration: David, whom ἔχρισα (*I have anointed* [v. 21]; cf. v. 39, τὸν χριστόν σου [*your anointed one* = *your Christ*]), would call on God as "my Father" (v. 26), and God thus would make him his πρωτότοκον (*firstborn* [v. 27]). In so doing, he was reflecting the reality that the king stood in for the people, the original "son and firstborn" (Exod 4:22–23), who as "son" is also his "anointed one" (= his Christ).

The Story of Jesus in the Gospels

The next step in Israel's narrative brings us to Jesus, who according to the Synoptic tradition took unto himself all of these themes except "firstborn" when he presented himself to Israel as its long-expected messianic king. Indeed, the primary themes are already put in place at his baptism, first with the voice from heaven ("You are my Son, whom I love") and second with his use of Deut 8 and 6 to respond to the tempter in the wilderness. Here is Jesus stepping into the role of Israel as God's Son, going through the waters, followed by forty days in the wilderness, but succeeding precisely at the points where Israel failed when they were tested forty years in the wilderness. And this is followed immediately in the NT narrative by Jesus' going forth to pronounce the advent of the kingdom of God.

All of this happened to Jesus himself, without others around to be observers. So how do the Gospel writers know about this event in which Jesus steps into the role of *Israel* as God's son and by implication into the messianic role of Israel's *king* as God's son? The possible answers are two: this is the creation of the later church that had come to believe this about him, or he himself disclosed it to the inner circle. My point is that in either case, this narrative is quite in keeping with what Paul had come to believe about Christ some years before the Gospels had been written. And since Paul, by his own testimony, had little association with the early Aramaic-speaking followers of Jesus, he can hardly be accused of creating this view of the historical Jesus.

It is of more than a little interest, therefore, that the series of conflict stories between Jesus and the Jewish leaders, as they come to us in the Gospel tradition, also presents the picture that emerges in Paul's letters. This comes out especially in the way these stories are arranged in Mark's Gospel (12:1–37 // Matt 21:33–22:46 // Luke 20:9–47). One can scarcely miss the nature of the disclosure. The central part of this series of five pericopes offers three different kinds of conflict between Jesus and the Jewish leaders: on paying the imperial tax to Caesar (vv. 13–17); on the question of the resurrection of the dead (vv. 18–27); on the question of the greatest commandment (vv. 28–34). But these are framed by two stories in which Jesus takes the initiative. The first one, the parable of the Tenants in the Vineyard, openly asserts a Son of God Christology, where God's final envoy to Israel is his beloved Son. Nor can one easily miss how the messianic Ps 118:22–23 is embedded in the story. Equally significant is the way the series concludes: with an exalted-Lord Christology, where Jesus' point is that he is more than merely a son of David. The Son of God is none other that the exalted Lord of Ps 110:1.

My point in this rehearsal of the basic narrative of Israel, of Israel's king as God's son, and of Jesus as the true Israel as well as God's true Son is that this is where all Son of God Christology in the NT must begin. And so it does with Paul. It is not, in fact, the creation of the later church as it gets tampered with by Greek modes of thought. It is biblical at its very core— although the way the story turns out is a surprise to everyone: the messianic king of Israel, God's true Son, is not simply one more in the line of David; he turns out in fact to be the incarnate Son, who in his incarnation reveals true sonship and true kingship.

If all of this is not found in Paul's writings in this way, it is arguable that such an understanding of the Jewish Messiah, and of Jesus as that Messiah, lies behind the telling moments when Paul does momentarily lift the veil. Indeed, this is the very first thing up in Romans, the letter whose ultimate concern is Jew and Gentile *together* as the one eschatological people of God. Thus, we start with this text, whose key words include "promised," "Son," and "David." And it emerges again at the beginning of the long exposition of God's faithfulness to Israel in 9:3–5, where Christ is specifically identified as the Jewish Messiah.[22]

---

[22] It is of particular interest to note that the two letters where "Son of God" is the dominant christological theme (Galatians and Romans) are the two letters dominated by more strictly Jewish concerns. Cf. Hurtado: "Paul's references to Jesus as God's Son are concentrated in Romans and Galatians . . . , where Paul is in most intense and sustained dialogue with the Jewish tradition" ("Paul's Christology," 191). Moreover, along with Col 1:13–17, Rom 1:2–4 holds together in unresolved tension the twin realities that the eternal Son of God entered human history as the messianic Son.

Jesus as the Eschatological King/Son of God

That leads us, then, to look once again at this theme in Paul's writings, because he stands in direct line between the disclosure by Jesus as found in the Synoptic tradition and the later, theologically insightful reflections on this reality found in John's Gospel. What happens with Son of God language in Paul's letters is very much like what happened with the messianic title ὁ Χριστός (*the Christ*). What at first was a messianic title, pure and simple (Jesus is the Christ, the Messiah), and still is found in such passages as Rom 9:5, soon became the Savior's primary *name*, "Christ." And it is used this way by Paul in his extant letters considerably more than what had now become the primary *title*, "the Lord."

The same thing can be seen in the use of Son of God language. It is still rooted in Jewish messianism; but because of Paul's conviction of the Son's *preexistence*, the language is also used to refer to him in his prior existence as God before he became one with us in his incarnation. This shift in perspective is seen most easily in three places in Paul's letters, where the relationship between Christ as kingly, thus messianic, Son of God easily merges with the greater reality that the kingly (messianic) Son is in fact the eternal Son of God, whom the Father sent into the world in order to make us his children.

Romans 1:2–4

My point in this long rehearsal has been that Son of God Christology in Paul's thought does not *begin* in eternity; rather, it begins with the OT narrative of God's dealings with Israel. But for Paul, this language has meaning far beyond its historical messianic origins. This is made especially clear in the prologue of Romans, where in vv. 2–4 Paul states that the gospel that he preaches was promised *beforehand* through the prophets and that the now fulfilled promise is essentially about God's Son, who in his earthly life was a descendant of David but who is now to be known as "the Son of God with power," predicated on resurrection from the dead.

Although perhaps not intended as such, here is the one certain place in Paul's letters where Davidic Son and eternal Son merge. And although it is true that if this were the only text of its kind in the corpus, one could easily settle for an adoptionist Christology—Jesus becomes the "eternal" Son at his resurrection and subsequent exaltation—the rest of Romans itself will not allow such a view. Rather, Rom 1:4 should be understood as the Father's and Spirit's vindication of the eternal Son, who had previously been sent by the Father "in the likeness of our sinful flesh" (8:3) so as to be the divine sin offering, which would be the starting point of our becoming children of God as well.

So when Paul in Gal 1:15–16 says that God was pleased to reveal his Son in Paul himself, Paul is no longer thinking of the Son's origins as the heir to the Davidic throne. Here, as elsewhere, he is expressing himself in terms of eternal realities. God's Son is not simply the messianic king, sent by God to deliver Israel from bondage; God's Son is the one whom the Father sent to earth to redeem his people and give them adoption as "sons" so that they, too, become full heirs—not now of a strip of land on the eastern Mediterranean shore but of eternity itself. Indeed, Paul urges, the redeemed themselves are joint-heirs with the "firstborn" into whose image they are being re-created (8:17, 29).

1 Corinthians 15:24–28

In this second text, Paul again blends Jesus as the kingly Messiah with his being the eternal Son, but in this case in a quite different, and most remarkable, way. The thrust of the passage involves the eschaton, when the Son turns over his rule to the Father. Currently, Paul affirms, everything is under his rule; indeed, he continues, the heavenly Messiah must rule until all his enemies are subdued, including especially the final enemy, death. In so doing, Paul merges two texts that had been long understood as messianic, Ps 110:1 (109:1 LXX) and Ps 8:6 (8:7 LXX). Thus, the exalted Messiah must rule on high until "all his enemies are under his feet" (Ps 110:1); for, Paul goes on in the language of Ps 8:6, "he [God] has subjected all things under his [the Son's] feet." Thus, when the currently reigning messianic Son has, by life, destroyed the final enemy, death, that marks the end of the Son's messianic functions. So he in turn returns to his prior "role" as eternal Son.

Colossians 1:13–15

That brings us back once more to the thanksgiving-turned-narrative in Col 1:12–15, where Paul refers to the Colossians' Redeemer as God's beloved Son and to their redemption in terms of being brought into "the kingdom of his Son." It is easy to see, as noted above, that this language has its roots in Israel's essential story—redemption into a kingdom ruled by God's Son. But when we come to vv. 15–17, even though Paul is still echoing OT language about the Son's relationship to the Father, his concern now moves far beyond the OT story as such to eternal verities. This Son preexisted with the Father, whose image he bears; this Son has the rights of primogeniture with regard to the whole created order, and that is because this Son is both the agent and the goal of the whole created order. Moreover, this Son is the head over all the powers for the sake of his body, of whom he is also the head from which all the forces of life are drawn. Indeed, he is also both Redeemer and Creator of the new creation (3:10–11).

These passages thus indicate that Paul could hold both dimensions of his Son of God Christology in some tension. The eternal Son entered our history in the role of the messianic Son, becoming incarnate so as to redeem us. The rest of this chapter will offer an interpretation of Paul's understanding of the eternal Son and his relationship to the Father; this will be done first by an examination of the various ways Paul presents his Son of God Christology.

Jesus as the Preexistent, Eternal Son of God

At issue for us is how we are finally to understand Paul's designation of Jesus as "the Son of God," especially in terms of his understanding of the relationship of the Son to the Father. To get there, we begin by noting the nature and extent of the data.

The Linguistic Data

Here are the bare data with regard to usage (the texts are given in the appendix to this chapter):

1. Paul refers to Christ as Son seventeen times, sixteen of which are directly qualified in relationship to God (either "of God," "his," or "his own");[23] all of these appear in the church corpus.

2. In the same corpus Paul refers to God as "Father" thirty times,[24] plus three in the Pastoral Epistles. Except for 1 Cor 15:23–28 and Col 1:12–13, where mention of the Son is separated from mention of the Father by twenty-six words or more, "Son" and "Father" do not otherwise occur in the same sentence or clause. That is, Jesus is "the Son of God" or "his [God's] Son" but never explicitly "the Son of the Father."

3. Of the thirty appearances of "Father," twenty-three occur in the combination "God and Father," of which eleven are qualified by "our" ("our God and Father").

4. Of the remaining twelve instances of this combination, three are qualified by "of our Lord Jesus Christ" (2 Cor 1:3; 11:31; Eph 1:3), while the same combination occurs in Col 1:3 but without the καί (*and*). As was noted in the exegesis of this latter passage (ch. 7, pp. 292–93), this appositional usage (i.e., "thanks be to God, the Father of our Lord Jesus Christ") serves as the clue that the καί in the other occurrences is also appositional (= "God, even the Father").

5. Emphasis on the relational aspect of the Son to God the Father occurs four times: twice with the language of "beloved" (Col 1:13; Eph 1:6), once with the reflexive ἑαυτοῦ (Rom 8:3), where it serves as an intensive (= "his

---

[23] The only instance where the divine genitive qualifier does not occur is in 1 Cor 15:28, where Paul says αὐτὸς ὁ υἱός ὑποταγήσεται (*the Son himself will be subject*); but even here the intensive αὐτός takes us back to v. 24, where Paul says that "he [Christ] will hand over the kingdom τῷ θεῷ καὶ πατρί [either *to his God and Father* or *to God, even the Father*]."

[24] This includes only the uses of πατήρ, not the 2 occurrences of Αββα, since πατήρ occurs in both cases as the Greek translation of this transliterated Aramaic word.

own"), and once as an intensive (Rom 8:32) in a passage that reflects the unique sonship of Isaac in Gen 22:1–19.

What emerges from this analysis of the data is that Christ as "Son of God" occurs in contexts that have to do with his relationship both to believers and to God the Father. To these two dimensions of the Son's relationships we now turn.

God's Son as Savior

Paul uses Son of God language in at least three kinds of settings, when speaking of human redemption. First, and not surprisingly, Son of God Christology emerges when Paul reflects on Christ's present reign as king, which we noted in the examination of Col 1:12–15 and 1 Cor 15:23–28. Especially in the latter passage, the Son now reigns and will do so until the final enemy, death, is destroyed and all things are restored to their pre-fallen, now eternal destiny. This usage almost certainly belongs to the tradition traced above in the sections "Jesus as the Messianic Son of God" and "Jesus as the Eschatological King/Son of God."[25]

Second, Paul often thinks of Christ as "Son of God" when he reflects on what it means for the redeemed to be in relationship with the eternal God as Father. This comes out especially in the twin passages in Gal 4:4–7 and Rom 8:14–18. In Galatians we are told that human redemption is the direct result of God's sending forth his Son and that the evidence for us of that redemption is his sending forth the Spirit of his Son into our hearts, whereby we use the Son's own language, *Abba*, which means in turn that we ourselves are God's children and heirs.

Here especially Christ as the messianic and the eternal Son of God merge in Paul's thinking. The Son who was sent into the world to redeem does so in the context of the basic biblical story (born under the law). But the story works precisely because the redeemer is the eternal Son of God, thus a fully divine Savior. It was the One who was eternally in the form of God, and thus equal with God and fully divine, whose humble obedience to his Father in his incarnation led to his death on a cross (Phil 2:6–8).[26]

This understanding of salvation—we have become God's children through redemption by God's Son—is what lies behind Paul's utter devotion to Christ the Son. This comes out especially in Gal 2:20, "The life I now live in the body I live by faith in the Son of God, who loved me and gave himself

---

[25] On the suggestion by O. Cullmann (*Christology*, 293) that Christ's sonship has a terminal point, see in the present volume n. 81 in ch. 3 (on 1 Cor 15:28). Cf. Ridderbos: "One will have to judge the 'post-existence' of the Son intended here in the light of what is elsewhere so clearly stated of his preexistence [Gal 4:4]" (*Paul*, 69).

[26] Cf. R. Bauckham: "Christology may not isolate Jesus' mission from his being. A purely functional Christology of God's action in Jesus' mission is inadequate, for his mission is rooted in his being the Son in his personal intimacy with the Father" ("The Sonship of the Historical Jesus in Christology," *SJT* 31 [1978]: 258–59).

for me," where the emphasis is on the Son's love as demonstrated in his re-deeming sacrifice. But it is also reflected in a much more relational way in the four passages where he speaks of God as "the Father of our Lord Jesus Christ" (2 Cor 1:3; 11:31; Col 1:3; Eph 1:3). The coming of the Son forever radicalized Paul's understanding of God, who is now blessed not in the lan-guage of Jewish transcendentalism, where God is blessed for his attributes of power and glory and otherness, but rather is blessed as the Father of our Lord Jesus Christ, the God whom we now know through his Son.

Third, Paul reflects a Son of God Christology when he thinks of our re-demption in terms of the new creation, whereby children of Adam, who bear the image of their fallen forebear, are now being transformed back into God's own image. This is effected by the Son, who, on the one hand, himself perfectly bears that image (2 Cor 4:4) and, on the other hand, bears the true, perfect image of our humanity (Rom 8:29). Through the Son we are ever being transformed into the image of the eternal God as we are being shaped into the image of the Son, the one perfect human being who most truly bore the image of God.[27]

In this regard it is of some importance for us briefly to note how Son of God Christology frames the whole of Rom 8. It begins in v. 3, with God send-ing his own Son in the likeness of our sinful humanity in order to condemn sin in human flesh. It is picked up again at the beginning of the application in vv. 14–17, whereby the Spirit of the Son brings about our adoption as "sons," the same Spirit who bears witness with our spirits that we are indeed God's children and, if children, then heirs of God as joint-heirs with Christ the Son. At the end of this section, in vv. 29–30, the final purpose of the Son's redemption is expressed in terms of our being conformed into the Son's own image so that he might be the firstborn of many brothers and sis-ters. And at the end, in vv. 32–34, where Paul now echoes the story of Abra-ham and Isaac in Gen 22, he returns to the theme of God's redeeming us through the gift of his Son: "He did not spare his own Son, but freely gave him up for us all."

All of this is to say, then, that Paul's Son of God Christology, with its roots deep in Israel's story, finds its grand expression in human redemption that transforms the redeemed into "sons" and heirs of God as well. No won-der, then, that when Paul bursts into doxology, it is expressed in terms of "the God [who is now known as] the Father of our Lord Jesus Christ," the eternal Son.

---

[27] Kim (*Origin of Paul's Gospel*, 133–36) reads the Pauline evidence in a quite dif-ferent way. Based on what he calls "the two definitions of the gospel" in Rom 1:2–4, 16, he makes the startling claim that "for Paul the 'Son of God' means, when used in definition of the gospel, the one who has brought the law to an end, redeemed the believer from sin and the law, and therefore superseded the law as the means of sal-vation" (p. 133). But this is to read "Son of God" into Rom 1:16 by the circuitous path of the so-called two definitions and thus also to miss the *relational* aspect of this christological perspective.

As has been pointed out regularly in the exegetical chapters, one should note again here how "unrehearsed" all of this is. There is no attempt to persuade (after all, the Colossians passage, e.g., flows out of the thanksgiving), and there is no need to call attention to the source of this language and imagery. This kind of thing just flows out of Paul. So Jesus as the Son of God has inherent in it that Jesus is the kingly Messiah who in his case *redeems* his people through sacrificial death and subsequent resurrection.

Jesus as Son of the Father

All that has been said to this point again simply draws out the christological implications that emerge in Paul's primarily soteriological concerns. We need to conclude by pointing out Paul's thoroughly presuppositional understanding of Christ the eternal Son's relationship to God the Father, an understanding that is embedded in several of these soteriological moments and that finally accounts for Paul's thoroughgoing Christ devotion.[28]

The *Abba*-Cry

As was pointed out in the exegesis of Gal 4:4–7, despite some attempts to do so, one can scarcely minimize the christological significance of Paul's appeal to believers' use of the *Abba*-cry (Gal 4:6; Rom 8:15) as evidence that they themselves are God's children through the gift of the Spirit and therefore do not need to observe Torah. But what must not be overlooked is the significance this has for Paul's understanding of Christ as Son of God.

First, Paul makes a considerable point that the cry comes from human hearts because God the Father sent the *Spirit of his Son* into their hearts, thus eliciting the cry. Just as the Son himself was sent into the world to effect redemption, so also the Spirit of the Son has been sent into the hearts of believers to effect the experienced realization of that redemption.

Second, there can be little question that this prayer was retained in the early believing community, and continued to be used several decades later in the Greek-speaking communities, because Jesus himself prayed thus and so taught his followers to pray. And however one might view the significance of this prayer for the earthly Jesus, these two passages in Paul's letters demonstrate that he understood it as the earthly prayer of the eternal Son of God. After all, they are both Son of God passages, and one does not need to move toward spiritual sentimentality to recognize that such usage by the Son of God points to a relational understanding of the Son with the Father.

Thus, the way Paul speaks of this cry points to an understanding of the risen Jesus as the Son of God that moves well beyond a merely titular matter.

---

[28] These are the texts that also give the lie to Cullmann's assertion that "it is only meaningful to speak of the Son in view of God's revelatory action, not in view of his being" (*Christology*, 293); cf. the critique in Ridderbos, *Paul*, 68–69.

We might note, therefore, that what becomes even more explicit in the Gospel of John is inherently present much earlier in Paul's letters; indeed, Pauline usage is very much in keeping with the Son of God Christology that appears in 1 John, even though the latter's concern is explicitly related to some who are "denying the Son of God," which is later explicated in terms of their denying the reality of the incarnation. But much that is said in this "epistle" about the Son of God could just as easily have appeared in the letters of Paul.

The Echoes of Abraham and Isaac (Gen 22)

This same relational understanding of Jesus as the eternal Son of God emerges in Paul's thought in his several echoes of the Abraham/Isaac narrative in Gen 22. This echo appears first in Rom 8, which, as noted above, is both framed and carried along by a strong Son of God Christology. The "frame" occurs in vv. 3 and 32. Here only in the corpus Paul emphasizes that God sent his "own" Son to effect redemption, which is then picked up in v. 32 with language about the Son taken directly out of Gen 22, that "God spared not his 'own' Son," just as Abraham had been willing to spare not his "own" son—even though Paul's verb is not used in the Genesis narrative. Paul's "own" (both the reflexive ἑαυτοῦ of v. 3 and the intensive ἴδιος in v. 32) are a nicely rabbinic understanding of the Genesis narrative. For what God was asking Abraham to do was to sacrifice his "own" son in the sense that he was the special son of promise. In a moment of inspired insight, Paul recognizes that the Son whom the Father both sent into the world and then offered up as a sacrifice for all was similarly and uniquely God's only Son.

This same background should be kept in mind in the two places where Paul refers to the Son as "God's beloved" (Col 1:13; Eph 1:6), since this is in fact the language used in the Septuagint to refer to Isaac in Gen 22:2 (cf. v. 16), where the unique position of Isaac is emphasized: λαβὲ τὸν υἱόν σου τὸν ἀγαπητόν, ὃν ἠγάπησας (*Take your son, the beloved one, whom you love*). It is not simply theological insight but theological reality that leads Paul in 8:32 to refer to the Father "sparing not his 'only' Son" so as to effect eternal redemption for all others who will become his υἱοί (*sons = children* [vv. 14, 17]). These echoes push us beyond a merely positional understanding of the eternal Son of God to a relational one. It is *this* Son, the one who is eternally with the Father, the one whom the Father "sent in the likeness of our (sinful) flesh so as to condemn sin in our flesh" (v. 3), whom he "gave up [παρέδωκεν] for us all" (v. 32). And even though Paul himself does not emphasize the relational aspect of the Son to the Father, the language itself pushes us to think in these terms.

Galatians 2:20

Finally, we turn to the very personal, and very rare, way Paul expresses his own relationship to the Son of God in Gal 2:20 and note how thoroughly interchangeable between the Father and the Son Paul understands the divine nature and activity to be. For here we have a total transfer of the Father's activity as expressed in Rom 8:32 to that of the Son.

In his more theologically reflective narrative in Rom 5:6–8, Paul emphasizes that the Son's death on our behalf is especially the evidence for, and the outflow of, God the Father's love for the fallen human race, who are in enmity against him. But here, in a sudden outburst about Christ's death, it is "the Son of God" himself who "loved me"; and it was the Son of God himself who "gave himself up [παραδόντος] for me." It is this same Son whom the Father *sent* into the world to redeem. This is especially personal and relational; and lying behind it is an understanding of the Son and the Father that is likewise personal and relational.

The Son as God's Image-Bearer

In the various twists and turns of NT scholarship, one of the more remarkable twists is the identification of "image" with personified Wisdom[29] when Paul himself, as one should well expect, uses the term primarily in terms of Christ being God's *Son*. I have already made this point at some length in ch. 13.[30] I return to it here simply to point out its significance for Paul's basic understanding of the relationship of the Son with the Father. The emphasis with regard to this usage goes in both directions: the Son as the perfect image-bearer in his humanity; the Son as able to do this because he is first of all the Son of the Father, whose image he perfectly bears. Here, then, is the true expression of the adage "Like Father, like Son." It is therefore of some christological significance that in one of the "image" passages (2 Cor 4:4) the emphasis is on Christ bearing the divine image as such, while in the two later passages (Rom 8:29; Col 1:15) the emphasis is on Christ as the (beloved) Son who bears the divine image.

God's Son as Creator

Finally, we need to return to the twin (and key) christological passages found in 1 Cor 8:6 and Col 1:13–17 to point out how Paul not only presupposes the preexistence of the Son but also emphasizes his *prior role in creation* before speaking of his role in redemption. The basic story is expressed in poetic shorthand in the 1 Corinthians text. The one θεός of the Jewish Shema is now identified as "the Father," who is the source (ἐξ αὐτοῦ) and goal (εἰς αὐτόν) of both creation (πάντα [*all things*]) and redemption. The one κύριος of the Shema is Jesus Christ (the Son of the Father), who is the divine agent (δι' αὐτοῦ) of both creation and redemption. Although Christ is not specified as Son in this passage, that is implied by the identification of God as Father.

---

[29] See the excursuses on 2 Cor 4:4, 6 in ch. 4 (pp. 186–87) and Col 1:15 in ch. 7 (pp. 321–25); see also appendix A (pp. 601–2).

[30] See ch. 13, pp. 518–32.

What is clear in this brief recital of the larger picture of God's work in the world is that the one Lord, Christ the Son, was eternally preexistent and partner with the Father in both creation and redemption. If the Father is the source and goal of all things, the Son is the divine agent of all things, including especially the creation itself. All of this is then spelled out even more explicitly and thoroughly in the Colossians passage.

Thus, when Paul turns from the story of redemption in Col 1:12–14 to the story of creation in vv. 15–17, he begins by specifically identifying the Son as the one who in his incarnation bore the Father's image and holds all the rights of primogeniture. He has these rights precisely because he is the one through whom and for whom and in whom all things were created. The expansive nature of this passage can be attributed primarily to Paul's desire to put "the powers" in their rightful place as both created by the Son and thus ultimately subservient to him. And as we noted in the preceding chapter, as the ἀρχή (*beginning*) of the new creation (v. 18), he himself is the one who is currently "re-creating" fallen humanity back into the divine image, which he alone has perfectly borne (3:10–11).

Here the preexistence of the eternal Son of God is spelled out in such explicit fashion that the only way one can get around the text is either to import foreign matter (personified Wisdom) or to deny Pauline authorship. But both of these moves are counsels of despair. Not only does this letter purport to be by Paul and have a thoroughly Pauline touch everywhere, but also the present passage is ultimately an elaboration of 1 Cor 8:6, which no one would deny to Paul.

All of this, then, is to say that Paul's Son of God Christology is his way of expressing not only the relationship of Christ to God the Father but also his eternal preexistence, including his role in both the original creation and the new creation. As Son of God, he bears the image of the Father, and he did so in his humanity; and it is the same Son of God who is re-creating a newly formed people of God back into the divine image.

Conclusion: The Question of "Origins"

By way of conclusion, we need finally to return to the question of "origins." Where did Paul come by this understanding of Christ as the messianic Son of God who at the same time is the eternal Son? And the first point to make is that the *reality* exists, whatever the *source* of Paul's understanding.

It should be noted at the outset that the evidence from Paul himself indicates that the origin of the *language* "Son of God" is to be found in a Jewish messianism that traces its roots back to the Davidic covenant. So the real question of origins is not with the terminology; that lay ready at hand with Jewish end-time expectations that a greater David would appear and "redeem" his people from their present bondage.[31] Rather, the real question has to do with how the messianic Son came to be understood as *the eternal Son, who preexisted* in "the form of God" and is thus "equal with God" (Phil 2:6).

First, of course, it is altogether possible that its origins for Paul can be traced back to his encounter with the risen and exalted Lord himself. This is in fact the position taken by many, but it is usually done so on the unfortunately untenable grounds of a quite mistaken reading of Gal 1:15–16.[32] There are simply no exegetical grounds, especially no Pauline grounds, for reading Paul's plain grammar that the Son was "revealed ἐν ἐμοί [*in me*]" as though Paul really intended "revealed *to* me." Paul apparently (obviously?) intended his own "conversion" to be a place of revelation for others: in his own "conversion" from a Christ hater to a Christ devotee, others could see Christ at work in the world. But one does not need this text in order to surmise that Paul's encounter with the risen Christ may have led him finally to understand Christ to be the preexistent Son. Indeed, I tend to think so, even though we have no tangible evidence from Paul himself for thinking so.

Second, there are no exegetical, linguistic, theological, or historical grounds for thinking that the answer lies with Jewish Wisdom. Those who would move in this direction must downplay or deny altogether the Son of God motif in the key passages, especially Col 1:13–17. The real problem with this view is that the reason for going this route is that it gave scholarship a "source" not only for preexistence but also especially for the preexistent One to be the agent of creation. However, as pointed out in appendix A, this reflects a quite misguided reading of Prov 8 and of the Wisdom of Solomon. Moreover, it is difficult to imagine how one such as Paul could come by an unquestionable *Son of God* Christology, with its certain roots in Jewish messianism, by way of a personified female figure. Whatever else is true of personified Wisdom, she played no redemptive role in Jewish wisdom speculation.

Third, what is often overlooked, or again downplayed, is that Paul himself bears evidence through his use of the Aramaic *Abba* as an address to God the Father that some form of Son of God Christology existed in the Aramaic Christian community before Paul became a believer. So Paul's understanding of Christ as preexistent Son very likely had its origins within the community that preceded him.

But in the end, we all must admit that we simply do not know the answer to the question "Where did Paul come by his understanding of Christ as the preexistent eternal Son of God?" I am attracted to the suggestion by Martin Hengel, who concludes on the basis of careful analysis of the available evidence that "this development in christology [including κύριος Christology] progressed *in a very short time*."[33] Then, citing *Barn.* 6:13 ("Behold, I make the last things as the first things"), he extrapolates the possibility that

---

[31] As, e.g., in *Pss. Sol.* 17–18.
[32] See the discussion of this passage in ch. 5, pp. 220–22.
[33] See Hengel, *Son of God*, 77.

such a view should also be seen in reverse: the first things must be viewed in light of the last things. In his words, "The beginning *had* to be illuminated by the end" (p. 69).

In any case, however an understanding of the preexistence of the Son of God arose in the earliest communities—whether by revelation, remembrance of Jesus himself, or thoughtful reflection—the reality exists in Paul; and together with his κύριος Christology it presupposes, as well as expresses, the kind of "high" Christology that finds very open, articulate expression in the Gospel of John. Paul and John are on the same christological page in the story. And whatever else, Son of God Christology is not peripheral to Paul's theological enterprise but rather is an essential part of it, and the part that will help to make sense of the rest, both in terms of finding a proper beginning point and in terms of Paul's essential theology.

Appendix: Son of God/God as Father Texts in Paul's Letters

Son and Father in the Same Context

1 Cor 15:24, 28 ²⁴εἶτα τὸ τέλος, ὅταν **παραδιδῷ τὴν βασιλείαν** <u>τῷ θεῷ καὶ πατρί</u>, ὅταν **καταργήσῃ** πᾶσαν ἀρχὴν καὶ πᾶσαν ἐξουσίαν καὶ δύναμιν. . . . ²⁸ὅταν δὲ **ὑποταγῇ αὐτῷ** τὰ πάντα, τότε καὶ **αὐτὸς ὁ υἱὸς** ὑποταγήσεται <u>τῷ ὑποτάξαντι</u> αὐτῷ τὰ πάντα, ἵνα ᾖ <u>ὁ θεὸς</u> τὰ πάντα ἐν πᾶσιν.

Gal 4:4–7 ⁴ὅτε δὲ ἦλθεν τὸ πλήρωμα τοῦ χρόνου, ἐξαπέστειλεν <u>ὁ θεὸς</u> **τὸν υἱὸν** <u>αὐτοῦ</u>, **γενόμενον ἐκ γυναικός, γενόμενον ὑπὸ νόμον, ἵνα τοὺς ὑπὸ νόμον ἐξαγοράσῃ**, ἵνα τὴν υἱοθεσίαν ἀπολάβωμεν. ⁶Ὅτι δέ ἐστε υἱοί, <u>ἐξαπέστειλεν ὁ θεὸς</u> **τὸ πνεῦμα τοῦ υἱοῦ αὐτοῦ** εἰς τὰς καρδίας ἡμῶν κρᾶζον· <u>ἀββα ὁ πατήρ</u>. ⁷ὥστε οὐκέτι εἶ δοῦλος ἀλλὰ υἱός· εἰ δὲ υἱός, καὶ κληρονόμος <u>διὰ θεοῦ</u>.

Col 1:12–15 ¹²εὐχαριστοῦντες <u>τῷ πατρὶ τῷ ἱκανώσαντι</u> ὑμᾶς εἰς τὴν μερίδα τοῦ κλήρου τῶν ἁγίων ἐν τῷ φωτί· ¹³<u>ὃς ἐρρύσατο</u> ἡμᾶς ἐκ τῆς ἐξουσίας τοῦ σκότους <u>καὶ μετέστησεν</u> **εἰς τὴν βασιλείαν τοῦ υἱοῦ** <u>τῆς ἀγάπης αὐτοῦ</u>, ¹⁴**ἐν ᾧ** ἔχομεν τὴν ἀπολύτρωσιν, τὴν ἄφεσιν τῶν ἁμαρτιῶν· ¹⁵**ὅς ἐστιν εἰκὼν** <u>τοῦ θεοῦ τοῦ ἀοράτου</u>, **πρωτότοκος** πάσης κτίσεως,

Christ as Son

1 Thess 1:10 καὶ ἀναμένειν **τὸν υἱὸν** <u>αὐτοῦ</u> ἐκ τῶν οὐρανῶν, ὃν ἤγειρεν ἐκ τῶν νεκρῶν, **Ἰησοῦν τὸν ῥυόμενον** ἡμᾶς ἐκ τῆς ὀργῆς τῆς ἐρχομένης.

1 Cor 1:9 πιστὸς <u>ὁ θεός, δι' οὗ</u> ἐκλήθητε εἰς κοινωνίαν **τοῦ υἱοῦ** <u>αὐτοῦ</u>
Ἰησοῦ Χριστοῦ τοῦ κυρίου ἡμῶν.

2 Cor 1:18–20 [18]<u>πιστὸς δὲ ὁ θεὸς</u> ὅτι ὁ λόγος ἡμῶν ὁ πρὸς ὑμᾶς οὐκ ἔστιν ναὶ
καὶ οὔ. [19]**ὁ** <u>τοῦ θεοῦ</u> γὰρ **υἱὸς Ἰησοῦς Χριστὸς** ὁ ἐν ὑμῖν δι' ἡμῶν
κηρυχθείς, . . . [20]ὅσαι γὰρ ἐπαγγελίαι <u>θεοῦ</u>, **ἐν αὐτῷ τὸ ναί· διὸ
καὶ δι' αὐτοῦ τὸ ἀμὴν** <u>τῷ θεῷ</u> πρὸς δόξαν δι' ἡμῶν.

Gal 1:15–16 [15]Ὅτε δὲ <u>εὐδόκησεν ὁ ἀφορίσας με ἐκ κοιλίας μητρός μου</u> καὶ
καλέσας διὰ τῆς χάριτος αὐτοῦ [16]ἀποκαλύψαι **τὸν υἱὸν αὐτοῦ ἐν
ἐμοί,** ἵνα εὐαγγελίζωμαι αὐτὸν ἐν τοῖς ἔθνεσιν,

Gal 2:20 ζῶ δὲ οὐκέτι ἐγώ, ζῇ δὲ ἐν ἐμοὶ Χριστός· ὃ δὲ νῦν ζῶ ἐν σαρκί, ἐν
πίστει ζῶ τῇ **τοῦ υἱοῦ τοῦ θεοῦ τοῦ ἀγαπήσαντός με καὶ
παραδόντος ἑαυτὸν** . . .

Rom 1:3–4 [3]περὶ **τοῦ υἱοῦ αὐτοῦ** τοῦ γενομένου ἐκ σπέρματος Δαυὶδ κατὰ
σάρκα, [4]τοῦ ὁρισθέντος **υἱοῦ** <u>θεοῦ</u> **ἐν δυνάμει** κατὰ πνεῦμα
ἁγιωσύνης ἐξ ἀναστάσεως νεκρῶν, **Ἰησοῦ Χριστοῦ τοῦ κυρίου
ἡμῶν,**

Rom 1:9 μάρτυς γάρ μού ἐστιν <u>ὁ θεός</u>, ᾧ λατρεύω ἐν τῷ πνεύματί μου **ἐν τῷ
εὐαγγελίῳ τοῦ υἱοῦ** <u>αὐτοῦ</u>, ὡς ἀδιαλείπτως μνείαν ὑμῶν ποιοῦμαι

Rom 5:10 εἰ γὰρ ἐχθροὶ ὄντες κατηλλάγημεν τῷ θεῷ **διὰ τοῦ θανάτου τοῦ
υἱοῦ** <u>αὐτοῦ</u>, πολλῷ μᾶλλον καταλλαγέντες σωθησόμεθα ἐν τῇ ζωῇ
αὐτοῦ·

Rom 8:3 Τὸ γὰρ ἀδύνατον τοῦ νόμου ἐν ᾧ ἠσθένει διὰ τῆς σαρκός, <u>ὁ θεὸς</u>
τὸν <u>ἑαυτοῦ</u> **υἱὸν** <u>πέμψας</u> ἐν ὁμοιώματι σαρκὸς ἁμαρτίας καὶ περὶ
ἁμαρτίας κατέκρινεν τὴν ἁμαρτίαν ἐν τῇ σαρκί,

Rom 8:29, 32 [29]ὅτι οὓς προέγνω, καὶ προώρισεν συμμόρφους **τῆς εἰκόνος
τοῦ υἱοῦ** <u>αὐτοῦ</u>, εἰς τὸ εἶναι αὐτὸν **πρωτότοκον ἐν πολλοῖς
ἀδελφοῖς·** . . . [32]<u>ὅς</u> γε **τοῦ** <u>ἰδίου</u> **υἱοῦ** <u>οὐκ ἐφείσατο ἀλλὰ ὑπὲρ
ἡμῶν πάντων παρέδωκεν</u> **αὐτόν**, πῶς οὐχὶ καὶ σὺν αὐτῷ τὰ πάντα
ἡμῖν χαρίσεται;

Eph 1:6 εἰς ἔπαινον δόξης τῆς χάριτος αὐτοῦ ἧς ἐχαρίτωσεν ἡμᾶς **ἐν τῷ
ἠγαπημένῳ** [see v. 3 for the antecedent].

Eph 4:13 μέχρι καταντήσωμεν οἱ πάντες εἰς τὴν ἑνότητα τῆς πίστεως καὶ
τῆς ἐπιγνώσεως τοῦ υἱοῦ <u>τοῦ θεοῦ</u>, εἰς ἄνδρα τέλειον, εἰς μέτρον
ἡλικίας τοῦ πληρώματος τοῦ Χριστοῦ,

God as Father

1 Thess 1:1 Παῦλος καὶ Σιλουανὸς καὶ Τιμόθεος τῇ ἐκκλησίᾳ
Θεσσαλονικέων <u>**ἐν θεῷ πατρὶ**</u> καὶ **κυρίῳ Ἰησοῦ Χριστῷ**, χάρις
ὑμῖν καὶ εἰρήνη.

2 Thess 1:1–2 ¹Παῦλος καὶ Σιλουανὸς καὶ Τιμόθεος τῇ ἐκκλησίᾳ
Θεσσαλονικέων <u>ἐν θεῷ πατρὶ ἡμῶν</u> καὶ **κυρίῳ Ἰησοῦ Χριστῷ**,
²χάρις ὑμῖν καὶ εἰρήνη ἀπὸ <u>θεοῦ πατρὸς</u> καὶ **κυρίου Ἰησοῦ
Χριστοῦ**.

1 Cor 1:3 χάρις ὑμῖν καὶ εἰρήνη ἀπὸ <u>θεοῦ πατρὸς ἡμῶν</u> καὶ **κυρίου Ἰησοῦ
Χριστοῦ**.

1 Cor 8:6 ἀλλ᾿ ἡμῖν <u>εἷς θεὸς ὁ πατὴρ ἐξ οὗ</u> τὰ πάντα καὶ ἡμεῖς <u>εἰς αὐτόν</u>,
καὶ **εἷς κύριος Ἰησοῦς Χριστὸς δι᾿ οὗ** τὰ πάντα καὶ ἡμεῖς **δι᾿
αὐτοῦ**.

2 Cor 1:2 χάρις ὑμῖν καὶ εἰρήνη ἀπὸ <u>θεοῦ πατρὸς ἡμῶν</u> καὶ **κυρίου Ἰησοῦ
Χριστοῦ**.

2 Cor 1:3 Εὐλογητὸς <u>ὁ θεὸς καὶ πατὴρ</u> **τοῦ κυρίου ἡμῶν Ἰησοῦ Χριστοῦ**, ὁ
πατὴρ τῶν οἰκτιρμῶν καὶ θεὸς πάσης παρακλήσεως,

2 Cor 11:31 <u>ὁ θεὸς καὶ πατὴρ</u> **τοῦ κυρίου Ἰησοῦ** οἶδεν, ὁ ὢν εὐλογητὸς εἰς
τοὺς αἰῶνας, ὅτι οὐ ψεύδομαι.

Gal 1:1 Παῦλος ἀπόστολος οὐκ ἀπ᾿ ἀνθρώπων οὐδὲ δι᾿ ἀνθρώπου ἀλλὰ διὰ
Ἰησοῦ Χριστοῦ καὶ <u>θεοῦ πατρὸς</u> τοῦ ἐγείραντος αὐτὸν ἐκ νεκρῶν,

Gal 1:3–5 ³χάρις ὑμῖν καὶ εἰρήνη ἀπὸ <u>θεοῦ πατρὸς ἡμῶν</u> καὶ **κυρίου Ἰησοῦ
Χριστοῦ** ⁴**τοῦ δόντος ἑαυτὸν** ὑπὲρ τῶν ἁμαρτιῶν ἡμῶν, ὅπως
ἐξέληται ἡμᾶς ἐκ τοῦ αἰῶνος τοῦ ἐνεστῶτος πονηροῦ κατὰ τὸ
θέλημα <u>τοῦ θεοῦ καὶ πατρὸς ἡμῶν</u>, ⁵ᾧ ἡ δόξα εἰς τοὺς αἰῶνας τῶν
αἰώνων, ἀμήν.

Rom 1:7 πᾶσιν τοῖς οὖσιν ἐν Ῥώμῃ ἀγαπητοῖς θεοῦ, κλητοῖς ἁγίοις, χάρις
ὑμῖν καὶ εἰρήνη ἀπὸ <u>θεοῦ πατρὸς ἡμῶν</u> καὶ **κυρίου Ἰησοῦ
Χριστοῦ**.

Rom 8:15–17 ¹⁵οὐ γὰρ ἐλάβετε πνεῦμα δουλείας πάλιν εἰς φόβον ἀλλὰ
ἐλάβετε πνεῦμα υἱοθεσίας ἐν ᾧ κράζομεν· <u>αββα ὁ πατήρ</u>. ¹⁶αὐτὸ τὸ
πνεῦμα συμμαρτυρεῖ τῷ πνεύματι ἡμῶν ὅτι ἐσμὲν τέκνα θεοῦ. ¹⁷εἰ
δὲ τέκνα, καὶ κληρονόμοι· κληρονόμοι μὲν θεοῦ, **συγκληρονόμοι
δὲ Χριστοῦ**, εἴπερ συμπάσχομεν ἵνα καὶ συνδοξασθῶμεν.

Col 1:3 Εὐχαριστοῦμεν <u>τῷ θεῷ πατρὶ</u> **τοῦ κυρίου ἡμῶν Ἰησοῦ Χριστοῦ**
πάντοτε περὶ ὑμῶν προσευχόμενοι,

Col 3:17 καὶ πᾶν ὅ τι ἐὰν ποιῆτε ἐν λόγῳ ἢ ἐν ἔργῳ, πάντα ἐν ὀνόματι
κυρίου Ἰησοῦ εὐχαριστοῦντες <u>τῷ θεῷ πατρὶ</u> **δι᾿ αὐτοῦ**.

Phlm 3 χάρις ὑμῖν καὶ εἰρήνη ἀπὸ <u>θεοῦ πατρὸς ἡμῶν</u> καὶ **κυρίου Ἰησοῦ
Χριστοῦ**.

Eph 1:2 χάρις ὑμῖν καὶ εἰρήνη ἀπὸ <u>θεοῦ πατρὸς ἡμῶν</u> καὶ **κυρίου Ἰησοῦ
Χριστοῦ**.

Eph 1:3 Εὐλογητὸς <u>ὁ θεὸς καὶ πατὴρ</u> **τοῦ κυρίου ἡμῶν Ἰησοῦ Χριστοῦ**, ὁ εὐλογήσας ἡμᾶς ἐν πάσῃ εὐλογίᾳ πνευματικῇ ἐν τοῖς ἐπουρανίοις ἐν Χριστῷ,

Eph 1:17 ἵνα <u>ὁ θεὸς</u> **τοῦ κυρίου ἡμῶν Ἰησοῦ Χριστοῦ**, <u>ὁ πατὴρ τῆς δόξης</u>, δώῃ ὑμῖν πνεῦμα σοφίας καὶ ἀποκαλύψεως ἐν ἐπιγνώσει αὐτοῦ,

Eph 2:18 ὅτι **δι᾽ αὐτοῦ** ἔχομεν τὴν προσαγωγὴν οἱ ἀμφότεροι ἐν ἑνὶ πνεύματι <u>πρὸς τὸν πατέρα</u>.

Eph 3:14–15 [14]Τούτου χάριν κάμπτω τὰ γόνατά μου <u>πρὸς τὸν πατέρα</u>, [15]ἐξ οὗ πᾶσα πατριὰ ἐν οὐρανοῖς καὶ ἐπὶ γῆς ὀνομάζεται,

Eph 4:6 <u>εἷς θεὸς καὶ πατὴρ πάντων</u>, ὁ ἐπὶ πάντων καὶ διὰ πάντων καὶ ἐν πᾶσιν.

Eph 5:20 εὐχαριστοῦντες πάντοτε ὑπὲρ πάντων ἐν ὀνόματι **τοῦ κυρίου ἡμῶν Ἰησοῦ Χριστοῦ** <u>τῷ θεῷ καὶ πατρί</u>.

Eph 6:23 Εἰρήνη τοῖς ἀδελφοῖς καὶ ἀγάπη μετὰ πίστεως ἀπὸ <u>θεοῦ πατρὸς</u> καὶ **κυρίου Ἰησοῦ Χριστοῦ**.

Phil 1:2 χάρις ὑμῖν καὶ εἰρήνη ἀπὸ <u>θεοῦ πατρὸς ἡμῶν</u> καὶ **κυρίου Ἰησοῦ Χριστοῦ**.

Phil 2:11 καὶ πᾶσα γλῶσσα ἐξομολογήσηται ὅτι **κύριος Ἰησοῦς Χριστὸς** <u>εἰς δόξαν θεοῦ πατρός</u>.

Phil 4:20 <u>τῷ δὲ θεῷ καὶ πατρὶ ἡμῶν</u> ἡ δόξα εἰς τοὺς αἰῶνας τῶν αἰώνων, ἀμήν.

1 Tim 1:2 . . . χάρις ἔλεος εἰρήνη ἀπὸ <u>θεοῦ πατρὸς</u> καὶ **Χριστοῦ Ἰησοῦ τοῦ κυρίου ἡμῶν**.

Titus 1:4 . . . χάρις καὶ εἰρήνη ἀπὸ <u>θεοῦ πατρὸς</u> καὶ **Χριστοῦ Ἰησοῦ τοῦ σωτῆρος ἡμῶν**.

2 Tim 1:2 . . . χάρις ἔλεος εἰρήνη ἀπὸ <u>θεοῦ πατρὸς</u> καὶ **Χριστοῦ Ἰησοῦ τοῦ κυρίου ἡμῶν**.

15

Jesus: Jewish Messiah and Exalted Lord

WITH THIS CHAPTER, WE COME to the most significant of the christological motifs that emerge in Paul's letters and thus to the absolute heart of Pauline Christology: Jesus as ὁ κύριος (*the Lord*). This title occurs less often overall than the title-turned-name Χριστός. In part, that is because κύριος is, as we will see below, a name-turned-title that in Paul's letters functions only as a title whereas (ὁ) Χριστός functions as both. Even so, the κύριος title predominates in the first two letters, as well as in the last ones in both the church corpus (Philippians) and the Pastoral Epistles (2 Timothy). Moreover, it plays a major role in every letter in the church corpus except 2 Corinthians and Galatians.[1]

Indeed, the significance for Paul of this name-turned-title can hardly be overstated. It is consistently the first thing up in every letter ("the Lord Jesus Christ"; i.e., "the Lord, namely, Jesus the Messiah"), always in conjunction with "God the/our Father." It is the language of the earliest Christian communities, which in Aramaic prayed *Marana tha* ("Come, Lord"). It is the language that Paul uses of his Damascus Road experience ("Have I not seen Jesus our Lord?"); and it is the primary confession of those who become believers and thus followers of the risen One ("the Lord is Jesus [Christ]" [1 Cor 12:3; Rom 10:9; Phil 2:11]). Moreover, in the sixty-five occurrences of the full designation, where all three names/titles appear together, κύριος always appears in either the first or last position (either "the Lord Jesus Christ [or, 'Christ Jesus']" or "Jesus Christ [or, 'Christ Jesus'] the Lord."

---

[1] In this case, the statistics have their own story to tell. Although, as pointed out in the preceding chapter, the title-turned-name Χριστός is Paul's most frequent referent to Jesus, a little over half of these stand alone, whereas two-thirds of Paul's references to κύριος stand alone. The figures:

κύριος	252	(alone, 164 = 66%)
Χριστός	376	(alone, 211 = 56%)
Ἰησοῦς	205	(alone, 18 = 9%)

In the same way as "Son of God" (see ch. 14),[2] the christological implications of this name-turned-title are considerable; and they force us toward
an understanding of Christ that can best be expressed in terms of full
deity—of a kind similar to that found in John's Gospel and in Hebrews under
the rubric "Son." This usage in particular is what requires theologizing on
our part, since (1) the divine Lord shares every kind of divine prerogative
with God the Father, except for "initiating" the saving event itself, but does
so (2) within the context of absolute monotheism and therefore (3) in his redemptive and mediatorial roles always with God the Father as the first and
last word. The data of this chapter demand that we either give up the
monotheism, which is what Paul will *not* do,[3] or find a way to include the
Lord Jesus Christ within the divine identity of the one God, which is what
Paul *has* done.[4]

Also as noted of "Son of God" in the preceding chapter, this title is laden
with messianic implications; but it is so in this case in terms of the eschatological dimension of Christ's messiahship, where the messianic Lord, in "fulfillment" of Ps 110:1, is seated at the right hand of God. Thus, as in the
preceding chapter, here is an appropriate place to begin the discussion.

Jesus Christ, Exalted Messianic Lord—Psalm 110:1

We begin again with Paul's own life-changing encounter with the risen
Christ. And here especially his own language is significant. Of this experience Paul says in 1 Cor 9:1, in defense of his apostleship, "I saw the Lord."
This is then clarified in 15:8 as referring to Christ's appearing to him after the
ordinary time of resurrection appearances had passed.

Paul's use of language in this latter passage indicates (quite clearly, it
would seem) that he thought of his "seeing the Lord" not as a visionary experience but as one in kind with those that the earliest disciples had experienced. The risen Christ appeared to him, Paul says in the same language,
and therefore in presumably the same way, as he appeared to all the others.
Paul did indeed have visionary experiences, as he reveals in 2 Cor 12:1–5;
however, of these he refers not to "seeing" the Lord but to "hearing" things
that cannot be expressed below. In our present text (1 Cor 15:8), the one difference that Paul readily points out between his experience of the risen

[2]For the close connection between these two major "titles" (Son and Lord), see
Hengel, *Son of God*, 13–14.
[3]Nor will some contemporary NT scholars, who thus put most of their emphasis
on the subordinating role that the Son plays in the story of redemption. See, e.g.,
Tuckett (*Christology*, 54–60), who acknowledges his indebtedness to Dunn.
[4]Despite Dunn to the contrary (*Christology in the Making*). Dunn clearly recognizes the force of what is said here and gets around it by trying to eliminate
preexistence and incarnation from the Pauline corpus. But to do so, he must repeatedly do exegesis whose aim is to get around what the texts affirm.

Christ and that of the others is that his was abnormal, in the sense of occurring well after the time when such appearances had ceased.[5] But his sentence leaves us with little doubt that he considered his the last in a series of such appearances of the risen Lord to his followers.[6]

The significance of this experience and language for Paul needs to be noted because it was upon "seeing the Lord" that Paul first received his commission to apostleship. That seems to be the intent of the juxtaposition of the three clauses that occur in the form of rhetorical questions in 1 Cor 9:1. First, he asks, "Am I not an apostle?" and from what follows, there can be little question that there was some doubt among the Corinthians on this score, since some of them have been calling into question Paul's "right" to forbid their attendance at the feasts in the pagan temples (1 Cor 8:1–13).

So he follows up this question with the two primary kinds of evidence that substantiate his apostleship. "Have I not seen Jesus our Lord?" Here is the first requirement for apostleship in Paul's view. Having seen, and thus having been commissioned by, the Lord himself is the first standard of apostleship, which is further evidenced in the condensed, second-hand version of this commissioning in Paul's speech before Agrippa in Acts 26:16–18. But for Paul, the third question serves equally as evidence: "Are you not the result of my work in the Lord?" Thus from Paul's perspective, his apostleship was based on the two factors of his having seen and been commissioned by the risen Lord and of his founding churches.

These very tight sentences undoubtedly compress a lot more than is here expressed, but the basic realities are in place. Paul saw, and was commissioned by, the risen Christ Jesus. But his language for this experience is expressed in terms of "seeing *the Lord*." At issue in Pauline Christology, therefore, is how Paul came by this use of language, this calling the risen Jesus "Lord." The answer in part is that this was the language of the earliest believers from the very beginning—before Paul became one of them—as evidenced by the Aramaic-speaking community's prayer, *Marana tha* ("Come, Lord"), perhaps in conjunction with the Lord's Table.

In keeping with others in the earliest community, Paul most likely understood this new title for Jesus in light of Jesus' own interpretation of Ps 110:1, which had been passed down among the earliest believers: "*The Lord says to my lord* [ὁ κύριος τῷ κυρίῳ μου], 'Sit at my right hand until I make your enemies a footstool for your feet,'" a passage that for many reasons had become a significant *messianic* text in Second Temple Judaism.[7] It is in fact the OT text most frequently cited or alluded to in the NT, including by Jesus

---

[5] For the full discussion of this meaning of the text, see G. D. Fee, *The First Epistle to the Corinthians* (NICNT; Grand Rapids: Eerdmans, 1987), 732–34.

[6] See, e.g., D. Garland, *1 Corinthians* (BECNT; Grand Rapids: Baker Academic, 2003), 691; R. Hays, *First Corinthians* (Interpretation; Louisville: John Knox, 1997), 257.

[7] See the evidence in D. Hay, *Glory at the Right Hand: Psalm 110 in Early Christianity* (SBLMS 18; Nashville: Abingdon, 1973), 21–33.

himself in controversy with the Jewish leaders (Mark 12:35–37 and pars.). It is found in four passages in the Pauline corpus.

In 1 Cor 15:27 this psalm text is brought forward to speak of Christ's present reign that will last until the final enemy, death, is brought under his feet at the time when those in Christ are raised from the dead. It is used in a somewhat similar way in Eph 1:20 to refer to Christ's present lordship over all the demonic powers. In both of these texts, especially 1 Cor 15:27, the usage has clear messianic implications, since "the Lord"—even though not called that in any of Paul's allusions to this passage—is the one who currently *reigns* on high.

In Rom 8:34 the psalm allusion takes on the interesting dimension of reference to Christ's present ministry of heavenly intercession for us, so that here it picks up in a larger metaphorical sense the fact that the one at the right hand of a king was regularly recognized as having the most influence with the king. Finally, in Col 3:1 it is used simply as a reference point regarding Christ's present position and is intended, as in Romans, to serve as both encouragement and exhortation.

That this is Paul's primary way of understanding Christ's present reign, and its significance for Pauline Christology, can be seen in the way he uses κύριος language in a whole variety of other settings in his letters, which is what much of the rest of this chapter will examine. But first we need to make three further important and interrelated observations about Paul's referring to the risen Christ as "at the right hand" of God the Father.

First, in none of these allusions does Paul use the title "Lord," the actual language of the psalm in the Septuagint. Although this could simply be accidental, having to do in each case with the issue at hand, nonetheless this phenomenon also fits well with Pauline usage elsewhere, especially in light of the next point.

Second, although κύριος occurs throughout the Septuagint both as a reference to Yahweh and especially as a translation of the Divine Name, Paul uses this title exclusively of Christ and never as a reference to God,[8] for whom he equally exclusively reserves the term θεός.[9]

Third, although there are a few exceptions,[10] ὁ κύριος is also used predominantly of Christ's *present* reign and anticipated *coming*, rarely of his earthly life.[11] Thus, Jesus died for us, or Christ died for us, but never "the

---

[8]For the several "exceptions" found in citations where the mention of God is irrelevant to the point of the citation as such, see n. 7 in ch. 3.

[9]For the two instances where many would take exception to this, see discussion on Rom 9:5 in ch. 6 (pp. 272–77) and Titus 2:13 in ch. 10 (pp. 442–46); see also discussion on 2 Thess 1:12 in ch. 2 (pp. 62–63), which has had fewer advocates.

[10]See, e.g., 1 Thess 1:6; 2:15, both of which refer to the suffering (or death) of the earthly Jesus. But these are rare and do not occur after this first letter.

[11]The primary exceptions are when he refers to something said by Jesus—e.g., 1 Cor 7:10, 12; 11:23; 1 Thess 4:15 (probably).

Lord died for us"—although, in 1 Thess 2:14–15 they "killed the Lord Jesus"; but this clause seems to be deliberately full of irony and in any case is looking back on what Paul's own people did: they killed the Jesus whom God would reinstate as Lord of all.

The probable reason, therefore, for Paul's using Χριστός rather than κύριος when echoing Ps 110:1 is that in each case the emphasis is on Christ's redemptive, including present intercessory, activity on behalf of his people, not on his lordship as such. So it is the Messiah, Christ, who is seated at the right hand, which seems to reflect the intent of the psalmist. Paul's use of the title "Lord," on the other hand, is quite unrelated to the messianic referent involved; this is presupposed by the use of the passage at all. Rather, "Lord" is the title by which Paul regularly includes Christ in the divine identity.[12] But it is a "title" that for Paul is first of all the Greek form of the Divine Name itself, now bestowed on Christ. Thus the "title" always carries a degree of ambiguity because of its initial reference point, even though for Paul it is used altogether in a titular sense. To this matter we now turn.

The "Name" above Every Name

The place to begin the present discussion is by returning to three crucial passages that offer us the clues to our theological understanding of this name-turned-title given to the risen Christ Jesus. Indeed, what is stated explicitly in these three texts serves as the presuppositional basis for our understanding of Paul's consistent and regular use of (ὁ) κύριος with reference to Christ and therefore of his basic understanding of "who" Christ is.

Jesus, the Lord of the Shema (1 Cor 8:6) [pp. 89–94]

Early on in the extant corpus, and in a quite presuppositional way, Paul uses the Jewish Shema, the fundamental expression of Jewish monotheism, to include Christ in the identity of the one God.[13] What occasions this moment is that some Corinthian believers, in the name of γνῶσις (knowledge), had laid hold of this monotheistic reality so as to argue that since there is only one God, then the "gods" and "lords" of the pagan temples do not exist. Thus they have concluded that attendance at temple feasts should be a matter of indifference, since there is no "god" in the temple.

---

[12] Whether intentional or not, by doing this, Paul stays consistent with his actual use of κύριος when citing or echoing the Septuagint. As we will note momentarily, Paul's regular reference is to Christ when he cites or echoes the Septuagint in places where κύριος is a gloss for Yahweh, by way of the substitution of *Adonai* in oral reading.

[13] The presentation here and for the rest of this chapter is a condensed version of the full exegesis found earlier. In each case the bracketed page numbers in the heading are for easy reference to the more complete discussion.

In countering this *gnōsis* of theirs, Paul first accepts the correctness of the basic theological presupposition, "There is only one God." However, he vehemently rejects what they are doing with it, ultimately for two reasons: such an action on the part of the "knowing ones" plays havoc with other believers for whom Christ died but who cannot make these fine distinctions; moreover, they have misunderstood the demonic nature of idolatry. So Paul will eventually argue that although there are no "gods" or "lords" as such, the pagan temples are the dwelling place of demons, and believers in Christ as Lord cannot eat at the Lord's Table and at the table of demons (10:13–22).

In his initial rejection of their reasoning in 8:4–6, Paul does a most remarkable thing. He allows for the moment that for others there are "gods many and lords many." But "for us," he goes on, there is only "one God" and "one Lord." *How* Paul does this is one of the striking moments in early Christian theology. He divides the Shema itself into two parts, something available to him only in the Septuagint, which itself offers evidence of a growing tradition within Second Temple Judaism of substituting *Adonai* ("Lord") for Yahweh in the sacred texts so as not to take Yahweh's name in vain. Thus, in the Septuagint the Shema reads, κύριος ὁ θεὸς ἡμῶν κύριος εἷς ἐστιν (*[the] LORD our God, [the] LORD is one*). And because the risen Christ had "the Name" κύριος bestowed on him at his exaltation (see the following discussion), Paul now applies the two words of the Shema, θεός and κύριος, to God the Father and Christ the Son respectively.

What seems clear in this passage is that the exalted Son of God is understood to be included in the divine identity, as the efficient agent of both creation and redemption, of which God the Father is seen as the ultimate source and goal. And Paul does this in a way that does not impinge on the understanding of his basic monotheism. What can be shown to be true for Paul is that when he is citing or echoing the OT where κύριος = *Adonai* = Yahweh, the κύριος consistently and exclusively is applied to the risen Lord Jesus. The clue as to *how* this came about is to be found in the next text.

But before that, we need to note what is said about the one Lord: he is the preexistent divine agent of creation as well as the historical agent of redemption. Since nothing further is made of creation in this immediate context, the affirmation may simply be nothing more than a typically Jewish affirmation about God vis-à-vis all other so-called gods and lords.[14] But it is also very likely that this affirmation about the one Lord as agent of creation prepares the way for Paul's later affirmation in 1 Cor 10:25–26, at the beginning of the next section of the argument (10:23–11:1). Here, with regard to food *sold in the marketplace* and in contrast to his absolute prohibition against eating in the pagan temples, Paul takes the opposite stance. Now they are encouraged to "buy and eat." The reason? Because, and now citing Ps 24:1 with Christ as the Lord = Yahweh of the psalm, "the earth and everything in

---

[14]On this matter, see esp. Bauckham, *God Crucified*, 1–16; Hurtado, *Lord Jesus Christ*, 42–50.

it belongs to the Lord," since the one Lord was the divine agent of creation in the first place.[15]

Thus, Paul not only presuppositionally places Christ the Lord as the preexistent agent of creation, but also he sees him as the Lord of Ps 24:1, to whom the whole of creation belongs.

The Bestowal of the Name (Phil 2:10–11) [pp. 396–401]

In this passage, Paul concludes his narrative of the essential Christ story by narrating God the Father's vindication of the Son: the One who was *equal* with God (v. 6) demonstrated Godlikeness by pouring himself out so as to become servant of all and by humbling himself in obedient death on the cross. The divine vindication took the form of God's having "bestowed" on Christ *the Name*, which is then identified as "the Name above every name."

As was pointed out in the exegesis of this passage (ch. 9, pp. 396–401), this language can only refer to the Divine Name, which functions as a central feature of Israel's self-understanding. The name of their God, Yahweh, first revealed to Moses at Horeb/Sinai in Exod 3:1–6, was to be their primary identity symbol. They were people of "the Name"—that is, of their God, Yahweh, who eventually chose Jerusalem as the place where "my Name shall dwell," and in whose name all Israel were to make and carry out their oaths.

This is "the Name" that has been bestowed on the risen Christ at his exaltation, not in its original Hebrew form, *Yahweh*, but (now by one of the happy "accidents of history") rather, for Paul and the early church, in its Greek expression κύριος, which had been consistently used by the Septuagint translators[16] to render the Divine Name. So the risen Christ is not Yahweh, who is always referred to by Paul as θεός (*God*); rather, the preexistent Son of God returns to receive the honor of having bestowed on him the *substitute name* for God, which for Paul then becomes *a title* for Christ as "Lord."

This was the reality already in place when Paul made his assertion regarding the Shema in 1 Cor 8:6. In the present passage it is made certain by Paul's intertextual use of Isa 45:23 as the means of identifying "the Name."[17] In place of Isaiah's "to/before me," referring to Israel's one God, Yahweh,

---

[15]Not all are of one mind as to whether κύριος here refers to Christ or to God; but why, one wonders, should Paul's consistent usage not be the deciding factor here, especially in light of what is said in 8:6?

[16]On this issue, see the discussion in ch. 1, pp. 21–23.

[17]In what appears to be in the interest of downplaying the significance of this passage for Paul's Christology, Tuckett (*Christology*, 59–60) tends to minimize the significance of Paul's use of Isaiah here, where both the language and eschatological context suggest that Paul was quite aware of its OT context. On the other hand (pp. 62–63), he opts to find "Wisdom" behind both 1 Cor 8:6 (where neither Paul's language nor content have any relationship to the Wisdom of Solomon) and the "sending" language in Rom 8:3 and Gal 4:4, which does in fact share a verbal similarity with Wis 9:10. Thus he shows considerable confidence that Paul echoes a text that he

Paul insists that the promise of every knee bowing before him and every tongue confessing him as God alone has now been transferred to the risen and exalted Lord Jesus Christ. And not satisfied with just the text of Isaiah as it stands, Paul elaborates the "every knee and tongue" to include all created beings: heavenly, earthly, and (probably) demonic. Thus, in the eschaton even κύριος καὶ σωτήρ (*lord and savior*) Nero Caesar, who is ultimately responsible for present suffering in Philippi, will acknowledge the lordship of the Messiah, whom the empire had once slain.

This passage thus serves as a classic example of this transfer of every kind of divine privilege to the risen Lord, as demonstrated throughout the corpus, including the Pastoral Epistles. In Paul's repeated citations and intertextual use of the Septuagint he consistently identifies the κύριος = Yahweh of the Septuagint with the risen Lord Jesus Christ.[18]

But this passage also has a singularly eschatological perspective to it; that is, this universal acknowledgment will take place at the eschaton. So we turn to our third significant text to point out that this phenomenon serves also as the *entry point* for all who would embrace Christ as Savior and thus become part of the newly formed people of God.

Confessing the Name (Rom 10:9–13) [pp. 255–59]

In the middle of a long passage in which Paul argues that God is not finished with his ancient people Israel, even though in the present time the newly formed people now (probably) includes more Gentiles than Jews, he makes a typically bold move with regard to an important OT passage: Deut 30, with its promised covenant renewal. In v. 9 Paul picks up and applies the language of "mouth" and "heart" from Deut 30:14, where God says that the word will not be too difficult for Israel or too distant for them. This, Paul says, is how Jew and Gentile together become the one eschatological people of God: by confessing with the *mouth* that κύριος Ἰησοῦς (*the Lord is Jesus*) and by believing with the *heart* that he is the risen (and thus exalted) One. And we must not miss this juxtaposition of what is believed with the heart and confessed with the mouth. What is believed is that God has raised the crucified Messiah from the dead and exalted him to the highest place, having bestowed on him "the Name" (Phil 2:9–11). Thus the confession of Jesus as Lord is predicated on this prior believing with the heart that through resurrection and exaltation Christ has assumed his present role as Lord of all.

---

may not even have known (see appendix A in the present volume), but he is ready to express doubt regarding the significance of a passage that Paul quite certainly knew and refers to on two different occasions in his letters (cf. Rom 14:11). And Tuckett is only popularizing what he finds in others. One wonders whether this is a methodological problem per se or whether it reflects a desire to downplay Paul's Christology in Philippians and to find Wisdom where it is not as part of this downplaying. See further the discussion in appendix A in the present volume.

[18] That is, he does so whenever κύριος is the reason for, or otherwise an important part of, the citation. For the exceptions, see n. 7 in ch. 3.

That the confession of the mouth refers to the same phenomenon as in Phil 2:10–11 is made certain by the follow-up citation in v. 13 of Joel 2:32 (3:5 LXX). There is no distinction between Jew and Greek on this matter, Paul says, for πᾶς ὃς ἂν ἐπικαλέσηται τὸ ὄνομα κυρίου σωθήσεται (*everyone who calls on the name of the Lord will be saved*). Here again, just as in the preceding passages, Paul has taken a very important eschatological text from the Septuagint, where "the name of the Lord" = "the name of Yahweh," and applied it directly to the risen Christ.

Thus, the same phenomenon as the eschatological "confessing" of the Name (in Phil 2:10–11) is, by "confessing Jesus as Lord" in the present, the way of entry into the new-covenant people of God.

But what happens at the entry point as well as at the eschatological conclusion serves further for Paul as a common way to identify God's newly formed people. Thus, this usage also plays itself out in Paul's letters in a variety of other ways that reflect this total transfer to Christ of the "name" of Yahweh in its Greek form, κύριος, in which the Name now functions altogether as Christ's title.

Calling on the Name (1 Cor 1:2, etc.)

The actual language of the Joel passage occurs in two other instances in the corpus (1 Cor 1:2; 2 Tim 2:22), in both cases as a way of identifying all of God's new-covenant people. In 1 Corinthians it appears in the salutation in an elaborated form that is almost certainly intended to catch the Corinthians' attention that they belong to a much larger network of believers and therefore need to keep in step with the larger community. Thus he refers "to the church in Corinth, called to be 'saints' along with all those in every place who *call on the name of the Lord, both their Lord and ours.*"[19] Here, then, for Paul is the biblical language that emphasizes the universalizing aspect of the work of Christ and the Spirit.

In the second passage, Timothy himself is being urged to join with others who "call on the name of the Lord" with a pure heart and thus to live in keeping with the Name, on which they call. In this latter case, the command to Timothy is a clear pickup of the second "sure foundation" of the newly formed temple of God (2 Tim 2:19). Thus Timothy is being encouraged first to remember that "the Lord knows those who are his";[20] but the second "foundation," he is reminded, is that those who belong to the Lord, who

---

[19] Thus with one stroke Paul accomplishes three matters by way of reminder: their conversion was to becoming a part of God's *holy* people; they join a much wider network of believers, all of whom "call on the name of the Lord"; and they are under the "lordship" of the One on whom they call. See further Fee, *First Epistle to the Corinthians*, 32–34; and in the present volume the discussion in ch. 3, pp. 127–29, plus n. 111.

[20] On this bit of intertextuality, where "the Lord" of the OT text is Yahweh, see ch. 10, pp. 455–58.

"name the name of the Lord" (thus echoing Isa 26:13), must "turn away from wickedness."[21]

Thus in each of these cases, the "name of the Lord" that was to be the identifying symbol of God's people Israel has been transferred to the newly formed people of God, where "the Lord" whose "name" now identifies them is the risen and exalted Christ Jesus.

Very likely, this is also how we are to understand the more unusual usage of "the name of the Lord Jesus" in 1 Cor 6:11. Here Paul says that in contrast to the kinds of sins noted in vv. 9–10, the believers in Corinth have been "washed, sanctified, and justified *in the name of the Lord Jesus Christ*" as well as by "the Spirit of our God." This fourth occurrence of the phrase in this letter (the most in the corpus) is most likely intended once more as their primary identity marker. Just as with Israel of old, who were identified as a people of the Name, so it is with believers in the new covenant. At their conversion they "call on the name of the Lord" precisely because that is the name by which they are now to be identified. Thus the Lord Jesus Christ has for Paul now assumed a role that belongs exclusively to Yahweh in the Jewish tradition, of which Paul had been, and still considers himself to be, a part.

Closely related to this usage is Paul's prayer for the Thessalonians in his second letter to them (2 Thess 1:12). After a series of intertextual echoes in the thanksgiving, where Christ the Lord (= Yahweh) will mete out judgment on their opponents (echoing esp. Isa 66:4–6 [see ch. 2, pp. 57–61]), Paul continues in this vein in his prayer for them, again echoing the same passage from Isaiah. What Paul desires for them is that by the way they live, "the *name of our Lord*, Jesus, *might be glorifie*d among you" (the italicized words are taken directly from Isa 66:5). Thus, not only are God's newly formed people to be identified as people of "the Name," but also they are urged to live so as to bring glory to that Name, which at the same time picks up the theme of Christ's being "glorified" in his people from v. 9.

Similarly, at the conclusion of his great eschatological oracle in Mic 4:1–5, the prophet contrasts eschatological Israel with the surrounding nations, which "walk in the name of their gods" (= live by the authority of and in keeping with their gods). Israel, Micah says, will do the same: "We will walk in the name of the LORD [Yahweh] our God forever." Even though Paul does not use the metaphor "to walk" as such, he reflects this usage in a couple of passages where he assumes that everything believers do is done "in the name of the Lord Jesus."

Thus, in Col 3:17, in concluding a context of worship while at the same time bringing the entire paraenesis of 3:12–17 to a fitting conclusion, Paul urges the believers in Colossae (and indirectly in Laodicea [4:15–16]) to do *everything*, whether word or deed, "in the name of the Lord Jesus." Thus what identifies them as God's new people is also the context in which they

---

[21] Thus, whether 2 Timothy is "Pauline" in a more direct sense or less direct sense, the "author" here fully represents Paul's usage.

are to live out that identification in its entirety (= walk in the Lord's name). In the companion passage in Eph 5:20, believers are urged especially in the context of worship to offer their thanksgiving to God "in the name of our Lord Jesus Christ."

The next group of passages in which this idiom occurs is especially, and directly, tied to what Yahweh had commanded Israel to do: take their oaths in Yahweh's name only (Deut 6:13). Thus in a variety of ways and circumstances Paul reflects this usage of "the Name" as that name has been bestowed on Christ. The phenomenon occurs first in 1 Thess 5:27, where Paul charges the Thessalonian believers "in the Lord" to have the letter read to all the brothers and sisters. When similar language is picked up again in 2 Thess 3:6, Paul "commands them in *the name* of the Lord Jesus Christ" to avoid the disruptive idle,[22] which command is "enclosed" by v. 12, where it is now given "in the Lord" directly to the disruptive idle themselves. The same kind of thing happens in 1 Cor 1:10 and 5:4–5, where again Paul commands and passes judgment "in the name of the Lord."

The point to make again, by way of conclusion, is that in every one of these instances where Paul uses the OT term "the name of the Lord," the Divine Name is now "the Name" that was bestowed on Christ at his exaltation. Thus all of these passages reflect various ways whereby the Divine Name that belonged to God alone in ancient Israel has now been transferred across the board to the One to whom that Name has now been given in its Greek form, κύριος. It is in light of this reality that we turn to examine a whole variety of phenomena whereby Paul understands the Lord Jesus also to have assumed roles that belonged historically to God alone.

Jesus the Lord: Eschatological Judge

We begin with a large group of texts that have to do with Christ the Lord's role as the Coming One, a role that includes both final salvation and divine judgment. Several texts fit this category, many of which reflect considerable intertextual echoes of the Septuagint and all of which make plain that the role traditionally assigned to Yahweh in Israel's worldview is now attributed to Christ as κύριος (= Yahweh). We begin with the basic designation for the final eschatological event.

The Day of the Lord

One of the ways the prophetic tradition spoke of God's eschatological future was with the expression "the Day of the Lord," a "day" that included

---

[22]This gloss is an attempt to catch the larger sense of ἀτάκτως, which carries little of the sense of "indolent" but more of their being "disorderly" in the process of not working for their own living.

both divine judgment and salvation. Indeed, in this tradition a day of the Lord that held promise for a bright future was seen first as a day of impending doom.[23] In the early Christian community the exaltation of the risen Christ carried with it an eager expectation of his return, the Parousia (coming again) of Christ in full glory. It was to this coming that they attached this OT eschatological terminology. The language itself appears six times in Paul's letters, all with reference to Christ's return (1 Thess 5:2; 2 Thess 2:2; 1 Cor 1:8; 5:5; Phil 1:6, 10). In the first two instances and in 1 Cor 5:5 Paul has the precise language of the prophets, "the Day of the Lord." In 1 Cor 1:8 "the Lord" is further identified as "Jesus Christ," and in the two later passages simply as "the Day of Christ [Jesus]."

This is a certain instance where Paul has altogether appropriated language that belonged to God alone and applied it to the risen Lord, Jesus Christ. As before, this language transfer is the result of Christ's having "the Name" bestowed on him, so that the Day of Yahweh is now the Day of the Lord Jesus Christ's Parousia.

The Parousia of the Lord

One may assume that the primary reason for the shift of language regarding the Day of the Lord was not intentionally christological; rather, it was the logical outcome of the church's expectation that the Lord who had ascended and had been seated at "the right hand" was going to return again in power and glory. Thus, the coming (Parousia) of the Lord would be the chief event of the new understanding of the Day of the Lord; and as in the OT, this Parousia would be an event of both salvation and judgment. For Paul, everything about this event, once the exclusive prerogative of God, is now focused on Christ the Lord (= Yahweh) of the Septuagint texts. Our first interest is with Paul's various descriptions of the event itself.

1 Thessalonians 3:13 (Zech 14:5) [pp. 43–44]; 4:16 (Ps 47:5) [pp. 44–45]

In keeping with one of the predominant concerns in both of his letters to the Thessalonian believers, Paul concludes his prayer for them (3:11–13) by expressing concern for, and thus reminding them of, their need to be blameless before God the Father at the Parousia of the Lord. He then goes on to describe the Parousia in language taken directly from Zech 14:5: the "coming of *the Lord* [ὁ κύριος]," now identified as "Jesus," will be μετὰ πάντων τῶν ἁγίων αὐτοῦ (*accompanied by all his holy ones*).[24] The christological import of this bit

---

[23] On this matter, see esp. Amos 5:20, but it is also reflected in, e.g., Isa 2:6–22; Joel 1:15; 2:1–11.

[24] To water this down by suggesting, as is frequently done, that the ἅγιοι in this case refers to Christian "saints" who will accompany Jesus (based on 4:14) not only imports foreign matter into this text (the word ἅγιοι does not appear in ch. 4) but

of intertextuality is that the Zechariah passage describes the παρουσία (*coming*) of Yahweh himself to the Mount of Olives when he carries out his eschatological victory over the nations. Thus the future coming of Yahweh, Paul implies, is now to be understood in terms of the παρουσία of the present reigning Christ, who *alone* is "Lord" in Paul's new understanding.

In an equally striking bit of intertextuality, Paul in 1 Thess 4:16 borrows language from the "ascent" of Yahweh in one of the enthronement psalms and applies it to the "descent" of Christ, when "the *Lord* himself will descend from heaven, accompanied by *the voice* of an archangel and *the trumpet* of God," where the italicized language is a direct echo of Ps 47:5. Again, with this bold stroke Paul applies to *the Lord*, Jesus, the language of the psalm that refers to Yahweh. Christ is not Yahweh; but as the exalted Lord, he is understood by Paul to assume the role of Yahweh at his coming.

2 Thessalonians 1:7–8 (Isa 66:15, 4) [pp. 58–60]

In another remarkable moment of intertextuality, Paul uses the opening thanksgiving in his second letter as a way of encouraging the suffering Thessalonians, by reassuring them that at Christ's coming not only will they be "glorified" but also their present enemies will be duly punished. Since their suffering is very likely related to their acknowledgment of the risen Jesus as κύριος in the context of a free city with deep loyalties to the Roman emperor as κύριος, Paul highlights the role that their heavenly κύριος will play in the final judgment. Thus, with a series of intertextual moments, all taken from OT judgment passages, Paul reassures these new believers that the future is theirs, not Caesar's or pagan Thessalonica's. We will look at most of these echoes in the next two sections, but we begin with the initial depiction of Christ's coming in vv. 7–8.

With a combination of language from the final oracle(s) in the book of Isaiah, where the prophet's words of judgment and hope for Jerusalem are placed in a kind of summary fashion for the whole collection, Paul deliberately places the risen Lord in the role that Yahweh is to play throughout. This begins with his description of the Parousia itself. Along with echoes of his own language from the first letter ("from heaven . . . with his powerful angels"), Paul describes the "revelation" of *the Lord* Jesus as "*in flaming fire, giving punishment* to those who do not know God *and do not obey* the gospel of our *Lord* Jesus Christ."

The italicized language is taken directly from Isa 66:15, 4, where the "Lord" is Yahweh. But for Paul, it is the Lord Jesus who will come with blazing fire to mete out justice; and in place of those "who do not obey *me*" in the Isaiah oracle, the judgment will be the result of their not obeying "the

---

also misses the import of the Zechariah text, which will be spelled out in greater detail in 2 Thess 1:7, where the "holy ones" are clearly stipulated to be angels.

gospel of our *Lord* Jesus Christ." Thus, as before, the risen Lord is not identified as Yahweh; rather, by his having had "the Name" bestowed on him, he assumes Yahweh's divine roles when he comes as judge, to which matter we now turn. And for Paul, the Lord Jesus assumes the role of judge for both his own people and his enemies.

Jesus the Lord: Present and Eschatological Judge of His People

One of the more significant instances of "shared divine prerogatives" (see the section "Jesus the Lord: Sharer of Divine Prerogatives" below), but not surprising given Paul's understanding of Christ as the presently exalted Lord, is the fact that Jesus as "Lord" also assumes the divine role of Yahweh as the One who will judge his own people.[25] This occurs several times in the corpus, always in passages where Paul is again echoing Septuagint texts where κύριος = Yahweh is now attributed to the risen Lord.

1 Thessalonians 4:6

In this passage Paul picks up the unusual language of the Lord (= Yahweh) as a God of vengeance from Ps 94:1. In a context where a brother is being abused by another in a matter of sexual immorality, Paul assures the offender that "the Lord [Christ] is an avenger in all these things" (NRSV). Despite the views of some to the contrary, here is a case where Paul very easily transfers to Christ biblical language that belongs to Yahweh (as "Lord") alone.[26]

1 Corinthians 4:4–5

Equally significant is what Paul says in 1 Cor 4:4–5. At the conclusion of a passage where he has been taking exception to some of the Corinthians sitting in judgment on him, he makes it plain that the only one with the right to do this is "the Lord," whose servant he is. So even though he knows of nothing that would be the cause for such judgment, that certainly does not mean final "justification" for him, since, he asserts, "it is the Lord who examines me." But with that, and typically, he concludes by including them in this final "examination" by the Lord. So they must be careful not to judge anything "before the time when the Lord himself comes and brings to light the things of the dark and will lay bare the plans of all hearts." At that time, when Christ has exercised his "judgment of light," the role of God the Father is to "praise" those found worthy by the Lord's judgment. This combination makes it quite clear that Paul understands the final judgment of believers to be the divine prerogative of the risen Lord, Jesus Christ.

---

[25] For fuller discussion, see Kreitzer, *Jesus and God*, 93–163.
[26] See the discussion in ch. 2, p. 47.

2 Corinthians 5:9–11 [pp. 190–92]

Equally significant are the various ways Christ as Lord in this passage is seen to assume the prerogative of God as judge at the final assize, but in this case without intertextual use of the Septuagint. Toward the end of a considerable narrative and appeal, and especially to conclude his reflection on the future of the present body that is destined to decay but to be "reclothed" in the eschaton, Paul uses himself as an example that serves as a couched appeal to the Corinthians. First, he expresses his desire to live so as "to please the Lord" (v. 9), an OT idea that Paul ordinarily expresses in terms of "pleasing God."[27] But here, as in 1 Cor 7:32, "the Lord" Christ is the one whom he seeks to please.

The reason for this, second, is that "we must all appear before the *bēma* of Christ" (v. 10), the place where Christ will assume God's role in issuing final judgment on his own people, "so that everyone may receive what is due them for the things done in the body, whether good or evil." Here is a case where Paul, without argumentation, places Christ the risen Lord in the role that every Jew considered to be the absolute prerogative of God alone. For whatever else is true of the late Jewish understanding of God, his own justice and his role as the absolute ruler of the universe meant that he, and he alone, would mete out eschatological judgment on all people at the end. And Paul simply attributes such judgment to Christ, the Lord whom he strives to please for that very reason.

Third, the ultimate appeal for the Corinthians to follow his own example comes in v. 11, where Paul speaks of "knowing the fear of the Lord," where a distinctive OT phrase regarding Yahweh is applied directly (here only, as it turns out) to Christ, the exalted Lord before whom both Paul and the Corinthians must appear at the end. This is not cringing or fearful "fear"; rather, it has to do with living with proper reverence and awe of the Lord (Christ), before whom all will appear finally for judgment.

As has been noted repeatedly in the exegesis chapters, what is striking about this usage is how easily and (apparently) unself-consciously Paul attributes to the risen Lord what are absolute prerogatives of Yahweh, the God of Israel.[28] Equality with God is not argued for by Paul; it is simply taken for granted and expressed in these various ways as a matter of course.

Jesus the Lord: Eschatological Judge of the Wicked

Perhaps even more telling than the preceding passages is this final divine prerogative that is also in a matter-of-fact way attributed by Paul to the

---

[27] See n. 76 in ch. 4.

[28] It is this feature that makes the exegesis of Rom 14:10–12 so difficult and thus not included in the summary assessment of this reality in Paul. But as was pointed out in the exegesis (see ch. 6, pp. 261–67), the very fact that the exegetical issue is so difficult to resolve occurs precisely because Paul can so easily make this kind of interchange between the exalted Lord and God the Father.

Lord (= Yahweh) in two passages in 2 Thessalonians. It is one thing for the believers' Lord to be "judge" in matters pertaining to them; but for Paul, Christ the Lord is also the final judge of those who have rejected him and who have caused grief for the Lord's people.

2 Thessalonians 1:9–10 (Isa 2:10; Ps 89:7; 68:35) [pp. 60–61]

After the description of Christ's coming as eschatological judge in 2 Thess 1:7–8, noted above, where Paul echoes significant language from Isa 66, he turns next to focus on the judgment of the wicked mentioned in v. 8. The description itself occurs in v. 9, where Paul says that they "will pay the penalty of everlasting destruction *from the face of the Lord and from the glory of his might.*" The apparent awkwardness of this clause is the direct result of the fact that the italicized words are taken directly from the Septuagint of Isa 2:10, a "Day of the Lord" oracle of judgment against Judah. Just as in the Isaiah passage, the judgment results in being cut off from the divine Presence ("the face of the Lord"), which is now assumed to be the risen Lord, Christ Jesus. The fact that the Isaianic oracle is fully attributed to Christ is made the more remarkable by the (in this case, seemingly unnecessary) inclusion of the final phrase, "from the glory of his might," a thoroughly Yahwistic moment in the prophet that Paul includes in the description of Christ's judgment on the Thessalonians' present enemies.

In v. 10, appropriately enough, the now very long sentence concludes on a note about the Lord's own people when he judges the wicked. Again Paul dips into the Septuagint for this description, this time from the Psalter and from texts where the referent is Elohim ("God"), not Yahweh. Nonetheless, in Paul's sentence "the Lord" (= *Adonai*/Yahweh) is still the subject of the verb, "when he comes." Thus, using language from Ps 89:7 and 68:35, Paul contrasts the preceding judgment of their enemies with the greater reality that Christ the Lord will be "glorified in [ἐν] his saints"[29] and "marveled at among all who believe."

Thus, this whole sentence (vv. 6–10) is one of the more significant moments in Paul's letters of intertextual attribution of several ΟΤ κύριος (= *Adonai*/Yahweh) texts, all now attributed to the Lord Christ. It is Christ the risen Lord who is now the Coming One; it is Christ the risen Lord who assumes the role of divine judge of the wicked; and it is Christ the risen Lord who will be glorified in his people at the Coming. Again, even though Paul stops short of calling Christ either Yahweh or God, this intertextual use of the Septuagint's κύριος (= *Adonai*/Yahweh) allows him to predicate his conviction of Christ's full deity without calling him θεός, who is always the Father of the Son in Pauline usage.

---

[29] For this as the probable meaning of Paul's ἐν, see n. 65 in ch. 2.

2 Thessalonians 2:8 (Isa 11:4) [pp. 56–57]

This final passage of the many that place Christ, the risen Lord, in the role of eschatological judge is the only one in Paul's letters where Christ "fulfills" an actual messianic passage from the prophetic tradition. In keeping with the expected Messiah's role of meting out God's justice on earth when he comes, Paul uses the language of Isa 11:4, but he puts it into the eschatological future, when "the Lord [not in Isaiah's text] *will slay [the wicked] with the breath of his mouth.*" Here Paul has it both ways: the exalted Lord is also the Messiah. And now the crucified One as the risen Lord fulfills the role of Isaiah's messianic figure in executing God's now final judgment against the wicked.

Jesus the Lord: Invoked in Prayer

In ch. 11 we noted that Paul's "Christ devotion" included both worship and prayer. Here we will see in a bit more detail the christological implications that lie behind the several texts noted there. Indeed, nowhere in the corpus is Paul's understanding of the Son's "equality with God" (Phil 2:6) more telling than in the fact that Paul can so easily, and in a considerable variety of ways, offer prayer to the risen Lord as one would ordinarily offer it to God alone. Here we note the various ways this happens, concentrating on the reality that such prayer is in every case addressed to the "Lord," who received *that* "Name" at his exaltation/vindication.

Prayer to "the Lord" in the Thessalonian Correspondence

On no less than four occasions in 1–2 Thessalonians Paul reports to the believers how he is praying for them (1 Thess 3:11–13; 2 Thess 2:16–17; 3:5; 3:16). In each case he uses the optative mood—what grammarians in such cases refer to as a "wish-prayer," which is simply a form of indirection, indicating to others the content of prayer made to God in their behalf. The most remarkable thing about these four prayers is how the Deity is addressed in each case.

In the first one (1 Thess 3:11) God the Father is mentioned first and intensified by means of an αὐτός (*himself*), with the Lord Jesus Christ in the second position, which in turn is followed by a verb in the singular, indicating that both are being addressed together. This is then followed in vv. 12–13 by a prayer addressed to *the Lord alone,* asking him for divine favors that only God himself could bestow: that their love increase and abound for one another and for all with the goal that their hearts be "strengthened" in holiness so that they will be blameless before God the Father at Christ's Parousia. Thus, although one might be able to get around the natural implications of the two divine persons being addressed with a verb in the singular,[30] the follow-up prayer report makes that nearly impossible.

---

[30] As attempted by, e.g., Wiles, *Paul's Intercessory Prayers,* 54–55; cf. E. J. Richard, *First and Second Thessalonians* (SP 11; Collegeville, Minn.; Liturgical, 1995), 167–68.

In the second prayer report (2 Thess 2:16–17) all of this is played in reverse. The prayer is still addressed to both divine persons, but it begins in this case as prayer addressed to "the Lord Jesus Christ αὐτός [himself]," while the elaboration that follows has to do with the Father. Nonetheless, the two actual verbs that form the content of the prayer are used elsewhere in these letters with regard to the work of the Father ("encourage your hearts") and of the Son ("strengthen you"). So both prayers seem intentionally addressed to both God the Father and the Lord Jesus.

But more remarkable still are the two final prayers, both of which are addressed to "the Lord" alone (2 Thess 3:5, 16). First, with what appears to be a deliberate echo of the prayer in 1 Thess 3:11, but now using language from David's prayer in 1 Chr 29:18, Paul addresses the One who has been given "the Name," that the Lord (Jesus) direct the believers' hearts into God's love and Christ's patience. In the second instance, and as the formal conclusion to the letter, Paul requests Christ, "the Lord of peace," to grant them his *shalom*. Everything about this echoes a divine appellation and prerogative now addressed to the risen Lord. To deny that these latter two are really prayers directed to Christ either is to miss by far Pauline usage of κύριος or is itself an exercise in theological prejudice. It could perhaps go without saying that had the two prayers been addressed to God the Father, nothing would have been said to the contrary, and the attempt on the part of some to make "the Lord" here refer to God the Father is moot evidence of how truly these are prayers to a deity.[31]

As noted at the end of the discussion of these prayers in ch. 2, the data from all of them together point to an especially high understanding of the person and role of Christ. Paul is addressing prayer, a prerogative that Jews reserved for God alone, to the present reigning Lord, Jesus Christ. And that he does this so matter-of-factly suggests that this has long been a part of his life of devotion.[32]

Other Prayer Addressed to "the Lord"

It is of interest that the kind of prayer reports that Paul mentions in the Thessalonian correspondence do not occur elsewhere in the corpus except for the benedictory "grace" that concludes all of the letters in the church corpus, most often in the form "May the grace of our Lord Jesus Christ be with you." It takes a different form altogether in Ephesians and lacks "of our

---

[31] In fact, these two passages serve as primary examples of the basically two different ways of approaching the Pauline texts. On the one hand, some start with the fact that this is prayer, and prayer is ordinarily addressed to God the Father; hence, God is "the Lord" in this case. Thus the exegetical issue is resolved on the basis of prior expectations and theological considerations. On the other hand, in the exegetical chapters I have argued that we should let Paul's own identification markers dictate our understanding of κύριος in passages such as this (since Paul himself has consistently identified Christ as κύριος in both of these letters and in this case especially has repeated the identification in the immediately preceding prayer [2:16–17]).

[32] See further Hurtado, *Lord Jesus Christ*, 138–40.

Lord Jesus Christ" in Colossians. That this is a form of prayer addressed to Jesus as Lord is made plain by two factors.

First, all one would have to do is insert any other name in the place of "the Lord." It would work perfectly for "God our Father": May the grace of God our Father be with you. And if this were the case, it would be universally recognized as prayer. But Paul, interestingly enough, never does that. Moreover, it simply does not work for any other kind of being. No one would think of saying, "May the grace of the great archangel Michael be with you"; more unthinkable yet would be such a "grace benediction" in the name of a mere human being, even a divinely exalted one.

Second, that this is intended as a benedictory prayer is confirmed by the singular triadic elaboration found at the conclusion of our 2 Corinthians. Here Paul begins with the standard "May the grace of our Lord Jesus Christ," but then, for reasons not at all clear, he adds, "and the love of God and the κοινωνία of [participation in/fellowship with] the Holy Spirit."[33] All agree that this triadic benediction is a form of prayer. It surely is no less so when it lacks the addition that includes God the Father.

The other instances of prayer reports occur in the Corinthian correspondence. In the one instance, *Marana tha* ("Come, Lord"), we are given the actual content of the earliest known prayer to be used among followers of Christ. By any definition, this is a prayer—addressed to Christ as Lord. The second instance occurs in 2 Cor 12:8–10, which has the twofold unique feature that (1) it is prayer addressed to "the Lord" for a very personal matter and (2) Paul also reports the answer, which was not in fact what he prayed *for.* The Lord's response was, "My grace is sufficient for you." Again, this clearly is prayer, and clearly it is addressed to Christ as Lord for something that only God could do for him. And the answer received was quite in keeping with what Paul had come to know of Christ his Lord. Paul had already learned that God's power is evident in the "weakness" of a crucified Messiah. He was also in the process of learning that discipleship means to live cruciform. Thus, "*my* grace is sufficient" because "*my* strength is perfected in [your] weakness." Such prayer with its recorded answer would seem to put considerable theological pressure on a monotheist who had not included the Lord in the divine identity.

Furthermore, and as we have noted with some frequency, these various prayer reports are stated quite matter-of-factly to believers in Paul's churches, whom he does not expect to be shocked by them. The fact that none of this is something that he sets out to prove is what makes the christological point so compelling.

Jesus the Lord: Sharer of Divine Prerogatives

To conclude this examination of Paul's understanding of Jesus as the one who in his exaltation was given "the Name," I present here a catch-all group-

---

[33]For further discussion, see Fee, *God's Empowering Presence,* 362–65.

ing of the various instances noted throughout the exegetical chapters where Christ "the Lord" shares all kinds of prerogatives that in the Jewish worldview belong exclusively to God. I begin with several further instances where the risen Lord has assumed the role of κύριος (= Yahweh) and where he is also thereby seen to have assumed the divine privileges inherent in the Septuagint text.

Christ, the "Lord" of Septuagint Texts

Boast in the Lord—1 Corinthians 1:31 (Jer 9:23–24) [pp. 129–30]

The language of "boasting"[34] occurs frequently enough in the Corinthian letters (39 of 55 occurrence in Paul's letters) to give one confidence that this was a considerable problem in the church in Corinth—at least from Paul's point of view. But Paul's own use of the language in response is drawn from the very important text Jer 9:23–24, on which Paul makes a considerable play in 1 Cor 1:26–31.[35] The argument of the paragraph concludes with an "in order that even as it is written," where Paul rephrases the Jeremiah text to fit his specific argument. What is "written" is "Let the one who boasts boast in the Lord." In Jeremiah, of course, κύριος glosses *Adonai* = Yahweh; but for Paul, the "Lord" in whom the Corinthians are to "boast" is Christ himself—a most remarkable reworking of the Jeremiah passage indeed, and especially so since the "boast" is to be in the crucified One (cf. Phil 3:3, 8, 10).

The Mind of the Lord—1 Corinthians 2:16 (Isa 40:13) [pp. 130–31]

After arguing vigorously with the Corinthians that God's true wisdom and power are to be found in the crucified Messiah (1:18–2:5), Paul feels the need to explain further (and perhaps somewhat ironically to those confident of their Spirit gifting) that the only way he and they can know this is by a revelation from the Spirit (2:6–16). He concludes the argument by citing Isaiah's poignant query: "Who has known the mind of the LORD? Who has been his counselor?" (Isa 40:13). Taken on its own terms, one could argue that "the Lord" in the citation is still God the Father. But Paul offers his own "interpretation," which indicates that yet another OT Yahweh passage is now to be understood in terms of Christ. "And we have the *mind of Christ*," he concludes, thus indicating still further that our ways are not God's ways.

Beloved of the Lord—2 Thessalonians 2:13 (Deut 33:12) [pp. 63–65]

Another remarkable moment of intertextuality in Paul's letters occurs in his second thanksgiving in 2 Thessalonians, where in the vocative in 2:13

---

[34] Gk. καυχάομαι, καύχημα, καύχησις (verb, abstract noun, verbal noun). These words occur 59 times in the NT, 55 of them in Paul's letters, thus 71 percent of them in these two letters.

[35] That Paul intends to be "citing" this passage in v. 31 is evident from vv. 26–28, where his categories for what people put their boast (= confidence) in are "wise," "powerful," and "well-born"; Jeremiah's categories are "wisdom," "power," and "riches."

he addresses the Thessalonian believers as "brothers and sisters *loved by the Lord.*" Paul's language is precisely that of Moses' blessing of the tribe of Benjamin in the Septuagint of Deut 33:12: "Benjamin, *the beloved of the Lord* [Yahweh], shall dwell safely in him." Thus, in a moment of needed reassurance, those whom Paul described as loved by God in 1 Thess 1:4 are here addressed in the language of Paul's own family crest: "beloved of the Lord" = Jesus Christ (cf. 2 Thess 2:16).[36]

The Lord Be with You—2 Thessalonians 3:16 (Ruth 2:4) [pp. 76–77]

In one final, and equally remarkable, moment of intertextuality in the Thessalonian correspondence, Paul signs off 2 Thessalonians with a clear echo of the personal greeting that thrived among Yahwists in ancient Israel, found in Ruth 2:4: "The LORD be with you" (cf. the angelic greetings in Judg 6:12; Luke 1:28). That this is another instance where κύριος = *Adonai* = Yahweh is verified by all the surrounding matter, plus the twofold identification of Christ as "Lord" in this letter in conjunction with θεός as Father (1:2; 2:16) and the consistent use of κύριος to refer to Christ. Just as Christ in his incarnation was *with us* when he came among us in our likeness in order to redeem, so now Paul concludes the letter with this historic greeting as a wish-prayer that the exalted Lord may continue to be present with the believers in Thessalonica. And he would be so, one might add, by the Spirit, who is at one and the same time known by Paul as the Spirit of God and the Spirit of Christ.[37]

The Lord Is Near—Philippians 4:5 (Ps 145:18)

In one of the more puzzling affirmations in his letters, in terms of what it is doing here, Paul picks up David's precise language from Ps 145:18 (*"The LORD is near* to all who call on him") as a means of encouragement to the Philippians. The puzzle is, first, whether it is a word about the present or an affirmation about the future and, second, whether it goes with what precedes or follows, most likely the latter: "The Lord is near, [so] be anxious about nothing."[38] In any case, this is yet another instance where Paul has adopted language about Yahweh from the Septuagint and applied it to Christ.

Κύριος and Θεός Share Prerogatives

In several other instances in his letters, Paul interchanges a variety of divine attributes or activities between God (ὁ θεός) and Christ (ὁ κύριος). Not

---

[36] And this is so in this case even if the Thessalonians themselves may not have caught the reference.

[37] See esp. discussion on Rom 8:9–11 in ch. 6, pp. 269–70.

[38] See the full discussion in G. D. Fee, *Paul's Letter to the Philippians* (NICNT; Grand Rapids: Eerdmans, 1995), 407–8.

all of these are strictly divine prerogatives; but what is striking is how easily, and without deliberation, Paul makes these interchanges. Rather than group or prioritize them in any way, I have chosen simply to list them in their (supposed) chronological order; and I have limited myself to the first four letters, since after that it is mostly repetition.

Christian Existence as Being in Christ/in God

The first mention of θεός (*God*) and κύριος (*Lord*) together in the corpus appears as the first thing up in the very first letter (1 Thess 1:1; cf. 2 Thess 1:1), in this case as the double objects of a single prepositional phrase. But it is also a phrase unlike any other in the letters, where Paul designates the church of the Thessalonians as existing ἐν θεῷ πατρὶ καὶ κυρίῳ Ἰησοῦ Χριστοῦ (*in God the Father and the Lord Jesus Christ*). In later letters he will speak of believers as being "in Christ," but only here does he speak of them as also being "in God."

The christological significance of this phrase is twofold. First, God and Christ are together understood as the sphere in which believers exist; they are simultaneously in God and in the Lord. And thus, second, to exist *in God* means at the same time to exist *in Christ*. And it is not as though they lived in a twofold sphere of existence. For Paul, to be "in Christ" means to be "in God," and vice versa—hence the reason Paul can later place them "in Christ" alone.

The Grace of the Lord/of God

Paul's prayer for "grace" for his churches is one of the places where the divine prerogatives are equally shared between God and the Lord. Almost all the letters begin with the doublet "grace and peace," which are then invariably from both "God the Father and the Lord Jesus Christ." On the other hand, most of the letters sign off with the singular benedictory prayer "May the grace of the Lord [= Christ Jesus] be with you," beginning with 1 Thessalonians (5:28). However, in the body of the letters "grace" is most often expressed as coming from God the Father, with the notable exceptions 2 Cor 8:9; 12:9; 1 Tim 1:14, where it is an attribute of the Christ the Lord.

The Peace of the Lord/of God; the God/Lord of Peace

The same interchangeability between θεός (*God*) and κύριος (*Lord*) regarding "grace" is also true of its companion "peace," which appears together with "grace" in all of the salutations. Elsewhere in the body of the letters there is again an interesting expression of interchangeability. On the one hand, the phrase "the peace of God" occurs only once in the corpus (Phil 4:7), as does its counterpart, "the peace of the Lord" (2 Thess 3:16). On the other hand, the descriptor, "the God of peace" occurs six times,[39] but in

---

[39] The precise phrase ὁ θεὸς τῆς εἰρήνης occurs 4 times (1 Thess 5:23; Rom 15:33; 16:20; Phil 4:9); it occurs with the compound "God of love and peace" in 2 Cor 13:11, and it is implied in the contrast with "disorder" in 1 Cor 14:33.

its second occurrence in the Thessalonian correspondence (2 Thess 3:16) Paul prays that "the Lord of peace" will "himself give you peace at all times." The ease with which Paul does this is what is so striking.

Walk Worthy of the Lord/of God

In 1 Thess 2:12 Paul, with a triple compounding of nearly identical verbs,[40] urges these new believers, even in the midst of present difficulties, to walk worthy of *the God* who called them. In a similar moment in Col 1:10, this time in prayer, he urges that "you walk worthy of *the Lord* so as to please him in every way." This is an interchange that most readers would scarcely notice, since either one fits well within one's expectations in reading Paul.

The Divine Presence at the Parousia

Closely associated with the divine glory in the OT is the concept of God's presence, as the interchange between these two ideas regarding the tabernacle and temple makes clear. Picking up the latter theme, and depending on the point of emphasis at a given moment, Paul can speak interchangeably of being in the presence of the Lord or of God. Thus in 1 Thess 2:19, in the first mention of Christ's Parousia in his letters, Paul speaks of Thessalonians as his joy and crown of boasting when together they appear "in the presence of *the Lord* Jesus Christ." A few sentences later, at the conclusion of his prayer in 3:11–13, he speaks of being "in the presence of *our God and Father* at the Parousia of our Lord Jesus."

The Lord/the God Who Strengthens Believers

In the same prayer in 1 Thess 3:13 Paul prays that *"the Lord* will 'strengthen' your hearts blameless in holiness." Similarly in 2 Thess 3:3, he assures them that *"the Lord* will 'strengthen' you and keep you from the evil one." But in between these two words of affirmation, in 2 Thess 2:17, he prays that "God our Father . . . may 'strengthen' your hearts." Again, just as he prays to both God the Father and Christ the exalted Lord, so also he very easily uses some identical language for both the Father and the Son when mentioning the content of his prayer.

The Word of the Lord/of God

The phrase "the word of God" occurs eight times in the Pauline corpus,[41] always as a subjective genitive, meaning a word that God has spoken, either inscripturated or with reference to the gospel. Although in some cases the nature of this genitive with the phrase "the word of the Lord" is less easy

---

[40] With the compounding of three (somewhat) synonymous participles, παρα-καλοῦτες (*urge, exhort, encourage*), παραμυθούμενοι (*console, cheer up*), μαρτυρόμενοι (*urge, implore*).

[41] See 1 Cor 14:36; 2 Cor 2:17; 4:2; Rom 9:6; Col 1:25; Titus 2:5; 2 Tim 2:9.

to determine,[42] there can be little question that in 1 Thess 4:15 Paul uses the phrase as a subjective genitive in precisely the same way as with "the word of God": "This we say to you by a word from the Lord."

The Faithfulness of the Lord/of God

One of the more consistent ways Yahweh reveals himself in the OT is in his faithfulness. It is not surprising, therefore, that Paul in 1 Thess 5:24 should appeal to such faithfulness with regard to God's carrying out his divine purposes in the lives of the Thessalonians. But what is surprising is that he should say the same of Christ in 2 Thess 3:3: "Faithful is *the Lord*, who will strengthen you and keep you from the evil one." So much is this so, that many commentators suggest that ὁ κύριος in this passage actually refers to God. But as was pointed out in the exegesis of this passage (ch. 2, pp. 71–72), that goes against not only Paul's own identifications and consistent usage elsewhere but also against the immediate context, where two sentences earlier (2 Thess 2:16–17) Christ has been specifically identified as "the Lord." Thus, despite the surprising (to us)[43] nature of this description of Christ as Lord, it is quite in keeping with what Paul does regularly elsewhere, as this present list of items indicates.

The Gospel of Our Lord Jesus Christ

Reading Paul's letters, one gets used to the easy interchange between "the gospel of God" (1 Thess 2:2, 8–9), where the emphasis is on its source, and "the gospel of Christ" (1 Thess 3:2), where the emphasis is on Christ as its basic content. However, in the long thanksgiving-turned-announcement of judgment against the Thessalonians' persecutors in 2 Thess 1:3–10, Paul refers to the latter as "not knowing God and not obeying the gospel *of our Lord Jesus*" (v. 8). This unique moment in the NT seems obviously shaped to fit the immediate context. This phrase is but one more adaptation of common language to fit the setting of Christ carrying out God's just judgment against those who are persecuting the Thessalonian believers. In this case, "the gospel of our Lord Jesus" is most likely intended as an explanation of what "knowing God" means in the present era. In any case, it is a remarkable adaptation of a common phrase, with the emphasis now on the gospel that has to do with the currently reigning Lord.

The Glory of the Lord/of God

On several occasions in his letters Paul speaks of "the glory of God" as the final goal of all things. The phrase itself is used both to describe the

---

[42] See, e.g., 1 Thess 1:8, where "Lord" is most likely "objective." What is spreading rapidly is "the word about the Lord." The same is very likely the case in 2 Thess 3:1, where he desires for "the word of the Lord" to spread rapidly.

[43] This is in fact the only instance in the corpus where Paul does this. He speaks of God's faithfulness elsewhere in 1 Cor 1:9; 10:13; 2 Cor 1:18.

infinite, indescribable greatness of God as such (we are to do all things with that glory in view [e.g., 1 Cor 10:31; Phil 1:11]) and to describe the sphere in which God dwells (Rom 5:2; Phil 4:19). Both of these nuances of the phrase are also used of Christ the Lord. In 2 Thess 2:14, the final goal of our salvation is the obtaining of "the glory of the Lord," having to do with our being together with him in the sphere of his glory; in 2 Cor 3:18 (cf. 4:4), when believers turn to Christ by the Spirit, they behold "the glory *of the Lord*," where the immediate context makes plain that Christ's glory is that of Yahweh, which Moses was *not* allowed to behold. Again, Paul does this kind of thing apparently without conscious reflection.

Paul Sent/Commissioned by Christ

In the Septuagint the verb ἀποστέλλω is regularly used for God's "sending/commissioning" of his messengers to his people. So much is this so that Paul can ask rhetorically, "How can anyone preach, unless they are sent [ἀποσταλῶσιν]?" (Rom 10:15). Thus, when Paul speaks of his own ministry, one is not surprised that he says, "Christ ἀπέστειλέν με to preach the gospel" (1 Cor 1:17); and even though "the Lord" is not here the subject of the verb, Paul himself considered this "sending" to be part of his experience related in 9:1, when he "saw the Lord."

The Power of the Lord/of God

One of the constants in the OT understanding of Yahweh is that he is a God of great and unlimited power. Thus, both creation and the redemption of Israel are regularly celebrated in the Psalter in terms of God's great love and power (e.g., Ps 89:5–18; 145:3–13). It is not surprising, therefore, to find this kind of language in Paul's letters. For example, in ch. 1 of Romans, Paul celebrates God's power revealed in redemption (v. 16) and creation (v. 20).

Given Paul's high Christology, neither is it surprising to find him using similar language with regard to the person and work of Christ. In the difficult situation of the incestuous man in 1 Cor 5, Paul urges the church in vv. 3–5 to carry out the judgment that he has pronounced "in the Name of the Lord, Jesus" (see ch. 3, p. 136) in the context of the gathered assembly, when "the *power* of the Lord Jesus" is also present. Although this is probably an oblique reference to the Spirit, it is of christological import that God's Spirit and power are understood to be present as the power of the exalted Lord, Jesus. Similarly in 2 Cor 12:8–10, Christ the Lord's answer to Paul's prayer concerning his "thorn in the flesh" is that "my *power* is made perfect in weakness" (cf. 1 Cor 1:22–25). Thus, Paul goes on, he will gladly bear with his weaknesses "so that Christ's *power* may rest on me."

Again, with perfect ease Paul interchanges the language and reality of an attribute intrinsic to God with the risen Lord, Jesus Christ.

The Lord/God Has Given

In the Septuagint narrative of the creation of the tabernacle (Exod 31:2–5; 36:1–2), we are told that "God gave to [Bezalel]" the wisdom and skill for the task (ᾧ ἔδωκεν ὁ θεὸς ἐπιστήμην [36:2]). Paul uses this same language for his own gifting for apostolic ministry in 2 Cor 5:18. But in 1 Cor 3:5, he refers to his and Apollos's gifting in terms of "as *the Lord* has given to each"—yet one more example of Paul picking up biblical phraseology and applying it to both God and the Lord.

God/the Lord Wills

Paul begins 1 Corinthians by noting that his apostleship is "by the will of God," a phrase that occurs some 13 times in his letters.[44] But in two remarkable moments in 1 Corinthians (4:19; 16:7), he refers to his coming to Corinth in terms of "if ὁ κύριος wills." The very fact that this absolute prerogative of God can be so easily transferred to Christ the Lord points up the presuppositional nature of Paul's understanding of Christ as divine.

Pleasing the Lord/God

In his discussion of what he perceives as the advantages of singleness over marriage, Paul asserts that a single person is able to be entirely devoted to one thing: πῶς ἀρέστη τῷ κυρίῳ (*how to please the Lord* [1 Cor 7:32]). In most other such moments, Paul speaks of "pleasing τῷ θεῷ [*God*]."[45] Here is yet another OT concern[46] that has been taken over by Paul and is directly applied to the Lord = Christ (cf. 2 Cor 5:9).

The Assembly(ies) of God/of Christ

In what is less a divine prerogative and more a matter of divine possession, Paul regularly refers to the believing communities with the term ἐκκλησία, a happy choice of term because it does double duty, picking up the language for the local "assembly" of people in the Greek city-states, language that had been conveniently used by the Septuagint translators to speak of the gathered "congregation" of Israel. Paul's genitive descriptor (used as a possessive) for this "assembly" is ordinarily "the assembly/ies *of God*"; but in Rom 16:16 he just as easily refers to the churches that are sending greetings to Rome as "the assemblies *of Christ*." Thus an obviously divine prerogative is shared by the risen Christ.

---

[44] See n. 133 in ch. 3.

[45] See 1 Thess 2:15; 4:1; Rom 8:8; 12:1–2; 14:18; Phil 4:18.

[46] See, e.g., Exod 33:13, 17; Num 14:8; Job 34:9; Ps 41:11; 69:13.

The Fear of the Lord

The penultimate example of this kind of interchange between "God" and "the Lord" is one of the more significant ones in the corpus, and it is a sure indicator not only of the ease with which Paul does this but also of the understanding of Christ as fully divine and therefore as one who can regularly stand in a role that is biblically otherwise assigned only to God. Although the phrase "the fear of the Lord" occurs most often in the Wisdom literature, it is a common perspective of Israel's understanding of God and of their relationship to God. In a passage in which Paul puts emphasis on Christ the Lord as the eschatological judge of his people (2 Cor 5:10), he follows up by referring to his "knowing *the fear of the Lord*," by which he undoubtedly means Christ. In so doing, he demonstrates once more how easily he can interchange references to God and to Christ, which should not surprise us at all in light of the foregoing discussion.

The Spirit of the Lord

This rehearsal of divine prerogatives shared by God and the Lord concludes with the only one that does not occur in the first four letters, and which will be taken up in some detail in the final chapter: for Paul, the one Holy Spirit is an easily interchangeable reality regarding the Father and the Son. Thus the Spirit, who is most often referred to as "the Spirit of God," is on three occasions specifically identified as "the Spirit of Christ." In Gal 4:6 Paul stipulates that God "sent *the Spirit of his Son* into our hearts," thus eliciting the *Abba*-cry. In Rom 8:9–10 this interchange is specific and thoroughgoing. What identifies the believer as one who does not live "according to the flesh" is the fact that "the *Spirit of God* lives in you." The immediate pickup of this phrase makes the interchange: "If one does *not* have *the Spirit of Christ*," such a person is not a believer at all.

Since for Paul there is only "one Holy Spirit" (1 Cor 12:4; Eph 4:4), this kind of interchange is a crowning expression of Paul's understanding of the full deity of Christ; and along with other Pauline texts, it serves as the basis for his triadic understanding of God that, along with John and Hebrews, eventually led the church to express this understanding in Trinitarian terms. Moreover, however one is finally to articulate the relationship between the one God and the one Lord, this kind of thing can be said by Paul only because he believed that the incarnate Son and now exalted Lord was eternally preexistent and thus fully equal with the Father. And this leads us to our final chapter.

Conclusion

The evidence of this chapter seems to put the capstone on the high Christology in Paul's thought that we have regularly observed in the preceding chapters. And it does so by way of the rich possibilities for Paul of the "title" for Jesus that had found expression in the earliest Aramaic-speaking communities, the confession that Jesus is "the Lord." It probably is not accidental, therefore, that in its three appearances in Paul's letters (1 Cor 12:3; Rom 10:9; Phil 2:11), this confession always occurs in the order "the Lord is Jesus." While it was indeed the earthly, incarnate Jesus who had been raised from the dead, it was at his exaltation that God the Father bestowed on his preexistent Son the Divine Name of "the Lord" itself.

Thus, through the happy circumstance that the Divine Name had been translated in the Septuagint by way of the Aramaic *Adonai*, Paul was able to have it both ways. The preexistent Son, who became incarnate as Jesus of Nazareth, received the "Name" at his vindication. But at the same time, by using "the Lord" exclusively to refer to the risen Christ, Paul could include the Son in the divine identity in a complete way, but without absolute identification (merging the two into one) and without the Son "usurping" the role of God the Father.

Thus, given the evidence that has been rehearsed in this chapter, I emphasize by way of conclusion the two matters that have been repeated throughout the discussion. First, one can hardly miss the rich variety of ways Paul has included Christ in the divine identity by means of the name-turned-title "the Lord." This phenomenon occurs repeatedly in the earliest letters in the corpus and is maintained throughout, to be highlighted again at the end in 2 Timothy; and it happens regularly in two ways: OT *texts* that refer to Yahweh and *phrases* that in the OT are primarily the exclusive province of Yahweh are, by means of the Septuagint, regularly attributed in Paul's writings to the exalted Lord, Jesus Christ.

Second (and what some may by now see as repetition ad nauseum), one can scarcely miss how theologically unself-consciously—what might be described as nearly off-handedly—Paul does this. Here is a man not trying to *assert* anything unusual about the role of the presently exalted Lord but a man who simply *assumes* it in every way and equally assumes that this understanding is shared by his readers. Furthermore, his appropriation of OT Yahweh language to refer to the divine activity of the reigning Lord has inherent in it an understanding of Christ as assuming roles that traditionally and exclusively belong to God alone.

It is therefore not at all difficult to see why Paul was used, along with John, by the orthodox to express their Trinitarianism a couple of centuries later. For whatever else is true for Paul, he is a thoroughgoing monotheist all the way through. Yet at the same time, Paul's devotion to Christ and his way of speaking about Christ are such that he, without argument, attributes to Christ Jesus his Lord many of what are strictly divine prerogatives. And finally, as we noted in ch. 11, Paul's devotion to Christ is that reserved by his Jewish heritage for God alone. Early Christian Christology hardly gets any higher than that.

16

Christ and the Spirit: Paul as a Proto-Trinitarian

EVEN A CASUAL READING OF the preceding pages forces on one the theological necessity of trying to come to terms with the twin realities of Paul's high Christology (preexistent Son, exalted Christ who is given "the Name") and absolute monotheism. What does it mean for a monotheist to envision the Deity as Father and Son? Yet there is more; for the one element generally avoided so far in this analysis, and which was picked up as the final item in the preceding chapter, is the role of the Spirit and his relationship to the Son and the Father. For it was not just the data of the Gospel of John but equally that of Paul's letters, that caused the later church to express itself in Trinitarian, not binitarian, terms. In this final chapter, therefore, we will pursue these several theological matters, not with "solution" in view but with some measure both of awareness and of discussion of the issues.

The first aim of this chapter is to point out the considerable christological implications found in Paul's many and varied statements that conjoin the Spirit with Christ (and the Father) in the economy of salvation. That is, what are the christological implications of Paul's understanding of the relationship of Christ and the Spirit, as much as that can be discovered in his various, not intentionally theological, statements? At the same time, I am interested in examining where Paul fits into a trajectory that caused these early, thoroughgoing monotheists to speak of Christ and the Spirit and their relationship to God the Father in such a way that finally resulted in the Trinitarian resolution of the early fourth century.

In order to pursue these two matters, we need first to look briefly at Paul's basic understanding of the person and role of the Spirit in the divine economy. Then we will briefly examine Paul's understanding of Christ's relationship with the Spirit, which points to an especially high Christology for Paul and at the same time pushes us toward a triadic understanding of the one God in Paul's thought. This in turn suggests that Paul held to a kind of proto-Trinitarian view of God, even though he never comes close to explaining how a strict monotheist could talk about God in this triadic way.

The Person and Role of the Spirit in Paul's Thought

We begin this discussion with a brief note about Paul's use of the word πνεῦμα as a referent to the Holy Spirit, which occurs approximately 120 times in the corpus.[1] Of these, the most common referent is simply to "the Spirit," while 17 times the fuller name "the Holy Spirit" appears. But 12 times Paul speaks of the Spirit as "the Spirit of God"[2] and 4 times as "the Spirit of [Christ]."[3] Our primary interest lies with these latter 16 instances. But first, three things about Paul's understanding of the Spirit need to be highlighted.

1. Although Paul obviously understood the Spirit to be intimately related both to God the Father and to Christ, it is also seems certain that he understood the Spirit to have personhood in his own right. Besides the many texts where the Spirit is the subject of actions that belong to personhood[4] three texts make it clear that Paul understood the Spirit not only as "person," but also at the same time as distinct from the Father and the Son.

First, in Rom 8:16 the Spirit who gives us "adoption as 'sons,'" attested by his prompting within us the *Abba*-cry, in turn, and for this very reason, becomes the *second (necessary) witness*[5] along with our own spirits to the reality of our being God's children. Of necessity, such a "witness" must be personal. Likewise in Rom 8:26–27, not only does the Spirit intercede on our behalf, thus "knowing us" being implied, but also we can be assured of the effectiveness of his intercession because "God knows *the mind* of the Spirit," who in turn thus prays "according to God['s will]." Whatever else, this is the language of personhood, not that of an impersonal influence or power. So also with 1 Cor 2:10–12, where Paul uses the analogy of human interior

---

[1]For the complete analysis, including the statistics, see Fee, *God's Empowering Presence*, ch. 2. The one difference between that analysis and the exegesis presented in this volume is with regard to τὸ πνεῦμα κυρίου in 2 Cor 3:17. For my change of perspective on this clause, see ch. 4, pp. 177–80, 190.

[2]See 1 Cor 2:11, 14; 3:16; 6:11; 7:40; 12:3; 2 Cor 3:3; Rom 8:9, 14; 15:19; Eph 4:30; Phil 3:3; this count does not include the further instances where Paul speaks of "his Spirit," where God is the antecedent to "his."

[3]The modifier varies: "the Spirit of the Lord" (2 Cor 3:17); "the Spirit of his Son" (Gal 4:6); "the Spirit of Christ" (Rom 8:9); "the Spirit of Jesus Christ" (Phil 1:19).

[4]For example, the Spirit *searches* all things (1 Cor 2:10), *knows* the mind of God (1 Cor 2:11), *teaches* the content of the gospel to believers (1 Cor 2:13), *dwells* among or within believers (1 Cor 3:16; Rom 8:11; 2 Tim 1:14), *accomplishes* all things (1 Cor 12:11), *gives life* to those who believe (2 Cor 3:6), *cries out* from within our hearts (Gal 4:6), *leads* us in the ways of God (Gal 5:18; Rom 8:14), *bears witness* with our own spirits (Rom 8:16), *has desires* that are in opposition to the flesh (Gal 5:17), *helps* us in our weakness (Rom 8:26), *intercedes* on our behalf (Rom 8:26–27), *works* all things *together* for our ultimate good (Rom 8:28), *strengthens* believers (Eph 3:16), and *is grieved* by our sinfulness (Eph 4:30). Furthermore, the fruits of the Spirit's indwelling are the personal attributes of God (Gal 5:22–23).

[5]That is, Paul is reflecting his biblical heritage that everything must be established by two or three witnesses (Deut 19:15); cf. 2 Cor 13:1.

consciousness (only one's "spirit" knows one's mind) to insist that the Spirit alone knows the mind of God. The Spirit "searches all things," even "the depths of God";[6] and because of this singular relationship with God, the Spirit alone knows and reveals God's otherwise hidden wisdom (1 Cor 2:7).

2. Despite attempts by some to conflate the risen Christ and the outpoured Spirit into a Spirit Christology,[7] it seems certain that for Paul the Spirit has personhood in his own right and that even though he is intimately related to both the Father and the Son, he is also quite clearly "distinct from" them. This is made plain especially by the many triadic statements in Paul's letters where the roles, noted below, of the Father, Christ, and the Spirit in our salvation are distinct and unique, even though everything is seen ultimately to come from the one God.

3. It is precisely Paul's triadic way of speaking about our human salvation that will not allow us to confuse or conflate either the person or the work of the Son and the Spirit. In Paul's present worldview—"between the times," as it were—*the Son* is now seated "at God's right hand in the heavenly realms" (Eph 1:20), where he currently makes intercession for us (Rom 8:32). Significantly, just a couple of sentences earlier in Romans, Paul refers to *the Spirit* as indwelling us and as helping us in our times of weakness by interceding from within, speaking for us what is inexpressible, which God knows because he "knows the mind of the Spirit" (8:26–27). Thus, to put it in different terms: in the present "geography" of heaven and earth, both Father and Son are seen as dwelling in heaven, while the Spirit is seen as (in)dwelling on earth.

So, in the language of the later creeds, what is certain about Paul's thought is that he understood the Spirit both as personal and "distinct from" the Father and the Son, although intimately related to both as God's and Christ's own personal presence within and among us, carrying on the ministry of Christ in the present age.

---

[6] An idea that reflects Paul's background in the OT and Jewish apocalyptic thought (cf. Dan 2:22–23).

[7] This is one of the idiosyncratic moments in twentieth century NT scholarship. For a critique, see G. D. Fee, *To What End Exegesis? Essays Textual, Exegetical, and Theological* (Grand Rapids: Eerdmans, 2001), 218–39. Not only do the various triadic passages currently under consideration speak strongly against it, but also it is of some interest to note that the two primary texts that have been used for this idea, 2 Cor 3:17 and 1 Cor 15:45, are both the result of Paul's using texts from the Septuagint to further other concerns in each passage. And whatever else, as I have pointed out in the exegesis of these texts (ch. 4, pp. 177–80; ch. 3, 116–18), Paul has no intention of identifying the risen Christ as the Spirit. The same is true with Rom 8:9–11, noted below, where Paul follows up "the Spirit of Christ dwells in you" with "if Christ is in you." In context, this simply means, "if Christ by his Spirit is in you," and it has nothing to do with equating the Spirit with Christ. At the end of the day, one senses that the advocacy for a Spirit Christology is predicated less on the Pauline data as such and more on a desire to avoid the triadic implications of Paul's way of talking about the one God.

Christ and the Spirit in Paul's Thought

Just as the coming of the Son has forever marked our understanding of God, who is henceforth known as "the Father of our Lord Jesus Christ"[8] who "sent his Son" into the world to redeem us (Gal 4:4–5), likewise the coming of Christ has forever marked our understanding of the Spirit. The Spirit of God is also the Spirit of Christ (2 Cor 3:17; Gal 4:6; Rom 8:9; Phil 1:19), who carries on the work of Christ following his resurrection and subsequent assumption of the place of authority at God's right hand. To have received the Spirit of God (1 Cor 2:12) is to have access to the mind of Christ (v. 16), meaning to understand what Christ was all about in bringing us salvation.

For Paul, therefore, Christ gives a fuller definition to the Spirit: people of the Spirit are God's children, fellow heirs with God's Son (Rom 8:14–17); at the same time, Christ is the absolute criterion for what is truly Spirit activity (e.g., 1 Cor 12:3). Indeed, Paul says, to have the Spirit of Christ indwelling us means that Christ himself is present with us (Rom 8:9–10). Thus it is fair to say, with some, that Paul's doctrine of the Spirit is Christ-centered, in the sense that Christ and his work help define the Spirit and his work in the Christian life.

For the most part, the relationship between the *role* of Christ and the Spirit in the new covenant era is fairly straightforward. This comes out most often in the many instances where Paul speaks of our salvation in triadic terms.[9] Thus for Paul, human redemption is the combined activity of Father, Son, and Spirit, in that (1) it is predicated on the love of God, whose love sets it in motion; (2) it is effected historically through the death and resurrection of Christ the Son; and (3) it is actualized in the life of believers through the power of the Holy Spirit. This is expressed in any number of ways in Paul, of which Rom 5:5, 8 offers a typical example. The love of God that found expression historically in Christ's dying for us (v. 8) is what the Holy Spirit has poured out in our hearts (v. 5).

Thus, in one of the most revealing of these passages (Gal 4:4–7), Paul speaks in identical terms, first, of God's "sending his Son" (v. 4) and, second, of his "sending the Spirit of his Son" (v. 6). In the first instance, the sending was for the purposes of effecting salvation in the course of human history: sent by the Father, the Son "was born of a woman" in the context of historic Judaism ("born under the law") for the express purposes of

---

[8]See the discussion of the first occurrence of this language in 2 Cor 1:3 (ch. 4, pp. 169–71).

[9]Among these many passages, see esp. the semicreedal soteriological passages, such as 1 Thess 1:4–6; 2 Thess 2:13–14; 1 Cor 6:11; 2 Cor 1:21–22; Gal 4:4–7; Rom 8:3–4; 8:15–17; Titus 3:4–7. But see also many other such texts, soteriological or otherwise: 1 Cor 1:4–7; 2:4–5; 2:12; 6:19–20; 2 Cor 3:16–18; Gal 3:1–5; Rom 5:5–8; 8:9–11; 15:16; 15:18–19; 15:30; Col 3:16; Eph 1:3; 1:17–20; 2:17–18; 2:19–22; 3:16–19; 5:18–19; Phil 1:19–20; 3:3.

human redemption. It is likewise clear from the broader context of Galatians that the first sending concluded with the Son's resurrection and exaltation.[10] So the "sending of the Spirit of the Son" occurred after the ascension, and from Paul's point of view it occurred precisely to put into effect the "life" that Christ had secured for us by his death. This presence of the Son by means of the Spirit of the Son actualizes our own "sonship."

The net result of all this is that in his incarnation, the Son of God came into our human history bearing the divine image and thus he was the divine Presence on earth. What the Son came to effect was the restoration of the divine image in those who would become God's children through faith in him. What the Spirit of the Son came to effect was the actual re-creating of that image in those who through Christ and the Spirit are themselves "the 'sons' [children] of God."[11]

These various data push us in two directions theologically. First, as already noted, there is in Paul's view a clear distinction between the risen Christ and the Holy Spirit whom God the Father sent into the world. Indeed, the narrowly focused data presented in the preceding chapters could perhaps be seen as part of a larger NT picture in which God's activity in our redemption is expressed basically in terms of the Father and the Son. But for Paul, that is obviously not the whole picture. In the end, it is the *triadic experience* of God and of God's effecting our salvation, the so-called economic Trinity, that led the later church to express this divine Triad in terms of the ontological Trinity: Father, Son, and Holy Spirit as one God in his being.

Second, what is striking for *Pauline Christology* is the ease with which Paul can, with regard to the Spirit, shift language between the Father and the Son. Nowhere does this happen in a more telling way than in Rom 8:9–11. Here in successive clauses the presently indwelling Spirit is spoken of in a most casual, off-handed manner as the way both the Father and the Son, who "dwell" in heaven, are seen to be present on earth, now "dwelling" in the heart of the believer. If the data of the preceding two chapters do not carry their own conviction about Paul's view of Christ as fully divine, then surely the ease with which Paul here refers to the Spirit should carry conviction. In the space of two clauses, where the second is obviously picking up what was said in the first, the *one Spirit* (cf. 1 Cor 12:4; Eph 4:4) is expressed by Paul first as "the Spirit of God who indwells you" and then immediately in the following pickup clause as our "having the Spirit of Christ." Since for Paul there are not two Spirits nor is there more than one God, sentences such as these call for some kind of theological/christological resolution on our part.

Thus, rather than thinking of Paul as either "confused" or "confusing" by what he does in Rom 8:9–11, it is the role of the Spirit—simultaneously

---

[10] Although only the resurrection is explicitly expressed in this way (1:1), the reality of Christ's present exaltation, expressed literally in Phil 2:9–11, e.g., is assumed in a variety of ways throughout the letter.

[11] See ch. 11, pp. 484–88; ch. 13, 519–20.

the Spirit of God and the Spirit of Christ—that both emphasizes the full deity of Christ and forces us in the end to think of the one God in triadic terms.

Paul and the Divine Triad

One of the more interesting phenomena regarding Paul's letters, given that he is writing to Gentile converts who would have been primarily polytheistic, is how seldom he puts any emphasis on the basic Jewish theological reality that there is only one God.[12] Since this is so presuppositional for Paul, the need seldom arises to make a point of it. But what is even more interesting is the fact that in five of the seven occurrences of this term or concept, Paul's affirmation of his consistent monotheism occurs in conjunction with equal emphasis on either Christ (1 Cor 8:6; Gal 3:20; 1 Tim 2:5) or Christ and the Spirit (1 Cor 12:6; Eph 4:6). Three of these texts (1 Cor 8:6; 12:6; Eph 4:6) call for special attention because, even though in each case the "work" of the divine Dyad or Triad is expressed, the emphasis is on the reality of the oneness of God in the context of emphasis on the "oneness" of Christ and, when included, the "oneness" of the Spirit.

Along with the more than a score of passages where the divine "three" are mentioned in their roles regarding human redemption,[13] the present texts are constant reminders that Paul's experience of Christ and the Spirit caused him to think of the "one God" in terms that included the Son and the Spirit. We have had reason to look carefully at the most important of the dyadic passages, 1 Cor 8:6,[14] where Paul deliberately expands the Shema to affirm the Father as the "one God [θεός]" and to include Christ the Son as "the one Lord [κύριος]." Here I simply note the significance of three triadic passages for Pauline Christology and emphasize again that these passages sound a death knell to all forms of Spirit Christology.

1. The remarkable grace-benediction of 2 Cor 13:13(14) offers us all kinds of theological keys to Paul's understanding of salvation and of God himself.[15] The fact that the benediction is composed and intended for the occasion,[16] rather than as a broadly applicable formula, only increases its

---

[12]The actual language εἰς θεός occurs in 1 Cor 8:4, 6; Gal 3:20; Rom 3:30; Eph 4:6; 1 Tim 2:5; it is implied in 1 Cor 12:6, where "the same" means "one and the same," as v. 11 makes clear about the Spirit, and is expressed in terms of μόνος (only) in 1 Tim 1:17.

[13]See the summarizing list of these passages in Fee, God's Empowering Presence, 841–42.

[14]See the extended discussion in ch. 3, pp. 89–94.

[15]For a more thorough analysis of this text, see Fee, God's Empowering Presence, 362–65.

[16]That it is both ad hoc and Pauline is demonstrated by the twofold reality that it functions precisely as do all of his other grace-benedictions, which all *begin* exactly this way, with "the grace of our Lord Jesus Christ," and that this beginning point thus determines the unusual order of Christ, God, the Spirit.

importance for hearing Paul. Thus, what he says here in prayer appears in a thoroughly presuppositional way—not as something that Paul argues for but as the assumed, experienced reality of Christian life.

First, it summarizes the core elements of Paul's unique passion: the gospel, with its focus on salvation in Christ, equally available by faith to Gentile and Jew alike. That the *love of God* is the foundation of Paul's view of salvation is stated with passion and clarity in passages such as Rom 5:1–11; 8:31–39; Eph 1:3–14. The *grace of our Lord Jesus Christ* is what gave concrete expression to that love; through Christ's suffering and death on behalf of his loved ones, God accomplished salvation for them at one moment in human history.

The *participation in the Holy Spirit* continually actualizes that love and grace in the life of the believer and the believing community. The κοινωνία *(fellowship/participation in) of the Holy Spirit* is how the living God not only brings people into an intimate and abiding relationship with himself, as the God of all grace, but also causes them to participate in all the benefits of that grace and salvation—that is, by indwelling them in the present with his own presence and guaranteeing their final eschatological glory.

Second, this text also serves as our entrée into Paul's understanding of God himself, which had been so radically affected for him by the twin realities of the death and resurrection of Christ and the gift of the Spirit. Granted, Paul does not here *assert* the deity of Christ and the Spirit. What he does is to *equate the activity of the three divine Persons* (to use the language of a later time) *in concert and in one prayer,* with the clause about God the Father standing in second place (!). This suggests that Paul was at least proto-Trinitarian: the believer knows and experiences the one God as Father, Son, and Spirit, and when dealing with Christ and the Spirit, one is dealing with God every bit as much as when one is dealing with the Father.

Thus this benediction, while making a fundamental distinction between God, Christ, and Spirit, also expresses in shorthand form what is found throughout Paul's letters: "salvation in Christ" is the cooperative work of God, Christ, and the Spirit.

2. The same proto-Trinitarian implications also appear in 1 Cor 12:4–6. Here Paul is urging the Corinthians to broaden their perspective and to recognize the rich diversity of the Spirit's manifestations in their midst (over against their apparently singular interest in speaking in tongues). He begins in vv. 4–6 by noting that *diversity reflects the nature of God* and is therefore the true evidence of the work of the one God in their midst. Thus the divine Triad is presuppositional to the entire argument, and these opening foundational words are all the more telling precisely because they are so unstudied, so freely and unself-consciously expressed. Just as there is only one God, from whom and for whom are all things, and one Lord, through whom are all things (1 Cor 8:6), so there is only one Spirit (1 Cor 12:9), through whose agency the one God manifests himself in a whole variety of ways in the believing community.

3. In Eph 4:4–6 one finds the same combination as in 2 Cor 13:13(14): a creedal formulation expressed in terms of the distinguishable activities of the triune God. The basis for Christian unity is the one God. The *one body* is the work of the *one Spirit* (cf. 1 Cor 12:13), by whom also we live our present eschatological existence in *one hope*, since the Spirit is the "down payment on our inheritance" (Eph 1:13–14). All of this has been made possible for us by our *one Lord*, in whom all have *one faith*, to which faith all have given witness through their *one baptism*. The source of all these realities is the *one God* himself, "who is over all and through all and in all." Again, because at issue is the work of the Spirit ("the unity the Spirit creates" [v. 3]), the order is the same as in 1 Cor 12:4–6—Spirit, Lord, God—which works from present, experienced reality to the foundational reality of the one God.

If the last phrase in this passage reemphasizes the unity of the one God, who is ultimately responsible for all things—past, present, and future—and subsumes the work of the Spirit and the Son under that of God, the entire passage at the same time puts into creedal form the affirmation that God is *experienced* as a triune reality. Precisely on the basis of such experience and language the later church maintained its biblical integrity by expressing all of this in explicitly Trinitarian language. And Paul's formulations, which include the work of both Christ and the Spirit, form a part of that basis.

The first significant point to make about these latter two passages is that in each case Paul is emphasizing, and thus not giving up, the basic theological reality of his tradition: there is only one God, and the one God is God alone. But the second point to note is that this emphasis occurs *primarily in contexts where he is deliberately expanding the identity of the one God to include the "one Lord" and the "one Spirit."* And it is the recognition of this reality that led the early church to wrestle with the biblical data so profoundly.

At the end of our study, therefore, we need to note that even though many feel especially uncomfortable with the Nicene "settlement" that spoke of Christ as "one Being with the Father," it is not difficult to see how this was the natural result of trying to come to terms with the biblical revelation as it existed now on predominantly Greek soil. What seems to be certain from the Pauline data is the inevitability of speaking of God at least in terms of the "economic Trinity."

And however one finally settles for oneself this divine mystery, to lower Paul's Christology to fit either patterns of development or the dictates of logic seems to miss Paul by too wide a margin. What Paul forces on us are the twin realities that must be held tenaciously—if one is to be true to the apostle himself—and must be so held even if in not fully resolved tension: there is only *one God*, and the one God includes, as simultaneously fully divine, the Father, the Son, and the Holy Spirit.

═══════ Appendix A ═══════

Christ and Personified Wisdom

IN THE PAST HALF CENTURY there has been a veritable groundswell in the NT academy both asserting and assuming that Paul's Christology is to be understood at least in part in terms of personified Wisdom, as "she" appears in three places in the Septuagint (Prov 8:22–31; Sir 14:3–22; Wis[1] 7:21–10:21). This appendix proposes to critique this view on the basis of the Pauline data and thus to explain why it has been given no place at all in the preceding synthesis and otherwise only in the three exegetical excursuses in chs. 3, 4, and 7.[2]

To be sure, this view had a previous history in the church. Although somewhat dubiously traced back as early as Justin Martyr (*Dial.* 100),[3] it had nonetheless by the fourth century become a common view—so much so that it was a central feature of the Arian controversy of the early fourth century. Since the Septuagint translator had rendered Prov 8:22, κύριος ἔκτισέν με ἀρχὴν ὁδῶν αὐτοῦ εἰς ἔργα αὐτοῦ (*The LORD created me as the beginning of his ways for his works*), Arius seized on this passage to argue for Christ as a created being. Given the general acceptance in the early church of the identification of Christ with Wisdom, Arius seems to have had Scripture on his side. But rather than rejecting the identification itself, as they well might have done, the Nicenes, especially Athanasius, responded in two ways: by arguing, first, that the Son was "created" when he became incarnate and, second, that Wisdom's "creation" was actually to be found in her "image" being "created" in the creatures who were brought into being.[4]

---

[1] To help the reader through the maze of language necessary for this chapter: I use "wisdom" generically, "Wisdom" to refer to wisdom personified, "wisdom tradition" for that locution, and "Wisdom literature" for that corpus; also, "Wisdom of Solomon" for that book of the Apocrypha, abbreviated "Wis" in chapter/verse citations.

[2] See pp. 102–5, 186–87, 317–25.

[3] Justin, however, offers only a hint of what was to come. In his sentence, "Wisdom" appears first in a list of things that Christ is "called" in the OT (Wisdom, the Day, the End, Sword, Stone, Rod, Jacob, Israel).

[4] For this history, see esp. the unpublished PhD dissertation by A. L. Clayton, "The Orthodox Recovery of a Heretical Proof-Text: Athanasius of Alexandria's Interpretation of Proverbs 8:22–30 in Conflict with the Arians" (Southern Methodist

Although the Arians seem to have had the better of this skirmish, the fact that they lost the battle itself is probably what caused this view eventually to fall out of favor for most of the succeeding centuries. And although it was reintroduced in the NT academy toward the end of the nineteenth century, its new life really began with Hans Windisch's contribution to the Heinrici Festschrift in 1914.[5] Even so, this view was found primarily in German scholarship until the second half of the last century,[6] when it finally became rooted also in the French- and English-speaking worlds.[7]

This perspective got a considerable boost from Martin Hengel, who set forth the steps that Paul himself took to adopt it.[8] First, it is argued that Paul very early had come to hold to God's having sent the Son, in which was in-

University, 1988). I am indebted to Bruce Waltke for calling this study to my attention (see Waltke, *The Book of Proverbs 1–15* [NICOT; Grand Rapids: Eerdmans, 2003], 127).

[5] H. Windisch, "Die göttliche Weisheit der Jüden und die paulinische Christologie," in *Neutestamentliche Studien: Georg Heinrici zu seinem 70. Geburtstag* (ed. H. Windisch; WUNT 6; Leipzig: Hinrichs, 1914), 220–34. For a convenient overview of this history, see esp. E. J. Schnabel, *Law and Wisdom from Ben Sira to Paul: A Tradition History Enquiry into the Relation of Law, Wisdom, and Ethics* (WUNT 2/16; Tübingen: Mohr Siebeck, 1985), 236–63. For a brief, helpful overview, see E. E. Johnson, "Wisdom and Apocalyptic in Paul," in *In Search of Wisdom: Essays in Memory of John C. Gammie* (ed. L. G. Perdue, B. B. Scott, and W. J. Wiseman; Louisville: Westminster John Knox, 1993), 263–83.

[6] It is noteworthy that the year before Windisch's essay appeared, W. Bousset had argued vigorously against any contact between Paul's understanding of Christ as κύριος and the OT (*Kyrios Christos*, 153–210, esp. 200), and thus one finds no suggestion of personified Wisdom as having any influence on Paul. This perhaps also accounts for Oscar Cullmann's basic lack of interest here as well; Wisdom receives only a passing note in his *Christology of the New Testament* (trans. S. C. Guthrie and C. A. M. Hall; Philadelphia: Westminster, 1959), 257.

[7] Although my search was by no means complete, the earliest referent to it in English-speaking scholarship that I found was by C. H. Dodd in his contribution, "The History and Doctrine of the Apostolic Age," to T. W. Manson's *Companion to the Bible* (Edinburgh: T&T Clark, 1947), 390–417. Dodd broaches the subject with due caution: "It seems probable also, though the proof is not complete, that some teachers, independently of Paul, had associated [Christ's] authority as the revealer of God with the Old Testament idea of the divine Wisdom" (p. 409); but then he cites 1 Cor 1:24 quite out of context to the effect that Paul considered Christ to be the Wisdom of God. He finally asserts, without giving the evidence, that "in Col. 1:15–19, without mentioning the word 'wisdom,' he [Paul] uses language which can be traced *in every point* (except the one word 'fullness') to Jewish Wisdom theology" (italics mine). Nonetheless, when starting his next paragraph, Dodd is content to put the term in quotation marks: "This 'Wisdom-Christology' made it possible for Paul to give a more adequate account of what was meant by calling Christ the Son of God." In French, see A. Feuillet, *Le Christ: Sagesse de Dieu d'après les épîtres pauliniennes* (EBib; Paris: Gabalda, 1966); Feuillet's position is so extreme that one wonders whether he is actually reading Paul, and his reading of Wisdom of Solomon is full of exegetical errors (e.g., arguing that Wisdom is present with Israel in chs. 10–12 [pp. 105–6] when clearly she has dropped out of the text at 11:1 and everything is done by God himself).

[8] See Hengel, *Son of God*, 66–76. Cf. Kim, *Origin of Paul's Gospel*, 102–36; Kim tends to carry this program to its extreme.

herent the concept of his preexistence, and eventually included his mediatorial role in creation; second, in the Jewish tradition Torah itself was also
considered to preexist before being given to Moses on Sinai; and third, since
Paul also belonged to a tradition that had long before equated wisdom with
Torah, it was a natural step for him, with the demise of Torah, to equate the
preexistent Son with preexistent Wisdom,[9] particularly because of her
alleged role as mediator of creation.

But even though this perspective has today become the unquestioned coin
of the realm—usually asserted without argumentation[10]—there is nonetheless every good reason to pause,[11] since it fails at the crucial point of being
substantiated in Paul's own thought. Indeed, since the actual exegetical basis
for this identification is so weak as to essentially not exist, one wonders how
and why such a view has become so commonplace in Pauline studies.

In the literature itself, the answer is related to two assumed "needs": to
find "biblical" background for the *idea of preexistence* in Paul's thought and
to find precedent for believing that Christ was the *agent of creation,* as Paul
plainly asserts in 1 Cor 8:6 and Col 1:15–17. Since Paul's understanding of
Christ seems to have no other possible "background," either Jewish or Greek,
personified Wisdom has been found to serve this purpose.[12] But this puts the

---

[9] Cf., e.g., Kim: "Paul obtained the insight that Christ was the end of the law at
the Damascus revelation and therefore was forced from then on to reflect upon
Christ's relationship to Wisdom" (*Origin of Christology,* 126). This is remarkable indeed, since there is not a single moment in Paul's letters where such "identification"
as such actually takes place.

[10] Cf., e.g., C. M. Tuckett: "One category not considered so far but which clearly
[!] is an important one for Paul's Christology is that of Wisdom" (*Christology and the
New Testament,* 62). This should amaze the reader of Paul, since Wisdom is not a
"category" at all. It is striking how often "clearly" emerges in these frequent assertions about Wisdom, which is not *clearly* in the texts, whatever else. The "folly" of
going this way can be seen in the lengths to which this has been carried by Ziesler in
his *Pauline Christianity,* 32–35, 45, where he simply asserts that in Wisdom of Solomon "wisdom virtually appears as . . . [God's] agent in revelation" and proffers as (a
rejected) option for the background of Phil 2:6–11 "a descending and ascending Wisdom story." The idea of "ascending Wisdom" is simply created *ex nihilo.*

[11] Indeed, it is refreshing to read in Douglas Moo's overview of the Christology of
Paul's earlier letters that "the influence of wisdom thought on Paul might be exag-
gerated"; he then goes on to note that "the evidence for wisdom influence on the
christology in the early Pauline Letters is slight and allusive" ("The Christology of
the Early Pauline Letters," in *Contours of Christology in the New Testament* [ed. R. N.
Longenecker; Grand Rapids: Eerdmans, 2005], 178). One might add that the same
holds true of the later letters as well.

[12] This becomes evident in James Dunn's arrangement of his chapter on
"preexistence" in his *Theology of Paul,* 266–93, which he begins not with the *Pauline*
texts themselves but with a disquisition on "Divine Wisdom" (pp. 267–72) before
looking at 1 Cor 8:6, where actual preexistence is dismissed by way of wisdom. The
same point was brought home to me in the strongest possible way when, after I had
given a public lecture on this topic, one of its strongest advocates and a personal
friend asked me to the effect, "Since there is no hint of preexistence in other possible

cart (the needed conclusion) before the horse (its exegetical basis); and very likely it is precisely because the alleged "biblical" base is so weak that one finds no exegesis of the basic wisdom texts in the literature. Rather, this view is usually simply asserted and then footnoted with references, as though these references should be plain to all.

But taking that route leaves a number of matters standing in unrelieved tension in the literature itself. For example, primary to this view is the constantly repeated assertion that Paul's "idea of [Christ's] mediation of the creation [was] derived from Wisdom speculation."[13] What is of interest here is that much is made of the fact that in the two places where Paul speaks thus of Christ, he uses the preposition διά (*through*), thus indicating mediatorial agency. But when one turns to the Wisdom literature itself, this is the one preposition that is consistently missing with regard to Wisdom's relationship to creation.[14] So how long, one wonders, can NT scholarship continue to argue thus when the one crucial preposition for this connection between Paul and Wisdom, not to mention *any other explicit linguistic tie*, does not occur at all in the literature that Paul is allegedly indebted to.

The purpose of this appendix, therefore, is to visit this issue once again,[15] and since what follows is filled with detailed examination at several points, I begin by noting the "logic" that has determined the presentation. I begin by briefly bringing forward the exegetical conclusions found in the earlier chapters regarding the basic Pauline texts. Although this in itself might have brought the discussion to a proper conclusion, the fact is that not all exegetes read these texts in the same way. So that leads to the second section, which is intended to lay bare what is perceived to be the *central exegetical fallacy* involved in the identification of Christ with personified Wisdom: arguing from what is obtuse as a way of setting aside what seems to be

---

'backgrounds' to Paul's thinking on this matter, where did this idea come from in Paul, if not from Wisdom?" Only half-facetiously, I reminded him of the possibility of "revelation." But the question itself again indicated where this speculation about Paul and Wisdom had its origins. It would never have happened simply by exegeting the Pauline texts themselves in their respective contexts.

[13]Kramer, *Christ, Lord, Son of God*, 222; cf., e.g., Hengel: "The Son of God [took] on the all-embracing functions of Wisdom as mediator" (*Son of God*, 73); Kim: "Thus it is clear [!] that . . . [Paul's] ideas of Christ's preexistence and mediatorship in creation are a result of his transferring the characteristics of the divine Wisdom to Christ" (*Origin*, 117).

[14]This point is conveniently overlooked in the literature by going with an English translation either of the straight dative (τῇ σοφίᾳ [Prov 3:19; Wis 9:2]) or the dative with ἐν (Ps 104:24) that assumes agency (e.g., Wis 9:2); but as pointed out in the exegesis below, that will hardly do here.

[15]Some of the content of this chapter first appeared in the Festschrift for my long-time colleague and friend Bruce Waltke (*The Way of Wisdom: Essays in Honor of Bruce K. Waltke* [ed. J. I. Packer and S. Soderlund; Grand Rapids: Zondervan, 2000), 251–79; it was reprinted as ch. 21 in G. D. Fee, *To What End Exegesis? Essays Textual, Exegetical, and Theological* (Grand Rapids: Eerdmans, 2001).

clear. To point out the difficulty involved, Paul's own demonstrable use and nonuse of the wisdom tradition is brought under careful examination. Here it is noted that Paul's actual (very limited) use of this tradition is always in keeping with the point of the tradition itself. More important still is the examination of Paul's use (actually *nonuse*) of Wisdom of Solomon, the one source without which this view would not exist at all.[16] And that leads to the third section, which is an examination of all the texts in the wisdom tradition that might even remotely suggest that personified Wisdom was perceived by these writers as the *agent* of creation. Since a crucial part of this task is to ask how the writers themselves might have understood the personification, this section begins with this question and asks whether there is any substantial relationship between their (apparent) understanding and Paul's own presentation of Christ as eternally preexistent.

Did Paul Identify Christ with Wisdom?

Since Paul's alleged identification of Christ with Wisdom has been dealt with in some detail in the exegetical chapters,[17] my purpose here is simply to lay out the primary texts and summarize the reasons they do not support a "Wisdom Christology." We start with the two texts where Paul both assumes and asserts that Christ is the divine agent of creation, 1 Cor 8:6 and Col 1:15–18, and conclude with 2 Cor 4:4–6, where Christ is called God's image and glory.

1 Corinthians 8:6 (and 1:24, 30)

It takes a bold step indeed to find personified Wisdom lying behind 1 Cor 8:6,[18] since there is nothing in the text itself that remotely suggests as much.[19] In the process of dividing the Jewish Shema into two parts, Paul explicitly identifies the one θεός (*God*) as "the Father" and the one κύριος as "Jesus Christ," with "the Son" being implied by the designation of God as Father. Yet it is frequently asserted that Paul actually intends us to understand Christ here in

---

[16]Even a casual look at the scholarly literature makes this clear. That is, since the recent expression of this view can hardly have arisen from either the Hebrew or Greek texts of Prov 8, the rhetoric of this position constantly uses phrases such as "the Wisdom tradition" or "Jewish Wisdom." But when the dust clears, even though Prov 8:22 and 24 are sometimes appealed to as indicating that Lady Wisdom was the *agent* of creation (which is simply *not* the case), the one book that advocates of this view could not do without is Wisdom of Solomon.

[17]See n. 2 above.

[18]For the full exegesis of these texts, see ch. 3, pp. 89–94, 106–7. Since what follows is simply a brief summation of the exegesis found there, I will not repeat here the documentation that would otherwise be necessary.

[19]Hurtado puts it bluntly: "The problem with this [identification with Wisdom] is that it is not what the Pauline passage says" (*Lord Jesus Christ*, 126).

terms of Lady Wisdom. And how does one come by this assertion? By being reminded that Paul himself has already made this identification in 1:24, 30.

But that is patently not true. Paul's identification of the crucified Messiah as "God's power and God's wisdom" in 1:24 not only has nothing to do with *personified* Wisdom but also actually stands quite over against such an understanding. After all, the occurrence of "Christ" in this clause (v. 24) is an appositional pickup of "Christ crucified" in the same sentence (v. 23). And since "Christ crucified" is folly to the *Greeks*—those who actually "pursue wisdom"—Paul now asserts (ironically) that a crucified Messiah is in fact the ultimate display of *God's* wisdom for those seeking wisdom. To extract personified Wisdom out of this deliberate irony is a form of irony itself, since it is not the "person" of Christ as such that is in view. Rather, God's presentation of his Messiah as the crucified One is alone what is in view.

This is made all the clearer by the pickup of this theme in 1:30, where in apposition to "wisdom" Paul places three metaphors of conversion, all resulting from the crucifixion: justification, sanctification, and redemption. All of this is said in such plain speech that ordinary readers could find Lady Wisdom in the passage only by being told that they should find "her" here, which, of course, the original recipients—the Corinthians themselves—could not possibly have done, since Paul here stands so adamantly opposed to "wisdom."

Furthermore, there is not an allusion of any kind in this passage to a text or motif from the Wisdom literature. Rather, the entirety of 1:26–31 is a Pauline "midrash" on a key *prophetic* text (Jer 9:23–24), which has in it the key word "wisdom" that Paul applies in an ironic way to the Corinthians' own fascination with wisdom. But theirs is a fascination with Greek wisdom, not Jewish—after all, it is the "Greeks" who seek "wisdom," and it is clear that this "wisdom" has nothing to do with the Bible. Thus the entire argument of this passage is an application of Jeremiah's prophecy to their own situation, which concludes by Paul's citing Jeremiah, "let the one who boasts, boast in *the Lord*," meaning in this instance in the exalted Lord, who in his earthly life had been set forth as the "crucified Messiah." It takes scholarly boldness of a unique kind to transfer all of this to Lady Wisdom!

So not only does Paul himself *not* make this identification in 1:24, 30, but also the nature of Paul's argument itself disallows that the Corinthians themselves would—not to mention "could"—have made such a connection. Furthermore, the sentence in 8:6 is so far removed from, and so totally unrelated to, what is said in 1:24 that it seems to be an exegetical jump of enormous proportions to argue that Paul in 8:6 has personified Wisdom in view. Paul himself in fact identifies the (now exalted) Son as the κύριος of the Shema and thereby assumes his preexistence as the Son of θεός the Father. How, one wonders, could this masculine imagery have been seen by the Corinthians as referring to *Lady* Wisdom?[20] So it is scholarly boldness, not

---

[20] It should be noted here that Philo, who does include personified Wisdom in the divine identity, recognizes the need to wrestle with the gender issue. Thus in *Fug.*

scholarly wisdom, that asserts without any exegetical basis in this passage it-self that κύριος should actually be read as referring to σοφία.

Colossians 1:15–18

Finding Wisdom in the Colossian "hymn" takes even more help for the uninitiated reader. After all, the grammatical antecedent to the "who" in v. 15 is "the Father's beloved Son" in v. 13. Furthermore, neither the *word* "wisdom" nor *language* from the wisdom tradition is to be found in this passage. The common assertion, for example, that " 'image' is a word that belongs to the Wisdom tradition" is simply not true. The word occurs but once in the entire tradition (Wis 7:26), as the third line of a triplet that is playing on mirror imagery. And despite oft-repeated assertions to the contrary, Wisdom is *not* alluded to as "God's image"; rather, based on the mirror imagery, Wisdom is "an image of his goodness," meaning that God's wisdom is "reflected" in his goodness (as in the first line of the triplet). This imagery, therefore, has no connection whatever with Gen 1–2, which Paul's usage demonstrably does.

The same is true with πρωτότοκος (*firstborn*), a word that does not occur in the wisdom tradition at all, despite repeated assertions to the contrary.[21] And the appeal often made to Philo's use of πρωτόγονος simply will not do, since (1) Philo himself does not use this word regarding *wisdom* and (2) Philo's word appears but once in the wisdom tradition, and not with reference to personified Wisdom.[22]

Finally, as was pointed out in the excursus on this passage (ch. 7, pp. 319–25), since none of the other alleged words "that belong to the wisdom tradition" actually do belong to that tradition, the identification of the Son of God with personified Wisdom should be a cause for wonder, not acceptance. This is all the more so when one considers that in the immediately preceding letter, Paul himself had already explicitly identified *the Son of God* as God's *image* and *firstborn* (Rom 8:29).

2 Corinthians 4:4–6

This is the only other text that could meaningfully be brought into this discussion, and that only because the two words "glory" and "image" appear together in this passage; and although "image" in the sense of Gen 1–2 is not used of personified Wisdom, the word "glory" is—in Prov 8:18 and Wis 7:25,

---

51–52 he identifies Bethuel, Rebecca's father, with Wisdom and then proceeds to ask, "How, pray, can Wisdom, the daughter of God, be rightly spoken of as a father?" to which he gives a typically convoluted answer.

[21] See the discussion in the excursus in ch. 7, pp. 319–25.

[22] It is used only in Sir 36:17 (36:11 LXX), to refer to Israel as God's "firstborn" (its other biblical occurrence is in the plural in Mic 7:1, regarding eating the "firstfruits" of crops).

where in the latter "she" is described as "a pure emanation of the glory of the Almighty." Given that Wisdom is alluded to in mirror imagery as "the image of his goodness" in the next triplet (v. 26), this collocation may look more promising. But in fact, as was noted in the excursus on this passage (ch 7, pp. 317–25), nothing in Paul's sentences specifically suggests personified Wisdom as being in the background; and the verbal proximity in both texts is purely coincidental, based on Paul's own use of mirror imagery in 3:18 in a context where he is expounding Exod 34:29–35, where "glory" is the presenting word.

Two final points need to be made regarding these texts. First, Paul clearly asserts that Christ is the *agent* of creation and thereby assumes his preexistence; and nothing in the Pauline texts that refer to the Son of God comes close to the assertions in the wisdom tradition that Wisdom was the "first of God's creations." Second, in making this affirmation about Christ, Paul never uses the language of the wisdom tradition, despite assertions to the contrary. Indeed, the straightforward exegesis of the Pauline texts would not lead one to include personified Wisdom in the discussion at all. How, then, is it that "she" appears in so many of the discussions, not as a matter that needs to be demonstrated but as one that can be simply asserted and then footnoted with references to the Wisdom literature? The answer lies not in the Pauline texts themselves but with the need that many have felt to find a possible background in Paul's Jewish tradition for his assertions about Christ's preexistence and Christ's role as the agent of creation. So to these questions we turn, beginning with the basic exegetical fallacy involved in this "discovery."[23]

Paul and the Wisdom Tradition

The place to begin any such investigation is with a basic methodological consideration: one begins with what is certain, not with what is merely speculative. In the present case, this fundamental methodological axiom translates into starting *not* with (merely possible but highly improbable) distant echoes of the wisdom tradition but rather with Paul's unquestionable, demonstrable use of this tradition. And here we will look at texts where Paul actually cites the tradition (which in fact he does but rarely) or in any case alludes to it in ways that seem almost certain.[24] Here three important conclusions can be drawn: (1) Paul's certain citations and allusions to this tradition are quite limited; (2) when he does cite the tradition, it is

---

[23] On this language, and especially on the matter at hand, see D. A. Carson, *Exegetical Fallacies* (2d ed.; Grand Rapids: Baker, 1996), 91–126.

[24] On the basically pejorative or corrective use of the language σοφία (*wisdom*) and σόφος (*wise*) in Paul, see the excursus on 1 Cor 1:17–2:16 in ch. 3, pp. 102–5.

invariably in keeping with the point made in the cited text; and (3) these citations/allusions are limited to the canonical Hebrew Bible and thus include neither Sirach nor Wisdom of Solomon. We take up each of these matters in turn.

Paul's Citations of the Wisdom Tradition

We begin this inquiry with Paul's use of the OT in general, where several matters are plain. If we limit ourselves momentarily to clear citations, what stands out is that Paul's primary interest lies with the central features of Israel's story: creation, Abraham (with the promise of Gentile inclusion), the exodus (including both deliverance from bondage and gaining the inherited land), the giving of the law (especially Deuteronomy, with its anticipation of Israel's failure regarding the law), the Davidic kingship, and the promised restoration, which especially included Gentiles. It is not surprising, therefore, that although Paul cites texts from all over the Greek Bible, the majority come from Genesis, Deuteronomy, Isaiah, and the Psalter. Furthermore, although he adapts some passages to the grammar and concerns of his own sentences, he nonetheless usually stays quite faithfully with the language of the Septuagint, even when it differs from the Hebrew text. This is probably due to the fact that this is the Bible that he and his churches had in common.

It is in light of this large use of the Greek Bible that we need to note the considerable paucity of texts from the wisdom tradition in the Pauline corpus: one "citation" and one (conceptual, but not linguistic) echo from Ecclesiastes; two probable echoes from Job; and two citations from Proverbs. Here are the texts themselves (**boldface** = citation of or common wording between Paul and the LXX):

(1) 1 Cor 3:19   γέγραπται γάρ· ὁ δρασσόμενος τοὺς **σοφοὺς**
                                        ἐν τῇ **πανουργίᾳ** αὐτῶν·

    Job 5:12–13 ¹²διαλλάσσοντα βουλὰς **πανούργων**, . . .
                                        ¹³ὁ καταλαμβάνων **σοφοὺς**
                                        ἐν τῇ φρονήσει

    1 Cor 3:19   *For it is written:*   *He catches*   *the*   ***wise***
                                        in their ***craftiness;***

    Job 5:12–13   ¹²*frustrating the counsels of* ***the crafty,*** . . .
                                        ¹³*who overtakes the*   ***wise***
                                        in their intelligence

(2) 2 Cor 9:7   **ἱλαρὸν** γὰρ **δότην** ἀγαπᾷ ὁ θεός.

    Prov 22:8a LXX ἄνδρα **ἱλαρὸν** καὶ **δότην** εὐλογεῖ ὁ θεός,

    2 Cor 9:7   *For*   ***God*** *loves*   ***a cheerful giver.***

    Prov 22:8a LXX   ***God*** *blesses a man who is*   ***cheerful and giving,***

(3) Rom 3:10   οὐκ ἔστιν δίκαιος οὐδὲ εἷς,

Eccl 7:20 ὅτι ἄνθρωπος οὐκ ἔστιν δίκαιος ἐν τῇ γῇ,

Rom 3:10   **there is no righteous** (person), not even one,

Eccl 7:20 because   **there is no righteous** man on the earth,

(4) Rom 12:20 ἀλλὰ ἐὰν πεινᾷ ὁ ἐχθρός σου, ψώμιζε **αὐτόν·**
                              ἐὰν διψᾷ, πότιζε **αὐτόν·**

Prov 25:21   ἐὰν πεινᾷ ὁ ἐχθρός σου, τρέφε **αὐτόν**
                              ἐὰν διψᾷ, πότιζε **αὐτόν·**

Rom 12:20 But   **if your enemy hungers,** feed **him**
                         if he thirsts, give him drink;

Prov 25:21   **If your enemy hungers,** feed **him**
                         if he thirsts, give him drink;

Beyond these four, more obvious citations/echoes, there is one other in-stance in the corpus where Paul seems to echo the Hebrew text, in a text that is translated quite differently in the Septuagint (or that gives evidence of a different Hebrew text):

(5) Rom 11:35 τίς προέδωκεν αὐτῷ, καὶ ἀνταποδοθήσεται αὐτῷ;

Job 41:11 מִי הִקְדִּימֵנִי וַאֲשַׁלֵּם (41:3 MT)

LXX (41:3) ἢ τίς ἀντιστήσεταί μοι καὶ ὑπομενεῖ, εἰ πᾶσα ἡ ὑπ᾽
           οὐρανὸν ἐμή ἐστιν;

Rom 11:35 *Who has given to him, and he should repay him?*

Job 41:11 *Who has a claim against me, that I must pay?* (TNIV)[25]

LXX (41:3) *Or who shall confront me and remain, since everything under heaven is mine?*

(6) Rom 11:33. Finally, there is one place where a single word is echoed in a passage that reflects a perspective similar to that of the author of Job. In the encomium at the end of Rom 11 (vv. 33–36), Paul declares that at the end of the day, God's greatness is both inexpressible and past finding out. In doing so, Paul patterns himself after biblical precedents; but except for the "citation" of Isa 40:13 in v. 34, all the rest appears to be a Pauline creation, in which he constantly echoes biblical *ideas* but the actual *language* of the Septuagint only once, in v. 33 with the word ἀνεξιχνίαστος (*not to be traced out*), which in the Septuagint occurs only in Job (5:9; 9:10; 34:24) and the

---

[25]The English Bible tradition is mixed here, depending altogether on the philoso-phy of translation, whether to go with the Hebrew text in moments like these (TNIV, ESV, NASB) or with the Septuagint when it seemed to the translators to have the better of it *ad sensum* (REB, NJB, NAB). In the present passage, one cannot tell in the end whether Paul was simply echoing the Hebrew text or whether he had a different Greek text from that of the Septuagint as it has come down to us.

Prayer of Manasseh 1:6. It is the unusual nature of this word that might make one think that Paul is using "biblical language" here.

Finally, it should be noted that apart from these six instances, the wisdom tradition as such simply cannot be found in the Pauline Letters.[26] Nonetheless, a careful analysis of these texts in their Pauline contexts makes it clear that Paul knew this tradition well, since his echoes in particular give evidence of a knowledge of the tradition that lies deep within him.

The Nature of Paul's Use of This Tradition

It is of some importance for our purposes to point out that although Paul actually cites the tradition only four times, in each case he makes the very point being made in the OT passage. For example, his citations of Eccl 7:20 in Rom 3:10 and of Prov 25:21–22 in Rom 12:20 come at moments where human sin and Christian ethics are at issue. Ecclesiastes 7:20 thus stands at the beginning of the long catena of texts from all over the OT that Paul uses in Rom 3:10–18 to demonstrate Scripture's witness to the universality of human sinfulness.[27] Similarly, the citation of Prov 25:21–22 comes at the end of the long series of ethical exhortation in Rom 12, in this case bringing closure to the section that has to do with the Christian response to those who intend to do evil.

Likewise, Paul's two citations from Job reflect the awe and wonder that believers experience when reflecting on the greatness and glory of God. The "citation" of/allusion to Job 5:12 in 1 Cor 3:19 is one of three OT texts Paul uses in this passage that I have dubbed "Don't match wits with God" texts (cf. his use of Isa 29:14 in 1:19; and Ps 94:11, immediately following the present one, in 1 Cor 3:20). In this passage he is trying to set the Corinthians straight regarding their overenthusiasm for wisdom, which they appear to treasure highly as one of the giftings of the Spirit. The allusion to Job 41:11 in Rom 11:35, on the other hand, is a reflection of the sheer wonder and majesty of God, whose ways are beyond tracing out. "Who has ever given to God, that God should repay them?"

Thus, regarding Paul's actual use of the wisdom tradition, our two summary conclusions can be reiterated: first, in comparison to his use of the rest of the OT, Paul has very few citations or echoes from Jewish wisdom; second, when he does cite this tradition, he does so quite in keeping with the actual points being made in the tradition itself.

Paul's Nonuse of Sirach and Wisdom of Solomon

Finally, we should note that if Paul actually were dependent on Wisdom of Solomon for his language and understanding of Christ as the mediator of

---

[26] The other exception might be 1 Tim 6:7, which echoes the sentiment of Eccl 5:14 but not the language of the Septuagint.

[27] Eccl 7:20 probably stands in first place because it has the key word: "there is none δίκαιος [righteous]."

creation, one might reasonably expect some sort of linguistic echo from Wisdom of Solomon to be found in his letters. But that is not the case. The evidence for this is found in addendum I at the end of this chapter, where all thirty-eight passages from Wisdom of Solomon in the Nestle-Aland[27] margins of the Pauline corpus are listed. Several things about this list are of specific interest.

1. Even the most casual, let alone carefully studied, walk through this list of alleged "echoes" demonstrates that there is not a single one that carries conviction that Paul knew or used this work. Some of the references are simply too obtuse to be of any use at all, and the others are either conceptual[28] or incidentally similar.

2. Not surprisingly, given the nature of Wisdom of Solomon, the large majority of these linguistic echoes occur *outside* the crucial central section (7:22–9:18), where (now personified) Wisdom is praised and desired through prayer. That is, most of the alleged "echoes" occur in passages where the author of Wisdom of Solomon is reflecting on the Jewish story as such and that have no relationship to personified Wisdom.

3. Given the obtuseness of some of these "parallels," it is of high interest that the Nestle-Aland text does not have a single marginal note pointing to Wisdom of Solomon for any of the passages that are crucial to the current discussion: 1 Cor 8:6; 2 Cor 4:4–6; Col 1:15–18. And this, of course, for good reason: there are neither linguistic *nor conceptual* parallels between this document and the Pauline texts. Furthermore, a careful look at the Pauline passages in addendum I below reveals that not one of them is a christological text of any kind.

All of this is to say that Paul's certain use of the wisdom tradition and the lack of any evidence that he even knew Wisdom of Solomon does not instill a great deal of confidence that here is the place to look for "background" for such a central christological assumption as that Christ preexisted and was the divine agent of creation.

Wisdom as the "Agent" of Creation

With these several realities in hand, we now turn to the texts that are often brought forward to support a Wisdom Christology in Paul's thought;

---

[28] These are quite legitimately included in Nestle-Aland, of course, for the sake of noting similarities between otherwise diverse authors. Thus, Wisdom of Solomon's description of the suddenness of God's destruction of the Egyptian firstborn is conceptually similar to Paul's "day of the Lord coming as a thief in the night" (1 Thess 5:2); but otherwise there is no relationship of any kind. And this is the case with most of these "parallels"; what might look like borrowing (e.g., the combination of ἐνδυσάμενοι θώρακα [1 Thess 5:8 // Wis 5:18]) is evidence that both authors knew Isa 59:17.

and in this case we focus on what is central for all the discussions in the literature. We begin by reiterating that Paul nowhere uses the *language* of this tradition when speaking about Christ as the divine agent of creation. The issue at hand, then, is whether there is a *conceptual* relationship between Christ's role in creation according to Paul and Wisdom's role in Wisdom of Solomon. Two issues face us here: first, how the writers of the wisdom tradition understood their personifications of wisdom; and second, whether they ever present personified Wisdom as the actual *agent* of creation.[29]

The Question of the Nature of Personification

The first issue is whether, by the various personifications found in Prov 8:22–31; Sir 24:3–12; Wis 6:12–25; 7:21–10:21, these authors had a divine hypostasis in view—that is, an actual divine (or quasi-divine) *being* who exists alongside (or in relationship with) God in some unique way.[30] Or are these merely literary moments in which the feminine nouns חכמה and σοφία are made powerfully present to the author's readers by means of the *literary* device of personification? The significance of this, as Dunn's work demonstrates, is that one may draw quite different conclusions if σοφία is more a literary device than a divine hypostasis.[31]

Although there has been considerable debate on this matter, the consensus of those who have worked closely with these texts without the present agenda in view is that in Proverbs and Sirach we are dealing with a literary device, pure and simple.[32] And although the personification of wisdom in

---

[29] For convenience, the various texts discussed in this section are found in addendum II at the end of the chapter.

[30] A point made by Dunn (*Christology in the Making*, 168–76; cf. idem, *Theology of Paul*, 270–72) that seems to have fallen on deaf ears.

[31] And because of this distinction, Dunn, while regularly using the language of "identification," sometimes speaks in a more nuanced way of "attributing her role" to Christ (see n. 66 in ch. 7 of the present volume). But this, of course, creates its own set of difficulties for Dunn's view, since he can scarcely avoid using more hypostatic personification as the basis for this "attribution." Thus he says that "it is entirely consistent with the evidence to conclude that Paul was tacitly *identifying* [italics mine] Christ with Wisdom, indeed *as* [italics his] Wisdom. In thinking of preexistent Wisdom Paul now thought of Christ" (*Theology of Paul*, 270). He then goes on to deny that this means a divine "hypostasis"; but his own language seems to betray him. And in the end, he resorts to a form of meaningless circularity when he asserts, "Is there a thought of preexistence in 1 Cor. 8.6 . . . ? Of course there is. But it is the preexistence of divine Wisdom. That is, the preexistence of God" (*Theology of Paul*, 274–75). Which means that there is no preexistence for the one κύριος in the text, since the one κύριος really means σοφία, and σοφία = θεός. Even worse exegetically is what is said in the material that I omitted in the preceding quotation: "not to mention 1.24 and 30." Thus Dunn posits that preexistent Wisdom is to be found in these two passages. But in fact, as the exegesis in ch. 3 has shown, divine Wisdom is not the purview of this passage in any way.

[32] For Proverbs, see the commentary by R. B. Y. Scott, *Proverbs and Ecclesiastes* (AB 18; Garden City, N.Y.: Doubleday, 1965), 69–72; for Sirach, see the commentary

Wisdom of Solomon seems to move much more toward some kind of hypostasis, this happens only at the author's more intense encomium of Wisdom in 7:22–8:18. When he turns toward Solomon's request for wisdom from God (8:19–21), the personification is much less hypostatic in appearance; and this less intense personification carries on through the prayer (ch. 9) and the following narrative of her role in the history of Israel from Adam to Israel's experience in the desert (ch. 10). And with that, even though she is still the (assumed) subject of the verb that begins ch. 11, Wisdom herself simply drops off the stage (except for a momentary cameo appearance in 14:2). It is this other role (or nonrole) that Wisdom plays in *most of the book* that would lead one to believe that the personification throughout is to be understood as a literary device, pure and simple. Thus the consensus here is to be found in this oft-quoted definition: "a quasi-personification of certain attributes proper to God, occupying an intermediate position between personalities and abstract beings."[33]

The nature of this "intermediate position," however, is taken by scholars each in their own way, depending on the degree to which they perceive the author to regard Wisdom as both personified and separate from her originator.[34] The question for us is this: Even if Paul were dependent on this

---

by P. W. Skehan and A. A. di Lella, *The Wisdom of Ben Sira* (AB 39; Garden City, N.Y.: Doubleday, 1987), 332. This is also affirmed in the commentary on Wisdom of Solomon by D. Winston (see the next note), who sees Philo and Pseudo-Solomon in contrast to Proverbs and Sirach at this very point (p. 34).

[33] W. O. E. Oesterley and G. H. Box, *The Religion and Worship of the Synagogue* (London: Pitman, 1911), 169, cited by, e.g., D. Winston both in his commentary (*The Wisdom of Solomon* [AB 43; Garden City, N.Y.: Doubleday, 1979], 34) and in his contribution to the Gammie memorial volume ("Wisdom in the Wisdom of Solomon," in Perdue, Scott, and Wiseman, *In Search of Wisdom*, 150); cf. R. Marcus, "On Biblical Hypostases of Wisdom," *HUCA* 23 (1950–1951): 159, cited by Witherington, *Jesus the Sage*, 109. But see also the cautions raised by Dunn, *Theology of Paul*, 272.

[34] This ambivalence can be found especially in Winston, who in his commentary cites the Oesterley-Box definition but in the footnote goes on to aver, "In Philo and Wisd . . . where Sophia is considered to be an eternal emanation of the deity, we undoubtedly have a conception of her as a divine hypostasis, coeternal with him" (34). This seems to go beyond Oesterley-Box by some margin (one wonders how "coeternal" fits in light of 6:22, καὶ πῶς ἐγένετο ["and how she came to be"], or 7:14, "for God is the guide even of wisdom"). Winston's commitment to a much more hypostatic understanding, as well as to this preexistent hypostasis as being God's agent of creation, can be found in the introduction, where he asserts, "The central figure in Wisd is Sophia, described as an 'effluence' or 'effulgence' of God's glory, and his agent in creation (7:25–6; 8:4; 9:1–2)," the reference in 7:25–26 being to Sophia: "while remaining in herself she renews all things (*ta panta kainizei*)" (59). But in the commentary on this passage he does not so much as mention creation—for good reason, one might add, since it simply is not in the text. The same ambivalence is to be found in the attempt to distinguish between wisdom as God's attribute and Wisdom in the NJB, especially in its handling of the three occurrences of σοφία in Wis 1:4–6, as well as in 3:11. Its consistent use of the capitalized "Wisdom" in 6:9–10:21 (except for 9:1–2!) seems especially prejudicial.

tradition—doubtful as that is—would he have understood wisdom in terms of *personal preexistence in the same way that he so considered Christ?*[35]

This matter becomes especially acute at a singularly crucial point: the way the wisdom writers themselves handle this personification in the context of their absolute monotheism. For it is of some interest that these monotheists resist the possibility that personified Wisdom is another quasi-divine *being* alongside the one God; they do this by referring to "her" as the first of God's own "creations"[36]—and this by writers who well understand that God by his very nature has *eternal wisdom.* Why, then, the guise of "creation" with regard to Lady Wisdom? Most likely this allowed them to use the literary device without at the same time encroaching on their basic monotheism.

In any case, there is no real similarity between what they did in creating personified Wisdom and what Paul asserts regarding the role of Christ in creation. What is clear from his few statements that assert or assume preexistence is that the Son was never thought of in terms of his being "created" himself so that he could be the agent of creation. Paul's assumption is quite the opposite: Christ is the agent of creation because as God's Son he was present with the Father *before* anything else came into existence. Indeed, it is plainly asserted in Col 1:15–17 that all creation was both "through him" and "for him" and subsists "in him." As we will see in what follows, there is nothing that remotely resembles this in the personification of Wisdom in the Jewish wisdom tradition.

The Texts: Wisdom and Creation

At issue ultimately in this discussion is the relationship of Wisdom to creation. For despite some attempts at finding other echoes of Wisdom in Paul's writings, it is singularly this one point at which the whole enterprise found its origins and continues to find support in the literature. Thus, to these texts we now turn.

As we noted at the outset, one of the common *assertions* in the NT academy that has now become an *assumption* is that personified Wisdom was understood by the writers of the wisdom tradition to be the mediator of creation. But a close look at the texts themselves gives one plenty of reason for pause. Indeed, nowhere in the tradition is it *explicitly* stated that personified Wisdom was the *mediating agent* of creation. At least, in none of the passages brought forward to defend such a view does one find language similar

---

[35] After all, the author of Wisdom of Solomon, who may well have been an older contemporary of Paul himself (Winston, e.g., dates the work within the reign of Caligula [37–41 C.E.]), is most likely merely heightening the effect of the personification rather than thinking of an actual being distinguishable from God. As will be pointed out below, the latter seems to be an unfortunate misreading of our author's text, not to mention his theology.

[36] See esp. Prov 8:22–26; Sir 1:4; 24:3, 9.

to that found in Paul's writings; these authors do *not* say that God created τὰ πάντα <u>διὰ</u> σοφίας (*all things <u>through</u> Wisdom*), nor do all things exist "for her" or subsist "in her."[37] Rather, "wisdom" is personified as present in another sense, as *the attribute of God that is manifest through the masterful design exhibited in creation,* or as Larry Hurtado puts it, "God's Wisdom [is] pictured as God's companion in creation";[38] but at no point is "she" ever seen as the *mediating agent* of creation. This is the consistent and invariable point of view of all our authors, even in the most intense moments of personification found in Wisdom of Solomon. Thus, let us look at the texts themselves.

Psalm 104:24

This way of speaking about creation finds its first expression in the exalted poetry of Ps 104:24 (103:24 LXX). After reflecting on the heavens, the earth, the living creatures on the earth, and the sun and moon, the author bursts forth in praise:

ὡς ἐμεγαλύνθη τὰ ἔργα σου, κύριε·
   πάντα ἐν σοφίᾳ ἐποίησας,
   ἐπληρώθη ἡ γῆ τῆς κτήσεώς σου.

How many are your works, LORD!
   In wisdom you made them all;
   the earth is full of your creatures.

Wisdom here is obviously "neither instrument nor agent but the attribute displayed by Yahweh in creating."[39]

Careful examination of the remaining texts indicates that all of our subsequent authors are guided by this same theology, so that even when they express in a heightened personified way Wisdom's presence with Yahweh at creation, σοφία is never the *agent* but rather is the *attribute,* being manifested in God's own creative work. Nor is it likely that Paul would himself have understood such language in terms of personal agency; so it would never have occurred to him to identify the historical, now exalted κύριος, Jesus Christ, with a merely literary personification.

Proverbs 3:19–20

The perspective of the psalmist is echoed in a very similar way in the prologue of the book of Proverbs. In a passage exhorting the young to pur-

---

[37] The closest thing to it in the Septuagint is Ps 103:24 (104:24 MT), πάντα ἐν σοφίᾳ ἐποίησας, which not only is in a nonwisdom passage but also reflects what the wisdom tradition does indeed affirm: "God in his own wisdom created" things so that they reflect his wisdom of design and purpose, which is not the same as mediation.

[38] See Hurtado, *Lord Jesus Christ,* 125.

[39] Quoting Scott (*Proverbs and Ecclesiastes,* 70), who applies these words to the companion passage in Prov 3:19.

sue wisdom, the author begins, "Blessed are those who find wisdom, those who gain understanding" (3:13). In the midst of a series of couplets that extol wisdom's greatness, he adds,

¹⁹ὁ θεὸς τῇ σοφίᾳ ἐθεμελίωσεν τὴν γῆν,
 ἡτοίμασεν δὲ οὐρανοὺς ἐν φρονήσει·
²⁰ἐν αἰσθήσει ἄβυσσοι ἐρράγησαν,
 νέφη δὲ ἐρρύησαν δρόσους.

¹⁹*God in wisdom laid the earth's foundations,*
 and he prepared the heavens with understanding;
²⁰*with discernment the deeps were divided,*
 and the clouds let drop their dew.

This is the same literary understanding of creation offering evidence of God's wisdom as in Ps 104. That the first line could not possibly refer to personified Wisdom is made plain by the second and third lines of the quatrain, which are clear examples of "synonymous parallelism": "he prepared the heavens with *understanding*; with *discernment* the deeps were divided."

Proverbs 8:22–31

The significance of the preceding passasge, which occurs early on in the prologue, is that in its present form the prologue has all the earmarks of a carefully constructed introduction to the proverbs that begin in 10:1;[40] this suggests that one should understand the personification in ch. 8 as a poetic elaboration of this text.[41] And indeed, that is exactly what one finds in this marvelous poetry, where Wisdom is now personified, but in a purely literary way.[42] This is also the passage from which both Sirach and the author of Wisdom of Solomon take their lead; and here she is pictured as *present* at creation, but as in 3:19, Wisdom is *not* its mediator: "I was there when [God] set the heavens in place, when he marked out the horizon on the face of the deep" (8:27).

Thus, Prov 8:22–26 asserts in a variety of ways that Wisdom was the first of God's creation, emphasizing her priority in time, so that her being *present* with God when he alone created the universe would thus reflect—as it actually does—God's wise blueprint. This, then, is the matter picked up in vv. 27–31, which further depict Wisdom as present at creation, again precisely in the sense of 3:19. But missing altogether in the Septuagint of this passage is any prepositional phrase that even remotely implies agency in the

---

[40] On this matter see, e.g., Waltke, *Proverbs 1–15*, 10–13.

[41] Here it is of some interest to point out that somewhere along the line, Prov 8:23–28 came into the margin of Nestle's Greek NT at Col 1:15! Paul's sentence does not have even a conceptual echo of Proverbs here, let alone a linguistic one.

[42] See Scott (*Proverbs and Ecclesiastes*, 70–71), who argues convincingly that this poem was written by the same author as 3:19.

creating process itself. Rather, she is depicted (in keeping with the Hebrew text) as παρ' αὐτῷ (*by his side*).

Those who think otherwise find their hope in the very ambiguous Hebrew term אמון in v. 30 (possibly "artisan"; but with a different pointing, "constantly" [TNIV]), which was translated in the Septuagint by the equally ambiguous ἁρμόζουσα (*being in harmony with*). Despite the probability that the author of Wisdom of Solomon knew no (or little) Hebrew, it is sometimes suggested in the literature that his use of τεχνῖτις (*fashioner, designer*) in 7:21 (7:22 NRSV); 8:6; 14:2 reflects this passage in Proverbs. But the difficulty lies with reading this usage from Wisdom of Solomon back into the *Hebrew* of Proverbs. In another context the author's poetry might be remotely stretched to mean "that the author sees Wisdom as preexisting and probably as having an active role in the work of creation."[43] But that is scarcely possible here, no matter how much its proponents might wish it to be so.

Indeed, this assumes a more hypostatic view of Wisdom than can be demonstrated in Proverbs, not to mention that it fails to take the point of the poetry seriously in the context of Prov 8 itself. Wisdom may indeed be "the master worker at his side," but she is not the mediator *through whom* creation *came into being*. Rather, for our author, the whole created order is so full of evidences of design and glory that God's own wisdom, now personified in a literary way, can be the only possible explanation for it.[44] This, of course, falls considerably short of Paul's understanding of Christ's role in creation as expressed in 1 Cor 8:6 and Col 1:16.

Sirach 24:1–22

The next appearance of these ideas is in "The Praise of Wisdom" in Sir 24:1–22. While creating his own (equally magnificent) poem, Sirach at the same time remains absolutely faithful to the understanding of his predecessor in Proverbs, on whom he is obviously dependent. For Sirach, who delights in the literary personification of wisdom, God alone is nonetheless the sole Creator of all things, including Wisdom herself: "Before the ages, from the beginning, he created me" (ἀπ' ἀρχῆς ἔκτισέν με [24:9]; cf. v. 8: "my Creator").

Those who find preexistent, personified Wisdom as having a role in creation appeal to v. 3: "I came forth from the mouth of the Most High, and covered the earth like a mist."[45] But that is to come to the text with an agenda in hand, not to read it on its own terms.[46] This passage reflects Sirach's view

---

[43] Witherington, *Jesus the Sage*, 44.

[44] See the full discussion in Waltke, *Proverbs 1–15*, 406–23.

[45] Cf. Witherington (*Jesus the Sage*, 95), who appeals to H. Ringgren, *Word and Wisdom: Studies in the Hypostatization of Divine Qualities and Functions in the Ancient Near East* (Lund: Ohlssons, 1947), 108–9.

[46] Cf. Skehan and di Lella (*Wisdom of Ben Sira*, 332–33), who do not so much as mention a view that reads this passage as Wisdom's having a role in creation itself.

that Wisdom is there "before the ages," since "from the first, he created me" (24:9); thus it is Sirach's own interpretation of "the Spirit of God . . . hovering over the waters" in Gen 1:2. His referent is *not* to her *creative* agency but rather to her having "sought a resting place" (v. 5), which took place historically in her presence with Israel in the Exodus!

It is hard to imagine that any ordinary reader of these texts from Proverbs and Sirach could ever suppose that their authors actually perceived personified Wisdom as the divine *agent* of creation. Present at creation, yes; but for other reasons, not for the actual act of creation itself.

Wisdom of Solomon 6:12–9:18

That brings us, then, to Wisdom of Solomon, which by everyone's reckoning has the crucial texts (found in the adulation of and prayer for wisdom in 7:21–9:18).[47] But here especially one needs to read what the author says in the context of the entire poetic narrative.

Wisdom of Solomon: An Overview

Our Alexandrian author's concern seems ultimately to be semiapologetic (both toward the Greeks and for the Jewish community's encouragement),[48] since the opening section (1:1–6:11), allegedly written by one who is himself a king, is framed by appeals to "the rulers of the earth," variously called "kings" or "despots." This opening appeal also sets forth the author's basic agenda: "living well" (doing justly and living righteously) is rewarded by immortality, whereas death awaits those who are evil. The way one lives well in this sense is to emulate Solomon and his own request for wisdom— a theme that is taken up in the crucial central section of the narrative (6:1–9:18; "if you delight in thrones and scepters, you monarchs over the peoples, honor wisdom, so that you may reign forever" [6:21]),[49] where "Solomon" sets out "to tell you [the monarchs] what wisdom is and how she came to be" (6:22).

---

[47] One of the problematic features of "dependency" on the part of Paul with regard to Wisdom of Solomon, of course, is its date. If Winston is correct that it should be dated during the reign of Caligula, then there seems almost no chance that Paul, who had become a follower of Christ by this time, would have known about this work—or, for that matter, given it the time of day if he had known of it. But since this dating (which I think is to be preferred for the reasons Winston sets forth) is much debated, I have chosen to enter this discussion on a level playing field.

[48] This begins in 1:1 ("Love righteousness, you rulers of the earth"); it is the recurrent theme of 6:1–11, which serves as transiton between the prologue and the praise of Wisdom that comes next.

[49] Unless otherwise noted, this and other translations will be from the NRSV, in part because, in keeping with its translation style, it tends to be close to the Greek text and in part because it consistently translates σοφία in the lower case (just as in Proverbs and Sirach), thus not prejudicing the reader toward any view of personification.

One can easily trace the author's progression of thought in this central section. He begins with Solomon's adulation of (now personified) Wisdom (6:12–21), which he proposes to describe (vv. 22–25). But before doing so, he reminds his readers of Solomon's ordinary humanity (7:1–6), so that he can appeal to the great things that happened to Solomon when he received wisdom (vv. 7–21), the secret to which he now hopes to "pass on liberally" (v. 13 [NJB]). That leads to his "eulogy of Wisdom" (7:22–8:1), which the note in the New Jerusalem Bible describes as "the peak of OT writings on Wisdom." Because of Wisdom's undoubted greatness—both for understanding and uprightness, which alone leads to immortality—the author returns to Solomon's own love for Wisdom (8:2–18), which he knows that he could never have had unless it was given by God (vv. 19–21). Thus, this author's own version of "In Praise of Wisdom" concludes with Solomon's prayer for wisdom/Wisdom (9:1–18).

And right at this point, true to his own narrative and historical tradition, our author rather significantly tempers the guise of personification, as the prayer is addressed to God and the desire is for the king to possess God's own wisdom, not a personified, quasi-divine being. Thus, even though "she sits by your throne" in v. 4, the main thrust of 9:1–9 is simply "the wisdom that comes from you" (v. 6). When the author picks up the personificaton again in v. 10, the primary concern is expressed in v. 11 ("For she understands and knows all things, and she will guide me wisely in my actions and guard me with her glory").

Following the prayer, the rest of the narrative is an intriguing mixture of reflection on God's goodness to Israel in its history—especially in the exodus, with several antitheses between this goodness received and the opposites that befell Israel's opponents—with theological reflections both on God's forbearance in dealing with these opponents and on the folly of their idolatry. What is noteworthy structurally is that this narrative begins with Wisdom playing the leading role (10:1–11:1) from Adam (10:1–2) to the exodus (10:15–11:1). Toward the end of the narrative of Israel's history in ch. 10, the author in v. 20 makes note of the people's singing of the Song of Moses in Exod 15. And with that, he himself addresses God in the second person singular ("and they sang hymns, *Lord*, to *your* holy name; and praised with one accord *your* defending hand"); and though he returns momentarily to the role that Wisdom plays in the story (10:21), at that point she simply drops out of the story. Thus, after the first antithesis—a contrast between Israel's gift of water from the rock and the water that punished their enemies (11:4–14)—the entire remainder of the poetry (through 19:22) takes the form of personal address to God, while Wisdom makes only a cameo appearance as the "artisan" of boats in 14:2, 5.[50]

---

[50] Some would see this text as supporting a view of Wisdom as agent of creation, but that is to make too much of almost nothing. Verse 5 offers the author's perspec-

It is in this last section in particular, all of it addressed to God and quite apart from reference to wisdom, that the author's basic "theology" emerges in true Jewish fashion over and again. Whatever else, he argues repeatedly, God's judgments are just. But God's love for what he has created causes him to show mercy even when he must judge. For God's people, this means punishment with mercy; for Egypt, it happens slowly so that they might learn of his mercy and that "they might learn that one is punished by the very things by which one sins" (11:16). This final section thus evolves into a constant round of condemning Egypt for its idolatry but showing mercy on Israel, even when it fell into similar sins. At the heart of it all is the author's scathing rebuke of idolatry; indeed, ch. 13 picks up Isa 44:9–20 (see 13:10–19), which in ch. 14 turns directly on the Egyptian (Roman) idolatry of his own day (especially emperor worship). And so he concludes in chs. 17–19 with the "reasonableness" of the plagues, since it is the God of the Jews who is the sole Creator and Ruler of all that is (11:17, 24–25; 13:3–5; 16:24).

My reason for rehearsing this narrative and its structure is that it must affect the way one reads the eulogy of Wisdom in the brief central section. Our author's concern about wisdom is not theological per se but rather practical and ethical. Only by having wisdom will rulers rule well, and only by having wisdom will people live well. This concern leads to his expansive praise of Wisdom and her "works." At issue is whether "agency" in the original creation of the world is seen by the author as part of these works. As indicated, and quite in keeping with the traditions to which he is indebted and despite his enthusiasm for Wisdom's greatness, he sees Wisdom as only *present* at creation (again because creation's wise design reflects God's attribute of wisdom), not as its divine agent.

Before we examine the texts themselves, some preliminary linguistic observations are in order. In the narrative of the creation in Gen 1–2, the Septuagint translators used ποιεῖν (*make*) as their primary verb for all the activity of creation, while the verb κτίζω (*create*) appears only in Gen 14:19, 22 and Deut 4:32 with regard to God being the Creator of all that is. After these few instances in the Pentateuch, κτίζω occurs only rarely with regard to creation (once each by the translators of Proverbs and Ecclesiastes). The author of Wisdom of Solomon, on the other hand, uses κτίζω as his primary verb to refer to God as Creator (1:14; 2:23; 10:1; 11:17; 13:3), but in his actual reference to the creation narrative itself (9:1, 9) he uses the Septuagint's ποιεῖν, as well as in two references to the creation of humankind in 2:23; 6:7. Paul himself consistently and exclusively refers to God's creating activity with the verb κτίζω. These various data will be important for the discussion that follows.

---

tive on the personification of v. 2, and it has nothing to do with creation of the world as such: "It is your will that works of your wisdom should not be without effect" (God's wisdom is seen in the fact that ships float!). Here the usage is simply in keeping with the whole sapiential tradition.

What is important for our present purposes is that the activity of personified Wisdom in Wisdom of Solomon is never associated with *any* of these verbs. That is, she may be present at creation, as in Proverbs and Sirach, but she is never mentioned as partner in God's act of creating. Since our authors consistently see her as present at, but not as agent of, creation, the preposition that Paul uses of the Son's role in creation (διά) *never emerges in any of the Wisdom literature*—including Wisdom of Solomon—to refer to Wisdom's relationship to creation. This is easily demonstrated by simply looking at each of the texts in turn.

Wisdom 7:22 (7:21 LXX)

This first text that broaches the subject of the relationship of Wisdom to the created order is usually also the first one brought into the discussion. Here our author says:

ἡ γὰρ πάντων τεχνῖτις ἐδίδαξέν με σοφία
for wisdom, the fashioner of all things, taught me

Here is the first instance where the key word τεχνῖτις occurs, and as the context makes clear, Wisdom is not here thought of as the agent of the whole created order; rather, her presence is in evidence by the way the creation has been "fashioned," as though by a master designer. Paul obviously cares for none of this when speaking of Christ.

Wisdom 8:4–6

Although at one level this set of doublets looks more promising than the previous one, it is in fact simply an elaboration of 7:22:

⁴μύστις γάρ ἐστιν τῆς τοῦ θεοῦ ἐπιστήμης
    καὶ <u>αἱρετὶς τῶν ἔργων αὐτοῦ</u>.
⁵εἰ δὲ πλοῦτός ἐστιν ἐπιθυμητὸν κτῆμα ἐν βίῳ,
    τί σοφίας πλουσιώτερον τῆς <u>τὰ πάντα ἐργαζομένης</u>;
⁶εἰ δὲ φρόνησις <u>ἐργάζεται</u>,
    τίς αὐτῆς <u>τῶν ὄντων μᾶλλόν ἐστιν τεχνῖτις</u>;
⁴*For she is an initiate in the knowledge of God,*
    and <u>an associate in his works</u>.
⁵*If riches are a desirable possession in life,*
    what is richer than wisdom, <u>who works all things</u>?[51]
⁶*If understanding <u>is effective</u>,*
    who more than she is <u>fashioner of what exists</u>?

Here is a text that may look as if Wisdom is placed at least within the general context of *creation;* but a closer look makes it certain that this is not

_____
   [51] This final clause is my own (more literal) translation to show the pickup of "works" from v. 4.

so. The triplet is noticeably held together by the recurrence of the verb ἐργάζομαι and its associated noun ἔργον, which is simply not biblical language for creation. In fact, our author's interest here is altogether with Wisdom's role in God's ongoing "works" in the world. Moreover, Paul himself never uses this verb or noun with God as subject except for what God does with and among his people. It takes a considerable stretch to think that Paul could have been influenced by this language and thought of it in terms of creation, even if he had known Wisdom of Solomon.

Wisdom 9:1–2, 9

We now come to the crucial texts at the beginning of Solomon's prayer. Precisely because he is now *praying* for Wisdom—not *describing* her—and thus in v. 1 addressing God in the second person, Solomon says to God,

ὁ ποιήσας τὰ πάντα ἐν λόγῳ σου
who have made all things by your word

This reflects the Genesis narrative by way of both the verb ποιέω from Gen 1:1 and the loaded Greek term λόγος. At this point, our author is merely putting Gen 1:1 into poetic form. The next phrase is where the issues lie, for in v. 2 he goes on to say,

καὶ τῇ σοφίᾳ σου κατασκευάσας ἄνθρωπον,
ἵνα δεσπόζῃ τῶν ὑπὸ σοῦ γενομένων κτισμάτων
and in your wisdom (you) fashioned humankind,
to have dominion over the creatures you have made

With these words, the author adds his own take on the Genesis narrative, asserting that the "man" whom God created to have dominion over all other creatures was thus "fashioned" by God's wisdom so as to play this role. Although it may be argued that this still refers to creation as such, there are at least four factors that suggest otherwise.

First, this is not biblical language for creation, since nowhere in the Septuagint does this verb appear in connection with creation itself.

Second, this is poetic narrative; and it is spoken about the *second stage* of the Genesis narrative, having to do not with the *creation* of humankind but rather with the role that human beings are to have on earth. They are first to have dominion over the creatures and thus to "rule the world in holiness and righteousness" (v. 3a) but also—and now the role of Solomon himself emerges in the narrative—to "pronounce judgment in uprightness of soul" (v. 3b).

Third, and most damaging of all to the case for Wisdom's role in creation, our author here is not referring to Lady Wisdom at all but to God's own attribute of wisdom. Indeed, this is so obviously not a personification, either of a divine *logos* or divine *sophia*, that even the New Jerusalem Bible, with its clear bias toward personified Wisdom throughout this work, translates these in the lower case. The grammar alone disallows such a view, since the dative phrase τῇ σοφίᾳ σου, with its articular σοφία and second-person possessive pronoun, shows that the author has clearly abandoned personification at this point and is referring simply to the divine attribute itself.

In fact, the only way one can find hypostatic Wisdom as the agent of creation in this passage is by bringing to the text a prior disposition to do so and by a misreading of the parallelism so as to make λόγος and σοφία interchangeable. Our author's obvious concern is not with Wisdom's role in creation as such but rather with God's own wisdom in "equipping/constructing" (κατασκευάσας) human beings for their life in the world that God had created by his word. And it is because the world is so wondrously arrayed by the God who created it that the author goes on to add in v. 9, "With you is wisdom, she who knows your works and was present when *you* made the world." This text is a straightforward reflection of Prov 8:27–31. And as with Prov 8, our author is not suggesting that Wisdom had a role in the actual creation of the world; rather, the world (and human beings in particular) is (are) so marvelously designed that only infinite wisdom could have made it so.

Fourth, in the third part of the book, when the guise of personified Wisdom has been given up altogether, the author repeatedly reveals his basic theology of creation—and Wisdom is nowhere to be found. Thus, in 11:17 he says, "For your all-powerful hand, which created the world out of formless matter, did not lack the means to send upon them . . ." Similarly, in 11:24, but now with the third line using the verb that had previously been attributed to Wisdom, "For you love all things that exist, and detest none of the things *you have created* [ἐποίησας], nor do you hate what *you have fashioned* [κατεσκεύασας]" (translation mine). This indicates that the strong appeal to Lady Wisdom in the earlier part of the book was for effect only, not to present hypostatic Wisdom as co-creator with God himself.

So not only does our author not attribute to Wisdom the high honor of mediating creation in the way Paul attributes such to Christ, but also nothing in these texts even approximates the use of the crucial prepositions διά (*through*) or ἐν (*by*) with Wisdom as the object of the preposition. In short, the role of Wisdom as agent of creation in the Wisdom literature is the creation of scholarship, not a disclosure based on the texts themselves.[52]

Conclusion

At the end of this lengthy analysis of texts in both Paul and the Wisdom literature, we may conclude with a considerable degree of confidence that

---

[52] I have avoided all mention of the alleged role of "preexistent Wisdom" as associated with the "flinty rock" in the desert (Wis 11:4), since this is a most unfortunate reading of the text of Wisdom. On this matter, see the discussion on 1 Cor 10:4 in ch. 3, pp. 95–97.

Paul neither knew nor articulated anything that might resemble a Wisdom Christology. I now emphasize this conclusion by summarizing the various points that have been made throughout.

1. This view could never have arisen on the basis of the Pauline texts alone. On no occasion does Paul say, or hint at the possibility, that Wisdom was involved in God's creation of the world. On this matter, he does not even echo the wisdom texts that speak of creation reflecting God's *attribute* of wisdom.

2. What Paul says, rather, is that all things that God created came into being through the agency of Christ, either as the Lord or as the divine Son.

3. Furthermore, there is nothing in Paul's use of the wisdom tradition that would lead anyone to look for personified Wisdom in what he does say either about Christ or about creation. A careful analysis of Paul's actual use of the wisdom tradition would scarcely cause one to look there for a christological resolution to Paul's understanding of Christ.

4. The absolutely crucial document for finding a tie to Paul and the Wisdom literature is Wisdom of Solomon. But an analysis of all possible allusions to this work in Paul's letters offers little confidence in this regard. Indeed, nothing in Paul's letters indicates that he knew of its existence; and even if he did know of it, he made no obvious use of it.

5. On the other crucial matter—whether in the wisdom tradition itself there is a tendency to view personified Wisdom as the *agent* of creation— careful exegesis of the various texts in the context of the whole document does not lead one to think that this was the view of any of the authors of these books.

6. What is startling when one reads the literature on this matter is the nature of the advocacy for such a view, where everything brought forward in support requires a methodology totally unlike anything else that one would use for constructing a Pauline theology, which ordinarily is constructed on *the basis of what Paul actually says on a subject* and recognizes the value of OT supporting evidence. But here, by way of contrast, every bit of "evidence" brought forward is by way of secondary (or even tertiary) allusions. That is, Paul himself never even remotely associates Christ with personified Wisdom. The only possible instance (1 Cor 1:24) has nothing to do with personified Wisdom but rather with "wisdom" at the human level, which has caused the Corinthians to reject the reality of a crucified Messiah. So when Paul says that all things were created "through [the Lord]" (1 Cor 8:6) and "through [the Son]" (Col 1:15) regarding his role in creation, it is certainly not *Paul* who intends us to read "Wisdom" for "Lord" or "Son," but rather some NT scholars in their wishfulness to see it so.

7. In light of the evidence, therefore, both in Paul's letters and in the Wisdom literature, we must conclude that Wisdom Christology is *not* found in Paul's letters and thus has no role in the reconstruction of Paul's Christology.

Addendum I: Nestle-Aland^{27} Margins

Allusions to Wisdom of Solomon

(P = Paul; W = Wisdom of Solomon)

1. Rom 1:19–23 // Wis 13–15

2. Rom 1:21 // Wis 13:1

(P) διότι γνόντες τὸν θεὸν οὐχ ὡς θεὸν ἐδόξασαν ἢ ηὐχαρίστησαν, ἀλλ᾽ **ἐματαιώθησαν** ἐν τοῖς διαλογισμοῖς αὐτῶν καὶ ἐσκοτίσθη ἡ ἀσύνετος αὐτῶν καρδία.

(W) **Μάταιοι** μὲν γὰρ πάντες ἄνθρωποι φύσει, οἷς παρῆν θεοῦ ἀγνωσία καὶ ἐκ τῶν ὁρωμένων ἀγαθῶν οὐκ ἴσχυσαν εἰδέναι τὸν ὄντα οὔτε τοῖς ἔργοις προσέχοντες ἐπέγνωσαν τὸν τεχνίτην,

3. Rom 1:23 // Wis 11:15; 12:24

(P) καὶ ἤλλαξαν τὴν δόξαν τοῦ ἀφθάρτου θεοῦ ἐν ὁμοιώματι εἰκόνος φθαρτοῦ ἀνθρώπου καὶ πετεινῶν καὶ τετραπόδων καὶ **ἑρπετῶν**.

(W) ἀντὶ δὲ λογισμῶν ἀσυνέτων ἀδικίας αὐτῶν, ἐν οἷς πλανηθέντες ἐθρήσκευον ἄλογα **ἑρπετὰ** καὶ κνώδαλα εὐτελῆ, ἐπαπέστειλας αὐτοῖς πλῆθος ἀλόγων ζῴων εἰς ἐκδίκησιν, καὶ γὰρ τῶν πλάνης ὁδῶν μακρότερον ἐπλανήθησαν θεοὺς ὑπολαμβάνοντες τὰ καὶ ἐν ζῴοις τῶν αἰσχρῶν ἄτιμα νηπίων δίκην ἀφρόνων ψευσθέντες.

4. Rom 2:4 // Wis 11:23

(P) ἢ τοῦ πλούτου τῆς χρηστότητος αὐτοῦ καὶ τῆς ἀνοχῆς καὶ τῆς μακροθυμίας καταφρονεῖς, ἀγνοῶν ὅτι τὸ χρηστὸν τοῦ θεοῦ εἰς μετάνοιάν σε ἄγει;

(W) ἐλεεῖς δὲ πάντας ὅτι πάντα δύνασαι καὶ παρορᾷς ἁμαρτήματα ἀνθρώπων εἰς μετάνοιαν.

5. Rom 2:15 // Wis 17:10

(P) οἵτινες ἐνδείκνυνται τὸ ἔργον τοῦ νόμου γραπτὸν ἐν ταῖς καρδίαις αὐτῶν, **συμμαρτυρούσης αὐτῶν τῆς συνειδήσεως** καὶ μεταξὺ ἀλλήλων τῶν λογισμῶν κατηγορούντων ἢ καὶ ἀπολογουμένων,

(W) δειλὸν γὰρ ἰδίῳ πονηρίᾳ **μάρτυρι** καταδικαζομένη, ἀεὶ δὲ προσείληφεν τὰ χαλεπὰ συνεχομένη **τῇ συνειδήσει**·

6. Rom 5:12 // Wis 2:24

(P) Διὰ τοῦτο ὥσπερ δι᾽ ἑνὸς ἀνθρώπου ἡ ἁμαρτία **εἰς τὸν κόσμον εἰσῆλθεν** καὶ διὰ τῆς ἁμαρτίας ὁ **θάνατος**, καὶ οὕτως εἰς πάντας ἀνθρώπους ὁ θάνατος διῆλθεν, ἐφ᾽ ᾧ πάντες ἥμαρτον·

(W) φθόνῳ δὲ διαβόλου **θάνατος εἰσῆλθεν εἰς τὸν κόσμον** πειράζουσιν δὲ αὐτὸν οἱ τῆς ἐκείνου μερίδος ὄντες.

7. Rom 9:19 // Wis 12:12

(P) Ἐρεῖς μοι οὖν· **τί** [οὖν] ἔτι μέμφεται; τῷ γὰρ βουλήματι αὐτοῦ **τίς ἀνθέστηκεν;**

(W) τίς γὰρ **ἐρεῖ Τί** ἐποίησας; ἢ **τίς ἀντιστήσεται** τῷ κρίματί σου;

8. Rom 9:21 // Wis 15:7

(P) ἢ οὐκ ἔχει ἐξουσίαν ὁ **κεραμεὺς** τοῦ πηλοῦ **ἐκ τοῦ αὐτοῦ** φυράματος ποιῆσαι ὃ μὲν εἰς τιμὴν **σκεῦος** ὃ δὲ εἰς ἀτιμίαν;

(W) Καὶ γὰρ **κεραμεὺς** ἁπαλὴν γῆν θλίβων ἐπίμοχθον πλάσσει πρὸς ὑπηρεσίαν ἡμῶν ἓν ἕκαστον· ἀλλ᾽ **ἐκ τοῦ αὐτοῦ πηλοῦ** ἀνεπλάσατο τά τε τῶν καθαρῶν ἔργων δοῦλα **σκεύη** τά τε ἐναντία, πάντα ὁμοίως· τούτων δὲ ἑτέρου τίς ἑκάστου ἐστὶν ἡ χρῆσις κριτὴς ὁ πηλουργός.

9. Rom 9:31 // Wis 2:11

(P) Ἰσραὴλ δὲ διώκων **νόμον δικαιοσύνης** εἰς νόμον οὐκ ἔφθασεν.

(W) ἔστω δὲ ἡμῶν ἡ ἰσχὺς **νόμος τῆς δικαιοσύνης**, τὸ γὰρ ἀσθενὲς ἄχρηστον ἐλέγχεται.

10. Rom 11:33 // Wis 17:1

(P) Ὦ βάθος πλούτου καὶ σοφίας καὶ γνώσεως θεοῦ· ὡς ἀνεξεραύνητα **τὰ κρίματα αὐτοῦ** καὶ ἀνεξιχνίαστοι αἱ ὁδοὶ αὐτοῦ.

(W) Μεγάλαι γάρ σου **αἱ κρίσεις** καὶ δυσδιήγητοι·

11. Rom 13:1 // Wis 6:3

(P) . . . οὐ γὰρ ἔστιν ἐξουσία εἰ μὴ ὑπὸ θεοῦ, αἱ δὲ οὖσαι ὑπὸ θεοῦ τεταγμέναι εἰσίν.

(W) ὅτι ἐδόθη παρὰ κυρίου ἡ κράτησις ὑμῖν καὶ ἡ δυναστεία παρὰ ὑψίστου,

12. Rom 13:10 // Wis 6:18

(P) ἡ ἀγάπη τῷ πλησίον κακὸν οὐκ ἐργάζεται· πλήρωμα οὖν **νόμου ἡ ἀγάπη.**

(W) **ἀγάπη δὲ τήρησις νόμων** αὐτῆς, προσοχὴ δὲ νόμων βεβαίωσις ἀφθαρσίας,

13. 1 Cor 1:24 // Wis 7:24–25

(P) αὐτοῖς δὲ τοῖς κλητοῖς, Ἰουδαίοις τε καὶ Ἕλλησιν, Χριστὸν **θεοῦ δύναμιν καὶ θεοῦ σοφίαν·**

(W) ²⁴πάσης γὰρ κινήσεως κινητικώτερον **σοφία**, διήκει δὲ καὶ χωρεῖ διὰ πάντων διὰ τὴν καθαρότητα· ²⁵**ἀτμὶς γάρ ἐστιν τῆς τοῦ θεοῦ δυνάμεως** καὶ ἀπόρροια τῆς τοῦ παντοκράτορος δόξης εἰλικρινής·

14. 1 Cor 2:16 // Wis 9:13

(P) **τίς γὰρ ἔγνω** νοῦν κυρίου, ὃς συμβιβάσει αὐτόν; ἡμεῖς δὲ νοῦν Χριστοῦ ἔχομεν.

(W) **τίς γὰρ** ἄνθρωπος **γνώσεται** βουλὴν θεοῦ; ἢ τίς ἐνθυμηθήσεται τί θέλει ὁ κύριος;

15. 1 Cor 4:14 // Wis 11:10

(P) Οὐκ ἐντρέπων ὑμᾶς γράφω ταῦτα ἀλλ᾽ **ὡς** τέκνα μου ἀγαπητὰ **νουθετῶ[ν]**.

(W) τούτους μὲν γὰρ **ὡς** πατὴρ **νουθετῶν** ἐδοκίμασας,

16. 1 Cor 6:2 // Wis 3:8

(P) ἢ οὐκ οἴδατε ὅτι **οἱ ἅγιοι τὸν κόσμον κρινοῦσιν;** καὶ εἰ ἐν ὑμῖν κρίνεται ὁ κόσμος,

(W) **κρινοῦσιν ἔθνη** καὶ κρατήσουσιν λαῶν, καὶ βασιλεύσει αὐτῶν κύριος εἰς τοὺς αἰῶνας.

17. 1 Cor 9:25 // Wis 4:2

(P) πᾶς δὲ ὁ **ἀγωνιζόμενος** πάντα ἐγκρατεύεται, ἐκεῖνοι μὲν οὖν ἵνα φθαρτὸν **στέφανον** λάβωσιν, ἡμεῖς δὲ ἄφθαρτον.

(W) . . . καὶ ἐν τῷ αἰῶνι **στεφανηφοροῦσα** πομπεύει τὸν τῶν ἀμιάντων ἄθλων **ἀγῶνα** νικήσασα.

18. 1 Cor 10:1 // Wis 19:7–8

(P) Οὐ θέλω γὰρ ὑμᾶς ἀγνοεῖν, ἀδελφοί, ὅτι οἱ πατέρες ἡμῶν πάντες ὑπὸ τὴν **νεφέλην** ἦσαν καὶ πάντες διὰ τῆς θαλάσσης διῆλθον

(W) ⁷ἡ τὴν παρεμβολὴν σκιάζουσα **νεφέλη**, ἐκ δὲ προϋφεστῶτος ὕδατος ξηρᾶς ἀνάδυσις γῆς, ἐθεωρήθη, ἐξ ἐρυθρᾶς θαλάσσης ὁδὸς ἀνεμπόδιστος καὶ χλοηφόρον πεδίον ἐκ κλύδωνος βιαίου· ⁸δι᾽ οὗ πανεθνεὶ διῆλθον οἱ τῇ σῇ σκεπαζόμενοι χειρὶ θεωρήσαντες θαυμαστὰ τέρατα.

19. 1 Cor 11:7 // Wis 2:23

(P) Ἀνὴρ μὲν γὰρ οὐκ ὀφείλει κατακαλύπτεσθαι τὴν κεφαλὴν **εἰκὼν** καὶ δόξα **θεοῦ** ὑπάρχων· ἡ γυνὴ δὲ δόξα ἀνδρός ἐστιν.

(W) ὅτι ὁ θεὸς ἔκτισεν τὸν ἄνθρωπον ἐπ᾽ ἀφθαρσίᾳ καὶ **εἰκόνα** τῆς ἰδίας ἀϊδιότητος ἐποίησεν αὐτόν·

20. 1 Cor 11:24 // Wis 16:6

(P) . . . τοῦτο ποιεῖτε **εἰς τὴν ἐμὴν ἀνάμνησιν**.

(W) εἰς νουθεσίαν δὲ πρὸς ὀλίγον ἐταράχθησαν σύμβολον ἔχοντες σωτηρίας **εἰς ἀνάμνησιν** ἐντολῆς νόμου σου·

21. 1 Cor 15:32 // Wis 2:5–6

(P) εἰ κατὰ ἄνθρωπον ἐθηριομάχησα ἐν Ἐφέσῳ, τί μοι τὸ ὄφελος; εἰ νεκροὶ οὐκ ἐγείρονται, φάγωμεν καὶ πίωμεν, αὔριον γὰρ ἀποθνήσκομεν.

(W) ⁵σκιᾶς γὰρ πάροδος ὁ καιρὸς ἡμῶν, καὶ οὐκ ἔστιν ἀναποδισμὸς τῆς τελευτῆς ἡμῶν, ὅτι κατεσφραγίσθη καὶ οὐδεὶς ἀναστρέφει. ⁶δεῦτε οὖν καὶ ἀπολαύσωμεν τῶν ὄντων ἀγαθῶν καὶ χρησώμεθα τῇ κτίσει ὡς ἐν νεότητι σπουδαίως·

22. 1 Cor 15:34 // Wis 13:1

(P) ἐκνήψατε δικαίως καὶ μὴ ἁμαρτάνετε, **ἀγνωσίαν γὰρ θεοῦ** τινες ἔχουσιν, πρὸς ἐντροπὴν ὑμῖν λαλῶ.

(W) Μάταιοι μὲν γὰρ πάντες ἄνθρωποι φύσει, οἷς παρῆν **θεοῦ ἀγνωσία** καὶ ἐκ τῶν ὁρωμένων ἀγαθῶν οὐκ ἴσχυσαν εἰδέναι τὸν ὄντα οὔτε τοῖς ἔργοις προσέχοντες ἐπέγνωσαν τὸν τεχνίτην,

23. 2 Cor 5:1, 4 // Wis 9:15

(P) ¹Οἴδαμεν γὰρ ὅτι ἐὰν ἡ ἐπίγειος ἡμῶν οἰκία **τοῦ σκήνους** καταλυθῇ, . . . ⁴καὶ γὰρ οἱ ὄντες **ἐν τῷ σκήνει** στενάζομεν βαρούμενοι, ἐφ᾽ ᾧ οὐ θέλομεν ἐκδύσασθαι ἀλλ᾽ ἐπενδύσασθαι, ἵνα καταποθῇ τὸ θνητὸν ὑπὸ τῆς ζωῆς.

(W) φθαρτὸν γὰρ σῶμα βαρύνει ψυχήν, καὶ βρίθει τὸ γεῶδες **σκῆνος** νοῦν πολυφρόντιδα.

24. 2 Cor 12:12 // Wis 10:16

(P) τὰ μὲν σημεῖα τοῦ ἀποστόλου κατειργάσθη ἐν ὑμῖν ἐν πάσῃ ὑπομονῇ, **σημείοις τε καὶ τέρασιν** καὶ δυνάμεσιν.

(W) . . . καὶ ἀντέστη βασιλεῦσιν φοβεροῖς **ἐν τέρασι καὶ σημείοις**.

25. Gal 6:1 // Wis 17:17

(P)   . . . ἐὰν καὶ προλημφθῇ ἄνθρωπος ἔν τινι παραπτώματι, ὑμεῖς οἱ
πνευματικοὶ καταρτίζετε τὸν τοιοῦτον ἐν πνεύματι πραΰτητος,
σκοπῶν σεαυτὸν μὴ καὶ σὺ πειρασθῇς.

(W)   εἴ τε πνεῦμα συρίζον ἢ περὶ ἀμφιλαφεῖς κλάδους ὀρνέων ἦχος
εὐμελὴς ἢ ῥυθμὸς ὕδατος πορευομένου βίᾳ ἢ κτύπος ἀπηνὴς
καταρριπτομένων πετρῶν

26. Eph 1:17 // Wis 7:7

(P)   . . . ὁ θεὸς τοῦ κυρίου ἡμῶν Ἰησοῦ Χριστοῦ, ὁ πατὴρ τῆς δόξης, δώῃ
ὑμῖν **πνεῦμα σοφίας** καὶ ἀποκαλύψεως ἐν ἐπιγνώσει αὐτοῦ,

(W)   διὰ τοῦτο εὐξάμην, καὶ φρόνησις ἐδόθη μοι· ἐπεκαλεσάμην, καὶ ἦλθέν
μοι **πνεῦμα σοφίας**.

27. Eph 4:24 // Wis 9:3

(P)   καὶ ἐνδύσασθαι τὸν καινὸν ἄνθρωπον τὸν κατὰ θεὸν κτισθέντα **ἐν
δικαιοσύνῃ καὶ ὁσιότητι** τῆς ἀληθείας.

(W)   καὶ διέπῃ τὸν κόσμον **ἐν ὁσιότητι καὶ δικαιοσύνῃ** καὶ ἐν εὐθύτητι
ψυχῆς κρίσιν κρίνῃ,

28. Eph 6:13 // Wis 5:17

(P)   διὰ τοῦτο ἀναλάβετε **τὴν πανοπλίαν τοῦ θεοῦ**, ἵνα δυνηθῆτε
ἀντιστῆναι ἐν τῇ ἡμέρᾳ τῇ πονηρᾷ καὶ ἅπαντα κατεργασάμενοι
στῆναι.

(W)   λήμψεται **πανοπλίαν** τὸν ζῆλον αὐτοῦ καὶ ὁπλοποιήσει τὴν κτίσιν εἰς
ἄμυναν ἐχθρῶν·

29. Eph 6:14 // Wis 5:18

(P)   στῆτε οὖν περιζωσάμενοι τὴν ὀσφὺν ὑμῶν ἐν ἀληθείᾳ καὶ
ἐνδυσάμενοι τὸν θώρακα τῆς δικαιοσύνης

(W)   **ἐνδύσεται θώρακα δικαιοσύνην** καὶ περιθήσεται κόρυθα κρίσιν
ἀνυπόκριτον·

30. Eph 6:16 // Wis 5:19, 21

(P)   ἐν πᾶσιν ἀναλαβόντες τὸν θυρεὸν τῆς πίστεως, ἐν ᾧ δυνήσεσθε πάντα
τὰ βέλη τοῦ πονηροῦ [τὰ] πεπυρωμένα σβέσαι·

(W)   [19]λήμψεται ἀσπίδα ἀκαταμάχητον ὁσιότητα, . . . [21]πορεύσονται
εὔστοχοι βολίδες ἀστραπῶν καὶ ὡς ἀπὸ εὐκύκλου τόξου τῶν νεφῶν
ἐπὶ σκοπὸν ἁλοῦνται,

31. Phil 4:5 // Wis 2:19

(P) τὸ ἐπιεικὲς ὑμῶν γνωσθήτω πᾶσιν ἀνθρώποις. ὁ κύριος ἐγγύς.

(W) . . . ἵνα γνῶμεν τὴν ἐπιείκειαν αὐτοῦ

32. Phil 4:13 // Wis 7:23

(P) πάντα ἰσχύω ἐν τῷ ἐνδυναμοῦντί με.

(W) ἀκώλυτον, εὐεργετικόν, φιλάνθρωπον,
βέβαιον, ἀσφαλές, ἀμέριμνον,
παντοδύναμον, πανεπίσκοπον
καὶ διὰ πάντων χωροῦν πνευμάτων
νοερῶν καθαρῶν λεπτοτάτων.

33. 1 Thess 4:13 // Wis 3:18

(P) . . . ἵνα μὴ λυπῆσθε καθὼς καὶ οἱ λοιποὶ οἱ μὴ ἔχοντες ἐλπίδα.

(W) ἐάν τε ὀξέως τελευτήσωσιν οὐχ ἕξουσιν ἐλπίδα οὐδὲ ἐν ἡμέρᾳ
διαγνώσεως παραμύθιον·

34. 1 Thess 5:1 // Wis 8:8 [on "signs and wonders," see 2 Cor 12:12;
Rom 15:19]

(P) Περὶ δὲ τῶν χρόνων καὶ τῶν καιρῶν, ἀδελφοί, οὐ χρείαν ἔχετε ὑμῖν
γράφεσθαι,

(W) . . . σημεῖα καὶ τέρατα προγινώσκει, καὶ ἐκβάσεις καιρῶν καὶ
χρόνων.

35. 1 Thess 5:2 // Wis 18:14–15 [on the suddenness of God's judgment of
Egypt]

(P) αὐτοὶ γὰρ ἀκριβῶς οἴδατε ὅτι ἡμέρα κυρίου ὡς κλέπτης ἐν νυκτὶ
οὕτως ἔρχεται.

(W) [14]ἡσύχου γὰρ σιγῆς περιεχούσης τὰ πάντα καὶ νυκτὸς ἐν ἰδίῳ τάχει
μεσαζούσης [15]ὁ παντοδύναμός σου λόγος ἀπ᾽ οὐρανῶν ἐκ θρόνων
βασιλείων ἀπότομος πολεμιστὴς εἰς μέσον τῆς ὀλεθρίας ἥλατο γῆς
ξίφος ὀξὺ τὴν ἀνυπόκριτον ἐπιταγήν σου φέρων

36. 1 Thess 5:3 // Wis 17:14

(P) . . . τότε αἰφνίδιος αὐτοῖς ἐφίσταται ὄλεθρος ὥσπερ ἡ ὠδὶν τῇ ἐν
γαστρὶ ἐχούσῃ, καὶ οὐ μὴ ἐκφύγωσιν.

(W) . . . αἰφνίδιος γὰρ αὐτοῖς καὶ ἀπροσδόκητος φόβος ἐπεχύθη.

37. 1 Thess 5:8 // Wis 5:18

(P)   . . . ἐνδυσάμενοι θώρακα πίστεως καὶ ἀγάπης καὶ περικεφαλαίαν ἐλπίδα σωτηρίας·

(W)   ἐνδύσεται θώρακα δικαιοσύνην καὶ περιθήσεται κόρυθα κρίσιν ἀνυπόκριτον·

38. Titus 3:4 // Wis 1:6

(P)   ὅτε δὲ ἡ χρηστότης καὶ ἡ φιλανθρωπία ἐπεφάνη τοῦ σωτῆρος ἡμῶν θεοῦ,

(W)   φιλάνθρωπον γὰρ πνεῦμα σοφία

Addendum II: The Wisdom Texts

1. Job 12:13

παρ᾽ αὐτῷ σοφία καὶ δύναμις,
   αὐτῷ βουλὴ καὶ σύνεσις.

Belonging to him are wisdom and power;
   counsel and understanding are his.

2. Psalm 104:24 (103:24 LXX)

ὡς ἐμεγαλύνθη τὰ ἔργα σου, κύριε·
   πάντα ἐν σοφίᾳ ἐποίησας,
   ἐπληρώθη ἡ γῆ τῆς κτήσεώς σου.

How many are your works, LORD!
   In wisdom you made them all;
   the earth is full of your creatures.

3. Proverbs 3:19–20

^{19}ὁ θεὸς τῇ σοφίᾳ ἐθεμελίωσεν τὴν γῆν,

ἡτοίμασεν δὲ οὐρανοὺς ἐν φρονήσει·

^{20}ἐν αἰσθήσει ἄβυσσοι ἐρράγησαν,

νέφη δὲ ἐρρύησαν δρόσους.

^{19}God in wisdom laid the earth's
   foundations,
with understanding he set the heavens in
   place;
^{20}in his knowledge the deeps were
   divided,
and the clouds let drop the dew.

4. Proverbs 8:22–31

^{22}κύριος ἔκτισέν με ἀρχὴν ὁδῶν αὐτοῦ
   εἰς ἔργα αὐτοῦ,
^{23}πρὸ τοῦ αἰῶνος ἐθεμελίωσέν με ἐν
   ἀρχῇ,
^{24}πρὸ τοῦ τὴν γῆν ποιῆσαι
   καὶ πρὸ τοῦ τὰς ἀβύσσους ποιῆσαι,
   πρὸ τοῦ προελθεῖν τὰς πηγὰς τῶν
      ὑδάτων,

The LORD made me the beginning of his
   ways for his works,
   before the ages he established me in
      the beginning;
before he created the earth,
   and before he created the depths,
   before the fountains of water came
      forth,

²⁵πρὸ τοῦ ὄρη ἑδρασθῆναι,
   πρὸ δὲ πάντων βουνῶν γεννᾷ με.
²⁶κύριος ἐποίησεν χώρας καὶ ἀοικήτους

   καὶ ἄκρα οἰκούμενα τῆς ὑπ' οὐρανόν.

²⁷ἡνίκα ἡτοίμαζεν τὸν οὐρανόν,
   συμπαρήμην αὐτῷ,
   καὶ ὅτε ἀφώριζεν τὸν ἑαυτοῦ θρόνον
     ἐπ' ἀνέμων.
²⁸ἡνίκα ἰσχυρὰ ἐποίει τὰ ἄνω νέφη,

   καὶ ὡς ἀσφαλεῖς ἐτίθει πηγὰς τῆς ὑπ'
     οὐρανὸν
²⁹καὶ ἰσχυρὰ ἐποίει τὰ θεμέλια τῆς γῆς,

³⁰ἤμην παρ' αὐτῷ ἁρμόζουσα,
   ἐγὼ ἤμην ᾗ προσέχαιρεν.

   καθ' ἡμέραν δὲ εὐφραινόμην
     ἐν προσώπῳ αὐτοῦ ἐν παντὶ
     καιρῷ,
³¹ὅτε εὐφραίνετο τὴν οἰκουμένην
   συντελέσας
   καὶ ἐνευφραίνετο ἐν υἱοῖς ἀνθρώπων.

before the mountains were settled,
   and before all the hills he begot me.
The LORD made countries and uninhabited places,
   and the highest inhabited places
     under heaven.
When he prepared the sky I was with
   him,
   and when he prepared his throne on
     the winds;
when he gave strength to the clouds
   above,
   and when he secured the fountains
     under heaven,
and when he strengthened the foundations of the earth,
I was with him arranging [things],
   I was the one in whom he took
     delight,
   and daily I rejoiced
     in his presence continually.

When he rejoiced, having completed the
   world,
   he also rejoiced among the sons of
     men.

5. Sirach 1:4, 9

⁴προτέρα πάντων ἔκτισται σοφία

   καὶ σύνεσις φρονήσεως ἐξ αἰῶνος.

⁹κύριος αὐτὸς ἔκτισεν αὐτὴν
   καὶ εἶδεν καὶ ἐξηρίθμησεν αὐτὴν
   καὶ ἐξέχεεν αὐτὴν ἐπὶ πάντα
     τὰ ἔργα αὐτοῦ,

⁴Wisdom was created before all other
things,
   and prudent understanding from
     eternity.
⁹The Lord himself created her;
   he saw her and took her measure;
   he poured her out upon all his works.

6. Wisdom of Solomon 7:21–28 (versification: Greek, LXX; English, NRSV)

²¹ὅσα τέ ἐστιν κρυπτὰ καὶ ἐμφανῆ ἔγνων·

   ἡ γὰρ πάντων τεχνῖτις ἐδίδαξέν με
     σοφία.
²²Ἔστιν γὰρ ἐν αὐτῇ πνεῦμα νοερόν,
   ἅγιον,
     μονογενές, πολυμερές, λεπτόν,
     εὐκίνητον, τρανόν, ἀμόλυντον,

²¹I learned both what is secret and what
   is manifest,
²²*for wisdom, the fashioner of all things,*
   taught me.
For there is in her a spirit: intelligent,
   holy,
     unique, manifold, subtle,
     mobile, clear, unpolluted,

σαφές, ἀπήμαντον, φιλάγαθον,
ὀξύ,
23 ἀκώλυτον, εὐεργετικόν,

φιλάνθρωπον,
βέβαιον, ἀσφαλές, ἀμέριμνον,

παντοδύναμον, πανεπίσκοπον
καὶ διὰ πάντων χωροῦν
πνευμάτων νοερῶν,
καθαρῶν, λεπτοτάτων.
²⁴πάσης γὰρ κινήσεως κινητικώτερον
σοφία,
διήκει δὲ καὶ χωρεῖ διὰ πάντων διὰ
τὴν καθαρότητα·
²⁵ἀτμὶς γάρ ἐστιν τῆς τοῦ θεοῦ δυνάμεως
καὶ ἀπόρροια τῆς τοῦ παντοκράτορος
δόξης εἰλικρινής·
διὰ τοῦτο οὐδὲν μεμιαμμένον εἰς
αὐτὴν παρεμπίπτει.
²⁶ἀπαύγασμα γάρ ἐστιν φωτὸς ἀιδίου
καὶ ἔσοπτρον ἀκηλίδωτον τῆς τοῦ
θεοῦ ἐνεργείας
καὶ εἰκὼν τῆς ἀγαθότητος αὐτοῦ.
²⁷μία δὲ οὖσα πάντα δύναται

καὶ μένουσα ἐν αὑτῇ τὰ πάντα
καινίζει
καὶ κατὰ γενεὰς εἰς ψυχὰς
ὁσίας μεταβαίνουσα
φίλους θεοῦ καὶ προφήτας
κατασκευάζει·
²⁸οὐθὲν γὰρ ἀγαπᾷ ὁ θεὸς
εἰ μὴ τὸν σοφίᾳ συνοικοῦντα.

distinct, invulnerable, loving the
good, keen,
irresistible, ²³beneficent,
humane,

steadfast, sure, free from
anxiety,
all-powerful, overseeing all,
and penetrating through the
spirits that are intelligent,
pure, and altogether subtle.
²⁴For wisdom is more mobile than any
motion;
she pervades/penetrates all things because of purity.
²⁵For she is a breath of the power of God,
and a pure emanation of the glory of
the Almighty;
therefore nothing defiled gains entrance into her.
²⁶For she is a *reflection* of eternal light,
a spotless mirror of the working of God;

and *an image of his goodness.*
²⁷Although but one, she can do all
things;
and while remaining in herself, she
renews all things;
in every generation she passes
into holy souls
and makes them friends of God,
and prophets.
²⁸For God loves nothing so much
as the person who lives with wisdom.

8:4–6

⁴μύστις γάρ ἐστιν τῆς τοῦ θεοῦ ἐπιστήμης
καὶ *αἱρετὶς τῶν ἔργων αὐτοῦ.*
⁵εἰ δὲ πλοῦτός ἐστιν ἐπιθυμητὸν κτῆμα
ἐν βίῳ
τί σοφίας πλουσιώτερον τῆς τὰ πάντα
ἐργαζομένης;
⁶εἰ δὲ φρόνησις ἐργάζεται,
τίς αὐτῆς τῶν ὄντων μᾶλλόν ἐστιν
τεχνῖτις;

⁴For she is an initiate in the knowledge of
God,
and *an associate in his works.*
⁵If riches are a desirable possession
in life,
*what is richer than wisdom, who works
all things?*
⁶If understanding is effective,
*who more than she is fashioner of what
exists?*

9:1–2

¹θεὲ πατέρων καὶ κύριε τοῦ ἐλέους
ὁ ποιήσας τὰ πάντα ἐν λόγῳ σου
²καὶ τῇ σοφίᾳ σου κατασκευάσας
ἄνθρωπον,
ἵνα δεσπόζῃ τῶν ὑπὸ σοῦ γενομένων
κτισμάτων

¹God of our fathers and Lord of mercy,
who created all things by your word,
²and *in your wisdom fashioned humankind,*

to have dominion over the creatures
you have made,

9:9–10

⁹καὶ μετὰ σοῦ ἡ σοφία ἡ εἰδυῖα τὰ ἔργα
σου
καὶ παροῦσα, ὅτε <u>ἐποίεις</u> τὸν κόσμον,

καὶ ἐπισταμένη τί ἀρεστὸν ἐν ὀφθαλμοῖς
σου
καὶ τί εὐθὲς ἐν ἐντολαῖς σου.

¹⁰ἐξαπόστειλον αὐτὴν ἐξ ἁγίων οὐρανῶν
καὶ ἀπὸ θρόνου δόξης σου πέμψον
αὐτήν,
ἵνα συμπαροῦσά μοι κοπιάσῃ
καὶ γνῶ τί εὐάρεστόν ἐστιν παρὰ σοί.

⁹*With you is wisdom, she who knows your*
works,
and was present when <u>you created</u> the
world;
she understands what is pleasing in your
sight
and *what is right according to your*
commandments.

¹⁰Send her forth from the holy heavens,
and from the throne of your glory
send her,
that she may labor at my side,
and that I may learn what is pleasing
to you.

10:20–11:4

²⁰διὰ τοῦτο δίκαιοι ἐσκύλευσαν ἀσεβεῖς

καὶ <u>ὕμνησαν</u>, <u>κύριε</u>, τὸ ὄνομα τὸ
ἅγιόν <u>σου</u>
τήν τε ὑπέρμαχόν <u>σου</u> χεῖρα ᾔνεσαν
ὁμοθυμαδόν·
²¹ὅτι ἡ σοφία ἤνοιξεν στόμα κωφῶν

καὶ γλώσσας νηπίων ἔθηκεν τρανάς.

¹¹:¹Εὐόδωσεν τὰ ἔργα αὐτῶν ἐν χειρὶ
προφήτου ἁγίου.
²διώδευσαν ἔρημον ἀοίκητον

καὶ ἐν ἀβάτοις ἔπηξαν σκηνάς·

³ἀντέστησαν πολεμίοις καὶ ἐχθροὺς
ἠμύναντο.
⁴ἐδίψησαν καὶ ἐπεκαλέσαντό <u>σε</u>,

²⁰Therefore, the righteous plundered the
ungodly
and *hymned,* <u>Lord</u>, <u>your</u> holy name,

and praised with one accord <u>your</u> *defend-*
ing hand;
²¹because wisdom opened the mouth of
the mute,
and made the tongues of infants
speak clearly.

¹¹:¹She prospered their works by the hand
of a holy prophet.
²They journeyed through an uninhabited
wilderness,
and pitched their tents in untrodden
places.
³They withstood their enemies and
fought off their foes.
⁴When they were thirsty, they called upon
<u>you</u>,

καὶ ἐδόθη αὐτοῖς ἐκ πέτρας
ἀκροτόμου ὕδωρ
καὶ ἴαμα δίψης ἐκ λίθου σκληροῦ.

and water was given them out of
flinty rock,
and from hard stone a remedy for
their thirst.

11:17, 24

[17]οὐ γὰρ ἠπόρει ἡ παντοδύναμός σου χεὶρ
καὶ κτίσασα τὸν κόσμον
ἐξ ἀμόρφου ὕλης
ἐπιπέμψαι αὐτοῖς πλῆθος ἄρκων ἢ
θρασεῖς λέοντας . . .
[24]ἀγαπᾷς γὰρ τὰ ὄντα πάντα
καὶ οὐδὲν βδελύσσῃ ὧν ἐποίησας·

οὐδὲ γὰρ ἂν μισῶν τι κατεσκεύασας.

[17]For your all-powerful hand,
which created the world
out of formless matter,
did not lack the means to send upon
them . . .
[24]For you love all things that exist,
and detest none of the things that you
have created;
nor do you hate what you have
fashioned.

16:24

Ἡ γὰρ κτίσις σοὶ τῷ ποιήσαντι
ὑπηρετοῦσα
ἐπιτείνεται εἰς κόλασιν κατὰ τῶν
ἀδίκων
καὶ ἀνίεται εἰς εὐεργεσίαν ὑπὲρ τῶν
ἐπὶ σοὶ πεποιθότων.

For creation, serving you who made it,

exerts itself to punish the unrighteous

and in kindness relaxes for those who
trust you.

Appendix B

Paul's Use of Κύριος for Christ in Citations and Echoes of the Septuagint

THE FIRST PURPOSE OF THIS appendix is, for the convenience of the reader, to gather all the citations and allusions discussed in chs. 2–10 in which Paul is most likely using the language of the Septuagint in referring to Christ (mostly κύριος but sometimes where Paul's κύριος stands in the place of "God"). They are listed in two groups: first, actual citations and apparent allusions to the Septuagint; second, Yahweh phrases from the Septuagint that have been applied to Christ. Here they are given in the order of the preceding chapters but in canonical order within each letter. The third group in this appendix lists the twelve citations of the Septuagint that include the name Κύριος where the reference is almost certainly to God the Father (see ch. 3, n. 7). As is noted in the texts below, the OT references reflect the chapter/ verse numbering of the Septuagint when it differs from the English Bible.

The second purpose here is to demonstrate the point made in the introduction (p. 21) as to both the ubiquity and the importance of this phenomenon in setting forth a Pauline Christology.

Citations and Allusions to the Text of the Septuagint

1 Thessalonians

1 Thess 3:13	ἐν τῇ παρουσίᾳ **τοῦ** **κυρίου** ἡμῶν Ἰησοῦ **μετὰ** **πάντων**
	τῶν ἁγίων αὐτου,
Zech 14:5	καὶ ἥξει **κύριος** ὁ θεός μου καὶ **πάντες**
	οἱ ἅγιοι **μετ'** **αὐτοῦ**.

1 Thess 4:6   διότι   **ἔκδικος**   *κύριος* περὶ πάντων τούτων,

Ps 93:1 LXX   ὁ θεὸς   **ἐκδικήσεων**   *κύριος*,

1 Thess 4:16   ὅτι αὐτὸς **ὁ** *κύριος* ἐν κελεύσματι, **ἐν φωνῇ** ἀρχαγγέλου
                            καὶ ἐν   **σάλπιγγι** θεοῦ,
                      καταβήσεται ἀπ᾽ οὐρανοῦ

Ps 46:6 LXX   ἀνέβη ὁ θεὸς ἐν ἀλαλαγμῷ,
                           κύριος   **ἐν φωνῇ**
                                  σάλπιγγος.

1 Thess 5:27   **ἐνορκίζω** ὑμᾶς **τὸν κύριον** ἀναγνωσθῆναι τὴν ἐπιστολὴν
                                      πᾶσιν τοῖς ἀδελφοῖς.

Gen 24:3   καὶ **ἐξορκιῶ   σε**   **κύριον** τὸν θεὸν τοῦ οὐρανοῦ
                                      [cf. Neh 13:25]

2 Thessalonians

2 Thess 1:7–8   [7]τοῦ **κυρίου Ἰησοῦ** . . . [8]**ἐν φλογὶ πυρός,**
                            διδόντος ἐκδίκησιν τοῖς μὴ εἰδόσιν θεὸν
                καὶ τοῖς μὴ ὑπακούουσιν τῷ εὐαγγελίῳ
                                      τοῦ κυρίου ἡμῶν Ἰησοῦ,

Isa 66:15   **κύριος** ὡς πῦρ ἥξει καὶ ὡς καταιγὶς τὰ ἅρματα αὐτοῦ
                        ἀποδοῦναι ἐν θυμῷ **ἐκδίκησιν**
                   καὶ ἀποσκορακισμὸν **ἐν φλογὶ πυρός.**

Isa 66:4   λέγει **κύριος** [v. 2] . . . **ἀνταποδώσω** αὐτοῖς ὅτι ἐκάλεσα
                   αὐτοὺς **καὶ οὐχ ὑπήκουσάν μου,**

2 Thess 1:9   οἵτινες . . .   **ἀπὸ προσώπου τοῦ**   **κυρίου καὶ ἀπὸ**
                                  τῆς δόξης τῆς ἰσχύος αὐτοῦ,

Isa 2:10   κρύπτεσθε . . . **ἀπὸ προσώπου τοῦ** φόβου **κυρίου καὶ ἀπὸ**
                                  τῆς δόξης τῆς ἰσχύος αὐτοῦ,

2 Thess 1:10   ὅταν **ἔλθῃ ἐνδοξασθῆναι   ἐν τοῖς**   **ἁγίοις αὐτοῦ**

Ps 88:8 LXX   ὁ θεὸς   **ἐνδοξαζόμενος ἐν** βουλῇ **ἁγίων,**

2 Thess 1:10   καὶ   **θαυμασθῆναι   ἐν πᾶσιν** τοῖς πιστεύσασιν,

Ps 67:36 LXX   **θαυμαστὸς** ὁ θεὸς **ἐν τοῖς   ἁγίοις αὐτοῦ·**

2 Thess 1:12   ὅπως   **ἐνδοξασθῇ**   τὸ ὄνομα τοῦ **κυρίου** ἡμῶν Ἰησοῦ
                                               ἐν ὑμῖν,

Isa 66:5   ἵνα   **τὸ ὄνομα κυρίου**   **δοξασθῇ**

2 Thess 2:13   εὐχαριστεῖν τῷ θεῷ πάντοτε περὶ ὑμῶν, ἀδελφοὶ
                            ἠγαπημένοι ὑπὸ κυρίου,

Deut 33:12   καὶ τῷ Βενιαμιν εἶπεν,
                       ἠγαπημένος ὑπὸ κυρίου κατασκηνώσει

2 Thess 3:5   ὁ δὲ **κύριος**   **κατευθύναι** ὑμῶν **τὰς καρδίας**
                                   εἰς τὴν ἀγάπην τοῦ θεοῦ

1 Chr 29:18   **κύριε** ὁ θεὸς . . . καὶ **κατεύθυνον**   **τὰς καρδίας**
                                   αὐτῶν πρὸς σέ.

2 Thess 3:16   ὁ **κύριος**   **μετὰ** πάντων **ὑμῶν.**

Ruth 2:4   **κύριος**   **μεθ'**   **ὑμῶν·**

1 Corinthians

1 Cor 1:31   ἵνα καθὼς γέγραπται· ὁ **καυχώμενος, ἐν κυρίῳ καυχάσθω.**

Jer 9:23 LXX   ἐν τούτῳ **καυχάσθω** ὁ **καυχώμενος,** συνίειν καὶ γινώσκειν
                                  ὅτι **ἐγώ εἰμι κύριος**

1 Cor 2:16   **τίς** γὰρ **ἔγνω**   **νοῦν κυρίου, ὃς συμβιβάσει αὐτόν;**
                  ἡμεῖς δὲ   **νοῦν Χριστοῦ** ἔχομεν.

Isa 40:13   **τίς**   **ἔγνω**   **νοῦν κυρίου,** καὶ τίς αὐτοῦ σύμβουλος
                           ἐγένετο,   **ὃς συμβιβᾷ αὐτόν;**

1 Cor 10:20   ἀλλ᾽ ὅτι ἃ **θύουσιν, δαιμονίοις καὶ οὐ θεῷ θύουσιν·**

Deut 32:17   **ἔθυσαν**   **δαιμονίοις καὶ οὐ θεῷ,**

1 Cor 10:22   ἢ   **παραζηλοῦμεν τὸν κύριον;**

Deut 32:21   αὐτοὶ   **παρεζήλωσάν**   **με**   ἐπ᾽ οὐ θεῷ,

1 Cor 10:26   τοῦ **κυρίου** γὰρ   ἡ γῆ **καὶ τὸ πλήρωμα αὐτῆς.**

Ps 23:1 LXX   τοῦ **κυρίου**   ἡ γῆ **καὶ τὸ πλήρωμα αὐτῆς,**

1 Cor 15:25   ἄχρι οὗ **θῇ** πάντας **τοὺς ἐχθροὺς**   **ὑπὸ**
                                                     τοὺς πόδας αὐτοῦ.

Ps 109:1 LXX   ἕως ἂν **θῶ**   **τοὺς ἐχθρούς** σου **ὑποπόδιον**
                                                 τῶν ποδῶν σου.

1 Cor 15:27   **πάντα** γὰρ **ὑπέταξεν**   **ὑπὸ**   **τοὺς πόδας αὐτοῦ.**

Ps 8:7 LXX   **πάντα**   **ὑπέταξας**   **ὑποκάτω τῶν ποδῶν αὐτοῦ,**

2 Corinthians

2 Cor 3:16   **ἡνίκα** δὲ ἐὰν <u>ἐπιστρέψῃ</u>   <u>πρὸς</u> **κύριον,**
                        περιαιρεῖται τὸ **κάλυμμα.**

Exod 34:34   **ἡνίκα** δ᾿ ἂν   <u>εἰσεπορεύετο</u> Μωυσῆς <u>ἔναντι</u> **κυρίου**
               λαλεῖν αὐτῷ, **περιῃρεῖτο**   τὸ **κάλυμμα**
                                  ἕως τοῦ ἐκπορεύεσθαι.

2 Cor 8:21   **προνοοῦμεν** γὰρ **καλὰ** οὐ μόνον   **ἐνώπιον κυρίου**
                        ἀλλὰ **καὶ** ἐνώπιον   **ἀνθρώπων.**

Prov 3:4   καὶ   **προνοοῦ**   **καλὰ**   **ἐνώπιον κυρίου**
                  καὶ   **ἀνθρώπων.**

Romans

Rom 10:13   **πᾶς** γὰρ **ὃς ἂν ἐπικαλέσηται τὸ ὄνομα κυρίου**
                                               σωθήσεται.

Joel 3:5 LXX   καὶ ἔσται **πᾶς**   **ὃς ἂν ἐπικαλέσηται τὸ ὄνομα κυρίου**
                                               σωθήσεται.

Rom 14:11   **ζῶ ἐγώ, λέγει κύριος**, **ὅτι ἐμοὶ κάμψει πᾶν γόνυ** καὶ **πᾶσα**
              γλῶσσα ἐξομολογήσεται   <u>τῷ θεῷ.</u>

Isa 49:18   **ζῶ ἐγώ, λέγει κύριος,**

Isa 45:23   **ὅτι ἐμοὶ κάμψει πᾶν γόνυ** καὶ
              ἐξομολογήσεται πᾶσα γλῶσσα <u>τῷ θεῷ.</u>

Ephesians

Eph 1:20   καὶ **καθίσας** ἐν **δεξιᾷ αὐτοῦ** ἐν τοῖς ἐπουρανίοις

Ps 109:1 LXX   εἶπεν ὁ κύριος τῷ κυρίῳ μου
         κάθου   **ἐκ δεξιῶν μου,**

Eph 4:8   **ἀναβὰς εἰς ὕψος ᾐχμαλώτευσεν αἰχμαλωσίαν,**
         ἔδωκεν **δόματα** τοῖς **ἀνθρώποις.**

Ps 67:19 LXX   **ἀνέβης εἰς ὕψος ᾐχμαλώτευσας αἰχμαλωσίαν,**
         ἔλαβες **δόματα** ἐν   **ἀνθρώπῳ.**

Philippians

Phil 2:10–11   [10]**πᾶν γόνυ κάμψῃ** ἐπουρανίων καὶ ἐπιγείων καὶ
                               καταχθονίων
         [11]**καὶ πᾶσα γλῶσσα ἐξομολογήσηται** ὅτι **κύριος**
                               Ἰησοῦς Χριστὸς

Isa 45:23   ὅτι ἐμοὶ   **κάμψει πᾶν γόνυ**
         καὶ ἐξομολογήσεται πᾶσα γλῶσσα τῷ θεῷ.

Phil 4:5b   **ὁ κύριος ἐγγύς.**

Ps 144:18 LXX   **ἐγγὺς κύριος**   πᾶσιν τοῖς ἐπικαλουμένοις αὐτόν,

Titus

Titus 2:14   ὃς ἔδωκεν ἑαυτὸν . . . ἵνα **λυτρώσηται** ἡμᾶς ἀπὸ
                πάσης   **ἀνομίας**
      καὶ καθαρίσῃ   ἑαυτῷ λαὸν περιούσιον,

Ps 129:8 LXX   καὶ   αὐτὸς   **λυτρώσεται** τὸν Ισραηλ ἐκ
         πασῶν τῶν   **ἀνομιῶν** αὐτοῦ.

Ezek 37:23   καὶ   ῥύσομαι αὐτοὺς ἀπὸ
         πασῶν τῶν   **ἀνομιῶν** αὐτῶν, . . . αὐταῖς,
      καὶ καθαριῶ αὐτούς, καὶ ἔσονταί **μοι εἰς λαόν,**

2 Timothy

2 Tim 2:7   **δώσει** γάρ σοι **ὁ κύριος**   **σύνεσιν** ἐν πᾶσιν.

Prov 2:6   ὅτι   **κύριος δίδωσιν** σοφίαν, . . . γνῶσις καὶ
                          σύνεσις·

2 Tim 2:19   ἔγνω κύριος τοὺς ὄντας αὐτοῦ,

Num 16:5   ἔγνω ὁ θεὸς τοὺς ὄντας αὐτοῦ

2 Tim 2:19   ἀποστήτω ἀπὸ ἀδικίας πᾶς ὁ ὀνομάζων   τὸ ὄνομα κυρίου.

Isa 26:13   κύριε, ἐκτὸς σοῦ ἄλλον οὐκ οἴδαμεν,   τὸ ὄνομά σου

                                      ὀνομάζομεν.

2 Tim 4:14   ἀποδώσει αὐτῷ ὁ κύριος κατὰ τὰ ἔργα αὐτοῦ·

Ps 61:13   κύριε, ... σὺ ἀποδώσεις ἑκάστῳ   κατὰ τὰ ἔργα αὐτοῦ.

Prov 24:12 κύριος ... ὃς ἀποδίδωσιν ἑκάστῳ   κατὰ τὰ ἔργα αὐτοῦ.

2 Tim 4:17   ὁ δὲ   κύριός μοι   παρέστη

Exod 34:5   καὶ κατέβη κύριος ... καὶ παρέστη αυτῷ ἐκεῖ·

Κύριος Phrases

1. ἐν λόγῳ κυρίου (1Thess 4:15, etc.) [by the word of the Lord]

2. ἡμέρα κυρίου (1 Thess 5:2, etc.) [the day of the Lord]

3. τὸ ὄνομα τοῦ κυρίου (1 Cor 1:2, etc.) [the name of the Lord]

4. κυρίου ἐντολή (1 Cor 14:37) [the command of the Lord]

5. τὸ πνεῦμα κυρίου (2 Cor 3:17) [the Spirit of the Lord]

6. ἡ δόξα κυρίου (2 Cor 3:18; 4:[4], 6) [the glory of the Lord]

7. ὁ φόβος τοῦ κυρίου (2 Cor 5:11) [the fear of the Lord]

Septuagint Citations Where Κύριος = God the Father

The following twelve citations of the Septuagint include the name Κύριος, where the reference is almost certainly to God the Father (which can be determined because Paul makes no point of the Divine Name, which sits as part of the text cited for other purposes); see especially the inclusion of the παντοκράτωρ in 2 Cor 6:18. The twelve texts, briefly mentioned in n. 7 in ch. 3, are given here for the sake of convenience.

1 Cor 3:20   κύριος γινώσκει τοὺς διαλογισμοὺς τῶν σοφῶν
              ὅτι εἰσὶν μάταιοι

Ps 93:11 LXX   κύριος γινώσκει τοὺς διαλογισμοὺς τῶν ἀνθρώπων
              ὅτι εἰσὶν μάταιοι

1 Cor 14:21   ἐν ἑτερογλώσσοις καὶ ἐν χείλεσιν ἑτέρων
          λαλήσω   τῷ λαῷ τούτῳ
             καὶ οὐδ᾽ οὕτως εἰσακούσονταί μου, λέγει κύριος.

Isa 28:11 LXX   διὰ φαυλισμὸν χειλέων διὰ γλώσσης ἑτέρας ὅτι
          λαλήσουσιν   τῷ λαῷ τούτῳ

2 Cor 6:17   διὸ ἐξέλθατε ἐκ μέσου αὐτῶν καὶ ἀφορίσθητε, λέγει κύριος,
             καὶ ἀκαθάρτου μὴ ἅπτεσθε·

Isa 52:11   ἐξέλθατε ἐκεῖθεν καὶ ἀκαθάρτου μὴ ἅπτεσθε ἐξέλθατε ἐκ
             μέσου αὐτῆς ἀφορίσθητε

2 Cor 6:18   καὶ ἔσομαι ὑμῖν εἰς πατέρα καὶ ὑμεῖς ἔσεσθέ μοι εἰς υἱοὺς
             καὶ θυγατέρας, λέγει κύριος παντοκράτωρ.

2 Sam 7:14   ἐγὼ ἔσομαι αὐτῷ εἰς πατέρα καὶ αὐτὸς ἔσται μοι εἰς υἱόν

Rom 4:8   μακάριος ἀνὴρ οὗ οὐ μὴ λογίσηται κύριος ἁμαρτίαν

Ps 31:2 LXX   μακάριος ἀνήρ οὗ οὐ μὴ λογίσηται κύριος ἁμαρτίαν

Rom 9:28   λόγον γὰρ συντελῶν καὶ συντέμνων ποιήσει κύριος
             ἐπὶ τῆς γῆς.

Isa 28:22   διότι συντετελεσμένα καὶ συντετμημένα πράγματα ἤκουσα
             παρὰ κυρίου σαβαωθ ἃ ποιήσει
             ἐπὶ πᾶσαν τὴν γῆν

Rom 9:29   εἰ μὴ κύριος σαβαὼθ ἐγκατέλιπεν ἡμῖν σπέρμα ὡς
             Σόδομα ἂν ἐγενήθημεν καὶ ὡς Γόμορρα ἂν ὡμοιώθημεν

Isa 1:9   καὶ εἰ μὴ κύριος σαβαωθ ἐγκατέλιπεν ἡμῖν σπέρμα ὡς
             Σοδομα ἂν ἐγενήθημεν καὶ ὡς Γομορρα ἂν ὡμοιώθημεν

Rom 10:16   κύριε, τίς ἐπίστευσεν τῇ ἀκοῇ ἡμῶν;

Isa 53:1   κύριε, τίς ἐπίστευσεν τῇ ἀκοῇ ἡμῶν;

Rom 11:3   κύριε, τοὺς προφήτας σου ἀπέκτειναν,
1 Kgs 19:10   τοὺς προφήτας σου ἀπέκτειναν,

Rom 11:34   τίς γὰρ ἔγνω νοῦν κυρίου; ἢ τίς σύμβουλος αὐτοῦ ἐγένετο;
Isa 40:13   τίς   ἔγνω νοῦν κυρίου, καὶ τίς αὐτοῦ σύμβουλος ἐγένετο,

Rom 12:19   ἐμοὶ ἐκδίκησις, ἐγὼ ἀνταποδώσω, λέγει κύριος
Deut 32:35   ἐν ἡμέρᾳ ἐκδικήσεως ἀνταποδώσω

Rom 15:11   αἰνεῖτε πάντα τὰ ἔθνη τὸν κύριον
Ps 116:1 LXX αἰνεῖτε τὸν κύριον πάντα τὰ ἔθνη

Bibliography

THIS BIBLIOGRAPHY INCLUDES WORKS CONSULTED, most of which are cited in footnotes.

I. Commentaries on the Pauline Epistles

A. 1–2 Thessalonians

Beale, G. K. *1–2 Thessalonians.* IVP New Testament Commentary 13. Downers Grove, Ill.: InterVarsity Press, 2003.

Best, Ernest. *A Commentary on the First and Second Epistles to the Thessalonians.* Harper's New Testament Commentaries. New York: Harper & Row, 1972.

Bruce, F. F. *1 and 2 Thessalonians.* Word Biblical Commentary 45. Waco, Tex.: Word, 1982.

Ellicott, Charles John. *Commentary on the Epistles of St. Paul to the Thessalonians.* 2d ed. 1861. Repr., Grand Rapids: Zondervan, 1957.

Findlay, G. G. *The Epistles of Paul the Apostle to the Thessalonians.* 1904. Repr., Grand Rapids: Baker, 1982.

Frame, James E. *A Critical and Exegetical Commentary on the Epistles of St. Paul to the Thessalonians.* International Critical Commentary. Edinburgh: T&T Clark, 1912.

Green, Gene L. *The Letters to the Thessalonians.* Pillar New Testament Commentary. Grand Rapids: Eerdmans, 2002.

Holmes, Michael W. *1 and 2 Thessalonians.* NIV Application Commentary. Grand Rapids: Zondervan, 1998.

Lightfoot, J. B. *Notes on Epistles of St. Paul from Unpublished Commentaries.* London: Macmillan, 1904.

Malherbe, Abraham J. *The Letters to the Thessalonians.* Anchor Bible 32B. New York: Doubleday, 2000.

Marshall, I. Howard. *1 and 2 Thessalonians.* New Century Bible. Grand Rapids: Eerdmans, 1983.

Milligan, George. *St. Paul's Epistles to the Thessalonians: The Greek Text with Introduction and Notes.* London: Macmillan, 1908.

Morris, Leon. *The First and Second Epistles to the Thessalonians.* 2d ed. New International Commentary on the New Testament. Grand Rapids: Eerdmans, 1991.

Richard, Earl J. *First and Second Thessalonians.* Sacra pagina 11. Collegeville, Minn.; Liturgical, 1995.

Rigaux, Béda. *Saint Paul: Les épîtres aux Thessaloniciens.* Études bibliques. Paris: Gabalda, 1956.

Wanamaker, Charles A. *The Epistle to the Thessalonians: A Commentary on the Greek Text.* New International Greek Testament Commentary. Grand Rapids: Eerdmans, 1990.

B. 1 Corinthians

Barrett, C. K. *The First Epistle to the Corinthians.* Harper's New Testament Commentaries. New York: Harper & Row, 1968.

Blomberg, Craig. *1 Corinthians.* NIV Application Commentary. Grand Rapids: Zondervan, 1994.

Collins, Raymond E. *First Corinthians.* Sacra pagina 7. Collegeville, Minn.: Liturgical, 1999.

Fee, Gordon D. *The First Epistle to the Corinthians.* New International Commentary on the New Testament. Grand Rapids: Eerdmans, 1987.

Garland, David. *1 Corinthians.* Baker Exegetical Commentary on the New Testament. Grand Rapids: Baker Academic, 2003.

Grosheide, F. W. *Commentary of the First Epistle to the Corinthians.* New International Commentary on the New Testament. Grand Rapids: Eerdmans, 1953.

Hays, Richard. *First Corinthians.* Interpretation. Louisville: John Knox, 1997.

Horsley, Richard A. *1 Corinthians.* Abingdon New Testament Commentaries. Nashville: Abingdon, 1998.

Keener, Craig S. *1–2 Corinthians.* New Cambridge Bible Commentary. Cambridge: Cambridge University Press, 2005.

Thiselton, Anthony T. *The First Epistle to the Corinthians: A Commentary on the Greek Text.* New International Greek Testament Commentary. Grand Rapids: Eerdmans, 2000.

Witherington, Ben, III. *Conflict and Community in Corinth: A Socio-Rhetorical Commentary on 1 and 2 Corinthians.* Grand Rapids: Eerdmans, 1995.

C. 2 Corinthians

Barnett, Paul W. *The Second Epistle to the Corinthians.* New International Commentary on the New Testament. Grand Rapids: Eerdmans, 1997.

Barrett, C. K. *A Commentary on the Second Epistle to the Corinthians.* Black's New Testament Commentary. Peabody, Mass.: Hendrickson, 1973.

Betz, Hans Dieter. *2 Corinthians 8 and 9: A Commentary on Two Administrative Letters of the Apostle Paul.* Edited by G. W. MacRae. Hermeneia. Philadelphia: Fortress, 1985.

Bruce, F. F. *1 and 2 Corinthians.* New Century Bible. Grand Rapids: Eerdmans, 1971.

Bultmann, Rudolf. *The Second Letter to the Corinthians.* Translated by R. A. Harrisville. Minneapolis: Augsburg, 1985.

Carson, Donald A. *From Triumphalism to Maturity: An Exposition of 2 Corinthians 10–13.* Grand Rapids: Baker, 1988.

Collange, J.-F. *Énigmes de la deuxième épître de Paul aux Corinthiens: Étude exégétique de 2 Cor 2:14–7:4.* Society for New Testament Studies Monograph Series 18. Cambridge: Cambridge University Press, 1972.

Furnish, Victor P. *II Corinthians.* Anchor Bible 32A. Garden City, N.Y.: Doubleday, 1984.

Harris, Murray L. *The Second Epistle to the Corinthians.* New International Greek Testament Commentary. Grand Rapids: Eerdmans, 2005.

Héring, Jean. *La seconde épître de Saint Paul aux Corinthiens.* Commentaire du Nouveau Testament 8. Neuchâtel: Delachaux & Niestlé, 1958.

Hughes, Philip E. *Paul's Second Epistle to the Corinthians.* New International Commentary on the New Testament. Grand Rapids: Eerdmans, 1962.

Lambrecht, Jan. *Second Corinthians.* Sacra pagina 8. Collegeville, Minn.: Liturgical, 1999.

Martin, Ralph P. *2 Corinthians.* Word Biblical Commentary 40. Waco, Tex.: Word, 1986.

Matera, Frank J. *II Corinthians.* New Testament Library. Louisville: Westminster John Knox, 2003.

Plummer, Alfred. *A Critical and Exegetical Commentary on the Second Epistle of St. Paul to the Corinthians.* International Critical Commentary. Edinburgh: T&T Clark, 1915.

Strachan, R. H. *The Second Epistle of Paul to the Corinthians.* Moffat New Testament Commentary. London: Hodder & Stoughton, 1935.

Tasker, R. V. G. *The Second Epistle of Paul to the Corinthians: An Introduction and Commentary.* Tyndale New Testament Commentaries. London: Tyndale, 1958.

Thrall, Margaret. *A Critical and Exegetical Commentary on the Second Epistle to the Corinthians.* 2 vols. International Critical Commentary. Edinburgh: T&T Clark, 1994–2000.

Windisch, Hans. *Der zweite Brief des Paulus an die Korinther.* 9th ed. Kritischexegetischer Kommentar über das Neue Testament. Göttingen: Vandenhoeck & Ruprecht, 1970.

D. Galatians

Betz, Hans Dieter. *Galatians.* Hermeneia; Philadelphia: Fortress, 1979.

Bruce, F. F. *The Epistle of Paul to the Galatians: A Commentary on the Greek Text.* New International Greek Testament Commentary. Grand Rapids: Eerdmans, 1982.

Burton, E. D. *A Critical and Exegetical Commentary on the Epistle to the Galatians.* International Critical Commentary. Edinburgh: T&T Clark, 1921.

Dunn, James D. G. *The Epistle to the Galatians.* Black's New Testament Commentary. Peabody, Mass.: Hendrickson, 1993.

Fung, R. Y. K. *Galatians.* New International Commentary on the New Testament. Grand Rapids: Eerdmans, 1988.

Hansen, G. Walter. *Galatians.* IVP New Testament Commentary 9. Downers Grove, Ill.: InterVarsity Press, 1994.

Lightfoot, J. B. *The Epistle of St. Paul to the Galatians.* Rev. ed. 1865. Repr., Grand Rapids: Zondervan, 1957.

Longenecker, Richard N. *Galatians.* Word Biblical Commentary 41. Dallas: Word, 1990.

Martyn, Louis. *Galatians.* Anchor Bible 33A. New York: Doubleday, 1997.

Matera, Frank J. *Galatians.* Sacra pagina 9. Collegeville, Minn: Liturgical, 1992.

Morris, Leon. *Galatians: Paul's Charter of Christian Freedom.* Downers Grove, Ill.: InterVarsity Press, 1996.

E. Romans

Achtemeier, Paul J. *Romans.* Interpretation. Atlanta: John Knox, 1985.

Barrett. C. K. *A Commentary on the Epistle to the Romans.* Black's New Testament Commentary. Peabody, Mass.: Hendrickson, 1971.

Barth, Karl. *The Epistle to the Romans.* Translated by E. C. Hoskyns. London: Oxford University Press, 1968.

Byrne, Brendan. *Romans.* Sacra pagina 6. Collegeville, Minn.: Liturgical, 1996.

Cranfield, C. E. B. *A Critical and Exegetical Commentary on the Epistle to the Romans.* 2 vols. 6th ed. International Critical Commentary. Edinburgh: T&T Clark, 1975–1979.

Denney, James. "St. Paul's Epistle to the Romans." Pages 556–725 in vol. 2 of *The Expositor's Greek Testament.* Edited by W. R. Nicoll. 5 vols. 1897–1910. Repr., Grand Rapids: Eerdmans, 1976.

Dunn, James D. G. *Romans.* 2 vols. Word Biblical Commentary 38A, 38B. Dallas: Word, 1988.

Fitzmyer, Joseph A. *Romans.* Anchor Bible 33. New York: Doubleday, 1993.

Godet, Frederic L. *Commentary on the Epistle to the Romans.* Translated by A. Cusin. 1883. Repr., Grand Rapids: Zondervan, 1951.

Hendriksen, William. *Romans.* 2 vols. New Testament Commentary. Edinburgh: Banner of Truth Trust. 1980–1981.

Hodge, Charles. *Commentary on the Epistle to the Romans.* 1835. Repr., Grand Rapids: Eerdmans, 1969.

Käsemann, Ernst. *Commentary on Romans*. Translated by G. W. Bromiley. Grand Rapids: Eerdmans, 1980.

Lietzmann, Hans. *An die Römer: Einführung in die Textgeschichte der Paulus-briefe*. 5th ed. Handbuch zum Neuen Testament 8. Tübingen: Mohr Siebeck, 1971.

Lightfoot, J. B. *Notes on the Epistles of St. Paul*. 1895. Rev. ed. Grand Rapids: Zondervan, 1957.

Moo, Douglas J. *The Epistle to the Romans*. New International Commentary on the New Testament. Grand Rapids: Eerdmans, 1996.

Morris, Leon. *The Epistle to the Romans*. Grand Rapids: Eerdmans, 1988.

Murray, John. *The Epistle to the Romans*. New International Commentary on the New Testament. Grand Rapids: Eerdmans, 1965.

Sanday, William, and Arthur C. Headlam. *A Critical and Exegetical Commentary on the Epistle to the Romans*. 5th ed. International Critical Commentary. Edinburgh: T&T Clark, 1911.

Schlatter, Adolf. *Romans: The Righteousness of God*. Translated by S. S. Schatzmann. Peabody, Mass.: Hendrickson, 1995.

Schreiner, Thomas R. *Romans*. Baker Exegetical Commentary on the New Testament. Grand Rapids: Baker, 1998.

Stuhlmacher, Peter. *Paul's Letter to the Romans: A Commentary*. Translated by S. J. Hafemann. Louisville: Westminster John Knox, 1994.

Ziesler, John. *Paul's Letter to the Romans*. Philadelphia: Trinity Press International, 1989.

F. Colossians

Barth, Markus, and Helmut Blanke. *Colossians*. Translated by A. B. Beck. Anchor Bible 34B. New York: Doubleday, 1994.

Bruce, F. F. *The Epistles to the Colossians, to Philemon, and to the Ephesians*. New International Commentary on the New Testament. Grand Rapids: Eerdmans, 1984.

Dunn, J. D. G. *The Epistles to the Colossians and to Philemon: A Commentary on the Greek Text*. New International Greek Testament Commentary. Grand Rapids: Eerdmans, 1996.

Eadie, J. *Commentary on the Epistle of Paul to the Colossians*. 1883. Repr., Grand Rapids: Zondervan, 1957.

Garland, David E. *Colossians and Philemon*. NIV Application Commentary. Grand Rapids: Zondervan, 1998.

Haupt, Erich. *Die Gefangenschaftsbriefe*. Kritisch-exegetischer Kommentar über das Neue Testament 8. Göttingen: Vandenhoeck & Ruprecht, 1902.

Hendriksen, William. *New Testament Commentary: Exposition of Colossians and Philemon*. Grand Rapids: Baker, 1964.

Lightfoot, J. B. *St. Paul's Epistles to the Colossians and to Philemon*. 3d ed. London: Macmillan, 1879.

Lohse, Eduard. *Colossians and Philemon.* Hermeneia. Philadelphia: Fortress, 1971.

MacDonald, Margaret Y. *Colossians and Ephesians.* Sacra pagina 17. Collegeville, Minn.: Liturgical, 2000.

Martin, Ralph P. *Colossians and Philemon.* New Century Bible. London: Oliphants, 1974.

Moule, H. C. G. *Colossian Studies.* London: Hodder & Stoughton, 1902.

O'Brien, P. T. *Colossians, Philemon.* Word Biblical Commentary 44. Waco, Tex.: Word, 1982.

Pokorný, Petr. *Colossians: A Commentary.* Peabody, Mass.: Hendrickson, 1991.

Schweizer, Eduard. *The Letter to the Colossians.* Translated by A. Chester. London: SPCK, 1982.

Wright, N. T. *Colossians and Philemon.* Tyndale New Testament Commentaries. Grand Rapids: Eerdmans, 1986.

G. Ephesians

Abbott, T. K. *A Critical and Exegetical Commentary on the Epistles to the Ephesians and to the Colossians.* International Critical Commentary. Edinburgh: T&T Clark, 1897.

Alford, Henry. *The Greek Testament.* 4 vols. 1845–1860. Repr., 4 vols. in 2.. Chicago: Moody, 1958.

Barth, Markus. *Ephesians.* 2 vols. Anchor Bible 34, 34A. Garden City, N.Y.: Doubleday, 1974.

Best, Ernest. *A Critical and Exegetical Commentary on Ephesians.* International Critical Commentary. Edinburgh: T&T Clark, 1998.

Bruce, F. F. *The Epistles to the Colossians, to Philemon, and to the Ephesians.* New International Commentary on the New Testament, Grand Rapids: Eerdmans, 1984.

Eadie, J. A. *A Commentary of the Greek Text of the Epistle of Paul to the Ephesians.* 3d ed. Edinburgh: T&T Clark, 1883.

Ellicott, C. J. *A Critical and Grammatical Commentary on the Epistle to the Ephesians.* 4th ed. Andover, Mass.: W. F. Draper, 1865.

Hendriksen, W. *Ephesians.* New Testament Commentary. Grand Rapids: Baker, 1967.

Hoehner, Harold W. *Ephesians: An Exegetical Commentary.* Grand Rapids: Baker, 2002.

Lincoln, Andrew T. *Ephesians.* Word Biblical Commentary 42. Dallas: Word, 1990.

MacDonald, Margaret Y. *Colossians and Ephesians.* Sacra pagina 17. Collegeville, Minn.: Liturgical, 2000.

Mitton, C. L. *Ephesians.* New Century Bible. London: Oliphants, 1976.

O'Brien, Peter T. *The Letter to the Ephesians.* Pillar New Testament Commentary. Grand Rapids: Eerdmans, 1999.

Robinson, J. Armitage. *St. Paul's Epistle to the Ephesians*. London: Macmillan, 1904.

Scott, Ernest F. *The Epistles to the Colossians, to Philemon, and to the Ephesians*. London: Hodder & Stoughton, 1930.

Snodgrass, Klyne. *Ephesians*. NIV Application Commentary. Grand Rapids: Zondervan, 1996.

Westcott, B. F. *Saint Paul's Epistle to the Ephesians*. London: Macmillan, 1906.

H. Philippians

Barth, Karl. *The Epistle to the Philippians*. Translated by J. W. Leitch. London: SCM Press, 1962.

Beare, Francis Wright. *The Epistle to the Philippians*. 3d ed. Black's New Testament Commentary. London: A. & C. Black, 1973.

Bockmuehl, M. *Philippians*. Black's New Testament Commentary. Peabody, Mass.: Hendrickson, 1997.

Bruce, F. F. *Philippians*. New International Biblical Commentary. Peabody, Mass.: Hendrickson, 1989.

Caird, George B. *Paul's Letters from Prison*. New Century Bible. Oxford: Oxford University Press, 1976.

Calvin, J. *The Epistles of Paul the Apostle to the Galatians, Ephesians, Philippians and Colossians*. Vol. 11 of *Commentaries*. Translated by T. H. L. Parker. Edited by D. W. Torrance and T. F. Torrance. Edinburgh: Oliver & Boyd, 1965.

Collange, Jean-François. *The Epistle of Saint Paul to the Philippians*. Translated by A. W. Heathcote. London: Epworth, 1979.

Craddock, Fred B. *Philippians*. Interpretation. Louisville: Westminster John Knox, 1984.

Dibelius, Martin. *An die Thessalonicher I, II; An die Philipper.* 3d ed. Handbuch zum Neuen Testament 11. Tübingen: Mohr Siebeck, 1937.

Ellicott, C. J. *A Critical and Grammatical Commentary on St. Paul's Epistles to the Philippians, Colossians, and to Philemon.* Andover, Mass.: Warren F. Draper, 1876.

Fee, Gordon D. *Paul's Letter to the Philippians*. New International Commentary on the New Testament. Grand Rapids: Eerdmans, 1995.

Fowl, Stephen. *A Commentary on Philippians*. Two Horizons New Testament Commentary. Grand Rapids: Eerdmans, 2005.

Gnilka, Joachim. *Der Philipperbrief.* Herders theologischer Kommentar zum Neuen Testament. Freiburg: Herder, 1968.

Hawthorne, Gerald F. *Philippians*. Word Biblical Commentary 43. Waco, Tex: Word, 1983.

Hendriksen, William. *Philippians*. New Testament Commentary. Grand Rapids: Baker, 1962.

Houlden, J. L. *Paul's Letters from Prison: Philippians, Colossians, Philemon, Ephesians*. Pelican New Testament Commentaries. Philadelphia: Westminster, 1977.

Jones, Maurice. *Philippians.* Westminster Commentaries. London: Methuen, 1918.

Kennedy, H. A. A. "The Epistle to the Philippians." Pages 398–473 in vol. 3 of *The Expositor's Greek Testament.* Edited by W. R. Nicoll. Repr., Grand Rapids: Eerdmans, 1976.

Kent, Homer H. "Philippians." Pages 95–159 in vol. 11 of *The Expositor's Bible Commentary.* Edited by F. E. Gaebelein. 12 vols. Grand Rapids: Zondervan, 1979–1992.

Lightfoot, J. B. *Saint Paul's Epistle to the Philippians.* 4th ed. London: Macmillan, 1896.

Lohmeyer, Ernst. *Die Briefe an die Philipper, an die Kolosser und an Philemon.* 13th ed. Kritisch-exegetischer Kommentar über das Neue Testament 9. Göttingen: Vandenhoeck & Ruprecht, 1964.

Martin, Ralph P. *The Epistle of Paul to the Philippians.* Rev. ed. Tyndale New Testament Commentaries. Grand Rapids: Eerdmans, 1987.

Melick, R. R. *Philippians, Colossians, Philemon.* New American Commentary 32. Nashville: Broadman, 1991.

Meyer, H. A. W. *Critical and Exegetical Handbook to the Epistles to the Philippians and Colossians.* Translated by J. C. Moore and W. P. Dickson. New York: Funk & Wagnalls, 1875.

Michael, J. Hugh. *The Epistle of Paul to the Philippians.* Moffat New Testament Commentary. London: Hodder & Stoughton, 1936.

Müller, Jacobus J. *The Epistles of Paul to the Philippians and to Philemon.* New International Commentary on the New Testament. Grand Rapids: Eerdmans, 1955.

O'Brien, Peter T. *Commentary on Philippians.* New International Greek Testament Commentary. Grand Rapids: Eerdmans, 1991.

Plummer, Alfred. *A Commentary on St. Paul's Epistle to the Philippians.* London: Macmillan, 1919.

Silva, Moisés. *Philippians.* Baker Exegetical Commentary on the New Testament. Grand Rapids: Baker, 1992.

Vincent, M. R. *A Critical and Exegetical Commentary on the Epistles to the Philippians and to Philemon.* International Critical Commentary. Edinburgh: T&T Clark, 1897.

I. The Pastoral Epistles

Bernard, J. H. *The Pastoral Epistles.* Cambridge Greek Testament for Schools and Colleges. Cambridge: Cambridge University Press, 1899.

Collins, Raymond F. *I and II Timothy and Titus: A Commentary.* New Testament Library. Louisville: Westminster John Knox, 2002.

Dibelius, M., and H. Conzelmann. *The Pastoral Epistles.* Hermeneia. Philadelphia: Fortress, 1972.

Fairbairn, Patrick. *The Pastoral Epistles.* 1874. Repr., Grand Rapids: Zondervan, 1956.

Fee, Gordon D. *1 and 2 Timothy, Titus.* New International Biblical Commentary. Peabody, Mass.: Hendrickson, 1989.

Hanson, Anthony T. *The Pastoral Epistles.* New Century Bible Commentary. London: Marshall, Morgan & Scott, 1982.

Johnson, Luke Timothy. *The First and Second Letters to Timothy.* Anchor Bible 35B. New York: Doubleday, 2001.

Kelly, J. N. D. *A Commentary on the Pastoral Epistles.* Black's New Testament Commentary. Peabody, Mass.: Hendrickson, 1963.

Knight, George W., III. *Commentary on the Pastoral Epistles.* New International Greek Testament Commentary. Grand Rapids: Eerdmans, 1992.

Lea, T. D., and H. P. Griffin Jr. *1, 2 Timothy, Titus.* New American Commentary 34. Nashville: Broadman. 1992.

Lock, Walter. *A Critical and Exegetical Commentary on the Pastoral Epistles.* International Critical Commentary. Edinburgh: T&T Clark, 1924.

Marshall, I. Howard. *A Critical and Exegetical Commentary on the Pastoral Epistles.* International Critical Commentary. London: T&T Clark, 1999.

Mounce, William D. *The Pastoral Epistles.* Word Biblical Commentary 46. Dallas: Word, 1997.

Quinn, J. D. *The Letter to Titus.* Anchor Bible 35. New York: Doubleday, 1990.

Quinn, J. D., and W. C. Wacker. *The First and Second Letters to Timothy.* Eerdmans Critical Commentary. Grand Rapids: Eerdmans, 1999.

Scott, Ernest F. *The Pastoral Epistles.* Moffat New Testament Commentary. London: Hodder & Stoughton, 1936.

Spicq, C. *Saint Paul: Les épîtres pastorales.* 2 vols. in 1. 4th ed. Études bibliques. Paris: Gabalda, 1969.

Towner, Philip H. *The Letters to Timothy and Titus.* New International Commentary on the New Testament. Grand Rapids: Eerdmans, 2006.

II. Other Works

Abbott, E. A. *Johannine Grammar.* London: A. & C. Black, 1906.

Achtemeier, P. J. "*Omne verbum sonat:* The New Testament and the Oral Development of Late Western Antiquity." *Journal of Bibilical Literature* 109 (1990): 3–27.

Arnold, Clinton E. *The Colossian Syncretism: The Interface between Christianity and Folk Belief at Colossae.* Grand Rapids: Baker, 1996.

Aus, R. "The Relevance of Isaiah 66:7 to Revelation 12 and 2 Thessalonians 2." *Zeitschrift für die neutestamentliche Wissenschaft und die Kunde der älteren Kirche* 67 (1976): 252–68.

Baillie, Donald. *God Was in Christ: An Essay on Incarnation and Atonement.* London: Faber & Faber, 1961.

Balchin, J. F. "Colossians 1:15–20: An Early Christian Hymn? The Argument from Style." *Vox evangelica* 15 (1985): 65–93.

Bandstra, Andrew J. "'Adam' and 'The Servant' in Philippians 2:5ff." *Calvin Theological Journal* 1 (1966): 213–16.

Barclay, John M. G. *Obeying the Truth: A Study of Paul's Ethics in Galatians.* Edinburgh: T&T Clark, 1988.

———. "Ordinary but Different: Colossians and Hidden Moral Identity." *Australian Biblical Review* 49 (2001): 34–52.

Barr, James. "'Abba, Father' and the Familiarity of Jesus' Speech." *Theology* 91 (1988): 173–79.

———. "'Abba' Isn't 'Daddy.'" *Journal of Theological Studies* 39 (1988): 28–47.

Barrett, C. K. *Paul: An Introduction to His Thought.* Louisville: Westminster John Knox, 1994.

Bassler, Jouette M. "A Plethora of Epiphanies: Christology in the Pastoral Letters." *Princeton Seminary Bulletin* 17 (1996): 310–25.

Bauckham, R. "The Sonship of the Historical Jesus in Christology." *Scottish Journal of Theology* 31 (1978): 245–60.

———. *God Crucified: Monotheism and Christology in the New Testament.* Grand Rapids: Eerdmans, 1999.

Baugh, S. M. "The Poetic Form of Col 1:15–20." *Westminster Theological Journal* 47 (1985): 227–44.

Baumgarten, J. *Paulus und die Apokalyptik: Die Auslegung apokalyptischer Überlieferungen in den echten Paulusbriefen.* Wissenschaftliche Monographien zum Alten und Neuen Testament 44. Neukirchen-Vluyn: Neukirchener Verlag, 1975.

Becker, J. "Erwägungen zu Phil. 3,20–21." *Theologische Zeitschrift* 27 (1971): 16–29.

Behm, J. "μορφή." Pages 759–62 in vol. 4 of *Theological Dictionary of the New Testament.* Edited by G. Kittel and G. Friedrich. Translated by G. W. Bromiley. 10 vols. Grand Rapids: Eerdmans, 1964–1976.

Behr, J. "Colossians 1:13–20: A Chiastic Reading." *St. Vladimir's Theological Quarterly* 40 (1966): 247–64.

Beker, J. Christiaan. *Paul the Apostle: The Triumph of God in Life and Thought.* Philadelphia: Fortress, 1980.

Belleville, Linda L. *Reflections of Glory: Paul's Use of the Moses-Doxa Tradition in 2 Corinthians 3.1–18.* Journal for the Study of the New Testament: Supplement Series 52. Sheffield: Sheffield Academic Press, 1991.

Benoit, P. "Body, Head and *pleroma* in the Epistles of the Captivity." Pages 51–92 in vol. 2 of *Jesus and the Gospel.* Translated by B. Weatherhead. 2 vols. London: Darton, Longman & Todd, 1973–1974.

Black, Matthew. "The Pauline Doctrine of the Second Adam." *Scottish Journal of Theology* 7 (1954): 70–79.

———. "The Christological Use of the Old Testament in the New Testament." *New Testament Studies* 18 (1971–1972): 1–14.

Bornkamm, G. "Zum Verständnis des Christus-Hymnus, Phil. 2.6–11." Pages 177–87 in *Studien zu Antike und Urchristentum.* Beiträge zur evangelischen Theologie 28. Munich: Kaiser, 1959.

Bousset, W. *Kyrios Christos: A History of the Belief in Christ from the Beginnings of Christianity to Irenaeus.* Translated by J. E. Steely. Nashville: Abingdon, 1970.

Brandenburger, E. *Adam und Christus: Exegetisch-religionsgeschichtliche Untersuchung zu Röm. 5, 12-21 (1.Kor 15).* Wissenschaftliche Monographien zum Alten und Neuen Testament 7. Neukirchen-Vluyn: Neukirchener Verlag, 1962.

Buchanan, George W. "Jesus and the Upper Class." *Novum Testamentum 7* (1964): 195–209.

Bugg, Charles. "Philippians 4:4–13." *Review and Expositor* 88 (1991): 253–57.

Bultmann, Rudolf. *Jesus and the Word.* Translated by L. P. Smith and E. Huntress. New York: Charles Scribner's Sons, 1934.

———. *Theology of the New Testament.* 2 vols. New York: Charles Scribner's Sons, 1952–1955.

Burkitt, F. C. "On Romans ix 5 and Mark xiv 61." *Journal of Theological Studies* 5 (1904): 451–55.

Burton, Ernest de Witt. *Syntax of the Moods and Tenses in New Testament Greek.* 3d ed. Edinburgh: T&T Clark, 1898.

Byrne, Brendan. "Christ's Pre-existence in Pauline Soteriology." *Theological Studies* 58 (1997): 308–30.

Caird, G. B. "The Descent of the Spirit in Ephesians 4:7–11." Pages 535–45 in *Studia evangelica II.* Edited by F. L. Cross. Texte und Untersuchungen zur Geschichte der altchristlichen Literatur 87. Berlin: Akadamie, 1964.

Capes, D. B. *Old Testament Yahweh Texts in Paul's Christology.* Wissenschaftliche Untersuchungen zum Neuen Testament 2/47. Tübingen: Mohr Siebeck, 1992.

Carmignac, Jean. "L'importance de la place d'une négation: ΟΥΧ ΑΡΠΑΓΜΟΝ ΗΓΗΣΑΤΟ (Philippiens II.6)." *New Testament Studies* 18 (1971–1972): 131–66.

Carr, Wesley. *Angels and Principalities: The Background, Meaning and Development of the Pauline Phrase "Hai Archai kai Hai Exousiai."* Society for New Testament Studies Monograph Series 42. Cambridge: Cambridge University Press, 1981.

Carson D. A. *Exegetical Fallacies.* 2d ed. Grand Rapids: Baker, 1996.

Carson, D. A., Douglas J. Moo, and Leon Morris. *An Introduction to the New Testament.* Grand Rapids: Zondervan, 1992.

Casey, Maurice. "Monotheism, Worship and Christological Developments in the Pauline Churches." Pages 214–33 in *The Jewish Roots of Christological Monotheism: Papers from the St. Andrews Conference on the Historical Origins of the Worship of Jesus.* Edited by C. C. Newman, J. R. Davila, and G. S. Lewis. Supplements to the Journal for the Study of Judaism 63. Leiden: Brill, 1999.

Cerfaux, Lucien. "'Kyrios' dans les citations pauliniennes de l'Ancien Testament." *Ephemerides theologicae lovanienses* 20 (1943): 5–17.

————. "L'hymne au Christ-Serviteur de Dieu (Phil 2,6–11 = Is 52,13–53,12)." Pages 425–37 in vol. 2 of *Recueil Lucien Cerfaux: Études d'exégèse et d'histoire religieuse.* 2 vols. Bibliotheca ephemeridum theologicarum lovaniensium. Leuven: Peeters, 1954.

————. *Christ in the Theology of St. Paul.* Translated by G. Webb and A. Walker. New York: Herder & Herder, 1959.

Chester, A. "Jewish Messianic Expectations and Mediatorial Figures and Pauline Christianity." Pages 17–89 in *Paulus und antike Judentum.* Edited by M. Hengel and U. Heckel. Wissenschaftliche Untersuchungen zum Neuen Testament 58. Tübingen: Mohr Siebeck, 1991.

Cheung, A. T. *Idol Food in Corinth: Jewish Background and Pauline Legacy.* Journal for the Study of the New Testament: Supplement Series 176. Sheffield: Sheffield Academic Press, 1999.

Collins, Raymond F. "Paul's Early Christology." Pages 253–84 in *Studies on the First Letter to the Thessalonians.* Bibliotheca ephemeridum theologicarum lovaniensium 66. Leuven: Leuven University Press, 1984.

————. "The Theology of Paul's First Letter to the Thessalonians." Pages 230–52 in *Studies on the First Letter to the Thessalonians.* Bibliotheca ephemeridum theologicarum lovaniensium 66. Leuven: Leuven University Press, 1984.

Clayton, A. L. "The Orthodox Recovery of a Heretical Proof-Text: Athanasius of Alexandria's Interpretation of Proverbs 8:22–30 in Conflict with the Arians." PhD diss. Southern Methodist University, 1988.

Craddock, F. *The Pre-Existence of Christ in the New Testament.* Nashville: Abingdon, 1968.

Cullmann, Oscar. *Die Christologie des Neuen Testaments.* Tübingen: Mohr Siebeck, 1957. ET, *The Christology of the New Testament.* Translated by S. C. Guthrie and C. A. M. Hall. Philadelphia: Westminster, 1959.

Dahl, Nils A. *Jesus the Christ: The Historical Origins of Christological Doctrine.* Minneapolis: Fortress, 1991.

Dahl, Nils A., and Alan Segal. "Philo and the Rabbis on the Names of God." *Journal for the Study of Judaism in the Persian, Hellenistic, and Roman Periods* 9 (1979): 1–28.

Davis, J. A. *Wisdom and Spirit: An Investigation of 1 Corinthians 1.18–3.20 against the Background of Jewish Sapiential Traditions in the Greco-Roman Period.* Lanham, Md.: University Press of America, 1984.

Dean, H. "Christ's True Glory." *Expository Times* 71 (1960): 189–90.

deLacey, D. R. " 'One Lord' in Pauline Christology." Pages 191–203 in *Christ the Lord: Studies in Christology Presented to Donald Guthrie.* Edited by H. H. Rowdon. Leicester: Inter-Varsity Press, 1982.

Deissmann, Adolf. *Die neutestamentliche Formel "In Christo Jesu."* Marburg: N. G. Elwert, 1892.

————. *Light from the Ancient East: The New Testament Illustrated by Recently Discovered Texts from the Greco-Roman World.* Translated by L. R. M. Strachan. London: Hodder & Stoughton, 1910.

Dodd, C. H. "The History and Doctrine of the Apostolic Age." Pages 390–417 in *A Companion to the Bible*. Edited by T. W. Manson. Edinburgh: T&T Clark, 1947.

Donfried, K. P. *Paul, Thessalonica, and Early Christians*. Grand Rapids: Eerdmans, 2002.

Donfried, K. P., and I. H. Marshall. *The Theology of the Shorter Pauline Letters*. New Testament Theology. Cambridge: Cambridge University Press, 1993.

Dunn, James D. G. "2 Corinthians iii.17—'The Lord Is the Spirit.'" *Journal of Theological Studies* 21 (1970): 309–20.

———. "1 Corinthians 15:45—Last Adam, Life-Giving Spirit." Pages 127–41 in *Christ and Spirit in the New Testament: Studies in Honour of Charles Francis Digby Moule*. Edited by B. Lindars and S. S. Smalley. London: Cambridge University Press, 1973.

———. "Jesus—Flesh and Spirit: An Exposition of Romans i:3–4." *Journal of Theological Studies* 24 (1973): 40–68.

———. *Christology in the Making: A New Testament Inquiry into the Origins of the Doctrine of the Incarnation*. 2d ed. Grand Rapids: Eerdmans, 1989.

———. "Once More, ΠΙΣΤΙΣ ΧΡΙΣΤΟΥ." Pages 730–44 in *The Society of Biblical Literature 1991 Seminar Papers*. Society of Biblical Literature Seminar Papers 30. Edited by E. H. Lovering Jr. Atlanta: Scholars Press, 1991.

———. "Prayer." Pages 617–25 in *Dictionary of Jesus and the Gospels*. Edited by J. B. Green and S. McKnight. Downers Grove, Ill.: InterVarsity Press, 1992.

———. *The Theology of Paul the Apostle*. Grand Rapids: Eerdmans, 1998.

———. *A New Perspective on Jesus: What the Quest for the Historical Jesus Missed*. Grand Rapids: Baker Academic, 2005.

Durham, J. *Exodus*. Word Biblical Commentary 3. Dallas: Word, 1987.

Elliott, J. K. *The Greek Text of the Epistles to Timothy and Titus*. Studies and Documents 36. Salt Lake City: University of Utah Press, 1968.

Ellis, E. Earle. *Paul's Use of the Old Testament*. Edinburgh: Oliver & Boyd, 1957. Repr., Grand Rapids: Baker, 1981.

Eriksson, A. *Traditions as Rhetorical Proof: Pauline Argumentation in 1 Corinthians*. Coniectanea biblica: New Testament Series 29. Stockholm: Almqvist & Wiksell, 1998.

Evans, Craig A. "Ascending and Descending with a Shout: Psalm 47.6 and 1 Thessalonians 4.16." Pages 238–53 in *Paul and the Scriptures of Israel*. Edited by C. A. Evans and J. A. Sanders. Journal for the Study of the New Testament: Supplement Series 83. Sheffield: Sheffield Academic Press, 1993.

Fee, Gordon D. *God's Empowering Presence: The Holy Spirit in the Letters of Paul*. Peabody, Mass.: Hendrickson, 1994.

———. *Paul, the Spirit and the People of God*. Peabody, Mass.: Hendrickson, 1996.

———. "Paul and the Trinity: The Experience of Christ and the Spirit for Paul's Understanding of God." Pages 49–72 in *The Trinity: An Interdisciplinary*

Symposium on the Trinity. Edited by S. T. Davis, D. Kendall, and G. O'Collins. Oxford: Oxford University Press, 1999.

———. "ΧΑΡΙΣ in 2 Corinthians 1:15: Apostolic Parousia and Paul-Corinth Chronology." Pages 99–104 in *To What End Exegesis? Essays Textual, Exegetical, and Theological.* Grand Rapids: Eerdmans, 2001.

———. "Christology and Pneumatology in Romans 8:9–11—and Elsewhere: Some Reflections on Paul as a Trinitarian." Pages 218–39 in *To What End Exegesis? Essays Textual, Exegetical, and Theological.* Grand Rapids: Eerdmans, 2001.

———. "2 Corinthians 6:14–7:1 and Food Offered to Idols." Pages 142–43 in *To What End Exegesis? Essays Textual, Exegetical, and Theological.* Grand Rapids: Eerdmans, 2001.

———. "Εἰδωλόθυτα Once Again—An Interpretation of 1 Corinthians 8–10." Pages 105–28 in *To What End Exegesis? Essays Textual, Exegetical, and Theological.* Grand Rapids: Eerdmans, 2001.

———. "Philippians 2:5–11: Hymn or Exalted Pauline Prose?" Pages 175–91 in *To What End Exegesis? Essays Textual, Exegetical, and Theological.* Grand Rapids: Eerdmans, 2001.

———. "Pneuma and Eschatology in 2 Thessalonians 2:1–2: A Proposal about 'Testing the Prophets' and the Purpose of 2 Thessalonians." Pages 290–308 in *To What End Exegesis? Essays Textual, Exegetical, and Theological.* Grand Rapids: Eerdmans, 2001.

———. "Textual-Exegetical Observations on 1 Corinthians 1:2, 2:1, and 2:10." Pages 43–56 in *To What End Exegesis? Essays Textual, Exegetical, and Theological.* Grand Rapids: Eerdmans, 2001.

———. *To What End Exegesis? Essays Textual, Exegetical, and Theological.* Grand Rapids: Eerdmans, 2001.

———. "Wisdom Christology in Paul: A Dissenting View." Pages 367–75 in *To What End Exegesis? Essays Textual, Exegetical, and Theological.* Grand Rapids: Eerdmans, 2001.

———. "The Cultural Context of Ephesians 5:18–6:9." *Priscilla Papers* 16 (Winter 2002): 3–8.

———. "St. Paul and the Incarnation: A Reassessment of the Data." Pages 62–92 in *The Incarnation: An Interdisciplinary Symposium on the Incarnation of the Son of God.* Edited by S. T. Davis, D. Kendall, and G. O'Collins. Oxford: Oxford University Press, 2002.

———. "1 Corinthians 11:2–16." Pages 149–55 in *Discovering Biblical Equality: Complementarity without Hierarchy.* Edited by R. W. Pierce and R. M. Groothuis. Downers Grove, Ill.: InterVarsity Press, 2004.

———. "Paul and the Metaphors of Salvation: Some Reflections on Pauline Soteriology." Pages 43–67 in *The Redemption: An Interdisciplinary Symposium on Christ as Redeemer.* Edited by S. T. Davis, D. Kendall, and G. O'Collins. Oxford: Oxford University Press, 2004.

———. "Praying and Prophesying in the Assemblies: 1 Corinthians 11:2–16." Pages 142–60 in *Discovering Biblical Equality: Complementarity without*

Hierarchy. Edited by R. W. Pierce and R. M. Groothuis. Downers Grove, Ill.: InterVarsity Press, 2004.

———. "Old Testament Intertextuality in Colossians: Reflections on Pauline Christology and Gentile Inclusion in God's Story." Pages 203–23 in *History and Exegesis: New Testament Essays in Honor of E. Earle Ellis on His Eightieth Birthday*. Edited by S. A. Son. London: T&T Clark, 2006.

Fee, Gordon D., and Douglas Stuart. *How to Read the Bible for All Its Worth*. 3d ed. Grand Rapids: Zondervan, 2002.

Feinberg, Paul D. "The Kenosis and Christology: An Exegetical-Theological Analysis of Phil 2:6–11." *Trinity Journal* 1 (1980): 21–46.

Feuillet, André. *Le Christ: Sagesse de Dieu d'après les épîtres pauliniennes*. Études bibliques. Paris: Gabalda, 1966.

Fitzmyer, Joseph F. "The Semitic Background of the New Testament *Kyrios*-Title." Pages 115–42 in *A Wandering Aramean: Collected Aramaic Essays*. Society of Biblical Literature Monograph Series 25. Missoula, Mont.: Scholars Press, 1979.

———. "Abba and Jesus' Relation to God." Pages 16–38 in *À cause de l'évangile: Mélanges offerts à Dom Jacques Dupont*. Edited by R. Gantoy. Lectio divina 123. Paris: Cerf, 1985.

———. "The Aramaic Background of Philippians 2:6–11." *Catholic Biblical Quarterly* 50 (1988): 470–83.

Foerster, Werner. "σωτήρ." Pages 1010–12 in vol. 7 of *Theological Dictionary of the New Testament*. Edited by G. Kittel and G. Friedrich. Translated by G. W. Bromiley. 10 vols. Grand Rapids: Eerdmans, 1964–1976.

Fowl, Stephen D. *The Story of Christ in the Ethics of Paul: An Analysis of the Function of the Hymnic Material in the Pauline Corpus*. Journal for the Study of the New Testament: Supplement Series 36. Sheffield: Sheffield Academic Press, 1990.

Francis, Fred O. "The Christological Argument of Colossians." Pages 192–208 in *God's Christ and His People: Studies in Honour of Nils Alstrup Dahl*. Edited by J. Jervell and W. A. Meeks. Oslo: Universitetsforleget, 1977.

Fuller, Reginald H. *The Foundations of New Testament Christology*. New York: Scribner, 1965.

Furness, J. M. "Ἁρπαγμός . . . ἑαυτὸν ἐκένωσε." *Expository Times* 69 (1957–1958): 93–94.

———. "The Authorship of Philippians ii.6–11." *Expository Times* 70 (1958–1959): 240–43.

———. "Behind the Philippian Hymn." *Expository Times* 79 (1967–1968): 178–82.

Gärtner, Bertil. *The Temple and the Community in Qumran and the New Testament*. Society for New Testament Studies Monograph Series 1. Cambridge: Cambridge University Press, 1965.

Gamble, Harry Y. *The Textual History of the Letter to the Romans: A Study in Textual and Literary Criticism*. Studies and Documents 42. Grand Rapids: Eerdmans, 1977.

————. *Books and Readers in the Early Church: A History of Early Christian Texts.* New Haven: Yale University Press, 1995.

Gaston, Lloyd. *Paul and the Torah.* Vancouver: University of British Columbia Press, 1987.

Giblin, Charles H. "Three Monotheistic Texts in Paul." *Catholic Biblical Quarterly* 37 (1975): 527–47.

Gibbs, John G. "The Relation between Creation and Redemption according to Phil. II.5–11." *Novum Testamentum* 12 (1970): 170–83.

Giles, Kevin. "The Subordination of Christ and the Subordination of Women." Pages 334–52 in *Discovering Biblical Equality: Complementarity without Hierarchy.* Edited by R. W. Pierce and R. M. Groothuis. Downers Grove, Ill.: InterVarsity Press, 2004.

Glasson, T. F. "Two Notes on the Philippians Hymn (ii.6–11)." *New Testament Studies* 21 (1974–1975): 133–39.

Greenspoon, Leonard. "The Use and Misuse of the Term 'LXX' and Related Terminology in Recent Scholarship." *Bulletin of the International Organization for Septuagint and Cognate Studies* 20 (1987): 21–29.

Habermann, Jürgen. *Präexistenzaussagen im Neuen Testament.* Europäische Hochschulschriften 23/362. Frankfurt am Main: Peter Lang, 1990.

Hagner, D. A., "Paul's Christology and Jewish Monotheism." Pages 19–38 in *Perspectives on Christology.* Edited by M. Shuster and R. Muller. Grand Rapids: Zondervan, 1991.

Hahn, Ferdinand. *Christologische Hoheitstitel: Ihre Geschichte im frühen Christentum.* Forschungen zur Religion und Literatur des Alten und Neuen Testaments 83. Göttingen: Vandenhoeck & Ruprecht, 1963. ET, *The Titles of Jesus in Christology: Their History in Early Christianity.* Translated by H. Knight and G. Ogg. London: Lutterworth, 1969.

Hamerton-Kelly, R. G. *Pre-existence, Wisdom, and the Son of Man: A Study of the Idea of Pre-existence in the New Testament.* Society for New Testament Studies Monograph Series 21. Cambridge: Cambridge University Press, 1973.

Hamilton, Neill Q. *The Holy Spirit and Eschatology in Paul.* Scottish Journal of Theology Occasional Papers 6. Edinburgh: Oliver & Boyd, 1957.

Hammerich, L. L. "An Ancient Misunderstanding (Phil. 2:6 'Robbery')." *Expository Times* 78 (1967): 193–94.

Hannah, Darrell. *Michael and Christ: Michael Traditions and Angel Christology in Early Christianity.* Wissenschaftliche Untersuchungen zum Neuen Testament 2/109. Tübingen: Mohr Siebeck, 1999.

Hanson, Anthony T. *The Image of the Invisible God.* London: SCM Press, 1982.

Harris, Murray J. *Jesus as God: The New Testament Use of Theos in Reference to Jesus.* Grand Rapids: Baker, 1992.

Harris, W. H. "The Ascent and Descent of Christ in Ephesians 4:9–10." *Bibliotheca sacra* 151 (1994): 198–214.

————. *The Descent of Christ: Ephesians 4:7–11 and Traditional Hebrew Imagery.* Grand Rapids: Baker, 1998.

Hasler, V. "Epiphanie und Christologie in den Pastoralbriefe." *Theologische Zeitschrift* 33 (1977): 193–209.

Hay, David. *Glory at the Right Hand: Psalm 110 in Early Christianity.* Society of Biblical Literature Monograph Series 18. Nashville: Abingdon, 1973.

Hays, Richard B. *The Faith of Jesus Christ: An Investigation of the Narrative Substructure of Galatians 3:1–4:11.* Society of Biblical Literature Dissertation Series 56. Chico, Calif,: Scholars Press, 1983.

———. "Christology and Ethics in Galatians: The Law of Christ." *Catholic Biblical Quarterly* 49 (1987): 268–90.

———. *Echoes of Scripture in the Letters of Paul.* New Haven: Yale University Press, 1989.

———. "ΠΙΣΤΙΣ and Pauline Christology: What Is at Stake?" Pages 714–29 in *The Society of Biblical Literature 1991 Seminar Papers.* Society of Biblical Literature Seminar Papers 30. Edited by E. H. Lovering Jr. Atlanta: Scholars Press, 1991.

Helyer, L. L. "Colossians 1:15–20: Pre-Pauline or Pauline?" *Journal of the Evangelical Theological Society* 26 (1983): 167–79.

———. "Arius Revisited: The Firstborn over All Creation (Col 1:15)." *Journal of the Evangelical Theological Society* 31 (1988): 59–67.

———. "Recent Research on Col 1:15–20 (1980–1990)." *Grace Theological Journal* 12 (1992): 61–67.

———. "Cosmic Christology and Col 1:15–20." *Journal of the Evangelical Theological Society* 37 (1994): 235–46.

Hengel, Martin. *Judaism and Hellenism: Studies in Their Encounter in Palestine during the Early Hellenistic Period.* Translated by J. Bowden. London: SCM Press, 1974.

———. *The Son of God: The Origin of Christology and the History of Jewish-Hellenistic Religion.* Philadelphia: Fortress, 1976.

———. " 'Christos' in Paul." Pages 65–77 in *Between Jesus and Paul: Studies in the Earliest History of Christianity.* Translated by J. Bowden. Philadelphia: Fortress, 1983.

———. "Hymns and Christology." Pages 78–96 in *Between Jesus and Paul: Studies in the Earliest History of Christianity.* Translated by J. Bowden. Philadelphia: Fortress, 1983.

———. " 'Sit at My Right Hand!' The Enthronement of Christ at the Right Hand of God and Psalm 110:1." Pages 119–225 in *Studies in Early Christology.* Edinburgh: T&T Clark, 1995.

Heriban, Josef. *Retto φρονεῖν e κένωσις: Studio esegetico su Fil 2,1–5,6–11.* Rome: LAS, 1983.

Hermann, Ingo. *Kyrios und Pneuma: Studien zur Christologie der paulinischen Hauptbriefe.* Studien zum Alten und Neuen Testaments 2. Munich: Kösel, 1961.

Hewett, J. A. "1 Thessalonians 3.13." *Expository Times* 87 (1975–1976): 54–55.

Hofius, O. *Der Christushymnus Philipper 2,6: Untersuchungen zu Gestalt und Aussage eines urchristlichen Psalms.* Wissenschaftliche Untersuchungen zum Neuen Testament 2/17. Tübingen: Mohr Siebeck, 1976.

Hooke, S. H. *Alpha and Omega: A Study in the Pattern of Revelation*. London: J. Nisbet, 1961.

Hooker, Morna D. "Philippians 2:6–11." Pages 151–64 in *Jesus und Paulus: Festschrift für Werner Georg Kümmel zum 70. Geburtstag*. Edited by E. E. Ellis and E. Grässer. Göttingen: Vandenhoeck & Ruprecht, 1978.

———. *Pauline Pieces*. London: Epworth, 1979.

———. "ΠΙΣΤΙΣ ΧΡΙΣΤΟΥ." *New Testament Studies* 35 (1989): 321–42.

Hoover, Roy W. "The HARPAGMOS Enigma: A Philological Solution." *Harvard Theological Review* 64 (1971): 95–119.

Horbury, William. *Jewish Messianism and the Cult of Christ*. London: SCM Press, 1998.

———. *Messianism among Jews and Christians: Twelve Biblical and Historical Studies*. Edinburgh: T&T Clark, 2003.

———. "Jewish Messianism and Early Christology" Pages 3–24 in *Contours of Christology in the New Testament*. Edited by R. N. Longenecker. Grand Rapids: Eerdmans, 2005.

Horsley, R. A. "The Background of the Confessional Formula in 1 Kor 8:6." *Zeitschrift für die neutestamentliche Wissenschaft und die Kunde der älteren Kirche* 69 (1978): 130–35.

Hort, F. J. A. *Judaistic Christianity*. 1894. Repr., Grand Rapids: Baker, 1980.

Howard, George. "The Tetragram and the New Testament." *Journal of Biblical Literature* 96 (1977): 63–83.

———. "Philippians 2:6–11 and the Human Christ." *Catholic Biblical Quarterly* 40 (1978): 368–87.

Hudson, D. F. "A Further Note on Philippians ii:6–11." *Expository Times* 77 (1965–1966): 29.

Hultgren, A. J. "The *PISTIS CHRISTOU* Formulation in Paul." *Novum Testamentum* 22 (1980): 248–63.

Hunter, A. M. *The Gospel according to Paul*. Philadelphia: Westminster, 1966.

Hunzinger, C. H. "Zur Struktur der Christus-Hymnen in Phil 2 und 1. Petr 3." Pages 142–56 in *Der Ruf Jesu und die Antwort der Gemeinde: Exegetische Untersuchungen; Joachim Jeremias z. 70 Geburtstag gewidmet von seinen Schülern*. Edited by E. Lohse, C. Burchard, and B. Schaller. Göttingen: Vandenhoeck & Ruprecht, 1970.

Hurst, L. D. "Re-enter the Pre-existent Christ in Philippians 2:5–11?" *New Testament Studies* 32 (1986): 449–57.

Hurtado, L. W. "The Doxology at the End of Romans." Pages 185–99 in *New Testament Textual Criticism—Its Significance for Exegesis: Essays in Honour of Bruce M. Metzger*. Edited by E. J. Epp and G. D. Fee. Oxford: Clarendon, 1981.

———. "Jesus as Lordly Example in Philippians 2:5–11." Pages 113–26 in *From Jesus to Paul: Studies in Honour of Francis Wright Beare*. Edited by P. Richardson and J. C. Hurd. Waterloo, Ont.: Wilfred Laurier University Press, 1984.

———. "God." Pages 275–76 in *Dictionary of Jesus and The Gospels*. Edited by J. B. Green and S. McKnight. Downers Grove, Ill.: InterVarsity Press, 1992.

———. "Lord." Pages 560–69 in *Dictionary of Paul and His Letters*. Edited by G. F. Hawthorne and R. P. Martin. Downers Grove, Ill.: InterVarsity Press, 1993.

———. "Pre-existence." Pages 743–46 in *Dictionary of Paul and His Letters*. Edited by G. F. Hawthorne and R. P. Martin. Downers Grove, Ill.: InterVarsity Press, 1993.

———. "Jesus' Divine Sonship in Paul's Epistle to the Romans." Pages 217–33 in *Romans and the People of God: Essays in Honor of Gordon D. Fee on the Occasion of His 65th Birthday*. Edited by S. K. Soderlund and N. T. Wright. Grand Rapids: Eerdmans, 1999.

———. *Lord Jesus Christ: Devotion to Jesus in Earliest Christianity*. Grand Rapids: Eerdmans, 2003.

———. "Paul's Christology." Pages 185–98 in *The Cambridge Companion to Paul*. Edited by J. D. G. Dunn. Cambridge: University Press, 2003.

Jaeger, W. W. "Eine stilgeschichtliche Studie zum Philipperbrief." *Hermes* 50 (1915): 537–53.

Jeremias, Joachim. "Zu Phil. ii 7: ΕΑΥΤΟΝ ΕΚΕΝΩΣΕΝ." *Novum Testamentum* 6 (1963): 182–88.

———. *The Prayers of Jesus*. Studies in Biblical Theology 2/6. London: SCM Press, 1967.

Jervell, J. *Imago Dei: Gen 1,26f. im Spätjudentum, in der Gnosis und in den paulinischen Briefen*. Forschungen zur Religion und Literatur des Alten und Neuen Testaments 58. Göttingen: Vandenhoeck & Ruprecht, 1960.

Jewett, R. "A Matrix of Grace: The Theology of 2 Thessalonians as a Pauline Letter." Pages 63–70 in *Thessalonians, Philippians, Galatians, Philemon*. Vol. 1 of *Pauline Theology*. Edited by J. M. Bassler. Minneapolis: Fortress, 1991.

Johnson, E. Elizabeth, "Wisdom and Apocalyptic in Paul." Pages 263–83 in *In Search of Wisdom: Essays in Memory of John C. Gammie*. Edited by L. G. Perdue, B. B. Scott, and W. J. Wiseman. Louisville: Westminster John Knox, 1993.

Johnson, Luke T. *The Writings of the New Testament: An Interpretation*. Philadelphia: Fortress, 1986.

Juel, Donald. *Messianic Exegesis: Christological Interpretation of the Old Testament in Early Christianity*. Philadelphia: Fortress, 1988.

Käsemann, Ernst. "A Critical Analysis of Philippians 2:5–11." *Journal for Theology and the Church* 5 (1968): 45–88.

Kasper, W. *Jesus the Christ*. Translated by V. Green. New York: Paulist Press, 1976.

Keck, Leander E. "Toward the Renewal of New Testament Christology." *New Testament Studies* 32 (1986): 362–77.

———. "Christology of the New Testament: What, Then, Is New Testament Christology?" Pages 185–200 in *Who Do You Say I Am? Essays on Christology*. Edited by M. A. Powell and D. R. Bauer. Louisville: Westminster John Knox, 1999.

Kerst, R. "1 Kor 8.6—Ein vorpaulinisches Taufbekenntnis?" *Zeitschrift für die neutestamentliche Wissenschaft und die Kunde der älteren Kirche* 66 (1975): 130–39.

Kiley, Mark C. *Colossians as Pseudepigraphy.* Biblical Seminar 4. Sheffield: JSOT Press, 1986.

Kim, Seyoon. *The Origin of Paul's Gospel.* Wissenschaftliche Untersuchungen zum Neuen Testament 2/4. Tübingen: Mohr Siebeck, 1981.

———. *Paul and the New Perspective: Second Thoughts on the Origin of Paul's Gospel.* Grand Rapids: Eerdmans, 2002.

Klöpper, A. "Zur Christologie der Pastoralbriefe." *Zeitschrift für wissenschaftliche Theologie* 45 (1902): 339–61.

Koperski, V. "The Meaning of *Pistis Christou* in Philippians 3:9." *Louvain Studies* 18 (1993): 198–216.

Kovach, S. D., and P. R. Schemm Jr. "A Defense of the Doctrine of the Eternal Subordination of the Son." *Journal of the Evangelical Theological Society* 42 (1999): 44–76.

Kramer, Werner. *Christ, Lord, Son of God.* Translated by B. Hardy. Studies in Biblical Theology 50. London: SCM Press, 1966.

Kreitzer, L. J. *Jesus and God in Paul's Eschatology.* Journal for the Study of the New Testament: Supplement Series 19. Sheffield: Sheffield Academic Press, 1987.

Krinetzki, L. "Der Einfluss von Is 52,13–53,12 Par auf Phil 2,6–11." *Theologische Quartalschrift* 139 (1959): 157–93, 291–336.

Küng, Hans. *On Being a Christian.* Garden City, N.Y.: Doubleday, 1976.

Kurz, William S. "Kenotic Imitation of Paul and of Christ in Philippians 2 and 3." Pages 103–26 in *Discipleship in the New Testament.* Edited by F. F. Segovia. Philadelphia: Fortress, 1985.

Kuschel, K.-J. *Born before All Time? The Dispute over Christ's Origin.* Translated by J. Bowden. London: SCM Press, 1992.

Kuss, Otto. "Zu Römer 9,5." Pages 291–303 in *Rechtfertigung: Festschrift für Ernst Käsemann zum 70. Geburtstag.* Edited by J. Friedrich, W. Pöhlmann, and P. Stuhlmacher. Tübingen, Mohr Siebeck, 1976.

Läger, Karoline. *Die Christologie der Pastoralbriefe.* Hamburger theologische Studien 12. Münster: LIT, 1996.

Lambrecht, J. "Paul's Christological Use of Scripture in 1 Cor 15:20–28." *New Testament Studies* 28 (1982): 502–27.

Lau, Andrew Y. *Manifest in the Flesh: The Epiphany Christology of the Pastoral Epistles.* Wissenschaftliche Untersuchungen zum Neuen Testament 2/86. Tübingen: Mohr Siebeck, 1996.

Lee, Aquila H. I. *From Messiah to Preexistent Son: Jesus' Self-Consciousness and Early Christian Exegesis of Messianic Psalms.* Wissenschaftliche Untersuchungen zum Neuen Testament 2/192. Tübingen: Mohr Siebeck, 2005.

Leivestad, R. " 'The Meekness and Gentleness of Christ': II Cor. X.1." *New Testament Studies* 12 (1965–1966): 156–64.

Levie, J. "Le chrétien citoyen du ciel (Phil 3,20)." Pages 81–88 in vol. 2 of *Studiorum paulinorum congressus internationalis Catholicus*. 2 vols. Analecta biblica 17–18. Rome: Pontifical Biblical Institute, 1963.

Lincoln, Andrew T. *Paradise Now and Not Yet: Studies in the Role of the Heavenly Dimension in Paul's Thought with Special Reference to His Eschatology*. Society for New Testament Studies Monograph Series 43. Cambridge: Cambridge University Press, 1981.

Lohmeyer, Ernst. *Kyrios Jesus: Eine Untersuchung zu Phil. 2,5–11*. Heidelberg: C. Winter, 1928.

Longenecker, Richard N., ed. *Contours of Christology in the New Testament*. Grand Rapids: Eerdmans, 2005.

MacDonald, William G. "Christology and 'The Angel of the Lord.'" Pages 324–35 in *Current Issues in Biblical and Patristic Interpretation: Studies in Honor of Merrill C. Tenney Presented by His Former Students*. Edited by G. F. Hawthorne. Grand Rapids: Eerdmans, 1975.

Marcus, Ralph. "On Biblical Hypostases of Wisdom." *Hebrew Union College Annual* 23 (1950–1951): 157–71.

Marshall, I. Howard. "The Christ-Hymn in Philippians 2:5–11." *Tyndale Bulletin* 19 (1968): 104–27.

———. *The Origins of New Testament Christology*. Issues in Contemporary Theology. Downers Grove, Ill.: InterVarsity Press, 1976.

———. "Incarnational Christology in the New Testament." Pages 1–16 in *Christ the Lord: Studies in Christology Presented to Donald Guthrie*. Edited by H. H. Rowdon. Leicester: Inter-Varsity Press, 1982.

———. "The Christology of the Pastoral Epistles." *Studien zum Neuen Testament und seiner Umwelt* 13 (1988): 157–77.

———. *Beyond the Bible: Moving from Scripture to Theology*. Acadia Studies in Bible and Theology. Grand Rapids: Baker, 2004.

Martin, Ralph P. "Μορφή in Philippians ii.6." *Expository Times* 70 (1959): 183–84.

———. *Carmen Christi: Philippians 2:5–11 in Recent Interpretation and in the Setting of Early Christian Worship*. Society for New Testament Studies Monograph Series 4. Cambridge: Cambridge University Press, 1967. Repr., *A Hymn of Christ: Philippians 2:5–11 in Recent Interpretation and in the Setting of Early Christian Worship*. Downers Grove, Ill.: InterVarsity Press, 1997.

———. "The Christology of the Prison Epistles." Pages 193–218 in *Contours of Christology in the New Testament*. Edited by R. N. Longenecker. Grand Rapids: Eerdmans, 2005.

Matera, Frank. *New Testament Christology*. Louisville: Westminster John Knox, 1999.

Mawhinney, A. "God as Father: Two Popular Theories Reconsidered." *Journal of the Evangelical Theological Society* 31 (1988): 181–89.

Menken, M. J. J. "Christology in 2 Thessalonians: A Transformation of Pauline Tradition." *Estudios biblicos* 54 (1996): 501–22.

Metzger, Bruce M. "The Punctuation of Rom. 9:5." Pages 95–112 in *Christ and Spirit in the New Testament: Studies in Honour of Charles Francis Digby Moule*. Edited by B. Lindars and S. S. Smalley. London: Cambridge University Press, 1973.

———. *A Textual Commentary on the Greek New Testament*. 2d ed. New York: United Bible Societies, 1994.

Moo, Douglas J. "The Christology of the Early Pauline Letters." Pages 169–92 in *Contours of Christology in the New Testament*. Edited by R. N. Longenecker. Grand Rapids: Eerdmans, 2005.

Morris, Leon. *1, 2 Thessalonians*. Word Biblical Themes. Dallas: Word, 1989.

Moule, C. F. D. *An Idiom Book of New Testament Greek*. 2d ed. Cambridge: Cambridge University Press, 1963.

———. "Further Reflexions on Philippians 2:5–11." Pages 264–76 in *Apostolic History and the Gospel: Biblical and Historical Essays Presented to F. F. Bruce on His 60th Birthday*. Edited by W. W. Gasque and R. P. Martin. Grand Rapids: Eerdmans, 1970.

———. "2 Cor 3.18b, καθάπερ ἀπὸ κυρίου πνεύματος." Pages 233–37 in *Neues Testament und Geschichte: Historisches Geschehen und Deutung im Neuen Testament*. Edited by H. Baltensweiler and B. Reicke. Zurich: Theologischer Verlag, 1972.

———. "The Manhood of Jesus in the New Testament." Pages 95–110 in *Christ, Faith and History: Cambridge Studies in Christology*. Edited by S. W. Sykes and J. P. Clayton. Cambridge: Cambridge University Press, 1972.

———. *The Origin of Christology*. Cambridge: Cambridge University Press, 1977.

Müller, Ulrich B. "Der Christushymnus Phil 2.6–11." *Zeitschrift für die neutestamentliche Wissenschaft und die Kunde der älteren Kirche* 79 (1988): 17–44.

Murphy-O'Connor, Jerome. "Christological Anthropology in Phil. II,6–11." *Revue biblique* 83 (1976): 25–50.

———. "I Cor. VIII,6: Cosmology or Soteriology?" *Revue biblique* 85 (1978): 253–67.

Neugebauer, F. *In Christus: Eine Untersuchung zum paulinischen Glaubensverständnis*. Göttingen: Vandenhoeck & Ruprecht, 1961.

Newman, C. C. *Paul's Glory-Christology: Tradition and Rhetoric*. Novum Testamentum Supplements 69. Leiden: Brill, 1992.

Obeng, E. "Abba, Father: The Prayer of the Sons of God." *Expository Times* 99 (1988): 363–66.

O'Day, Gail R. "Jeremiah 9:22–23 and 1 Corinthians 1:26–31: A Study in Intertextuality." *Journal of Biblical Literature* 109 (1990): 259–67.

Oesterley, W. O. E., and G. H. Box. *The Religion and Worship of the Synagogue*. London: Pitman, 1911.

Oesterreicher, J. M. "'Abba, Father!' On the Humanity of Jesus." Pages 119–36 in *The Lord's Prayer and Jewish Liturgy*. Edited by J. J. Petuchowski and M. Brocke. New York: Seabury, 1978.

O'Neill, J. C. "Hoover on *Harpagmos* Reviewed, with a Modest Proposal concerning Philippians 2:6." *Harvard Theological Review* 81 (1988): 445–49.

Osburn, Carroll D. "The Text of 1 Corinthians 10:9." Pages 201–12 in *New Testament Textual Criticism—Its Significance for Exegesis: Essays in Honour of Bruce M. Metzger.* Edited by E. J. Epp and G. D. Fee. Oxford: Clarendon, 1981.

Pate, C. M. *The Reverse of the Curse: Paul, Wisdom, and the Law.* Wissenschaftliche Untersuchungen zum Neuen Testament 2/114. Tübingen: Mohr Siebeck, 2000.

Perkins, Pheme. "Philippians: Theology for the Heavenly Politeuma." Pages 89–104 in *Thessalonians, Philippians, Galatians, Philemon.* Vol. 1 of *Pauline Theology.* Edited by J. M. Bassler. Minneapolis: Fortress, 1991.

Pietersma, Albert. "Kyrios or Tetragram: A Renewed Quest for the Original Septuagint." Pages 85–101 in *De Septuaginta: Studies in Honour of John William Wevers on His Sixty-Fifth Birthday.* Edited by A. Pietersma and C. Cox. Mississauga, Ont.: Benben, 1984.

Pohlmann, W. "μορφή." Pages 442–43 in vol. 2 of *Exegetical Dictionary of the New Testament.* Edited by H. Balz and G. Schneider. 3 vols. Grand Rapids: Eerdmans, 1990–1993.

Reid, Jennings B. *Jesus, God's Emptiness, God's Fullness: The Christology of St. Paul.* New York: Paulist Press, 1990.

Renwick, D. A. *Paul, the Temple, and the Presence of God.* Brown Judaic Studies 224. Atlanta: Scholars Press, 1991.

Richardson, N. *Paul's Language about God.* Journal for the Study of the New Testament: Supplement Series 99. Sheffield: Sheffield Academic Press, 1994.

Ridderbos, H. *Paul: An Outline of His Theology.* Grand Rapids: Eerdmans, 1975.

Ringgren, H. *Word and Wisdom: Studies in the Hypostatization of Divine Qualities and Functions in the Ancient Near East.* Lund: Ohlssons, 1947.

Rissi, Mathias. "Der Chistushymnus in Phil 2,6–11." *ANRW* 25.4:3314–26. Part 2, *Principat,* 25.4. Edited by H. Temporini and W. Haase. New York: de Gruyter, 1987.

Robbins, Charles J. "Rhetorical Structure of Philippians 2:6–11." *Catholic Biblical Quarterly* 42 (1980): 73–82.

Robbins, Vernon K. *Exploring the Texture of Texts: A Guide to Socio-Rhetorical Interpretation.* Valley Forge, Pa.: Trinity Press International, 1996.

Robinson, D. W. B. "Ἁρπαγμός: The Deliverance of Jesus Refused?' *Expository Times* 80 (1968–1969): 253–54.

Robinson, John A. T. *The Body: A Study in Pauline Theology.* Studies in Biblical Theology 5. London: SCM Press, 1952.

Robinson, William C., Jr. "Christology and Christian Life: Paul's Use of the Incarnation Motif." *Andover Newton Quarterly* 12 (1971): 108–17.

Ross, J. "ΑΡΠΑΓΜΟΣ (Phil. ii.6)." *Journal of Theological Studies* 10 (1909): 573–74.

Rousseau, François. "Une disposition des versets de Philippiens 2,5–11." *Studies in Religion* 17 (1988): 191–98.

Sanders, J. T. *The New Testament Christological Hymns: Their Historical Religious Background.* Society for New Testament Studies Monograph Series 15. Cambridge: Cambridge University Press, 1971.

Schelkle, K. H. "σωτήρ." Pages 325–27 in vol. 3 of *Exegetical Dictionary of the New Testament.* Edited by H. Balz and G. Schneider. 3 vols. Grand Rapids: Eerdmans, 1990–1993.

Schnabel, Eckhard J. *Law and Wisdom from Ben Sira to Paul: A Tradition History Enquiry into the Relation of Law, Wisdom, and Ethics.* Wissenschaftliche Untersuchungen zum Neuen Testament 2/16. Tübingen: Mohr Siebeck, 1985.

Schnelle, Udo. *Apostle Paul: His Life and Theology.* Grand Rapids: Baker Academic, 2005.

Schweizer, Eduard. *Lordship and Discipleship.* Studies in Biblical Theology 28. London: SCM Press, 1960.

———. "Zum religionsgeschichtlichen Hintergrund der 'Sendungsformel' Gal 4,4f., Rm 8,3f., Joh 3,16f., 1 Joh 4,9." *Zeitschrift für die neutestamentliche Wissenschaft und die Kunde der älteren Kirche* 57 (1966): 455–68.

———. "Paul's Christology and Gnosticism." Pages 115–23 in *Paul and Paulinism: Essays in Honour of C. K. Barrett.* Edited by M. D. Hooker and S. G. Wilson. London: SPCK, 1982.

Scott, James M. *Adoption as Sons of God: An Exegetical Investigation into the Background of ΥΙΟΘΕΣΙΑ in the Pauline Corpus.* Wissenschaftliche Untersuchungen zum Neuen Testament 2/48. Tübingen: Mohr Siebeck, 1992.

Scott, R. B. Y. *Proverbs and Ecclesiastes.* Anchor Bible 18. Garden City, N.Y.: Doubleday, 1965.

Scroggs, Robin. *The Last Adam: A Study in Pauline Anthropology.* Philadelphia: Fortress, 1966.

Simonsen, H. "Christologische Traditionselemente in den Pastoralbriefen." Pages 51–62 in *Die paulinische Literatur und Theologie—skandinavische Beiträge: Anlässlich der 50. jährigen Gründungs-Feier der Universität von Aarhus.* Edited by S. Pedersen. Teologiske studier 7. Århus: Forlaget Aros, 1980.

Singer, S., trans. *The Authorized Daily Prayer Book of the United Hebrew Congregations of the British Empire.* London: Eyre & Spottiswoode, 1935.

Skehan, Patrick W. "The Divine Name at Qumran, in the Masada Scroll, and in the Septuagint." *Bulletin of the International Organization for Septuagint and Cognate Studies* 13 (1980): 14–44.

Skehan, Patrick W., and Alexander A. di Lella. *The Wisdom of Ben Sira.* Anchor Bible 39. Garden City, N.Y.: Doubleday, 1987.

Smith, G. V. "Paul's Use of Psalm 68:18 in Ephesians 4:8." *Journal of the Evangelical Theological Society* 18 (1975): 181–89.

Soards, Marion L. "Christology of the Pauline Epistles." Pages 88–109 in *Who Do You Say I Am? Essays on Christology.* Edited by M. A. Powell and D. R. Bauer. Louisville: Westminster John Knox, 1999.

Spicq, C. "Note sur ΜΟΡΦΗ dans les papyrus et quelques inscriptions." *Revue biblique* 80 (1973): 37–45.

Standhartinger, A. "The Origin and Intention of the Household Code in the Letter to the Colossians." *Journal for the Study of the New Testament* 79 (2001): 117–30.

Stanley, Christopher D. *Paul and the Language of Scripture: Citation Technique in the Pauline Epistles and Contemporary Literature.* Society for New Testament Studies Monograph Series 74. Cambridge: Cambridge University Press, 1992.

————. " 'Pearls Before Swine': Did Paul's Audiences Understand His Biblical Quotations?" *Novum Testamentum* 41 (1999): 124–44.

Stanley, David M. *Boasting in the Lord: The Phenomenon of Prayer in Saint Paul.* New York: Paulist Press, 1973.

Stanton, Graham N. *Jesus of Nazareth in New Testament Preaching.* Society for New Testament Studies Monograph Series 27. London: Cambridge University Press, 1974.

Steele, E. S. "The Use of Jewish Scriptures in 1 Thessalonians." *Biblical Theology Bulletin* 14 (1984): 12–17.

Steenburg, Dave. "The Case against the Synonymity of *MORPHE* and *EIKON.*" *Journal for the Study of the New Testament* 34 (1988): 77–86.

Stettler, H. *Die Christologie der Pastoralbriefe.* Wissenschaftliche Untersuchungen zum Neuen Testament 2/105. Tübingen: Mohr Siebeck, 1998.

Strecker, Georg. "Redaktion und Tradition im Christushymnus Phil 2 6–11." *Zeitschrift für die neutestamentliche Wissenschaft und die Kunde der älteren Kirche* 55 (1964): 63–78.

Strimple, Robert B. "Philippians 2:5–11 in Recent Studies: Some Exegetical Conclusions." *Westminster Theological Journal* 41 (1979): 247–68.

Talbert, Charles H. "The Problem of Pre-existence in Philippians 2:6–11." *Journal of Biblical Literature* 86 (1967): 141–53.

Thekkekara, M. "A Neglected Idiom in an Overstudied Passage (Phil 2:6–8)." *Louvain Studies* 17 (1992): 306–14.

Thielman, Frank. *Theology of the New Testament: A Canonical and Synthetic Approach.* Grand Rapids: Zondervan, 2005.

Thompson, Marianne Meye. *The Promise of the Father: Jesus and God in the New Testament.* Louisville: Westminster John Knox, 2000.

Thompson, Michael B. *Clothed with Christ: The Example and Teaching of Jesus in Romans 12:1–15:13.* Journal for the Study of the New Testament: Supplement Series 59. Sheffield: JSOT Press, 1991.

Towner, Philip H. *The Goal of Our Instruction: The Structure of Theology and Ethics in the Pastoral Epistles.* Journal for the Study of the New Testament: Supplement Series 34. Sheffield: Sheffield Academic Press, 1989.

————. "Christology in the Letters to Timothy and Titus." Pages 219–44 in *Contours of Christology in the New Testament.* Edited by R. N. Longenecker. Grand Rapids: Eerdmans, 2005.

Tuckett, Christopher M. "Paul, Scripture and Ethics: Some Reflections." *New Testament Studies* 46 (2000): 403–24.

———. *Christology and the New Testament: Jesus and His Earliest Followers*. Louisville: Westminster John Knox, 2001.

Turner, M. M. B. "The Significance of Spirit Endowment for Paul." *Vox evangelica* 9 (1975): 58–69.

Turner, Nigel. *Syntax*. Vol. 3 of J. H. Moulton, *A Grammar of New Testament Greek*. Edinburgh: T&T Clark, 1963.

Uprichard, R. E. H. "The Person and Work of Christ in 1 Thessalonians." *Evangelical Quarterly* 53 (1981): 108–14.

Vermès, Géza. *Jesus and the World of Judaism*. London: SCM Press, 1983.

Vokes, F. E. "'Απαργμος in Phil. 2:5–11." Pages 670–75 in *Studia evangelica II*. Edited by F. L. Cross. Texte und Untersuchungen zur Geschichte der altchristlichen Literatur 87. Berlin: Akadamie, 1964.

Wagner, G. "Le scandale de la croix expliqué par le chant du Serviteur d'Isaïe 53: Réflections sur Philippiens 2/6–11." *Études théologiques et religieuses* 61 (1986): 177–87.

Wallace, Daniel B. *Greek Grammar Beyond the Basics: An Exegetical Syntax of the New Testament*. Grand Rapids: Zondervan, 1996.

Wallace, D. H. "A Note on *morphé*." *Theologische Zeitschrift* 22 (1966): 19–25.

Waltke, Bruce. *The Book of Proverbs 1–15*. New International Commentary on the Old Testament. Grand Rapids: Eerdmans, 2003.

Wanamaker, Charles A. "Philippians 2.6–11: Son of God or Adamic Christology?" *New Testament Studies* 33 (1987): 179–93.

Watson, Francis. *Paul and the Hermeneutics of Faith*. London: T&T Clark International, 2004.

Warren, W. "On ἑαυτὸν ἐκένωσεν." *Journal of Theological Studies* 12 (1911): 461–63.

Wedderburn, A. J. M. "Some Observations on Paul's Use of the Phrases 'in Christ' and 'with Christ.'" *Journal for the Study of the New Testament* 25 (1985): 83–97.

Weima, Jeffrey A. D. *Neglected Endings: The Significance of the Pauline Letter Closings*. Journal for the Study of the New Testament: Supplement Series 101. Sheffield: JSOT Press, 1994.

Wiles, Gordon P. *Paul's Intercessory Prayers: The Significance of the Intercessory Prayer Passages in the Letters of St. Paul*. Society for New Testament Studies Monograph Series 24. Cambridge: Cambridge University Press, 1974.

Windisch, Hans. "Die göttliche Weisheit der Jüden und die paulinische Christologie." Pages 220–34 in *Neutestamentliche Studien: Georg Heinrici zu seinem 70. Geburtstag*. Edited by H. Windisch. Untersuchungen zum Neuen Testament 6. Leipzig: Hinrichs, 1914.

———. "Zur Christologie der Pastoralbriefe." *Zeitschrift für die neutestamentliche Wissenschaft und die Kunde der älteren Kirche* 34 (1935): 213–38.

Winston, David. *The Wisdom of Solomon*. Anchor Bible 43. Garden City, N.Y.: Doubleday, 1987.

———. "Wisdom in the Wisdom of Solomon." Pages 149–64 in *In Search of Wisdom: Essays in Memory of John C. Gammie*. Edited by L. G. Perdue, B. B. Scott, and W. J. Wiseman. Louisville: Westminster John Knox, 1993.

Witherington, Ben, III. "Christology." Pages 100–115 in *Dictionary of Paul and His Letters*. Edited by G. F. Hawthorne and R. P. Martin. Downers Grove, Ill.: InterVarsity Press, 1993.

———. *Jesus the Sage: The Pilgrimage of Wisdom*. Minneapolis: Fortress, 1994.

———. *Paul's Narrative Thought World: The Tapestry of Tragedy and Triumph*. Louisville: Westminster John Knox, 1994.

Wong, T. Y.-C. "The Problem of Pre-existence in Philippians 2,6–11." *Ephemerides theologicae lovanienses* 62 (1986): 167–82.

Woyke, J. *Götter, "Götzen," Götterbilder: Aspekte einer paulinischen "Theologie der Religionen."* Beihefte zur Zeitschrift für die neutestamentliche Wissenschaft 132. Berlin: de Gruyter, 2005.

Wrede, Wilhelm. *Die Echtheit des zweiten Thessalonicherbriefs*. Texte und Untersuchungen zur Geschichte der altchristlichen Literatur 9/2. Leipzig: Hinrichs, 1903.

Wright, N. T. "Adam in Pauline Christology." Pages 359–89 in *The Society of Biblical Literature 1983 Seminar Papers*. Society of Biblical Literature Seminar Papers 22. Edited by K. H. Richards. Chico, Calif.: Scholars Press, 1983.

———. "Ἁρπαγμός and the Meaning of Philippians 2:5–11." *Journal of Theological Studies* 37 (1986): 321–52.

———. "ΧΡΙΣΤΟΣ as 'Messiah' in Paul: Philemon 6." Pages 41–55 in *The Climax of the Covenant: Christ and the Law in Pauline Theology*. Minneapolis: Fortress, 1992.

———. *The Climax of the Covenant: Christ and the Law in Pauline Theology*. Minneapolis: Fortress, 1992.

———. "Monotheism, Christology and Ethics: 1 Corinthians 8." Pages 120–36 in *The Climax of the Covenant: Christ and the Law in Pauline Theology*. Minneapolis: Fortress, 1992.

———. *Jesus and the Victory of God*. Minneapolis: Fortress, 1996.

Yates, R. "A Re-examination of Ephesians 1:23." *Expository Times* 83 (1972): 146–51.

Young, Frances. *The Theology of the Pastoral Letters*. New Testament Theology. Cambridge: Cambridge University Press, 1994.

Ziesler, John. *Pauline Christianity*. Rev. ed. Oxford Bible Series. Oxford: Oxford University Press, 1990.

Index of Modern Authors

Index of Subjects

Index of Ancient Sources

NOTE: Items in bold indicate significant discussion of the passage.